PATTERNS OF EVOLUTION IN

GALAPAGOS ORGANISMS

Edited by
Robert I. Bowman
San Francisco State University
Margaret Berson
California Academy of Sciences
and
Alan E. Leviton
Pacific Division, AAAS and
California Academy of Sciences

Pacific Division, AAAS
San Francisco, California
1983

Library of Congress Catalog No. 83-062392
ISBN 0-934394-05-9

This volume has been typeset in *Press Roman* type on an IBM Mag Card Composer in the Department of Herpetology, California Academy of Sciences

c/o California Academy of Sciences
Golden Gate Park
San Francisco, California 94118

Manufactured in the United States of America by the Allen Press, Lawrence, KS 66044

TABLE OF CONTENTS

PREFACE

According to legend as set forth by Peruvian cosmographer Captain Pedro Sarmiento de Gamboa, some time in the second half of the 15th century the Inca king, Tupac Yupanqui, embarked from Manta, near Guayaquil, on a voyage that lasted more than a year. During the voyage, the expedition is said to have encountered two islands, which the king named Nina-Chumba (island of fire) and Hahua-Chumbi (outer island). These islands may have belonged to the Galapagos group. In 1535, Emperor Carlos V ordered Fray Tomás de Berlanga to go to Peru to settle a dispute between Spanish conquistadors Pizarro and his lieutenant, Diego de Almagro, over territorial acquisitions. Bishop Tomás left Panama on February 23rd, but a week later his vessel became trapped in an equatorial calm, and it slowly drifted westward in the equatorial current. On the 10th of March, an island was sighted, and, being short of provisions, the ship's crew made a landing. Berlanga finally arrived in Puerto Viejo, Peru, in late April. On April 26th he wrote a letter to Emperor Carlos V, in which he gave an account of the voyage. This letter included a description of the island and the first written descriptions of Galapagoan animals, like the giant land tortoises, "such big tortoises, that each could carry a man on top of itself," and iguanas "that are like serpents" (see Slevin 1959:13-15).

For the balance of the 16th and 17th centuries, the islands served largely as a haven and reprovisioning site for buccaneers, mostly British, who raided the coastal towns of Central and northern South America and plundered captured Spanish ships. During the 18th century the islands were visited by other vessels, such as the French frigate *Philippeaux*, HMS *Discovery*, and HMS *Rattler*, on voyages of exploration or as whalers, again for the purpose of replenishing ship's stores of water, fresh meat, and fuel. It was not until the arrival of HMS *Beagle*, under the command of Captain Robert Fitz-Roy, on the 15th of September, 1835, that a serious effort was made to explore and chart the Archipelago.

Although the islands were sighted by the Beagle's crew on the 15th of September, the ship did not make landfall until two days later when its crew, including the ship's naturalist, Charles Darwin, went ashore on Chatham Island (San Cristóbal). Of his first encounter with this strange new world, Darwin recorded in his *Journal*, "The natural history of this archipelago is very remarkable: it seems to be a little world within itself; the greater number of its inhabitants, both vegetable and animal, being found nowhere else" (Darwin 1839:454-455). The *Beagle* spent less than two months in Galapagoan waters, but during that time more was accomplished cartographically and scientifically than had been done during the preceding 300 years or was to be done for many years thereafter. For instance, Captain Fitz-Roy's hydrographic charts were used by all countries for more than one hundred years, until 1942, when the Archipelago was resurveyed by the USS *Bowditch*. And, suffice to say, apart from his collections and notes on natural history, Darwin's Galapagos experience was in time to alter the way we think about ourselves and the world in which we live.

Although one hundred and fifty years have passed since the *Beagle* dropped anchor off Chatham Island, the Archipelago has lost none of its charm and fascination. Indeed, scores of scientists continue to visit and revisit the islands and, following in Darwin's footsteps, discover this "little world within itself" to be a veritable living museum and laboratory for the study of evolutionary processes and patterns, unmatched anywhere in the world. The papers in this volume incorporate the results of much exciting current research on the animals and plants of the Galapagos Archipelago, as well as summaries of recent, tantalizing discoveries found among the submarine hotsprings that lie offshore and new ideas on the ages of the islands. The Pacific Division, AAAS, through the authorization of its Executive Committee, takes pride in bringing these papers to the attention of scientists and others who continue to be intrigued by these "Enchanted Islands."

LITERATURE CITED

Darwin, Charles. 1839. Journal of researches in the geology and natural history of the various countries visited by H.M.S. Beagle, under command of Captain FitzRoy, R.N. Henry Colburn, London. 615 pp., 16 pls. (Fascsimile reprint by Hafner Publ. Co., New York & London, 1952).

Slevin, Joseph Richard. 1959. The Galapagos Islands: A history of their exploration. Occ. Pap. Calif. Acad. Sci. 25. 150 pp.

Alan E. Leviton
Pacific Divison, AAAS, and
California Academy of Sciences
San Francisco, CA

Michele L. Aldrich
American Association for the
Advancement of Science
Washington, D.C.

August 23, 1983

DEDICATION

ROBERT CUNNINGHAM MILLER

This volume is dedicated to Robert C. Miller in recognition of his distinguished career and accomplishments in science; his contributions to the Pacific Division, American Association for the Advancement of Science, of which he was Secretary 1944-72 and President 1973-74; and his service to the California Academy of Sciences as Director 1938-63 and since then as Senior Scientist and Director Emeritus.

Robert Miller was born in Blairsville, Pennsylvania, July 3, 1899. He graduated from Greenville College in 1920. He did his graduate work at the University of California under Joseph Grinnell, which possibly accounts for his lifelong interest in birds, and received his Ph.D., with a major in marine biology, in 1928. While a graduate student, and immediately following, he was concerned with marine boring organisms, which were causing San Francisco's piers to fall into the Bay. That was another research interest that has been continued throughout his life.

Miller was Assistant Professor of Zoology and Oceanography at the University of Washington 1924-30, Associate Professor 1930-36, and Professor 1936-38. He was Visiting Professor at Lingnan University, China, 1929-31. Those were productive years, with Miller, in his quiet way, stimulating the interest and motivation of hundreds of students. The discipline with which he was involved had practical application. He was a staff member of the University of Washington's Oceanography Laboratory. Victor B. Scheffer, in his book *Adventures of a Zoologist*, tells how Miller offered him an unpaid job on the 1932 Alaskan cruise of the Laboratory's top-heavy vessel, the *Catalyst*, and says that experience opened his eyes to his career in marine research.

In 1937 Robert Miller married a lovely fellow faculty member, Lea Van Puymbroeck. This was most fortunate for the California Academy of Sciences. University of Washington regulations prohibited a man and wife both serving on its faculty. Robert Miller appealed for a waiver of the regulation, to no avail. In the meantime he was offered a professorship at the University of California, and prepared to move to Berkeley. However, the Academy was searching for a Director, and Joseph Grinnell, a trustee, recommended his former student. Robert Miller did not apply for the position, but he did accept it, and remained at the Academy's helm for 25 years. Under his leadership the institution prospered and matured. It also became the headquarters for the Pacific Division of the American Association for the Advancement of Science with Miller guiding it, as Secretary, for 28 years before he retired to become its President.

Robert Miller is a man of keen wit, and the old Executive Committee meetings of the AAAS, PD, in the Board Room of the Mechanic's Library, were occasions none of the past officers will forget. Serious matters were considered, but roars of laughter, escaping from the Board Room, puzzled and sometimes irritated the serious readers in the Mechanic's Library. The meeting went on from four p.m. until seven or eight, when we adjourned downstairs to Post Street and into the Gold Nugget (and after its demise to The Old Poodle Dog) for dinner. Bob Miller's stories continued. They were always sophisticated and pertinent, and he approached them in a ponderous but straightforward way—and they always worked.

Miller continued his own research while administering the Academy and directing the activities of others. He was a director of the California State Marine Research Commission, President of the Oceanographic Society of the Pacific, and was involved with many aspects of commercial fisheries investigation.

I was invited to succeed Robert C. Miller when he retired from the directorship of the Academy in 1963, and was fully aware that no other person could fill the position he had developed. Bob asked me to come, gave me his full support, and we became closest friends.

The 1964 Galapagos International Scientific Expedition was our first fully shared experience. Unable to sail with most of the scientists aboard the *Golden Bear*, we made our way to

Quito, Guayaquil, and to the islands. There it was hot, and somewhat confused. Diplomats, distinguished scientists, two members of Ecuador's military junta, American naval officers, a Royal Navy captain who was Charles Darwin's grandson, and amazed natives of Academy Bay, Santa Cruz Island, were mixed in a grand potpourri.

The Charles Darwin Research Station, which we had come to dedicate, was some distance from the village and the only source of cold drinks. Bob made the trek often, carrying a folding canvas bucket to be filled with large bottles of excellent Ecuadorian Pilsener. The equatorial sun was hot and the white coral trail long, and stops in scant shade were not infrequent. By the time he reached the station, the thirsty stevedores, all scientists, quickly finished the remaining bottles. Bob, resigned and heroic, would return to the trail to Bud Divine's Bar, to resupply.

Dedication ceremonies completed, Bob and I felt obliged to return to California, and the one way to do it was aboard a vessel called the *Cristóbal Carrier*, which in those days was the connecting link with the mainland. The *Carrier* was a surplus LST with the bow doors welded closed, a deck of cabins added on the stern, and one still-operable engine. It was half a ship wide and three ships high, with a permanent ten-degree list to the starboard. David Balfour took us out to the *Carrier* at midnight, and we scrambled over sleeping deck passengers to reach our cabin, which measured six feet by six feet six inches, had an upper and lower berth, and a wash basin and pitcher of water. We were out of sight of land the next morning, when cocks crowing and cattle lowing awakened us—they were among our fellow passengers. Bob declared he had sailed in almost everything in the China Sea, but this was a new kind of adventure. Among his many attributes is the important one of being a good sport. The *Carrier* made the crossing successfully, and three days later we left her, at three a.m., in Guayaquil.

Robert Miller is a person of sophistication, as was lovely Lea. Their beautiful home, at the head of Dwight Way in Berkeley, reflects their wide-ranging cultural interests. It was a place where stimulating people came and shared views and experiences.

Robert Miller did not retire from the professional staff of the California Academy of Sciences, and he still visits regularly. His name remains on the masthead of the magazine *Pacific Discovery*, which he started 35 years ago. His book, *The Sea*, was translated and published in four additional languages. Biological and general oceanography, the biology of woodboring organisms, photobiology, and bird behavior and flight continue to be among his principal interests. Robert Cunningham Miller received the highest honor the California Academy of Sciences can bestow, its Fellow's Medal, in 1969.

The dedication of a Pacific Division, AAAS publication about the Galapagos Islands to Robert Cunningham Miller is particularly appropriate. It is an expression of the esteem in which he is held by the members of both the Pacific Division and the California Academy of Sciences.

George E. Lindsay
Director Emeritus
California Academy of Sciences

San Francisco, California
August, 1983

INTRODUCTION

This volume brings together many of the scientific papers first presented at a one-day symposium on the Galapağos Islands, convened by the Pacific Division of the American Association for the Advancement of Science on the campus of San Francisco State University, San Francisco, California, June 13, 1977. These expanded and updated research reports cover such varied topics as the origin and antiquity of the islands, the nature of submarine rift hydrothermal systems, and the evolutionary significance of structural and behavioral diversity in terrestrial plants and animals. The reports should interest scientists from diverse disciplines, including geologists, chemical oceanographers, biogeographers, geneticists, population ecologists, ethologists, and systematists.

The book appears at a propitious time, at the close of the worldwide celebration of the life and works of Charles Robert Darwin. This notorious Englishman brought the concept of organic evolution to the attention of thinking people in a manner that ultimately compelled its almost universal acceptance, certainly among scientists. The revolution of thought that followed publication of the *Origin of Species* in 1859 has been described by Ernst Mayr as perhaps the most fundamental of all intellectual revolutions in the history of humankind. It changed our view of ourselves in the evolutionary scheme of things and gave reason for a retreat from the established anthropocentric view of the world. Darwin also argued that adaptation in organisms results from "blind rules" of Nature, without recourse to "divine intelligence." He opined that variation produces novelties *at random*, but natural selection—biology's most persuasive and pervasive paradigm, first voiced by Alfred Russell Wallace—determines which are preserved. Today, more than a century after the appearance of the *Origin*, biochemical and population genetics are filling in the gaps in Darwin's work by providing the observations and paradigms that make the causes of evolution accessible to reason. Although it was Wallace's genius that unlocked the door to "natural selection," the way in which Darwin melded observation and theory made the notion of "organic evolution" a compelling doctrine, the "pièce de résistance" of human thought.

Darwin's early discoveries about evolution stemmed from observations he made during his world cruise aboard H.M.S. *Beagle*, especially on fossil mammals of Patagonia and the living mockingbirds, finches, and tortoises of the Galapagos Islands. These classic examples of organic evolution are today familiar to laypeople and specialists alike.

The papers assembled in this volume demonstrate how scientists fruitfully continue to study many of the living materials that captivated Darwin's imagination more than a century ago. Surely, no one would be more pleased than Darwin were he able to survey the momentous scientific accomplishments of the last few decades, which have expanded our understanding of the physical and biological forces that shape biotic communities not only in the Galapagos, but everywhere else as well. The Galapagos, a "satellite of the Americas," displays in microcosm the effects of plate tectonics on the formation of volcanic edifices and the appearance of ocean-floor hot springs with their aphotic biological communities of bizarre organisms. The discovery of these communities ranks among the most spectacular scientific surprises of the twentieth century. In the marine and terrestrial zones of photosynthetic activity, a panorama of esthetically pleasing patterns of organic structure and ecological interdependencies has evolved, as deeply impressive to Darwin in 1835 as to those of us today who have been privileged to explore these "treasure islands."

The editors are grateful for the advice given by those scientists who peer-reviewed the papers or who otherwise helped in this volume's own "organic evolution": Michele L. Aldrich, Luis F. Baptista, George A. Bartholomew, Dennis E. Breedlove, Peter R. Grant, Sylvia Hope, Donald E. Kroodsma, Eugene S. Morton, James L. Patton, Frank A. Pitelka, Laurene Ratcliffe, Peter U. Rodda, G. Ledyard Stebbins, and John W. Wright. To them we offer our sincere thanks. For permission to use plant illustrations from *Flora of the Galápagos* by Ira. L. Wiggins and Duncan M. Porter, we thank Mr. William Carver of the Stanford University Press. Penultimately, we appreciatively acknowledge the Executive Committee of the Pacific Division, American Association for the Advancement of Science, for authorizing and funding publication of this volume. And finally to the authors, first for your participation in the symposium and next for your indulgence and faithful weathering of the long process of publication, thank you!

Robert I. Bowman
Margaret Berson
Alan E. Leviton

San Francisco, California
September, 1983

AGES OF THE GALAPAGOS ISLANDS

ALLAN COX

Department of Geophysics, Stanford University, Stanford, CA 94305

The Galapagos Islands are volcanoes that comprise the top of the Carnegie Ridge, a submarine mountain range extending eastward from the Galapagos Islands almost to the mainland. The ridge rests on the Nazca Plate, which grows by accretion along its western and northern edges where it faces the Pacific and Cocos plates. The Galapagos Islands are the youngest part of the Carnegie Ridge and the islands themselves are progressively younger to the west, suggesting that the ridge and the islands reflect the passage of the Nazca Plate over a column of magma rising from deep in the mantle. The first island to emerge above sea level was probably Española or San Cristóbal, although it may have been Santa Cruz, and the date of emergence was probably 3 to 5 million years ago. There is no geologic evidence to suggest that the islands were ever linked to the mainland by an isthmus or chain of islands. In fact, when the first islands emerged above sea level they were located about 200 km farther from the mainland than they are now. The present islands are destined to disappear 20 million years from now as they are subducted into the Chile-Peru Trench.

Isolated islands such as the Galapagos are ideal natural laboratories in which to measure the rate of evolutionary divergence, provided the ages of the islands are known and provided the islands have not been intermittently connected to the mainland by a land bridge or island chain. However, the accuracy with which a rate can be determined depends on the accuracy with which a time interval can be measured. Until the past decade geologists have not known the ages of the islands accurately, nor have we had a theoretical tectonic framework within which to investigate questions such as the relative ages of the islands or whether the islands as a group were once closer to the mainland. The theory of plate tectonics has revolutionized our way of thinking about these problems, and nowhere has plate tectonics served to illuminate the geologic history of a complex part of the globe more successfully than in the Galapagos Islands.

PLATE TECTONIC HISTORY

The geologic history of the Galapagos Islands is closely linked to the history of the Nazca Plate, on which the islands rest, and that of the Cocos Plate a few hundred kilometers to the north (Fig. 1). The Cocos Plate is known from the spacing of dated magnetic anomalies to be moving northward relative to the Nazca Plate at a rate of 60 mm per year (60 km per million years) at the longitude of the Galapagos Islands (Hey et al. 1977). Every million years, a strip of new basaltic sea floor 30 km wide is added to the north edge of the Nazca Plate and a second strip 30 km wide is added to the south edge of the Cocos Plate. The Galapagos rift valley and volcanic spreading center lies between. The process of north-south plate divergence and generation of new ocean floor has been going on here for the past 25 million years (my), prior to which the Cocos and Nazca plates were joined together as the single, unbroken Farallon Plate (Hey 1977).

The rate of divergence between the two plates decreases to the west, the movement being scissors-like with a pivot point located at (0°N, 126°W) (Hey et al. 1977). During the past 25 my as the Cocos and Nazca plates have rotated apart about this pivot point (or "pole of relative

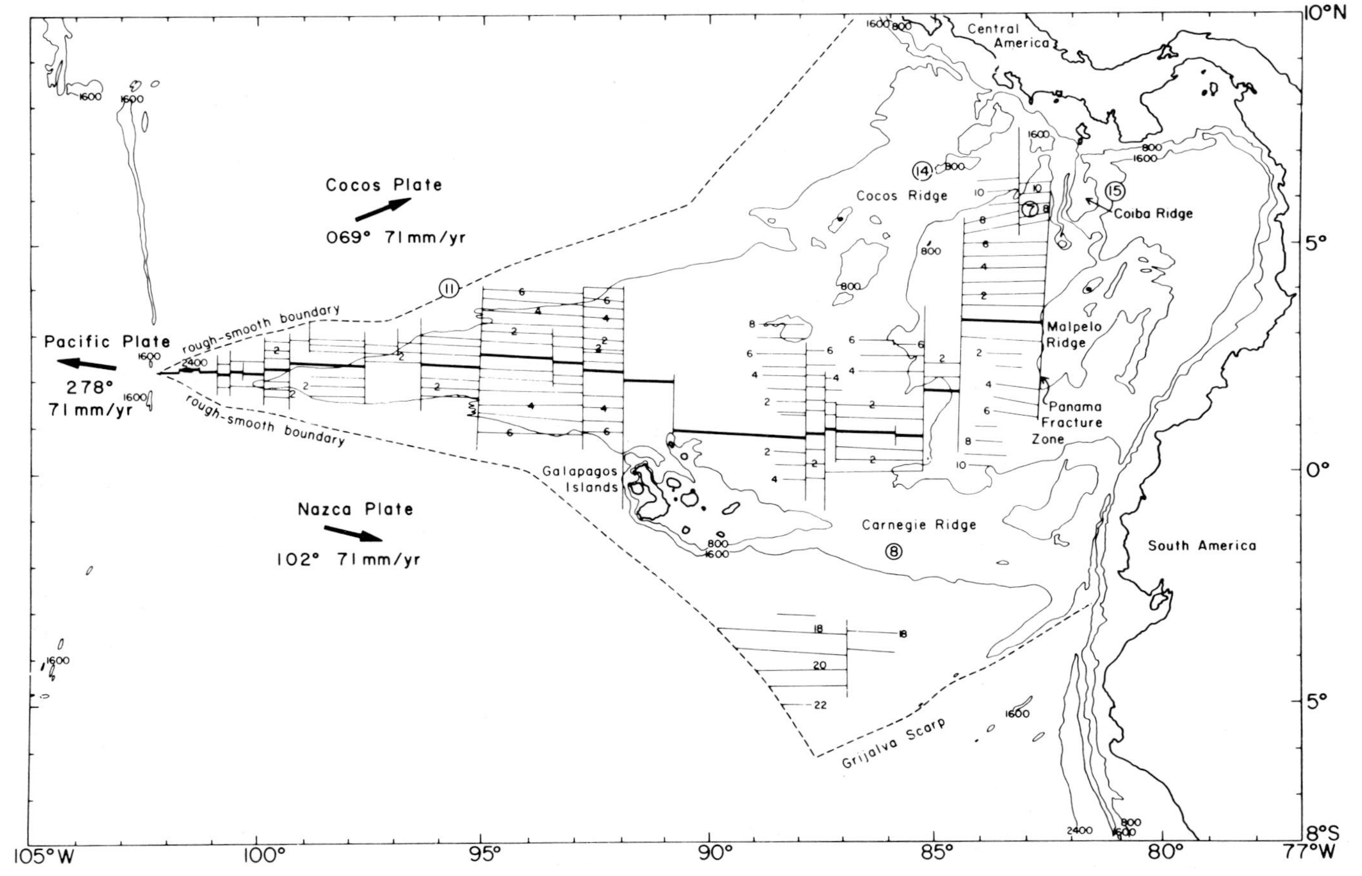

Fig. 1. Tectonic setting of the Galapagos Islands. The heavy, nearly east-west lines north of the Galapagos mark the spreading boundary between the Cocos and Nazca plates, along which new ocean floor is being generated. The light east-west lines are isochrons along which the ocean floor is of constant age, shown in millions of years. (Note that age increases both north and south of the spreading center.) The dashed lines delineate the boundary of the wedge-shaped portion of ocean floor formed as the Nazca and Cocos plates have moved apart during the past 25 million years. From Hey (1977).

motion"), a wedge-shaped segment of basaltic ocean floor 1600 km wide at its base has been generated with its apex toward the west (Fig. 1). Since the Galapagos Islands are located on this wedge of ocean floor, it is not surprising that the history of the islands is linked to that of the Cocos and Nazca plates.

THE CARNEGIE RIDGE, THE COCOS RIDGE, AND HOT SPOTS

The Galapagos Islands are volcanic edifices rising above the Galapagos platform, which comprises the western part of the Carnegie Ridge. The latter is the southern limb of a large V-shaped topographic high with its apex toward the west. The northern limb of the V is the Cocos Ridge. The possibility that these striking geologic features are a subsided land bridge to South and Central America has long intrigued biologists.

The western third of the Carnegie Ridge is the rather flat Galapagos platform, which has an average depth of 600 meters. The ridge terminates steeply on the west along a volcanic escarpment 2800 meters high. Submerged or emergent volcanoes are concentrated toward the western ends of the Cocos and Carnegie ridges but are absent or rare toward the east. Both ridges have gently undulating crests bordered by steep flanks shown by seismic profiling to consist of a sequence of down-faulted blocks with sediment-covered terraces up to 100 km long and 20 km wide (Heath and Van Andel 1973). Extensive oceanographic surveys in this area have found no evidence that the Carnegie and Cocos ridges were ever emergent above sea level nor have the surveys found a chain of submerged, flat-topped volcanoes (guyots) along the ridges, as would be expected of a chain if island steppingstones had once linked the Galapagos Islands to the mainland. Plate tectonic analysis shows that the Nazca Plate is moving eastward into the trench adjacent to the coast of Ecuador at a rate of 50 km per million years, so in the past the islands were somewhat farther from the mainland than they are at present. The islands and their unique fauna will disappear into the trench about 20 million years from now.

Of the theories advanced to explain the origin of the Carnegie and Cocos ridges (Van Andel et al. 1971; Sclater and Klitgord 1973), the one most consistent with my own geologic studies on the Galapagos Islands is the "hot spot" hypothesis. The Cocos and Carnegie ridges are viewed as marking the voluminous outpouring onto the Cocos and Nazca plates of basalt from a deep mantle convective basaltic plume or "hot spot" that remained centered near the Cocos-Nazca spreading center (Morgan 1972; Holden and Dietz 1972; Anderson et al. 1975; Hey 1977). As a plate moves past a plume or hot spot, volcanic eruptions onto the ocean floor build a topographic ridge commonly (but not always) capped by volcanic islands. The age of the ridge increases with distance from the presently active center of volcanism, the archetypical example of a hot spot trace being the submarine ridge and chain of islands extending west from Hawaii. The two diverging hot spot traces, the Carnegie and Cocos ridges, are thought to be a consequence of (1) the proximity of the hot spot to a spreading center and (2) the northeastward and southeastward motions of the two plates. During the past few million years the northern edge of the Nazca Plate has grown as the spreading center has migrated northward, so at present all of the hot spot volcanism in the Galapagos Islands is on the Nazca Plate. The twin hypotheses of plate motions and hot spots predict that the Galapagos Islands should be youngest toward the west and that the Carnegie Ridge is growing by volcanic activity in a westerly direction at a rate of 50 or 60 km per million years. We will see that the geologically determined ages of the Galapagos Islands are consistent with this model.

AGES AND PALEOMAGNETISM OF GALAPAGOS ISLANDS

Field Work

The purpose of the present study was to determine the age relations of the Galapagos Islands using potassium-argon dating, paleomagnetism, and geomorphology. During field trips in 1964,

1965, and 1973, 16 islands were visited including all of the larger islands and most of the smaller ones. In collecting samples for paleomagnetic and dating studies, from six to eight oriented samples were collected from each site visited, using a portable diamond drill. All of the samples collected at one site were from the same lava flow. Most of the sampling was done along the coasts where wave erosion had stripped off the rubbly surfaces of lava flows to expose fresh, undisturbed rock in the interior of the flows, which is ideal material for paleomagnetic purposes. In the following list, the number opposite the name of an island is the number of sites sampled on that island, which in most cases is the number of individual lava flows that was sampled. In a few instances, the same lava flow appears to have been sampled several times inadvertently.

San Salvador	28	Española	15	Pinzón	2
San Cristóbal	27	Pinta	12	Rábida	2
Santa Cruz	21	Isabela	5	Wolf	2
Genovesa	19	Santa Fe	5	Darwin	1
Fernandina	18	Marchena	3		

Determinations of paleomagnetic polarity of all of these sites and potassium-argon dating of a few of them provide the main body of data used in the present study.

Extensive use was also made of air photos and field observations to determine the amount of weathering and erosion, the growth of vegetation, and the development of faulting as measures of the relative ages of the volcanic units. Extensive petrologic and geochemical studies on Galapagos basalts have been made by other workers (McBirney and Williams 1969; Swanson et al. 1974) and were not pursued in the present research. The age relationships determined in the present study are relevant to several of the regional tectonic questions discussed above. When did island-forming volcanic activity begin in the Galapagos? In what direction and at what rate did the center of volcanic activity move? Is this consistent with current estimates of movement of the Nazca Plate? How long did volcanism last on individual islands? This report helps to answer some of these questions and, while reconnaissance in nature, may prove useful in planning more intensive geologic studies of individual islands, such as that of Swanson et al. (1974) on Rábida and Pinzón.

METHODS USED FOR AGE DETERMINATIONS

Magnetic Reversals

The main stratigraphic tool used in determining the ages of the islands was geomagnetic reversal stratigraphy. It is now widely recognized that the earth's magnetic field switches between so-called normal polarity states when it is directed toward the north and reversed polarity states when it is directed toward the south (Cox 1969). The most recent intervals (or epochs) of normal and reversed polarity have the following time boundaries (McDougall 1977).

0.00 million years	
Brunhes Normal Polarity Epoch	Age Group 4 Age Group 3 Age Group 2
0.72 million years	
Matuyama Reversed Polarity Epoch	Age Group 1
2.47 million years	
Gauss Normal Polarity Epoch	Age Group 0

In the present study the six to eight samples collected at each site were all found after suitable magnetic cleaning to invariably have the same magnetic polarity, so that in all cases the magnetic polarity of the site was determined unambiguously. However, lava flows that formed during the time of the Gauss Normal Epoch are identical in their magnetic polarity to lava flows that formed during the Brunhes Normal Polarity Epoch. Potassium-argon dating and geomorphology were used to remove the resultant stratigraphic ambiguity. Within the Brunhes Polarity Epoch, three age subdivisions were made on the basis of the amount of vegetation cover, the degree of weathering and erosion, and the extent of faulting. The basis for assigning lava flows to the individual age groups is as follows, the groups being listed in order of increasing age.

Age Group 4. The coastline where the flow has entered the sea is irregular. Erosion by the surf has been minor, removing only loose debris and, at most, 0.5 m of the flow surface. The color of the flow surface is dark grey or black. There is no vegetation on the flow other than a few solitary small cactus plants on the flow surface and at most a few mangrove trees along the coast.

Age Group 3. The front of the flow where it entered the sea has been moderately trimmed by the sea to form a small scarp 0.5 m to 2 m high. Color of rock surface is brown. There is scattered to moderately dense vegetation, but 20% or more of the original flow surface appears as bare rock on the air photos. Original flow surfaces are generally preserved beneath the vegetation, and there is no indication of stream erosion or soil formation.

Age Group 2. Along the coast, the original irregular outline of the flow has been trimmed by the surf to form a rather smooth coastline. Sea cliffs may have been formed, and small cones near the coast are truncated. The flow may be faulted. On the surface of the lava, original flow features are largely obliterated by small stream channels, or, more commonly, by development of patterned ground produced by wetting and drying of expansive clay. Soil may be present and vegetation is well developed. Magnetic polarity is normal.

Age Group 1. Similar to 2, but the magnetic polarity is reversed; the flow belongs to the Matuyama Reversed Polarity Epoch (2.4 to 0.7 my ago).

Age Group 0. Similar to 1 and 2, but on the basis of geomorphology, stratigraphy or radiometric dating, the flow appears to be older than the Matuyama Reversed Polarity Epoch.

There is a subjective element in assigning lava flows to Groups 2-4, and some overlapping may occur between groups, especially where environmental conditions vary. Rainfall is greater at higher elevations, for example, so that rates of erosion, soil formation, and vegetation growth are greater there. Similarly, lava flows on the south coasts of islands have obviously undergone more wave erosion than flows of the same age on north coasts because the surf runs strongest from the south. An attempt was made to allow for these variations subjectively in assigning flows to age groups. This task was simplified by the fact that most sites were along the arid coast where erosion rates, soil formation, and plant growth are uniformly slow—so slow, in fact, that flows with ages of 0.7 my are distinctly more youthful in appearance than are flows of greater age.

Patterned Ground on Older Surfaces

In flows of Age Groups 2, 1, and 0, the progressive obliteration of small-scale flow-surface morphology is clearly displayed both in air photos and in the field. On young flows (Age Groups 4 and 3) typical volcanic features such as the lateral dikes of channels, arcuate transverse bands, small splatter cones, pahoehoe textures, small collapse pits, and intricate lobate fronts are all visible in sharp relief. The main process by which these volcanic landforms are destroyed in older flows is not erosion by surface run-off, at least not along the arid coastal belt where stream channels are rare and poorly developed. The dominant erosional process appears to be an unusual combination of chemical and mechanical weathering. The first step is formation of an expansive red clay. Because of the low rainfall and porosity of the lava flows, the clay is not eroded. It slowly develops in place until local pockets are sufficiently large to displace jointed blocks of unweathered basalt as the clay wets and expands. The result is the development of patterned ground very similar in its morphology to that formed in the Arctic by the expansion of water on freezing. Stone nets, stone stripes, and terraces all are well developed on the surfaces of older flows in the Galapagos. On Santa Cruz at South Channel, for example, well-developed stone nets occur on the surfaces of two normally magnetized flows sampled (sites G28 and G29) which appear to be nearly contemporaneous. The older flow (G28) has a potassium-argon age of 0.74 ± 0.22 my (Cox and Dalrymple 1966). Both flows are in Age Group 2, having formed near the beginning of the Brunhes Normal Polarity Epoch. The stone nets on the flat surfaces of the flows are up to 50 meters across; high centers consisting almost entirely of red clay are surrounded by linear arrays of basalt boulders up to 1.5 meters long. The normal flows terminate toward the east, exposing an underlying flow (G27) that is reversely magnetized and has a potassium-argon age of 1.47 ± 0.40 my, placing it in Age Group 1. Stone stripes and terraces very similar morphologically to those found in the Arctic are well developed in the gently sloping surface of this older flow. In general the average boulder size is smaller on this than on the adjacent younger flows, and the topography is more subdued. On the air photos the surface patterns have less contrast than on the younger flow. Similar patterns are common on many islands. Wherever there is independent dating evidence, the age of patterned ground is early Brunhes or older. Apparently, half a million years is required to develop enough clay to initiate this process. The time required for development of patterned ground in the arid environment of the Galapagos is thus two orders of magnitude greater than that required in areas with periglacial climates.

RESULTS AND DISCUSSION

Ages of the Islands

Radiometric ages, magnetic polarities, and assignments to age groups are summarized in Table 1. The oldest potassium-argon ages were found in rocks from Española (3.3 my), Santa Fe (2.7 my), and Santa Cruz (4.8 ± 1.8 my), the latter being from the tuff formation on Plazas. On San Cristóbal the oldest radiometric date is 0.7 my; however, erosion is so extensively developed on the southeast part of the island (which was not sampled) that San Cristóbal most likely is a member of the older group of islands erupted prior to 2.4 million years ago.

Islands of intermediate age on which volcanism probably began during the Matuyama Reversed Polarity Epoch are Floreana, Rábida, Pinzón, and Wolf. All of the rocks collected for paleomagnetic and radiometric dating analysis on the remaining islands were extruded during the Brunhes Normal Polarity Epoch, which began 0.7 million years ago. However, as will be discussed later, it is possible that the central cores of some of these islands formed slightly earlier than this.

The age group assignments for all of the islands are shown in Fig. 2, where one symbol is commonly used to represent many different sites of the same polarity. The older group of sites (diamonds) is located toward the east, the intermediate group (open circles) toward the central part of the Galapagos Islands, and the youngest group (solid circles) toward the west. The exception to this generalization is Wolf Island, which together with Darwin lies near the end of a long ridge extending northwest from the Galapagos platform. Quite possibly these two islands and this ridge have a tectonic history different from that of the main group of islands and the Galapagos platform. On the platform, the geologic evidence clearly indicates that volcanic island building migrated westward during the past 3 or 4 million years, as predicated by the hypothesis that the Galapagos Islands are a hot spot trace.

The biologically important question of the time when the islands emerged from the ocean and subsequently remained emergent cannot be answered with assurance for several reasons. One is that the oldest lava flows on some of the islands such as Baltra and Española are nearly flat flows extruded onto wave-planed surfaces. In some cases, the flows were probably emplaced below sea level (McBirney and Williams 1969), and in others the sea may have risen above them after emplacement. The age of the oldest rock presently found on some islands may therefore be older than the age of final emergence of the island above sea level. In other cases, a frosting of young lava may completely mask a core of older rocks inaccessible to the geologists today. In this regard

TABLE 1. RESULTS OF AGE DETERMINATION

Radiometric Age[a]	Magnetic Polarity	Sample Numbers	Paleomagnetic and Geomorphological Age Groups	References
Española			0,1	
3.31±0.36	R	5C987		2
3.04±0.11	N	5C959		2
2.12±0.38	R	5C316		2
San Cristóbal			0(?),1,2,3,4	4
0.66±0.08	R	5C748		2
	N			4
Santa Fe			0,1(?)	2
2.85±0.06		JD1088		2
2.56±0.08		JD1088		2
	N&R			
Santa Cruz and Plazas			0,1,2,3,4(?)	
4.21±1.81		4C238		
1.03±0.78		H70-130		
0.98±0.43		H70-130		2
1.47±0.40	R	G27		1
0.74±0.22	N	G28		1
0.28±0.30	N	G23		1
Baltra			1	
1.37±0.16	R	G11		1
Floreana (Santa Maria)			1,2,3,4,(?)	
0.72±0.40	R	G43		1
	N			
Pinzón			1	
1.09±0.14	N	DH-6J		3
0.98±0.12	N	DH-18B		3
0.94±0.11	R	DH-10B		3
0.93±0.14	R	DH-8B		3
Rábida			1	
1.06±0.17	R	HR-17A		3
1.03±0.05	N	R-2L		3
0.92±0.09	N	HR-14E		3
San Salvador			2,3,4	
0.77±0.12		JL-25		3
0.22±0.15	N	G21		1
0.18±0.04		JL-39		3
0.14±0.21		JL-39		3
	N (all sites)			

[a] Ages in millions of years, ± standard deviations.

TABLE 1. (Continued)

Radiometric Age[a]	Magnetic Polarity	Sample Numbers	Paleomagnetic and Geomorphological Age Groups	References
Genovesa			2,3,4	
	N (all sites)			
Marchena			2,3,4	
0.30±0.10	N	G4		1
	N (all sites)			
Pinta			2,3,4	
	N (all sites)			1
Isabela			2,3,4	
0.09±0.04	N	G14		1
	N (all sites)			
0.50±0.08				5
Fernandina			2(?),3,4	
	N (all sites)			1
Wolf			1	
0.72±1.10	R (2 sites)	4CO75		2
				1
Darwin			2	
	N			1

References:
1. Cox and Dalrymple 1966.
2. Bailey 1976.
3. Swanson et al. 1974.
4. Cox 1971.
5. Nordlie 1973 (no analytical data given).

[a] Ages in million of years, ± standard deviations.

it is interesting to note that both Floreana and Santa Cruz are almost completely covered with lavas younger than 0.7 million years. Fortunately for the geologist, at a few localities along the coasts, older rock strata are presently exposed. It seems likely that islands such as San Salvador (which so far as we know is completely covered with lavas of Brunhes age) emerged from the sea at a time prior to the age of the oldest lavas exposed on the islands today. The conclusions of geologists, like those of other natural historians, are always subject to uncertainty because of the incompleteness of the available historical record.

Duration of Volcanism on Individual Islands

The geologic record is unambiguous about the duration of volcanism on individual islands: in most cases it has continued from the time the volcano first emerged from the sea up to the present time. San Cristóbal, for example, consists of an older volcanic edifice on the south that is probably older than 2.4 million years, joined on the north by an irregular apron of lava flows and

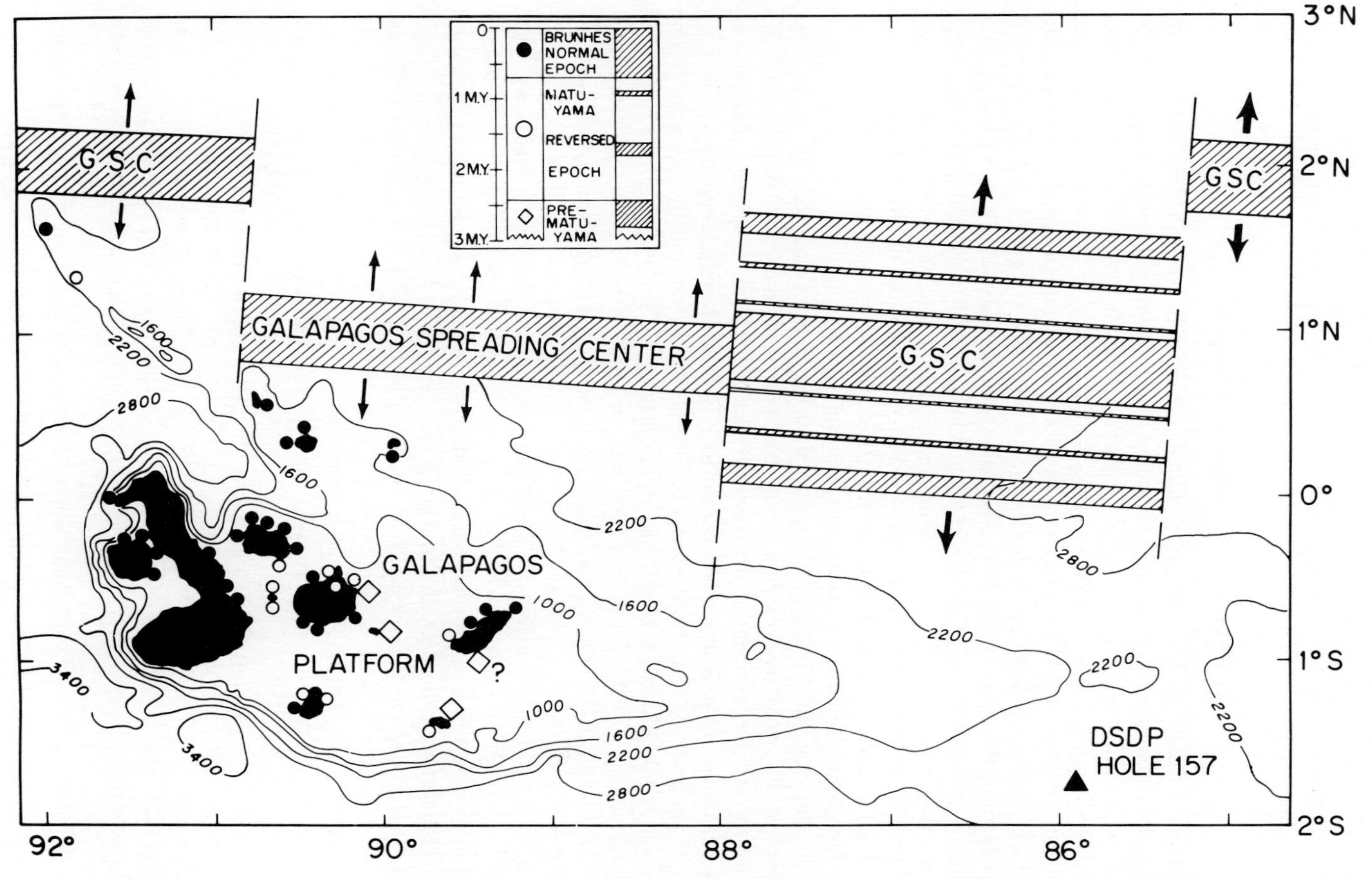

Fig. 2. Ages of Galapagos Islands. Each symbol represents the age of one or more lava flows, with age assignments as indicated in the inset. *Inset*: Times in millions of years (m.y.) when the field was of normal polarity (shaded) and of reversed polarity (unshaded). *GSC*: Central shaded band is the area of new ocean floor formed along the Galapagos Spreading Center between the Nazca and Cocos plates during the Brunhes Normal Polarity Epoch (after Anderson et al. 1975). The adjacent shaded bands shown between 85°W and 88°W are parts of the ocean floor that formed during the two short intra-Matuyama normal polarity intervals shown in the inset. Contour intervals are in meters.

small cones with ages ranging from 0.7 million years up to the present (Cox 1971). The only islands on which volcanism has been extinguished for at least 1 million years are Española, Santa Fe, Rábida, and Pinzón. On the other islands, although the time required for volcano building may be relatively short, volcanic activity has continued for a million years or more. In this regard, the volcanism of the Galapagos Islands is similar to volcanism elsewhere.

Island Ages and the Galapagos Hot Spot

Some additional insight into the probable ages of the islands is provided by the hot spot hypothesis. Consider a point on the deep ocean floor immediately west of the steep escarpment on the western end of the Galapagos platform (Fig. 2). What volcanic history will this point experience if the hot spot theory is correct? As the volcanic escarpment sweeps westward past the point, the onset of volcanic activity will occur quickly. The cessation of volcanic activity will probably occur over a much longer period of time. Considerable irregularity is to be expected in the pattern of volcanism because of the finite width of the hot spot, probably about 150 km in this area, and because the larger volcanic vents are spaced irregularly. However, despite these irregularities, as the process continues the age of the onset of volcanism on individual volcanic islands should systematically increase with distance from the advancing edge of the volcanic platform. Conversely, if the hot spot model is correct, present distance from the western edge of the platform can be used to estimate the age of the onset of volcanism at any point on the platform.

The rate of motion of the Galapagos hot spot as determined from plate tectonic analysis has been 55 mm per year in a westerly direction for the past several million years (Hey et al. 1977). This would place the steep escarpment at the west end of the platform 38 km east of its present position at the beginning of the Brunhes Normal Polarity Epoch. Although reversely magnetized rocks have not as yet been reported from Isabela or Fernandina, it seems likely that some of the large volcanoes which comprise these islands had emerged from the sea by this time, as suggested in Fig. 3, although perhaps not all of them had. However, we know with certainty that Rábida and Pinzón existed as islands 0.7 million years ago, so the edge of the platform lay to the west of these two islands.

Again assuming a hot spot velocity of 55 mm per year, the location of the edge of the platform 2.4 million years ago was 132 km east of its present position, which would place it near Santa Cruz Island as shown in Fig. 4. Note that at that time, the older islands were much closer to the Galapagos Spreading Center (GSC in Fig. 4).

It is instructive to explore the consequences of assuming that the hot spot model works on the micro as well as the macro scale, so that given the distance x of an island from the advancing volcanic front and given the hot spot velocity v, one can find the age of the island simply as $t=x/v$. Using a velocity of 55 mm per year gives the following ages in millions of years for the islands.

	Calculated Age	Oldest Measured Age
San Cristóbal	4.5	(0.7)
Española	4.1	3.3
Santa Fé	3.3	2.7
Santa Cruz	2.7	4.2 ± 1.8

A better fit to the oldest ages on Española and Santa Fe is obtained by setting v=68 mm per year:

	Calculated Age	Oldest Measured Age
San Cristóbal	3.7	(0.7)
Española	3.4	3.3
Santa Fe	2.7	2.7
Santa Cruz	2.2	4.2 ± 1.8

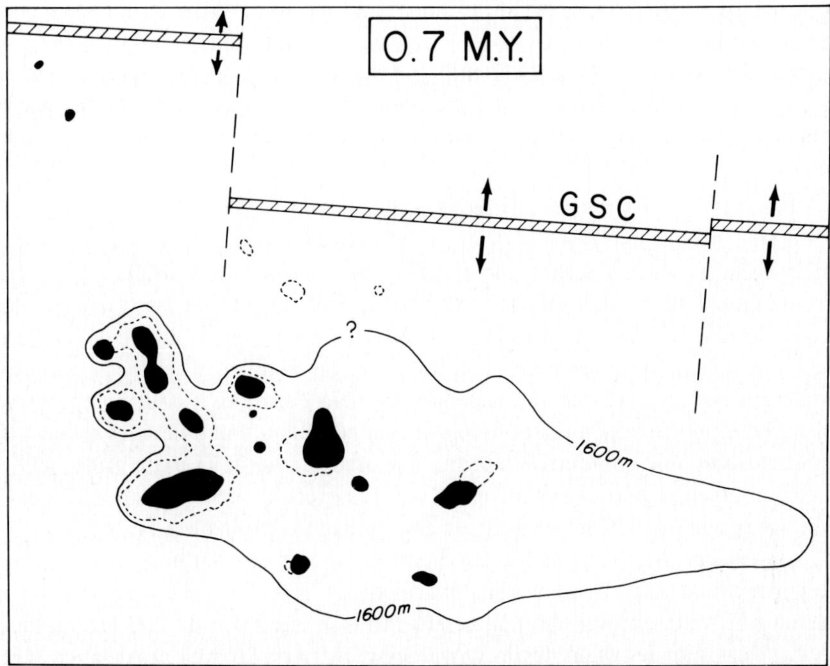

Fig. 3. Cartoon showing the estimated location of the 1600-meter isobath around the Galapagos platform as it may have appeared 0.7 million years ago. Whether any or all of the volcanoes of Fernandina and Isabela were emergent above sea level at this time is uncertain.

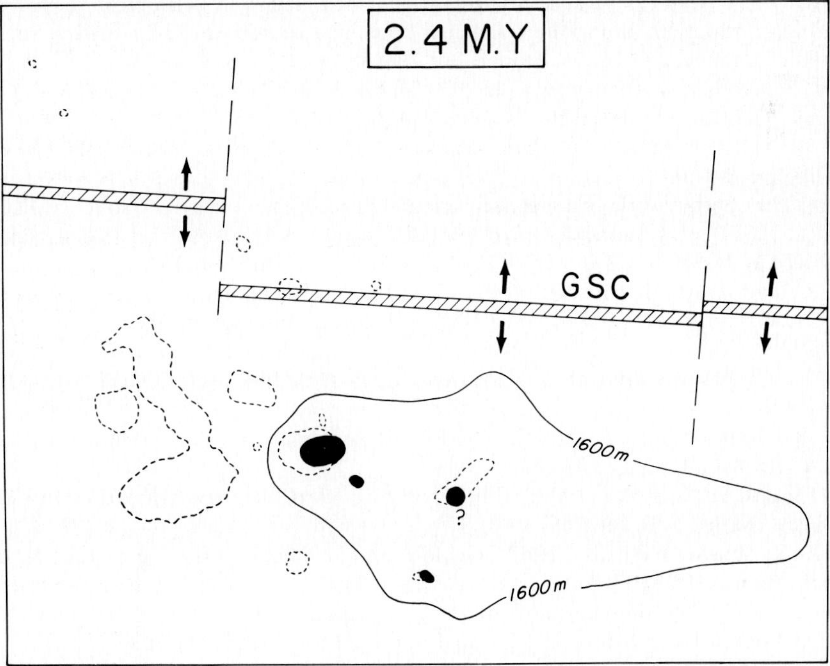

Fig. 4. Cartoon showing the estimated location of the 1600-meter isobath 2.4 million years ago. Note that the ocean floor on which the younger, more northerly islands presently rest did not exist at this time.

Although 68 mm per year is faster than the rate of 55 mm per year inferred from recent plate motions, it falls within the range of 61 to 133 mm per year inferred (Hey 1977) from the age of basalt encountered in Hole 157 (Fig. 2) (Heath and Van Andel 1973), assuming that the hot spot moved at a constant rate from Hole 157 to the present western edge of the Galapagos platform. The two sets of calculated ages bracket what I regard as the most likely ages of the oldest rocks on these islands.

RESUMEN

Las Islas Galápagos son volcanes que constituyen la cima de la Cordillera Carnegie, esta es una cadena montañosa submarina que se extiende hacia el oriente de las Galápagos, casi hasta tierra firme. La cordillera descansa en la Placa de Nazca, la cual crece por adición a lo largo de sus lados occidental y boreal en donde limita con las placas del Pacífico y de Cocos respectivamente. Las Islas Galápagos son la parte más joven de la Cordillera Carnegie, las islas son progresivamente más jovenes hacia el poniente, sugiriendo que tanto la cordillera como las islas reflejan el paso de la placa de Nazca sobre una columna de magma que asciende desde la parte profunda del manto. La primera isla en emerger por sobre el nivel del mar fué probablemente Española ó San Cristóbal, aunque pudo haber sido Santa Cruz, la fecha de emergencia fué probablemente hace 3 a 5 millones de años. No hay evidencias geológicas que sugieran que las islas estuvieron alguna vez conectadas a tierra firme por medio de algún istmo ó alguna cadena de islas. En realidad, cuando las primeras islas emergieron por sobre el nivel del mar, se encontraban alrededor de 200 km más alejadas de tierra firme. Las islas actuales estan destinadas a desaparecer en 20 millones de años al subducirse en la trinchera Chile-Peru.

LITERATURE CITED

Anderson, R. N., D. A. Clague, K. D. Klitgord, M. Marshall, and R. K. Hishimori. 1975. Magnetic and petrologic variations along the Galapagos spreading center and their relation to the Galapagos melting anomaly. Geol. Soc. Amer. Bull. 86:683-694.

Bailey, K. 1976. Potassium-argon ages from the Galapagos Islands. Science 192:465-467.

Cox, A. 1969. Geomagnetic reversals. Science 163(3864):237-245.

Cox, A. 1971. Paleomagnetism of San Cristobal Island, Galapagos. Earth and Planetary Sci. Letters 11(2):152-160.

Grim, P. J. 1970. Bathymetric and magnetic anomaly profiles from a survey south of Panama and Costa Rica: U.S. Dept. Commerce, Environmental Science Services Administration, ESSA Tech. Memo. ERLTM-AOML 9:1-87.

Heath, G. R., and Tj. H. Van Andel. 1973. Tectonics and sedimentation in the Panama basin: Geologic results of Leg 16. Deep Sea Drilling Project, Washington, D.C. U.S. Govt. Printing Office 16:899-913.

Hey, R. 1977. Tectonic evolution of the Cocos Nazca spreading center. Geol. Soc. Amer. Bull. 88:1404-1420.

Hey, R. G., L. Johnson, and A. Lowrie. 1977. Recent plate motions in the Galapagos area. Geol. Soc. Amer. Bull. 88:1385-1403.

Holden, J. C., and R. S. Dietz. 1972. Galapagos gore, NazCoPac triple junction and Carnegie/-Cocos ridges. Nature 235:266-269.

McBirney, A. R., and H. Williams. 1969. Geology and petrology of the Galapagos Islands. Geol. Soc. Amer. Mem. 118:1-197.

McDougall, I. 1977. The present status of the geomagnetic polarity time scale. Publ. No. 1288, Research School of Earth Sciences, Australian National University. 34 pp.

Morgan, W. J. 1972. Plate motions and deep mantle convection. Geol. Soc. Amer. Mem. 132: 7-22.

Nordlie, B. E. 1973. Morphology and structure of the western Galapagos volcanoes and a model for their origin. Geol. Soc. Amer. Bull. 84:2931-2956.

Sclater, J. G., and K. D. Klitgord. A detailed heat flow, topographic and magnetic survey across the Galapagos spreading center at 96°W. J. Geophys. Res. 87:6951-6975.

Swanson, F. J., H. W. Baitis, J. Lexa, and J. Dymond. 1974. Geology of Santiago, Rabida, and Pinzon Islands, Galapagos. Geol. Soc. Amer. Bull. 85:1803-1810.

Van Andel, Tj. H., G. R. Heath, B. T. Malfait, D F. Heinrichs, and J. I. Ewing. 1971. Tectonics of the Panama basin, eastern equatorial Pacific. Geol. Soc. Amer. Bull. 82:1489-1508.

THE THERMAL SPRINGS OF THE GALAPAGOS RIFT: Their Implications for Biology and the Chemistry of Sea Water

JOHN B. CORLISS
School of Oceanography, Oregon State University, Corvallis, OR 97331

Exploration of submarine hydrothermal activity on and near the Galapagos Rift, involving the use of the Deep Submersible ALVIN, has provided a wealth of new information regarding these hydrothermal systems. Analysis of water samples from these vents reveals that the process provides significant sources and sinks for several components of sea water. Studies of conductive and convective heat transfer suggest that in the first million years, two-thirds of the heat loss from the oceanic lithosphere at the Galapagos Rift may have been vented from thermal springs, predominantly along the axial high within the rift valley. The vent areas are populated by unique animal communities, which, rather than photosynthesize, appear to chemosynthesize by using sulfur-oxidizing bacteria to derive their energy supply from seawater-rock reactions at high temperature.

An important feature of the tectonic fabric of that part of the oceanic crust in which the Galapagos Islands have evolved is the Galapagos Rift, an ocean crust spreading center that trends across the Panama Basin between the Cocos Ridge and the Carnegie Ridge (Fig. 1). Along this spreading center, the two adjacent crustal plates are separating at a combined rate of 7 cm per year. This spreading is accompanied by the upwelling, from some 60 to 100 km below, of viscous rock that makes the "low-velocity" layer, which decouples the rigid lithospheric plates of the earth's surface from the mantle beneath. The release of pressure on this material as it rises leads to the melting of the low-melting components of these rocks, producing liquid of basaltic composition that separates to form the ~5-km thick oceanic crust. The oceanic crust is remarkably uniform in composition and structure, both in the oceans and wherever it is exposed for study, primarily in ophiolite complexes on the continents. To a significant extent, this structure, presented in Fig. 2, is determined by the process that removes most of the heat from this crust: the convective circulation of sea water through fissures and fractures that form as the magma solidifies and cools. The convective cooling and fracturing are in fact coupled in a feedback cycle (cooling induces fracturing, which enhances cooling) that produces a striking phenomenon, a transient flow of warm water from the ocean floor–the ascending plumes of these convective systems, which accompany episodes of active volcanism along the rift. Evidence suggests that these thermal springs are essentially ubiquitous along the global mid-ocean rift system.

In early 1977, an expedition utilizing the deep submersible ALVIN first explored these submarine hydrothermal systems and carried out a broad-based study of several aspects of the phenomena (Corliss et al. 1979), as exemplified by the hot springs along the Galapagos Rift (Fig. 1). Venting of heated sea water was found in four vent areas along the axial ridge within the axial valley. The hydrothermal fluids flow from the rocks at temperatures from 10 to 17°C, with measured flow rates of 20 to 10 cm/sec, and form large plumes that drift horizontally in the bottom currents. These were detected up to 150 m above the bottom where the temperature anomaly had dropped to 0.01°C.

Samples of the fluids were collected and results of the extensive analytical program have

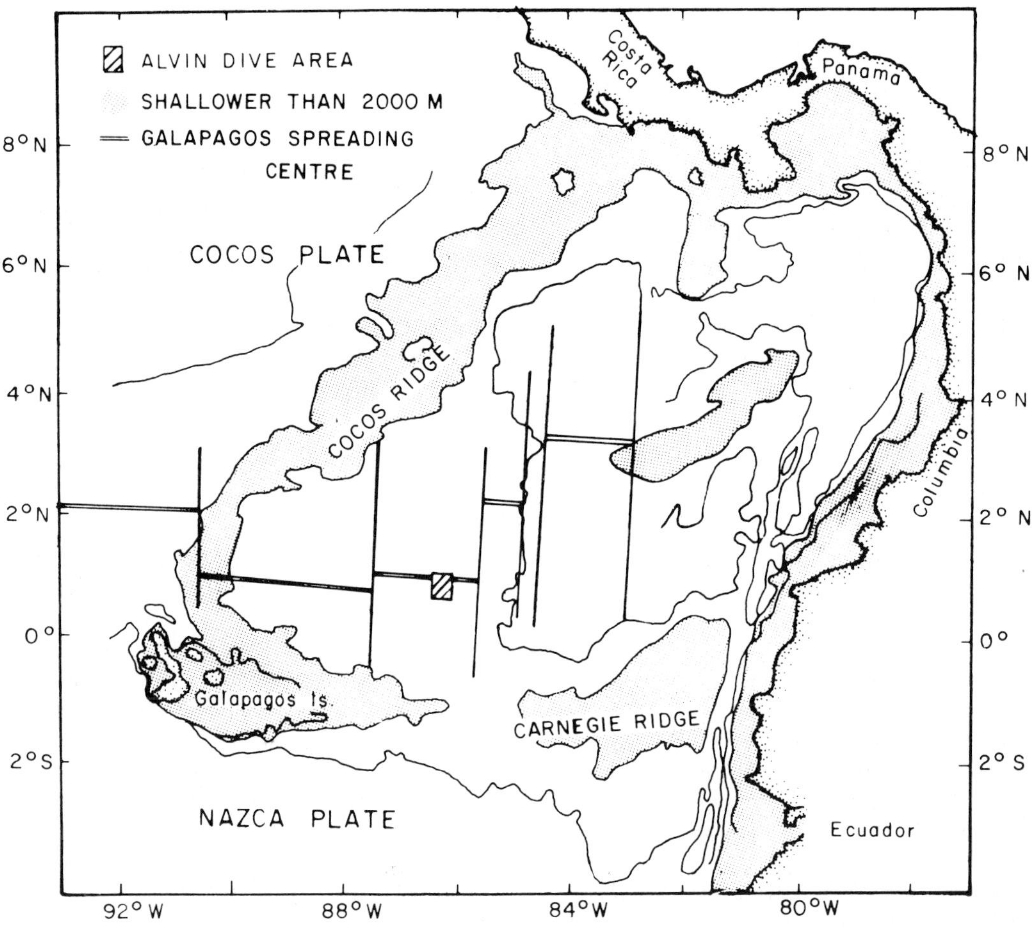

Fig. 1. Index map to Galapagos Rift Thermal Springs. The ALVIN dives were made to the 2500-meter deep axis of the Galapagos Rift 200 miles from the Galapagos Islands. The Cocos and Nazca plates are separating along this line where new oceanic crust is forming.

been reported (Corliss et al. 1979a; Jenkins et al. 1978; Edmond et al. 1979a,b; Corliss et al. 1979b). Jenkins et al. (1978), assuming that the known global flux of primordial ^{3}He from the oceans to the atmosphere and into space is all from the mid-ocean ridges and that the Galapagos springs are representative, used the nearly constant ratio of heat to ^{3}He in the Galapagos Rift fluids to deduce the global flux of heat extracted from the newly forming oceanic crust by circulating sea water. The result, 5×10^{19} calories per year, is in surprising agreement with estimates made from heat flow measurements, which range from 2.4 to 6.5×10^{19} calories per year (Anderson et al. 1977; Williams and von Herzen 1974; Wolery and Sleep 1976).

Given this relationship, the heat-to-mass ratios for various components in the hydrothermal fluids can be used to deduce the global hydrothermal fluxes of several elements (Corliss et al. 1979a; Edmond et al. 1979a). These data indicate that submarine hydrothermal activity plays a dominant role in regulating the steady-state composition of sea water for magnesium, sulfate, manganese, lithium and rubidium, and contributes significantly to the sea-water concentrations of calcium, potassium, barium, and silicon. Magnesium is removed from sea water and stored in the crust by the process, resolving the long-standing problem of balancing in river flux of this element into the oceans (Corliss et al. 1979a). Sulfur is reduced to hydrogen sulfide by reactions with the

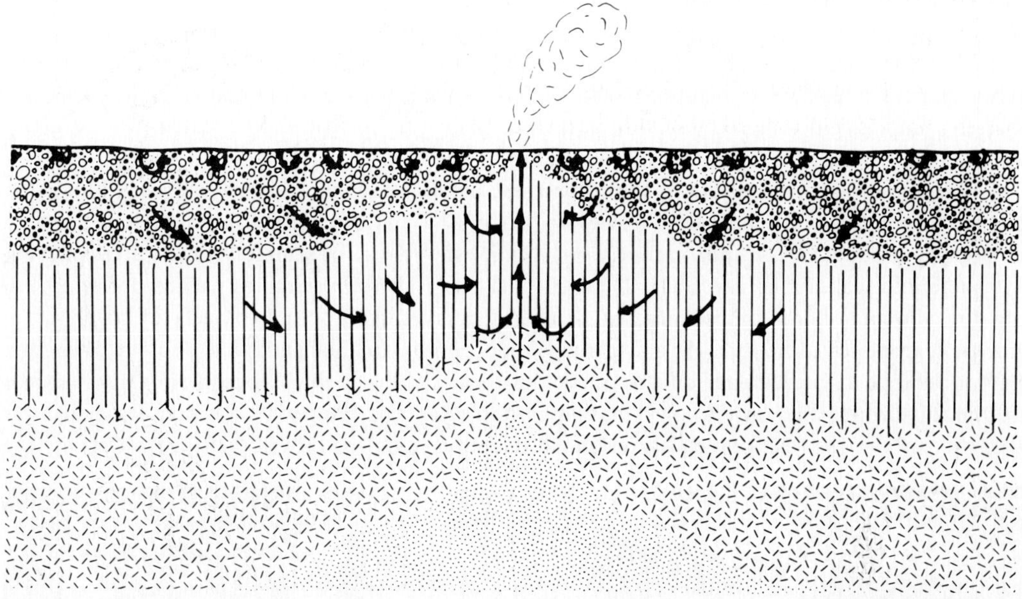

Fig. 2. Cross section of oceanic crust at a spreading center. The upper layer of basaltic lava flows, increasing in thickness away from the spreading axis, is underlain in turn by the dike complex, gabbro, and the magma chamber (stippled). An eruption is initiated by upward doming of magma and horizontal tension in the direction of spreading, resulting in the opening of fissures that fill with lava (forming dikes) and extrusion onto the surface. Sea water in the permeable crust is heated to form convective circulation, which cools the dikes and the underlying magma chamber, plating the gabbro out on its upper surface.

ferrous iron in silicate minerals in the basalt. This reaction commonly produces a montmorillonite-type clay mineral, saponite, which incorporates magnesium and hydroxl ion from the sea water, reducing its pH (Bischoff and Dickson 1975). Saponite is abundant in hydrothermally altered mid-ocean ridge basalts (Humphris and Thompson 1978), and particles of saponite have tentatively been identified in samples filtered *in situ* from the Galapagos Rift vent waters. The remaining elements are leached from the crust and added to sea water.

Three different geochemical indicators suggest that the fluids last equilibrated with the rocks at depth at a temperature of approximately 300°C (Corliss et al. 1979a; Edmond et al. 1979a,b). The data for silica, magnesium, and sulfate fall on mixing lines with temperature that can be extrapolated to high temperatures. Both the magnesium and sulfate extrapolate to zero concentration at about 300°C, while the silica intersects the silica saturation curve at the same temperature. We can use this result, along with the estimate of the total global flux of heat from mid-ocean ridge hydrothermal systems and the heat capacity of the water, to estimate mass of water per year equilibrating with rock at 300°C. This mass is 1.67×10^{17} gm/year. Given the ocean volume, $1.35 \times 10^9 km^3$, this means that a mass of water equal to the mass of the ocean cycles through the crust and is heated to 300°C every 8 million years at the present rate. Thus in the history of the oceans, if we assume they have existed for at least 3.5 billion years, at the present rate they have cycled through the oceanic crust over 400 times.

While the importance of the chemistry of the fluids was anticipated, it took some time to acquire the data and interpret it. The impact of the biological observations, on the other hand, was more immediate and more profound. On the first dive, as we entered the first area of thermal vents, we discovered that the fluids streamed up from the natural openings between the rocks, and that these spaces were occupied by living animals, large brown mussels 10 to 15 cm long, and white clams 15 to 30 cm in length (Fig. 3). On subsequent dives we located three additional vent areas (Fig. 4), each of which had a unique active population of animals. We made collections of those animals amenable to sampling with ALVIN's mechanical arm, primarily large clams and mussels, limpets and tube worms; took numerous photographs; and also collected water samples and filtered suspended water for biological studies.[1]

Many important observations regarding these communities must await studies by biologists, but we can provide a reasonable answer to the most significant question: what is the source of primary productivity supporting these communities? Analysis of samples of the water collected for bacteriological studies revealed 10^8 to 10^9 per cm^3. These bacteria, as well as bacteria from the gut contents of frozen specimens of clams and mussels, were found to be facultatively autotrophic, capable of utilizing H_2S, and perhaps reduced iron and manganese, as a source of energy. Carbon isotope measurements on the mussel soft parts showed them to contain carbon that is isotopically lighter than any known marine carbon (Rau and Hedges 1979), suggesting strongly that the carbon was fractionated bacteriologically, supporting the notion that the bacteria are the

Fig. 3. ALVIN photograph in the Clambake vent area. The submarine's mechanical arm is inserting the water sampling probe, with attached thermistor, into the flow of 10°C water coming from the vent. The milky suspended precipitate is elemented sulfur; the waters are also heavily laden with bacteria. The large clams and mussels dominate the Clambake area, filtering bacteria from the warm water flowing past them. Nearly all of the animals found are new species, genera, or families (photo by ALVIN automatic camera).

[1] The clams were classified by K. Boss, Harvard University; the mussels by V. Kenk, San Jose State University; the limpets by J. McLean, Los Angeles County Museum of Natural History; the pogonophorans by M. Jones, National Museum of Natural History; and the fish photographs were examined by D. Cohen, National Fisheries Service, NOAA. Bacteriological studies were carried out by John Baross, Oregon State University.

Fig. 4. Sampling hydrothermal fluids in the Oyster Bed. Large Pogonophora are attached to the rocks surrounding the vent, and live in the streams of warm bacteria-laden water. These tube worms, the limpets and serpulid worms on the rocks, and small mussels of the same species as in the Clambake are the dominant filter feeders here. Each of the four vent areas, separated by 200-700 meters, had a unique community of organisms (photo by John Edmond).

basic food source for these communities. The source of the carbon is also unique. Mid-ocean ridge basalt magmas have been shown to contain from 800 to 2300 ppm of dissolved CO_2, primordial carbon, which accreted into the earth's mantle from the solar nebula. During the cooling and interaction of these magmas with sea water, the CO_2 is extracted into the water, and appears in the hydrothermal fluids (Corliss et al. 1979). (It is important to note that this carbon [$\delta C^{13} \simeq -5$, (J. O'Neil, pers. comm.)] is isotopically lighter than sea water CO_2 [$\delta C^{13} = 0$], but this difference is not large enough to account for the fractionation observed in the mussels.) Several aspects of the problem are being investigated further, but it seems likely that these are the first known animal communities that do not depend on solar energy photosynthesis for their primary production. Rather they derive their energy from the products of chemical reactions between the sea water and rocks driven by heat from the interior of the earth (Corliss et al. 1979).

An interesting question for further speculation regarding these submarine hydrothermal systems concerns their possible role, early in the earth's history, in providing a site for the abiotic synthesis of complex carbon compounds necessary for the origin of life (Oparin 1957). Though the existence of plate tectonic processes in the first billion years of the earth's history cannot be established, the occurrence of submarine volcanic activity is likely. Cooling by convective circulation of sea water is an integral part of the process emplacing volcanic rocks on the sea floor.

The following conditions within the hydrothermal system seem relevant:

1. The high temperature fluids at depth are highly reducing and may reach

temperatures approaching the magma temperatures (~1000°C) in isolated zones. Reduced gases including hydrogen sulfide and hydrogen (Corliss et al. 1979) are present in the fluids. Methane may be produced by reduction of carbon dioxide; perhaps ammonia could be produced by the reaction of hydrogen and sea-water nitrate. Thus these mid-ocean ridge systems provide an extensive reducing environment in the presence of an oxidizing atmosphere. The existence of oxygen in the atmosphere has been thought to preclude such abiotic synthesis (Urey 1952).

2. This fluid rises and mixes with cold oxygen-bearing sea water as it percolates through the fractured permeable crustal rocks. Thus a continuous gradient of temperature (down to ~2°C) and chemistry is established in these systems, and removal of the products from the site of reaction is provided for. Both of these latter conditions are considered essential for abiotic synthesis (Fox and Dose 1979).

3. The walls of these fractures are lined with alteration minerals, the most common of which is saponite. Anders et al. (1973) have shown that such montmorillonite minerals can serve as effective catalysts in a special set of reactions designed to reproduce the condensation behavior of carbon from the solar nebula. They produced a wide range of relevant compounds including amino acids. Although the specific reactions they studied (Fischer-Tropsch synthesis, reactions of carbon monoxide with hydrogen) may not be relevant to submarine thermal springs, the behavior of the clay mineral that is ubiquitous in such systems as an effective catalyst may well be.

The possibility of abiotic synthesis of "organic" compounds in sea-water hydrothermal systems in the primitive ocean remains to be established. The influence of hydrogen sulfide in the systems is not clear; our understanding of the abiotic carbon and nitrogen chemistry of such systems is complicated by the presence of extensive colonization of the walls of the modern systems by bacteria; and the chemistry and physics of the high temperature regions of the systems remain to be clarified. Future studies of these systems can be designed to answer many of these questions.

RESUMEN

Las exploraciones submarinas de la actividad hidrotérmica realizadas, incluyendo el uso del sumergible ALVIN, sobre y en los alrrededores de la grieta de Galápagos han contribuido con nueva información acerca de estos sistemas hidrotérmicos. Los análisis de las muestras de agua de estas grietas submarinas revelan que la actividad hidrotérmica da origen a muchos de los compuestos existentes en el agua del mar. Los estudios de la transferencia de calor de conducción y de convección sugieren que en los primeros millones de años, las dos tercera parte de la pérdida de calor de la litosfera oceánica en la grieta de Galápagos pudo haberse originado de los manantiales térmicos, localizados principalmente a lo largo de la cima de la cresta en el valle de la grieta. Estas grietas estan pobladas por comunidades de animales únicas, las cuales parecen utilizar quimosintesis en lugar de fotosintesis para la obtención de energía, por medio de bacterias que oxidan el azufre de reacciones a alta temperatura de las rocas y del agua de mar.

LITERATURE CITED

Anders, E., R. Hayatsu, and M. H. Studier. 1973. Organic compounds in meteorites. Science 182:781-790.

Anderson, R. M., M. G. Langseth, and J. G. Sclater. 1977. The mechanism of heat transfer through the floor of the Indian Ocean.

Bischoff, J. L., and F. W. Dickson. 1975. Seawater-basalt interaction at 200 C and 500 bars:

Implications for origin of sea floor heavy-metal deposits and regulation of seawater chemistry. Earth Plan. Sci. Lett. 25:385-397.

Corliss, J. B., J. Dymond, L. I Gordon, J. M. Edmond, R. P. von Herzen, R. D. Ballard, K. Green, D. Williams, A. Bainbridge, K. Crane, and Tj. H. van Andel. 1979a. Science 203:1073-1083.

Corliss, J. B., M. Edmond, and L. I. Gordon. 1979b. Some implications of heat/mass ratios in Galapagos Rift hydrothermal fluids for models of seawater rock interaction and the formation of oceanic crust. Pages 391-402 *in* Deep Drilling Results in the Atlantic Ocean. Proc. 2nd Ann. Ewing Symp. Amer. Geophys. Union 2.

Edmond, J. M., C. Measures, R. E. McDuff, L. H. Chan, R. Collier, B. Grant, L. I. Gordon, and J. B. Corliss. 1979a. Ridge crest hydrothermal activity: The Galapagos data. Earth. Plan. Sci. Lett. 46:19-30.

Edmond, J. M., C. Measures, B. Magrum, B. Grant, F. R. Sclater, R. Collier, A. Hudson, L. I. Gordon, and J. B. Corliss. On the formation of metal rich deposits at ridge crests. Earth Plan. Sci. Lett. 46:1-18.

Fox, S. W., and K. Dose. 1979. Molecular evolution and the origin of life. Marcel Dekker Inc., New York, N. Y.

Humphris, S. E., and G. Thompson. 1978. Hydrothermal alteration of oceanic basalts by seawater. Geochim. Cosmochim. Acta 42:107-125.

Jenkins, W. J., J. M. Edmond, J. B. Corliss. 1978. Excess He-3 and He-4 in Galapagos submarine hydrothermal waters. Nature (London) 272:156-158.

Rau, G. M., and G. I. Hedges. 1979. Carbon-13 depletion in a hydrothermal vent mussel: Suggestion of a chemosynthetic food source. Science 203:648-649.

Urey, H. C. 1952. On the early chemical history of the earth and the origins of life. Proc. Nat'l. Acad. Sci. U.S.A. 38:351-363.

Williams, D. L., and R. P. von Herzen. 1974. Heat loss from the earth: New estimate. Geology 2:327-328.

Wolery, T. J., and N. H. Sleep. 1976. Hydrothermal circulation and geochemical flux at mid-ocean ridges. J. Geol. 84:249-275.

ADDENDUM

A more complete description of this model for the origin of life is presented in Corliss et al. (1981). These hot springs are beautiful examples of powerful natural dissipative structures (Prigogine 1978), the spaces in our second law of thermodynamics universe where order is created.

LITERATURE CITED

Corliss, J. B., J. A. Baross, and S. E. Hoffman. 1981. An hypothesis concerning the relationship between submarine hot springs and the origin of life on Earth. Oceanologica Acta 1981:59-69.

Prigogine, I. 1978. Time, structure, and fluctuations. Science 201:777-785.

VASCULAR PLANTS OF THE GALAPAGOS: ORIGINS AND DISPERSAL

DUNCAN M. PORTER
Dept. of Biology, Virginia Polytechnic Institute & State University, Blacksburg, VA 24061

An attempt is made to quantify the geographical relationships of the Galapagos vascular plants and to determine their most likely methods of dispersal. The affinities of the vascular flora are mainly with adjacent South America. Birds probably have played the most important role in the dispersal of vascular plants to the islands, with man, wind, and oceanic drift playing lesser roles.

The close relationship of the Galapagos biota to continental America was recognized from the beginning of biological studies on the archipelago: "From the presence of the Opuntias and some other plants, the vegetation partakes more of the character of that of [South] America than of any other country . . . I will not here attempt to come to any definite conclusions, as the species have not yet been accurately examined; but we may infer, that, with the exception of a few wanderers, the organic beings found on this archipelago are peculiar to it; and yet their general form strongly partakes of an [South] American character." (Darwin 1839:460, 474).

The first paper to study the geographic relationships of the flora in detail was that of J. D. Hooker (1847b), which was based on Darwin's collections. Discussion of the flora's relationships in the second edition of the "Voyage of the *Beagle*" (Darwin 1845:395), in fact, was based on information supplied by Hooker. Hooker's flora (1847a) described 253 species of flowering plants and ferns from the archipelago, the majority collected by Darwin. His insights into floristic relationships and dispersal mechanisms remain impressive to this day. If more attention had been paid to Hooker's indication of the basic disharmony of the flora, the long controversy over whether the islands are oceanic or were attached to the continents by land bridges (see Vinton 1951; Croizat 1952:254) might have been avoided.

In essence, Hooker (1847b:235) found that the flora could be divided into two elements: "the peculiar or new species being for the most part allied to plants of the cooler parts of America, or the uplands of the tropical latitudes, whilst the non-peculiar are the same as abound chiefly in the hot and damper regions, as the West Indian islands and the shores of the Gulf of Mexico . . ." Hooker's "peculiar" element corresponds to what in the present paper is termed the Andean element, while his "non-peculiar" element corresponds to the Tropical American and Pantropical elements. These are the three largest indigenous elements in the vascular flora (Table 1). Hooker also pointed out the importance of man as a vector for plant introductions. He concluded (Hooker 1847b:253) that, "The means of transport which may have introduced these plants are, oceanic and aërial currents, the passage of birds, and man." These four methods of introduction also are concluded to be of importance in the present paper, although herein the importance of natural methods is reversed.

N. J. Andersson (1855) indicated that a number of species in the flora have pantropical distributions, an element not stressed by Hooker. In general, however, he corroborated Hooker's findings as to geographical relationships and methods of dispersal. Andersson's study was based on his own collections, which swelled the known angiosperm flora of the islands to 333 species.

Following these two pioneer papers on the ecology and relationships of Galapagos vegetation, botanical studies to the present (Robinson and Greenman 1895; Robinson 1902; Stewart

TABLE 1. GEOGRAPHICAL RELATIONSHIPS OF THE INDIGENOUS VASCULAR PLANTS OF THE GALAPAGOS ISLANDS[1,2]

	Endemic	Tropical America	Pantropical	Andean	Caribbean	Mexico and Central America	North America	South America	Total
Pteridophytes	8	52 (3)[3]	18 (2)	22 (1)	6	1 (2)			107
Monocots	18 (12)	35 (4)	23 (1)	5 (5)	4 (1)			(1)	85
Dicots	205 (96)	64 (26)	35 (1)	39 (43)	6 (4)	2 (3)	(3)	(1)	351
Total	231	151	76	66	16	3			543
Percentage	43%	28%	14%	12%	3%	1%			

[1] Geographical areas are defined as follows: Endemic (occurring only in the Galapagos Islands); Tropical America (distributed generally in the American tropics); Pantropical (distributed in both the Old and New World tropics); Andean (occurring only in western South America from Venezuela to Chile, generally or in part); Caribbean (occurring in the West Indies and often also on the edges of the surrounding continents); Mexico and Central America (occurring only in Mexico and/or Central America, rarely also to northern Colombia and Venezuela); North America (occurring in the southwestern United States and adjacent northern Mexico); South America (occurring only in extra-Andean South America).

[2] The figures in Table 1 differ in some respects from those in my previous paper (Porter 1976). This is due to several factors: (1) more taxa have been added from the reports of Adsersen (1976a, 1976b) and van der Werff (1977) and from my own research on the flora; (2) the endemics have not been considered separately from the rest of the indigenous flora, thus giving a more accurate account of geographical relationships; and (3) the geographical distributions of many taxa have been refined. Two examples of the latter may be given. In my previous paper, species that occur in the West Indies and northern South America were placed in the Tropical American category; now they are placed there only if their distributions extend southward to Ecuador. Secondly, species originally from the American tropics that have been spread by man to become pantropical in distribution were placed in the Pantropical category; now they are reckoned as Tropical American. Such changes serve to more accurately represent the flora's relationships.

[3] Figures in parentheses indicate the number of introductions from each geographic area that have resulted in the present endemic flora.

1911, 1915; Svenson 1935, 1942, 1946a; van Balgooy 1960; Wiggins 1966; Porter 1976) have continued to provide evidence for Hooker's hypotheses. In a series of papers, Svenson (1935, 1942, 1946a) documented the close relationship of the islands' plants to the adjacent mainland of Ecuador and Peru, a relationship borne out by the present study. Additionally, researchers from Svenson on have placed an important emphasis on West Indian relationships, relationships that prove to be slight (Robinson 1902:239; Porter 1979).

Few researchers, however, have speculated to any great extent on the methods by which the present flora reached the archipelago. Following Hooker and Andersson, Robinson (1902:254) mentioned that "the flora of the Galapagos Islands is assumed to have been brought to them by the ordinary agents of plant-distribution, namely, the wind, oceanic currents, and migratory birds." However, only wind and oceanic drift are mentioned in any detail by Robinson, and that only in a few sentences. Stewart (1911:239) added some more detail to the efficacy of these three natural agents of dispersal, while Svenson (1942) mentioned only wind and drift. In a study based on Stewart's (1911) flora, Carlquist (1967:144; 1974:78) determined that the flora had been derived 73% by bird dispersal, 23% by oceanic drift, and 4% by wind. In a paper preliminary to the present one, I reported (Porter 1976) that the indigenous flora has been derived by the agents of birds, wind, and drift in a ratio of 6:3:1. This was the first effort to quantify the geographic relationships of the vascular plant flora since that of Stewart (1911:245). Further refinements in this study are discussed below.

FLORISTIC RELATIONSHIPS

The vascular flora of the Galapagos Islands consists of 543 indigenous taxa (species, subspecies, or varieties) plus 192 weeds and garden escapes introduced by man, for a total of 735 vascular plants. These figures are slightly higher than those of Porter (1976), reflecting the recent reports of Adsersen (1976a, 1976b) and van Der Werff (1977).

The known extra-Galapagoan distributions for the archipelago's indigenous vascular plants are given in Table 1. Numbers to the left in each column show indigenous species with the given distribution. Those in parentheses give the presumed number of introductions from the area in question that have given rise to the present endemics. I estimate that a minimum of 413 introductions of plant disseminules can account for the 543 indigenous vascular plants of the archipelago, 312 introductions for 312 indigenes, 101 introductions for 231 endemics. It must be emphasized that this is a *minimum* number of introductions. Chances are that the actual number is higher, but 413 introductions is the absolute minimum that will account for the indigenous flora. The archipelago has a probable maximum age of three million (Bailey 1976) to a possible five million years (Cox, this volume). This means that the arrival and establishment of one successful disseminule every 7,300 to 12,100 years would account for the present indigenous flora.

The Andean, Tropical American, and Pantropical elements overlap in that all three occur across the Andean area. Thus, there is the possibility that 92% of the introductions have come from this area, from adjacent South America. At a minimum, only 34 introductions have come from elsewhere. The main differences between the categories of Table 1 and those of my previous paper are in the presence of Caribbean and North American elements. Their recognition results from more information on distributions and on not considering the endemics as a category separate from the other indigenes. The endemics are discussed in detail in a separate paper. The most liberal estimate of endemism in the vascular flora is 43%, the most conservative 37% (Porter 1979).

DISPERSAL

"An island rises out of the sea : within a year some plants appear on it, first those that have sea-borne seeds or rhizomes, then wind-borne seeds, then those borne on the feet and plumage of wandering sea-fowl, and when the vegetation is tall enough, come land birds bringing seeds of the baccate or drupaceous fruits which they had eaten before their flight. Finally appears man with seeds of his food crops and the weeds which accidentally accompany them, or are carried by his domestic animals." (Ridley 1930:xii). This succinct scenario accurately describes what has happened in the Galapagos Islands, with the exception that seabird-borne disseminules probably were the first to arrive (Thornton 1971:36).

The basic weediness of the vascular plant flora of the Galapagos has been commented upon many times since Darwin's (1839:460) first observations. The indigenous flora is full of taxa particularly well adapted to crossing the sea barrier between the archipelago and the mainland. It is a disharmonic assemblage of species adapted to long-distance dispersal. Their open, naturally disturbed habitats make volcanic islands the ideal places for the disseminules of weedy plants to gain a foothold. The Galapagos essentially are a jumble of open and pioneer habitats. Each habitat can become pioneer in an instant through volcanic eruption (e. g. the 1968 eruption on Fernandina; see Colinvaux et al. 1968). The plants that have invaded these habitats are those of open and marginal habitats elsewhere. Characteristics of such colonizers are discussed in detail by Carlquist (1966a, 1974). "The question is no longer whether overseas dispersal occurs, but rather its probability in different taxa over various distances and routes." (Sauer 1969:583).

Unless one is there when it happens, it is almost impossible to determine exactly how a specific plant arrived in a specific spot. However, there are certain obvious clues that can be used in interpreting introductions. Fleshy fruits like berries and drupes are eaten by birds and the seeds are regurgitated or passed in their feces. Granivorous birds are efficient in seeking out small seeds, which occasionally pass through their alimentary tracts undigested and germinable (Gillham 1970: 94). Other fruits or seeds are mucilaginous or have processes that serve to attach them to the surfaces of animals. Many fruits and seeds have wings or trichomes that catch the wind and bear them elsewhere. Wind dispersal of spore-bearing plants is well known. Oceanic drift is not so common a dispersal mechanism, but a few species such as mangroves have exploited it very well. Man has become a dominant force in making many plants almost cosmopolitan in distribution, either as weeds of agriculture or as escapes from cultivation. All these methods have proved important in the derivation of the Galapagos flora, with birds and men playing the most important roles (Table 2). Tables 3, 4 and 5 give the geographic sources for the disseminules of the indigenous pteridophytes, monocots, and dicots. Dispersal by birds, wind, oceanic drift, and man is discussed below.

Dispersal is only half the battle; establishment is the other half. Establishment is more of a bottleneck to migration than is dispersal. Many disseminules may reach an island, but only those that fall in habitats in which they can grow have any chance of becoming established. Weedy plants again are at an advantage here, in that they are more easily established in open habitats. Flowering plants of open habitats that do not have specialized requirements for pollination seem to be especially favored for establishment (Carlquist 1966:252, 1974:13). This has been important

TABLE 2. ORIGINAL INTRODUCTIONS THAT HAVE RESULTED IN THE VASCULAR PLANT FLORA OF THE GALAPAGOS ISLANDS

	Birds	Man	Wind	Oceanic drift	Total
Pteridophytes	1		106		107
Monocots	63	39	14	2	118
Dicots	180	155	14	33	382
Total	244 (40%)	194 (32%)	134 (22%)	35 (6%)	607
Total for natural introductions	244 (59%)		134 (32%)	35 (8%)	413

TABLE 3. GEOGRAPHICAL SOURCES
OF PTERIDOPHYTE INTRODUCTIONS

	Tropical America	Pantropical	Andean	Caribbean	Mexico and Central America	North America	South America	Total
Wind	51 (3)[1]	18 (2)	22 (1)	6	1 (2)			98 (8)
Birds	1							1

[1] Figures in parentheses indicate the number of introductions from each geographic area that have resulted in the present endemic pteridophytes.

TABLE 4. GEOGRAPHICAL SOURCES
OF MONOCOT INTRODUCTIONS

	Tropical America	Pantropical	Andean	Caribbean	Mexico and Central America	North America	South America	Total
Birds	27 (4)[1]	21 (1)	3 (3)	3			(1)	54 (9)
Wind	7	1	2 (2)	1 (1)				11 (3)
Oceanic drift	1	1						2

[1] Figures in parentheses indicate the number of introductions from each geographic area that have resulted in the present endemic monocots.

TABLE 5. GEOGRAPHICAL SOURCES
OF DICOT INTRODUCTIONS

	Tropical America	Pantropical	Andean	Caribbean	Mexico and Central America	North America	South America	Total
Birds	56 (21)[1]	18	35 (34)	6 (3)	2 (2)	(3)	(1)	116 (63)
Oceanic drift	5 (2)	16	3 (5)	1	(1)			25 (8)
Wind	3 (3)	1 (1)	1 (4)	(1)				5 (9)

[1] Figures in parentheses indicate the number of introductions from each geographic area that have resulted in the present endemic dicots.

for the colonization of the Galapagos, where the number of pollinating insects is quite small (Linsley 1966; Linsley et al. 1966).

Ferns with bisexual gametophytes capable of self-fertilization (Smith 1972:6) and angiosperms that are capable of self-pollination and self-fertilization (Baker 1955) would seem to be at an advantage in the colonization of the islands. The one field study that has been performed on self-compatibility of Galapagos angiosperms (Rick 1966) showed that 13 of 17 species tested were autogamous. The disadvantages of long-term self-fertilization discussed by Carlquist (1966a:263, 1974:30) may be circumvented by continued introduction from elsewhere or by the arrival of several simultaneous disseminules, as on the foot of a bird (or birds) or in its (their) feces.

In a series of critical papers, Carlquist (1966a, 1966b, 1966c, 1966d, 1967; revised as several chapters in Carlquist 1974) has discussed in detail long-distance dispersal to islands and resultant phenomena characteristic of island floras. Two of these phenomena, loss of dispersibility (perhaps better expressed as change in dispersal mechanism) and change to the dioecious condition, have proved important in the evolution of the Hawaiian and other Pacific island floras (Carlquist 1966b, 1966c, 1966d). However, only a few Galapagos endemics exhibit either phenomenon. A number of monoecious endemics are found, but only *Baccharis steetzii, Bursera malacophylla, Castela galapageia*, and the three varieties of *Croton scouleri* are dioecious. In none of these cases has dioecism been evolved autochthonously in the Galapagos. All six taxa belong to genera that are dioecious elsewhere.

Carlquist (1966b) pointed out the changes in dispersal mechanisms that have taken place in the endemic genera *Lecocarpus, Macraea*, and *Scalesia*. However, the first to discover this phenomenon in Galapagos plants was Robinson (1902:238), who attributed the "decided reduction in the spines of most of the species of *Cenchrus*, and in a variety of *Tribulus cistoides*, as well as in *Acanthospermum microcarpum*" to the "paucity of indigenous mammals." The most interesting of Robinson's examples is *Tribulus cistoides*, an African species introduced by man. Most of the specimens collected above Tagus Cove, Isla Isabela, since the first was made in 1825, have partially or totally spineless fruits. Spineless individuals are known from South Africa, but are unknown from the New World tropics, where this species is a common weed of drier areas. Selection for the spineless condition either has been quite successful at Tagus Cove, or the original introduction was spineless. The latter is unlikely, in that such a fruit would be dispersed with difficulty. Specimens collected elsewhere in the archipelago have fruits with normal spines.

To the former examples may be added *Froelichia juncea* subsp. *juncea* and *F. nudicaulis* subsp. *lanigera* (perianth-tubes have become wingless or nearly so in fruit), *Gossypium klotzschianum* (seed trichomes reduced to an inconspicuous coat of fine fuzz), and *Opuntia megasperma* var. *megasperma* (seeds have become enlarged to 8-13 mm long, 6-10 mm wide, and 4-6 mm thick), var. *mesophytica* (7-10 X 5-8 X 2-4 mm), and var. *orientalis* (5-10 X 4-9 X 2-4 mm). In *Froelichia* the change has been from wind to bird (internal) dispersal, in *Gossypium* from oceanic drift to bird (internal) dispersal, and in *Opuntia* from bird to reptile (land iguana and tortoise) dispersal (both internal). *Opuntia* is the only example of "gigantism" evolved in Galapagos seeds, a phenomenon that is so important in the endemic Hawaiian angiosperm flora (Carlquist 1966c). In these five taxa the change has been from a wider means of dispersal to a narrower means. That is, they are now most likely to be dispersed by endemic animals with restricted distributions.

Bird Dispersal (Figs. 1-6)

There is no question that dispersal of plants by birds to islands and within archipelagos is important. Recent reviews of seed and fruit dispersal by birds (Gillham 1970) and plant dispersal to islands (Carlquist 1974) give many examples of this process. In addition, studies on captive birds (deVlaming and Proctor 1968; Proctor 1968) have shown that migrant shore birds may retain viable seeds in their digestive tracts for as long as 340 hours. "There is evidence that seeds of many species can remain viable in the intestinal tract of some shorebirds long enough to be transported several thousand miles." (Proctor 1968:321).

The Galapagos Archipelago spans an area of approximately 304 km east to west and 341 km northwest to southeast, roughly 103,700 km^2. The land area of the islands is about 7900 km^2. This is a reasonably large target for such vagile organisms as birds to hit (Livingston and Sinclair 1966:15). The Galapagos target probably was even larger during the Pleistocene glaciations (Simpson 1974:699), when sea level dropped to 100 m lower than at present. Because of the large amount of seismic and volcanic activity in the archipelago, however, it is difficult to predict how much larger it might have been.

The common and scientific names of Galapagos birds that follow, and the order in which they appear in the different groups discussed, are after Harris (1974).

Plant dispersal by birds between and within islands probably is mainly by the endemic seed and fruit eaters such as the Galapagos dove (*Zenaida galapagoensis*), mockingbirds (*Nesomimus parvulus, N. trifasciatus, N. macdonaldi, N. melanotis*), and finches (*Geospiza fuliginosa, G. fortis, G. magnirostris, G. difficilis, G. scandens, G. conirostris, Platyspiza crassirostris, Camarhynchus parvulus, C. pauper, C. psittacula, Cactospiza pallida, C. heliobates*). Seed- and fruit-eating migrants also may play the same roles. The resident white-cheeked pintail (*Anas bahamensis*) certainly plays an important role in the dispersal of aquatics and semi-aquatics within the archipelago, and perhaps between the mainland and the islands as well. The latter species occurs not only in the lagoons and crater lakes of the islands, but also in small temporary freshwater ponds (Townsend 1928:147).

It is not impossible that the predators (Galapagos hawk, *Buteo galapagoensis*; peregrine falcon, *Falco peregrinis*, a migrant; barn owl, *Tyto alba*; short-eared owl, *Asio flammeus*) may play a minor role by eating seed-containing birds, then eliminating the seeds in their regurgitated pellets. Such a situation, involving finches and short-eared owls, has recently been described by Grant et al. (1975:252). Indeed, it is not inconceivable that the osprey (*Pandion haliaetus*, a migrant) might catch fish that had eaten seeds and disperse them to land, as hypothesized by Darwin (1859:362). Such a role has been proposed for Galapagos boobies by Grant et al. (1975: 255).

External transport of disseminules within and between the islands also may be accomplished by the endemic (marked *) and resident animal feeders:

Great Blue Heron (*Ardea herodias*)
Common Egret (*Casmerodius albus*)
*Lava Heron (*Butorides sundevalli*)
Striated Heron (*B. striatus*)
Yellow-crowned Night Heron (*Nyctanassa violacea*)
Greater Flamingo (*Phoenicopterus ruber*)
*Galapagos Rail (*Laterallus spilonotus*)
Paint-billed Crake (*Neocrex erythrops*)
Common Gallinule (*Gallinula chloropus*)
Common Stilt (*Himantopus himantopus*)
*Lava Gull (*Larus fuliginosus*)
Dark-billed Cuckoo (*Coccyzus melacoryphus*)
Vermilion Flycatcher (*Pyrocephalus rubinus*)
*Large-billed Flycatcher (*Myiarchus magnirostris*)
*Galapagos Martin (*Progne modesta*)
Yellow Warbler (*Dendroica petechia*)
Warbler Finch (*Certhidea olivacea*)

In addition, it is well known that "many so-called insectivorous birds will, on occasions, eat seeds." (Wickens, 1976:120). Such occasions have been documented in the endemic large-billed flycatcher (Amadon 1966:22) and in the "insectivorous" Darwin's finches of the genus *Camarhynchus* (Bowman 1961:36-37). Thus, many of these primarily zoophagous birds also are potential dispersers of internally carried seeds.

By far the most important vectors for plant disseminules to the islands from elsewhere, however, probably are the migrants. Shore birds, land birds, and sea birds, in order of importance, have played significant roles in transporting disseminules. Lévêque et al. (1966:98) have recognized three groups of migrants, which they termed the charadriiform group, the American mainland group, and the petrel group. It may be assumed that members of the first two groups have brought in disseminules, either internally or externally.

The charadriiforms constitute the largest group both in terms of species and of individuals (Lévêque et al. 1966:98). They also are likely to be the most important for plant dispersal. A number (marked *) are known to ingest seeds and fruits (Ridley 1930; Martin et al. 1951). Common migrants to the archipelago are:

*Black-bellied Plover (*Squatarola squatarola*)
*Semipalmated Plover (*Charadrius semipalmatus*)
Ruddy Turnstone (*Arenaria interpres*)
Spotted Sandpiper (*Actitis macularia*)
Wandering Tattler (*Heteroscelus incanum*)
Willet (*Catoptrophorus semipalmatus*)
Least Sandpiper (*Erolia minutilla*)
Sanderling (*Crocethia alba*)
Whimbrel (*Numenius phaeopus*)
Northern Phalarope (*Lobipes lobatus*)
Wilson's Phalarope (*Steganopus tricolor*)
*Franklin's Gull (*Larus pipixcan*)
Royal Tern (*Sterna maxima*)

The following have been seen or collected only rarely:

Surfbird (*Aphriza virgata*)
Solitary Sandpiper (*Tringa solitaria*)
Lesser Yellowlegs (*Totanus flavipes*)
Greater Yellowlegs (*Totanus melanoleucus*)
*Semipalmated Sandpiper (*Ereunetes pusillus*)
Western Sandpiper (*Ereunetes mauri*)
Baird's Sandpiper (*Erolia bairdii*)
*Pectoral Sandpiper (*Calidris melanotos*)
*Stilt Sandpiper (*Micropalama himantopus*)
*Marbled Godwit (*Limosa fedoa*)
*Short-billed dowitcher (*Limnodromus griseus*)
Red Phalarope (*Phalaropus fulicarius*)
Laughing Gull (*Larus atricilla*)
Common Tern (*Sterna hirundo*)

The following have been recorded only once:

Golden Plover (*Pluvialis dominica*)
Thick-billed Plover (*Charadrius wilsonia*)
*Killdeer (*Charadrius vociferus*)
Black Turnstone (*Arenaria melanocephala*)
*Knot (*Calidrus canutus*)
*White-rumped sandpiper (*Erolia fuscicollis*)

Fairy Tern (*Gygis alba*)

Many of the foregoing species also feed along the edges of freshwater ponds and streams, and in grassy areas, and in other open habitats, especially when migrating (Bond 1971; Harris 1974; Ridgely 1976).

"The American mainland group is a heterogenous group of widely distributed aquatic and terrestrial species that are distinguished by long-distance migrations." (Lévêque et al. 1966:98). A few members of this group (marked *) are known to eat seeds or fruits as part of their diet (Ridley 1930; Martin et al. 1951). They and the others also could carry external disseminules. Common migrants are:

Cattle Egret (*Bubulcus ibis*)
*Blue-winged Teal (*Anas discors*)
*Barn Swallow (*Hirundo rustica*)
*Bobolink (*Dolichonyx oryzivorus*)

The following have been seen or collected only rarely:

Pied-billed Grebe (*Podilymbus podiceps*)
Snowy Egret (*Leucophoyx thula*)
*Purple Gallinule (*Porphyrula martinica*)
Common Nighthawk (*Chordeiles minor*)
Belted Kingfisher (*Ceryle alcyon*)
Purple Martin (*Progne subis*)
Bank Swallow (*Riparia riparia*)

The following have been recorded only once:

Brown Booby (*Sula leucogaster*)
Black-crowned Night Heron (*Nycticorax nycticorax*)
*Black-bellied Tree Duck (*Dendrocygna autumnalis*)
Black-billed Cuckoo (*Coccyzus erythropthalmus*)
Cliff Swallow (*Petrochelidon pyrrhonota*)
*Summer Tanager (*Piranga rubra*)

Members of the petrel group are not likely to have played more than a minor role in plant dispersal to and between the islands. They are pelagic birds which do not visit land except when nesting. While it is improbable that any of the petrels, shearwaters, or storm petrels which migrate through Galapagos waters have played a role in dispersal, it is not impossible that those which nest in the archipelago may spread externally attached disseminules, as has been described by Falla (1960) for petrels and shearwaters in the Antarctic. The Hawaiian Petrel (*Pterodroma phaeopygia*), Audubon's shearwater (*Puffinus lherminieri*), White-vented Storm Petrel (*Oceanites gracilis*), Band-rumped Storm Petrel (*Oceanodroma castro*), and Wedge-rumped Storm Petrel (*O. tethys*) thus may play a limited role in interisland dispersal. The Hawaiian petrel is the best candidate for this group, as it nests in the thickly vegetated uplands of the largest islands.

Other sea birds that nest in the Galapagos also may play limited roles in plant dispersal. The following can be added to our list of possible vectors:

Waved Albatross (*Diomedea irrorata*)
Red-billed Tropic Bird (*Phaethon aethereus*)
Brown Pelican (*Pelecanus occidentalis*)
Blue-footed Booby (*Sula nebouxii*)
Masked Booby (*Sula dactylatra*)
Red-footed Booby (*Sula sula*)
Great Frigatebird (*Fregata minor*)
Magnificent Frigatebird (*Fregata magnificens*)
Swallow-tailed Gull (*Creagrus furcatus*)

Brown Noddy (*Anous stolidus*)

Sooty Tern (*Sterna fuscata*)

Disseminules may become attached to any of these species while they are in the vicinity of their nests. This is especially true for the Brown Pelican, frigate birds, and Red-footed Booby, which nest in trees or shrubs and collect plant material to build their nests. In addition, boobies are known to pick up floating objects, including seeds, and convey them to their nests (Carlquist 1967:148). Seabirds, banded as young in the Galapagos, have been captured on the mainland of Ecuador (Waved Albatross, Blue-footed Booby, Red-billed Tropic Bird), off Peru and in the Gulf of Panama (Red-billed Tropic Bird), and in Costa Rica (Magnificent Frigatebird) (Harris 1976:20), indicating the possibility of regular long-distance wanderings on the part of these species as well.

Thus, most of the known members of the Galapagos avifauna may serve as vectors for the disseminules of vascular plants. In addition, there must be other migrants that have passed through the archipelago in the past for which we have no records; indeed, some may still visit that have not yet been recorded. It is not impossible that some once-common shore birds that have been hunted nearly to extinction, such as the Eskimo Curlew (*Nemenius borealis*), were past migrants through the islands.[1]

Wind Dispersal (Figs. 7-8)

Wind dispersal to the Galapagos has been accomplished only by members of a few groups that are eminently suited for this mode of dispersal (i.e. pteridophytes, Orchidaceae, Asteraceae, etc.). However, with the notable exception of the ferns and the so-called "fern allies," it has not been as successful an introductory mechanism as oceanic drift. Pteridophyte spores have a high dispersal capacity, and their ability to colonize islands through long-distance dispersal is well documented (Tryon 1970). Most of those pteridophyte taxa that have become established in the archipelago (83 of 99 indigenes, seven of eight endemics) are widely distributed or have widely distributed progenitors in contental America. Relatively frequent dispersal to islands may take place at distances of about 800 km (Tryon 1972:121), the minimum distance of the Galapagos from the mainland. Endemism in Galapagos pteridophytes (8%, as compared with 51% in the angiosperms) probably is so low because of continuous spore arrival from the source areas. Orchid seeds probably are regularly introduced via wind dispersal as well. However, relatively few species have become established, either because of the absence in the Galapagos of their specialized pollinators or mycorrhizal symbionts, or of suitable sites for germination and growth.

Very few groups of angiosperms have disseminules that are adapted for long-distance wind dispersal as their normal process of dissemination (Wickens 1976:111). Indeed, following a review of the mechanics and mathematics of wind dispersal, Wickens (1976:115) concludes that long-distance dispersal to islands has a low probability of success.

Oceanic Drift (Fig. 9)

With the exception of the endemic cottons (*Gossypium* spp.; see Stephens 1958), the taxa that have arrived and become established in the Galapagos via oceanic drift are plants of the littoral zone. They are mangroves or plants of the beaches, strands, sand dunes, and salt flats. All are plants that can tolerate salt or brackish water.

Other species certainly have arrived by drift. Large, unidentified trees, bamboos, sugar cane, and palm fruits are reported as frequently being found in beach drift on the southeastern shores of the islands (Fitz-Roy 1839:505). Stewart (1915:195) was the first to recognize that "these could hardly be brought hence by the Humboldt Current." Seventeen out of the 35 introductions that apparently have arrived through drift have been of pantropical taxa that probably have come with

[1] I am indebted to my colleague C. S. Adkisson for this suggestion.

the warm currents out of the Gulf of Panama. Such currents are especially common from February through April (Abbott 1966:110).

Large amounts of floating vegetation originating on the mainland have been reported from the vicinity of the archipelago (Beebe 1926:52; Townsend 1928:149). The sources for this material, however, are for the most part mesic lowland habitats. Species of mesic lowland habitats have not become established in the Galapagos because such habitats are not available to them. As Scharff (1912:309) was the first to indicate, "A point of great importance in connection with the theory of dispersal of seeds by marine currents is the condition of the coasts of the Galapagos Islands."

For the same reason, there is no evidence that any disseminules not adapted to drift dispersal have arrived as colonists on rafts of vegetation originating on the mainland. Most likely, these would be epiphytic plants of more mesophytic habitats than are available anywhere on the islands. Such plants are particularly inappropriate for becoming established at sea level in these islands. Except for *Peperomia*, which is bird-dispersed, the small Galapagos epiphytic flora has been derived through wind dispersal.

The small number of species that have been derived through oceanic drift is not surprising. Although drift-dispersed taxa have relatively high immigration rates in comparison with those that are dispersed by birds or wind, very few are adapted to this mode of introduction. In addition, their high immigration rates and the small number of habitats available to them in the Galapagos also reduce the opportunities for endemism in this group (Johnson and Raven 1973:895). Only 4% (10 taxa) of the vascular plant endemics occur in the littoral zone.

Man

European man first discovered the archipelago in 1535, and Heyerdahl (1963:51) hypothesized that the islands served as an aboriginal fishing outpost for hundreds of years before this. The history of their exploration and exploitation is well documented (Slevin 1959). There has been a progression of buccaneers, whalers, farmers, and fishermen to the Galapagos since 1535. Each group has added its share of plants to the flora. The importance of man in plant dispersal to the islands is underlined by the large number of species on them that are weeds of his environs (133 species) or escapes from cultivation, which are naturally reproducing themselves (59 species).

Today, humans have replaced birds as the most important factor in the dispersal of plants to the Galapagos. Except for ferns most of the plants reported from the archipelago in recent years have been introduced by man. The deleterious effects of some of these man-introduced species on the native flora are just beginning to be appreciated (Weber 1971:9; Thornton 1971:272; Eckhardt 1972; Schofield 1973; Porter 1973; Hamann 1974c:313, 1975). Increased visits to the islands by tourists who fly in directly from the Ecuadorian mainland will affect the vegetation not only by increasing human pressure, but also by increasing the numbers of plant and animal disseminules being introduced.

DISCUSSION AND CONCLUSIONS

In spite of recent speculation to the contrary (Holden and Dietz 1972; Croizat et al. 1974: 282; Rosen 1974:453), there is no geological evidence to indicate that the Galapagos Islands were ever any closer to the mainland than they are today. Any drift movement of the islands that may have taken place would have been in a southerly direction from the Galapagos Rift Zone, which is slightly north of the geographical equator. The sea floor surrounding the islands is from five to ten million years old (Hey et al. 1977:1386; Cox, this volume), which sets a maximum limit for their age. From geophysical data, it has been estimated that the Galapagos Islands and the subsurface Carnegie Ridge to their east originated three to four million years ago (Anderson et al. 1975:6921).

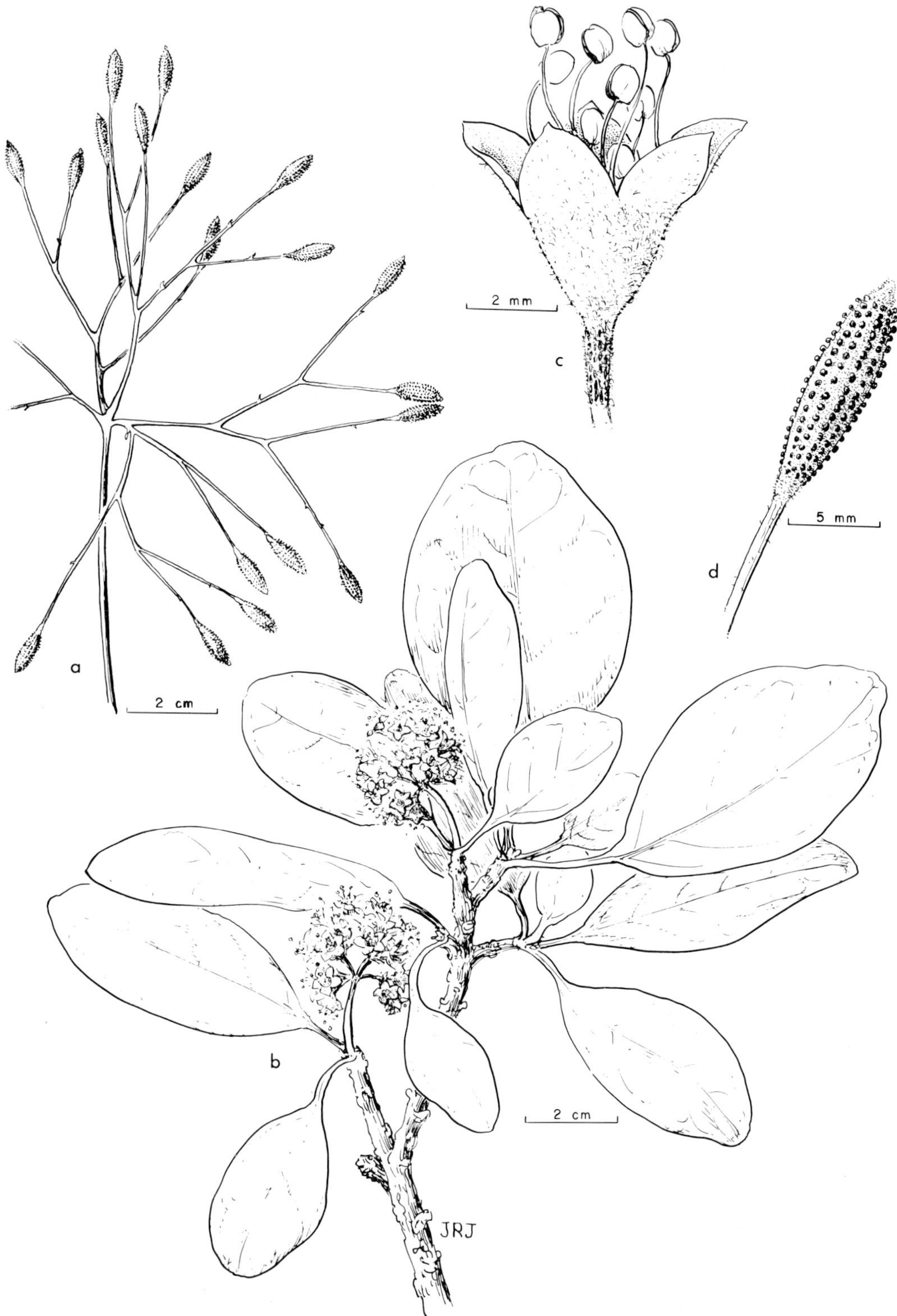

Fig. 1. Bird dispersal (external). *Pisonia floribunda*. Endemic.

Fig. 2. Bird dispersal (external). *Scalesia affinis*. Endemic.

Fig. 3. Bird dispersal (internal). *Bursera graveolens*. Andean.

Fig. 4. Bird dispersal (internal). *Psidium galapageium* var. *galapageium*. Endemic.

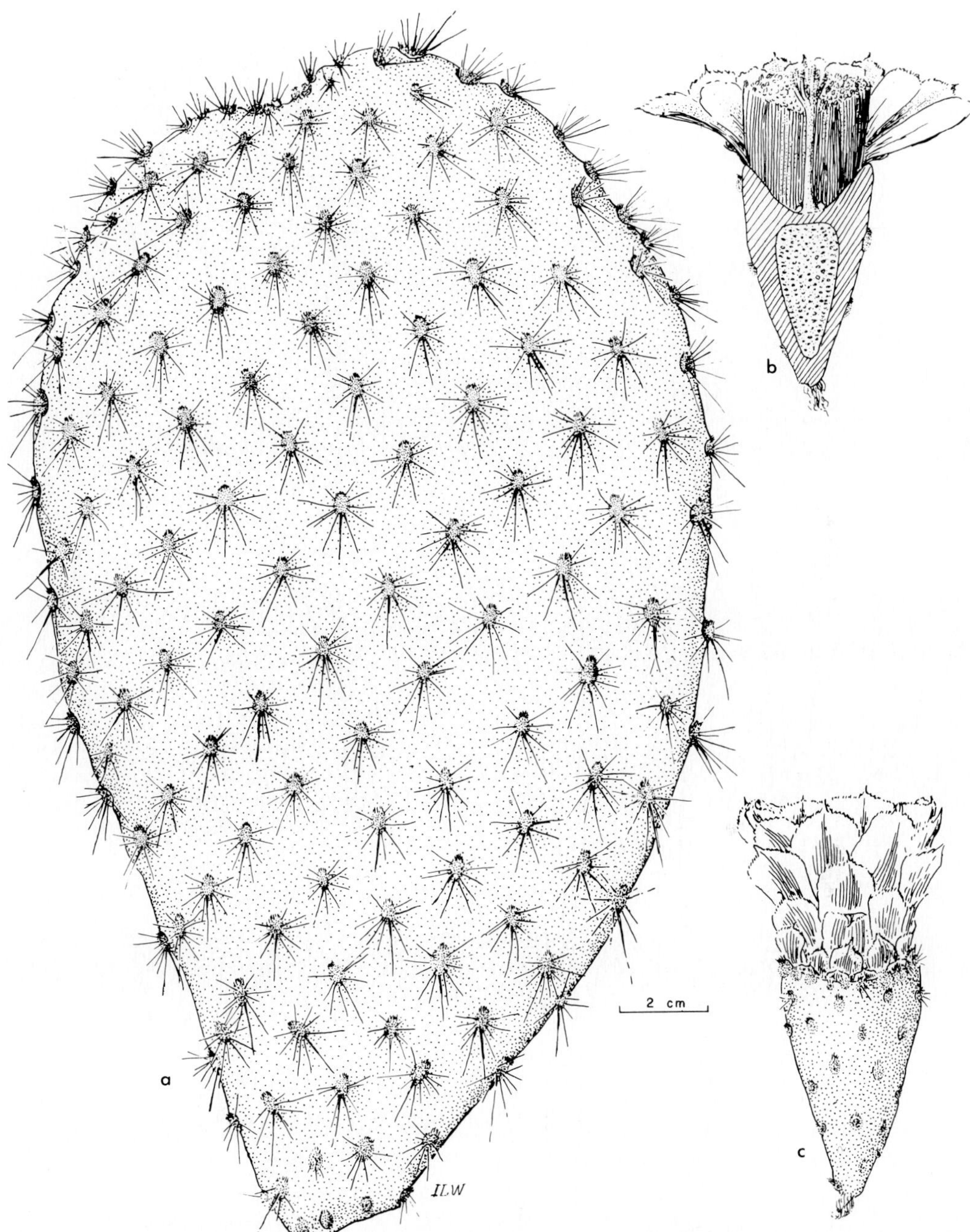

Fig. 5. Bird dispersal (internal). *Opuntia echios* var. *echios*. Endemic.

Fig. 6. Bird dispersal (external). *Cenchrus platyacanthus*. Endemic.

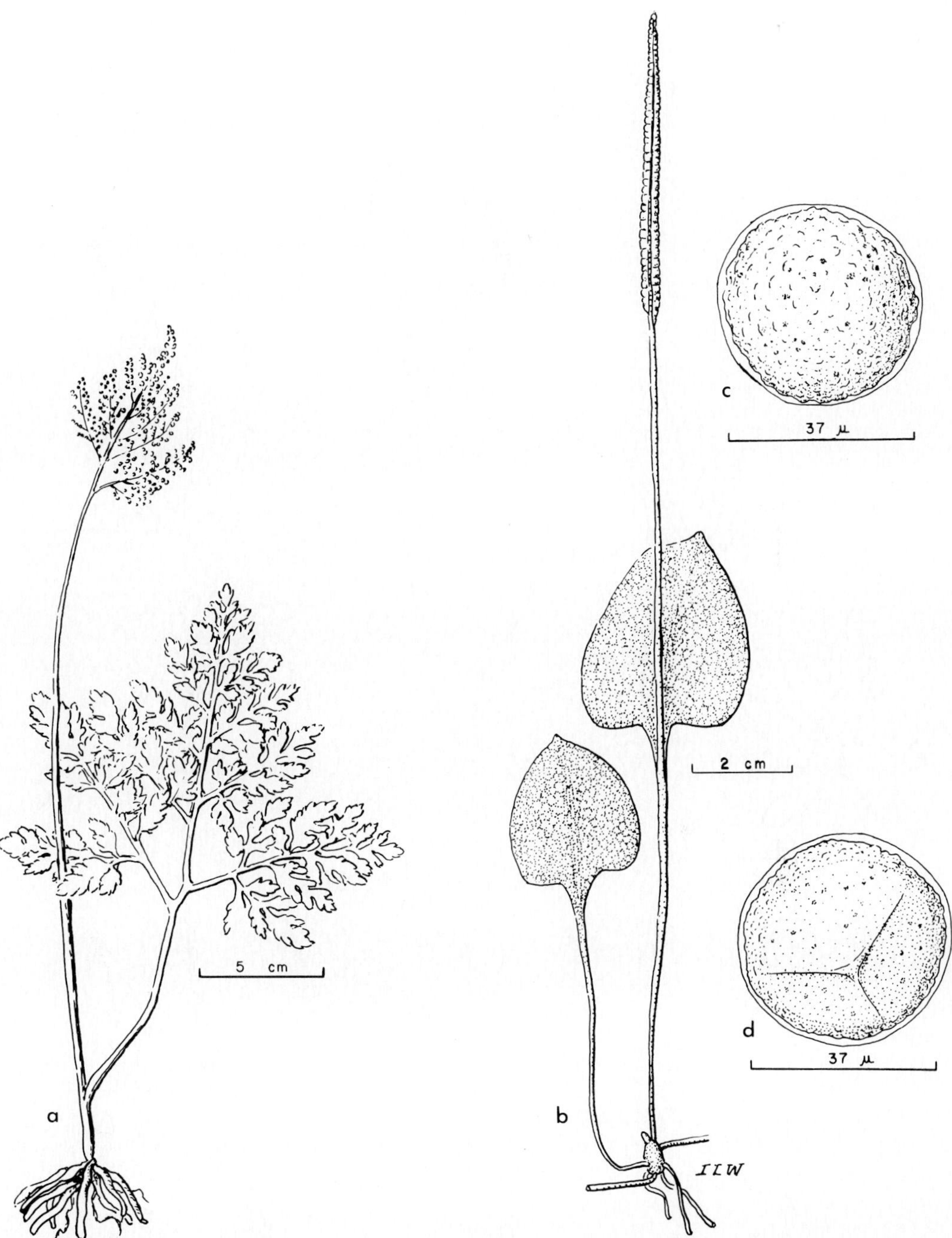

Fig. 7. Wind dispersal (spores). *Botrychium underwoodianum* (a), Caribbean. *Ophioglossum reticulatum* (b-d), Pantropical. (Fig. 7a drawn from halftone in Bot. Notisser 121:630-32, 1968).

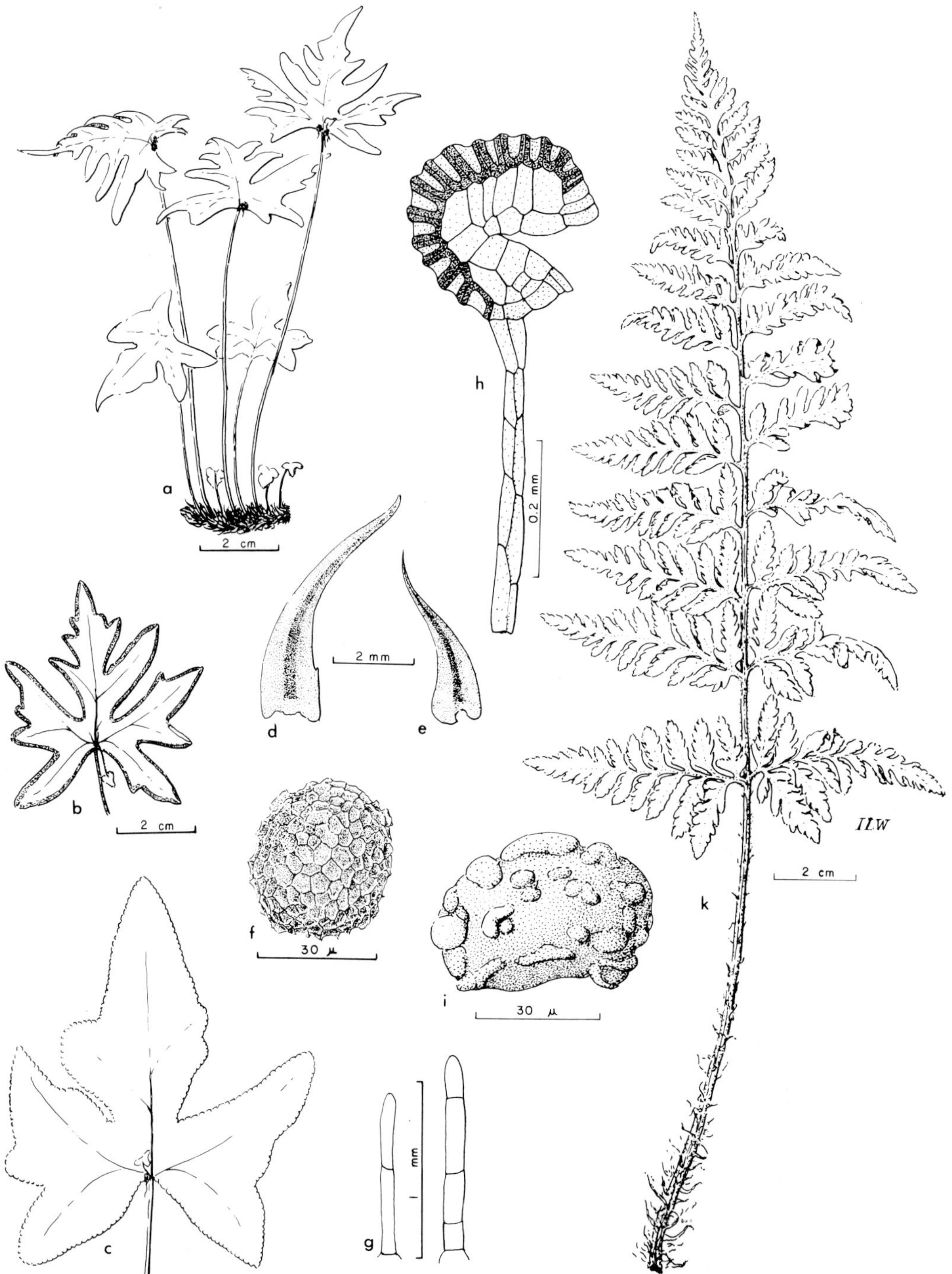

Fig. 8. Wind dispersal (spores). *Doryopteris pedata* var. *palmata* (a-g). *Dryopteris patula* (h-k). Tropical America.

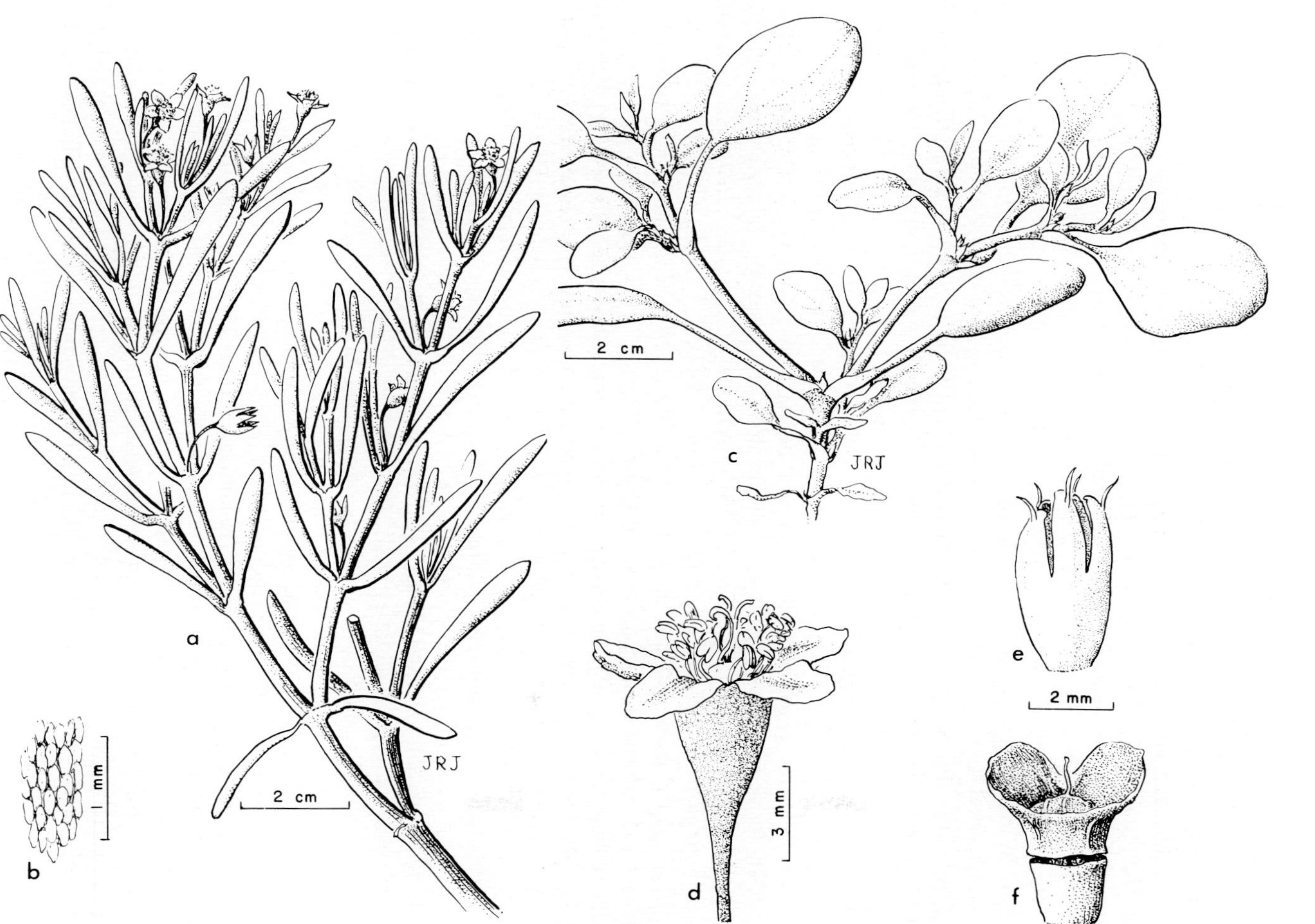

Fig. 9. Oceanic drift. *Sesuvium edmonstonei* (a,b): b, epidermal vesicles on stems; Endemic. *Trianthema portulacastrum* (c-f), Pantropical.

Most potassium-argon datings for Galapagos rocks formed above sea level are in the vicinity of one million years (Cox and Dalrymple 1966; Swanson et al. 1974:1807; Bailey 1976). Their maximum age may be three (Bailey 1976) to five (Cox, this volume) million years.

Holden and Dietz date the beginning of the rift, which formed the plate whereon the archipelago lies, as 40 million years ago, during the late Eocene. They admit, however, that their figures may be as much as twice as high as some of their geophysical evidence indicated (Holden and Dietz 1972:267). According to Malfait and Dinkelman (1972:254), on the other hand, rifting began in the middle Miocene, and they figure (1972:260) the Galapagos as being no older than late Pliocene in age. Hey et al. (1977) have reduced the magnitude of Holden and Dietz' dates about one-half, bringing them more into line with those of Malfait and Dinkelman.

Holden and Dietz concluded (1972:269) that, "The Galapagos Islands contain many endemic birds and bizarre animals which have required many millions of years for their evolution in isolation. By our model, the modern Galapagos Islands may have inherited faunas from a whole series of ancestral 'Galapagos islands' which existed over a span of 40 m.y. Presumably the animals would have little difficulty negotiating the short span of water to a new volcanic island as an older extinct volcanic island drifted eastward and subsided beneath the sea (a subsiding 'stepping stone'), adding itself to the end of the Cocos and Carnegie ridges. To date no guyots have been reported from either the Carnegie or Cocos chains, but this still is not conclusive evidence that these ridges were not subareal at some time in their history." However, there is no geological evidence (McBirney and Williams 1969:109) for either continental connections via landbridges (cf. Croizat 1952:254), for former "stepping stone" islands along the Cocos or Carnegie ridges (cf. Rosen 1974:459), or that they are the result of the subsidence of an earlier land mass, an argument favored by some earlier biogeographers (cf. Baur 1891, 1897).

In spite of Holden and Dietz' hypothesis as to the age of the Galapagos biota, evidence from the plants and animals themselves, no matter how "bizarre" they may seem to some, indicate that the archipelago is a young one. Speciation and subspeciation appear to have taken place fairly recently even in those groups of terrestrial animals that have undergone radiation in the islands. In the land snails, the "fauna probably came from South America during Pleistocene time and perhaps earlier" (Smith 1966:240), and Valvolgyi (1974:474) argues that they have resulted from two colonizations by aerial dispersal during the past one million years. The cryptozoic fauna is at least a million years of age (Thornton 1971:87), while the orsilline insects represent "an early stage in the evolution of island faunas" (Usinger and Ashlock 1966:233). Butterflies and hawkmoths also are recent arrivals (Linsley et al. 1966:15).

The situation is similar in the endemic vertebrates. In the reptiles, the two species of land iguanas (*Conolophus*, an endemic genus) (Thornton 1971:97), five species (eight taxa) of geckos (*Phyllodactylus*) (Thornton 1971:96), seven forms of marine iguana (*Amblyrhynchus*, an endemic genus) (Thornton 1971:110), nine species of lava lizards (*Tropidurus*) (Carpenter 1966:273), and 15 subspecies of tortoise (*Geochelone*) (Hendrickson 1966:252) are allopatric, while the three species (eight taxa) of snakes (*Dromicus*) are sympatric to some extent (Thornton 1971:95). This suggests that the reptiles are sufficiently recent in the Galapagos so that the different taxa in each genus, except for the snakes, have not yet diverged enough so that sympatry has resulted from reinvasion of an already occupied island. It may be that the sympatric snakes are isolated ecologically. Five successful introductions during the past one million years "would suffice to account for the existence of the present Galapagos reptiles" (Thornton 1971:197).

In the birds, two groups have undergone radiation. There are four species of mockingbirds (*Nesomimus*, an endemic genus), which are allopatric (Harris 1974:127). The five endemic genera (fide Bowman 1961) and 13 species of Galapagos finches, which to a large extent are sympatric, are reproductively isolated, and song is their principal isolating mechanism (Bowman, this volume). Again, fairly recent introduction for both groups is indicated. The same is true for the three genera (one endemic) and seven species of rice rats (Patton, this volume). In a paper published before the recent geological studies on the islands discussed above, Kuschel (1963:94) concluded prophetically: "the Galapagos fauna, including the terrestrial vertebrates, might go back only to the Pliocene, or even, to the end of the Pliocene and to the Pleistocene."

In spite of the large amount of endemism (43%) in the vascular plant flora, the botanical evidence also indicates a relatively recent age for the archipelago. A substantial number of endemics are subspecies and varieties, indicating that radiations in such genera as *Acalypha* and *Alternan thera* have begun fairly recently. The close relationships among species in a large genus like *Scalesia* show this as well. The population structure of plants growing under arid or semiarid conditions is likely to be more favorable for evolutionary change that that of those in more mesic habitats (Stebbins 1952). The frequent isolation of small populations offers many situations for change through natural selection and chance gene fixation. Occasional gene flow between populations further increases their genetic diversity and offers new gene combinations to the selective action of the environment. Such a population structure is that most favorable for rapid evolution (Wright 1940). Most likely, Galapagos vascular plants have evolved under such circumstances.

The vegetation of the archipelago may be divided into three major ecological zones, littoral, arid, and mesic (Johnson and Raven 1973:895). The arid zone not only has the highest amount of species diversity, it is also the area in which most of the evolutionary radiation has taken place in the endemic flora (Porter 1979). The fossil pollen and spore records (Colinvaux and Schofield 1976a:1011, 1976b:1027) indicate that on Isla San Cristóbal over the past 25,000 years there was a dry period for the first 15,000 years, followed by 10,000 years when more mesic habitats were available. The dry period was preceded by an earlier mesic period, probably less wet than the present one (Colinvaux 1972:20). This situation in the Galapagos is consistent with the contemporary climate elsewhere in the eastern tropical Pacific (Simpson 1975). Thus, the arid zone is not only the most widespread zone today, it probably was even more so in the past. Diversity in the littoral zone is low for reasons mentioned previously. It is not any higher in the mesic zone because mesic habitats have been both fewer and available for disseminules for a shorter period of time than have arid habitats. The resultant flora is one of weedy groups of drier habitats well-adapted to long-distance dispersal.

The Plants

Taxa in the following list are given first by division (Psilophyta, Equisetophyta, Lycopodophyta, Pteridophyta, and Magnoliophyta). Within each division, the list is alphabetical by family, genus, and species. The Magnoliophyta are further divided into the classes Monocotyledonae and Dicotyledonae. In the tables and the text, the ferns (Pteridophyta) and the so-called "fern allies" (Psilophyta, Equisetophyta, Lycopodophyta) are referred to collectively as teridophytes, while the two classes of flowering plants (Magnoliophyta) are referred to as monocots and dicots respectively. References are given to the places of publication of taxa reported since Wiggins and Porter (1971). Nomenclatural changes from those names used in Wiggins and Porter are followed by a reference leading to a discussion of the reasons for such changes. In addition, the following taxa are newly reported: *Ergarostris pilosa* (Poaceae), *Galium canescens* (Rubiaceae), and *Datura innoxia, Jaltomata* aff. *procumbens*, and *Physalis cordata* (Solanaceae); while the following likewise are deleted: *Paspalum paniculatum* (Poaceae), *Iresine edmonstonei* (Amaranthaceae), *Crotalaria incana* var. *nicaraguensis* (Fabaceae), *Malachra capitata* (Malvaceae), *Cissampelos galapagensis* and *C. tropaeolifolia* (Menispermaceae), *Solanum edmonstonei* (Solanaceae), and *Duranta repens* var. *microphylla* (Verbenaceae).

Listed for each taxon are its extra-Galapagoan distribution, relationships (if endemic), and known or presumed method of dispersal and part(s) dispersed (if indigenous). Where two methods of dispersal are given, that which is most likely is given first. I echo Carlquist (1967:129) in that, "Fruit and seed morphology are used as evidence for mode of dispersal interpreted in the light of known dispersal methods." Ridley (1930), Martin et al. (1951), and van der Pijl (1972) have been most helpful in this regard, but the final interpretations are my own, just as they are for classifying a specific taxon as indigenous or introduced. Endemics are discussed in more detail elsewhere (Porter 1979). Introduced weeds and cultivated escapes are followed by the date of their first known collection in the Galapagos.

Figures in parentheses to the right of the taxa in the list give the *minimum* number of introductions that could have given rise to the taxon in question. For each non-endemic indigene this will be one. For most endemics there is a single presumed introduction for each genus or species group. In a few cases, one introduction is reckoned to have resulted in both an indigene and an endemic taxon that has been derived from it.

ACKNOWLEDGMENTS

Field studies in the Galapagos Islands in 1967 and 1977 were made possible through the National Science Foundation and the Friends of the Museum of Comparative Zoology, Harvard University. The American Philosophical Society and the Virginia Polytechnic Institute and State University Education Foundation provided funds so that Galapagos collections at the Royal Botanic Gardens, Kew and at Cambridge University could be consulted. H. van der Werff, H. Adsersen, O. Hamann, and U. Eliasson generously provided valuable information on distribution and ecology, as did W. G. D'Arcy (Scrophulariaceae and Solanaceae), L. A. Garay (Orchidaceae), J. R. Reeder (Poaceae), L. B. Smith (Bromeliaceae), R. M. Tryon (pteridophytes), and B. L. Turner (*Chrysanthellum*) on their respective specialties. My colleagues D. A. West, C. S. Adkisson, and R. D. Ross provided valuable comments on parts of this paper. All are most gratefully acknowledged.

RESUMEN

Se hace un presupuesto tentativa sobre las relaciones geográficas de las plantas vasculares del Archipiélago de Colón, y para determinar sus méthodos de la dispersión. Las afinidades de la flora vascular son principalmente de la Sudamera adyacente. Los pájaros probablemente representaban un papel mas importante en la dispersión de las plantas vasculares a las islas, con el hombre, el viento, y las corrientes océanicas representando unos papales menores.

CHECKLIST
OF THE VASCULAR PLANTS
OF THE GALAPAGOS ISLANDS

PSILOPHYTA

Psilotaceae

Psilotum nudum L.
Pantropical. Wind (spores). (1)

EQUISETOPHYTA

Equisetaceae

Equisetum bogotense HBK.
Andean (Venezuela to Chile and Argentina). Wind (spores). (1)

LYCOPODOPHYTA

Lycopodiaceae

Lycopodium cernuum L.
Pantropical. Wind (spores). (1)

L. clavatum L.
Pantropical. Wind (spores). (1)

L. complanatum L. (as *L. thyoides* Willd.)
Pantropical. Wind (spores). (1)

L. dichotomum Jacq.
Tropical America (Mexico and the West Indies to Brazil). Wind (spores). (1)

L. passerinoides HBK.
Andean (Venezuela to Peru). Wind (spores). (1)

L. phylicaefolium Desv. (Adsersen 1976b:432)
Andean (Ecuador and Peru). Wind (spores). (1)

L. reflexum Lam.
Tropical America (Mexico and the West Indies to Bolivia and Paraguay). Wind (spores). (1)

L. setaceum var. *galapagense* O. Hamann (Hamann 1974b; Adsersen 1976b:432)
Endemic; *L. setaceum* is pantropical in distribution; Proctor (1977) places it in synonomy under *L. verticillatum* L. f. Wind (spores). (1)

PTERIDOPHYTA

Adiantaceae

Adiantum concinnum Willd.
Tropical America (Mexico and the West Indies to Peru). Wind (spores). (1)

A. henslovianum Hook. f.
Andean (Venezuela to Peru). Wind (spores). (1)

A. macrophyllum Sw.
Tropical America (Mexico and the West Indies to Bolivia and Brazil). Wind (spores). (1)

A. patens Willd.
Tropical America (Mexico to Bolivia). Wind (spores). (1)

A. villosum L.
Tropical America (Mexico and the West Indies to Peru and Brazil). Wind (spores). (1)

Aspidiaceae

Arachniodes denticulata (Sw.) Ching (van der Werff 1977:89)
Tropical America (Mexico and the West Indies to Peru). Wind (spores). (1)

Ctenitis pleiosoros (Hook. f.) Morton
Endemic; apparently most closely related to the tropical American *C. subincisa* (Willd.). Ching. Wind (spores). (1)

C. sloanei (Spreng.) Morton
Tropical America (Guatemala and Florida to Bolivia). Wind (spores). (1)

Dryopteris parallelogramma (Kunze) C. Alston (van der Werf 1977:90)
Andean (Colombia to Argentina). Wind (spores). (1)

D. patula (Sw.) Underw.
Tropical America (Mexico and the West Indies to Ecuador and Brazil). Wind (spores). (1)

Polystichum gelidum (Kunze) Fée
Andean (Venezuela and probably Ecuador). Wind (spores). (1)

P. muricatum (L.) Fée
Tropical America (Mexico and the West Indies to Bolivia and Brazil). Wind (spores). (1)
Rumohra adiantiformis (Forst.) Ching
Pantropical. Wind (spores). (1)
Tectaria aequatoriensis (Hieron.) C. Chr.
Andean (Ecuador). Wind (spores). (1)
Woodsia montevidensis (Spreng.) Hieron. (Adsersen 1976b:434)
Pantropical. Wind (spores). (1)

Aspleniaceae

Asplenium auritum var. *auriculatum* (Hook. f.) Morton & Lellinger
Andean (Venezuela to Ecuador). Wind (spores). (1)
A. cristatum Lam.
Tropical America (Mexico and the West Indies to Bolivia and Brazil). Wind (spores). (1)
A. feei Fée
Tropical America (Mexico and the West Indies to Bolivia and Brazil). Wind (spores). (1)
A. formosum var. *carolinum* (Maxon) Morton
Endemic; *A. formosum* Willd. is pantropical. Wind (spores). (1)
A. otites Link
Tropical America (Honduras to Peru). Wind (spores). (1)
A. praemorsum Sw.
Tropical America (Mexico and the West Indies to Bolivia and Brazil). Wind (spores). (1)
A. pumilum Sw.
Tropical America (Mexico and Florida to Brazil). Wind (spores). (1)
A. serra var. *imrayanum* Hook.
Pantropical. Wind (spores). (1)

Athyriaceae

Diplazium subobtusum Rosenst.
Andean (Ecuador). (1)

Azollaceae

Azolla microphylla Kaulf.
Tropical America (West Indies to Peru and Brazil). Birds (external in mud or viscid attachment; spores, sporangia, or vegetative parts). (1)

Blechnaceae

Blechnum falciforme (Liebm.) C. Chr.
Caribbean (Mexico to Colombia). Wind (spores). (1)
B. lehmanii Hieron.
Caribbean (Costa Rica to Colombia, Venezuela, Brazil). Wind (spores). (1)
B. occidentale var. *puberulum* Sodiro
Tropical America (Mexico and Florida to Argentina). Wind (spores). (1)
B. polypodioides Raddi
Tropical America. Wind (spores). (1)

Cyatheaceae

Cyathea weatherbyana (Morton) Morton
Endemic; most closely related to the tropical American *C. andina* (Karst.) Domin. Wind (spores). (1)

Dennstaedtiaceae

Dennstaedtia cicutaria (Sw.) Moore
Tropical America (Mexico and the West Indies to Bolivia and Brazil). Wind (spores). (1)
D. dissecta (Sw.) Moore (van der Werff 1977:90)
Tropical America (Mexico and the West Indies to Bolivia and Brazil). Wind (spores). (1)
D. globulifera (Poir.) Hieron.
Tropical America (Texas and the West Indies to Argentina and Uruguay). Wind (spores). (1)

Histiopteris incisa (Thunb.) J. E. Sm.
Pantropical. Wind (spores). (1)
Hyolepis hostilis (Kunze) Presl
Andean (Colombia to Bolivia and Brazil). Wind (spores). (1)
Pteridium aquilinum var. *arachnoideum* (Kaulf.) Herter
Tropical America (Mexico and the West Indies to Argentina and Uruguay). Wind (spores). (1)

Gleicheniaceae

Dicranopteris flexuosa (Schrad.) Underw.
Tropical America (West Indies to Peru and Brazil). Wind (spores). (1)

Grammitidaceae

Grammitis delitescens (Maxon) Proctor (Adsersen 1976b:429)
Caribbean (Mexico and the West Indies to Colombia). Wind (spores). (1)
G. serrulata (Sw.) Sw.
Pantropical. Wind (spores). (1)

Gymnogrammaceae

Anogramma chaerophylla (Desv.) Link
Tropical America (Mexico and the West Indies to Argentina). Wind (spores). (1)
Hemionitis palmata L.
Tropical America (Mexico and the West Indies to Bolivia and Brazil). Wind (spores). (1)
Pityogramma calomelanos (L.) Link var. *calomelanos*
Pantropical (originally tropical America). Wind (spores). (1)
P. calomelanos var. *aureoflava* (Hook.) Bailey
Pantropical (originally tropical America). Wind (spores). (1)
P. tartarea (Cav.) Maxon
Tropical America (Mexico and the West Indies to Bolivia and Brazil). Wind (spores). (1)
Trachypteris pinnata (Hook. f.) C. Chr.
Andean (Peru to Argentina and Brazil). Wind (spores). (1)

Hymenophyllaceae

Hymenophyllum hirsutum (L.) Sw.
Tropical America (Mexico and the West Indies to Brazil). Wind (spores). (1)
H. lehmannii Hieron.
Andean (Colombia). Wind (spores). (1)
H. plumieri Hook & Grev. (van der Werff 1977:89)
Andean (Ecuador). Wind (spores). (1)
H. polyanthos (Sw.) Sw.
Pantropical. Wind (spores). (1)
Trichomanes reptans Sw.
Tropical America (Guatemala and the West Indies to Bolivia and Brazil). Wind (spores). (1)

Lomariopsidaceae

Elaphoglossum engelii (Karst.) Christ
Andean (Colombia and Venezuela to Bolivia). Wind (spores). (1)
E. firmum (Kuhn) Urban
Caribbean (West Indies to Colombia). Wind (spores). (1)
E. glossophyllum Hieron.
Andean (Colombia). Wind (spores). (1)
E. minutum (Fée) Moore
Tropical America (Costa Rica and northern South America). Wind (spores). (1)
E. tenuiculum (Fée) Christ
Andean (Colombia and Venezuela to Bolivia). Wind (spores). (1)
E. yarumalense Hieron.
Andean (Colombia). Wind (spores). (1)

Oleandraceae

Nephrolepis biserrata (Sw.) Schott
Pantropical. Wind (spores). (1)
N. cordifolia (L.) Presl
Pantropical. Wind (spores). (1)

Ophioglossaceae

Botrychium underwoodianum Maxon
Caribbean (Costa Rica, Jamaica, Colombia, Venezuela). Wind (spores). (1)
Ophioglossum palmatum L. (Adsersen 1976b:433)
Pantropical. Wind (spores). (1)
O. reticulatum L.
Pantropical. Wind (spores). (1)

Polypodiaceae

Polypodium angustifolium var. ***amphostenon*** (Klotzsch) Hieron.
Tropical America (Mexico and Florida to Argentina). Wind (spores). (1)
P. astrolepis Liebm. (van der Werff 1977:90)
Tropical America (Mexico to Brazil). Wind (spores). (1)
P. aureum var. ***areolatum*** (Willd.) Baker
Tropical America (Mexico and Florida to Argentina). Wind (spores). (1)
P. dispersum A. M. Evans
Tropical America (Mexico and Florida to Bolivia and Brazil). Wind (spores). (1)
P. insularum (Morton) de la Sota
Endemic; probably related to the Andean ***P. bombycinum*** Maxon or ***P. balaonense*** Hieron. Wind (spores). (1)
P. lanceolatum L.
Pantropical. Wind (spores). (1)
P. phyllitidis L.
Tropical America (Mexico and Florida to Uruguay). Wind (spores). (1)
P. polypodioides var. ***burchellii*** (Baker) Weatherby
Tropical America (Guatemala to Bolivia and Brazil). Wind (spores). (1)
P. steirolepis C. Chr.
Andean (Venezuela and Ecuador). Wind (spores). (1)
P. tridens Kunze
Endemic; apparently most closely related to Mexican and Central American species. Wind (spores). (1)

Pteridaceae

Pteris quadriaurita Retz.
Pantropical. Wind (spores). (1)

Sinopteridaceae

Cheilanthes microphylla (Sw.) Sw.
Tropical America (Mexico and Florida to Ecuador). Wind (spores). (1)
C. myriophylla Desv.
Tropical America (Mexico and the West Indies to Chile, Argentina, and Brazil). Wind (spores). (1)
Doryopteris concolor (Langsd. & Fisch.) Kuhn
Tropical America. Wind (spores). (1)
D. pedata var. ***palmata*** (Willd.) Hicken
Tropical America (Mexico to Bolivia). Wind (spores). (1)
Mildella intramarginalis (Link) Trev.
Mexico and Central America (Mexico to Panama). Wind (spores). (1)
Notholaena aurea (Poir.) Desv.
Tropical America (southwestern U.S. and the West Indies to Chile and Argentina). Wind (spores). (1)

N. galapagensis Weatherby & Svens.
Endemic; most closely related to the Mexican and Central American (Texas to Honduras) *N. candida* (Mart. & Gal.) Hook. Wind (spores). (1)
Pellaea sagittata (Cav.) Link
Tropical America (Mexico to Guatemala and Colombia to Bolivia). Wind (spores). (1)

Thelypteridaceae

Thelypteris balbisii (Spreng.) Ching
Tropical America (Mexico and the West Indies to Bolivia and Brazil). Wind (spores). (1)
T. cheilanthoides (Kunze) Proctor (van der Werff 1977:92)
Tropical America (Mexico and the West Indies to Bolivia and Brazil). Wind (spores). (1)
T. conspersa (Schrad.) A. R. Smith (*T. kunthii* [Desv.] Morton, in part; van der Werff 1977:92)
Andean (Panama to Bolivia, Argentina, Uruguay, and Brazil). Wind (spores). (1)
T. gardneriana (Baker) Reed (van der Werff 1977:91)
Andean (Colombia, Ecuador, and Brazil). Wind (spores). (1)
T. aff. *glandulosolanulosa* (C. Chr.) Tryon (van der Werff 1977:92)
Andean (Peru). Wind (spores). (1)
T. grandis var. *pallescens* (C. Chr.) A. R. Smith (Smith 1971:113; as *T. invisa* var. *aequitorialis* [C. Chr.] Morton and *T. kunthii* [Desv.] Morton, in part; van der Werff 1977:93)
Tropical America (Costa Rica and the West Indies to Bolivia and Brazil). Wind (spores). (1)
T. linkiana (Presl) Tryon
Tropical America (Mexico to Bolivia and Brazil). Wind (spores). (1)
T. oligocarpa (Willd.) Ching (van der Werff 1977:92)
Tropical America (Mexico and the West Indies to Bolivia and Brazil). Wind (spores). (1)
T. pachirachis (Mett.) Ching (van der Werff 1977:92)
Tropical America (Panama and the West Indies to Ecuador and Brazil). Wind (spores). (1)
T. patens (Sw.) Small (Smith [1971] cites no collections of this species from the archipelago, but van der Werff [1977:91] includes it in his "Key to the species of *Thelypteris* known from the Galapagos Islands.")
Tropical America (Mexico and Florida to Chile and Argentina).Wind (spores). (1)
T. pilosula (Mett.) Tryon
Andean (Venezuela to Bolivia). Wind (spores). (1)
T. poiteana (Bory) Proctor
Tropical America (Guatemala and the West Indies to Peru and Brazil). Wind (spores). (1)
T. quadrangularis (Fée) Schelpe (Smith [1971] cites no collections from the archipelago, but van der Werff [1977:91] includes this species in his key)
Pantropical. Wind (spores). (1)
T. tetragona subsp. *aberrans* Morton
Endemic; *T. tetragona* (Sw.) Small is tropical American. Wind (spores). (1)
T. thomsonii (Jenm.) Proctor (van der Werff 1977:92)
Caribbean (Jamaica, Hispaniola, and Colombia). Wind (spores). (1)
T. torresiana (Guad.) Alston (van der Werff 1977:91)
Pantropical (originally tropical Asia). Wind (spores). (1)

Vittariaceae

Polytaenium lineatum (Sw.) J. E. Sm. (as *Antrophyum lineatum* [Sw.] Kaulf.)
Tropical America (Mexico and the West Indies to Bolivia). Wind (spores). (1)

MAGNOLIOPHYTA

Monocotyledonae

Agavaceae

Furcraea hexapetala (Jacq.) Urban (as *F. cubensis* [Jacq.] Vent.; Adams 1972:81)
Cultivated escape (1906; Caribbean).

Araceae

Colocasia esculenta (L.) Schott
Cultivated escape (1967; tropical Asia, now pantropical).

Bromeliaceae

Tillandsia insularis Mez (includes var. ***latilamina*** Gilmartin; van der Werff 1977:98).
Endemic; closest relative (***T. multiflora*** Benth.) Andean (Ecuador and Peru).
Wind (seeds plumose). (1)

Cannaceae

Canna lambertii Lindl.
Tropical America (West Indies to Brazil). Birds (internal; seeds 5-7 mm in diameter). (1)
C. ***lutea*** Mill.
Cultivated escape (1964; tropical America).

Commelinaceae

Commelina diffusa Burm. f.
Tropical America (Mexico and Florida to Peru). Birds (internal; seeds ca 3 mm long). (1)

Cyperaceae

Bulbostylis hirtella (Schrad.) Urban
Tropical America (widespread). Birds (internal or external in mud; achenes 0.6 mm long). (1)
Cyperus anderssonii Boeck.
Endemic; perhaps related to the tropical American *C.* ***hermaphroditis*** (Jacq.) Standl. Birds (internal or external in mud; achenes 1-1.25 mm long). (1)
C. ***aristatus*** Rottb.
Pantropical. Birds (internal or external in mud; achenes 0.6-0.7 mm long). (1)
C. ***brevifolius*** (Rottb.) Hassk.
Pantropical. Birds (internal or external in mud; achenes 1.5 mm long). (1)
C. ***compressus*** L.
Introduced weed (1932; pantropical).
C. ***confertus*** Sw.
Caribbean (West Indies to coasts of Colombia and Venezuela). Birds (internal or external in mud; achenes 1-1.2 mm long). (1)
C. ***densicaespitosus*** Mattf. & Kuekenth. (van der Werff 1977:99)
Pantropical. Birds (internal or external in mud; achenes 1 mm long). (1)
C. ***distans*** L. f.
Pantropical. Birds (internal or external in mud; achenes 1-1.2 mm long). (1)
C. ***elegans*** subsp. ***rubiginosus*** (Hook. f.) Eliass.
Endemic, subsp. ***elegans*** is tropical American. Birds (internal or external in mud; achenes 1.2-1.5 mm long). (1)
C. ***esculentus*** L.
Pantropical. Birds (internal or external in mud; achenes 1.5-1.75 mm long). (1)
C. ***grandifolius*** Anderss.
Endemic; perhaps related to the tropical American *C.* ***meyenianus*** Kunth. Birds (internal or external in mud; achenes 1.5-2 mm long). (1)
C. ***laevigatus*** L.
Pantropical. Birds (internal or external in mud; achenes 1.5 mm long). (1)
C. ***ligularis*** L.
Pantropical. Birds (internal or external in mud; achenes 1.5 mm long). (1)
C. ***odoratus*** L. (van der Werff 1977:99)
Introduced weed (1974/75; pantropical).
C. ***polystachyos*** subsp. ***holosericeus*** (Link) T. Koyama
Tropical America (eastern U.S. to Ecuador). Birds (internal or external in mud). (1)
C. ***rivularis*** subsp. ***lagunetto*** (Steud.) Kuekenth.
Tropical America (Central America to Chile and Argentina). Birds (internal or external in mud; achenes 1 mm long). (1)
C. ***rotundus*** L.
Introduced weed (1967, pantropical).
C. ***virens*** subsp. ***drummondii*** (Torr. & Hook.) T. Koyama
Tropical America (southern U.S. to Ecuador and Brazil). Birds (internal or external in mud; achenes 1.25 mm long). (1)
Eleocharis atropurpurea (Retz.) Presl
Pantropical. Birds (internal or external in mud; achenes 0.5 mm long). (1)

E. fistulosa (Poir.) Link
Pantropical. Birds (internal or external in mud; achenes 1.5-2 mm long). (1)

E. maculosa (M. Vahl) Roem. & Schult.
Tropical America (Guatemala to tropical South America). Birds (internal or external in mud; achenes 1 mm long). (1)

E. mutata (L.) Roem. & Schult.
Tropical America (Central America and the West Indies to Paraguay). Birds (internal or external in mud; achenes 1.5-2 mm long). (1)

E. nodulosa (Roth) Schult.
Tropical America (southern U.S. to Argentina). Birds (internal or external in mud; achenes 1 mm long). (1)

E. sellowiana Kunth.
Tropical America (central U.S. to Uruguay). Birds (internal or external in mud; achenes 0.8-1 mm long). (1)

Fimbristylis dichotoma (L.) M. Vahl
Pantropical. Birds (internal or external in mud; achenes 0.8-1.2 mm long). (1)

F. littoralis Gaud.
Introduced weed (1932; pantropical).

Hemicarpha micrantha (M. Vahl) Britt.
Introduced weed (1891; tropical America).

Rhynchospora corymbosa (L.) Britt.
Pantropical. Birds (internal or external in mud; achenes 3-3.5 mm long). (1)

R. minutiflora (Spreng.) C. D. Adams (as *R. micrantha* M. Vahl; Adams 1971:70)
Tropical America (Mexico and the West Indies to Brazil). Birds (internal or external in mud; achenes 0.5-0.7 mm long). (1)

R. nervosa (M. Vahl) Boeck. subsp. *nervosa*
Introduced weed (1953; tropical America).

R. nervosa subsp. *ciliata* (M. Vahl) T. Koyama
Tropical America (Central America and the West Indies to Brazil). Birds (internal or external in mud; achenes 1-1.3 mm long). (1)

R. rugosa (M. Vahl) Gale
Caribbean (West Indies to Colombia, Venezuela and the Guianas; also in the Old World tropics). Birds (internal or external in mud; achenes 2 mm long). (1)

R. tenuis Link
Tropical America (Mexico and the West Indies to Argentina). Birds (internal or external in mud; achenes 1 mm long). (1)

Scleria hirtella Sw.
Pantropical. Birds (internal; achenes 1-1.75 mm long). (1)

S. pterota Presl
Tropical America (Mexico and the West Indies to Argentina). Birds (internal; achenes 1.5-2.5 mm long). (1)

Hypoxidaceae

Hypoxis decumbens L.
Tropical America (Mexico and the West Indies to Paraguay). Birds (internal; seeds ca 1 mm in diameter). (1)

Iridaceae

Sisyrinchium macrocephalum Graham
Andean (Colombia to Argentina). Birds (internal; seeds 1.5 mm in diameter). (1)

Lemnaceae

Lemna aequinoctialis Welw.
Pantropical. Birds (external in mud or by viscid attachment; thalli 1-2.5 mm long, 0.6-2 mm wide). (1)

Najadaceae

Najas guadalupensis (Spreng.) Morong
Tropical America (western U.S. to Uruguay). Birds (internal or external; nutlets or vegetative parts). (1)

N. marina L.
Pantropical. Birds (internal or external; as above). (1)

Orchidaceae

Cranichis lichenophila D. Weber (Weber 1973:18)
Endemic; related to the West Indian *C. tenuis* complex. Wind (minute seeds). (1)
C. schlimii Rchb. f.
Andean (Colombia to Peru). Wind (minute seeds). (1)
Epidendrum spicatum Hook. f.
Endemic; related to the Andean (Ecuador) *E. neglectum* Schltr. Wind (minute seeds). (1)
Erythrodes weberiana Garay
Andean (Ecuador). Wind (minute seeds). (1)
Govenia utriculata (Sw.) Lindl.
Tropical America (Mexico and Florida to Argentina). Wind (minute seeds). (1)
Habenaria alata Hook.
Tropical America (Mexico and the West Indies to Bolivia). Wind (minute seeds). (1)
H. distans Griseb. (Weber 1973:29; as *H. distans* var. *jamaicensis* [Fawc. & Rendle] Cogn.)
Tropical America (Central America and Florida to Bolivia and Brazil). Wind (minute seeds). (1)
H. monorrhiza (Sw.) Rchb. f.
Tropical America (Guatemala and the West Indies to Peru and Brazil). Wind (minute seeds). (1)
Ionopsis utricularioides (Sw.) Lindl.
Tropical America (throughout). Wind (minute seeds). (1)
Liparis nervosa (Thunb.) Lindl.
Pantropical. Wind (minute seeds). (1)
Ponthieva maculata Lindl.
Tropical America (Mexico to Ecuador). Wind (minute seeds). (1)
Prescottia oligantha (Sw.) Lindl.
Tropical America (Mexico and Florida to Argentina). Wind (minute seeds). (1)
Tropidia polystachya (Sw.) Ames
Caribbean (Mexico and Florida to Costa Rica and the Greater Antilles).
Wind (minute seeds). (1)

Poaceae

Anthephora hermaphrodita (L.) Kuntze
Introduced weed (1932; tropical America).
Aristida. The Galapagos species appear to be most closely related to the South America (Brazil) *A. doelliana* Henr. and *A. setifolium* HBK. (1 for genus)
A. divulsa Anderss.
Endemic. Birds (external, mechanical attachment; awns minutely scabrous, 10-12 mm long).
A. repens Trin.
Endemic. Birds (external, mechanical attachment; awns minutely scabrous, 7-10 mm long).
A. subspicata Trin. & Rupr.
Endemic. Birds (external, mechanical attachment; awns minutely scabrous, 10-15 mm long).
A. villosa Robins. & Greenm.
Endemic. Birds (external, mechanical attachment; awns minutely scabrous, 10-12 mm long).
Axonopus compressus (Sw.) Beauv. (van der Werff 1977:99)
Introduced weed (1974/75; pantropical).
Bouteloua disticha (HBK.) Benth.
Introduced weed (1825; tropical America).
Cenchrus echinatus L.
Introduced weed (1899; pantropical, originally tropical America).
C. platyacanthus Anderss.
Endemic; most closely related to the pantropical *C. incertus* M. A. Curtis. Birds (external, mechanical attachment; burs with spines 3-6 mm long, retrorsely barbed near apices). (1)
Chloris mollis (Nees) Swallen
Introduced weed (1891; tropical America).
C. pycnothrix Trin. (Anderson 1974:116)
Introduced weed (1932; pantropical).

C. radiata (L.) Sw.
Introduced weed (1891; tropical America).
C. virgata Sw.
Introduced weed (1906; pantropical).
Coix lacryma-jobi L.
Cultivated escape (1932; pantropical, originally tropical Asia).
Cynodon dactylon (L.) Pers.
Cultivated escape (1964; pantropical).
Dactyloctenium aegyptium (L.) Beauv.
Introduced weed (1891; pantropical, originally Old World).
Digitara ciliaris (Retz.) Koeler (as *D. adscendens* [HBK.] Henrard; Reeder, pers. comm.)
Introduced weed (1899; pantropical).
D. decumbens Stent (van der Werff 1977:99)
Cultivated escape (1974/75; pantropical; originally South African).
D. horizontalis Willd.
Introduced weed (1846; pantropical).
Echinochloa colonum (L.) Link
Introduced weed (1835; pantropical, originally Old World).
Eleusine indica (L.) Gaertn.
Introduced weed (1852; pantropical, originally Old World).
E. ciliaris (L.) R. Br.
Pantropical. Birds (internal; caryopses). (1)
Eragrostis major Host. (as *E. cilianensis* [All.] Lutati; Reeder, pers. comm.)
Introduced weed (1923; pantropical, originally European).
E. mexicana (Hornem.) Link
Tropical America (southwestern U.S. to Chile). Birds (internal; caryopses). (1)
E. pilosa (L.) Beauv. (not hitherto reported with certainty)
Introduced weed (1835; pantropical).
Eriochloa pacifica Mez
Andean (Ecuador and Peru). Birds (internal; caryopses). (1)
Ichnanthus nemorosus (Sw.) Doell
Introduced weed (1932; tropical American).
Leptochloa filiformis (Lam.) Beauv.
Introduced weed (1899; tropical America).
L. virgata (L.) Beauv.
Introduced weed (1852; tropical America).
Melinis minutiflora Beauv. (van der Werff 1977:99)
Cultivated escape (1974/75; pantropical, originally tropical Africa).
Muhlenbergia microsperma (DC.) Kunth
Tropical America (southwestern U.S. to Guatemala and Colombia and Venezuela to Peru). Birds (external, mechanical attachment; lemma awn 1-3 cm long). (1)
Oplismenus setarius (Lam.) Roem. & Schult.
Introduced weed (1891; tropical America).
Panicum arundinariae Fourn.
Tropical America (Mexico to Ecuador). Birds (internal; caryopses). (1)
P. dichotomiflorum Michx.
Tropical America (U.S. to Argentina). Birds (external in mud or internal; caryopses). (1)
P. fasciculatum Sw.
Tropical America (southern U.S. to Peru and Brazil). Birds (external in mud or internal; caryopses). (1)
P. geminatum Forsk.
Pantropical. Birds (external in mud or internal; caryopses). (1)
P. glutinosum Sw.
Tropical America (Mexico and the West Indies to Argentina). Birds (external in mud or internal; caryopses). (1)
P. hirticaule Presl
Tropical America (southwestern U.S. and the West Indies to Argentina). Birds (internal or external in mud; caryopses). (1)

P. laxum Sw.
Tropical America (Mexico and the West Indies to Argentina). Birds (external in mud or internal; caryopses). (1)
P. maximum Jacq.
Cultivated escape (1964; pantropical, originally African).
P. muticum Forsk. (as *P. purpurascens* Raddi; Reeder, pers. comm.)
Cultivated escape (1906, pantropical, originally African).
Paspalum. The three endemics are most closely related to Andean species. (1 for endemics)
P. conjugatum Bergius
Cultivated escape (1852; pantropical).
P. distichum L. (as *P. vaginatum* Sw.; Adams 1972:182).
Pantropical. Birds (external in mud or internal; caryopses). (1)
P. galapageium Chase var. *galapageium*
Endemic. Birds (internal or external in mud; caryopses).
P. galapageium var. *minoratum* Chase
Endemic. Birds (internal or external in mud; caryopses).
(*P. paniculatum* L. The two Edmonston collections of this taxon discussed by Reeder and Reeder [in Wiggins & Porter 1971:873] most likely were collected in mainland Ecuador.)
P. pasploides (Michx.) Scriber (as *P. distichum* L.; Adams 1972:182)
Pantropical. Birds (external in mud or internal; caryopses). (1)
P. penicillatum Hook. f.
Andean (Ecuador to Bolivia). Birds (internal or external in mud; caryopses). (1)
P. redundans Chase
Endemic. Birds (internal or external in mud; caryopses).
Pennisetum pauperum Steud.
Endemic; perhaps related to the Andean (Ecuador and Peru) *P. intectum* Chase. Birds (external, mechanical attachment; spikelets subtended by bristles ca 4-6 mm long). (1)
P. purpureum Schum.
Cultivated escape (1966; pantropical, originally African).
Setaria geniculata (Lam.) Beauv.
Tropical America (eastern U.S. to Argentina).
Birds (internal or external in mud; caryopses). (1)
S. setosa (Sw.) Beauv.
Caribbean (West Indies to Colombia). Birds (internal; caryopses). (1)
S. vulpisecta (Lam.) Roem. & Schult.
Introduced weed (1932; tropical America).
Sporobolus indicus (L.) R. Br.
Tropical America (southeastern U.S. to Paraguay).
Birds (internal; caryopses 1-1.2 mm long). (1)
S. pyramidatus (Lam.) Hitchc.
Tropical America (southern U.S. to Argentina). Birds (internal or external in mud; caryopses 1 mm long or less). (1)
S. virginicus (L.) Kunth
Pantropical. Oceanic drift (rhizomes or caryopses). (1)
Stenotaphrum secundatum (Walt.) Kuntze
Pantropical. Birds (internal or external in mud; caryopses). (1)
Trichoneura. The Galapagos taxa apparently are most closely related to the Andean (Peru) *T. weberaueri* Pilger. (1 for genus)
T. lindleyana (Kunth) Ekman var. *lindleyana*
Endemic. Birds (external, mechanical attachment; lemmas 3-3.5 mm long, ciliate marginally, awned apically, with a sharp callus basally).
T. lindleyana var. *albemarlensis* (Robins. & Greenm.) J. & C. Reeder
Endemic. Birds (as for var. *lindleyana*).
Trisetum howellii Hitchc.
Endemic; apparently most closely related to the tropical American *T. deyeuxioides* (HBK.) Kunth. Birds (external, mechanical attachment; lemmas 4-5 mm long, with a geniculate twisted awn 5-6 mm long apically). (1)
Uniola pittieri Hack.
Tropical America (Mexico to Ecuador). Oceanic drift (caryopses, culms, or stolons). (1)

Potamogetonaceae

Potamogeton pectinatus L.
Pantropical. Birds (internal or external; drupelets, tubers, or vegetative parts). (1)

Ruppiaceae

Ruppia maritima L.
Pantropical. Birds (internal or external; nutlets or vegetative parts). (1)

Dicotyledonae

Acanthaceae

Blechum pyramidatum (Lam.) Urban (as ***B. brownei*** f. ***puberulum*** Leonard; Adams 1972:689)
Pantropical (originally tropical America). Birds (external, viscid attachment; seeds ca 1.5 mm long, with dense gelatinous band of trichomes on margins when wetted). (1)

Dicliptera peruviana (Lam.) Juss.
Andean (Ecuador and Peru). Birds (external, viscid attachment; seeds 1-1.25 mm in diameter, presumably becoming mucilaginous when wetted). (1)

Elytraria imbricata (M. Vahl) Pers.
Introduced weed (1939; pantropical, originally tropical America).

Justicia galapagana Lindau
Endemic; apparently most closely related to the Andean (Bolivia) ***J. kuntzii*** Lindau. Birds (external, viscid attachment; seeds 2.5 mm in diameter, trichomes presumably becoming mucilaginous when wetted). (1)

Ruellia floribunda Hook.
Andean (Ecuador and Peru). Birds (external, viscid attachment; seeds 2 mm long, becoming mucilaginous-pubescent when wetted). (1)

Tetramerium nervosum Nees
Tropical America (Central America to northern South America).
Birds (external, viscid attachment; seeds 1.5 mm long, presumably becoming mucilaginous when wetted). (1)

Aizoaceae

Sesuvium edmonstonei Hook f.
Endemic, presumably most closely related to the following. Oceanic drift (vegetative parts or seeds). (1 for genus)

S. portulacastrum L.
Pantropical. Oceanic drift (vegetative parts or seeds).

Trianthema portulacastrum L.
Pantropical. Oceanic drift (vegetative parts or seeds). (1)

Amaranthaceae

Achyranthes aspera L. (van der Werff 1977:93)
Introduced weed (1974/75; pantropical, perhaps originally Old World).

Alternanthera. The endemics are most closely related to Andean species. (4 for endemics)

A. echinocephala (Hook. f.) Christoph.
Andean (Peru). Birds (external in mud; utricles). (1)

A. filifolia (Hook. f.) Howell subsp. ***filifolia***
Endemic, most closely related to ***A. flavicoma***. Birds (external in mud; utricles).

A. filifolia subsp. ***glauca*** Howell
Endemic. Birds (external in mud; utricles).

A. filifolia subsp. ***glaucescens*** (Hook. f.) Eliass.
Endemic. Birds (external in mud; utricles).

A. filifolia subsp. ***microcephala*** Eliass.
Endemic. Birds (external in mud; utricles).

A. filifolia subsp. ***nudicaulis*** (Hook. f.) Eliass.
Endemic, perhaps also occurring in Chile. Birds (external in mud; utricles).

A. filifolia subsp. ***pintensis*** Eliass.
Endemic. Birds (external in mud; utricles).

A. filifolia subsp. ***rabidensis*** Eliass.
Endemic. Birds (external in mud; utricles).

A. flavicoma (Anderss.) Howell
Endemic. Birds (external in mud; utricles).
A. galapagensis (Stewart) Howell
Endemic. Birds (external in mud; utricles).
A. halimifolia (Lam.) Standl.
Tropical America (Mexico and the West Indies to Chile). Birds (internal or external in mud; utricles). (1)
A. helleri (Robins.) Howell
Endemic. Birds (external in mud; utricles).
A. lehmannii Hieron. (Eliasson 1972:320).
Introduced weed (1971; Andean).
A. nesiotes I. M. Johnston.
Endemic. Birds (external in mud; utricles).
A. rugulosa (Robins.) Howell
Andean (Peru). Birds (internal; utricles). (1)
A. sessilis (L.) R. Br. (van der Werff 1977:93)
Introduced weed (1974/75; pantropical).
A. snodgrassii (Robins.) Howell
Endemic; closely related to *A. vestita*. Birds (external in mud; utricles).
A. vestita (Anderss.) Howell
Andean (Chile). Birds (external in mud; utricles). (1)
Amaranthus. The endemics presumably are related to Andean species. (2 for endemics)
A. anderssonii Howell
Endemic; apparently related to *A. squamulatus*. Birds (internal or external in mud; seeds ca 0.8 mm long).
A. dubius Mart.
Introduced weed (1835; pantropical).
A. furcatus Howell
Endemic closely related to *A. sclerantoides*. Birds (internal or external in mud; seeds ca 1 mm in diameter).
A. gracilis Desf.
Introduced weed (1906; pantropical).
A. lividus L.
Introduced weed (1906, pantropical).
A. quitensis HBK.
Cultivated escape (1835; Andean).
A. sclerantoides (Anderss.) Anderss.
Endemic. Birds (internal or external in mud; seeds ca 1 mm in diameter).
A. spinosus L.
Introduced weed (1852; pantropical, originally probably tropical America).
A. squamulatus (Anderss.) Robins.
Endemic. Birds (internal or external in mud; seeds 0.9-1.11 mm in diameter).
Froelichia. The Galapagos taxa perhaps are related to the tropical American *F. interrupta* (L.) Moq. (1 for genus)
F. juncea Robins. & Greenm. subsp. *juncea*
Endemic. Wind (perianth-tubes with wings ca 0.5 mm wide in fruit).
F. juncea subsp. *alata* Howell
Endemic. Wind (perianth-tubes with wings ca 1 mm wide in fruit).
F. nudicaulis Hook. f. subsp. *nudicaulis*
Endemic. Wind (perianth-tubes with wings ca 1 mm wide in fruit).
F. nudicaulis subsp. *curta* Howell
Endemic. Wind (perianth-tubes with wings ca 0.7 mm wide in fruit).
F. nudicaulis subsp. *lanigera* (Anderss.) Eliass.
Endemic. Wind (perianth-tubes more or less wingless in fruit).
(*Iresine edmonstonei* Hook. f. The type collection of Edmonston, reputedly from the Galapagos Islands, most likely was made in mainland Ecuador.)
Lithophila. The relationships of the Galapagos endemics are with Caribbean species. (1 for genus)
L. radiata (Hook. f.) Standl.
Endemic. Wind (floral bracts and bractlets 2.5-3 mm long, tepals ca 3 mm long).

L. subscaposa (Hook f.) Standl.
Endemic. Wind (floral bracts and bractlets 2-2.5 mm long, tepals ca. 3 mm long).
Philoxerus rigidus (Robins. & Greenm.) Howell
Endemic; the genus is pantropical. Wind (bracts ca 2 mm long, woolly-pubescent basally, bractlets 2.5-2.7 mm long, tepals 2.6-3 mm long). (1)
Pleuropetalum darwinii Hook. f.
Endemic; probably most closely related to the tropical American ***P. sprucei*** (Hook. f.) Standl. Birds (internal; seeds 1-1.5 mm in diameter). (1)

Anacardiaceae

Spondias purpurea L.
Cultivated escape (1964; pantropical, originally tropical America).

Annonaceae

Annona cherimola Mill.
Cultivated escape (1906; pantropical, originally Andean).
A. muricata L.
Cultivated escape (1906; pantropical, originally tropical America).

Apiaceae

Apium laciniatum (DC.) Urban
Andean (Ecuador to Chile). Birds (internal; schizocarps 1.5-2.5 mm long). (1)
A. leptophyllum (Pers.) F. Muell.
Introduced weed (1835; pantropical, originally tropical America).
Bowlesia palmata Ruiz & Pav. (Eliasson 1970:352)
Andean (Ecuador and Peru). Birds (external, mechanical attachment; schizocarps 2.5-4 mm long, stellate-pubescent and glochidiate). (1)
Centella asiatica (L.) Urban
Pantropical. Birds (external in mud or internal; schizocarps 2-4 mm long, 3-5 mm wide). (1)
Hydrocotyle galapagensis Robins.
Endemic; closely related to, and perhaps only a form of, ***H. umbellata***. Birds (external in mud or internal; schizocarps). (1 for genus)
H. umbellata L. (van der Werff 1977:98)
Pantropical; originally tropical America. Birds (external in mud or internal; schizocarps 1-2 mm long, 2-3 mm wide).
Petroselinum crispum (Mill.) A. W. Hill
Cultivated escape (1852; pantropical, originally Europe).

Apocynaceae

Vallesia glabra (Cav.) Link var. *glabra*
Tropical America (Mexico and the West Indies to Argentina). Birds (internal; drupes or berries 8-12 mm long, seeds 6-10 mm long). (1 for genus)
V. glabra var. *pubescens* (Anderss.) Wiggins
Endemic; perhaps only a pubescent form of var. ***glabra***, not worthy of taxonomic recognition.

Asclepiadaceae

Asclepias curassavica L.
Cultivated escape (1906; tropical America).
Sarcostemma angustissimum (Anderss.) R. W. Holm (as ***S. angustissima***)
Endemic; probably related to an Andean or South American species. Wind (seeds 6-7 mm long, 2.5-3 mm wide, wing 0.5-0.8 mm wide, coma ca 2 cm long). (1)

Asteraceae

Acanthospermum microcarpum Robins.
Introduced weed (1899; Andean).
Adenostemma platyphyllum Cass. (as ***A. lavenia*** [L.] Kuntze; King & Robinson 1975:892)
Introduced weed (1964; Andean).
Ageratum conyzoides L. subsp. *conyzoides*
Introduced weed (1906; pantropical, originally tropical America).
A. conyzoides subsp. *latifolium* (Cav.) M. F. Johnson (Johnson 1971:33)
Introduced weed (1835; tropical America).

Ambrosia artemisiifolia L.
Introduced weed (1906, pantropical, originally New World).
Baccharis. The Galapagos species appear to be closely related. (1 for genus)
B. gnidiifolia HBK.
Andean (Ecuador). Wind (pappus of achenes 2-3 mm long).
B. steetzii Anderss.
Endemic. Wind (pappus of achenes 2-3 mm long).
Bidens cynapiifolia HBK.
Introduced weed (1932; tropical America).
B. pilosa L.
Introduced weed (1852; pantropical, originally Caribbean).
B. riparia HBK.
Tropical America (Mexico to Peru and Brazil). Birds (external; achenes 10-15 mm long, pappus of 3-5 retrorsely-barbed awns). (1)
Blainvillea dichotoma (Murr.) Stewart
Pantropical.
Birds (external; achenes 2-3.5 mm long, pappus awns 0.5-1.5 mm long, hirtellous). (1)
Brickellia diffusa (M. Vahl) A. Gray
Introduced weed (1899; tropical America).
Chrysanthellum pusillum Hook. f.
Endemic; most closely related to the Mexican *C. mexicanum* Green. (B. L. Turner, pers. comm.). Birds (external; achenes 1-2 mm long, irregularly tuberculate). (1)
Conyza bonariensis (L.) Cronq.
Introduced weed (1891, pantropical, originally tropical America).
Darwiniothamnus. An endemic genus, most closely related to *Erigeron*, its nearest relatives probably being the Andean (Chile) *E. berterianus* DC. and *E. litoralis* (Phil.) Skottsb. (Harling 1962: 108). (1 for genus)
D. lancifolius (Hook. f.) Harling subsp. *lancifolius* (as *D. tenuifolius* var. *glabriusculus* [Stewart] Cronq.).
Endemic. Wind (pappus).
D. lancifolius subsp. *glandulosus* Harling (as *D. tenuifolius* var. *glandulosus* [Harling] Cronq.).
Endemic. Wind (pappus).
D. tenuifolius (Hook. f.) Harling subsp. *tenuifolius* (as var. *tenuifolius*).
Endemic. Wind (pappus).
D. tenuifolius subsp. *santacruzianus* Harling (as var. *tenuifolius*).
Endemic. Wind (pappus).
Delilia. The Galapagos endemics are closely related to *D. biflora*, the only other member of the genus. (1 for endemics)
D. biflora (L.) Kuntze (van der Werff 1977:94)
Introduced weed (1975/75, tropical America).
D. inelegans (Hook f.) Kuntze (as *Elvira inelegans* [Hook. f.] Robins.)
Endemic. Wind (achenes included within persistent involucral bracts, dispersed as a unit).
D. repens (Hook. f.) Kuntze (as *Elvira repens* [Hook. f.] Robins.)
Endemic. Wind (achenes included within persistent involucral bracts, dispersed as a unit).
Eclipta alba (L.) Hassk.
Pantropical (originally tropical America). Birds (external in mud or internal; achenes 2-2.5 mm long). (1)
Encelia hispida Anderss.
Endemic; closely related to the Andean (Peru) *E. canescens* Lam.
Wind (achenes 4-5 mm long, densely pubescent, upper trichomes surpassing achene body by more than 1 mm). (1)
Enydra maritima (HBK.) DC.
Andean (Pacific Coast of tropical South America). Birds (external in mud or internal; achenes ca 2 mm long). (1)
Erechtites hieracifolia var. *cacaloides* (Spreng.) Griseb. (van der Werff 1977:94)
Introduced weed (1974/75; pantropical, originally tropical America).
Flaveria bidentis (L.) Kuntze
Introduced weed (1852; tropical America).

Fleischmannia pratensis (Klatt) King & Robins. (as *Eupatorium pycnocephalum* Less.; King & Robinson 1975:945)
Introduced weed (1905; tropical America).
Galinsoga urticaefolia (HBK.) Benth. (van der Werff 1977:94)
Introduced weed (1974/75, pantropical, originally tropical America).
Gnaphalium purpureum L.
Introduced weed (1963; tropical America).
G. vira-vira Molina
Introduced weed (1906, Andean).
Jaegeria gracilis Hook. f. (including *J. crassa* Torres; van der Werff 1977:94-95)
Endemic; closely related to the tropical American *J. hirta* (Lag.) Less.
Birds (external in mud; achenes ca 1 mm long). (1)
Jungia hirsuta Cuatr.
Introduced weed (1967; Andean).
Koanophyllon solidaginoides (HBK.) King & Robins. (as *Eupatorium solidaginoides* HBK.; King & Robinson 1971:151)
Tropical America (Mexico to Ecuador). Wind (achenes 1.5-2.5 mm long, pappus abundant, longer than achenes). (1)
Lecocarpus. An endemic genus most closely related to the tropical American *Acanthospermum* and *Melampodium*. (1 for genus)
L. lecocarpoides (Robins. & Greenm.) Cronq. & Stuessy
Endemic. Birds (external, mechanical attachment; achenes; see Carlquist 1966:41-42).
L. leptolobus (Blake) Cronq. & Stuessy
Endemic. Birds (as in *L. lecocarpoides*).
L. pinnatifidus Decne.
Endemic. Birds (as in *L. lecocarpoides*).
Macraea laricifolia Hook. f.
Endemic; monotypic, apparently most closely related to tropical American species of *Wedelia*.
Birds (external, mechanical attachment; achenes; see Carlquist 1966:41) (1)
Pectis. The Galapagos endemics appear to be most closely related to Andean species. (1 for endemics)
P. linifolia L.
Introduced weed (1852; Caribbean).
P. subsquarrosa (Hook. f.) Schultz-Bip.
Endemic. Birds (external, mechanical attachment; achenes 2.5-3.5 mm long, minutely hispidulous, minutely barbed pappus 2-3 mm long).
P. tenuifolia (DC.) Schultz-Bip.
Endemic. Birds (external, mechanical attachment; achenes 3-4 mm long, minutely hispidulous, minutely barbed pappus 3-5 mm long).
Porophyllum ruderale var. *macrocephalum* (DC.) Cronq.
Introduced weed (1852; tropical America).
Pseudelephantopus spicatus (Aubl.) C. F. Baker
Introduced weed (1932; pantropical, originally tropical America).
P. spiralis (Less.) Cronq.
Introduced weed (1967, tropical America).
Scalesia. An endemic genus apparently most closely related to Andean species of *Helianthus* and *Viguiera*. The treatment below follows that of Eliasson (1974). The original introduction of the genus most likely was by birds (Carlquist 1966:40-41). (1 for genus)
S. affinis Hook. f. subsp. *affinis*
Endemic. Birds (external, mechanical attachment; achenes 2.5-4 mm long, pappus absent or rudimentary).
S. affinis subsp. *brachyloba* Harling (as *S. affinis*; Eliasson 1974:77)
Endemic. Birds (as in subsp. *affinis*).
S. affinis subsp. *gummifera* (Hook. f.) Harling (as *S. affinis*; Eliasson 1974:77)
Endemic. Birds (external, mechanical attachment; achenes 2.5-4 mm long, pappus rarely forming an awn to ca as long as achene).
S. aspera Anderss.
Endemic. Birds (external, mechanical attachment; achenes 4-5 mm long, pappus rarely prolonged into 2 awns to ca 4 mm long).

S. atractyloides Arn. var. ***atractyloides***
Endemic. Birds (external, mechanical attachment; achenes 3-4 mm long, pappus sometimes forming 1-2 short awns).
S. atractyloides var. ***darwinii*** (Hook. f.) Eliass. (as ***S. atractyloides***; Eliasson 1974:60)
Endemic. Birds (as in var. ***atractyloides***).
S. baurii Robins. & Greenm. subsp. ***baurii*** (as ***S. incisa***; Eliasson 1974:93).
Endemic. Birds (external, mechanical attachment; achenes 3.5-4 mm long, pappus absent or rudimentary and forming 1-2 small callosities).
S. baurii subsp. ***hopkinsii*** (Robins.) Eliass. (as ***S. incisa***; Eliasson 1974:94)
Endemic. Birds (as in subsp. ***baurii***).
S. cordata Stewart
Endemic. Birds (external, mechanical attachment; achenes ca 3.5 mm long, pappus generally of 2 laciniate-margined awns to 2 mm long).
S. crockeri Howell
Endemic. Birds (external, mechanical attachment; achenes 4-5 mm long, pappus apparently absent).
S. divisa Anderss. (as ***S. incisa***; Eliasson 1974:66)
Endemic. Birds (external, mechanical attachment; achenes ca 4-5 mm long, pappus rarely present as 1-2 pointed callosities to ca 0.5 mm long).
S. helleri Robins. subsp. ***helleri***
Endemic. Birds (external, mechanical attachment; achenes 2-4 mm long, pappus absent or present as low callosities).
S. helleri subsp. ***santacruziana*** Harling (as ***S. helleri***; Eliasson 1974:89)
Endemic. Birds (as in subsp. ***helleri***).
S. incisa Hook. f.
Endemic. Birds (external, mechanical attachment; achenes 4-4.5 mm long, pappus apparently absent).
S. microcephala Robins. var. ***microcephala***
Endemic. Birds (external, mechanical attachment; achenes 3-4 mm long, pappus rarely present, of 1-2 awns to ca 1.5 mm long).
S. microcephala var. ***cordifolia*** Eliass. (Eliasson 1974:55)
Endemic. Birds (as in var. ***microcephala***).
S. pedunculata Hook. f. (includes var. ***parviflora*** Howell; Eliasson 1974:69)
Endemic. Birds (external, mechanical attachment; achenes ca 4-6 mm long, pappus rarely forming a short awn).
S. retroflexa Hemsley (as ***S. incisa***; Eliasson 1974:88)
Endemic. Birds (external, mechanical attachment; achenes ca 4 mm long, pappus absent).
S. stewartii Riley
Endemic. Birds (external, mechanical attachment; achenes 3-4 mm long, pappus apparently absent).
S. villosa Stewart
Endemic. Birds (external, mechanical attachment; achenes 3-4 mm long, pappus apparently absent).
Sonchus oleraceus L.
Introduced weed (1899; pantropical, originally Old World).
Spilanthes acmella (L.) Murr.
Introduced weed (1846; pantropical).
S. darwinii D. M. Porter (as ***S. diffusa*** Hook. f.; Porter 1978)
Endemic; apparently most closely related to tropical American species. Birds (external, mechanical attachment; achenes 1.4-1.5 mm long, pappus absent or of 1 small awn). (1)
Synedrella nodiflora (L.) Gaertn.
Introduced weed (1963; pantropical, originally tropical America).
Tridax procumbens L. (van der Werff 1977:95)
Introduced weed (1974/75; pantropical, originally Central America).

Avicenniaceae

Avicennia germinans (L.) L.
Tropical America (Texas and Florida to Peru and Brazil).
Oceanic drift (capsule 1.2-5 cm long). (1)

Balanophoraceae

Ombrophytum peruvianum Poepp. & Endl. (Adsersen 1976a)
Andean (Ecuador, Peru, Brazil). Birds (internal; drupes 3-4 mm long, red-violet). (1)

Basellaceae

Anredera ramosa (Moq.) Eliass.
Mexico and Central America (Mexico, Guatemala, Costa Rica).
Birds (internal, small drupes). (1)

Batidaceae

Batis maritima L.
Pantropical.
Oceanic drift (ovaries coalescent to form fleshy compound fruits 5-20 mm long). (1)

Bixaceae

Bixa orellana L.
Cultivated escape (1906; pantropical, originally South America).

Bombacaceae

Ochroma pyramidale (Lam.) Urban
Cultivated escape (1964; tropical America).

Boraginaceae

Cordia. The four Galapagos endemics are most closely related to Andean species, three being related to *C. polyantha* Benth. (Colombia to Peru) and the fourth (*C. revoluta*) having its relationships elsewhere. (2 for endemics)

C. anderssonii (Kuntze) Guerke
Endemic. Birds (internal; drupes 6-10 mm long, flesh thin, reddish).

C. leucophlyctis Hook. f.
Endemic. Birds (internal; drupes 4-6 mm long, scarlet).

C. lutea Lam.
Andean (Ecuador and Peru; introduced into Marquesas Islands).
Birds (internal; drupes 8-12 mm wide, fleshy). (1)

C. revoluta Hook. f.
Endemic. Birds (internal; drupes 5-6 mm long, reddish).

C. scouleri Hook. f.
Endemic. Birds (internal; drupes 3-5 mm long).

Heliotropium anderssonii Robins.
Endemic; relationships are with Andean species. Birds (internal; schizocarps 1-1.2 mm long, 2-3 mm wide). (1)

H. angiospermum Murr.
Tropical America (Florida to Argentina). Birds (internal; schizocarps 1.8-2 mm high, 2-2.8 mm wide, mericarps 2). (1)

H. curassavicum L.
Pantropical. Birds (internal or external in mud; schizocarps 1.5-2 mm long, 2-2.5 mm wide). (1)

H. indicum L.
Pantropical. Birds (internal or external in mud; schizocarps 2.5-3.5 mm long, mericarps 4). (1)

H. rufipilum var. *anademum* I. M. Johnst.
Introduced weed (1932; Andean).

Tiquilia. The Galapagos species are most closely related to the Andean (Ecuador to Chile) *T. paronychioides* (Phil.) A. Richardson. (1 for genus)

T. darwinii (Hook. f.) A. Richardson (as *Coldenia darwinii* [Hook. f.]. A. Gray; Richardson 1977:565)
Endemic. Birds (internal; mericarps 0.7-0.8 mm long).

T. galapagoa (Howell) A. Richardson (as *Coldenia fusca* [Hook. f.] A. Gray and *C. galapagoa* Howell; Richardson 1977:565)
Endemic. Birds (internal; mericarps 0.7-0.8 mm long).

T. nesiotica (Howell) A. Richardson (as *Coldenia nesiotica* Howell)
Endemic. Birds (internal; mericarps 0.75-0.85 mm long).

Tournefortia. The endemics apparently are related to the tropical American (Florida to South America) *T. volubilis* L. (1 for endemics)

T. psilostachya HBK.
Andean (Colombia to Peru and Brazil). Birds (internal; berries 5-6 mm long, flesh thin, yellowish to yellow-orange). (1)

T. pubescens Hook. f.
Endemic. Birds (internal; berries 3-6 mm long, flesh thin, white).

T. rufo-sericea Hook. f.
Endemic. Birds (internal; berries 5-6 mm in diameter, flesh white-translucent).

Brassicaceae

Brassica campestris L.
Introduced weed (1899, pantropical, originally Europe).

Coronopus didymus (L.) J. E. Smith
Introduced weed (1835, pantropical, originally Europe).

Lepidium virginicum L.
Introduced weed (1906; pantropical, originally North America).

Raphanus sativus L.
Cultivated escape (1852; pantropical, originally Europe).

Burseraceae

Bursera. The two Galapagos species are closely related. (1 for genus)

B. graveolens (HBK.) Trian. & Planch.
Andean (Venezuela to Peru). Birds (internal; drupes 9-12 mm long, reddish).

B. malacophylla Robins.
Endemic. Birds (internal; drupes 8-13 mm long, reddish).

Cactaceae

Brachycereus nesioticus (K. Schum.) Backbg.
Endemic (a monotypic genus); most closely related to the Andean (Ecuador) *Armatocereus cartwrightianus* (Britt. & Rose) Backb. Birds (internal; berries dark, 1.5-3.5 cm long, seeds 1-1.5 mm long). (1)

Jasminocereus. An endemic genus most closely related to the Andean (Ecuador) *Monvillea maritima* Britt. & Rose. (1 for genus)

J. thouarsii (Weber) Backbg. var. *thouarsii*
Endemic. Birds (internal; berries 2.8-5 cm long, olive-green, seeds 1 mm long).

J. thouarsii var. *delicatus* (Dawson) Anderson & Walkington
Endemic. Birds (internal; berries 1.5-4.4 cm long, usually reddish, seeds ca 1 mm long).

J. thouarsii var. *sclerocarpus* (K. Schum.) Anderson & Walkington
Endemic. Birds (internal; berries 4-7 cm long, green suffused with red, seeds ca. 1.5 mm long).

Opuntia. Relationships of the Galapagos endemics are Andean. (2 for genus)

O. echios Howell var. *echios*
Endemic. Birds (internal; berries 4-6 cm long, green to brown, seeds 2-3 mm long).

O. echios var. *barringtonensis* Dawson
Endemic. Birds (internal; berries 7.2-11.7 cm long, seeds 3-5 mm long).

O. echios var. *gigantea* (Howell) D. M. Porter
Endemic. Birds (internal; berries 5.5-7.5 cm long, seeds 2-3 mm long).

O. echios var. *inermis* Dawson
Endemic. Birds (internal; berries 4-5.2 cm long, seeds 2-3 mm long).

O. echios var. *zacana* (Howell) Anderson & Walkington
Endemic. Birds (internal; berries 4-8.5 cm long, seeds 3-4 mm long).

O. galapageia Hensl. var. *galapageia*
Endemic. Birds (internal; berries 2-6 cm long, green, seeds 2.5-3.3 mm long).

O. galapageia var. *macrocarpa* Dawson
Endemic. Birds (internal; berries 3.2-5 cm long, green, seeds 3.5-5 mm long).

O. galapageia var. *profusa* Anderson & Walkington
Endemic. Birds (internal; berries 1.7-2.5 cm long, yellow-green to brown, seeds 2-3 mm long).

O. helleri K. Schum.
Endemic. Birds (internal; berries 4-7 cm long, green, seeds 4-6 mm long).

O. insularis Stewart
Endemic. Birds (internal; berries 2-4.2 cm long, greenish, seeds 2.5-3.5 mm long).
O. megasperma Howell var. *megasperma*
Endemic. Birds (internal; berries 8-17 cm long, yellowish-green, seeds 8-13 mm long).
O. megasperma var. *mesophytica* J. Lundh
Endemic. Birds (internal; berries 4-6 cm long, seeds 7-10 mm long).
O. megasperma var. *orientalis* (Howell) D. M. Porter
Endemic. Birds (internal; berries 6-13 cm long, seeds 5-10 mm long).
O. saxicola Howell
Endemic. Birds (internal; berries 2.5-3.9 cm long, green seeds 2-3 mm long).

Caesalpiniaceae

Caesalpinia bonduc (L.) Roxb.
Pantropical. Oceanic drift (seeds). (1)
Cassia bicapsularis L.
Introduced weed (1964; pantropical, originally tropical America).
C. hirsuta L.
Introduced weed (1888; pantropical, originally tropical America).
C. occidentalis L.
Pantropical. Birds (internal; capsules 8-10 cm long; seeds). (1)
C. picta G. Don
Andean (Ecuador and Peru). Birds (internal; capsules 7-11 cm long, seeds many). (1)
C. tora L.
Introduced weed (1930; pantropical).
C. uniflora Mill.
Caribbean (Mexico and the West Indies to Venezuela). Birds (internal; capsules 6-7 cm long, seeds). (1)
Parkinsonia aculeata L.
Pantropical (originally tropical America).
Oceanic drift (seeds to ca 1 cm long). (1)

Calltrichaceae

Callitriche deflexa Hegelm. (Eliasson 1972:320)
Introduced weed (1966; tropical America).

Capparidaceae

Cleome viscosa L.
Introduced weed (1963; pantropical, originally tropical Asia).

Caricaceae

Carica papaya L.
Cultivated escape (1852; pantropical, originally Andean).

Caryophyllaceae

Drymaria cordata (L.) Willd.
Pantropical. Birds (internal; seeds ca 1 mm in diameter). (1)
D. monticola Howell
Endemic; closely related to several Andean species.
Birds (internal; seeds ca 1 mm in diameter). (1)
D. rotundifolia A. Gray
Andean (Ecuador to Bolivia). Birds (internal; seeds ca 0.8 mm in diameter). (1)
Stellaria media (L.) Vill.
Introduced weed (1967; pantropical).

Celastraceae

Maytenus octogona (L'Her.) DC.
Andean (Ecuador to Chile). Birds (internal; seeds 5-7 mm long, covered by pulpy bright red aril). (1)

Ceratophyllaceae

Ceratophyllum llerenae Fassett (Hamann 1974a:245)
Caribbean (Guatemala to Colombia, Trinidad, Surinam, and Brazil). Birds (internal; achenes ca 3.5 mm long). (1)

Chenopodiaceae

Atriplex peruviana Moq.
Andean (Peru and Chile). Birds (external in mud; nutlets enclosed in accrescent bractlets 4-8 mm long and 3-6 mm wide). (1)

Chenopodium ambrosioides L.
Introduced weed (1932; pantropical, originally perhaps Mexico and Central America).

C. murale L.
Introduced weed (1932; pantropical, originally probably Old World).

Salicornia fruticosa L.
Pantropical. Oceanic drift (utricles enclosed by spongy perianth; vegetative parts). (1)

Combretaceae

Conocarpus erecta L.
Pantropical. Oceanic drift (pseudocarps 3-3.5 mm long). (1)

Laguncularia racemosa (L.) Gaertn. f.
Pantropical. Oceanic drift (pseudocarps 15-21 mm long). (1)

Convolvulaceae

Convolvulus soldanella L.
Pantropical. Oceanic drift (capsules 1-1.5 cm in diameter, enclosed by accrescent bracts and sepals; seeds 5-6 mm long). (1)

Dichondra repens var. *microcalyx* Hallier f.
Andean (Colombia and Brazil to Peru and Argentina).
Birds (internal; seeds 1.8-2.2 mm long. (1)

Evolvulus convolvuloides (Willd.) Stearn (as *E. glaber* Spreng.; Adams 1972:789)
Tropical America (Mexico and Florida to Paraguay).
Birds (internal; seeds 1.8-2.2 mm long). (1)

E. simplex Anderss.
Andean (Ecuador and Peru). Birds (internal; seeds ca 1.5 mm long). (1)

Ipomoea alba L.
Cultivated escape (1899; pantropical, originally tropical America).

I. batatas (L.) Lam. (Hamann 1974a:248)
Cultivated escape (1972; pantropical, originally tropical America).

I. habeliana Oliv.
Endemic; relationships presumably with tropical America. Oceanic drift (seeds 8-10 mm long, marginally pubescent with trichomes 4-5 mm long). (1)

I. linearifolia Hook. f.
Endemic; closely related to, or perhaps conspecific with, the basically Andean (Dutch West Indies, Venezuela, Ecuador, Peru) *I. incarnata* (Vahl) Choisy.
Oceanic drift (seeds 6-7 mm long). (1)

I. nil (L.) Roth
Introduced weed (1899; pantropical).

I. pes-caprae (L.) R. Br.
Pantropical. Oceanic drift (seeds 8-10 mm long, densely pubescent with spreading trichomes 0.5-1 mm long). (1)

I. pulchella Roth (van der Werff 1977:95)
Introduced weed (1974/75, pantropical).

I. stolonifera (Cyrill.) Gmel. (van der Werff 1977:95)
Pantropical. Oceanic drift (seeds). (1)

I. triloba L.
Pantropical (originally tropical America). Oceanic drift (seeds). (1)

I. tubiflora Hook. f.
Endemic; relationships presumably with tropical America. Oceanic drift (seeds). (1)

Merremia aegyptica (L.) Urban
Pantropical (originally tropical America). Oceanic drift (seeds 4-5 mm long). (1)
M. umbellata (L.) Hallier f. (van der Werff 1977:95)
Introduced weed (1974/75 pantropical).
Strictiocardia campanulata (L.) Merrill (as *S. tiliifolia* [Desr.] Hallier f.; Gunn 1972:169)
Pantropical. Oceanic drift (seeds).

Crassulaceae

Kalanchoe pinnata (Lam.) Pers.
Cultivated escape (1932; pantropical, probably originally from Africa or Madagascar).

Cucurbitaceae

Citrullus lanatus (Thunb.) Mats. & Nakai
Cultivated escape (1852, pantropical, originally tropical Africa).
Elaterium. The two Galapagos taxa differ only in minor characters of leaf shape and are questionably distinct. (1 for genus)
E. carthagenense Jacq. var. *carthagenense*
Andean (Ecuador and Peru). Birds (internal; seeds 5-6 mm long).
E. carthagenense var. *cordatum* (Hook. f.) Svens.
Endemic. Birds (internal; seeds 5-6 mm long).
Luffa astorii Svens.
Andean (Ecuador and Peru). Oceanic drift (capsules 5-8 cm long). (1)
Momordica charantia L.
Cultivated escape (1891, pantropical).
Sicyocaulis pentagonus Wiggins
Endemic; a monotypic genus presumably most closely allied to the mostly tropical American *Sicyos*. Birds (external, mechanical attachment; capsules 12.5-18 mm long, with several basal upright retrorsely-barbed spines ca 1/3 as long). (1)
Sicyos villosa Hook. f.
Endemic; perhaps related to the Andean *S. chaetocephalus* Harms (Peru) or *S. malvifolius* Griseb. (Peru, Bolivia, and Argentina). Birds (external, viscid attachment; capsules 9-11 mm long, moderately prickly with acicular bristles 5-7 mm long and villous with glandular trichomes. (1)

Cuscutaceae

Cuscuta acuta Engelm.
Endemic (possibly present in Peru); closely related to the South American (Brazil and Fernando Noronha) *C. globosa* Ridley.
Birds (internal; seeds 1-1.2 mm long). (1)
C. gymnocarpa Engelm.
Endemic; closely related to the Andean (Argentina) *C. stuckertii* Yuncker. Birds (internal; seeds 0.8-1.2 mm long). (1)

Ericaceae

Pernettya howellii Sleumer
Endemic; apparently most closely related to the Andean (Chile) *P. mucronata* (L. f.) Gaud. Birds (internal; berries 4-5 mm in diameter, white to delicate pink). (1)

Euphorbiaceae

Acalypha. The Galapagos endemics are most closely related to tropical American species. (1 for genus)
A. flaccida Hook. f.
Endemic. Birds (internal; seeds ca 1.2 mm long).
A. parvula Hook. f. (including var. *chathamensis* [Robins.] Webster, var. *reniformis* [Hook. f.] Muell.-Arg., and var. *strobilifera* [Hook. f.] Muell.-Arg.; van der Werff 1977:97)
Endemic. Birds (internal; seeds 0.7-1.6 mm long).
A. sericea Anderss. var. *sericea*
Endemic. Birds (internal; seeds 1-1.1 mm long).

A. sericea var. *baurii* (Robins. & Greenm.) Webster (including var. *indefessus* Webster; van der Werff 1977:97)
Endemic. Birds (internal; seeds 1.2-1.3 mm long).
A. velutina Hook. f.
Endemic. Birds (internal; seeds 1-1.1 mm long).
A. wigginsii Webster
Endemic. Birds (internal; seeds 1.3-1.5 mm long).
Chamaesyce. The endemics presumably are related to tropical American species. (1 for endemics)
C. abdita Burch
Endemic. Birds (internal; seeds to 0.7 mm long).
C. amplexicaulis (Hook. f.) Burch
Endemic. Birds (internal; seeds to 1.2 mm long).
C. bindloensis (Stewart) Burch
Endemic. Birds (internal; seeds ca 0.7 mm long).
C. galapageia (Robins. & Greenm.) Burch
Endemic. Birds (internal; seeds to 1 mm long).
C. hirta (L.) Millsp.
Introduced weed (1835; pantropical).
C. lasiocarpa (Kl.) Arthur (van der Werff 1977:97)
Introduced weed (1974/75; tropical America).
C. nummularia (Hook. f.) Burch var. *nummularia*
Endemic. Birds (internal; seeds to 1 mm long).
C. nummularia var. *glabra* (Robins. & Greenm.) Burch
Endemic. Birds (internal; seeds to 1 mm long).
C. opthalmica (Pers.) Burch
Introduced weed (1899; tropical America).
C. punctulata (Anderss.) Burch
Endemic. Birds (internal; seeds to 0.8 mm long).
C. recurva (Hook. f.) Burch
Endemic. Birds (internal; seeds to 1.4 mm long).
C. viminea (Hook. f.) Burch
Endemic. Birds (internal; seeds).
Croton. The Galapagos taxa appear to be closely related to the Andean (Ecuador) *C. rivinifolius* HBK. (1 for genus)
C. scouleri Hook. f. var. *scouleri*
Endemic. Birds (internal; seeds carunculate, 2.6-4.1 mm long).
C. scouleri var. *brevifolius* (Anderss.) Muell.-Arg.
Endemic. Birds (internal; seeds carunculate, 2.8-3 mm long).
C. scouleri var. *darwinii* Webster
Endemic. Birds (internal; seeds carunculate, 3.9-4.5 mm long).
C. scouleri var. *grandifolius* Muell.-Arg.
Endemic. Birds (internal; seeds carunculate, 3.7-4.7 mm long).
Euphorbia equisetiformis Stewart
Endemic; apparently most closely related to tropical American species.
Birds (internal; seeds). (1)
Hippomane mancinella L.
Caribbean (Mexico and Florida to Panama, Colombia, and Venezuela).
Oceanic drift (capsules ca 3 cm in diameter). (1)
Jatropha curcas L.
Cultivated escape (1906; pantropical, originally Mexico and Guatemala).
Phyllanthus caroliniensis Walt.
Tropical America (eastern U.S. to Argentina). Birds (internal; seeds 0.6-1 mm long). (1)
Ricinus communis L.
Cultivated escape (1852; pantropical, originally Old World).

Fabaceae

Canavalia dictyota Piper (Hamann 1974c:312)
Introduced weed (1972; tropical America).
C. maritima (Aubl.) Thouars
Pantropical. Oceanic drift (seeds ca 15-18 mm long). (1)

Crotalaria incana L. (including var. *nicaraguensis* Senn)
Pantropical (originally tropical America). Birds (internal; seeds 2.5-4 mm long). (1)
C. pumila Gomez Ortega
Pantropical (originally tropical America). Birds (internal; seeds 2-2.5 mm long). (1)
Dalea tenuicaulis Hook. f.
Endemic; perhaps related to the Andean (Colombia to Peru) *D. coerulea* (L. f.) Schinz & Thell. Wind (legume indehiscent, included in calyx). (1)
Desmodium canum (J. F. Gmel.) Schinz & Thell.
Introduced weed (1899; pantropical, originally tropical America).
D. glabrum (Mill.) DC.
Introduced weed (1852; tropical America).
D. limense Hook.
Introduced weed (1835; Andean).
D. procumbens (Mill.) Hitchc.
Pantropical (originally tropical America). Birds (external, mechanical attachment; articles uncinate-pubescent, ca 2.5-5 mm long). (1)
Erythrina velutina Willd.
Tropical America (West Indies to Peru and Brazil). Birds (internal; seeds 11-17 mm long). (1)
Galactea striata (Jacq.) Urban
Caribbean (West Indies to Venezuela). Birds (internal; seeds 3-4 mm long). (1)
G. tenuifolia (Willd.) Wight & Arn.
Introduced weed (1899; pantropical).
Geoffroea spinosa Jacq.
Cultivated escape (1899, Andean).
Glycine max (L.) Merr.
Cultivated escape (1926; pantropical, originally Asia).
Lablab purpureus (L.) Sweet
Cultivated escape (1957; pantropical, originally tropical Africa).
Mucuna rostrata Benth.
Cultivated escape (1906; tropical America).
Phaseolus adenanthus G. F. W. Mey.
Pantropical (originally tropical America). Birds (internal; seeds ca 5 mm long). (1)
P. atropurpureus DC.
Tropical America (southwestern U.S. to Bolivia). Birds (internal; seeds 2-4 mm long). (1)
P. lathyroides L.
Introduced weed (1852; pantropical).
P. mollis Hook. f.
Endemic; possibly only a variant of the pantropical (originally tropical America) *P. lunatus* L. Birds (internal; seeds). (1)
Piscidia carthagenensis Jacq.
Tropical America (Mexico and the West Indies to Peru). Wind (legumes winged, 5-11 cm long, wings 4, 13-18 mm wide). (1)
Rhynchosia minima (L.) DC.
Pantropical. Birds (internal; seeds ca 3 mm long). (1)
Stylosanthes sympodialis Taub.
Andean (Ecuador and Peru). Oceanic drift (lower article usually 3-4.5 mm long, upper article 5-6.5 mm long). (1)
Tephrosia decumbens Benth.
Mexico and Central America. Birds (internal; seeds 3-4.5 mm long). (1)
Vigna luteola (Jacq.) Benth.
Pantropical. Birds (internal; seeds 4-5 mm long). (1)
Zornia curvata Mohlenbrock
Introduced weed (1932; Caribbean).
Z. piurensis Mohlenbrock
Introduced weed (1906; Andean).

Goodeniaceae

Scaevola plumieri (L.) M. Vahl
Pantropical. Oceanic drift (berries 1-1.8 mm long). (1)

Hydrophyllaceae

Nama dichotomum (R. & P.) Choisy
Tropical America (southwestern U.S. to Guatemala and Ecuador to Chile and Argentina). Birds (internal; seeds 0.5-0.6 mm long). (1)

Hypericaceae

Hypericum uliginosum var. *pratense* (Cham. & Schlecht.) Keller
Tropical America (Mexico to northern South America). Birds (external in mud or internal; seeds 0.4-0.5 mm long). (1)

Lamiaceae

Hyptis gymnocaulis Epling
Endemic; apparently related to Andean species. Birds (external, viscid attachment; nutlets presumably mucilaginous when wetted). (1)
H. rhomboidea Mart. & Gal.
Introduced weed (1906; pantropical, Mexico and Central America in New World).
H. sidaefolia (L'Her.) Briq.
Introduced weed (1932; Andean).
H. spicigera Lam.
Pantropical (originally tropical America). Birds (external, viscid attachment; nutlets ca 1.2-1.4 mm long, presumably mucilaginous when wetted). (1)
Mentha piperita L.
Cultivated escape (1932; temperate Old World).
Salvia. The Galapagos endemics apparently are most closely related to Caribbean species. (1 for endemics)
S. insularum Epling
Endemic. Birds (external, viscid attachment; nutlets presumably mucilaginous when wetted).
S. occidentalis Sw.
Tropical America (Mexico and Florida to Bolivia). Birds (external, viscid attachment; nutlets 1.5-1.7 mm long, presumably mucilaginous when wetted). (1)
S. prostrata Hook. f.
Endemic. Birds (external, viscid attachment; nutlets presumably mucilaginous when wetted).
S. pseudoserotina Epling
Endemic. Birds (external, viscid attachment; nutlets presumably mucilaginous when wetted).
Teucrium vesicarium Mill.
Tropical America (Mexico and the West Indies to Argentina).
Birds (external, viscid attachment or in mud; nutlets 2.5-3 mm long, presumably mucilaginous when wetted). (1)

Lauraceae

Persea americana Mill.
Cultivated escape (1967; pantropical, originally Mexico and Central America).

Lentibulariaceae

Utricularia foliosa L.
Pantropical. Birds (external in mud; vegetative parts, turions, or seeds). (1)

Linaceae

Linum. The two Galapagos species apparently are closely related to the Andean (Peru) *L. oligophyllum* Willd. (1 for genus)
L. cratericola Eliass.
Endemic. Birds (external, viscid attachment; seeds ca 1.5 mm long, presumably mucilaginous when wetted).
L. harlingii Eliass.
Endemic. Birds (external, viscid attachment; seeds 1.5 mm long, presumably mucilaginous when wetted).

Loasaceae

Mentzelia aspera L.
Tropical America (Mexico and the West Indies to Bolivia and Brazil).
Birds (external, mechanical attachment; capsules 5-11 mm long, pubescent with short retrorsely barbed trichomes). (1)

Sclerothrix fasciculata Presl
Tropical America (Mexico to Bolivia and Brazil). Birds (internal; seeds ca 0.5 or 1 mm long). (1)

Lobeliaceae

Lobelia xalapensis HBK.
Tropical America (Mexico to Peru and Argentina). Birds (external in mud; seeds 0.4-0.5 mm long). (1)

Lythraceae

Cuphea carthagenensis Jacq.
Introduced weed (1884; pantropical, originally tropical America).

C. racemosa (L. f.) Spreng. (van der Werff 1977:97)
Introduced weed (1974/75; tropical America).

Malvaceae

Abelmoschus manihot (L.) Medic.
Cultivated escape (1906; pantropical, originally tropical Asia).

Abutilon depauperatum (Hook. f.) Robins.
Endemic; closely related to, or conspecific with, the tropical American *A. umbellatum* (L.) Sweet. Birds (internal; seeds to 1.7 mm long). (1)

Anoda acerifolia DC.
Introduced weed (1888; pantropical, originally tropical America).

Bastardia viscosa (L.) HBK.
Tropical America (Mexico and the West Indies to Peru and Argentina).
Birds (external in mud; seeds ca 2 mm long, silky-pubescent). (1)

Gossypium barbadense var. *darwinii* (Watt) J. B. Hutch.
Endemic; two other varieties are Andean (Ecuador and Peru). Oceanic drift (seeds densely tomentose and with longer lint). (1)

G. klotschianum Anderss.
Endemic; most closely related to the Mexican *G. davidsonii* Kellogg.
Oceanic drift (seeds densely tomentulose). (1)

Herissantia crispa (L.) Brizicky
Pantropical (originally tropical America). Birds (internal; seeds). (1)

Hibiscus diversifolius Jacq.
Cultivated escape (1906; pantropical, originally Old World tropics).

H. rosa-sinensis L.
Cultivated escape (1964; pantropical, originally probably tropical Asia).

H. tiliaceus L.
Pantropical. Oceanic drift (seeds). (1)

Malachra alceifolia Jacq. (including *M. capitata* [L.] L. reported by Hooker 1847a:231)
Introduced weed (1835; pantropical, originally tropical America).

Malva parviflora L.
Introduced weed (1932; pantropical, originally temperate Old World).

Malvastrum americanum (L.) Torrey
Introduced weed (1906; pantropical, originally tropical America).

M. coromandelianum (L.) Garcke
Introduced weed (1852; pantropical, originally tropical America).

M. scoparium (L'Her.) A. Gray
Introduced weed (1906; Andean).

Sida acuta Burm. f.
Introduced weed (1852; pantropical).

S. glutinosa Cav. (van der Werff 1977:98)
Introduced weed (1974; pantropical, originally Caribbean).
S. hederifolia Cav.
Pantropical. Birds (internal; seeds to 2 mm long). (1)
S. paniculata L.
Introduced weed (1894; pantropical).
S. rhombifolia L.
Introduced weed (1846; pantropical).
S. rupo Ulbr.
Andean (Peru). Birds (external, mechanical attachment; mericarps to 6 mm long, with 2 retrorsely armed apical spines). (1)
S. salviifolia Presl.
Caribbean (Mexico and the West Indies to Colombia and Venezuela).
Birds (external, mechanical attachment; mericarps 2-3.5 mm long, retrorsely pubescent apical beaks 0.1-2.5 mm long). (1)
S. spinosa L.
Pantropical. Birds (external, mechanical attachment; mericarps to 4 mm long, upper half stellate-pubescent, antrorsely pubescent apical awns to 1 mm long). (1)
Urocarpidium insulare (Kearney) Krapov.
Endemic; related to the Andean (Argentina) *U. pentandrum* Krapov. Birds (internal; mericarps to 1.3 mm long). (1)

Melastomataceae

Miconia robinsoniana Cogn.
Endemic; related to a group of Andean (Colombia and Venezuela) species, also reported from Panama. Birds (internal; berries 5-6 mm long). (1)

Meliaceae

Melia azedarach L.
Cultivated escape (1967; pantropical, originally tropical Asia).

Menispermaceae

Cissampelos glaberrima St. Hil. (including *C. galapagensis* Stewart; Rhodes 1975:429)
Tropical America (Guatemala to Brazil). Birds (internal; drupes 4-5 mm long). (1)
C. pareira L.
Pantropical. Birds (internal; drupes 4-5 mm long, salmon to scarlet). (1)
(*C. tropaeolifolia* DC. Reported from the archipelago by Rhodes 1978:425. The specimens cited are *C. pareira*).

Mimosaceae

Acacia insulae-iacobi Riley
Andean (Ecuador, Bolivia, Argentina). Oceanic drift (legume 10-17 cm long). (1)
A. macracantha Willd.
Tropical America (Mexico and Florida to Bolivia). Oceanic drift (legumes 8-14 cm long). (1)
A. nilotica (L.) DeLisle
Cultivated escape (1964; pantropical, originally northwestern Africa).
A. rorudiana Christoph.
Endemic; possibly also in Chile. Oceanic drift (legumes 7-16 cm long). (1)
Desmanthus virgatus var. *depressus* (Willd.) B. L. Turner
Pantropical (originally tropical America). Birds (internal; seeds ca 3 mm long). (1)
Inga edulis Mart.
Cultivated escape (1906; tropical America).
I. schimpfii Harms
Cultivated escape (1964; Andean).
Mimosa acantholoba (Willd.) Poir.
Cultivated escape (1932; Andean).
M. albida var. *aequatoriana* Rudd
Cultivated escape (1932; Andean).

M. pigra L.
Cultivated escape (1932; tropical America).
Neptunia plena (L.) Benth.
Pantropical (originally tropical America). Birds (internal; seeds). (1)
Prosopis juliflora (Sw.) DC.
Pantropical (originally tropical America). Oceanic drift (legumes 9-25 cm long). (1)

Molluginaceae

Mollugo. The Galapagos taxa are closely related to the pantropical (originally probably tropical America) *M. verticillata* L. (1 for endemics)
M. cerviana (L.) Ser.
Pantropical. Birds (internal or external in mud; seeds 0.3 mm long). (1)
M. crockeri Howell
Endemic. Birds (internal or external in mud; seeds 0.5-0.6 mm in diameter).
M. flavescens Anderss. subsp. *flavescens*
Endemic. Birds (internal or external in mud; seeds 0.5-0.6 mm in diameter).
M. flavescens subsp. *gracillima* (Anderss.) Eliass.
Endemic. Birds (internal or external in mud; seeds 0.4-0.5 mm in diameter).
M. flavescens subsp. *insularis* (Howell) Eliass.
Endemic. Birds (internal or external in mud; seeds 0.5-0.6 mm in diameter).
M. flavescens subsp. *striata* (Howell) Eliass.
Endemic. Birds (internal or external in mud; seeds 0.5-0.6 mm in diameter).
M. floriana (Robins.) Howell subsp. *floriana*
Endemic. Birds (internal or external in mud; seeds 0.4-0.6 mm in diameter).
M. floriana subsp. *gypsophiloides* Howell
Endemic. Birds (internal or external in mud; seeds ca 0.4 mm in diameter).
M. floriana subsp. *santacruziana* (Christoph.) Eliass.
Endemic. Birds (internal or external in mud; seeds ca 0.5 mm in diameter).
M. snodgrassii Robins.
Endemic. Birds (internal or external in mud; seeds 0.5-0.6 mm in diameter).

Myrtaceae

Psidium. The endemic species is most closely related to the basically Mexico and Central America (Mexico to northern Colombia and Venezuela) *P. sartorianum* (Berg) Ndzu. (1 for endemics)
P. galapageium Hook. f. var. *galapageium*
Endemic. Birds (internal; berries 6-13 mm in diameter).
P. galapageium var. *howellii* D. M. Porter
Endemic. Birds (internal; berries 8-11 mm in diameter).
P. guajava L.
Cultivated escape (1932; pantropical, originally tropical America).

Nolanaceae

Nolana galapagensis (Christoph.) I. M. Johnst.
Endemic; most closely related to Andean (Chile) species. Oceanic drift (mericarps 1-2 or 2-3 mm long). (1)

Nyctaginaceae

Boerhaavia caribaea Jacq.
Tropical America (southern U.S. to Bolivia). Birds (external, viscid attachment; anthocarps ca 2.5 mm long, glandular-puberulant). (1)
B. coccinea Mill.
Introduced weed (1906; pantropical, originally tropical America).
B. erecta L.
Pantropical (originally tropical America). Birds (external in mud or internal; anthocarps ca 3 mm long). (1)
Commicarpus tuberosus (Lam.) Standl.
Andean (Ecuador and Peru). Birds (external, viscid attachment; anthocarps 6-10 mm long, with 5 subapical viscid glands). (1)

Cryptocarpus pyriformis HBK.
Andean (Ecuador and Peru). Birds (external in mud; anthocarps ca 1.5 mm long). (1)
Mirabilis jalapa L.
Cultivated escape (1906; pantropical, originally tropical America).
Pisonia floribunda Hook. f.
Endemic; apparently related to the pantropical (probably originally tropical America) *P. aculeata* L. Birds (external, viscid attachment; anthocarps ca 1 cm long, with stalked glands). (1)

Onagraceae

Ludwigia erecta (L.) Hara
Pantropical (originally tropical America).
Birds (external in mud; seeds 0.3-0.5 mm long). (1)
L. leptocarpa (Nutt.) Hara
Pantropical. Birds (external in mud; seeds 1-1.2 mm long). (1)
L. peploides (HBK.) Raven
Pantropical. Birds (internal; capsules 1-2.5 cm long). (1)

Oxalidaceae

Oxalis corniculata L.
Introduced weed (1891; pantropical, originally Old World).
O. corymbosa DC.
Cultivated escape (1967; pantropical, originally South America).
O. dombeyi St. Hil. (as *O. cornellii* Anderss.)
Andean (Panama, Ecuador, Peru). Birds (external, viscid attachment; seeds ca 1 mm long). (1)
O. megalorrhiza Jacq.
Andean (Peru, Bolivia, Chile). Birds (external, viscid attachment; seeds). (1)

Papaveraceae

Argemone mexicana L.
Introduced weed (1967; pantropical, probably originally Caribbean).

Passifloraceae

Passiflora colinvauxii Wiggins
Endemic; presumably related to tropical American species. Birds (internal; seeds ca 2 mm long, enclosed in mucilaginous arils). (1)
P. foetida var. *galapagensis* Killip
Endemic; the other 36 varieties are tropical American. Birds (internal; seeds 3-4 mm long, enclosed in grayish arils). (1)
P. suberosa L.
Pantropical (originally tropical American). Birds (internal; seeds 3-4 mm long). (1)

Phytolaccaceae

Phytolacca octandra L.
Tropical America (Mexico to Peru). Birds (internal; fruits berry-like, dark purple to nearly black). (1)
Rivinia humilis L.
Introduced weed (1906; pantropical, originally tropical America).

Piperaceae

Peperomia. The Galapagos endemics are most closely related to tropical American species. (1 for endemics)
P. galapagensis Miq. var. *galapagensis*
Endemic. Birds (external, viscid attachment; drupes 0.5-0.7 mm long).
P. galapagensis var. *ramulosa* (Anderss.) Yuncker
Endemic. Birds (external, viscid attachment; drupes 0.5-0.7 mm long).
P. galioides HBK.
Tropical America (Mexico and the West Indies to South America).
Birds (external, viscid attachment; drupes ca 1 mm long). (1)

P. obtusilimba C. DC.
Endemic. Birds (external, viscid attachment; drupes 0.5-0.6 mm long).
P. petiolata Hook. f.
Endemic. Birds (external, viscid attachment; drupes 0.7-0.8 mm long).
P. tequendamana Trel. (van der Werff 1977:93)
Andean (Colombia and Venezuela). Birds (external, viscid attachment; drupes). (1)
Pothomorphe peltata (L.) Miq. (Hamann 1974a:247)
Introduced weed (1971; tropical America).

Plantaginaceae

Plantago galapagensis Rahn (as *P. paralias* var. *pumila* [Hook. f.] Wiggins; Rahn 1974:135)
Endemic; closely related to the North American (Southwestern U. S. and northern Mexico) *P. rhodosperma* Decne. Birds (external, viscid attachment; seeds 1.8-2.2 mm long, markedly mucilaginous when wetted). (1)
P. major L.
Introduced weed (1884; pantropical, originally Old World).

Plumbaginaceae

Plumbago coerulea HBK.
Andean (Peru). Birds (external, viscid attachment; capsules surrounded by persistent stipitate-glandular 6-7 mm long calyx). (1)
P. scandens L.
Tropical America (Arizona and Florida to Argentina). Birds (external, viscid attachment; capsules surrounded by persistent stipitate-glandular 8-11 mm long calyx). (1)

Polemoniaceae

Phlox sp. (Schofield 1973:49)
Cultivated escape (1973; North America).

Polygalaceae

Polygala. The Galapagos species appear to be most closely related to the tropical American *P. paludosa* St.-Hil. or *P. paniculata* L. (1 for genus)
P. anderssonii Robins.
Endemic; perhaps not distinct from *P. galapageia*. Birds (internal; seeds 2.5-3 mm long, arillate).
P. galapageia Hook. f. var. *galapageia*
Endemic. birds (internal; seeds 2-2.5 mm long, arillate).
P. galapageia var. *insularis* (A. W. Bennett) Robins.
Endemic. Birds (internal; seeds 2-2.5 mm long, arillate).
P. sancti-georgii Riley var. *sancti-georgii*
Endemic. Birds (internal; seeds 2.5-3 mm long, arillate).
P. sancti-georgii var. *oblanceolata* Howell
Endemic. Birds (internal; seeds 2.5 mm long, arillate).

Polygonaceae

Antignon leptopus Hook. & Arn. (Hamann 1974a:246)
Cultivated escape (1972; pantropical, originally Mexico and Central America).
Polygonum acuminatum HBK.
Tropical America (mexico and the West Indies to Argentina). Birds (external in mud or internal; achenes 2-2.5 mm long). (1)
P. galapagense Caruel
Endemic; perhaps related to the tropical American *P. hydropiperoides* Michx. Birds (external in mud or internal; achenes ca 3 mm long). (1)
P. hydropiperoides var. *persicarioides* (HBK.) Stanford
Tropical America (central U.S. to southern South America). Birds (external in mud or internal; achenes 2.5-3 mm long). (1)
P. opelousanum Small
Tropical America (Mexico and southeastern U.S. to northern South America). Birds (external in mud or internal; achenes 1.5-2 mm long). (1)

P. punctulatum Ell.
Tropical America (Canada to Paraguay). Birds (external in mud or internal; achenes 2.2-2.5 mm long). (1)
Rumex crispus L.
Introduced weed (1967; pantropical, originally Old World).

Portulacaceae

Calandrinia galapagosa St. John
Endemic; closest to the Andean (Chile) *C. splendens* Barn. Birds (internal; seeds 1-1.3 mm in diameter). (1)
Portulaca howellii (Legr.) Eliass.
Endemic; most closely related to the Andean (Argentina) *P. fulgens* Griseb. Birds (internal; seeds ca 1 mm in diameter). (1)
P. oleracea L.
Introduced weed (1852; pantropical, originally Old World).
P. umbraticola HBK.
Tropical America (southern U.S. to Argentina).
Birds (internal; seeds ca 0.8 mm in diameter). (1)
Talinum paniculatum (Jacq.) Gaertn.
Introduced weed (1964; pantropical, originally tropical America).

Ranunculaceae

Ranunculus flagelliformis J. E. Sm. (Hamann 1974c:309; Wiggins 1975:62)
Tropical America (Mexico to Chile and Argentina). Birds (external in mud or internal; achenes 1.6-2 mm long). (1)

Rhamnaceae

Gouania polygama (Jacq.) Urban
Introduced weed (1926; tropical America).
Scutia spicata var. *pauciflora* (Hook. f.) M. C. Johnst. (as *S. pauciflora* [Hook. f.] Weberb.; Johnston 1974:70)
Endemic; the typical variety occurs in Ecuador and Peru. Birds (internal; berries slightly fleshy, bright red, ca 5 mm long). (1)

Rhizophoraceae

Rhizophora mangle L.
Pantropical. Oceanic drift (berries viviparous, becoming 15-25 cm long before dropping). (1)

Rubiaceae

Borreria. The endemics probably are most closely related to Andean species. (1 for endemics)
B. dispersa Hook. f.
Endemic. Birds (internal; seeds 1.6-1.8 mm long).
B. ericaefolia Hook. f.
Endemic. Birds (internal; seeds 1.6-1.8 mm long).
B. laevis (Lam.) Griseb.
Introduced weed (1891; pantropical, originally tropical America).
B. linearifolia Hook. f.
Endemic. Birds (internal; seeds 1.6-2 mm long).
B. perpusilla Hook. f.
Endemic. Birds (internal; seeds 0.8-1 mm long).
B. rotundifolia Anderss.
Endemic. Birds (internal; seeds).
B. suberecta Hook. f.
Endemic. Birds (internal; seeds 1.6-2 mm long).
Chiococca alba (L.) Hitchc.
Tropical America (Mexico and Florida to Peru and Brazil). Birds (internal; drupes white, 4-8 mm long). (1)
Cinchona succiruba Klotzsch (Hamann 1974c:313)
Cultivated escape (1971; Andean).

Coffea arabica L.
Cultivated escape (1906; pantropical, originally East Africa).
Diodia radula (Roem. & Schult.) Cham. & Schlecht.
Introduced weed (1891; Andean).
Galium canescens HBK. (hitherto not reported from the archipelago)
Introduced weed (1835; Andean).
G. galapagoense Wiggins
Endemic; probably most closely related to Andean species. Birds (internal; schizocarps reddish to orange, slightly juicy, 1.5-2 mm in diameter). (1)
Oldenlandia corymbosa L. (van der Werff 1977:95)
Introduced weed (1974/75; pantropical).
Psychotria. The Galapagos species are most closely related to Andean species. (1 for genus)
P. angustata Anderss.
Endemic. Birds (internal; berries 4-6 mm in diameter).
P. rufipes Hook. f.
Endemic. Birds (internal; berries red, juicy, 7-9 mm long).
Spermacoce confusa Rendle
Introduced weed (1932; tropical America).

Rutaceae

Citrus limetta Risso
Cultivated escape (1932; pantropical, originally Asia).
Zanthoxylum fagara (L.) Sarg.
Tropical America (Mexico and Florida to Peru). Birds (internal; seeds 4 mm in diameter). (1)

Sapindaceae

Cardiospermum halicacabum L. (as *C. corindum* L.)
Pantropical. Birds (internal; seeds 3 mm in diameter). (1 for genus)
C. galapageium Robins. & Greenm.
Endemic; perhaps only a narrow-leaved form of *C. halicacabum*. Birds (internal; seeds 4 mm in diameter).
Dodonaea viscosa var. *galapagensis* (Sherff) D. M. Porter
Endemic; relationships are with taxa in tropical America. Wind (capsules 2-3-winged, 12-16 mm long, 18 mm wide including wings). (1)
D. viscosa var. *spatulata* (J. E. Sm.) Benth.
Pantropical. Wind (capsules 2-3-winged, 8-13 mm long, 10-18 mm wide including wings). (1)
Sapindrus saponaria L.
Pantropical (originally tropical America). Birds (internal; schizocarps 1-2.5 cm in diameter). (1)

Scrophulariaceae

Calceolaria meistantha Pennell
Andean (Colombia to Peru). Birds (external in mud; seeds minute). (1)
Capraria biflora L.
Pantropical (originally tropical America).
Birds (external in mud; seeds 0.4-0.5 mm long). (1)
C. peruviana Benth.
Andean (Colombia to Peru). Birds (external in mud; seeds 0.3-0.4 mm long). (1)
Castilleja arvensis Cham. & Schlecht.
Tropical America (Mexico to Bolivia and Brazil). Wind (seeds 0.8-1 mm long, testa papery, finely reticulate). (1)
Galvezia. The Galapagos taxa are most closely related to the Andean (Peru) *G. fruticosa* Gmelin. (1 for genus)
G. leucantha Wiggins subsp. *leucantha*
Endemic. Birds (external in mud; seeds 0.4-0.5 mm long).
G. leucantha subsp. *pubescens* Wiggins
Endemic. Birds (external in mud; seeds 0.4-0.5 mm long).
Lindernia anagallidea (Michx.) Pennell
Tropical America (northern U.S. to southern South America). Birds (external in mud; seeds ca 0.3 mm long).

Mecardonia procumbens (Mill.) Small (as *M. dianthera* [Sw.] Pennell; D'Arcy 1979)
Tropical America (Arizona and Florida to southern South America).
Birds (external in mud; seeds ca 0.2 mm long). (1)

Scoparia dulcis L.
Pantropical (originally tropical America). Birds (external in mud; seeds 0.3-0.4 mm long). (1)

Stemodia verticillata (Mill.) Sprague
Introduced weed (1964; tropical America).

Simaroubaceae

Castela galapageia Hook. f.
Endemic; most closely related to the Caribbean (Lesser Antilles to northern Colombia and Venezuela) *C. erecta* Turp. and North American (Texas to southern Mexico) *C. tortuosa* Liebm. Birds (internal; drupes fleshy, bright red, 8-12 mm long). (1)

Solanaceae

Acnistus ellipticus Hook. f.
Endemic; relationships Andean. Birds (internal; berries 10-25 mm in diameter). (1)

Browallia americana L.
Introduced weed (1964; tropical America).

Brugmansia candida Pers. (as *Datura arborea* L.)
Cultivated escape (1964; pantropical, originally Andean).

Capsicum frutescens L.
Cultivated escape (1852; pantropical, originally tropical America).

C. galapagense Heiser & Smith (as *C. galapagoense* Hunziker)
Endemic; apparently most closely related to Andean species. Birds (internal; berries orange-red, 5-7 mm in diameter). (1)

C. pendulum Willd.
Cultivated escape (1932; Andean).

Datura innoxia Mill. (not hitherto reported)
Introduced weed (1960; pantropical, originally Andean).

D. stramonium L. (including var. *tatula* (L.) Torr.; D'Arcy, pers. comm.)
Introduced weed (1899; pantropical, originally tropical America).

Exedeconus miersii (Hook. f.) D'Arcy (as *Cacabus miersii* [Hook. f.] Wettst.)
Endemic; most closely related to an Andean (Ecuador and Peru) taxon.
Oceanic drift (berries). (1)

Grabowskia boerhaaviaefolia (L. f.) Schlecht.
Andean (Peru). Birds (internal; berries blue-black, glaucous, 6-8 mm long). (1)

Jaltomata aff. *procumbens* (Cav.) J. L. Gentry (D'Arcy, pers. comm., not hitherto reported)
Tropical America (southwestern U.S. to Bolivia). Birds (internal; berries purple). (1)

Lycium minimum C. L. Hitchc.
Endemic; apparently most closely related to the North American (Sonoran Desert) *L. californicum* Nutt. Birds (internal; berries red-orange, 5-6 mm long). (1)

Lycopersicon. The Galapagos taxa are most closely related to the Andean (Ecuador and Peru) *L. pimpinellifolium* Mill. (1 for genus)

L. cheesmanii Riley var. *cheesmanii*
Endemic. Birds (internal; berries greenish to golden yellow, 8-12 mm in diameter).

L. cheesmanii var. *minor* (Hook. f.) D. M. Porter (as *L. cheesmanii* f. *minor* [Hook. f.] Muller)
Endemic. Birds (internal; berries orange-red, 8-12 mm in diameter).

Nicandra physalodes (L.) Gaertn.
Introduced weed (1932; pantropical, originally Andean).

Nicotiana glutinosa L.
Andean (Ecuador and Peru). Birds (external in mud; seeds ca 0.6 mm long). (1)

N. tabacum L.
Cultivated escape (1884; pantropical, originally tropical America).

Physalis angulata L.
Pantropical (originally tropical America). Birds (internal; berries 10-12 mm in diameter). (1)

P. cordata Mill. (not hitherto reported)
Introduced weed (1964; tropical America).

P. galapagoensis Waterfall
Endemic; apparently most closely related to *P. cordata*. Birds (internal; berries 12-15 mm in diameter). (1)
P. peruviana L. (van der Werff 1977:95)
Cultivated escape (1974/75; pantropical, originally Andean).
P. pubescens L.
Pantropical (originally tropical America). Birds (internal, berries 10-18 mm in diameter). (1)
Solanum americanum Mill. (as *S. nodiflorum* Jacq.; D'Arcy, pers comm.)
Introduced weed (1835; pantropical).
(*S. edmonstonei* Hook. f. The type collection of Edmonston, reputedly from the Galapagos Islands, most likely was made in mainland Ecuador.)
S. erianthum D. Don
Caribbean (Mexico and Florida to Venezuela and the Guianas). Birds (internal; berries yellow, 10-12 mm in diameter). (1)
S. quitoense Lam.
Cultivated escape (1906; Andean).

Sterculiaceae

Waltheria ovata Cav.
Andean (Peru). Birds (internal; capsules 2-3 mm long). (1)

Tiliaceae

Corchorus orinocensis HBK.
Tropical America (Texas and the West Indies to Bolivia). Birds (external in mud; seeds 1.2-1.4 mm long). (1)
Triumfetta semitriloba Jacq.
Introduced weed (1899; tropical America).

Ulmaceae

Trema micrantha (L.) Blume
Cultivated escape (1964; tropical America).

Urticaceae

Laportea aestuans (L.) Chew (as *Fleurya aestuans* [L.] Gaud.; Adams 1972:236)
Pantropical. Birds (external in mud; achenes ca 1.5-2 mm long). (1)
Parietaria debilis Forst.
Pantropical. Birds (internal; achenes ca 1 mm long). (1)
Pilea baurii Robins.
Endemic; relationships are with Andean species. Birds (external in mud or internal; achenes 0.3-0.4 mm long). (1)
P. microphylla (L.) Liebm.
Introduced weed (1835; pantropical).
P. peploides (Gaud.) Hook & Arn.
Pantropical (originally Andean).
Birds (external in mud or internal; utricles 0.6-0.8 mm long). (1)
Urera caracasana (Jacq.) Griseb.
Introduced weed (1906; tropical America).

Valerianaceae

Astrephia chaerophylloides (Sm.) Dc.
Introduced weed (1964; Andean).

Verbenaceae

Clerodendrum molle HBK. var. *molle*
Andean (Panama to Peru). Birds (internal; fruits drupaceous, less than 1 cm in diameter). (1 for genus)
C. molle var. *glabrescens* Svens.
Endemic; questionably distinct from var. *molle*. Birds (internal; fruits drupaceous, less than 1 cm in diameter).

Duranta dombeyana Moldenke
Andean (Ecuador and Peru). Birds (internal; fruits drupaceous, to 1 cm in diameter). (1)
D. mutisii L. f.
Andean (Colombia and Venezuela to Peru). Birds (internal; berries fleshy, yellow or orange). (1)
D. repens L. (including var. ***microphylla*** [Desf.] Moldenke)
Pantropical (originally tropical America). Birds (internal; fruits drupaceous, yellow, 7-11 mm in diameter, enclosed by accrescent yellowish calyx). (1)
Lantana. The Galapagos taxa are closely related to the Andean (Ecuador and Peru) *L. sprucei* Hayek. (1 for genus)
L. peduncularis Anderss. var. ***peduncularis***
Endemic. Birds (internal; fruits drupaceous, white, fleshy).
L. peduncularis var. ***macrophylla*** Moldenke
Endemic; questionably distinct from var. ***peduncularis***. Birds (internal; fruits drupaceous, white, fleshy).
Lippia. The Galapagos endemics apparently are most closely related to Andean species. (1 for endemics)
L. reptans (Spreng.) HBK. (as ***Phyla nodiflora*** var. ***reptans*** [HBK.] Moldenke; Gibson 1970:212)
Introduced weed (1906; pantropical, originally tropical America).
L. rosmarinifolia Anderss. var. ***rosmarinifolia*** (including var. ***stewartii*** Moldenke; van der Werff 1977:96)
Endemic. Birds (internal; mericarps 1 mm long).
L. rosmarinifolia var. ***latifolia*** Moldenke
Endemic; questionably distinct from var. ***rosmarinifolia***.
Birds (internal; mericarps 1 mm long).
L. salicifolia Anderss.
Endemic. Birds (internal; mericarps ca 2 mm long).
L. strigulosa Mart. & Gal. (as ***Phyla strigulosa*** [Mart. & Gal.] Moldenke; Adams 1972:631)
Tropical America (Texas and the West Indies to Peru and Bolivia).
Birds (external in mud or internal; mericarps). (1)
Priva lappulacea (L.) Pers.
Introduced weed (1906; pantropical, originally tropical America).
Stachytarpheta cayennensis (L. C. Rich.) M. Vahl
Introduced weed (1884; pantropical, originally tropical America).
Verbena. The Galapagos endemics are related to tropical American species. (2 for endemics)
V. brasiliensis Vell. (van der Werff 1977:96)
Introduced weed (1974/75; pantropical, originally tropical America).
V. grisea Robins. & Greenm.
Endemic. Birds (external in mud or internal; mericarps).
V. litoralis HBK.
Introduced weed (1835; pantropical, originally tropical America).
V. sedula Moldenke var. ***sedula***
Endemic; Birds (external in mud or internal; mericarps).
V. sedula var. ***darwinii*** Moldenke
Endemic; questionably distinct from var. ***sedula***. Birds (external in mud or internal; mericarps).
V. sedula var. ***fournieri*** Moldenke
Endemic; questionably distinct from var. ***sedula***. Birds (external in mud or internal; mericarps).
V. townsendii Svens. (including *V. galapagosensis* Moldenke, *V. glabrata* var. ***tenuispicata*** Moldenke, *V. stewartii* Moldenke; van der Werff 1977:96)
Endemic. Birds (external in mud or internal; mericarps 1.5 mm long).

Viscaceae

Phoradendron henslovii (Hook. f.) Robins.
Endemic; apparently most closely related to the Caribbean (Cuba) *P. dichotomum* Krug & Urb. Birds (internal; drupes 4-6 mm in diameter). (1)

Vitaceae

Cissus sicyoides L.
Tropical America (Mexico and Florida to South America). Birds (internal; berries black, 5-8 mm in diameter). (1)

Zygophyllaceae

Kallstroemia adscendens (Anders.) Robins.
Endemic; most closely related to the North American (southwestern U.S. and northern Mexico) *K. californica* (S. Wats.) Vail. Birds (external or internal, viscid attachment; mericarps ca 3 mm long, becoming mucilaginous when wetted). (1)

Tribulus cistoides L.
Introduced weed (1825; pantropical, originally tropical Africa).

T. terrestris L.
Introduced weed (1906; pantropical, originally Old World).

LITERATURE CITED

Abbott, D. P. 1966. Factors influencing the zoogeographic affinities of the Galápagos inshore marine fauna. Pages 108-122 *in* R. I. Bowman, ed. The Galápagos. University of California Press, Berkeley and Los Angeles, Calif.

Adams, C. D. 1971. Miscellaneous additions and revisions of the flowering plants of Jamaica. Phytologia 21:65-71.

Adams, C. D. 1972. Flowering plants of Jamaica. University of the West Indies, Mona, Jamaica. 848 pp.

Adsersen, H. 1976a. *Ombrophytum peruvianum* (Balanophoraceae) found in the Galápagos Islands. Bot. Not. 129:113-117.

Adsersen, H. 1976b. New records of pteridophytes from the Galápagos Islands. Bot. Not. 129: 429-436.

Amadon, D. 1966. Insular adaptive radiation among birds. Pages 18-30 *in* R. I. Bowman, ed. The Galápagos. University of California Press, Berkeley and Los Angeles, Calif.

Anderson, D. E. 1974. Taxonomy of the genus *Chloris* (Gramineae). Brigham Young Univ. Sci. Bull., Biol. Ser. 19(2):1-133.

Anderson, R. N., et al. 1975. Magnetic and petrologic variations along the Galapagos spreading center and their relation to the Galapagos melting anomaly. Bull. Geol. Soc. Amer. 86:683-694.

Andersson, N. J. 1855. Om Galapagos öarnes Vegetation. Kongl. Vetensk. Akad. Handl. 1853: 61-120.

Bailey, K. 1976. Potassium-Argon ages from the Galápagos Islands. Science 192:465-467.

Baker, H. G. 1955. Self-compatibility and establishment after "long-distance" dispersal. Evolution 9:347-349.

Van Balgooy, M. M. J. 1960. Preliminary plant-geographical analysis of the Pacific as based on the distribution of Phanerogam genera. Blumea 10:384-430.

Baur, G. 1891. On the origin of the Galapagos Islands. Amer. Nat. 25:217-299, 307-326.

Baur, G. 1897. New observations on the origin of the Galapagos Islands, with remarks on the geological age of the Pacific Ocean. Amer. Nat. 31:661-680, 864-896.

Beebe, W. 1926. The Arcturus adventure. Putnam, New York, N. Y. 439 pp.

Bond, J. 1971. Birds of the West Indies. 2nd ed. Collins, London. 256 pp.

Bowman, R. I. 1961. Morphological differentiation and adaptation in the Galápagos finches. Univ. Calif. Publ. Zool. 58:1-302.

Carlquist, S. 1966a. The biota of long-distance dispersal. I. Principles of dispersal and evolution. Quart. Rev. Biol. 41:247-270.

Carlquist, S. 1966b. The biota of long-distance dispersal. II. Loss of dispersibility in Pacific Compositae. Evolution 20:30-48.

Carlquist, S. 1966c. The biota of long-distance dispersal. III. Loss of dispersibility in the Hawaiian flora. Brittonia 18:310-335.

Carlquist, S. 1966d. The biota of long-distance dispersal. IV. Genetic systems in the floras of oceanic islands. Evolution 20:433-455.

Carlquist, S. 1967. The biota of long-distance dispersal. V. Plant dispersal to Pacific Islands. Bull. Torr. Bot. Club. 94:129-162.

Carlquist, S. 1974. Island biology. Columbia University Press, New York and London. 660 pp.

Carpenter, C. C. 1966. Comparative behavior of the Galápagos lava lizards (*Tropidurus*). Pages 269-273 *in* R. I. Bowman, ed. The Galápagos. University of California Press, Berkeley and Los Angeles, Calif.

Colinvaux, P. A. 1972. Climate and the Galapagos Islands. Nature 240:17-20.

Colinvaux, P. A., and E. K. Schofield. 1976a. Historical ecology in the Galápagos Islands. I. A Holocene pollen record from El Junco Lake, Isla San Cristobal. J. Ecol. 64:989-1012.

Colinvaux, P. A., and E. K. Schofield. 1976b. Historical ecology in the Galápagos Islands. II. A Holocene spore record from El Junco Lake, Isla San Cristobal. J. Ecol. 64:1013-1028.

Colinvaux, P. A., E. K. Schofield, and I. L. Wiggins. 1968. Galápagos flora: Fernandina (Narborough) caldera before recent volcanic event. Science 162:1144-1145.

Cox, A., and G. B. Dalrymple. 1966. Paleomagnetism and potassium-argon ages of some volcanic rocks from the Galapagos Islands. Nature 209:776-777.

Croizat, L. 1952. Manual of phytogeography. Dr. W. Junk, The Hague. 558 pp.

Croizat, L., G. Nelson, and D. E. Rosen. 1974. Centers of origin and related concepts. Syst. Zool. 23:265-287.

D'Arcy, W. G. 1979. Scrophulariaceae. Flora of Panama, Part IX, Family 171. Ann. Missouri Bot. Gard. 66:173-272.

Darwin, C. 1839. Narrative of the surveying voyages of His Majesty's ships *Adventure* and *Beagle,* between the years 1826 and 1836, describing their examination of the southern shores of South America, and the Beagle's circumnavigation of the Globe. Vol. 3. Journal and remarks. 1832-1836. Henry Colburn, London. 629 pp.

Darwin, C. 1845. Journal of researches into the natural history and geology of the countries visited during the voyages of H.M.S. Beagle 'round the world, under the Command of Capt. Fitz Roy, R. N. 2nd rev. ed. John Murray, London. 520 pp.

Darwin, C. 1859. On the origin of species by natural selection, or the preservation of favoured races in the struggle for life. John Murray, London. 502 pp.

Eckhardt, R. C. 1972. Introduced plants and animals in the Galápagos Islands. Bioscience 22:585-590.

Eliasson, U. 1970. Studies in Galápagos plants. IX. New taxonomical and distributional records. Bot. Not. 123:346-357.

Eliasson, U. 1972. Studies in Galápagos plants. XIII. Three new floristic records and two supplementary remarks. Bot. Not. 125:320-322.

Eliasson, U. 1974. Studies in Galápagos plants. XIV. The genus *Scalesia.* Opera Bot. 36:1-117.

Falla, R. A. 1960. Oceanic birds as dispersal agents. Proc. Roy. Soc. Lond, Ser. B. 152:655-659.

Fitz-Roy, R. 1839. Narrative of the surveying voyages of His Majesty's ships *Adventure* and *Beagle,* between the years 1826 and 1836, describing their examination of the southern shores of South America, and the Beagle's circumnavigation of the globe. Vol. 2. Proceedings of the second expedition, 1831-1836, under the command of Captain Robert Fitz-Roy, R. N. Henry Colburn, London. 695 pp.

Gibson, D. N. 1970. Flora of Guatemala. Verbenaceae. Fieldiana: Bot. 24(pt. IX, 1/2):167-236.

Gillham, M. E. 1970. Seed dispersal by birds. Pages 90-98 *in* F. Perring, ed. The Flora of a Changing Britain. F. Classey, Hampton, Middlesex. 157 pp.

Grant, P. R., et al. 1975. Finch numbers, owl predation and plant dispersal on Isla Daphne Major, Galápagos. Oecologia 19:239-257.

Gunn, C. R. 1972. Notes on *Strictocardia campanulata* (L.) Merrill and *S. jucunda* (Thw.) C. R. Gunn (Convolvulaceae). Brittonia 24:169-176.

Hamann, O. 1974a. Contributions to the flora and vegetation of the Galápagos Islands. I. New floristic records from the archipelago. Bot. Not. 127:245-251.

Hamann, O. 1974b. Contributions to the flora and vegetation of the Galápagos Islands. II. A new subspecies of *Lycopodium* from the Archipelago. Bot. Not 127:252-255.

Hamann, O. 1974c. Contributions to the flora and vegetation of the Galápagos Islands. III. Five new floristic records. Bot. Not. 127:309-316.

Hamann, O. 1975. Vegetational changes in the Galápagos Islands during the period 1966-73. Biol. Conserv. 7:37-59.

Harling, G. 1962. On some Compositae endemic to the Galápagos Islands. Acta Hort. Bergiana 20:63-120.

Harris, M. P. 1974. A field guide to the birds of Galapagos. Collins, London. 160 pp.

Harris, M. P. 1976. Ringing of Galápagos seabirds. Noticias de Galápagos 25:20-22.

Hendrickson, J. D. 1966. The Galápagos tortoises, *Geochelone* Fitzinger 1835 (*Testudo* Linnaeus 1758 in part). Pages 252-257 *in* R. I. Bowman, ed. The Galápagos. University of California Press, Berkeley and Los Angeles, Calif.

Hey, R., G. L. Johnson, and A. Lowrie. 1977. Recent plate motions in the Galapagos area. Bull. Geol. Soc. Amer. 88:1385-1403.

Heyerdahl, T. 1963. Archaeology in the Galápagos Islands. Occas. Pap. Calif. Acad. Sci. 22:45-51.

Holden, J. C., and R. S. Dietz. 1972. Galapagos gore, NazCoPac triple junction and Carnegie/Cocos Ridges. Nature 235:266-269.

Hooker, J. D. 1847a. An enumeration of the plants of the Galapagos Archipelago; with descriptions of those which are new. Trans. Linn. Soc. Bot. 20:163-233.

Hooker, J. D. 1847b. On the vegetation of the Galapagos Archipelago as compared with that of some other tropical islands and of the continent of America. Trans. Linn. Soc. Bot. 20:235-262.

Johnson, M. F. 1971. A monograph of the genus *Ageratum* L. (Compositae-Eupatorieae). Ann. Missouri Bot. Gard. 58:6-88.

Johnson, M. P., and P. H. Raven. 1973. Species number and endemism: The Galápagos Archipelago revisited. Science 179:893-895.

Johnston, M. C. 1974. Revision of *Scutia* (Rhamnaceae). Bull. Torr. Bot. Club 101:64-72.

King, R. M., and H. Robinson. 1971. Studies in the Eupatorieae (Asteraceae). LXIV. The genus, *Koanophyllon*. Phytologia 22:147-152.

King, R. M., and H. Robinson. 1975a. Compositae. 10. *Adenostemma.* Flora of Panama, Part IX, Family 184. Ann. Missouri Bot. Gard. 62:891-892.

King, R. M., and H. Robinson. 1975b. Compositae. 21. *Fleischmannia*. Flora of Panama, Part IX, Family 184. Ann. Missouri Bot. Gard. 62:937-948.

Kuschel, G. 1963. Composition and relationships of the terrestrial faunas of Easter, Juan Fernández, Desventuradas, and Galápagos Islands. Occas. Pap. Calif. Acad. Sci. 44:79-95.

Lévêque, R., R. I. Bowman, and S. I. Billeb. 1966. Migrants in the Galápagos area. Condor 68: 81-101.

Linsley, E. G. 1966. Pollinating insects of the Galápagos Islands. Pages 225-232 *in* R. I. Bowman, ed. The Galápagos. University of California Press, Berkeley and Los Angeles, Calif.

Linsley, E. G., C. M. Rick, and S. G. Stephens. 1966. Observations on the floral relationships of the Galápagos carpenter bee (Hymenoptera: Apidae). Pan-Pacific Entomol. 42:1-18.

Livingston, J., and L. Sinclair. 1966. Darwin and the Galapagos. Canadian Broadcasting Corporation, Toronto. 58 pp.

Malfait, B. T., and M. G. Dinkelman. 1972. Circum-Caribbean tectonic and igneous activity and the evolution of the Caribbean plate. Bull. Geol. Soc. Amer. 83:251-271.

Martin, A. C., H. S. Zim, and A. L. Nelson. 1951. American wildlife and plants. McGraw-Hill, New York, N. Y. 500 pp.

McBirney, A. R., and H. Williams. 1969. Geology and petrology of the Galapagos Islands. Mem. Geol. Soc. Amer. 118:1-197.

Van der Pijl, L. 1972. Principles of dispersal in higher plants. 2nd ed. Springer-Verlag, Berlin, Heidelberg, and New York. 162 pp.

Porter, D. M. 1973. The Galápagos Islands (letter). BioScience 23:276.

Porter, D. M. 1976. Geography and dispersal of Galapagos Islands vascular plants. Nature 264: 745-746.

Porter, D. M. 1978. Nomenclatural changes in *Spilanthes, Lycopersicon,* and *Opuntia* for the Galápagos Islands. Madroño 25:58-59.

Porter, D. M. 1979. Endemism and evolution in Galápagos Islands vascular plants. Pages 225-256 *in* D. Bramwell, ed. Plants and Islands. Academic Press, London.

Proctor, G. R. 1977. Flora of the Lesser Antilles. Vol. 2. Pteridophyta. Arnold Arboretum, Jamaica Plain, Massachusetts.

Proctor, V. W. 1968. Long-distance dispersal of seeds by retention in digestive tract of birds. Science 160:321-322.

Rahn, K. 1974. *Plantago* section *Virginica*. A taxonomic revision of a group of American plantains, using experimental, taximetric and classical methods. Dansk Bot. Ark. 30(2):1-180.

Rhodes, D. G. 1975. A revision of the genus *Cissampelos*. Phytologica 30:415-484.

Richardson, A. Monograph of the genus *Tiquilia* (*Coldenia*, sensu lato), Boraginaceae: Ehretioideae. Rhodora 79:467-572.

Rick, C. M. 1966. Some plant-animal relationships on the Galapagos Islands. Pages 215-224 *in*

R. I. Bowman, ed. The Galápagos. University of California Press, Berkeley and Los Angeles, Calif.

Ridgely, R. S. 1976. A guide to the birds of Panama. Princeton University Press, Princeton, N. J. 394 pp.

Ridley, H. N. 1930. The dispersal of plants throughout the world. Reeve, Ashford, Kent. 744 pp.

Robinson, B. L. 1902. Flora of the Galapagos Islands. Proc. Amer. Acad. 38:77-269.

Robinson, B. L., and J. M. Greenman. 1895. On the flora of the Galapagos Islands as shown by the collection of Dr. Baur. Amer. J. Sci. 150:135-149.

Rosen, D. E. 1974. A vicariance model of Caribbean biogeography. Syst. Zool. 23:431-464.

Sauer, J. D. 1969. Oceanic islands and biogeographical theory: A review. Geogr. Rev. 59:582-593.

Scharff, R. F. 1912. Distribution and origin of life in America. Constable, London.

Schofield, E. K. 1973. Galápagos flora: The threat of introduced plants. Biol. Conserv. 5:48-51.

Simpson, B. B. 1974. Glacial migrations of plants: Island biogeographical evidence. Science 185: 698-700.

Simpson, B. B. 1975. Glacial climates in the eastern tropical South Pacific. Nature 253:34-36.

Slevin, J. R. 1959. The Galápagos Islands, a history of their exploration. Occas. Pap. Calif. Acad. Sci. 25:1-150.

Smith, A. G. 1966. Land snails of the Galápagos. Pages 240-251 *in* R. I. Bowman, ed. The Galápagos. University of California Press, Berkeley and Los Angeles, Calif.

Smith, A. R. 1971. Systematics of the Neotropical species of *Thelypteris* section *Cyclosorus*. Univ. Calif. Publ. Bot. 59:1-136.

Smith, A. R. 1972. Comparison of fern and flowering plant distributions with some evolutionary interpretations for ferns. Biotropica 4:4-9.

Stebbins, G. L. 1952. Aridity as a stimulus to plant evolution. Amer. Nat. 86:33-44.

Stephens, S. G. 1958. Salt water tolerance of seeds of *Gossypium* species as a possible factor in seed dispersal. Amer. Nat. 92:83-92.

Stewart, A. 1911. A botanical survey of the Galapagos Islands. Proc. Calif. Acad. Sci., ser. 4, 1:7-288.

Stewart, A. 1915. Further observations on the origin of the Galapagos Islands. Pl. World 18: 192-200.

Svenson, H. K. 1935. Plants of the Astor Expedition, 1930 (Galapagos and Cocos Islands). Amer. J. Bot. 22:208-277.

Svenson, H. K. 1942. Origin of plants on the Galapagos Islands. Proc. 8th Amer. Sci. Congr. 3:285-286.

Svenson, H. K. 1946. Vegetation of the coast of Ecuador and Peru and its relation to the Galapagos Islands. I. Geographical relations of the flora. Amer. J. Bot. 33:394-426.

Swanson, F. J., H. W. Baitis, J. Lexa, and J. Dymond. 1974. Geology of Santiago, Rábida, and Pinzón Islands, Galápagos. Bull. Geol. Soc. Amer. 85:1803-1810.

Thornton, I. 1971. Darwin's islands. Natural History Press, New York, N. Y. 322 pp.

Townsend, C. H. 1928. The Galapagos Islands revisited. Bull. N. Y. Zool. Soc. 31:148-168.

Tryon, R. 1970. Development and evolution of fern floras of oceanic islands. Biotropica 2:76-84.

Tryon, R. 1972. Endemic areas and geographic speciation in tropical American ferns. Biotropica 4:121-131.

Usinger, R. L., and P. D. Ashlock. 1966. Evolution of orsilline insect faunas on oceanic islands (Hemiptera, Lygaeidae). Pages 233-235 *in* R. I. Bowman, ed. The Galápagos. University of California Press, Berkeley and Los Angeles, Calif.

Vagvolgyi, J. 1974. Body size, aerial dispersal, and origin of the Pacific land snail fauna. Syst. Zool. 23:465-488.

Vinton, K. W. 1951. Origin of life on the Galapagos Islands. Amer. J. Sci. 249:356-376.

De Vlaming, V. L., and V. W. Proctor. 1968. Dispersal of aquatic organisms: Viability of seeds recovered from the droppings of captive killdeer and mallard ducks. Amer. J. Bot. 55:20-26.

Van der Werff, H. 1977. Vascular plants from the Galápagos Islands: New records and taxonomic notes. Bot. Not. 130:89-100.

Weber, D. 1971. Pinta, Galápagos: Une ile à sauver. Biol. Conserv. 4:8-12.

Weber, D. 1973. Deux orchidacées nouvelles pour la flore des Iles Galapagos. Bull. Soc. Neuchateloise Sci. Nat. 96:17-30.

Wickens, G. E. 1976. Speculations on long distance dispersal and the flora of Jebel Marra, Sudan Republic. Kew Bull. 31:105-150.

Wiggins, I. L. 1975. *Ranunculus flagelliformis* discovered in the Galápagos Islands. Madroño 23: 62-64.

Wiggins, I. L., and D. M. Porter. 1971. Flora of the Galápagos Islands. Stanford University Press, Stanford, Calif. 998 pp.

Wright, S. 1940. Breeding structure of populations in relation to speciation. Amer. Nat. 74:232-248.

GENETIC VARIATION AND EVOLUTION OF GALAPAGOS TOMATOES

CHARLES M. RICK
Department of Vegetable Crops, University of California, Davis, CA 95616

The nature of genetic variation in both gross morphological and allozymic characters was investigated in natural populations of the Galapagos tomato, *Lycopersicon cheesmanii* Riley. Individuals in the progeny of single plants in the wild invariably agreed in genotype. Likewise, but with rare exceptions, members of the same wild population exhibited the same genotype. Thus, the great majority of tested populations behaved like essentially pure lines. The data accrued from both character series are consistent in pointing to a very high degree of autogamy. This conclusion is also compatible with the observations that the flower structure is adapted for self-pollination and the flowers do automatically self-pollinate in tests made in the wild and in experimental cultures.

Certain wild populations are characterized by the presence in all members of certain unique morphs, of either allozymic or gross morphological nature. Each of these morphs, some apparently defective, is determined by a single mutant gene. The fixation of each of these genes throughout a given population, a unique situation amongst tomato species, is considered to reflect genetic drift and a relatively low pressure of natural selection on the Galapagos Islands.

In contrast to the genetic relationship between plants within populations, much variation was observed between populations. The widespread f. *minor* is well distinguished from other forms of *L. cheesmanii* in one or more of a series of eight morphological characters. No other prevailing subspecific type can be identified, although certain populations exhibit the opposite extremes for the same eight morphs. F. *minor* is not distinctive in its allozymes.

Amongst the other tomato species, certain biotypes of *L. pimpinellifolium* from NW Peru show the closest relationships with *L. cheesmanii*, according to comparisons of genotype and habitat preferences. It is therefore suggested that the ancestral *cheesmanii* migrated from that region to the Galapagos, a course that would have been favored by the flow of the Humboldt Current. The existence of but one known bee species in the archipelago (perhaps only in recent history) severely limits the extent of insect cross-pollination. Therefore, in addition to the many other drastic exigencies faced by the founding populations, extreme selection presumably took place in entomophilous plants for autogamy and ability of the genoytpe to tolerate the resulting inbreeding. The consequent fixation of genotypes and accumulation of mutant genes would have led to rapid differentiation. Field tests of the mating system in other endemic angiosperm species and a survey of the relative abundance of groups that are anemophilous, obligately, or facultatively entomophilous suggest that the pattern of establishment and evolution of the mating system in *L. cheesmanii* might be typical of many other components of the Galapagos flora.

The presence of *Lycopersicon* on the Galapagos Islands was first documented by Darwin in the collections of his memorable visit in 1835. As interest of the scientific world became aroused, collections were made subsequently by various explorers at an increasing rate. Interest first focused on the systematics of these collections. For a review of the taxonomic history of this material, the reader is referred to papers by Muller (1940) and Rick (1963, 1971).

In the rapidly accelerated research in tomato breeding during the present century, investigators understandably screened germplasm of all potential kinds that might serve their purposes. In this sphere of activity, they eventually extended their testing to available wild species of *Lycopersicon* and have succeeded admirably in breeding desirable traits from them to the cultivated tomato, *L. esculentum*. As this work progressed, their curiosity became piqued by the Galapagos material, which was not experimentally cultured until 1951.

We are aware of several unsuccessful attempts made in the 1940s to acquire and study Galapagos tomatoes. Undoubtedly, similar attempts unknown to us were made by other workers. Although the history of these ventures is not well known, it is likely that seed germination was the stumbling block. Mature seeds of all of the 60+ accessions in our collection prove to have severe seed dormancy that requires for its abatement the drastic removal of the testa by chemical or mechanical treatment. Passage through the gut of the giant Galapagos tortoises also promotes germination, suggesting that such a mutualism might serve as a natural means for both establishment and dispersal (Rick and Bowman 1961). Subsequent studies showed that digestion by the Galapagos mockingbird can also facilitate germination (Rick 1966), but action by the gizzard of all other tested bird species demolishes the ingested seeds.

Once established, the accessions proved amenable to experimental culture, thereby permitting studies on their genetics, biochemistry, evolution, and practical utilization in tomato improvement programs. Ample genetic variation, including such characteristics as jointless pedicel, thick pericarp, and high β-carotene content, was encountered to stimulate the further interests of tomato breeders. Complete genetic compatibility with the cultivated tomato expedited this utilization (Rick 1963, 1967, 1968).

The group was also analyzed biosystematically from the standpoints of cytogenetics, crossability, and genetic variation. According to the early studies (Rick 1963), the coherence in these respects of all available accessions led to the treatment of all as a single species. Distinctness and geographic isolation from all other known Lycopersici, as well as other potential biosystematic barriers to interbreeding, substantiate recognition of this unit as a separate species, *L. cheesmanii* Riley.

It is the purpose here to review briefly the recent literature, to present the results of some new research on morphological variation in Galapagos tomatoes, to reassess their biosystematic relationships, and to compare their population dynamics with that of the angiosperm flora as a whole.

MATING SYSTEM

In the course of these early investigations of *L. cheesmanii*, evidence of the following categories was encountered for certain unusual aspects of population dynamics (Rick 1963): (1) Progenies of single plants, often whole populations, exhibited extreme uniformity in gross morphology. (2) Such drastic deviations as jointless pedicel, lutescent foliage, and complete anthocyanin deficiency, each determined by a single recessive gene, were found to be fixed throughout certain wild populations. (3) Substantial interplant variation was found in only one population, yet individual plant progenies from this population displayed the same uniformity observed in other accessions. (4) The structural arrangement of floral parts promotes automatic self-pollination. (5) Fruits are set abundantly by automatic self-pollination in experimental cultures and in the wild (Rick 1966). All of these phenomena allude to strict autogamy throughout the species, leading to rapid fixation of alleles and differentiation between populations.

VARIATION IN GROSS MORPHOLOGY

The observations summarized above provide the premises for analysis of genetic variation in the species as a whole. The extreme uniformity of wild populations greatly simplifies the presentation of data, since the great majority of populations can be accurately represented by a single phenotype. Genetic variation was investigated in this manner for gross morphological characters and allozymes. This section is devoted to the morphological aspects. A preliminary classification of this type was presented earlier (Rick 1963) but was handicapped by the limited number of available living accessions. That survey also included herbarium specimens, but they proved to be unsatisfactory for the assessment of certain morphs. The present survey is based on comparisons of living plants of 46 accessions either in wild populations, in cultures grown at Davis, California from seeds harvested in the wild, or from both.

The following eight characters epitomize the nature of gross morphological variation in *L. cheesmanii*. According to breeding experiments (Rick 1956, 1963, and unpublished), these characters are highly heritable. Despite environmental variables and wide segregation in certain hybrid progenies, the phenotypes are relatively stable and can be simply and accurately characterized. Where known, inheritance of these morphs is summarized below; determination is relatively simple, in certain cases apparently monogenic. Variants of most of these morphs have been illustrated previously (Rick 1956); references for the others are cited below.

Internode length. Most accessions fall into two categories of mean internode lengths of 2-4 cm and 6-8 cm. Intermediate forms are rare.

Epidermal hairs. The herbage of all biotypes is amply invested with a mixture of small glandular and unicellular non-glandular hairs. But great differences are seen in the larger, multicellular trichomes, ranging in density from complete absence to thick pubescence, and in length from 1-4 mm. The incompletely dominant *h* gene plays a major role in determining these hair phenotypes.

Leaf subdivision. A remarkable break is detected between leaves that have lst-2nd order pinnate subdivisions and those of 3rd-4th order. Extremes of the latter type in forma (f.) *minor* present a picture of magnificent complexity with hundreds of segments of 4th order. According to our unpublished findings, the difference between these two groups is regulated by alleles of a single locus.

Corolla shape. Corolla segments vary markedly in width of segments and corresponding depth of segmentation. Wide segments are associated with more condensed and more ramified inflorescences, narrow ones consistently with more elongate, unbranched inflorescences.

Calyx size. The calyx of f. *minor* expands rapidly as the fruit develops and far exceeds the diameter of the fruit. In other races the calyx may expand to the diameter of the fruit or slightly exceed it.

Calyx shape. A qualitative difference can be observed in all stages of post-anthetic development of calyx form: in nearly all accessions of f. *minor* the calyx is accrescent to the fruit, whereas in most other accessions the calyx segments radiate in one plane. Intermediate types have not been found.

Pericarp thickness. The fruit wall varies from a very thin structure, lending a softness to the ripe fruit invariably found in f. *minor*, to the contrasting, unique, thick walls, and firm ripe fruit at the other extreme (Rick 1967). Intermediate types are known. According to our inheritance studies (Rick 1967), genetic control is probably monogenic.

Fruit color. The *B* gene, determining the synthesis of β-carotene (MacKinney et al. 1954), is universal in *L. cheesmanii*. Differences are seen, however, in the intensity of pigmentation of the flesh and in the presence vs. absence of yellow-orange flavonoids in the epidermis, the latter difference known to be governed by alleles at the *y* locus. In external aspects fruit color varies from pale straw-yellow through dull orange-yellow to the deep orange-red typical of f. *minor*.

To summarize, the well-defined subspecific type f. *minor* is characterized by short internode length, dense hairiness of herbage, highly compound leaf, wide corolla segment and condensed, compound inflorescence, large accrescent calyx, thin pericarp, and dark orange-red fruit color. The contrasting type, which is arbitrarily labelled f. *typicum* with no taxonomic significance, displays the opposite extremes.

The qualitative or near qualitative expression of these eight morphs greatly facilitates classification into finite categories and permits the bulk of the data to be presented in simple diagrammatic fashion as in Fig. 1.

The relatively high level of uniformity in f. *minor* is evident in the symbolic representation in Fig. 1 (solid circle with seven long appendages), departures from this type being found in only two of the eight characters. The impression of near monomorphy thus given is false, however, because accessions do differ genetically in the extent of anthocyanin pigmentation, degree of complexity of leaf subdivision (although never less than 3rd order), length of internodes (although seldom longer than 4 cm), and other features.

The opposite situation prevails in the remainder of this species. The assortment of these and other characters in this group is too heterogeneous to permit rational classification into subgroups. As seen in Fig. 1, *minor*-type variations appear in various accessions of this group for all characters except leaf subdivision. The association of opposite extremes from f. *minor* in all morphs as defined for f. *typicum* is found in a few accessions from Santa Cruz and San Cristóbal, but these populations are not homogeneous for other morphs.

In a few localities (Villamil, Isabela; NE shore, Fernandina), f. *minor* intermingles with other biotypes, but still maintains its morphological integrity. Intergradation between f. *minor* and f. *typicum* for these morphs was discovered in only one population (W of Villamil), but even in this

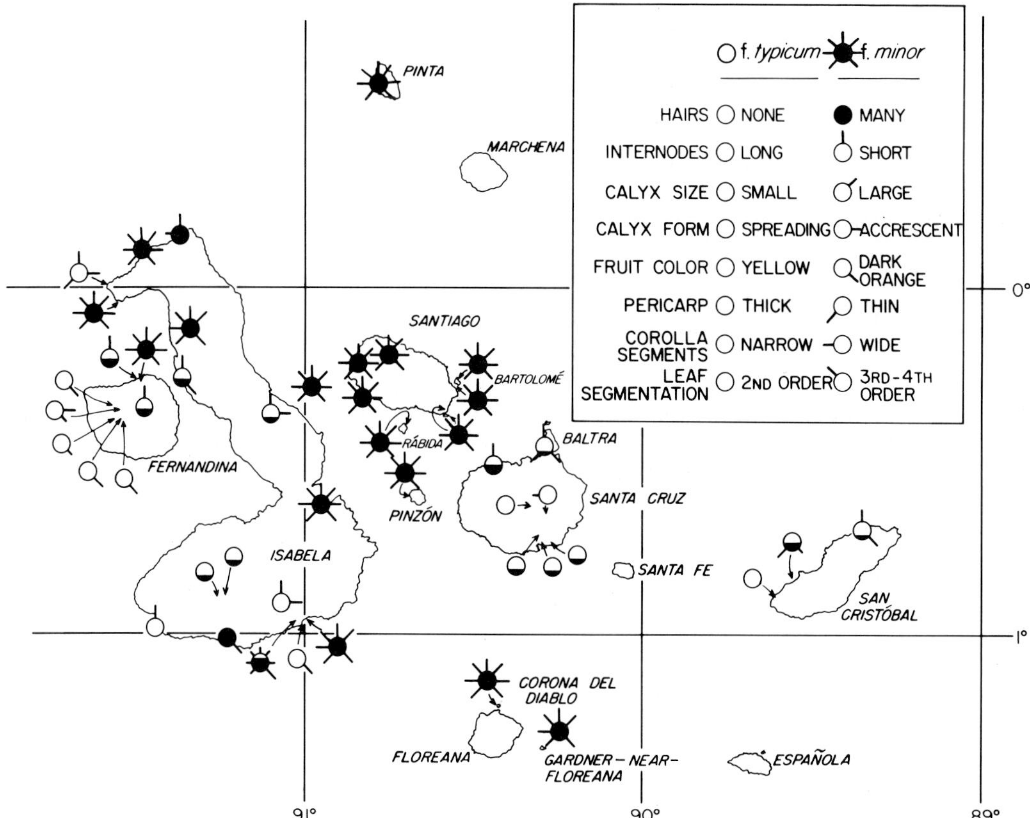

Fig. 1. Distribution of variation for eight morphs in accessions of *L. cheesmanii*. Symbols represent the characteristic phenotype of each accession; extent of deviation from f. *typicum* indicated by the length of appendages and extent of black area in circles.

exception, each of the variant types was homozygous, as verified by progeny tests (Rick 1963).

The accessions also exhibit variability in the appearance of various mutant recessive genes for very clearly distinguished morphological characters. Examples of these include: (1) ag^2 (complete lack of anthocyanin) in all accessions from San Cristóbal and from Corona del Diablo and Gardner-near-Charles, islets offshore from Isla Floreana. (2) Very dark purple pigmentation of the subepidermal cell layers of unripe fruit (*atv*) is found in occasional plants in populations behind Puerto Ayora, Santa Cruz, and, curiously, fixed in accessions from the W caldera rim of Fernandina and E slope of Cerro Azul, Isabela. (3) The distinctive absence of pedicel articulation (*j*-2) is characteristic of accessions in the vicinity of Puerto Ayora, Santa Cruz and in the collection from Bahía San Pedro on the southern shore of Isabela. (4) Early senescence leading to premature yellowing of foliage (*l*) and the orange-yellow fruit pigmentation diospyros (*dps*) variant are widespread in accessions from San Cristóbal and elsewhere. (5) A weak, partial chlorophyll deficiency (*glg*) segregated in progenies grown from one of the lowland accessions from Fernandina.

This array of mutant genes, some determining phenotypes of considerably reduced vigor, is unique amongst tomato species and is considered to be evidence of the rapid, fortuitous fixation of genes (genetic drift) and the relatively relaxed intensity of natural selection on the Galapagos.

As illustrated in Fig. 1, f. *minor* prefers the low arid and littoral zones, the other biotypes tending to prefer more mesophytic conditions, but with great diversity in their ecology as manifested by occasional sympatry with f. *minor*. The widespread distribution of f. *minor* certainly testifies to its mobility.

The morphological distinctiveness of f. *minor* deserves further comment. The consistent appearance of the aforementioned syndrome permits unequivocal identification. Yet, the extensive leaf segmentation, a monogenic character (*Pts*, Rick 1980), is the only unique feature not found in the remainder of the species. All other *minor*-like characters appear in one of several non-*minor* accessions. The complete intercompatibility between f. *minor* and other *L. cheesmanii* biotypes, as well as the suggestion of introgression in the Villamil population, argue against classification of the former as a separate species.

ALLOZYME VARIATION

Seeking additional genetic information concerning population structure and dynamics, Rick and Fobes (1975) subjected the available living accessions to allozyme analysis. The components of four enzyme systems were dispersed by standard, horizontal, starch-gel electrophoresis. Many studies in diverse organisms have demonstrated the merits of this method for providing precise data on the genotypes of parents and progeny for various genes that code for simply detected, soluble enzymes. Seedlings of 54 accessions distributed over the archipelago and representing the known races of *L. cheesmanii* were grown and samples were analyzed for genotypes of four enzyme systems.

Of the 14 loci tested, eight proved to be polymorphic, with a total of 21 allozymes. Breeding experiments in this and related species clearly established the bands corresponding to alleles of the same or different loci. Genetic variation was exhibited by only two single-plant progenies, in each of which only a single locus segregated: the data imply that both parent plants were homozygotes, outcrossing probably having been responsible for the observed variability. Thus, no case of heterozygosity in a wild plant was encountered and intrapopulation genetic variation was minimal. These results are therefore concordant with the survey of gross morphological variation in implying that reproduction is almost completely autogamous and that natural populations often approach a pure-line constitution.

This reconfirmed simple genetic constitution of populations greatly facilitates comparisons and analyses of interpopulation and racial variation. Figure 2 presents a summary of these results in relation to geographic distribution. The regional and particularly the ecological distribution of

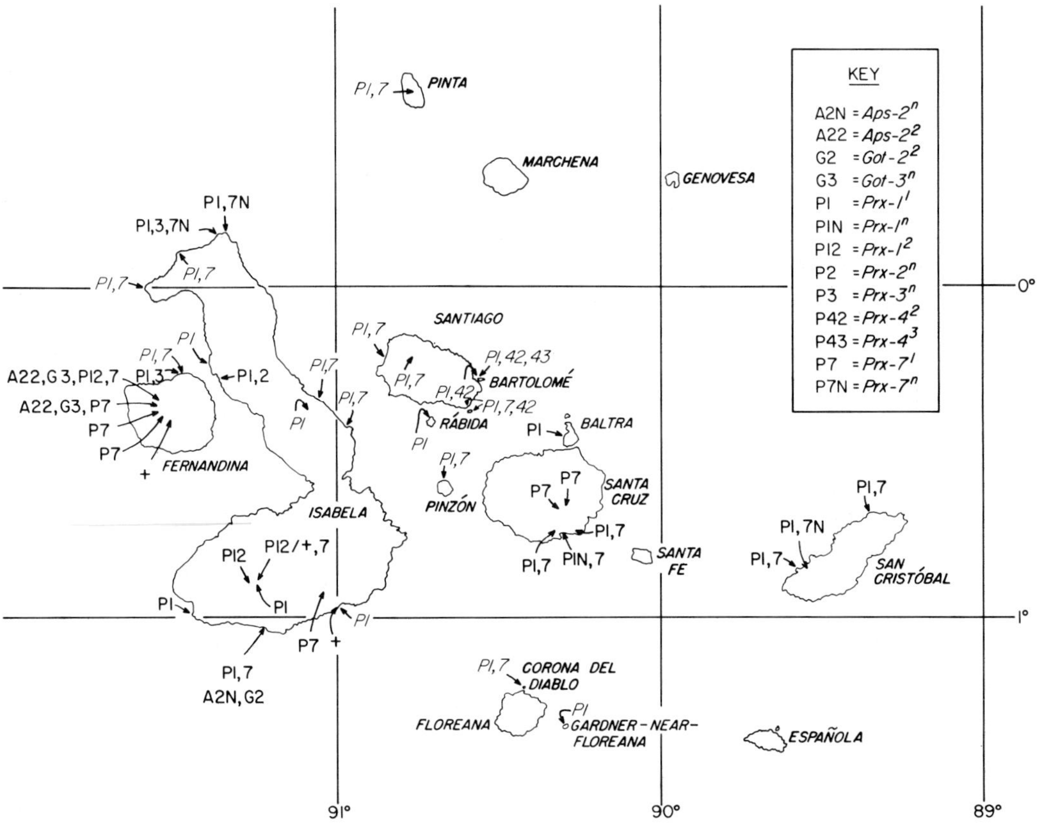

Fig. 2. Distribution of allozymes in accessions of *L. cheesmanii*: f. *minor* in italics, f. *typicum* in boldface (redrawn from Rick and Fobes 1975).

certain common alleles suggests adaptive significance. The commonest genotype is $Prx\text{-}1^1$, $Prx\text{-}7^1$, which is found on all major islands and on some of the lesser islands. In keeping with the survey of gross morphological variation, f. *minor* was found to be relatively invariable, being mostly of the aforementioned genotype. The degree of interpopulation variation in other races is greater, mostly reflecting the existence of various rare alleles, which tend to be distributed on the western slopes of the western islands. Except for these rare alleles, the tendency toward island endemism, so clearly demonstrated in other organisms (*Scalesia*, for example), is not evident in *L. cheesmanii*.

The proportion of null alleles amongst all variant alleles is much greater in *L. cheesmanii* (63%) than in the other congeneric species, all from continental South America; for example, 10% in *L. pimpinellifolium* and in values reported for other organisms in general. Comparisons between these species in respect to reproductive systems and null allele frequency reinforce the concept that *L. cheesmanii* may have evolved under conditions of less intense natural selection.

Zymotypes of *L. cheesmanii* were compared with those of the most closely related, highly polymorphic *L. pimpinellifolium* (Rick and Fobes 1975; Rick et al. 1977). The closest resemblance in zymotype is with accessions from Depto. Lambayeque, Peru. The tomato habitats of the two regions are remarkably similar in flora, topography, and general ecology. The hypothesized origin of the *L. cheesmanii* precursor in northern Peru is also compatible with the flow direction of the Humboldt Current, which might have facilitated drift of the founder stocks thence to the Galapagos Islands.

RELATIONSHIPS WITH THE GALAPAGOS FLORA

The results of the investigations summarized here tend to reinforce the generalizations reached in previous studies (Rick 1966) concerning the circumstances of the founding and origin of the Galapagos flora. In those studies of the pollination relations in a sample of the present flora, all but one of the 13 effectively tested species, representing seven angiosperm families, reproduce autogamously and the remaining species set fruit and seeds when artificially self-pollinated. Although only a tiny experimental sample, it was taken at random from available flowering species and the results are remarkably consistent. *L. cheesmanii* is therefore typical, not exceptional, of the angiosperm flora in respect to mating system. This widespread ability to self-pollinate automatically contrasts markedly with the bulk of species from adjacent continental areas, which, by virtue of various inherent devices, depend on pollen vectors for pollination, hence reproduction.

The implications of these observations and generalizations for the origin of the Galapagos flora are profound. They suggest that rigid selection for autogamy or at least for the tolerance of autogamy took place during the founding and early evolution of the surviving immigrants. One very important factor in these considerations is the paucity of native insects on the islands, which is epitomized by the existence of only a single species of bee, *Xylocopa darwini* Cockerell, in the entire archipelago. This overworked carpenter bee must attend to all the pollination for the reproduction and maintenance of genetic variability of certain plant species, if indeed it is necessary at all (Linsley et al. 1966). This situation stands in stark contrast to the hundreds of bee species in several families on the adjacent mainland. There the floral apparatus of a high proportion of the flora reveals elaborate and extensive entomophily.

Xylocopa darwini requires wood for its nesting sites, a fact that emphasizes the concept of a harsh fate for pioneer plant species requiring bee pollination. Presumably the founding populations of this bee could not have survived without the widespread presence of woody plants on the Galapagos. Now, since trees and shrubs appear relatively late in the ecological sequence in an entirely new habitat, the ancestral carpenter bee would not have arrived on the scene until still later, and its role in the establishment and evolution of the flora might consequently have been minor. In pursuing this argument, the possibility must be admitted that other species of bees or other insects, that are now extinct, might have participated in pollination earlier in the evolution of the flora. However valid this idea, certainly no strong mutualism could have evolved between the extinct insects and elements of the flora unless it permitted the subsequent substitution of *X. darwini*.

A less important role of *X. darwini* in the evolution of the endemic flora is also implied by the studies of Linsley et al. (1966). Their observations that the proportion of endemic plant species visited by this bee is significantly smaller than the proportion of endemics in the total flora led to the conclusion " . . .that the Galápagos carpenter bee probably played a greater role in the establishment of immigrant plant species than of ancestors of the older endemic species and that evolution among at least some of the endemic elements could have taken place without the aid of the carpenter bee."

The consequences of these considerations would be that the Galapagos environment was extraordinarily forbidding for the establishment of flowering plants. The absence of insect pollinators would have added one more hurdle to the number of extreme exigencies faced by immigrating plants. Clearly any obligately entomophilous species could not have survived, and those species that were automatically self-pollinating and could tolerate inbreeding would have enjoyed a much better opportunity for survival.

The consequences of such extreme selection can be observed in the present Galapagos flora. In their floral display, the native species are anything but spectacular; furthermore, the drabness of flowering is vastly more extreme in the endemic than in the pantropic species. Thus, the species that evolved on the Galapagos without benefit of pollinating bees would have lost their floral showiness by lack of selection pressure. The pantropic species, probably more recent immigrants, differ little from their conspecific representatives elsewhere. Many of the latter group are, in fact, known to have been introduced by man (Wiggins and Porter 1971).

Such drastic circumstances have wrought the expected impact on the composition of the flora: those families and genera that are largely entomophilous are poorly represented. A dramatic example is found in the Orchidaceae. According to Wiggins and Porter's flora (1971), only 11 species of orchids are known in the archipelago, and they tend to lack the flower size, color, fragrance, and other insect-attracting devices so typical of the group. In contrast, on adjacent continental Ecuador, many hundreds of orchid species are known; they display a bewildering array of mechanisms to promote insect pollination, often by bizarre mutualisms (van der Pijl and Dodson 1966); and in many instances reproduction depends upon the visits of a single bee species. This enormous difference exists despite the fact that, since orchid seeds are minute enough to be windborne, conditions for transport to the islands would have been far more favorable than for other flowering plants. On the other hand, plant groups that are equally mobile, yet not dependent upon animal pollen vectors, are well represented; to wit, the relatively rich fern and lichen flora of the Galapagos.

In contrast to the evolution of entomophilous plants, the dearth of bees would not have obstructed the establishment of wind-pollinated plants. Thus, it is not surprising that such anemophilous groups as the Gramineae and Euphorbiaceae are well represented in the flora.

CONCLUSIONS

It is evident from this summary of research on *L. cheesmanii* that it is a useful species for analysis of population structure and interspecific relationships. This species is a good representative of the endemic flora in that its mode of pollination and consequent effects on population dynamics and evolution may be typical of many other endemic species.

L. cheesmanii is likewise not exceptional in its phytogeographical relationships: in its probable derivation from ancestral stocks on the nearby mainland of South America, it conforms to the pattern of the great majority of Galapagan flowering plant species (Porter 1975).

ACKNOWLEDGMENTS

Research support for this study was provided in part by grant DEB 80-05542 and in part by previous grants of the National Science Foundation. The author also gratefully acknowledges the editorial assistance of Dora G. Hunt and Dr. Jon F. Fobes, and the assistance of Moira Tanaka in the preparation of the figures.

RESUMEN

Se he investigado la naturaleza de la variabilidad genética de caracteres morfológicos crasos, así como de aloenzimas, en poblaciones naturales del tomate de las Islas Galápagos, *Lycopersicon cheesmanii* Riley. Todos los miembros de la progenie de plantas individuales silvestres mostraron invariablemente el mismo genotipo. Por lo tanto, aunque con raras excepciones, miembros de una misma población silvestre exhibieron el mismo genotipo. La gran mayoría de las poblaciones investigadas se comportaron esencialmente como lineas puras y los resultados procedentes de ambos grupos de caracteres indican un nivel muy alto de autofecundación. Esta conclusión es compatible con las observaciones procedentes de estudios realizados en ambientes naturales y controlados; en ambos casos se observó que la estructura floral está adaptada para la autopolinización y de hecho las flores se autopolinizan.

Ciertas poblaciones silvestres se caracterizan por la presencia, en todos sus individuos, de ciertas formas singulares, tanto de las aloenzimas como de los caracteres morfológicos crasos. Cada una de estas formas, algunas de las cuales son aparentemente defectuosas, está determinada por un solo gene mutante. La fijación de cada uno de estos genes en una población dada, una condición única entre las especies de *Lycopersicon*, se considera debida a la deriva genética y a una presión relativamente baja de la selección natural en las Islas Galápagos.

En contraste con la uniformidad genética encontrada dentro de cada población, se observó mucha variabilidad genética entre poblaciones. La forma abundante f. *minor* se distingue bien de las otras formas de *L. cheesmanii* en una o más de una serie de ocho caracteres morfológicos. No se ha podido identificar ninguna otra forma subespecifica abundante, aunque ciertas poblaciones muestran valores extremos opuestos para los mismos ocho caracteres morfológicos. F. *minor* no se distingue de las demás formas en lo que se refiere a sus aloenzimas.

Entre las otras especies de tomates, ciertos biotipos de *L. pimpinellifolium* del noroeste del Perú se muestran estrechamente relacionados con *L. cheesmanii* de acuerdo a comparaciones de sus genotipos y de sus preferencias ecológicas. Por lo tanto, se sugiere que las formas ancestrales de *L. cheesmanii* proceden de dicha región y que de allí migraron a las Islas Galápagos–rumbo que habría sido favorecido por la corriente de Humboldt. El hecho de que exista una sola especie de abeja en el archipiélago (quizás restringuida a tiempos recientes) limita severamente las posibilidades de polinazación cruzada. Por lo tanto, las poblaciones colonizadoras de plantas entomófilas se vieron probablemente sometidas entre muchas exigencias, hacia una selección extrema a la autogamía y hacia la habilidad de tolerar la consanguinidad resultante. La fijación consiguiente de genotipos y la acumulación de genes mutantes habría conducido a una diferenciación rápida. Ensayos realizados en el campo para estudiar los sistemas de apareamiento de otras especies endémicas de angiospermas, y un estudio de la abundancia relativa de grupos anemófilos y entomófilos obligados o facultivos, sugieren que el modelo de establecimiento y evolución de los sistemas de apareamiento en *L. cheesmanii* podría ser el típico de muchos otres componentes de la flora galapagueña.

LITERATURE CITED

Linsley, E. G., C. M. Rick, and S. G. Stephens. 1966. Observations on the floral relationships of the Galápagos carpenter bee. Pan-Pac. Entomol. 42:1-18.

MacKinney, G., C. M. Rick, and J. A. Jenkins. 1954. Carotenoid differences in *Lycopersicon:* hybrids of an unusual race of *L. pimpinellifolium*. Proc. Nat. Acad. Sci. 40:695-699.

Muller, C. H. 1940. A revision of the genus *Lycopersicon*. U. S. Dept. Agr. Misc. Publ. 382.

van der Pijl, J., and C. H. Dodson. 1966. Orchid flowers: Their pollination and evolution. University of Miami Press, Coral Gables, Fla.

Porter, D. M. 1975. Geography and dispersal of Galápagos Islands vascular plants. Nature (London) 264:745-746.

Rick, C. M. 1956. Genetic and systematic studies on accessions of *Lycopersicon* from the Galápagos Islands. Amer. J. Bot. 43:687-696.

Rick, C. M. 1963. Biosystematic studies on Galápagos tomatoes. Occas. Pap. Calif. Acad. Sci. 44: 59-77.

Rick, C. M. 1966. Some plant-animal relations on the Galápagos Islands. Pages 214-224 *in* R. I. Bowman, ed. The Galápagos. University of California Press, Berkeley and Los Angeles, Calif.

Rick, C. M. 1967. Fruit and pedicel characters derived from Galápagos tomatoes. Econ. Bot. 21: 171-184.

Rick, C. M. 1968. El mejoramiento del tomate mediante el empleo de formas silvestres. Agron. Trop. 18:143-150.

Rick, C. M. 1971. *Lycopersicon.* Pages 468-471 *in* I. L. Wiggins and D. M. Porter, eds. Flora of the Galápagos Islands. Stanford University Press, Stanford, Calif.

Rick, C. M. 1980. Petroselinum (*Pts*), a new marker for chromosome 6. Rep. Tomato Genet. Coop. 30:32.

Rick, C. M., and R. I. Bowman. 1961. Galápagos tomatoes and tortoises. Evolution 15:407-417.

Rick, C. M., and J. F. Fobes. 1975. Allozymes of Galápagos tomatoes: polymorphism, geographic distribution, and affinities. Evolution 29:443-457.

Rick, C. M., J. F. Fobes, and M. Holle. 1977. Genetic variation in *Lycopersicon pimpinellifolium*: evidence of evolutionary change in mating systems. Plant Syst. Evol. 127:139-170.

Wiggins, I. L., and D. M. Porter. 1971. Flora of the Galápagos Islands. Stanford University Press, Stanford, Calif.

MORPHOMETRICS OF GALAPAGOS TORTOISES: EVOLUTIONARY IMPLICATIONS

THOMAS H. FRITTS[1]

Department of Zoology, San Diego State University, San Diego, CA 92182

The giant tortoises that inhabit a diversity of insular environments throughout the Galapagos Archipelago are among the largest of living terrestrial reptiles. In order to investigate the evolutionary relationships of Galapagos tortoises, morphological variation within living populations in the Galapagos and in museum collections is examined. Factor analysis and discriminant function analysis of morphometric data indicate considerable divergence of populations. Two major trends describing size and carapace shape appear to be related to environmental characteristics of the individual islands inhabited. Comparison of young tortoises from different islands reared under identical conditions suggests that morphological divergence is not environmentally controlled.

Carapace size correlates with a combination of altitudinal relief and dryness throughout the archipelago. The shape of the anterior margin of the carapace correlates with the area of the volcanoes or islands inhabited. Concurrent variation in these trends results in extreme divergence within the Galapagos. It is hypothesized that the elevation of the anterior carapace and related changes in neck and limb length simultaneously function to increase the vertical feeding range and individual success in aggressive encounters in dry habitats where inter- and intraspecific competition would be maximized during xeric climatic periods. Tortoises are poorly known in relation to other elements of the Galapagos biota.

During the historic visit of Charles Darwin to the Galapagos in 1834-35, he was informed by the Vice Governor of the archipelago that it was possible to tell from which island a tortoise came on the basis of its appearance (Darwin 1889). This so impressed Darwin that he began recording from which islands specimens came instead of labeling them as being from "Galapagos," as had many of his predecessors and as others would continue to do for many years. Although giant tortoises may have played an important role in prompting Darwin to compare island faunas, for the most part he chose to ignore tortoises in his writings except for a few notes on their natural history and habits. The diversity and divergence of tortoises in the Galapagos suggested by the Vice Governor was confirmed when additional material was studied by Günther (1875, 1877), Rothschild (1915), and Van Denburgh (1914).

Rothschild and Van Denburgh provided the last thorough reviews of taxonomic relationships of Galapagos tortoises, recognizing 13 species, with two other populations left unnamed because of inadequate material. Subsequent authors, such as Hendrickson (1966), Thornton (1971), MacFarland et al. (1974), and others have, without benefit of morphological or taxonomic review, tended to group all nominal taxa of tortoises from the Galapagos under *Geochelone elephantopus* (Harlan).

Van Denburgh (1914) diagnosed the taxa that he recognized on the basis of characteristics of the carapace and plastron, as well as a complex formulation of morphometric variables. Such characteristics are amenable to analysis using presently available statistical methods and current evolutionary theory. Thus it is now appropriate to ask if significant differences do occur within tortoises from the archipelago and what this variation can tell us about the evolutionary history of

[1] Present address: U.S. Fish and Wildlife Service, Denver Wildlife Research Center, Belle Chasse, LA 70037

tortoises in insular ecosystems. The extent of speciation of tortoises in the Galapagos and the systematic relationships of the group are parts of a larger evolutionary study still in progress and will not be treated in this report. Instead, I shall review current morphological studies and examine the possible evolutionary implications of morphological and ecological variation.

To determine if significant interpopulational variation existed in samples available to Van Denburgh (1914), an oblique factor analysis was computed on the basis of 26 morphometric characteristics recorded from 139 tortoises collected by the 1905-06 expedition of the California Academy of Sciences. By using factor analysis to obtain an overview of morphometric variation, it is possible to view major trends and compare inter- and intra-populational similarities without *a priori* assumptions as to affinities or subjective selection of primary characteristics. Thus not until factor scores were computed for each specimen and the order of specimens determined on the major trends of variation (i.e. the vectors) was geographic origin of the samples taken into account. Oblique factor rotation was used in lieu of orthogonal rotation because the data set is entirely morphometric and even major trends are likely to show intercorrelations in such situations. A visual examination of the bivariate plot of factors 1 and 2 (Fig. 1) allows consideration of general

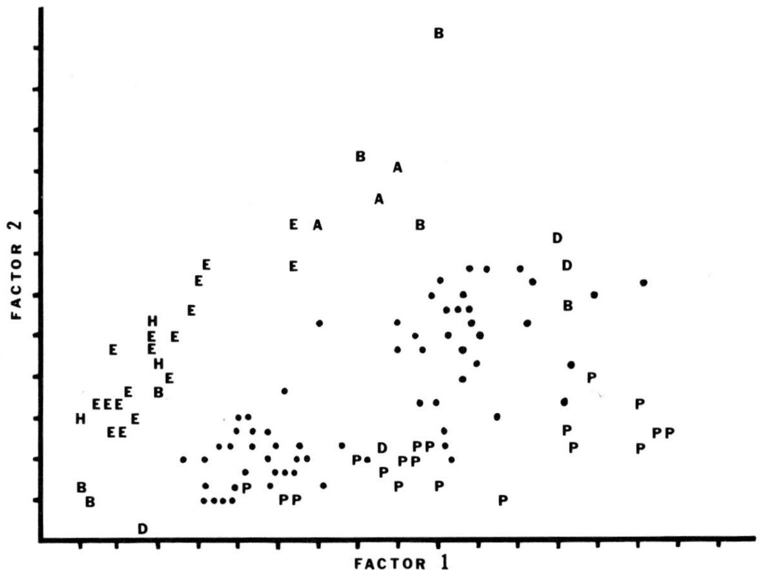

Fig. 1. Distribution of tortoises on the first and second principal components extracted from the data set described in the text. Symbols follow the taxonomic groupings of Van Denburgh (1914) except for the four southern volcanoes of Isabela. A=*Geochelone abingdoni*; B=*G. becki*; D=*G. darwini*; E=*G. epphipium*; and P=*G. porteri*. Dots represent tortoises of *G. vicina, guentheri,* and *microphyes.*

morphological relationships, and even from the conservative viewpoint of factor analysis, interpopulational variation can be noted, warranting further study.

Discriminant function analyses of the same data set result in increased separation of most populations and facilitate identification of the most divergent populations. Not all populations can be distinguished using these techniques, and some similarity can be noted between geographically distant populations. The question of how many species of tortoises occur in the Galapagos is an important one, but it must be dealt with in greater detail than possible at this time.

Van Denburgh recognized two major assemblages of tortoises, although there is no indication in his writings that he considered these as single evolutionary lines. "Saddle-backed" tortoises, heretofore referred to as saddles, named for their similarity in shape to ancient Spanish saddles, have carapaces highly elevated anteriorly, proportionately longer necks and limbs, and usually are smaller in size (Fig. 2). Van Denburgh recorded taxa of this body form from Pinzón, Española, Volcán Wolf of Isabela, Fernandina and Pinta. It can now be shown that the extinct tortoises from Floreana (=Santa María) and Santa Fé also exhibited this body form. "Non-saddle-backed tortoises," herein called domes, have highly rounded carapaces, attain large body sizes, and in general possess a carapace similar in shape to tortoises living in other parts of the world (Fig. 3). Van Denburgh considered only the tortoises from Santa Cruz and Volcán Alcedo of Isabela to be consistently dome shaped. He considered tortoises from Santiago (=San Salvador), San Cristóbal and the volcanoes of Sierra Negra, Cerro Azul, and Volcán Darwin on Isabela to be intermediate between the two extremes. The single specimen collected on Isla Rábida was also considered intermediate, but this specimen was probably introduced by man from southern Isabela. It is doubtful that tortoises ever successfully colonized Isla Rábida (MacFarland and Reeder 1975).

Any attempt to systematically compare morphological variation in giant tortoises must consider ontogenetic and sexual variation, as well as populational and environmentally determined variation. To allow concurrent consideration of these aspects, the emphasis in this report will be on local populations rather than hypothesized taxonomic or island groupings. In general, the five large volcanoes of Isabela are treated as discrete entities in the comparison of ecological conditions. For present purposes, all individuals encountered in the same general vicinity (usually a radius of 2-3 km) are considered to comprise a local population or deme. Although museum specimens have been studied, analyses of size and shape relationships presented here are based on data that I recorded from living specimens in the Galapagos during 1976 and 1977, except where noted. Because some populations are represented by small samples and poorly known, it was not possible to include all samples in each analysis.

As noted by Van Denburgh (1914), populations appear to differ in size and shape. In order to distinguish components of evolutionary divergence, it is desirable to consider separately aspects of size and shape that vary. Thus, I have attempted to identify one morphometric variable that measures size and that is minimally influenced by variation in carapace shape. Such a variable would be one that correlates highly with most morphometric variables in both inter- and intrapopulational correlation analyses. The rationale for selection of an independent estimator of size is presented by Kluge (1974).

Of 20 morphometric variables from the carapace and plastron of living tortoises, and 26 such variables from museum specimens, the curved width of the carapace (CW), a measurement also studied by Van Denburgh, was consistently highly correlated with most variables in both inter- and intra-populational correlation matrices. It is also significant that in principal component analyses CW is heavily emphasized on the first factor, which is hypothesized to measure size relationships.

Comparison of living populations of tortoises is facilitated by using CW as a measurement of size (Fig. 4). Because of the varying effects of man and introduced mammals on the natural population structure of individual tortoise populations (reproduction and survivorship), the range of size variation is more likely to depict previous populational differences than are populational means or variances. It can be noted that individuals from Española and Pinzón are relatively small in relation to most other populations, and that individuals from San Cristóbal and Pinta are intermediate in size, based on present samples. Size ranges evident in museum samples are similar, and it can be hypothesized that significant size differences do occur.

From the factor matrix of the principal component analyses, it can be determined that the second factor emphasizes three variables measuring vertical distortion of the anterior carapace: the height of the anterior carapace (FH), the height of the first marginal (H1M), and the height of the second marginal (H2M) were most strongly emphasized. Since this is an orthogonal vector, the trend it describes is independent of size considerations, and it can be considered to be a vector measuring the shape of the anterior carapace. By selecting the most heavily weighted of these variables (FH) as an indication of height, we can confine our preliminary comparisons

Fig. 2. Anterior view of an adult male from Pinta (CW = 931mm) showing a saddled shape of the carapace.

Fig. 3. Anterior view of a male from Volcán Alcedo, Isabela, showing a domed shape of the carapace.

to bivariate relationships of height (FH) and of size (CW) in investigating shape relationships.

It is apparent from Figs. 5-10, which depict shape relationships for individual populations, that adult males are consistently larger than females. With the possible exception of tortoises from Santiago, shape relationships are similar for both sexes within the population (i.e. populations can be represented as a continuous straight line). The shape relationships for the sexes from Santiago, in contrast, form two parallel lines, suggesting increased sexual dimorphism in this population. Comparison of the slopes (b) of the regression lines of Figs. 5-10 reflects populational differences in carapace shape. Specifically, populations from Pinzón, Española and San Cristóbal have larger slopes, indicating an increase in the height of the anterior carapace in relation to overall size. Of the populations considered here, the two judged to be of the saddle-backed type by Van Denburgh have the largest slopes (Española 0.479 and Pinzón 0.514). The population from San Cristóbal has a smaller slope (0.414), and other populations range from 0.209 to 0.313. This relationship provides a quantitative measure of carapace shape and allows comparison of populations. A high value for the slope indicates a high anterior carapace relative to size, whereas a low value reflects a low anterior carapace. Tortoises from Pinzón and Española have anterior carapaces nearly equal in height to those of much larger tortoises from other populations. Tortoises from San Cristóbal are intermediate in slope values as well as in overall size.

Gould (1971) pointed out that allometric changes in shape were the rule rather than the exception in groups with significant size variation. Such allometry presumably facilitates the maintenance of functional relationships (usually structural or physiological) of individual morphological components. Thus it might be expected that the size variates within a single population might reflect some of the same functional shifts seen in interpopulational comparisons. Frazzetta

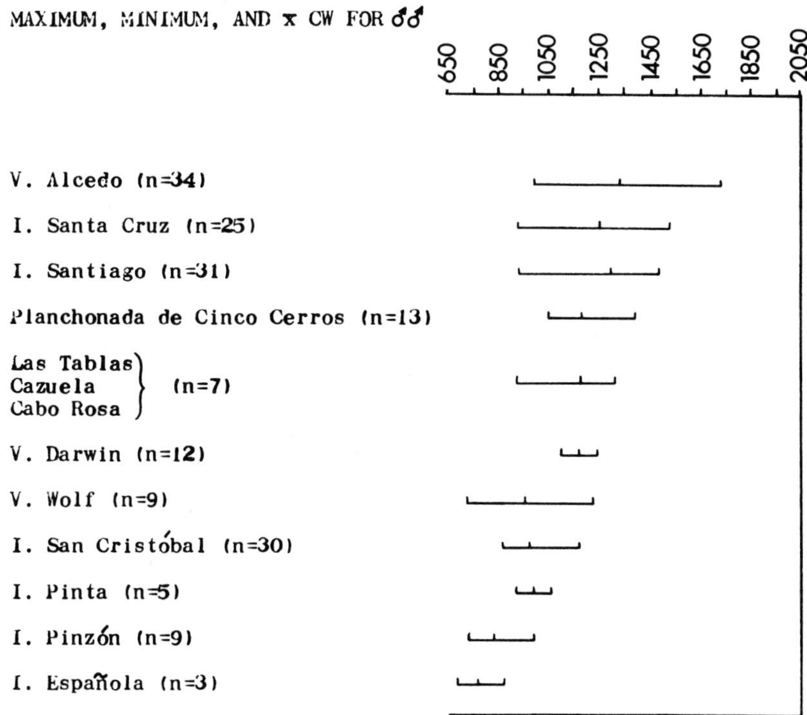

Fig. 4. Minimum, maximum, and mean curved widths of tortoises in living populations in Galapagos.

(1975:198) discussed a hypothetical example of size variation involving such relationships. This model predicts that individuals of two divergent taxa would be similar in shape at comparable sizes irrespective of age or life stage. On the basis of available data from Galapagos tortoises, such a model appears to be inappropriate. Shape differs between some populations throughout the entire range of adult sizes. In addition, individuals from populations with the largest body sizes differ less in shape from juveniles than do adults from populations with smaller body sizes. Instead of the giant differing from other life stages, extreme divergence in shell shape appears in populations not attaining large adult sizes. The possibility that the allometry of tortoises is adaptive in preserving an ecological function is considered later in this paper.

In the relationship between FH and CW, only two populations (Santiago and Planchonada de Cinco Cerros) appear to have curvilinear size relationships in adult samples. A logarithmic transformation ($\log^{10}$) of the frontal height was employed to investigate the possible curvilinearity of all populations. Table 1 compares correlation coefficients of transformed and untransformed values of FH with CW. Coefficients for populations hypothesized to be linear either decreased in value when transformed data were used or varied insignificantly, whereas those for Santiago and Planchonada de Cinco Cerros (PCC) appeared to increase. Using a *t*-test for comparison of correlation coefficients, it can be shown that the difference observed for SNT is insignificant whereas that for PCC is significant at $P<0.05$ level. Thus it appears that only the tortoises from PCC on the eastern slopes of Cerro Azul show curvilinear relationships between FH and CW. In this population, larger individuals tend to have a disproportionately high frontal height, but since this exaggeration of FH occurs at a much larger size than in the populations from Pinzón, Española and San Cristóbal, a distinct carapace shape results. It is possible that paedomorphism has played an important role in the evolution of carapace shapes in Galapagos tortoises.

As a means of investigating the possibility of environmental effect on carapace size and

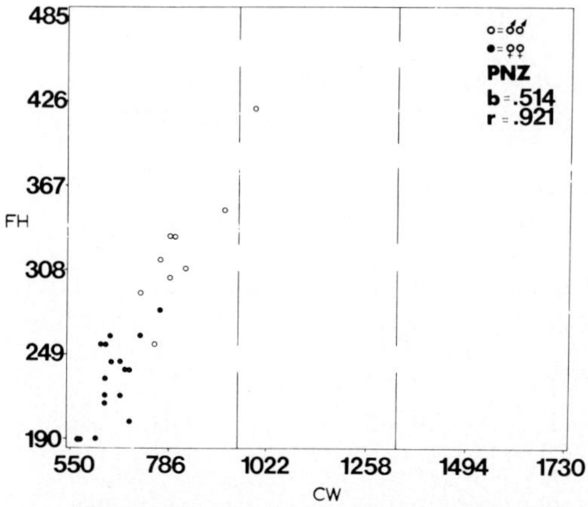

Fig. 5. Bivariate plot showing regression of FH on CW for tortoises from Isla Pinzón.

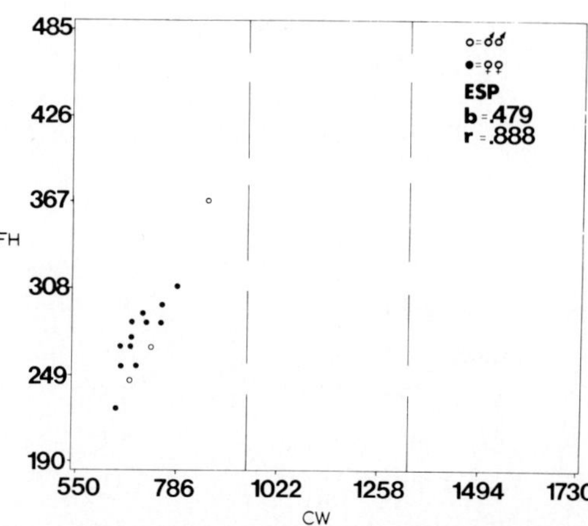

Fig. 6. Bivariate plot showing regression of FH on CW for tortoises from Isla Española.

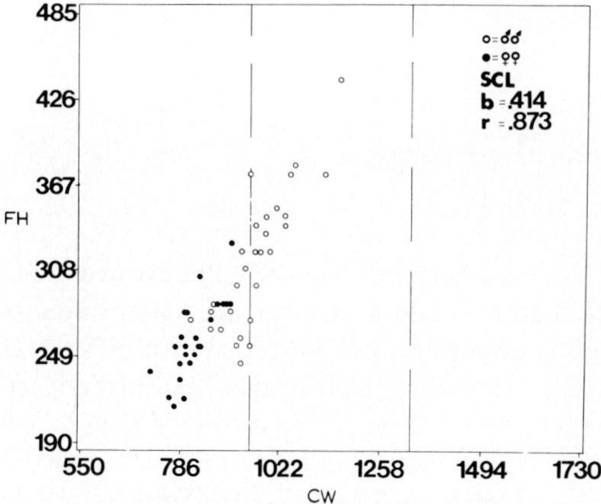

Fig. 7. Bivariate plot showing regression of FH on CW for tortoises from Isla San Cristóbal.

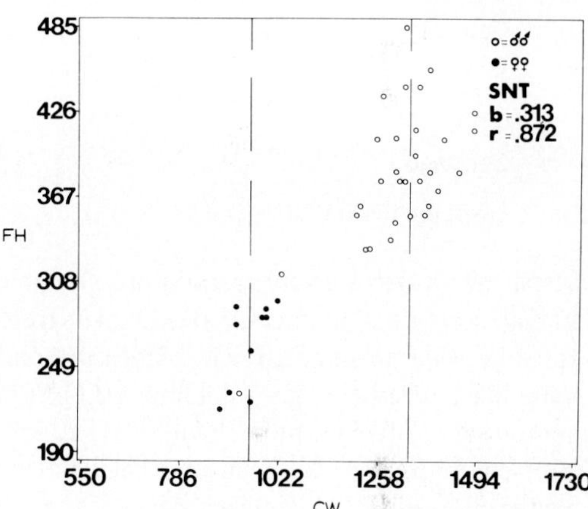

Fig. 8. Bivariate plot showing regression of FH on CW for tortoises from Isla Santiago.

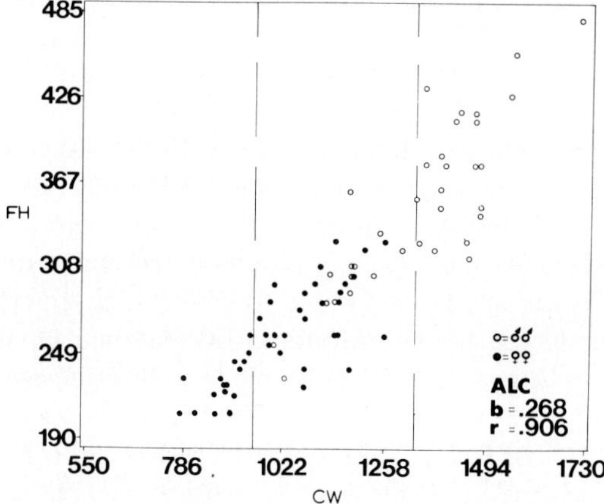

Fig. 9. Bivariate plot showing regression of FH on CW for tortoises from Volcán Alcedo, Isla Isabela.

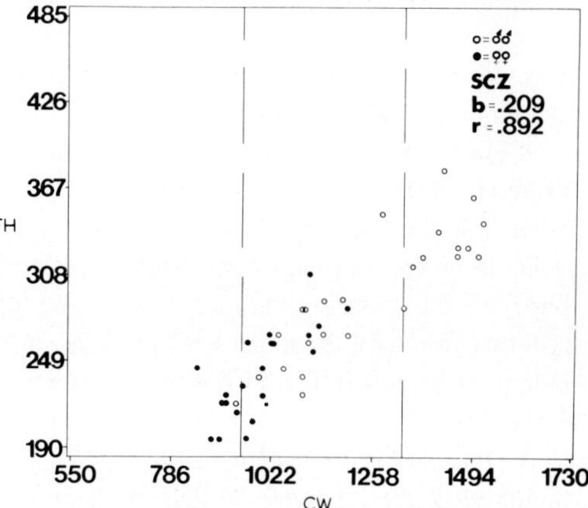

Fig. 10. Bivariate plot showing regression of FH on CW for tortoises from Isla Santa Cruz.

TABLE 1. CORRELATION COEFFICIENTS OF CURVED WIDTH (CW) WITH FRONTAL HEIGHT (FH) AND THE LOG OF FH, ILLUSTRATING VARIATION IN SEVERAL POPULATIONS AND THE CURVILINEARITY OF THE POPULATION FROM PLANCHONADA DE CINCO CERROS, CERRO AZUL

	N	*r*FH/CW	*r*logFH/CW	Significance of Difference
V. Alcedo	81	.9236	.9250	ns[1]
Cazuela	15	.9829	.9675	ns
V. Darwin	16	.9808	.9694	ns
Española	14	.8881	.8745	ns
Las Tablas	31	.9821	.9779	ns
Planchonada de Cinco Cerros	31	.9460	.9690	$P<0.05$
Pinzón	30	.9499	.9519	ns
Cabo Rosa	10	.9736	.9825	ns
San Cristóbal	55	.8732	.8663	ns
Santa Cruz	54	.9384	.9213	ns
Santiago	43	.8725	.8878	ns

[1] Not significant.

shape, two sources of comparison are available. The young tortoises hatched and/or reared under similar conditions at the Charles Darwin Research Station (CDRS), as a part of conservation efforts, provide an opportunity to measure phenotypic divergence with environmental differences minimized. Even though hatchling tortoises from all populations are similar in external appearance, four- to five-year-old young from Española show an elevation of the anterior carapace and light coloration on the head and neck not present in young of the same age from Santiago or southern areas of Isabela. This suggests that there is an underlying genetic control of these phenotypic differences, which will be examined in detail in a later paper. I have not included juveniles in the present analyses for three reasons: (1) except for a few populations, few data are available from young; (2) the present comparison of variation in adult populations is not intended to describe ontogenetic variation although patterns may be similar; (3) young tortoises from all populations are quite similar at hatching and apparently only show interpopulational differences after varying periods of development. A precise method of aging young tortoises would facilitate comparative studies of young in the field.

Preliminary comparisons of museum specimens collected during the period 1890-1910 with specimens found living in Galapagos in 1976 and 1977 indicate that populational differences are stable and do not vary with short-term climatic or ecological fluctuations. Thus on the basis of available morphological data, we can note that: (1) individual populations differ in size and in the shape of the anterior carapace; (2) these differences are probably due to differential growth patterns; and (3) these growth patterns do not appear to be environmentally determined. It remains to be resolved whether these differences can be related to selective trends in the Galapagos environment.

Domed tortoises such as those from the islands of Santa Cruz, southern Isabela, and other populations, are relatively similar in shape to other tortoises of the genus *Geochelone* and related genera in South America, Africa, Asia and North America. Nearly all are capable of retracting the head and neck within the carapace and protecting the anterior opening of the carapace by pulling up the forelimbs, which are covered with thick scales. Nearly all such tortoises passively protect themselves from vertebrate predators in this manner. However, the elevation of the anterior carapace of saddles is found nowhere outside of the Galapagos and is unknown in the fossil record. Such a morphology presents a proportionately large opening of the anterior carapace which cannot be effectively covered by the forelimbs (Fig. 2). Since this deviation from a "typical" tortoise shape has evolved only in the Galapagos where there are no large native terrestrial predators, I suggest that predation pressure may have prevented such innovations in more complex ecosystems. This hypothesis is supported by the effect of predators introduced in the Galapagos by man. Dogs have been used to hunt tortoises since colonization of the islands by man and now, as feral populations, prey on tortoises on islands supporting both saddled and domed tortoises. The domed populations on Cerro Azul, Sierra Negra, and Santa Cruz have been reduced by a variety of factors, including predation by feral dogs and man, but they still persist in viable populations. In contrast, the saddled populations on the islands of Santa Fe and Floreana (=Santa María) became extinct soon after the arrival of man.

Darwin (1889) noted that in 1835, only four years after the island was colonized, the tortoises were sufficiently rare on Floreana to necessitate hunters traveling to other islands to secure tortoises for meat and oil. Tortoises were extinct on Santa Fe prior to 1905. It is probable that both populations were reduced by man, with feral dogs attacking and killing the remaining individuals. That at least adults of domed populations are more resistant to dog attacks is evidenced by their survival on Sierra Negra and Cerro Azul, both of which have large feral dog populations. Several specimens collected on Sierra Negra by the California Academy of Sciences' expedition in 1905-06 show severe scars from dog or pig attacks. Some individuals survived complete removal of scutes and underlying bone of all anterior marginals and had initiated regeneration of scales prior to being collected by the Academy expedition (pers. obs.).

Thus the saddle morphology appears to be unique to the Galapagos and to be an adaptation that is most likely to persist only in an environment devoid of large terrestrial predators. This, however, does not tell us why saddled tortoises evolved in the Galapagos, but rather suggests why they did not evolve or survive in continental faunas.

In order to consider the adaptive nature of the saddled morphotype, it is necessary to scrutinize the individual islands and habitats where these tortoises occur. No island with a maximum elevation below 800 m has a native domed population, even though domed tortoises do occur below 800 m on other islands. In contrast, six of eight saddled populations occur on islands with a maximum elevation of less than 800 m (Table 2). If islands and major volcanoes are ranked by surface area, six of eight with the largest areas are inhabited by domed tortoises. The exceptions are Fernandina and San Cristóbal, both of which had native saddled tortoises. All six of the smallest tortoise islands have or have had in historical times saddled tortoises. Only three of the Galapagos islands that exceed 15 km^2 in area lack native tortoises, and all of these fail to exceed 400 m in maximum elevation. Apparently both island area and elevation are related to environmental conditions of humidity, temperature, and plant diversity, which affect tortoise distributions. And since the large islands usually have higher volcanoes than do the small islands, they also have larger areas that tend to be cooler and more mesic than any habitats on the small, low islands. These climatic differences are due to cloud capture and "garua" (fog drip or drizzle) produced by inversion layers and predominant winds from southeastern coordinates (Bowman 1961; Thornton 1971). The moisture-bearing clouds tend to build up against southeastern facing slopes at elevations of 300 to 800 m, increasing available moisture and moderating temperatures; at the same time, terrain above 800 m and below 300 m and northern exposures may be sunny and dry. These local climatic extremes, as well as volcanic activity, are possibly the most important factors maintaining the diversity of the archipelago's fauna and flora.

Since carapace size differences have been recognized within both saddled and domed populations, the possibility of correlation between carapace size and maximal altitude of the volcano inhabited was investigated. A preliminary analysis, based on the mean length of museum specimens,

TABLE 2. COMPARISON OF ENVIRONMENTAL CHARACTERISTICS WITH THE CARAPACE MORPHOLOGY OF POPULATIONS OCCUPYING ISLANDS WITHIN THE GALAPAGOS

		Area km^2	Altitude (in m)	Carapace Shape	Slope FH/CW
Sierra Negra		1590	1486	dome	–
Santa Cruz	(SCZ)	985	864	”	.209
Fernandina		642	1494	saddle	–
Volcán Alcedo	(ALC)	615	1113	dome	.268
Santiago	(SNT)	584	907	dome	.313
San Cristóbal	(SCL)	558	730	saddle	.414
Volcán Darwin	(DAR)	530	1311	dome	–
Cerro Azul		530	1689	dome	.291
Volcán Wolf	(WOL)	380	1707	saddle/dome	.305
Floreana		172	640	saddle	–
Española	(ESP)	60	206	”	.479
Pinta		59	777	”	–
Santa Fe		24	259	”	–
Pinzón	(PNZ)	18	458	”	.514

indicated a significant correlation of size with terrain elevation (Fig. 11). Subsequent analyses using curved widths of the carapace determined from living populations resulted in a significant correlation between carapace size and maximum terrain elevation for females ($r = .66$, $P<0.05$) but not for males ($r = .47$, $P<0.1$). Since the elevational effect was hypothesized to result from cooler and more mesic climates of higher zones, and since such effects are also dependent upon exposure to winds from southeastern coordinates, the location of major tortoise populations was included in the analysis. Dry, warm zones extend much higher on northern slopes than they do on southern slopes (Thornton 1971). Accordingly an elevational divisor was devised based on a simplistic model of exposure to the southeast. Populations occupying slopes in the southeastern quarter of an island or major volcano were assigned divisors of one, those in northeastern, southwestern or central areas two and those in the northwestern quarter three. The analysis was repeated using maximal elevations divided by the appropriate divisor and correlations for female and male samples were $r = .76$, $P<0.01$ and $r = .68$, $P<0.05$ respectively (Fig. 12).

A parallel situation can be seen in size variation within the tortoises related to *Geochelone chilensis* in Argentina (Freiberg 1973) where tortoises in dry, warm northern regions of the range are significantly smaller than those from southern extremes of the range where moister and more temperate conditions prevail. On the basis of a variety of evidences, it can be shown that saddled tortoises in the Galapagos occupy drier habitats with more extreme temperatures than do domed forms. This is true even of the three exceptional saddled populations from San Cristóbal, Fernandina, and Volcán Wolf; all are volcanoes that are drier than other large land masses in the Galapagos. In the case of Volcán Wolf, tortoises are restricted to the drier northern and western slopes by volcanic formations. At present only saddled tortoises remain on San Cristóbal, and these are confined to a low dry area occupying the half of the island to the northeast. Whether the extinct tortoises that occupied the higher and wetter regions on the rest of San Cristóbal were domed or saddled is not known. Fernandina, despite its large size and extremely high altitude, is quite

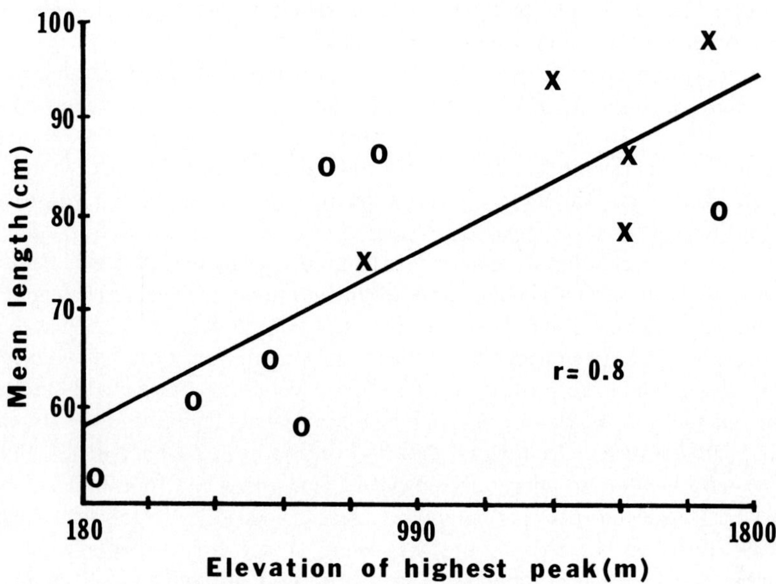

Fig. 11. Bivariate plot showing correlation of mean size (length of carapace) with the maximum elevation of volcanoes inhabited by 12 populations of tortoises represented in museum collections.

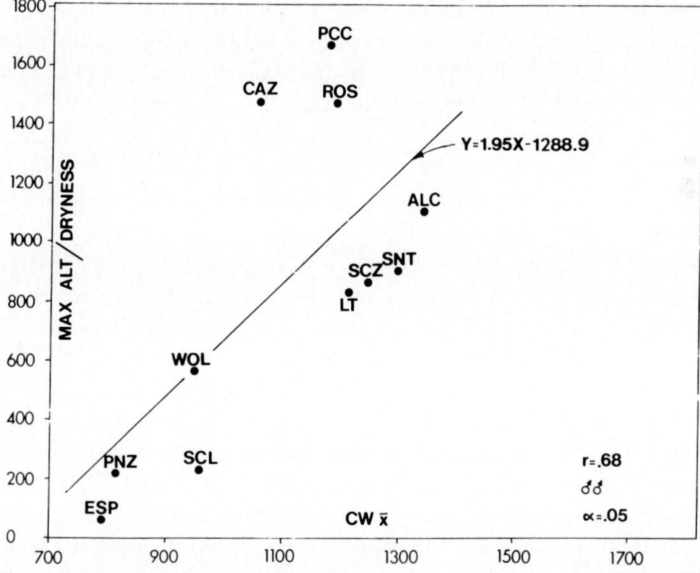

Fig. 12. The relationship of mean size of males with maximum altitude of volcanoes inhabited modified for exposure to moist southeastern winds. See text for explanation of altitude/dryness index (ordinate).

xeric, in part due to being in a partial rain shadow of Isabela, in part to the porosity of the recent volcanic ash and other materials that blanket the island.

It is, therefore, important to ask why smaller tortoises with an elevated anterior carapace should occupy xeric habitats on small islands and localized areas of large islands whereas larger domed forms predominate on larger islands with increased altitudinal relief and more mesic habitats. Clearly some of the hypotheses addressed to this question may be tested only after future investigations are completed. However, it may be instructive to examine the various alternatives upon which projected studies may be based.

In considering size in relation to temperature and moisture gradients, it may be hypothesized that smaller tortoises have several physiological advantages in warm, xeric environments. For instance: 1) A small- to medium-sized tortoise could use the limited shade of small shrubs and trees found in dry areas, as well as the irregular cavities found in volcanic rock, to avoid intense heat. The number of sites adequate to protect larger tortoises would be extremely limited in dry areas, and as pointed out by Ian Swingland (pers. comm.), the availability of shade is a significant limiting factor to giant tortoises *Geochelone gigantea* of the atoll Aldabra in the Indian Ocean. 2) Smaller body size would also allow survival on reduced water and food budgets in extremely xeric habitats where both resources are limited on a seasonal basis, if not for much longer periods. Conversely, large tortoises occupying more mesic and cooler environments would seldom be subject to limited food or water resources. This is true even in undisturbed populations in the Galapagos because the availability of nest sites is probably a major population-limiting factor, which normally maintains population levels below the carrying capacities of food or water supplies. At the same time, a large body size might function to prevent excessive heat loss during intermittent fogs and cool periods associated with higher elevations. The importance of these factors in the physiology of giant tortoises is amenable to further study.

The preceding hypotheses attempt to explain size differences in different island environments, but what is the significance of the saddle morphology in dry and hot areas? On the basis of observations of both captive tortoises at the San Diego Zoo and CDRS, and tortoises in the field, it has been noted that saddles are able to extend their heads higher than similarly sized or even larger domes. This is confirmed by Van Denburgh's measurements (1914), which indicate that saddles have proportionately longer limbs, a higher positioning of the neck on the anterior carapace opening and a longer neck (Fig. 13).

Two hypotheses can be offered to explain the adaptive significance of increased reach of the head in saddled populations in the Galapagos: 1) Increased head reach in relation to size could function to increase the vertical feeding strata available to a tortoise. Since plant density and palatability are reduced in xeric environments where saddled tortoises occur, such an increase could enable animals to reach the upper stems of *Opuntia* and other plants in areas where food and water resources are limited. Tortoises are known to depend on *Opuntia* for sources of water during prolonged dry periods (Craig MacFarland pers. comm.). 2) Increasing head reach may also confer an advantage in aggressive encounters related to intraspecific, and potentially interspecific, competition. Although aggressive interactions are infrequently observed in the reduced population densities in the Galapagos today, they are frequently observed under captive or crowded conditions. During these encounters, the tortoises extend their heads and necks as high as possible, and with limbs fully extended, they ultimately resort to lifting one forelimb, thereby gaining added height (Fig. 13). Extended to their maximum height, the tortoises may threaten each other with a "gaping" display of the mouth. Occasionally the highest tortoise will strike or bite the head of the other tortoise. The victor, or dominant individual, is nearly always the one that extends its head the highest. The loser, or subordinate, will acknowledge defeat by retracting its head into the carapace, simultaneously emitting a loud hiss, and turn or crawl away. Such encounters have been observed during feeding, drinking, and mating activities and occasionally when two tortoises move toward the same area for undetermined motives. These behaviors resemble ritualistic dominance

Fig. 13. Aggressive interaction of tortoises of divergent carapace shapes at the Charles Darwin Research Station. Male domed tortoise of unknown origin (CW=1198 mm) on right and male saddle-backed tortoise from Española (CW=860 mm) on left. Note height of head in relation to size.

interactions, well known in other animals, which function during intraspecific competition. The degree of intraspecific competition in undisturbed populations of tortoises in the Galapagos is unknown, but it is expected to be greater in xeric areas where food, water, and shade may be limited.

Both hypotheses attempt to relate the saddle morphology to increased fitness in intraspecific competition and subsistence in extreme xeric environments. No quantitative measurements of food abundance in the Galapagos are available; however, tortoises in xeric habitats on Pinzón, San Cristóbal and Volcán Wolf were rarely observed feeding during the dry periods of 1976, and the areas inhabited were largely devoid of living forbs and preferred food plants. In contrast, during the same period, tortoises in mesic habitats on other islands were often observed feeding, and the plants available as food plants did not appear reduced in relation to tortoise browsing.

The advantage of an increased feeding range and the ability to protect resources during intraspecific competition would be accentuated even more during extreme dry periods that span more than one year. Colinvaux (1972) and Colinvaux and Schofield (1976) have provided evidence that the Galapagos region was much drier during the late Pleistocene than during the Holocene. On the basis of Colinvaux's interpretation of sediments, the 15,000-year dry period was due to reduced rainfall in the wet season, with little change in present garua patterns. Since seasonal rains provide nearly all of the available moisture to lowland areas, small islands with minimal altitudinal relief would have been much more severely affected by this dry period than higher areas on large islands with the potential for cooler temperatures and significant moisture derived from garua and fog. While the exact mechanism accounting for the drying during Pleistocene times is open to dispute, the effect on some tortoise populations is more certain.

If tortoises inhabited lowland areas during drier periods when food and water resources were limited, two results could be expected: 1) animals might migrate to higher elevations where more mesic conditions persisted; or 2) on islands without sufficient altitudinal relief, there should have been a marked increase in intraspecific competition among the inhabitants for food, water and resting places.

An important factor influencing the survival of tortoises and any resultant evolutionary response during dry climatic periods would be the degree of ecological amplitude on the volcanoes inhabited by tortoises. Although the degree of evolutionary change would be related to both the amount of genetic variation in the original population and the intensity of selective pressures, we can estimate only the latter, using physical parameters of the volcanoes inhabited. Using the slopes (b), listed in Table 2, as a measure of the extent of morphological change and the areas (in km^2) of the individual volcanoes as measures of ecological amplitude, a negative correlation ($r = -.73$, $P<0.05$) is evident. Islands and volcanoes with small areas show an increased tendency toward a saddle morphology and vice versa.

Upon examining all populations of tortoises for tendencies toward increasing the vertical reach of the head, several differences in carapace morphology were noted that may represent independent adaptations to similar selective pressures. (For examples of various populations, see the photos published by Van Denburgh [1914]). Inasmuch as the ability to extend the head vertically is governed by several aspects of carapace morphology, simple measurements of the height of the anterior carapace (FH) do not provide adequate insight into factors limiting head movement. For instance, tortoises from Santa Cruz tend to have the lowest anterior carapace. This is in part due to the extremely large convex anterior marginals, which slope ventrally toward their anterior margins. This results in a horizontal shelf that limits the elevation of the basal portion of the neck. Alternatively, tortoises from various populations on Volcán Alcedo, Cerro Azul, and Sierra Negra, Isabela have anterior marginals that are horizontal, or slope only slightly, which effectively raises the anterior margin of the carapace.

Individuals from Planchonada de Cinco Cerros, Isabela and Pinzón are quite distinct in appearance, but both tend to have anterior marginals that are reduced in size and less convex on their anterior edges. This results in a shorter shelf above the basal neck, which possibly affects the angle at which the basal neck can be elevated. Tortoises from Española and Santiago have respectively large, recurved or dorsally flared anterior marginals. Both marginal types appear to reduce restriction of neck elevation. Such a diversity of anterior marginal types may provide evidence of similar selective trends during dry periods within a variety of insular populations.

An evaluation of evolutionary relationships of living and extinct populations of giant tortoises in the Galapagos is underway. Following analyses of morphological, ecological, and reproductive data, an estimate of the number of species within the archipelago will be possible. However, evidence is accumulating to suggest that tortoises, within the Galapagos Archipelago, have evolved in several directions. Clearly, our knowledge of giant tortoises presently lags far behind that of other elements of the Galapagos biota, but future studies promise to contribute significantly to an understanding of the evolutionary history of the Galapagos.

ACKNOWLEDGMENTS

Funds for the study of giant tortoises have been provided by the National Science Foundation (DEB 76-10003) and the San Diego Zoological Society. The personnel of the Charles Darwin Research Station and Servicio Parque Nacional Galápagos assisted field work in innumerable ways. Michael J. McCoid, Susan F. Palko, Howard L. Snell, and Patricia R. Fritts assisted in the collection and compilation of data. I am grateful to the curators of the following museums for permitting study of material in their collections: American Museum of Natural History, British Museum (Natural History), California Academy of Sciences, Museum of Comparative Zoology—Harvard University, Oxford University Museum, and the National Museum of Natural History. Access to computer facilities was provided by San Diego State University.

I am grateful to Craig G. MacFarland, Director of the Charles Darwin Research Station, for providing logistic support, encouragement, and country music during my field work in the Galapagos.

RESUMEN

Las tortugas gigantas del Archipielago del Colón son unas de las más grandes de los reptiles terrestres. Estos animales tienen varias formas morfológicas y ocurren en una variedad de ambientes en Galápagos. Análices estadísticas como *factor analysis* y *discriminant function* indican que unas poblaciones insulares parecen distintas especies por su morfología. Hay dos fuentes mayores de variacíon: el tamaño y la forma del carapacho anterior. Las dos tendencias tienen relaciones con la ecología de las poblaciones y características ambientales. Estudios comparativos de tortugas criadas en condiciones iguales en la Estacion Darwin indican que las diferencias morfológicas tienen bases geneticas y que probablemente no sean efectos ambientales.

El tamaño del carapacho de una poblacíon tiene relaciones adaptivas con la altura maxima del volcán en que viven y características de la humedad (lluvia y garúa). La forma del carapacho varía con la área del volcán o isla habitada y la humedad del ambiente. La variación de las dos tendencias resulta en la divergencia conocida en las tortugas de Galápagos.

Asumo una hipótesis que en zonas secas las características de un cuello largo, piernas largas y un carapacho alto anteriormente permitan a las tortugas alcanzar más alto con la cabeza. Con esta altura comen sobre una zona vertical más amplia y defienden recursos limitados (agua, comida y sombra) de otras individuales. La conducta de tortugas de Galapagos incluye una pelea con cabezas verticales; él que alcanza más alto domina al otro. Se encuentran estas adaptaciones extremas en las ambientes más secas del archipielago donde la competición entre individuales es lo más grande.

LITERATURE CITED

Bowman, R. I. 1961. Morphological differentiation and adaptation in the Galápagos finches. Univ. Calif. Publ. Zool. 58:1-302.

Colinvaux, P. A. 1972. Climate and the Galápagos Islands. Nature (London) 240:17-20.

Colinvaux, P. A., and E. K. Schofield. 1976. Historical ecology in the Galápagos Islands. 1. A Holocene pollen record from El Junco Lake, Isla San Cristóbal. J. Ecol. 64:989-1012.

Darwin, C. 1889. A naturalist's voyage. Journal of researches into the natural history and geology of the countries visited during the voyage of H.M.S. Beagle round the world, under the Command of Capt. Fitz Roy, R. N. 2nd ed. rev. John Murray, London. 520 pp. (reprint of 1845 ed.)

Frazzetta, T. H. 1975. Complex adaptations in evolving populations. Sinauer Associates Inc. Sunderland, Mass. 267 pp.

Freiberg, M. A. 1973. Dos nueva tortugas terrestres de Argentina. Bol. Soc. Biol. Concepción. 46:81-93.

Gould, S. J. 1971. Geometric similarity in allometric growth: A contribution to the problem of scaling in the evolution of size. Amer. Natur. 105:113-136.

Günther, A. 1875. Description of the living and extinct races of gigantic land tortoises. Parts I-II. Phil. Trans. Roy. Soc. London 165:251-284, pls. 33-45.

Günther, A. 1877. The gigantic land tortoises in the collection of the British Museum. British Museum (Natural History), London. 96 pp.

Hendrickson, J. D. 1966. The Galápagos tortoises, *Geochelone* Fitzinger 1835 (Testudo Linnaeus 1758 in part). Pages 252-257 *in* R. I. Bowman, ed. The Galápagos. University of California Press, Berkeley and Los Angeles, Calif.

Kluge, A. 1974. A taxonomic revision of the lizard family Pygopodidae. Misc. Publ. Mus. Zool. Univ. Michigan (147):1-221.

MacFarland, C. G., and W. G. Reeder. 1975. Breeding, raising and restocking of giant tortoises (*Geochelone elephantopus*) in the Galápagos Islands. Pages 13-37 *in* R. D. Martin, ed. Breeding Endangered Species in Captivity. Academic Press, New York, N. Y.

MacFarland, C. G., J. Villa, and B. Toro. 1974. The Galápagos giant tortoises (*Geochelone elephantopus*). Part I: Status of the surviving populations. Biol. Conserv. 6:118-133.

Rothschild, Lord. 1915. The giant land tortoises of the Galápagos Islands in the Tring Museum. Nov. Zool. 22:403-417.

Thornton, I. 1971. Darwin's islands. A natural history of the Galápagos. Natural History Press, New York, N. Y. 322 pp.

Van Denburgh, J. 1914. Expedition of the California Academy of Sciences to the Galápagos Islands 1905-1906. X. The gigantic land tortoises of the Galápagos Archipelago. Proc. Calif. Acad. Sci., Ser. 4, 2(1):203-374, pls. 12-124.

THE EVOLUTION AND BIOGEOGRAPHY OF THE LIZARDS OF THE GALAPAGOS ARCHIPELAGO: EVOLUTIONARY GENETICS OF *PHYLLODACTYLUS* AND *TROPIDURUS* POPULATIONS

JOHN W. WRIGHT

Section of Herpetology, Natural History Museum of Los Angeles County, Los Angeles, CA 90007

Population samples representing the geographical and taxonomic diversity of lizards of the genera *Phyllodactylus* and *Tropidurus* in the Galapagos were subjected to allozyme electrophoresis. Rogers' genetic similarity values ranged to a low of 0.38 in *Phyllodactylus* and 0.29 in *Tropidurus*. UPGMA clustering identified two divergent phenads in *Tropidurus*, one containing only the San Cristóbal and Marchena samples. Within the larger phenad, the Española sample is the most distinct. The samples from the central group of islands are united at values averaging higher than 0.84. Clustering of the *Phyllodactylus* data revealed four strongly divergent populations: San Cristóbal (D), Wolf, San Cristóbal (L), and Española. Most samples from the central group of islands clustered at levels averaging higher than 0.81.

The allozyme data were used to test Van Denburgh's Galapagos Land hypothesis. For the purpose of comparison, simulated Rogers' S values were generated and assigned to Van Denburgh's estimates of relationships based on his morphological analyses. There is general concordance between the levels of morphological and allozyme divergence in the *Phyllodactylus* populations but little between those in *Tropidurus*. Van Denburgh's hypothesis is not sufficient to explain the patterns of genetic divergence found in the lizard populations.

The allozyme data and the geological data are generally concordant. The older eastern islands have the genetically more divergent populations. The populations from the younger, more centrally located islands are genetically more similar.

The molecular clock calibrations of Nei and Sarich for electrophoretic data were applied to the allozyme data sets. Sarich's calibration yielded time estimates that exceed the time frame of both the archipelago and most of the individual islands, while Nei's calibration tended to provide underestimates. New calibrations of 8.9 million years for *Phyllodactylus* and 10.2 million years for *Tropidurus* for a Nei distance of 1.0 were calculated using the Galapagos allozyme and geological data. Using these calibrations, divergence times were calculated for the clustering nodes in the phenograms for Rogers' genetic similarity.

The ancestors of the Galapagos lizards probably came from the deserts of western South America by means of the Humboldt Current. Considering the allozyme and geological data, the island populations most likely stem from three separate foundings by mainland *Phyllodactylus* and two by *Tropidurus*.

Since the time of Charles Darwin, the biota of the Galapagos Archipelago has been accorded special consideration in the continuing development of evolutionary biology. For its geographic size, it is unrivaled by any other area in its impact on the foundations of evolutionary principles. Despite such a prominent role, there remain both many groups of organisms that are either unstudied or understudied and many unresolved, intriguing evolutionary and biogeographic questions. Some of the more fundamental unanswered questions relate to the origin and history of the islands and their biota. Modern geological studies have provided possible answers, but as usual, such studies serve to raise new biological questions that can be addressed only with additional biological data.

The reptiles of the archipelago are a good example of an understudied group of higher organisms. Since the pioneering work of Van Denburgh (1912, 1912b, 1914, and 1913 with Slevin), most of the study of the terrestrial reptilian fauna of the islands has been focused on the "unusual," "bizarre," or "spectacular" giant tortoises, land iguanas, and marine iguanas. Comparatively little attention has been accorded the snakes or the drab, but much more common and diverse, geckos (*Phyllodactylus*) and lava lizards (*Tropidurus*). Van Denburgh's studies remain not only as the sole comprehensive analyses of these genera, but as the data base for his hypotheses concerning the origin and evolution of the lizards and of the archipelago in general. His "Galapagos Land" hypothesis (a single island formerly connected to the mainland), though not widely accepted, has always received some attention from biologists. In more recent times it has been embraced, in large part, by the founder of the Vicariance Biogeography sect (Croizat 1958) and advocated, in a modified form, by some of his recent disciples (e.g. Rosen 1975). To date, however, Van Denburgh's evolutionary and biogeographic hypotheses have not been subjected to critical analyses. A primary goal of this paper is to provide such analyses by using allozyme data from population samples representing the range of diversity in the archipelago in both *Phyllodactylus* and *Tropidurus*, the pivotal groups for Van Denburgh's hypotheses. The allozyme data sets are also used to examine in a critical sense the goodness of fit of current geological hypotheses (Cox, this volume) for the development of the archipelago in terms of the sequence and timing of events. Furthermore, by coupling the allozyme data with the geological data, one of the more critical tests is provided for the two prominent calibrations of the "molecular clock" (Nei 1975; Sarich 1977).

METHODS AND MATERIALS

For allozyme analyses, a total of 222 geckos and 231 lava lizards representing, respectively, 17 and 18 locality samples from 14 and 15 islands were obtained (Fig. 1). At least one sample of each lizard group was collected from each of the major islands of known occurrence (see below for specimens examined). The lizards were secured alive and processed aboard the *R/V Beagle III.* Tissue samples consisting primarily of heart and liver were placed in "Nunc" vials and frozen and transported in liquid nitrogen. Mixed tissue homogenates were subjected to horizontal gel electrophoresis as described by Selander et al. (1971). Thirteen proteins coded by 20 presumptive loci were analyzed in the samples of *Phyllodactylus* (Table 1) and 16 coded by 23 in the samples of *Tropidurus* (Table 2). Only 3 of the total of 23 protein loci were not analysed in samples of both groups: albumin (Alb), protein 1 (Pt-1) and sorbital dehydrogenase (SDH). The following 20 were analyzed in all samples: esterase (Est-1 and 2), lactate dehydrogenase (LDH-1 and 2), peptidase (Pept-1 and 2), fumarase (Fum), glutamate oxalate dehydrogenase (GOT-1 and 2), glutamate dehydrogenase (GDH), 6-phosphogluconate dehydrogenase (6PGD), malate dehydrogenase (MDH-1 and 2), isocitrate dehydrogenase (IDH-1 and 2), malic enzyme (ME), mannose phosphate isomerase (MPI), phosphoglucose isomerase (PGI-), and phosphoglutamase (PGM 1+ and 2-).

Electromorphs (putative alleles) at each presumptive gene locus were scored relative to their mobilities (i.e. slow to fast). The most common allele was scored as medium (M). The levels of heterozygosity per locus, per individual, and per population were determined by direct counts from scored gels (see Soule and Yang 1976). To assess levels of interpopulational divergence, both Rogers' coefficient of genetic similarity (S; Rogers 1972) and Nei's coefficient of genetic distance (D; Nei 1972) were calculated from allele frequency data. The matrices of Rogers' S values were clustered by both the unweighted pair group method using arithmetic averages

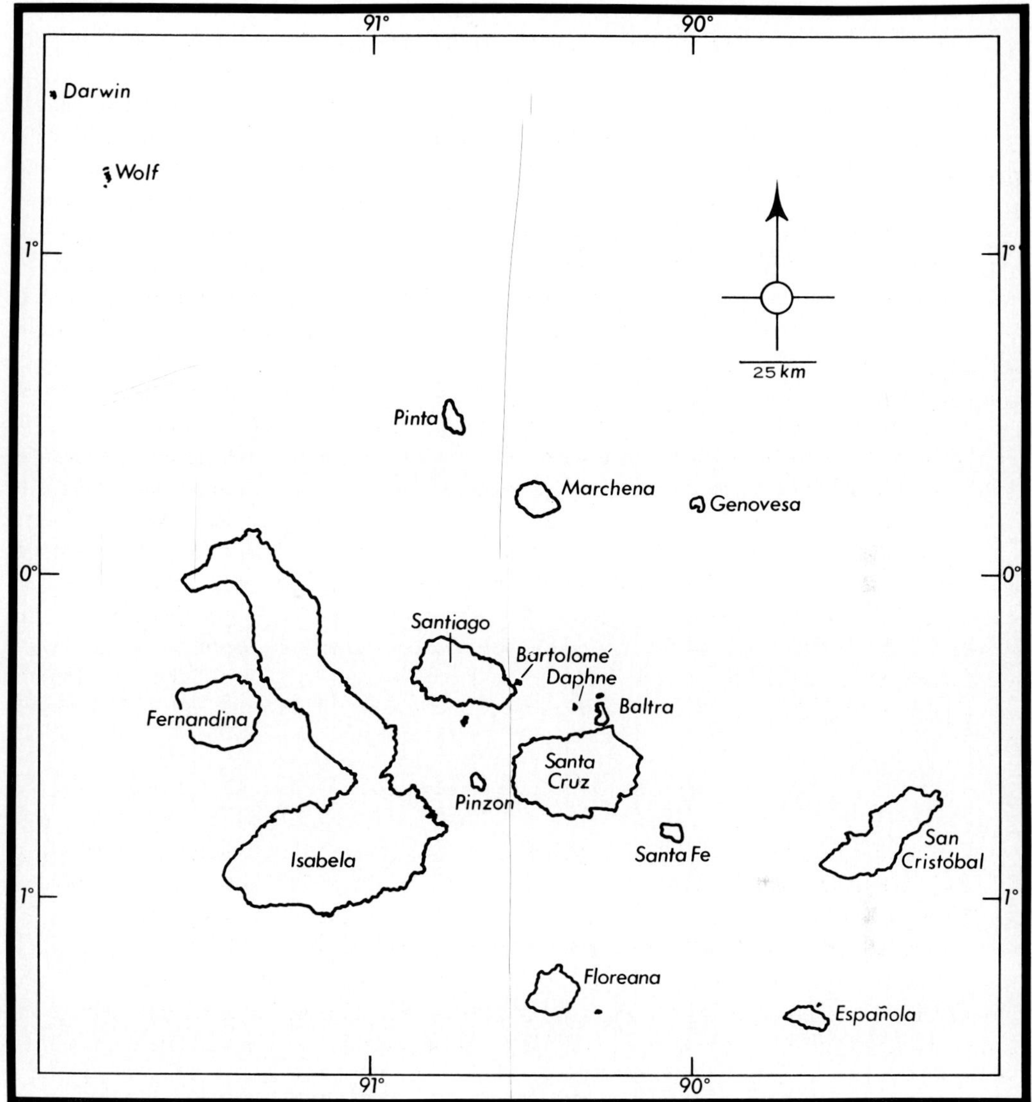

Fig. 1. Map of the Galapagos Archipelago with the names of the islands as used in the text.

(UPGMA) and the complete linkage method. No significant differences between the two methods were obtained; thus, only the results of the UPGMA method are presented. Nei's D values were used in the "clock setting" exercise.

Estimates of the numbers of species of *Phyllodactylus* and *Tropidurus* in the Galapagos range from a low of six in the former to as many as nine in the latter (Van Denburgh 1912b, 1913; Peters and Donoso-Barros 1970; Lanza 1973, 1974; Dixon and Wright 1975; Werner 1978), each with variable numbers of subspecies. Most workers, however, have followed Van Denburgh and have recognized six species of *Phyllodactylus*, one with three subspecies, and seven species of *Tropidurus*, one with two subspecies. Regardless, with the exception of two subspecies of *P. galapagoensis* described by Lanza (1973), allozyme data were obtained for all named populations of the two genera in the archipelago. For the purposes of this analysis, however, I have disregarded all estimates of the number of taxonomic units (species and subspecies) and have treated the data

TABLE 1. ALLELE FREQUENCIES AND GENETIC VARIABILITY IN SAMPLES OF *PHYLLODACTYLUS* FROM THE GALAPAGOS ISLANDS

Protein locus and allele		Sample locality and number of individuals																
		Academy Bay (10)	Conway Bay (14)	Baltra (15)	Daphne (16)	Sullivan Bay (6)	Bartolomé (12)	James Bay (15)	Tagus Cove (11)	Pinzón (11)	Fernandina (9)	Marchena (14)	Santa Fe (13)	S. Cristóbal L (14)	S. Cristóbal D (15)	Española (14)	Floreana (13)	Wolf (20)
Est-1	S														0.93			
	S+														0.07			
	M-			0.07									0.35					
	M	0.05	1.00	0.93	1.00	1.00	1.00	1.00	1.00	1.00	1.00	1.00	0.65			0.18	0.96	0.22
	F-	0.95												1.00		0.82	0.04	
	F																	0.78
Est-2	S														1.00			
	M-								1.00		1.00		0.15	1.00				
	M	1.00	1.00	1.00	1.00	1.00	1.00	1.00		1.00		1.00	0.85			1.00	1.00	1.00
LDH-1	S-																	0.98
	S					0.08									0.03			
	M	1.00	0.96	1.00	1.00	0.92	1.00	1.00	0.86	1.00	1.00	1.00	1.00	1.00	0.97	1.00	1.00	0.02
	F		0.04						0.14									
LDH-2	S																	
	M	0.95	1.00	1.00	1.00	1.00	1.00	1.00	1.00	1.00	0.72	1.00	1.00	1.00	1.00	1.00	1.00	1.00
	F	0.05									0.28							
Pept-1	S		0.89	0.04	0.25	1.00	1.00	1.00	1.00	0.86	1.00	1.00	1.00	0.93		1.00	1.00	1.00
	M	1.00	0.11	0.96	0.75					0.14				0.07				
	F														1.00			
Pept-2	S				0.12								0.69					
	M	1.00	0.93	1.00	0.88	0.42	0.12	0.33	1.00	1.00			0.31					
	F-															1.00		
	F		0.07			0.58	0.88	0.67			1.00	1.00		1.00	1.00		1.00	1.00
Fum	M	1.00	1.00	1.00	1.00	1.00	1.00	1.00	1.00	1.00	0.94	1.00	1.00		1.00	0.89	1.00	
	F										0.06			1.00		0.11		1.00
GOT-1	S														1.00			
	M-												1.00					
	M	1.00	1.00	1.00	1.00		0.08		1.00		1.00			0.86				1.00
	M+													0.14		0.03	0.08	
	F-															0.97	0.92	
	F					1.00	0.92	1.00		1.00		1.00						
GOT-2	S							0.07										
	M	1.00	1.00	1.00	1.00	1.00	1.00	0.93	1.00	1.00	1.00	1.00	1.00	1.00	1.00	1.00	1.00	

TABLE 1.
(Continued)

		Academy Bay (10)	Conway Bay (14)	Baltra (15)	Daphne (16)	Sullivan Bay (6)	Bartolomé (12)	James Bay (15)	Tagus Cove (11)	Pinzón (11)	Fernandina (9)	Marchena (14)	Santa Fe (13)	S. Cristóbal L (14)	S. Cristóbal D (15)	Española (14)	Floreana (13)	Wolf (20)
GDH	S																1.00	
	M	1.00	1.00	1.00	1.00	1.00	1.00	1.00	1.00	1.00	1.00	1.00	1.00	1.00	1.00	1.00		
	F																	
6 PGD	S							0.03	0.05					0.36	0.33			
	M	0.95	0.93	0.93	1.00	0.67	0.88	0.87	0.91	1.00	0.78	1.00	0.35	0.61	0.67	1.00	1.00	1.00
	F	0.05	0.07	0.07		0.33	0.12	0.10	0.05		0.22		0.65	0.03				
MDH-1	M	1.00	1.00	1.00	1.00	1.00	1.00	1.00	1.00	1.00	1.00	1.00	1.00		1.00	1.00	1.00	0.75
	F													1.00				0.25
MDH-2	M	1.00	1.00	1.00	1.00	1.00	1.00	1.00	1.00	1.00	1.00	1.00	0.95	1.00		1.00	1.00	1.00
	F												0.05		1.00			
IDH-1	S						0.08											
	M	1.00	1.00	1.00	1.00	1.00	0.92	0.97	1.00	1.00	1.00	1.00	0.21	1.00	0.90	0.96	1.00	1.00
	M+							0.03										
	F												0.79		0.10	0.04		
IDH-2	S										1.00				1.00			
	M	1.00	1.00	1.00	1.00	1.00	1.00	1.00	1.00	1.00		1.00	1.00	1.00		1.00	1.00	1.00
ME	S					0.92	1.00	1.00				1.00			0.23			
	M	1.00	1.00	1.00	1.00	0.08			1.00	1.00	1.00		1.00	1.00	0.77	1.00	1.00	
	F																	1.00
MPI	S-														0.03			
	S														0.97			
	S+		0.04															1.00
	M-																	
	M	1.00	0.96	1.00	1.00	1.00	1.00	1.00	1.00	1.00				1.00		1.00	1.00	
	F-										1.00							
	F											1.00						
PGI	M	1.00	1.00	1.00	1.00	1.00	1.00	1.00	1.00	1.00	1.00	1.00	1.00	1.00	1.00	1.00	1.00	1.00
PGM+	M	1.00	0.89	1.00	1.00	1.00	1.00	0.80	0.95	1.00	1.00	1.00	1.00				1.00	
	M+		0.11											1.00		1.00		0.72
	F							0.20										0.28
	F+								0.05						1.00			
PGM-	S							0.03			0.28							
	M	1.00	0.96	0.93	1.00	1.00	1.00	0.97	0.93	1.00	0.67	1.00	1.00	1.00			1.00	
	M+		0.04	0.07					0.07		0.05							
	F-														0.17	1.00		
	F														0.80			1.00
	F+														0.03			

as though they were derived from population samples of single, large gene pools of *Phyllodactylus* sp. and *Tropidurus* sp. Thus, the samples are referenced by locality (see below) and not taxon. Systematic analyses incorporating additional data sets are the subjects of future reports.

Voucher specimens were prepared from all individuals used in the analyses and are deposited in the Section of Herpetology, Natural History Museum of Los Angeles County (LACM). Abbreviated locality data are presented here for each sample; more complete data are available on request. Sample sizes are shown in Tables 1 and 2. The sample localities (Fig. 1) are as follows:

Phyllodactylus. Academy Bay (near Darwin Research Station, S side of Isla Santa Cruz); Conway Bay (NW side of Isla Santa Cruz); Baltra (near muelle, Isla Baltra); Daphne (main crater, Isla Daphne); Sullivan Bay (E end of Isla Santiago, opposite Isla Bartolomé); Bartolomé (Isla Bartolomé, see preceding); James Bay (NW end of Isla Santiago); Tagus Cove (W side of Isla Isabela); Pinzón (NW side Isla Pinzón); Fernandina (Punta Espinosa, E side of Isla Fernandina); Marchena (NE side of Isla Marchena); Santa Fe (vicinity of cove, N side of Isla Santa Fé); San Cristóbal L and D (sympatric populations, NE edge of Wreck Bay, W end of Isla San Cristóbal); Española (beach opposite Isla Gardner, NE side of Isla Española); Floreana (Black Beach, W end of Isla Floreana); and Wolf (N end of Isla Wolf).

Tropidurus. Sample localities the same except Cartago Bay (E side of Isla Isabela); Wreck Bay (Isla San Cristóbal); Marchena (S end of Isla Marchena); Gardner (Isla Gardner, satellite island NE of Isla Española); and Pinta (S side Isla Pinta).

RESULTS

Phyllodactylus

The number of putative alleles per locus at the 20 loci analysed (Table 1) ranged from one (PGI) to seven (MPI). The modal number of alleles per locus is four (at 6 loci), with three alleles at 5 loci, two at 4, six at 2, and none with 5. The maximum number of alleles per locus per population was three.

The levels of interpopulation similarity as indicated by the Rogers' S values (Table 2) ranged from a low of 0.38 (between San Cristóbal D and Wolf) to a high of 0.97 (between Daphne and Baltra and between Bartolomé and James Bay on Isla Santiago). The matrix of S values was subjected to the UPGMA clustering technique (Figs. 2 and 3). With the exception of the samples (L and D, sympatric) from San Cristóbal, all samples from the same island clustered with high average similarities (e.g. Academy Bay and Conway Bay on Santa Cruz, 0.92; James Bay and Sullivan Bay on Santiago, 0.96), as did samples from satellite or nearby islands (e.g. Baltra and Daphne 0.98, to Santa Cruz, 0.95; Bartolomé to the samples from Santiago, 0.96). The samples from the group of central and western islands tended to have high average similarities (S=0.80), with the notable exceptions of Fernandina and Santa Fe (Fig. 3), but all clustered at levels greater than 0.70. The more distant islands (San Cristóbal, Española, and Wolf) have the most divergent populations. This is true for both populations on San Cristóbal. The sample from Floreana is surprisingly more similar to those from the central islands than would be suggested by its relative geographic position; in contrast, the Fernandina sample is more dissimilar from the Tagus Cove sample from Isabela (S=0.80) relative to their proximity. The clustering analysis revealed only two multi-island groups with high levels of average similarity, Isabela to Pinzón to Santa Cruz, Daphne, and Baltra (S=0.88) and Marchena to Santiago and Bartolomé (S=0.92), with a more remote cluster including Floreana (S=0.86).

Tropidurus

The number of putative alleles per locus in the 23 loci analysed (Table 3) ranged from one (GOT-2 and MDH-1) to six (Est-2). The modal number of alleles per loci was three (at 10 loci),

TABLE 2. COEFFICIENTS OF GENETIC SIMILARITY (ROGERS' S) AMONG SAMPLES OF *PHYLLODACTYLUS* FROM THE GALAPAGOS ISLANDS

	Academy Bay	Conway Bay	Baltra	Daphne	Sullivan Bay	Bartolomé	James Bay	Tagus Cove	Pinzón	Fernandina	Marchena	Santa Fe	San Cristóbal (L)	San Cristóbal (D)	Española	Floreana	Wolf
Academy Bay	1.000	0.890	0.945	0.929	0.757	0.752	0.747	0.835	0.855	0.664	0.698	0.692	0.674	0.472	0.732	0.801	0.495
Conway Bay		1.000	0.939	0.948	0.847	0.840	0.842	0.926	0.930	0.753	0.786	0.757	0.677	0.484	0.747	0.883	0.559
Baltra			1.000	0.973	0.803	0.798	0.794	0.887	0.898	0.710	0.742	0.722	0.630	0.478	0.704	0.844	0.507
Daphne				1.000	0.819	0.815	0.809	0.889	0.913	0.722	0.765	0.735	0.643	0.480	0.717	0.865	0.520
Sullivan Bay					1.000	0.959	0.960	0.800	0.898	0.691	0.904	0.735	0.612	0.477	0.692	0.862	0.521
Bartolomé						1.000	0.966	0.790	0.885	0.707	0.930	0.720	0.627	0.494	0.699	0.886	0.543
James Bay							1.000	0.790	0.887	0.682	0.911	0.708	0.616	0.484	0.704	0.861	0.535
Tagus Cove								1.000	0.876	0.802	0.733	0.722	0.715	0.475	0.694	0.833	0.507
Pinzón									1.000	0.700	0.843	0.759	0.631	0.475	0.745	0.893	0.498
Fernandina										1.000	0.707	0.650	0.648	0.564	0.587	0.756	0.489
Marchena											1.000	0.706	0.581	0.495	0.652	0.850	0.555
Santa Fe												1.000	0.550	0.449	0.635	0.759	0.434
S. Cristóbal (L)													1.000	0.441	0.676	0.685	0.575
S. Cristóbal (D)														1.000	0.478	0.525	0.375
Española															1.000	0.801	0.539
Floreana																1.000	0.558
Wolf																	1.000

TABLE 3. ALLELE FREQUENCIES AND GENETIC VARIABILITY IN SAMPLES OF *TROPIDURUS* FROM THE GALAPAGOS ISLANDS

Enzyme		Sample locality and number of individuals																	
		Academy Bay (9)	Conway Bay (11)	Baltra (10)	Daphne (14)	James Bay (16)	Bartolomé (10)	Sullivan Bay (10)	Cartago Bay (11)	Black Cove (7)	Fernandina (19)	Santa Fe (7)	Pinzón (20)	Wreck Bay (16)	Marchena (16)	Gardner (10)	Española (14)	Floreana (17)	Pinta (14)
Est-1	S													1.00					
	M	1.00	1.00	0.90	0.89	0.78	0.90	0.80	1.00	1.00	1.00	1.00	1.00		1.00	1.00	1.00	1.00	1.00
	F			0.10	0.11	0.22	0.10	0.20											
Est-2	S	0.28				0.12		0.10											
	M-	0.67	1.00	1.00	1.00	0.88	1.00	0.90	0.82	0.86	1.00	1.00							
	M	0.06							0.18	0.14			0.92		0.03	1.00	1.00		0.97
	F													1.00	0.97				0.03
	F+												0.08						
	A																	1.00	
Alb	S												1.00	1.00	0.03				
	M					1.00	1.00	1.00	1.00	1.00	1.00	1.00			0.97	1.00	1.00	1.00	1.00
	F	1.00	1.00	1.00	1.00														
Pt-1	S													1.00					
	M	1.00	1.00	1.00	1.00	1.00	1.00	1.00	1.00	1.00	1.00	1.00	1.00		1.00			1.00	1.00
	F															1.00	1.00		
LDH-1	S	0.06												1.00	1.00				
	M	0.94	1.00	1.00	1.00	1.00	1.00	1.00	1.00	1.00	1.00	1.00	1.00			1.00	1.00	1.00	1.00
LDH-2	S								0.18	0.14	0.13			0.12					
	M	1.00	1.00	1.00	1.00	1.00	1.00	1.00	0.82	0.86	0.87			0.88	1.00	1.00	1.00	1.00	1.00
	F											1.00	1.00						
Pept-1	S																		
	M	1.00	1.00	1.00	1.00	1.00	1.00	1.00	1.00	1.00	1.00	1.00	1.00	1.00		1.00	1.00	1.00	1.00
	A														1.00				
Pept-2	S							0.05											
	M	1.00	1.00	1.00	1.00	1.00	1.00	0.95	1.00	1.00	1.00	1.00	1.00	1.00	1.00			1.00	1.00
	F															1.00	1.00		
Fum-1	S													1.00	1.00				
	M	1.00	1.00	1.00	1.00	1.00	1.00	1.00	1.00	1.00	1.00	1.00	1.00			1.00	1.00	1.00	1.00
GOT-1	S-			0.10															
	S		0.05			0.03													
	M	1.00	0.95	0.90	1.00	0.97	1.00	1.00	1.00	1.00	1.00	1.00	1.00	1.00	1.00	1.00	1.00	0.91	1.00
	F																	0.09	
GOT-2	M	1.00	1.00	1.00	1.00	1.00	1.00	1.00	1.00	1.00	1.00	1.00	1.00	1.00	1.00	1.00	1.00	1.00	1.00

TABLE 3. (Continued)		Academy Bay (9)	Conway Bay (11)	Baltra (10)	Daphne (14)	James Bay (16)	Bartolomé (10)	Sullivan Bay (10)	Cartago Bay (11)	Black Cove (7)	Fernandina (19)	Santa Fe (7)	Pinzón (20)	Wreck Bay (16)	Marchena (16)	Gardner (10)	Española (14)	Floreana (17)	Pinta (14)
GDH	S							0.06		0.07									
	M	1.00	0.90	1.00	1.00	0.97	1.00	0.94	1.00	0.93	1.00	1.00	1.00			1.00	1.00	1.00	1.00
	M+					0.03								1.00	1.00				
	F		0.10																
6 PGD	S-													1.00					
	S														1.00				
	M-	0.11	0.05			0.72	1.00	0.80	0.55	0.64	0.21					0.90	0.89	0.97	1.00
	M	0.78	0.95	0.85	1.00	0.28		0.20	0.45	0.36	0.79	1.00	1.00			0.10	0.11		
	F	0.11		0.15														0.03	
SDH	S	0.92	0.95	0.95	1.00				0.09										
	M	0.08	0.05	0.05		1.00	1.00	1.00	0.91	1.00	1.00	1.00	1.00			1.00	1.00	1.00	1.00
	M+													1.00	1.00				
MDH-1	M	1.00	1.00	1.00	1.00	1.00	1.00	1.00	1.00	1.00	1.00	1.00	1.00	1.00	1.00	1.00	1.00	1.00	1.00
MDH-2	S													1.00	1.00	0.15	0.04		
	M		0.05															1.00	1.00
	F	1.00	0.95	1.00	1.00	1.00	1.00	1.00	1.00	1.00	1.00	1.00				0.85	0.96		
IDH-1	M	1.00	0.77	1.00	1.00	1.00	1.00	1.00	1.00	1.00	1.00	1.00	1.00	1.00	1.00	1.00	1.00	1.00	1.00
	F		0.23																
IDH-2	S													1.00	1.00				
	M	0.17	1.00	0.95	0.71	0.69	1.00	0.80	0.55	0.67	1.00	1.00	1.00			1.00	1.00	1.00	1.00
	F	0.83		0.05	0.29	0.31		0.20	0.45	0.33									
ME	S													1.00	1.00				
	M	1.00	1.00	1.00	1.00	1.00	1.00	1.00	0.91	1.00	1.00	1.00	1.00			1.00	1.00	1.00	1.00
	F								0.09										
MPI-1	S															0.05			
	M	1.00	1.00	1.00	1.00	1.00	1.00	1.00	1.00	1.00	1.00	1.00	1.00	1.00	1.00	0.95	1.00	1.00	1.00
MPI-2	S													1.00	1.00				
	M	1.00	1.00	1.00	1.00	1.00	1.00	1.00	1.00	1.00	1.00	1.00	1.00			1.00	1.00	1.00	1.00
PGI-	S								0.05					0.03		0.85	0.93		
	M-															0.15	0.07		
	M	1.00	1.00	1.00	1.00	1.00	1.00	0.90	0.95	1.00	1.00	1.00	1.00	0.97	1.00			1.00	1.00
	F							0.10											
PGM(+)	S					0.03													
	M	1.00	1.00	1.00	1.00	0.97	1.00	0.95	1.00	0.86	1.00	1.00	1.00	1.00		1.00	1.00	0.97	1.00
	F							0.05		0.14					1.00	0.72		0.03	
	F+															0.28			
PGM(-)	S													0.03					
	M	0.11												0.97	1.00				
	F	0.89	1.00	1.00	1.00	1.00	1.00	1.00	1.00	1.00	1.00	1.00			1.00	1.00	1.00	1.00	

TABLE 4. COEFFICIENTS OF GENETIC SIMILARITY (ROGERS' S) AMONG SAMPLES OF *TROPIDURUS* FROM THE GALAPAGOS ISLANDS

	Academy Bay	Conway Bay	Baltra	Daphne	James Bay	Bartolomé	Sullivan Bay	Cartago Bay	Black Cove	Fernandina	Santa Fe	Pinzón	Wreck Bay	Marchena	Gardner	Española	Floreana	Pinta
Academy Bay	1.000	0.920	0.934	0.942	0.847	0.826	0.832	0.861	0.847	0.856	0.816	0.796	0.390	0.443	0.682	0.688	0.761	0.794
Conway Bay		1.000	0.969	0.961	0.846	0.857	0.841	0.844	0.845	0.889	0.857	0.817	0.362	0.416	0.696	0.701	0.780	0.820
Baltra			1.000	0.977	0.864	0.874	0.858	0.856	0.854	0.895	0.860	0.820	0.371	0.419	0.701	0.707	0.786	0.819
Daphne				1.000	0.872	0.863	0.861	0.865	0.863	0.886	0.858	0.818	0.376	0.422	0.690	0.696	0.771	0.817
James Bay					1.000	0.961	0.979	0.950	0.966	0.942	0.897	0.823	0.385	0.465	0.797	0.803	0.880	0.864
Bartolomé						1.000	0.964	0.934	0.947	0.957	0.912	0.831	0.371	0.458	0.819	0.824	0.906	0.871
Sullivan Bay							1.000	0.939	0.958	0.938	0.893	0.818	0.380	0.460	0.807	0.813	0.881	0.858
Cartago Bay								1. 000	0.970	0.948	0.903	0.836	0.390	0.470	0.789	0.795	0.861	0.866
Black Cove									1.000	0.953	0.906	0.836	0.394	0.476	0.794	0.800	0.874	0.868
Fernandina										1.000	0.952	0.870	0.378	0.460	0.794	0.799	0.874	0.903
Santa Fé											1.000	0.918	0.335	0.420	0.749	0.754	0.829	0.876
Pinzón												1.000	0.378	0.383	0.745	0.751	0.789	0.872
Wreck Bay													1.000	0.772	0.297	0.293	0.367	0.370
Marchena														1.000	0.347	0.343	0.460	0.464
Gardner															1.000	0.990	0.786	0.798
Española																1.000	0.785	0.797
Floreana																	1.000	0.913

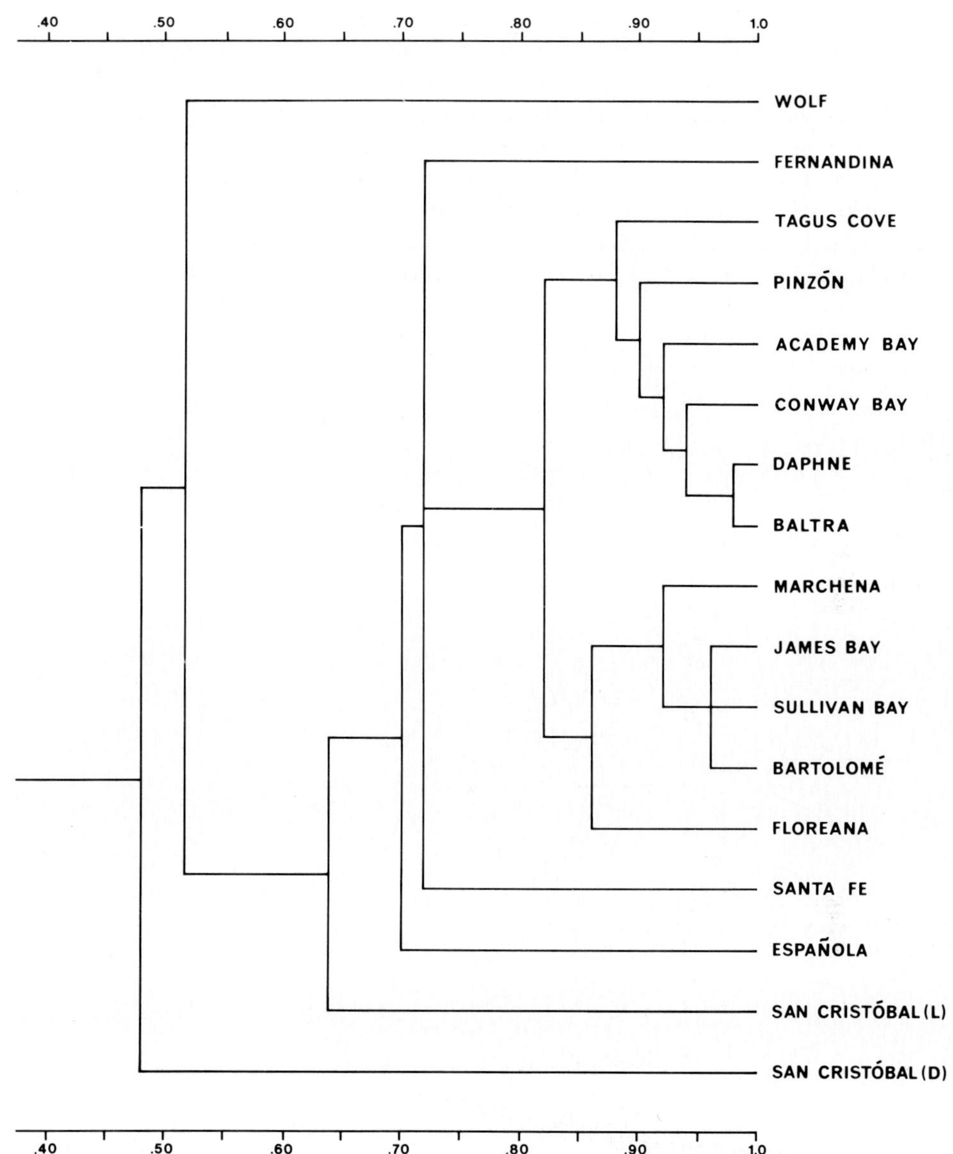

Fig. 2. Phenogram for Galapagos *Phyllodactylus* populations produced by UPGMA clustering of Rogers' genetic similarity coefficients for allozyme data (Tables 1 and 2).

with two alleles at 5 loci, four at 4, and five at 1 locus. Fixed null alleles were found at 2 loci (Est-2 and Pept-1), each in one sample (Pinta and Marchena, respectively). The maximum number of alleles per locus per population was three.

The levels of interpopulation similarity as estimated by S values (Table 4) ranged from a low of 0.29 (between the San Cristóbal and Española samples) to a high of 0.99 (between Española and its satellite, Gardner). The UPGMA clustering analysis and resultant phenogram (Figs. 4 and 5) revealed two groups of samples with low average between-group similarity (S=0.40), the San Cristóbal and Marchena samples in one group and all other samples in the other. The genetic similarity of the samples within these two phenads is relatively high, 0.78 in the former and 0.76 in the latter. Within the larger phenad, Española and its satellite together have the most divergent populations, while the remaining cluster contains all samples in the central group of islands as well as those of the more distant Pinta and Floreana. Within this cluster, there are four units each having within-cluster average similarities greater than 0.90. All samples from the same islands and from immediately adjacent satellites have high levels of similarity (S=0.94). The samples from Fernandina and Santa Fe have greater similarity to each other than would be expected from their geographic positions. The sample from Pinzón, on the other hand, is relatively more divergent than its geographic position would suggest. As in the case of the *Phyllodactylus*, the southeasternmost islands (San Cristóbal and Española) have the more divergent populations, while those of the western and central group (except for Marchena) have relatively high levels of similarity (>0.84).

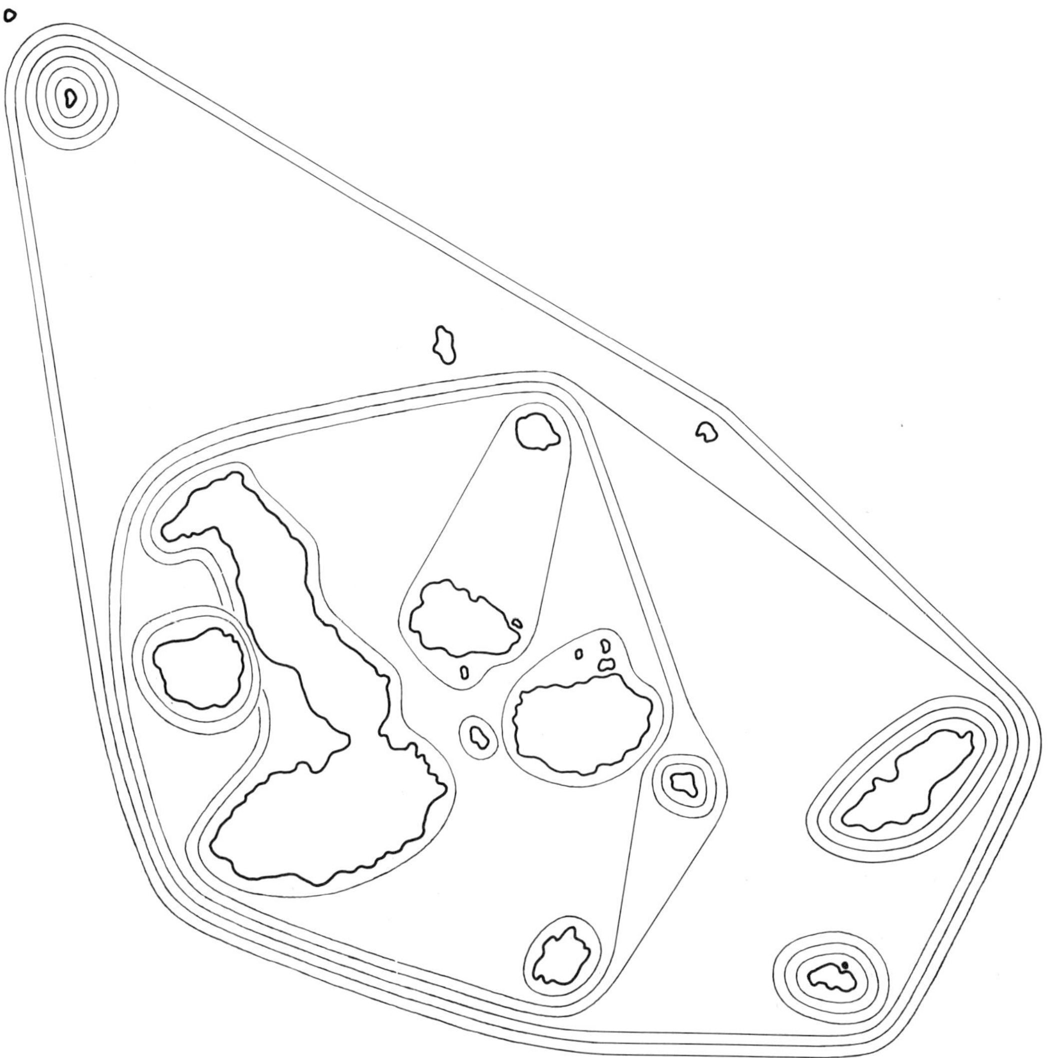

Fig. 3. Map of Galapagos Archipelago with isograms of similarity among *Phyllodactylus* populations. Isograms represent 0.10 intervals of Rogers' genetic similarity coefficients (S) as clustered by the UPGMA (Fig. 2). The innermost rings are S=0.90, the outermost S=0.40. All islands with *Phyllodactylus* populations are ringed at S=0.50, but an additional ring is required to enclose both populations on San Cristóbal.

DISCUSSION

Before proceeding into the following discussions of the allozyme analysis, I would like to emphasize that the results obtained are viewed in light of two biases or assumptions: 1) the primary factors contributing to allozymic variation are mutation rate, population size, and time, with little or no contribution from selection (see Sarich 1977 for a recent discussion of the neutral alleles hypothesis); and 2) the genetic similiarity values are indicative of the degree or level of overall genetic relatedness among the populations of each of the two genera.

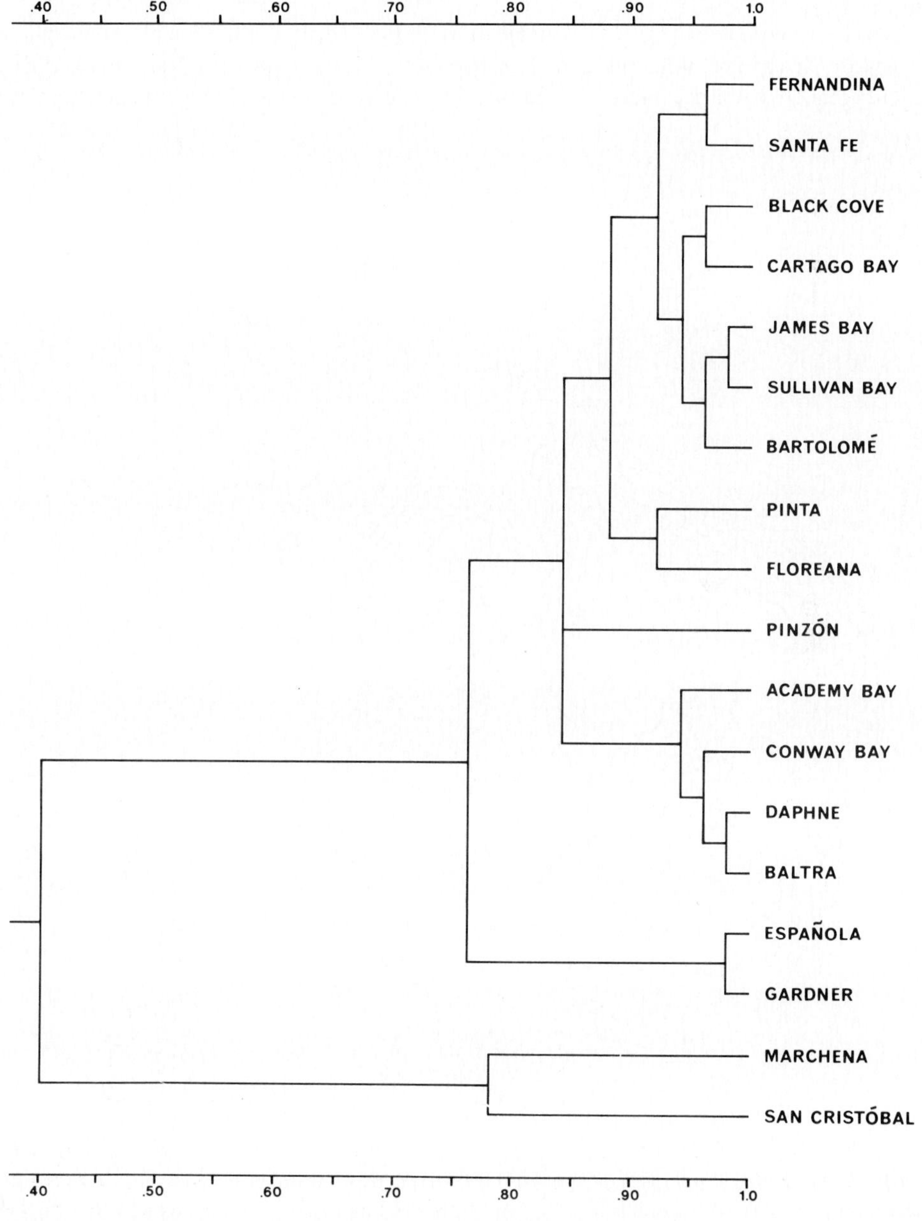

Fig. 4. Phenogram for Galapagos *Tropidurus* populations produced by UPGMA clustering of Rogers' genetic similarity coefficients for allozyme data (Tables 3 and 4).

To facilitate the evaluation and interpretation of the allozyme analyses, the following discussion has been divided into four parts: (1) a comparison of the allozyme analyses and Van Denburgh's evolutionary scenarios for both *Phyllodactylus* and *Tropidurus*, and an evaluation of his "Galapagos Land" hypothesis; (2) a comparison of the allozyme analyses with available geological data as summarized by Cox (this volume); (3) applications of the molecular clock hypotheses and calibrations of Nei (1975) and Sarich (1977) to the allozyme data sets; (4) biogeographic scenarios incorporating the geological and allozyme data.

Van Denburgh's "Galapagos Land" Hypothesis

In order to compare effectively Van Denburgh's (1912b, 1913) statements of morphological or systematic divergence with the allozyme data sets, I have converted Van Denburgh's statements into genetic similarity values. To do this, I have used the general ranges in genetic similarity

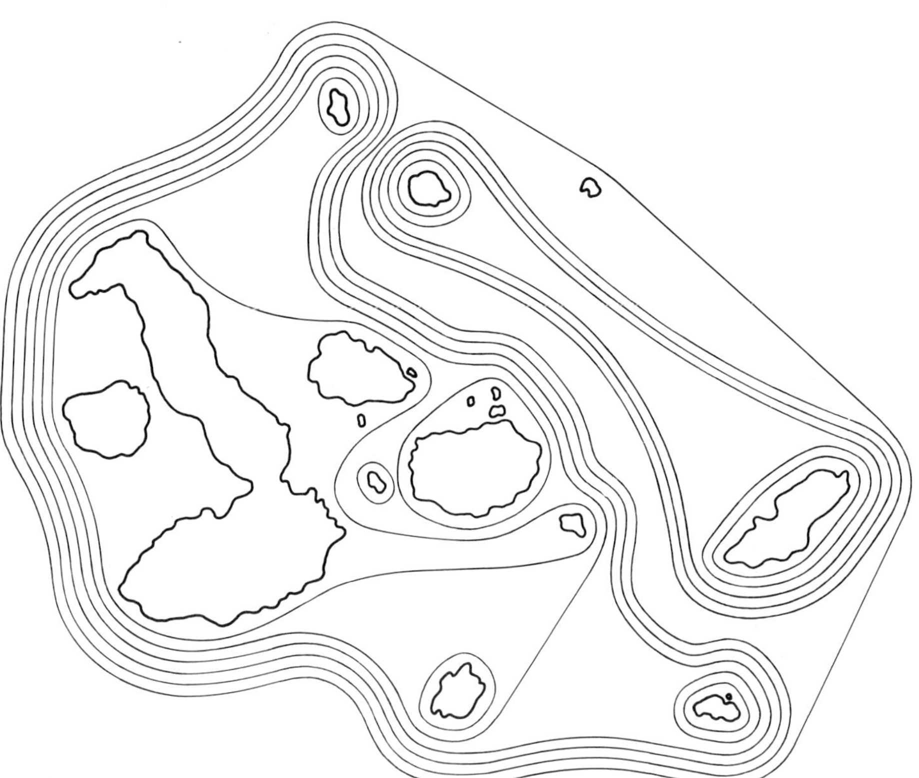

Fig. 5. Map of Galapagos Archipelago with isograms of similarity in *Tropidurus* populations. Isograms represent 0.10 intervals of Rogers' genetic similarity coefficients (S) as clustered by the UPGMA method (Fig. 4). The innermost rings represent S=0.90; the outermost, S=0.40. The isogram linking Floreana and Pinta at S=0.90 has been omitted.

for organisms of differing levels of relationship summarized by Selander and Johnson (1973) and Avise (1974), as follows:

Relationship[1]	*Rogers' Genetic Similarity (S)*
Same population, or nearly so	0.95-1.00
Different populations or subspecies	0.90-0.95
Different species	0.85 or <
Same species subgroup	0.70 or >
Same species group	0.60 or >
Different species groups	0.50 or <
Different genera	0.40 or <

To generate simulated genetic similarity values, each statement of relationship between populations would be assigned an S value. For example, where two populations were said to be undifferentiated, I would insert an S of 0.95. Van Denburgh began his narrative on the relationships within *Phyllodactylus* by stating that one of the geckos on San Cristóbal is a non-Galapagoan species. In In other words, it is not in the same species group, and its relationship to the other geckos would accordingly be assigned an S of between 0.50 and 0.60 or 0.55. Thus, all other S values would range from 0.55 to 0.95 with each value being relative to the stated degree of relationship.

The following accounts are, in large part, direct quotes from Van Denburgh's narratives on the relationships of Galapagoan *Phyllodactylus* (1912b:407-409) and *Tropidurus* (1913:139-142). However, to assist the reader, I have taken the liberty of modifying the accounts. I have omitted all references to the various specific names and other inappropriate sections. I also substituted the Ecuadorian for the English names of the islands. Wherever a statement of relationship between lizards or islands occurs, I have inserted a corresponding Rogers' S value. These "simulated S values" have been used to construct dendrograms (Figs. 6 and 7) which can be compared with dendrograms derived from nonsimulated or "real" genetic data (Figs. 2 and 4). The narratives have also been used to construct a series of maps (Fig. 8), which present graphically Van Denburgh's view of the sequence of events that led to the formation of the archipelago.

Phyllodactylus Narrative

San Cristóbal is the only island upon which there occurs more than one species of *Phyllodactylus*. Here, two very distinct species have been found. One of these has been regarded as identical with one on the North and South American continents. It has no close relatives on any of the other islands of the archipelago [S = 0.55], and may have been introduced on San Cristóbal since the plantation was established there.

The other Galapagoan geckos are all closely related [S=0.60]. There can be little doubt that all are directly descended from a single species which formerly occupied this entire area. We must believe that the isolation resulting from the separation of an original large island into the various small islands which now exist, has made possible the differentiation which we now find in these geckos.

If this be true, we should expect to find that the greatest differentiation exists where isolation has been longest maintained, and, conversely, that separation has existed longest where the greatest differentiation is found. Thus we may proceed to sketch the history of the Galapagos Islands as indicated by the geckos of the genus *Phyllodactylus.*

ORIGIN AND HISTORY OF THE GALAPAGOS ISLANDS

One species has been found only on Wolf. It is the most distinct of all the Galapagoan geckos [S=0.60], except the introduced species, which we shall not consider

[1] By using these values, I do not wish to imply that there is more than a very general relationship between genetic similarity and systematic status. See Avise (1974) for a full discussion of the utility of allozyme analyses in systematic studies.

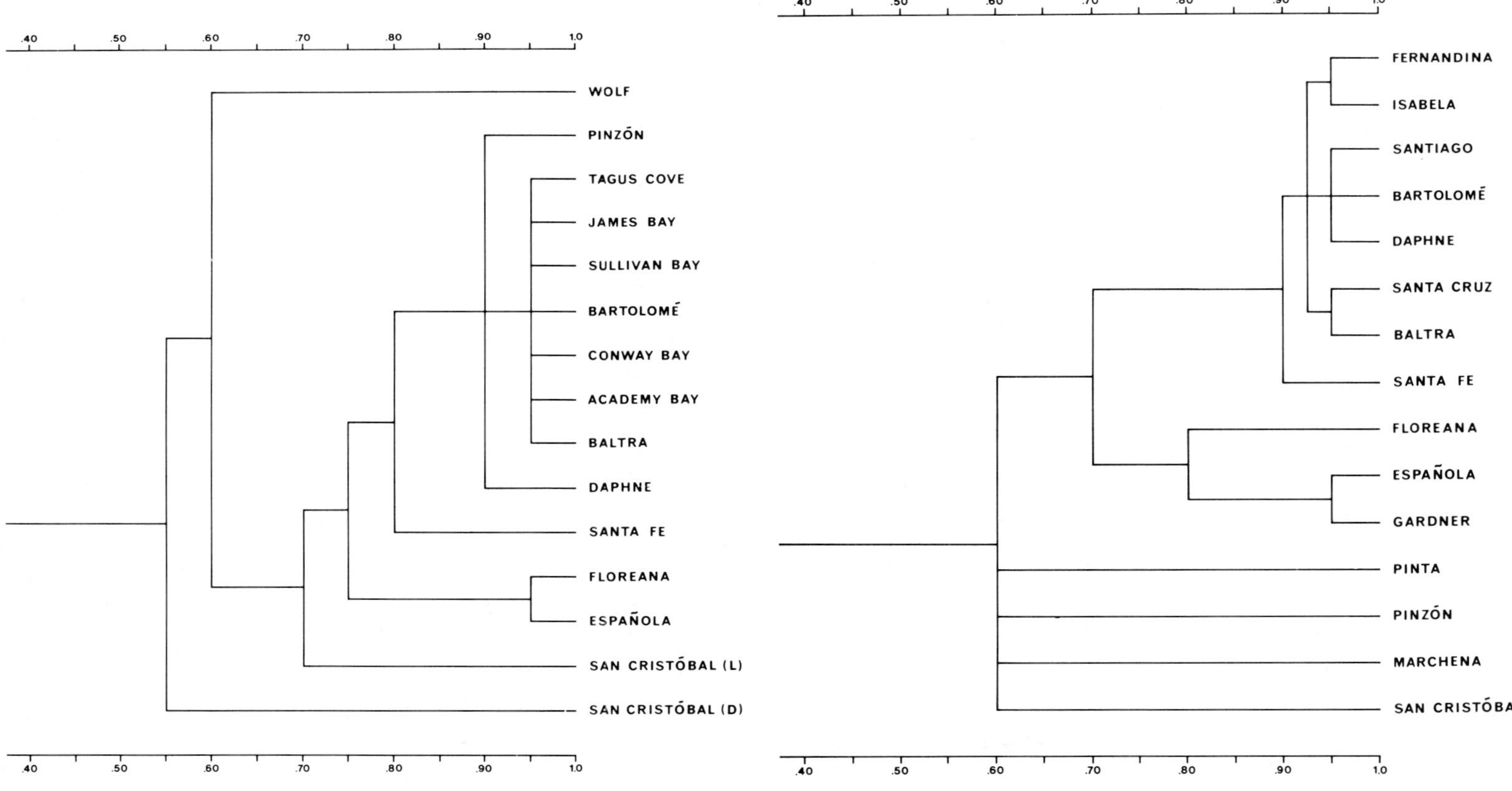

Fig. 6. Phenogram for Galapagos *Phyllodactylus* populations.

Fig. 7. Phenogram for Galapagos *Tropidurus* populations.

Both figures are based on "simulated" Rogers' genetic similarity coefficients (S). Data are derived from assignments of S values to statements of relations in Van Denburgh's (1912, 1913) narratives of the origin and history of the Galapagos *Phyllodactylus* and *Tropidurus*. See text for the method and rationale.

farther [S=0.55]. Hence, we may infer that Wolf has had an individual existence longer than any of the other gecko-bearing islands of the archipelago. No geckos have ever been found on Darwin, Pinta, Marchena or Genovesa.

The next gecko in point of distinctness is the other *Phyllodactylus* of San Cristóbal. This leads us to believe that San Cristóbal became a separate island at a time when the other central and southern islands still were connected [S=0.70].

There may be some difference of opinion as to whether the *Phyllodactylus* of Española-Floreana or of Santa Fe is the more differentiated form. Nevertheless, I believe that the differences found in the former, involving as they do changes in arrangement as well as in number, are of greater import than the mere reduction in dorsal tubercles which characterizes the latter. This view of the case leads to the conclusion that Española and Floreana probably were the next to become separated in the breaking up of the original large island [S=0.75], and that the isolation of Santa Fe occurred soon after [S=0.80].

The same species inhabits both Española and Floreana, with their outlying islets. Since we cannot believe that this species has been independently evolved in two separate islands, and do not think that it has been carried across the water from one island to the other, we are forced to conclude that Española and Floreana were connected, and formed parts of a single large southern island, for a considerable time after their separation from the rest of the land area which later became the present archipelago [S=0.95].

The relationship which exists between the geckos of San Cristóbal and Santa Fe perhaps may indicate that the last connection of San Cristóbal with the central island was by way of Santa Fe.

The geckos of the remaining islands have undergone much less differentiation than those which we have thus far considered. For the present, we must refer them all to one species [S=0.85], although it is quite possible that more abundant material might enable us to recognize differences which now are hidden.

From this we may conclude that these islands all remained connected, and formed a single island, for a long time after their separation from those islands already considered, where distinct species have been evolved.

While it is true that all these geckos from the central islands are so closely related they are not all identical. Those of Pinzón and Daphne islands differ sufficiently to enable us to recognize them as distinct subspecies [S=0.90]; from which we may conclude that these two islands have had an independent insular existence longer than the others of the central group, which doubtless remained connected until a still later period [S=0.95].

Farther than this we cannot go, and it is evident that differentiation in the geckos of the Galapagos Islands has progressed neither so rapidly nor so far as it has in the case of the snakes of the archipelago. The older and more stable organization of these lizards has not changed so quickly. For this reason, the geckos throw but little light upon the more recent history of the islands. They, as it were, have not kept up to date. Their story stops before the separation of Floreana from Española at a time when the central islands, excepting Pinzón and Daphne, yet were one. But so far as it goes, the story of the geckos agrees completely with that of the snakes, except on one minor point. Our study of the snakes indicated that Santa Fe only recently became separated from Santa Cruz. The evidence afforded by the geckos would lead us to place the separation of Santa Fe at a more remote period. In other respects there is complete agreement.

Tropidurus Narrative

The fact that these lizards occur on nearly every island of the archipelago can be explained only in one of two ways. These *Tropiduri* must have reached these island either by land or by water. Either they have been carried to each island, islet, and rock by some such means of dispersal as floating driftwood driven by the winds and currents, or else they were already on each island at the time when it became separated from a larger land-mass. The former view has been held by those who believe that these islands never have been connected, but have been independently thrust above the surface of the ocean. The latter explanation finds favor with those who believe that these islands all formerly were connected, and formed part of a single large island which, sometime, must have been connected with continental America.

We can see but little to commend the former view, for the means of dispersal from continent to island or from island to island over the intervening water must, in the nature of things, be but accidental or occasional, and must seem quite inadequate to account for the wide distribution of these lizards in the archipelago. Again, Wolf and Darwin lie directly in the path of the currents from the other islands, yet both are without *Tropiduri*. Furthermore, were such means of dispersal sufficient to bring about the wide distribution of these reptiles, we must believe that the interchange of lizards between the islands would result either in preventing differentiation on the various islands, or in the transportation of differentiated races from island to island. Thus we should expect to find either one kind of lizard on all the islands, or a tendency toward the distribution of all kinds of lizards to each island. But many of the islands have each its peculiar kind of *Tropidurus*, and no island has more than one kind. Even in the case of Pinzón, almost surrounded as it is by other close-lying islands, the evidence all points to complete isolation during a long period of time.

ORIGIN AND HISTORY OF THE GALAPAGOS ISLANDS

We therefore, adopt the other theory: that there formerly was a single large island inhabited by one species of *Tropidurus*; that through partial and gradual submersion this island became divided into the many islands of the present archipelago; that each island after its separation was occupied by those animals which inhabited it before; and that the present fauna of each island is directly descended from its original inhabitants.

It is probable that the separation of the various islands occurred at different times rather than simultaneously.

If it be admitted that the degree of differentiation in a single group, under conditions such as obtain in these islands, may be regarded as an index to the period of isolation, we may proceed to sketch the history of the archipelago as indicated by the lizards of this genus.

The *Tropiduri* of Pinta, Marchena, Pinzón, and San Cristóbal show the greatest differentiation. Accordingly, we may believe that these islands early became separated from each other and from the remaining portions of the group, and have maintained independent existence ever since [S=0.60].

Fig. 8. Graphic representation of the origin and history of the Galapagos Archipelago as described by Van Denburgh (see text and Figs. 6 and 7). Each map contains the outline of the major islands as they are at present. The heavier lines around the islands represent the hypothetical extent of former land masses. A. Van Denburgh's "Galapagos Land" with all islands forming a single land mass connected to continental America (via arrow). The entire mass was occupied by a single species each of *Phyllodactylus* and *Tropidurus*. B. The islands as they appeared after the first series of subsidences. "Galapagos Land" is now separate from the mainland and the two northernmost islands (Darwin and Wolf) are separated from the large island. C. The next series of subsidences resulted in the formation of five new islands. The remaining northern islands (Pinta, Marchena, and Genovesa) are now distinct. The isthmus connecting San Cristóbal to the large island (via Santa Fe) is gone. Pinzón is now separated from the remaining large island by an extensive bay. D. Additional subsidence removed the isthmus that connected the Española-Floreana island to the large island via Santa Fe. E. Subsidence separated Santa Fe from the large island. F. A major wave of subsidence resulted in the break-up of the remaining large island, leaving Fernandina connected with Isabela, Santiago with Rabida and Bartolomé, and Santa Cruz with Baltra. Española and Floreana were separated. The next wave of subsidences left the island composition of the Archipelago as it appears today.

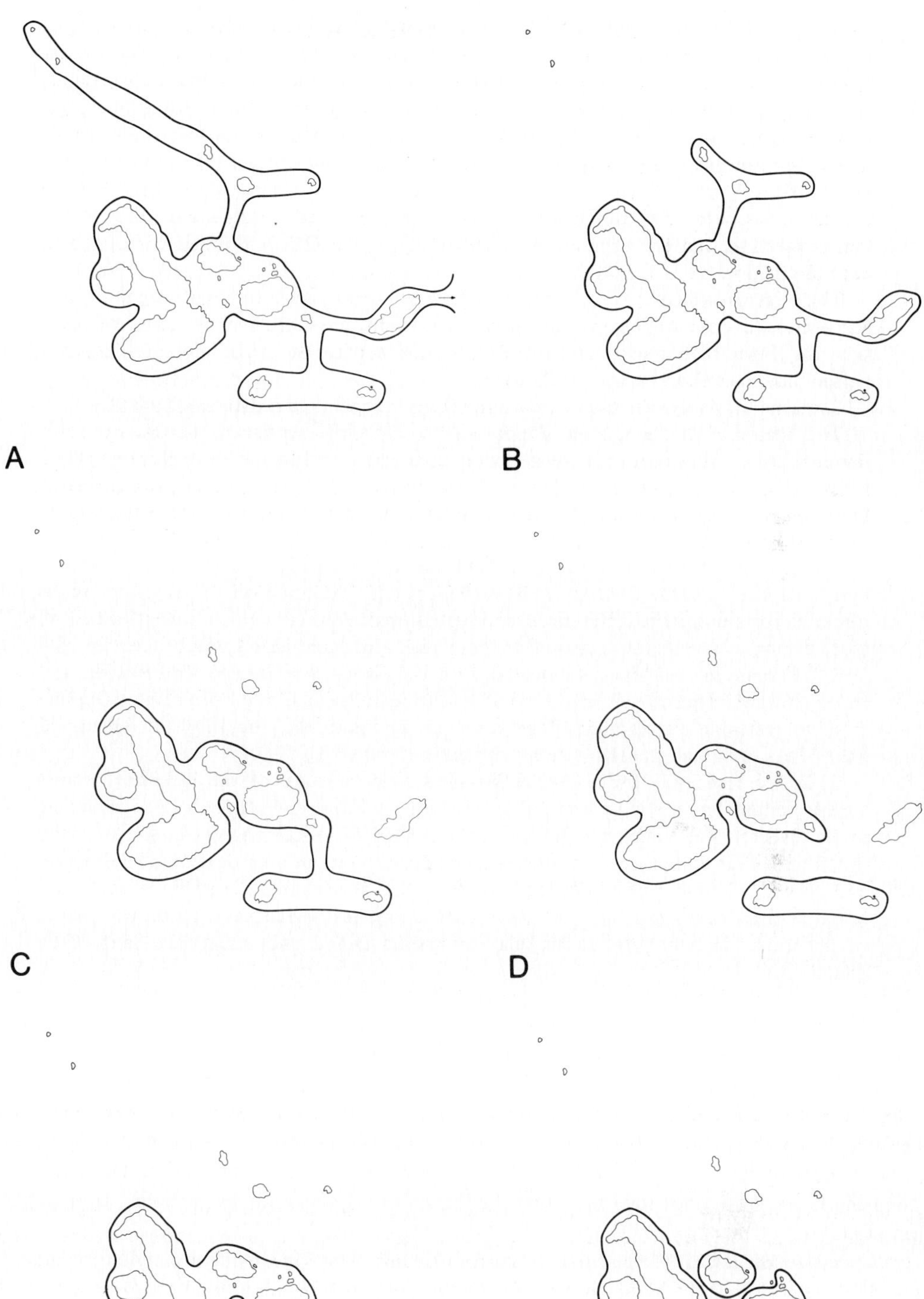
A
B
C
D
E
F

> The next lizard, in point of distinctness, is that of Española. Hence it would seem probable that this southern island was the one next separated [S=0.70]. The closest relationship of this *Tropidurus* seems to be with that of Floreana. This relationship is not nearly so striking as in the case of the snakes and geckos of these two islands, but it nevertheless may be interpreted as indicating some connection between these islands in the past, probably subsequent to their separation from the rest of the archipelago [S=0.80].
>
> The *Tropidurus* of Gardner-near-Española appears to be identical with that of the main island, so that the separation of this islet from Española doubtless is of recent date [S=0.95].
>
> The Floreana lizard is, in a sense, intermediate between those of Española and Santa Fe. This apparent relationship with the Santa Fe form inclines one to believe that the former connection of Española-Floreana with the remainder of the archipelago may have been by way of Santa Fe.
>
> Santa Fe probably was the next to assume an independent existence [S=0.90].
>
> The lizards of the remaining islands show so little differentiation that we are led to the conclusion that all of these islands were connected, and formed a single large island for some time after the separation of Santa Fe [S=0.90]. It is probable that a large bay extended from the south toward the center of this island, completely surrounding Pinzón with water.
>
> The history of this large central island cannot be clearly traced farther from evidence afforded by the *Tropiduri*. Nevertheless, the examination of very large series discloses certain average differences, and certain resemblances, which lead us to believe that, during a considerable period of time after this large island was broken up [S= 0.92], Fernandina remained connected with Isabela, as did Santiago with Rábida, and Santa Cruz with Baltra [all with S= 0.95]. Curiously enough, the *Tropiduri* of Daphne seem to resemble those of Santiago more closely than they do those of Baltra and Santa Cruz, although the latter lie much nearer [S=0.95].
>
> Thus we find that the evidence gathered from a study of the *Tropiduri* points to the gradual depression and partial submersion of a former Galapagos Land, resulting in its division into many smaller islands and islets. The story agrees in almost every detail with that which we have previously gathered from an investigation of the snakes and geckos. The chief points of difference are that the snake of Santa Fe is less differentiated than the lizard, and the *Tropiduri* afford less evidence than do the snakes of a former division into an Isabela-Fernandina Island and a Santiago-Santa Cruz Island.

In general the array of simulated and genetic similarity values for *Phyllodactylus* are remarkably similar. The four most divergent phenads are the same and in the same relative order in both clusters (San Cristóbal D, L, Wolf, and Española). Fernandina geckos were unknown to Van Denburgh. The placement of the Floreana sample is quite different and may reflect a bias carried over by Van Denburgh from his analysis of the snakes. The placement of the Santa Fe sample is similar in both. The presence of two multisample terminal phenads is not indicated in the simulated array. The genetic array does not separate either the Pinzón or Daphne samples as distinct from adjacent samples.

The two clusters of *Tropidurus* are more different. The San Cristóbal sample is separated at low levels in both, but the Marchena sample clusters at a much higher level in the genetic array. No hint of a close relationship between the San Cristóbal and Marchena samples is contained in the simulated array. Neither the Pinta nor the Pinzón samples are separated very remotely from adjacent samples in the genetic array. There is no special relationship in the genetic cluster between Floreana and Española. The relative position of the Santa Fe sample is different in that it is not separated from the samples from the central group of islands by the genetic data. These latter samples are arranged into subgroupings not detectable in the simulated data.

In Van Denburgh's Galapagos Land hypothesis, the archipelago originated as a single island connected to mainland South America. The island broke away from the continent and, through a series of differential subsidences, broke apart to form the present configuration of islands (Fig. 8). As formulated, the hypothesis is a vicariant model, subsequently elaborated by Croizat (1958) and modified by Rosen (1975). At first, only a single species each of *Tropidurus* and *Phyllodactylus* reached the islands via the mainland connection. Each species then diversified as the island broke up into smaller islands, ending with a series of species in each genus arrayed over the islands. Populations from more recently separated island pairs should therefore be genetically more similar. Furthermore, if the hypothesis were valid, members of both genera on each island would have shared a common history, and one would expect that they would have undergone comparable or similar levels of genetic divergence from populations on adjacent islands. For the most part this seems to be the case. Good examples can be found on San Cristóbal, Española, Santa Cruz and its adjacent satellites, Santiago and Isabela. However, there are some notable exceptions, e.g. Marchena, Santa Fe, and Fernandina. The amount of apparent concordance between Van Denburgh's analyses and hypothesis and the allozyme analysis undoubtedly reflects the history of the islands, but not necessarily his version.

Geological History of the Galapagos Archipelago

Cox (this volume) has summarized the available geological data for the origin and development of the islands. These data are primarily from four kinds of studies: plate tectonics, paleomagnetism, potassium-argon (K-Ar) dating, and geomorphology. The tectonic data indicate that the archipelago rests on the Nazca Plate. This plate is sliding southeastward and is subducting under the South American Plate at the Peru-Chile Trench. The archipelago is now closer to the South American continent than it has ever been. Furthermore, the sea floor upon which the archipelago rests is no older than 10 my and was probably formed close to 9 my ago. Needless to say, the islands must be younger than the sea floor under them.

Paleomagnetic data and potassium-argon dates indicate a general trend in island age from east to west in the archipelago with the easternmost islands being older (Fig. 9). Briefly, there are rocks on the eastern islands that formed and cooled during Gauss Normal Polarity Epoch (2.4-3 my) with K-Ar ages in general slightly more than 3 my (Fig. 9). The oldest data from Española (3.31 ± 0.36 my) is from a sample with reversed polarity. This could indicate that it hardened during Gilbert Reversed Polarity Epoch (3.3 to 5.1 my), and if so, would constitute the oldest aerial lava sampled in the archipelago. The oldest lavas on most of the western islands erupted during Brunhes Normal Polarity Epoch and are less than 0.7 my. The geographically intermediate islands and the northwesternmost (Wolf and Darwin) have rocks that were formed during Matuyama Reversed Polarity Epoch with ages between 0.7 and 2.4 my. Most of the K-Ar dates are in the range of 0.8 to 1.2 my. This age trend is sufficiently linear to substantiate a "hot spot model," where the volcanic plume zone is stationary and the plate slowly moves over it (Cox, this volume) as has also been proposed for the Hawaiian chain. Cox has used the rate of plate movement over the stationary plume zone to calculate estimated ages of the islands. Using a rate of 68 mm/year, the calculated dates correspond closely to those derived from the paleomagnetic, K-Ar, and geomorphologic analyses and indicate a maximum age of the islands of less than 4 my (ca. 3.7).

As emphasized by Cox (this volume), locating the oldest rocks on volcanic islands is difficult at best as these rocks are frequently covered by younger lava or ash, so there remains the question of whether the oldest rocks have been analysed. Another complicating factor, from a biological standpoint, is whether or not the "island" was aerial when the rocks were deposited or cooled. For example, some of the oldest rocks dated are submarine lavas that subsequently have been thrust above the surface. Thus, biologically speaking, these islands have to be younger than the rocks.

Keeping in mind the various qualifications of the geological data, it is safe to assume that from 3 to 4 and certainly not more than 5 my ago the first island formed and that by at least 3

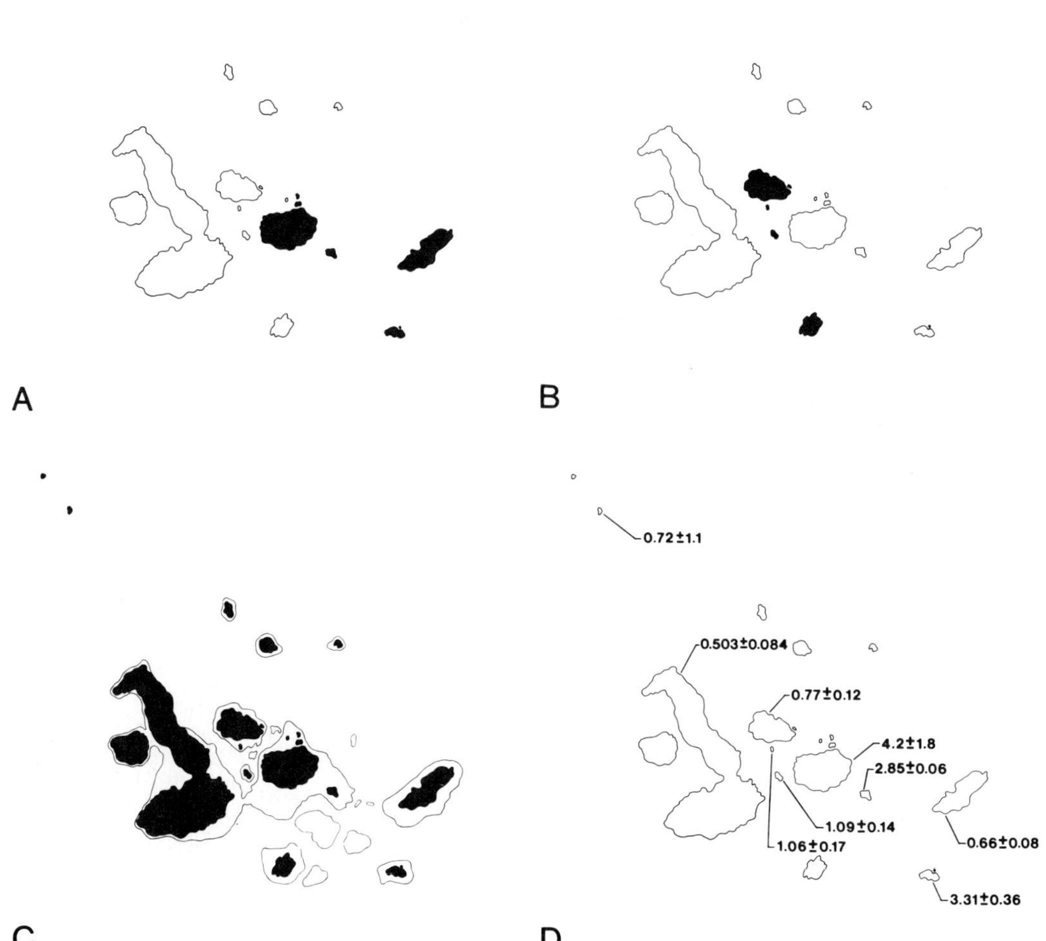

Fig. 9. Graphic summary of the geological history of the Galapagos Archipelago (see text and Cox, this volume). Each map contains the outlines of all major islands as they appear today, for the purposes of orientation only. These outlines should be viewed with caution, as the islands have only recently assumed their modern shapes, and it is extremely difficult, if not impossible, to determine what the shapes might have been during a particular time interval (see Cox, this volume). Islands (solid only) present during: A. Gauss Normal Polarity Epoch (3.3-2.4 my); B. Matuyama Reversed Polarity Epoch (2.4-0.7 my); and C. Brunhes Normal Polarity Epoch (0.7-0.0 my). Contour lines around islands (D) represent approximately 100 fathoms (200 m) in the archipelago. Maximum eustatic drop in sea level during Pleistocene glaciations is considered to have been ca. 100 m. E. Outline of the islands with the oldest potassium-argon date available for each. All dates are from Bailey (1976) except those from Santiago, Rábida, and Pinzón (Swanson et al. 1974) and that from Isabela (Nordlie 1973). See Cox (this volume) for additional dates.

my ago there were three islands: San Cristóbal, Española, and Santa Cruz (Fig. 9). Isla Santa Fe came into existence at about 2.7 my ago; there was a considerable time lag before the next islands were formed at a little more than 1 my ago (Floreana, Pinta, Santiago, Wolf, and Darwin). By 1 my ago, parts of Isabela may have existed, but the present island and parts if not all of the other major islands (Fernandina, Pinta, Marchena, and Genovesa) formed during the last 0.7 my (Fig. 9).

Assuming there was no appreciable time delay between the formation of an island and its colonization by lizards, the geological data would allow for several predictions. For example, the greatest genetic divergence should exist amongst the lizards on the islands that have been in existence and separated the longest. This is clearly the case with the three oldest islands, San Cristóbal, Española, and Santa Cruz, in the *Tropidurus* data set (Figs. 4 and 5). It is also true of the *Phyllodactylus* data set, if it is assumed, as discussed below, that the geckos on Isla Wolf and the D sample from San Cristóbal were the result of introductions independent of the remainder of the samples and that the within-Galapagos genetic divergence began with Node 3 and San Cristóbal L (Fig. 2). With these assumptions, the two data sets become remarkably similar. In both data sets the two most divergent phenads contain lizard samples from San Cristóbal and Española in that order. The Santa Cruz samples in each case are in the third phenad opposite Española. Except for the Marchena *Tropidurus* sample, all remaining samples in both data sets are genetically more similar to the Santa Cruz samples. This undoubtedly reflects the colonization sequences (see discussion below under Biogeographical Scenarios) and the fact that Santa Cruz is geographically more central to these other islands and may have been the source of the colonizing lizards.

A more extensive discussion of time, geology, and genetic divergence is contained in the following discussion. It is sufficient to conclude this section with the observation that the geological data provide no support for Van Denburgh's Galapagos Land hypothesis.

Molecular Clock Hypothesis

Both Nei (1972, 1975) and Sarich (1977) agree that genetic distance estimates (Nei's D) from analyses of protein electrophoresis can be used to calculate divergence times of organisms or lineages by linking D to a protein molecular clock. There is, however, great difference between the setting or calibration of their individual clocks. Roughly speaking, for D=1.0, Nei's clock would read 5 my, whereas Sarich's would read some four times as much or approximately 20 my. It is beyond the intent or scope of this paper to present the assumptions, data, and/or rationale for molecular clocks or their calibration. It is, however, appropriate and desirable to attempt to "test" the calibration of these clocks by using the data from the electrophoretic analyses of Galapagos lizards. Such an attempt is made possible only by the fact that as of now there are probably few, if any, areas on earth with better control, geologically speaking, over real or absolute time than that represented by the data set for development of the Galapagos Archipelago (see above discussion and Cox, this volume). Needless to say, even with rather rigorous control over absolute time, there remain numerous biological qualifications or conditions that should be satisfied or met before such a "test" would have great significance. As these have been all but ignored by most users of molecular clocks, I will do likewise and focus the discussion on D values, geology, and time, and sidestep lizard biology.

For the purposes of this discussion, I have calculated Nei's genetic distance estimates (D) and the corresponding divergence time estimates (Table 5) of Nei (T_n) and Sarich (T_s) for the clustering nodes on the phenograms of Rogers' S values for the samples of both *Phyllodactylus* (Fig. 2) and *Tropidurus* (Fig. 4). Comparing these values for the *Tropidurus* data set for Node 1, T_n (4.65 my) is just outside the range of time for the archipelago (4 my) as determined by the geological data, but T_s (18.6 my) is over four times older and represents a time interval twice that of the age of the underlying sea floor. Thus, both T estimates suggest that some of the divergence at this node could have (T_n) or must have (T_s) occurred on the mainland prior to the establishment of island populations. The T estimates for Node 2 both fall within the age frame of the region, except that T_s (4.8 my) is beyond the time range for the archipelago. The T_n value (1.2 my) is well within the time range for the separate existence of Española (ca. 3 my) and the two oldest islands in the other cluster (Santa Cruz, > 3 my and Santa Fe, 2.8). Both T estimates for Node 3 (San Cristóbal-

Marchena) yield dates older than the 0.7 my or younger for Marchena. However, T_n (1.2 my) is closer to the geological data, while T_s (4.8 my) is many times greater and beyond the geological age for the islands.

When the *Phyllodactylus* data sets (Fig. 2) are analyzed in a comparable fashion, it is clear that all T_s values for Nodes 1 through 5 (14.4-5.6 my) dictate more time than is allowable for the archipelago by the geological data. Furthermore, the values for Nodes 1 and 2 exceed the age of the underlying sea floor. All T_n values are within the geological time range of the archipelago, but that for Node 2 exceeds the geological age of Wolf by a considerable amount (3.1 vs 1.0 or from 0.7 to 2.4 my). From Node 3 on, all divergence time represented by T_n values could have taken place within the islands. At T_n of 2.1 my there should have been four islands (geologically speaking), but the T_n indicates only two islands (San Cristóbal and Española) with *Phyllodactylus* populations or a 50% underestimate. By T_n of 1.7 (Node 4) there would have been geckos on three of the four islands, but by this time there should have been more islands and gecko populations. Thus, it would appear that while T_s greatly overestimates the potential ages of the islands and gecko populations, T_n tends to provide underestimates.

If the T_n and T_s estimates are viewed from a different vantage point, i.e. from what these divergence times can predict about lizard evolution and biogeography, some interesting implications are revealed. For example, if we accept as real or final the ages in the geological data set, then the T_n values would indicate that all genetic diversity in both lizard groups *could* have resulted from a single ancestral island population or from at most two separate introductions from an extra-island source for *Tropidurus*. On the other hand, the T_s values would indicate that the genetic diversity in all Galapagoan *Tropidurus* and *Phyllodactylus* resulted from at least nine separate introductions from a non-island source for each genus (*Tropidurus* at Node 6 and *Phyllodactylus* at Nodes 8 and 9).

Clearly the divergence time estimates from the calibration of Nei's clock provide the best "fit" with both the geological and biological data, but could there be a better "fit" or calibration more directly derivable from just the allozyme and geological data sets? What follows is an effort to calibrate a molecular clock on this basis. The geological data indicate that San Cristóbal is one of the oldest islands in the archipelago. This is consistent with the allozyme data, which indicate that the most distantly related lizard populations in both genera are found on this island. However, both sets of biological data suggest that much of this observed genetic distance may be due to separate or independent introduction of lizards in each genus to San Cristóbal.[2] With this in mind, San Cristóbal and its lizard populations have been excluded from this "clock-setting exercise." Considering the remaining islands and data, it is reasonably clear that two other islands were present by 3 my ago, Española and Santa Cruz. If the distance values between the respective populations of *Phyllodactylus* and *Tropidurus* from Santa Cruz (actually a cluster for Santa Cruz: Academy Bay, Conway Bay, Baltra, and Daphne), and Española (i.e. *Phyllodactylus*, $\bar{D}_n$=0.295, range 0.257-0.330, N=4; and *Tropidurus*, $\bar{D}_n$=0.337, range 0.345, N=4) are set on a clock as 3 my, then D=1.0 for *Phyllodactylus* would read 8.9 (8.7-9.1) my and for *Tropidurus*, 10.2 (9.1-11.6 my). When these settings are superimposed on the Rogers' S clustering nodes (see Table 5 and Figs. 2 and 4), certain relationships become apparent. As might be expected in the *Phyllodactylus* set, Nodes 1 (6.4 my) and 2 (4.7 my) dictate more divergence time than is available in the geological data, and some of the divergence in these populations must have occurred while their ancestors were still on the mainland. Node 3 (3.7 my) divergence is possible and perhaps consistent with the relative greater age of Isla San Cristóbal. The time at Node 4 (2.9 my) is only slightly less than the 3.0 my used to set the *Phyllodactylus* clock. Part of Node 5 divergence is very close to the

[2] A preliminary allozyme analysis comparing mainland and Galapagos populations of *Tropidurus* revealed that the populations on San Cristóbal and Marchena are genetically more similar to three mainland species than they are to the other Galapagos populations.

TABLE 5. GENETIC DISTANCE ESTIMATES (NEI'S D) FOR THE CLUSTERING NODES IN FIGS. 2 AND 4, WITH CORRESPONDING DIVERGENCE TIME ESTIMATES[1]

NODE (S)[2]	Nei's D	T_n(my)	T_s(my)	T_w(my)
Phyllodactylus				
1 (0.48)	0.72	3.6	14.4	6.4
2 (0.52)	0.62	3.1	12.4	4.7
3 (0.64)	0.42	2.1	8.4	3.7
4 (0.70)	0.33	1.7	6.6	2.9
5 (0.72)	0.28	1.4	5.6	2.5
6 (0.82)	0.14	0.7	2.8	1.25
7 (0.86)	0.12	0.6	2.4	1.1
8[3] (0.88)	0.05	0.25	1.0	0.4
9[4] (0.92)	0.06	0.3	1.2	0.5
Tropidurus				
1 (0.40)	0.93	4.65	18.6	9.5
2 (0.78)	0.24	1.2	4.8	2.45
3 (0.76)	0.24	1.2	4.8	2.45
4 (0.84)	0.15	0.75	3.0	1.5
5 (0.88)	0.12	0.6	2.4	1.2
6 (0.92)	0.09	0.45	1.8	0.9

[1] Clustering nodes as shown in the phenograms of genetic similarity (Rogers' S) of samples of *Phyllodactylus* (Fig. 2) and *Tropidurus* (Fig. 4); divergence time estimates in millions of years as calculated from the molecular clock calibrations of Nei [1975; $T_n = D(5 \times 10^6)$], Sarich [1977; $T_s = D(20 \times 10^6)$], and Wright [this paper; $T_w = D\ (8.9 \text{ or } 10.2 \times 10^6)$].

[2] Nodes are read from left to right or low to high S.

[3] Tagus Cove, etc., cluster.

[4] Marchena, etc., cluster.

geological data, e.g., T_w of 2.5 vs 2.7 my for Santa Fe, but the date for the Fernandina populations presents a problem that would remain unresolved with any "clock setting." For the divergence time for Node 6, at least two islands in each phenad would have been present. Thus, the *Phyllodactylus* clock or calibration allows the identification of recurrent "inconsistencies," especially related to the more divergent populations (i.e. San Cristóbal D and Wolf) and Fernandina, but provides a better "fit" to the geological and biological data than the T_n or T_s calibrations.

The T_w data set for *Tropidurus* provides perhaps a little better fit with the geological and biological data than does the setting for *Phyllodactylus*. It clearly separates the divergence at Node 1 (9.5 my) from the time frame of the archipelago, and again suggests independent introduction from extra-island populations. The divergence at Node 2 (2.45) is considerably less than the predicted time (3.0 my) used to calibrate the clock. Node 3 (2.45 my) presents a different problem and tends to again indicate either that Marchena is older than the 0.7 my granted in the geological data or, at the other extreme, that the *Tropidurus* on both Marchena and San Cristóbal diverged separately from some extra-island population. The T_w at Node 4 is consistent with the geological data, where at 1.5 my ago each phenad would have been represented by at least one island. The T_w values for the remaining nodes provide similar "good fits."

In double-checking the T_w calibrations for both groups with specific D values rather than nodal averages, certain different relationships are revealed. For example, if Santa Fe did indeed begin existence some 2.7 my ago and received lizards from some source shortly thereafter, it should be possible to identify the most likely source by computing the actual D values from all intra-archipelago potential sources. In the case of *Phyllodactylus*, at 2.7 my, there could have been five other island populations, two of which (San Cristóbal-D and Wolf) were excluded from clock calibrations, but as might be expected, the genetic distance values and separation times between these two and Santa Fe (7.0 and 7.1 my, respectively) exceed the available time. The other times are as follows: San Cristóbal (L), 5.1 my; Española, 3.6 my; and Santa Cruz complex, 2.3 my. This suggests a scenario where the Española and Santa Cruz geckos diverged some 3+ my ago (generally consistent with other data) and that after Santa Fe (at 2.7 my) became an island, it most likely received geckos from Santa Cruz shortly thereafter (at 2.3 my). Using comparable data for divergence times for *Tropidurus* on Santa Fe to those of San Cristóbal (11.2 my), Española (2.8 my), and Santa Cruz complex (1.5 my), the following are suggested: a) lizards on Santa Fe and San Cristóbal last shared a common ancestor somewhere on the "mainland"; b) the Santa Fe and Española lizards could have diverged at 2.8 my or just about the time that Santa Fe came into existence; and c) the Santa Fe *Tropidurus* most likely shared a more recent divergence time with lizards of the Santa Cruz island complex than with the other islands. Thus, the most likely scenario is that the *Tropidurus* of Española and Santa Cruz diverged some 3.0 my ago and that the Santa Fe and Santa Cruz lizards diverged at ca. 2.5 my ago; and that the slightly lesser amount of genetic distance and time between Santa Fe and Española (0.275, 2.8 my) vs Santa Cruz and Española (0.337, 3.0 my) must be the results of the usual and ever-present stochastic events.

Biogeographical Scenarios

To develop biogeographical scenarios for the sequence of founder events that led to the modern populations of *Phyllodactylus* and *Tropidurus* in the Galapagos, I have attempted to couple the allozyme and geological data. In general such analyses are risky, for if even one data set contains errors, then a house of cards has fallen. In this instance, it is already known that there is something unusual about the fit of the two data sets regarding Marchena and Fernandina samples. In both cases, one of the lizard populations appears older than the geological data, and these islands could be older—or something may have differentially affected the allozyme data. A candidate of first choice for the latter might be the Founder Principle (Mayr 1942), where the founders of a new population contain only a small portion of the genetic diversity contained in the source population. From the onset of the new population, there is at least an average genetic difference between the populations. This can have a dramatic effect where one is concerned with large variable populations giving rise to one or a few founders, but should have little consequence in island populations where variation is characteristically truncated or absent (Gorman et al. 1975). In the case of the Galapagos lizards, the majority of gene loci are homozygous (Tables 1 and 2) and where variability does exist, it involves very few alleles. A second major evolutionary factor could be drift to fixation of alleles resulting from mutations in the small island or founder populations. Both factors could result in significant changes in gene frequencies and in seemingly different evolutionary rates, but their actual consequences in a real situation, such as in the Galapagos, are virtually impossible to evaluate. Given these reservations, I have intertwined the two data sets in hopes of unraveling the sequence of evolutionary events in the history of these lizards.

The geological data indicate that the islands are the result of separate volcanic events and that there were no connections to the mainland or between any of the major islands. Hence the lizards presently occupying these islands must have traveled over water from the mainland and/or from an adjacent island. Undoubtedly the sources of origin of the Galapagos lizards were from populations that occupied the desert areas of western South America (southeastern Ecuador to northern Chile) where some 13 species of *Phyllodactylus* and 9 of *Tropidurus* are now known to occur (Dixon and Huey 1970; Dixon and Wright 1975; Wright, ms.). The transport of the lizards to the islands was probably facilitated by the wind and ocean currents associated with the Humboldt Current. This current has its origin in Antarctic waters, sweeps along the west coast of South America as far north as southern Ecuador where it bends to the northwest towards the

Galapagos, and dissipates in equatorial waters a short distance beyond the archipelago (Wyrtki 1967; Wyrtki et al. 1976). It has been a prominent feature in the eastern Pacific for the past 40 my (Wright, ms.). Undoubtedly the long-term effects of this current have produced the redundant distributional tracks that prompted Croizat (1958) to hypothesize a former land connection between the Galapagos and South America, and Rosen (1975) to hypothesize the existence of now-submerged steppingstones or coyats. As discussed above, there is no geological evidence for a land connection nor for steppingstones.

In order to make the following scenarios most parsimonious, the number of independent foundings of island populations from continental sources was minimized.

Phyllodactylus. The *Phyllodactylus* of the archipelago most likely have been derived from three extra-island founders (Fig. 10). The population on Isla Wolf and one on San Cristóbal (D) are the results of two of these foundings. They are not otherwise closely related genetically to each other or to the remaining island populations. The San Cristóbal (D) population may have been recently introduced by man, as believed by Van Denburgh (1912b). The third founding was to San Cristóbal, perhaps the oldest island in the archipelago. This population gave rise to San Cristóbal L, the genetically most distinct of the remaining geckos, and may have provided founders

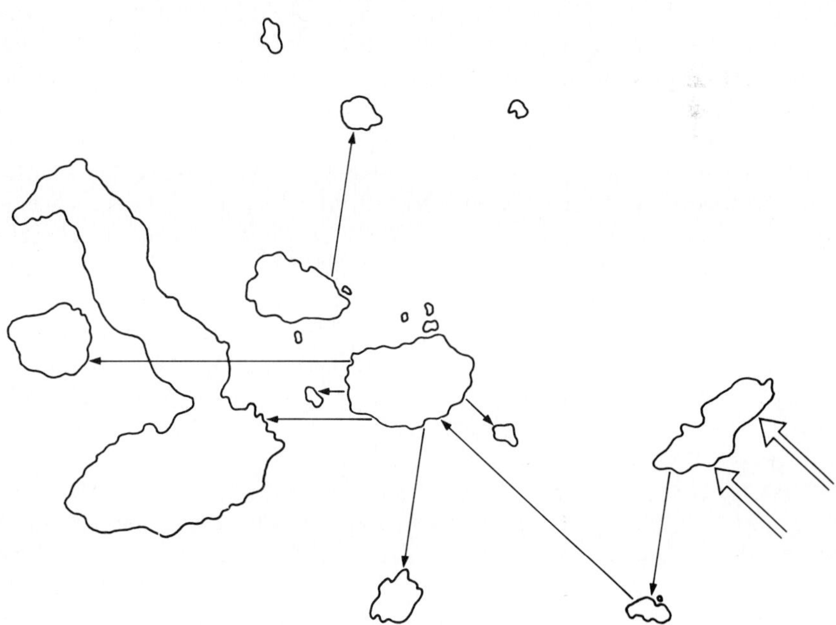

Fig. 10. Map of the Galapagos Archipelago with the probable sequence of founder events for populations of *Phyllodactylus*, based on allozyme electrophoretic and available geological data. Arrows indicate directions of colonizations. Open arrows represent foundings from extra-Galapagos sources.

for the populations on Española. The population on Santa Cruz was derived from geckos on either San Cristóbal or Española, but more likely from the latter. The population on Santa Cruz gave rise early to the lizards on Santa Fe (and perhaps to those on Fernandina). Later, it provided founders for the populations on Isabela, Pinzón, and Santiago and then to those of its satellite islands. Santiago served as the source of the founders for the Marchena geckos.

Tropidurus. The *Tropidurus* of the Galapagos were undoubtedly derived initially from two separate dispersal events from western South America, one each to San Cristóbal and Española (Fig. 11). Later the lizards on Marchena were founded from the population on San Cristóbal. No other island lizards were derived from this lineage. The population on Española gave rise to the founders for the lizards on Santa Cruz. All of the remaining island population appear to have ultimately been derived from the Santa Cruz population, but the sequence is unclear—perhaps a reflection of the relatively short time span over which the foundings occurred. It appears that

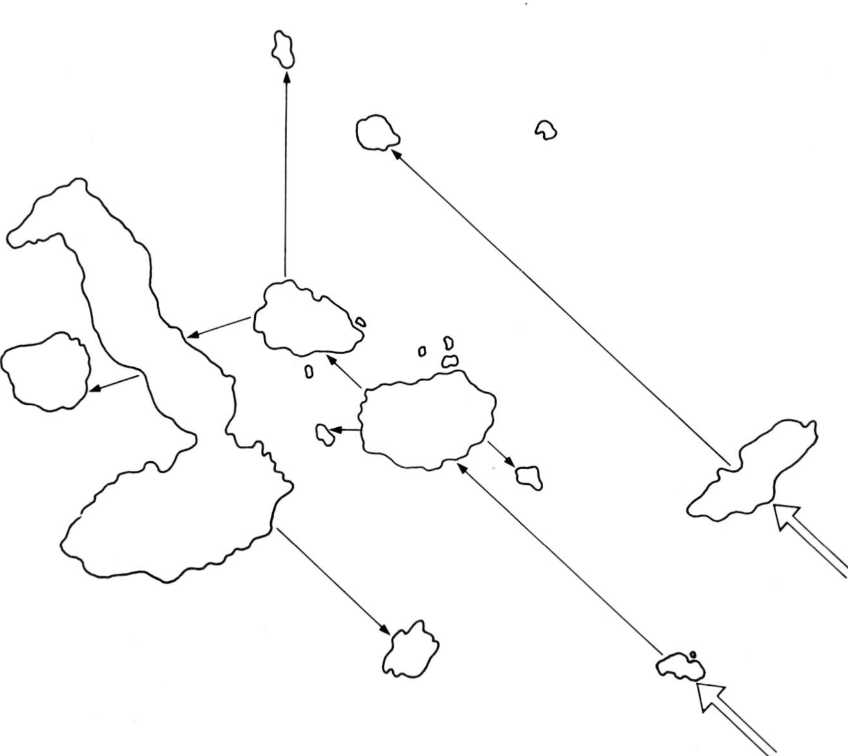

Fig. 11. Map of the Galapagos Archipelago with the probable sequence of founder events for populations of *Tropidurus*, based on allozyme electrophoretic and available geological data. Arrows indicate directions of colonizations. Open arrows represent foundings from extra-Galapagos sources.

the populations on Pinzón and Santiago were founded early and that the remainder of the populations on the major islands may have been founded from the Santiago population. The various populations on the satellite islands were derived from their adjacent major island.

SUMMARY AND CONCLUSIONS

Tissue samples of the lizard genera *Phyllodactylus* and *Tropidurus* obtained from 17 and 18 populations from 14 and 15 islands, respectively, were subjected to electrophoretic analyses of allozymes. A total of 20 presumptive loci were analyzed in the *Phyllodactylus* samples and 23 in the *Tropidurus* samples. The levels of interpopulation genetic similarity as measured by Rogers' S values ranged to a low of 0.38 in *Phyllodactylus* and 0.29 in *Tropidurus*. The most divergent populations in both genera occur on San Cristóbal. Samples from the same islands or from adjacent satellite islands have high levels of genetic similarity, with the exception of the sympatric geckos on San Cristóbal. The genetic similarity between these two is 0.44. The UPGMA clustering method identified two very divergent phenads in the *Tropidurus* samples with an average similarity of 0.40 between them. One phenad contained only the San Cristóbal and Marchena samples. Within the larger phenad, Española is the most divergent population. The samples from the more central group of islands are united at values averaging higher than 0.84. Clustering of the *Phyllodactylus* data revealed four strongly divergent populations: San Cristóbal (D), Wolf, San Cristóbal (L), and Española. With the exception of Fernandina and Santa Fe, all samples from the central group of islands clustered at values averaging higher than 0.81.

The results of the allozyme analyses were used to test the Galapagos Land hypothesis of Van Denburgh, which was developed primarily from morphological analyses of Galapagos *Phyllodactylus* and *Tropidurus*. Simulated genetic similarity values were generated and assigned to Van Denburgh's statements of relationships among the lizard populations. These simulated Rogers' values were then used to construct phenograms for comparison with those for the allozyme data. The two phenograms for *Phyllodactylus* are markedly similar with respect to the relative placements of the five most divergent populations: San Cristóbal (D), Wolf, San Cristóbal (L), Española, and Santa Fe. The close relationship between the geckos on Española and Floreana in Van Denburgh's analysis is not indicated in the allozyme data. Within the clusters for the central group of islands, the populations on Pinzón and Daphne are not genetically distinct from those on adjacent islands, as indicated by the morphological analysis.

While there is considerable concordance between the relative levels of morphological and allozyme similarity in the phenograms for *Phyllodactylus* populations, there is much less between those of *Tropidurus* populations. Only one (either San Cristóbal or Marchena) of four populations considered to be morphologically most distinct is strongly divergent genetically. The two phenograms are similar in the relative placement of the Española population, but differ markedly in the placement of the Pinta, Pinzón, and Floreana populations. If Van Denburgh's Galapagos Land hypothesis were true, there should have been greater similarity between the simulated and actual phenograms for *Tropidurus* populations. Furthermore, if both the *Tropidurus* and *Phyllodactylus* in the islands shared the same history as suggested by Van Denburgh, there should be even more similarity in the relative placement of the respective populations of each genus from an island in the phenograms for the genetic data. Despite some general similarity between the morphological and allozyme data, Van Denburgh's hypothesis is not sufficient to explain the patterns of genetic divergence found in the lizard populations.

The geological history of the Galapagos indicates that the sea floor under the islands is approximately 9 my old and that the oldest island was formed about 4 my ago. There is a general east-to-west age trend, with the eastern islands being older. For the most part the allozyme data and the geological data are concordant. The older eastern islands have the more genetically divergent populations, while the populations from the younger, more centrally located islands are genetically more similar.

The molecular clock calibrations proposed by Nei and Sarich for electrophoretic data were applied to the allozyme data sets. Sarich's calibration yielded time estimates that exceed the geological time frame for both the archipelago and most of the individual islands, whereas Nei's calibration tended to provide underestimates. A coupling of the allozyme and geological data yielded calibrations of 8.9 my for *Phyllodactylus* and 10.2 my for *Tropidurus* for a Nei distance of 1.0. Using these calibrations, divergence times were calculated for the clustering nodes in the phenograms for Rogers' genetic similarity. Divergence time estimates for Nodes 1 and 2 of the *Phyllodactylus* phenogram dictate more time than is available in the geological data, indicating that some of the divergence must have occurred on the mainland. From Node 3 up (3.8 my), all divergence times are within the time frame for the islands and are consistent with the relative age of the individual islands, with the exception of the Fernandina population. The divergence times indicate three separate invasions of the islands by *Phyllodactylus* founders: San Cristóbal (D) and (L), and Wolf; all of the remaining populations could have been derived from San Cristóbal (L).

The divergence time estimates for the *Tropidurus* data compare favorably with both the geological and biological information. The divergence time for Node 1 (9.5 my) is beyond the time frame for the archipelago and suggests independent introductions from an extra-island source. The divergence times from Node 2 up (2.45 my) are within the age frame for the islands. The time for Node 3 (2.45 my) indicates that Marchena is either older than the 0.7 my granted by the geological data or that both Marchena and San Cristóbal were founded separately from an extra-island population. From the standpoint of the geographical age trend of the islands, Marchena should be older than 0.7 my. With this in mind, the divergence times indicate two foundings of *Tropidurus* to the islands: San Cristóbal and Española. The Marchena population was derived early from the San Cristóbal lizards, and all of the remaining populations could have been established from the Española geckos.

The source of the original Galapagos lizards was probably the deserts of western South America (southeastern Ecuador to northern Chile) where some 13 species of *Phyllodactylus* and 9 of *Tropidurus* now occur. The long-term existence of the Humboldt Current must have been critical in the over-water transport of founder lizards. The *Phyllodactylus* in the Galapagos most likely have been derived from three founder populations from the mainland: San Cristóbal (D) and (L), and Wolf. San Cristóbal (D) and Wolf are not closely related to each other or to any other island geckos. The population on Española may have been founded from the San Cristóbal population; Española in turn provided founders for the Santa Cruz lizards. All remaining gecko populations in the archipelago were at least indirectly derived from the Santa Cruz population. The populations on Santa Fe and Fernandina were established early, and the populations of Floreana, Isabela, Pinta, and Santiago later. The geckos on Marchena were derived from the Santiago population.

The *Tropidurus* of the Galapagos most likely were established from two founder populations, one each to San Cristóbal and Española. San Cristóbal served as the source of founders for the Marchena population. No other island lizards are closely related to this lineage. Española provided founders for the Santa Cruz lizards, which in turn provided founders for the Pinzón and Santiago populations. All remaining island populations may have been established from the Santiago population.

The Galapagos Archipelago is a truly unique laboratory for biological research. Few places have such a large volume of information available on both biotic and physical aspects of the environment. This study of the evolutionary genetics of *Phyllodactylus* and *Tropidurus* utilizes to advantage such information, not only to provide useful new insights into the complex biogeographic history of the islands but also to allow a direct test of the calibrations of the molecular clock, which is of broad topical interest in biology.

ACKNOWLEDGMENTS

This study received financial support from the Janss Foundation; the Museum of Vertebrate Zoology, University of California, Berkeley; the Natural History Museum of Los Angeles County Foundation; and the American Philosophical Society (Penrose Fund 7557). The field work was accomplished by joint logistical cooperation of the Museum of Vertebrate Zoology and the Natural History Museum of Los Angeles County during the second expedition to the Galapagos in January-February, 1974. I sincerely thank Janet S. Dock, Mary Bergen, Dorothy Woods, Helen Chin, Judith Mesa, Philip Myers, and James L. Patton for valuable assistance in the field. Jar Fee Yung, Julie Feder, Margaret F. Smith, Suh Y. Yang, and James L. Patton rendered invaluable assistance in the laboratory phases. The cooperation from the staff of the Charles Darwin Research Station, especially from Peter Kramer, Tjitter De Vries, and the captain, Bernhard Schreyer, and crew of the *Beagle III* is gratefully acknowledged. The field work was made possible by permits granted through the Servicio Forestal and the Parque Nacional Galápagos, Quito, Ecuador. Robert L. Bezy and James L. Patton provided editorial comments. I wish especially to acknowledge the efforts of five individuals, whose contributions to this study were so significant that it could not have been accomplished otherwise: Janet S. Dock, Mary Bergen, and Philip Myers during the field phase of both expeditions, and James L. Patton and Suh Y. Yang in the laboratory phase. Patricia Luisa Serrano translated the abstract into Spanish.

Last but not least, appreciation is extended to the crews of the *R/V Searcher* and the *M/B Toluca*, the former for their assistance during the first attempt at this project and the latter for their rescue efforts in May of 1972, permitting the second, and thankfully successful and uneventful, attempt to complete the field phase of this project.

RESUMEN

Muestras de la población que representan la diversidad geográfica y taxonómica de los lagartos de los géneros *Phyllodactylus* y *Tropidurus* en las Islas Galápagos fueron sometidas a estudios electroforéticos de alozima. Los valores de similitud genético de Rogers llegaron a 0.38 en *Phyllodactylus* y 0.29 en *Tropidurus.* Las agrupaciones UPGMA identificaron dos fenades divergentes en *Tropidurus*, una que contiene sólamente las muestras de San Cristóbal y Marchena. Dentro del fenad mayor, la muestra de Española es la más característica. Las muestras del grupo central de las islas están unidas por valores que tienen un promedio más alto que 0.84. Agrupaciones de los datos de *Phyllodactylus* revelaron cuatro poblaciones divergentes muy fuertes: San Cristóbal (D), Wolf, San Cristóbal (L), y Española. La mayor parte de las muestras del grupo central de las islas se agruparon a niveles que alcanzaron promedios más altos que 0.81.

Los datos de las alozimas se usaron para probar la hipótesis de Van Denburgh sobre la tierra de las Islas Galápagos. Con el objeto de comparar, los valores simulados de Rogers fueron generados y asignados a los estimados de las relaciones de Van Denburgh basadas en sus análisis morfológicos. Hay una concordancia general entre los niveles de divergencias morfológicas y alozimas en las poblaciones de *Phyllodactylus*, pero hay una más pequeña entre aquellos niveles en *Tropidurus*. La hipótesis de Van Denburgh no es suficiente para explicar los patrones de divergencias genéticas encontradas en las poblaciones de los lagartos.

Los datos alozimicas y geológicos generalmente concuerdan. Las islas más viejas del este poseen la población que tiene más divergencias genéticas. La población de las islas más jovenes localizadas más al centro del archipiélago es geneticamente más similar.

Las calibraciones del reloj molecular de Nei y Sarich para los datos electroforéticos fueron aplicados a los grupos de datos de las alozimas. La calibración de Sarich produjo calculos de tiempo que exedieron el tiempo trazado tanto para el archipiélago como para la mayoría de las islas, mientras que la calibración de Nei tiene la tendencia de proveer datos subestimados. Nuevas calibraciones de 8.9 millones de años para *Phyllodactylus* y 10.2 millones de años para *Tropidurus* para una distancia Nei de 1.0 se calcularon usando los datos alozimicas y geológicos de las Islas Galápagos. Usando estas calibraciones, las divergencias en el tiempo fueron calculadas para los grupos nodos en los fenogramas para la similitud genética de Rogers.

Los progenitores de los lagartos de las Islas Galápagos probablemente vinieron de los desiertos del oeste de Sud América a través de la Corriente de Humboldt. Considerando los datos alozimicas y geológicos, es probable que la población de las islas nazca de tres orígenes diferentes del continente para *Phyllodactylus* y dos para *Tropidurus.*

LITERATURE CITED

Avise, J. C. 1974. Systematic value of electrophoretic data. Syst. Zool. 23:465-481.

Bailey, K. 1976. Potassium-argon ages from the Galapagos Islands. Science 192:465-467.

Cox, A. 1983. Ages of the Galapagos Islands. Pages 11-23 *in* Patterns of Evolution in Galapagos Organisms. Pacific Division, Amer. Assoc. Advance. Sci., San Francisco, Calif.

Croizat, L. 1958. Panbiogeography. Published by the author, Caracas.

Dixon, J. R., and R. B. Huey. 1970. Systematics of the lizards of the gekkonid genus *Phyllodactylus* of mainland South America. Contrib. Sci. 192:1-78.

Dixon, J. R., and J. W. Wright. 1975. A review of the lizards of the iguanid genus *Tropidurus* in Peru. Contrib. Sci. 271:1-39.

Gorman, G. C., M. Soule, S. Y. Yang, and E. Nevo. 1975. Evolutionary genetics of insular Adriatic lizards. Evolution 29(1):52-71.

Lanza, B. 1973. On some *Phyllodactylus* from the Galapagos Islands (Reptilia, Gekkonidae). Mus. Zool. Univ. Firenze 1-34.

Lanza, B. 1974. Le Isole Galapagos. Con la Spedizione mares–G.R.S.T.S. all'Arcipelago de Colombo. Parte seconda. L'Universo (Florence) 56(6):817-918.

Mayr, E. 1942. Systematics and the origin of species. Columbia University Press, New York, N. Y.

Nei, M. 1971. Interspecific gene differences and evolutionary time estimated from electrophoretic data on protein identity. Amer. Nat. 105:385-398.

Nei, M. 1972. Genetic distance between populations. Amer. Nat. 106:283-292.

Nei, M. 1975. Molecular population genetics and evolution. American Elsevier Publ. Co., Inc., New York, N. Y.

Nordlie, B. E. 1973. Morphology and structure of the western Galapagos volcanoes and a model for their origin. Bull. Geol. Soc. Amer. 84:2931-2956.

Peters, J. A., and R. Donoso-Barros. 1970. Catalogue of Neotropical Squamata: Part II. Lizards and amphisbaenians. U.S. Nat. Mus. Bull. 297:1-293.

Rogers, J. S. 1972. Measures of genetic similarity and genetic distance. Studies in Genetics VII, Univ. Texas Publ. 7213:145-153.

Rosen, D. E. 1975. A vicariance model of Caribbean biogeography. Syst. Zool. 24(4):431-464.

Sarich, V. M. 1977. Rates, sample sizes, and the neutrality hypothesis for electrophoresis in evolutionary studies. Nature 265:24-28.

Selander, R. K., and W. E. Johnson. 1973. Genetic variation among vertebrate species. Ann. Rev. Ecol. Syst. 4:75-92.

Selander, R. K., M. H. Smith, S. Y. Yang, W. E. Johnson, and J. B. Gentry. 1971. Biochemical polymorphism and systematics in the genus *Peromyscus*. I. Variation in the old-field mouse (*Peromyscus polionotus*). Studies in Genetics VI, Univ. Texas Publ. 7103:49-90.

Swanson, F. J., H. W. Baitio, J. Lexa, and J. Dymond. 1974. Geology of Santiago, Rabida, and Pinzon Island, Galapagos. Bull. Geol. Soc. Amer. 85:1803-1810.

Soule, M., and S. Y. Yang. 1976. Genetic variation in side-blotched lizards on islands in the Gulf of California, Mexico. Evolution 27:593-600.

Van Denburgh, J. 1912a. Expedition of the California Academy of Sciences to the Galapagos

Islands, 1905-1906. IV. The snakes of the Galapagos Islands. Proc. Calif. Acad. Sci. (4)1:323-374.

Van Denburgh, J. 1912b. Expedition of the California Academy of Sciences to the Galapagos Islands, 1905-1906. VI. The geckos of the Galapagos Archipelago. Proc. Calif. Acad. Sci. (4)1: 405-430.

Van Denburgh, J., and J. R. Slevin. 1913. Expedition of the California Academy of Sciences to the Galapagos Islands, 1905-1906. IX. The Galapagoan lizards of the genus *Tropidurus* with notes on the iguanas of the genera *Conolophus* and *Amblyrhynchus*. Proc. Calif. Acad. Sci. (4)2:132-202.

Van Denburgh, J. 1914. Expedition of the California Academy of Sciences to the Galapagos Islands, 1905-1906. X. The gigantic land tortoises of the Galapagos Archipelago. Proc. Calif. Acad. Sci. (4)2:203-374.

Werner, D. I. 1977. On the biology of *Tropidurus delanonis* Baur (Iguanidae). Z. Tierpsychol. 47:337-395.

Wright, J. W. Biogeography of the herpetofauna of the deserts of western South America. In ms.

Wyrtki, K. 1967. Circulation and water masses in the eastern Equatorial Pacific Ocean. Internat'l. J. Oceanol. Limnol. 1:117-147.

Wyrtki, K., E. Stroup, W. Patzert, R. Williams, and W. Quinn. 1976. Predicting and observing El Niño. Science 191(4225):343-346.

AN ECOLOGICAL STUDY OF THE GALAPAGOS MARINE IGUANA

P. DEE BOERSMA
Institute for Environmental Studies, University of Washington, Seattle, WA 98195

The size of adult Galapagos marine iguanas varies from island to island. Iguanas measured on six islands were largest on Isla Isabela and smallest on Isla Genovesa. Marine iguanas from aggregations tend to be faithful to the aggregation where they were marked. Some of the largest aggregations occur at Punta Espinosa, Fernandina, where this study took place. Censuses of Punta Espinosa between 1964 and 1978 show that iguana numbers have been stable. The sex ratio of groups of iguanas varies widely, with female aggregations predominating near tidal reefs. Iguanas forage during low tide, but feeding is more intense at the lowest monthly tides. Males are significantly longer and heavier than females, and forage on submerged reefs. Females forage on exposed reefs, and young forage in crevices on algae unavailable to adults.

Gravid females are eaten by hawks during the breeding season, and a variety of predators eat eggs and young. Synchronous egg laying and hatching may be adaptations to predation. Egg laying follows the lowest tides of the year, when food is most available, occurring first in the western, more productive, waters of the archipelago. Females are aggressive during egg laying when competition for quality nesting sites is intense. Young grow slowly and avoid open areas because of predators.

The marine iguana (*Amblyrhynchus cristatus*) feeds primarily on marine benthic algae, and is confined to the Galapagos Islands where it lives along rocky coasts. Iguanas are abundant and moderately dense; thus, their foraging may affect the structure of the intertidal algae community. Their unique diet and habitat have led to many studies on their thermoregulatory behavior and physiology (MacKay 1964; Bartholomew 1966; Bennett et al. 1975; Bartholomew et al. 1976; Dawson et al. 1977). On land, body temperature is regulated behaviorally by altering posture and orientation to the sun (Bartholomew 1966). Blood flow is controlled by a cardiovascular mechanism that minimizes heat loss in the water and regulates heat gain from solar radiation on land (Bartholomew and Lasiewski 1965; Morgareidge and White 1969; White 1973). Feeding at depths of 12 meters (Hobson 1965), iguanas can stay submerged for over an hour (Darwin 1845). One physiological adaptation to their maritime existence is the presence of salt glands, which allow iguanas to drink salt water and later excrete excess salt through the nostrils (Schmidt-Nielsen and Fange 1958; Dunson 1969). Iguanas go to sea to feed at any time of day (Bartholomew 1966), but do so most actively at low tide (Beebe 1924; Eibl-Eibesfeldt 1960). Carpenter's discussion of the breeding biology (1966) is the only major natural history study that has been conducted on this species. This paper is a quantitative study of the ecology and behavior of the marine iguana population on Isla Fernandina.

METHODS

Marine iguanas were systematically watched from 10 January to 14 March and 24 June to 20 September 1972, with casual observations in previous years and during August 1978, on Isla Fernandina, with additional observations from Islas Santa Cruz, San Cristóbal, Española, Santa Fe,

Genovesa, and Isabela. Males were recognized by brighter coloration, larger femoral pores, longer spines on the nuchal crest, and bulges around the vent. Iguanas were captured and marked with paint, or tagged with Scotch Brand magic mending tape of varied colors attached by monofilament fish line through the nuchal crest. Adults retained both types of markings for over three months, but young had to be repainted weekly because they sloughed their skin so frequently.

In general, all study groups of iguanas were checked for marked individuals at least once daily at Punta Espinosa. All iguanas on the point were counted within an hour of high or low tide. During low tide, foraging males and females were counted on the exposed reefs. From 10 January to 4 March, the study groups were also checked between 0700 hours and 0800 hours. Whenever possible, observations were made on behavior, nesting, growth, and predation.

Adult iguanas were weighed with a hand-held spring scale with 25g graduations, while young were weighed on a scale with 1g graduation. Body dimensions (cm) were taken with a metal measuring tape.

RESULTS

Distribution and Abundance

My observations and those reported by Dowling (1962), Carpenter (1966), and Thornton (1971) indicate that marine iguanas occur along the shores of most islands, islets, and rocky outcroppings of the Galapagos Archipelago. Large groups on Isla Fernandina occur at Punta Espinosa (Carpenter 1966) and also at Cabo Hammond. By contrast, on nearby Isla Isabela large aggregations (10 or more) are relatively uncommon.

Estimates (but no censuses) of the total iguana population of the Galapagos Archipelago have been made. Dowling (1962) estimated hundreds of thousands of iguanas. Tiny Isla Jensen, only 2 hectares in extent in Bahia Academy, Isla Santa Cruz, was estimated to have a population of 1800 to 2000 (Dowling 1962; Carpenter 1966). From walking the coastline and counting individuals on Isla Fernandina, I estimate that between 7,000 and 10,000 iguanas occur within 1600 m of Punta Espinosa, and 1650 iguanas along 400 m of coastline at Cabo Douglas. Although iguanas may be somewhat more concentrated along the shore of Punta Espinosa than elsewhere on the island, by using the lower figure and extrapolating, Fernandina may have approximately 385,000 marine iguanas.

Local residents state that iguanas are rare on Isla San Cristóbal except in remote coastal locations. Carpenter (1966) reports seeing none at Wreck Bay in 1964, where Dowling (1962) found only one in the early 1960s. In August 1978, there were none in the town of Wreck Bay. I found two iguanas 2 km south and two aggregations of 75 iguanas within 3 km of the settlement.

Iguanas are still commonly found around Academy Bay, Isla Santa Cruz. Although marine iguanas were not found at the public boat landing in 1972, over 20 young and 2 adult iguanas were there in 1978, presumably because of national park protection. On both San Cristóbal and Santa Cruz, iguanas are more common away from human habitation.

Published descriptions of marine iguana abundance (Darwin 1845; Beebe 1924; Pinchot 1931; Slevin 1959; Eibl-Eibesfeldt 1960), including photographs of large concentrations (Beebe 1924; Peterson 1967; Cousteau and Diolé 1973), and individual counts of colonies (Carpenter 1966), all indicate that the marine iguana has been abundant over the past 150 years and has occurred in large assemblages at Punta Espinosa since at least 1906.

Carpenter (1966) made two censuses of marine iguanas at Punta Espinosa in January 1964. The average number of basking iguanas he counted at medium tide was 1722. I made six censuses (three counts at high tide and three at low tide) in the same area and determined the mean number of individuals in July 1972 to be 1784. On 20 August 1978, three hours after low tide there were 1210 iguanas, indicating no significant changes in population size from 1964 to 1978 (Tables 1 and 2). Descriptions and censuses of marine iguanas on Isla Jensen, Bahia Academy, and Punta

TABLE 1. NUMBERS OF IGUANAS ON LAND AT PUNTA ESPINOSA DURING HIGH AND LOW TIDES[a]

Location at Pta. Espinosa[b]	HIGH TIDE No. of Censuses	Mean No. of Animals	± SE	LOW TIDE No. of Censuses	Mean No. of Animals	± SE
A	7	432.71	20.88	8	187.12	37.33
B	6	198.17	18.61	4	184.75	23.19
C	8	1094.88	43.83	12	408.42	37.11
D	6	157.50	11.77	8	55.00	7.53
E	4	48.25	5.34	4	41.50	3.28
F	7	75.71	8.57	10	39.80	4.09
G	6	62.83	7.48	7	42.57	4.09
H	6	139.83	5.27	7	76.71	10.65
Total Number of Iguanas:		2209.88			1035.87	

[a] S.E. = standard error.
[b] Locations shown in Fig. 1.

Espinosa also suggest that marine iguana populations have been relatively stable over the last 60 years. On Isla Isabela, however, Slevin (1935) reported a large population at Iguana Cove in 1905-1906. When I visited Iguana Cove in August 1972, fewer than 50 individuals were present.

Iguanas are patchily distributed along the coast, and their concentration varies with water depth, bottom gradient, and algal production. For example, iguanas are abundant at Punta Espinosa, Cabo Hammond, and Cabo Douglas where shallow reefs occur, but are scarce where reefs are rare along cliff edges. Within areas with exposed reefs, aggregations are found near shallow water but not where depth changes abruptly. Furthermore, aggregations persist adjacent to the reef, rarely shifting much more than 30 m along the coast. Carpenter (1966) identified aggregations A and C, both of which still occupied the same locations from 1970 through 1978.

At Punta Espinosa, iguanas are found in aggregations of from 10 to over 1000 individuals, usually within 30 meters of the sea and on a variety of substrates, including sand, lava, and the trunks or branches of mangrove trees. Figure 1 shows the distribution of basking aggregations and tidal reefs around Punta Espinosa. Not all iguanas aggregate: one adult male basked and slept alone in the same lava fissure about 45 m from shore for over three months. During the breeding season, a few new aggregations of fewer than fifty males formed inland between C and D, and females grouped adjacent to the sandy beaches where they nest. The new all-male groups were composed of individuals excluded from the predominantly female aggregations near the tidal reefs.

TABLE 2. NUMBER OF MARINE IGUANAS AT PUNTA ESPINOSA DURING HIGH AND LOW TIDES

Census Date	Total number of marine iguanas, all locations combined: HIGH TIDE	LOW TIDE
4 July 1972		1591
5 July 1972	2372	
6 July 1972	2046	1304
7 July 1972	2035	1358

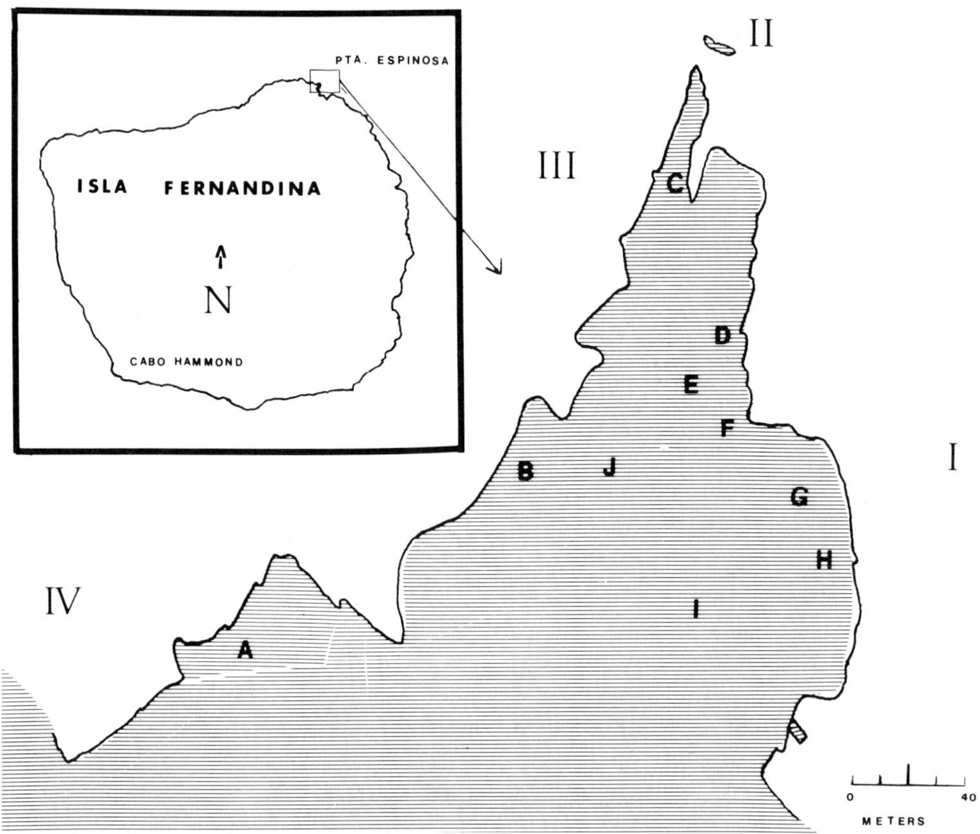

Fig. 1. Map of Punta Espinosa, Isla Fernandina, showing location of basking aggregations and foraging reefs.

Fidelity to an Aggregation

Marine iguanas remain for long periods in the aggregation where they were marked, moving to other aggregations only temporarily (Table 3). Because none of the animals were observed to change aggregations immediately after marking, changing locations does not appear to be a response to handling. Foraging at sites adjacent to the basking aggregation, they generally return to the same location. Iguanas marked at location A foraged at reef IV. Iguanas marked at locations D, E, F, G, and H foraged at reef I. Aggregation B foraged at reef III (Fig. 1). Only once was a marked iguana found foraging in a location not adjacent to its "home" aggregation.

When individuals did move (Table 3), they remained in another aggregation from half a day to over 20 days before returning to the "home" location. Typically they remained only a day or two in an alternate site. These individuals probably stopped over at a different aggregation after an extended foraging trip—an interpretation supported by the fact that most movements occur between aggregations that share a foraging area.

Movement to a new site is most likely to occur when feeding bouts are of longer duration, as occurs during the lowest tides. During the breeding season of 1972 (7 January to 28 February), one male had moved from F to an aggregation 2 km northwest of Punta Espinosa (on 12 February 1972), and another male moved from F to an aggregation 2 km west of Punta Espinosa (on 14 February 1972). Both sightings were within three days after a very low tide. On 13 July 1972, during the lowest tide of the month, one male iguana was seen foraging at location IV; two days before, I had marked it 2 km northwest of Punta Espinosa.

TABLE 3. EXTENT OF TEMPORARY MOVEMENT OF IGUANAS BETWEEN AGGREGATIONS AT PUNTA ESPINOSA

Marking Location	No. of Individuals marked	Observation Period	No. of individuals observed at locations[a] B	C	D	E	F	G	H	I	J
A	15	7/01/72–26/2/72								1	1
A	31	27/06/72–23/9/72	6	4							
F	25	7/01/72–26/2/72		2				1	3	5	1
F	22	27/06/72–23/9/72		6	8	2	4	4	12		
H	17	27/06/72–23/9/72		1	7	4	3	10			

[a] Locations shown in Fig. 1.

Individuals in groups that move more frequently share a foraging site with an adjacent aggregation. Individuals in these aggregations move more frequently than individuals in other groups. Males and females move similarly between aggregations, but move less frequently during the breeding period (7 January to 7 February) when males are territorial (Table 4).

Differences in Sex Composition of Aggregations

The sex ratio varies between aggregations (Table 5), with more females than males in four (A, D, E, and F), but more males than females in four others (B, C, G, and H) of the eight aggregations most thoroughly studied. However, the largest aggregation, C, which could not be readily counted at high tide, had a ratio of six males to one female at low tide (Fig. 2). The sex ratio of aggregations A, B, D, and G changed significantly from one high tide to another and that of D, F, and H from one low tide to another (Table 5). Group composition may vary because of movement between aggregations after foraging or because of differences in foraging frequencies of males and females.

Size and Sexual Dimorphism

The average size of marine iguanas differs dramatically between islands. The largest animals are found on Isla Isabela. Slevin (1935) reported males as long as 1.5m and weighing 9-10kg. One large male that I captured at Bahia Elizabeth, Isla Isabela, greatly exceeded the capacity of the 6kg scale available. Snout-vent length of this individual was .56m and the total length was 1.17m, which is almost twice the mean size of adult males on Isla Santa Cruz. Smaller iguanas are found on the more northerly islands. Adult iguanas on Genovesa are smaller (S-V = 20.4cm, σ = 2.3 [N = 22]; wt = 0.47kg, σ =.1 [N = 22]) than adult iguanas on Fernandina, Isabela, Santa Cruz, San Cristóbal, or Española.

The mean measurements of six adult males on San Cristóbal were S-V = 44.0cm, σ = 2.0; wt = 4.8kg, σ = 1.1. The mean length of 58 male (34.35cm) and 64 female (20.45 cm) iguanas, and the mean weight of 24 male (2.26kg) and 26 female (1.37kg) iguanas at Punta Espinosa are similar to Carpenter's (1966) values. Female iguanas at Punta Espinosa are larger than females at Bahia Academy, Isla Santa Cruz (t = 5.06, P<.001). Weights and measurements indicate that males are longer and heavier than females (t = 8.82 and 7.47 respectively and P<.001 [see Fig. 3]).

Male and Female Foraging Patterns

Foraging groups on exposed reefs at low tide have more females proportionately than the nearest basking aggregation in 58% of the comparisons (Table 6). Basking aggregation A did not

TABLE 4. COMPARISON OF TEMPORARY MOVEMENTS OF MARINE IGUANAS AT PUNTA ESPINOSA BY SEX, SEASON, AND AGGREGATION

Marking Locations (No. Marked)	Males	Females	Total No. of moves	Total No. moved	Observation Period (1972)	Degrees of Freedom	Chi Square Comparison[a]	Chi Square
D and F (13)	3	5	0	8	7 Jan.-12 Feb.	1	A	.7
	3	2	2 or more	5				
D and F (39)	8	3	0 - 2	11	30 June-23 Sept.	3	A	1.8
	3	3	3	6				
	7	3	4	10				
	6	6	5 or more	12				
A (31)	5	16	0	21	10 July-23 Sept.	1	A	0
	2	8	1 or more	10				
D and F (52)	Sex not Determined		0	8	7 Jan.-7 Feb.	1	B	22.0[b]
			1 - 10	5				
			0	1	1 July-31 July			
			1 - 10	38				
A (46)			0	14	11 Feb.-28 Feb.	1	B	.8
			1 or more	1				
			0	26	11 July-28 July			
			1 or more	5				
F (28)			0	8	7 Jan.-7 Feb.	1	C	4.1[b]
			1 or more	5				
			0	14	11 Feb.-28 Feb.			
			1 or more	1				
F (70)			0	1	30 June-23 Sept.	3	C	40.8[c]
			1 - 10	38				
A			0	21	30 June-23 Sept.			
			1 - 10	10				

[a] Null hypotheses being tested: A. Movements between aggregations are independent of the sex of the migrant. B. Movements between sites are not influenced by season. C. Different sites have similar patterns of migration.

[b] Significant at .05 probability level.

[c] Significant at .005 probability level.

Fig. 2. The large aggregation of marine iguanas at Punta Espinosa, Isla Fernandina at Location C during low tide in July, 1972.

TABLE 5. DEVIATION FROM 50/50: SEX RATIO OF MARINE IGUANAS AT BASKING AND FORAGING SITES DURING HIGH AND LOW TIDES, PUNTA ESPINOSA[a]

	HIGH TIDE			LOW TIDE				LOW TIDE		
Basking location[a]	No. of censuses	Mean sex ratio[b]	χ^2 values	No. of censuses	Mean sex ratio	χ^2 values	Foraging location	No. of censuses	Mean sex ratio	χ^2 values
A	6	.32	35.9[d]	5	.23	1.7	I	6	.52	11.2[c]
B	5	3.00	21.7[d]	2	16.6	1.1	III	2	4.58	26.5[d]
C				1	6.6		IV	6	.25	20.5[d]
D	9	.85	89.4[d]	6	.68	44.8[d]				
E	4	.07	1.6	3	.09	4.5				
F	6	.26	8.2	6	.17	12.7[c]				
G	6	1.67	21.3[d]	6	3.21	6.3				
H	6	5.17	4.6	5	7.7	15.7[d]				

[a] Locations shown in Fig. 1.
[b] Males/females.
[c] Null hypothesis rejected at .05 probability level.
[d] Null hypothesis rejected at .005 probability level.

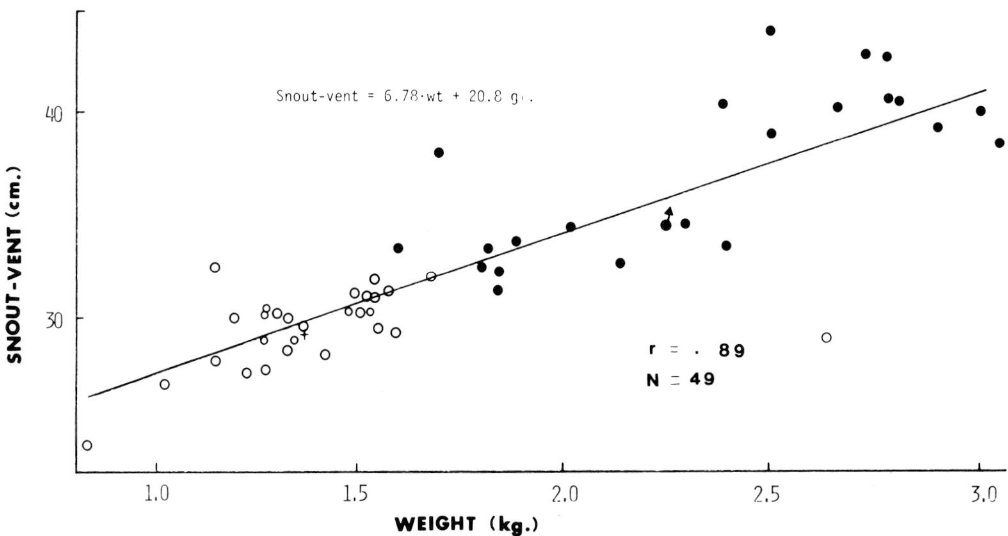

Fig. 3. Weight/length relationship of male (●) and female (○) marine iguanas at Punta Espinosa, Isla Fernandina. Mean body size for females and males is indicated by sex symbols.

have a significantly higher male/female ratio than the group of iguanas foraging at the nearby reef (IV) in five of the six censuses made. Foraging area IV is isolated from aggregations other than A, explaining why the foraging and basking composition is similar. However, on a very low tide (1.0 feet) on 14 July 1972, the sex ratio of even this foraging group (IV) had more females than the basking aggregation at location A on 9 July. Individuals from basking aggregations 2 km away by water and approximately 3 km by land came to foraging area IV during this extremely low tide. If these movements are by swimming and not walking, they would appear to require substantial swimming ability—contrary to the Dawson et al. (1977) interpretation. In all cases, when the sex ratios of the basking and foraging areas were dissimilar, this was due to the presence of more females on the exposed reef.

Because females are more likely to forage on reefs exposed at low tide, predominantly female aggregations should be found near tidal reefs and predominantly male aggregations near submerged reefs. Ranking of the basking aggregations according to their proximity to deep water is as follows (those closest given first): C, B, H, G, A, D, F, E. The first four colonies are composed of more males than females, and the last four, more females than males. These data are consistent with the hypothesis that females are found nearer exposed tidal reefs on which they forage, and males are found closer to deeper water where they forage on submerged reefs.

Foraging Tides and Lunar Rhythms

Previous authors have not agreed on the foraging cycle of the iguanas. Beebe (1924) suggests that they feed exclusively on algae-covered rocks exposed at low tide. Bartholomew (1966) thought feeding was more intense at low tide than at high tide, but that iguanas feed at any stage of the tide. He further suggested that feeding was minimal in the late afternoon irrespective of the tidal stage because the amount of solar radiation was important in determining the time of foraging. After many hours of observing marine iguanas, I realized that individual iguanas do not forage every day. During periods when they are fasting or digesting, they move inland to crevices, trees, or some other place out of the direct rays of the sun. When tidal fluctuations were minimal —the middle of the lunar cycle—iguanas formed an aggregation inland at E, and the basking aggregation at location A also moved away from the sea into crevices.

TABLE 6. COMPARISON OF SEX RATIOS IN AGGREGATIONS OF BASKING IGUANAS WITH THOSE AMONG FORAGING GROUPS AT NEAREST FEEDING AREAS AT PUNTA ESPINOSA

Location of census	Date of census	Males	Females	Sex Ratio[a]	Chi Square Values
A	3 July	80	376	.21	2.9
IV	2 July	60	204	.29	
A	4 July	149	396	.38	3.0
IV	4 July	38	144	.26	
A	6 July	87	322	.27	0
IV	6 July	55	206	.27	
A	7 July	84	314	.27	1.3
IV	7 July	63	189	.33	
A	9 July	90	315	.28	.4
IV	10 July	66	263	.25	
A	9 July	90	315	.28	14.7[b]
IV	14 July	37	288	.13	
G, H	3 July	175	41	4.27	33.3[b]
I	2 July	14	24	.58	
G, H	4 July	102	23	4.43	56.9[b]
I	4 July	13	43	.30	
G, H	6 July	158	56	2.82	59.0[b]
I	6 July	32	77	.42	
G, H	7 July	157	57	2.75	58.3[b]
I	7 July	33	79	.42	
G, H	9 July	159	51	3.12	41.6[b]
I	14 July	72	95	.76	
G, H	6 July	497	75	6.63	81.1[b]
III	6 July	257	156	1.76	

[a] Males/females.
[b] Significant at .005 probability level.

The number of basking iguanas occurring around Punta Espinosa at high and low tides in February, June, July, August, and September of 1972 was noted. The effect of tides on the foraging behavior of marine iguanas was determined using a two-way analysis of variance (Table 7). There is no significant difference in foraging activity according to the times of the high or low tides. The time of tidal occurrence during the day (i.e. low tide in the morning compared to low tide at noon) is not significantly correlated with the amount of foraging activity, thereby suggesting that foraging is not regulated by solar radiation. The number of individual iguanas in basking groups is significantly different at high and low tides ($P < .001$). Thus, the state of the tide, not solar radiation, is the most important factor determining foraging activity.

Additional evidence suggesting that foraging occurs primarily during low tides comes from

TABLE 7. TWO-WAY ANALYSIS OF VARIANCE OF THE NUMBER OF MARKED IGUANAS PRESENT AT HIGH AND LOW TIDES IN THE MORNING AND AFTERNOON AT PUNTA ESPINOSA, ISLA FERNANDINA
(DF = Degrees of Freedom; SS = Sums of Squares, and MS = Mean Squares)[a]

HIGH TIDE/LOW TIDE/AM/PM	DF	SS	MS	F VALUE
Subgroups	3	2219.42	739.81	
B [Row (Time a.m., p.m.)]	1	20.09	20.09	.17
A [Columns (Tides high, low)]	1	2127.39	2127.39	17.71[b]
A X B (interactions)	1	71.94	71.94	.60
Within subgroups (error)	46	5526.34	120.14	
Total	49			

[a] Method of analysis according to Sokal and Rohlf (1969).
[b] Significant at .001 probability level.

data collected during the breeding and rainy season of January and February 1972. A one-way analysis of variance (Table 8) shows fewer marine iguanas basking at low tide than at high tide. Breeding activities do not appear to modify the pattern of foraging at low tide.

A further test of the effects of tides on foraging can be made by determining the number of basking iguanas present throughout the tide cycle. The number of marked iguanas counted on a given day was expressed as a percentage of the total number of marked individuals. The maximum height of the tide for each day of the count was ranked from lowest high tide to highest high tide. The correlation coefficient (Sokal and Rohlf 1969) between percentage of basking, marked iguanas present at high tide and high tide height was -.40 ($P<.05$), indicating that the largest numbers of marine iguanas were basking on days with the highest tides. Thus, marine iguanas are least likely to forage on days when the tidal height is greatest. Next, the percentage of basking, marked iguanas at low tide was ranked from lowest to highest, and the low tidal height was ranked from lowest to highest. The correlation between percentage of marine iguanas and low tide height was .7 ($P< .001$). Marked marine iguanas bask less on days of the lowest tide, and therefore probably forage more. Observations support this view: iguanas were often wet in basking aggregations on those days with the lowest tides, suggesting that they had recently returned from foraging.

TABLE 8. ONE-WAY ANALYSIS OF VARIANCE OF THE NUMBER OF MARKED IGUANAS PRESENT AT HIGH AND LOW TIDE IN JANUARY AND FEBRUARY 1972 AT PUNTA ESPINOSA, ISLA FERNANDINA
(DF = Degrees of Freedom, SS = Sums of Squares)[a]

HIGH TIDE/LOW TIDE	DF	SS	F VALUE
Groups	1	1065.36	11.75[b]
Error	38	3446.20	
Total	39	4511.56	

[a] Method of analysis according to Sokal and Rohlf (1969).
[b] Significant at .001 probability level.

Breeding Season

The breeding season of marine iguanas on Isla Fernandina commences in December, when males begin to defend territories, and extends until March. From the limited data available, it appears that egg laying may commence as much as a month earlier (Carpenter 1966). On Isla Fernandina in 1972, egg laying continued for more than a month, but was highly synchronous at individual sites. Eggs were probably laid first at Cabo Hammond and Punta Espinosa, followed by Cabo Douglas. Figure 4 depicts the synchrony of egg laying at two sand beaches at Punta Espinosa, Isla Fernandina. The majority of females laid eggs within a six-day period.

Growth of Young and Adults

Young iguanas are found among the adults in most basking aggregations. Unlike adults, they spend a great amount of time in cracks and crevices. Even when they bask, they are never far from a hiding place such as a crevice or a rock pile, and they forage only at low tide. In addition, they are faithful to the aggregation where first marked. For at least three months, 45 marked young never moved to another aggregation. At low tide, young follow the fissures or crevices in the lava from the basking aggregation down to the water level where they forage in hidden recesses on algae that adults cannot reach because of their larger head size. Young do forage in the open but rarely far from a hiding place. Only rarely do they enter the water, and then only to cross narrow stretches to reach a foraging site.

The first young hatch in May. In July 1972 I marked 24 young with snout-vent lengths from 10.5 cm to 16.9 cm ($\bar{x}$ = 12.4 cm). Recapture was attempted weekly, but was not entirely

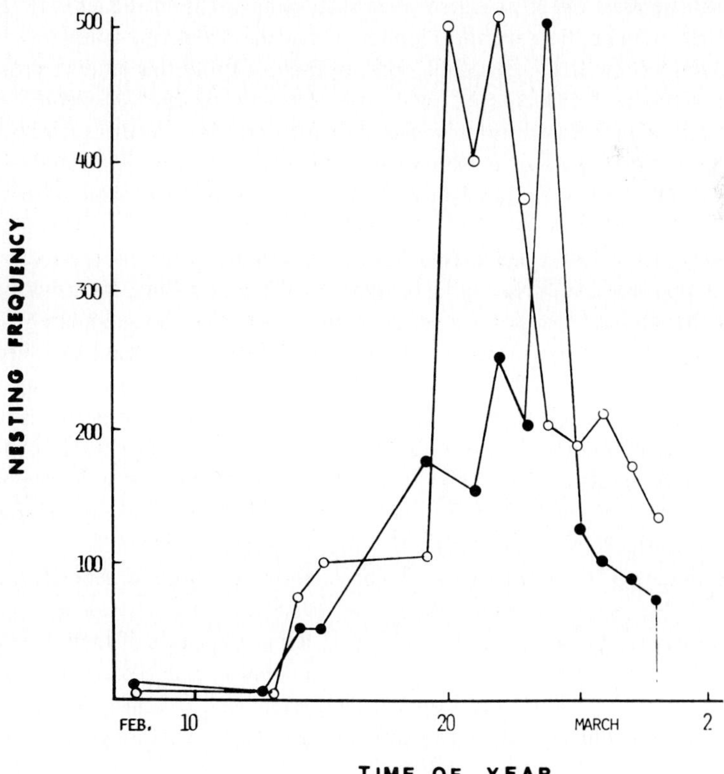

Fig. 4. Frequency of occurrence of female marine iguanas on or adjacent to two egg-laying beaches on Punta Espinosa, Isla Fernandina, 8-28 February, 1972.

successful. The average weight gain of the 24 hatchlings (recapture = 58) was .5 grams per day (S. E. ± .1) over a three-week period.

Relative growth rates, measured as a percentage of increase per day, were calculated using the formula derived by Brody (1945), and used by Ricklefs and Cullen (1973) to compare the growth of young green iguanas (*Iguana iguana*), which are herbivorous (Rand, pers. comm.), with the growth of the young herbivorous marine iguanas. The average postnatal growth rate of the green iguana is 1.05%/day, decreasing to .012% during their third year (Ricklefs and Cullen 1973). Galapagos marine iguanas, at least for the first two months, grow at a still lower rate (.004%/day; N = 24). This is probably a result of food scarcity, as evidenced by young foraging on rocks that appeared bare from 1 m away. No *ulva*, a primary food for adults, is found in most of the crevices where young forage. Adults also gnaw on rocks with little algae. One adult iguana showed a mean loss of 25.6 gm in 14 days, yet another iguana lost 300 gm within 7 days. The fluctuating weights of adults are in part due to irregular foraging and not to food availability.

Mortality

Potential predators of marine iguanas on Isla Fernandina include hawks, owls, snakes, mockingbirds, sally lightfoot crabs, gulls, frigates, herons, sharks, and native rats. On other islands introduced cats, rats, pigs, dogs, and humans prey upon iguanas (Beebe 1924; Blomburg 1951; Dowling 1962; Hatch 1965; Carpenter 1966; Hobson 1969; Thornton 1971). The abundance of marine iguanas and the comparatively few observations of predation upon them have led some authors to conclude that marine iguanas have no significant predators (Carpenter 1966; Bartholomew 1966). The Galapagos Hawk (*Buteo galapagoensis*) has been reported to feed on marine iguanas, although deVries (1973) suggests that such behavior is infrequent. It is not surprising that the influence of predation on the number of iguanas would be underestimated, since few scientists have resided on Isla Fernandina for very long. During this study I observed predation on adults and young by the Galapagos Hawk, Lava Heron (*Butorides sandevalli*), Striated Heron (*Butorides striatus*), Great Blue Heron (*Ardea herodias*), and Frigate Birds (*Fregata minor* and *F. magnificens*). Short-eared Owls (*Asio flammeus*) probably eat young, while crabs, rats, and mockingbirds eat eggs. Of these predators, only the Galapagos hawk is capable of capturing an adult iguana.

In February 1972, three Galapagos hawks (two adults and one juvenile) frequented the beach at Punta Espinosa and preyed on adult iguanas. When attacking, the hawk typically grasped the iguana by the neck and back. A struggle ensued, and after approximately 20 minutes the marine iguana expired. The hawk pressed the iguana against the hot sand so it could not raise its body to keep cool as it usually does. Death appeared to be caused by overheating, as there was no external sign of bleeding or evidence of injury. The hawk panted during the capture, suggesting that it and possibly the marine iguana were heat stressed (Fig. 5). The hawk rolled the iguana on its back, opened the throat area, drew out the viscera, and ate them. The muscles were sometimes eaten, but the carcass was generally left intact. All three hawks observed in February 1972 shared their kills. Not all attacks were successful. On one occasion, an iguana was able to turn its head enough to bite the leg of the hawk holding its back, and after about 30 seconds the hawk released the iguana.

During the breeding season, hawks prey upon females because of their exposed situation on the sand beaches from where they can neither scramble away nor hold onto rocks. Nonetheless, even on a sandy substrate, when caught the iguana does manage to crawl around, thrashing its tail. On a rock substrate, an adult iguana is probably strong enough to escape by crawling into a crevice and dislodging the hawk. Normally, basking iguanas do not pay attention to hawks, but nest-constructing females on the beach are skittish. As far as I could ascertain, only gravid females were preyed upon by the hawks. On the average, one adult female iguana, captured on the beach

Fig. 5. A Galapagos hawk with its booty, a pregnant marine iguana on a nesting beach. The hawk is panting.

during egg laying, was eaten every two days by the three hawks. Thus, approximately 3% of the laying females were eaten by hawks. Predation on adult iguanas is highest during the egg-laying season. I never saw an adult eaten outside the breeding season.

Sharks and other fish may on occasion prey on iguanas, as evidenced by missing tails (Heller 1903), but the importance of shark predation may be overestimated (Hobson 1969). Unlike some lizards, marine iguanas never "drop" their tails, but the tips are often missing, suggesting that tails or parts thereof, when lost, are not regenerated. I have seen land iguanas (*Conolophus subcristatus*), which under normal circumstances could not be attacked by a shark, missing part of their tails; tails of marine iguanas, therefore, may also be lost for reasons other than shark attack. The lack of tail regeneration in land and marine iguanas is consistent with the Vitt et al. (1977) findings that lizards that are long-lived and late-maturing with restricted breeding seasons regenerate tails at low rates.

The leathery eggs of marine iguanas are destroyed by a variety of predators. Carpenter (1966) noted one nest with eggs infested with maggots. I found flies around every nesting burrow during the day. I do not know the percentage of iguana eggs lost to flies, but several nests had fly eggs. Unattended and exposed eggs may fall prey to mockingbirds (Hatch 1965). An incidental cause of death is the collapse of nesting burrows. Three females were found dead in nesting burrows that had collapsed either naturally or forcibly by the weight of sea lions.

Some females did dig burrows at night. Short-eared owls and barn owls (*Tyto alba*) may take hatching young and females that are digging nests. Native rice rats (*Oryzomys*) that frequent the nesting beaches at night prey upon eggs and young.

DISCUSSION

Sexual Dimorphism

Male iguanas prefer to feed on submerged algae or at a greater distance from the shore, whereas females generally forage intertidally on exposed algae-covered reefs. Because of their larger size, males have slower rates of cooling in the water, greater forward thrust from their long tails, larger lung capacity (Bartholomew et al. 1976), and greater strength. Despite their greater strength, even large iguanas have some difficulty swimming through the surf (Dawson et al. 1977). All of these are important adaptations, reducing the cost of submerged foraging for large individuals. One of the consequences of size dimorphism is separation of foraging niches by the sexes, which may reduce intraspecific competition for food (Selander 1966; Schoener 1967, 1974; Hogstad 1976). Foraging at low tide is beneficial to both males and females because the expenditure of energy in reaching the feeding site and in diving for food is minimized. Foraging adaptations include both the synchrony of foraging with low tide and partitioning of feeding areas.

Competition and Food Resources

Interactions with other species may be an important determinant of body size. Sea urchins are known to be major cropping agents (Paine and Vadas 1969), and other invertebrate grazers (Nicotri 1977) can also alter the resource base in intertidal communities. Competition with grazers may not only affect iguana size, but also their abundance. On Isla Fernandina, crabs (*Grapsus grapsus*) forage predominantly at low tide on the exposed reefs, eating at least some of the same algae as the iguanas. Because larger body size facilitates diving in marine iguanas (Bartholomew 1966; Morgareidge and White 1969), grazing pressure may have favored larger body size on Isla Fernandina than on Santa Cruz. Large size may allow access to resources not exploited by crabs, but it also places greater demand on the resources. Conflict between these adaptive problems has not been resolved, nor is it known whether body size is genetically or ecologically controlled.

The location of the food resource may also act as a determinant of body size. There are no submerged reefs around Darwin Bay, Isla Genovesa, and iguanas are small. Where there are submerged reefs and heavy surf around Isabela, at Tortuga Bay, Santa Cruz and south of Wreck Bay, San Cristóbal, iguanas are large. Selection may favor small size where there are no offshore reefs and large size when reefs are submerged at low tide.

Breeding Cycles

Most terrestrial vertebrates in the Galapagos breed irregularly and frequently, but marine iguanas breed once a year in February and March. Penguins, cormorants, and pelicans on Isla Fernandina have flexible and frequent breeding schedules (Boersma 1976, 1978). Galapagos hawks (de Vries 1973), Galapagos finches (Downhower 1976), and undoubtedly other species also have flexible and irregular breeding patterns.

The subsurface east-flowing Cromwell Current, which upwells along the western side of the Galapagos platform, is one of the principal means of transport of cold, nutrient-rich waters to the Galapagos (Maxwell 1974; Pak and Zaneveld 1973). Surface water temperature fluctuates irregularly as upwell from the Cromwell Current intensifies or diminishes (Boersma 1976). Breeding in some species follows an increase in food supply associated with lower surface water temperatures (Boersma 1978). The rigid breeding cycle of the marine iguana suggests that breeding is not adapted to current fluctuations. Fluctuations in upwelling have no effect on whether algae are exposed at low tide and are therefore available. Either changes in ocean nutrients must be insignificant in altering the availability of algae, or other events are more important for breeding success.

Carpenter (1966) suggests that the annual breeding cycle of the marine iguana may be adapted to avoid the cool and dry garua season, because the eggs may become too cold or dry to hatch. (During the garua season, generally June to October, light mist and rain frequently occur inland, but little precipitation occurs in coastal areas, and rainfall is noticeably absent on Isla Fernandina, which is in a rain shadow.) A flexible, not a rigid, breeding schedule would be expected if iguanas are avoiding the garua season, because seasons vary greatly from year to year (Boersma 1974). Furthermore, egg laying should be more extended on Isla Fernandina, which is in a rain shadow, than on Isla Española or the eastern islands. In 1964, egg laying was in February on Isla Fernandina and probably in April on Isla Española (Carpenter 1966), the opposite of what would be expected.

During breeding, males defend territories and females produce eggs, requiring additional energy. Each female lays two to three eggs (N = 7), which weigh 87 gm (N = 2). One female's eggs were 18% of her body weight.

If food resources are periodically scarce, breeding should take place when food resources are most available to females for egg production. Food should be most available at the least cost to the individual when the tidal water is at its lowest ebb because more algae will be exposed for a longer period of time. The lowest spring tides are in January (Baker 1964). Thus, food availability should be the greatest during the early part of the year. A breeding cycle coordinated with the lowest tides of the year would have the fixed regularity characteristic of the marine iguana breeding cycle.

If the onset of the breeding cycle is adapted to the period of lowest tides of the year, then why should there be variation in the timing of breeding within the archipelago? The littoral zone of the more nutrient-rich waters of the western islands should have more algal growth than the littoral zones in the relatively nutrient-poor eastern region of the archipelago. The largest and densest aggregations of iguanas are founds on islands in the nutrient-rich western archipelago. Disparities in productivity may also account for the differences in timing of the breeding season. Where algal production is lower, animals may need to forage longer at the lowest tides of the year to gain sufficient resources to lay eggs. If ocean productivity is influencing the timing of egg laying, nesting should occur first around Isla Fernandina and slightly later in the less productive eastern region of the archipelago—which it does.

Hatching occurs after the period of maximum food availability, unlike hatching in many species. Because of predators, young normally remain near the basking aggregations and do not forage on nearby reefs. An increase in reef exposure, while irrelevant to food resources or survival of the young, provides additional algae at a lower energetic cost for adults.

Predation

Predation has probably been the causal force for local synchrony in nesting and hatching. Although an increase in the availability of food may be a major selective pressure determining the timing of breeding, food availability does not explain synchrony in egg laying at a nesting area. Synchrony is known to reduce predation (Tinbergen 1953; Morton 1971). If predators are preying heavily on young or adults, selection should favor synchronous breeding because predators would be less effective in capturing large numbers of prey during the limited time when they are vulnerable (Lloyd and Dybas 1966). Hatching synchrony, group foraging, and activity coordination among hatching green iguanas are probably adaptations to reduce predation (Burghardt et al. 1977). Synchrony of breeding and hatching likewise minimizes predation on marine iguanas. Female iguanas saturate the sandy beaches during nesting; individual females are thus less vulnerable to hawk predation. Similarly, the young, which are heavily preyed upon by hawks and other birds, hatch synchronously.

Predation pressure probably also affects the quality of nesting sites. Sandy beaches located near exposed lava flows appear to offer the best egg-laying sites because the time required for females to arrive and depart from the nest site, when they are vulnerable to hawk attack, will be minimized.

The quality of the nesting beaches depends not only upon the predation risk for the female, but for the young as well. Because young iguanas have a variety of predators, the "best" nesting sites should be those closest to the protective cover of lava crevices and reefs where young can forage by following the irregularities and crevices in the lava flow. The young's survival and growth depend on the amount of algae that is available near these protected feeding sites until the young become too large for most predators.

Availability of nesting sites may be a limiting factor on some islands, as evidenced by disputes over nesting sites, which are common on Española but rare on Fernandina and Santa Cruz (Eibl-Eibesfelt 1961, 1962, 1966a, 1966b). Digging sites are not limited, but because the quality of nesting sites varies greatly, sites where adults and young have higher survival rates must be limited. Females should be aggressive and territorial on all islands if the survival of young is closely correlated to the quality of the nesting site. Contrary to Eibl-Eibesfeldt's observation, females regularly fight over burrows on Fernandina (Figs. 6, 7).

Burrow digging takes several hours, and females frequently leave and return to dig later in the day, thus making it possible for another iguana to steal the burrow. Rand and Rand (1976) describe aggressive encounters of green iguanas similar to those of marine iguanas over nesting burrows. They conclude that energy costs are minimized by aggressive displays for nesting female green iguanas. Because of the behavioral similarity of these species, marine iguanas are probably also minimizing the cost of digging a burrow. Grappling over nest burrows may also be advantageous because a female may displace another female from a nearly completed burrow, reducing the time the winner will be exposed to predators. Fighting over burrows and the adjacent sand may

Fig. 6. Two female iguanas grappling over a nesting burrow on a beach at Punta Espinosa, Isla Fernandina, March, 1972.

Fig. 7. One of the two major nesting beaches at Punta Espinosa, Isla Fernandina. Females are more or less evenly spaced out and the depressions indicate nesting sites. Many of the females are digging burrows or investigating burrows. March, 1972.

have a secondary consequence of increasing the distance between nesting burrows and thereby reducing accidental uncovering of eggs.

In conclusion, body size is extremely variable between sites. Whether size is determined ecologically or genetically by resource competition with invertebrates, enhanced diving effectiveness, or location and quality of the food resource is unknown. All could contribute. Marine iguanas are abundant, and their numbers appear numerically stable through time. The ecological pressures responsible for population size are unknown, but predation on females and young seems to be of paramount importance. Because few young are recruited into the population each year, any increase in the death rate of the adults will reduce population size rather quickly. Conservation management must, therefore, concentrate on maintaining high adult female survival. Measures designed to increase hatching success or juvenile survival will be largely useless or cost-prohibitive because of predation pressure. Thus, conservation programs and policies that enhance female survival will be the most useful in maintaining and preserving the population.

ACKNOWLEDGMENTS

I am grateful to Sally Cloninger, who filmed the research and helped in the field. Paul Colinvaux, principal investigator of the grant GB-29065X, which funded this study, has given generously of his ideas, while acting as a mentor, friend, and colleague. I thank Mary Nerini and Jerry Downhower for helpful discussion. S. Cloninger, P. Colinvaux, J. Downhower, R. Huey, M. Nerini, G. Orians, and R. T. Paine read the drafts of the manuscript and made valuable suggestions for its improvement. Barbara C. Peterson typed the manuscript. I am grateful to the many people in the Galapagos who were helpful in the field. The crews of the *Liña A* and the *Golden Cachalot* and the staff of the Charles Darwin Research Station made our stay comfortable. Chris Kjolhede and Nancy Jo provided field assistance during parts of this study. This paper is Contribution No. 204 of the Charles Darwin Foundation.

RESUMEN

Estudio ecológico de la iguana marina de las Islas Galápagos (*Amblyrhynchus cristatus*) fue realizada en Punta Espinosa, Isla Fernandina, donde se encuentran en grandes agregaciones durante todo el año. Los machos son significativamente más largos y pesados que las hembras. La proporción de sexos en poblaciones coloniales es bien variable, con las agregaciones de hembras predominantemente cerca de los arrecifes de la zona de marea. Los machos buscan alimento en los arrecifes sumergidos, las hembras en los arrecifes expuestos, y los jóvenes en grietas, alimentándose de algas inaccesibles para los adultos. Todos se alimentan predominantemente durante la bajamar. La búsqueda de alimento es mas intensa durante las mareas más bajas de cada mes. Las iguanas se desplazan entre agregaciones pero tienden a retornar al lugar donde fueron marcadas. La depredación sobre los jóvenes, hembras preñadas y huevos juega un papel importante en la regulación de la población y determina una sincronización en la puesta y eclosión de los huevos. La oviposición sigue a las mareas más bajas del año, cuando hay mayor cantidad de alimento, occurriendo primero en las aguas del oeste, las más productivas del Archipiélago. Las hembras son agresivas durante la puesta de huevos, momento de intensa competencia por los mejores sitios para anidar. Los jóvenes crecen lentamente y eluden las areas abiertas a cause de los depredadores.

LITERATURE CITED

Baker, R. H. 1964. Astronomy. D. van Nostrand and Co., Inc., Princeton, N. J. 528 pp.

Bartholomew, G. A. 1966. A field study of temperature relations in the Galápagos marine iguana. Copeia 2:241-250.

Bartholomew, G. A., and R. C. Lasiewski. 1965. Heating and cooling rates, heart rate and simulated diving in the Galapagos marine iguana. Comp. Biochem. Physiol. 16:573-582.

Bartholomew, G. A., A. F. Bennett, and W. R. Dawson. 1976. Swimming, diving and lactate production of the marine iguana, *Amblyrhynchus cristatus*. Copeia 4:709-720.

Beebe, W. 1924. Galapagos, world's end. G. P. Putnam's Sons, New York, N. Y. 443 pp.

Bennett, A. F., W. R. Dawson, and G. A. Bartholomew. 1975. Effects of activity and temperature on aerobic and anaerobic metabolism in the Galapagos marine iguana. J. Comp. Physiol. 100: 317-329.

Blomburg, R. 1951. Strange reptile of the Galapagos. Nat. Hist. 60:234-239.

Boersma, P. D. 1974. The Galapagos penguin: Adaptation to life in an unpredictable environment. Ph.D. Thesis. Ohio State University, Columbus, Oh. 222 pp.

Boersma, P. D. 1976. An ecological and behavioral study of the Galapagos penguin. Living Bird 15:43-93.

Boersma, P. D. 1978. Galápagos penguins as indicators of oceanographic conditions. Science 200:1481-1483.

Brody, S. 1945. Bioenergetics and growth. Reinhold, New York, N. Y. 1023 pp.

Burghardt, G. M., H. W. Greene, and A. S. Rand. 1977. Social behavior in hatching green iguanas: Life at a reptile rookery. Science 195:689-691.

Carpenter, C. C. 1966. The marine iguana of the Galápagos Islands, its behavior and ecology. Proc. Calif. Acad. Sci., Ser. 4, 34:329-376.

Cousteau, J., and P. Diolé. 1973. Three adventures, Galápagos–Titicaca–The blue holes. Doubleday and Co., Inc. New York, N. Y. 304 pp.

Darwin, C. 1845. Journal of researches into the natural history and geology of the countries visited during the voyage of H.M.S. Beagle round the world, under the Command of Capt. Fitz Roy,

R. N., 2nd rev. ed. John Murray, London. 520 pp.

Dawson, W. R., G. A. Bartholomew, and F. F. Bennett. 1977. A reappraisal of the aquatic specializations of the Galapagos marine iguana (*Amblyrhynchus cristatus*). Evolution 31:891-897.

de Vries, T. 1973. The Galapagos hawk: An eco-geographical study with special reference to its systematic position. Ph.D. Thesis. Vrije Universiteit te Amsterdam, Amsterdam. 108 pp.

Dowling, H. G. 1962. Sea dragons of the Galápagos: The marine iguanas. Animal Kingdom 65: 169-174.

Downhower, J. F. 1976. Darwin's Finches and the evolution of sexual dimorphism in body size. Nature 263:558-563.

Dunson, W. 1969. Electrolyte excretion by the salt gland of the Galápagos marine iguana. Amer. J. Physiol. 216:995-1002.

Eibl-Eibesfeldt, I. 1960. Galapagos. MacGibbon and Kee, London. 192 pp.

Eibl-Eibesfelt, I. 1961. The fighting behavior of animals. Sci. Amer. 205:112-121.

Eibl-Eibesfelt, I. 1962. Neue unterarten der Meerechse *Amblyrhynchus cristatus*, nebst weiteren Angaben zur Biologie besonderer Art. Senckenberg. biol. 43:177-199.

Eibl-Eibesfeldt, I. 1966a. Marine iguanas. Animals 9:150-153.

Eibl-Eibesfeldt, I. 1966b. Das verteideben den Einablageplatze Bei Der Hood-Meereschse (*Amblyrhynchus cristatus venustissimus*). Tierpsychol. 23:49-62.

Hatch, J. 1965. Only one species of Galapagos mockingbird feeds on eggs. Condor 67:354-355.

Heller, E. 1903. Papers from the Hopkins Stanford Galápagos Expedition, 1898-1899. XIV. Reptiles. Proc. Wash. Acad. Sci. 5:39-98.

Hobson, E. S. 1965. Observations on diving in the Galapagos marine iguana, *Amblyrhynchus cristatus* (Bell). Copeia 2:249-250.

Hobson, E. S. 1969. Remarks on aquatic habits of the Galapagos marine iguana, including submergence times, cleaning symbiosis, and the shark threat. Copeia 2:401-402.

Hogstad, O. 1976. Sexual dimorphism and divergence in winter foraging behavior of three-toed woodpeckers *Picoides tridactylus*. Ibis 118:41-49.

Lloyd, M., and H. S. Dybas. 1966. The periodical Cicada problem. 1. Population ecology. Evolution 20:134-149.

MacKay, S. 1964. Galapagos tortoise and marine iguana deep body temperatures measured by radio telemetry. Nature 204:355-358.

Maxwell, D. C. 1974. Marine productivity of the Galapagos Archipelago. Ph.D. Thesis. Ohio State University, Columbus, Oh. 167 pp.

Morgareidge, K. R., and F. N. White. 1969. Cutaneous vascular changes during heating and cooling in the Galapagos marine iguanas. Nature 223:587-591.

Morton, E. S. 1971. Nest predation affecting the breeding season of the clay-colored robin, a tropical song bird. Science 171:920-921.

Nicotri, M. E. 1977. Grazing effects of four marine intertidal herbivores on the microflora. Ecology 58:1020-1032.

Paine, R. T., and R. L. Vadas. 1969. The effects of grazing by sea urchins, *Strongylocentrotus* spp., on benthic algal populations. Limnol. Oceanogr. 14:710-719.

Pak, H., and J. R. V. Zaneveld. 1973. The Cromwell Current on the east side of the Galapagos Islands. J. Geophys. Res. 78:7845-7859.

Peterson, R. T. 1967. The Galápagos: Eerie cradle of new species. Nat'l. Geogr. 131:541-585.

Pinchot, G. 1931. To the South Seas. Hutchinson, London. 500 pp.

Rand, W. M., and A. S. Rand. 1976. Agonistic behavior in nesting iguanas: A stochastic analysis of dispute settlement dominated by the minimization of energy cost. Z. Tierpsychol. 40: 279-299.

Ricklefs, R. E., and J. Cullen. 1973. Embryonic growth of the green iguana, *Iguana iguana*. Copeia 2:296-305.

Schmidt-Nielson, K., and R. Fange. 1958. Salt glands in marine reptiles. Nature 182:783-785.

Schoener, T. W. 1974. Resource partitioning in ecological communities. Science 185:27-39.

Schoener, T. W. 1974. Sexual dimorphism and differential niche utilization in birds. Condor 68:

113-151.

Slevin, J. R. 1935. An account of the reptiles inhabiting the Galápagos Islands. Bull. N. Y. Zool. Soc. 38:3-14.

Slevin, J. R. 1959. The Galápagos Islands: A history of their exploration. Occas. Pap. Calif. Acad. Sci. 25:1-150.

Sokal, R. R., and F. J. Rohlf. 1969. Biometry. W. H. Freeman and Co., San Francisco, Calif. 776 pp.

Thornton, I. 1971. Darwin's islands: A natural history of the Galápagos. Natural History Press, New York, N. Y. 322 pp.

Tinbergen, N. 1953. Social behavior of animals. Oxford University Press, London. 150 pp.

Vitt, L. S., J. D. Congdon, and N. A. Dickson. 1977. Adaptive strategies and energetics of tail autotomy in lizards. Ecology 58:326-337.

White, F. N. 1973. Temperature and the Galapagos marine iguana—insights into reptilian thermoregulation. Comp. Biochem. Physiol. 45A:503-513.

ARE THE GALAPAGOS IGUANAS OLDER THAN THE GALAPAGOS?
Molecular Evolution and Colonization Models for the Archipelago

JEFF S. WYLES[1,2] AND VINCENT M. SARICH[2,3]
[1] Department of Biology, University of California, Los Angeles, CA 90024
[2] Department of Biochemistry and [3] Department of Anthropology,
University of California, Berkeley, CA 94720

Molecular phylogenetic studies of the Galapagos iguanas support two main evolutionary hypotheses: (1) the marine and land iguanas represent two separate invasions from the mainland; and (2) the Galapagos fauna may be older than most conventional estimates. Colonization models based upon these and other taxa are discussed.

The marine iguana (*Amblyrhynchus*) and the land iguana (*Conolophus*) are genera endemic to the Galapagos Islands; they are generally assumed to share a common Galapagos ancestor and to have evolved from a common stock *in situ* (Dawson et al. 1977). Our molecular comparisons indicate monophyly relative to other iguanines, but albumin differences suggest a divergence time of 15-20 million years (my). This is in contrast to current geological evidence that there are no reliable core samples from the Galapagos with an age greater than about two my (Cox 1971).

The islands (Fig. 1) are situated in the Pacific Ocean some 1000 kilometers from the coast of Ecuador and an equal distance from the east rise of the Pacific Plate. The marine iguana (*Amblyrhynchus cristatus*) is found on virtually all of these islands and rock piles. In contrast, the land iguanas are limited today to just a portion of the archipelago. Two species are currently recognized, *Conolophus pallidus*, which is only found on Santa Fé Island, and *C. subcristatus*, which occurs on Fernandina, Isabela, Santiago, Baltra, and Santa Cruz (Thornton 1971).

MOLECULAR STUDIES OF GALAPAGOS IGUANAS

We have placed the Galapagos iguanas phylogenetically through immunological comparisons of serum albumins (Sarich and Wilson 1967; Champion et al. 1974; Maxson et al. 1975; Carlson et al. 1978) and polyacrylamide electrophoresis of plasma proteins (Davis 1964; Cronin 1975). The protein data have been calibrated against the fossil record, establishing a reasonably accurate molecular clock (Maxson et al. 1975; Carlson et al. 1978).

Results of immunological comparisons are given in Table 1. Antisera to the albumins of *Ambyrhynchus* and *Conolophus* were used to measure the distance to the albumins of 13 iguanid genera (ten iguanine, one oplurine, one basiliscine, and one crotaphytine). It is clear that the average *Amblyrhynchus-Conolophus* immunological distance of 30 is only slightly less than distances between either of these two and several mainland iguanines. The predicted divergence time is 15-20 my. A cladistic analysis using outside reference species such as *Basiliscus* and *Crotaphytus* (Wyles, unpublished) indicates that albumin evolution in the Galapagos iguanas has proceeded at rates similar to those in other iguanines. Therefore *Amblyrhynchus* and *Conolophus* can share no more than a brief period of common ancestry subsequent to their divergence from other iguanines. Furthermore, reciprocal measures with other antisera are consistent with this interpretation. A morphological study (Avery and Tanner 1971) agrees with this phylogenetic picture. They considered *Amblyrhynchus* and *Conolophus* to be a sister group but quite distinct

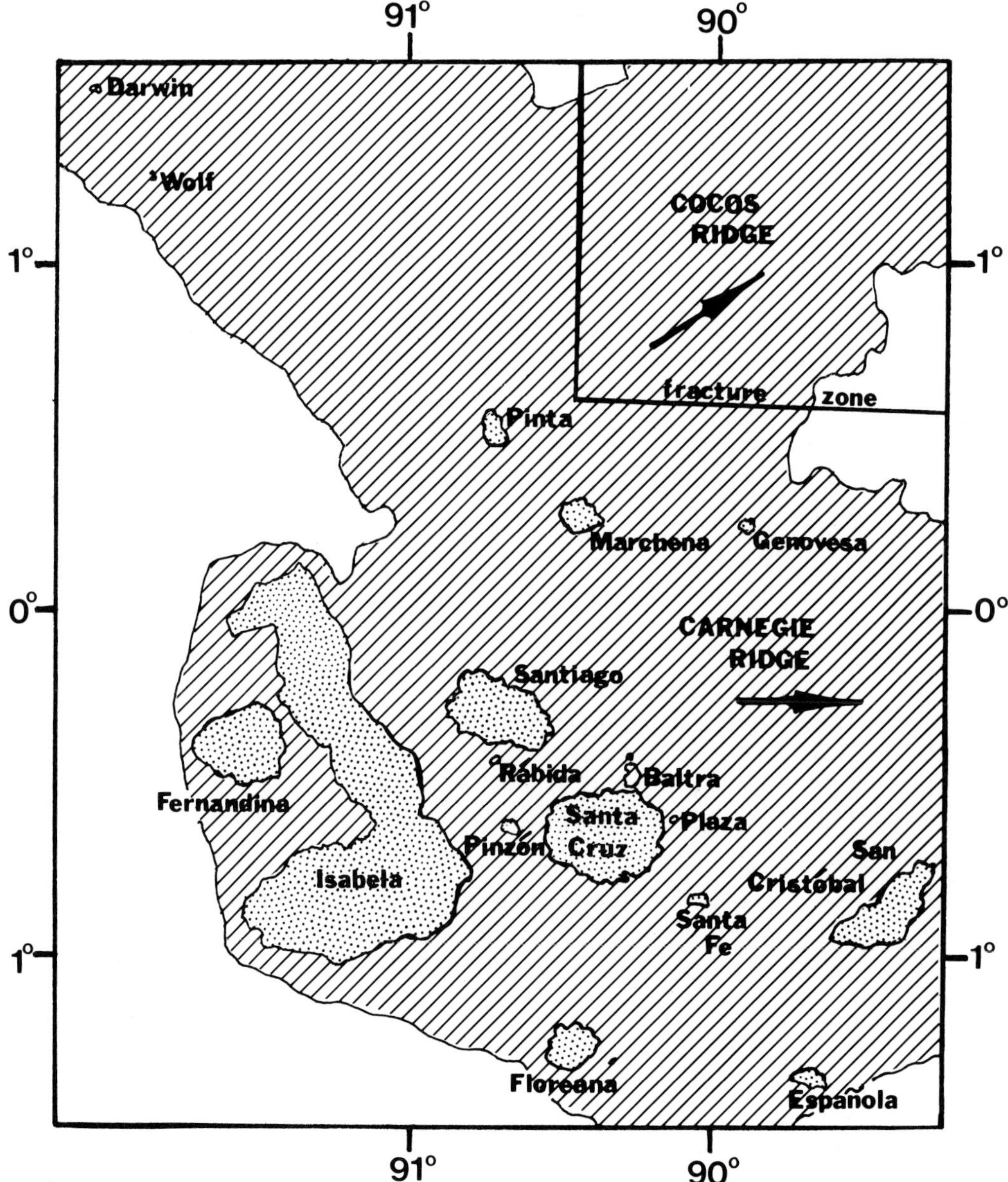

Fig. 1. Principal islands of the Galapagos Archipelago. The area that represents the Cocos and Carnegie ridges is shown with diagonal lines. Arrows indicate pathways to mainland Central and South America.

from one another. The recognized iguanine genera all have average distances of less than 50 to the Galapagos iguanas except for *Dipsosaurus* (75) and *Brachylophus* (80).

Polyacrylamide electrophoresis of plasma proteins of *Amblyrhynchus* and *Conolophus* substantiates the schematic representations of Higgins and Rand (1974) that definite plasma protein mobility differences differentiate the land and marine iguanas. These investigators utilizing somewhat less sensitive molecular techniques showed little genetic divergence among island populations of *Amblyrhynchus* (Higgins et al. 1974; Higgins and Rand 1974, 1975).

TABLE 1. IMMUNOLOGICAL DISTANCES TO VARIOUS IGUANID LIZARDS[a]

Albumin Source	Antiserum to *Amblyrhynchus* albumin	Antiserum to *Conolophus* albumin	Mean
Iguanines:			
1. *Amblyrhynchus cristatus*	0	30	
2. *Conolophus subcristatus*	31	0	30
3. *Conolophus pallidus*	34	0	
4. *Enyaliosaurus clarki*	42	29	36
5. *Iguana iguana*	44(38)[b]	34(28)	36
6. *Ctenosaura hemilopha*	44(51)	39(50)	46
7. *Sauromalus obesus*	46	38	42
8. *Cyclura stejnegeri*	40	52	46
9. *Dipsosaurus dorsalis*	76	73	75
10. *Brachylophus fasciatus*	72	87	80
Crotaphytine:			
11. *Crotaphytus wislizenii*	82(82)	76(72)	78
Basiliscine:			
12. *Basiliscus vittatus*	78(106)	89(88)	90
Oplurine:			
13. *Oplurus sebae*	100(150)[c]	117(110)	119

[a] Obtained from antisera against purified albumin from Galapagos iguanas.
[b] Numbers in parentheses indicate reciprocal measurements.
[c] Approximate values.

Starch gel electrophoresis studies comparing enzymatic proteins in the Galapagos iguanas are in progress at the Museum of Vertebrate Zoology, U.C. Berkeley, by Drs. R. Sage and J. Patton and Mr. R. Marlow. These investigators have kindly allowed us to use their preliminary data to calculate Nei distances (Nei 1972) for the iguanas. For 26 presumptive genetic loci examined, a Nei distance of 0.761 was calculated between *Amblyrhynchus* and *Conolophus*. Molecular differences between the two species of *Conolophus* were found to be very small (D=0.036). The *Amblyrhynchus-Conolophus* distance is consistent with the immunological data (Sarich 1977) and indicates a separation time approaching 20 my.

The two species of *Conolophus* can be distinguished using our antisera to *Amblyrhynchus* albumin but not with antisera to *Conolophus* albumin. In addition, they can be distinguished by polyacrylamide gel electrophoreses of their plasma proteins. The differences found are more in the range of between-population rather than between-species differences (Ayala 1975; Bezy et al. 1977). It can be safely assumed that the species shared a common ancestor within the last one my. The two nominal *Conolophus* species are also very similar in aggressive posture, but rather different in their display action patterns (Carpenter 1969). It is then questionable whether these forms should be considered species rather than geographic races—but as they are completely allopatric, it is futile to argue the point.

Other Molecular Data

Other studies of the Galapagos fauna (J. Patton, pers. comm.) indicate different evolutionary patterns. The Galapagos tortoises (*Geochelone*) (Patton, in press) and finches show very small Nei distances among populations, races, species, and even genera (less than 0.1 among tortoise races and less than 0.15 among finch genera). Conversely, among the native rats, *Oryzomys* and *Nesoryzomys*, the genetic distances are large.

COLONIZATION MODELS

These patterns can be best explained by several colonization models for the Galapagos Islands (Fig. 2). Figure 2A represents the evolutionary pattern of the Galapagos iguanas. Neither genus has significantly speciated within the Galapagos Islands, and no closely related mainland representatives exist today. The model predicts either (1) two recent colonizations from now extinct mainland stocks or (2) evolution within the islands for a long period of time, accompanied by very little speciation.

Figure 2B is a model for the Galapagos finches and tortoises. The Nei distances for both are small among all species represented on the islands. The process of colonization for tortoises and finches when calibrated to the albumin clock (Sarich 1977) suggests invasions over the last one to two my. If genetic distances to mainland forms are small, then support exists for recent origin of the island fauna through colonization from the mainland. This observation, however, does not negate multiple recolonization from older, now-submerged islands. If mainland relatives are only distantly related, two possibilities seem likely: (1) the islands themselves are very old and populations surviving volcanic activity have undergone rapid speciation over relatively short periods of time or (2) the islands are young and the nearest mainland relatives of the Galapagos have become extinct.

Figure 2C is a model of speciation within the islands over a long period of time. It can alternatively be interpreted to represent multiple colonizations of taxa that had common ancestors on the mainland (e.g. the rice rats, *Oryzomys-Nesoryzomys*).

Figure 2D is the most divergent picture of colonization, and no taxa at this point seem to fit this model. It represents a single invasion with one lineage speciating over a long period of time.

ANALYSIS OF BIOTIC DISTRIBUTIONS

One may ask, what do present-day biotic distributions tell us about the process of colonization of these islands? To answer this question, a phenogram was constructed from a matrix of relative island biotic dissimilarities (Fitch and Margoliash 1967). It was based on 22 groups representing a broad spectrum of the endemic flora and fauna of the Galapagos Islands (Thornton 1971). The results, presented in Fig. 3, indicate that: (1) the islands of Isabela, Santa Cruz, Santiago, and Fernandina all are biotically similar, and (2) Pinzón Island has biotic affinities with all four islands.

Interestingly, it has been postulated (Van Denburgh and Slevin 1913) that some of the larger central islands were once part of an even bigger island, which later split apart due to volcanic activity. Furthermore, Pinzón Island seems to be part of a central volcanic cone whose activity gave rise to the present-day islands (Van Denburgh and Slevin 1913; Thornton 1971).

It is difficult to assess the relative importance of geographic distance, dispersal ability, island size, niche availability, and extinction rates on biotic similarity. However, we feel that this kind of analysis might provide insight into the ancestry of the islands and the evolutionary history of their colonization.

Fig. 2. Colonization models for the Galapagos Islands. (A). Low frequency of speciation (few lineages) with long divergence times. This model best fits the pattern in the Galapagos iguanas. (B). High frequency of speciation with either a close or distant mainland ancestor (Galapagos finches and tortoises). (C). High frequency of speciation and old lineages. (D). One lineage does all of the speciating.
Dotted lines represent hypothetical ancestors.

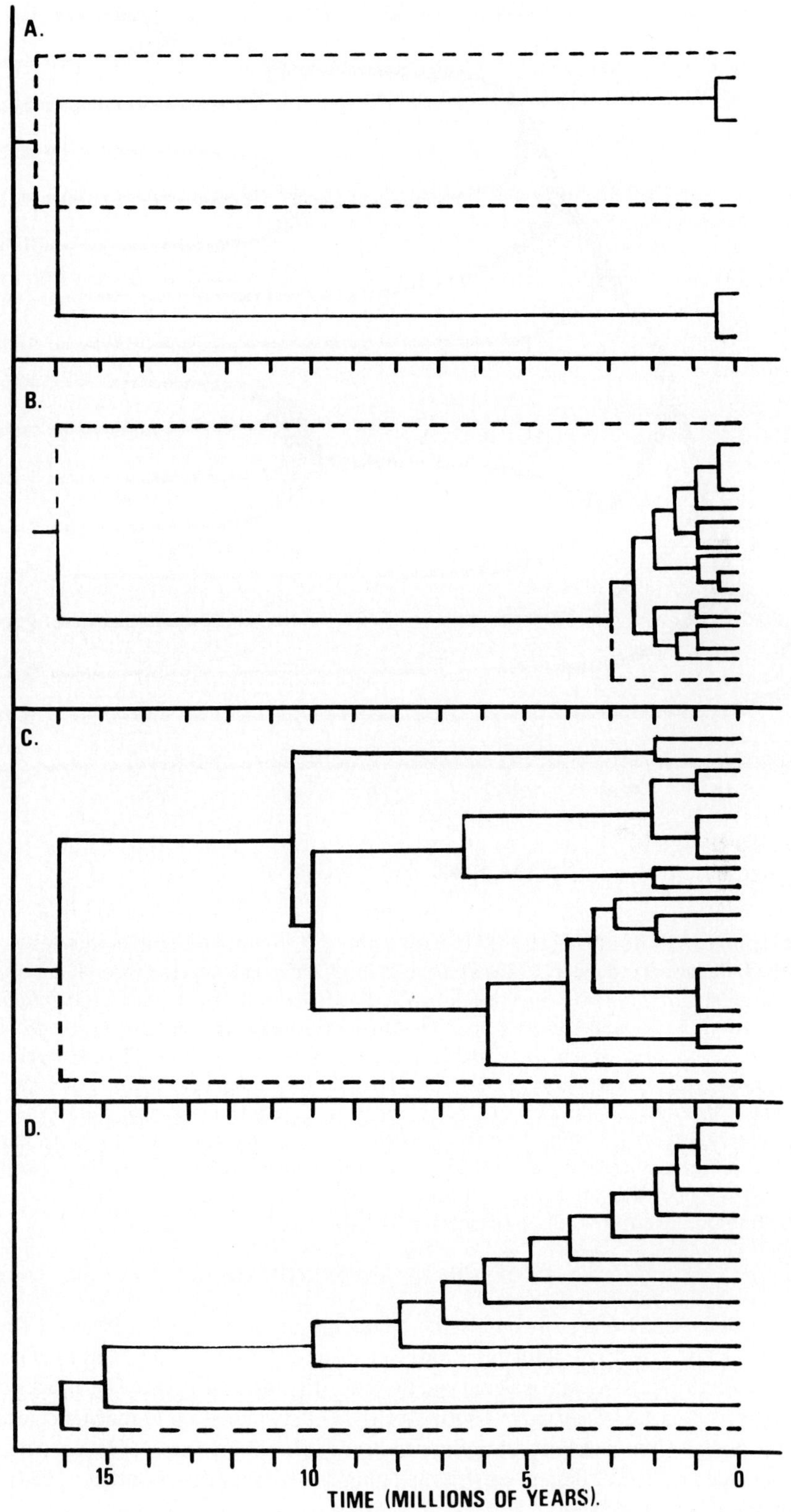
A.
B.
C.
D.
15
10
5
0
TIME (MILLIONS OF YEARS).

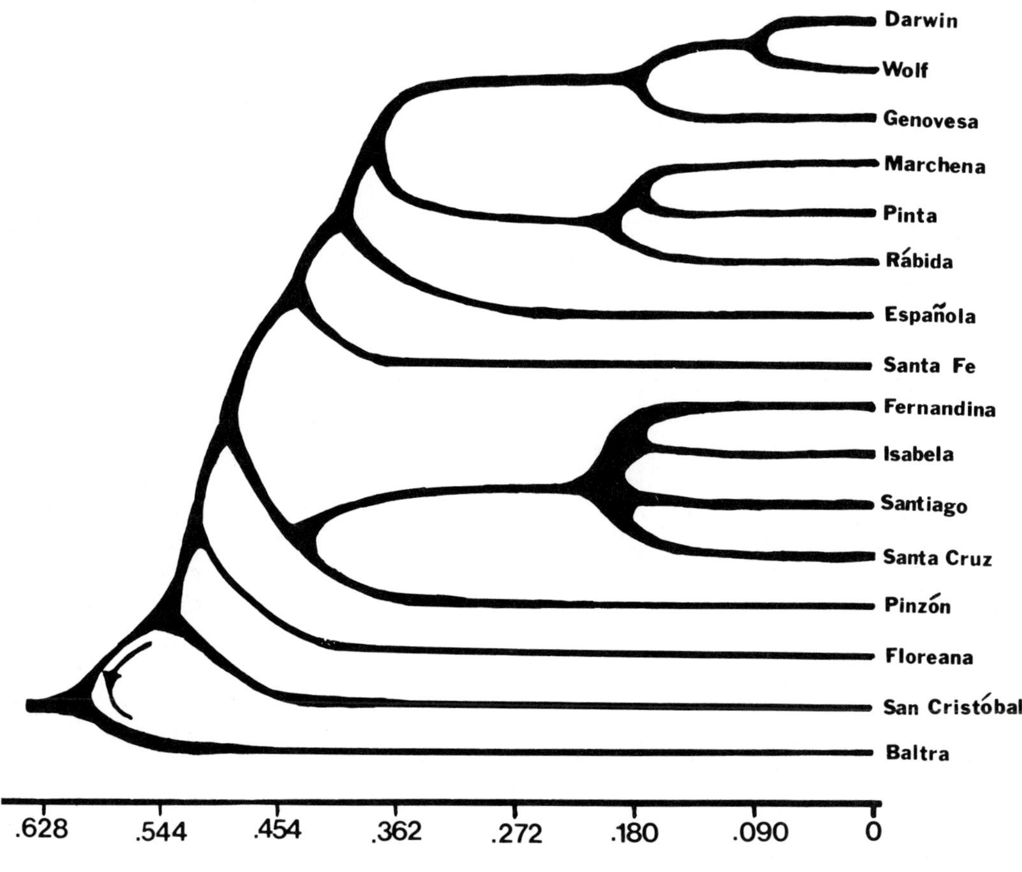

Fig. 3. Phenetic analysis of the Galapagos Island endemic fauna and flora. The raw data for this figure come from Thornton (1971). The following 22 phyletic categories were used: (A). Reptiles: lizards (Galapagos land iguana, *Conolophus*, 2 spp.; Galapagos marine iguana, *Amblyrhynchus*, 1 sp.; lava lizards, *Tropidurus*, 7 spp.; geckos, *Phyllodactylus*, 6 spp.), snakes (*Dromicus*, 3 spp.), tortoises (*Geochelone elephantopus*, 1 sp.). (B) Birds (vermilion flycatchers, *Pyrocephalus*, 2 spp.; mockingbirds, *Nesomimus*, 4 spp.; Galapagos finches, 5 genera represented). (C). Mammals (native rats, *Oryzomys*, 2 spp.; *Nesoryzomys*, 4 spp.). (D). Plants (sunflower, *Scalesia*, 15 spp.; *Alternanthera*, 10 spp.; *Mollugo*, 7 spp.; cactus, *Jasminocereus*, 3 spp.; palo santo, *Bursera*, 2 spp.). (E). Insects (ants, *Camponotus*, 2 spp.; flightless grasshoppers, *Halmenus*, 2 spp.; winged grasshoppers, *Schistocerca*, 2 spp.). Numbers that follow each island name refer to their geographic position shown in Fig. 1. The branching order follows Fitch and Margoliash (1967). Tree statistics are F=13.5%; standard deviation=20.2% (Prager and Wilson 1978).

GEOLOGICAL BACKGROUND

Considerable controversy surrounds the exact age of the Galapagos Islands (Vinton 1951; Banfield et al. 1956; Cox 1971; Williams 1966; Herron and Heirtzler 1967; McBirney and Williams 1969; Hey et al. 1977). K-Ar and paleomagnetic dates for the extant islands give ages of between 0.22 and 2.4 my (Cox and Dalrymple 1966; Cox 1971). Extrapolation of magnetic anomalies and dating of the S. San Cristóbal Island sea floor indicate a maximum age of 9-10 my for the islands, and available paleontological data suggest a maximum 10-15 my origin (Durham 1964; Cox 1971; Durham and McBirney 1975).

DISCUSSION

There seems to be some consensus that the Galapagos Islands are young (i.e. about two my old). However, the sea floor ridge appears to be old, 10-15 my, according to shallow water marine fossils (Durham 1964; Durham and McBirney 1975; Durham, pers. comm.). In the present study, we have predicted a divergence time among the endemic iguanine genera of 15-20 my. This would require either two separate recent colonizations of already differentiated, and now extinct, mainland stocks (if the Galapagos are younger than the divergence between the taxa) or the existence of land areas harboring these stocks during the last 15 my even if these islands were not in the present position of the Galapagos.

It has been proposed that the Galapagos Islands were created by plate movement over a hot spot (Wilson 1963; Holden and Dietz 1972; Dalrymple et al. 1973; Hey 1977; Hey et al. 1977). We still need to explain how possible land bridges might have existed between the Galapagos and the mainland. One explanation is furnished by the Cocos and Carnegie ridges once being above sea level (see Fig. 1). It is difficult to substantiate this point in the absence of any known seamounts or submarine guyots that might represent the eroded islands in the ridges. We know that the sea floor at the time of the origin of the hot spot was about 600m, a depth that corresponds to the present-day depth of the Galapagos platform. Nevertheless, Detrick and Crough (1978) have shown that hot spots can modify previous estimates of ocean floor subsidence rates. Applied to our problem, land positive areas might have existed during the Miocene in these ridges and connected the Galapagos Islands to the mainland.

Further evidence is needed to support a land bridge via the Cocos and Carnegie ridges (but see Vinton 1951; Shumway 1954; Shumway and Chase 1963; Rosen 1975). The validity of a large hypothetical island splitting up from volcanic activity should also be subjected to a careful examination (Van Denburgh and Slevin 1913; Thornton 1971).

A concerted effort should be made to assess the validity of present fossil age estimates from the Galapagos Islands. Deeper underlying core samples should be obtained from the vicinity of these islands. An effort should especially be made on the portions of San Cristóbal Island that still remain uninvestigated, because it is thought to be the oldest island. Recent geological evidence (Hey 1979, pers. comm.) indicates that some islands can be at least five my old.

A Galapagos iguana-like fossil has also been found on Barbuda in the Caribbean (Etheridge 1964). This fossil may represent the remains of a once more widespread iguanine stock that existed in Central American and colonized the Galapagos Islands via the Cocos Ridge.

Additional experiments could be conducted to test the possibility of rafting events from the mainland via floating land masses, logs, or pumice (Richards 1958; Holden and Dietz 1972). If the Humboldt and El Niño currents were much the same in the past, the odds would shift in favor of multiple colonization events.

We feel such multidisciplinary efforts should provide robust tests of the colonization hypotheses discussed here.

ACKNOWLEDGMENTS

Thanks are given to Dr. J. Patton and Mr. R. Marlow, who collected marine iguanas (*Amblyrhynchus cristatus* on Isla Coamaño, Academy Bay, Santa Cruz Island), and land iguanas (*Conolophus subcristatus* on Cerro Dragon [antiserum] and S. Plaza, near Santa Cruz Island and *C. pallidus* on Santa Fé Island). Dr. R. Sage ran the starch gel electrophoreses and allowed us to calculate preliminary Nei distances from them. Dr. J. van Andel was most helpful with geological interpretations, and Drs. A. C. Wilson, G. Gorman, J. Wyatt Durham, H. Williams, M. Benado, and J. Patton provided helpful discussion and constructive criticism of the manuscript. Dr. J. Patton graciously allowed us to cite some of his unpublished molecular data on some Galapagos fauna. This work was partially supported by grants to G. C. Gorman (NSF-DEB-77-03259), A. C. Wilson

(NSF-74-11866A03), and V. M. Sarich (NSF-GB-20750). All of the work was conducted in the laboratory of Dr. A. C. Wilson, Department of Biochemistry, U.C. Berkeley.

RESUMEN

Estudios filogenéticos moléculares de las iguanas de las Islas Galápagos sustentan dos hipótesises evolutivas: (1) Las iguanas marinas y terrestres representan dos invasiónes diferentes desde el continente; (2) La fauna de las Islas Galápagos puede ser más antigua que los cálculos convencionales. Se presentan modelos de colonización en base de estas y otras especies.

LITERATURE CITED

Avery, D. F., and W. W. Tanner. 1971. Evolution of the iguanine lizards (Sauria, Iguanidae) as determined by osteological and myological characters. Brig. Young Univ. Sci. Bull. Biol. Ser. 12(3):1-79.

Ayala, F. J. 1975. Genetic differentiation during the speciation process. Pages 1-78 *in* T. Dobzhansky, M. K. Hecht, and W. C. Steere, eds. Evolutionary Biology. Plenum Press, New York, N. Y.

Banfield, A. F., C. H. Behre, Jr., and D. St. Clair. 1956. Geology of Isabela (Albemarle) Is. Geol. Soc. Amer. Bull. 67:215-234.

Bezy, R., G. Gorman, Y. Kim, and J. Wright. 1977. Chromosomal and genetic divergence in the fossorial lizards of the family Anniellidae. Syst. Zool. 26(1):57-71.

Carlson, S. S., A. C. Wilson, and R. D. Maxson. 1978. Do albumin clocks run on time? Science 200:1183-1185.

Carpenter, C. 1969. Behavioral and ecological notes on the Galapagos land iguanas. Herpetologica 25(3):155-164.

Champion, A. B., E. M. Prager, D. Wachter, and A. C. Wilson. 1974. Pages 397-416 *in* C. A. Wright, ed. Biochemical and Immunological Taxonomy of Animals. Academic Press, New York, N. Y.

Cox, A. 1971. Paleomagnetism of San Cristóbal Island, Galapagos. Earth Plan. Sci. Letts. 11: 152-160.

Cox, A., and G. B. Dalrymple. 1966. Paleomagnetism and Potassium-Argon ages of some volcanic rocks from the Galapagos Islands. Nature 209:776-777.

Cronin, J. 1975. Molecular systematics of the order primates. Ph.D. Thesis. University of California, Berkeley, Calif.

Dalrymple, G. B., E. A. Silver, and E. D. Jackson. 1973. Origin of the Hawaiian Islands. Amer. Sci. 61:294-308.

Davis, B. J. 1964. Disc electrophoresis II. Methods and application to human serum proteins. Ann. N. Y. Acad. Sci. 121:404-427.

Dawson, W. R., G. A. Bartholomew, and A. F. Bennett. 1977. A reappraisal of the aquatic specializations of the Galapagos marine iguana (*Amblyrhynchus cristatus*). Evolution 31:891-897.

Detrick, W. R., and S. T. Crough. 1978. Island subsidence, hotspots, and lithospheric thinning. J. Geophys. Res. 83(B3):1236-1244.

Durham, W. 1964. The Galapagos Islands expedition of 1964. Page 53 *in* Ann. Rep., Amer. Malacol. Un.

Durham, W., and A. R. McBirney. 1975. Pages 285-290 *in* R. W. Fairbridge, ed. Encyclopedia of World Regional Geology, Part I. Dowden, Hutchinson and Ross, Inc., New York, N. Y.

Etheridge, R. 1964 Late Pleistocene lizards from Barbuda, British West Indies. Bull. Florida State Mus. Biol. Sci. 9:1-75.

Fitch, W. H., and E. Margoliash. 1967. Construction of phylogenetic trees. Science 155:279-284.

Herron, E. M., and J. R. Heirtzler. 1967. Sea-floor spreading near the Galapagos. Science 158: 775-780.

Hey, R. 1977. Tectonic evolution of the Cocos-Nazca spreading center. Geol. Soc. Amer. Bull.

88:1404-1420.
Hey, R., G. L. Johnson, and A. Lowrie. 1977. Recent plate motions in the Galapagos area. Geol. Soc. Amer. Bull. 88:1385-1403.
Higgins, R. J., C. S. Rand, and J. L. Haynes. 1974. Galapagos iguanas: *Amblyrhynchus* and *Conolophus*. Serum protein relationships. J. Exp. Zool. 189(2):255-259.
Higgins, R. J., and C. S. Rand. 1974. A comparative immunochemical study of the serum proteins of several Galapagos iguanids. Comp. Biochem. Physiol. 49A:347-355.
Higgins, and C. S. Rand. 1975. Comparative immunology of Galapagos iguana hemoglobins. J. Exp. Zool. 193(3):391-397.
Holden, J. C., and R. S. Dietz. 1972. Circum-Pacific tectonic and igneous activity and the evolution of the Caribbean plate. Geol. Soc. Amer. Bull. 83:251-272.
Marlow, R., and Patton, J. 1981. Biochemical relationships of the Galapagos giant tortoises (*Geochelone elephantopus*). J. Zool. (London) 195:413-422.
Maxson, L. R., V. M. Sarich, and A. C. Wilson. 1975. Continental drift and the use of albumin as an evolutionary clock. Nature 255:397-400.
McBirney, A. R., and H. Williams. 1969. Geology and petrology of the Galapagos Islands. Geol. Soc. Amer. Mem. 118:1-197.
Nei, M. 1972. Genetic distance between populations. Amer. Nat. 106:283-292.
Prager, E. M., and A. C. Wilson. 1978. Construction of phylogenetic trees for proteins and nucleic acids: empirical evaluation of alternative matrix methods. J. Mol. Evol. 11:129-142.
Richards, A. 1958. Transpacific distribution of floating pumice from Isla San Benedicto, Mexico. Deep Sea Res. 5:29-35.
Rosen, E. E. 1975. A vicariance model of Caribbean biogeography. Syst. Zool. 24(4):431-464.
Sarich, V. M. 1977. Rates, sample sizes and neutrality hypothesis for electrophoresis in evolutionary studies. Nature 265:24-28.
Sarich, V. M., and A. C. Wilson. 1967. Immunological time scale for hominoid evolution. Science 158:1200-1203.
Shumway, G. 1954. Carnegie Ridge and Cocos Ridge in the east equatorial Pacific. J. Geol. 62: 573-586.
Shumway, G., and T. E. Chase. 1963. Bathymetry in the Galapagos region. Occas. Pap. Calif. Acad. Sci. 44:11-19.
Thornton, J. 1971. Darwin's islands: A natural history of the Galapagos. Natural History Press, Garden City, N.Y. 322 pp.
Van Denburgh, J., and J. R. Slevin. 1913. The Galapagoan lizards of the genus *Tropidurus*; with notes on the iguanas of the genera *Conolophus* and *Amblyrhynchus*. Proc. Calif. Acad. Sci., Ser. 4, 2:133-202.
Vinton, K. 1951. Origin of life on the Galapagos Islands. Amer. J. Sci. 249:356-376.
Williams, H. 1966. Geology of the Galapagos Islands. Pages 65-70 *in* R. I. Bowman, ed. The Galápagos. University of California Press, Berkeley and Los Angeles, Calif.
Wilson, J. T. 1963. Continental drift. Sci. Amer. 208:86-100.

ADDENDUM

Since this symposium took place, new evidence has come to the foreground supporting the idea that the situation for the Galapagos Islands could be analogous to that in Hawaii (Diamond 1982). Biochemical dating methods for *Drosophila* (Beverley 1980) and honeycreepers (Sibley and Ahlquist 1982) suggest that these species diverged from mainland ancestors 15-42 my ago, long before the existing Hawaiian Islands rose above sea level. The explanation here is that the present Hawaiian Islands are merely the most recent islands formed from volcanic activity by motion of the Pacific Plate over a hot spot. In the case of Hawaii, the submerged Emperor Seamounts (37-70 my old) could be the remnants of islands on which the ancestors of modern *Drosophila* and the honeycreepers started their initial colonizations and from which they later diverged *in situ*.

LITERATURE CITED

Beverley, S. M. 1980. A molecular view of the age and origin of the Hawaiian *Drosophila*. 2nd Int'l. Congr. Syst. Evol. Biol. Abstr. 112.

Diamond, J. 1982. The biogeography of the Pacific Basin. Nature 298:604-605.

Sibley, C., and J. Ahlquist. 1981. The relationship of the Hawaiian honeycreepers (Drepaninini) as indicated by DNA-DNA hybridization. Auk 99:130-140.

THE ROLE OF INTERSPECIFIC COMPETITION IN THE ADAPTIVE RADIATION OF DARWIN'S FINCHES

P. R. GRANT
Department of Biology, McGill University, Montreal, PQ, Canada H3A 181[1]

There is lack of agreement on the role of interspecific competition for food in the adaptive radiation of Darwin's finches. To assess the significance of competition, food supply and feeding ecology of the six species of ground finches (*Geospiza*) were studied at eight sites on seven islands in the wet and dry seasons of 1973. Two sets of observations support the hypothesis that competition in the past has governed which species can coexist, and their ecological differences. First, the allocation of species to congeneric pairs, triplets and quadruplets is non-random. Species which do not occur together are very similar in diet. Second, sympatric species are spaced approximately regularly on a beak-size gradient, and associated with this their diets differ. Ongoing competition is suggested by decreased diet breadths and decreased interspecific overlaps in diet during the subsequent dry season.

More than forty years ago, the British geneticist J. B. S. Haldane wrote: "There are still a number of people who do not believe in the theory of evolution. Scientists believe in it, not because it is an attractive theory, but because it enables them to make predictions which come true" (Haldane 1937). Not all scientists would agree about its predictive capacity, but then there are two interrelated functions of prediction which tend to get confused in discussions of whether evolutionary theory can predict or not. These are (a) forecasting, and (b) testing. The first is anticipating what one will find if one searches in a field of the unknown, either forward (prediction) or backward (postdiction) in time. The second is testing whether the theory sufficiently accounts for organic diversity or not. Of course these two functions are not entirely separable. I have contrasted them for emphasis. The distinction between them arises from the fact that the domain of testability of evolutionary theory, in which predictions are potentially falsifiable, is a restricted segment of the total range of conditions to which the theory applies. More in the spirit of forecasting than of testing, I am going to apply the predictive approach to the question of whether interspecific competition has played an important role in the evolution of Darwin's finches.

Consider the following hypothetical and unlikely circumstance. The number, size, location, climate and vegetation of the Galapagos are all known, approximately, but the land bird fauna is unknown, perhaps because landing on the islands is almost impossible. Could we predict what we would find were a landing finally achieved? To a limited extent we could.

For a start, the seasonal aridity of the islands would be expected to favor land birds capable of exploiting seeds and fruits for most of the year and arthropods for the relatively short period when rain falls. It would be a reasonable suggestion, therefore, that finches would be well represented on the islands, since this is the most diverse granivorous taxon on the adjacent mainland. Furthermore, we would need no detailed information about the islands to predict the occurrence of several species in this taxon. It would be enough to know that the islands are well isolated from the South American continent, yet numerous. These conditions are known to favor speciation among the few taxa that are capable of reaching isolated archipelagos.

Beyond that we could predict the minimum number of seed-eating finch species on the

[1] Present address: Division of Biological Sciences, University of Michigan, Ann Arbor, MI 48109

Galapagos. Our prediction is seven. These should occur together on the same island. Many other species might occur in allopatry, but predicting their number is not possible at present.

Seven finch species are predicted from a knowledge of the finch species on the adjacent mainland, and from a knowledge of the "rules" that govern community membership, more specifically guild membership, on islands. This is where interspecific competition enters the picture. Closely related species with similar feeding niches may compete for food when some or all kinds of food are in short supply. Theory tells us that the similarity in feeding niches of closely related species varies directly with food diversity, as mediated by natural selection (MacArthur 1972; May 1972). Food diversity is lower on islands than on mainlands (Abbott 1976; Allan et al. 1973; Janzen 1973), consequently niche similarity is less. The feeding niche similarity of island bird species has never been studied adequately, but is indexed by the similarity in functionally related morphology. For many species of birds, body size (weight) seems to be the most appropriate measure (Diamond 1973; Hespenheide 1973), but for granivorous birds, whose bill-related "handling" skills determine whether a seed can or cannot be exploited, bill size is the appropriate measure. Empirical studies have shown that the limiting similarity of feeding niches of island bird species, as indexed by bill morphology, is 15% (Grant 1968). This is the rule that governs guild membership. The number of species in the guild is determined by this spacing-rule, and by the range of bill sizes permitted by the spectrum of food resources.

Marchant's (1958) study of birds on the Santa Elena Peninsula of coastal Ecuador, a region of climatic and vegetational similarity to the arid zone of the Galapagos (Grant and Boag 1980; Svenson 1946), enables us to calculate the potential bill-size spectrum. The minimum average beak length is 7.1 mm (*Sporophila telasco*) and the maximum is 17.4 mm (*Pheucticus chrysopeplus*). Starting with 7.1 and multiplying iteratively by 1.15 until 17.4 is reached, we generate seven bill lengths (including the starting one).

A visit to the islands at this point would reveal a total of six species of seed-eating finches in the genus *Geospiza*. This is close to the predicted seven. But not all occur together, a point to which I will return later. Measurements of the six species throughout the archipelago would reveal two additional facts. First, the missing species is the smallest. This is deduced from the observation that the mainland and island's largest species (*Pheucticus chrysopeplus* and *Geospiza magnirostris* respectively) are more similar to each other in size than are their smallest species (*Sporophila telasco* and *Geospiza fuliginosa*). Second, beak sizes of the six species are well predicted (Fig. 1); the multiplier rule works well. The most discrepant species is *Geospiza magnirostris*. Observed beak length in this species is below the predicted value by about 7%. But observed beak depth is above the predicted value by about the same amount. This indication of mutual compensation suggests that beak shape rather than a single dimension is important in determining coexistence (cf. Grant 1972). In fact, deviation of observed values of all six species from those predicted is smaller when $[\text{length x depth}]^{1/2}$ is used than when either length or depth is used alone.

The absence of a very small seed-eating ground finch calls for an explanation. Three obvious explanations are: (1) there is no food niche for it; (2) there is a food niche but it is restricted, it varies in time and space and can only be exploited by a highly nomadic species; and (3) there has not been enough time for this finch species to evolve.

The first hypothesis, taken at face value, is not likely to be correct. Unless the smallest species on the Ecuadorian mainland is adapted to exploiting certain seed-bearing plants which have not been able to colonize the Galapagos, the hypothesis is probably wrong because there is an abundance of small seeds on the islands (Abbott et al. 1977; Smith et al. 1978). Of course, it is always possible to fall back on an argument of diffuse competition; i.e., the depletion of small seeds by the combined efforts of *Geospiza fuliginosa, Zenaida galapagoensis* (dove) and others (e.g. *Tropidurus* lizards and native rats [*Oryzomys* and *Nesoryzomys*]) renders impossible the occupation of a small-seed niche by a micro-*Geospiza*. But it is not obvious why the hypothetical *Geospiza* species would be the competitively inferior one. However, detailed information on the way

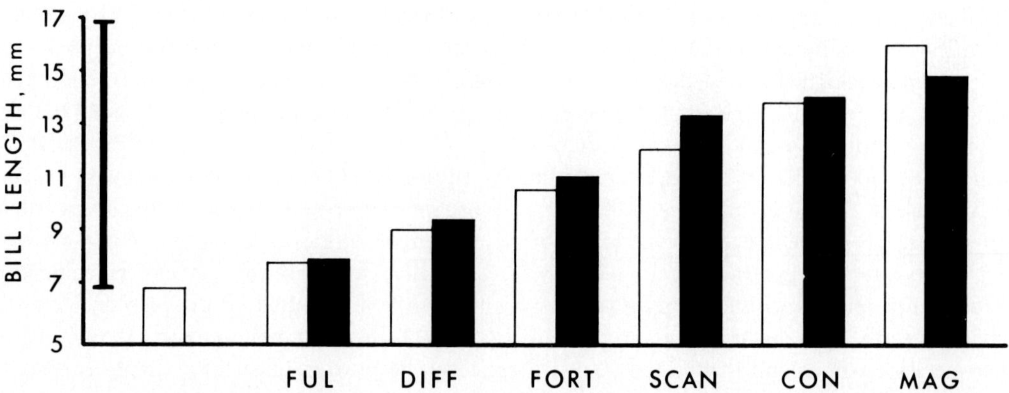

Fig. 1. Predicted bill lengths (open bars) for species on the Galapagos. Solid bars show the mean male bill lengths of the six species of *Geospiza: fuliginosa* (FUL), *difficilis* (DIFF), *fortis* (FORT), *scandens* (SCAN), *conirostris* (CON) and *magnirostris* (MAG). The vertical line close to the ordinate shows the range of male beak lengths spanned by finches on Marchant's (1958) study area on the Santa Elena Peninsula (based on measurements of five male specimens of each species in the American Museum of Natural History).

in which the supply of small seeds varies among years may show the hypothesis to be plausible.

The second hypothesis could be correct because *Sporophila telasco*, the smallest species in the comparable mainland, apparently was resident in Marchant's study area only in the breeding season. Moreover the smallest year-round resident in that area, *Neorhynchus peruvianus,* has a bill about as long as that of *Geospiza fuliginosa*, the smallest member of the *Geospiza* guild. However, there is a difficulty with this hypothesis. Isla Isabela in the Galapagos is roughly 150 km long and 50 km wide and would appear to be large enough to accommodate the nomadic movements and niche requirements of a micro-*Geospiza*. Like several other large islands in the archipelago, it also offers a diversity of habitats along an altitudinal gradient. It is therefore not obvious why a particularly small finch species could not meet its requirements on Isabela, and perhaps on other large islands as well.

The third hypothesis is the one to fall back on if all else fails (cf. Pianka 1966). No direct information can be brought to bear upon it. This is one reason why the predictions cannot be used as a critical test of the theory of guild organization. Another reason is that there is no non-arbitrary operational distinction between departures from prediction attributable to chance and departures attributable to incorrect theory. Nevertheless, the insufficient-time hypothesis may be correct since the Galapagos are relatively young (Bailey 1976) and presumably the adaptive radiation is distinctly younger.

If we found a convincing reason for the absence of a seventh *Geospiza* species, we would still be left with a difficulty. The six (or seven) species are predicted to coexist, yet a maximum of four or five do so (depending on whether *G. fuliginosa* and *G. difficilis* are sympatric; see later). Why? Without detailed information on food resources, and their variation in time and space, we are not in a strong position to account for discrepancies such as this. Pulliam (1975) has been able successfully to predict the number and identity of species of sparrows in even simpler communities from a knowledge of food production. On the Galapagos, food diversity is known at 11 sites (Abbott et al. 1977; Grant 1975, unpublished data; Smith et al. 1978), but we are ignorant of annual production. We also have no quantitative estimate of variation in annual production, either here or on the mainland. Variation in production may be an important determinant of finch coexistence.

The predictive approach has given only partial satisfaction, and has raised several questions which fieldwork on the mainland and islands might answer. I see refinements and elaboration of the theory and its application as one extension of this approach. For example, it might be expanded to the total radiation of the finches, i.e. both ground-dwelling and tree-dwelling members, for which a more detailed knowledge of mainland communities is required. Another possible extension is to set up a no-competition, or neutral (Caswell 1976), model in opposition to guild theory, and allow the data to choose between them. Another model already exists, but unfortunately it makes the same prediction as does the guild theory. Mezhzherin (1971) employed a theory of hierarchical use of "potential quasi-energy," whose correspondence with properties of the real world is not very clear, to predict that a maximum of six congeneric species of any taxon could coexist.

One final point: although guild theory is essentially, although not entirely, an ecological theory, I have put it to work to predict evolution. In this role it is limited. It does not enable us to predict specific evolutionary events (e.g. see Mayr 1961). Thus we cannot say with any confidence that species *A* will colonize the islands and give rise to species *B* to *F*. Instead the theory enables us to predict general evolutionary trends concerning the morphological and ecological characteristics of species derived from a common ancestor.

RECENT STUDIES: SINGLE SEASON

In order to keep the reasoning as uncontaminated by prior knowledge as possible, I have so far avoided referring to recent work. But it is recent work that raised the question of the importance of interspecific competition in the first place.

Lack (1947), following Darwin (1859), attached considerable importance to the process of interspecific competition in the evolution of the finches. Observing that the vegetation of the islands he visited appeared to be very similar, Lack wondered how differentiation of the species could have occurred. His answer to this dilemma was that genetic sampling effects (founder effect and drift) produced the initial differences between populations in allopatry; and that later, when sympatry was established, natural selection enhanced these differences and thereby minimized inter-specific competition. In fact Lack was led astray by the apparent similarity of the habitats on different islands. As Beebe (1924) aptly put it, "The most astonishing thing about the various islands of the Galápagos is their superficial similarity and their actual diversity." Bowman (1961) pointed this out and documented it with a list of plant species on each island. Our studies at eight sites on seven islands in 1973 fully confirm the point. Not only do islands differ in plant species, they differ in the frequency distribution of seeds and fruits classified in functionally meaningful size-hardness categories. Bowman (1961) concluded, and our studies confirm, that inter-island differences in vegetation could account for the initial steps in finch differentiation, i.e. they are adaptive and not necessarily just the result of genetic sampling.

But Bowman (1961) went further and suggested that it was no longer necessary to invoke interspecific competition as the cause, and associated natural selection as the means, of further differentiation. In his view, all of the differentation could be explained by the initial adaptations to different food conditions in different island environments. Our studies do not support this conclusion. The detailed explanations are published elsewhere (Abbott et al. 1977). Here I shall concentrate on the two main reasons.

First, the occurrence of particular combinations of *Geospiza* species on islands is non-random (Table 1). Certain pairs, triplets and quadruplets occur more frequently than expected by chance, and correspondingly others occur less frequently than expected by chance, or never. Furthermore there is pattern in the missing combinations. Missing combinations comprise species which are size-neighbors on a bill-size spectrum (Table 2). *G. difficilis* does not coexist with the smaller *G. fuliginosa* (Lack 1945, 1947 [but see Bowman 1961]) or with the larger *G. scandens* where they occur on the same island; *G. conirostris* does not occur with *G. fortis*, which it resembles in bill depth, or with *G. scandens*, which it resembles in bill length. It is a reasonable inference that these species do not occur together for reasons of ecological incompatibility; i.e. whenever these

TABLE 1. PROBABILITY THAT COMBINATIONS OF *GEOSPIZA* SPECIES ARE RANDOM[1]

No. *Geospiza* spp. per island	No. islands	No. types of combinations: possible	observed	Probability
1	2	6	1	.330
2	7	15	4	.054
3	8	20	2	.0002
4	3	15	1	.0044
5	3	6	1	.556

[1] See Abbott et al. (1977) for further details.

species have met, one has been competitively excluded. It is a reasonable inference because size-neighbors have very similar diets. Diet similarity is a simple function of beak size similarity (r = 0.62, df = 16, P<0.01) and is not simply determined by what food is available (Abbott et al. 1977).

Second, there is pattern in the bill size frequency distributions of coexisting species that is consistent with the theory of guild composition and with the empirical rule of 15% difference between species-pairs. This is manifested as a tendency towards regular spacing of the species along a bill-size axis, and non-overlap of the frequency distributions (Abbott et al. 1977). Exceptions are only apparent and disappear when more than one bill dimension is considered (Fig. 2; Table 3). Minimum differences and the tendency towards regular spacing are not predicted by Bowman's floristic hypothesis, but they are predicted by competition theory.

TABLE 2. PRESENCE (X) AND ABSENCE (0) OF JOINT OCCURRENCES OF SPECIES OF *GEOSPIZA*[1]

	fuliginosa	*difficilis*	*scandens*	*fortis*	*conirostris*	*magnirostris*
fuliginosa	*					
difficilis	0	*				
scandens	X	0	*			
fortis	X	X	X	*		
conirostris	X	X	0	0	*	
magnirostris	X	X	X	X	X	*

[1] Species are ordered in a sequence of increasing size, so entries adjacent to the diagonal apply to size-neighbors.

Following up the last point, I have since done a multivariate analysis of bill sizes and have found that pairs of species tend to be more different in bill size in sympatry than in allopatry. The multivariate difference in bill size between any two species on an island is measured as the distance between their positions on a canonical variates plot (Fig. 3). The average distance for sympatric populations of a given pair of species is then compared with the average distance for all of the populations of those species, both sympatric and allopatric. This is repeated for all pairs of

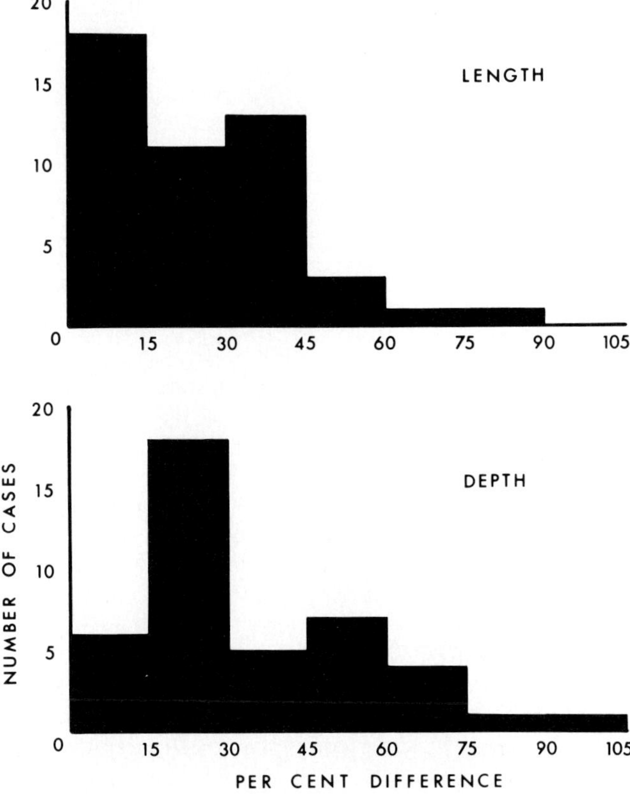

Fig. 2. Frequency distributions of male beak size differences among all pairs of coexisting *Geospiza* species. Original measurements of more than 90% of known museum specimens were made and supplied by I. J. Abbott. The six pairs differing in bill depth by less than 15% (*scandens* with *fortis* or *difficilis*) all differ in bill length more than 15% (e.g. see Table 3).

TABLE 3. PER CENT DIFFERENCE IN ADULT MALE BILL SIZE BETWEEN COEXISTING *G. SCANDENS* AND *G. FORTIS*

Island	Length	Depth	Width
Rábida	16.7	26.7	18.9
Marchena	31.2	**1.2**[1]	**2.8**
Isabela	21.7	19.6	**14.7**
Santa Cruz	24.6	19.3	**13.3**
Pinta	30.6	**6.2**	**0.2**
San Salvador	**13.6**	39.5	19.5
San Cristóbal	**8.9**	31.8	20.3
Santa Fe	**14.5**	19.0	**14.7**
Pinzón	34.5	**10.8**	**2.0**
Champion	**14.2**	30.6	15.8
Gardner/Floreana	**11.3**	21.3	17.2
Floreana	18.9	22.2	**13.5**
Baltra	29.0	17.9	**11.7**
Daphne Major	37.0	**1.9**	**1.0**

[1] Differences of less than 15% are in bold.

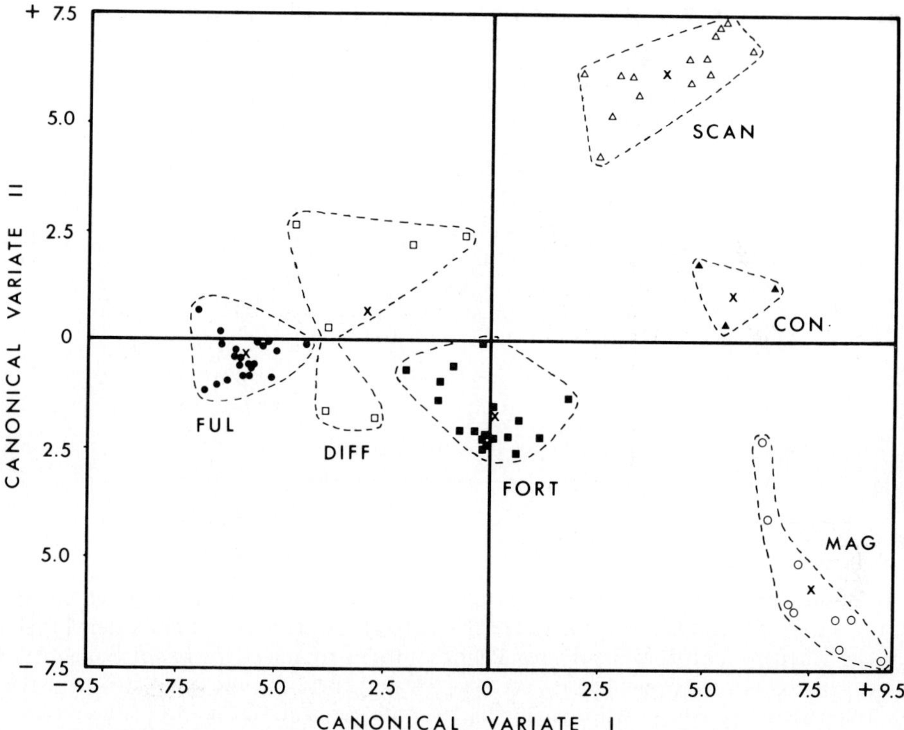

Fig. 3. Canonical variates of male beak length, depth and width for all populations of the six *Geospiza* species represented in museum collections by at least five specimens. Symbols as in Fig. 1. Mean position of each species is shown by a cross.

species. The result (Fig. 4) is that 11 of the 13 pairs of species are more different when sympatric than would be expected on the basis of randomly combining populations (Sign Test: $P = 0.022$). The implication is that character displacement has occurred in some of the situations.

Surprisingly, the two exceptions are the two most similar pairs of species; these are *G. difficilis* with *G. fuliginosa* and *G. difficilis* with *G. fortis*. They seem to be more similar when co-occurring than expected by chance. Here convergence may be due to responses to some environmental factor which varies latitudinally. The three islands where these pairs occur (or occurred), Santa Cruz, Santiago and Pinta, are located somewhat centrally in the archipelago. *G. difficilis* occurs in the more northern islands in the absence of the other two species, and *G. fuliginosa* and *G. fortis* occur on the southern islands in the absence of *G. difficilis.* Moreover, one of these pairs should probably be deleted because it is doubtful that the species coexist even though they occur on the same island. *G. difficilis* and *G. fuliginosa* have become spatially isolated to a large, and possibly complete, extent through occupying different altitudinal zones, perhaps in part because they are ecologically too similar to coexist. It is also possible that *G. fortis* is to a large extent allopatric with *G. difficilis.*

RECENT STUDIES: SEASONAL COMPARISON

If competition is a potent force we should be able to detect its effects by studying the finches at contrasting times of food abundance and scarcity. The wet season, when we did our initial work (Abbott et al. 1977), is a time of abundance. We therefore returned at the end of the dry season of the same year (1973), a time of food scarcity. We found that there had been an adjustment of finch numbers to food supply. Whereas there was no correlation between finch numbers

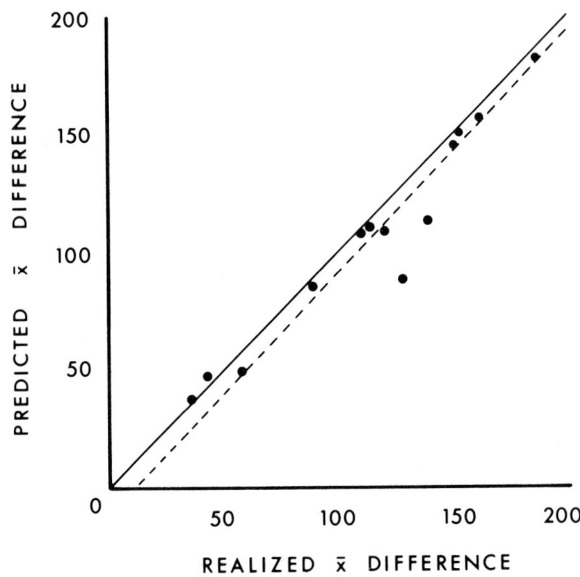

Fig. 4. Prediction of multivariate beak differences, in arbitrary units, between co-occurring *Geospiza* congeners. Predicted differences are the differences between species means for all island populations, whether they coexist or not. Realized differences are averages of the actual differences between co-occurring populations of those species; these include populations on the same island but apparently separated altitudinally, e.g. *G. fuliginosa* and *G. difficilis*. If predictions were correct in all cases, all points would lie along the solid line; the broken line is a least squares best fit to the points. *G. conirostris* and *G. scandens* are predicted to co-occur with a multivariate difference of 67 units, whereas in fact they never occur on the same island. Based on data in Fig. 3, *G. conirostris* and *G. scandens* also do not occur together; the predicted multivariate difference of this pair of species is 78 units.

and seed numbers at eight sites in the wet season, there was now a positive correlation at five sites in the dry season (Smith et al. 1978). This suggests that food was the limiting factor in the dry season but not in the wet season. Competition for food occurred, and the result was death or emigration. Such competition could be intraspecific, interspecific or both. How might we recognize interspecific competitive effects?

We reasoned that in a patterned heterogeneous environment competition between species with overlapping diets should lead to restriction of diets. Finches would be expected to concentrate on food items that they are best adapted to handle, and on the patches where those particular food items are found in greater than average numbers.

In accordance with expectation, we found that diversity of diets decreased and interspecific diet overlaps decreased from wet to dry season. These changes were the result of a shift from a common wet season diet of soft, easy-to-handle seeds and fruits to divergent diets, each reflecting the morphological and behavioral specializations of the respective species (Smith et al. 1978). The results are the opposite of what is predicted by several simple models of optimal diets in a competitive environment, perhaps because those models do not take adequate account of the co-variation of food diversity, food abundance and patch distribution over a long period of time. Our results can be interpreted as indicating increasing patch specialization as food abundance decreases. Because patches do not contain the total variety of food types, diets are restricted even though finches may forage in a generalized fashion within those patches.

FUTURE STUDIES

I have established a case for the role of interspecific competition, but I have avoided the question of whether it is still an ingredient of natural selection. The adaptive radiation may have been guided by interspecific competition in the past, but perhaps the radiation is finished, and now whenever interspecific competition occurs it is relatively transitory, non-selective and without enduring effects. This may be true, but I think the case for the evolutionary role of interspecific competition will be strengthened if it can be shown that directional selection occurs now, even though it is oscillatory between phenotypic optima (Grant et al. 1976), and that it occurs in a direction and at a time predicted by an hypothesis of interspecific competition for food.

A program of research being conducted by P. T. Boag on Daphne Major island is partly directed towards this possibility. Daphne Major is a suitable island because it is small (32 ha), it has no mockingbirds, which are nest predators, and it has manageable populations of about 1500 *G. fortis* and 400 *G. scandens* (Grant et al. 1975), which are size-neighbors and hence potential competitors. We have measured beak and body dimensions, banded and released more than 1000 finches. We have the opportunity of making crude estimates of the heritabilities of these traits by relating offspring measurements to parental measurements (Boag and Grant 1978). This will tell us something about the additive genetic variance underlying the traits. We also have the opportunity of following the fates of cohorts to see who survives best and who reproduces most. With this information we should be in a position to (a) assess the significance of population variation in these phenotypic traits; (b) detect selection on those traits, if it occurs; (c) estimate the intensity of selection; and (d) test the prediction that under conditions of severe food limitation in a heterogeneous environment, selection favors divergent individuals of *G. fortis* and *G. scandens*. We predict that this will occur in a year when rains fail and, as a result, the plants produce a sparse seed crop. We are poised in readiness to test the prediction immediately, inasmuch as the rains have failed to materialize on Daphne Major this year [editor's note: 1977].

For symmetry I shall end, as I began, with a quotation from Haldane (1937): "No scientific theory is worth anything unless it enables us to predict something which is actually going on. Until that is done, theories are a mere game with words, and not such a good game as poetry."

ACKNOWLEDGMENTS

Our research has been supported by NRC (Canada) and McGill University and has been facilitated by P. Kramer and C. MacFarland of the Charles Darwin Research Station. Mary LeCroy kindly measured the Ecuadorian finches in the American Museum of Natural History in exactly the same way as Ian Abbott measured museum specimens of Darwin's finches, and I am grateful to both for making their measurements available. I appreciate comments on an earlier manuscript and various other forms of help from I. J. Abbott, P. T. Boag, J. N. M. Smith, and my wife.

RESUMEN

Según una teoría importante, el máximo número de especies en una comunidad está determinado por la competencia interspecífica por alimentos. Es posible aplicar esta teoría para predecir el número de especies de pinzones terrestres de Darwin en las Islas Galápagos, basándose en el conocimiento de dos tipos de informaciones: 1) la provisión de alimentos de las islas y 2) la mínima diferencia en la dieta entre los competidores. Se predecinía que ocurran siete especies, pero en realidad hay sólamente seis y no más de cinco occurren en una misma isla. Hay varías razones possibles que explicanían la discrepancia entre el número de especies observado y el predicho. Se necesitan estudios adicionales sobre la provisión de alimentos en las islas (y en el continente) y acerca de la dieta de los pinzones.

La competencia entre pinzones conduce a la evolución de grandes diferencias morfológicas. Los pinzones de Darwin proveen evidencia de esto: las especies coexistentes se diferencian más entre sí de lo que se esperara si la competencia no existiera. Estudios recientes de los pinzones terrestres han demostrado que el tamaño de las poblaciones esta limitado por la cantidad de alimento disponible en la época seca; que, durante dicha época, están sujectos a una selección natural, y que la competencia interspecífica podría ser un componente importante en las fuerzas selectivas que operan en los pinzones.

LITERATURE CITED

Abbott, I. 1976. Comparisons of habitat structure and plant, arthropod and bird diversity between mainland and island sites near Perth, Western Australia. Austr. J. Ecol. 1:275-280.

Abbott, I. J., L. K. Abbott, and P. R. Grant. 1977. Comparative ecology of Galápagos ground finches (*Geospiza* Gould): Evaluation of the importance of floristic diversity and interspecific competition. Ecol. Monogr. 47(2):151-184.

Allan, J. D., L. W. Barnthouse, R. A. Prestbye, and D. R. Strong. 1973. On foliage arthropod communities of Puerto Rican second growth vegetation. Ecology 54:628-632.

Bailey, K. 1976. Potassium-argon ages from the Galápagos Islands. Science 194:465-467.

Beebe, W. 1924. Galápagos: World's end. G. P. Putnam's Sons, New York, N. Y.

Boag, P. T., and P. R. Grant. 1978. Heritability of external morphology in Darwin's finches. Nature 274:793-794.

Bowman, R. I. 1961. Morphological differentiation and adaptation in the Galápagos finches. Univ. Calif. Publ. Zool. 58:1-302.

Caswell, H. 1976. Community structure: A neutral model analysis. Ecol. Monogr. 46(3):327-354.

Darwin, C. 1859. On the origin of species by means of natural selection, or the preservation of favoured species in the struggle for life. John Murray, London.

Diamond, J. M. 1973. Distributional ecology of New Guinea birds. Science 179:759-769.

Grant, P. R. 1968. Bill size, body size, and the ecological adaptations of bird species to competitive situations on islands. Syst. Zool. 17:319-333.

Grant, P. R. 1972. Bill dimensions of the three species of *Zosterops* on Norfolk Island. Syst. Zool. 21:289-291.

Grant, P. R. 1975. Four Galápagos Islands. Geogr. J. 141:76-87.

Grant, P. R., and P. T. Boag. 1980. Rainfall on the Galápagos and the demography of Darwin's finches. Auk 97:227-244.

Grant, P. R., J. N. M. Smith, B. R. Grant, I. J. Abbott, and L. K. Abbott. 1975. Finch numbers, owl predation and plant dispersal on Isla Daphne Major, Galápagos. Oecologia (Berlin) 19: 239-257.

Grant, P. R., B. R. Grant, J. N. M. Smith, I. J. Abbott, and L. K. Abbott. 1976. Darwin's finches: Population variation and natural selection. Proc. Nat'l. Acad. Sci. USA 73:257-261.

Haldane, J. B. S. 1937. Adventures of a biologist. Harper and Bros., New York, N. Y.

Hespenheide, H. A. 1972. Ecological inferences from morphological data. Ann. Rev. Ecol. Syst. 4:213-229.

Janzen, D. H. 1973. Sweep samples of tropical foliage insects: Effects of seasons, vegetation types, elevation, time of day, and insularity. Ecology 54:687-708.

Lack, D. 1945. The Galápagos finches (Geospizinae): A study in variation. Occas. Pap. Calif. Acad. Sci. 21:1-159.

Lack, D. 1947. Darwin's finches. Cambridge University Press, Cambridge.

MacArthur, R. 1972. Geographical ecology. Harper and Row, New York, N. Y.

Marchant, S. 1958. The birds of the Santa Elena Peninsula, S. W. Ecuador. Ibis 100:349-387.

May, R. M. 1972. Stability and complexity in model ecosystems. Princeton University Press, Princeton, N. J.

Mayr, E. 1961. Cause and effect in biology. Science 134:1501-1506.

Mezhzherin, V. A. 1971. Energetic structure of zoological systems. Nature 231:461-462.

Pianka, E. R. 1966. Latitudinal gradients in species diversity: A review of concepts. Amer. Nat. 100:33-46.

Pulliam, H. R. 1975. Coexistence of sparrows: A test of community theory. Science 189:474-476.

Smith, J. N. M., P. R. Grant, B. R. Grant, I. J. Abbott, and L. K. Abbott. 1978. Seasonal variation in feeding habits of Darwin's ground finches. Ecology 59:1137-1150.

Svenson, H. K. 1946. Vegetation of the coast of Ecuador and Peru and its relation to the Galápagos Archipelago. Amer. J. Bot. 33:394-426.

ADDENDUM

Since early 1977, when this paper was prepared, two developments have occurred that make it out of date in places. First, we have accomplished some of the tasks heralded in the paper. Second, a minor explosion of papers dealing with the question of interspecific competition among Darwin's finches has occurred. I will comment on these two developments in turn.

Our earlier work had yielded estimates of high heritabilities of bill and body size traits in *G. fortis* on Isla Daphne Major (Boag and Grant 1978), and subsequent work showed *G. scandens* heritabilities to be generally high also (Boag 1981). In the present paper I predicted that selection, favoring divergent individuals of *G. fortis* and *G. scandens*, would occur during the drought of 1977 and its aftermath. As predicted, agents of selection did act on both species, and the intensity of selection was particularly high in *G. fortis* (Boag 1981; Boag and Grant 1981; Grant and Price 1981).

However, during 1977 we realized that the prediction of divergence was unrealistically simple. It was based on the unstated assumption that the ecological relationship of the two species conformed to the standard pattern of overlapping niches. In fact *G. scandens*, a feeding specialist, has a niche included in that of *G. fortis*, which is a feeding generalist (Grant and Grant 1980). Under these circumstances it is to be expected that *G. scandens* would undergo stabilizing selection and *G. fortis* would undergo directional selection. This is what did happen (Boag 1981; Boag and Grant 1981; Grant and Price 1981). An expectation of competition theory is that as food abundance declines, the overlap in niches of the two species should decrease. This also happened in 1977 during a period of apparently strong food limitation and high finch mortality (Boag 1981), with a reversal of the trend in niche divergence occurring only after the resurgence of a single resource, *Opuntia* flowers (Boag 1981; Grant and Grant 1980). This provides indirect evidence that competition between the species for a diminishing food supply contributed to the selective mortality experienced by each species.

The issue of whether interspecific competition has had a detectable influence on the structuring of *Geospiza* communities (guilds) in the past has been taken up by Connor and Simberloff (1978), Simberloff (1978, 1983), Simberloff and Boecklin (1981), Simberloff and Connor (1979, 1981), Strong and Simberloff (1981), and Strong et al. (1979). The main point of these papers is methodological. The authors argue that morphological and distributional data should not be taken as evidence for competition until they are tested against, and found to reject, null hypotheses of no interaction among species. They show how, in their view, null hypotheses should be constructed. They have applied numerous statistical tests to published data, and in almost all cases have found no reason to reject the null hypotheses. Simberloff (1983) lists seven exceptions to the trend, including three reported in the present paper.

While unexceptionable in calling for the rigorous testing of hypotheses, these studies have themselves been criticized on methodological grounds (Case 1983; Case and Sidell 1982; Colwell and Winkler 1983; Grant and Abbott 1980; Grant and Schluter 1983; Hendrickson 1981; Schoener 1983). The random colonization models have been criticized on the grounds of inappropriate species pools and sampling procedures (Grant and Abbott 1980). Case (1983), Case and Sidell (1982), and Colwell and Winkler (1983) have explicitly shown how the use of these particular models does not detect the effects of competition even when competition is known to have occurred. The tests of minimum or regular morphological differences between coexisting species have been criticized on analogous grounds; the assumption of a uniform distribution of morphological traits for the null model is not realistic (Schoener 1983). The net effect of all of the artificialities in the models is to bias the results towards accepting the null hypothesis when it is false, i.e. making a statistical type II error (Grant and Abbott 1980). Therefore, the large number of negative results produced from a plethora of tests in these studies is not surprising. The effort underscores once again the difficulties of devising and conducting realistic tests of the competition hypothesis in the absence of detailed ecological information and experimental studies (Abbott 1980).

Several but not all of our own efforts to test the competition hypothesis, following the approach of Abbott et al. (1977), have resulted in support for the hypothesis and rejection of alternatives (Grant and Grant 1982; Grant and Schluter 1983). Moreover there is agreement that some of the distributional and morphological data from the *Geospiza* species support the competition hypothesis (Grant and Schluter 1983; Simberloff 1983). We now have the more difficult task of assessing just how important competition is and has been in structuring species assemblages.

I conclude by identifying some errors in this paper. First, the probability values for *Geospiza* species occurrences on islands given in Abbott et al. (1977) and repeated in Table 1 of the present paper are slightly wrong. Correct values are given in Grant and Schluter (1983). The errors are conservative, and the conclusion on non-randomness amongst the species has actually been strengthened (Grant and Schluter 1983). Second, extensive fieldwork by Schluter (1982a,b) has shown that *G. difficilis* is not altitudinally separated from *G. fuliginosa* and *G. scandens* on Isla Pinta, in contrast to what we previously reported (Abbott et al. 1977). Moreover on San Salvador also, where *G. scandens* is rare, *G. difficilis* and *G. fuliginosa* have overlapping distributions. These new observations necessitate corrections to details in the text of this paper, but not to the overall conclusion.

LITERATURE CITED

Boag, P. T. 1981. A population study of two species of Darwin's finches (Geospizinae) on the Galápagos Islands. Unpubl. Ph.D. Thesis. McGill University, Montreal, Can.

Boag, P. T., and P. R. Grant. 1978. Heritability of external morphology in Darwin's finches. Nature 274:793-794.

Boag, P. T., and P. R. Grant. 1981. Intense natural selection on a population of Darwin's finches (Geospizinae) in the Galápagos. Science 214(4516): 82-85.

Case, T. J. 1983. Geographical ecology of sex and size in *Cnemidophorus* lizards. *In* R. B. Huey, E. R. Pianka and T. W. Schoener, eds. Lizard Ecology: Studies on a Model Organism. Harvard University Press, Cambridge, Mass.

Case, T., and R. Sidell. 1982. Pattern and chance in the structure of model and natural communities. Evolution 36.

Colwell, R. K., and D. Winkler. 1983. A null model for null models in evolutionary ecology. *In* D. R. Strong, D. S. Simberloff, and L. G. Abele, eds. Ecological Communities: Conceptual Issues and the Evidence. Princeton University Press, Princeton, N. J.

Connor, E. F., and D. Simberloff. 1978. Species number and compositional similarity of the Galápagos flora and avifauna. Ecol. Monogr. 48:219-248.

Grant, P. R., and I. Abbott. 1980. Interspecific competition, null hypotheses and island biogeography. Evolution 34:332-341.

Grant, P. R., and B. R. Grant. 1980. Annual variation in finch numbers, foraging and food supply on Isla Daphne Major, Galápagos. Oecologia (Berl.) 46:55-62.

Grant, P. R., and B. R. Grant. 1982. Niche shifts and competition in Darwin's finches: *Geospiza conirostris* and congeners. Evolution 36:637-657.

Grant, P. R., and T. D. Price. 1981. Population variation in continuously varying traits as an ecological genetics problem. Amer. Zool. 21:795-811.

Grant, P. R., and D. Schluter. 1983. Interspecific competition inferred from patterns of guild structure. *In* D. R. Strong, D. S. Simberloff, and L. G. Abele, eds. Ecological Communities: Conceptual Issues and the Evidence. Princeton University Press, Princeton, N. J.

Hendrickson, J. A., Jr. 1981. Community-wide character displacement reexamined. Evolution 35:794-809.

Schluter, D. 1982a. Seed and patch selection by Galápagos ground finches: Relation to foraging efficiency and food supply. Ecology 63:1106-1120.

Schluter, D. 1982b. Distributions of Galápagos ground finches along an altitudinal gradient: The importance of food supply. Ecology 63:1504-1517.

Schoener, T. W. 1983. Size-differences among sympatric, bird-eating hawks: A worldwide survey. *In* D. R. Strong, D. S. Simberloff and L. G. Abele, eds. Ecological Communities: Conceptual Issues and the Evidence. Princeton University Press, Princeton, N. J.

Simberloff, D. 1978. Using island biogeographic distributions to determine if colonization is stochastic. Amer. Natur. 112:713-726.

Simberloff, D. 1983. Morphological and taxonomic similarity and combinations of coexisting birds in two archipelagoes. *In* D. R. Strong, D. S. Simberloff, and L. G. Abele, eds. Ecological Communities: Conceptual Issues and the Evidence. Princeton University Press, Princeton, N. J.

Simberloff, D., and W. Boecklen. 1981. Santa Rosalia reconsidered: Size-ratios and competition. Evolution 35:1206-1228.

Simberloff, D. S., and E. F. Connor. 1979. Q-mode and R-mode analyses of biogeographic distributions: null hypotheses based on random colonization. Pages 123-138 *in*: G. P. Patil and M. L. Rosenzweig, eds. Contemporary Quantitative Ecology and Related Ecometrics. Statistical Ecology Ser. 12.

Simberloff, D., and E. F. Connor. 1981. Missing species combinations. Amer. Natur. 115:215-239.

Strong, D. R., and D. Simberloff. 1981. Straining at gnats and swallowing ratios: Character displacement. Evolution 35:810-812.

Strong, D. R., L. A. Szyska, and D. Simberloff. 1979. Tests of community-wide character displacement against null hypotheses. Evolution 33:897-913.

KARYOTYPIC ANALYSIS OF DARWIN'S FINCHES

NANCY JO
Department of Biological Sciences, San Francisco State University, San Francisco, CA 94132

The chromosomes of 138 individuals of Darwin's finches, including 12 species, were examined. The analysis of the karyotypes has demonstrated a striking similarity among the species in the number (mean = 76) and gross morphology of the chromosomes. From six well-defined metaphase figures from each species, the seven largest pairs of chromosomes were measured. The sex chromosomes of females from 11 species were found to be heteromorphic. In a comparison of the karyotypes of 5 species of the family Fringillidae, viz. *Zonotrichia albicollis* and *Junco hyemalis* of the subfamily Emberizinae, *Geospiza magnirostris* of the subfamily Geospizinae, and *Serinus canarius* and *Fringilla coelebs* of the subfamily Fringillinae, three possible interpretations of phylogenetic relationships have emerged.

With the development of new cytogenetic methods, there has been a significant increase in the number of studies of avian chromosomes. Made possible by the introduction of the hypotonic pretreatment, which was first applied to the study of mammalian chromosomes by Hsu and Pomerat (1953), adaptations of mammalian techniques to avian tissues have been made by Sandnes (1954), Krishan (1962, 1963) and Shoffner et al. (1967). Several in vitro and in vivo colchicine-hypotonic citrate methods are currently in use, including feather-pulp culture (Sasaki et al. 1968), peripheral blood culture (Takagi et al. 1972), embryo culture (Piccini and Stella 1970) and the in vivo method of Patton (1967).

Although these techniques have made possible the analysis of the morphology of chromosome complements in the class Aves, exact determination of the total chromosome number (2*N*) is still difficult, due to the high number of microchromosomes in their complements (Ohno 1961; Ray-Chaudhuri 1973). According to Shields (1982), the karyotypes of only about 3% of the living species of birds have been described. Ohno et al. (1964) have demonstrated that the karyotypes of some orders of the subclass Carinatae are quite similar. Subsequent work by Hammar (1966, 1970), Ray-Chaudhuri et al. (1969), Piccini and Stella (1970), and Ray-Chaudhuri (1973) suggests that bird karyotypes are markedly conservative in both number and morphology. Indeed, the apparent similarity of bird karyotypes led Shoffner (1974), Stock et al. (1974) and Takagi and Sasaki (1974) to question whether the application of karyological data would be fruitful in determining phylogenetic relationships of birds. Stock, Takagi, and their respective collaborators independently arrived at the application of the G-banding technique to determine whether the morphologically similar chromosomes are homologous. Thus, for example, these workers found that the three largest chromosomes of *Gallus domesticus* (order Galliformes), *Columba livida,* and *Streptopelia risoria* (order Columbiformes) are homologous (Stock et al. 1974; Takagi and Sasaki 1974; but see Shields 1982). These findings led the latter authors to conclude that the three homologous chromosomes were transmitted from a common ancestor.

Although the application of modern techniques has permitted cytogeneticists to explore the vast field of avian cytotaxonomy, much remains to be investigated. The present study is a preliminary quantitative analysis of the chromosome morphology of Darwin's finches, using standard karyotypic techniques. Its purpose is to attempt to correlate the chromosomal findings with the known structural patterns (Lack 1947; Tordoff 1954; Bowman 1961; Cutler 1970) and to assess this information in the light of the various phylogenetic relationships proposed within the family Fringillidae. Future findings using G-, R-, and C-banding techniques are likely to be of greatest value in elucidating the chromosomal picture in birds.

MATERIALS AND METHODS

A total of 257 Darwin's finches were captured in the field with the use of mist nets. This sample includes 12 species from 12 islands of the Galapagos Archipelago (Fig. 1). Preliminary identification of the finches was made at the time of collection and later verified by examination of the carcasses, which were preserved in formalin. Specimens were deposited in the Vertebrate Museum of San Francisco State University.

Of the specimens collected, a total of 138 were processed for chromosomal analysis. Reference to these materials is made by field catalogue number, preceded by the collector's initials, NJ. All 257 specimens have been electrophoretically assayed (Polans, this volume).

In general, chromosomes were prepared using the colchicine-hypotonic citrate technique of Ford and Hamerton (1956), modified by Patton (1967). Slides were examined under a phase contrast Carl Zeiss microscope with Neofluar objective. Metaphase plates were photographed at magnification of 800x, and final prints were enlarged to 4000x. All measurements and counts were made at this magnification. The relative length (=RL) was determined for each chromosome, and the centromeric index (=CI) calculated using the seven largest pairs of chromosomes from six

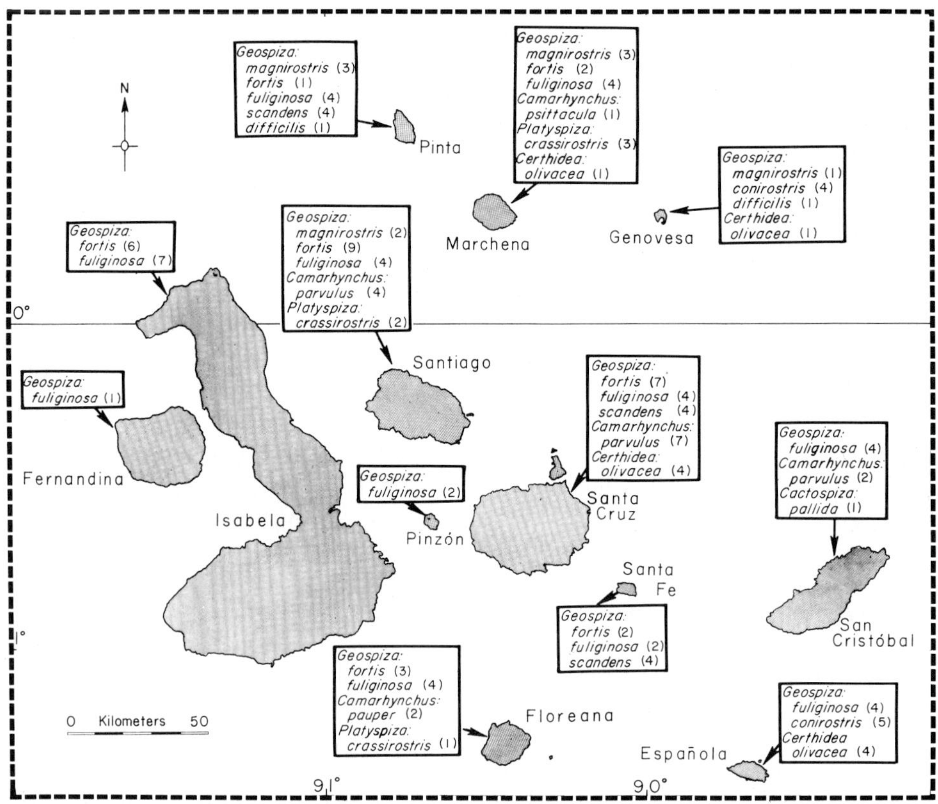

Fig. 1. Island sources of 138 individuals of Darwin's finches from the Galapagos Archipelago used in determining karyotypes.

well-defined metaphase figures of each species. Measurements of relative length were made following the method of Takagi and Sasaki (1974). The relative length of the chromosome was defined as percent of the total length of the haploid set excluding the microchromosomes after the seventh pair. Mean difference in relative length and centromeric index was tested by analysis of variance (ANOVA). All chromosomes are arranged in the karyograms according to size, including the sex chromosomes. Chromosome designation follows Levan (1964): median (m, centromeric index from 37.5 to 47.5, sub-median (sm, CI from 25.0 to 37.5), subterminal (st, CI from 12.5 to 25.0), telocentric or acrocentric (t, CI from 2.5 to 12.5).

For chromosomal comparison among members of the family Fringillidae, measurements, as described above, were taken from published photographs of the particular species under consideration. The measurements were used in the construction of a comparative ideogram. The following species were compared: subfamily Fringillinae (vide Sibley 1970)–*Serinus canarius* (Fig. 10 of Ohno et al. [1964]), *Fringilla coelebs* (Fig. 1 of Piccina and Stella [1970]); subfamily Emberizinae–*Zonotrichia albicollis* (standard karyotype A in Fig. 1 of Thorneycroft [1975]), *Junco hyemalis* (standard karyotype A in Fig. 5 of Shields [1973]).

In addition to the above, the following specimens were examined:

Geospiza magnirostris. Isla Pinta (N=3), NJ 131-132, 163. Isla Marchena (N=3), NJ 173, 175, 179. Isla Genovesa (N=1), NJ 183. Isla Santiago: Bahía James (N=2), NJ 239, 241.

Geospiza fortis. Isla Santa Cruz: Bahía Academy (N=6), NJ 2-3, 28-31; Transition zone, road from Puerto Ayora to Bellavista (N=1), NJ 252. Isla Santa Fé (N=2), NJ 44-45. Isla Floreana: Black Beach, road to Chacras (N=3), NJ 98-99, 102. Isla Isabela: Tagus Cove (N=6), NJ 117-118, 122-125. Isla Pinta (N=1), NJ 135. Isla Marchena (N=2), NJ 167, 174. Isla Santiago: Bahía James (N=9), NJ 205-206, 236, 238, 240, 243-246.

Geospiza fuliginosa. Isla Santa Cruz: Bahía Academy (N=4), NJ 1, 32-34. Isla Santa Fe (N=3), NJ 38, 49-50. Isla San Cristóbal: El Progreso (N=4), NJ 52, 54-56. Isla Española: Bahía Gardner (N=4), NJ 76-79. Isla Floreana: Black Beach, road to Chacras (N=4), NJ 100-101, 103-104. Isla Isabela: Tagus Cove (N=6), NJ 119-121, 126-128; Bahía Cartago (N=1), NJ 199. Isla Fernandina (N=1), NJ 129. Isla Pinta (N=4), NJ 136, 141, 165-166. Isla Marchena (N=4), NJ 176-178, 180. Isla Santiago: Bahía James (N=4), NJ 202-204, 242. Isla Pinzón (N=2), NJ 197-198.

Geospiza conirostris. Isla Española: Bahía Gardner (N=5), NJ 93-97. Isla Genovesa (N=4), NJ 181, 184-186.

Geospiza scandens. Isla Santa Cruz: Bahía Academy (N=4), NJ 14-17. Isla Santa Fe (N=4), NJ 42, 43, 47, 48. Isla Pinta (N=4), NJ 137, 138, 140, 164.

Geospiza difficilis. Isla Pinta (N=1), NJ 139. Isla Genovesa (N=1), NJ 182.

Camarhynchus psittacula. Isla Marchena (N=1), NJ 171.

Camarhynchus pauper. Isla Floreana: Black Beach (N=2), NJ 105, 107.

Camarhynchus parvulus. Isla Santa Cruz: Bahía Academy (N=4), NJ 4, 35-37; Claudia Chastain's farm (highlands) (N=1), NJ 250; Transition Zone, road from Puerto Ayora to Bellavista (N=2), NJ 254, 255. Isla San Cristóbal: El Progreso (N=2), NJ 53, 57. Isla Floreana: Black Beach, road to Chacras (N=2), NJ 106, 108. Isla Santiago: Bahía James (N=4), NJ 201, 247-249.

Cactospiza pallida. Isla San Cristóbal: El Progreso (N=1), NJ 60.

Platyspiza crassirostris. Isla Floreana: Black Beach, road to Chacras (N=1), NJ 109. Isla Marchena (N=3), NJ 168-170. Isla Santiago: Bahía James (N=2), NJ 235, 237.

Certhidea olivacea. Isla Santa Cruz: Claudia Chastain's farm (highlands) (N=1), NJ 251; Transition Zone, road from Puerto Ayora to Bellavista (N=3), NJ 253, 256, 257. Isla Española: Gardner Bay (N=4), NJ 68-70, 73. Isla Marchena (N=1), NJ 172. Isla Genovesa (N=1), NJ 187.

RESULTS

The nearly identical karyotypes of 12 species (five genera) of Darwin's finches are illustrated in Figures 3-5. A summary of the number of metaphase cells counted and the observed range of the diploid number for each species is given in Fig. 2. Data on sample sizes (random sampling),

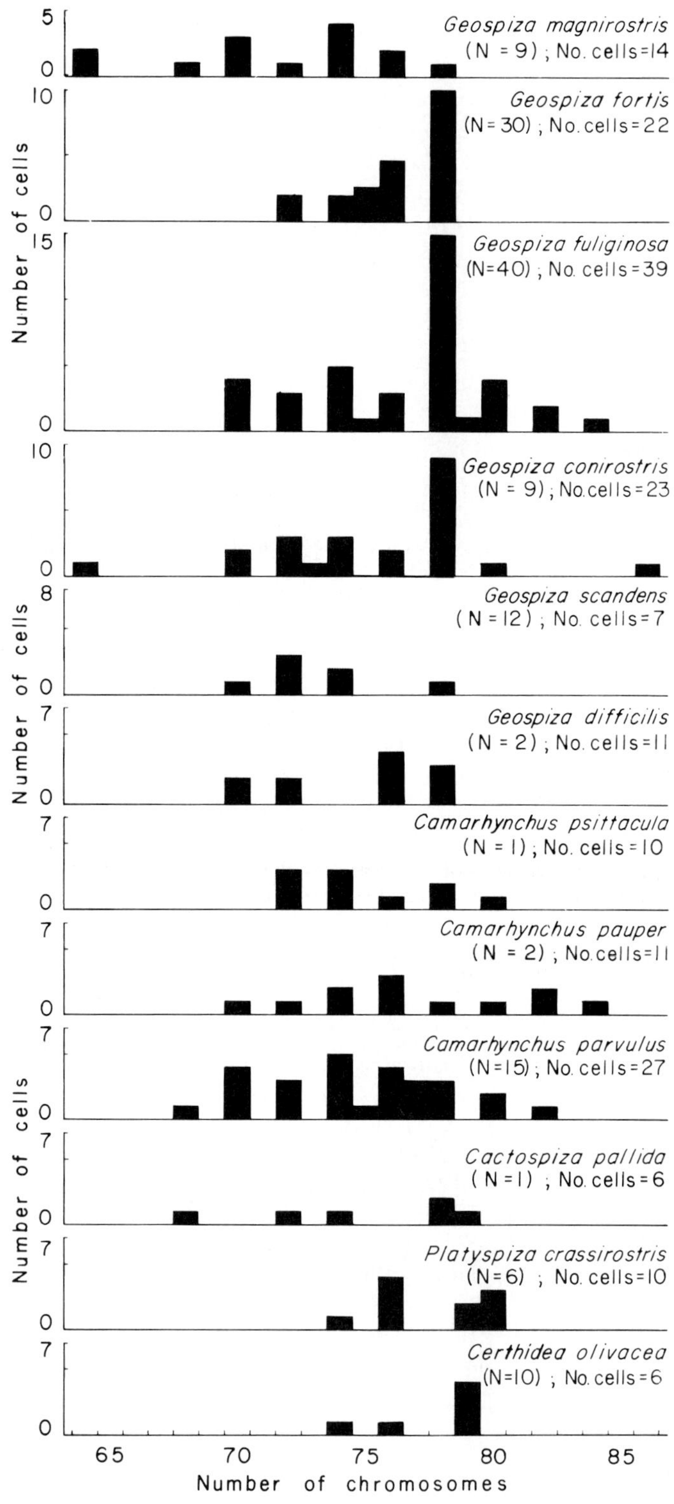

Fig. 2. Variation in the diploid number of chromosomes in twelve species of Darwin's finches.

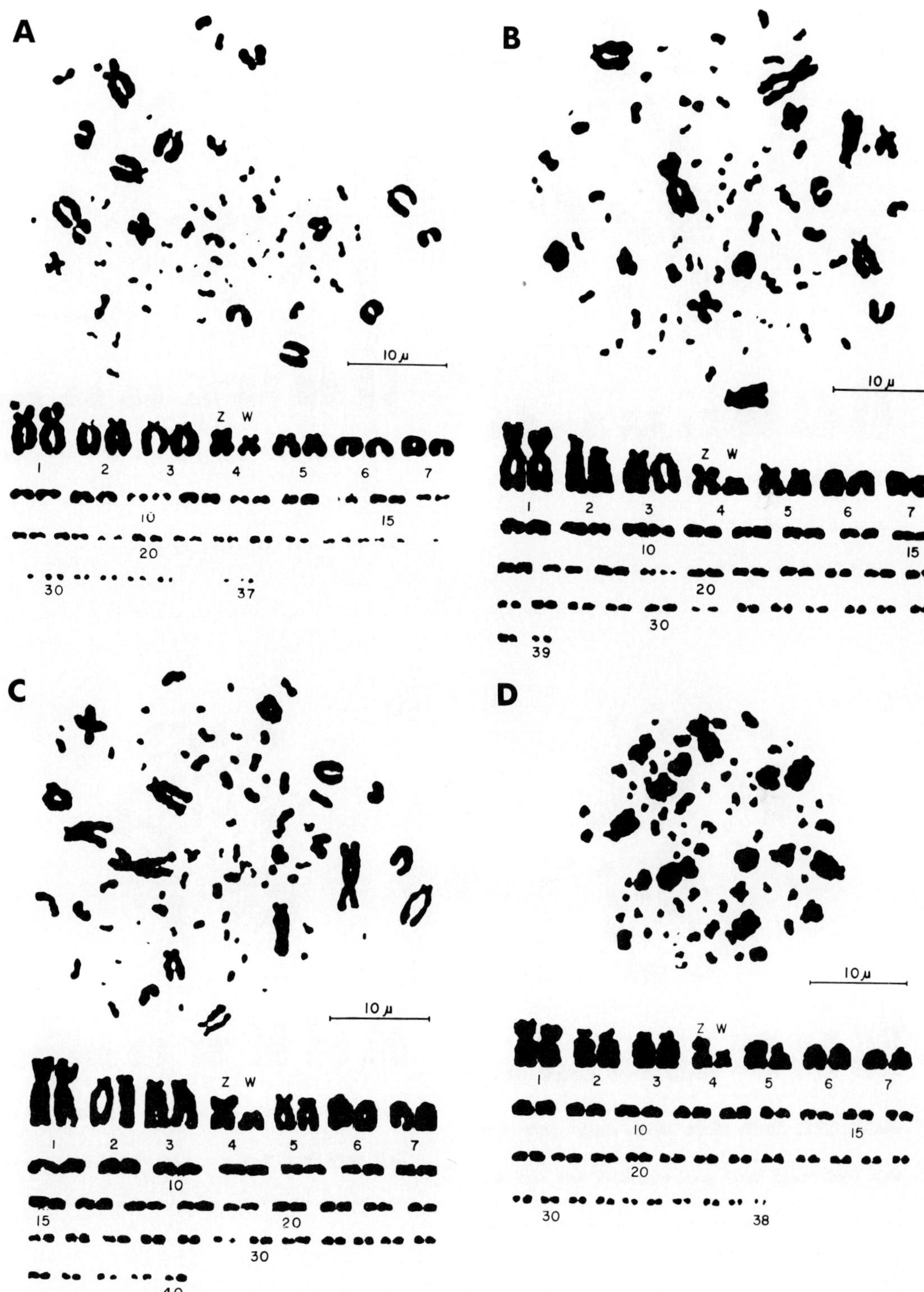

Fig. 3. Karyotypes of four species of Darwin's finches. A, *Geospiza magnirostris*, Isla Marchena (female, NJ 179); B, *Geospiza fortis*, Isla Santiago (female, NJ 236); C, *Geospiza fuliginosa*, Isla Santiago (female, NJ 204); D, *Geospiza difficilis*, Isla Genovesa (female, NJ 182).

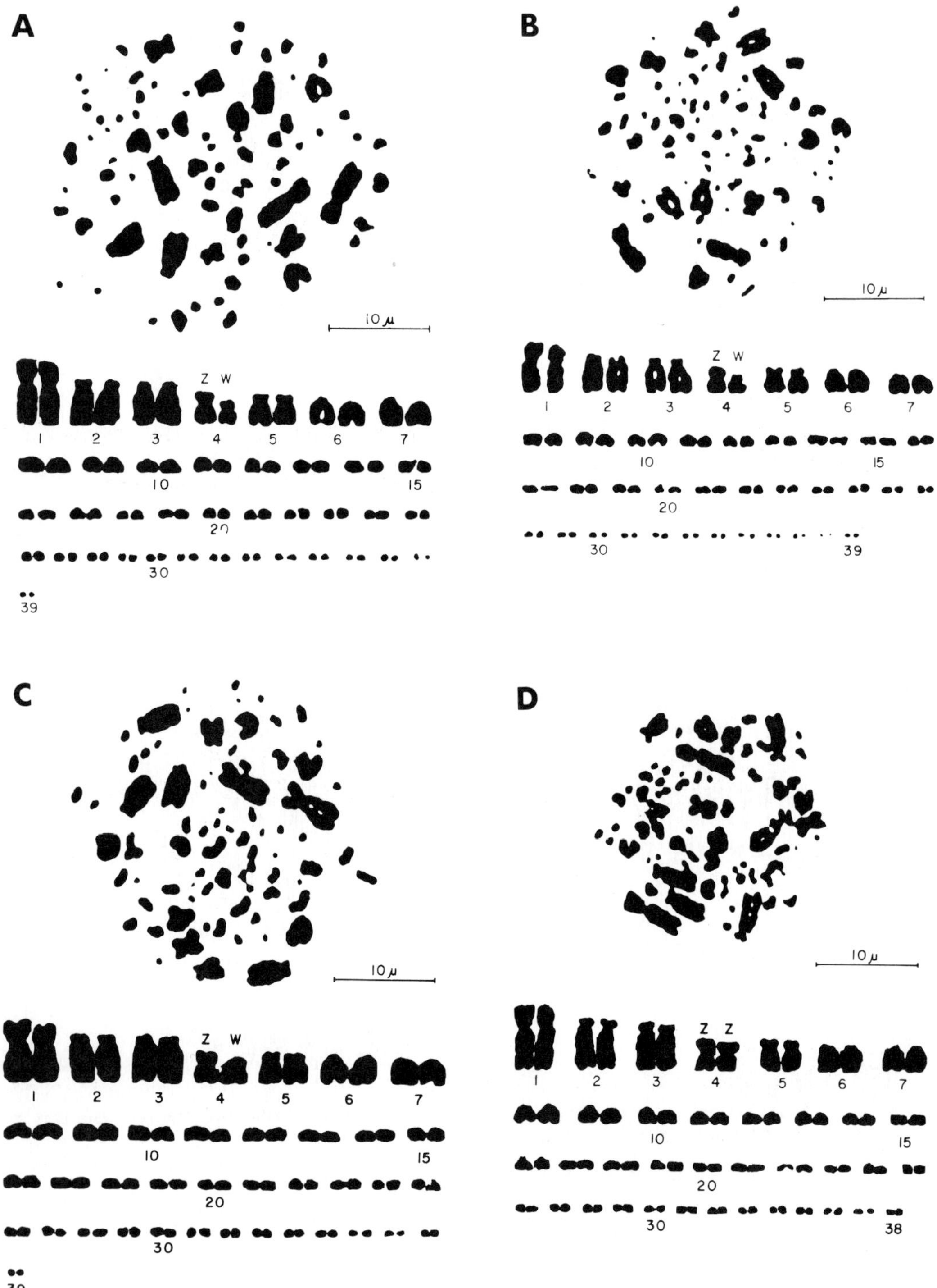

Fig. 4. Karyotypes of four species of Darwin's finches. A, *Geospiza conirostris*, Isla Genovesa (female, NJ 185); B, *Geospiza scandens*, Isla Pinta (female, NJ 137); C, *Cactospiza pallida*, Isla San Cristóbal (female, NJ 60); D, *Certhidea olivacea*, Isla Española (male, NJ 70).

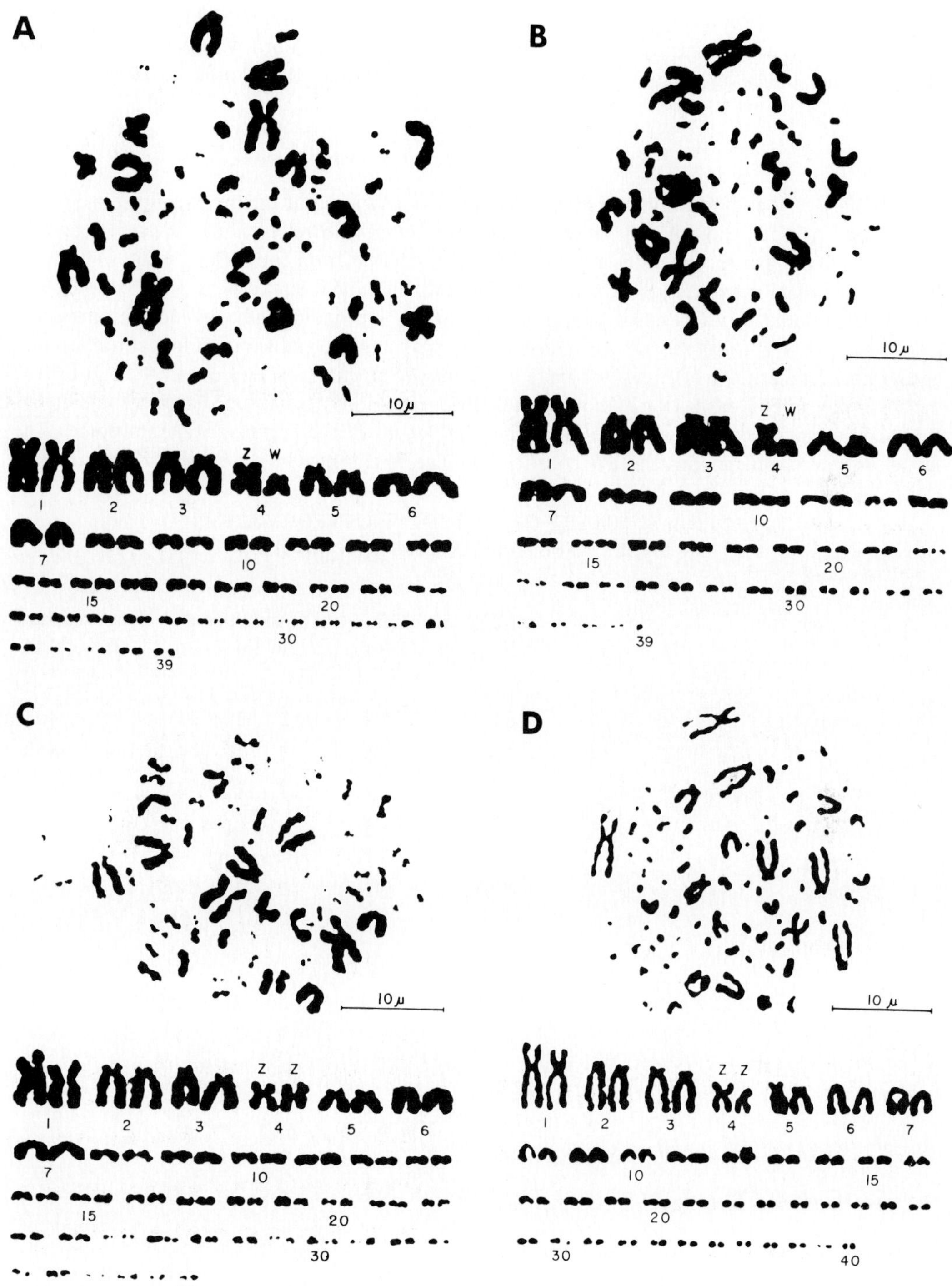

Fig. 5. Karyotypes of four species of Darwin's finches. A, *Platyspiza crassirostris*, Isla Santiago (female, NJ 235); B, *Camarhynchus psittacula*, Isla Marchena (female, NJ 171); C, *Camarhynchus pauper*, Isla Floreana (male, NJ 107); D, *Camarhynchus parvulus*, Isla Santiago (male, NJ 201).

diploid numbers and chromosome morphology are summarized in Table 1. In Table 2, the mean values of relative chromosome length and centromeric index are summarized and compared; no significant differences in the ANOVA, except for the relative length of the first chromosome pair (Table 2), are indicated. A follow-up multiple-range test (Woolf 1968) showed no significance between any of the means.

Karyotype of *Geospiza magnirostris*

In view of the uniformity in the karyotypes of the 12 species of finches examined, a detailed description is given below for only one species, *Geospiza magnirostris.* (Compare Figs. 3, 4, and 5.)

A total of nine specimens (four males and five females) from four islands (Fig. 1) was analyzed. The diploid number ranged from 64 to 78 with the modal count 74 (Fig. 2; Table 1). The macrochromosome series is composed of seven pairs of morphologically distinct chromosomes (Fig. 3A). Pair I is a sub-median chromosome; pairs II and III and sub-terminal chromosomes, and ordinal arrangement of these two pairs is arbitrary. Sex chromosomes constitute pair IV; the male is homogametic and has the ZZ constitution. Both chromosomes have median centromere position and average a little more than 50% of the total length of the first pair of chromosomes. The female is heterogametic with the ZW constitution. The W chromosome is a median chromosome,

TABLE 1. SUMMARY OF KARYOTYPIC INFORMATION ON TWELVE SPECIES OF DARWIN'S FINCHES

Species	Sex		2*N*	2*N*	Autosomes[1]			Sex Chromosomes	
	M	F	Range	Mode	sm	st	t	Z	W
Geospiza									
magnirostris	4	5	64-78	74	2	2	34±	m[1]	m
fortis	16	14	72-78	78	2	2	34±	m	m
fuliginosa	20	20	70-84	78	2	2	37±	m	m
conirostris	4	5	64-86	78	2	2	38±	m	m
scandens	6	6	70-78	72	2	2	34±	m	m
difficilis	1	1	70-78	76	2	2	34±	m	m
Camarhynchus									
psittacula	–	1	72-80	72 & 74	2	2	35±	m	m
pauper	2	–	70-84	76	2	2	37±	m	–
parvulus	6	9	68-82	74	2	2	36±	m	m
Cactospiza									
pallida	–	1	68-79	78	2	2	34±	m	m
Platyspiza									
crassirostris	3	3	74-80	76	2	2	35±	m	m
Certhidea									
olivacea	6	4	74-78	78	2	2	34±	m	m

$F = 0.74^{ns}$

[1] m=median centromere; sm=submedian centromere; st=subterminal centromere; t=terminal centromere; ns=not significant ($P = 0.05$).

TABLE 2. MEANS AND STANDARD ERRORS OF RELATIVE LENGTH (RL) AND CENTROMERIC INDEX (CI) OF SEVEN LARGEST PAIRS OF CHROMOSOMES FROM TWELVE SPECIES OF DARWIN'S FINCHES (^{s} significant [P=0.05]; ^{ns} not significant)

Species		Chromosome number							
		1	2	3	4 (Z)	4 (W)	5	6	7
Geospiza magnirostris	RL	22.23 ±0.39	17.69 ±0.34	16.69 ±0.19	12.27 ±0.24	5.91 ±0.34	11.44 ±0.28	10.37 ±0.55	9.01 ±0.37
	CI	35.42 ±1.16	21.20 ±1.56	23.00 ±0.68	46.23 ±1.34	37.21 ±2.54	30.16 ±1.31	-- --	-- --
fortis	RL	23.81 ±0.67	17.87 ±0.47	16.22 ±0.23	11.16 ±0.46	6.71 ±0.65	11.36 ±0.69	10.31 ±0.26	9.37 ±0.38
	CI	37.45 ±1.58	23.60 ±1.59	23.92 ±0.70	43.14 ±2.20	39.02 ±2.49	29.27 ±0.62	-- --	-- --
fuliginosa	RL	21.41 ±0.62	17.04 ±0.55	16.95 ±0.49	12.16 ±0.55	6.43 ±1.95	11.85 ±0.36	11.13 ±0.39	9.91 ±0.36
	CI	35.84 ±0.64	23.64 ±3.97	19.56 ±1.46	45.17 ±2.68	37.05 ±1.72	31.52 ±1.19	-- --	-- --
conirostris	RL	21.05 ±0.20	17.12 ±0.22	16.31 ±0.27	12.18 ±0.38	7.17 ±1.17	11.48 ±0.34	11.60 ±0.26	9.86 ±0.36
	CI	35.16 ±1.02	20.40 ±1.24	23.46 ±1.18	43.75 ±0.99	39.86 ±1.98	32.85 ±1.57	-- --	-- --
scandens	RL	21.24 ±0.32	17.90 ±0.90	16.35 ±0.25	11.82 ±0.25	5.51 --	11.37 ±0.46	11.12 ±0.36	9.96 ±0.31
	CI	36.10 ±0.85	21.91 ±1.84	20.18 ±1.02	41.91 ±1.91	42.92 --	33.23 ±1.39	-- --	-- --
difficilis	RL	21.42 ±0.68	17.72 ±0.18	16.48 ±0.30	12.88 ±0.38	6.06 --	11.88 ±0.45	10.33 ±0.38	9.38 ±0.34
	CI	36.10 ±0.63	17.22 ±2.41	21.59 ±0.77	42.93 ±2.12	41.15 --	31.18 ±2.43	-- --	-- --
Camarhynchus psittacula	RL	21.30 ±0.54	17.59 ±0.18	15.67 ±0.44	12.32 ±0.54	5.17 --	11.76 ±0.24	11.44 ±0.27	10.02 ±0.42
	CI	36.18 ±0.99	18.91 ±1.86	22.90 ±4.23	44.92 ±1.80	33.36 --	26.91 ±1.92	-- --	-- --
pauper	RL	21.15 ±0.08	17.62 ±0.30	16.45 ±0.20	13.09 ±0.48	-- --	11.78 ±0.31	10.89 ±0.31	9.36 ±0.25
	CI	37.15 ±0.72	22.60 ±2.65	19.96 ±1.09	46.76 ±2.01	-- --	31.01 ±1.37	-- --	-- --
parvulus	RL	21.96 ±0.82	18.67 ±0.52	16.99 ±0.50	12.37 ±0.37	5.18 --	11.18 ±0.19	10.15 ±0.80	8.68 ±0.81
	CI	36.22 ±0.41	19.71 ±1.57	20.97 ±1.75	44.57 ±0.84	49.26 --	33.44 ±1.92	-- --	-- --
Cactospiza pallida	RL	22.92 ±0.64	16.75 ±0.26	16.02 ±0.25	12.22 ±0.10	-- --	11.47 ±0.38	11.43 ±0.13	9.19 ±0.50
	CI	36.51 ±0.81	20.68 ±1.50	22.23 ±0.84	42.61 ±1.47	-- --	31.98 ±1.88	-- --	-- --
Platyspiza crassirostris	RL	21.48 ±0.53	17.94 ±0.65	16.41 ±0.64	12.21 ±0.69	6.06 ±0.39	11.72 ±0.50	10.83 ±0.47	9.38 ±0.39
	CI	36.74 ±0.86	23.77 ±0.84	24.74 ±2.16	46.73 ±1.47	33.06 ±0.94	30.50 ±1.42	-- --	-- --
Certhidea olivacea	RL	22.71 ±0.74	17.19 ±0.37	16.42 ±0.14	11.90 ±0.41	-- --	11.44 ±0.35	10.99 ±0.37	9.29 ±0.39
	CI	34.82 ±1.14	19.29 ±0.72	20.77 ±0.77	45.85 ±2.22	-- --	28.95 ±1.88	-- --	-- --
	RL	$F = 2.34^{s}$	$F = 1.21^{ns}$	$F = 1.05^{ns}$	$F = 1.49^{ns}$	$F = 0.70^{ns}$	$F = 0.31^{ns}$	$F = 1.43^{ns}$	$F = 0.93^{ns}$
	CI	$F = 0.66^{ns}$	$F = 1.06^{ns}$	$F = 1.00^{ns}$	$F = 1.04^{ns}$	$F = 2.28^{ns}$	$F = 1.10^{ns}$	--	--

approximately 50% of the total length of the Z chromosome. The fifth pair are sub-median chromosomes. The sixth and seventh pairs are acrocentric chromosomes; they appear identical to each other and their placement also is arbitrary. The remaining microchromosomes (average 32 pairs) are acrocentrics. The pairing of these elements is arbitrary.

Atypical Karyotypic Variation in Darwin's Finches

Only one somatic cell from each of three species of finch was found to show significant variation in karyotype. These variants are illustrated in Fig. 6A, B, and C and described below.

Geospiza magnirostris (Isla Pinta). Among the metaphase plates examined, one was found to contain an extra chromosome with a rare configuration. For convenience of comparison, this chromosome has been placed together with the sex chromosome (ZZ) complement due to its resemblance, except for size, to the W chromosome of the female constitution (Fig. 6A).

Geospiza difficilis (Isla Pinta). One metaphase figure was observed with an apparent pericentric inversion in one chromosome of the second pair (Fig. 6B).

Certhidea olivacea (Isla Genovesa). One metaphase plate, found to vary from the standard karyotype, has one of the first pair of chromosomes with a terminal deletion and an apparent trisomy of the sixth or seventh pair (Fig. 6C).

Comparison of gross morphology of karyotypes of *Geospiza magnirostris* (chosen randomly from among the 12 species examined) and two members of the subfamily Fringillinae, *Serinus canarius* and *Fringilla coelebs,* for which karyotypes are known, show that the three species have similar karyotypes (Fig. 7). The first five pairs of chromosomes, including the sex chromosome pair, show striking similarity with only slight differences in their relative length and centromeric indices (Table 3). Differences, however, do exist from the sixth chromosome down. In *G. magnirostris* the sixth chromosome is acrocentric whereas in *S. canarius* and *F. coelebs* it is sub-median. The seventh pair is similar in *G. magnirostris* and *S. canarius,* with both having an acrocentric chromosome, and contrasting with the sub-median chromosome in *F. coelebs.* In *G. magnirostris* the remaining chromosomes from the eighth pair down (not shown in ideogram) are acrocentrics. In *S. canarius* and *F. coelebs*, chromosomes eight and nine are also acrocentrics. After the ninth pair, the chromosomes are not presented in the karyograms of the published photographs (Ohno et al. 1964; Piccini and Stella 1970, respectively).

When comparing *G. magnirostris* (subfamily Geospizinae) with members of the subfamily Emberizinae (*Zonotrichia albicollis* and *Junco hyemalis*), more differences are evident among their respective karyotypes (Fig. 7; Table 3). Only the first three pairs of chromosomes resemble each other closely. The sex chromosomes are quite distinct. The Z chromosomes of the three species have almost the same relative length, but differ in centromeric position. In *G. magnirostris* the Z is a median chromosome, but it is sub-median in *Z. albicollis* and *J. hyemalis*. Differences are also found in the W chromosome, which is a median chromosome in *G. magnirostris* and acrocentric in *Z. albicollis* and *J. hyemalis*. The relative length among these three W chromosomes also varies, being smallest in *Z. albicollis*, increasing in *J. hyemalis*, and is largest in *G. magnirostris*. Chromosome five is a sub-median chromosome in *G. magnirostris* and subterminal in *Z. albicollis* and *J. hyemalis*. Chromosome six is acrocentric in *G. magnirostris,* median in *Z. albicollis,* sub-median in *J. hyemalis,* and in the latter species it resembles that of *S. canarius* and *F. coelebs.* Chromosome seven is notably similar among *Z. albicollis, J. hyemalis,* and *F. coelebs,* in all of which it is sub-median, whereas in *G. magnirostris* and *S. canarius* it is acrocentric.

DISCUSSION AND CONCLUSIONS

Birds, unlike most vertebrates, exhibit high chromosome numbers. Bloom (1969) in his review of 91 species, reported a mode of 80 chromosomes, with 77% of the chromosome numbers

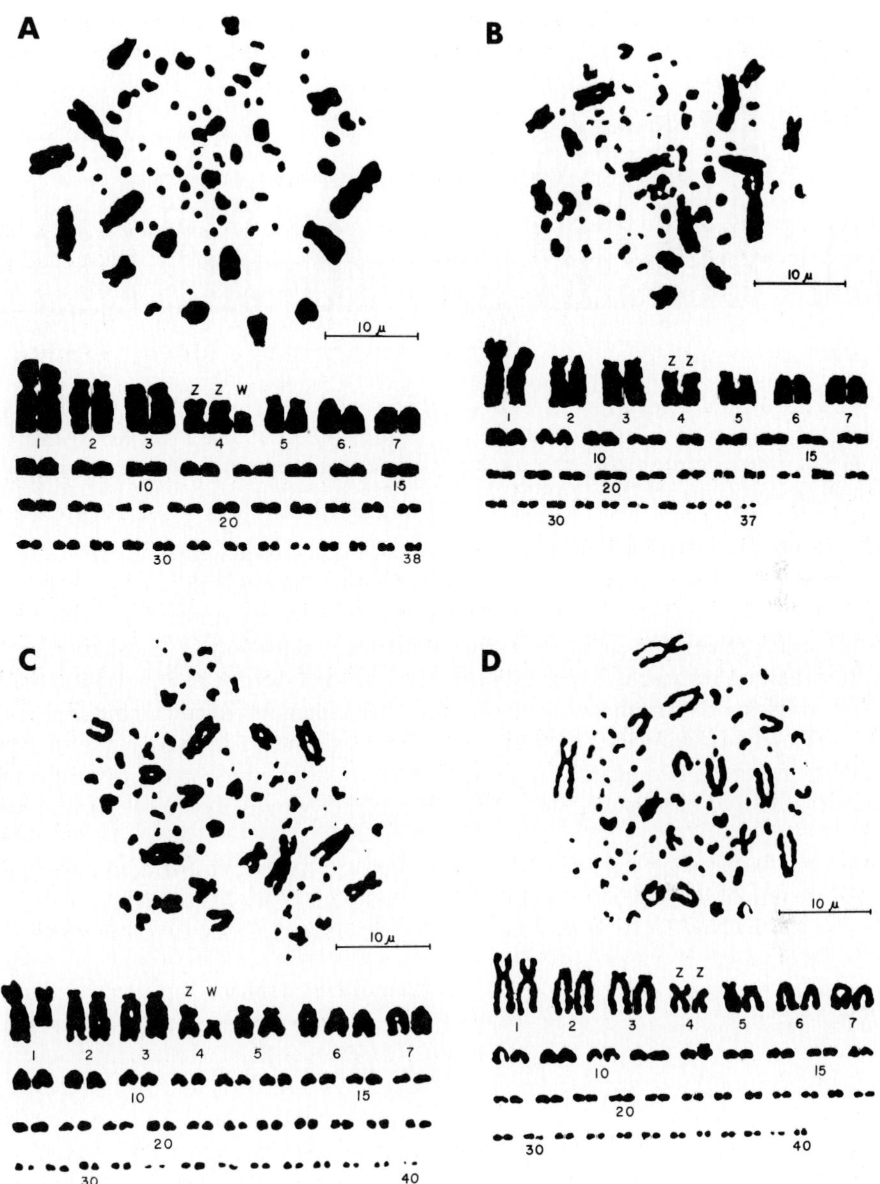

Fig. 6. Karyotypes of four species of Darwin's finches. A, *Geospiza magnirostris*, Isla Pinta (male, NJ 163), showing an unidentifiable chromosome marked with a "W"; B, *Geospiza difficilis*, Isla Pinta (male, NJ 139), showing an apparent pericentric inversion in chromosome pair II; C, *Certhidea olivacea*, Isla Genovesa (female, NJ 187) showing terminal deletion in the first pair of chromosomes and a trisomic configuration in pair VI; D, *Camarhynchus parvulus*, Isla Santiago (male, NJ 201), showing normal chromosomal configurations throughout.

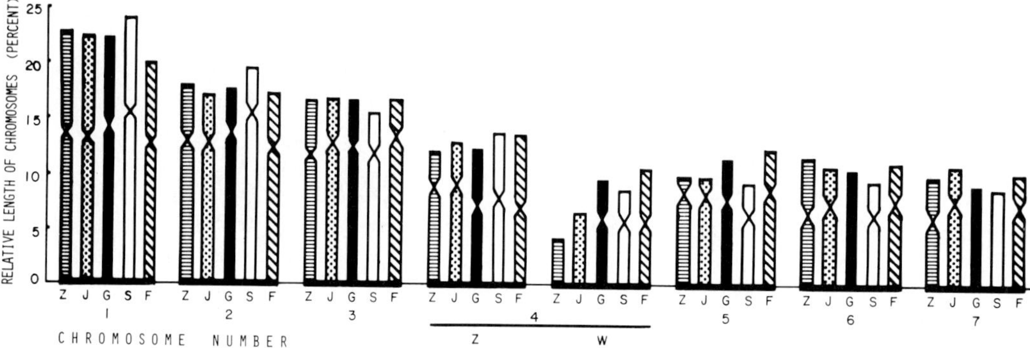

Fig. 7. Ideogram comparing the first seven pairs of macrochromosomes from five species of the family Fringillidae. Z = *Zonotrichia albicollis* (Thorneycroft 1975); J = *Junco hyemalis* (Shields 1973); G = *Geospiza magnirostris* (present study); S = *Serinus canarius* (Ohno et al. 1964); and F = *Fringilla coelebs* (Piccina and Stella 1970).

in the 76 to 80 range. Darwin's finches also show high chromosome numbers with a mode at 78. Sixty-three percent of the chromosome numbers fall within the range of 74 to 78 (Fig. 2).

Like most birds, Darwin's finches have a typical avian karyotype with two well-marked groups of chromosomes, the so-called macrochromosomes and the microchromosomes. Members of the former group are usually recognizable by their size and distinct morphology; there are seven pairs. The remaining chromosomes belong to the latter group. All microchromosomes show acrocentric configurations. Ohno et al. (1962) have described the microchromosomes of the chicken to be nucleolus-organizing. A similar function is accorded to the microchromosomes in the fibroblasts of Japanese quail by Comings and Mattoccia (1970). These writers also found microchromosomes

TABLE 3. MEANS OF RELATIVE LENGTH (RL) AND CENTROMERIC INDEX (CI) OF *ZONOTRICHIA ALBICOLLIS, JUNCO HYEMALIS, GEOSPIZA MAGNIROSTRIS, SERINUS CANARIUS,* AND *FRINGILLA COELEBS*

Species		Chromosome number 1	2	3	4(Z)	4(W)	5	6	7
Zonotrichia	RL	22.66	17.98	16.50	11.92	4.14	9.79	11.53	9.76
albicollis	CI[1]	40.82	27.55	28.82	27.62	--	15.75	44.25	33.33
Junco	RL	22.27	17.18	16.70	12.73	6.26	9.76	10.63	10.72
hyemalis	CI	40.49	24.51	22.42	26.48	--	17.51	32.05	29.33
Geospiza	RL	22.23	17.69	16.69	12.27	9.47	11.44	10.37	9.01
magnirostris	CI	35.42	21.20	23.00	46.23	38.94	30.16	--	--
Serinus	RL	24.05	19.49	15.48	13.70	8.47	9.13	9.35	8.69
canarius	CI	37.31	19.57	23.31	44.64	38.76	35.46	30.12	--
Fringilla	RL	19.96	17.18	16.59	13.33	10.31	12.21	10.91	9.99
coelebs	CI	34.84	24.69	25.25	48.54	44.44	30.40	28.90	30.03

[1] The centromeric index (CI) is a measure of the relative position of the centromere on the chromosome. Chromosomal nomenclature is based on Leval et al. (1964) as follows: 2.5-12.5 = telocentric; 12.5-25.0 = sub-terminal; 25.0-37.5 = sub-median; and 37.5-47.5 = median.

to be heterochromatic and late-replicating, whereas this seems not to be true for the chicken (*Gallus domesticus*), according to a study by Ohno (1961).

The sex chromosomes of Darwin's finches occupy fourth place according to relative size in the macrochromosome series. The female is heteromorphic with a ZW constitution, and the male is homomorphic with a ZZ constitution. Unlike mammals, birds do not exhibit dosage compensation (Cock 1964). Stefos and Arrighi (1971), using C-banding (constitutive heterochromatin) technique, showed the presence of a heterochromatic W chromosome in the domestic chicken, parakeet, domestic pigeon, ringed turtle dove, pheasant, duck, quail, and chukar. The W chromosome is largely repetitive DNA, and it has been suggested that it is genetically inactive. However, Mittowock (1971) proposed that the W chromosome may play a role in inducing a faster growth rate of the left gonadal rudiment, which develops into an ovary.

Aberrant metaphase figures have been found in three species of Darwin's finches. In each case, only one metaphase plate was observed in the abnormal configuration, and the others were normal. In the case of *Geospiza magnirostris* (Isla Pinta), an unidentifiable extra chromosome was found (Fig. 6A). Its morphology resembles that of the W chromosome of the heterogametic female, but a more feasible explanation might be that two microchromosomes are overlapping each other, and partly obscuring their form. Since other metaphase figures of the same individual were observed to carry the typical ZZ constitution, the latter interpretation is more likely. An attempt to obtain finer resolution of this "chromosome" under the scanning electron microscope was unsuccessful. Another variation was found in one chromosome of Pair II of a male *G. difficilis* (Isla Pinta), possibly indicating a pericentric inversion (Fig. 6B). In a female *Certhidea olivacea* (Isla Genovesa), two pairs of chromosomes were involved. In the first pair, one chromosome shows terminal deletion. In the sixth pair, a mitotic anaphase lag could explain the presence of the trisomic configuration (Fig. 6C). Failure to find more abnormal configurations in metaphase plates, such as described in the three species, suggests that these abnormalities are rare and may be due simply to mishaps during somatic mitosis. A triploid diploid mosaic chicken embryo has been reported by Bloom and Buss (1966), and other chromosomal aberrations are known. For example, Fechheimer et al. (1968) described trisomy and haploid embryos in *Gallus domesticus* chicks; Ohno et al. (1963) reported an adult triploid chicken with a left ovotestis; and Shoffner et al. (1973) describe trisomy and abnormal segregation in the hybrid Ross goose X Emperor goose.

Hammar (1966, 1970) concluded that closely related bird species often have the same karyotype. Darwin's finches are a classical example of this situation; 12 species in five genera exhibit nearly identical karyotypes (Figs. 3-5). The differences among the mean values of the relative length of the first pair of chromosomes in the 12 species are insignificant at $P = 0.05$. However, the F value of 2.34 is only marginally significant. The striking chromosomal uniformity in the karyotypes of Darwin's finches may be explained as follows. First, if chromosomal rearrangements have occurred, they are of the paracentric inversion type or are symmetrical translocations, which are not detectable with the karyotyping technique used in this study. Application of differential staining techniques, such as G-banding or C-banding, will be necessary to spot the presence or absence of the possible differences concealed by seemingly gross similarities. Second, the apparent uniformity in Darwin's finches' chromosomes suggests that they might have been transmitted with comparatively little karyotypic change from a common ancestor, yet with significant evolutionary changes at the structural gene level. Polans (this volume) found "fast" esterase bands that are almost completely species-specific among the 12 species examined.

A parallel situation seems to exist in Darwin's finches and the Hawaiian drosophilids. In both cases there is a general uniformity within each of their group karyotypes in spite of phenotypic divergences following adaptive radiation. This led Carson et al. (1967:1285) to conclude that ". . . it is possible for speciation and evolution to be based entirely on mutational changes occurring at the submicroscopic level." It remains to be determined whether Darwin's finches likewise possess fully stable chromosomes at the microscopic level. Data presented here certainly suggest that this might be the case.

Comparative analysis of the gross karyotypic characteristics of Darwin's finches with those of four members of the family Fringillidae yields three possible interpretations. One interpretation suggests that the chromosomal similarity (homology?) of Darwin's finches to the two members of the subfamily Fringillinae, *Serinus canarius* and *Fringilla coelebs,* is due to their lineage. In partial support of this view, a structural analysis of the unfused palato-maxillary bones (Tordoff 1954) also suggests an affinity between New World Darwin's finches and the genus *Fringilla* (Table 4). However, Tordoff's study did not show a relationship between *S. canarius* (considered by Tordoff to be a member of the subfamily Carduelinae) and *F. coelebs* (subfamily Fringillinae), and these findings contrast with the karyotypic data herein presented. However, Tordoff no longer holds this view of relationships (*vide* Sibley 1970: 101).

Another interpretation of the karyotypic similarities between Geospizinae and Fringillinae has to do with the possibility of convergence. Support for this notion comes from electrophoretic banding data on egg-white proteins (Sibley 1970; Table 4). This study, which included two species of Darwin's finches, *Geospiza magnirostris* and *G. fortis,* shows close protein similarities to certain New World members of the subfamily Emberizinae. If we assume that the Geospizinae and the Emberizinae are genetically closely allied, the karyotypic data from the present study suggest major chromosomal divergence between Darwin's finches and the two species of the subfamily Emberizinae, *Zonotrichia albicollis* and *Junco hyemalis,* and are additional evidence in support of the suggestion made by Beecher (1953) and Bowman (1961) that Darwin's finches constitute a group significantly distinct from the subfamily Emberizinae. Cutler (1970) found characteristic syringeal structures that could justify setting these birds apart from the Emberizinae as a distinct systematic group.

Tordoff (1954) presented the hypothesis that several genera of the family Fringillidae, possessing primitive unfused or partially fused palato-maxillary bones, have persisted in remote or isolated areas that form a ring at the periphery of the central land mass of North America. The West Indies at the southeast part of the ring, Cocos Island, the Galapagos Archipelago, and the volcanoes of Central America in the southern part of the ring harbor the "primitive" genera of Fringillidae, i.e., those with unfused palato-maxillary bones. Present karyotypic data might be interpreted as favoring Tordoff's hypothesis since the geospizine finches, which show unfused palato-maxillary bones, survive today in two of those southerly isolated locations. Geospizine finches of the Galapagos show only slight chromosomal divergence from the presumed ancestral stock (subfamily Fringillinae) of the family Fringillidae. Moreover, Cutler (1970) suggested that the geospizines possess an "unspecialized" type of syringeal structure possibly characteristic of the ancestral oscine group, now surviving mainly in isolated locations such as the Galapagos Islands, Cocos Island, Cuba, and Santa Lucia Island.

TABLE 4. SIMILARITIES AMONG SPECIES OF THE SUBFAMILY GEOSPIZINAE (NEW WORLD), THE SUBFAMILY FRINGILLINAE (OLD WORLD), AND THE SUBFAMILY EMBERIZINAE (NEW WORLD)

Character	Geospizinae	Fringillinae	Emberizinae
Chromosomes[1]	X	X	
Bony palate[2]	X	X	
Egg proteins[3]	X		X

[1] Present study.
[2] Unfused palato-maxillary bones: Tordoff (1954).
[3] Electrophoretic banding of egg-white proteins: Sibley (1970).

Additional investigations of the various members of the family Fringillidae, using such methods as chromosomal banding, are needed to guide our interpretations of these karyotypic data. Stock (1975), using banding pattern methods in phyllostomatic bats of the genera *Choeroniscus* and *Carollia,* concludes that some of the phylogenetic affinities reported by earlier authors, who used only gross karyotypic similarities, are not warranted. Patton and Gardner (1971) are of the same opinion.

Application of advanced cytological techniques to the study of avian chromosomes could further our understanding of their phyletic relationships.

RESUMEN

Los cromosomas de 138 individuos de pinzones de Darwin (Darwin's finches), incluyendo 12 especies, fueron examinados. El análisis de los cariotipos muestra bastante similitud entre las especies en el número de cromosomas (promedio = 76) y en la morfología de los mismos. Las medidas de la longitud relativa de los siete pares de cromosomas más grandes de cada especie fueron tomadas de seis fotografías de células en metafase. Los cromosomas de sexo de los pinzones femeninos son heterogaméticos. De la comparación de los cariotipos de cinco especies de la familia Fringillidae, *viz. Zonotrichia albicollis* y *Junco hyemalis* de la subfamilia Emberizinae, *Geospiza magnirostris* de la subfamilia Geospizinae y *Serinus canarius* y *Fringilla coelebs* de la subfamilia Fringillinae, ha surgido tres interpretaciones sobre la relacíon filogenética de estas especies.

ACKNOWLEDGMENTS

I wish to thank Robert I. Bowman, John W. Wright, and James L. Patton for their advice, encouragement and technical assistance. For field assistance I am grateful to Tjitter DeVries, the staff of the Charles Darwin Research Station, Philip Myers, Carol Patton, Helen Chin, and Janet Dock. The cooperation of the Director General de Desarrollo Forestal, Ministerio de Agricultura y Ganadería, Sr. Ing. Teodoro Suárez M., and members of the Parque Nacional Galápagos is gratefully acknowledged. I wish to acknowledge the Organization of American States for fellowship support of my graduate studies at San Francisco State University. This study was supported by the National Science Foundation (GB-7059 to Robert Bowman), the Committee on Research and Exploration of the National Geographic Society, and the Chapman Fund of the American Museum of Natural History.

LITERATURE CITED

Beecher, W. J. 1953. A phylogeny of the oscines. Auk 70:270-333.

Bowman, R. I. 1961. Morphological differentiation and adaptation in the Galápagos finches. Univ. Calif. Publ. Zool. 58:1-302.

Bloom, S. E. 1969. A current list of chromosome numbers and variations for species of avian subclass Carinatae. J. Hered. 60:217-220.

Bloom, S. E., and E. G. Buss. 1966. Triploid-diploid mosaic chicken embryo. Science 153:759-760.

Carson, H. L., F. Clayton, and H. D. Stalker. 1967. Karyotypic stability and speciation in Hawaiian *Drosophila*. Proc. Nat'l. Acad. Sci. 57:1280-1285.

Cock, A. G. 1964. Dosage compensation and sex chromatin in non-mammals. Genet. Res. 5:354-365.

Comings, D. E., and E. Mattoccia. 1970. Studies of microchromosomes and a G-C rich DNA satellite in the quail. Chromosoma 30:202-214.

Cutler, B. D. 1970. Anatomical studies on the syrinx of Darwin's finches. Master's Thesis. San Francisco State University, San Francisco, Calif.

Fechheimer, N. S., D. L. Zartman, and R. G. Jaap. 1968. Trisomic and haploid embryos of the chick. J. Reprod. Fert. 17:215-217.

Ford, C. E., and J. L. Hamerton. 1956. A colchicine, hypotonic-citrate, squash sequence for mammalian chromosomes. Stain Technol. 31:247-254.

Hammar, B. 1966. The karyotype of nine birds. Hereditas 55:367-385.

Hammar, B. 1970. The karyotype of thirty-one birds. Hereditas 65:29-58.

Hsu, T. C., and C. M. Pomerat. 1953. Mammalian chromosomes *in vitro* II. A method for spreading the chromosomes of cells in tissue culture. J. Hered. 44:23-29.

Krishan, A. 1962. A cytological method for sexing young chicks. Experientia 18:100-101.

Krishan, A. 1963. Mitotic and meiotic chromosomes of the domestic duck. J. Hered. 54:91-95.

Lack, D. 1947. Darwin's finches. Cambridge University Press, Cambridge.

Levan, A., K. Fredga, and A. A. Sandberg. 1964. Nomenclature for centromeric position on chromosomes. Hereditas 52:201-220.

Mittwoch, V. 1971. Sex determination in birds and mammals. Nature 231:432-434.

Ohno, S. 1961. Sex chromosomes and microchromosomes of *Gallus domesticus.* Chromosoma 11:484-498.

Ohno, S., L. C. Christian, and C. Stenius. 1962. Nucleolus-organizing microchromosomes of *Gallus domesticus.* Exp. Cell Res. 27:612-614.

Ohno, S. W., A. Kittrell, L. G. Christian, C. Stenius, and G. A. Witt. 1963. An adult triploid chicken (*Gallus domesticus*) with a left ovotestis. Cytogenetics 2:42-49.

Ohno, S., C. Stenius, L. C. Christian, W. Becak, and M. L. Becak. 1964. Chromosomal uniformity in avian subclass Carinatae. Chromosoma 15:280-288.

Patton, J. L. 1967. Chromosome studies of certain pocket mice, genus *Perognathus* (Rodentia: Heteromyidae). J. Mammal. 48:27-37.

Patton, J. L., and A. L. Gardner. 1971. Parallel evolution of multiple sex-chromosome systems in the phyllostomatid bats, *Carollia* and *Choeroniscus.* Experientia 27:105-106.

Piccini, E., and M. Stella. 1970. Some avian karyograms. Caryologia 232:189-202.

Ray-Chaudhuri, R. 1973. Cytotaxonomy and chromosome evolution in birds. Pages 425-483 *in* A. B. Chiarelli and E. Capanna, eds. Cytotaxonomy and Vertebrate Evolution. Academic Press, New York, N. Y.

Ray-Chaudhuri, R., T. Sharma, and S. P. Ray-Chaudhuri. 1969. A comparative study of the chromosomes of birds. Chromosoma 26:148-168.

Sandnes, G. C. 1954. A new technique for the study of avian chromosomes. Science 119:508-509.

Sasaki, M., T. Ikeuchi, and S. Makino. 1968. A feather pulp culture technique for avian chromosomes, with notes on the chromosomes of the peafowl and the ostrich. Experientia 24:1292-1293.

Scherz, R. G. 1962. Blaze-drying by igniting the fixative, for improved spreads of chromosomes in leucocytes. Stain Technol. 37:386.

Shields, G. F. 1982. Comparative avian cytogenetics: A review. Condor 84:45-58.

Shields, G. F. 1973. Chromosomal polymorphism common to several species of *Junco* (Aves). Can. J. Genet. Cyto. 15:461-471.

Shoffner, R. N. 1974. Chromosomes of birds. Pages 223-261 *in* H. Busch, ed. The Cell Nucleus, vol. 2. Academic Press, New York, N. Y.

Shoffner, R. N., J. C. Otis, and F. Lee. 1973. Trisomy and abnormal chromosome segregation in Ross' X Emperor goose hybrids. Genetics 74:253 (Abstr.).

Shoffner, R. N., A. Krishan, G. J. Haiden, B. K. Bammi, and J. S. Otis. 1967. Avian chromosome methodology. Poultry Sci. 46:333-344.

Sibley, C. G. 1970. A comparative study of the egg-white proteins of passerine birds. Bull. Peabody Mus. Nat. Hist. 32.

Stefos, K., and F. E. Arrighi. 1971. The heterochromatic nature of the W chromosome in birds. Exp. Cell Res. 68:228-231.

Stock, A. D. 1975. Chromosome banding pattern homology and its phylogenetic implications in the bat genera *Carollia* and *Choeroniscus.* Cytogenet. Cell Genet. 14:34-41.

Stock, A. D., F. E. Arrighi, and K. Stefos. 1974. Chromosome homology in birds: Banding patterns of the chromosomes of the domestic chicken, ring-necked dove, and domestic pigeon. Cytogenet. Cell Genet. 13:410-418.

Takagi, N., M. Itoh, and M. Sasaki. 1972. Chromosome studies in four species of Ratitae (Aves). Chromosoma 36:281-291.

Takagi, N., and M. Sasaki. 1974. A phylogenetic study of bird karyotypes. Chromosoma 46:91-120.

Thorneycroft, H. B. 1975. A cytogenetic study of the white-throated sparrow, *Zonotrichia albicollis* (Gmelin). Evolution 29:611-621.

Tordoff, H. B. 1954. A systematic study of the avian family Fringillidae based on the structure of the skull. Misc. Publ. Mus. Zool. Univ. Mich. 81.

Woolf, C. M. 1968. Principles of biometry. D. Van Nostrand Co., Princeton, N. J.

ENZYME POLYMORPHISMS IN GALAPAGOS FINCHES

NEIL O. POLANS
Department of Biology, San Francisco State University, San Francisco, CA 94132[1]

Enzyme polymorphisms of 257 Darwin's finches, representing 12 species from 12 islands of the Galapagos Archipelago, are analyzed electrophoretically on polyacrylamide slabs. Electrophoretic bands of supernatant malate dehydrogenase, alpha-glycerophosphate dehydrogenase, and esterases are grouped into band patterns, and band frequencies are determined. A putative genetic scheme is also proposed from which allelic frequencies are estimated by the method of maximum likelihood. The average and median percentage of polymorphic loci found among the 12 species are both estimated to be 30%, while the average proportion of heterozygous loci per individual is estimated to be 0.054 ± 0.022 across all species. Band data mainly demonstrate only subtle differences among the finches. With but a few possible exceptions, location-specific bands and/or band patterns are not found. Genetic distance, as well as other measures of taxonomic similarity, is also considered; and, with some notable exceptions, the previous classification of the finches is upheld.

Thirteen species of Darwin's finches occur in the Galapagos Archipelago, with one additional species confined to nearby Cocos Island, Costa Rica. The birds are generally classified as a sub-familial group, the Geospizinae, of the family Fringillidae, and separated into six genera (Bowman 1961; Swarth 1931). Based on feeding habits, the Galapagos species may be grouped into four categories as follows: (1) almost completely insectivorous (two species of *Cactospiza* and one species of *Certhidea*); (2) mostly insectivorous, but partly gramnivorous (three species of *Camarhynchus*); (3) mainly gramnivorous, but partly insectivorous (six species of *Geospiza*); and (4) almost completely herbivorous/gramnivorous (one species of *Platyspiza*) (Bowman 1963).

Distributional data on the finches have been summarized recently by Harris (1973). The large central islands of the Galapagos, such as Santiago and Santa Cruz, support as many as nine species, whereas the smaller, lower-lying islands, such as Española and Genovesa, support only three and four species, respectively. The absence of species from any island probably is due more to ecological unsuitability than to inaccessibility of the island (Bowman 1961; Lack 1969). In some instances, the ecological dissimilarities between islands have resulted in significant structural and behavioral variations between island populations of the same species (Bowman 1961; Bowman and Billeb 1965).

The finches have been classified chiefly on the basis of structural characters, namely, size and shape of bill and plumage coloration. The close resemblances among the finches have suggested to some (Ford, Ewing, and Parkin 1974) that the birds have had insufficient time for major evolutionary divergences to occur. The possibility also exists, however, that the more limited ecological opportunities of the islands have helped to restrict adaptive divergences (Bowman 1961). Several of the ground and tree finches of the genera *Geospiza* and *Camarhynchus*, respectively, are considered to be sibling species (Lack 1947); furthermore, on Isla Santa Cruz, and several other islands as well, they are sympatric. Recent studies by Bowman (pers. comm.) indicate that species recognition is primarily by means of song, although some other clues, such as subtle differences in bill size and shape (cf. Lack 1947), may at times be used.

[1] Present address: Dept. of Plant Biology, Carnegie Institution of Washington, Stanford, CA 94305-1297

A critical investigation of evolutionary change in Darwin's finches must consider not only the more obvious phenotypic variation, as did those of Charles Darwin (1845) and most subsequent workers, but also the hidden genetical variation, the latter now possible through the techniques of gel electrophoresis. The pioneering studies in this field can be traced to the research of Hubby (1963), Hubby and Throckmorton (1965), Hubby and Lewontin (1966), Lewontin and Hubby (1966), and Harris (1966).

In the present study, tissues from a total of 257 Galapagos finches, comprising 12 species, were examined electrophoretically for enzyme polymorphisms. Assays include the esterases, alpha-glycerophosphate dehydrogenase, and malate dehydrogenase. Data from these assays, consisting of various protein bands and their grouping into specific band patterns or band phenotypes, are used to: (1) characterize the genotypes of the enzyme bands; (2) estimate the degree of polymorphism and heterozygosity existing in natural populations of the finches; (3) measure the degree of affinity between the 12 species of finches grouped into five genera. The characterization of genotypes is complicated by the difficulty of performing classical transmission genetics crosses in birds necessary for the complete elucidation of these enzyme systems.

The Galapagos finches are particularly well suited for a study of biochemical variation because collectively they breed in and seasonally occupy virtually all the habitats found in the Galapagos Archipelago. And because Darwin's finches constitute one of the best avian examples of adaptive radiation, and presumably are of monophyletic origin, it would be particularly interesting to discover the underlying genetic changes that have occurred along with the structural and behavioral adaptations. Furthermore, the comparison of interspecific and intergeneric differences among the birds, according to band patterns, is a useful means by which traditional taxonomic designations can be independently evaluated.

MATERIALS AND METHODS

Collection of Specimens. Between 19 January and 13 February 1974, 257 specimens of Galapagos finches, representing 12 species of the subfamily Geospizinae, were collected from 12 islands of the Galapagos Archipelago (Table 1). The birds were captured alive by means of mist nets and held in cotton sacks until transported to a shipboard laboratory. If circumstances did not allow immediate access to the ship, the birds were held in temporary cages and fed water and rice. Aboard ship, each finch was injected with colchicine, as part of a karyotyping experiment, three hours prior to sacrificing by forcible lung collapse. Excised liver, kidney, and heart tissues from each bird were placed in a plastic "Nunc" vial, covered with 0.85% saline solution, capped, and immediately frozen in liquid nitrogen. Vials were stored in liquid nitrogen for approximately six weeks after their collection. Upon return, vials were transferred to a laboratory Revco freezer and stored at -70°C. The finch carcasses were preserved in formalin and the original field identifications checked by Robert I. Bowman.

Homogenization. Liver, kidney, and heart tissues of each bird were homogenized by the following method: each Nunc vial, containing tissues from a single finch, was thawed, as much saline as possible removed, and the net weight of the combined organs determined. Once the weight of the three tissues was determined (usually between 0.5 and 1.0 grams), they were homogenized together for approximately one minute in an Evelejhm-Potter glass tissue grinder with Teflon motor-powered pestle in two volumes of the homogenizing buffer, 0.1M Tris-chloride–0.001M EDTA in 0.04% (v/v) mercaptoethanol (adjusted to pH 6.8 at 4°C with hydrochloric acid). The actual homogenization step was performed in a 4°C cold room with the glass tissue grinder packed in ice. Immediately following homogenization, the crude homogenate was transferred to a polypropylene tube and spun at 16,000 rpm (31,500g) in a Sorvall RC2-B centrifuge at approximately 10°C for 30 minutes to pellet debris and mitochondria. The resulting supernatant was carefully collected with a Pasteur pipette to avoid as much floating lipid material as possible and

TABLE 1. POPULATION SAMPLES OF GALAPAGOS FINCHES BY SPECIES AND ISLAND

Islands / Species	Pinta	Isabela	Santa Fe	Marchena	San Cristóbal	Floreana	Pinzón	Española	Santa Cruz	Santiago	Fernandina	Genovesa	Totals
Geospiza													
magnirostris	7			3						5		1	16
fortis	3	6	2	3		4			14	23			55
fuliginosa	11	7	6	4	10	9	2	9	10	14	1		83
difficilis	1									2		2	5
scandens	11		5						10				26
conirostris								17				4	21
Platyspiza													
crassirostris	1			4	1					2			8
Camarhynchus													
psittacula				1									1
pauper						3							3
parvulus					2	2			8	10			22
Cactospiza													
pallida					1								1
Certhidea													
olivacea				2				8	4			2	16
TOTALS:	34	13	13	17	14	18	2	34	46	56	1	9	257

placed in a calibrated tube. Glycerol was next added to equal 10% (v/v). The glycerol (10%) allows for easy sample application to polyacrylamide gel slabs by underlaying and is also a satisfactory medium for long-term storage of proteins at subzero temperatures. The final homogenate was then divided into several tubes and stored, until needed, at -70°C. Portions of this procedure were modified versions of a procedure outlined in Selander, Smith, Yang, Johnson, and Gentry (1971).

Polyacrylamide Gel and Buffer Preparation. Two different gel and gel-buffer systems were employed. Esterases were run on a system modified from Selander et al. (1971), the original system having been derived for use on starch gels. Malate dehydrogenase and alpha-glycerophosphate dehydrogenase were run on a system slightly modified from Hubby (1963).

For esterases, a 5% stacking gel and 7.5% resolving gel were used. In all cases, gel percentage denotes a weight-to-total-volume measurement of acrylamide plus Bis at 5% of the acrylamide mass. The gel and electrophoresis buffers employed for the esterase run were both twice as concentrated as stipulated by Selander et al. (1971). This was found to provide better band resolution on polyacrylamide slabs. The electrophoresis buffer (Stock Solution A) was 0.06M lithium hydroxide–0.38M boric acid, pH 8.1. The gel buffer, for both stacking and running gels, was a 1:9 mixture of Stock Solutions A and B, where Stock Solution B was 0.1M Tris-chloride–0.016M citric acid, pH 8.4.

For malate dehydrogenase and alpha-glycerophosphate dehydrogenase, a simple 7.5% resolving gel, without a stacking gel, was used. The gel and electrophoresis buffers employed for these assays were, once again, twice as concentrated as stipulated in the literature (Hubby 1963). In this case, both buffers were 0.2M Tris-chloride–0.003M EDTA–0.2M boric acid. The gel buffer was adjusted to pH 8.4 and the electrophoresis buffer was adjusted to pH 8.9.

Gel mixtures contained a final polyacrylamide concentration of 7.5%, a final TEMED concentration of 0.12% (v/v), and a final ammonium persulfate concentration of 0.2 mg/ml.

Sample Preparation. The esterases were run separately on one gel, while the other two enzymes were run on the same gel, which was cut in half prior to functional staining. In this fashion, all three assays could be undertaken for a given sample in the course of a single electrophoretic run using a single power supply and two slab gel apparatuses. On gel number one, homogenate from the various birds was inserted into every other slot to obtain esterase bands so that there would not be interference from adjacent samples due to either insertion runover or the lateral spread of very concentrated bands. Each esterase sample was also run at two different dilutions, at 1:5 in one slot and 1:100 in a second slot. The lower dilution allowed resolution of the more weakly staining upper bands, while rendering the more concentrated lower bands amorphous. The higher dilution, while usually eliminating detection of the upper bands altogether, permitted fine resolution of the lower bands. On gel number two, malate dehydrogenase bands were able to be assayed in contiguous slots, but alternate slots were again used for alpha-glycerophosphate dehydrogenase. The former enzyme was diluted 1:20, while the latter was inserted at full strength. All dilutions were made with the corresponding gel buffer (normal strength) in 10% glycerol. All slots received a 10-microliter sample.

Slab electrophoresis of the finch homogenate was accomplished using a device designed originally by Reid and Bieleski (1968) and modified by Studier (1973). The slab gel apparatus used in these experiments was fabricated from plans supplied by personal communication from Studier. For additional information regarding the slab apparatus, refer to Studier (1973) or Ames (1974).

Staining. Of the three functional stains employed, all reported by Selander et al. (1971), only the esterase stain was not light-sensitive. All three, however, were incubated in a Psycotherm controlled environment incubator-shaker in total darkness at 37°C with shaking action for approximately 15 minutes prior to bathing the gels. In the cases of malate dehydrogenase and alpha-glycerophosphate dehydrogenase, extra precautions were taken against light contamination by covering these staining dishes with aluminum foil.

Data Collection. Measurements of band migration distance were taken immediately following the completion of staining procedures using a Starret caliper with finely ground tips. Measurements were taken to the nearest thousandths of an inch with the top of the gel, not including the comb-like "fingers," serving as the fixed point from which measurements could be derived. In addition to measuring sample bands, internal standards were employed to supply reference bands for comparison of band migrations occurring on different gels. On the esterase gel, electric eel cholinesterase (Sigma) was used as the internal standard, best results being obtained with 0.04 units of enzyme per 10-microliter sample. On the other gel, rabbit muscle alpha-glycerophosphate dehydrogenase (Sigma) yielded a somewhat less stable, but nonetheless acceptable band. Approximately 0.1 units of enzyme per 10-microliter sample seemed to provide the best band here. Both standards were lyophilized, salt-free preparations that were dissolved with homogenizing buffer (to every 100 ml of which was added 0.04 ml mercaptoethanol) in 10% glycerol. In addition to the internal standards, a 1-mg/ml solution of Bromophenol Blue served as tracking dye for both gels.

RESULTS

Comparison of bands, on the same gel and between gels, and the labeling of each band were accomplished by measuring the relative distances between the bands and the most common invariant band of the particular assay. This method was found to be both as accurate and as facile as the comparison of a band against an internal standard (see Table 2).

Following the designation of each band with a letter, each bird was scored for particular

TABLE 2. RELATIVE MOBILITY OF ENZYME BANDS IN GALAPAGOS FINCHES

Bands[a]	Esterases[b]	Alpha-glycerophosphate dehydrogenase[c]	Malate dehydrogenase[c]
A	–[d]	1.63	.58
B	4.04	1.38	
C	3.93	1.15	
D	3.87	.97	
E	3.68	.37	
F	3.63		
G	3.57		
H	3.42		
I	3.31		
J	3.26		
K	3.14		
L	3.06		
M	1.66		
N	1.23		
O	–[e]		

[a] Bands listed in order of migration distance from the anode.
[b] Band migration distance relative to electric eel cholinesterase migration distance.
[c] Band migration distance relative to rabbit muscle alpha-glycerophosphate dehydrogenase migration distance.
[d] Presence of band only weakly suggested.
[e] Relative mobility not accurately determined.

band patterns or band phenotypes. In the case of malate dehydrogenase, only a single band (A) appeared for every finch. In the cases of alpha-glycerophosphate dehydrogenase and the "slow" esterases (the group of esterase bands located distinctively near the cathode after electrophoresis), five bands (A-E) and three bands (M-O), respectively, appeared. The same four-banded alpha-glycerophosphate dehydrogenase pattern (ACDE) appeared in 241 of the finches (see Table 3).

TABLE 3. PATTERN OF VARIATION IN BANDS OF ALPHA-GLYCEROPHOSPHATE DEHYDROGENASE AND "SLOW" ESTERASES

Band pattern	No. of birds[a]	Species	Island
ACDE	241	All 12 species examined	
ABCDE	1	*Platyspiza crassirostris*	Pinta
	1	*Geospiza fortis*	Pinta
	3	*Geospiza fuliginosa*	Pinta
ABDE	1	*Geospiza fortis*	Santa Fe
	2	*Geospiza fuliginosa*	Santa Fe
	1	*Geospiza fuliginosa*	Española
	1	*Certhidea olivacea*	Española
ADE	1	*Geospiza magnirostris*	Marchena
	1	*Certhidea olivacea*	Genovesa
MN	253	All 12 species examined	
MNO	1	*Geospiza fortis*	Santa Cruz
	1	*Geospiza fuliginosa*	San Cristóbal
	2	*Geospiza conirostris*	Española

[a] Accurate scores could not be determined for four out of the 257 birds.

Five of the finches displayed a four-banded pattern (ABDE) that differed from the most common phenotype by only one band. Another five finches displayed the same five-banded pattern (ABCDE) that contained, in addition to the four most common bands (ACDE), a fifth band (B) similar to the one variant band already mentioned. Two of the birds assayed for alpha-glycerophosphate dehydrogenase possessed only the three most common bands (viz. bands ADE, which are present in all finches examined), while at least four of the finches could not be accurately scored. Two "slow" esterase bands (MN) also appeared in each bird examined, accompanied by a third band (O) in only a small number of the finches. The "fast" esterases (the group of esterase bands located distinctively near the anode after electrophoresis), however, displayed the greatest degree of both band variation and band pattern variation. Eleven bands (viz. B-L), distributed throughout the 12 species, yielded 32 different patterns. These patterns, as well as those for alpha-glycerophosphate dehydrogenase and malate dehydrogenase, are pictured in Figs. 1 and 2. A summary of the variation found in the slow esterases and alpha-glycerophosphate dehydrogenase is presented in Table 3.

The following relationships, based upon band data, were studied: the number of bands species share in common (Table 4); the number of bands common to several island locations; the frequency distribution of bands among species (Table 5) and among island locations; interspecific band correlations (Table 6); the frequency distribution of putative alleles (based upon maximum likelihood estimates) among species (Table 7) as well as among island locations; genetic identity and genetic distance (Table 8). The more relevant of these comparisons are presented in Tables 4-8. Comparisons involving band data and locality revealed that the presence of a particular band at a given location generally results from the presence of a particular species or species. Band frequency and distribution, consequently, appear to be much more a function of species than species location.

DISCUSSION AND CONCLUSIONS

Enzyme Analysis

The electrophoretic evidence accrued to date, virtually without exception, characterizes the NAD-specific supernatant malate dehydrogenases of birds as extremely conservative, the enzyme almost always appearing as a single anodal band (Kitto and Wilson 1966; Karig and Wilson 1971; Nottebohm and Selander 1972; Corbin et al. 1974; Aspinwall 1974). Among closely related birds, and often among birds only distantly related, the enzyme bands possess an identical mobility, suggesting an identical or nearly identical enzyme. The evidence collected from this study

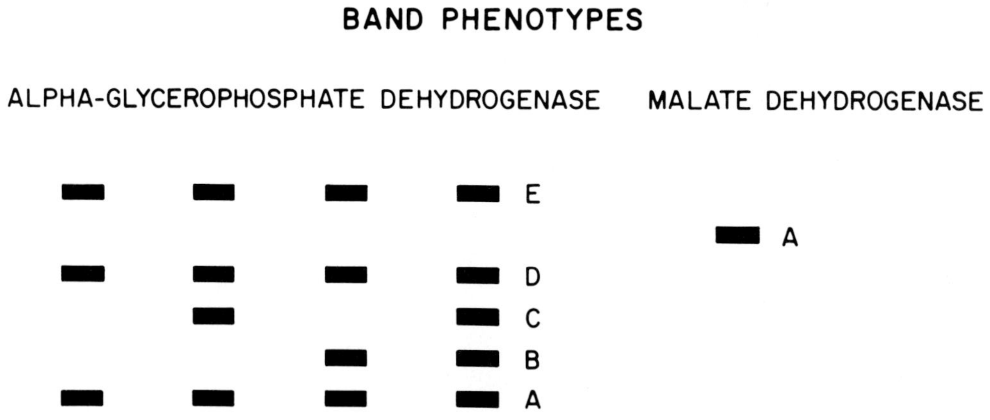

Fig. 1. Enzyme band phenotypes in Galapagos finches.

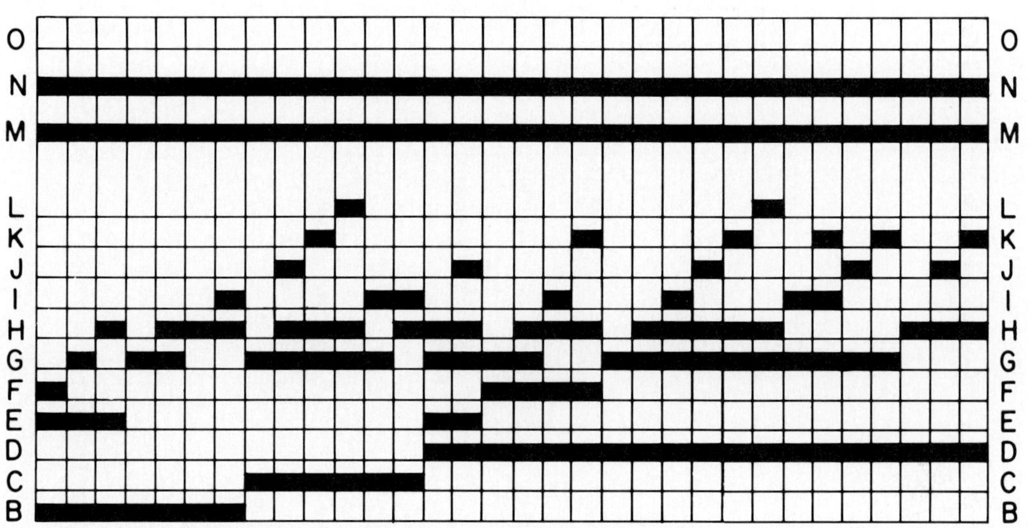

Fig. 2. Esterase band phenotypes in Galapagos finches.

TABLE 4. ENZYME BANDS COMMON TO SEVERAL SPECIES OF GALAPAGOS FINCH

Species	Bands: Number/Identity[a]	*C. oliv.*	*C. pall.*	*C. parv.*	*C. paup.*	*C. psitt.*	*P. crass.*	*G. conir.*	*G. scand.*	*G. diff.*	*G. fulig.*	*G. fort.*	*G. mag.*
Geospiza													
magnirostris	14/ CDGHJKL	9	10	11	10	10	10	11	12	13	14	14	–
fortis	17/a^B CDGHIJKLO	11	10	11	10	10	12	12	13	13	17	–	
fuliginosa	19/a^B CDEFGHIJKLO	13	10	12	10	11	13	12	13	13	–		
difficilis	13/ CDGHJK	9	10	11	10	10	10	11	12	–			
scandens	13/ DGHIJK	10	10	11	10	10	11	11	–				
conirostris	12/ DGHKO	9	10	10	10	10	9	–					
Platyspiza													
crassirostris	12/a^B DFHIJ	11	9	11	9	10	–						
Camarhynchus													
psittacula	11/ DFGH	10	10	11	10	–							
pauper	10/ DGH	9	10	10	–								
parvulus	12/ DFGHJ	10	10	–									
Cactospiza													
pallida	10/ DGH	9	–										
Certhidea													
olivacea	13/a^B BEFGHI	–											

[a] Bands M^A, a^A, a^C, a^D, a^E, E^M and E^N are present in all species.

TABLE 5. NUMBER AND FREQUENCY DISTRIBUTION OF ELECTROPHORETIC BANDS IN 12 SPECIES OF GALAPAGOS FINCH[a]

Species	No. of birds	M^A	a^A	a^B	a^C	a^D	a^E	E^B	E^C	E^D	E^E	E^F
Geospiza magnirostris	16	16 (100%)	16 (100%)	0 (0%)	15 (93.8%)	16 (100%)	16 (100%)		2[b] (12.5%)	14 (87.5%)		
fortis	54	54 (100%)	54 (100%)	2 (3.7%)	53 (98.1%)	54 (100%)	54 (100%)		4 (7.4%)	50 (92.6%)		
fuliginosa	83	83 (100%)	83 (100%)	6 (7.2%)	80 (96.4%)	83 (100%)	83 (100%)		1 (1.2%)	82 (98.8%)	2 (2.4%)	1 (1.2%)
difficilis	5	5 (100%)	5 (100%)	0 (0%)	5 (100%)	5 (100%)	5 (100%)		1 (20%)	4 (80%)		
scandens	26	26 (100%)	26 (100%)	0 (0%)	26 (100%)	26 (100%)	26 (100%)			26 (100%)		
conirostris	21	21 (100%)	21 (100%)	0 (0%)	21 (100%)	21 (100%)	21 (100%)			21 (100%)		
Platyspiza crassirostris	8	8 (100%)	8 (100%)	1 (12.5%)	8 (100%)	8 (100%)	8 (100%)			8 (100%)		1 (12.5%)
Camarhynchus psittacula	1	1 (100%)	1 (100%)	0 (0%)	1 (100%)	1 (100%)	1 (100%)			1 (100%)		1 (100%)
pauper	3	3 (100%)	3 (100%)	0 (0%)	3 (100%)	3 (100%)	3 (100%)			3 (100%)		
parvulus	22	22 (100%)	22 (100%)	0 (0%)	22 (100%)	22 (100%)	22 (100%)			22 (100%)		10 (45.5%)
Cactospiza pallida	1	1 (100%)	1 (100%)	0 (0%)	1 (100%)	1 (100%)	1 (100%)			1 (100%)		
Certhidea olivacea	16	16 (100%)	16 (100%)	1 (6.3%)	14 (87.5%)	16 (100%)	16 (100%)	16[c] (100%)			4 (25%)	2 (12.5%)

[a] Band frequency was determined by multiplying by 100 the quotient derived by dividing the number of times a particular band appears in a species sample by the number of individuals in the sample.

[b] C band found exclusively in four sibling species of *Geospiza*.

[c] B band found exclusively in *Certhidea olivacea*.

TABLE 5. Continued.

Species	No. of birds	E^G	E^H	E^I	E^J	E^K	E^L	E^M	E^N	E^O
Geospiza magnirostris	16	15 (93.8%)	15 (93.8%)		2 (12.5%)	10[d] (62.5%)	3[e] (18.8%)	16 (100%)	16 (100%)	0 (0%)
fortis	54	52 (96.3%)	48 (88.9%)	5 (9.3%)	20 (37%)	24 (44.4%)	2 (3.7%)	54 (100%)	54 (100%)	1 (1.9%)
fuliginosa	83	79 (95.2%)	63 (75.9%)	1 (1.2%)	37 (44.6%)	7 (8.4%)	1 (1.2%)	83 (100%)	83 (100%)	1 (1.2%)
difficilis	5	5 (100%)	5 (100%)		2 (40%)	2 (40%)		5 (100%)	5 (100%)	0 (0%)
scandens	26	24 (92.3%)	21 (80.8%)	3 (11.5%)	11 (42.3%)	1 (3.8%)		26 (100%)	26 (100%)	0 (0%)
conirostris	21	21 (100%)	18 (85.7%)			2 (9.5%)		21 (100%)	21 (100%)	2 (9.5%)
Platyspiza crassirostris	8		8 (100%)	1 (12.5%)	7 (87.5%)			8 (100%)	8 (100%)	0 (0%)
Camarhynchus psittacula	1	1 (100%)	1 (100%)					1 (100%)	1 (100%)	0 (0%)
pauper	3	3 (100%)	3 (100%)					3 (100%)	3 (100%)	0 (0%)
parvulus	22	21 (95.5%)	19 (86.4%)		2 (9.1%)			22 (100%)	22 (100%)	0 (0%)
Cactospiza pallida	1	1 (100%)	1 (100%)					1 (100%)	1 (100%)	0 (0%)
Certhidea olivacea	16	11 (68.8%)	12 (75%)	1 (6.3%)				16 (100%)	16 (100%)	0 (0%)

[d] K band found exclusively in all species of *Geospiza.*

[e] L band found exclusively in three of the four sibling species of *Geospiza.*

TABLE 6. INTERSPECIFIC BAND CORRELATIONS
IN GALAPAGOS FINCHES

Species	*C. oliv.*	*C. pall.*	*C. parv.*	*C. paup.*	*C. psitt.*	*P. crass.*	*G. con.*	*G. scan.*	*G. diff.*	*G. fulig.*	*G. fort.*	*G. mag.*
Geospiza												
magnirostris	.710	.955	.923	.955	.840	.777	.961	.939	.978	.942	.983	
fortis	.712	.969	.944	.969	.852	.837	.973	.980	.993	.981		
fuliginosa	.722	.974	.961	.974	.869	.866	.977	.997	.973			
difficilis	.732	.964	.937	.964	.850	.829	.964	.971				
scandens	.725	.977	.962	.977	.872	.874	.978					
conirostris	.748	.997	.975	.997	.897	.801						
Platyspiza												
crassirostris	.610	.812	.814	.812	.734							
Camarhynchus												
psittacula	.677	.905	.969	.905								
pauper	.755	1.000	.977									
parvulus	.736	.977										
Cactospiza												
pallida	.755											
Certhidea												
olivacea												

corroborates these previous findings. Within the limits of the technique employed, no variant supernatant malate dehydrogenase band appeared in the five genera of Galapagos finches.

With regards to alpha-glycerophosphate dehydrogenase, it is not possible to fully understand what the various bands represent genetically. Three of the bands, A, D, and E, appear in all of the birds assayed. It is proposed that each of these bands is controlled at a separate genetic locus, each of the loci being monomorphic. If this is the case, the bands represent either monomers or homopolymers. Alternatively, these three bands might be controlled at only two loci. Bands A and E would represent the homopolymers for each of two alleles coded by different loci, while Band D would represent a heteropolymer. Although control by two or three loci seems likely here, other less obvious alternatives are also possible. The presence of conformational isomers, post-translational tailoring, electrophoretically silent alleles, or heterogeneous tissue samples could radically alter the characterization of any pattern. A separate locus is thought to be controlling Bands B and C.

The presence of band pattern ABCDE exclusively on Isla Pinta and of band pattern ABDE only on Islas Santa Fé and Española *may* suggest an ecological/environmental influence. Evidence for this derives from a categorization of the Galapagos Islands by Bowman (1961) into groups according to size, flora, elevation and number of vegetation zones. Isla Pinta, a large island with a diverse flora, areas of moderate elevation, and multiple vegetation zones, would seemingly offer a varied environment in which enzymatic variation might be advantageous. Both Isla Santa Fe and Isla Española, on the other hand, are smaller, have less diverse flora, are generally of low elevation, and have only an arid coastal vegetation zone. Perhaps, within the constraints of these less variable environments, there is less of a need for enzyme variablity. Selection might favor the homozygous condition over the heterozygous condition. The presence of Band B, exclusively with Band C present, in finches of Isla Pinta, and the presence of Band B, always with the absence of Band C, in finches of Islas Santa Fe and Española, support this contention. It is important to note, however, that this same relationship does not hold for the island classification scheme of Bowman (1961) and heterozygosity levels in general. In fact, heterozygosity levels are remarkably similar in all species, irrespective of degree of floristic and topographic diversity on the host island.

The only other readily observable correlation between electrophoretic data and the ecology of the finches is the differentiation between the four individuals of *Certhidea olivacea* sampled from the higher transition and *Scalesia* forest zones of Isla Santa Cruz and the remaining 12 individuals of *C. olivacea* from Islas Marchena, Española and Genovesa, the Isla Santa Cruz finches having an unusually high frequency of esterase Bands E and F. The inadequacy of the small number of birds involved in this comparison is obvious.

The electrophoretic analysis of bird esterases has been the subject of several studies of biochemical variation. Baker and Hanson (1966), investigating the blood proteins of 11 species of geese, discovered esterase variation to be primarily individual, rather than species-specific. No one esterase band was found to be confined to a single species or genus, disallowing even generic separation on the basis of serum esterases. The researchers concluded that these species of geese are closely related. An examination of the blood proteins of the house sparrow (*Passer domesticus*) by Bush (1967), revealed 21 or 22 nonspecific esterase bands. Bush found as many as 16 to 18 of these bands in single individuals. A detailed study of the genetic polymorphisms of esterases of the blood plasma in two species of doves, their hybrids and backcross hybrids, as well as in other species of Columbidae, was undertaken by Boehm and Irwin (1970). Extensive examination revealed nine esterase phenotypes (15 bands in all) for one species, with but a single phenotypic pattern for the other. From the study of backcrosses and hybrids of the more variable species, Boehm and Irwin (1970) postulated that the nine observed band patterns were controlled by nine separate alleles. A clear division of all the esterase bands into a fast zone and a slow zone was also observed. The results of this investigation, unlike that of the 11 species of geese, showed each of the species examined distinguishable on the basis of esterase polymorphism. A study of esterase polymorphism in the Chingolo sparrow (*Zonotrichia capensis*) by Nottebohm and Selander (1972) revealed three separate esterase systems, none of which can be characterized. Examination of two species of New Guinea starlings (Corbin et al. 1974) also revealed some difficulties with regard to accurate band scoring, although it was possible to score accurately one region of the esterase activity. This major esterase was polymorphic in both species of starlings, with one species displaying three phenotypes and the other species displaying six phenotypes. Corbin et al. explained these patterns by postulating two codominant alleles at the esterase locus of the first species and three codominant alleles at the esterase locus of the second species.

A study of the blood proteins from five species of Galapagos finches, using starch gel electrophoresis, was done by Ford, Ewing, and Parkin (1974). As in the study of doves and pigeons (Boehm and Irwin 1970), the esterases were clearly divided into a fast zone and a slow zone. All of the finches examined had the same slow-running bands; however, in contrast to the findings of Boehm and Irwin, the fast-running bands were *not* species-specific. According to Ford, Ewing, and Parkin, as a rule "Considerable variation in electrophoretic patterns of esterases is normally found both between and within species. However, species-specific patterns are usual." In support of this contention, they cite, in addition to the study of Boehm and Irwin, the work of Beckman and Nilson (1965). They postulate that this apparent exception to the rule perhaps is indicative of a situation in which complete reproductive isolation between the species has occurred only recently and there has been insufficient time for the evolution of species-specific esterase patterns. They further state that their investigation indicates ". . . that, in the Geospizinae, the rates of protein evolution may be much slower than those for morphological characters associated with feeding." It appears that more than one phenotype or band pattern is found in three finch species. Of the eight patterns observed, though, consisting of five slow-running bands and eight fast-running bands, four of these phenotypes *do* appear to be species-specific. Three of these four patterns, however, are represented by a single individual. The fourth is present in three birds. Of the four patterns that are present in more than a single species, one consists of three birds belonging to two different species. The remaining three phenotypes apparently are distributed as follows: 10 birds belonging to three species, 13 birds belonging to three species, and 47 birds belonging to

TABLE 7. ALLELIC FREQUENCIES IN ENZYME LOCI OF GALAPAGOS FINCHES[a]

Alleles	*G. mag.*	*G. fort.*	*G. fulig.*	*G. diff.*	*G. scand.*	*G. conir.*	*P. crass.*	*C. psitt.*	*C. paup.*	*C. parv.*	*C. pall.*	*C. oliv.*
MDH-1^{A}	1.000	1.000	1.000	1.000	1.000	1.000	1.000	1.000	1.000	1.000	1.000	1.000
α-1^{A}	1.000	1.000	1.000	1.000	1.000	1.000	1.000	1.000	1.000	1.000	1.000	1.000
α-2^{B}	0	.028	.054	0	0	0	.063	0	0	0	0	.033
α-2^{C}	.750	.972	.946	1.000	1.000	1.000	.938	1.000	1.000	1.000	1.000	.669
α-2^{null}	.250	0	0	0	0	0	0	0	0	0	0	.298
α-3^{D}	1.000	1.000	1.000	1.000	1.000	1.000	1.000	1.000	1.000	1.000	1.000	1.000
α-4^{E}	1.000	1.000	1.000	1.000	1.000	1.000	1.000	1.000	1.000	1.000	1.000	1.000
E-1^{B}	0	0	0	0	0	0	0	0	0	0	0	1.000
E-1^{C}	.125	.074	.012	.200	0	0	0	0	0	0	0	0
E-1^{D}	.875	.926	.988	.800	1.000	1.000	1.000	1.000	1.000	1.000	1.000	0
E-2^{E}	0	0	.012	0	0	0	0	0	0	0	0	.130
E-2^{F}	0	0	.006	0	0	0	.065	.500	0	.227	0	.063
E-2^{G}	.750	.808	.785	1.000	.723	1.000	0	.500	1.000	.667	1.000	.473
E-2^{null}	.250	.192	.197	0	.277	0	.935	0	0	.106	0	.334
E-3^{H}	.500	.542	.462	.700	.493	.607	.500	1.000	1.000	.616	1.000	.492
E-3^{I}	0	.019	.006	0	.062	0	.063	0	0	0	0	.031
E-3^{J}	.063	.144	.228	.100	.192	0	.438	0	0	.045	0	0
E-3^{K}	.344	.247	.042	.200	.019	.048	0	0	0	0	0	0
E-3^{L}	.094	.019	.006	0	0	0	0	0	0	0	0	0
E-3^{null}	0	.029	.256	0	.234	.345	0	0	0	.339	0	.477
E-4^{M}	1.000	1.000	1.000	1.000	1.000	1.000	1.000	1.000	1.000	1.000	1.000	1.000
E-5^{N}	1.000	.991	.994	1.000	1.000	.952	1.000	1.000	1.000	1.000	1.000	1.000
E-5°	0	.009	.006	0	0	.048	0	0	0	0	0	0

[a] Estimated by the method of maximum likelihood.

TABLE 8. MEASURES OF GENETIC IDENTITY/GENETIC DISTANCE[a]

Species	*C. oliv.*	*C. pall.*	*C. parv.*	*C. paup.*	*C. psitt.*	*P. crass.*	*G. con.*	*G. scan.*	*G. diff.*	*G. fulig.*	*G. fort.*	*G. mag.*
Geospiza												
magnirostris	.866	.968	.972	.968	.951	.919	.972	.980	.982	.981	.992	
fortis	.856	.982	.985	.982	.963	.924	.986	.993	.993	.993		.008
fuliginosa	.862	.975	.992	.975	.958	.929	.991	.999	.982		.007	.019
difficilis	.853	.989	.977	.989	.962	.883	.987	.979		.018	.007	.018
scandens	.863	.975	.992	.975	.961	.940	.988		.021	.001	.007	.020
conirostris	.852	.986	.990	.986	.959	.881		.012	.013	.009	.014	.028
Platyspiza												
crassirostris	.820	.879	.920	.879	.906		.127	.061	.125	.073	.079	.084
Camarhynchus												
psittacula	.833	.975	.980	.975		.099	.042	.040	.039	.043	.038	.050
pauper	.835	1.000	.978		.026	.129	.014	.026	.011	.025	.018	.033
parvulus	.864	.978		.022	.020	.083	.010	.008	.023	.008	.015	.028
Cactospiza												
pallida	.835		.022	.000	.026	.129	.014	.026	.011	.025	.018	.033
Certhidea												
olivacea		.181	.146	.181	.182	.199	.160	.148	.160	.148	.155	.144

[a] By the method of Nei (1975).

four species. The problem here obviously is one of insufficient sample size. Furthermore, of the five species of Galapagos finches examined, two species are represented by a single individual. Ford et al. conclude that the restricted biochemical divergence found between species of Galapagos finches hinders the elucidation of their phylogenetic relationships.

In the present study of 12 species of Galapagos finches, esterase bands were distinctly divided into "fast" and "slow" zones. As in the findings of Ford, Ewing, and Parkin, all of the finches examined possessed the same slow-running bands, although a third band (O) was recorded in a small number of birds (see Table 3). What appears to be a similar type of variant band is recorded by Ford et al. with a dashed line. Unlike the slow esterase bands, the fast esterase bands of this study revealed a wealth of band and band pattern variation. The various combinations of 11 fast esterase bands produced 32 separate band patterns (Fig. 2). That Ford et al. found fewer might be attributed, as with the slow esterases, to several different possibilities. Differences in tissues sampled, method of tissue storage, sample preparation technique, polyacrylamide gel and starch gel electrophoresis, electrophoretic conditions, type of stain, number of species examined, and sample size are just a few of the possible explanations for the differences between the results of Ford et al. and those reported here.

Limited information presently does not allow an absolute understanding of what the 14 esterase bands characterized in this study represent genetically. The two common slow esterase bands are thought to be coded by separate loci, with the rarer Band O being the product of an allele of the same locus coding for Band N. Other explanations are possible. When interpreting these data, however, it should be emphasized that, although Bands M and N appear in each of the finches examined, Band N is normally thin, strongly stained, and consistent in migration distance, while Band M is often diffuse, irregularly shaped, and somewhat less consistent in migration distance.

With reference to the fast esterases, the data suggest that Bands B, C, and D are controlled by one locus; that Bands E, F, and G may be controlled by a second locus; and that still a third locus may be controlling Bands H, I. J, K, and L. Null alleles are also proposed to exist, one in each of the latter two loci.

In the case of Bands B, C, and D, only one of the bands is ever expressed in any of the finches (see Fig. 2). The high frequency of Band D suggests the homozygous form of a common allele. The presence of Band B in the 16 specimens of *Certhidea olivacea*, and in none of the other species, suggests the homozygous form of a less common allele, either particularly advantageous to the "warbler" finch or fixed in this species through genetic drift. Band C is also characterized as the homozygous form of a third allele; however, as it never appears together with either Band D or Band B, heterozygosity for this locus becomes more difficult to explain, even though the presence of Band C is limited to eight birds.

Percentage of Polymorphic Loci

The three enzyme assays undertaken in this study are presumed to involve ten genetic loci, including one malate dehydrogenase locus, four alpha-glycerophosphate dehydrogenase loci, and five esterase loci. Across all 12 species, 50% of these loci are polymorphic (an allele being designated as such if it occurs with a frequency of $\geqslant 0.01$); although, within the seven species represented by ten or more individuals, the percentage of polymorphic loci ranges between 20% and 40%, with a median and mean of 30%.

Average Proportion of Heterozygous Loci per Individual

The weighted average proportion of heterozygous loci per individual, $\overline{H}$, is 0.054 ± 0.022 across all 12 species of Galapagos finch. This estimate of $\overline{H}$ is similar to those found in the literature for other bird species (see Selander 1976:35).

PHYLOGENETIC RELATIONSHIPS

In this study of the Galapagos finches, individual band patterns are found to occur in more than one species. The same applies to individual bands. Ford, Ewing, and Parkin (1974), in their investigation of Galapagos finch blood proteins, discovered a similar situation (although, unlike this investigation, they were unable to find any species-specific bands or band patterns). There are several possible explanations of these results, some of which have already been proposed. Perhaps the variation existed before adaptive radiation of the finches occurred. Another explanation, although an unlikely one, is that the different species independently selected for parallel mutations in response to similar environmental needs. Perhaps, if speciation has been relatively recent (see below), the evolution of species-specific bands and/or band patterns may only now be occurring. Furthermore, according to Prager and Wilson (1975), birds have lost the potential for interspecific hybridization slowly. The accessibility of any of the islands of the Galapagos Archipelago, coupled with the possibility of interspecific mating, could also account for the spread of bands and band patterns throughout most of five genera and 12 islands. The absence of strict geographical isolation might certainly be construed as a mitigator of species-specific proteins. Of course, it would also be desirable to have data from more assays in addition to that from the esterases, alpha-glycerophosphate dehydrogenase and malate dehydrogenase data alone (see addendum).

A study by Prager and Wilson (1975) has shown that birds, in general, are evolutionarily conservative creatures. They have undergone a slow loss of hybridization potential, a slow anatomical evolution and a slow chromosomal evolution. Prager and Wilson attribute slow avian evolution to the slow evolution of regulatory systems, to slowly changing patterns of gene expression. The underlying reason behind slow evolution in birds, however, may very well stem from those constraints that characterize the bird. In other words, the metabolism, anatomy, and behavior of flight may be highly resistant to change. In any event, none of the species of Galapagos finches examined in this study differ from the other species by a very significant degree. In most cases, whether comparisons are made on the basis of individual band frequency, the number of bands in common, specific band patterns, or genetic similarity, differences between species are established on the basis of small and subtle differences in the data. These differences, however, although small and subtle, are consistent and not so biochemically restricted as to be unable to provide insights into Galapagos finch phylogenetic relationships. In fact, the results from all the comparison tests lead to much the same conclusions; and, generally, these conclusions support most of the previous work done on the classification of the subfamily Geospizinae.

The most nebulous classification assignments must involve those species with the smallest sample sizes. *Platyspiza crassirostris* and *Geospiza difficilis* are presented despite their representation by less than ten birds. Because *Camarhynchus pauper* is represented by only three birds, however, and *Camarhynchus psittacula* and *Cactospiza pallida* by only one bird each, these three species cannot be given serious consideration in the following treatment.

The most obvious relationships established by these phylogenetic comparison schemes are intergeneric. The species of *Geospiza* are most closely related to each other. The other three genera for which reasonably good sample size is available are less closely related to *Geospiza* or to each other. This fact would seem to reinforce the validity of existing generic classification (Bowman 1961; Swarth 1931). *Camarhynchus* seems to be the closest of the three genera to *Geospiza*, followed by *Platyspiza* (*crassirostris*). *Certhidea* (*olivacea*) is the most distantly related. *Camarhynchus parvulus* is particularly close to the six species of *Geospiza* on the basis of electrophoretic information and, allowing for the exclusion of a vast array of anatomical, behavioral, and ecological data, might easily be placed among them. Within the genus *Geospiza*, several interesting relationships are presented. In keeping with prior classification schemes, *Geospiza magnirostris, Geospiza fortis,* and *Geospiza fuliginosa* appear to be very closely related, although *fuliginosa* and *fortis* seem to be closer to each other than to *magnirostris*. An unexpected finding is the close relationship between *Geospiza fuliginosa* and *Geospiza scandens,* a propinquity more than rivaling that of *fuliginosa* to *fortis* and *magnirostris*. Ford, Ewing, and Parkin (1974), having observed this same unexpected relationship, referred to Lack's (1947) belief that the seed-eating small-billed ground finch, *G. fuliginosa*, and the more specialized cactus finch, *G. scandens*, are a subgenus apart.

Previous studies (notably those of Lack, 1947) have indicated *Geospiza difficilis* to be close to the base of the Darwin finch phylogenetic series. Bowman (this volume) has indicated that *Platyspiza crassirostris, Certhidea olivacea*, and *Pinaroloxias inornata* (of Cocos Island) have basic songs remarkably similar to the song of *Geospiza difficilis* (on Isla Genovesa), and that this resemblance may be correlated with similarities in their respective environments. The findings of this investigation can only demonstrate a relative measure of the relationships among the finches and, therefore, cannot realistically address the questions of which species are most ancestral. The electrophoretic data collected, however, do not indicate a close relationship among *Geospiza difficilis, Platyspiza crassirostris,* and *Certhidea olivacea*.

Based upon measures of genetic distance (Table 8) and the rough estimation of parameters of protein biochemistry, such as the rate of amino acid substitution, etc. (see Nei 1975), approximate divergence times are established for species of Galapagos finches that range from 5,000 years to nearly one million years (Table 9). Recent evidence (Cox, this volume) gives geological support to these crude estimates, extracted solely from electrophoretic data. According to Cox, the geological age of the oldest islands of the Galapagos Archipelago, the central and southeastern islands, is likely four million years or less—for some, it may be two million years or less. The more recently formed islands of the chain may be less than 500,000 years old. If these figures are at all accurate, the notion is upheld that most of the speciation among the finches has occurred within the order of one million years or so, as predicted by electrophoretic analysis.

TABLE 9. APPROXIMATE INTERSPECIFIC DIVERGENCE TIME BETWEEN SPECIES OF GALAPAGOS FINCHES (IN THOUSANDS OF YEARS)[a]

Species	*C. oliv.*	*C. pall.*	*C. parv.*	*C. paup.*	*C. psitt.*	*P. crass.*	*G. con.*	*G. scan.*	*G. diff.*	*G. fulig.*	*G. fort.*	*G. mag.*
Geospiza												
magnirostris	720	165	140	165	250	420	140	100	90	95	40	
fortis	775	90	75	90	190	395	70	35	35	35		
fuliginosa	740	125	40	125	215	365	45	5	90			
difficilis	800	55	115	55	195	625	65	105				
scandens	740	130	40	130	200	305	60					
conirostris	800	70	50	70	210	635						
Platyspiza												
crassirostris	995	645	415	645	495							
Camarhynchus												
psittacula	910	130	100	130								
pauper	905	–	110									
parvulus	730	110										
Cactospiza												
pallida	905											
Certhidea												
olivacea												

[a] By the method of Nei (1975).

ACKNOWLEDGMENTS

I am especially grateful to Dr. John Stubbs for technical advice and helpful criticism, and to Dr. Robert I. Bowman for the opportunity to undertake this study. For their many services I wish to thank Dr. John Wright, Dr. Suy Yang, Mr. Mike Rivers, Ms. Susan Wong, Dr. Sarane Bowen, Mr. Craig MacFarland, and Dr. T. E. Reed (for the use of his "Maxlik" computer program). For invaluable help in collecting tissue samples in the field, special thanks are due Ms. Nancy Jo, Dr. James Patton, and Dr. Philip Meyers. Permits to carry out this work in the Galapagos National Park were provided by Director General de Desarrollo Forestal, Ministerio de Agricultura y Ganaderia (Sr. Ing. Teodora Suarez M.). For grants in aid I am grateful to the Frederic Burk Foundation for Education (through a faculty research award to Dr. Stubbs) and to both the Committee on Research and Exploration of the National Geographic Society and the Chapman Fund of the American Museum of Natural History (through grants to Dr. Bowman).

RESUMEN

Estudio del polimorfismo enzimático de 257 pinzones de Darwin (Darwin's finches), representando 12 especies de 12 islas del Archipiélago de Galápagos, fue realizado por medio del análisis electroforético en tablas de poliacrilamide. Las bandas electroforéticas de supernatant malate dehidrogenase, alpha-glycerophosphate dehidrogenase, y esterases fueron agrupadas en formas de patrones de bandas y las frequencias de bandas fueron determinadas. Se propuso también un esquema genético hipotéticamente, del cual frequencias de alelos fueron estimados por medio del método de probabilidad máxima. El promedio y el porcentaje medio de los loci polimórficos entre las 12 especies fueron calculados aproximadamente como 30%, mientras que el promedio de la proporción de loci heterocigota por individuo fue calculado entre 0.054 ± 0.022 a través de todas las especies. Los datos de las bandas muestran generalmente pequeñas diferencias entre los pinzones diferencias que en cierto grado son de especie-específica. Posiblemente con la excepción de algunos casos, no se han encontrado bandas relacionadas a localidad-específica o a patrones de bandas. Distancia genética, asi como otras medidas de similitud taxonómica fueron también consideradas; pero con algunas excepciones estos resultados apoya a la clasificación previa de los pinzones de Darwin.

LITERATURE CITED

Ames, G. 1974. Resolution of bacterial proteins by polyacrylamide gel electrophoresis on slabs. J. Biol. Chem. 249:634-644.

Aspinwall, N. 1974. Genetic analysis of duplicate malate dehydrogenase loci in the pink salmon, *Oncorhynchus gorbuscha*. Genetics 76:64-72.

Baker, C. M. A., and H. C. Hanson. 1966. Molecular genetics of avian proteins-6. Evolutionary implications of blood proteins of eleven species of geese. Comp. Biochem. Physiol. 17:997-1006.

Beckman, L., and L. R. Nilson. 1965. Variations of serum enzyme in bird species and hybrids. Hereditas 53:221-230.

Boehm, L. G., and M. R. Irwin. 1970. Genetic polymorphisms of esterase isozymes of the plasma in two species of doves, their hybrids and backcross hybrids, and in other species of Columbidae. Comp. Biochem. Physiol. 32:377-386.

Bowman, R. I. 1961. Morphological differentiation and adaptation in the Galapagos finches. Univ. Calif. Publ. Zool. 58:1-302.

Bowman, R. I. 1963. Evolutionary patterns in Darwin's finches. Occas. Pap. Calif. Acad. Sci. 44: 107-140.

Bowman, R. I., and S. L. Billeb. 1965. Blood-eating in a Galapagos finch. Living Bird 4:29-44.

Bush, F. M. 1967. Developmental and population variation in electrophoretic properties of dehydrogenases, hydrolase and other blood proteins of the house sparrow, *Passer domesticus*. Comp. Biochem. Physiol. 22:273-287.

Corbin, K. W., C. G. Sibley, A. Ferguson, A. C. Wilson, A. H. Brush, and J. E. Ahlquist. 1974. Genetic polymorphism in New Guinea starlings of the genus *Alponis*. Condor 76:307-318.

Darwin, C. 1845. Journal of researches into the natural history and geology of the countries visited during the voyage of H. M. S. "Beagle" round the world, under the command of Capt. Fitz Roy, R. N. 2nd rev. ed. John Murray, London. 520 pp.

Ford, H. A., A. W. Ewing, and D. T. Parkin. 1974. Blood proteins in Darwin's finches. Comp. Biochem. Physiol. 47B:369-375.

Harris, H. 1966. Enzyme polymorphisms in man. Proc. Roy. Soc. London B 164:298-310.

Harris, M. P. 1973. The Galapagos avifauna. Condor 75:265-278.

Hubby, J. L. 1963. Protein differences in *Drosophila*. 1. *Drosophila melanogaster*. Genetics 48:871-879.

Hubby, J. L., and R. C. Lewontin. 1966. A molecular approach to the study of genic heterozygosity in natural populations. 1. The number of alleles at different loci in *Drosophila pseudoobscura*. Genetics 54:577-594.

Hubby, J. L., and L. H. Throckmorton. 1965. Protein differences in *Drosophila*. 2. Comparative species genetics and evolutionary problems. Genetics 52:203-215.

Karig, L. M., and A. C. Wilson. 1971. Genetic variation in supernatant malate dehydrogenase of birds and reptiles. Biochem. Genet. 5:211-221.

Kitto, G. B., and A. C. Wilson. 1966. Evolution of malate dehydrogenase in birds. Science 153: 1408-1410.

Lack, D. 1947. Darwin's finches. Cambridge University Press, Cambridge. 208 pp.

Lack, D. 1969. Subspecies and sympatry in Darwin's finches. Evolution 23:252-263.

Lewontin, R. C., and J. L. Hubby. 1966. A molecular approach to the study of genic heterozygosity in natural populations. 2. Amount of variation and degree of heterozygosity in natural populations of *Drosophila pseudoobscura*. Genetics 54:595-609.

Nei, M. 1975. Molecular population genetics and evolution. North-Holland/American Elsevier, Amsterdam. 288 pp.

Nottebohm, F., and R. K. Selander. 1972. Vocal dialects and gene frequencies in the Chingolo sparrow (*Zonotrichia capensis*). Condor 74:137-143.

Prager, E. M., and A. C. Wilson. 1975. Slow evolutionary loss of the potential for interspecific hybridization in birds: a manifestation of slow regulatory evolution. P.N.A.S. 72:200-204.

Reid, M. S., and R. L. Bieleski. 1968. A simple apparatus for vertical flat-sheet polyacrylamide gel electrophoresis. Anal. Biochem. 22:374-381.

Selander, R. K. 1976. Genic variation in natural populations. Pages 21-45 *in*: F. J. Ayala, ed. Molecular Evolution. Sinauer, Sunderland, Mass.

Selander, R. K., M. H. Smith, S. Y. Yang, W. E. Johnson, and J. B. Gentry. 1971. Biochemical polymorphism and systematics in the genus *Peromyscus*. 1. Variation in the old-field mouse. Stud. in Genet. 6:49-90.

Studier, F. W. 1973. Analysis of Bacteriophage T7 early RNAs and proteins on slab gels. J. Molec. Biol. 79:237-248.

Swarth, H. S. 1931. The avifauna of the Galapagos Islands. Occas. Pap. Calif. Acad. Sci. 18. 299 pp.

ADDENDUM

This manuscript was submitted for publication in the summer of 1977. Subsequently, another treatment of electrophoretic variability in the Galapagos finches, based on the same tissue samples used in this study, appeared in the literature (Yang and Patton 1981). Following the initial survey, the tissue samples were supplied to Yang and Patton for the purpose of extending the number of assays performed (and, hence, loci examined) on this valuable collection of birds. The results of the second survey generally corroborate the original study, particularly as regards the estimate of $\bar{H}$ across all taxa and overall taxonomic relationships. However, the close relationship between *Cactospiza* and *Platyspiza* (as opposed to *Camarhynchus*) found by these authors was not suggested by the original data set.

LITERATURE CITED

Yang, S. Y., and J. L. Patton. 1981. Genic variability and differentiation in the Galapagos finches. Auk 98:230-242.

THE EVOLUTION OF SONG IN DARWIN'S FINCHES

ROBERT I. BOWMAN
Department of Biological Sciences, San Francisco State University, San Francisco, CA 94132

This study of the singing patterns of Darwin's finches was conducted over a 20-year period and has involved the spectrographic analysis of several thousand field recordings of the songs of all 14 species of the avian tribe Geospizini. Experiments were conducted on the progeny of captive finches to determine the relative importance of heredity and learning in the development of definitive vocalizations. Sound-pressure levels of the songs were measured in four species of free-living finches. Patterns of sound transmission were determined in various Galapagos environments and correlated with energy spectra of songs as well as with anatomical, ecological, and behavioral features of the birds.

Three types of "vocal expression" (Darwin 1872) are associated with reproductive behavior. High-frequency "whistle" song is given during courtship and is structured so as to impede binaural localization of its source by nest predators, including short-eared owls and mockingbirds. "Basic" and "derived" songs are used in mate attraction and territorial defense, and appear in a variety of patterns associated with differing motivational states, transmission distances, and vegetation formations.

It is hypothesized that in the evolution of territorial vocal communication in Darwin's finches, natural selection has shaped the signal structure so as to minimize transmission loss of acoustical energy and thereby maximize the energetic response of the intended participants. Each Galapagos plant community transmits sound frequencies differently, i.e. exhibits a distinctive pattern of frequency-dependent attenuation. Regional differences in songs (dialects) reflect regional differences in sound transmission and ecology of the finches. Thus there is evidence that natural selection has shaped song form.

This study provides no evidence for "character displacement" in the songs of the finches. Song convergences (and parallelisms) are thought to be the result of sympatric or allopatric occupation of identical or very similar acoustical environments. Song divergences are the result of the occupation of different acoustical environments by different populations of the same or different species. Vocal convergences between Darwin's finches and their ecological counterparts in other regions of the world are apparent and indicate a correspondence between ecological niche and acoustical form. As in the feeding behaviors of the finches, there is a strong positive correlation in their vocal behaviors between structural and environmental diversity, i.e. the more variable the song, the broader the "acoustical aperture" of the transmission field, wherein differential frequency-dependent loss of sound energy is minimal at any given transmission distance.

Song-learning experiments, along with observations on heterospecific matings in the wild, suggest that specific adult mating preferences are conditioned early in life (age 10-40 days) through imprinting on the song of the attending parental male with whom a strong social bond has developed as a result of feeding. Should vocal misimprinting result from a heterospecific foster-father adoption, interspecific pairings may result in adulthood. Some experimental evidence indicates that female finches also imprint early in life on the songs of the attending adult male, and they vocalize this song as reproductive preparedness approaches. Thus heterosexual pairing may be the result of mutual recognition (matching) of conspecific song imprints. One wild male intergeneric hybrid ("*Camarhynchus conjunctus*") successfully backcrossed with a typical wild female *Camarhynchus parvulus*, producing three nestlings, thus proving that hybrids among Darwin's finches may be fertile and contribute to introgression of structural and vocal characteristics.

Inasmuch as vocal dialects in Darwin's finches appear to be local adaptations to prevailing acoustical environments, and since dialects are known to be culturally transmitted, they could, theoretically, be the initial cause and not the consequence of genic diversification. If local habitats are imprinted as are local song dialects, early in life, adult mobility could be reduced and genetic divergences affecting feeding and morphological adaptations enhanced.

The great ecological diversity of the Galapagos Islands, with their numerous insular worlds within a world, all differing in their florae and geospizine faunae, seems to have led to a rapid and varied proliferation of vocal (and feeding) adaptations, for which Darwin's finches are justly famous.

Ecological (acoustical) conditions that have made possible the remarkable radiation in Darwin's finches are not unique to insular settings such as the Galapagos Islands, but occur in differing degrees in all regions of the world where birds sing.

TABLE OF CONTENTS

Largely due to the classical writings of Darwin (1945) and Lack (1947), the 14 species of endemic songbirds of the Galapagos and Cocos islands have become famous as a textbook example of adaptive radiation in the class Aves (Sulloway 1982a,b). Although Darwin's finches are best known for their diversity of bill structure (Fig. 1) and associated feeding behavior (Bowman 1961), the present study has revealed an equally varied adaptive radiation in their song signals (Fig. 2). Like the feeding behaviors, finch vocal behaviors show clear correlations with the ecological conditions under which the birds live.

Following the methodology of ethologists (Eibl-Eibesfeldt and Kramer 1958), this study on the evolution of vocal communication in Darwin's finches was carried out in three stages. Initially, a large number of field recordings of songs were catalogued according to structure and behavioral context. Secondly, using aviary-bred, hand-reared individuals, the ontogeny and filial transmission of songs were studied under controlled acoustical enviroments. Thirdly, contributions to fitness of observed vocal characters were assessed from additional studies on sound attenuation in various Galapagos environments. Concurrently, a detailed investigation of the anatomy of the geospizine syrinx (Cutler 1970) made it possible to correlate certain details of syringeal structure with distinctive features of songs.

The results of these investigations are numerous and varied. New insights have been gained into the role of the acoustical environment in shaping vocal signal structure (Bowman 1979), the possible causes of convergence and parallelism in bird songs generally, the relative importance of nature and nurture in normal song development, and the role of song in mate selection.

For a number of reasons, Darwin's finches have been ideal subjects for behavioral studies. Genetic relationships among most members of the group are fairly well known (Polans, this volume; Yang and Patton 1981). All available evidence (Table 1) points to a monophyletic origin of the finches, with major features of their adaptive radiation having arisen in their present oceanic island settings. The finches occur abundantly in most of the insular habitats, many of which are distinctive both floristically and vegetatively (Figs. 4-18). Because conditions on many of the islands are virtually pristine, correlations between the prevailing vegetation and local song dialects can be made directly, with little or no concern for the effects of past ecological disturbances by man or his domesticates. Sound pollution resulting from human activities is minimal. All finches sing at least two types of song, with a few singing three or more, all of which show some degree of geographic variation (Figs. 42-47). Collectively, the songs of Darwin's finches display structural convergences with those of ecological equivalents on continents (Figs. 2, 39-41). Interisland differences in the composition of geospizine faunas (Fig. 3, Table 2) provide natural experiments in coexistence; the effects of these differences on song diversity can be readily evaluated. Except possibly *Certhidea olivacea* and *Cactospiza heliobates*, which have not been studied in captivity, all species adapt quickly to aviary conditions and thrive on simple diets consisting of millet seed, fresh greens, and occasional live insects. The birds are long-lived and may remain reproductively active for as long as 8 years in the wild (pers. comm., P. R. Grant) and over 15 years in captivity (Fig. 176). But surely one of the most important features that make the finches such a treasured resource is their extraordinary tameness toward humans (Darwin 1845), which facilitates the recording of their songs and of other aspects of their natural history. Such unbashful behavior should command our highest respect and our never-failing concern for its preservation.

The principal aims of this paper are as follows: (1) to describe the variability in song patterns of all species of Darwin's finches; (2) to explain the probable adaptive significance of the patterns in the context of environmental differences in vegetation structure and sound transmission; and (3) to demonstrate that cultural transmission of song has led to the persistence of the widespread dialect phenomenon and the occasional hybridization of species.

METHODS AND MATERIALS

Because many biologists may be unfamiliar with the basic equipment and techniques employed in bioacoustical research, the following descriptions are presented in considerable detail in order to facilitate independent evaluation of our findings.

Field Recordings

Tape recordings of the songs of Darwin's finches were made exclusively on Nagra III-B and IV single-track tape recorders operating at tape speeds of 19.05 cm/s and 38.1 cm/s and using the

"HI-FI" record setting. Frequency response characteristics of the Nagra III-B recorders are presented in Fig. 19. In most cases the signal-to-noise ratios at 19.05 and 38.1 cm/s were essentially the same, i.e. 45 dB for Nagra No. 1, and 43 dB for Nagra No. 2.

In the early stages of song recording (1961, 1962, and 1964), American D-33 microphones were mounted in 24-inch diameter unpolished aluminum reflectors, but these were subsequently replaced, and the bulk of the finch song recordings were made with Sennheiser "ultradirectional" microphones (models MKH 805 and 815U) equipped with windscreens (Models MZW 815 or 804). Frequency response characteristics of the model MKH 805 are shown in Fig. 20 and are similar for the model MKH 815U. No individual response curves are available for the D-33 microphones.

Several types of "3M" brand, quarter-inch, polyester base, magnetic recording tape were used, including Nos. 200, 202, and 207.

Because of the extraordinary tameness of the finches, most song recordings were made within 15 feet of the singing bird. "Playback" technique was often used to attract a distant bird and cause it to sing close to our microphone. Despite the close-range work, under certain conditions it was necessary to collect the bird in order to verify our field identification. Such was the case when we started recording sympatric species of tree-finch (*Camarhynchus*) on Isla Floreana and sympatric species of ground-finch (*Geospiza*) on islas Santa Cruz and Santiago. Specimen vouchers for these species are deposited in the Vertebrate Museum, San Francisco State University.

Laboratory Analyses of Songs

For the analysis of song variation in *Certhidea olivacea* (Billeb 1968), recordings were played on a Magnecord PT6-6A tape deck and fed into a Kay Electric "Sona-graph" model 6061-A using the "high-shape" circuit and the "wide band" filter settings.

Frequency/temporal parameters of the audiospectrograms were measured on a graduated clipboard similar to that described by Marler and Isaac (1960). For all other song analyses three types of spectrographic displays were prepared, namely, narrow band, wide band, and amplitude contour, by means of the Kay Elemetrics Spectrum Analyzer ("Sona-graph" model 6061-B, range 85-16,000 Hz) equipped with an Amplitude Display (model 6070-A) tuned to the "flat" response setting (Fig. 21). Recordings were played on either Nagra III-B or Ampex tape deck model AG-500.

The amplitude contour accessory to the sound spectrograph converts the sound signal into a display in which amplitude distribution is defined according to frequency by six contour lines, each with a 6-dB interval. Only the four highest contour areas, namely 6, 5, 4, and 3 (Fig. 21), were used in this study, because the perimeter of amplitude area 3 approximates that normally obtained when preparing wide- and narrow-band displays of the same song and probably delimits most if not all of the critical sound energy used in song transmission. The automatic gain control (AGC) is normally adjusted to its minimal setting (near zero) when making amplitude displays, whereas the AGC is usually adjusted upwards (approximately 2.5) when making normal narrow- and wide-band displays. This difference in settings accounts for the "disappearance" on narrow- and wide-band displays of the low-amplitude sound contained within the contour areas 1 and 2 of the amplitude contour display.

Because of the approximate doubling of sound amplitude with each 6-dB pressure increment (Peterson and Gross 1972), numerical values of 1, 2, 4, and 8 were assigned to contour levels 3, 4, 5, and 6, respectively, in order that logarithmic values (decibels) of the amplitude contour display could be converted proportionately to linear values of the amplitude grid score. This permitted adding the linear values when calculating relative amplitude distributions (i.e. energy spectra) for entire songs (Fig. 21).

Over each amplitude display to be "read" was placed a transparent plastic sheet on which a black grid was printed (see Fig. 21). Each square of the grid spanned 250 Hz on the vertical scale and 25 msec. on the horizontal scale.

Within the confines of any given square of the grid, the amplitude shading with the highest numerical value determined the value assigned to the entire square, even though shades of lesser value may also have been present. Thus, the machine-generated amplitude contour display of a song is translated into a mosaic composed of four numbers: 1, 2, 4, and 8. The total relative energy contained within a 250-Hz bandwidth across the song was obtained by summating all linear values of the grid squares in the band. Using the band totals of all songs, histograms were constructed, showing the amplitude distribution (i.e. energy spectrum) according to frequency for individuals and populations.

Measurement of Decibel Level of Song

Published sound intensity values for vertebrate vocalizations are very few. For lower vertebrates, the study of Australian anurans by Loftus-Hill and Littlejohn (1970), and for birds, the studies on oscines by Witkin (1977), Heuwinkel (1978), Brackenbury (1979), and Dabelsteen (1981) are notable for their use of modern instrumentation under field conditions.

In the Galapagos we have been successful in measuring sound-pressure levels of advertising song of four species of Darwin's finches on islas Genovesa and Wolf (see Fig. 3). Playback of a tape recording of an individual's song was used to attract the bird to within 3 feet or less of a hand-held microphone (Brüel and Kjaer type 4131) equipped with a random-incidence corrector (B & K type UA 0055) and windscreen (B & K type UA 0082). The entire transducer system was mounted on a Sennheiser microphone boom (model MZS 805) and connected to a sound-level meter (B & K type 2203) with octave filter set (B & K type 1613) by means of a 10-foot long extension cable (B & K type AO 0033). The microphone output was calibrated with a pistonphone (B & K type 4220). The nonweighted signal from the sound-level meter was fed into a Nagra III-B tape recorder (operating at 38.1 cm/s at the HI-FI record setting), the two instruments previously having been "matched" by using the dB level of the approximately 1-kHz calibration tone of the sound-level meter as a reference standard (Wilson 1968).

In the field an estimate was made of the distance between the bill of a singing bird and the end of the microphone. This estimate, the nature of the alignment between bird and microphone, the readings of the attenuator setting on the sound-level meter, the date, time, temperature, and relative humidity were recorded on the sound tapes. In the laboratory, recordings were analyzed using essentially the same equipment, and arrangement thereof, as employed in the analysis of sound transmission (see below, and Fig. 22).

The all-pass dB-level readings on the output of the graphic level recorder (B & K type 2305) were adjusted for each song recording because of differences in subject-to-microphone distance. When recordings of singing birds were made in the field to measure absolute amplitude of sound, it was assumed that at a bill-to-microphone distance of 30 to 36 inches, sounds were diverging spherically—an assumption that is not founded on preliminary research and therefore may be incorrect (cf. Witkin 1977). As Dr. E. S. Morton has pointed out (pers. comm.), much depends upon the shape of the mouth/air interface and the frequency of the sound, with higher frequencies "beaming" more than lower frequencies. If the sound source is very small compared to the wavelengths contained in the song, then the sound will probably diverge spherically from the source outward. Since sound-pressure level diminishes with increasing distance at the rate of about 6 dB with each doubling of distance from the sound source ("inverse square law," Wood 1947), the recording distance of a singing bird was "halved" enough times to bring the effective distance between bird and microphone to about 1 inch (actual range 0.9 - 1.5 inches). With each halving of distance, a factor of 6 dB was added to the dB value shown on the output of the graphic level recorder. For example, if the dB level of the song was 75 dB, and the estimated recording distance was 36 inches, then, as a result of dividing 36 inches by 2, and each successive quotient by 2 through a series of five such divisions, we arrived at an effective working distance of 1.125 inches between bird bill and front end of microphone. To the level recorder output of 75 dB was added

30 dB (i.e. 5 times 6 dB), thereby making a total song pressure level of 105 dB at a point very close to the source of the sound. Most of the dB values of song were arrived at by averaging comparable data points from two or more song recordings from the same individual (see Table 18).

Physical Factors Affecting Sound Transmission

The singing bird and the listening bird are coupled by an acoustical transmission path. Loss of sound energy along that path may be caused by (1) spherical divergence, (2) air losses, and (3) terrain losses. Spherical divergence is the result of sound propagation in all directions from a point source, and dominant at short distances. Because of the almost universal occurrence of spherical divergence, it is customary for acoustical engineers, whose example has been followed by some biologists (cf. Morton 1970, 1975; Marten and Marler 1977; Marten, Quine and Marler 1977; Marten 1980) to subtract from the measured sound pressure levels (SPL's) the 6 dB per doubling of distance. Values less than zero are the "excess attenuations" (EA) values, which are often used to compare sound transmission characteristics of different environments. Although Marten and Marler (1977) and Waser and Waser (1972) state that EA comes close to having a linear relationship with distance, both theory and empirical data indicate that it does not (Marton 1981).

Air losses are due principally to molecular absorption and dispersion (both of which are frequency-, temperature-, and humidity-dependent), and amount to a few decibels per 100 feet in the frequency range of 500-2000 Hz (Lyon 1973). Additionally, refractive effects of temperature and wind gradients may cause appreciable loss of sound energy along a linear pathway.

Terrain losses are those due to scattering of sound energy by vegetation and ground surface. Exposed soil affects sound attenuation chiefly in frequencies between 200 and 1000 Hz; this range is below that of most bird song. Leaves and branches on the ground have little effect on sound transmission (Aylor 1972a; Ingård 1953). Sound sources close to the ground may be attenuated as much as 6 dB in excess of that resulting from spherical divergence, especially in the very low frequency range. At 1.0 to 1.8 M above ground level, excess attenuation in the range of 10-18 dB between 200 and 800 Hz has been detected (cf. Bowman 1979; Morton 1975).

For present purposes, it seems unnecessary and undesirable to manipulate the field data (SPL's) in order to accommodate the effects on sound transmission theoretically attributable to spherical diverence, since it is the net behavior of sound transmission under natural conditions that we wish to study (Tables 3, 4, 5).

Selective attenuation of sound frequencies by vegetation is probably the most important environmental factor shaping the vocal signals of many songbirds, including Darwin's finches (cf. Marten 1980; Morton 1975). The way vegetation affects sound transmission is complex, and a detailed analysis of the phenomena involved is beyond the scope of the present paper (see reviews in Michelson 1978 and Wiley and Richards 1978).

A visual assessment of vegetation density was attempted by Aylor (1972b) and Yeocum (1975) to predict sound transmission characteristics of habitats. The results of both studies show that visibility is not a good measure of the attenuating capacity of vegetation because it is diminished by small objects, such as narrow branches and twigs, which do not scatter much sound except at very high frequencies. Morton (1970) has correctly noted that predicting the degree of sound scattering by vegetation cannot be handled analytically unless the acoustic impedances of the component plants are known (cf. Embleton 1966).

Studies by Beranek (1971) and Aylor (1972a) on sound attenuation by shrubbery produced different equations, both of which failed to consider such variables in the sound transmission pathway as differential leaf size, leaf orientation, etc. Lyon (1973) reviewed the sound propagation studies up to 1972 and found that researchers differed in their results up to a factor of ten. These discrepancies were due partly to the great variability of sound transmission by vegetation, and partly to surface meteorological factors. Embleton (1963) found that a comparatively small effect of vegetation on sound attenuation is caused by oscillation of tree branches 8 to 15 feet above ground level, in the frequency range of 1200 and 2400 Hz, and well within the lower frequency ranges of the songs of many birds (Bondesen 1977).

Except for linear dispersion, as noted above, and within the linear distances and the frequency ranges wherein most terrestrial vocalizations of songbirds must function, habitat differences in sound transmission are attributable mainly to vegetation structure (Bowman 1979; Embleton 1963; Morton 1970; Weiner and Keast 1959; Yeocum 1975). Vegetations differing in growth-form, species and foliage densities, stem diameter, and leaf/stem surface impedances may alter differently the frequency-dependent amplitude characteristics of sound by shifting the optimal transmission bandwidth upward or downward, broadening or narrowing it. Natural selection has modified vocal signals to make the best fit with concordant sound environments (Bowman 1979).

Although physical perturbations caused by wind, heat stratification, and leaf reflectancy may seriously affect the intelligibility of information encoded in amplitude and frequency modulation, it appears that for most species of songbirds, the problem of signal degradation during sound transmission may be circumvented through a number of behavioral adjustments affecting time and location of signaling, signal structure, and, most importantly, by territorial cruising accompanied by oft-repeated song (see Richards and Wiley 1980).

Measurement of Sound Transmission

In the Galapagos Archipelago, sound transmisson in song environments of the finches was measured on islas Santa Cruz, Española, Genovesa, and Santiago (Fig. 23), and also on Isla Wolf (Fig. 3). Depending on the length of the sound transect, measurements were made over a 30-90 minute period and as soon as possible after sunrise (6 a.m.) when the air was most calm and relatively free of heat stratification (Table 6), which significantly shortens transmission distance of sound by mid-day, when singing subsides. An amplified "pink noise" spectrum, originating from a battery-powered noise generator (custom built for this study by the acoustical consulting firm of Wilson, Ihrig and Associates of Oakland, California) was broadcast through a speaker system (Altec Lansing driver model 802D and horn model 811H) mounted on a metal Tiltall tripod 1 meter above ground level (Fig. 24). The transmitted noise was recorded through a sound-level meter equipped as described above for measurement of song dB level, using the nonweighted network. The meter was also mounted 1 meter above ground level on a tripod positioned at six stations along a straight line transect, 25, 50, 100, 150, 200, and 300 feet from the front of the speaker.

In all sound-transmission measurements, the sound source (horn) was positioned within the vegetation so as to avoid the "boundary effect" generated when the horn is situated outside the plant formation (cf. Aylor 1972b; Linskens et al. 1976).

Because of the equipment limitations in 1968, when sound-transmission experiments were run, our instrument level for all environments was standardized at 1 meter. Singing heights of the finches were as variable as the vegetation heights. Darwin's finches live in a wide variety of habitats ranging from low-growing coastal scrub (Figs. 9, 12A, and 14), to humid forest (Figs. 6, 8, 10A, 16, and 17), herbaceous uplands (Figs. 7A and 13B), and intermediate types (Bowman 1961; Wiggins and Porter 1971; Reeder and Riechert 1975; Svenson 1930a,b and 1935). Nests and singing perches may be close to ground level (as for *Geospiza difficilis* on islas Darwin, Genovesa, Pinta, Santiago, and Wolf; see Fig. 15A; and for *Certhidea olivacea* on islas Española and Wolf; see Figs. 10 and 14B), at 3-15 feet for most species (Fig. 9B), and up to 50 feet in the highlands of the larger islands (e.g. Cocos, San Cristóbal, Santiago, and Santa Cruz; see Figs. 6B and 17A) for arboreal species of *Camarhynchus, Cactospiza, Certhidea,* and *Pinaroloxias*. Because of the obvious difficulty in measuring sound transmission in the leaf canopy of forest trees such as *Scalesia pedunculata* (Fig. 6), a compromise was worked out whereby measurements were made through the foliage of a dense second-growth stand (4-8 feet tall) at 1 meter above ground level. Leaf structure and branching of these young *Scalesia* trees was quite similar to those of mature trees nearby at heights of 50 feet.

The Wilson/Ihrig random noise generator used a zener diode as the source of the white noise. The signal was enhanced by two voltage amplifiers in order to provide sufficient level for driving a power amplifier and loudspeaker. Between the two voltage amplifiers, a filter network was inserted to provide various noise spectra for the specific requirements of the project. Three noise spectra provided were white, pink, and red. Their characteristics are indicated in Table 7 and graphed in Fig. 25. The noise generator was equipped with a voltage-regulated power supply to maintain the noise level constant in amplitude and spectrum as the battery voltage decayed.

The Nagra power amplifier (model DH-66 997) was used as portable power source for the horn-speaker. The maximum power capability of the amplifier was eight watts. The fidelity of the power amplifier was high, having a uniform response from 20 Hz to 20,000 Hz. The output connection to the external speaker was through a series capacitor and an autotransformer. The series capacitor served to block low frequencies, thereby avoiding damage to the high-frequency Altec speaker, which could occur from switching transients of low-frequency noise signals in the amplifier. The output autotransformer was provided so as to better match the 4-ohm output impedance of the speaker. The impedance characteristic of the speaker with its associated horn is shown in Fig. 26. Also shown is the overall electrical response from the input of the power amplifier to the speaker terminals, with the speaker as load on the amplifier. This represents the electrical response of the system as a function of frequency rather than the acoustical output of the speaker.

The frequency response of the B & K sound level meter (Type 2203), measured between the microphone input and the output of the SLM, was perfectly flat between 20 and 20,000 Hz on the linear scale (i.e. nonweighted network), the only one used in this study.

In all measurements with the B & K sound level meter, the normal microphone protection grid was replaced with the B & K incidence corrector (Type UA 0055). This made it possible to accurately measure sound frequencies (up to 10 kHz) having a variable or random incidence, such as may occur when working with pink noise transmission in vegetation with highly reflectant qualities.

The B & K windscreen (Type UA 0082) shields the microphone from very low-frequency noise in outdoor measurements. With the angle of incidence of the sound on the windscreen zero degrees, the response is linear with an error of ± 0.5 dB between 1 and 15 kHz (Brüel and Kjaer 1967).

Recordings of transmitted pink noise were analyzed by means of a sound filter (General Radio Sound and Vibration Analyzer model 1564) at one-third octave intervals from 500 Hz to 10,000 Hz. Sound-pressure levels (dB values) were obtained from the strip chart of the graphic level recorder (Fig. 22B). The frequency-response characteristics of the combined acoustical and electronic pathways leading to the output of the graphic level recorder are shown in Fig. 22C, which indicates an essentially flat frequency response under controlled test conditions. The latter consisted of a one-third octave filter analysis of a pink noise spectrum, broadcast over the Altec driver/horn combination, recorded at a distance of 10 feet from the speaker, using a Nagra III-B tape recorder at a speed of 38.1 cm/s and 3M recording tape type 207 (Fig. 22).

A random "pink noise" spectrum was used for measuring sound transmission because of the availability of a one-third octave constant percentage bandwidth sound filter (GenRad model 1564). Before filtering, the pink noise spectrum between 1 and 20 kHz is characterized by a sound-pressure level (SPL) decrease of 3 dB per octave (see Fig. 25A and Table 7). After one-third octave filtering, the pink noise spectrum is converted to a "white noise" spectrum, characterized by a constant energy distribution per octave (see Fig. 25B).

In our analyses the tape-recorded pink noise signals were electronically separated into 14 frequency bands, i.e. one-third octave bands with center frequencies at 500, 620, 790, 1000, 1240, 1580, 2000, 2480, 3160, 4000, 4960, 6320, 8000, and 9920 Hz. This process yielded a series of one-third octave sound-pressure levels (dB's) as shown in Tables 3, 4, and 5. The effective bandwidth of the 1000 Hz one-third octave center frequency extends from about 884 Hz to 1116 Hz, i.e. the bandwidth is about 23% of the center frequency (Peterson and Gross 1972). Because the GenRad 1564 sound filter is of the "constant percentage" bandwidth type, the bandwidth becomes increasingly broader as the center frequency becomes higher, resulting in an energy increase of 3 dB per octave (see Fig. 27A,B). This feature of the one-third octave filter, namely a 3 dB per octave *increase*, is equally offset by the 3 dB per octave *decrease* of the pink noise spectrum, and results in a "flat" frequency response curve for filtered pink noise, shown in Fig. 25B.

One-third octave bands below 500 Hz were not examined because the random noise generator was limited to the 500 to 20,000 Hz range. Also, none of the songs of Darwin's finches contained fundamental frequencies below 500 Hz (see Fig. 128). Proof of performance of our GenRad sound filter type 1564 is shown in Fig. 27C.

In many of the present considerations of sound transmission, it has been assumed that transmission efficiencies of identical frequencies composing the filtered noise spectra and song spectra are the same.

Display of Sound-Transmission Data

One-third octave absolute sound-pressure levels (Tables 3, 4, and 5) have been plotted on graph paper having frequency (kHz) on the vertical axis and distance in feet from the sound source on the horizontal axis (see Fig. 28). Points of equal absolute sound pressure were connected to produce an "isodecibel" contour line. Contour lines were plotted at 3-dB intervals, with their dB values shown near the top or bottom of each line (see Figs. 133-134). In this way a "sound-transmission isopleth" was generated, showing the frequency-dependent pattern of sound attenuation in a given environment. In practice the results obtained from the analyses of two or more sample "sound lines" were averaged before the data were plotted as an isopleth (mean data are given in Tables 3, 4, and 5). This was done because any single microphone placement will lie in a null for some frequencies and in a maximum for others. Thus, by averaging the results of several broadcast lines, which involve different microphone and horn placements, we can minimize the effects of frequency-dependent stationary wave shifts (cf. Wiley and Richards 1978).

Shown along the right vertical axis of each isopleth are average dB levels of one-third octave filtered background noise for selected one-third octave frequencies (Fig. 28).

The energy spectra (frequency/amplitude histograms) of song may be "projected" onto the corresponding "song fields" (sound-transmission isopleths) to allow for visual detection of possible correlations between the most intensively used frequencies in the songs and the most energy-conserving transmission channels in the environment (e.g. Figs. 130, 142).

As indicated in Fig. 128, only a very small percentage of the geospizine song frequencies occur below 1 kHz (cf. Konishi 1970a). Consequently, we need have little concern here for the poor transmission efficiency that characterizes all the isopleths below 1 kHz, presumably due to ground attenuation (Ingård 1953; Aylor 1971) and varying according to the height of instrumentation above ground level (Marten and Marler 1977). In those Galapagos environments so far tested (Figs. 127, 133-134), the most energy-efficient channels for sound transmission occur in the frequency range of 1.5 to 2.0 kHz (i.e. the "sound window" of Morton 1970 and 1975, or the "ground effect window" of Marten 1980). This is below the frequencies of modal amplitudes but within the lower ranges of most geospizine songs (e.g. see Fig. 136). According to Marten (1980), this window is a ground-related phenomenon, occurring only near the ground below 1 meter, and in all habitats (cf. Morton 1970), although it is more pronounced in "open" habitats than in forests, a condition not found to be true in all cases for Galapagos habitats.

Sound-transmission data (Tables 3-5) are presented in somewhat different form in Fig. 29. Here differences in cumulative dB losses, at standard distances from the sound source, are plotted according to frequency, with points having equal cumulative dB-loss values connected by an isodecibel contour line. The resulting "cumulative dB-loss isopleth," like the "sound-transmisssion isopleth," graphically displays different vegetation-induced "acoustic climates" (Linskens et al. 1976) over which song spectra (i.e. modal amplitude/frequency bands containing approximately 80-85% of the song energy) can be laid (e.g. Fig. 131).

Description of "Fish" Sound-Isolation Chamber and Measurement of Acoustical Insulation

Hand-reared finches were housed in modified Hartshorne sound-isolation chambers manufactured by Dr. William Fish of Carmichael, California. Each unit consists of three plywood boxes, the smaller ones nested within the larger ones, like Chinese boxes. Interior dimensions of the smallest (inner) box are as follows: 20" wide, 19" deep, and 13" high. Each of the inner two boxes was seated on a H-shaped double-bevelled wooden frame that maintained a 2-inch separation of the boxes on all six surfaces and helped to minimize sound conduction between them.

Fan-driven exterior air was forced into the inner box through an insulated baffled conduit, which also channeled wires to the ceiling-mounted fluorescent lamp, rear wall-mounted microphone connector, and 3-inch diameter speaker. Two wooden dowel perches were wedged between side walls, on which were mounted water and seed dispensers. A drawer on the floor of the innermost box was filled with fine sand to a depth of about an inch.

Provision was made for servicing the center box through a door on the front of each box. Visual monitoring of birds was possible through the glass windows in the doors (see Fig. 30). A roller blind over the exterior window shielded a bird from room light during its 12-hour darkness period. Automatic timers were programmed to switch the light, microphone, tape recorder, and speaker on and off as needed.

Sound-attenuation characteristics were determined for one of 10 isolation chambers used in the song-development experiments. The test was performed in an open level grassy playfield with the chamber standing 24 inches above ground. A sound-level meter was placed inside the innermost box and aligned with the horn. The latter was positioned 36 inches above ground at a distance of 10 feet from the exterior vertical surface of the chamber (Fig. 30). During sound tests of front, side, and rear walls of the isolation chamber, the alignment of horn and sound-level meter microphone were always maintained. The meter was connected by shielded cable through an insulated passageway to a Nagra III-B tape recorder located outside the chamber. Full-track recordings were made at 38.1 cm/s on 3M type 207 magnetic tape.

Differences in sound attenuation between front, side, and rear walls were less than 7 dB at 500 Hz and less than 2 dB from 1.5 to 20 kHz. Attentuation values for the three walls were averaged and compared to attenuation over 10 feet of open air in the same testing field. Differences between the absolute dB values represent the relative dB attenuation effected by the walls of the sound chamber.

As shown in Fig. 30, the isolation chamber attenuates sound by about 50 dB in the 2-7 kHz range and by about 60-70 dB between 8 and 20 kHz. Thus the attenuation between the interiors of two adjacent chambers would be on the order of 100 dB in the frequency range carrying most of the sound energy of songs (i.e. 2-7 kHz for Darwin's finches).

Skull Measurements

"Interaural distance" was measured with fine-pointed dial calipers along the ventral surface of the skull, across the basisphenoid plate between the medial-most edges of the left and right tympanic recesses (Fig. 108).

"Maximal diameter of skull" was measured with dial calipers at the greatest width of the skull, i.e. between lateral surfaces of left and right quadrato-jugal bars near their joints with the quadrates (as in larger species), or from left to right lateral surfaces of the parietals (as in smaller species).

Times and Location of Field Work

Between 1961 and 1979, nine visits were made to the Galapagos Islands and two to Cocos Island, Costa Rica for purposes of studying vocal communication in Darwin's finches. One visit to St. Lucia, West Indies was made in 1967 to study *Melanospiza richardsoni* (see Table 8). Out of a total of 342 days spent on this study in the Galapagos Archipelago, 30 days were consumed in interisland travel. A total of 313 days was spent on 20 Galapagos islands (Table 9).

Song Spectrograms

Unless otherwise indicated in the caption, song figures have been prepared using the wide-band display of the sound spectrograph (Fig. 21B). Individual songs are identified by the author's field catalogue number, e.g. R-126/6, which designates the reel (126) and cut (6) numbers. Other songs are identified by the name or initials of the recorder, e.g. CURIO for Dr. Eberhard Curio, JLG for Dr. James L. Gulledge, RATCLIFFE for Dr. Laurene Ratcliffe, or LOR for the Laboratory of Ornithology, Cornell University. Original recordings by the author are housed in the Bioacoustics Laboratory, Vertebrate Museum, San Francisco State University. Copies will be available from the Library of Natural Sounds, Laboratory of Ornithology, Cornell University.

GENERAL DESCRIPTION OF GEOSPIZINE SONG

Subjective Descriptions

Before the widespread use of tape recorders and sound spectrographs in vocalization studies, definitive adult songs of Darwin's finches were variously described as follows: "Of primitive pattern, unmusical, and with no complex phrases" (Lack 1945); by no means do they "rank with those of even ordinary singing birds, and indeed anywhere else would scarcely pass for songs. One never hears from the Geospizas such songs as are uttered by the song-sparrow or house-finches" (Snodgrass and Heller 1904); their utterances, like those of all the finches, were monotonous, a series of double syllables, two notes apart (Beebe 1924). Whereas the sounds of most songbirds are generally narrow-band and tonal (Marler 1977), the songs of most of Darwin's finches are "drab," i.e. punctuated with repetitious "buzzy" wide-band unmusical syllables. Some populations are as variable in their vocalizations as they are in their bill dimensions, e.g. *Geospiza fortis* on Isla Santa Cruz (Fig. 31). As Harris (1974) has pointed out, intrapopulational variation in song may be as great as, if not greater than, interpopulational variation (cf. Figs. 31 and 32). Seemingly rampant variability in the songs of some species is accompanied by pronounced interspecific parallel resemblances within the geospizine tribe (Figs. 33-38). At the same time, vocal divergences associated with various foraging niches would seem to have led to vocal convergences with ecologically equivalent species of songbirds on continents (Figs. 2, 39-41). Despite the relatively colorless song character overall, some geospizine populations have given rise to what, in human terms, may be described as melodious rhythmical productions (Figs. 52G,H; 82A,B).

Charles Darwin did not describe the songs of Galapagos finches because, at the time of his visit (September-October, 1835), the birds were not in breeding condition. Later explorers have provided song descriptions which, despite their subjective characterization, do nevertheless provide useful information on song stability and also on geographic variation (including dialects) in populations for which audiospectrographic data are not yet available.

In an attempt to integrate subjective (syllabic) and objective (audiospectrographic) representations of songs, Fig. 42 was prepared, wherein some typical song spectrograms of Darwin's finches are "interpreted" by means of English language syllables. Because tonal impurities are so widespread in finch songs, no neat correspondence between avian audiospectrographic "syllables" and human phonetic syllables is possible.

Song Classification

Each geospizine song may be assigned to one of the following three categories: "whistle," "basic," or "derived" (see Fig. 42). Whereas basic and derived songs are used in territorial advertisement, whistle songs are not. Additional details on song structure and function are given in subsequent sections.

Whistle song (Fig. 42A). There are two forms of this song type: a long continuous hissing note (e.g. "hisssssssssssssssss") or a series of short hiss-like notes (e.g. "see-see-see-see-see-see"), both starting at a very high frequency (often inaudible to humans), descending gradually or rather precipitously, and ending at a lower (more audible) frequency.

Basic song (Fig. 42B). There are three forms of this song type: basic song proper, special basic song, and abbreviate basic song. The "basic song proper" (hereafter designated simply as "basic song") can be described syllabically by the city name "Chicago," with emphasis on the drawn-out middle, buzzy, "a" syllable (e.g. "chic-a.a.a.a.a.a.-go"). There is also a tremolant form of the basic song characteristic of *Geospiza magnirostris* on Isla Santa Cruz and other islands (e.g. "too-chee-oo-oo-oo-oo-oo-oo-oo-oo"). The "special basic song" consists of a drawn-out rasping syllable (e.g. "bizzzzzzzzzzzzzzzz"), as in the first syllable of the word "*bus*iness." It is a rather high-pitched "growl." The "abbreviate basic song" is, in effect, a contracted form of the "basic song" in which the extended middle buzzy syllable has been much shortened (e.g. "ree-search, ree-search").

Derived song (Fig. 42C). There are essentially two forms of this song type: the polysyllabic form (e.g. "tee-you, tee-you"; "chee-tee, chee-tee") and the repetitive monosyllabic form (e.g. "churr-churr-churr-churr-churr-churr").

The distribution of the various song forms among the 14 species of Darwin's finches is presented in Table 10.

Song Descriptions and Song Parallelisms

Geospiza fuliginosa (Figs. 43, 46, 48)

The single bisyllabic set of songs is the fundamental element of all singing in this species (Snodgrass and Heller 1904), and is more common than the monosyllabic song (Lack 1945). The song of this species is weaker than in other ground-finches (Harris 1974).

Polysyllabic form (Fig. 42B, abbreviate basic song; Fig. 42C, derived song; Fig. 45D, basic song).

Tagus Cove (Isla Isabela). Accent on the first syllable: *teeur'-wee* or *tur'-wee* or *tee'-twur* or *tee'-ul-tee* (lengthening of first syllable) or *tu'-dl* or *ee'-zert*. Accent on the second syllable: *teur-wee'* or *teur-lee---e'* (lengthening of second syllable) or *tur-lee'* (Snodgrass and Heller 1904).

Iguana Cove (Isla Isabela). Accent on first syllable: *tul'-wee* or *tu...u-twur* (two syllables with the first syllable much prolonged) or *tee'-twur* or *tu'-wee*. Accent on second syllable: *tu-lee'* or *tu-twee'* (Snodgrass and Heller 1904).

Islas Seymour, Baltra, and north Santa Cruz. Accent on second syllable: *teur-lee'* (nearly always consisting of four sets; Snodgrass and Heller 1904).

Black Beach to highlands (Isla Floreana). Accent on first syllable: *skee'-wee*. Accent on second syllable: *teu-wink'*, the second syllable decidedly different in sound from anything heard elsewhere (Snodgrass and Heller 1904).

Isla San Cristóbal. Accent on first syllable: *see'-urr* (Snodgrass and Heller 1904).

Isla Santiago. Accent on first syllable: *chee'see-chee'see* (Beebe 1924).

Islas San Cristóbal, Isabela, and Pinzón. *Kee-week* (Rothschild and Hartert 1902).

Isla Baltra. *Cu-wee* (Beebe 1924).

Monotypic form (Figs. 37, 46D, derived song).

Tagus Cove (Isla Isabela). *Tew--twee-twee-twee-twee* with the "twee" syllable generally repeated four times, but often only once or twice (Snodgrass and Heller 1904); *che-che che-chee cheet* (Rothschild and Hartert 1902).

West side, Perry Isthmus (Isla Isabela). Song consisted of a repetition of a single note resembling *t'wer-t'wer-t'wer-t'wer*. Each note had a double sound, the "t" being slightly separated, as if composed of a bisyllabic sound condensed into a single syllable. The note was usually repeated three or four times (Snodgrass and Heller 1904).

Iguana Cove (Isla Isabela). *Tul-twee-twee-twee* or *tee'-twur-twur-twur* or *twee-twee-twee* or *tu wee'-twee-twee-twee* (Snodgrass and Heller 1904).

Islas Seymour, Baltra, and north Santa Cruz. *Teur'-lee-hee* or *teur-lee'-hee* (the same individual sometimes alternating between these two types) or *tee'-wee-wee* (Snodgrass and Heller 1904).

Many individuals of *Geospiza fuliginosa* have songs so similar to those of other species of Darwin's finches that field identification on the basis of song alone is often impossible. Examples of parallel song types are as follows: *Geospiza fuliginosa* with *Geospiza fortis* (Figs. 35A,B; 36); with *Geospiza scandens* (Fig. 34K,L); with *Camarhynchus parvulus* (Fig. 33J,K; Lack 1945); with *Cactospiza heliobates* in the region of Elizabeth Bay, Isla Isabela (Snodgrass and Heller 1904); with *Camarhynchus psittacula* (Figs. 34C,D; 35C,D); and with *Geospiza difficilis* (Fig. 34E,F).

Among species of ground-finch, the problem of field identification by means of song alone is greatest wherever *Geospiza fuliginosa* and *G. fortis* occur together as they do at Academy Bay, Isla Santa Cruz (see Fig. 36). In general, the songs of smaller-billed species of ground-finch have a faster delivery and a somewhat higher modal frequency in their energy spectra than do those of the larger species (Fig. 49).

The whistle songs of all species of *Geospiza* are virtually indistinguishable in the field, although on the average, larger species tend to have more extended songs than smaller species (see Fig. 43; Table 13).

Geospiza fortis (Figs. 31, 32, 43, 50, 51)

The songs of this species are among the most variable of the geospizine finches, e.g. compare intra- and inter-populational differences in Figs. 31 and 32, respectively.

Polysyllabic form (Fig. 32, basic, abbreviate basic, and derived songs; Fig. 36, basic song; Fig. 42B, abbreviate basic song; Fig. 46C, abbreviate basic song; Fig. 50, basic, abbreviate basic and derived songs).

Tagus Cove (Isla Isabela). Accent on the first syllable: *tee'-up twee'u* or *zee'-u twee-u* (the difference between the initial consonants of the two parts was very marked, and scarcely ever did the bird make any variation). Accent on the second syllable: *ter-r-r-r-wee'* (first syllable much prolonged by an *r*-like trill, while the second has a long *e* sound carrying the accent); Snodgrass and Heller (1904).

Isla Floreana. Accent on first syllable: *teur'-wee*, resembling almost one song of *G. fuliginosa* of Tagus Cove (Snodgrass and Heller 1904).

Isla Daphne Major. Accent on second syllable: *kah-lee'* (Beebe 1924).

Monosyllabic form (Figs. 36, 46C).

Tagus Cove (Isla Isabela). Accent on first syllable: *teur'-wee-wee* (often all notes resembled the first, or the first only slightly differed from the other two), or *tee'-wer-wer* (nearly always three sets were uttered in succession), or *tur'-we-wee* or *tur'-wur-wur* (Snodgrass and Heller 1904).

Iguana Cove (Isla Isabela). *Twee'-ur'r'r'*, uttered generally twice in succession, often only once, sometimes three times (Snodgrass and Heller 1904).

Isla Daphne Major. *Kak-kah-kah-kah* (Beebe 1924).

Individual songs of *G. fortis* were sometimes indistinguishable from those of *G. magnirostris, G. fuliginosa, G. scandens,* and *Cactospiza pallida* (Lack 1945). (Compare Figs. 35A,B; F,

G; J,K). Parallel songs are known between *G. fortis* and *Camarhynchus pauper* (Fig. 34I, J) and *Camarhynchus psittacula* (Fig. 35A,D). According to Snodgrass and Heller (1904), a *G. fortis* at Tagus Cove (Isla Isabela) sang very much like *Cactospiza heliobates* of Elizabeth Bay and Turtle Point (Isla Isabela).

In the field the song of *G. fortis* is most likely to be confused with that of *G. fuliginosa* on those islands where the two species co-exist: it is often very similar, and always constructed on the same plan (Snodgrass and Heller 1904). On Isla Santa Cruz the higher-pitched songs of the smaller-billed individuals of *G. fortis* bear the closest resemblance to *G. fuliginosa* songs. As Lack (1945) has correctly pointed out, the song of *G. fortis*, although harsh, is on occasion more melodious and forceful than the song of *G. fuliginosa. G. fortis* songs tend to be lower-pitched (Fig. 36), with the modal frequency of the energy spectrum slightly lower than in *G. fuliginosa* (Fig. 49). Larger individuals of *G. fortis* deliver their songs at a slightly slower pace than the smaller-billed individuals do, and the latter, in this regard, are virtually indistinguishable from *G. fuliginosa.* As in the case of *G. fuliginosa*, the polysyllabic song of *G. fortis* is much more commonly heard than the monosyllabic song (Fig. 46C).

Geospiza magnirostris (Figs. 36, 42B, 43, 45, 52, 53)

The song of *G. magnirostris* is a "very pleasing sound," differing considerably from the ordinary *Geospiza* notes (Snodgrass and Heller 1904). It is of a slower tempo than in other species of *Geospiza* and more melodious and forceful (Lack 1945). There is considerable divergence in song on several of the islands (notably islas Genovesa and Wolf), resulting in well-marked dialects (Figs. 52, 53).

Polysyllabic form (Figs. 36, 42B, 45, 52, 53, basic song; Figs. 94, 166, derived song).

James Bay (Isla Santiago). Accent on the first syllable: *teu'u.......e.....e-leur* (basic song). The first greatly prolonged syllable was indistinctly divided into two parts, the second one with the "e" sound especially prolonged. The sound of the first syllable was smooth and continuous, but the second syllable was abruptly different from the preceding. It was slightly prolonged, had a very pure tone, and ended with a rising inflection (Snodgrass and Heller 1904). The song is a distinctive *teu...e...e...leur*, slower and lower-pitched than in other species (Harris 1975). Accent not indicated: *witchee-witchee* (Beebe 1924).

Isla Pinta. Accent not indicated: *keu, keu*, like song of *Geospiza fortis*, but louder and clearer. It sometimes has a pleasing trill on the last syllable (Rothschild and Hartert 1902). Compare Figs. 52E and 53.

Isla Genovesa. Accent indicated: *kah-lee' kah-luh'* or *ker-dee' ker-dah'*. A monotonous series of double syllables, two musical notes apart, the first often being "C" (Beebe 1924). This description is somewhat at odds with the impression of the writer gained from field audition and spectrographic analyses (see Figs. 52 and 124B). When heard close-up, Beebe's *kah-lee'* would seem to be more appropriately represented by *kah kah-lee lee*, that is, each of his syllables is two-parted, sometimes subtly so, and the first syllable may actually be a staccato-like "trill" (Fig. 52G). The difference in pitch between the first pair of syllables and the second may be as much as four musical notes apart, the second usually higher than the first, but sometimes just the reverse (Fig. 166B). In the former case, the terminal rise in pitch seems to be accentuated by the fact that the closing syllables are of greater amplitude than the opening syllables (Fig. 124B), thereby producing the psychological effect of a rise in pitch (Armstrong 1963). Beebe (1924) correctly identified the pitch of the first syllable as "often being C." The musical quality of the Genovesa and Wolf island songs is due to their relatively pure tones, not typical of most geospizine songs.

Monosyllabic form (Figs. 36, 45D, 166B).

The "churr" note (derived song) was very infrequently encountered on Isla Santa Cruz

(Fig. 45D), rarely on Isla Genovesa (Fig. 166B), and not at all on other islands visited, the latter possibly the result of a sampling error.

On Isla Santa Cruz, *G. magnirostris* and large-billed forms of *G. fortis* have confusingly similar songs. But, in general, the songs of these sibling species can be distinguished on the basis of greater length and lower pitch in *G. magnirostris* (Figs. 36, 49). Lack (1945) was unable to distinguish between some songs of *G. magnirostris* and *G. scandens*, presumably on Isla Santa Cruz and in reference to monosyllabic song. This is understandable if the birds were not in view while singing (cf. derived songs in Figs. 45D and 46B). Lack's impression (1945), that *G. magnirostris* (basic?) song on Isla Genovesa is indistinguishable from that on Isla Santa Cruz, cannot be substantiated on the basis of the writer's field experience and available audiospectrograms (Figs. 52, 53). Certain of the songs of *G. conirostris*, Isla Española (Fig. 56), resemble fairly closely those of *G. magnirostris* on Isla Santa Cruz, Marchena, and Santiago (Fig. 52), largely because of their similar length, elongated trill, and overall quality.

There is a parallelism between certain of the songs of *G. magnirostris*, Isla Wolf (Fig. 52H), *G. fuliginosa*, Isla Santa Cruz (Fig. 35C), and *Camarhynchus psittacula*, Isla Santa Cruz (Fig. 35D).

Geospiza conirostris (Figs. 43B, 44B, 46A, 54-59)

This species regularly breeds on islas Española and Genovesa. Curio and Kramer (1965) have reported breeding on islas Wolf and Pinta, and a sample of *G. conirostris* song from a Pinta bird was generously provided by Dr. Eberhard Curio (Fig. 54B).

G. conirostris song on Isla Española is decidedly different from that of other species of *Geospiza* (*magnirostris* excepted) and in itself presents a large amount of variation (Snodgrass and Heller 1904). There can be little doubt that the Española song is more variable than that of any other species population of Darwin's finches, including *Geospiza fortis* (cf. Figs 31, 50, and 54-58). Many of the songs have extended trills; a few are nearly the reverse of others (Fig. 59, derived songs); and all are more or less musical in quality. They closely resemble the songs of the redwing blackbird of North America (Fig. 30). Although Lack (1945) correctly noted that the songs (basic) of Española birds do not bear any particular resemblance to those of Genovesa birds or those of *Geospiza scandens*, this is not true for the derived songs of these species (cf. Figs 46A,B, 59, and 60A). On Isla Genovesa the (derived) song consists of a rapid succession of notes (Lack 1945) and is far less variable than its conspecific song on Isla Española.

Polysyllabic form (Figs. 45E, 46A, 54B, 55, 56, basic song; Figs. 54B, 57, 58, abbreviate basic song).

Isla Osborn. *Chuckel-low* (basic song), Beebe (1926).

Isla Española. *Twee'-u'r'r'r'r-rwu* (basic song), the "r" sound of the second syllable is trilled; *tlee-lee-oo* (consonant sound variable and difficult to represent by the sound of letters) or *chee'-you-hoo* (the space between the second and the third syllable in each set is longer than between the first and second [Snodgrass and Heller 1904]). Accent on first syllable: *chee'-woo* (Snodgrass and Heller 1904); *tlee-oo* (Harris 1975).

Monosyllabic form (Figs. 45E, 46A, and 57-59).

Islas Española and Genovesa. Well developed.

Lack (1945) was unable to distinguish between the song of Genovesa *G. conirostris* and that of Santa Cruz *G. scandens*. This is particularly true of the derived songs, less so of the basic songs. The very close parallel between Genovesa *G. conirostris* (Fig. 54, R-84/21) and one Santa Fe *G. scandens* (Fig. 34M,N) is noteworthy. Although B. N. Grant and P. R. Grant (1979) claim that the song types of *G. conirostris* on Isla Genovesa are unlike those on Isla Española, the occasional resemblance between derived songs on Española (Fig. 59A,C) and Genovesa (Fig. 46, R-666/6) is strikingly good. Lack (1945) found that certain individuals of Española *G. conirostris* "were perhaps indistinguishable" from *G. fortis* (cf. Figs. 39A,C and 60A), and *Platyspiza crassirostris* (cf. Figs. 45, 56, and 64). Many of the songs of *G. magnirostris* on islas Marchena, Santa Cruz, and Santiago (Fig. 52D,I,F) resemble closely certain songs of *G. conirostris* on Isla Española (Fig. 56).

Geospiza scandens (Figs. 38, 43, 46B, 51)

On the larger central islands, the song of *G. scandens* is typically a rapid succession of strongly accentuated notes similar to that of *G. conirostris* on Isla Genovesa. Some versions have a banjo-like quality to the sound. A distinctive disyllabic song (Fig. 38) was reported by Lack (1945) and by others (see below). On the northern islands of Marchena and Pinta, portions of the song have a trill-like quality (Fig. 60A).

Polysyllabic form (Figs. 46B, 60).

James Bay (Isla Santiago). Accent on the first syllable: *teu'-lee*, set of two syllables repeated four times in succession (Snodgrass and Heller 1904).

Isla Baltra. *Clee-wick, clee-wick, ke-wick* (Rothschild and Hartert 1902); *chur-wee' chur-wee' chur-wee'* (Beebe 1924).

Isla Santa Cruz. *Teu-lee, teu-lee* (Harris 1975).

Monosyllabic form (Figs. 46B, 60).

James Bay (Isla Santiago). Accent on the first syllable: *teur'-wee-wee,* first syllable separated from the second by a longer interval than that between the second and the third; *bur-tee-tee-tee* (Snodgrass and Heller 1904).

Isla Baltra. *Tlee-tlee-tlee,* consisting sometimes of only three or four notes, but generally a larger number, such as six or seven (Beebe 1924); *teur'-wer-wer, teur'-wer-wer, teur'-wer wer* (Snodgrass and Heller 1904).

On Isla Santa Cruz, Certain of the monosyllabic (derived) songs of *G. scandens, G. magnirostris, G. fortis, G. fuliginosa*, and *Cactospiza pallida* were judged to be so similar that they could not assuredly be field identified to species on the basis of song alone (cf. Figs. 45D, 46B,C,D, and 47A). Comparison of certain song spectrograms of *G. scandens* from Isla Santa Fe (Fig. 60A, R-82/1X) and of *G. conirostris* from Isla Genovesa (Fig. 54) provides convincing evidence in support of the impressions of Snodgrass and Heller (1904) and Lack (1945) that the songs of these two species are sometimes very similar. Bisyllabic (derived) songs of certain individuals of *G. scandens, Camarhynchus parvulus,* and *Camarhynchus psittacula* in the region of Academy Bay, Isla Santa Cruz, likewise can be remarkably alike (Fig. 38).

Geospiza difficilis (Figs. 43F, 46E, 47F, 61, 62)

One of the few published descriptions of the song of *Geospiza difficilis* is that given by Lack (1945) for the Isla Genovesa population (*G. d. difficilis*): ". . . distinctive, consisting of short and more feebles notes [than *Geospiza fuliginosa*], often with a hissing note in the middle, so that in timbre it approaches the [basic] song of *Certhidea*" (cf. Figs. 61E and 78). Writing in his field notebook in the early 1930s about the then-extant Isla Santa Cruz population (*G. d. debilirostris*), Swarth (1932) described the song as distinctive, "like a tiny siren running down." In view of what we now know about the vocalizations of this species on other islands, it is likely that he was describing the "whistle song," which is presently known only from islas Genovesa and Darwin populations (Fig. 62D,E). Harris (1974) describes what is probably the basic song of *G. difficilis* on Isla Genovesa as "rather feeble with short notes . . . somewhat like Warbler Finch" (cf. Figs. 46E and 61E, and description of Lack 1945, above).

With the possible exception of *Geospiza conirostris*, no other species of Darwin's finches shows such remarkable interisland differences in song structure as does *Geospiza difficilis*. Whereas some populations (e.g. islas Darwin, Genovesa) have what might be considered a typical five-parted basic song (Fig. 61A,E) and a typical *Geospiza*-like whistle song (Fig. 62D,E), other populations have not only somewhat unusual five-parted basic songs (Fig. 61C,D) but also a special basic three-parted song (Fig. 62B,C), yet lack the typical *Geospiza*-like whistle song. Possibly unique among *G. difficilis* is the Isla Wolf population (*G. d. septentrionalis*), which sings not only the typical five-parted basic song (known only from a few individuals recorded in the field; see Fig. 61B), but also a more common derived song and a secondary three-parted "special basic" song (Fig. 62A). The terminal segment of the latter song consists of a unique high-pitched "whistle" that seems not to be homologous to the "whistle song" of other populations (see pp. 271-272). A similar, but much lower-pitched, terminal whistle is known from the Isla Santiago population (Fig. 62B), but none has yet been reported from the Isla Pinta population (Fig. 62C), in which a "normal" terminal syllable (song region 5) of the special basic song appears to be all that occurs. These marked interisland populational differences in vocalizations are to be correlated in part with differences in the habitats of the birds on the various islands. As yet unknown are the songs of *G. difficilis* in the higher regions of Isla Fernandina where the species is moderately abundant (personal observations of Dagmar Werner and R. I. Bowman; observations of Beck [Gifford 1919]).

Several workers have remarked upon the fact that, despite the great superficial similarity in bill size and shape between *G. difficilis* and *G. fuliginosa*, these sibling species show great dissimilarity in their songs (whistle song excepted). Only one moderately good example of song parallelism has been recognized for these species (Fig. 34E,F). Closer parallelisms are known between *G. difficilis* (Genovesa) and *Certhidea olivacea* (Santa Cruz) in their basic songs (cf. Figs. 35B and 46E), between the song of *G. difficilis* (Wolf) and the special basic song of *Camarhynchus parvulus* (Santiago) (Fig. 34O,P), and between the derived songs of *G. difficilis* (Wolf) and *Camarhynchus parvulus* (Floreana) (Fig. 34G,H).

Camarhynchus parvulus (Figs. 33-35, 38, 43, 63-70)

The advertising songs of *C. parvulus* are highly variable wherever encountered (Fig. 63). Lack (1945) has described the songs of this species on Isla Santa Cruz as follows: "Two main types of song, one a rapidly repeated succession of similar harsh notes [abbreviate basic song], the second, various combinations of two types of harsh notes succeeding each other rapidly, the phrasing and accenting being extremely variable [derived song]. The second type is usually harsher and shorter than the disyllabic type in *Camarhynchus psittacula* [Fig. 38, Type 1] but musical varieties occur. A "churr" [special basic song] and a long-drawn-out "see" [whistle song] may be added to the song . . ." (Fig. 64). The very varied vocalizations of this species show convergences with many of the songs of the Plain Titmouse, *Parus inornatus* (Fig. 40) and other parids of North America (cf. Dixon 1969; Dixon and Stefanski 1970) and Europe (cf. Lack 1945; Latimer 1977). On Isla Santa Cruz greater song diversity is found in the coastal zone than in the *Scalesia* forest highlands (cf. Figs. 65-66 and 68), with the most commonly heard song in the latter region sounding much like the *chick-a-dee* song of *Parus gambeli* of western North America, i.e. *chit'a-tee, chit'-a-tee, chit'-a-tee* (Fig. 68). The most common song of the coastal zone sounds very much like the "trill" of *Junco oreganus* of North America, and spectrographically resembles it (cf. Marler, Kreith, and Tamura 1962, Fig. 1B,H and Fig. 65). Lack (1945) remarked that "near the summit of Indefatigable Island [Isla Santa Cruz] nearly all the *parvulus* had musical songs [Fig. 68] whereas in the intermediate zone they were normally harsher" (Figs. 66, 67). The whistle song of all species of *Camarhynchus* is not a drawn-out "see" as suggested by Lack (1945), but rather a rapidly delivered series of distinct "see"-like notes, gradually decreasing in frequency (see Figs. 44A,B,C and 64B).

On Isla Santa Cruz some songs of *C. parvulus* are similar to those of *C. psittacula* (Fig. 38), but as Lack (1945) has pointed out, the notes of *parvulus* are usually shorter and sung more rapidly (Fig. 38, song type 2). In the coastal zone of Isla Santa Cruz, *C. parvulus, C. psittacula,* and *Geospiza scandens* show a remarkable parallel in two forms of their songs, i.e. two notes at about the same interval (Fig. 38). In the *Scalesia* forest highlands of the same island, three of the arboreal finches, *Certhidea olivacea, Camarhynchus parvulus,* and *Cactospiza pallida*, sing very similar songs, albeit different in amplitude and modal frequency, among other things (Fig. 70). Certain of the derived songs of *parvulus* on Isla Floreana are acoustically and spectrographically very similar to certain derived songs of *Geospiza difficilis* on Isla Wolf (Fig. 34G,H). A special basic song of *C. parvulus* recorded on Isla Santiago is almost identical to an atypical basic song of *Geospiza difficilis* recorded on Isla Wolf (Fig. 34O,P). Certain of the vocalizations of *C. parvulus* (Isla Santa Cruz) bear a striking resemblance (except in modal frequency) to those of *Cactospiza pallida* (islas Santa Cruz and San Cristóbal); see Fig. 33A,B; C,D; and H,I. Some of the derived songs of *C. parvulus* on coastal Isla Santa Cruz and *Certhidea olivacea* on Isla Española show close parallel construction (Fig. 33F,G). On Isla Floreana at intermediate elevations where all three species of *Camarhynchus* may co-exist, it is often difficult to distinguish between them in the field, using the character of the song (see Fig. 69) or relative differences in size and shape of their bills.

The whistle songs of all species of *Camarhynchus* are indistinguishable (Fig. 44B,C,D and Table 13), but all are notably distinguishable from the whistle songs of *Cactospiza* "tree-finches" and the "vegetarian-finch" *Platyspiza* (Fig. 44D,E,F and G). On the basis of protein electrophoresis, Yang and Patton (1981) have shown that there is a closer relationship between *Cactospiza* and *Platyspiza* than between either of them and *Camarhynchus.*

Camarhynchus pauper (Figs. 44, 47, 68, 71, 72)

Occurring only on Isla Floreana (Table 2), this medium-sized tree finch has been little studied in the field. Gifford (1919) briefly described the song as being very distinctive and readily distinguished from that of *Camarhynchus parvulus* and other finches. This impression was not fully confirmed by our field studies in 1962 (Table 9). In the transition forest of the interior of Isla Floreana (i.e. admixture of exotic sweet lime, guava and endemic species; Fig. 8), *C. pauper* was the most abundant of the three tree-finches. Some of its songs were so similar to those of *C. parvulus* (cf. Figs. 63B and 71) and *C. psittacula* (cf. Figs. 69, 71, and 73) that we routinely collected all species of *Camarhynchus* whose songs were recorded, in order to verify our field observations. Harris (1974) has provided the following helpful descriptions of *C. pauper* song: five-syllabic *tju-tju-tju-tju-tju* and also *dzi-dzi-dzi.*

In general, the notes of the derived songs of *C. parvulus* are sung somewhat faster than those of *C. pauper* (cf. Figs. 63B and 69). Timing is a less reliable feature when used to distinguish between the songs of *C. psittacula* and *C. pauper* (Fig. 69). Whereas the frequency spread of the songs of the three species is about the same, distribution of the song energy peaks is somewhat different, with progressively more energy occurring in the lower frequencies in passing from small (*parvulus*), to medium (*pauper*), to large (*psittacula*) species (see Fig. 69). Special basic songs of these same "sibling" species were often too similar to permit their use for certain field identification to species (cf. Figs. 47, 64, 71, and 73). Whistle songs were virtually indistinguishable (cf. Figs. 44B,C,D, 64, 72, and 74).

A few striking similarities in song structure were detected between *C. pauper* and *Geospiza fortis* (Isla Santiago; Fig. 34I, J) and *C. psittacula* (Isla Floreana; Fig. 69).

Camarhynchus psittacula (Figs. 44B, 47C, 69, 73)

The songs of this species, according to Lack (1945) are of two main types: one soft, rather slow disyllabic (Fig. 73, R-150/8), and a second, a rapidly repeated succession of harsh notes (Fig. 73C, B-75/2). A "churr" (Fig. 73B) and a high-pitched, rapid succession of "see" notes (Fig. 73A) are often added to the song phrase. Harris (1974) described the song of *C. psittacula* as "soft and low, sometimes a bell-like note '*turelu, turelu*' or '*tui-tui, tui-tui*' [Fig. 73C, R-438/7 and R-159/5], often followed by a high-pitched '*e-e-e-e-*' " (Fig. 73A). At James Bay, Isla Santiago, Beebe (1924) represented a song as "*chee-chee-chee-chee-chee-chee-chee,*" uttered more rapidly than the human imitation can give it. At Iguana Cove, Isla Isabela, during June, Snodgrass and

Heller (1904) described a song as *twir'-e-twee-twee-ee-ee*, which could represent subsong, to judge from its atypical character and the time of year that it was given.

On Isla Santa Cruz some derived songs of *C. psittacula* were not clearly distinguishable from those of *Geospiza fuliginosa* (Fig. 34C,D), *Camarhynchus parvulus*, and *Geospiza scandens* (Figs. 33E, 38), and *Cactospiza pallida* (cf. Figs. 73 and 77). The special basic songs of *C. psittacula* are not readily distinguishable from some songs of *C. parvulus, C. pauper*, and *Cactospiza pallida*, except that the latter species is usually somewhat lower pitched (cf. Figs. 64A, 71, 73B, and 78A). The whistle song of *psittacula* is indistinguishable from that of other members of the genus *Camarhynchus*, but readily distinguishable from *Cactospiza* (Fig. 44).

Platyspiza crassirostris (Figs. 44G, 45C, 74)

According to Rothschild and Hartert (1902), this species has a song very similar to that of the redwing blackbird (*Agelaius phoeniceus*) in California (Fig. 74), sounding like *kon-quer-ee*. It should be noted, however, that many of the songs of *Geospiza conirostris* on Isla Española also show striking convergences with those of redwings (cf. Figs. 39, 55, and 66). Snodgrass and Heller (1904) state that the song of *Platyspiza* is very different from any of the typical *Geospiza* songs (but see below), and according to Lack (1945) has the most specialized and constant song of any form, with no particular resemblance to the song of *Camarhynchus*! Nevertheless, there is a strong kinship with the songs of all other genera, including *Camarhynchus*, as shown in Figs. 85 and 89. Lack (1945) also considered the song of *Platyspiza* to be more distinctive than that of most species, with several rather musical notes run into a grinding *churr* (Fig. 74). This phrasing is remarkably constant and specific, although in quality it varies slightly, particularly the vigor of the *churr*. As in other species, a descending "hiss" (whistle song) is sometimes added to the song phrases, often ending with a disjunct loud, short whistle note of slightly lower pitch (Figs. 75, 76). On Isla Pinta the introductory notes of the basic song are of much greater amplitude and of purer tone than the following *churr*, with the latter almost inaudible except at very close range (see Figs. 45C and 74F). Gifford (1919) made a similar observation on Pinta. This variation is the only significant one detected in the island populations examined thus far. On Isla Fernandina, according to Snodgrass and Heller (1904), the song sounded like *cher-ke-ree-zee-ee-e*, beginning low and gradually coming up to a climax at the finish. Harris (1974) described the song as "distinctive," composed of several loud, "musical notes running into a harsh churring" (cf. Lack 1945).

Contrary to the opinion of Lack (1945) and Snodgrass and Heller (1904), *Platyspiza* song is not "the most specialized" or "very different from" *Geospiza* song. The five-parted basic song is probably the most generalized of geospizine song, and essentially the same in overall patterning as the five-parted songs of *Certhidea olivacea, Pinaroloxias inornata, Geospiza magnirostris, Geospiza difficilis* (Genovesa), and *Geospiza conirostris* (Española), as shown in Figs. 85 and 89.

Except as noted above, the whistle song of *Platyspiza* is also typically constructed as in species of *Geospiza, Cactospiza*, and *Pinaroloxias* (cf. Figs. 43A-G and 44E-G).

Cactospiza pallida (Figs. 44, 77, 78)

The songs of *Cactospiza pallida* have been described by Lack (1945) as follows: a rapid succession usually of seven to eight notes, often more, with either all of one type or of two (abbreviate basic and derived songs; Fig. 77). Typically loud, and usually more musical than in other species, but harsher in some individuals. Phrasing and tone extremely variable. A "churr" (special basic song) and long-drawn-out "see" (whistle song) were joined with the main song much more frequently than in other species (Fig. 78). On Isla Santiago, Snodgrass and Heller (1904) described the song phonetically as *chir-kee e-e-e-* (special basic song). Harris (1974) contributes a phonetic transcription of *C. pallida* vocalizations as *tchur-tchur-tchur e-e-e-e-* (derived or abbreviate basic plus special basic songs), remarking that one note succeeds the other with no pause between them (cf. Fig. 77). A musical variant of the typical punctuated derived song of *C. pallida* was recorded on Isla Santiago (Fig. 67A). The ending consisted of a three-noted flourish, the last note of which was a strongly accented whistle-like slur.

Our field studies do not indicate that the special basic and whistle songs in this species are more frequently associated with each other than in other species (Lack 1945), or that the apparent lack of a pause between the special basic and whistle songs is distinctive of *Cactospiza pallida* (Harris 1974). Close linkage of these two songs in *C. pallida*, as in all species of *Camarhynchus*, is greatest during the nest-building stage, when the male bird is establishing territory and interacting most vigorously with other competitive conspecific males.

The songs (i.e. special basic and derived) of *Cactospiza pallida* and *C. heliobates* are very different (Snodgrass and Heller 1904), as shown in Fig. 47A,B. These congenerics cannot be distinguished on the basis of their whistle song, which does serve, however, to separate *Cactospiza* from *Camarhynchus* (Fig. 44). There is unmistakable similarity between the derived song of *C. pallida* and the vocalizations of a variety of forest- and treetrunk-dwelling birds of North America, particularly woodpeckers, nuthatches, and jays (Fig. 41). The song units are chevron-shaped "barks," which, according to the structural-motivational rules of Morton (1977), are long-distance communication signals symbolizing "neutral or adaptively indecisive motivation" (Morton 1983).

The derived song of *Cactospiza pallida* parallels in pattern, but not in pitch, the territorial vocalizations of *Camarhynchus parvulus* and *Certhidea olivacea* in the highlands of Santa Cruz, where all three species are sympatric in the *Scalesia* forest (see Figs. 33H,I and 70). In the coastal zone of Isla Santa Cruz, the derived song is reminiscent in amplitude and quality of the derived song of *Geospiza scandens* (Fig. 34A,B) and other species of *Geospiza* and *Camarhynchus* (Figs. 46, 47). The special basic song of all species of *Camarhynchus* is very similar to that of *Cactospiza pallida*, but the latter is usually of lower pitch and greater amplitude (cf. Figs. 47, 70, 71, 73, and 78). The whistle songs of *C. pallida* and *C. heliobates* are essentially alike (cf. Figs. 78B and 79). Such likeness does not extend to the derived songs, where we find that *C. heliobates* generally has a di- or tri-syllabic song, with each syllable repeated three times over in sequence (see below).

Cactospiza heliobates (Figs. 44E, 47B, 79)

Few biologists have heard the song of this relatively rare species because it is confined to the mangrove forests of islas Isabela and Fernandina. There exist only two published reports of original observations. Snodgrass and Heller (1904) encountered singing birds at two locations. At Turtle Point, just north of Tagus Cove (Isabela), the song resembled *tur-tur, tur-tur, tur-tur,* the set of two syllables being generally repeated three times in succession, although sometimes more and sometimes only twice. The sound was somewhat varied and often resembled *twer-twer, twer-twer*. The notes are uttered rather loudly and have a striking effect when heard issuing from the depths of a dense and apparently otherwise uninhabited mangrove forest. West of Elizabeth Bay (Isabela), they report, the song was repeated two or three times just as with the others. Hence, the song resembled *tur-tur-tur, tur-tur-tur, tur-tur-tur*. Only infrequently were bisyllabic sets heard. A common note very characteristic of the species is a rather harsh prolonged sound, declining toward the end. Presumably, these authors were describing the whistle song (Fig. 79).

More recently, Curio and Kramer (1964) visited the same regions and described the vocalizations of *C. heliobates* (using German language phonetic symbols). The two-syllable *dschedde* (preumably the equivalent of "tur-tur" of Snodgrass and Heller 1904), was given one to three times (but mostly three). The sound was fuller and slower than the sequence of monosyllabic notes characteristic of the territorial song of *C. pallida* (Fig. 77). Curio and Kramer (1964) did not hear *C. heliobates* give a special basic song (see Fig. 47), nor did any of the earlier explorers report it. Presumably, then, it does not occur in this species. But should this turn out to be a sampling error, I predict that it would resemble the special basic song of *C. pallida* (Fig. 47).

Snodgrass and Heller (1904) confused the song of *Geospiza fuliginosa* with that of *Cactospiza heliobates*, as did this writer, where the two species come together at the edge of the mangrove forests. They described the confusing song of *G. fuliginosa* as *t'wer-t'wer-t'wer-t'wer*, each note having a double sound. The same authors report that certain songs of *Geospiza fortis* at Tagus Cove (Isabela) resembled those of *C. heliobates.*

Certhidea olivacea (Figs. 44A, 45B, 70A, 80-82, 96-100, 109-115, 155-160)

Upon first hearing the derived song of *Certhidea olivacea* on Isla Genovesa (Fig. 82A), Beebe (1924) was prompted to describe it as "a sweet, simple warble, eight notes run and jumbled together, no one distinct, and impossible to transcribe. Rarely a variation was given—a long-drawn-out wheezy note, followed by the usual vocal tangled knot" (basic song; Fig. 80D). Lack (1945) had the following impressions of the derived song of *Certhidea*: a rapid succession of notes thinner than any other geospizine song except *Geospiza d. difficilis* from Isla Genovesa (cf. Figs. 85C,E). In *C. o. luteola* of Isla San Cristóbal the song was reminiscent of the European wren, *Troglodytes troglodytes* (Fig. 81C). In *C. o. olivacea* on Isla Santa Cruz there were typically fewer notes in the phrase (Fig. 81A), with greater loudness and harshness than in the San Cristóbal birds, being not unlike the song of *Camarhynchus parvulus* (Fig. 70A). Without specifying any island source, Harris (1974) describes *Certhidea olivacea* as having a "melodious song, often ending in a high-pitched buzz" (presumably, the latter in reference to the basic song). On Isla Osborn (near Isla Española) Beebe (1926) described *Certhidea* derived song as "of the simplest, a sibilant *Sip-sip-sip-sip-chew-chew-chew*" (Figs. 33G, 81B).

It is clear from the descriptions given above that most authors have been more or less aware of the fact that at least two elaborate songs are sung by *Certhidea*: basic and derived. However, none seems to have commented upon the sometimes very elaborate whistle song that always precedes the basic song and is invariably united with it (see Fig. 80).

The marked vocal dialects of *Certhidea olivacea* affect not just derived song but also whistle and basic songs (cf. Figs. 80-82). Within the framework of insular dialects there is notable intrapopulational variation in all three song forms (cf. Figs. 99-100, 109-115, and 155-160).

Lack (1945) mentioned the resemblance of the derived song of *Certhidea olivacea* to that of *Camarhynchus parvulus* on Isla Santa Cruz (Fig. 33K,L), but the parallel extends to other island populations as well (Figs. 33F,G; 35H,I), and should also include *Cactospiza pallida* (Fig. 70A). The five-parted pattern of *Certhidea* basic song reappears in remarkably similar form in *Pinaroloxias inornata, Geospiza conirostris,* and *G. difficilis*, and *Platyspiza crassirostris* (cf. Figs. 84-86).

Pinaroloxias inornata (Figs. 83-86)

The songs of this most peripheral member of the Darwin's finch assemblage have never been described in the literature. Gifford (1919) heard only a "sort of chip, in spite of the fact the nuptial season was on, as attested by the testes of the adult males skinned." Beebe (1926), Slud (1967), and Smith and Sweatman (1976) did not hear the species in song during their respective visits. Two brief stopovers by the writer during the breeding season (Table 8) made it possible to record the songs of *Pinaroloxias* for the first time. Our field recordings of the birds were unsatisfactory because of the extreme height of the rainforest canopy in which the species spends much of its time foraging (Fig. 17A), and where, in my early March visit, the calls of the nesting fairy terns and roosting brown boobies masked the "thin" basic songs of *Pinaroloxias*. However, a number of adults and immatures were mist-netted in the dense edge shrubbery (Fig. 17B) and brought to our San Francisco State University aviaries, where they sang liberally and were successfully tape-recorded (Fig. 83).

The whistle and basic songs of the Cocos honeycreeper-finch are typically geospizine in character (Fig. 83) and closely resemble the songs of *Geospiza conirostris* (Española), and the basic song of *Certhidea olivacea, Geospiza difficilis* (Genovesa), and *Platyspiza crassirostris* (see Figs. 84-86). *Pinaroloxias* was never heard to sing derived song; in this respect it resembles *Platyspiza* (Table 10). In the general form of the whistle song *Pinaroloxias* resembles *Platyspiza, Cactospiza,* and *Geospiza*, in which there is no obligate connection to the basic song, as there is in *Certhidea.*

Generic Distinctiveness of Geospizine Song

"If song could be more objectively recorded, it might be a valuable guide to classification." This prophetic statement about the vocalizations of Darwin's finches was written by Lack (1945) shortly after his return from the Galapagos in 1939. It is now clear that on the basis of songs, it is possible to distinguish between the six genera of Geospizini (see Table 10 and Figs. 43 and 47) and to link them morphologically, via *Certhidea*, with *Melanospiza richardsoni* of St. Lucia, West Indies, as follows.

1. *Certhidea.* The only genus in which the whistle song is always linked to the basic song proper.

[*Melanospiza.* One of the few, if not the only known closely related genus outside the Galapagos-Cocos area that has a single-note whistle song confluent with the basic song proper, as in *Certhidea* (Fig. 104).]

2. *Pinaroloxias.* The only genus (except for *Platyspiza*) having a single-note whistle song and a basic song proper, occurring outside the Galapagos, only on Cocos Island, Costa Rica.

3. *Platyspiza.* The only genus (except for *Pinaroloxias*) having a single-note whistle song and a basic song proper, and occurring only in the Galapagos.

4. *Geospiza.* The only genus in which there is a single-note whistle song, a basic song proper, and a derived song. (True whistle song is absent from some populations of *G. difficilis*, but these have also a special basic song that may, in part, be functionally equivalent to it. See Table 10).

5. *Camarhynchus.* The only genus with a multi-note whistle song, showing no obligate linkage to the basic song.

6. *Cactospiza.* The only genus with a single-note whistle song and a special basic song (the latter possibly absent in *C. heliobates*).

These vocal distinctions, when evaluated along with features of plumage and bill, suggest the correctness of the six generic groupings championed by Ridgway (1896), Swarth (1931), and Bowman (1961), and originally adopted by Lack (1945), because they delineate major ecological divergences within the tribe Geospizini (cf. Lack 1947, 1968; Paynter and Storer 1970). Recent studies on the anatomy of the cerebellum (St. Jules 1977) and on allozymes (Yang and Patton 1981; Polans, this volume) also give support to these generic groupings. According to Yang and Patton (1981), genic similarity indices indicate a closer relationship between *Cactospiza* and *Platyspiza* as opposed to *Camarhynchus* (cf. Lack 1947).

Except for Güttinger (1970), who studied the phylogeny and systematic position of four genera of estrildid finches using song and other behavioral features, ornithologists have had only limited success in delineating taxonomic relationships by means of vocalizations (Marler 1957; Stein 1958, 1963; Thorpe and Lade 1961; Selander and Giller 1961; Traylor 1967; Lanyon 1969; Thielcke 1969a,b; Payne 1973). Hope (1980) has suggested that perhaps this may be due to the use of too gross a perspective or the wrong kind of characters. She has pointed to the possibility that subcomponents of design should be carefully examined (see below).

SONG PATTERNS IN DARWIN'S FINCHES

Song Homology

Despite the seemingly endless diversity of song structure in Darwin's finches, it is possible to identify an underlying pattern of uniformity, a condition which derives from the fact that the birds are, in all probability, of monophyletic origin: the basic song behavior of their common ancestor was inherited by the descendant forms. Evidence that the 14 species of finches are closely related comes from studies on the anatomy, behavior, and genetics of the group (Table 1). In all studies of kinship, "A cautious man should above all be on his guard against resemblances; they are a very slippery sort of thing" (Plato, *fide* Cornford 1973).

In this study of song homology in Darwin's finches, three main criteria have been used extensively: position, special quality of the structure, and interconnections by intermediate forms, i.e. continuity (Atz 1970; Remane 1961; Tembrock 1963; Tinbergen 1962; Wickler 1961).

Recognition of Song Patterns

The results of a detailed examination of thousand of audiospectrograms of geospizine songs suggest that the ancestral song pattern was probably composed of five temporal regions (see examples of the "basic scheme" in Figs. 84 to 86). This five-parted pattern makes its appearance not only in the songs of all 14 species of Darwin's finches, but also in a presumed close relative of the group living outside the Galapagos-Cocos area, *Melanospiza richardsoni*, the Black Finch of St. Lucia, West Indies (Fig. 104). Song regions are the result of (a) real temporal separations due to a discontinuous signal, (b) changes in frequency or frequency modulation in one or both signals emanating from the syrinx, i.e. one from each internal tympaniform membrane, and (c) asynchrony in onset and termination of the two signals (see Figs. 87 and 88), possibly attributable to asymmetries in certain ventral syringeal muscles or membranes or both (see Cutler 1971).

Variations in Pattern

Differences in song patterns between individuals, populations, and species are due to one or more of the following alterations in the basic five-parted signal (see Figs. 89-103): (1) Repetition of structural units of region 4 (e.g. patterns B, E; Figs. 90, 93, respectively). (2) Abbreviation of region 4 (e.g. patterns C, E in part, and J; Figs. 91, 93, 103, respectively). (3) Splitting apart of basic song to form two distinct songs (e.g. patterns D, E, F, H, I, J; Figs. 92, 93, 101, 102, 103, respectively). (4) Loss of a region (e.g. patterns G, H; Figs. 95, 100, respectively).

Eleven song patterns (viz. A through J) have thus far been identified, and the number may be expected to increase as populations become better known.

The distribution of song patterns among the species of Darwin's finches is summarized in Table 11. Collectively, the six species of *Geospiza* have the greatest diversity (eight patterns); the six species of *Camarhynchus, Cactospiza,* and *Certhidea* show a modest diversity (six patterns); and the two species of *Platyspiza* and *Pinaroloxias* have essentially no pattern diversity (only one pattern is present). In the last group can be included the St. Lucia Black Finch, *Melanospiza richardsoni.*

Description of Song Patterns

Pattern A (Fig. 89). This probably represents the ancestral song pattern of the Darwin's finch group (subfamily Geospizinae of Lack 1945; tribe Geospizini of Grzimek 1973). The five regions are generally very distinct, with region 4 (i.e. the frequency-modulated "buzz") forming over 50% of the total song duration. It is the most widely distributed pattern, occurring in all genera except *Cactospiza* and *Camarhynchus* (cf. Figs. 85-86). *Melanospiza* shows a basic pattern directly comparable to the "basic" pattern A of *Certhidea* (Fig. 104).

Pattern B (Fig. 90). This "basic" pattern differs from pattern A essentially in having region 4 dissected into a number of similar repeated units (syllables). Region 4 constitutes at least 50% of the total song duration.

Pattern C (Fig. 91). Described as an "abbreviate basic" song, this pattern includes all five regions, with region 4 constituting less than 50% of the entire song duration. Thus, pattern C is essentially the same as pattern A, except for a much shortened region 4, which makes for a shorter overall song length. As shown in Fig. 91, some birds, such as *Geospiza conirostris* (Isla Española), may sing both patterns A and C.

Pattern D (Fig. 92). This pattern includes two song types, the "derived" song, consisting of the detached first two regions of the abbreviate basic song (pattern C), and the "abbreviate basic" song itself. Individuals of *Geospiza conirostris* (Isla Española) are known to sing both types of song, delivering the abbreviate basic at times of most intense territorial defense–in pursuing an intruder from its territory–and the derived song during the hotter times of the day or whenever the amplitude of maintenance activities was much reduced (see p. 276). In a nonhomologous way, *Certhidea* (Isla Genovesa) may, under differing motivational states, delete the second half of the advertising song (see Fig. 99A,B, derived song type 2). Similar kinds of variation in song length have been reported in individual singing birds of *Passerina cyanea* in Michigan (Thompson 1972, Fig. 1), and in infinite variety in the house finch (*Carpodacus mexicanus*), *fide* S. Hope.

Pattern E (Fig. 93). Essentially the same as pattern D, this pattern differs from it in having region 4 of the abbreviate basic song dissected into two more or less identical units (syllables). Derived and abbreviate basic songs are combined in a manner that is species-distinctive. For example (see Fig. 93), one form of the song of *Cactospiza pallida* groups the abbreviate basic (AB) and derived (D) songs into couplets, i.e. D-AB, D-AB, D-AB, etc., whereas in *Camarhynchus parvulus*, one form of singing consists of a trill-like succession of derived songs (regions 1 and 2), followed by a succession of five-parted abbreviate basic songs, yielding a song format such as D-D-D-D-D, AB-AB-AB-AB-AB (Fig. 93). "Bilingual" birds (i.e. those with two song themes) singing pattern E are typically tree-finches of the genera *Cactospiza* and *Camarhynchus*. (Bilingual birds of the genus *Geospiza* typically sing pattern F songs, Fig. 94; see below.) On the basis of observations on captive *C. parvulus*, it is known that bilingual singing continues minimally through age five years; during this period, black head plumage, considered typical of full adult condition in this species (Bowman 1961), may not yet have been acquired. The ecological and behavioral significance of bilingual singing is discussed on pp. 274-275.

Pattern F (Fig. 94). Pattern F consists of two songs, a "derived" and a "basic," but differs from patterns D and E in having a full basic song (pattern A or B) rather than an "abbreviate basic" song (pattern C). "Bilingual" birds singing pattern F are typically "ground-finches" or "cactus-finches" of the genus *Geospiza*. A more or less typical bilingual cycle of singing in *Geospiza magnirostris* or *G. conirostris* (Fig. 94), and also occurring in *G. difficilis*, Isla Genovesa, combines the derived (D) and basic (B) songs in the following scheme: D-D-D, B. In Genovesa *G. conirostris*, adult males generally sing only the full basic song (pattern B) or the three-parted derived song, but occasionally subadults entering their first breeding season, and probably full adult birds as well (only very occasionally) may be bilingual singers, alternating basic and derived songs (Fig. 94). The significance of this behavior as it relates to mate selection and alleged sympatric speciation (cf. Grant and Grant 1979) is discussed below (p. 277).

Pattern G (Figs. 95-100). This song pattern is peculiar to some populations of *Certhidea olivacea* (typically those of islas Santa Cruz and Santiago) and consists of two songs, the full basic (pattern A) and a derived song (pattern G). The derived song (Figs. 95, 96) is composed of regions 1, 2, 3, and 5, with a tendency for these regions to cluster into a series of similarly structured syllables, each of which, in turn, may further divide into like syllables to form a staccato-like trill (see morphological sequence A-D-E in Fig. 97). The presumed loss of region 4 of the basic song is suggested by a morphological series illustrated in Fig. 98. For example, subsongs B, C, and D, sung by a subadult at Academy Bay, Isla Santa Cruz, when positioned between adult basic (A) and derived (E) songs recorded in the same locality, form a morphological series which we may interpret as an ontogenetic transformation. Essentially, this involves the shortening of song region 4 (Fig. 98B), the ultimate deletion of the region (Fig. 95C), and the closing of the gap (Fig. 98D), thereby bringing song regions 3 and 5 closer together. Refinement of details of song regions 1, 2, 3, and 5 leads to the definitive derived song of *Certhidea olivacea* (Fig. 97E).

To conclude that all island populations of *C. olivacea* develop their derived songs in this way would be erroneous. They probably do not. An example of a different developmental transformation may be seen in some individuals of the Genovesa population in which we find extraordinary variability in basic and derived songs (Fig. 99). A possible developmental series based entirely on adult morphological series is presented in Fig. 100. Here the starting point in the transmutational process includes two basic songs, both of pattern A type (Fig. 110A,B), followed by an atypical basic song type, pattern B, and this by a derived song type of more or less typical form (Fig. 100C,D). In song region 4, we may trace the transformation of a pure-frequencied signal into a frequency-modulated signal with rapid sweep-rate (Figs. 100A,B), and this in turn into a repetitive sequence of notes and complex syllables (Fig. 100C). In the absence of a true ontogenetic sequence, it is impossible to trace the syllable homologies between basic song (pattern B, Fig. 100C) and derived song (Fig. 100D). Nevertheless, there is a clear structural similarity in syllables between song regions 4 and 5 in the two songs, and a less clear relationship between other regions. In other words, region 4 of the basic song appears to have been retained, at least in part, during its transformation into the derived song of *Certhidea* on Isla Genovesa, unlike the condition on Isla Santa Cruz in which region 4 of the basic song seems to have been deleted from the derived song.

Pattern H (Figs. 86A-D, 101). This pattern is most frequently found in the songs of *Camarhynchus* and *Cactospiza* and rarely in *Geospiza fortis*. It consists of two songs, both resulting, presumably, from a fragmentation of the ancestral five-parted "basic" (pattern A) into the "derived" (composed of regions 1 and 2) and a so-called "special basic H" song (composed of a short region 3 and an extended monotonic "buzzy" region 4). Region 5 has been lost.

Pattern I (Figs. 62A-C, 102). Peculiar to *Geospiza difficilis* (islas Santiago, Pinta, and Wolf), this pattern is almost the same as pattern H, except for the addition of region 5 to the "special basic I" song. Region 5 is most unusual in that it may be of short duration (Isla Pinta) or of extended duration (islas Santiago and Wolf), and in the Isla Wolf population it is very high-pitched (circa 13 kHz), and almost inaudible to the human ear. Functionally, the "special basic I" song of Santiago and Wolf populations appears to be similar to the combined whistle and basic songs of *Certhidea olivacea* (as in the Isla Santa Cruz population). See page 272.

Pattern J (Fig. 103). Only one example of this song pattern has been discovered, in the Isla Santiago *Geospiza fuliginosa*. It consists of an abbreviate basic song (regions 1-5), followed by a two-syllabled derived song, uniquely formulated from regions 3, 4, and 5.

Uses of Song Homology Studies

Given the feasibility of relating most songs of Darwin's finches to an "idealized" basic signal pattern, it then becomes possible to trace evolutionary pathways not only between but also within species (Fig. 104B).

Interisland Population Differences

One of the more noteworthy characteristics of Galapagos finches is their tendency to show marked inter- and even intra-island dialects. The extent to which dialects are expressed appears to be most clearly related to inter- and intra-island differences in vegetation and their effect on sound transmission (see below). Homology studies allow us to identify regions of song that have undergone structural alterations of such magnitude that they seem to belie their true affinities, as illustrated by the following examples.

Geospiza magnirostris (Fig. 53). The five regions of the basic song of the species have undergone moderate changes in duration, modal frequency, and frequency modulation of the two syringeal oscillators, resulting in such extreme song dialects as occur on islas Santa Cruz, Genovesa, and Wolf.

Geospiza difficilis (Figs. 61, 62). This species is one of the most "ground bound" of Darwin's finches and displays some striking interisland dialects. All populations so far studied sing a five-parted basic song (Fig. 61), and the populations on islas Wolf, Santiago, and Pinta also sing a second kind of song (Fig. 62A,B and C, respectively) designated "special basic I" (Fig. 102). The latter consists of song regions 3, 4, and 5, with regions 1 and 2 deleted (Santiago and Pinta populations), or retained as a derived song (Wolf population).

The true whistle song of *Geospiza difficilis* is presently known only in Darwin and Genovesa populations, and is typically *Geospiza*-like (cf. Figs. 43 and 62). What at first appears to be a whistle song (but not serially homologous with that of other *Geospiza* populations), occurs as a specialized region 5 of the "special basic I" song on islas Wolf and Santiago.

Parallel Song Development in Closely Related Genera

The five-parted basic song in species of *Camarhynchus* and *Cactospiza* has been disarticulated between regions 2 and 3 (Fig. 86), resulting in song patterns E (Fig. 93) and H (Fig. 101), each with a derived song composed of regions 1 and 2. In the case of pattern E the abbreviate basic song is retained; in the case of pattern H, the five-parted basic song is abandoned and a "basic H" song substituted. The latter is formulated from song regions 3 and 4, with region 5 being dropped. Since derived and special basic songs are rather different in their structure, one might suspect that they serve different functions, as in fact they appear to do (see page 275 and Fig. 70).

Phylogenetic Affinities of Geospizine Song Patterns

Recent studies by Yang and Patton (1981; see also Polans, this volume) on genic variability and differentiation in Darwin's finches indicate that *Certhidea olivacea* was the earliest species among those examined to diverge from the ancestral stock, and this occurred about 570,000 years before the present, in contrast to 62,500 years ago for species of *Cactospiza* and *Platyspiza*.

There are acknowledged difficulties associated with the assumptions used in these calculations (based on the method of Nei 1975). Nevertheless, these divergences fall well within the dates established by Cox (this volume) for the emergence of the oldest islands, namely 3 to 5 million years ago.

Having identified *Certhidea olivacea* as the species with one of the oldest lineages relative to other species of Galapagos finches (Patton, pers. comm.; Yang and Patton 1981; Polans, this volume), it has been assumed that the vocalizations of this species embody most, if not all, of the essential features of the "idealized" (primitive?) geospizine song. Indeed, evidence presented in this report does support this notion.

The presence of (1) a whistle song invariably linked with (2) a five-parted basic song, (3) a derived song probably resulting from a transformation of the basic song, and (4) strongly differentiated insular dialects in all three song types is befitting a species that is the longest established, the most widely distributed, and possibly one of the most sedentary of all Galapagos finches, to judge from known reports of interisland wanderings (see Gifford 1919). These considerations make *Certhidea olivacea* pivotal to our formulation of a phylogenetic "search image" for mainland relatives.

One American species of songbird, the St. Lucia Black Finch (*Melanospiza richardsoni*) is known to share a number of important features with geospizine finches (see Table 12), to which we may now add advertising song (Fig. 104A). So remarkably similar is the song of *Melanospiza* to the combined whistle and basic songs of *Certhidea* of Isla Santa Cruz that on the basis of this feature alone it would not be unreasonable to classify the St. Lucia Black Finch as a species of Geospizini, as did Cory (1892), who described it as "*Geospiza richardsonii*." So far as is known, *Melanospiza* does not have a "derived" song, and in this respect it resembles *Pinaroloxias* (Isla Cocos) and *Platyspiza* (Fig. 85).

The basic (or abbreviate basic) song pattern makes its appearance in all species of Darwin's finches (Fig. 104B and Table 10), as well as in the black finch of St. Lucia Island in the Caribbean. There are probably numerous other passerine species also distributed in "peripheral" areas such as the volcanic highlands of Central and South America (e.g. slaty finch, *Spodiornis rustica*) whose songs, once known, may show a similar five-parted pattern. Such resemblances in vocal behavior, when paralleled by structural similarities in the syrinx, among other things (Table 12), point strongly in the direction of a genetic component involved in regulating the appearance of temporal division of song, i.e. regions 1 through 5.

Limited experiments with song development (p. 307 ff) suggest that details of both basic and derived songs are learned. This situation in Darwin's finches, wherein genetic control of vocalization is lessened and cultural control increased, has permitted extraordinary diversification of song within the five-parted temporal framework. These song patterns beautifully illustrate the biological principle of diversity amidst uniformity.

Song divergence has involved mainly the evolution of "derived" patterns (Figs. 2, 40, 41), many of which show convergences in structure with songs of ecologically equivalent species on mainlands. The magnitude of the divergence of song in Darwin's finches is probably regulated by the diversity of sound transmission environments in the Galapagos.

The pervasiveness of the basic song pattern throughout the geospizine tribe would seem to be a reflection of the pervasiveness of similar acoustical transmission environments to which the basic song is adapted (see p. 297 ff). Although the mainland and the Galapagos/Cocos islands are significantly different floristically and vegetatively (Fosberg and Klawe 1966; Fournier 1966; Wiggins 1966; Wiggins and Porter 1971), convergent and divergent patterns of sound transmission between insular vegetations and, presumably, between insular and mainland vegetations, are thought to be of paramount importance in explaining the divergent and convergent/parallel patterns, respectively, of song evolution in Darwin's finches.

FUNCTION AND ADAPTIVE MORPHOLOGY OF SONGS OF DARWIN'S FINCHES

Communication Defined

Biological communication, according to Wilson (1975), is the action on the part of one organism that alters the probability pattern of behavior in another organism in a fashion adaptive to either one or both of the participants. It is neither the signal by itself nor the response; it is instead the relation between the two. Dawkins and Krebs (1978) have characterized signaling (used synonymously for communication) as a means by which one animal makes use of another animal's muscle power. They reason that there is no need to think of signals as "meaning" anything at all, but rather as a device to manipulate successfully the behavior of other individuals (cf. Krebs and Kroodsma 1980). Like Wilson, Dawkins and Krebs are concerned with "average statistical benefits." Signaling is but one attribute of an animal, and it is not perfect in every situation. In fact, a particular action, e.g. vocalization, may turn out to be a mistake in a particular situation, but on the average, a signal will persist if it serves to propagate the signaler's genes, even though some individuals may fail as a direct result of the behavior (Dawkins and Krebs 1978).

Ecology of Song

The effectiveness of sound as a means of communication depends in part on the distance over which vocalizations can be heard. The broadcast range of the sound depends not only on the sensitivity of the ear, but also on the nature of the animal's environment (Suthers 1978) and source amplitude. The ability to localize a sound source in the environment plays a vital role in the lives of song birds and underlies many of their activities, including the attraction of a mate, the maintenance of territory, and the avoidance of predators (but see Morton 1983). It generally has been assumed that this ability depends on binaural cues, including interaural time and intensity differences (Marler 1955, 1961; Wilkenson and Howse 1975).

In the evolution of vocal communication in Darwin's finches, I hypothesize that selection has shaped the signal structure so as to minimize transmission loss of acoustical energy and thereby maximize the energetic response of the intended participant.

I. Whistle Songs

Characteristics

During the breeding season the males of all species of Darwin's finches sing a definitive "whistle" song consisting of a more or less pure (i.e. non-frequency-modulated) high-pitched tone, which, in quality, is somewhat reminiscent of the "lisping" note of the Cedar Waxwing, *Bombycilla cedrorum* (Fig. 105), and the whistle note in one of the songs of the cowbird, *Molothrus ater* (see King et al. 1981, Fig. 1). In species of *Geospiza, Cactospiza, Platyspiza,* and *Pinaroloxias* the song is a single continuous whistle, gradually descending in pitch (Figs. 43, 44), whereas in species of *Camarhynchus* and in most populations of *Certhidea olivacea*, the song consists of a variable number of discrete whistle notes (as many as 20 in *Camarhynchus parvulus* and 6 in *Certhidea olivacea*), of slightly differing duration, strung together as in a musical scale of rising and/or falling pitch (Table 13; Figs. 64, 72, 80). In some populations of *Geospiza difficilis* (notably on islas Santiago and Pinta, and possibly others), the whistle song has not yet been reported, although it is present in typical *Geospiza*-like form in populations on islas Darwin and Genovesa (Fig. 62). The Isla Wolf population of *G. difficilis* has evolved a high-pitched whistle-like note that is not strictly homologous with the true whistle song of its conspecifics on other islands, but rather appears to be a highly modified song region 5 of the "special basic" song, distinctive of this species population. Geographic variation in whistle songs is known only in *Certhidea olivacea*, producing distinctive dialects on some islands (cf. Figs. 109-115 and below).

Because of the high-frequency sound characteristic of the whistle song (mean high frequency 14 kHz; range 11.6 - 15.9 kHz; see Table 13), parts of it are barely audible to humans. In fact, the initiation of the whistle song can often only be inferred, in the absence of human auditory sensitivity to the frequencies involved, from the assumption of a singing posture (out-stretched neck with bill agape). Even the lowest frequencies of the whistle song may be difficult to hear (mean low frequency 10 kHz; range 6.9 - 14.1 kHz; see Table 13). However, even when the whistle song is audible and the bird is not visible, spatial localization of the sound source by (human) ears alone is in most cases difficult, if not impossible, to achieve.

All species confine their whistle songs, on the average, to between 14 and 10 kHz, despite marked differences in body weight. For example, the heaviest species (*Geospiza magnirostris*) has an average body weight of 38.3 g and a mean high frequency of its whistle song of 13.7 kHz (maximum range 15.4 kHz). The smallest species (*Certhidea olivacea*, on Isla Genovesa) has an average body weight of 8.0 g and a mean high frequency of its whistle song of 13.9 kHz (maximum range 15.3 kHz). See Table 13. The mean width of the internal tympaniform membrane is approximately 1.8 and 1.3 mm in *G. magnirostris* and *Certhidea*, respectively (Fig. 129). The whistle song has a mean duration of about two seconds (1891 msec.), with some individuals singing as briefly as 487 msec. or as long as 6190 msec. The whistle songs of larger-bodied species are generally of greater duration than those of smaller-bodied species (Fig. 106), certain populations of *Certhidea olivacea* excepted (see Table 13). This relationship is probably a simple functional consequence of a larger air sac system in the larger species, whose greater capacity permits a longer sustained air flow through the syrinx. The Genovesa *Certhidea* (wt. 8 g) has a whistle song eight times as long as that of the Santa Cruz *Certhidea* (wt. 9.5 g) and similar in mean song duration to *Geospiza conirostris,* a species that is over three times its body weight (Table 13). This disparity can probably best be explained by noting that the whistle song of Genovesa *Certhidea* is not a single continuous whistle, as in *G. conirostris* and Santa Cruz *Certhidea*, but rather consists of a series of discontinuous whistle notes (range 2 - 8 kHz, Fig. 115) with note intervals accounting for as much as 31% of the total song length. It is possible that the multi-note whistle song of certain small-bodied *Certhidea* (e.g. Genovesa bird, Fig. 115J) is not the result of a single evacuation of the air sac system, but due to a train of rapid inspirations (note intervals) and expirations (notes), i.e. mini-inhalations following each sound pulse (cf. Calder 1970). In species of *Camarhynchus*, however, the numerous short whistle notes comprising the song are, apparently, "beats" resulting from the rhythmical interaction of a frequency-modulated wave with an essentially non-frequency-modulated carrier wave, as the former periodically approaches the frequency of the latter (see Fig. 107).

Behavioral Context

The whistle song is most intimately associated with a state of high sexual motivation, and probably functions in pair-bond formation, nest-entry invitation, and breeding synchrony (Lehrman and Friedman 1969). See Table 17. In Darwin's finches, mated and unmated males on territory may deliver one or more whistle songs between bouts of territorial singing (using basic, special basic, and derived songs). As a nest-invitation signal, the whistle song may be uttered by the male within or atop the net, or while perched immediately adjacent to it. Never have I heard a finch sing "territorial" song inside the nest, only whistle song. Singing in or near the nest is known in other songbirds in which, unlike the geospizines, there is marked concealing coloration in male plumage, e.g. *Vireo gilvis* (Robbins et al. 1966) and *Pheucticus melanocephalus* (Weston 1947). During the drooped wing display, copulation, posturing with nesting material in the bill, and immediately after courtship feeding, geospizines may give whistle song. Under both captive conditions and in the wild, when the female is incubating, males may sing whistle song interspersed with territorial song, the latter generally precipitated when an alien male intrudes on his ground territory or flies over his aerial space. In general, the frequency of singing whistle song declines steadily as the nesting season progresses.

According to the "motivational-structural rules" described by Morton (1977), high-frequency pure-tone sounds are associated with friendly and appeasive (submissive) motivation at close range (cf. flute-like "quiet songs" of the New Zealand saddleback; Jenkins 1977). Accordingly, whistle songs indicate a nonaggressive state, a condition confirmed by field studies.

Lengthy and almost continuous field recording of singing birds, when analyzed according to the relative abundance of the various song types in the repertoire, reveals that the frequency of singing whistle, basic/special basic, and derived songs changes during vocal ontogeny (Table 14). During vocal maturation in first-year birds, the whistle song is sung with ever-decreasing relative frequency, while the basic/special basic and derived songs are sung with ever-increasing relative frequency. This shift in emphasis, noted in all species, reflects a gradual change from random vocalization to nonrandom and orderly focusing of whistle song on pair-bonding, with basic/special basic and derived songs focused on territorial proclamations, among other things.

Adaptive Significance of Whistle Song

To broadcast a pair-bonding and nest-invitation signal beyond those individuals of immediate concern (i.e. the mate) is to provide an unnecessary and dangerous homing beacon for predators (Wilson 1975). Those features of sound that make spatial localization difficult to achieve for humans, and presumably also for Darwin's finches, have been described by Marler (1955, 1961), and are as follows: (1) Tonal purity combined with imperceptible fade-in and fade-out of a sustained stable frequency sound, thereby providing no abrupt discontinuities in the signal that would allow the differences in the time of arrival of the sound at the near and far ear to be compared. (Green [1976] is of the opinion that timing information is not present in vertebrate nervous systems at very high frequencies; cf. Busnel 1963). (2) High frequencies whose wavelengths are somewhat larger than the width of the head or the intertympanic membrane distance, thus making the signal somewhat too low-pitched for ideal detection of intensity differences, the latter best discerned when frequencies are smaller than the diameter of the head that serves to absorb or block the sound on its course to the far ear. The use of moderately high frequencies also makes ineffective the detection of phase differences between near and far ears—a process otherwise operatively only at low frequencies. However, Knudsen (1980) claims that there are no behavioral data suggesting that birds do, in fact, exploit interaural phase differences for sound localization, which is most effective at low frequencies, according to Marler (1955, 1961). The use of high frequencies also promotes reflections from vegetation, resulting in a somewhat disorganized signal with high loss of sound pressure during transmission.

Based on these criteria, whistle songs of Darwin's finches appear to be ideally structured to hinder their auditory localization not only by the finches themselves, but also by sympatric passerine species, notably the mockingbirds. Whistles are largely sustained pure tones that have subtle intensity-graded beginnings and endings. They are high-frequencied and therefore with wavelengths that are not only small but also about 2 to 5 times greater than the interaural distances (Cocos finch excepted), which, presumably, makes them too high-pitched (i.e. wave-length too short) for effective detection of phase difference, yet too low-pitched (i.e. wavelengths too long) for effective detection of intensity difference (see Table 15). High frequencies, characteristic of the whistle songs, probably also promote rapid environmental attenuation of their small wavelengths with increasing distance from the sound source (see cumulative dB-loss isopleths in Fig. 29; cf. King et al. 1981). Even the *Asio* owl and the *Buteo* hawk possess interaural dimensions that probably forestall use of intensity differences at the two eardrums for signal localization. Skull diameter percentages (Table 15, Fig. 108) for these raptores do not substantiate this conclusion, but this parameter is probably not a true measure of the effective "frequency blocking" distance between left and right tympani.

In the light of recent neurophysiological studies on hearing and vocalizations in songbirds (e.g. Dooling 1980; Dooling, Mulligan, and Miller 1971; Konishi 1970a), one might have cause to wonder if the finches are capable of hearing the high frequencies of their whistle songs. Konishi (1970b) asserts that it is not at all necessary to assume that birds should be able to hear the entire range of frequencies in their vocalizations. He also points out that in those species studied so far, the dominant vocal frequencies do not seem to coincide with the most sensitive range of hearing, but are located above that range. Hearing thresholds are frequency-dependent, with higher (as well as lower) frequencies having dramatically higher thresholds than mid-frequencies, i.e. 2-4 kHz.

To judge from the single unit threshold plots of Konishi (1970a, Fig. 4), which generally match auditory threshold curves (Manley 1971), the effective upper limit of hearing and vocalization in songbirds generally is somewhat under 9 kHz, and Pumphrey (1961) and Dooling (1980) doubt that there is little useful sensitivity above 10 kHz in birds other than owls, parrots, and possibly a few finches. In a summary of high-frequency "cut-off" (i.e. highest frequency that a bird can hear at a sound pressure level of 60 dB), Dooling (1980) has shown that for fringillids as a group the range extends from as high as 12 kHz for the bullfinch (Schwartzkopff 1949) to as low as 7.2 kHz for the house finch (Dooling, Zoloth, and Baylis 1978), with the field sparrow at 11.0 kHz (Dooling, Peters, and Searcy 1979), the cowbird at 9.7 kHz (Hienz, Sinnot, and Sachs 1977), and the canary at 9.6 kHz (Dooling, Mulligan, and Miller 1971).

Absolute dB levels of the whistle song are known only for a single recording of *Certhidea olivacea*, Isla Genovesa (Figs. 121, 122), and when compared with absolute levels of the basic and derived songs (Figs. 122, 123), prove to be higher by 4 and 6 dB, respectively, at their maximum values, possibly due to the very narrowly beamed nature of the whistle song.

If the assumption is correct that bird songs are designed to function at distances appropriate for the territory size of the species (cf. contrasting views of Wiley and Richards 1978 and Morton 1983), then the amplitude of whistle songs of Darwin's finches—to judge solely on data for

Certhidea olivacea (Isla Genovesa)–would seem to be of sufficient magnitude for the most intimate situations of their use, even when allowances are made for massive energy losses due to attenuations from high hearing thresholds and environmental transmission, generally associated with such high frequencies (see Tables 19 and 22). For example, if we assume that the high-frequency cut-off of 60 dB is around 10-14 kHz in *Certhidea olivacea* (Schwartzkopff [1949] reports a 12 kHz cut-off for the bullfinch), and use an average amplitude value for the whistle song at the source of 95 dB (range is 80-105 dB; see Figs 121 and 122), then it is possible to determine from the cumulative dB isopleth for Isla Genovesa (Fig. 139) that a sound-pressure level of 35 dB (i.e. 95 dB minus 60 dB) would allow the bird to hear the whistle song at a distance of approximately 140 feet from the sound source. This distance is well within the range of maximal territory size for this species on Isla Genovesa, i.e. mean 184 ft.; range 85-282 ft.; see Table 23. (The 34 dB contour line in Fig. 139 continues on a vertical course from 10 to 15 kHz, although this range is not shown in the isopleth.) Furthermore, the marked similarity in the frequency characteristics of the whistle songs in several widely sympatric species, irrespective of body size (Table 13; Figs. 43 and 44, and cf. Fig. 140) suggests that the signal function and the structural basis of sound production are also similar.

Whistle songs, with their ultra-high frequencies, would seem to require a very special, if not unique, syrinx for such vocal productions. And, indeed, such is the case. In a thoroughly executed anatomical study of the geospizine syrinx, Cutler (1970) has uncovered a distinctive and remarkably uniform arrangement of muscles not previously described for oscines. Concerning the ten pairs of syringeal muscles of the geospizines, she states (p. 22): "The heavy syringeal musculature . . . may be able to create a considerable amount of tension on the internal tympaniform membrane and any other potentially vibratory parts, which should enable the birds to produce very high frequency sounds. . . ."

If, in fact, there is a functional relationship between the heavily muscularized syrinx of the geospizines and their ability to produce high-frequency vocalizations, then we must assume that such a structure would not have evolved, let alone prevailed, were the whistle songs they produce inaudible to the birds, or served no critical function in their lives.

The critical function of whistle songs seems to be pair-bonding, and nest-invitation, and in order not to unintentionally facilitate the visual clues that could reveal the location of the singer or its mate at critical times (e.g. nest construction, incubation), vocalizations should provide some degree of "acoustical camouflage." Lack (1945) has correctly stated that nest-building in the Geospizini is closely linked with display, as occurs in some other birds that have no enemies at the nest. But are there really no sources of danger for the finches, no nest predators?

It is now known that a number of species occasionally focus their depredatory activities at geospizine nests, including the centipede (*Scolopendra*), colubrid snake (*Dromicus*), short-eared owl (*Asio*), and mockingbird (*Mimus* [*Nesomimus*]) (Gifford 1919; Bowman 1961; and personal observations). From direct and circumstantial evidence, the abundant and ubiquitous mockingbirds appear to be one of the most widespread predators on geospizine eggs and nestlings (Bowman and Carter 1971; Downhower 1978; Grant and Grant 1979, 1980), although the short-eared owl may be a serious threat to nestlings only on some islands (e.g. Genovesa; Grant and Grant 1980) and not on others (e.g. Wolf; Curio 1965). This owl is unreported from, or very scarce on, several islands (Swarth 1931). Mockingbirds have been observed by the writer to inspect the interior of newly constructed finch nests on islas Genovesa (*G. magnirostris*), Santa Cruz (*G. fortis*), and Española (*G. conirostris*) (cf. Grant and Grant 1980), and although no finch eggs were seen to be looted, the nest owners vigorously attacked the marauders, even riding on their backs for several seconds of flight! Curio (1969) remarks that mockingbirds "viciously" hunt after finches.

Rats (*Rattus*), mice (*Mus*), and house cats (*Felis*) are known to occasionally plunder finch nests, but their presence could not have been a selective force in the evolution of whistle songs, because of their relatively recent introductions by man, to only some of the islands.

Predators on fledglings and adult finches include the endemic hawk (*Buteo galapagoensis*), short-eared owl (*Asio flammeus*), (Abs et al. 1965; de Vries 1976; Gifford 1919; Grant et al. 1975) as well as the migratory peregrine (*Falco peregrinus; fide* Harris 1975). The resident barn owl (*Tyto alba*) is not known to prey upon the finches (Bowman 1961).

Recent studies on the auditory sensitivity of the barn owl (Konishi 1973) state that it is unlikely that this avian predator is capable of locating pure tones above 9 kHz, where frequencies so typical of the whistle songs of the finches occur (Table 13). In studies by Schalter and Schleidt (1977) on barn owls, and Schalter (1978) on goshawks and pygmy owls, the high-pitched, pure-toned aerial predator alarm call ("seeet") of the European blackbird elicited fewer responses than did the lower-pitched non-pure-toned alarm calls of chaffinch and chicken (see critiques in Brown 1982 and Hailman 1978). Konishi (1973) noted that pure-tone signals are less accurately located by barn owls than wide-band noises. Thus, the qualities of pure-toneness and high frequency, as originally described by Marler (1955), do appear to impart a nonlocatable attribute to the aerial predator alarm notes of some passerine birds. Whereas "anti-predator" calls of the European blackbird and other songbirds have a maximal/minimal frequency range of approximately 9.5/7.5 kHz, the whistle songs of Darwin's finches show a mean maximal/minimal frequency range of 14/10 kHz (Table 13). The average 10 kHz cut-off frequency may indicate a critical auditory threshold level above which such finch predators as short-eared owls and Galapagos mockingbirds are incapable of binaurally locating the whistle songs of Darwin's finches.

On the basis of Marler's postulates (1955, 1961), Cutler's syringeal findings (1970), Konishi's auditory sensitivity studies on barn owls (1973), field observations of various workers, and lastly, inferences to be drawn from measurements of the interaural distances of the skulls in finches, mockingbirds, and owls (Fig. 108; Table 15), one may tentatively conclude the following: (1) *Asio* and *Buteo* do not hear the higher ranges of the whistle songs, or if they do, are incapable of locating their source binaurally. (2) Galapagos mockingbirds may or may not be capable of hearing the whistle songs, but if they do, like the finches which produce them, they probably would be incapable of locating their source binaurally. (3) Darwin's finches probably hear their own whistle songs within the limits of their territories, but most likely are incapable of spatial localization of their sources by auditory means alone. In other words, the public nature of sound communication has been circumvented and privacy achieved by the use of very high-frequency sound. Because of dispersion by vegetation, such small wavelengths are most vulnerable to amplitude reduction, and therefore would tend to reduce the probability of their reaching the ears of predators over moderate distances from the nest site.

Both the short-eared owl and the mockingbird are diurnal, visually oriented predators at the nests of the finches. On Isla Genovesa, Grant and Grant (1980) have made the significant discovery that owls prey more heavily on the larger of the four resident species of finch, *Geospiza magnirostris* and *G. conirostris*. They have attributed this behavior to the greater conspicuousness and landing stability of the larger nests, as well as to the larger nestling prey associated with them (see also Downhower 1978). By contrast, mockingbirds prey more heavily at the nests of smaller species (*Certhidea olivacea* and *Geospiza difficilis*), whose owners are more ineffectual than the larger species in warding off their predatory attacks.

Distributional data on short-eared owls and mockingbirds (Swarth 1931) indicate that the former species is less widespread and far less abundant than the latter species. The absence of mockingbirds from islas Pinzón and Floreana may be man-induced (Abbott and Abbott 1978, and D. W. Steadman, pers. comm.). Wherever mockingbirds occur they seem to be abundant and display aggressiveness, nearly insatiable curiosity, and group territoriality (Bowman and Carter 1971; Hatch 1966; Abbott and Abbott 1978; Grant and Grant 1979). Furthermore, since nestling periods of the finches and mockingbirds are relatively longer on the Galapagos Islands than they are for passerine species generally on the coastal mainland of Ecuador (Grant and Grant 1979, 1980), we may reasonably assume that the predatory threat by mockingbirds on nestling geospizines is also prolonged and could further enhance the need for a vocal pair-bonding signal that "conceals" its sender.

Long-range territorial song (mainly basic and derived) is known to diminish in amount from the time of egg-laying through nestling periods (Lack 1945; Downhower 1978). There appears to be a corresponding diminution in whistle song in the wild (L. Ratcliffe, pers. comm.), but it does not completely cease, to judge from our observations on captive birds in San Francisco. Territorial (advertising) song contains all the features that promote localization of the singer (cf. Marler 1955), whereas whistle songs bear no such features, at least in those populations where mockingbird predation pressures are high (see below).

Grant and Grant (1980) have suggested the possibility that on Isla Genovesa there is heavier owl predation on nestling *G. magnirostris* and *G. conirostris* during the second than the first week of age, presumably because the cries of the nestlings may be louder or more insistent, and hence more readily detected. Once alerted, a predator could initiate a visual search in nearby areas. In this sense, Grant and Grant (1980) suggest that calling nestlings are more vulnerable than silent ones. Also, it should be noted that the calls of nestling geospizines are about as high-pitched as the whistle songs and somewhat similarly structured (Fig. 116), thereby probably also making them less vulnerable to binaural detection by owls. Our experience in hand-rearing over 70 nestling geospizines has been that their food calls are extremely difficult to locate under conditions where the position of the youngster is not previously known to the listener. The only sound that we have been able to detect from a nestling geospizine is the high-pitched, binaurally unlocatable, presumably "predator-proof," whistle-like call. Even though the amplitude of this call increases as the nestling grows older, the sound structure does not undergo fundamental change until the time of fledging (12-14 days) when a radically different food call appears spontaneously (Fig. 116; Table 16). "Breaking" of the voice is probably the result of increased androgen secretion (Abs 1975; Abs et al. 1977). The begging call is much lower-pitched, almost growl-like in character (because of the wide-band, rapid frequency modulation of the signal) and therefore replete with auditory localization clues (Marler 1955; cf. Brosset and Chappuis 1969). The fledgling call is audible at a considerable distance because of its high overall amplitude (Fig. 117), and although it undoubtedly may attract the attention of the diurnal short-eared owl and *Buteo* hawk, and also the mockingbird, it is given mainly at times when the attending adults are nearby, and distraction of the predator from the juvenal prey is possible.

It is significant, I believe, that the nestling food call of species of *Geospiza* would seem to be a kind of diminutive whistle song of the adult male, and may have given rise to the adult whistle song. There is also a rather close resemblance to the adult female *Geospiza* subsong (Fig. 175C). In both instances the distinctive songs are intimately associated with breeding activity. Lorenz (1943) has pointed out that morphological features of infant animals are adapted for releasing parental responses such as feeding. In geospizine nestlings, as in some other altricial songbirds, vocalizations are very high-frequencied, and according to the motivational-structural rules of Morton (1977), would tend to attract the attending adult rather than repel it.

Morton (1977) has wondered why nestlings should vocalize at all in the "predation-vulnerable stage." In geospizine nestlings, it is likely that the food call is structured such that binaural localization of its source by predators is made difficult (Fig. 116). Both nestling food calls and adult whistle songs are given in the presence or absence of potential predators.

The broad-band structure of the fledgling calls of geospizines suggests hostile motivation, but the pitch is rather high (cf. Morton 1977). The calls are readily locatable (Fig. 116) and attract the adults in whose feeding territory the fledglings occur. Upon the approach of the parent, the fledgling assumes a crouched position, wings partly spread and quivering, head retracted and bill agape. In the context of a submissive posture, these calls are probably mildly assertive and bring about feeding behavior on the part of the attending adults.

Dialect Formation in Whistle Song

Certhidea olivacea, the smallest and phylogenetically the oldest of the 13 species of Galapagos finches (Yang and Patton 1981), is the only geospizine showing dialect formation in the true whistle song. There is some evidence to suggest that interisland differences in predatory pressure from mockingbirds may partly explain this phenomenon. An examination of Figs. 109 through 115 reveals that a similar form of whistle song occurs on the islands of Santa Cruz, Española, San Cristóbal, and Wolf: one or two notes with an average minimal frequency of about 10 kHz. On the islands of Marchena and Pinta, however, whistle songs contain several frequency-modulated notes of low mean frequency. Mockingbirds occur on both islands. On Isla Marchena, my impression from casual field observing is that mockingbird densities are not as high, for example, as on Española and Santa Cruz, where high-pitched frequencies prevail in the whistle songs, and binaural localization clues are few or entirely wanting. On Isla Pinta, mockingbirds are abundant in the arid and transition vegetation zones, but less so at higher elevations (L. Ratcliffe, pers. comm.) where *Certhidea* reaches its greatest density (Bowman, pers. obs.).

If the mockingbirds show preferential nest predation on small-bodied geospizines wherever they occur in the Galapagos, just as they do on Isla Genovesa (Grant and Grant 1980), then one might predict that any significant difference between islands in the relative density of mockingbirds and small geospizines, or in vegetation density affecting visibility, would affect the character of the whistle song, making its acoustical camouflage more or less effective, according to the intensity of prevailing selective predatory pressures from mockingbirds.

It is perhaps noteworthy that in the dense ground-vegetated highlands of islas Pinta and Santiago, where *Geospiza difficilis* abound, and mockingbirds are noticeably less common, the distinctive special basic songs of this ground-loving species lack a high-pitched terminal flourish (song region 5), so characteristic of the population on Isla Wolf where sympatric mockingbirds are plentiful and the ground vegetation is more open (see Fig. 62). Also, the true whistle song is lacking in these three populations of *G. difficilis* but present in islas Genovesa and Darwin populations where mockingbirds abound and the vegetation is comparatively "open" (see Table 17A).

It is not entirely clear why whistle and basic songs should be "linked" only in the species of Darwin's finch, *Certhidea olivacea*, with the longest lineage, as well as in the presumed closely related *Melanospiza richardsoni* of St. Lucia in the Caribbean (Fig. 104). In the population of *G. difficilis* on Isla Wolf, which lacks a true whistle song, there is what appears to be a functional equivalent in the form of a "linked" whistle-like region 5 of the special basic song (Fig. 62). There is an uncanny similarity between this special basic song of *Geospiza difficilis* and the combined whistle/basic song of *Certhidea olivacea* on the same island, one being a mirror image of the other (compare the special basic song of *G. difficilis*, Fig. 62A with *Certhidea olivacea*, Figs. 80G and 112B). Both vocalizations are associated with nest-invitation activities. These two small-bodied species have fairly high population densities and probably defend smaller territories, the latter judged from the study of Grant and Grant (1980) on Isla Genovesa (see Table 25). Both species routinely forage in the near vicinity of the nest. Because the near-nest feeding territory is comparatively small in these species, it is probably partially coincidental with the nest site itself, where whistle song or whistle notes are most often given. Thus, functional and spatial separations of the two sites are not achieved and the two contrasting vocal behaviors, otherwise nonlinked in other geospizines, are joined in what might be a contrasting, motivationally conflicting, two-parted vocal signal, namely, a friendly, submissive, pair-bonding, pure-tone "whistle song" or "whistle note" and a hostile, aggressive, territorial, basic or special basic "growl" signal (see Morton 1977).

Pinaroloxias *Whistle Song*

Why does the Cocos finch (*Pinaroloxias inornata*) also have a well-developed whistle song similar to that of *Geospiza* of the Galapagos (Fig. 43)? Although there are no mockingbirds endemic to Cocos Island, there is a rare endemic cuckoo (*Coccyzus ferrugineus*) that could be a nest predator. Very little is known about its behavior (Swarth 1931; Slud 1967), but two fairly close mainland relatives, *Coccyzus erythrophthalamus* and *C. americanus*, occasionally pirate nests of other songbirds for their eggs (Pearson 1940). Were the Cocos cuckoo to behave similarly, such a predatory pressure might be sufficient to cause *Pinaroloxias* to retain the whistle song, presumably present in its founding ancestor. It is possible, however, that whistle song could also be maintained in the absence of any selective force for it on Cocos Island, i.e. as an hereditary "heirloom" in a comparatively predation-free environment.

Female Whistle Song

Female geospizines do not normally sing definitive whistle, basic, or derived songs. It was discovered, however, that under the influence of testosterone propionate, an adult female *Geospiza magnirostris* (Isla Genovesa) could sing a whistle-like song bearing a strong resemblance in tonal purity, frequency spread, and maximal frequency (14 kHz), to the typical adult male whistle song of the same species (Fig. 118). Whistle song can be induced in both sexes under a high-level regime of male sex hormone, but under normal conditions the androgenic effect is "externalized" as song only in the male (cf. Kern and King 1972). The physical basis for species-specific song exists in both sexes, as evidenced by the presence of a uniform pattern of syringeal musculature in all geospizines, although of much less robust development in females (Cutler 1970).

II. Advertising Songs

Collectively, and in their various structural forms (Fig. 42), basic and derived songs are the "advertising" songs of Darwin's finches. It is assumed that they simultaneously attract potential mates and repulse conspecific neighboring territory holders among other things (see Morton 1983). They may be heard abundantly throughout the Galapagos Archipelago during an average rainy season, January through April (Bowman 1961; Grant and Boag 1980). During the remainder of the year ("garúa" season), less vigorous vocalizations occur sporadically in the highlands of the larger islands such as Floreana, Isabela, San Cristóbal, Santa Cruz, and Santiago, where some year-round breeding probably takes place. In years of heavy and prolonged rainfall ("El Niño" phenomenon), breeding may occur throughout the year at all elevations (pers. obs.). On Cocos Island, Costa Rica, *Pinaroloxias inornata* confines its breeding activity to the comparatively dry and sunny months of January through March, but the birds are essentially nonsinging throughout the rest of the year when persistent tropical rainshowers drench the island (pers. obs.; Gifford 1919; Slud 1967).

In contrast to "whistle" songs–which I interpret to be "concealingly" structured–basic, special basic, abbreviate basic, and derived songs are interpreted to be "revealingly" structured, i.e. designed to facilitate binaural localization of their source. Consequently, one should expect to find, as indeed we do, notable interpopulational variation, befitting the regional differences in vegetative cover that affect sound transmission.

Special Basic and Certhidea *Basic Songs*

Geospiza difficilis, Figs. 47F, 62A, 85F, 102; *Geospiza fortis*, Fig. 101; *Cactospiza pallida*, Figs. 47A, 70B, 78A, 86D, 101; *Camarhynchus psittacula*, Figs. 47, 73B, 86C; *Camarhynchus pauper*, Figs. 47D, 71, 86B, 101; *Camarhynchus parvulus*, Figs. 42, 47, 64A, 70B, 86A; *Certhidea olivacea*, Figs. 45, 80, 84, 85E, 86F, 90, 95, 98, 99, 104, 122, 128.

Characteristics. These songs are typically drawn-out, "buzzy," growl-like vocalizations of the "tree-finches" (*Certhidea olivacea, Cactospiza pallida, Camarhynchus psittacula, C. pauper*, and *C. parvulus*) and certain populations of "ground-finches" (*Geospiza difficilis* on islas Wolf, Pinta, Santiago, and possibly other islands; and a few individuals of *Geospiza fortis* on Isla Pinta; see Figs. 47, 101).

The duration of special basic and *Certhidea* basic songs is quite variable (mean 1.28 sec.; range 0.75-1.87 sec.), and to judge from the very limited song sample available, there appears to be no constant relationship between song duration and body size (as in the whistle song, Fig. 106). In general, larger species such as *Cactospiza pallida* have a lower fundamental song frequency than smaller species such as *Camarhynchus parvulus* and *Certhidea olivacea* (see Fig. 70), although there is considerable variation in this character depending upon the acoustical properties of the transmission environment in which the song is sung—populations show adaptations in their songs related to environmental factors. For example, in the coastal zone of Isla Santa Cruz, the special basic song of *C. parvulus* has a slightly higher fundamental frequency and a significantly broader bandwidth than in the *Scalesia* forest zone (cf. Figs. 119 and 120). On Isla Floreana, the special basic song of *Camarhynchus pauper* is typically a narrow-band frequency-modulated signal (Fig. 71) with a distinctive nasal quality that is not so strongly emphasized in the special basic songs of *Camarhynchus parvulus* and *C. psittacula*.

Behavioral context. There is a problem, as Hailman (1973) has correctly observed, in trying to determine the function of songs by studying the dynamics of behavior, since function is ultimately assessed by showing its selective advantage within populations, and an analysis of proximate factors does not "solve" the problem.

As summarized in Table 17, characteristically the special basic and *Certhidea* basic songs are delivered at their highest intensity near the nest site or in close proximity to an intruding conspecific male. In the case of *Cactospiza* and *Camarhynchus*, and depending on circumstances, songs may be interspersed with whistle and/or derived songs, and in the case of *Certhidea* (in which the whistle and basic songs are linked) they may be alternated with derived song. For example, on Isla Floreana, on one occasion a male *Camarhynchus pauper* on territory sang derived song antiphonally with a distant conspecific male. Upon the approach of the distant bird to within a few feet of the nest site of the near bird, the latter switched to the special basic song, which now dominated his vocalizing, as it pursued the intruder through the forest canopy.

On Isla Wolf, breeding male *Geospiza difficilis* sing their special basic song, with its distinctive terminal whistle-like note (see Fig. 126), close to the nest and/or the female. On one occasion in our aviary I saw a male sing inside its nest, which was nearing completion. According to Dr. L. Ratcliffe (pers. comm.), the special basic song, at least on Isla Pinta (Fig. 62C), is equivalent in function (nest-invitation) to the true whistle song of other populations (e.g. Genovesa, Fig. 62D). The special basic and *Certhidea* basic songs are rarely given during territorial pursuit.

There is a parallel between two Galapagos finches, *Certhidea olivacea* and certain populations of *Geospiza difficilis*, and species of New World warblers (F. Parulidae) through the possession in both groups of more or less distinct songs for territorial defense and courtship (cf. Lein 1972; Morse 1966, 1970), i.e different songs for transmitting different kinds of information in a way analogous to such capabilities with visual signals. For example, song "B" of *Dendroica virens* is given in the presence of the conspecific female, or when no conspecifics are present, near the center of the territory and during the nest-building and incubation periods. It functions in pair-bonding, and is composed mostly of whistle-like notes, with a terminal frequency-modulated note. Possibly it is convergent with the combined whistle and basic songs of *Certhidea* and with the partially homologous special basic song of *G. difficilis*. In *D. virens*, a song "A," given in the presence of neighboring conspecific males or when the bird is alone at its territorial boundary, would seem to be functionally similar to the derived songs of *Certhidea* and *G. difficilis*—in both groups they repel conspecific males. Structurally they are composed of frequency-modulated notes, but with a few whistle-like notes interspersed.

Adaptive significance of special basic song. A wide-band frequency spectrum is a distinctive feature of special basic songs and probably facilitates source locatability by providing a large spectrum of binaural intensity differences (Hope 1980; Konishi 1973; Marler 1955). According to

According to the motivation-structural rules of Morton (1977), "aggressive" sounds used for close-up ("face-to-face") confrontations (where the possibility and consequences of attack are immediate) are generally of low frequency, harsh or rasping quality, and broad frequency spread. Such a sound indicates that the sender is likely to attack if the receiver comes closer or remains at the same distance (Morton 1977). This accurately describes the puppy-dog-like "growl" of the special basic song, and its behavioral context in *Geospiza difficilis* (Isla Wolf), species of *Camarhynchus* and *Cactospiza*, and basic song of *Certhidea olivacea*. Since these songs are given at fairly close range both in the vicinity of the nest and in the more remote sections of the territory, but most frequently when another conspecific male is nearby, it is noteworthy that the decibel level of the special basic song of *G. difficilis* (Isla Wolf) averages about 10 to 12 dB lower than the level of the derived song of the same individual (see Fig. 126 and Table 18; compare regions 3, 4, and 5 with region 1). This initial source disparity in amplitude between the two songs, in conjunction with a relatively greater attenuation of very high frequencies through transmission loss and differential auditory sensitivity, results in a more rapid environmental decay of the special basic signal with increasing distance from the sound source, and is befitting its relatively close-range use, when compared to the derived song and its typical use for somewhat greater range (see p. 271 and Table 17). Similarly, the buzzy region 4, which constitutes the longest region of *Certhidea* basic song, is of somewhat lower amplitude (about 7 dB) than the loudest region of the derived song (cf. Figs. 122 and 123).

It is probably not fortuitous that a distinct, noisy, wide-band song occurs only in those species which forage and nest in comparatively dense foliage, where visibility is often severely restricted. Such frequency-modulated signals with their patterns, pulses, and spaces allow for easy encoding of essential information about individual and species identities (Marler 1960, 1969; Falls 1963; Greenewalt 1968; Emlen 1971b). Broadcasting over a broad range of frequencies is an effective device in situations where pure tone attenuation is highly variable (Morton 1970; see also Table 30), because it offers assurances that at least some of the frequencies composing the band will be transmitted, thereby permitting some binaural intensity and spectral comparisons (Konishi 1973), while temporal characteristics of the signal are maintained.

Seven species of Darwin's finches have a special basic song (see Table 10), and these birds live in habitats with significant vegetative stratification (leafy crown with branch understory; see Figs. 6A,B and 70). Each vocal signal would seem to be designed to most effectively meet the prevailing frequency-dependent transmission characteristics of the major vegetative strata or clusters occupied by the bird (see Spieth 1979).

An equal number of geospizine species, lacking a special basic song, occupy shrubby habitats in which there is greater overall internal structural uniformity in the vegetation, with less stratification or clustering, even though plant species diversity may be greater than in habitats where finches sing special basic songs (see Figs. 4B and 5B). The evolutionary consequence of structural uniformity in the vegetation (and concomitantly in the acoustical habitat) seems to be the development of a single "multipurpose," all-in-one song such as the widely occurring "basic song proper" (Fig. 89).

But why should the mangrove-finch, *Cactospiza heliobates*, have neither special basic nor derived songs in its repertoire, when its closest relative of the inland forests, *Cactospiza pallida*, has both? (See Figs. 45 and 127). The explanation would seem to be founded in the general vegetative uniformity of the mangrove forest (Fig. 16). The acoustical solution to the problem appears to have gone the route of vocal simplification: a "compromise," strongly pulsed, frequency-modulated, abbreviate basic song, with little internal diversity; these features are suited for long-distance communication in a vegetatively simple, more or less uniform arboreal setting where visibility is somewhat obscured (compare *C. pallida* and *C. heliobates* songs, Figs. 70 and 127).

Basic, Abbreviate Basic, and Derived Songs

Geospiza magnirostris, Figs. 36, 37, 42B, 45, 52, 53, 85G, 94, 133B; *Geospiza fortis*, Figs. 36, 42B, 46, 50, 85H, 91, 101, 128; *Geospiza fuliginosa*, Figs. 36, 37B, 42B,C, 46D, 48B, 103, 127; *Geospiza difficilis*, Figs. 42B,C, 46E, 47D, 61, 62A, 85C,F, 102, 146; *Geospiza scandens*, Figs. 46B, 60A, 94; *Geospiza conirostris*, Figs. 42C, 46A, 54B, 55-59, 84C, 85B, 89-92, 124A; *Platyspiza crassirostris*, Figs. 45, 74, 85D, 89; *Certhidea olivacea*, 81, 82, 95-99, 123, 155-160; *Pinaroloxias inornata*, Figs. 45, 83, 84, 85A, 86E; and *Melanospiza richardsoni*, Fig. 104.

Characteristics. Intrinsic to one's first impression of the Galapagos during the breeding season are the ubiquitous and acoustically diverse vocalizations of the finches (Fig. 42, Table 10). They exhibit geographic variation, often forming distinctive regional dialects. The "basic song proper," in its protracted form, closely resembles *Certhidea* basic song (Figs. 84-85): it is typically five-parted. Intra- and inter-specific variation in basic song patterning is extraordinary. Some appreciation of this variation can be obtained by scanning spectrograms of *Platyspiza crassirostris* (Fig. 64), *Geospiza difficilis* (Fig. 61), *Geospiza scandens* (Fig. 60), *Geospiza magnirostris* (Fig. 53), among other species. Basic song of shortest duration was found in *Geospiza magnirostris*, Isla Wolf (0.3 sec.), and of longest duration in *Geospiza conirostris*, Isla Española (1.3), which are two of the larger species of finch (Figs. 53, 55). The *Certhidea* basic song on islas Marchena and Wolf, exclusive of the "linked" whistle song, is the longest of any basic song hitherto encountered (1.87 sec on Isla Wolf), and this species is the smallest-bodied of the Darwin's finch assemblage (see Fig. 80F,G).

Two species, *Pinaroloxias inornata* and *Platyspiza crassirostris*, sing only one basic song of the protracted type (see Figs. 74 and 83 and Table 10). Another species, *Geospiza difficilis*, sings the protracted basic song exclusively on Isla Darwin; protracted basic and derived songs on Isla Genovesa; protracted basic (rarely), special basic, and derived songs on Isla Wolf; and protracted basic and protracted derived songs on islas Pinta and Santiago (see Figs. 46, 61, and 62). Each island population of finch seems to have its own constellation of song types; only further field studies can elucidate the reasons for this.

Many of the abbreviate basic forms of the basic song proper (those with a shortened region 4) are difficult to distinguish from certain derived songs. This situation can best be appreciated by examining the mixture of songs displayed in island population samples of *Geospiza fortis* (Figs. 31, 32, and 50).

As noted previously, individual birds may contract their basic song proper to form an abbreviate basic song (Fig. 91). Further shortening can occur by disarticulating regions 1 and 2 (Fig. 101) or regions 1, 2, and 3 (Figs. 92-94) from the remaining song regions. The result is a somewhat "simplified" song composed of the much-repeated, two- or three-regioned, staccato-like syllables, onomatopoetically represented by "tu-tu-tu-tu-tu . . . " or "churr-churr-churr-churr-churr . . ." (cf. Figs. 42C, 92-94, and 101).

Infrequently, several species of Darwin's finches are known to sing both basic and derived songs, for example *Camarhynchus parvulus*, Isla Santa Cruz. "Bilingual" individuals are known from field recordings (Fig. 93) and aviary auditions. As discussed further below, in this species the abbreviate basic song is preferentially, although not exclusively, sung in the *Scalesia* forest highlands (Fig. 68), whereas the derived song is preferentially, although not exclusively, sung in the arid coastal lowlands. They differ conspicuously in their frequency spread, with the bulk of the sound energy being confined to frequencies below 4 kHz in the highlands, and 7 kHz in the lowlands. Occasionally, free-living *Geospiza conirostris* and *G. magnirostris* have been recorded singing full basic and derived songs (Fig. 94). One hand-reared *G. magnirostris* ("JLG," Fig. 166), bred from wild Isla Genovesa parents, spontaneously sang what are interpreted to be derived and basic songs, even though the nestling was exposed to basic song only during the first five days of post-hatching life.

Displays of frequency spread and modal amplitudes of Darwin's finch vocalizations (Fig.

128) represent combined data on basic, abbreviate basic, and derived songs. These data, when plotted against mean body weight, support the conclusion of Greenewalt (1968) that there is little if any direct correlation between body size of songbirds and the highest frequencies of their songs. For example, *Geospiza magnirostris* on Isla Wolf (the second largest species of Darwin's finches) and *Geospiza difficilis* on Isla Genovesa (the second smallest species) sing some of the highest frequencies, whereas *Geospiza conirostris* on Isla Española (the third largest species) and *Certhidea olivacea* on Isla Santa Cruz (the smallest species) sing some of the lowest frequencies. (It was noted earlier [see p. 264] that the "whistle" songs of all species of Darwin's finches begin in the frequency range of approximately 11-16 kHz [see Table 13]).

Schwartzkopff (1955a,b) suggested that the vocalizations of birds show a strong dependence on body weight, and Simkin (1973) found a correlation between body size and "vocal cords" with a reduction in the former associated with a reduction in the latter. The possibility that lowest frequencies of songs may be correlated with the size of the internal tympaniform membrane of the syrinx was suggested by Konishi (1970a). A comparison of data in Figs. 128 and 129 shows that such a correlation is none too good for Darwin's finches. Rather, the correlation seems to be much better when the "modal frequency" of the song, i.e. frequency of the modal amplitude of the energy spectrum, is compared with average maximal membrane dimension.

Even though *Certhidea olivacea* (the smallest finch) is capable of membrane vibration at a fundamental frequency as low as in *Geospiza conirostris* (the third largest finch according to body weight), the smallest absolute size of the membrane in *Certhidea olivacea* presumably causes it to vibrate at a modal frequency that is considerably higher. However, as noted below, ecological requirements associated with sound transmission may cause modal frequency shifts that are somewhat independent of size (Simkin 1973; Bergmann 1976 ms; Wallschläger 1980). See Figs. 139 and 143. Thus, the ability to produce high modal frequencies need not necessarily symbolize size advantage or aggressive motivation (cf. Morton 1977).

Behavioral context. Since one of the principal functions of basic, abbreviate basic, and derived songs is advertisement by unmated males to females in search of mates, as well as to rival males (Lack 1945), we find that these songs are most vigorously delivered during the establishment of territory, although they continue to be sung throughout the reproductive season in varying degrees of intensity (see Downhower 1978). Mated and unmated males usually sing from conspicuous perches near their nest site, pursuing, preferentially, conspecific and, rarely, heterospecific males when they trespass (Ratcliffe 1981).

Singing has been observed at all heights within the vegetation, and notably at ground level, in *Geospiza difficilis* (islas Genovesa, Santiago, and Wolf) and *Certhidea olivacea* (islas Darwin, Española, and Wolf; see Fig. 10B). *Certhidea* has also been observed in flight song high above the *Scalesia* forest canopy of Isla Santa Cruz in company with the vermilion flycatcher. All species of Darwin's finches, except possibly *Cactospiza heliobates*, for which few observations are available, have been observed to sing advertising song while in flight. Some species of *Geospiza* vocalize more on the wing than others (e.g. Harris 1974 for *G. scandens*, and Ratcliffe 1981 for other species). Flight songs are most prevalent and possibly more frequent in the more operation terrain of the coastal zone. But careful observation may reveal frequent, although less prevalent, flights accompanied by song in other species, particularly the "tree-finches," which occupy the more leafy canopies of the trees and shrubs. "Flight song" is most often given just a few seconds before the bird alights and while executing a very slow flight, verging on an aerial stall, with wings broadly arched and quivering.

During the early phase of breeding, an unmated male on territory and in flight song makes himself more conspicuous to an overflying unmated female, which might thereby be attracted to him and perhaps mate with him. There is no way of assessing the costs versus benefits of flight singing (Gochfeld 1978), but conspicuous singing could be hazardous where swift-flying hawks (e.g. *Falco* and *Accipiter*) occur. Such agile aerial predators are absent from the Galapagos, but in

Europe, where they abound, particularly *Accipiter*, they cause the Great Tit (*Parus major*) to sing from high perches (above 2-6 meters, in the visually obfuscated zone), presumably thereby making themselves inconspicuous rather than facilitating long-distance transmission of their songs (Hunter 1980).

Nonoverlapping, interspecific song duetting has been noted by Beebe (1924) between *Geospiza magnirostris* and *Camarhynchus psittacula*, and interspecific countersinging has been tape-recorded in *G. magnirostris* (Isla Genovesa), *Camarhynchus pauper* (Isla Floreana), *Camarhynchus parvulus* (Isla Santa Cruz), *Cactospiza pallida* and *Certhidea olivacea* (*Scalesia* forest, Isla Santa Cruz). Grant and Grant (1979) report countersinging between male *Geospiza conirostris* (Isla Genovesa) of similar song morph, i.e. basic vs. basic or derived vs. derived, but never basic vs. derived. Songs of any given morph often differ in detail. On Isla Española I have recorded three adult-plumaged *G. conirostris* countersinging derived song while on nonadjacent territories. Although similar in morph, the internal structure of their songs was different, based on spectrographic analysis. Such countersinging situations are not analogous to "song matching" reported in other passerine species (e.g. Baptista 1975) because the individuals do not normally sing other variants (morphs) or otherwise alter the song form to more closely resemble that of a territorial neighbor. Were similar-songed individuals siblings, the close intrapopulation resemblance could be readily explained.

Darwin's finches are comparatively late morning risers. Whereas around Academy Bay, Isla Santa Cruz, the first morning song of the yellow warbler was occasionally heard about one-half hour before sunrise, first geospizine song sometimes was not audible until shortly before sunrise, and then a good deal of sun-bathing usually preceded full-intensity territorial singing. Singing diminishes in intensity by late morning, but picks up again by mid-afternoon at a time when cooling offshore winds frequently bring slight moderation of the temperature, especially in the coastal regions.

Downhower (1978) observed an appreciable decline in the frequency of male singing once incubation was initiated by the female, with a resurgence of male song as the nestlings approached their time for fledging. He does not comment upon "whistle song."

Several species, including *Geospiza magnirostris* (Fig. 94), *G. conirostris* (Figs. 91, 92, 94), *Camarhynchus parvulus* (Fig. 93), and *Certhidea olivacea* (Fig. 99A,B) are "graded" vocalizers. Field observations suggest that in certain situations the choice of a particular song may depend upon the bird's motivational state. For example, as noted in *Certhidea olivacea* and *Geospiza conirostris* on low-lying islas Genovesa and Española, respectively, full basic song was given preferentially in highly aggressive situations. During the mid-day heat, a territorial male frequently chooses a somewhat shaded perch from which to oversee his territory, often sitting quietly with feathers fluffed and bill agape. Foraging and patrol activities were minimal, and infrequent song was mostly of the abbreviate basic or derived type (as in *G. conirostris*) or "abbreviated derived" type (as in *Certhidea olivacea*). Were a conspecific male to fly overhead or to enter his territory, the resident male would make an almost immediate changeover to the "normal basic" or "abbreviate basic" song (as in *G. conirostris*, Isla Española; Figs. 91, 92), or nonabbreviated derived song (as in *Certhidea olivacea*, Isla Genovesa; Fig. 99A-3, B-3), usually accompanied by the drooped wing display or aerial pursuit.

Because abbreviate basic song in Española *G. conirostris* (pattern D, Fig. 92) is longer than the derived song and is usually accompanied by flight pursuit, it is probably more costly of energy than the shorter, and presumably lower-intensity, derived song. However, as Dawkins and Krebs (1978) point out, the cost to the bird could be more than the energetic cost of the display; it could be a risk of retaliation with escalated fighting by a rival.

In North America, Lein (1972, 1978) has shown that a graded series of vocal signals is given by the black-throated green and the chestnut-sided warblers. Songs of different "valence" encode for and transmit different messages concerning the location of the singer in its territory, as well as its level of aggressiveness. See also Kroodsma (1981).

Birds in less than full adult plumage distinctive of their species (see Bowman 1961), and presumably under two years of age, may alternately sing basic and derived songs (e.g. *Geospiza conirostris* and *G. magnirostris*, Fig. 94; *Camarhynchus parvulus*, Fig. 93). Such birds have not been systematically followed into adulthood (two or more years of age) to determine whether one or the other of the two songs becomes the sole definitive vocal advertising signal. Possibly birds choose a particular song that best contrasts with that of nearby conspecific males, thereby facilitating individual recognition (cf. Peters, Searcy, and Marler 1980). Many animals may learn the visual, auditory, or even olfactory characteristics of their immediate kin early in life and still opt to mate with an individual that is slightly different from those that are familiar from early life (Bateson 1978). In this way an animal is, presumably, able to strike an optimal balance between inbreeding and outbreeding. Petrinovitch, Patterson, and Baptista (1981) have found that male and female white-crowned sparrows (*Zonotrichia leucophrys nuttalli*) located on a dialect boundary tended to sing different songs, and Baptista (1975) also found that year-old males in juvenile crown plumage also sing two adjacent song dialects.

Grant and Grant (1979) describe a situation which, they suggest, could give rise to sympatric speciation in Darwin's finches. They found that on Isla Genovesa, *Geospiza conirostris* distributed their breeding territories such that no two breeding males of the same song type (i.e. basic or derived; see Fig. 94) shared a territory boundary. Although these authors detected no "bilingual" singing in their sample of adult males, one of their nestlings, color-banded in 1978 and holding a territory as a subadult male in 1979, was recorded by the writer singing both basic and derived songs (Fig. 94).

Kalamus and Maynard Smith (1966) have considered imprinting as a special form of sexual selection promoting assortative mating that is necessary for sympatric speciation to occur. In the case of *G. conirostris* on Isla Genovesa, we have a song polymorphism, i.e. basic and derived, that appears to be functional in mate discrimination. If there were "absolute" imprinting of the song, the population could, theoretically, become split into two distinct subpopulations, but if song imprinting were "partial," a balanced polymorphism would result, and the population would not be enduringly subdivided genetically. As yet we have no evidence from any "bilingual" species of Darwin's finch that the effect of imprinting on mate choice is absolute (cf. Seiger 1967), and in view of the fact that certain subadult males may sing both song types, it would appear that absolute imprinting does not prevail, and therefore full reproductive isolation of the two morphs, through sympatric speciation, is unlikely to occur. Indeed, Grant and Grant (1979) have indicated correctly that the reproductive "strategy" of *G. conirostris*, made necessary by the extreme environmental oscillations affecting food supply, might be one of alternating intra- and inter-morph mating behavior, thereby promoting heterozygous vigor. Intra-song morph, nonrandom mating might prevail when populations are large, whereas inter-song morph, random mating might predominate when populations are small and mate choice limited. During the latter condition, gene pool constriction resulting from "drift" might be offset by genetic enrichment resulting from random mating of song morphs (cf. Grant and Grant 1979 and Baker, Spitler-Nabors and Bradley 1982). Whereas the songs of the two morphs show discontinuous variation, the bill types show some degree of overlap in their dimensions. Foraging methods have been shown to differ in field situations, and may be looked upon as a subtle form of adaptive radiation within a population, somewhat similar in their ecological consequences to the consistent sexual dimorphisms in bill length reported by Lack (1947, Table 29) for most populations of *Certhidea olivacea*. As discussed on page 287, birds "fixed" on full basic song might, theoretically, be expected to possess larger breeding territories than birds "fixed" on derived song.

It is clear that we need to know a great deal more about the roles of imprinting and improvisation in the development and "fixation" of particular song morphs in male geospizines (and possibly females also; see below) showing bilingualism in their youth, if we are to understand its evolutionary significance, if any, in assortative matings and sympatric speciation (cf. Grant and

Grant 1979). Obviously, a particular "fixed" vocal phenotype may not necessarily be a good indicator of genotype (Baptista 1974; Petrinovitch et al. 1981), and "making genetic inferences from phenotypic data is fraught with difficulties" (Grant, Grant, Smith et al. 1976).

Adaptive Significance of Basic, Abbreviate Basic, and Derived Songs

The most striking feature of advertising song in Darwin's finches is its overall variability. In the following discussion an attempt is made to explain some of this variability (e.g. frequency, amplitude) in terms of regional differences in sound transmission through vegetation.

Sound Parameters

Several acoustical measurements were developed, including energy spectra and absolute sound-pressure levels of songs, and isopleths of sound transmission and cumulative dB loss for the environment (see p. 239 ff. and Figs. 21, 28, 29).

From the song energy spectra we determine the relative amplitude distribution, noting in particular the frequency(ies) at which peak energy occurs (i.e. "modal frequency"), and also the upper and lower frequencies that delimit a bandwidth containing approximately 80-85% of the sound energy of a song population (e.g. Fig. 130). These data may be "projected" onto the sound-transmission isopleths and cumulative dB-loss isopleths (see Figs. 130 and 131).

Acoustical Apertures

From the sound-transmission isopleths we determine the pattern formed by the amplitude contour lines (see Fig. 28), which are spaced at 3-dB intervals (e.g. Fig. 133). Where the lines are closely spaced, sound is strongly attenuated; where they are widely spaced, sound is not strongly attenuated by the environment at a particular distance from the sound source. If the slope of the contour line is more or less vertical across the bandwidth, it indicates that there is no frequency-dependent disparity in sound attenuation at that distance from the sound source, and we may speak of an *unbiased* "acoustical aperture" whose width is delimited by the upper and lower frequencies of the bandwidth exhibiting such a uniform transmission efficiency. (The term "acoustical aperture," here coined for the phenomenon just described, should not be confused with the term "sound window" of Morton [1970, 1975] or "ground effect window" of Marten [1980].) For example, in Fig.133B, the acoustical aperture has a width of 2 kHz, i.e. a bandwidth extending from approximately 2 kHz to 4 kHz over a distance of 300 feet from the ground source. We may arbitrarily delineate aperture width by specifying how much disparity in amplitude is to be allowed between highest and lowest frequencies in the song beyond which signal integrity, and presumably auditory intelligibility, are lost, i.e. the result of a *biased* acoustical aperture.

For species with comparatively small territories, the vocal signal need maintain its amplitude and frequency integrity over only a relatively short transmission range within which the acoustical aperture is usually quite broad. In Fig. 134B, for example, the unbiased acoustical aperture has a width of approximately 4 kHz, i.e. a bandwidth extending from 2 to 6 kHz over a range of approximately 50 feet from the sound source, whereas at a distance of 300 feet, the aperture has narrowed to approximately 2 kHz, between approximately 2 and 4 kHz. The "rate" of constriction of the acoustical aperture is determined by distance and vegetation type, as can be seen in Fig. 142, where differences between the isopleths of the *Scalesia* forest and outer coastal zone of Isla Santa Cruz are clearly evident.

In all Galapagos environments examined so far, the amplitude disparity between specific high and low frequencies is invariably of less magnitude, the shorter the transmission distance, and of greater magnitude, the longer the transmission distance. This condition probably explains why smaller birds with smaller territories frequently have wider song bandwidths, utilizing broad-band acoustical apertures, and larger birds with larger territories have narrower song bandwidths, utilizing more constricted acoustical apertures available to them largely in the lower frequency ranges (see Fig. 135).

In various examples described in detail below, Darwin's finches appear to be using acoustical apertures whose bandwidths, on the average, contain frequencies that attenuate more or less uniformly within a specific distance from the sound source. Unlike the "sound windows" of Morton (1970), which occur at very low frequencies (and below 2 kHz in Galapagos habitats), and are presumably the result of the so-called "ground-effect" (Ingärd 1953; Marten 1980, but see Roberts et al. 1979; Marton 1981), Galapagos "acoustical apertures" are almost certainly caused by vegetation-related, frequency-dependent sound attenuation, and are essentially unrelated to height above ground at which sound was transmitted (cf. Marten 1980). Also, according to the "acoustic rules" of Marten (1980), ground attenuation is supposed to be greater in open habitats than in forests. In no instance could this be shown to be true of Galapagos environments. For example, if we compare sound transmission in (a) the *Scalesia* forest of Isla Santa Cruz (Figs. 6, 142A) and the outer coastal zone (the only zone present) of Isla Española (cf. Figs. 9 and 134B, respectively), or in (b) the midget *Croton* "forest" of Isla Wolf (Figs. 14, 134A) and the "parkland" of Isla Genovesa (Figs. 11A, 134B), and focus our attention on the relative position of the 59-db isodecibel contour line in the sound-transmission isopleth, we find in every instance that more "open" habitats, with less ground vegetation cover, show less sound attenuation in the 1-2 kHz bandwidth than the more "closed" habitats, with the greater ground vegetation cover. In all Galapagos examples, sound transmission was measured at approximately 1 meter above ground level.

Debates in the literature concerning the cause and reality of Morton's "sound window" are judged to be irrelevant to the present investigation (see Roberts et al. 1979, 1981; Marton 1981; and compare with Marten 1980) and essentially beyond the scope of this study, largely because such windows occur in all our sound transmission isopleths and at frequencies below those at which the finches normally vocalize (Figs. 128, 133-134). Since islands of the Galapagos Archipelago differ in their plant species composition, relative abundance, and growth-form (Bowman 1961; Wiggins and Porter 1981; Hamann 1979, 1981), it is not surprising that we do find persistent differences in frequency-dependent attenuation of sound from habitat to habitat and island to island (cf. Morton 1970; Wiley and Richards 1978).

Loss of Amplitude

Using the cumulative dB-loss isopleths (e.g. Fig. 29), we may quickly determine from the distribution pattern of the contour lines (drawn at 3-dB intervals), the total loss of absolute amplitude as a function of frequency and distance from the sound source.

A particular vocalization is considered to be well adapted to the transmission characteristics of its acoustical environment if the upper and lower frequency limits of the song bandwidth show no great disparity in amplitude loss over a distance equivalent to about the mean width of the species' territory.

Effect of Body Size on Song

In Darwin's finches, and presumably in songbirds generally, there is a direct correlation between body size and diameter of the sound-producing vibratory membranes of the syrinx (Fig. 129). This results in a modal frequency of song that is inherently "natural" for a species of a particular body size. But adaptive radiation has resulted in an array of species and insular populations with rather different body sizes (e.g. Figs. 128-129), with concomitant differentiation of "modal" frequencies as a secondary event, and not without direct adaptive value in specific environments (cf. Bergmann 1976). Evidence reported below clearly indicates that birds have the capacity to adapt their vocalizations to ecological factors (cf. Wallschläger 1979), often producing modalities in the energy spectrum that are rather different from the modalities of the auditory sensitivity spectra of their ears (cf. Dooling et al. 1971; Konishi 1970a). Such fundamental disparities might be ameliorated in part by a source adjustment in the dB level of appropriate song frequencies (see discussion of *G. difficilis* below).

Song amplitude appears to be correlated with absolute body size, with larger birds singing more loudly than smaller birds (Figs. 122-126, Table 18).

Auditory Sensitivity Factors

In order to assess amplitude loss during transmission in the light of a songbird's auditory capabilities, auditory sensitivity factors were subtracted from the absolute dB values for cumulative transmission loss, in order to adjust for frequency-dependent differences in sensitivity of the songbird ear (Table 19). Since nothing is known about the auditory sensitivities of the geospizine ear, good data for the distantly related finch *Serinus canarius* (Dooling, Mulligan, and Miller 1971; Konishi 1970a) have been applied.

Significance of Dialects

According to Nottebohm (1972), vocal dialects are said to occur when the songs or calls of conspecific birds in an area are alike, but differ from those of conspecifics in other areas. In other words, "dialects" are defined by the greater local incidence of a particular song theme, which may occur less frequently or not at all elsewhere.

Song dialects in Geospiza conirostris. On islas Española and Genovesa the song populations of *Geospiza conirostris* differ in many ways, the most obvious of which is frequency spread, i.e. bandwidth (Figs. 128, 130). Considering only the song bandwidths containing 80-85% of the sound energy (shaded areas on sound-transmission isopleths and cumulative dB-loss isopleths, Figs. 130 and 131, respectively), we see that the frequency spread is 2.5 kHz (range 1.5-4.0 kHz) on Española and 1.0 kHz (range 2.0-3.0 kHz) on Genovesa. The frequency of the modal amplitude of song is 2.25 kHz and 2.75 kHz for islas Española and Genovesa, respectively. The greater frequency spread of the Española song appears to correlate with the broad "unbiased" acoustical aperture as evidenced by the more or less vertical orientation of the isodecibel contour lines between approximately 1.5 and 4.0 kHz (Figs. 130-131). The sound-transmission and cumulative dB-loss isopleths for Isla Genovesa suggest that the most efficient transmission bandwidth available to *G. conirostris* occurs between approximately 2 and 3 kHz, with very little latitude for variation into the higher frequencies without risk of developing a significant bias in the acoustical aperture, i.e. differential loss of amplitude between high and low frequencies in the bandwidth of such magnitude as to endanger signal intelligibility.

Perhaps a more revealing demonstration of the adaptiveness of the two *conirostris* song populations to their respective (concordant) environments can be made by "projecting" song dialects into discordant sound-transmission environments, as in Fig. 132 and Table 20. It should be noted, however, that in Table 20, transmission losses have been adjusted to the auditory sensitivity spectrum of the canary ear so as to reflect better the relative intensities of the songs as the birds might hear them in nature.

Now it can be seen that the acoustical aperture on Isla Española is broad enough to accommodate equally well both concordant song of *G. conirostris* from Isla Española and discordant song from Genovesa with no more than 1-dB amplitude disparity between upper and lower limits of their bandwidths at distances of 200 and 300 feet from the sound source. However, on Isla Genovesa the situation is rather different, for here the discordant song from Isla Española is at a significant disadvantage over its conspecific's concordant song from Isla Genovesa, especially between 200 and 300 feet from the sound source where the 5-dB amplitude disparity between upper and lower bandwidth frequencies of concordant song is close to the presumed maximal tolerance. As for the discordant song, the 10-12 dB amplitude disparity is probably in excess of the "intelligibility level."

On Isla Genovesa *G. conirostris* has an average maximal territorial width of about 256 feet

(Table 21-22), a distance that generates a 5-dB amplitude difference between high and low frequencies in its song. Territorial dimensions are unknown for the Española population, but if we assume them to be about the same as for the Isla Genovesa population, the discordant dialect develops a notable disparity (13 dB, Table 20) between upper and lower frequency components even during short-range transmission (100 feet), which probably results in a short-range loss of intelligibility.

Differences in the song ecology of the two island populations of *Geospiza conirostris* suggest that certain vagrant males might experience formidable difficulties in establishing themselves on another island because of possible mismatching of song structure and sound-transmission patterns. For example, in the vocally polymorphic song population on Isla Española (Figs. 55-59), certain song morphs, e.g. R-61/3 and R-73/10 (Fig. 130) might fare better than others, e.g. R-46/2 (Fig. 130), if accidentally transplanted to a "foreign" environment such as Isla Genovesa. Unless an immigrant flock of mixed sex were involved, we might speculate that none of the songs would be likely to pass the "acid test" of assortative mating (mate selection by a conspecific female) because field observations and laboratory experiments seem to indicate that geospizine song is culturally transmitted not only from "father-to-son" but also from "father-to-daughter" during the father-dependent fledgling stage (see p. 309 ff.). Thus, an autochthonous female probably would tend not to pair with an "exotic" male conspecific, because of her disharmonic fledgling-stimulated auditory template. Of course, factors other than vocal sympathy between sexes may be involved in successful assortative matings, and could emerge as significant determinants under conditions of interisland dislocation (cf. Ratcliffe 1981).

The adaptive relationship between song bandwidth (frequency spread) and the width of the acoustical aperture may be demonstrated further, as follows. The "cactus-finches," *Geospiza scandens* (Isla Santa Cruz) and *Geospiza conirostris* (Isla Española), are very variable in frequency spread (Fig. 130). Coincidentally, the sound-transmission isopleths and the cumulative dB isopleths (Fig. 131) show an energy-efficient acoustical aperture of broad bandwidth, within which there is very little frequency-dependent amplitude disparity with increasing distance from the sound source. Thus, within these frequency limits the songs may vary, and indeed they do, from narrowband to broadband. Whenever the transmission pecularities of a given sound environment permit the nondiscriminant use of higher frequencies over lower frequencies, the songs of the finches almost invariably move into high frequency ranges. On islands where such species are fairly common, as they surely are on islas Santa Cruz and Española, there is greater potential latitude for frequency variation, especially into higher frequencies, with their attendant advantage for sound localization through improved binaural intensity differences (see Table 22). On Isla Genovesa, very little energy is concentrated in what few high frequencies prevail in the songs of *G. conirostris*, and this seems clearly to be due to the very narrow acoustical aperture that is characteristic of this island's vegetation. Where such conditions prevail, song variability in the frequency parameter may give way to increased variability in the temporal pattern (compare song examples of *G. conirostris*, Isla Genovesa with those of *G. scandens*, Isla Santa Cruz, Fig. 130; also compare the songs of *Camarhynchus parvulus* in the coastal and *Scalesia* forest zones of Isla Santa Cruz, Fig. 142). Thus, the principal differences between narrowband songs of *G. conirostris* on Isla Genovesa occur in the temporal realm, as indicated in song pattern B (Fig. 90) and F (Fig. 94).

What emerges from an analysis of these data is a better understanding of the adaptiveness of song to specific environments. Dialects in concordant song environments are efficient in the sense that most of the song energy is concentrated within the acoustical aperture wherein there is no significant frequency-dependent disparity in amplitude loss over a specified distance. In other words, selection may have led to the evolution of songs with structural features that allow transmission over appropriate distances according to the function of the signal and the unique acoustical characteristics of the vegetative environment.

On first consideration it might seem that stabilizing selection on *Geospiza conirostris* song is less intense on Española than on Genovesa, but this is probably not the case. Rather, song variation appears to be operating within a broader acoustical aperture (sound niche) on the former island. Differences in overall frequency-bandwidth between the two island song populations would appear to have little if anything to do with differences in the state of balance between opposing forces of mutation and immigration affecting an increase in variation, and selection affecting a decrease, inasmuch as advertising song in Darwin's finches is culturally transmitted (cf. Grant and Price 1981). Rather, as explained below, song form within a population varies continuously and probably adapts individuals to various portions of the acoustical aperture according to territory size, body size, food availability, and song amplitude, among other things.

Marler (1957) suggested that individual and species distinctive features have been relegated to different regions of the song. In field studies of vocal communication in the spotted towhee (Richards 1978, 1981) and redwing blackbird (Brenowitz 1982), it has been shown that frequencies of the "trill" portion of the respective songs encodes species identity information, and that these same frequencies happen to be those that exhibit optimal sound transmission in the bird's particular breeding habitat. The introductory notes of the song, with their more or less consistent individual variability, are thought to be composed of individual recognition components in the redwing blackbird and "alerting" components in the spotted towhee (see also Shiovitz 1975). However, as indicated by Richards (1981) and Shiovitz (1975), there appears to be a "hierarchy of levels of song recognition" with different components of song serving to identify a singer to species at some distance and close up, and the bird is capable of using different aspects of the redundant information, depending on specific conditions of the transmission field that might distort the sound signal.

Although no experimental work has been done on Darwin's finches to identify functional specialization of song regions and their informational synergistic effects under different sound-transmission environments, it is here suggested that both individual and species-identifying features of advertising song, whatever their structure or location within the song, must be perceived at a distance more or less equal to mean territory breadth. As noted above, the advertising songs of Darwin's finches appear to be structured such that their bandwidths conform to the acoustical apertures of their specific transmission fields, and the amplitudes of the major temporal regions are sufficient to carry the signal to the limits of the territory (see p. 284). In this way, and under average conditions, signal "integrity" is maintained, and this involves the persistence of information on species and individual identities, undistorted by discriminatory (frequency-dependent) degradation of the transmission environment.

Geospizine dialects on islas Genovesa and Wolf compared. The geospizine faunae on islas Genovesa and Wolf are composed of four and three species, respectively (Table 2, Fig. 3). Both islands support resident populations of *Geospiza difficilis, Geospiza magnirostris,* and *Certhidea olivacea* (Figs. 146, 147). Additionally, *Geospiza conirostris* is a permanent resident on Isla Genovesa. Conspecifics on the two islands display marked song dialects (cf. Figs. 135 and 136). A comparison of energy spectra (amplitude distributions) of the songs shows that the largest species, *G. magnirostris*, has a monomodal energy peak at 2.5 kHz on Isla Genovesa, but a trimodal distribution on Isla Wolf at 2.5, 5.0, and 8.0 kHz. A similar shift into higher frequencies occurs in *Geospiza difficilis* where a bimodal distribution of energy occurs at 3.5 and 9.0 kHz on Isla Genovesa, and a trimodal distribution at 4.0, 9.5, and 14.0 kHz on Isla Wolf (cf. Figs. 135 and 136). *Certhidea olivacea*, the smallest species, has a monomodal energy peak at 6.0 kHz on Isla Genovesa, whereas on Isla Wolf there is a bimodal distribution at 5.0 and 7.5 kHz, once again showing a parallel shift to higher frequencies on Isla Wolf.

If we average the energy spectra for the songs of all species of each island (Fig. 134), we may quickly see the general correlation that exists between peak emphasis and the sound-transmission patterns. On Isla Genovesa (Fig. 134B), the summarial distribution of song energy, although quite broad, is nevertheless concentrated at the 2.75 kHz mode, whereas on Isla Wolf (Fig. 134A) the more broadly distributed energy spectrum has four modes, 2.0-2.5, 4.75, 8.5, and 13.0 kHz!

It should be noted that the song samples of *Certhidea olivacea* and *Geospiza magnirostris* are small, a true reflection of the comparative scarcity of these species on the northern mesas of Isla Wolf, to which our study was limited (see Fig. 14A). Because of the rarity of *Geospiza magnirostris*, pairs are not crowded and territories are very widely separated. Song energies are mostly concentrated in the two lower modal frequencies, 2.0 and 5.0 kHz, although a minor "invasion" of the higher frequencies at 8.0 kHz is attempted (Fig. 137). This may reflect the physical limitations of body size that prevent the species from making a more intensive use of the higher frequencies available in the acoustic aperture. *Certhidea* is less rare, and because of its small body size (9g) and the high availability of arthropod prey items, its territories are assumed to be quite small. *Geospiza difficilis* is unquestionably the most abundant geospizine on Isla Wolf where it feeds on the plentiful supply of seeds (e.g. *Alternanthera, Croton,* and *Opuntia*) and duff arthropods, and the seasonally available blood of nesting masked and red-footed boobies (Bowman and Billeb 1965), all of which probably promotes small territories. This, in turn, allows the species to use the broad bandwidth acoustical aperture associated with short-distance sound transmission (Fig. 138), within which a broad range of frequencies suffers no severe differential frequency-dependent attenuation.

Compared to the other islands, the Wolf environment most severely attenuates sound over the entire frequency scale (0.5-10.0 kHz), a fact that can most readily be appreciated by comparing cumulative dB isopleths (Fig. 29). On Isla Wolf a 40-dB loss in sound-pressure level occurs be-and 8.0 kHz at a distance of 100 feet from the sound source! This extraordinary transmission loss may be attributed to the high-density monotypic midget forest of *Croton scouleri* (Fig. 14B). As shown by Hamann (1979), the difference in leaf size and shape of this species is enormous within and between populations. On Wolf its leaves are near maximal size for the species and are probably responsible for much of the transmission loss that characterizes this island.

Although territorial song is most often perceived as a long-distance communication signal, on Wolf it is operating at close range and within an acoustical environment that shows no significant selective disadvantage in singing song punctuated with high frequencies. In fact, by "invading" a high-frequency spectrum in a visually obfuscated environment, the bird may be exploiting the inherent advantage that accrues for binaural localization of sound (Marler 1955; Konishi 1970b, 1973; Wiley and Richards 1978). Data on cumulative dB loss for Isla Wolf (Fig. 134A) would seem to contradict the statement by Richards and Wiley (1980) that "At no time is high frequency (above 8 kHz) advantageous for maximum [transmission] distance." For example, a frequency of 2.5 kHz will travel 300 feet in the Isla Wolf environment and experience approximately the same loss in amplitude as a frequency of about 9.5 kHz traveling the same distance!

The Acoustics Nexus

As noted by Nottebohm (1972), sound production and reception by songbirds are adaptively linked, and one can anticipate that there will be close correspondences between the properties of songs and those of hearing. Data on auditory sensitivity in the canary (Dooling, Mulligan, and Miller 1971), indicate maximum sensitivity at 2.8 kHz and an optimal range between 2.0 and 4.0 kHz. These authors hypothesize that songs will fall in the frequency region for which a songbird has maximum auditory sensitivity. All species of songbird so far studied have rather similar audibility curves (cf. Hienz et al. 1977). If we compare the average energy distribution of all geospizine songs on islas Genovesa and Wolf (Fig. 134), we note that the modal amplitude for Genovesa falls between 2.5. and 3.0 kHz, which is in remarkably good agreement with the maximum sensitivity data of Dooling et al. (1971). However, the same kind of coincidence does not occur for Isla Wolf songs. Are we to assume that conspecifics on Wolf have different hearing sensitivities than on Genovesa? Whatever advantages accrue to the Isla Wolf finches through intensive use of high frequencies in their songs (Table 22), they must surely be founded in the extraordinary acoustical conditions and/or the bountiful food resources affecting territory size that prevail on Isla Wolf.

Body size in birds and other animals is intimately related to various aspects of a species' ecology (Garnett 1981; Roff 1981; Roth 1981), including the structure of advertising song (see below). For example, on Isla Genovesa, the two smaller-sized species, *Certhidea olivacea* (8g) and *Geospiza difficilis* (11g) have much broader bandwidths and higher modal frequencies in their energy spectra than do the two larger-sized species, *G. conirostris* (25g) and *G. magnirostris* (35g).

This picture of adaptive radiation in vocal signals can be explained by interrelating available data on territory size, relative abundance, size of body and vibratory membrane of the syrinx, feeding habits, modal amplitudes, dB levels of songs, and sound transmission in the Genovesa environment (see Fig. 140).

The basic field studies of Abbott, Abbott, and Grant (1977) and Grant and Grant (1980) provide us with data in support of the generalization that the larger-bodied species such as *G. magnirostris* and *G. conirostris* hold larger territories than do the smaller species *G. difficilis* and *Certhidea olivacea* (see Table 21). The only minor exception concerns the order of arrangement of the latter two species (Fig. 140). *Geospiza difficilis* is 38% larger than *Certhidea*, yet holds a territory that is 29% smaller than that of *Certhidea*. Because it is known that insectivorous birds generally have larger territories than herbivorous species of the same weight (Schoener 1968; Harestad and Bunnell 1979) and that on Isla Genovesa *Certhidea* is more insectivorous than *G. difficilis* (Grant and Grant 1980), we may readily reconcile this seeming disparity in territory size.

The detailed anatomical studies of Cutler (1970) have shown that larger species generally have larger internal tympaniform membranes in the syrinx, which basically determines the modal frequency of song amplitude (Figs. 129, 128), with smaller species having higher average modal song frequencies than larger.

Field measurements of dB level of Genovesa songs (Figs. 121-126), and plots of the loudest songs according to body weight (Fig. 141) allow the generalization that songs of larger species are of greater amplitude than those of smaller species, thus permitting greater transmission distance appropriate to their generally larger territory size. But as Morton (1983) has correctly stated, "high source amplitude may be more important to our understanding of the functions and evolution of song than solely as an accouterment to increase propagation." For example, Morton (1983 points out that a larger bird might symbolize its size advantage or aggressive motivation by producing a higher frequency and higher amplitude signal than another bird.

Sound-transmission data for Isla Genovesa (Fig. 134B) clearly indicate that the acoustical aperture best suited for long-range vocal communication occurs between 2.0 and 3.0 kHz. It is significant that the two largest-bodied species, *G. magnirostris* and *G. conirostris*, concentrate more of their song energies in this narrow bandwidth that is characterized by minimal frequency-dependent disparity in amplitude levels between high and low frequencies (cf. Figs. 131 and 137). Furthermore, the effective transmission range of a sound signal can be significantly increased by utilizing a narrow-band FM signal of appropriate center frequency, thereby taking advantage of the greater amount of energy per Herz than is available in a wide-band FM signal. For the two smallest species, *Certhidea olivacea* and *G. difficilis*, with their smaller territories (28% and 49% less, respectively, than the larger species; Table 21), and songs of diminished amplitude, the acoustical apertures best suited to their needs have broader bandwidths and high modal frequencies (cf. Figs. 134, 138, and 139).

From field studies on Isla Genovesa we know dB levels of the advertising songs of the finches, background noise levels of their environments, and the amount of sound transmission loss caused by the vegetation. Transmission data have been adjusted to accommodate for the frequency-dependent auditory sensitivities of a "typical finch." Using these data we can calculate distances from the sound source at which the songs of the different species should be attenuated to a particular level (here selected at 30 dB) above the background noise level (Table 23).

Inasmuch as actual territory sizes of the finches are known (Grant and Grant 1980), we can compare these values with those estimated from data based on our acoustical studies. The comparison shows that all acoustical estimates of territory size fall well within the ranges of real values based on field studies. For example, from Table 23 we can see the following: the acoustical estimate of territory size of *G. magnirostris* is 300 feet. The actual range of territory size is 200 to 383 feet. Similar data for *G. conirostris, G. difficilis* and *Certhidea* are as follows: 300 feet vs. 170-341 feet, 100 feet vs. 72-171 feet, and 150 feet vs. 85-285 feet, respectively.

From this demonstration we may conclude that the use of the terms "long-distance" and "short-distance" communication is relative, and that their significance depends essentially on knowledge of absolute size (diameter) of the species' territory. When discussing signal adaptation we need to know not only the ecologically significant transmission distances involved (which could be greater than the maximal diameter of the territory, as would appear to be necessary according to the "ranging hypothesis" of song function [Morton 1983]), but also the specific pattern of frequency-dependent sound attenuation caused by the vegetation, which, in turn, shapes the acoustical aperture.

Whatever the distance required, natural selection has favored a signal structure capable of transmission with minimal distortion, i.e. "with the best retention of stimulus properties at the preferred communication distance" (Hansen 1979).

Intrapopulational Variation in the Songs of Camarhynchus parvulus

Breeding from the coastal cactus plains through the fog-drip *Scalesia* forest (Figs. 4B, 5, 6) on the south-facing slope of Isla Santa Cruz is the parid-like tree-finch, *Camarhynchus parvulus* (Fig. 1). Although the species exhibits no obvious morphological differentiation throughout this range, its galaxy of song shows a "clinal" shift along the lowland-highland vegetation transect (Lack 1945). Songs heard along the coast are reminiscent of certain vocalizations of *Parus inornatus* (Fig. 40), *Junco oreganus*, and *Spizella passerina* (Fig. 65) of western North America, whereas the highlands songs show some acoustical resemblance to the "chick-a-dee" utterances of *Parus atricapillus* and *P. inornatus* (Figs. 40D, 67, 68), also of western North America. Typical songs of the outer coastal zone (Fig. 65) were never heard in the interior highlands, but an occasional more or less typical song of the *Scalesia* forest zone (Fig. 65, B-430/4) was heard in the coastal zone. At intermediate elevations in the transition zone forest, the songs of *Camarhynchus parvulus* are of intermediate character (Figs. 66, 67, 142B).

An explanation of this rather remarkable song distribution may be found in the nature of sound transmission in the different vegetation zones (Fig. 142). In the outer coastal zone, the songs of *C. parvulus* have a very broad bandwidth (2.5 to 6.5 kHz) with 80-85% of the song energy concentrated around two modal frequencies, 3.25 and 6.25 kHz. Within this bandwidth the maximum disparity in amplitude loss between highest and lowest frequencies is never more than 4 dB, even up to a distance of 300 feet from the sound source (Fig. 143), as is evident from the nearly vertical orientation of contour lines in the cumulative dB isopleth.

In the *Scalesia* forest zone, the amplitude distribution of the songs is no longer bimodal as in the outer coastal zone, but rather monomodal, with an energy peak at 3.25 kHz, and a bandwidth that contains 80-85% of the song energy narrowed to between frequencies of 2.5 and 4.0 kHz (Fig. 142A). As indicated in the cumulative dB isopleth for the *Scalesia* forest zone (Fig. 143), attenuation of sound by branches, twigs, and leaves is more intensive at frequencies above 4 kHz than below this frequency (cf. Embleton 1963; Martens 1980). Dense vegetation has some of the effects of distance because the lower-frequencied sounds are less dampened by vegetative obstructions (Hartshorne 1973). Thus, the overall lowering of the upper limits of both basic and derived songs of *C. parvulus* in the *Scalesia* forest (cf. Figs. 119 and 120) appears to be due to the more severe attenuation of high frequencies by the vegetation and not necessarily to the "need" for escape from the "masking" effects of acoustic reverberations (cf. Richards and Wiley 1980).

Using actual sound-transmission loss figures, which have been adjusted to the auditory sensitivity spectrum of a "typical finch" (Table 24), we may accurately assess frequency-dependent disparities in amplitude for *C. parvulus* songs in concordant and discordant environments.

The typical bimodal song of the outer coastal zone (Fig. 142C) develops progressively more amplitude disparity between its highest and lowest frequencies at a distance of between 50 and 300 feet from the sound source, i.e. 0 dB at 50 feet, 1 dB at 100 feet, 3 dB at 200 feet, and 4 dB at 300 feet. By contrast, the typical monomodal song (Fig. 142A) of the highlands, when projected through the outer coastal zone environment, develops relatively less disparity in amplitude between its highest and lowest frequencies. Maximal disparity of 2 dB is attained at a distance of 300 feet from the sound source.

Although territory size for *C. parvulus* is not known, it is likely, on the basis of what is known about other small-bodied species (Table 23), that its maximal breadth is close to 150 feet in the coastal zone of Isla Santa Cruz. If we assume that such an estimate is close to reality, we may conclude that there is no particular transmission advantage of the highlands song over the coastal song in the outer coastal zone vegetation of Isla Santa Cruz (Table 24), although there may be psychological and other advantages (see Table 22). But why then is the slightly "disadvantaged" bimodal coastal song more commonly heard in the outer coastal zone than the monomodal highlands song? Possibly in the more "permissive" semi-open "edge" environment (Fig. 4B), a two-toned sound signal of alternating high and low notes is a more effective "acoustical flag" or "attention-getter" than is the typically more monotonous signal of the highlands population. While in humans there is a psychological advantage to using a two-parted repetitive sound ("hi-lo") over a continuous wailing sound (siren) for spatial location of emergency vehicles—the latter sound promoting fatigue and adaptation leading to an elevated auditory threshold displacement (Elliott and Fraser 1974)—birds appear to be relatively immune to such "acoustic trauma" (Dooling and Saunders 1974; cf. Pumphrey 1961). The wide-band, high-frequencied "alerting" notes of the coastal dialect (see Fig. 65) are essentially transients or "impact" sounds, with highest frequencies under 8 kHz, which allow the birds to exploit interaural arrival time differences for sound localization (Knudsen 1980). Because of the very short interaural distance (see Table 13) in the finches, high frequencies are inherently better suited than low frequencies for binaural localization of sound using intensity differences at the two ears.

In the *Scalesia* forest of Isla Santa Cruz, the typical monomodal song of *C. parvulus* (Fig. 142A) gradually develops a slight amplitude disparity between highest and lowest frequencies, reaching a maximum of 4 dB at a distance of 300 feet from the sound source (Table 24). By contrast, the bimodal coastal song when projected through the highlands environment acquires a 10-dB amplitude differential between highest and lowest frequencies of the signal at only 100 feet from the sound source, which, we may assume, results in sufficient loss of "intelligibility" within normal territorial limits to put it at a selective disadvantage over the typical concordant song. (Because food resources for *C. parvulus* are probably more abundant and dependable in the humid *Scalesia* forest than in the arid coastal zone, territories are probably smaller in the former habitat).

The fact that the highlands song of *C. parvulus* is well adapted for optimal sound transmission in both the *Scalesia* forest and the coastal lowlands makes it possible, in the absence of philopatry or habitat fidelity, for individuals from the humid interior of Isla Santa Cruz to move into the lower and normally drier regions of the island during years of exceptionally wet conditions, i.e. "El Niño" phenomenon. However, during extended droughts in the lowlands, the reverse movement, if it occurs in this species, brings the typical lowland dialect of *C. parvulus* into the highlands forest where it is not so well disposed to cope with the more restrictive conditions of sound transmission. There is the possibility that should such coastal birds be "bilingual" (see below and Fig. 93), an appropriate adjustment could be made, i.e. highlands mate secured and adequate territory size maintained. Song dialects then might not serve as effective barriers to dispersal (cf. Petrinovitch et al. 1981 and Baker and Mewaldt 1978). The existence of highland and lowland song dialects in *C. parvulus* does not by itself necessarily indicate that dispersal is insufficient to "swamp" the effects of local selection, and therefore too limited to forestall eventual subspeciation.

One of the puzzling aspects of song variation in *C. parvulus*, Isla Santa Cruz, is the condition known as "bilingual" vocalization, documented in the field for at least one individual (Fig. 180D). This bird was recorded singing both bimodal (coastal dialect) and monomodal (*Scalesia* forest dialect) songs in the lower transition zone. This region on Isla Santa Cruz is characterized by an admixture of plant species from higher (humid *Scalesia* forest) and lower (arid coastal) regions, combining environmental features (ecological and acoustical) of each (see Fig. 142B). Bilingualism has been detected so far mainly but not exclusively in subadult males (e.g. *C. parvulus, G. magnirostris* and *G. conirostris*; Figs. 93, 94). Such individuals would seem to have kept all their vocal communication options "open," thereby preadapting themselves to potential occupancy of environments with different acoustical properties and different food availabilities necessitating altered territory sizes. Perhaps such a vocal system would facilitate rapid colonization of locally devastated areas that periodically develop in unstable volcanic island ecosystems.

Source Compensation in Song Amplitude

Because of the nature of sound transmission, i.e. more attenuation, in general, at higher frequencies than at lower frequencies, two potential evolutionary pathways are open to birds: (a) to inject more source-generated energy into the higher frequencies, or (b) to reduce the frequency spread of the signal and concentrate most of the sound energy in lower frequencies. Darwin's finches appear to have exploited both pathways.

The latter pathway has been used most notably by *Camarhynchus parvulus* (see above). The *Scalesia* forest dialect concentrates its sound energies at a modal frequency of 3.25 Hz and with a bandwidth between 2.5 and 4.0 kHz. The coastal dialect concentrates its energy around two modal frequencies, 3.25 and 6.25 kHz, with a bandwidth between 2.5 and 6.5 kHz (Fig. 142). Waser and Waser (1977) report on a comparable evolutionary trend in the calls of tropical forest primates in which long-range vocalizations are structured so as to minimize attenuation losses through use of lower frequency transmission channels (see also Brenowitz 1982).

The former pathway, injection of more energy into higher frequencies, has been used by *Geospiza difficilis* on Isla Genovesa. The song has a bimodal energy distribution (Figs. 125, 138) with song region 4 having a source modal amplitude of approximately 94 dB at 9 kHz, and song regions 1 and 2 having a source modal amplitude of about 75 dB at approximately 3.5 kHz– a difference of 19 dB between modes.

Data on adjusted cumulative dB losses at 9 and 3.5 kHz on Isla Genovesa indicate that at a distance from the sound source of about 150 feet, the difference in amplitude between modes is somewhere between 8 and 15 dB (Table 19), i.e. in fairly good agreement with the 19-dB source modal amplitude difference (above). Apparently, the bird has made a source adjustment in the vocal signal so as to accommodate for the difference in frequency-dependent transmission loss between the two modal frequencies over a distance equal to the territory size of the species (72-171 ft.; Table 23), thereby maintaining the integrity of the *entire* vocal signal amplitude, and, presumably, other features of the signal containing individual and population-specific information.

Richards and Wiley (1978) have suggested that features of song that encode different kinds of information might propagate to different distances. There is some slight evidence in support of this idea from the songs of *Geospiza conirostris*, Isla Genovesa.

As noted (pp. 260 and 277) *Geospiza conirostris* and other species of Darwin's finches are bilingual singers (e.g. song pattern F, Fig. 94), i.e. they may alternate between basic and derived songs. The latter, consisting of song regions 1 to 3, is generally of broader frequency bandwidth and of somewhat greater amplitude than succeeding regions 4 and 5 to which they are joined in full basic song. In general, broad-band songs, with their higher modal frequencies, are associated with shorter transmission fields than are songs of narrow bandwidth and lower modal frequency (cf. Figs. 94, 123-125, 134, and 140; Table 21). This suggests that adult males "fixed" on full basic song may have somewhat larger territories than those "fixed" on derived song, where both song types are sung in the same general habitat. At first glance, data on approximated territory sizes segregated according to song type (Table 26) would seem to suggest that this relationship may indeed be real, but the numerical differences are totally wanting in statistical significance, as was also concluded by B. R. Grant and P. R. Grant (1979). Obviously, much more information is needed, particularly on song amplitude, in order that we may fully evaluate this suggestion. What difference, if any, there might be in the "information content," i.e. individual versus population-specific identity clues, between regions 1 to 3 and 4 to 5 of full basic song, is unknown.

Song Variability in Sympatric Species

A rather widely held notion about song variability in passerines is that environments harboring few species are more "permissive" (i.e. tolerate greater population variation) than environments with numerous closely related species, which are more "restrictive" (i.e. promote species stereotypy). This phenomenon, known as "character displacement," has been attributed to the absence or presence of one or more competitive, ecologically similar species (Lack 1947; Brown and Wilson 1956; Marler 1960; Thorpe and Lade 1961; Armstrong 1963; Mayr 1963; Grant 1966, 1972; Cody 1969, 1974a; Cody and Brown 1970; Hecklenlively 1970; Otte 1974; Latimer 1977; cf. Thielcke 1969a). For example, the songs of chaffinches are said to be "simpler" on Tenerife, Canary Islands (*Fringilla teydea*), where fewer species of songbird live than on the Azores (*F. coelebs*) or European mainland (*F. coelebs*), where many related species occur together. The insular song (Tenerife) is reminiscent of mainland birds raised in acoustical isolation, " . . . as though the circumstances favoring learned elaboration of the mainland song no longer exists in the simpler fauna of the islands" (Marler and Hamilton 1966), or that the ancestral colonizers were vocally immature birds whose song had not yet been fixed by learning and became divergent by chance in isolation (Thielcke 1973) or that the Tenerife songs resemble mainland (Moroccan) songs due to the "founder effect" (Thielcke 1969a). Spectrographic documentation on the songs of the chaffinch assembled by Knecht and Scheer (1968) indicates that Azorian songs are as complex as European song, and in certain areas where canaries are common, chaffinches may adopt some of their songs. Further, in Great Britain, the blue titmouse (*Parus caeruleus*) is sympatric with several other *Parus* species and its repertoire is species-specific, although smaller than on the Canary Islands where it is the only species present and produces a wide variety of distinctive sounds. Lack and Southern (1949) have claimed that on Tenerife the blue titmouse occupies food niches which in western Europe are divided among at least four species of *Parus* (viz. blue, great, coal, and crested titmice). Additionally, the island population has a larger bill than the continental population. According to Latimer (1977), where species live without congeners, more of the genetic potential of the genus may be "realized" and songs become more variable due to the diminished selective pressures exerted by the acoustic environment, i.e. vocal sounds produced by sympatric species.

Recently, Becker, Thielcke, and Wüstenberg (1980) have compared the songs of *P. caerulens* from Tenerife and Central Europe (Spain, Morocco). Their sound spectrograms clearly show that Morocco and Tenerife songs are somewhat similar and differ rather markedly from those of Central Europe and Spain in having a greater variety of notes and interindividual variation. Before one can confidently conclude that the "founder effect" is the cause of the similarity of Moroccan and Tenerifean songs, one must rule out the possibility of "habitat effect," i.e. parallelism due to similarities in vegetation structure (both regions have semiarid climates). To accomplish the latter, quantitative data are required on habitat utilization, sound transmission patterns, and energy spectra of songs, among other things.

Marler (1960) has noted that there is an "exception to the rule" that specific distinctiveness in territorial song is adaptive. When two or more species are in "competition" for the resources of a habitat, it may be advantageous for their utterances to have similarities so that they maintain mutually exclusive territories. Similarities in song serve to partition resources and discourage dysgenic hybridization through repulsion of heterospecific males, just as if they were conspecific males.

In a recent review of examples, Brown (1977) has concluded that important documentation is lacking for most of the supposed cases of character convergence in bird song. See also Murray and Hardy (1981). Let us examine the songs of Darwin's finches for evidence of convergent or divergent character displacement.

Example 1. Sympatric sibling species of Geospiza. Among the six species of *Geospiza*, none shows such striking parallel development of their advertising songs as do *magnirostris, fortis*, and *fuliginosa* in the region about Academy Bay, Isla Santa Cruz (Figs. 36, 37), a condition that is all the more impressive in the light of overall similarity in their plumage, behavior, and bill shape (Table 1, Bowman 1961).

The songs of these species, although quite "similar," are certainly not identical. Their principal differences concern overall duration, rate of delivery (faster in smaller species than in larger species), and modal frequency (larger species having somewhat longer songs and of lower modal frequency than smaller species; see Figs. 36, 49). These average character differences may be a direct consequence of their average body size differences, and their general similarities (parallelisms) may be explained most parsimoniously by assuming that because of their almost identical habitats and partially overlapping territories, their vocalizations are similarly constrained so as to conform to the sound transmission characteristics of their common acoustical environment (Fig. 133B). In other words, there is no evidence for or need to invoke the concept of "character displacement" in order to account for the rather modest vocalization differences between "sibling" or otherwise closely related sympatric species (see also Thielcke 1969).

Example 2. Sympatric species of "tree-inhabiting" finches. Three generically distinct species of finches, *Certhidea olivacea, Camarhynchus parvulus*, and *Cactospiza pallida* coinhabit the interior *Scalesia* forest of Isla Santa Cruz. Their territorial songs are quite similar, although differing in modal frequency, a condition correlated with differences in body size and territory size (Fig. 70). The sound transmission characteristic of their common habitat probably has been the most important selective factor bringing conformity in the overall structure of their songs. In parallelisms, equivalent selective forces act upon organisms having lineages of relatively recent common ancestry and more or less equivalent genetic potential, to produce behaviors that are both homologous and analogous.

Field observations on unmarked individuals suggest that (1) their territories are far from being mutually exclusive; (2) there is little or no overt reaction, such as territorial pursuit, upon hearing or seeing an heterospecific male nearby; and (3) antiphonal singing between sympatric heterospecific males does not occur. In other words, the birds seemingly do not misidentify their heterospecific coinhabitants of the *Scalesia* forest on the basis of singing or other behavior or structural features.

Although it is reasonable to assume that close genetic affinity of the species accounts for some sharing of song parameters, e.g. temporal division of their basic songs (cf. Figs. 93, 94, 101), it probably does not account for much of the parallel structural pattern and energy distribution, which is here assumed to be the result of their mutual occupation of ecologically similar "sound transmission environments."

Example 3. Geographic variation in Certhidea *song.* As yet there are few well-documented cases of bird songs evolving in relation to songs of other birds inhabiting the same region (Otte 1974). Lack (1947) suggested that selection tends to act against much variation when a number of species are interacting with one another, and that relaxation may have resulted in the greater song variation seen in Galapagos finches. The very broad distribution of the warbler-finch, *Certhidea olivacea*, with its different incidence of geospizine sympatry on various islands, provides an opportunity for testing the validity of this hypothesis.

Study of Table 27 reveals some slight correlation between song complexity (distinctiveness) and geospizine species richness. For example, the Santa Cruz dialect (Figs. 81A, 155, 156) shows modest diversity amidst one of the most diverse geospizine avifaunas, whereas the Genovesa dialect (Figs. 82A, 99, 159, 160) shows high diversity amidst one of the least diverse avifaunas. Song parameters for these two island dialects, and also for Isla Española, are shown in Table 31.

What is perhaps most significant is the difference in habitat diversity between the islands. On Isla Santa Cruz *Certhidea* is most abundant in the ecologically uniform dense *Scalesia* forest (Fig. 6), whereas on Isla Genovesa, the species is abundantly distributed in an open, patchy, coastal zone parkland habitat (Fig. 11).

Example 4. Comparison of variability in song bandwidth of Camarhynchus parvulus *in the coastal and* Scalesia *forest zones on the south side of Isla Santa Cruz.* As noted previously (see p. 285 ff.), advertising songs of *C. parvulus* show a considerably greater frequency spread in the patchy vegetation of the arid coastal zone than in the vegetationally uniform *Scalesia* forest zone, with the upper range of frequencies being much higher in the former population than in the latter population.

If one were to expect song distinctiveness, i.e. intraspecific variation in song bandwidth, to be correlated with species diversity, then the *Scalesia* forest population of *C. parvulus* should exhibit greater variation in this ecologically significant song parameter in an environment shared with four other geospizine species (*Camarhynchus psittacula, Certhidea olivacea, Platyspiza crassirostris*, and *Cactospiza pallida*), than does the arid coastal zone population of *C. parvulus* in an environment shared with eight geospizine species (the aforementioned species plus *Geospiza magnirostris, G. fortis, G. fuliginosa*, and *G. scandens*). But such is not the case (cf. Figs. 65, 68, 199, 120, and 142). What may also be significant in this connection is the parallel development of two types of song patterns in the south coastal region of Isla Santa Cruz in sympatric species of arboreal finches, namely, *C. parvulus, C. psittacula*, and *Geospiza scandens* (see Fig. 38).

Example 5. Overall distinctiveness of frequency and amplitude parameters in three species of Geospiza *on different islands.* The songs of *Geospiza magnirostris* (Table 28) on Isla Santa Cruz (where nine species of geospizines reside sympatrically) are more variable in bandwidth and less distinctive as a species (cf. Figs. 36, 37, 49, 52, 53, and 137) than are the songs on Isla Genovesa (where only three species occur). The songs on Genovesa and Wolf are very distinctive (cf. Figs. 52 and 53).

Songs of the cactus-finches, *G. scandens* on Isla Santa Cruz, where nine species reside sympatrically, and the ecologically allied *G. conirostris* on Isla Española, where three species occur, are more variable than they are in *G. conirostris* on Isla Genovesa where four species reside sympatrically (Table 28; Figs. 54, 60, 131).

One can best make ecological "sense" out of these data by considering the selective impact of the acoustical aperture, rather than the vocal environment, on song variability. It is here proposed that the acoustical parameter of the niches occupied by the species is fundamentally more significant in shaping vocal signals than is the diversity of vocal sounds produced by sympatric species. If we assume that each environmental niche generates its own distinctive pattern of sound attenuation (acoustical aperture), then it follows that the narrower the aperture, the greater the song stereotypy in the frequency dimension, and the broader the aperture, the less the song stereotypy. An important corollary of this proposition is that birds that occupy mosaic environments or edge habitats should, as a population, have more variable songs or, as individuals, have larger song repertoires than species inhabiting less patchy environments, if each patch of the mosaic generates a distinctive acoustical aperture (cf. Hunter and Krebs 1979).

Presumably, and solely from an ecological perspective, the advertising songs of birds occupying patchy environments accommodate to the different acoustical properties of each habitat patch in a variety of ways. (1) A species might evolve a continuous polymorphic song population, with each individual singing but one distinctive song that shows moderate qualitative differences from the songs of local conspecifics (e.g. *Geospiza fortis*, Isla Santa Cruz, and *Geospiza conirostris*, Isla Española). The song population may thereby be "sympathetic" to such variable needs as near versus far, individual versus species-specific recognition via song, or small versus large body size, among other things (Fig. 31). (2) A species might evolve a number of different stereotyped and discontinuously variable polymorphic songs, each with its distinctive time, frequency, and amplitude adaptations to the differing acoustical properties of the habitat patches (e.g. *Camarhynchus parvulus*, Isla Santa Cruz, and *Geospiza conirostris*, Isla Genovesa). In order for spatial environmental heterogeneity to maintain vocal polymorphisms, it is assumed that the various environmental conditions (e.g. acoustical apertures) encountered by the species result in a mosaic of contradictory selective regimes (Spieth 1979). (3) Species might also evolve song combining aspects of examples (1) and (2). Such a song is unknown among Darwin's finches but is characteristic of the vocal signals found in a variety of continental species of "edge" birds (Fig. 148), and typical of *Passerella iliaca* and *Chlorura chlorura* (Figs. 149, 150), each with their unique internal structural complexity. The question raised by these examples is whether particular song configurations (e.g. note, syllable, phrase), their duration and frequency of use in a repertoire, bear some direct relationship to the intensity of utilization, or relative abundance of a particular habitat patch for which a song region is acoustically adapted (Fig. 144). Geographic variation in vegetation, acoustical apertures, and habitat patch utilization by the birds, could be reflected in regional structural and programmatic differences in songs (dialects). Presumably, the greater the song diversity, the greater the diversity of interdigitating vegetation patches, and the better the territorial quality. In this regard it is perhaps significant that McGregor, Krebs, and Perrins (1981) have shown that in the British great tit (an edge-inhabiting species), birds having larger song repertoires tend to survive to breed in a second season and are more likely to father heavier offspring that survive to breed.

Just as the foraging niches of Darwin's finches differ according to species, island, and habitat, so do the accompanying acoustical niches differ in their patterns of sound transmission. Whereas feeding structures (bills) show regional adaptive "tuning" to their associated foraging niches (Bowman 1961; Abbott et al. 1977; Boag 1981), song dialects show regionally adaptive "tuning" to their associated acoustical niches. Environmental diversity and intraspecific habitat choice may be responsible for the great variety of vocal phenotypes. There is available to songbirds a great selection of microhabitats in which different song types might be favored (cf. Powell and Taylor 1979).

The Niche-variation Hypothesis of Van Valen (1965)

This proposition states that the extent of morphological variation in a given population results in part from the size of that organism's ecological niche. Although the theory was formulated with structural characters in mind, such as bird bills and trophic appendages (cf. Grant et al. 1976; Grant and Price 1981), and the validity of the theory has been seriously questioned, most recently by Beever (1979), it may similarly be applied to the structure of signals (i.e. frequency bandwidth of advertising song) and with width of "sound niches" (i.e. "acoustical apertures", see p. 277 ff.; also see Hurlbert 1981, for a review of the "niche concept."). When formulated in this way, the niche-variation hypothesis might state that the variability of song bandwidths is directly correlated with the width of the available and "appropriate" acoustical aperture, i.e. "appropriate" with respect to such variables as modal frequency of song and territory size of the species. Thus, species populations using wide acoustical apertures available in the environment should show greater variability in frequency bandwidth of song than populations utilizing narrow apertures. In all cases the width of the acoustical aperture is a function of sound-transmission characteristics of the vegetation composing the species' niche.

Thus, according to the "adaptive variation hypothesis" of Van Valen (1965), there would be no single optimal song phenotype, but rather an array thereof whose individual population variants would have more or less equivalent fitness through differential use of appropriate segments of the environment (i.e. acoustical aperture). In the case of Darwin's finches, this would result in a highly polymorphic song population.

The validity of this concept may be tested in part by examining the correlation between diversity of vegetational and acoustical habitats of species and the widths of acoustical apertures and song bandwidths.

In the three examples presented in Table 29, there is a clear and positive relationship between these four variables, and, not surprisingly, even with bill variability (cf. Grant et al. 1976). Wherever habitat diversity is greatest and foraging niche broadest, variability of bill structure, breadth of song bandwidth, acoustical diversity of habitat, and width of acoustical aperture are also broadest. For example, if we compare *Geospiza conirostris* populations on islas Española and Genovesa, we find that on Española the bill is substantially more variable in length, the habitat (as measured by plant species diversity) is more diverse, the variety of vegetation patches utilized is greater, the breadth of the song bandwidth is greater, the acoustical diversity of the habitat is greater, and the breadth of the acoustical window is greater.

Songbirds of low-latitude oceanic islands tend to be smaller in body size and relatively more abundant in a given area than songbirds with similar ecologies on mainlands (Grant 1965, 1968). On the basis of population size alone, insular species might be expected to present a broader spectrum of vocal variation in a given area simply because of the increased need for individual recognition. Thus, among species of Darwin's finches that are obviously the most abundant on their respective islands (pers. obs.), e.g. *Geospiza fortis* (Isla Santa Cruz), *Geospiza conirostris* (Isla Española), and *Geospiza difficilis* (Isla Wolf), we should find some of the greatest individual variations in song, and this we do (cf. Figs. 31, 55-59, 61B, 62A, respectively). These same populations exhibit the greatest extremes for their species in bill length (Bowman 1961, Table 61). Furthermore, the sympatric distribution of sibling species with their sibling-like songs (e.g. Fig. 36) provides additional evolutionary "justification" for individuality in vocal signals. Possibly the widespread occurrence of basic and derived song patterns in their various forms (cf. Figs. 89-95, 99-103) can be partly attributed to this "need."

Finally, by having songs of various length and of slightly different modal frequency (the latter largely a consequence of body size differences), we may escape the problem of masking and psychological delay, as described by Brémond (1973), who states that a very "noisy" environment arising from a large number of conspecific and heterospecific individuals hinders communication to a degree that depends mainly on the continuous character of the noise. For species of Darwin's finches, there appears to be a margin of safety, derived from frequency and quality discontinuities within songs, sufficiently large to permit the birds to distinguish successfully between each other's vocal signals in all situations, despite human difficulties in doing likewise.

Song Convergence

Mention has already been made of the remarkable similarity in song structure between various groups of Darwin's finches on the Galapagos Islands and their ecological counterparts on continental areas (see Figs. 2, 39-41). For example, "warbler-finches" (*Certhidea olivacea*) sing like New World warblers (family Parulidae); "blackbird-finches" (*Geospiza conirostris* and *G. scandens*) sing like New World blackbirds (family Icteridae); "tit-finches" (species of *Camarhynchus*) sing like New and Old World titmice (family Paridae); ("woodpecker-finches" (species of *Cactospiza*) sing like woodpeckers (family Picidae) and other trunk-foraging species (families Sittidae and Corvidae).

In song convergence, equivalent acoustical selective forces act in sympatry or allopatry upon species of differing genetical potential, so that analogous but not necessarily homologous song behaviors are produced. Convergence in bird songs between very different geographical areas containing genetically different bird faunas suggests that selection has reached optimal solutions in both areas, despite differences in histories, time scale, and genetic origins (Cody 1974b). Insofar as songbird vocalizations are concerned, there is no obvious reason why selective forces should operate in unique ways in isolated systems like the Galapagos, as suggested by Peet (1978) who states that "the more isolated a system, the less likely the eventual adaptive solution to an environmental situation will resemble that found in other parts of the world. Although there is little doubt that volcanic island ecosystems evolved unique environmental conditions, recent studies in Hawaii (Mueller-Dombois 1981) indicate that the ecological principles operating therein appear not to differ from those operating on continental ecosystems. Cody (1974a) has demonstrated that the foliage-insectivorous niche is present in the *Fagus-Acer* forests of north temperate regions (Japan, Denmark, Ohio) and in the *Nothofagus* forests of south temperate regions (New Zealand, Australia, Tasmania, Chile), although occupied by different and distantly related species. It appears that adaptations to titmouse, warbler, woodpecker, and other foraging niches are common to several habitats, and although different species may be involved in different regions, the ecological role remains essentially unchanged (Cody 1974a). Apparently the niche is not confined to a single type of habitat (vegetation), but remains relatively unaltered with minor or even major changes in structure and geographic location. Thus it appears that the niches of avian species showing convergences in their advertising songs offer not only foraging niches with resources of similar kind and location, but probably also acoustical niches with similar sound-transmission characteristics. There is, of course, an obvious need to demonstrate acoustical similarity between Galapagos and continental niches, as well as between various continental niches where song convergences are known to occur (cf. Crowder 1980; Carr and James 1975; see also Figs. 2, 145, 147-150).

Origin and Function of Song Dialects in Darwin's Finches

Differentiation of populations is most likely to occur where environmental factors vary greatly in space, but are relatively stable in time (Levins 1962, 1973; Maynard Smith 1966). As shown in an earlier section of this report, more or less consistent structural differences in certain song populations (dialect) of Darwin's finches are closely correlated with regional differences in their sound-transmission environments and are, therefore, clearly adaptive, i.e. the result of natural selection acting upon learned variations and not the result of "cultural drift" (cf. Andrew 1962; Thielcke 1969a; Lemon 1975; and Bonner 1980). In other words, each major dialect corresponds to a different acoustical habitat (cf. Nottebohm 1975 and Handford 1981).

Darwin's finches appear to show nongenetic mating preferences, i.e. sexual selection based on culturally transmitted song (see p. 315 ff.). Such a behavioral system probably has had a very significant effect upon the "population mechanism" of heritable characters (Cushing 1941). Preferential mating rests on a complex basis involving the interaction of many factors. In the finches, sexual preference based on early song conditioning becomes fixed (imprinted) considerably in advance of sexual maturity, and thereafter remains immutable.

If song learning varies—is not always a precise copy of the parental model—as sometimes is the case in the finches (see Figs. 164, 170) and other songbirds (Lemon 1975; Marler and Mundinger 1971; Kroodsma 1978), natural selection could shape the raw materials of vocal communication to "fit" the environmental transmission field and thereby cause locally adaptive song modalities to develop. Such variations should elicit different behavioral responses and result in some degree of geographic isolation. The greater the regional adaptive differences, the less apt the conditioned young would be to react to vocal stimuli of a cultural group other than its own.

Avian song dialects might arise, therefore, as a result of colonization followed by local adaptation to sound transmission characteristics, which subsequently restrict but do not absolutely prevent gene flow between populations. Since the songs of Darwin's finches are acquired by tradition (see Figs. 169-172) and probably play an important role in assortative mating, therefore dialects could be the initial cause and not a consequence of genic diversity (cf. Curio 1977; Cushing 1941; Konishi 1965; Marler and Tamura 1961; Nottebohm 1969; Nottebohm and Selander

1972). Concomitant reduction in mobility (through sedentary occupation of insular habitats, barrier bound in varying degrees) and strong philopatry (resulting from habitat imprinting in youth; see Lemaire 1977; Löhrl 1959; Petrinovitch, Patterson, Baptista, and Morton 1981) would enhance the opportunity for, but need not necessarily result in, genetic divergence affecting structural and behavioral adaptations for food-getting, among other things (see also Christian 1970; Udvardy 1970; Ford, Parkin and Ewing 1973; Grant and Grant 1980).

The "capacity for learning" that contributes to "teaching" the young to become habituated to their environment results in a rather strict localization of populations, and may cause rapid speciation (Mayr 1974; see also Marler and Mundinger 1971).

Marler (1970) has correctly noted that the employment of learned behavior patterns to accomplish a limited degree of reproductive isolation of local populations may have the valuable advantage of flexibility, so that populations faced with a change in their habitat, or forced to move to a new one (because of environmental catastrophes), could still regain access to the main gene pool of the species by shifting, in the space of a few generations, to another evolutionary adaptive vocal direction. The adaptive significance of such an "open-ended" program is almost axiomatic in notoriously unstable volcanic archipelagoes like the Galapagos.

Several schemes have been proposed to explain the origin of vocal dialects in songbirds, none of which appear to be fully applicable to Darwin's finches. For example, Lemon (1975) assumes that vocal dialects are ecologically nonadaptive or neutral vocal variants resulting from accidents of improper copying of male parental song during youth. Although "miscopying" does occur in geospizines, natural selection probably preserves only those variants that best fit local and transmission characteristics of the vegetation, and quickly rejects (through failure to obtain a conspecific mate) those that are acoustically nonadaptive. In other words, there is a disproportionate disappearance from the population of lineages less vocally adapted. Minor innovations are "tolerated" if they occur within the limits of the acoustical aperture and do not seriously alter species- and population-specific attributes of song. Since Darwin's finches do not seem to require vocal reinforcement of imprinted song in order to develop population-specific definitive song, dispersal of a juvenal bird after about 40 days of age, when song learning appears to be complete, would not necessarily give rise to atypical adult vocalizations (cf. Thielcke 1973). Hansen (1979) postulates that young males (and females?) in the "sensitive period" of song development choose the most clearly heard (nearby) species-specific songs or song elements as a model for copying. Ill-defined (more distant, faintly heard) songs would be difficult to copy and would be eliminated. In the Galapagos, however, many environments have as many as eight closely related coinhabiting species of finch, with varying degrees of territorial overlap (Fig. 3, Table 2). What is more critical for filial transmission of vocal dialects in Darwin's finches is a close social bond generated through parental feeding. Should this bond be accidentally changed, and foster-fathering occur, vocal misimprinting is likely to result (see below).

Song Structure as a Tracer of Species Derivation or Island Source

In the light of numerous examples of interspecific parallelism and intraspecific variability in songs (see Figs. 31, 33-36, 50), it would be hazardous to speculate on the evolutionary origin of any species or population from any other in the archipelago solely on the basis of vocal similarities. Similarly, caution is warranted, for the same reasons, when using bill characters (Swarth 1931; Bowman 1961). One is not likely to find convincing evidence from vocalizations to corroborate the speculation by Lack (1947) that *Camarhynchus pauper* and *C. psittacula* (on Isla Floreana) have resulted from two separate invasions by *C. psittacula*, one originating from Isla Isabela (and giving rise to *C. pauper* on Floreana) and another originating from islas Santa Cruz or Santiago (but giving rise to *C. psittacula* on Floreana).

In the present study, whenever a strange song was first encountered in the field, an immediate effort was made to identify the singer in order to determine if it might be a vagrant from another island, possibly a hybrid, or simply an anomalous vocalist. The songs of species popultions are rarely sufficiently distinctive in structural design to permit their independent use in identifying their island source, except possibly the following: *Geospiza difficilis*, Isla Wolf (special basic song); *G. magnirostris*, Isla Wolf; *G. scandens*, Isla Marchena; *Cactospiza heliobates* (islas Isabela and Fernandina), *Platyspiza crassirostris*, Isla Pinta; and *Certhidea olivacea* (basic and derived songs on islas Santa Cruz, Genovesa, Marchena, Pinta, and Wolf).

Evolutionary Trends in the Songs of Darwin's Finches: General Discussion and Conclusions

Bird songs are a product of compromise (Latimer 1977). As noted previously, evolution has proceeded with certain constraints on frequency and amplitude, as determined by the physical and functional aspects of the syrinx and the auditory mechanism. The acoustical environment has also imposed constraints on the signal structure to be used, depending upon density and dimensions of branches, twigs, and leaves, among other things. Vocal behavior in Darwin's finches is constantly the target of natural selection (cf. Mayr 1974).

One of the principal thrusts of this study has been to demonstrate a direct correlation between the physical properties of vocalizations and their acoustical environments. Essentially we have described patterns of adaptive radiation in the acoustical communication system. Some of these patterns may have arisen in advance of, others concurrently with, patterns of evolutionary divergence in feeding ecology.

Recent reviews of, and research reports on, the physical aspects of sound transmission in the atmosphere (Aylor 1971, 1972a, 1972b; Linskens et al. 1976; Lyon 1973; Marten and Marler 1977; Marten, Quine, and Marler 1977; Martin 1981; Michelsen 1978; Roberts et al. 1979, 1981; Wiley and Richards 1978; Richards and Wiley 1980) have focused attention on acoustics in natural environments, and these have paralleled landmark studies on the ecology of bird song by Chappuis (1971), Jilka and Leisler (1974), and Morton (1970, 1975, 1977).

Only fairly recently have biologists come to realize that vocal communication signals of higher vertebrates are no more free of the pressures of environmental selection or no more "conservative" than many morphological characters (cf. Tembrock 1973).

Homology studies have shown how a rather simple five-parted song (basic) can be transformed into an array of vocalizations that show structural convergences with mainland songs of ecologically equivalent species, belonging to rather diverse groups of continental families of birds. The range of song divergence in Darwin's finches is neither unlimited nor a match for the bounds established by oscine birds as a group. This is due to the rather restricted ecological opportunities available to the finches in their sharply circumscribed oceanic island environments (cf. Bowman 1961).

Although much is still to be learned, we now have a fairly comprehensive understanding of many ecological correlates of variation in avian song structure, and those that relate directly to the situation in Darwin's finches are summarized in Table 30 and below.

Within the distances and the frequency bandwidths wherein most territorial vocalizations of songbirds must function, habitat differences in sound transmission loss are attributable mainly to the structure of vegetation (Embleton 1963; Morton 1970; Bowman 1979). Scattering of sound waves by tree trunks, branches, stems and leaves brings about frequency-dependent differential amplitude attenuation in those frequencies that are abundantly present in the vocal signals of most songbirds.

The "need" for song seems to arise chiefly from two features (Hartshorne 1973): isolation or territoriality, and invisibility of the bird in its habitat. That a bird may sing in a conspicuous position does not necessarily make it conspicuous, if while foraging it is seldom visible to its conspecifics or other species. Much of the time other individuals of its kind will themselves be invisible in vegetation where they will be unable to see very far. Thus their principal means of keeping track of mate or rivals will be hearing vocal signals, and to the extent that a given vegetation affects visibility and differentially attenuates sound according to wavelength, we may expect, and indeed do find, that songs vary in frequency and amplitude modulation, bandwidth, frequency emphasis, and temporal characteristics. In this way natural selection arrives at an optimal signal structure, one that best fits the sound transmission field (Bowman 1979).

We know that geographic variation in territorial songs of the finches (see above and Bowman 1979) and other birds (Hunter and Krebs 1979; Handford 1981) are correlated with geographic variation in vegetation and in some cases with attendant differences in sound transmission spectra. Also, within a particular habitat the songs of species vary in quality, depending upon the vegetation stratum in which the species lives (see Fig. 70), among other things (see Fig. 140). Biomass stratification and life-form vary within and between vegetations (compare coastal vegetation of islas Santa Cruz and Wolf, Figs. 4B and 11, respectively). Darwin's finches differentially use these vegetative strata for foraging, singing, and nesting, depending on specific conditions prevailing on each island (see Bowman 1961; Grant and Grant 1980). As shown in Fig. 130, the arid coastal zone on islas Genovesa, Española and Santa Cruz displays three different acoustical environments, as revealed by dissimilarities in their sound transmission isopleths and visual "transparency" (cf. Figs 11, 9, and 4B-5B, respectively). Conditions such as these have led to dialects and interspecific song parallelisms.

Principal ways in which the songs of Darwin's finches differ from each other concern bandwidth, FM rate, and the percentage of the song that is frequency modulated. Indeed, not a single song of the finches (save the whistle song) is constructed entirely of pure tones (Fig. 146), a condition that correlates with the general shrubby character of the Galapagos vegetation. The relative degree of vegetative openness in which a species lives seems, ultimately, to determine the relative amount of frequency modulation contained in the signal.

A scheme is set forth in Figs. 144 and 145 to illustrate how the nature of the sound environment appears to be correlated with trends in frequency modulation of song. Under conditions of poor visibility, as in dense shrubby vegetation, the songs of Darwin's finches and many North American species (Fig. 147) have a high rate of frequency modulation, with uniform and repetitious notes, syllables and phrases of broad bandwidth. But under conditions of good visibility and vegetative openness, the songs are characterized by a low rate of frequency modulation, variable nonrepetitive notes and syllables of relatively narrow bandwidth. A comparison of selected advertising songs of *Geospiza fortis* and *G. fuliginosa* recorded in brushy coastal zone vegetation of Academy Bay with those recorded in the open parklands coastal zone of south James Bay (Figs. 151-152 and 4A,B) illustrates the effect of vegetative obfuscation on the structure of song signals in Darwin's finches. In the basic song of *Certhidea olivacea* (Fig. 153), the "texture" of the frequency modulation (i.e. fine-grained as in Isla Española and coarser-grained as in Isla Marchena, and differing combinations of each) varies from island to island and may reflect real differences in vegetative structure, such as diameter and density of branches, stems, and leaves.

As suggested by the songs illustrated in Fig. 146, those with marked frequency modulation are generally of greater duration than those that are not. Increased song length in visibly obfuscated environments has the obvious advantage of providing more time for binaural localization of the sound source in the absence of conspicuous visual clues. Under normal conditions such auditory signals are readily located because they contain abrupt changes in frequency (and often amplitude), for each of which binaural intensity and spectral comparisons can be made (Marler 1955; Konishi 1970). Where air turbulence and shadow zone (resulting from heat stratification of air masses) produce unpredictable frequency-dependent degeneration in time and space—a condition commonly afflicting the coastal zone of all islands—frequency-modulated songs will, nevertheless, have enduring temporal characteristics (Morton 1970), and allow for a certain amount of "prediction" of signal identity from hearing but a part of it (Richards and Wiley 1980). In contrast to the view of Morton (1975), Richards and Wiley (1980) claim that birds vocalizing in grassy habitats (as compared to forest habitats) use rapid frequency modulation in their songs because reverberations are less prevalent and therefore their tendency to mask repetitive frequency modulation in vocal signals is reduced.

"Redundancy" resulting from repetition of parts of the signal or the entire signal, or both (Fig. 42B), is one of the characteristic features of the songs of Darwin's finches and animal communication systems in general (Wilson 1975). Dawkins and Krebs (1978) have suggested that signal redundancy is a form of "hypnotic persuasion" on the part of males, the function of which is not to "convey information," but rather to "manipulate" the "motivational state" of others, i.e. repel rival conspecific males and attract potential conspecific females. But the songs of birds, repetitious or otherwise, do indeed contain "information" about individual and species identities (Marler 1960, 1969; Falls 1963; Greenewalt 1968; Emlen 1971b), and they generally do so by means of a constellation of song features (e.g. variation in bandwidth, amplitude, and frequency modulation) none of which, individually, are probably able to substitute for one another (see Peters et al. 1980). These are essentially the same song features that are molded by natural selection to conform to the acoustical requirements of a specific sound-transmission field.

Many species of Darwin's finches, and especially members of the genus *Geospiza*, live in habitats that might best be described as "edge" situations wherein the birds are "obliged" to direct their advertising songs into a variety of interdigitating habitat types (see Figs. 4, 9, 11, 12, 14, 15), each of which has its own distinctive sound-transmission characteristics. It is hypothesized here that differently structured vegetations require differently structured signals in order to achieve effective equivalence in sound penetration. A sound signal composed of a diversity of notes and syllables strung end to end, such as characterizes the five regions of geospizine basic song (Figs. 84-86), allows the bird to "address" almost simultaneously a variety of acoustical niches found within a territory. In "edge" or "patchy" environments, where conspecific territorial males and potential female mates are intermittently shielded from viewing each other as they move about their habitat, a richly polymorphic vocal signal, with diverse notes, syllables and phrases, might better project individual, population- and species-specific information through the acoustical discontinuities of the transmission field. On the average, one might expect that the relative abundance and utilization of different vegetation types composing a species' territory, each with its distinctive acoustical aperture, might correlate fairly well with the relative abundance, duration, bandwidth, modal amplitude and tonal purity of the different notes, syllables and phrases of the vocal signal.

Most songbirds encounter more than one type of sound-niche within their breeding territory. Those occupying fairly nondiverse habitats have the most uniform songs (Fig. 145). The fact that many species of songbirds, other than Darwin's finches, sing more than one song type during the breeding season (e.g. Figs. 45-47; cf. Kroodsma 1981; Martin 1977, 1979; and Morse 1966, 1970), each of which, as in the case of certain parulid warblers, serves a somewhat different function (territoriality, pair-bonding), suggests that the structural differences between songs may be related not only to differences in sound transmission within slightly different sound niches, but also to motivational states.

Working in Panamanian habitats, Morton (1970, 1975) compared the songs of edge-dwelling birds with those of grassland and forest, and he observed that the edge species have both pure tone-like sounds as well as frequency-modulated sounds in nearly equal amounts, whereas forest species predominating in pure tones and grassland species predominated in FM signals (cf. Emlen et al. 1975). Morton also noted that there seemed to be no "optimum" frequency range for sound propagation in "edge" habitats, where acoustical conditions and vegetative structure were also of intermediate character. He concluded, perhaps erroneously, that edge environments lack an ecological basis for selection of bird sounds.

In the Galapagos, intermediate type habitats (e.g. inner coastal and transition zones) on Isla Santa Cruz also show acoustical and vegetative intermediacy between the outer coastal and *Scalesia* forest zones, as do the advertising songs of *Camarhynchus parvulus* (Figs. 65-68, 142).

Perhaps a finer-grained analysis of sound transmission in Panamanian "edge" micro-habitats might reveal an ecological basis for avian song structure described by Morton (1970, 1975).

In North America the ultimate diversity in song is displayed by edge-inhabiting species (Fig. 148). Brilliant songsters such as the fox sparrow (*Passerella iliaca*) and green-tailed towhee (*Chlorura chlorura*), living in sympatry with partially overlapping territories (cf. Cody 1974a), perform bouts of conspecific and heterospecific antiphonal singing (Figs. 148A,B - 150A,B). Vocal bouts reveal repertoires whose individual songs show remarkable internal structural variation involving tonal purity, modal frequency, bandwidth, etc. (cf. Fig. 144). These various songs may serve to "test" the near and far surroundings of its territorial habitat with a suite of acoustical signals. Those most closely matching the transmission spectra of the different sound-niches might elicit the most advantageous responses from conspecific males and/or females, and would be the ones "favored" by the bird. In this way, possibly, geographically variable "theme-dialects" could arise in edge-inhabiting species. The larger and more diverse the repertoire, the greater the likelihood of matching the different sound-niches of the environment. In heterogeneous environments natural selection has the greatest potential for rapid generation of phenetic (= energetic) polymorphisms.

From these considerations it appears that "environmental sources of selection" (Morton 1970), resulting in effective long-distance transmission of song, may often override all other sources of selection in shaping the basic configuration of the vocal signal, even structural-motivational coding (Morton 1977, 1983). The fact that songs of sympatric "edge" birds show parallel construction in the Galapagos (e.g. *Geospiza* spp., Fig. 36), and possibly convergent construction in North America (e.g. *Passerella* and *Chlorura*, etc., Figs. 148-150), should perhaps be considered *prima facie* evidence in support of this phenomenon in birds, other explanations for song repertoires and convergences notwithstanding (e.g. "anti-monotony" principle and "musical enjoyment" hypothesis of Hartshorne [1973] and Krebs [1974], "character displacement" of Grant [1966, 1972] and Cody [1969, 1974a] but see Brown [1977], Murray and Hardy [1981] and Dobkin [1979], "Beau Geste" deceit hypothesis of Krebs [1978], status-signalling hypothesis of Yasukawa [1981], "vocal oratory strategy" of Dawkins and Krebs [1978], "ranging" hypothesis of Morton [1983]; see Krebs and Kroodsma [1980] for a recent review of proposed functions of song).

POPULATION VARIATION IN THE DERIVED SONGS OF *CERTHIDEA OLIVACEA*

Because of the controversial nature of the literature dealing with characteristics and causes of structural and behavioral variability in insular and continental species populations (e.g. Lack and Southern 1949; Van Valen 1965; Partridge and Pring-Mill 1977; Beever 1979; see also p. 290), the variability in advertising songs of *Certhidea olivacea* was studied in selected island populations in order to determine if variation on oceanic islands is of a different magnitude than on continents. Much of the information contained in this section is an updated version of the research of Billeb (1968) and is included here with permission.

Method of Selecting Songs

For measuring frequency/temporal parameters of songs, only continuous recordings of adult individuals were used. The first 10 "derived" songs on a "cut" were selected from populations of *Certhidea olivacea* on islas Genovesa and Española, but for Isla Santa Cruz, all songs were analyzed. In cases where songs on a cut were lacking in definition, 10 of the clearest ones were selected for analysis. When less than 10 songs were available, all were used if of acceptable quality. The number of individuals (and songs) analyzed is as follows: Isla Santa Cruz, 26 (217); Isla Genovesa 14 (132); and Isla Española, 13 (107). Adult male condition was judged on the basis of plumage, i.e. presence of tawny throat feathers (Swarth 1931), skull pneumatization, when bird was collected (Bowman 1961), and precise replication of songs in a cut, i.e. definitive song (Lanyon 1960).

Song Terminology

The terminology of Marler (1961) and Mulligan (1963) has been adapted to the study of *Certhidea* songs. Extensive application of their terms permits a direct comparison to be made between continental species and Darwin's finches.

Note. Any sound producing a continuous trace on the sound spectrograph. The complexity varies greatly. For example, each of the small units composing the syllables in phrase "B" may be termed a note (see Fig. 154).

Syllable. Any group of notes forming a cohesive unit. When syllables are repeated consecutively, they form a *trill* (see Phrase "B" in the song of Española *Certhidea*, Figs. 157-158). A syllable may be equivalent to a phrase (e.g. phrase "C" in the song of Española *Certhidea*, Figs. 157-158); likewise, a single although complex note may be equivalent to a phrase (e.g. phrase "A" in the song of Española *Certhidea*, Fig. 154B).

Phrase. Usually this consists of one or more unrepeated, dissimilar syllables or a series of repeated syllables or trill (e.g. phrases "A" and "C," respectively, in Genovesa *Certhidea*, Figs. 159-160).

Song type. One of the distinctive and frequently uttered songs in an individual's repertoire.

Interval. A silent period between notes, syllables, or phrases.

Measurements

The following frequency characteristics were measured on wide-band spectrograms of all *Certhidea* songs:

Maximal frequency. The highest point reached by a fundamental sound.

Minimal frequency. The lowest point reached by a fundamental sound.

Frequency spread. The range from maximal to minimal frequencies.

The following temporal characteristics were measured on spectrograms of all songs:

Song duration. The length of the song as measured from the beginning of the first trace to the end of the last trace of the fundamental sound.

Phrase duration. The length of the phrase as measured from the beginning of the first trace to the end of the last trace of a fundamental sound in each of the major subdivisions of the song.

Syllable duration. The length of the syllable as measured from the beginning of the first trace to the end of the last trace of a fundamental sound in the subunits comprising phrases and trills.

Interphrase and intersyllable intervals. The duration of the soundless period of time from the ending of the last fundamental sound of one unit to the beginning of the first trace of a fundamental sound of the next succeeding unit of the song. For trills, interval lengths were obtained by averaging the measurements of individual syllables and intersyllable intervals.

The following statistical parameters were determined for populations of songs:

Mean. A "mean of means" (Simpson et al. 1960) was obtained by averaging the means of all the birds of a given population. The reliability of this "short cut" method as compared to the "weighted mean" method was tested using the average minimal frequency of song of the Isla Santa Cruz sample. The result was as follows: weighted mean yielded 1.67 kHz and the mean-of-means yielded 1.68 kHz. The observed difference of 0.01 kHz is well within the limits of accuracy for this measurement. The use of the "mean of means" to exemplify the population may be preferable to selecting a "typical" audiospectrogram for each individual because the former method is probably less subjective and less liable to sampling errors than is the latter method.

Coefficient of variation. This measure represents the variation in a given parameter expressed as a percentage of the mean. Population variation in this index was arrived at by averaging the coefficients for each individual of a population. Nonhomologous variates, e.g. V values for frequency and temporal characteristics, have not been compared (cf. Simpson et al. 1960).

Describing and Comparing Complex Songs

In order to compare the songs of individuals and populations of birds, one must identify measurable units. When the songs of the various populations are variable and often markedly different in their structure (cf. Figs. 157-162), it is desirable to be able to demonstrate some relationship between the units being compared. There would seem to be two possible methods of approaching the analysis. The songs of the populations being compared could be divided into homologous or analogous units. In the case of homologous units, it would be necessary to demonstrate a developmental relationship between the song regions being compared involving studies of song ontogenesis in young birds. This has not been done. In the case of analogous units, the parts being compared should be functionally similar, assuming, in the absence of experimental evidence bearing on the problem, that regional differences do indeed exist. The subdivisions of song resulting from these two methods will not necessarily be the same. Our present lack of understanding of the development and assumed differences in function between temporal components of derived song in *Certhidea olivacea* would seem to restrict our analysis to the measurement of unambiguous parameters, such as total song duration and minimal song frequency, so different are the song dialects of the three populations under consideration (Fig. 154).

In the comparison of analogous (functionally similar) units, two criteria have been used to recognize "natural units." Units may be separated temporally by an interval of sufficient length to make them appear discrete and divorced from adjacent units of song. Or, they may be closely positioned but remain clearly identifiable because of their structure, as revealed by the sound spectrograms. The subdivisions of the song resulting from this kind of analysis are of differing character within the song pattern, and each unit by itself or in combination with adjacent units undoubtedly has functional significance (cf. Marler 1957). When the song pattern is the same in all individuals of a population, it is relatively easy to identify comparable subdivisions. Difficulties arise primarily when one attempts to compare songs from different populations, which often show structural variations of such magnitude that neither homologous nor functionally similar units can be readily recognized (cf. Figs. 81-82).

An hypothetical song, consisting of two major parts (A and B), each of which has many units (1, 2, 3, etc.), might be represented as follows: A(1-2-3-4) B(1′-2′-3′). The units composing part A are different in construction from the units composing part B, and the two parts are separated by an obvious pause. If this basic pattern appears throughout the population, then, presumably, the song is composed of two functionally and developmentally different parts. However, let us assume that a song of the following type is discovered: A(1-2-3) A(4)B(1′-2′-2′). If divided on the basis of homologues, A(4) is related to part one, and the interval separating part one (A) and part two (B) becomes indistinguishable from those intervals separating the other units of the song. If, on the other hand, the song is divided on the basis of functionally related parts, then the second part of the song becomes composed of two syllable types (A and B) and the basic song pattern remains the same. With or without knowledge of song homology, some difficulties remain because even though two units of the song may appear to be derived from the same basic component, there is no reason to assume that the derived units serve the same function as did their precursors. Subdividing song into functionally related parts is probably less subjective than dividing it by presumed homologies since in the former, we are attempting to recognize existing natural divisions of the song, as revealed by the sound spectrograph. When comparing highly divergent songs, it may be possible to recognize overall patterns, even if details of notes and syllables differ greatly. For example, a long introductory phrase in one song population (i.e. phrase "A" in Genovesa *Certhidea*, Figs. 159-160) may be compared to a short introductory phrase in a second population (i.e. phrase "A" in Española *Certhidea*, Figs. 157-158). A song unit following the introductory phrase may be compared in each population whether or not it is repetitive, inasmuch as it is merely the second functional unit of each song (cf. phrase "B" in Genovesa *Certhidea*, Figs. 161-162, in which the syllable is not repetitive in most songs, with phrase "B" in Española *Certhidea*, Figs. 157-158, in which the syllable is consistently repetitive). Those few song types that do not seem to fit the general pattern have been classified arbitrarily by comparing them with the most frequently occurring types. It must be kept in mind that in the statistical comparison of similar temporal and frequency parameters, we may be dealing with units serving different functions in each population.

Comparison is made below between analogous parts of the songs of three island populations of the warbler-finch, *Certhidea olivacea*, viz. *C. o. olivacea* of Isla Santa Cruz, *C. o. cinerascens* of Isla Española and *C. o. mentalis* of Isla Genovesa (see Swarth 1931).

Results

General Description of the Derived Songs of Three Island Populations of Certhidea

Isla Santa Cruz (*C. o. olivacea*), Figs. 155-156. All songs of the 26 birds comprising this population have been divided into two phrases, "A" and "B," with phrase "B" subdivided into as many as seven syllables. The major constituent of phrase "A" is a slurred, vibrato note (frequency-modulated wave train of "buzzy" quality) of variable duration. Phrase "B" usually consists of two similar syllables. The majority of the songs were three-parted, with phrase "B" composed of two similar syllables (see Fig. 155), although four-parted and seven-parted songs are also known (see Fig. 156).

Isla Española (*C. o. cinerascens*), Figs. 157-158. The songs of 13 birds comprising this population sample show considerably less variation in song type than was found in the Santa Cruz population. All songs are multiparted with a trill composing phrase "B." Several songs have a similar syllable construction in phrases "A" and "B" (see Fig. 157), and a few songs have a phrase "C" resembling the last syllable of phrase "B." Phrase "C" was lacking in one song (Fig. 158G). The main variation in Española song is brought about through varying the number of repeated parts in phrase "B," i.e. three to seven syllables.

Isla Genovesa (*C. o. mentalis*), Figs. 159-160. All but a few songs of this race are composed of three phrases in which the number of syllables and their form are quite variable. One song (i.e. Fig. 159B) is composed of only phrase "A," and is assumed to be a shortened version of a full-blown derived song containing three phrases (see Fig. 99A, song 4).

It is evident that the three island populations of *Certhidea* show more or less constant differences in their derived songs (Fig. 154). Española songs have a unique repetitive middle portion (phrase B), Genovesa songs begin with a complex phrase "A" consisting of a number of syllables, and Santa Cruz songs have generally longer frequency-modulated syllables in phrases "A" and "B," with phrase "C" apparently wanting.

In general, the three island dialects of *Certhidea olivacea* may be subjectively distinguished on the basis of phrase "A," although this does not preclude the possibility of separation on any other basis. Further, there is a good deal of sharing of syllable types and note types within each population, a phenomenon most evident in the songs of Española birds, slightly less so in Genovesa birds, and least evident in Santa Cruz birds.

Statistical Comparison of Certhidea *Populations on Islas Santa Cruz, Española and Genovesa*

As indicated in Table 31, frequency characteristics are the least variable of the song parameters measured in the populations. Both maximal and minimal frequencies show considerable overlap between populations (Fig. 161A,B) and are the least variable at the populational level (Table 31), with maximal frequency the least variable at the individual level (Table 32). This situation is probably correlated with ecological aspects of sound transmission on their respective islands (see Figs. 144-145). Thus frequency characteristics contribute to the subspecific distinctiveness of the songs of *Certhidea olivacea.* This then leaves available the temporal characteristics of the song to fulfill the requirements for individual recognition and to contribute to population distinctiveness. The duration of the introductory phrase "A" is the likely choice for the latter since this parameter shows an average coefficient of variation of 35.63, the highest value for any song characteristic measured (see Table 31), and shows no overlap between populations at the 95% confidence level (Fig. 162B), whereas total song duration lacks such distinctiveness. Furthermore, syllables comprising phrase "A" are structurally diverse or complex and virtually nonrepetitive. Coming as it does at the beginning of the song, phrase A may be construed as a "declarative" statement of population identity, and represents the best parameter for distinguishing subjectively (by humans and presumably by birds) and statistically (by humans) the three island populations of *Certhidea.*

It must always be kept in mind, however, that phrases "A, B, and C" of like designation in the three populations are not necessarily homologous and are used here only to represent a serial succession of units within each song type.

Discussion and Conclusions

Character Release versus Altered Acoustical Apertures

When comparing differences in songs of populations on mainlands and islands, it has been assumed by several authors that on islands, the vocal environment is somewhat simplified because of the more limited avifauna (Marler and Hamilton 1966; see also p. 288 ff.). Presumably, this lessens the need for specific distinctiveness in song and, as a result of "character release," the development of more variable song is fostered. As pointed out by Marler (1960), the effect of islands is usually to reverse the song trends in mainland populations of the same species (either from more elaborate to more simple or vice versa) rather than simply to relax the need for stereotypy. This situation is highly significant because it suggests that one of the most critical factors determining the direction of song shift on islands is not so much the relative richness or poorness of the vocal sounds produced by rich or poor avifaunas, but rather the nature of the ecological niche(s) now occupied by the island "species" as a consequence of its geographic displacement from a "harmonic" continental to a "disharmonic" insular milieu. The direction of this shift is unpredictable. Concomitant with an insular niche shift (i.e. to narrower or broader limits) is a vocalization shift to a narrower or broader bandwidth in order to accommodate (a) for differences in acoustical apertures that characterize the different vegetational types or strata, and (b) for differences in the ecological needs of the species that are related to the physical limitations of its altered body size, among other things (see p. 284).

In dealing with the songs of geospizine species, one is faced with a mainland-like series of populations living in vegetationally less varied insular environments, but not necessarily acoustically less varied, with respect to the number of different acoustical niches available (see Table 29). The relative species richness of insular avifaunas is a function of a number of factors such as island area, geological age, topographic diversity, etc. (MacArthur and Wilson 1967). Generalizations regarding the diversity of vocal environments (as opposed to acoustical environments) and their purported effect on song-shifts (character displacement) in insular populations of mainland species need to be better documented by means of song spectrographic and sound-transmission data for specific situations on islands and continental source areas (see pp. 288-291).

The bulk of the Galapagos passerine avifauna consists of closely related species of geospizine finches, and in this sense it is more similar to a mainland avifauna with its greater "harmonic" species diversity than to some insular avifaunas on which most vocalization studies have heretofore been made.

Variation in Insular and Continental Songs Compared

Insular dialects in *Certhidea olivacea* are of the same general magnitude as continental dialects of geographically adjacent populations of *Zonotrichia leucophrys* in western North America (Baptista 1975; Baptista and King 1980).

In order to relate the variability findings on the songs of *Certhidea olivacea* in the Galapagos to similar studies on mainland species of songbirds (Konishi 1965; Brown and Lemon 1979), data on all three island populations of warbler-finch have been grouped (Table 33).

In general, song variation exhibited collectively by *Certhidea olivacea* on islas Santa Cruz, Española and Genovesa is of the same magnitude as that shown by continental songbirds (Table 33). Relative variation in syllable duration and in the intersyllable interval in *Certhidea* is much less than would be expected when compared to mainland species songs, but all of the latter have a "trill" making up a considerable portion of their songs, while this is true only for the Española population of *Certhidea*. The variability in frequency characteristics is in agreement with all of the species except the Oregon Junco, the only bird showing minimal frequency to be less variable than maximal frequency. However, since each of the three populations of *Certhidea* represent what is probably a very strong race (Swarth 1931), if not an incipient species, it may be more meaningful to compare the individual columns of Table 31 with the corresponding figures for the mainland species listed in Table 33. When this is done, it becomes evident that each of the three island populations of *Certhidea olivacea* exhibit *less* variation in song than any of the mainland species populations considered here.

Since all populations contain elements in their songs that fulfill the criteria for easy binaural location in that they are short, repeated notes, covering a wide frequency range (Marler 1959), it can be assumed that the need for sound localization is not a primary cause of one island population differing from another. The effect of difference in habitat upon plumage of *Certhidea* has been pointed out by Bowman (1961). Most of the Isla Santa Cruz population lives year-round in a moist green environment (upper transition and *Scalesia* forest zones of the interior) that is quite different from that occurring on low-lying arid islands such as Española and Genovesa (compare Figs. 6, 9, and 11). On Isla Española during the rainy (breeding) season of the finches, visibility is greatly restricted by foliage. Of the three islands considered here, the most visibly open habitat for *Certhidea* occurs on Isla Genovesa where a parkland-like vegetation of scattered low trees (almost exclusively *Bursera graveolens*), prickly pear thickets, and shrubs (see Fig. 11) restricts visibility to a lesser extent than on Isla Española or the interior forests of Isla Santa Cruz.

Correlated with a lesser degree of visual obfuscation on Isla Genovesa are the increasing duration, syllable diversity, whistle-like quality, and modal frequency of *Certhidea* song. Virtually absent from the Genovesa songs are the broad-band, strongly frequency-modulated syllables so distinctive of the Santa Cruz and some Española songs (cf. Figs. 155-158 and 159-160). Presumably, the broad-band derived song of the Santa Cruz *Certhidea*, like the basic song of *Pinaroloxias* of Cocos Island, provides abundant auditory clues for sound localization in an environment where visual communication is impeded (Fig. 163).

Individual and Species Recognition

In any study of song variation it is important to distinguish, if possible, those parameters that might be useful in species and individual recognition. As pointed out by Marler (1957, 1959, 1960), there is conflicting need for both stereotypy and variability of characters for specific and individual recognition, respectively. The former need will favor a stereotyped song, and the latter a more variable song. Most species seem to have "solved" this "conflict" by relegating different characteristics to different parts of the song. For species recognition to be operative, a particular feature of one species must differ consistently in some manner from the same feature in another species, i.e. the feature must be stereotyped for each species.

Experimental playback studies with altered songs have provided information about the way messages are coded in communication signals. Discrimination of neighbors from strangers has been clearly demonstrated in those birds in which only one song type per male is sung, for example Emlen's work (1971b) with indigo buntings, and Fall's studies (1969) of white-throated sparrows. Experiments with ambiguous results are those involving birds with song repertoires, for example Kroodsma's study (1976b) with song sparrows, Pickstock and Krebs' work (1980) with the chaffinch, and Martin's experiments (1980) on fox sparrows. Thus, the earlier hypothesis of Marler (1957) that individual and species identification messages are coded in different parameters of the song has received partial confirmation.

In *Certhidea olivacea* it has been shown that maximal frequency is the least variable parameter of song at the species, population, and individual levels, suggesting that it could contribute to specific distinctiveness of songs. Although we are not justified in assuming that a feature of song is used in species recognition solely because it is relatively invariant in that species' song (Peters, Searcy, and Marler 1980), if that feature, e.g. maximal frequency, is the least variable of those parameters measured, and if it can be shown that this feature is adaptively involved in communication by the finches (see Fig. 139, Table 22), then our inference as to function is probably correct.

Psychological data indicate that songbirds can detect a smaller change in frequency than other birds with less elaborate vocalizations (Suthers 1978). If we assume that Darwin's finches have as good frequency discrimination as parakeets, cowbirds, and red-winged blackbirds, then they should be able to detect a frequency difference of less than 1%, which is nearly as good as that of man (Dooling and Saunders 1975; Hienz, Sinnott, and Sachs 1977). Such resolving power, which is more acute at lower than at higher frequencies, would allow individuals of one population of *Certhidea* to distinguish individuals of another population, on the average, using frequency differences alone (Table 32).

To establish parameters that might satisfy the needs for individual recognition, it is necessary to determine those features that are variable at the population level (Table 31) yet stereotyped at the individual level (Table 32). Also, if one assumes that island populations of *Certhidea olivacea* are distinct entities with little, if any, present-day interchange (Yang and Patton 1981), then it is clear that different parameters may be used for individual recognition of each population. The duration of the introductory phrase "A" shows considerable variability at the population level (Table 31) yet relatively little variability at the individual level (Table 32) in all *Certhidea* populations. Other possibilities includes syllable duration, and duration of phrase "B" (Isla Genovesa population only). Even so, it must be remembered that more than one factor in the song may contribute to individual recognition, and that *Certhidea olivacea*, specifically, and Darwin's finches in general, probably use an array of song features in species recogition–amplitude, cadence, duration, etc.–with no one feature unable to substitute for another (cf. Peters et al. 1980).

As shown in Table 32, those parts of the song of each population containing repetitive elements (phrase "B" for islas Santa Cruz and Española, and phrase "C" for Isla Genovesa) have the greatest variability at the individual level. Also, the intersyllable intervals for all populations are more variable than are the durations of syllables, indicating that this variable is primarily due to the spacing of the units rather than to their composition. This fact supports the contention that the song types (composition of an individual song) are consistent within each individual over time (see also Fig. 168). Marler and Tamura (1962) found similar kinds of individual variation in white-crowned sparrows in California, which species can be said to have a song similar to *Certhidea* in that it contains both repetitive and single temporal elements.

The intrapopulational similarities in *Certhidea* songs, particularly the sharing of note and syllable types, appear to indicate that filial learning may play an important role in the development of song, and that these populations are indeed distinct. As pointed out by Swarth (1931), the arguments for classifying island populations of *Certhidea olivacea* as races or species are equally valid. Data presented here suggest that isolation may be behavioral as well as spatial (see below).

Although derived songs of only three widely separated populations of *Certhidea* have been statistically analyzed here, preliminary data on other island populations indicate a notable degree of population distinctiveness, not only in derived songs but also in whistle and basic songs (cf. Figs. 80-82).

VOCAL LEARNING IN DARWIN'S FINCHES

Among songbirds, species differences in vocal ontogeny relate mainly to the relative importance of genetic control of motor development over dependence on auditory information from the external environment, including auditory feedback by reference to their own singing (Marler 1970; Nottebohm 1972).

When this study of song evolution in Darwin's finches was begun, there was already a large body of circumstantial evidence implicating a strong environmental component in vocal ontogeny. There were several reports of insular song dialects, parallel song development in sympatric and allopatric species, and interspecific matings judged to be heterospecific on the basis of bill structure but conspecific on the basis of song structure. Consequently, a concerted effort was made to document field examples of mismatings and accompanying song, and to perform a number of controlled vocal learning experiments using the offspring of wild-caught birds held captive in our San Francisco State University aviaries. The results of our laboratory experiments have been integrated with our field observations, as is desirable in such behavioral studies (Eibl-Eibesfeldt and Kramer 1958; Marler and Mundinger 1971).

Methods

Birds representing all species of Darwin's finches, except *Certhidea olivacea* and *Cactospiza heliobates*, were captured by means of mist-nets on various Galapagos and Cocos islands and transported to San Francisco, where they were housed in exterior aviaries for breeding. Nestlings and fledglings were isolated at various ages but none under the age of five days. "Orphaned" nestlings were maintained in a dark-interiored laboratory incubator until about 13 days of age (range 11-15 days), a time usually signalled by spontaneous fledging from the artificial nests as well as by marked changes in food-call structure (Fig. 116). Fledglings were immediately installed individually or in small groups within Fish Sound-Isolation Chambers (Fig. 30 and p. 246). Self-maintenance was attained on the average at 27 days of age (range 20-29 days, Table 16).

In most of the experiments reported below, we deprived the nestling or fledgling of normal parental influence (reinforcement through feeding, singing, etc.) and substituted human attention and often an inanimate sound model (tutor tape recording). Rigorous procedures were developed to forestall "sound contamination" of experimental birds. The sound environment within each chamber was remotely controlled through a built-in speaker system of mediocre quality and over which tutor-tape model recordings, on continuous loop "Cousino" tape cassettes, could be played. These "models" provided a heavy dosage of tutor song, which was broadcast to the bird during the first and last hours of a 12-hour artificial "day." Each 3-minute Cousino loop contained on the average 10 renditions of the song model taken from field recordings. During a 1-hour exposure to the tape loop, a bird would receive about 200 songs over the internal loudspeaker of the sound chamber. The inner atrium of the chamber was equipped with a fairly high-quality microphone (American D-33) through which vocalizations of the experimental birds could be systematically tape recorded.

Results

In this section I describe summarily several of our experiments on captive finches, the results of which illustrate the most salient points concerning vocal learning in the geospizine group (Figs. 164-175; Table 34).

I. Male Song

A. No acoustical isolation during parent-dependent stage

EXPERIMENT 1 (Fig. 164; Table 34): One male Isla Genovesa *Geospiza magnirostris* ("Junior").

Conditions:
a. "Junior" raised to complete independence by both parents under aviary conditions.
b. Exposed to parental male basic song (Fig. 164D) and whistle song from hatching to age 42 days.
c. Housed in sound isolation chamber from age 43 days on.
d. Exposed to tutor song of another conspecific Genovesa male (Fig. 164D) for 30 days, starting at age 150 days.

Results:
a. Whistle song (Fig. 164F) and definitive basic song (Fig. 164C) were developed by ages 256 and 270 days, respectively, both closely resembling father's songs.
b. None of the details of tutor song were learned (Fig. 164E).

Conclusions:
a. Learning of whistle and basic songs of *Geospiza magnirostris* (Genovesa), from and in the presence of the parental male, occurs within the "critical period" of 1-42 days of age.
b. Alteration of "learned" song, or acquisition of a new song, does not occur while in social isolation after age 42 days as a result of exposure to tutor song of a different conspecific male.

B. Acoustical isolation before the end of the parent-dependent nestling stage.

EXPERIMENT 2 (Fig. 165; Table 34): One male Isla Darwin *Geospiza difficilis* ("Perr").

Conditions:
a. "Perr" raised to age 12 days by "wild" parents, during which time he was exposed to parental male basic song (Fig. 165A).
b. Kept in total physical and acoustical isolation from age 13 days on.

Results:
a. Definitive basic song (Fig. 165B) was acquired by age 265 days.
b. Learned song is very similar to parental male song in its modal frequency, (3 kHz) but in other parameters, notably duration and frequency spread, it is approximately twice normal magnitude (cf. Fig. 165A,B).

Conclusion: The fundamental form of the definitive basic song of Darwin *Geospiza difficilis* is learned from the parental male during the first 12 days of nestling life, but some details of song structure, including frequency spread and duration, are not.

EXPERIMENT 3 (Fig. 166; Table 34): One male Isla Genovesa *Geospiza magnirostris* ("J.L.G.").

Conditions:
a. "J.L.G." raised to age 6 days by "wild" parents, during which time he was exposed to parental male song (Fig. 167A).
b. Bird kept in physical and acoustical isolation until age 23 days when he was exposed to tape-recorded tutor song of his father for a period of 46 days.

Results:
a. Subsong at age 153 days (Fig. 166D) composed of two parts, a derived song and an extended version of a poorly formed basic song. This song pattern is similar to Pattern F (Fig. 94), which is typically seen in its definitive form in several species of *Geospiza*.
b. Definitive learned song (Fig. 166C) was developed by age 206 days, but was a poor copy of the father's song, differing from it as follows: lower modal frequency, greater duration, and lack of clear regionalization (i.e. proper distinction between song regions 1, 2, 3, and 4,5 [see Fig. 53]).

Conclusions:
a. The fundamental form of the definitive basic song of Genovesa *Geospiza magnirostris* is imprecisely learned from the parental male during the first six days of nestling life, even when "reinforced" with tape-recorded tutor song of father from age 23 to 69 days. Nevertheless, song definition, such as it is, is probably better than it would have been were there no song reinforcement during the final days of the parent-dependent stage of the

young. (Compare these experimental results with "Eggbird-I," below). Thus, song reinforcement, if late in coming in the dependent stage of the young, is ineffective in improving copy fidelity when the initial song exposure is too brief and/or comes at too early a stage in vocal ontogeny.

b. The tendency for Genovesa *Geospiza magnirostris* to form derived song (Pattern F) without exposure to this pattern may indicate a predisposition (genetic basis) for such structuring in this species and possibly other geospizines as well (see p. 260 ff.).

EXPERIMENT 4 (Fig. 167; Table 34): One male Isla Santa Cruz *Geospiza scandens* ("Eggbird-I").

Conditions: a. "Eggbird-I" raised to age 7 days by parents, during which time he was exposed to parental male basic and whistle songs (Fig. 167K,L).

b. Bird kept in total physical and acoustical isolation from age 8 days on, with no recorded tutor song exposure.

Results: a. Definitive songs developed by age 179 days,

b. Typical whistle song developed (cf. J and L, Fig. 167).

c. Basic song is atypical, consisting of what appears to be a stereotyped form of fledgling food calls, yet differing from the latter in its frequency spread (fledgling calls are of broader bandwidth), and in duration (greater in atypical basic song). Compare H and C, Fig. 167.

d. Two innovative definitive sounds are produced, namely a "double-click" and whistle-like notes (Fig. 167I), with the former making its appearance in subsong at age 68 days, and the latter at age 129 days.

Conclusions: a. Population-specific definitive basic song is not acquired if exposure of young birds to parental male singing occurs only during the first seven days of nestling life.

b. In the absence of acoustical stimulation from parental male or tutor-tape model during the vocally sensitive learning period, the young male, using "auditory feedback," may "capture" certain elements of its self-generated sound environment, e.g. fledgling food calls and early subsong sounds, and "shape" them into innovative, stereotyped, definitive vocalizations.

c. Species-specific whistle song develops its normal definitive form even when exposure to parental male whistle song is restricted to the first seven days of nestling life. On the other hand, it is possible that no exposure whatsoever to parental male whistle song would still result in normal whistle song development, assuming that such development is totally genetically determined, i.e. innate.

EXPERIMENT 5 (Figs. 168-169; Table 34): One male Isla Darwin *Geospiza difficilis* ("Rollo").

Conditions: a. "Rollo" raised to age 3 days by "wild" parents, during which time he was exposed to parental male song (Fig. 168A).

b. Bird kept in physical and acoustical isolation until 27 and 93 days of age, when he was exposed to definitive derived tutor song of Wolf *Geospiza difficilis* for periods lasting 13 and 7 days, respectively.

Results: a. Definitive song is developed by age 166 days and is a nearly perfect copy of the derived tutor song of Wolf *Geospiza difficilis* (cf. F and G, Fig. 169).

b. A poor replication of the basic parental male song is also sounded by "Rollo" as part of the definitive vocal repertoire (cf. F and G, Fig. 169), but it lacks fidelity in modal frequency, frequency modulation bandwidth, and definition of song regions (see Fig. 61A).

c. Details of temporal and frequency parameters of the Wolf *G. difficilis* song copied by "Rollo" partially "faded" within two years of definitive acquisition, although most aspects of the song persisted for many years.

Conclusions: a. Racial dialects in *Geospiza difficilis* may be cross-culturally transmitted, and the "sensitive period" for some degree of learning of "foreign" persists beyond the parent-dependent fledgling stage.

b. Song learning can occur in *G. difficilis* solely by means of auditory tuning and in the total absence of a real or surrogate adult.

c. Significant differences in meter and bandwidth between concordant (Isla Darwin) and discordant (Isla Wolf) song dialects in *G. difficilis* seem not to impede song learning, but may affect long-term song retention.

d. Isla Darwin *G. difficilis* is capable of learning more than one definitive song, even when one of the songs is of a discordant (heterosubspecific) type.

EXPERIMENT 6 (Figs. 170-171; Table 34): Two male *Geospiza difficilis*, "George" (Isla Darwin and "Nureyev" (Isla Wolf).

Conditions: a. "George" and "Nureyev" raised separately by their respective parents to the same age (12-13 days), after which they were maintained together for 99 days in the same sound isolation chamber.

b. Between 33 and 94 days of age, while housed together and subsong singing had just begun, the birds were simultaneously exposed to the same heterospecific tutor-tape song.

c. After age 114 days, "George" and "Nureyev" were separated, each in his own isolation chamber.

Results: a. By age 144 days and 245 days for "George" and "Nureyev" respectively, the birds developed rather gross copies of their respective definitive male parent's song, i.e. for "George," Darwin "basic" song; for "Nureyev," Wolf "derived" and "special basic" songs (cf. D and F, Fig. 170; A, B, and E, Fig. 171).

b. Differences between definitive copies and original parental male songs relate to details of regional definition (cf. D and F, Fig. 170), frequency modulation (cf. A and B, Fig. 171), modal frequency, and song duration.

c. Both "George" and "Nureyev" developed poor imitations of the tutor-tape model of *Camarhynchus parvulus* (compare E and G, Fig. 170, and C and D, Fig. 171), but "George" was better able than "Nureyev" to duplicate the staccato-like character of its syllables, and to "crystallize" them more quickly, i.e. 192 versus 278 days.

d. "Nureyev" was remarkably successful at duplicating the high whistle note distinctive of region 5 of the special basic song of Wolf *G. difficilis* (Figs. 62A, 171A), but less successful in constructing the wide-band FM signal of region 4. Although song regions 3 and 4 are distinguished in Fig. 171E, the order of presentation of region 5 is incorrect (it precedes region 3 instead of following region 4). Typical whistle song (Fig. 43) did not appear in the repertoire of "Nureyev" (it is unknown in adult male Wolf birds), but its absence from the repertoire of "George" is abnormal since the bird was exposed to it during the first 12 days of nestling life. Possibly its absence is a sampling artifact of our monitoring system.

Conclusions: a. In *Geospiza difficilis* the gross aspects of song are learned from the parental males during the first 12 days of nestling life.

b. Song learning may continue beyond the parent-dependent stage and include totally new components acquired solely through hearing tutor-tape song.

c. *G. difficilis* may learn singularly different heterospecific song as readily as it does typical conspecific song.

II. Female Song

Previous workers familiar with the breeding habits of Darwin's finches (Snodgrass and Heller 1904; Gifford 1919; Lack 1945, 1947; Orr 1945) failed to notice or comment upon the fact made known to us through this study, that both subadult and adult females approaching ovulation and egg-laying pass through a period of vocalization, during which they produce sounds resembling male subsong (cf. Figs. 172, 175 with Figs. 167, 171). This behavior was discovered when hand-reared birds, which were assumed to be males in subsong, spontaneously laid eggs in their sound chambers! At about the same time it was noted that certain adult females would spontaneously sing subsong. Such black-beaked, brown-plumaged adult females were found to possess a tumid brood-patch on the belly (see Table 36).

These findings have prompted us to reinterpret some earlier field observations on subsong vocalizing by non-black-plumaged, black-beaked geospizines. It cannot be assumed that birds so marked or behaved are males. In the absence of other information, we now know that phenotypically and vocally, subadult/adult females cannot absolutely be distinguished from subadult males.

Song-learning experiments with female finches are reported below.

EXPERIMENT 1 (Fig. 172; Table 34): One female Isla Genovesa *Geospiza magnirostris* ("Thor").

Conditions:
a. "Thor" was raised to age 9 days by parents, during which time she was exposed to parental male basic song (Fig. 164D).
b. She was kept in physical and acoustical isolation from age 10 days until age 31 days, followed by 62 days (age 32 to 93 days) of exposure to tutor-tape song of Isla Santa Cruz *Geospiza magnirostris* (Fig. 172, lower right).

Results:
a. "Thor" laid one egg in sound chamber at age 177 days.
b. Voluminous subsong was recorded at age 179 days. (Presumably, bird was singing for some time before our monitors detected it.)
c. One subsong figure vaguely resembles the parental male song (compare Figs. 172, lower left, and 164D), while another more closely resembles the Isla Santa Cruz tutor song (compare Fig. 172, middle right and lower right figures). The terminal portion of the Santa Cruz tutor song imitation is composed of two whistle frequencies about 1 kHz apart. In most of the Santa Cruz definitive male songs of *Geospiza magnirostris*, the frequency separation is less, resulting in "beating" of the two oscillators (see Figs 36, 88B).

Conclusions:
a. First-year female Genovesa *G. magnirostris* spontaneously sing subsong at the time of egg-laying, if not earlier.
b. Some subsong sounds appear to be nascent forms of the parental male song or the tutor-tape model of *Geospiza magnirostris.*
c. Young females, like young males, apparently "pay attention to" (memorize) typical male vocal signals in their sound environments.
c. Since the "copy" of the tutor-tape song is better defined than that of the parental male song, the "sharper" reproduction may be due to:
   (i) greater learning sensitivity in the post-parent-dependent stage as compared to the prefledging stage, and/or
   (ii) a "heavier" dose of tutor-tape model song than of parental male song.

Thus, the apparent absence of selective learning of the population-specific song over the foreign dialect song could be due to an artifact of the experimental conditions.

EXPERIMENT 2 (Fig. 173; Table 34): One female Isla Española *Geospiza conirostris* ("Snodgrass").

Conditions:
a. "Snodgrass" was aviary-raised by her parents to the postfledging stage (age 31 days), during which time she was exposed to parental male basic song (Fig. 173D).
b. Bird kept in physical and acoustical isolation from age 32 days on, without recorded tutor song.

Results:
a. "Snodgrass" spontaneously laid one egg at age 284 days.
b. Spontaneous subsong was first detected at age 205 days (79 days before laying of first egg [Fig. 173A]). Subsong is characterized by great diversity

of signal structure and frequency spread, with some sounds resembling song regions 3, 4, and 5, of parental male song (Fig. 173D; cf. Fig. 84C). Wingfield and Farner (1978) have shown that in a migratory population of the white-crowned sparrow in western North America, maximal levels of plasma testosterone in both males and females are coincident with maximal gonadal weights, defense of territory courtship and nesting activity, and probably induce sexual and territorial behavior in both sexes. Possibly, in species of Darwin's finches, singing by females preparatory to egg-laying is likewise induced by high levels of testosterone. Certainly, injections of high doses of testosterone into a mature captive *Geospiza magnirostris* were followed by intense singing (see Experiment 4 below and Fig. 175).

c. Subsong at age 263 days–21 days before laying of first egg–is more uniformly structured, with slight variations on the "theme" that appeared in less stable form at age 205 days (cf. A and B, Fig. 173).

d. Eight days after laying of first egg, subsong had subsided and typical call notes of this species were all that remained (Fig. 173C).

Conclusions: a. First-year female Isla Española *G. conirostris* may spontaneously sing subsong as much as 79 days before egg-laying (at age 205 days).

b. As time for egg-laying approaches, subsong becomes more structured and stable, resembling what is termed "rehearsed" song in males (Lanyon 1960). See Fig. 173B.

c. The principal song form of "Snodgrass" at 21 days before egg-laying is remotely similar to the parent male song (cf. B and D, Fig. 123).

d. Shortly after egg-laying (8 days), subsong subsides and gives way to typical call notes. The close association of changes in vocal behavior and reproductive behavior suggests that both are under the influence of sex hormone(s). Probably the ovary produces androgens when mature (see Kern and King 1972), which stimulates song production.

EXPERIMENT 3 (Fig. 174A, Table 34): One female Isla Wolf *Geospiza difficilis* ("Duncan").

Conditions: a. "Duncan" was raised to age 8 days by parents, during which time she was exposed to parental male "derived" and "special basic" songs (Fig. 174E).

b. Bird kept in physical and acoustical isolation from age 9 days on, except for exposure to definitive song of *Geospiza fuliginosa* (Isla Española) via recorded tutor-tape model for five days at age 30-34 days.

Results: a. Singing was induced four days after testosterone propionate injection at age 153 days (Fig. 174A).

b. At age 160 days (11 days after hormone treatment), subsong was more structured and bore a fair resemblance in timing and overall structure to heterospecific tutor song (Fig. 174B,C).

c. Modal frequency of Duncan's subsong was about 1 kHz higher than the tutor-tape model song.

d. Only a remote resemblance developed between definitive derived and special basic songs of parental male in one or two song figures, i.e. compare last song figure in Fig. 174A,B with father's song in Fig. 174E.

Conclusions: a. Testosterone propionate induces subsong in female *Geospiza difficilis* at age 153-160 days.

b. Exposure to parental male songs during first eight days of nestling life is insufficient for full selective vocal imprinting to take place.

c. Five days of exposure to tutor tape recording of heterospecific *Geospiza* song at age 30-35 days is sufficiently long to permit a fair imitation thereof to develop.

EXPERIMENT 4 (Fig. 175): Vocalizations in a captive wild adult female Isla Genovesa *Geospiza magnirostris* ("006") under hormonal regimes associated with (a) normal brood patch development, and (b) under the influence of testosterone propionate.

Conditions:
a. A fully black-beaked, brown-plumaged, adult female *G. magnirostris*, captured on Isla Genovesa, was maintained in an open wire cage in a laboratory where she was occasionally exposed to call notes of nestlings, fledglings, and some juvenal subsong of Darwin's finches used in sound isolation experiments.
b. Occasionally, "006" was exposed to the sound of a manual typewriter, which stimulated the bird to sing. Presumably there was a resemblance to the impact sounds of raindrops (cf. Orr 1945).
c. The presence of a brood patch on "006" on June 21, 1968 was associated with spontaneous singing (Fig. 175A,B).
d. About eight months later, on February 10, 1969, when the brood patch and subsong singing had faded, "006" was injected with testosterone propionate (0.5 ml. of Schering "Oreton" containing approximately 12.5 mg. of propionic acid ester of testosterone in sesame oil solution).

Results:
a. Under the natural hormonal regime associated with the presence of a brood patch, "006" sang highly variable subsong (Fig. 175A,B).
b. Loss of the brood patch was associated with loss of subsong singing.
c. Some vocalizations appearing three days after testosterone treatment resembled naturally occurring "whistle" subsong of male *Geospiza* in both quality and frequency spread, i.e. 8-14 kHz (cf. Figs. 118 and 175C,D) and derived song of Isla Genovesa *G. magnirostris* (cf. Figs. 166B and 175E).
d. Other vocalizations induced by testosterone resembled early subsong figures of male *G. magnirostris* (e.g. those of "Junior," which are not illustrated in Fig. 164).
e. All testosterone-related vocalizations disappeared as the synthetic hormone effect wore off.

Conclusions:
a. Subsong vocalizations are associated with the presence of a brood patch in an adult female Genovesa *G. magnirostris*.
b. Under the influence of testosterone an adult female *G. magnirostris* may sing whistle and derived songs whose forms are similar to subsong verions of the same songs sung by male conspecifics from the same island source.
c. Subsong in an adult female *G. magnirostris* is due, presumably, to ovarian androgen synthesis associated with the onset of an endogeneous cycle (Hohn and Cheng 1967; Kern and King 1972). Biochemical transformation of androgen to estrogen is facilitated by their structural similarity (Turner 1966; Larsson 1979). Prolactin is known to induce brood patch formation in songbirds (Bailey 1952).
d. Subsong collapses with the waning of testosterone propionate levels (cf. De Voogd and Nottebohm 1981).

Function of Female "Subsong" in Darwin's Finches

Female subsong was heard from four species of captive *Geospiza*, namely, *magnirostris, conirostris, scandens* and *difficilis*. Circumstantial evidence from field observations indicate that female subsong also occurs in the wild in *Cactospiza pallida, Camarhynchus parvulus, Certhidea olivacea* and *Pinaroloxias inornata.* From these observations it is concluded that most female geospizines sing subsong with the onset of their first reproductive season, and probably with each ovarian recrudescence thereafter.

Vocal ontogenetic studies in Darwin's finches have indicated a close cause-and-effect relationship between approaching ovulation/egg-deposition and maximal subsong singing (Figs. 172, 173). Although female subsong may be an incidental "by-product" of her reproductive physiology, and an imperfect but recognizable copy of her parental male or tutor male song, it could increase the probability of successfully attracting a conspecific mate (Kern and King 1972) by signalling her reproductive readiness, and thereby ensure reproductive isolation between species and populations (see below for exceptions).

Mate attraction and pair-bonding. In most continental situations one of the functions of *male* advertising song is reputedly for species (and mate) recognition by conspecific males (and females). But this end cannot always be readily and invariably served, as in the Galapagos under conditions of high-density sympatry, by species showing marked similarities in song, courtship behavior, and body structure (Table 1). Under such circumstances, fidelity of conspecific recognition might be increased, and the probability of dysgenic hybridization decreased, by *reciprocal recognition* of key elements in the songs of conspecific males and females. On continents a combination of vocal and visual behaviors is effective in reducing interspecific pairings (Dilger 1956; Stein 1958, 1963; Lanyon 1960; Hinde 1959). In the absence of obvious and persistent species differences in the songs of some species of finch, Lack (1947) suggested that species may recognize each other by their bill size and shape, and so keep segregated. Preliminary experiments using stuffed specimens (Lack 1945, 1947) indicated that *Geospiza fuliginosa* could correctly distinguish members of its own group from those of the larger-sized *Geospiza fortis* by means of beak differences. Conspecific identification was presumed to occur when two birds "face off" and sometimes manipulate each other's bill. The latter behavior is of rare occurrence in the field and the aviary, to judge from my own experience in looking specifically for it over a 20-year period! When something akin to "billing" behavior was observed, it seemed to occur not in the context of species identification, but rather in conspecific and heterospecific male-to-male encounters in group feeding situations.

Thus, although subtle interspecific differences in patterns, modal amplitudes, and duration of songs often appear to be sufficiently distinctive to permit correct conspecific identification to be made, it remains to be demonstrated that, in most cases, interspecific differences in body structure and nonvocal behavior provide *all* the clues necessary for species recognition, even though such features may sometimes be no less variable than vocal attributes. Recently, Ratcliffe (1981) has studied species recognition in the field and has found that in all species of *Geospiza*, visual cues are used extensively.

Reproductive readiness. But how does a female finch approaching reproductive readiness indicate her physiological state to a prospective male mate and thereby initiate pair-bond formation? A singing male may cause such a female to enter his territory where he must be able to quickly identify her sex and species. How does the male distinguish between a female finch in song from a subadult female-plumaged male in subsong? Probably other behavioral features are utilized, notably, the nonaggressive stance of a receptive female, versus an aggressive stance, with or without "billing," of a subadult male. A singing female may be more attractive to a reproductively ready male than one that is silent, especially if the vocalizing female sings conspecific subsong, or otherwise behaves in a distinctively female manner.

Female subsong, signalling reproductive preparedness, may be a redundant behavior in regions where climatic conditions are less variable or extreme than in the Galapagos. But the vagaries of the Galapagos rainy season (Grant and Boag 1980) might confer a selective advantage on those birds that can most quickly procure a mate (facilitated by female subsong?) and reproduce in environments where the annual cycle of rainfall and resulting food resources are predictably irregular (cf. Downhower 1978).

Reproductive isolation. Female singing may facilitate conspecific pairing in populations composed of bewildering arrays of look-alikes, sing-alikes, and otherwise behave-alikes, if male and female recognize conspecific mates by their own kind of vocalizations.

Under reasonably controlled conditions in our aviaries, our frequent inability to induce pair bonding between single males and females of different island populations of the same species may have been due to mismatched song dialects. We experienced a similar difficulty in efforts to mate different island "species" of Galapagos mockingbirds (Bowman and Carter 1971). In all such examples, indications of reproductive readiness were fully in evidence, i.e. in the male, nest-building, definitive advertising song, fully black colored bill, full adult plumage, large cloacal protuberance; in the female, curiosity in the male-built nest, subsong singing, fully black bill, developing brood patch, participation in courtship feeding by the male. For example, a "wild" adult female *Geospiza magnirostris*, Isla Wolf, could not be induced to mate with a "wild" adult male of the same species from Isla Genovesa, even when she was under the influence of high levels of injected testosterone propionate, and like the male, showed all the normal signs of breeding preparedness. Advertising songs typical of these two island populations are distinctively different (see Fig. 53).

Our greatest success in breeding captive finches was realized with wild-caught paired individuals.

Clearly, vigorous (controlled) experimental studies in laboratory and field are called for if we are to better understand the significance of female singing in Darwin's finches.

Persistence of Individual Distinctiveness in Geospizine Song

Do individual male song patterns change over the years? The anwer to this question appears to be "no," and is based on evidence from song recordings of unmarked free-living individuals made years apart, and on long-lived captive birds. For example, songs of *Certhidea olivacea* and *Camarhynchus parvulus*, recorded in the field at intervals of three and seven years, respectively, in the same restricted area of *Scalesia* forest of Isla Santa Cruz, appear to be identical, and, presumably, were sung by the same individuals (Fig. 176A,C). Also, a fully black male *Geospiza scandens*, recorded in song on Isla Santa Cruz in 1963, was held captive in San Francisco until its death of natural causes in 1980. Songs recorded 17 years apart are virtually identical (Fig. 176B).

The only documented "change" in individual geospizine song that is known to be age-related is that of a hand-reared experimental bird, "Rollo," (Isla Darwin *Geospiza difficilis*). Twelve months after "misimprinting" on the song dialect of *G. difficilis*, Isla Wolf, its song showed evidence of "fading" of details (see Fig. 169F,H).

All available evidence, therefore, indicates that individual male geospizine song is durable, i.e. immutable throughout the life of the individual. This characteristic, in conjunction with long life and philopatry (McGregor 1980), so typical of songbirds on oceanic islands (cf. Berger 1980), encourages the development of persistent localized song dialects in Darwin's finches.

Unusual Songs of Darwin's Finches

Among the thousands of geospizine songs recorded in the field, a few are grossly aberrant and wanting in species-specific characteristics. Additionally, there are examples of birds singing heterospecific song, and one significant example of an intergeneric hybrid singing typical derived song of both parental species! Most, if not all, examples of atypical vocalizations are probably the result of "misimprinting" of song during the first six weeks of life.

One such bird was a full-plumaged male *Geospiza fortis* whose song had a plosive transient start followed by a 1-second-long, loud clear monotonous whistle with a modal frequency of 1.75 kHz (Fig. 177A). This unique vocalization is not a stereotyped true whistle song by virtue of its low uniform frequency. The absence of significant regional subdivisions makes it impossible to homologize it with other known *G. fortis* vocalizations. The closest parallel is to be found in the definitive subsongs of various experimental females (Fig. 177B,C). Some of these vocalizations may also include harmonically and nonharmonically related frequencies, but the fundamental, similar in frequency and purity if not in duration to that of the female subsong of the similar-sized *G. conirostris* (Fig. 177B), is probably a significant ontogenetic marker.

One possible "scenario" of song ontogenesis that might account for the strange *G. fortis* songs calls for the loss of the male parent during the early nestling stage. In our San Francisco State University aviaries, we have seen a female successfully rear her young from nestling stage to self-maintenance in the complete absence of the male parent. If, while the female is administering parental care, she enters into a new reproductive cycle, dependent male progeny would face exposure to their mother's subsong and possibly imprint upon it, resulting in a stereotyped definitive song similar to that shown in Fig. 177A.

Although Lack (1945) indicated that the role of feeding fledglings was entirely the responsibility of the male, this was not our experience with aviary captives, nor was it Orr's (1945). In fact, a female was often an active partner with the male in caring for nestlings and fledglings. Females feed fledglings in all five *Geospiza* species on islas Genovesa and Daphne Major (pers. comm. from P. R. Grant). Orr (1945) also noted that on several occasions females were seen to feed young while incubating a new clutch of eggs, and sometimes this behavior would continue to within a day or so of the hatching of the successive brood. Such a situation might, theoretically, lead to misimprinting on female subsong by the dependent young.

In the field near Academy Bay, Isla Santa Cruz, I have observed a family of fledgling *G. fuliginosa* being attended only by an adult female. During two hours of almost continuous observation, no male helper appeared on the scene. Thus, most of the conditions necessary for song learning via imprinting on maternal subsong have been observed in nature or in captivity, and, collectively, give some support for the proposed developmental sequence of female-like subsong in males.

Misimprinting of Male Song in Darwin's Finches

Interspecific matings. Among the curious behaviors for which Darwin's finches are noteworthy is the singing by certain males of heterospecific song (cf. Beebe 1926). We have documented this phenomenon on the islands of Española, Santa Cruz, and Santa Fe.

(1) *Geospiza fuliginosa*, Isla Española (Fig. 178). A fully black-plumaged territorial male *G. fuliginosa*, in the company of a presumed female *Certhidea olivacea*, sang typical derived song of the local *Certhidea* dialect (Fig. 169B). The nest of *G. fuliginosa* was without eggs.

(2) *Geospiza fuliginosa*, Isla Santa Fé (Fig. 179). Perched beside its nest, a fully black-plumaged *G. fuliginosa* was recorded singing typical basic song of *Geospiza scandens* (Fig. 170B). His singing attracted a female *G. scandens*. Both birds were observed carrying nesting material.

(3) *Geospiza fortis*, Isla Santa Cruz (Fig. 180). A male *Geospiza fortis* with a few black feathers on its head (i.e. plumage category 5 of Bowman 1961) was recorded singing basic song of *Geospiza scandens* (Fig. 180B). A nest was under construction in an *Opuntia* cactus, and on one occasion both the male *fortis* and the female *scandens* were seen to enter the nest cavity together. Presumably, the birds were mated. Between bouts of singing typical *G. scandens*-like basic song, the *G. fortis* male chased fully black-plumaged *G. scandens* from his territory. The "misimprinted" *G. fortis* showed no reaction to playback of his own recorded song.

Several features of these interspecific relationships should be noted.

(a) Heterospecific song of the male closely matched, in energy distribution and frequency spread, the species-specific male song of the population to which his female mate belonged.

(b) The male in such interspecific pairings is not always the larger (heavier) sex. For example, if we apply body weight data for Santa Cruz birds (Fig. 49) to other island populations of the same species, we find the following relations: on Isla Santa Fe, male *G. fuliginosa* (14 g) is smaller than female *G. scandens* (23 g); on Isla Santa Cruz, male *G. fortis* (25 g) is approximately the same size as female *G. scandens* (23 g) from the same island; and on Isla Española, male *G. fuliginosa* (14 g) is larger than female *Certhidea olivacea*.

(c) Differences between normal species-specific song and atypical heterospecific song of the male range from modest (Fig. 179) to great (Figs. 178, 180).

(d) Interspecific differences in bill shape between male and female range from modest (Fig.

180) to great (Figs. 178, 179).

(e) There is no evidence indicating that progeny resulted from any of these interspecific matings. However, in all cases, except the Isla Española example, both sexes were known to be involved in nesting activity.

Interspecific hybridization. It has long been known that morphological boundaries between species of Darwin's finches appear to be labile. Ranges and means of linear dimensions of bills, tarsi, and wings differ from island to island, and on islands where two or more sibling species occur in sympatry, overlap in several parameters may occur (see Swarth 1931; Lack 1947; Bowman 1961). Overlap in behavior, including feeding (Snodgrass 1902; Lack 1945; Bowman 1961, 1963; Grant et al. 1976; Abbott et al. 1977; Smith et al. 1979), singing (Snodgrass and Heller 1904; Gifford 1919; Beebe 1926; Lack 1945; Bowman 1979) and courting (Lack 1945; Orr 1945), is appreciable. Some authors (Rothschild and Hartert 1899) felt obliged to combine all geospizines into one genus, *Geospiza*, and Swarth (1931) suggested that one could "argue for the specific identity of all the forms concerned (from *Geospiza* to *Certhidea*), to regard them all as only subspecifically separate." Lowe (1936) even went so far as to propose that Galapagos finches represent one grand "hybrid swarm." Whereas Beebe (1924) gives the impression that hybridization is a common phenomenon in Galapagos finches, Lack (1945) thinks that it has played a very minor role in speciation.

The widespread occurrence (on at least eight islands) of "freak" specimens of intermediate character between two species (see Lack 1945 and his Table 32 for a summary) suggests that interspecific hybridization occasionally occurs. The last author to treat certain hybrid individuals as new species was Swarth (1929), who, for example, on the basis of two specimens from Isla Floreana, described a new tree-finch, which he named "*Camarhynchus conjunctus*," but which Lack (1947) concluded to be of hybrid origin between *Certhidea olivacea* and *Camarhynchus parvulus*, because of the intermediacy of its characters. New data described below provides rather convincing evidence that Swarth's "new species" is almost surely of intergeneric hybrid origin, and furthermore, that such hybrids may be fertile.

In 1957, a very cautious local naturalist, Alf Kastdalen, who at that time had already spent over 20 years in residence on Isla Santa Cruz, told this writer of having seen a finch that appeared to be intermediate in bill shape between *Certhidea olivacea* and *Camarhynchus parvulus*. The sighting was made in the lower transition forest north of Academy Bay. In the same general area in 1968, James L. Gulledge and the writer recorded a small finch singing derived song typical of *Camarhynchus parvulus*. As we pursued the bird for additional recordings, it suddenly switched vocalizations and sang typical derived song of *Certhidea olivacea* (Fig. 181A). This "bilingual" male was followed to its nest where we discovered its mate, a typical female *Camarhynchus parvulus* with three nestlings. Both adult birds were collected and when comparison was made with museum specimens, the male was found to match closely the intermediate condition of both type specimens of "*Camarhynchus conjunctus*" from Isla Floreana, and the female was found to be typical of *Camarhynchus parvulus* specimens of the same sex from Isla Santa Cruz (Table 38; Fig. 182).

Like the two "*Camarhynchus conjunctus*" taken on Isla Floreana (Swarth 1931), our Santa Cruz bird was a male in breeding condition. Thus, on the basis of the evidence presented above, it is concluded that interspecific hybrids between *Certhidea olivacea* and *Camarhynchus parvulus* can be fertile. What is not so immediately apparent is the origin of the "bilingual behavior" of the hybrid.

Interspecific and interracial hybrids have been produced in our aviaries (Table 37), but none of these survived long enough to test their fertility. On Isla Daphne Major, several hybridizations between *Geospiza fortis* males and *Geospiza fuliginosa* females have been documented (Boag 1981), but no information is yet available on the fertility of the hybrids.

The following features of "*Camarhynchus conjunctus*" are of special interest.

(1) "Bilingual" singing is typical of most geospizine species (*Pinaroloxias inornatus, Cactospiza heliobates*, and *Platyspiza crassirostris* excepted); in addition to whistle song, they sing basic, special basic, and derived song (see Figs. 45-47; 93-96).

(2) A bilingual *Camarhynchus parvulus* was recorded singing both basic and derived songs three days earlier and in the same general area where "*Camarhynchus conjunctus*" was discovered (Fig. 181D).

(3) "*C. conjunctus*" sang derived song of *Camarhynchus parvulus* more frequently than *Certhidea olivacea* derived song, and the latter was sung mostly in the vicinity of the nest.

(4) The "mixed" song of "*C. conjunctus*" provoked singing reactions from nearby individuals of both *Camarhynchus parvulus* and *Certhidea olivacea* (cf. Lemaire 1977).

(5) The basic song of Isla Santa Cruz *C. parvulus* sometimes parallels rather closely the derived song of *Certhidea olivacea* (cf. Figs. 33K,L and 70).

(6) "*C. conjunctus*" did not sing any songs resembling *Certhidea olivacea* basic, or *C. parvulus* special basic (cf. Figs. 64A, 96, and 181A), or the whistle song of either parental species (Figs. 64, 109). Our attention to the vocalizations of the hybrid was of sufficient focus and duration that these songs should have been heard and recorded had they been given.

(7) Average body weights of *C. parvulus* and *C. olivacea* from Isla Santa Cruz are 13 and 9 grams, respectively. On the basis of our aviary experiments (Table 37), and field observations of interspecific matings (Figs. 178-181), the larger species in such crosses is not always of the male sex.

(8) In spite of all the biological information at hand, it is not possible to determine which of the two possible parental crosses have yielded the "*Camarhynchus conjunctus*" hybrid (see Fig. 182A). The matter can only be resolved through careful long-term field and aviary studies, a research program with formidable practical difficulties, requiring much patience and skill (Lanyon 1979).

Importance of Song in Species Recognition

Lack (1945) was of the opinion that because of song overlap among geospizines, song could not be of fundamental importance in keeping these species apart. However, all the evidence now available from field and laboratory studies suggests that normal positive assortative (selective) mating in species of Darwin's finches is mediated predominantly, if not entirely, by advertising song. When male song of one species is misappropriated by a male of another species, as a result of foster fathering, the first consequence upon the approach of the mating season is heterospecific pairing, followed in some cases by interspecific hybridization.

The following sequence of events is proposed as a reasonably parsimonious explanation of misimprinting of song and interspecific hybridization in Darwin's finches. It presupposes that on the basis of the imprinting paternal song, a female preferentially selects a mate whose advertising song most closely matches her own learned "template." It also suggests that the male likewise shows some preferential selection of a female whose subsong not only indicates a physiological preparedness for breeding, but also shows some degree of matching his own territorial vocalizations. Evidence in support of the four stages is as follows:

STAGE 1. Parent-dependent fledgling is accidentally separated from its family group, thereby terminating song learning from its parental male. The orphan associates with a nearby heterospecific family group and develops a close social bond as a result of foster-parent feeding. Feeding reinforcement helps to insure adoption of the foster father's advertising song.

EVIDENCE FOR STAGE 1. There are several field observations on mixed species fledgling groups being attended by parents of only one species. Gifford (1919) saw two fledgling *G. fuliginosa* begging a *Geospiza fortis* adult (sex unspecified) to feed them. Lack (1945) noted that as soon as fledging occurs, the young geospizine tends to give food-begging posture at any moving bird, including any species of Darwin's finch that happens to come near. Young *G. fuliginosa* were seen to posture at an adult *G. magnirostris*, also vice versa, and young *G. scandens* were seen to posture at both. This writer observed two fledgling *G. fuliginosa* following a female *G. scandens* while begging to be fed. Moore (1980) saw a *G. fuliginosa* fledgling in company with two *G. scandens* fledglings being fed by an adult *G. scandens* (sex unspecified).

The ease with which heterospecific young are "adopted" by adult males is perhaps traceable to the remarkable interspecific uniformity in fledgling food calls (Fig. 116) and accompanying display (wings outstretched and quivered, or sometimes waved unilaterally) and their similarity to the calls and displays of adult females during courtship feeding. Such behavior almost invariably attracts an adult male, and often stimulates his singing.

STAGE 2. At sexual maturity the ex-orphan sings one or two songs, namely, the conspecific male song and/or the heterospecific foster male song. The fidelity of learned songs is a function of the length of exposure and the time at which it is presented to the young during its "sensitive" learning period.

EVIDENCE FOR STAGE 2. The results of song-learning experiments with "Rollo" indicate that an orphaned nestling can learn foster tutor song well, and even sing a poor imitation of its parental male song to which it was exposed for only eight days (see Fig. 165). "George" and "Nureyev" sang poor imitations of both parental male song (to which they were exposed during their entire nestling stage) and foster heterospecific tutor-tape song under the experimental conditions provided (see Figs. 170-171). Presumably, misimprinted heterospecific songs of free-living finches are the result of early exposure to a foster male parent (Figs. 178-181).

STAGE 3. Accidental appropriation (learning) of heterospecific song results in a breakdown of the principal ethological barrier to nonassortative mating. Breaching of the "sound barrier" results in interspecific matings between individuals differing in genetic lineage as reflected in discordant structure and behavior, but now excluding vocal behavior. This situation is different from that described by Emlen et al. (1975) for lazuli and indigo buntings, in which males singing mixed songs were correctly mated to females of their own species. The females must have made the appropriate choice of a male mate on the basis of some visual clues. By contrast, in Darwin's finches structural differences seem not to be overly significant in species recognition (the claim of Lack 1945, regarding the function of "billing," notwithstanding; see p. 312), or at least they seem not to be used to the same extent as in other species. This, of course, is not too surprising, in view of the notorious interspecific overlapping of characteristics (see Table 1). In both sexes, imprinting on certain essential features of the song of the conspecific attendant male parent during the "sensitive" period in youth normally provides the basis for the evolutionary continuity of the taxa through assortative mating, i.e. female selection of a mate singing song that matches her own vocal imprint because it elicits the strongest mating response (cf. Searcy and Marler 1981 and Baker et 1982).

EVIDENCE FOR STAGE 3. Examples in nature of heterospecific pairings are illustrated in Figs. 178-180, in which the male's song is "conspecific" with the female's bill structure and numerous other features of her biology (see Table 1).

Our failure to produce significant numbers of hybrids among our wild-caught finches, despite concerted attempts to do so (Table 37), may well have been due to the fact that assortative mating, based on female preference for a "compatible" song type, could not be fulfilled under our captive conditions.

STAGE 4. Progeny resulting from interspecific hybridization are intermediate in structure (bill) and behavior (two songs; presumably one of the paternal father and the other of the stepfather), and may be fertile.

EVIDENCE FOR STAGE 4. "*Camarhynchus conjunctus*" (Isla Santa Cruz) is clearly a hybrid between *Camarhynchus parvulus* and *Certhidea olivacea* (see Table 38, Fig. 182A). Other presumed hybrids are listed by Lack (1947). Song-learning experiments nos. 5 ("Rollo") and 6 ("George" and "Nureyev") suggest that two song types can be learned, namely, the paternal male and stepfather male songs. Fertility of interspecific hybrids is indicated by progeny from a backcross (Fig. 182B).

Discussion and Conclusions

These findings would seem to underline the claim of Alexander (1969) that nearly every intensive effort at hybridization in vertebrates has revealed widespread interfertility among congeneric species and supports the idea that sterility does not necessarily occur before secondary contact between populations in order for them to remain separate. Vocal differences between sympatric, synchronous, closely related species are seemingly sufficient to enable both males and females to distinguish their own conspecifics. In Darwin's finches, vocal signals may be more species-specific than any other aspect of the mating sequence probably because they represent the earliest sexually significant encounter between the sexes. According to Alexander (1969), behavioral phenotypic differences, if available to selection, will always be more efficient isolators in terms of conserving time and energy, because they operate before morphological or physiological differences.

Vocal learning plays an important role in the acquisition of normal adult song in Darwin's finches, and it may be the principal means by which reproductive isolation of populations occurs (cf. Cushing 1941). Field observations and laboratory experimentation strongly suggest that population-specific characteristics of advertising song, including pitch, pattern, tempo, and timbre, are learned in youth from singing adult males with which a social bond has been established. Like the bullfinch, *Pyrrhula pyrrhula* (Nicolai 1959), zebra finch, *Taeniopygia guttata* (Immelmann 1969), and white-crowned sparrow, *Zonotrichia leucophrys* (Marler and Tamura 1964), and parasitic indigo birds (Nicolai 1964; Payne 1973, 1980), Darwin's finches imitate the songs of the male with which the youngster established a "care-bond," be it father or foster father. In the wild the social bond determines the "correct" model to be copied, but in the laboratory, young Darwin's finches are capable of learning songs of birds with which they have had no social interaction during the most sensitive time within the critical learning period, i.e birds can imitate song heard over a loudspeaker in social isolation. As in the white-crowned sparrow (Marler 1970), in Darwin's finches there is no "enduring bond" between parent and young; rather parental dependency of young does not extend much beyond 35-40 days of age under experimental conditions. Downhower (1978) has reported that males of *Geospiza fuliginosa* and *G. conirostris* (both on Isla Española) stay with and care for the fledglings up to two weeks after they have left the nest. On the basis of our experience with experimental birds, fledging occurs, on the average, at age 13 days. Thus, in the wild fledgling independence is attained at age of 37 days. On islas Genovesa and Daphne Major, *Geospiza* fledglings have become independent of parents at 36-47 days after hatching (pers. comm. from P. R. Grant). Based on over 50 experiments on song learning in Darwin's finches (not all of which have been reported here), the "sensitive period" during which exposure to parental male and its song or to recorded song played over a loudspeaker results in a good imitation, occurs from about 10 to 40 days of age. It should be noted that in our experiments it was impossible to eliminate the possibility of learning (hearing) in the egg and up to about six days of nestling life. Perfect copying can occur without the need for subsequent extrinsic vocal or social reinforcement. Marler (1970) reports a similar sensitive period in white-crowned sparrows, namely 10 to 50 days of age, and 10 to 40 days of age for swamp sparrows (Marler and Peters 1981, 1982). In Darwin's finches, lack of exposure to a model song during the critical period results in first-year males singing only stereotyped fledgling food calls and peculiar innovative sounds unknown in any wild population.

Exposure to model song before 7 days of age or after 40 days of age results in little or no learning of the essential components, i.e. the sensitive period for song learning is age-dependent in most, if not all, Darwin's finches. (Whether the use of live tutors would have prolonged the sensitive period is unknown, although improbable. See Baptista and Morton 1981). Exposure of nestling birds to male song up to 12 days of age has a significant effect on song learning, that is, the bird acquired most of the essential elements of song. It should be noted that there is a marked change in the attentiveness of the parental male toward the young as the end of the nestling stage approaches. Working with aviary captives, Orr (1945) observed that by the time the young are ready to fledge, the male has assumed most of the nesting duties, but the female also continued in the work, although not as vigorously as the male (cf. Lack 1945). Downhower (1978) discovered that the intensity of male advertising song, which had diminished from a high prenesting level to a low level during brooding and early nestling stages, picked up shortly before nestlings were about to fledge and parental male care increased. Not only are social stimuli unessential for vocal imprinting to occur (i.e. auditory stimulation without associative visual and tactile stimulation), but also in experimental situations, heterospecific and "heteroracial" song models were learned almost as precisely as conspecific and "conracial" ones. The finches seemed to show no marked species-specific perceptual predisposition in their choice of model for learning. In our laboratory experiments, however, we did not have a "controlled choice situation" in which the fledgling was provided with both conspecific and heterospecific songs during the critical learning period. (Such an experiment was performed, but due to unforeseen circumstances, the young were lost before definitive song was sung.) In the wild, heterospecific song is occasionally learned in all its details. Marler and Peters (1977) have shown that the congeneric swamp and song sparrows of the eastern United States show marked differences in their selectivity of each other's song during vocal ontogeny. Among west coast races of white-crowned sparrows, young males exposed to dialects atypical of their regional population do learn ("misimprint" on) "foreign" songs if exposed to them in nature during the acoustically sensitive learning stage of their juvenal life (Baptista 1974, 1975; Baptista and Morton 1981). Marler (1970) found that under experimental conditions "song-sensitive" white-crowns did not learn the songs of other species normally occurring in their natural environment, i.e. white-crowned sparrows are selective in their song imitations (cf. Peters, Searcy and Marler 1980). However, L. F. Baptista (pers. comm.) has successfully tape-tutored white-crowned sparrows with junco song.

In Darwin's finches, conspecific advertising song, once imprinted, endures for the life of the individual, and this may be upwards of 15 years or more, based on longevity records of our aviary captives. In some cases, such as birds with misimprinted songs, there may be some loss of details by two years of age, but the essential components of the song remain intact for much longer periods of time.

Although experimental proof is available only for certain basic and derived songs, it is here assumed that population-specific patterns of all song types, excluding whistle songs, are learned by the youngster from the attendant paternal or foster-male parent. (The environmental/genetic determinants of whistle song are still unknown.) In species like the white-crowned sparrow (Marler 1970) and Darwin's finches, the "auditory template" (Konishi and Nottebohm 1969) may be construed, as it is by Dawkins and Krebs (1978), to be a kind of tape recording registered in the bird's nervous system as a result of hearing its conspecific song early in life (during the sensitive imprinting period). At a later period, when the young bird learns the motor patterns of song through "matching" (via subsong and rehearsed song) of its "recorded" song with that produced through neuromotor activation of the syringeal musculature, the template then functions as a complex "reinforcer."

We have not been able to determine an "innate" predisposition of the young geospizine to learn conspecific song, but we do not conclude from this that a genetic component is wanting (cf. Immelmann 1969). Nottebohm (1972) has suggested that in certain song-learning situations there is a "loosening of genetic control over motor development and an increasing dependence on auditory information." Darwin's finches appear to be an ultimate example of this phenomenon. The "improvisation" that we see in the diversification of song patterns in Darwin's finches is probably not without "genetic guidelines" (all derived songs are traceable to presumed genetically determined homologous units of the five-parted "basic song pattern"). Hence, species-specific songs remain in the absence of genetically based programs for each particular song type (cf. Marler and Tamura 1964; Marler and Mundinger 1971). The great "open program" (Mayr 1974) of vocal diversity in Darwin's finches, cast in a setting of pattern uniformity, suggests that maximal relaxation of genetic control (i.e. motor specification) and maximal development of auditory specification (through cultural evolution) has occurred in the vocal ontogeny of Darwin's finches. This condition seems to have facilitated rapid prolific speciation, and vocal behavior appears to be an important, if not the principal, species- and population-isolating barrier. In those cases where we have some information on hybridization and interspecific matings, it seems likely that normal conspecific song imprinting failed to occur. This has resulted in the disruption of the normal pattern of assortative mating, which leads to the development of a "filial" song dialect in populations.

There is no evidence to suggest that the cause of hybridization in Darwin's finches is the breakdown of habitat barriers separating species, since populations are largely sympatric in the Galapagos, with little or no evidence of interspecific territoriality (cf. Parkes 1951; Sibley 1957).

Female geospizines sing a form of subsong as the time for breeding approaches. These vocalizations reveal some of the rudiments of population-specific songs of the parental male from which she learned them (cf. Kern and King 1972). Kroodsma (1976a), Searcy et al. (1981), and Searcy and Marler (1981) have demonstrated in canaries, swamp sparrows, and song sparrows, respectively, that females are very attentive to various attributes of male song. If it is correct to assume that males are "aggressive sexual advertisers" and females "careful comparison shoppers" (Barish 1977), with the female showing a preference for males with a song dialect matching that from the area where she was raised, then male song could serve as a strong psychological attractant to unpaired females of similar genetic background (Marler 1957), thereby promoting the formation of song dialects (cf. Petrinovitch et al. 1981; Baker 1975a,b; Baker and Mewaldt 1978). Female fidelity in pairing with males that sing conspecific dialect may help to explain certain local and infrequent mixed species matings, despite sometimes marked differences in bills and plumages of their mates. (For a review of song parameters implicated in species recognition in birds, see Peters, Searcy, and Marler 1980).

Normally in Darwin's finches, species distinctiveness appears to be encouraged, if not principally maintained, by an invisible vocal barrier (cf. Lack 1947). Whereas among many continental species of songbirds visual as well as auditory stimuli are generally considered to be determinants of social attraction, with visual stimuli playing an important role in the maintenance of social group cohesion (Delsaut and Roy 1980), in Darwin's finches, the visual stimuli may be less important because of the apparently weak or totally wanting species distinctiveness in nonvocal courtship displays, certain bill anatomy, and karyotype. Interspecific hybrids may be fertile, as in the case of "*Camarhynchus conjunctus*" on Isla Santa Cruz. Presumably, backcrossing of the hybrid was facilitated by the ability of the hybrid to sing typical species-specific population dialect of its mate (cf. Lanyon 1966).

Our experimental studies on song learning have shown that timely substitution of paternal song with foster paternal song during the "vocally impressionable" fledgling stage of development can lead to "bilingual" singing and heterospecific pairing, and thereby begin the "psychological breakdown" of interspecific barriers, which the normal pattern of vocal behavior serves to forestall.

The high degree of intrapopulational variability in bill dimensions of *Geospiza fortis* at Academy Bay, Isla Santa Cruz (see Bowman 1961, Table 61) has prompted some authors (Lowe 1930, 1936; Lack 1947, 1969) to suggest that limited interspecific hybridization has occurred. Recently it has been shown that the sympatric sibling species of *Geospiza fuliginosa* and *G. fortis* at Academy Bay and James Bay (Isla Santiago) display more genic similarity to each other than either does to conspecific populations on other islands (Yang and Patton 1981). Vocalization studies also indicate that song variability within populations of *G. fortis* at Academy and James bays (Figs. 31 and 50, respectively) is greater than interisland variability (Fig. 32). In view of the reports of mixed fledgling groups of *G. fuliginosa* and *G. fortis*, which species are abundantly sympatric on several islands (Table 2), and the numerous "intermediate and freak specimens" (hybrids?) involving these same species (Lack 1947, Table 32), and the ease with which territorial song can be misimprinted interspecifically, the breeding biology of these species merits much closer scrutiny for direct field evidence of hybridization and subsequent genic introgression.

The genetic significance of a moderate degree of hybridization in insular groups is that it tends to encourage heterozygosity, permitting evolutionary flexibility despite loss of genetic contact with mainland relatives and fairly small land area (Carlquist 1974). In the face of catastrophic population reduction during extended droughts and concomitant dwindling of vegetated land area following periods of volcanic eruption, an heterozygous group may be better equipped to survive recurring "genetic constriction" of its gene pool (cf. Rattenbury 1962), and retain overall balance in its ecological adaptiveness.

Yang and Patton (1981) and Polans (this volume) have clearly demonstrated that the geospizines form a tightly knit assemblage of taxa, which share a high degree of overall genetic similarity. Indeed, they found that in species of ground-finch (*Geospiza*) for which they had good sample sizes from several islands, the amount of interspecific differentiation was not different from the degree of intraspecific variation, a condition which prompted them to suggest the possibility of limited interspecific hybridization. Heterospecific matings of the kinds described above lend support to this idea (fostered by others on the basis of bill structure; see Lowe 1930, 1936; Lack 1947, 1969).

Whatever the genetic advantages of hybridization may be for Darwin's finches in their insular setting, the integrity of the vocal signal remains intact, since there is no "blending" of songs (e.g. "*Camarhynchus conjunctus,*" Fig. 182). In Darwin's finches, energetic adaptations of songs have supplanted most, but not all, ancestral genetic adaptations. Presumably, learned dialects can develop quickly in the wild and remain homogeneous, even in the presence of substantial genetic variability affecting other aspects of the species' evolutionary success (Bonner 1980; Cavalli-Sforza and Feldman 1981; Nottebohm 1972; Wilson 1976; Yang and Patton 1981). Such a scheme is evolutionarily adaptive in the unstable environment that characterizes the volcanic island ecosystem. Mutual responsiveness of males and females to each other's singing of regionally generated vocal dialects, in conjunction with learned local habitat recognition (cf. Lemaire 1977), presumably increases the likelihood that males and females will settle in the same general area and habitat in which they were raised, and discourages major nonadaptive wanderings (Löhrl 1959). In other words, through faithful imprinting, female vocal preferences and population habitat preferences (philopatry), assortative matings would be fostered (cf. Mulligan and Verner 1971; Lemon 1975; Baptista 1977). As long as the level of copying precision is maintained, characteristics of song will be sufficiently consistent within the species for new individuals to associate with conspecifics. Large changes in the characteristics of the song might limit an individual's ability to secure a mate, whereas small changes could likely exist and spread throughout the species population if they are adaptive (Shiovitz 1975).

It should be pointed out that, in addition to song, several other behaviors of Darwin's finches may be acquired through cultural transmission. Field observations and laboratory studies suggest that the tool-using behavior of *Cactospiza pallida* may be acquired early in life through associative learning in the presence of experienced adults (Millikan and Bowman 1967). Similarly, the disjunct distributions of the blood-eating behavior of *Geospiza difficilis* on Isla Wolf (Bowman and Billeb 1965) and Isla Darwin (pers. comm. from D. Schluter), the tick-removing behavior of *Geospiza fuliginosa* on islas Isabela and Fernandina (Bowman, pers. obs.; Amadon 1967; MacFarland and Reeder 1974), and the "bill-bracing" excavation of *Geospiza conirostris* on Isla Española (De Benedictis 1966) and of *Geospiza fortis* on Isla Santa Cruz (Bowman pers. obs.), are probably also based in cultural tradition.

Krebs and Kroodsma (1980) have pointed out that it is helpful to consider the question of dialect function in two parts: (a) why birds learn to sing, and (b) why learned songs vary from place to place. Any attempt to answer the question of why Darwin's finches acquire their definitive songs through imitation of their father's song while under his paternal care must consider the specifics of their ecology. Presumably, were song entirely under genetic control, dialect formation would require more time to develop than it would if the major parameters of song are culturally transmitted from father to son (and daughter). The evolution of Darwin's finches is marked by rapid evolutionary change within a comparatively brief span of time (Yang and Patton 1981). The geospizine founders, presumably, brought with them the emerizine characteristics of cultural transmission of song. Rapid adaptive modification of feeding behaviors and structures in various parts of the Galapagos Archipelago was accompanied by selective pressures favoring vocalizations sympathetic to the acoustical apertures of the birds' varied environments. Cultural control of song lends itself to comparatively rapid selective modification, in contrast to genetic control. Indeed the ability may have facilitated rapid genetically based structural and behavioral evolution of feeding habits, and, perhaps, even preceded it (cf. Immelmann 1975). The inherent advantages of vocal signalling over visual or olfactory means in obfuscated environments make the former the ready target of selection, especially if it should vary (as it is known to do). Ecosystem instability through more or less regular catastrophic events, such as volcanic eruptions, geological uplifts, etc., destroy or alter vegetation, often on a grand scale (Simkin and Howard 1970), "forcing" behavioral accommodation or extinction. Song learning, via imprinting on parental male, may be accompanied by habitat imprinting, which reinforces philopatry, thereby promoting the development of songs among immediate neighbors that are more similar to each other than they are to distant birds.

The question of why learned songs of Darwin's finches vary from place to place seems clearly to be related to the sound transmission characteristics of each major habitat patch.

There is good evidence that dialects of Darwin's finches do, in fact, tend to promote assortative mating. Accidental exceptions indicate the pervasiveness of this rule (see Figs. 178-181). The tendency for females to vocalize (subsong or rehearsed-like song) may indicate that assortative mating involves a mutual matching of vocal signatures by male and female, and helps to assure conspecific segregation amidst a plethora of similar-sounding and appearing sympatric populations, especially on the larger islands.

Payne (1981) has set forth three models to explain the origin and maintenance of song dialects, the essentials of which are as follows. His "historical model" places emphasis on unique distributional events of the past. Regional differences in songs may be caused by unrelated, independent founding events, i.e. founders may bring a song variant that is rather different from that of the site of origin. Coupled with copy errors, changes in local (isolated) populations would occur and would ultimately spread to broad areas.

This model assumes that regional dialects are largely shaped by chance events, with ecological factors playing a very minor, if not irrelevant, role. It makes no assumptions about the genetic distinctiveness of populations or predictions of relationships between them. It predicts that population size and area are variable because of local differences in time between founding and population expansion. Some boundary changes due to local expansions and immigrations may occur but no rapid changes in song. The historical model makes no clear predictions regarding the function of song or social interaction between birds sharing a common song.

Although historical and often random events are assumed to be typical components of oceanic island colonization, establishment of transoceanic founders is a highly selective process in which genetic preadaptation and behavioral plasticity play significant roles. Most dialect distributions in Darwin's finches are coincident with specific habitat distributions. Ecological factors, i.e. sound transmission through vegetation, have markedly shaped vocal signals. Thus, whereas song seems not to be a good tracer of intra-archipelagic origin of finch populations (although it may be useful tracing continental origins of the geospizine tribe), the historical model does not help to explain prevailing song conditions and is, therefore, rejected.

A second model proposed by Payne (1981), designed to test the behavioral significance of song dialects, is termed the "social adaptation model." This behavioral model suggests, among other things, that local song differences result from intraspecific vocal mimicry, with the song mimic gaining an advantage over nonmimics in his ability to gain and hold territory and to attract a mate. Thus, birds that copy the song of an established male may have an advantage over other birds, resulting in local sharing of song, i.e. dialect formation.

There is no evidence from Darwin's finches that dialect areas correspond to social units (seemingly weakly defined in the finches), or that differences in song population are the result of behavior modification to social action. In fact, dialect boundaries neatly correspond to habitat boundaries. Song development studies suggest that definitive, population-specific song patterns of the finches are acquired during the first 40 days of post-hatching life and remain more or less constant during the life of the individual. Song mimicry, i.e. copying of sounds other than species-specific vocalizations (Krebs and Kroodsma 1980), is unknown in Darwin's finches, although the birds are very adept at learning the songs of their father during the sensitive period of their youth and vocalizing their imitation during the first and all subsequent breeding seasons. Populational differences in song are not due to the lack of social interactions, as suggested by the social adaptation model, but rather to local adaptations to sound transmission characteristics of the vegetative environment. Darwin's finches are remarkably sedentary, although relatively rare inter-island wanderings have been reported (Gifford 1919). There is no sure evidence that birds disperse between dialect areas. However, in *Camarhynchus parvulus* on Isla Santa Cruz, there may be some interchange of birds from the highland and coastal regions, whose dialects differ, but this difference could entail merely a switching between basic and derived songs (Fig. 181D). This phenomenon is poorly understood. Thus, the social adaptation model is also rejected, principally because its central feature, intraspecific vocal mimicry, is totally foreign to the vocal behavior of Darwin's finches.

A third model proposed by Payne (1981) is termed the "racial specialization" model, although with reference to Darwin's finches it might more appropriately be designated the "ecological specialization" model. It assumes that populations with distinctive dialects are genetically unique, not necessarily in regard to the development of song differences, but rather in local adaptations to environmental differences. Populations are specialized for particular habitats, and dispersal between dialect populations is ineffective. Population size and geographic area of a dialect are highly variable because the habitat patches of each population are likely to vary in size. Dialects and dialect boundaries are more or less stable over time; females choose mates with songs like those of their parents (or conspecific neighbors) that were heard when they were young. Song is a permanent marker of the home region of the bird, which does not change during the life of the individual, i.e. the bird cannot "lie about its past" (Payne 1981).

It should be noted, however, that the racial specialization model does not specify that local dialectal differences in song are adapted to local differences in sound transmission. Payne (1981) specifically states that "the process of speciation provides no adaptive explanation for the local differences in terms of natural selection." Except for this feature, the "racial specialization" model quite faithfully describes the dialect conditions in Darwin's finches. For example, structural differences between populations are probably related to local ecological conditions and are genetically based (Boag and Grant 1978). Interpopulational levels of genic (allozyme) differentiation range from slight to marked, the latter as in *Certhidea olivacea* (Yang and Patton 1981). Dialectal differences between finch populations are culturally transmitted and are not rigidly regulated by, or entirely free of, genetic factors. As previously described, regional dialects probably have resulted from natural selection "shaping" occasional errors in copying parental male song, so that they "match" the sound-transmission characteristics of the vegetations (i.e acoustical aperture) in the various colonial regions. A female finch probably mates selectively with males according to the song most closely resembling her father's type, thus assuring that she will be mated to a bird culturally and genetically specialized for the same local environment. Dispersal, leading to permanent residence, between dialect areas is probably of rare occurrence and largely ineffective. This is due to the improbability of an appropriate matching of male song with acoustical apertures, and/or mutual matching of songs of prospective mates. The finches probably remain in their home area or habitat type by attraction to the local dialect and environment on which they are imprinted. Such philopatry combined with individual longevity may account for the persistence of regional dialects over long periods of time. To judge from onomatopoeic descriptions made by Snodgrass and Heller (1904) in 1898-1899, the dialect of *Geospiza conirostris*, for example, on Isla Española is virtually unchanged after eight decades and an unknown number of finch generations later. The durability of individual song types and population dialects in time and space prevents concealment of the cultural lineage of song. Even intergeneric hybrids (Fig. 181A) can retain the male song characteristics of both parental species!

In conclusion, in Darwin's finches the cultural evolution of dialects under the guidance of natural selection is essentially a tracking of the local environments by differential preservation of populations whose vocal signals are designed for optimal transmission of identity and motivational information.

ACKNOWLEDGMENTS

Financial support for this research project was generously provided by the National Science Foundation through grants G-18103, GB-1457, GB-7059, and GE-2370. Additional support and encouragement was received from the National Geographic Society, Chapman Fund of the American Museum of Natural History, the New York Zoological Society, California Academy of Sciences, and "Earthwatch," for which I am most grateful. San Francisco State University awarded research leaves, arranged for the construction of aviaries, and made available spacious laboratory quarters. Dr. Peter Marler provided the initial stimulus for this study through his pioneering research on vocal communication in birds. Dr. William Fish and the late Dr. Peter Paul Kellog gave valuable advice on recording equipment and procedures. Methods of measuring sound transmission and acoustical analysis of our sound tapes were carefully prescribed in an operations manual expressly compiled for this research project by Dr. George Wilson of the acoustical consulting firm of Wilson, Ihrig and Associates, Inc. of Oakland, California. Without the kindly concerns and suggestions of Dr. Robert T. Orr and the late Eric C. Kinsey, our rearing of Darwin's finches in captivity might not have succeeded as well as it did.

The Government of Ecuador was always sympathetic to my requests for scientific collecting permits, and I wish to thank the following officials for facilitating the field work: Dr. Leonidas Bacquero, former Consul General of Ecuador in San Francisco; various Ministers of National Defense; Ing. Arturo Ponce, Chief of National Parks and Wildlife; Ing. Teodora Suárez, Head of the Forestry Directorate; and Lic. Miguel Cifuentes, former Superintendent of the Galapagos National Park. Mr. Heinz Jirsak arranged for temporary care of our live finches in Guayaquil and procured health certificates from the local authorities. On more than one occasion the United States Consul General and his staff in Guayaquil expedited customs clearance of our scientific equipment. Through the kind cooperation of Capt. Carl Bowman, formerly of the California Maritime Academy, I was permitted to transport caged finches aboard the training ship "Golden Bear." Mr. David Cavagnaro skillfully captured Galapagos tree-finches and arranged for their safe transportation to San Francisco. Through the generosity of Mrs. Sue Tishman it was possible for me to accompany the 1973 Smithsonian Institution/Darwin Foundation Galapagos cruise and obtain song recordings of rare populations of finches.

To Dr. George A. Bartholomew, Dr. Nathan Cohen, Mr. Clyde Smith and the late Mrs. Alice

Kermeen, all of the University of California, I express my sincere thanks for making possible one or more of my various Galapagos visits. Logistical support of the United States Navy made our helicopter landings on the higher elevations of islas Darwin and Wolf one of the highlights of the 1964 Galapagos International Scientific Project. The upper reaches of Isla Darwin had not previously been explored, and our visit provided a superb opportunity to determine the status of breeding populations of Darwin's finches, among other things. Many Galapagos residents assisted our field research through making the comforts of their homes available to us, by providing interisland boat transportation, or by relating valuable first-hand natural history information. I owe a debt of gratitude to Alf Kastdalen, Friedel Hornemann, Carmen, Fritz, and Karl Angemeyer, Forrest Nelson, Friedel Vonka, Miguel Castro, and the De Roy family, all of Isla Santa Cruz; and to Margret Wittmer and family of Isla Floreana. Past directors of the Charles Darwin Research Station, including Raymond Lévêque, Dr. David Snow, Roger Perry, Dr. Peter Kramer, Craig MacFarland, and Dr. Heinrik Hoeck, were always helpful in providing housing and research space at the station, as well as in many other ways, all of which allowed us to make the most of our limited time in the Galapagos. Edgar Potts and Rolf Sievers, former managers of the Darwin Research Station, were always ready and willing to help us solve logistical problems.

Special thanks are owing many of my former graduate students for their faithful assistance in one or more of the field, aviary, or laboratory projects, namely, Stephen L. Billeb, Dr. Michael Bentzien, Mrs. Betsey D. Cutler, Dr. James L. Gulledge, Ms. Nancy Jo, Mrs. Sylvia Hope, Dr. Bruce Manion, Dr. George Millikan, Arthur Rochester, Stephen Siegel, and Dr. Richard Tenaza. I especially wish to thank Betsey Cutler, Sylvia Hope, and Stephen Billeb for permission to use unpublished data from their graduate dissertations. Nancy Jo has volunteered untold hours for the painstaking task of "reading" sound spectrograms, for which I thank her profusely.

Drs. Laurene Ratcliffe, Dagmar Werner, and Eberhard Curio have graciously provided copies of some of their rare recordings of finch songs; Daphne Gemmill has made available the photograph of the Isla Santiago highlands vegetation. Dr. Peter Grant allowed me to use his data on body weight for finches on islas Genovesa and Wolf, and through his numerous publications on Darwin's finches provided essential natural history information helpful to my vocalization studies. Dr. G. C. Gorman advised me well on the logistics of field work in St. Lucia, and put me in touch with the inveterate local naturalist, Mr. Stanley John, whose knowledge of the behavior of *Melanospiza richardsoni* proved to be invaluable. Dr. James L. Gulledge recorded the song of *Melanospiza* and generously made available several formalin specimens for an anatomical study on the syrinx. Various officers of the Charles Darwin Foundation for the Galapagos Isles, including the late Sir Julian Huxley, the late Dr. Victor van Straelen, Dr. Harold J. Coolidge, Dr. Jean Dorst, Dr. S. Dillon Ripley, Dr. Tom Simkin, and Dr. Peter Kramer have, through their recommendations, helped to smoothen the way for me in various governmental circles.

For patiently tolerating my numerous long absences from home, and seemingly endless hours of isolation in my study and laboratory during the course of this research, I wish to express my deepest appreciation to my wife and sons. Paul Bowman has provided invaluable technical advice on the electronic analysis of the sound tapes and also assisted in the formulation of analytical procedures. Carl Bowman located the elusive breeding population of *Geospiza scandens* on Isla Marchena.

Prof. William Seto, Department of Mechnical Engineering at San Jose State University, kindly allowed me the use of his anechoic chamber for acoustical testing purposes. A penultimate draft of the manuscript was read by Luis Baptista, Betsey Cutler, Peter Grant, Sylvia Hope, Donald Kroodsma, Eugene Morton, and Laurene Ratcliffe. Their comments have helped to clarify many points in the discussion, for which I am most grateful. The Spanish summary was skillfully prepared by María-Alicia Barros, Nancy Jo, and John and Ligia Simmons. Dr. Alan Leviton, Executive Editor of the Pacific Division, AAAS symposium series, has been a very positive force in bringing the manuscript to completion. His persistence has been exceeded only by his executive acumen!

RESUMEN

Este estudio de los patrones del canto de los pinzones de Darwin ha sido conducido a lo largo de un período de veinte años, durante los cuales se han realizado análisis de miles de grabaciones hechas en el campo, en los cantos de 14 especies de la tribu de aves Geospizini. Con el propósito de determinar la importancia del aprendizaje y de la heredabilidad en el desarrollo de la vocalización final en el adulto, se condujeron experimentos en las progenies de los pinzones que se mantuvieron en cautividad. En cuatro especies de pinzones silvestres se midió el nivel de intensidad acústica. También se determinaron los modelos de transmisión acústica en distintos ambientes de las Islas Galápagos, los cuales posteriormente fueron correlacionados con los espectros de energía de los cantos, como también con aspectos ecológicos, anatómicos y del comportamiento.

Tres tipos de las "expresiones vocales" (Darwin 1872) estan asociados con el comportamiento reproductivo. Durante el cortejo, se produce un canto que tiene un silbido de alta frecuencia, el cual posee una estructura tal, que su fuente no es localizada por los predadores de los nidos, tales como el buho de orejas cortas y el cucube. Cantos "básicos" y "derivados" son utilizados para atracción sexual y en la defensa territorial, estos presentan una variedad de patrones, los cuales estan asociados con los diferentes estados de motivación, la distancia de transmisión del sonido y el tipo de vegetación.

La estructura de la señal acústica en los pinzones de Darwin presenta una forma en la cual la pérdida de energía acústica se encuentra minimizada. En cada comunidad vegetativa de las Islas Galápagos el sonido es transmitido en diferentes frecuencias, en otras palabras, este exhibe un patrón característico en su atenuación, dependiendo de la frecuencia. La amplia diferencia regional en los cantos (dialectos), es un reflejo de las diferencias regionales encontradas en la transmisión del sonido y en la ecología de los pinzones. Por lo tanto existe una evidencia de que la selección natural le ha dado forma al estilo del canto.

Este estudio no provee evidencias de la ocurrencia de "desplazamiento de caracteres" en el canto de los pinzones. Pero nos lleva a postular que la convergencia y el paralelismo de los cantos sean el resultado de que ambientes acústicos idénticos o similares presenten una distribución simpátrida o alopátrida. Diferentes poblaciones de la misma especie o de diferentes especies habitan diferentes ambientes acústicos. Entre los pinzones y sus equivalentes acústicos de otras regiones del mundo existe una convergencia vocal que nos indica una correlación entre el nicho ecológico y la forma acústica. También existe una gran correlación positiva entre el hábito alimenticio de los pinzones y su comportamiento vocal, con la diversidad estructural y del ambiente, en otras palabras, mientras exista una mayor variación en el canto la transmisión de la "apertura acústica" en el campo será mas amplia, en donde en cada distancia de transmisión la perdida diferencial dependiendo de la frecuencia de la energía del sonido sea mínima.

Tanto los experimentos realizados en el aprendizaje de los cantos, como las observaciones de apareamientos heteroespecíficos realizadas en el campo, sugieren que las preferencias específicas de apareamiento en los adultos ha sido conducionada a muy temprana edad (entre los 10 y 40 días de edad), a traves del aprendizaje del canto del macho que la ha dado cuidado, con el cual ha desarrollado una fuerte unión alimenticia (con el padre que le da de comer). Si ocurren apareamientos interespecíficos en adultos, estos pueden ser el efecto de haber adquirido un aprendizaje vocal erróneo en un macho como resultado de un padre adoptivo heteroespecífico. Algunas evidencias experimentales indican que los pinzones hembras también aprenden el canto a temprana edad del macho adulto que las nutre, y vocalizan este canto cuando se acercan a la etapa reproductiva. Por lo tanto el apareamiento heterosexual puede ser el resultado de un reconocimiento mutuo de aprendizajes de los cantos de la misma especie. Un macho silvestre híbrido intergenérico ("*Camarhynchus conjunctus*") se retrocruzo exitosamente con una silvestre (*Camarhynchus parvulus*), produciendo tres nidadas, comprobandose así que los híbridos entre los pinzones pueden ser fértiles y pueden así contribuir a la introgresión de caracteres vocales estructurales.

Puesto que el dialecto vocal de los pinzones parece ser una adaptación local a los ambientes acústicos dominantes y ya que se conoce que estos son transmitidos culturalmente, estos podrían ser teóricamente la causa inicial y no la consecuencia de la diversificacion génica entre poblaciones. Si en los ambientes locales como en los dialectos el aprendizaje ocurriera a temprana edad, esto reduciría la mobilidad de los adultos y podría aumentar las divergencieas genéticas que afectan la alimentación (nutrición) y las adaptaciones morfológicas.

La gran diversidad ecológica de las Islas Galápagos, cada una de las cuales representa un mundo aislado dentro de ese mundo, difiriendo estas en su flora y en su fauna de geospizini, parecen habaer conducido a una proliferación rápida y variada de las adaptaciones vocales (y alimenticias), y es precisamente por esto que los pinzones de Darwin son famosos.

Las condiciones ecológicas (acústicas) que han hecho posible la notable radiación vocal de los pinzones no son únicas del entorno insular de las Islas Galápagos, sino que también ocurren en mayor o menor grado en todas las regiones del mundo donde existen aves que cantan.

LITERATURE CITED

Abbott, I., and L. K. Abbott. 1978. Multivariate study of morphological variation in Galapagos and Ecuadorian mockingbirds. Condor 80:302-308.

Abbott, I., L. K. Abbott, and P. R. Grant. 1977. Comparative ecology of Galápagos ground finches (*Geospiza* Gould): Evaluation of the importance of floristic diversity and interspecific competition. Ecol. Monogr. 47:151-184.

Abs, M. 1975. Zur Entwicklung der Lautäusserungen bei der Haustauble (*Columba livia domestica*). Verh. Deut. Zool. Ges. 1974:347-350.

Abs, M., S. A. Ashton, and B. K. Follett. 1977. Plasma luteinizing hormone in juvenile pigeons around the time of breaking of the voice. Horm. Behav. 9:189-192.

Abs, M., E. Curio, P. Kramer, and J. Niethammer. 1965. Zur Ernahrungsweise der Eulen auf Galápagos. J. Orn. 106:49-57.

Alexander, R. D. 1969. Comparative animal behavior and systematics. Pages 494-520 *in* C. G. Sibley, ed. Systematic Biology. Nat'l. Acad. Sci. Publ. 1692. Washington, D.C.

Amadon, D. 1967. Galapagos finches grooming marine iguanas. Condor 69:311.

Andrew, R. J. 1962. Evolution of intelligence and vocal mimicking. Science 137:585-589.

Armstrong, E. A. 1963. A study of bird song. Oxford University Press, New York, N. Y.

Atz, J. W. 1970. Application of the idea of homology to behavior. Pages 53-74 *in* L. R. Aronson, E. Tobach, D. S. Lehrman and J. S. Rosenblatt, eds. Development and Evolution of Behavior. W. H. Freeman and Co., San Francisco, Calif.

Aylor, D. 1972a. Noise reduction by vegetation and ground. J. Acoust. Soc. Amer. 51:197-205.

Aylor, D. 1972b. Sound transmission through vegetation in relation to leaf area density, leaf width and breadth of canopy. J. Acoust. Soc. Amer. 51:411-414.

Bailey, R. E. 1952. The incubation patch of passerine birds. Condor 54:121-136.

Baker, M. C. 1975a. Song dialects and genetic differences in white-crowned sparrows with different song dialects. Condor 76:351-356.

Baker, M. C. 1975b. Song dialects and genetic differences in white-crowned sparrows (*Zonotrichia leucophrys*). Evolution 29:226-241.

Baker, M. C., and L. R. Mewaldt. 1978. Song dialects as barriers to dispersal in white-crowned sparrows, *Zonotrichia leucophrys nuttalli*. Evolution 32:712-722.

Baker, M. C., K. J. Spitler-Nabors, and D. C. Bradley. 1981. Early experience determines song dialect responsiveness of female sparrows. Science 214:819-821.

Baker, M. C., K. J. Spitler-Nabors, and D. C. Bradley. 1982. The response of female mountain white-crowned sparrows to songs from their natal dialect and an alien dialect. Behav. Ecol. Sociobiol. 10:175-179.

Baptista, L. F. 1974. The effects of songs of wintering white-crowned sparrows on song development in sedentary populations of the species. Z. Tierpsychol. 34:147-171.

Baptista, L. F. 1975. Song dialects and demes in sedentary populations of the white-crowned sparrow (*Zonotrichia leucophrys nuttalii*). Univ. Calif. Publ. Zool. 105:1-52.
Baptista, L. F. 1977. Geographic variation in song and dialects of the Puget Sound white-crowned sparrow. Condor 79:356-370.
Baptista, L. F., and J. R. King. 1980. Geographical variation in song and song dialects of montane white-crowned sparrows. Condor 82:267-284.
Baptista, L. F., and M. L. Morton. 1981. Interspecific song acquisition by a white-crowned sparrow. Auk 98:383-385.
Barash, D. P. 1977. Sociobiology and behavior. Elsevier North-Holland, Inc., New York, N. Y.
Bateson, P. P. G. 1978. Sexual imprinting and optimal outbreeding. Nature 273:659-670.
Becker, P.H., G. Thielcke, and K. Wüstenberg. 1980. Versuche zum angenommenen Kontrastverlust im Gesang der Blaumeise (*Parus caerulens*) auf Teneriffa. J. Orn. 121:81-95.
Beebe, W. 1924. Galapagos: World's end. G. P. Putnam's Sons, New York, N. Y.
Beebe, W. 1926. The Arcturus adventure. G. P. Putnam's Sons, New York, N. Y.
Beever, III. J. W. 1979. The niche-variation hypothesis: An examination of organisms. Evol. Theory 4:181-191.
Beranek, L. L. 1971. Noise and vibration control. McGraw-Hill, New York, N. Y.
Berger, A. 1980. Longevity of Hawaiian honeycreepers in captivity. Auk 92:263-264.
Bergmann, H-H. 1976. Konstitutionsbedingte Merkmale in Gesängen und Rufen europäischer Grasmücken (Gattung *Sylvia*). Z. Tierpsychol. 42:315-329.
Billeb, S. L. 1968. Song variation in three island populations of Galapagos warbler finch (*Certhidea olivacea* Gould). M. A. Thesis. San Francisco State University, San Francisco, Calif.
Boag, P. T. 1981. Morphological variation in Darwin's finches (Geospizinae) of Daphne Major Island, Galápagos. Ph.D. Thesis. McGill University, Montreal, Can.
Boag, P. T., and P. R. Grant. 1978. Heritability of external morphology in Darwin's finches. Nature 274:793-794.
Bond, J. 1961. Birds of the West Indies. Houghton Mifflin Co., Boston, Mass.
Bondenson, P. 1977. North American bird song—a world of music. Scandinavian Science Press Ltd., Klampenborg, Denmark.
Bonner, J. T. 1980. The evolution of culture in animals. Princeton Univ. Press, Princeton, N.J.
Bowman, R. I. 1961. Morphological differentiation and adaptation in the Galápagos finches. Univ. Calif. Publ. Zool. 58:1-302.
Bowman, R. I. 1979. Adaptive morphology of song dialects in Darwin's finches. J. Orn. 120: 353-389.
Bowman, R. I., and S. L. Billeb. 1965. Blood-eating in a Galápagos finch. Living Bird 4:29-44.
Bowman, R. I., and A. Carter. 1971. Egg-pecking behavior in Galápagos mockingbirds. Living Bird 10:243-270.
Brackenbury, J. H. 1979. Power capabilities of the avian sound producing system. J. Exp. Biol. 78:163-166.
Brémond, J. C. 1963. Acoustic behaviour in birds. Pages 709-750 *in* R.-G. Busnel, ed. Acoustic Behaviour of Animals. Elsevier Publishing Co., Amsterdam.
Brémond, J. C. 1973. Acoustic competition between the song of the wren (*Troglodytes troglodytes*) and the songs of other species. Behaviour 55:89-98.
Brenowitz, E. A. 1982. Long-range communication of species identity by song in the red-winged blackbird. Behav. Ecol. Sociobiol. 10:29-38.
Brosset, A., and C. Chappuis. 1969. Aspects écologiques de l'évolution des émissions sonores chez les Oiseaux. C. R. Acad. Sci. Paris, Ser. D.:1113-1114.
Brown, C. H. 1982. Ventroloquial and locatable vocalizations in birds. Z. Tierpsychol. 59:338-350.
Brown, R. N. 1977. Character convergence in bird song. Can. J. Zool. 55:1523-1527.
Brown, R. N., and R. E. Lemon. 1979. Structure and evolution of song in the wrens *Thryothorus sinaloa* and *T. felix*. Behav. Ecol. Sociobiol. 5:111-131.
Brown, Jr., W. L. and E. O. Wilson. 1956. Character displacement. Syst. Zool. 5:49-64.
Brüel and Kjaer. 1967. Precision sound level meter, Type 2203/1613. (Performance manual).

Brüel and Kjaer. Naeum, Denmark.
Busnel, R.-G. 1963. On certain aspects of animal acoustic signals. Pages 69-131 *in* R.-G. Busnel, ed. Acoustic Behaviour of Animals. Elsevier Publishing Co., Amsterdam.
Calder, W. A. 1970. Respiration during song in the canary (*Serinus canaria*). Comp. Biochem. Physiol. 32:251-258.
Carlquist, S. 1974. Island biology. Columbia University Press, New York, N. Y.
Carr, J. R., and F. C. James. 1975. Eco-morphological configurations and convergent evolution in species and communities. Pages 258-291 *in* M. L. Cody and J. M. Diamond, eds. Ecology and Evolution of Communities. Harvard University Press, Cambridge, Mass.
Cavalli-Sforza, L. L., and M. W. Feldman. 1981. Cultural transmission and evolution. Princeton University Press, Princeton, N. J.
Chappuis, C. 1971. Un exemple de l'influence du milieu sur les émissions vocales des oiseaux: l'évolution des chants en forêt équitoriale. Terre et Vie 25:183-202.
Christian, J. J. 1970. Social subordination, population density, and mammalian evolution. Science 168:84-90.
Cody, M. L. 1969. Convergent characteristics in sympatric species: a possible relation to interspecific competition and aggression. Condor 71:222-239.
Cody, M. L. 1974a. Competition and the structure of bird communities. Princeton University Press, Princeton, N. J.
Cody, M. L. 1974b. Optimization in ecology. Science 183:1156-1164.
Cody, M. L., and J. H. Brown. 1970. Character convergence in Mexican finches. Evolution 24: 304-310.
Cornford, F. M. 1973. Plato's theory of knowledge. Routledge and Kegan Paul, Ltd., London.
Cory, C. B. 1892. Catalogue of West Indian birds. Published privately. Boston, Mass.
Crowder, L. B. 1980. Ecological convergence of community structure. A neutral analysis. Ecology 61:194-204.
Curio, E. 1965. Zur geographischen Variation des Feinderkennens einiger Darwinfinken (Geospizinae). Verh. Dtsch. Zool. Ges. Kiel. 466-492.
Curio, E. 1969. Funktionsweide und Stammes geschichte des Flugfeinderkennens einiger Darwinfinken (Geospizinae). Z. Tierpsychol. 26:394-487.
Curio, E. 1977. Some aspects of individual variation in birds. Die Vogelwarte 29:111-120.
Curio, E., and P. Kramer. 1964. Vom Mangrovefinken (*Cactospiza heliobates* Snodgrass und Heller). Z. Tierpsychol. 21:223-234.
Cushing, E. J. 1941. Non-genetic mating preference as a factor in evolution. Condor 43:233-236.
Cutler, B. D. 1970. Anatomical studies on the syrinx of Darwin's finches. M. A. Thesis. San Francisco State University, San Francisco, Calif.
Dabelsteen, T. 1981. The sound pressure level in the dawn song of the blackbird *Turdus merula* and a method for adjusting the level in experimental song to the level in natural song. Z. Tierpsychol. 56:137-149.
Darwin, C. 1845. Journal of researches into the natural history and geology of the countries visited during the voyage of H. M. S. "Beagle" round the world, under the command of Capt. Fitz Roy, R. N. 2nd rev. ed. John Murray, London.
Darwin, C. 1872. The expression of the emotions in man and animals. Appleton Publ. Co., London.
Dawkins, R., and J. R. Krebs. 1978. Animal signals: information or manipulation? Pages 282-309 *in* J. R. Krebs and N. B. Davies, eds. Behavioural Ecology: An Evolutionary Approach. Blackwell Scientific Publs., London.
De Benedictis, P. 1966. The bill-brace feeding behavior of the Galapagos finch *Geospiza conirostris*. Condor 68:206-208.
De Voogd, T., and F. Nottebohm. 1981. Gonadal hormones induce dendritic growth in the adult avian brain. Science 214:202-204.
De Vries, Tj. 1976. Prey selection and hunting methods of the Galapagos hawk, *Buteo galapagoensis.* Le Gerfaut 66:3-24.

Delsaut, M., and J. C. Roy. 1980. Auditory and visual stimuli as reinforcers among lovebirds (*Agapornis roseicollis*). Behav. Neur. Biol. 28:319-334.

Diamond, A. W. 1973. Habitats and feeding stations of St. Lucia forest birds. Ibis 115:313-329.

Dilger, W. C. 1956. Adaptive modifications and ecological isolating mechanisms in the thrush genera *Catharus* and *Hylocichla*. Wilson Bull. 68:171-199.

Dixon, K. L. 1969. Patterns of singing in a population of the plain titmouse. Condor 71:94-101.

Dixon, K. L., and R. A. Stefanski. 1970. An appraisal of the song of the black-capped chickadee. Wilson Bull. 82:53-62.

Dobkin, D. S. 1979. Functional and evolutionary relationships of vocal copying phenomena in birds. Z. Tierpsychol. 50:348-363.

Dooling, R. J. 1980. Behavior and psychophysics of hearing in birds. Pages 261-288 *in* A. N. Popper and R. R. Fay, eds. Comparative Studies of Hearing in Vertebrates. Springer-Verlag, New York, N. Y.

Dooling, R. J., and J. C. Saunders. 1975. Auditory intensity discrimination in the parakeet (*Melopsittacus undulatus*). J. Acoust. Soc. Amer. 58:1308-1310.

Dooling, R. J., J. A. Mulligan, and J. D. Miller. 1971. Auditory sensitivity and song spectrum of the common canary (*Serinus canarius*). J. Acoust. Soc. Amer. 50:700-709.

Dooling, R. J., S. Peters, and M. H. Searcy. 1979. Auditory sensitivity and vocalizations of the field sparrow (*Spizella pusilla*). Bull. Psychonom. Soc. 14:106-108.

Dooling, R. J., S. R. Zoloth, and J. R. Baylis. 1978. Auditory sensitivity, equal loudness, temporal resolving powers and vocalizations in the house finch (*Carpodacus mexicanus*). J. Comp. Physiol. Psych. 92:867-876.

Downhower, J. F. 1978. Observations on the nesting of the small ground finch *Geospiza fuliginosa* and the large cactus ground finch *G. conirostris* on Española, Galapagos. Ibis 120:340-346.

Eibl-Eibesfeldt, I., and S. Kramer. 1958. Ethology, the comparative study of animal behavior. Quart. Rev. Biol. 33:181-211.

Elliott, D. N., and W. R. Fraser. 1970. Fatigue and adaptation. Pages 115-155 *in* Foundations of Modern Auditory Theory, vol. 1. Academic Press, New York, N. Y.

Embleton, T. E. W. 1963. Sound propagation in homogeneous deciduous and evergreen woods. J. Acoust. Soc. Amer. 35:1119-1125.

Embleton, T. E. W. 1966. Scattering by an array of cylinders as a function of surface impedance. J. Acoust. Soc. Amer. 40:667-670.

Emlen, S. T. 1971a. Geographic variation in indigo bunting song (*Passerina cyanea*). Anim. Behav. 19:407-408.

Emlen, S. T. 1971b. The role of song in individual recognition in the indigo bunting. Z. Tierpsychol. 28:241-246.

Emlen, S. T., J. S. Rising, and W. L. Thompson. 1975. A behavioral and morphological study of sympatry in the indigo and lazuli buntings of the Great Plains. Wilson Bull. 87:145-179.

Falls, J. B. 1963. Properties of bird song eliciting responses from territorial males. Pages 259-271 *in* Proc. XII Internat'l Orn. Cong.

Falls, J. B. 1969. Functions of territorial song in the white-throated sparrow. Pages 207-232 *in* R. A. Hinde, ed. Bird Vocalizations. Cambridge University Press, London.

Ford, H. A., D. T. Parkin, and A. W. Ewing. 1973. Divergence and evolution in Darwin's finches. Biol. J. Linn. Soc. 5:289-295.

Fournier, L. A. 1966. Botany of Cocos Island, Costa Rica. Pages 183-186 *in* R. I. Bowman, ed. The Galápagos. University of California Press, Berkeley, Calif.

Fosberg, F. R., and W. L. Klawe. 1966. Preliminary list of plants from Cocos Island. Pages 187-189 *in* R. E. Bowman, ed. The Galápagos. University of California Press, Berkeley, Calif.

Garnett, M. C. 1981. Body size, its heritability and influence on juvenile survival among great tits, *Parus major*. Ibis 123:31-41.

Gifford, W. E. 1919. Field notes on the land birds of the Galapagos Islands and of Cocos Island, Costa Rica. Proc. Calif. Acad. Sci. 2:189-258.

Gochfeld, M. 1978. Social facilitation of singing: Group size and flight song rates in the pampas meadowlark *Sturnella defilippi*. Ibis 120:338-339.

Grant, B. R., and P. R. Grant. 1979. Darwin's finches: population variation and sympatric speciation. Proc. Nat'l. Acad. Sci. USA 76:2359-2363.

Grant, P. R. 1965. The adaptive significance of some size trends in island birds. Evolution 19: 225-267.

Grant, P. R. 1966. Coexistence of two wren species of the genus *Thryothorus*. Wilson Bull. 78:266-278.

Grant, P. R. 1968. Bill size, body size, and the ecological adaptations of bird species to competitive situations on islands. Syst. Zool. 17:319-333.

Grant, P. R. 1972. Convergent and divergent character displacement. Biol. J. Linn. Soc. 4:39-68.

Grant, P. R., and P. T. Boag. 1980. Rainfall on the Galapagos and the demography of Darwin's finches. Auk 97:277-244.

Grant, P. R., and B. R. Grant. 1980. The breeding and feeding characteristics of Darwin's finches on Isla Genovesa, Galápagos. Ecol. Monogr. 50:391-410.

Grant, P. R., B. R. Grant, J. N. M. Smith, I. J. Abbott, and L. K. Abbott. 1976. Darwin's finches: Population variation and natural selection. Proc. Nat'l. Acad. Sci. USA 73:256-261.

Grant, P. R., and N. Grant. 1979. Breeding and feeding of Galapagos mockingbirds, *Nesomimus parvulus*. Auk 96:723-736.

Grant, P. R., J. N. M. Smith, B. R. Grant, I. J. Abbott, and L. K. Abbott. 1975. Finch numbers, owl predation and plant dispersal on Isla Daphne Major, Galápagos. Oecologia 19:239-257.

Grant, P. R., and T. D. Price. 1981. Population variation in continuously varying traits as an ecological genetics problem. Amer. Zool. 21:795-811.

Green, D. M. 1976. An introduction to hearing. Lawrence Erlbaum Associates, Hillsdale, N. J.

Greenlaw, J. S. 1977. Taxonomic distribution, origin, and evolution of bilateral scratching in ground-feeding birds. Condor 79:426-439.

Greenewalt, C. H. 1968. Bird song: Acoustics and physiology. Smithsonian Institution Press, Washington, D.C.

Grzimek, B. 1973. Grzimek's animal life encyclopedia. Birds, vol. III. Van Nostrand Reinhold Co., New York, N.Y.

Güttinger, H. R. 1970. Zur evolution von Verhaltensweisen und Lautäusserungen bei Prachtfinken. Z. Tierpsychol. 27:1011-1075.

Hailman, J. P. 1973. Territorial and courtship songs of birds. Bird-Banding 44:134-135.

Hailman, J. P. 1978. Localization of passerine seet and mobbing calls by goshawks and pygmy owls. Bird-Banding 49:375.

Hamann, O. 1979. On climatic conditions, vegetation types, and leaf size in the Galápagos Islands. Biotropica 11:101-122.

Hamann, O. 1981. Plant communities of the Galápagos Islands. Dansk Bot. Arkiv 34:13-163.

Handford, P. 1981. Vegetational correlates of variation in the song of *Zonotrichia capensis*. Behav. Ecol. Sociobiol. 8:203-206.

Hansen, P. 1979. Vocal learning: Its role in adapting sound structure to long-distance propagation, and a hypothesis on its evolution. Anim. Behav. 27:1270-1271.

Harestad, A. S., and F. L. Bunnell. 1979. Home range and body weight—a reevaluation. Ecology 60:389-402.

Harris, M. P. (1974) 1975. A field guide to the birds of Galapagos. Taplinger Publishing Co., Inc., New York, N. Y.

Hartshorne, C. 1973. Born to sing. Indiana University Press, Bloomington, Ind.

Hatch, J. J. 1966. Collective territories in Galápagos mockingbirds, with notes on other behavior. Wilson Bull. 78:198-207.

Heckenlively, D. B. 1976. Variation in cadence of field sparrow songs. Wilson Bull. 88:588-602.

Hienz, R. D., J. M. Sinnott, and M. B. Sachs. 1977. Auditory sensitivity of the redwing blackbird (*Agelaius phoeniceus*) and brown-headed cowbird (*Molothrus ater*). J. Comp. Physiol. Psychol. 91:1365-1376.

Henwood, K., and A. Fabrick. 1979. A quantitative analysis of the dawn chorus: Temporal selection for community optimization. Amer. Nat. 114:267-274.

Heuwinkel, H. 1978. Der Gesang des Teichrohrsängers (*Acrocephalus scirpaceus*) unter besonderer Berücksichtigung der Schalldruckpegel ("Lautstärke"-) Verhältnisse. J. Orn. 119:450-461.
Hinde, R. A. 1959. Behaviour and speciation in birds and lower vertebrates. Biol. Rev. 34:85-128.
Höhn, E. O., and S. C. Cheng. 1967. Gonadal hormones in Wilson's phalarope (*Steganopus tricolor*) and other birds in relation to plumage and sex behavior. Gen. Comp. Endocrinol. 8:1-11.
Hope, S. 1980. Call form in relation to function in the Steller's jay. Amer. Nat. 116:788-820.
Hunter, M. L. 1980. Microhabitat selection for singing and other behaviour in great tits, *Parus major*: Some visual and acoustical considerations. Anim. Behav. 28:468-475.
Hunter, M. L., and J. R. Krebs. 1979. Geographical variation in the song of the great tit (*Parus major*) in relation to ecological factors. J. Anim. Ecol. 48:759-785.
Hurlbert, S. H. 1981. A gentle depilation of the niche: Dicean resource sets in resource hyperspace. Evol. Theory 5:177-184.
Immelmann, K. 1969. Song development in the zebra finch and other estrildid finches. Pages 61-74 *in* R. H. Hinde, ed. Bird Vocalizations. Cambridge University Press, Cambridge.
Immelmann, K. 1975. Ecological aspects of imprinting and early learning. Ann. Rev. Ecol. Syst. 6:15-37.
Ingärd, U. 1953. A review of the influence of meteorological conditions on sound propagation. J. Acoust. Soc. Amer. 25:405-411.
Jenkins, P. F. 1977. Cultural transmission of song patterns and dialect development in a free-living population. Anim. Behav. 25:50-78.
Jilka, A., and B. Leisler. 1974. Die Einpassung drier Rohrsängerarten (*Acrocephalus schoenobaenus, A. scirpaceus, A. arundinaceus*) in ihre Lebensräume in bezug auf das Frequenspecktrum ihrer Reviergesänge. J. Orn. 115:192-212.
Kalamas, H., and J. Maynard Smith. 1966. Some evolutionary consequences of pegmatic mating systems (imprinting). Amer. Nat. 199:619-635.
Kern, M. D., and J. R. King. 1972. Testosterone-induced singing in female white-crowned sparrows. Condor 74:204-209.
King, A. P., M. J. West, D. H. Eastzer, and J. E. R. Staddon. 1981. An experimental investigation of the bioacoustics of cowbird song. Behav. Ecol. Sociobiol. 9:211-217.
Knecht, S., and U. Scheer. 1968. Lautäusserung und Verhalten des Azoren-Buchfinken (*Fringilla coelebs moreletti* Pucheran). Z. Tierpsychol. 25:155-169.
Knudsen, E. I. 1980. Sound localization in birds. Pages 289-322 *in* A. N. Popper and R. R. May, eds. Comparative Studies of Hearing in Vertebrates. Springer-Verlag, New York, N. Y.
Konishi, M. 1965. The role of auditory feedback in the control of vocalizations in the white-crowned sparrow. Z. Tierpsychol. 22:779-783.
Konishi, M. 1970a. Comparative neurophysiological studies of hearing and vocalizations in songbirds. Z. vergl. Physiol. 66:257-272.
Konishi, M. 1970b. Evolution of design features in the coding of species-specificity. Amer. Zool. 10:67-72.
Konishi, M. 1973. Locatable and nonlocatable acoustic signals for barn owls. Amer. Nat. 107: 778-785.
Konishi, M., and F. Nottebohm. 1969. Experimental studies in the ontogeny of avian vocalizations. Pages 29-48 *in* R. A. Hinde, ed. Bird Vocalizations. Cambridge University Press, Cambridge.
Krebs, J. R. 1974. Habituation and song repertoire in the great tit. Behav. Ecol. Sociobiol. 1:215-227.
Krebs, J. R. 1978. The significance of song repertoires: The Beau Geste hypothesis. Anim. Behav. 25:475-478.
Krebs, J. R., and D. E. Kroodsma. 1980. Repertoires and geographical variation in bird song. Pages 143-177 *in* J. S. Rosenblatt, R. A. Hinde, C. Beer, and M.-C. Busnel, eds. Advances in the Study of Behavior. Vol. 11. Academic Press, New York, N. Y.
Kroodsma, D. E. 1976a. Reproductive development in a female song bird: Differential

stimulation by quality of male song. Science 192:574-575.
Kroodsma, D. E. 1976b. The effect of large song repertoires on neighbor "recognition" in male song sparrows. Condor 78:77-79.
Kroodsma, D. E. 1978. Aspects of learning in the ontogeny of bird song: Where, from whom, when, how many, which, and how accurately? Pages 215-230 *in* G. Burghardt and M. Bekoff, eds. The Development of Behavior. Garland Publishing Co., New York, N. Y.
Kroodsma, D. E. 1981. Geographical variation and functions of song types in warblers (Parulidae). Auk 98:743-751.
Lack, D. 1945. The Galápagos finches (Geospizinae): A study in variation. Occ. Pap. Calif. Acad. Sci. 21:1-152.
Lack, D. 1947. Darwin's finches. Cambridge University Press, Cambridge.
Lack, D. 1969. Subspecies and sympatry in Darwin's finches. Evolution 23:252-263.
Lack, D., and H. N. Southern. 1949. Birds of Tenerife. Ibis 91:607-626.
Lanyon, W. E. 1960. The ontogeny of vocalizations in birds. Pages 321-367 *in* W. E. Lanyon and W. N. Tavolga, eds. Animal Sounds and Communication. Amer. Inst. Biol. Sci. Publ. 7. Washington, D.C.
Lanyon, W. E. 1966. Hybridization in meadowlarks. Bull. Amer. Mus. Nat. Hist. 132:1-25.
Lanyon, W. E. 1969. Vocal characters and avian systematics. Pages 291-310 *in* R. A. Hinde, ed. Bird Vocalizations. Cambridge University Press, Cambridge.
Lanyon, W. E. 1979. Hybrid sterility in meadowlarks. Nature 279:557-558.
Larsson, K. 1979. Features of the neuroendocrine regulation of masculine sexual behavior. Pages 77-163 *in* C. Beyer, ed. Endocrine Control of Sexual Behavior. Raven Press, New York, N. Y.
Latimer, W. 1977. A comparative study of the songs and alarm calls of some *Parus* species. Z. Tierpsychol. 45:414-433.
Lehrman, D. S., and M. Friedman. 1969. Auditory stimulation of ovarian activity in the ring dove (*Streptopelia risoria*). Anim. Behav. 17:494-497.
Lein, M. R. 1972. Territorial and courtship songs of birds. Nature 237:48-49.
Lein, M. R. 1978. Song variation in a population of chestnut-sided warblers (*Dendroica pensylvanica*): Its nature and suggested significance. Can. J. Zool. 56:1266-1283.
Lemaire, F. 1977. Mixed song, interspecific competition and hybridization in the reed and marsh warblers (*Acrocephalus scirpaceus* and *palustris*). Behaviour 63:215-240.
Lemon, R. E. 1975. How birds develop song dialects. Condor 77:385-406.
Levins, R. 1962. Theory of fitness in a heterogeneous environment. I. The fitness set and its adaptive function. Amer. Nat. 96:361-373.
Levins, R. 1963. Theory of fitness in a heterogeneous environment. II. Developmental flexibility and niche selection. Amer. Nat. 97:75-90.
Linskens, H. F., M. J. M Martens, H. J. G. M. Hendriksen, A. M. Rosetenberg-Sinnige, W. A. J. M. Brouwers, A. L. H. C. van der Staak, and A. M. J. Strik-Jansen. 1976. The acoustic climate of plant communities. Oecologia (Berl.) 23:165-177.
Loftus-Hill, J. J., and M. J. Littlejohn. 1970. Mating-call sound intensities of anuran amphibians. J. Acoust. Soc. Amer. 49:1327-1329.
Löhrl, H. 1959. Zur Frage des Zeitpunktes einer Prägung auf die Heimatregion beim Halsbandschnäpper (*Ficedula albicollis*). J. Orn. 100:132-140.
Lorenz, K. 1943. Die angeborenen Formen möglicher Erfahrung. Z. Tierpsychol. 5:235-409.
Lowe, P. R. 1930. Hybridization in birds and its possible relation to the evolution of the species. Bull. Brit. Orn. Club 50:22-29.
Lowe, P. R. 1936. The finches of the Galapagos in relation to Darwin's conception of species. Ibis 78:310-321.
Lyon, R. H. 1973. Propagation of environmental noise. Science 179:1083-1090.
MacArthur, R. H. 1958. Population ecology of some warblers of northeastern coniferous forests. Ecology 39:599-619.
MacArthur, R. A., and E. O. Wilson. 1967. The theory of island biogeography. Princeton University Press, Princeton, N. J.

MacFarland, C. G., and W. G. Reeder. 1974. Cleaning symbiosis involving Galápagos tortoises and two species of Darwin's finches. Z. Tierpsychol. 34:464-483.

Manley, G. A. 1971. Some aspects of the evolution of hearing in vertebrates. Nature 230:506-509.

Marler, P. 1955. Characteristics of some animal calls. Nature 176:6-7.

Marler, P. 1957. Specific distinctiveness in the communication signals of birds. Behaviour 11: 13-39.

Marler, P. 1959. Developments in the study of animal communication. Pages 150-206 *in* P. R. Bell, ed. Darwin's Biological Work, Some Aspects Reconsidered. J. Wiley and Sons, New York, N. Y.

Marler, P. R. 1960. Bird sounds and mate selection. Pages 348-367 *in* W. E. Lanyon and W. N. Tavolga, eds. Animal Sounds and Communication. Amer. Inst. Biol. Sci. Publ. 7. Washington, D. C.

Marler, P. R. 1961. The evolution of visual communication. Pages 96-121 *in* W. F. Blair, ed. Vertebrate Speciation. University of Texas Press, Austin, Tex.

Marler, P. R. 1969. Tonal quality of bird sounds. Pages 5-18 *in* R. A. Hinde, ed. Bird Vocalizations. Cambridge University Press, Cambridge.

Marler, P. 1970. A comparative approach to vocal learning: Song development in white-crowned sparrows. J. Comp. Physiol. Psychol. Monogr. 71:1-25.

Marler, P. R. 1977. The structure of animal communication sounds. Pages 17-35 *in* T. H. Bullock, ed. Recognition of Complex Acoustical Signals. Dahlem Konferenzen by Abakon Verlagsgesellschaft, Life Sciences Research Reports 5. West Berlin.

Marler, P. R., and W. J. Hamilton, III. 1966. Mechanisms of animal behavior. J. Wiley and Sons, New York, N. Y.

Marler, P. R., and D. Isaac. 1960. Physical analysis of a simple bird song as exemplified by the chipping sparrow. Condor 62:124-135.

Marler, P., and D. Isaac. 1961. Song variation in a population of Mexican juncos. Wilson Bull. 73:193-206.

Marler, P., M. Kreith, and M. Tamura. 1962. Song development in hand-raised Oregon juncos. Auk 79:12-30.

Marler, P., and P. Mundinger. 1971. Vocal learning in birds. Pages 389-450 *in* H. Moltz, ed. The Ontogeny of Vertebrate Behavior. Academic Press, Inc., New York, N. Y.

Marler, P., and S. Peters. 1977. Selective vocal learning in a sparrow. Science 198:519-521.

Marler, P., and S. Peters. 1981. Sparrows learn adult song and more from memory. Science 213: 780-782.

Marler, P., and S. Peters. 1982. Long-term storage of learned birdsongs prior to production. Anim. Behav. 30:479-482.

Marler, P., and M. Tamura. 1962. Song "dialects" in three populations of white-crowned sparrows. Condor 64:368-377.

Marler, P., and M. Tamura. 1964. Culturally transmitted patterns of vocal behavior in sparrows. Science 146:1483-1486.

Marten, K. L. 1980. Ecological sources of natural selection on animal vocalizations, with special reference to the African wild dog (*Lycaon pictus*). Ph.D. Thesis. University of California, Berkeley, Calif.

Marten, K., and P. Marler. 1977. Sound transmission and its significance for animal vocalization. I. Temperate habitats. Behav. Ecol. Sociobiol. 2:271-290.

Marten, K., D. Quine, and P. Marler. 1977. Sound transmission and its significance for animal vocalization. II. Tropical forest habitats. Behav. Ecol. Sociobiol. 2:291-302.

Martens, M. J. M. 1980. Foliage as a low-pass filter: Experiments with model forests in an anechoic chamber. J. Acoust. Soc. Amer. 67:66-72.

Martin, D. J. 1977. Songs of the fox sparrow. I. Structure of song and its comparison with song in other Emberizidae. Condor 79:209-221.

Martin, D. J. 1979. Songs of the fox sparrow. II. Intra- and inter-population vegetation. Condor 81:173-184.

Martin, D. J. 1980. Response by male fox sparrows to broadcast of particular conspecific songs. Wilson Bull. 92:21-32.

Marton, G. R. 1981. Avian vocalizations and the sound interference model of Roberts et al. Anim. Behav. 29:632-633.

Maynard Smith, J. 1966. Sympatric speciation. Amer. Nat. 100:637-650.

Mayr, E. 1963. Animal species and evolution. Harvard University Press, Cambridge, Mass.

Mayr, E. 1974. Behavior programs and evolutionary strategies. Amer. Sci. 62:650-659.

McGregor, P. K. 1980. Song dialects in the corn bunting (*Emberiza calandra*). Z. Tierpsychol. 54: 285-297.

McGregor, P. K., J. R. Krebs, and C. M. Perrins. 1981. Song repertoires and lifetime reproductive success in the great tit (*Parus major*). Amer. Nat. 118:149-159.

Mickelsen, A. 1978. Sound reception in different environments. Pages 345-373 *in* M. A. Ali, ed. Sensory Ecology: Review and Perspectives. Penium Press, New York, N. Y.

Mileaf, H. 1967. Electronics one-seven. Hayden Book Co., New York, N. Y.

Milligan, M. M., and J. Verner. 1971. Inter-populational song dialect discrimination in the white-crowned sparrow. Condor 73:208-213.

Millikan, G. C., and R. I. Bowman. 1967. Observations on Galapagos tool-using finches in captivity. Living Bird 6:23-41.

Moore, T. D. 1980. Darwin's finches. Pacific Discovery 33:1-11.

Morse, D. H. 1966. The context of songs in the yellow warbler. Wilson Bull. 78:444-455.

Morse, D. H. 1970. Territorial and courtship songs of birds. Nature 226:659-661.

Morton, E. S. 1970. Ecological sources of selection on avian sounds. Ph.D. Thesis. Yale University, New Haven, Conn.

Morton, E. S. 1975. Ecological sources of selection on avian sounds. Amer. Nat. 109:17-34.

Morton, E. S. 1977. On the occurrence and significance of motivational-structural rules in some birds and mammal sounds. Amer. Nat. 111:855-869.

Morton, E. S. 1983. Grading, discreteness, redundancy, and motivational-structural rules. *In* D. E. Kroodsma and E. H. Miller, eds. Acoustic Communication in Birds. Academic Press, New York, N. Y.

Mueller-Dombois, D. 1981. Island ecosystems: What is unique about their ecology? Pages 485-501 *in* D. Mueller-Dombois, K. W. Bridges, and H. L. Carson, eds. Island Ecosystems. Hutchinson Ross Publishing Co., Stroudsburg, Pa.

Mulligan, J. A. 1963. A description of song sparrow song based on instrumental analysis. Pages 272-284 *in* Proc. XIII Internat'l. Orn. Congr.

Murray, Jr., B. G. and J. W. Hardy. 1981. Behavior and ecology of four syntopic species of finches in Mexico. Z. Tierpsychol. 57:51-72.

Nicolai, J. 1959. Familientradition in der Gesangsentwicklung des Gimpels (*Pyrrula pyrrula* L.). J. Orn. 100:39-46.

Nicolai, J. 1964. Broodparasitism of the Viduinae as an ethological problem. Z. Tierpsychol. 21: 129-204.

Nottebohm, F. 1969. The "critical period" for song learning. Ibis 111:386-387.

Nottebohm, F. 1972. The origin of vocal learning. Amer. Nat. 106:116-140.

Nottebohm, F. 1975. Continental patterns of song variability in *Zonotrichia capensis*: Some possible ecological correlates. Amer. Nat. 109:605-624.

Nottebohm, F., and R. K. Selander. 1972. Vocal dialects and gene frequencies in the chingolo (*Zonotrichia capensis*). Condor 74:137-143.

Orr, R. T. 1945. A study of captive Galapagos finches of the genus *Geospiza*. Condor 47:177-201.

Otte, D. 1974. Effects and functions in the evolution of signalling systems. Pages 385-417 *in* R. F. Johnston, P. W. Frank, and C. D. Michener. Annual Review of Ecology and Systematics 5.

Parkes, K. C. 1951. The genetics of the golden-winged X blue-winged warbler complex. Wilson Bull. 63:5-15.

Partridge, L., and F. Pring-Mill. 1977. Canary Island blue tits and English coal tits: Convergent evolution? Evolution 31:657-665.

Payne, R. B. 1973. Behavior, mimetic songs and song dialects, and relationships of the parasitic indigobirds (*Vidua*) of Africa. Orn. Monogr. 11:1-333.

Payne, R. B. 1980. Behavior and songs of hybrid parasitic finches. Auk 97:118-134.

Payne, R. B. 1981. Population structure and social behavior: Models for testing the ecological significance of song dialects in birds. Pages 108-120 *in* R. D. Alexander and D. W. Tinkle, eds. Natural Selection and Social Behavior. Chiron Press, New York, N. Y.

Paynter, Jr., R. A. and R. W. Storer. 1970. Check-list of birds of the world. Vol. XIII. Mus. Comp. Zool., Cambridge, Mass.

Pearson, T. G., ed. 1940. Birds of America. Garden City Publishing Co., New York, N. Y.

Peet, R. K. 1978. Ecosystem convergence. Amer. Nat. 112:441-444.

Peters, S. S., W. A. Searcy, and P. Marler. 1980. Species song discrimination in choice experiments with terrestrial male swamp and song sparrows. Anim. Behav. 28:393-404.

Peterson, A. P. G., and E. E. Gross, Jr. 1972. Handbook of noise measurement. General Radio Co., Concord, Mass.

Petrinovitch, L., T. Patterson, and L. F. Baptista. 1981. Song dialects as barriers to dispersal: A re-evaluation. Evolution 35:180-188.

Pickstock, J. C., and J. R. Krebs. 1980. Neighbour-stranger song discrimination in the chaffinch (*Fringilla coelebs*). J. Orn. 121:105-108.

Powell, J. R., and C. E. Taylor. 1979. Genetic variation in ecologically diverse environments. Amer. Scientist 67:591-596.

Pumphrey, R. J. 1961. Sensory organs: Hearing. Pages 69-86 *in* A. J. Marshall, ed. Biology and Comparative Physiology of Birds, Vol. II. Academic Press, New York, N. Y.

Ratcliffe, L. 1981. Species recognition in Darwin's ground finches (*Geospiza*, Gould). Ph.D. Thesis. McGill University, Montreal, Can.

Rattenbury, J. A. 1962. Cyclic hybridization as a survival mechanism in the New Zealand forest flora. Evolution 16:348-363.

Reeder, W. G., and S. E. Riechert. 1975. Vegetation change along an altitudinal gradient, Santa Cruz Island, Galapagos. Biotropica 7:162-175.

Remane, A. 1952. Gedanken zum Problem: Homologie und Analogie, Praeadaption und Parallelität. Zool. Anz. 166:447-470.

Richards, D. G. 1978. Environmental acoustics and song communication in passerine birds. Ph.D. Thesis. University of North Carolina, Chapel Hill, N. C.

Richards, D. G. 1981. Alerting and message components in songs of rufous-sided towhees. Behaviour 76:223-249.

Richards, D. G., and R. H. Wiley. 1980. Reverberations and amplitude fluctuations in the propagation of sound in a forest: Implications for animal commmunication. Amer. Nat. 115:381-399.

Ridgway, R. 1896 (1897). Birds of the Galapagos Archipelago. Proc. U. S. Nat'l. Mus. 19:459-670.

Robbins, C. S., B. Brunn, and H. S. Zim. 1966. Birds of America: A guide to field identification. Golden Press, New York, N. Y.

Roberts, J., M. L. Hunter, and A. Kacelnik. 1981. The ground effect and acoustic communication. Anim. Behav. 29:633-634.

Roberts, J., A. Kacelnik, and M. L. Hunter. 1979. A model of sound interference in relation to acoustic communication. Anim. Behav. 27:1271-1273.

Roff, D. 1981. On being the right size. Amer. Nat. 118:405-422.

Roth, V. L. 1981. Constancy in the size ratios of sympatric species. Amer. Nat. 118:394-404.

Rothschild, W., and E. Hartert. 1899. A review of the ornithology of the Galapagos Islands. With notes on the Webster-Harris expedition. Novit. Zool. 6:85-205.

Rothschild, W., and E. Hartert. 1902. Further notes on the fauna of the Galapagos Islands. Novit. Zool. 9:373-418.

Schalter, M. D. 1978. Localization of passerine seet and mobbing calls by goshawks and pygmy owls. Z. Tierpsychol. 46:260-267.

Schalter, M. D., and W. M. Schleidt. 1977. The ability of barn owls, *Tyto alba*, to discriminate and localize avian alarm calls. Ibis 119:22-27.

Schoener, T. W. 1968. Sizes of feeding territories among birds. Ecology 49:123-141.

Schwartzkopf, J. 1949. Uber Sitz und Leistung von Gehor und Vibrationseinn bei Vogeln. Z. vergl. Physiol. 31:527-603.

Schwartzkopf, J. 1955a. On the hearing of birds. Auk 72:340-347.

Schwartzkopf, J. 1955b. Schallsinnesorgane, ihre Funktion und biologische Bedeutung bei Vogeln. Pages 189-207 *in* Acta XI Congr. Int. Orn. 1954.

Searcy, W. A., E. Balaban, R. A. Canady, S. J. Clark, S. Runfeldt, and H. Williams. 1981. Responsiveness of male swamp sparrows to temporal organization of song. Auk 98:613-615.

Searcy, W. A., and P. Marler. 1981. A test for responsiveness to song structure and programming in female sparrows. Science 213:926-928.

Seiger, M. B. 1967. A computer study of the influence of imprinting on population structure. Amer. Nat. 101:47-57.

Selander, R. K., and D. R. Giller. 1961. Analysis of sympatry of great-tailed and boat-tailed grackles. Condor 63:29-86.

Shiovitz, K. A. 1975. The process of species-specific song recognition by the indigo bunting, *Passerina cyanea*, and its relationship to the organization of avian acoustical behavior. Behaviour 55:128-179.

Sibley, C. G. 1957. The evolutionary and taxonomic significance of sexual dimorphism and hybridization in birds. Condor 59:166-191.

Simkin, G. 1973. Principles of acoustical transformation in calls and songs of birds. (Printsip akusticheskoi transformatsii v pozyvakhi ipesne ptit.) Z. Zhurn 52:1261-1263.

Simkin, T., and K. A. Howard. 1970. Caldera collapse in the Galapagos Islands, 1968. Science 169:429-437.

Simpson, G. G., A. Roe, and R. C. Lewontin. 1960. Quantititative zoology. Harcourt, Brace and Co., New York, N. Y.

Slud, P. 1967. The birds of Cocos Island (Costa Rica). Bull. Amer. Mus. Nat. Hist. 135:263-295.

Smith, J. N. M., P. R. Grant, B. R. Grant, I. J. Abbott, and L. K. Abbott. 1978. Seasonal variation in feeding habits of Darwin's ground finches. Ecology 59:1137-1150.

Smith, J. N. M., and H. P. A. Sweatman. 1976. Feeding habits and morphological variation in Cocos finches. Condor 78:244-248.

Snodgrass, R. E., and E. Heller. 1904. Papers from the Hopkins-Stanford Galapagos expedition, 1898-1899. XVI. Birds. Proc. Wash. Acad. Sci. 5:231-372.

Spieth, P. T. 1979. Environmental heterogeneity: A problem of contradictory selection pressures, gene flow, and local polymorphism. Amer. Nat. 113:247-260.

Steadman, D. W. 1981. Vertebrate fossils in lava tubes in the Galápagos Islands. Pages 549-540 *in* B. F. Beck, ed. Proc. Eighth Int'l. Congr. Speliology. Bowling Green, Ky.

Stewart, A. 1911. A botanical survey of the Galapagos Islands. Proc. Calif. Acad. Sci., ser. 4, 1:7-288.

St. Jules, R. S. 1977. Cerebellar evolution in Darwin's finches. M. S. Thesis. Texas A. & M. University, Lubbock, Tex.

Stein, R. C. 1958. The behavioral, ecological, and morphological characteristics of two populations of the Alder Flycatcher *Empidonax traillii* (Audubon). New York State Mus. Sci. Serv. Bull. 371.

Stein, R. C. 1963. Isolating mechanisms between populations of Traill's flycatchers. Proc. Amer. Phil. Soc. 107:21-50.

Sulloway, F. J. 1982a. Darwin and his finches: The evolution of a legend. J. Hist. Biol. 15:1-53.

Sulloway, F. J. 1982b. The *Beagle* collections of Darwin's finches (Geospizinae). Bull. Brit. Mus. Nat. Hist., Zool. Ser. 43:49-94.

Suthers, R. A. 1978. Sensory ecology of birds. Pages 217-251 *in* M. A. Ali, ed. Sensory ecology. Review and Perspectives. Plenium Press.

Svenson, H. K. 1930a. Report on a botanical exploration trip to the Galapagos Islands. Brooklyn Bot. Gard. Rec. 19:269-284.

Svenson, H. K. 1930b. The vegetation of Indefatigable Island. Bull. N. Y. Zool. Soc. 33:163-170.

Svenson, H. K. 1935. Plats of the Astor expeditions, 1930 (Galapagos and coastal islands). Amer. J. Bot. 22:208-277.

Swarth, H. S. 1929. A new bird family (Geospizidae) from the Galapagos Islands. Proc. Calif. Acad. Sci. 18:29-43.

Swarth, H. S. 1931. The avifauna of the Galapagos Islands. Occ. Pap. Calif. Acad. Sci. 18.

Swarth, H. S. 1932. (Field notes). Mar. 11 - July 6, 1932. On file at the California Academy of Sciences, San Francisco, Calif.

Tembrock, G. Acoustic behavior of mammals. Pages 777-778 *in* R.-G. Busnel, ed. Acoustic Behaviour of Animals. Elsevier Publishing Co., Amsterdam.

Thielcke, G. 1969a. Geographic variation in bird vocalizations. Pages 311-339 *in* R. A. Hinde, ed. Bird Vocalizations. Cambridge University Press, Cambridge.

Thielcke, G. 1969b. Die Reaktion von Tannen- und Kohlmeis (*Parus ater, P. major*) auf den Gesang nahverwandter Formen. J. Orn. 110:148-157.

Thielcke, G. 1973. On the origin of divergence of learned signals (songs) in isolated populations. Ibis 115:511-516.

Thompson, W. L. 1972. Singing behavior of the indigo bunting *Passerina cyanea*. Z. Tierpsychol. 31:39-59.

Thorpe, W. H., and Lade, B. I. 1961. The songs of some of the families of the Passeriformes. II. The songs of the buntings (Emberizidae). Ibis 103a:246-259.

Tinbergen, N. 1962. The evolution of animal communication–a critical examination of methods. Symp. Zool. Soc. London 8:1-6.

Tordoff, H. B. 1954. A systematic study of the avian family Fringillidae based on the structure of the skull. Misc. Publ. Mus. Zool. Univ. Michigan 81.

Traylor, M. A. 1967. *Cisticola aberdare* a good species. Bull. Brit. Orn. Club 87:137-141.

Tremaine, H. M. 1959. The audio cyclopedia. Bobbs-Merrill Co., Inc., New York, N. Y.

Turner, C. D. 1966. General endocrinology. Fourth ed. Saunders, Philadelphia, Pa.

Udvandy, M. D. F. 1970. Mammalian speciation: Is it due to social subordination? Science 170: 344-345.

Van Valen, L. 1967. Morphological variation and width of ecological niche. Amer. Nat. 99:377-390.

Wallschläger, D. 1980. Correlation of song frequency and body weight in passerine birds. Experientia 36:412.

Waser, P. M., and M. S. Waser. 1977. Experimental studies of primate vocalization specializations for long-distance propagation. Z. Tierpsychol. 44:239-263.

Weiner, F. M., and D. N. Keast. 1959. Experimental study of the propagation of sound over ground. J. Acoust. Soc. Amer. 31:724-733.

Weston, H. G. 1947. Breeding behavior of the black-headed grosbeak. Condor 49:54-73.

Wickler, W. 1961. Ökologie und Stammeageschichte von Verhaltensweisen. Fortschr. Zool. 13: 303-365.

Wiggins, I. L. 1966. Origins and relationships of the flora of the Galápagos Islands. Pages 175-182 *in* R. I. Bowman, ed. The Galapagos. University of California Press, Berkeley, Calif.

Wiggins, I. L., and D. M. Porter. 1971. Flora of the Galapagos Islands. Stanford University Press, Stanford, Calif.

Wilkenson, P., and P. E. Howse. 1975. Time resolution of acoustic signals by birds. Nature 258: 320-321.

Wiley, R. H., and D. G. Richards. 1978. Physical constraints on acoustic communication in the atmosphere: Implications for the evolution of animal vocalizations. Behav. Ecol. Sociobiol. 3: 69-94.

Wilson, A. C. 1976. Gene regulation in evolution. Pages 225-235 *in* F. J. Ayala, ed. Molecular Genetics. Sinauer Assoc. Inc., Sunderland, Mass.

Wilson, E. O. 1975. Sociobiology. Harvard University Press, Cambridge, Mass.

Wilson, G. P. 1968. Instruction book for Galápagos Islands project: Acoustical measuring equipment. Wilson, Ihrig & Assoc., Oakland, Calif.

Wingfield, J. C., and D. S. Farner. 1978. The annual cycle of plasma irLH and steroid hormones of Reproduction 19:1046-1056.

Witkin, S. R. 1977. The importance of directional sound radiation in avian vocalization. Condor 79:490-493.

Wood, A. 1947. Acoustics. Interscience Publ., Inc., New York, N. Y.

Yang, S. Y., and J. L. Patton. 1981. Genic variability and differentiation of the Galapagos finches. Auk 98:230-242.

Yasukawa, K. 1981. Song repertoires in the red-winged blackbird (*Agelaius phoeniceus*): A test of the Beau Geste hypothesis. Anim. Behav. 29:114-125.

Yeoman, E. 1975. The selective effect of vegetation density on songs of three races of wrentit (*Chamaea fasciata*) in central California. M. A. Thesis. San Francisco State University, San Francisco, Calif.

TABLES

TABLES

TABLE 1. FEATURES OF DARWIN'S FINCHES SUGGESTING A MONOPHYLETIC ORIGIN OF THE TRIBE GEOSPIZINI[1] (FAMILY FRINGILLIDAE)

Feature	Description	Authority
Anatomy	Uniformity of pattern in jaw musculature and skull pneumatization.	Bowman 1961
	Uniformity of pattern of bony palate, including presence of partially fused palatomaxillary processes.	Tordoff 1954
	Uniformity in the syringeal skeleton and musculature.	Cutler 1970
	Uniformity in structure of domed nest with lateral entrance (Fig. 10A). Pattern of color marking on eggs is uniform.	Swarth 1931; Lack 1945
	Feathers on lower back and rump are long, dense, and fluffy; tarsus and toes are long, with outstretched feet extending beyond tip of tail.	Swarth 1929
	Similar cerebellar structure.	St. Jules 1977
Behavior	All species use feet to hold objects against perch.	Bowman 1961; pers. obser.
	Bilateral scratching in most, if not all, species.	Greenlaw 1977; Bowman, pers. obser.
	Only female incubates eggs.	Orr 1945; Bowman, pers. obser.
	Male courtship pattern is uniform.	Lack 1945; Orr 1945; Bowman, pers. obser.
Vocalization	Five-parted basic song and high-frequency whistle song present in all genera; song dialects are culturally transmitted.	Bowman, this volume
Physiology	Seasonal change in color of bill in both sexes.	Swarth 1931; Bowman, pers. obser.
Genetics	Uniform karyotype.	Jo, this volume.
	High genic (allozyme) similarity.	Polans, this volume; Yang and Patton 1981
Distribution	Galapagos and Cocos islands	Swarth 1931

[1] Grzimek 1973.

TABLE 2. PRESENT-DAY DISTRIBUTION OF BREEDING POPULATIONS OF DARWIN'S FINCHES ON THE MAJOR ISLANDS OF THE GALAPAGOS ARCHIPELAGO AND ON COCOS ISLAND, COSTA RICA[1]

	Islands[2]																
Species	Cocos	Baltra	Darwin	Española	Fernandina	Floreana	Genovesa	Isabela	Marchena	Pinta	Pinzón	Rábida	San Cristóbal	Santa Cruz	Santa Fe	Santiago	Wolf
Geospiza magnirostris		x			x	[4]	x	x	x	x	x	x	[4]	x	?[3]	x	x
Geospiza conirostris				x			x										[5]
Geospiza scandens		x				x		x	x	x	x	x	x	x	x	x	
Geospiza fortis		x			x	x		x	x	x	x	x	x	x	x	x	
Geospiza fuliginosa		x		x	x	x		x	x	x	x	x	x	x	x	x	
Geospiza difficilis[6]			x		x		x	x		x				[7]		x	x
Platyspiza crassirostris					x	x		x	x	x	x	x	x	x		x	
Cactospiza pallida		x			?			x			x	x	x	x		x	
Cactospiza heliobates					x			x									
Camarhynchus psittacula		x			x	x		x	x	x	x	x		x	?	x	
Camarhynchus pauper						x											
Camarhynchus parvulus		x			x	x		x		x	x	x	x	x	?	x	
Certhidea olivacea		x	x	x	x	x	x	x	x	x	x	x	x	x	x	x	x
Pinaroloxias inornata	x																
Total no. of species:	1	8	2	3	9	8	4	10	7	9	9	9	7	9	4	10	3

[1] Data based on information in Bowman (1961) and subsequent field observations by the writer on remote islands and regions during the breeding season of the finches. See Tables 8 and 9. On the basis of historical information presented by Sulloway (1982) and fossils discovered by Steadman (1981), the distributional picture of Darwin's finches before the advent of man appears to have been somewhat different from that recorded here.

[2] See map, Fig. 3.

[3] "?" indicates that present status is uncertain due to rarity.

[4] Fossiliferous remains of *Geospiza magnirostris* have been found in lava tubes on Isla Floreana (Steadman 1981). Bowman (1961) also reported on a large-billed *G. magnirostris* collected by him on Floreana in 1957. Sulloway (1982a,b) has verified the fact that Darwin and members of the "Beagle" crew collected this species on Floreana and San Cristóbal islands (cf. Swarth 1931).

[5] The breeding of *Geospiza conirostris* on Isla Wolf has been reported only by Curio and Kramer (1965). Neither Bowman, who has visited the island during the breeding seasons of 1964, 1967, 1968 and 1979 (see Table 9), nor Peter R. Grant, who visited the island in 1978 (pers. obser.), has observed this species on Isla Wolf.

[6] According to the International Rules of Nomenclature, *Geospiza nebulosa* has priority over *G. difficilis* (see Sulloway 1982a,b).

[7] *Geospiza difficilis* was last reported alive on Isla Santa Cruz by Swarth (field notes) during the 1930s.

TABLE 3. SOUND-PRESSURE LEVELS (MINIMAL, MAXIMAL, MEAN) ALONG TRANSMISSION TRANSECTS ON ISLA SANTA CRUZ AT STATIONS 25, 50, 100, 150, 200 and 300 FEET FROM SOUND SOURCE[1]

ISLAND: SANTA CRUZ NO. OF TRANSECTS: 3 DESIGNATIONS: A, B, C
LOCALITY: BAHIA ACADEMIA, NORTH SIDE, INNER COASTAL ZONE DATE: MARCH 17, 1968

CENTER FREQUENCY IN HERZ (dB VALUES: ONE-THIRD OCTAVE FILTER)	25 FEET*			50 FEET			100 FEET			150 FEET			200 FEET			300 FEET		
	RANGE		MEAN	RANGE		MEAN	RANGE		MEAN	RANGE		MEAN	RANGE		MEAN	RANGE		MEAN
	MIN.	MAX.	N= 3	MIN.	MAX.	N= 3	MIN.	MAX.	N=3	MIN.	MAX.	N= 3	MIN.	MAX.	N= 2	MIN.	MAX.	N=1
9920	72	78	74	59	67	62	51	57	53	35	44	39	33	38	36	-	-	29
8000	72	82	81	65	73	68	54	66	60	40	50	46	38	43	41	-	-	29
6320	75	85	81	69	75	72	58	69	65	44	52	50	41	48	45	-	-	32
4960	82	87	85	72	77	75	64	70	67	49	57	53	44	53	48	-	-	36
4000	84	86	85	75	79	77	64	72	69	52	61	57	48	56	52	-	-	38
3160	81	84	83	73	79	75	63	70	67	52	62	57	48	54	51	-	-	38
2480	80	83	82	72	75	74	66	69	67	51	56	54	48	55	51	-	-	38
2000	82	85	83	76	77	77	67	70	69	53	57	55	49	56	52	-	-	37
1580	81	87	84	78	79	78	69	72	71	54	61	57	52	58	54	-	-	38
1240	83	85	84	75	82	77	67	72	69	56	58	57	51	57	54	-	-	40
1000	86	87	86	72	81	78	66	77	70	58	63	61	50	61	56	-	-	43
790	83	86	85	75	81	78	65	71	68	57	62	59	52	57	55	-	-	41
620	80	83	82	74	75	75	62	69	65	55	63	58	50	54	52	-	-	38
500	77	80	79	69	72	71	59	63	61	48	59	54	43	55	48	-	-	38

* DISTANCE FROM SOUND SOURCE

ISLAND: SANTA CRUZ NO. OF TRANSECTS: 2 DESIGNATIONS: X, Y
LOCALITY: BAHIA ACADEMIA, WEST SIDE. OUTER COASTAL ZONE DATE: APRIL 10, 1968

CENTER FREQUENCY IN HERZ (dB VALUES: ONE-THIRD OCTAVE FILTER)	25 FEET*			50 FEET			100 FEET			150 FEET			200 FEET			300 FEET		
	RANGE		MEAN	RANGE		MEAN	RANGE		MEAN	RANGE		MEAN	RANGE		MEAN	RANGE		MEAN
	MIN.	MAX.	N= 2	MIN.	MAX.	N= 2	MIN.	MAX.	N= 2	MIN.	MAX.	N=2	MIN.	MAX.	N= 2	MIN.	MAX.	N= 2
9920	71	73	72	66	66	66	54	55	55	45	49	47	39	44	42	30	34	32
8000	79	82	81	72	73	73	64	64	64	54	58	56	48	54	51	39	43	41
6320	83	83	83	77	77	77	64	65	65	59	62	61	51	58	55	43	46	45
4960	85	86	86	78	78	78	67	69	68	62	64	63	53	62	58	46	48	47
4000	84	86	85	79	79	79	68	70	69	62	65	64	56	61	59	48	50	49
3160	84	84	84	77	78	78	64	69	67	60	65	63	58	59	59	50	50	50
2480	83	85	84	76	76	76	65	66	66	64	67	66	57	62	60	48	51	50
2000	83	84	84	76	77	77	68	70	69	65	66	66	56	63	60	49	50	50
1580	83	83	83	78	79	79	70	72	71	68	68	68	58	65	62	50	53	52
1240	83	84	84	80	80	80	71	72	72	68	69	69	56	68	62	51	53	52
1000	82	84	83	77	77	77	66	70	68	64	65	65	55	61	58	48	50	49
790	81	89	85	77	83	80	68	71	70	63	69	66	57	60	59	51	55	53
620	77	79	78	70	73	72	59	67	63	57	59	58	54	57	56	47	49	48
500	73	77	75	69	70	70	60	62	61	51	59	55	53	56	55	47	47	47

* DISTANCE FROM SOUND SOURCE

[1] Means rounded to nearest whole decibel. Above: inner coastal zone. Below: outer coastal zone. Locations of transects shown in Fig. 23A.

TABLE 4. SOUND-PRESSURE LEVELS (MINIMAL, MAXIMAL, MEAN) ALONG TRANSMISSION TRANSECTS ON ISLAS SANTA CRUZ AND ESPANOLA AT STATIONS 25, 50, 100, 150, 200 and 300 FEET FROM SOUND SOURCE[1]

ISLAND: SANTA CRUZ — NO. OF TRANSECTS: 2 — DESIGNATIONS: F, G
LOCALITY: 1 KM NE BELLA VISTA. SCALESIA FOREST ZONE — DATE: MARCH 21, 1968

CENTER FREQUENCY IN HERZ (dB VALUES: ONE-THIRD OCTAVE FILTER)	25 FEET*			50 FEET			100 FEET			150 FEET			200 FEET			300 FEET		
	RANGE		MEAN	RANGE		MEAN	RANGE		MEAN	RANGE		MEAN	RANGE		MEAN	RANGE		MEAN
	MIN.	MAX.	N=2	MIN.	MAX.	N=2	MIN.	MAX.	N=2	MIN.	MAX.	N=2	MIN.	MAX.	N=2	MIN.	MAX.	N=2
9920	74	75	75	65	65	65	41	47	44	34	39	37	27	49	38	20	32	26
8000	78	78	78	69	78	74	52	54	53	40	40	40	31	48	40	23	32	28
6320	80	83	82	73	74	74	46	54	50	40	44	42	33	46	40	34	31	30
4960	84	84	84	73	77	75	51	59	55	42	45	44	37	45	41	30	35	33
4000	82	83	83	70	76	73	53	65	59	45	49	47	40	45	43	34	34	34
3160	81	83	82	75	77	76	56	64	60	47	54	51	43	46	45	36	37	37
2480	82	83	83	72	75	74	61	64	63	50	56	53	45	47	46	37	38	38
2000	83	87	85	70	79	75	64	68	66	58	60	59	52	52	52	44	45	45
1580	86	87	87	76	78	77	67	67	67	60	64	62	52	56	54	42	52	47
1240	83	84	84	77	79	78	66	68	67	60	64	62	56	57	57	44	52	48
1000	80	86	83	75	78	77	64	66	65	57	62	60	53	56	55	44	53	49
790	84	85	85	75	77	76	64	65	65	56	60	58	51	55	53	43	52	48
620	83	83	83	73	73	73	57	62	60	55	57	56	45	49	47	40	46	43
500	77	77	77	66	67	67	53	57	55	52	53	53	43	45	44	39	40	39

* DISTANCE FROM SOUND SOURCE

ISLAND: ESPAÑOLA — NO. OF TRANSECTS: 8 — DESIGNATIONS: A,B,C,D,E,F,G,H
LOCALITY: PUNTA SUAREZ, NORTH SHORE, BAHIA GARDNER — DATE: MARCH 10, 11, 13, 1968

CENTER FREQUENCY IN HERZ (dB VALUES: ONE-THIRD OCTAVE FILTER)	25 FEET*			50 FEET			100 FEET			150 FEET			200 FEET			300 FEET		
	RANGE		MEAN	RANGE		MEAN	RANGE		MEAN	RANGE		MEAN	RANGE		MEAN	RANGE		MEAN
	MIN.	MAX.	N=8	MIN.	MAX.	N=8	MIN.	MAX.	N=8	MIN.	MAX.	N=8	MIN.	MAX.	N=7	MIN.	MAX.	N=7
9920	64	79	71	59	69	64	51	62	57	44	55	49	34	52	42	24	47	34
8000	64	79	71	58	72	63	49	65	56	43	63	51	35	56	45	27	52	37
6320	70	83	75	63	76	68	54	71	61	48	63	55	41	59	50	32	57	42
4960	73	85	79	67	78	72	60	73	64	50	64	59	47	64	56	38	62	48
4000	77	85	82	70	79	74	62	71	67	59	70	64	47	68	59	42	64	52
3160	77	84	81	70	77	74	64	72	69	57	70	64	50	67	59	43	62	51
2480	77	83	81	73	76	74	67	73	70	60	70	64	55	56	60	42	62	52
2000	82	87	84	75	80	78	71	76	73	62	70	67	59	65	61	45	61	53
1580	83	86	85	78	82	80	72	76	75	62	70	67	55	66	61	46	63	54
1240	84	87	85	77	82	80	71	75	74	62	78	68	55	66	61	45	65	54
1000	83	87	85	76	81	79	68	73	72	61	67	65	52	64	58	45	65	52
790	82	93	86	76	85	80	66	76	71	60	65	64	54	63	59	45	66	52
620	79	86	83	72	79	74	62	70	66	56	61	58	48	58	44	40	64	47
500	75	81	78	66	74	70	55	65	61	49	61	54	43	55	48	37	57	42

* DISTANCE FROM SOUND SOURCE

[1] Means rounded to nearest whole decibel. Above: *Scalesia* forest zone, Isla Santa Cruz. Below: Isla Espanola. Locations of transects shown in Fig. 23A,B.

TABLE 5. SOUND-PRESSURE LEVELS (MINIMAL, MAXIMAL, MEAN) ALONG TRANSMISSION TRANSECTS ON ISLAS GENOVESA AND WOLF AT STATIONS 25, 50, 100, 150, 200 and 300 FEET FROM SOUND SOURCE[1]

ISLAND: GENOVESA — NO. OF TRANSECTS: 4 — DESIGNATIONS: A, B, C, D
LOCALITY: BAHIA DARWIN — DATE: MARCH 26, 27, 1968

CENTER FREQUENCY IN HERZ	25 FEET*			50 FEET			100 FEET			150 FEET			200 FEET			300 FEET		
	RANGE		MEAN	RANGE		MEAN	RANGE		MEAN	RANGE		MEAN	RANGE		MEAN	RANGE		MEAN
dB VALUES: ONE-THIRD OCTAVE FILTER	MIN.	MAX.	N= 4	MIN.	MAX.	N= 4	MIN.	MAX.	N= 4	MIN.	MAX.	N=4	MIN.	MAX.	N= 4	MIN.	MAX.	N= 2
9920	69	77	74	56	67	61	43	59	50	23	48	34	21	38	29	16	30	23
8000	74	83	80	62	72	67	49	60	53	36	48	40	29	38	35	20	30	25
6320	80	85	82	65	75	69	51	61	55	41	48	43	33	44	38	24	30	27
4960	79	86	84	67	76	72	55	61	58	46	50	47	39	44	42	31	34	33
4000	80	87	85	70	78	74	58	63	61	53	56	54	45	52	48	38	41	40
3160	80	84	83	71	78	74	61	66	64	52	59	56	46	59	53	42	43	43
2480	80	83	82	74	79	77	64	70	68	53	60	57	47	63	55	45	49	47
2000	83	84	84	74	82	77	70	75	73	60	65	63	53	63	59	48	50	49
1580	81	89	85	78	87	81	70	79	75	60	70	67	57	66	62	49	51	50
1240	83	87	85	78	82	80	70	79	74	58	73	66	54	68	61	47	48	48
1000	83	86	85	75	78	77	68	76	70	55	70	63	50	64	57	47	49	48
790	82	85	84	74	76	75	64	72	67	54	66	60	50	59	55	44	48	46
620	75	81	79	66	72	69	59	62	61	49	58	53	45	52	49	39	45	42
500	73	77	74	62	73	67	51	63	56	45	55	50	42	49	46	36	42	39

* DISTANCE FROM SOUND SOURCE

ISLAND: WOLF — NO. OF TRANSECTS: 2 — DESIGNATIONS: A, B
LOCALITY: NW MESA — DATE: APRIL 1, 1968

CENTER FREQUENCY IN HERZ	25 FEET*			50 FEET			100 FEET			150 FEET			200 FEET			300 FEET		
	RANGE		MEAN	RANGE		MEAN	RANGE		MEAN	RANGE		MEAN	RANGE		MEAN	RANGE		MEAN
dB VALUES: ONE-THIRD OCTAVE FILTER	MIN.	MAX.	N= 2	MIN.	MAX.	N=2	MIN.	MAX.	N=2	MIN.	MAX.	N=1	MIN.	MAX.	N= 2	MIN.	MAX.	N= 2
9920	66	75	71	53	55	54	33	38	36	-	-	38	32	35	34	25	38	32
8000	69	78	74	56	60	58	33	38	36	-	-	37	31	37	34	27	37	32
6320	74	80	77	58	63	51	35	38	37	-	-	36	32	33	33	25	36	31
4960	71	82	77	59	65	62	40	40	40	-	-	35	32	33	33	25	35	30
4000	82	83	83	63	68	66	46	47	47	-	-	39	33	38	36	28	36	32
3160	79	83	81	65	71	68	52	54	53	-	-	44	33	45	39	31	37	34
2480	78	79	79	63	71	67	57	58	58	-	-	47	40	47	44	36	41	39
2000	81	81	81	73	75	74	59	67	63	-	-	53	46	51	49	44	48	46
1580	83	84	84	77	78	78	67	68	68	-	-	60	53	53	53	50	52	51
1240	82	82	82	76	78	77	61	63	62	-	-	62	55	58	57	50	52	51
1000	81	81	81	75	77	76	54	63	59	-	-	64	56	60	58	51	55	53
790	83	84	84	75	76	76	59	64	62	-	-	66	58	63	61	55	57	56
620	79	80	80	69	70	70	58	58	58	-	-	60	53	59	56	50	52	51
500	73	74	74	61	61	61	55	56	56	-	-	55	46	52	49	43	48	46

* DISTANCE FROM SOUND SOURCE

[1] Means rounded to nearest whole decibel. Above: Isla Genovesa. Below: Isla Wolf. Isla Genovesa locations shown in Fig. 23D.

TABLE 6. ENVIRONMENTAL INFORMATION ON SELECTED SOUND TRANSMISSION TRANSECTS IN THE GALAPAGOS

Island	Locality[1]	Date	Line	START			END		
				Time	Temp. ° F.	% Rel. Humidity	Time	Temp. ° F.	% Rel. Humidity
Española	5 mi. E. Punta Suarez, N side, elevation 10-20 ft.	Mar. 10/68	A	0600	74	86	0735	80	80
	Gardner Bay, elevation, 50 ft.	Mar. 11/68	D	0645	77	88	0730	78	90
Santa Cruz	Outer coast, W Academy Bay, elevation 30 ft.	Apr. 10/68	X	0720	74	91	0815	77	92
	Lower transition zone, 2 mi. N Academy Bay, elevation 200 ft.	Mar. 18/68	D	0725	77	82	0800	78	79
	Scalesia forest, 0.5 mi. NE Bella Vista, elevation 750 ft.	Mar. 21/68	F	0845	78	79	1000	88	61
Genovesa	N side Darwin Bay, elevation 60 ft.	Mar. 26/68	B	0730	77	88	0825	82	76
Pinta	S slope, elevation 430 ft.	Mar. 29/68	A	0830	80	80	0915	79	81
Wolf	NW mesa, elevation 200 ft.	Apr. 1/68	A	0810	76	80	0930	81	80

[1] See Figs. 3 and 23.

TABLE 7. CHARACTERISTICS OF WHITE, PINK, AND RED NOISE SPECTRA BEFORE AND AFTER ONE-THIRD OCTAVE CONSTANT PERCENTAGE BANDWIDTH FILTERING, BETWEEN 1 kHz AND 20 kHZ[1]

Noise spectrum	Characteristics before filtering	Characteristics after filtering
White	Constant energy distribution per octave	Energy increase of 3 dB per octave
Pink	Energy decrease of 3 dB per octave	Constant energy distribution per octave
Red	Energy decrease of 6 dB per octave	Energy decrease of 3 dB per octave

[1] Graphic representation in Fig. 25.

TABLE 8. DATES OF VISITS BY THE AUTHOR TO THE GALAPAGOS ARCHIPELAGO (ECUADOR), COCOS ISLAND (COSTA RICA), AND ST. LUCIA (WEST INDIES) FOR BIRD VOCALIZATION STUDIES

Year	Inclusive Dates	No. Days	Total
Galapagos			
1961-62	November 6-March 11	126	
1964	January 19-February 28	41	
1967	January 25-February 19	26	
	July 10-August 18	40	
1968	March 5-April 11	38	
	July 4-26	23	
1973	April 28-May 11	14	
	August 13-24	12	
1979	February 5-26	22	342
Cocos			
1964	March 8-9	2	
1967	January 22-23	2	4
St. Lucia			
1967	February 28-March 6	7	7

TABLE 9. DATES OF VISITS BY THE AUTHOR TO VARIOUS ISLANDS OF THE GALAPAGOS ARCHIPELAGO, 1961-1979

Island	Inclusive Dates	No. Days	Total
Bartólome	August 14, 1967	1	
	July 21, 1968	1	
	May 4 & August 17, 1973	2	
	February 25, 1979	1	5
Baltra	May 2 & August 24, 1973	2	
	Feb. 26, 1979	1	3
Champion	January 18-20, 1962	3	
	February 13, 1967	1	
	May 8, 1973	1	5
Daphne Major	August 15, 1967	1	1
Darwin	January 29-30, 1964	2	2
Española	January 3-17, 1962	15	
	February 1-2, 1962	2	
	February 10-12, 1967	3	
	July 16-18, 1967	3	
	March 9-13, 1968	5	
	May 10 & August 22, 1973	2	30
Fernandina	January 26-27 & August 4-5, 1967	4	
	July 8-19, 1968	12	
	May 2 & August 18, 1973	2	18
Floreana	January 21-23, 1962	11	11
Gardner-near-Floreana	July 19, 1967	1	1
Genovesa	February 10-23, 1962	14	
	February 4-6, 1967	3	
	March 25-28, 1968	4	
	April 29 & August 15, 1973	2	
	February 14-16, 1979	3	26
Isabela	February 26-27, 1962	2	
	January 28-30, 1967	3	
	July 30-August 3, 1967	5	
	August 6, 1967	1	
	April 6, 1968	1	
	May 2-3, 1973	2	14
Marchena	April 30 & August 16, 1973	2	
	February 17, 1979	1	3

TABLE 9. Continued

Island	Inclusive Dates	No. Days	Total
Pinta	March 28-29, 1968	2	
	April 30, 1973	1	
	February 13 & 24, 1979	2	5
Pinzón	May 5, 1973	1	1
Plazas	May 6, 1973	1	1
Rábida	February 25, 1962	1	
	July 29, 1967	1	
	May 5, 1973	1	3
San Cristóbal	March 11, 1962	1	
	February 8-9, 1967	2	
	March 5 & July 26, 1968	2	
	May 9, 1973	1	6
Santa Cruz	November 6-December 16, 1961	41	
	December 25, 1961-January 2, 1962	9	
	February 3-9 & 28, 1962	8	
	January 19-27 & Feb. 2-28, 1964	36	
	February 16-20, 1967	5	
	July 11-14, 1967	4	
	August 10-17, 1967	8	
	March 6-7 & 14-23, 1968	12	
	April 7-10, 1968	4	
	July 5-6 & 22-25, 1968	6	
	May 7 & August 20-23, 1973	5	
	February 5-12, 1979	8	146
Santa Fe	December 16-22, 1961	7	
	February 2, 1962	1	
	February 14-15 & July 14-15, 1967	4	
	March 8 & 13, 1968	2	14
Santiago	January 31-February 3, 1967	4	
	April 4-5, 1968	2	
	May 1 & August 19, 1973	2	8
Wolf	January 31-February 1, 1964	2	
	January 25, 1967	1	
	March 30-April 2, 1968	4	
	February 21-23, 1979	3	10

TABLE 10. DISTRIBUTION OF WHISTLE, BASIC, AND DERIVED SONGS IN 14 SPECIES OF DARWIN'S FINCHES AND THE ST. LUCIA BLACK FINCH[1]

Species	Whistle song		Basic song		
	One note	Two or more notes	Basic and/or abbreviate basic	Special	Derived Song
Geospiza					
magnirostris	x		x		x
conirostris	x		x		x
fortis	x		x		x
fuliginosa	x		x		x
difficilis					
I. Darwin	x		x		?[2]
I. Genovesa	x		x		x
I. Wolf			x	x	x
I. Santiago			x	x	
I. Pinta			x	x	
scandens	x		x		x
Pinaroloxias					
inornata	x		x		
Platyspiza					
crassirostris	x		x		
Cactospiza					
pallida	x		x	x	x
heliobates	x		x	?[3]	
Camarhynchus					
psittacula		x	x	x	x
pauper		x	x	x	x
parvulus		x	x	x	x
Certhidea					
olivacea	[4] x[5]	x	x		
Melanospiza					
richardsoni	x		x		

[1] Song types of Darwin's finches are illustrated in Figs. 43-47. *Melanospiza* song is illustrated in Fig. 104.

[2] Question mark indicates that song status has not been conclusively established.

[3] Curio and Kramer (1964) did not hear the special basic song in any of the seven males of *Cactospiza heliobates* they recorded.

[4] Box contains those signals with an obligate linkage, i.e. whistle song is never sounded apart from basic song proper.

[5] The whistle song of *Certhidea olivacea* consists of a single note in Santa Cruz and Española populations, and occasionally so in San Cristóbal and Wolf populations. See Figs. 109-112.

TABLE 11. DISTRIBUTION OF 11 SONG PATTERNS IN 14 SPECIES OF DARWIN'S FINCHES AND *MELANOSPIZA RICHARDSONI*

Genus	Species	Patterns[1]										Total number of patterns
		A	B	C	D	E	F	G	H	I	J	10
Geospiza	*magnirostris* *fortis* *fuliginosa*	x			x				x	x	x	5
	conirostris *scandens*	x	x	x			x				x	5
	difficilis	x		x						x		3
Camarhynchus	*psittacula* *pauper* *parvulus*			x		x			x			3
Cactospiza	*pallida*			x		x			x			3
	heliobates					x						1
Certhidea	*olivacea*	x	x					x				3
Platyspiza	*crassirostris*	x										1
Pinaroloxias	*inornata*	x										1
Melanospiza	*richardsoni*	x										1

[1] Patterns illustrated in Figs. 89-95 and 101-103.

TABLE 12. FEATURES OF *MELANOSPIZA RICHARDSONI* (ST. LUCIA BLACK FINCH) SHARED WITH ONE OR MORE SPECIES OF DARWIN'S FINCHES

Feature	Authority
Short tail	Bond 1961; Bowman, pers. obser.
Bony palate structure	Tordoff 1954
Skull pneumatization pattern	Bowman 1961
Similar (but not identical) syringeal musculature	Cutler, ms.
Seasonal change in color of bill	Stanley John[1], pers. comm.
Whistle song confluent with five-parted basic song of *Certhidea*	Fig. 104a.
Females may sing "partial" male song	Stanley John, pers. comm.; Bowman, this vol., Figs. 173-176.
Domed nest with opening at one side, often built 2-3 feet off ground	Stanley John, pers. comm. (cf. Fig. 10A)
Young males acquire black plumage in blotches as in *Pinaroloxias*	Stanley John, pers. comm.; Swarth 1931
Birds forage close to ground as in *Geospiza*	Stanley John, pers. comm.
Live among the shrubs of *Psychotria, Croton*, and *Miconia*, and feed upon their fruits	Stanley John, pers. comm.; Bowman, pers. obser.; Diamond 1973

[1] The late Stanley John was an experienced long-time resident naturalist of St. Lucia.

Whistle song

TABLE 13. MEASUREMENTS OF INTERAURAL DISTANCE, SKULL WIDTH, AND FREQUENCIES AND WAVELENGTHS OF WHISTLE SONGS IN 14 SPECIES OF DARWIN'S FINCHES

Species	Mean body wt.[1] (g)	No. specimens		Mean (range) interaural distance[2] (mm)	Mean (range) skull diameter[3] (mm)	Mean (range) duration of song[4] (msec)	Mean (range) maximal song frequency[4] (kHz)	Approximate wavelength of mean maximal frequency[5] (mm)	Mean (range) minimal frequency of song[4] (kHz)	Approximate wavelength of mean minimal frequency[5] (mm)	Difference between mean high and mean low song frequencies (kHz)
		Skulls	Songs								
Platyspiza crassirostris	35.5	4	14	9.9 (9.5-10.0)	17.2 (16.9-17.8)	3792 (2060-6190)	13.2 (11.6-15.5)	26	7.0 (5.9-8.5)	49	6.2
Geospiza magnirostris	38.3	4	13	12.9 (12.5-13.0)	20.4 (19.9-20.5)	3051 (1915-3905)	13.7 (12.0-15.4)	25	9.2 (6.4-11.4)	37	4.5
Geospiza conirostris	27.5	6	30	10.4 (10.0-12.0)	18.7 (17.5-19.9)	3164 (1915-3940)	14.5 (13.0-16.0)	24	9.6 (8.5-12.3)	36	4.9
Geospiza fortis	22.0	5	22	10.0 (9.0-11.0)	17.2 (16.8-17.8)	2220 (1500-3200)	14.6 (12.3-16.5)	24	9.3 (7.6-12.0)	37	5.3
Geospiza fuliginosa	15.0	5	5	8.0 (8.0-8.0)	14.5 (14.4-14.6)	1624 (1200-1975)	14.5 (14.0-15.0)	24	12.1 (9.5-13.8)	28	2.4
Geospiza difficilis (I. Genovesa)	11.0	1	10	7.5 (7.5)	13.7 (13.7)	1749 (1270-2470)	14.1 (13.0-15.0)	24	10.9 (8.8-12.8)	32	3.2
(I. Wolf)	21.0	1	11	8.0 (8.0)	14.5 (14.5)	554 (370-835)	14.6 (13.6-16.0)	24	12.9 (12.0-15.0)	27	1.7
Geospiza scandens	22.8	2	9	9.0 (9.0-9.3)	15.5 (15.4-15.6)	2438 (1715-3200)	14.9 (12.9-16.5)	23	9.0 (7.5-11.9)	38	5.9
Cactospiza pallida	22.4	2	5	9.0 (9.0-9.0)	16.0 (15.9-16.2)	2028 (1560-2520)	13.9 (13.4-14.5)	25	9.0 (8.3-10.0)	38	4.9
Camarhynchus psittacula	18.3	4	2	8.7 (8.3-9.0)	15.0 (14.8-15.3)	2402 (1845-2960)	15.9 (15.6-16.3)	22	12.1 (11.2-13.0)	28	3.8
Camarhynchus pauper	18.4	2	9	8.3 (8.0-8.5)	14.9 (14.8-15.0)	2352 (1835-2745)	14.2 (13.0-15.5)	24	11.4 (9.8-12.5)	30	2.8
Camarhynchus parvulus	13.0	5	23	7.5 (7.3-7.8)	14.2 (13.9-14.5)	1823 (1135-2870)	15.3 (14.0-16.3)	23	11.9 (9.6-13.3)	29	3.4

TABLE 13. Continued

Species	Mean body wt.[1] (g)	No. specimens Skulls	Songs	Mean (range) interaural distance[2] (mm)	Mean (range) skull diameter[3] (mm)	Mean (range) duration of song[4] (msec)	Mean (range) maximal song frequency[4] (kHz)	Approximate wavelength of mean maximal frequency[5] (mm)	Mean (range) minimal frequency of song[4] (kHz)	Approximate wavelength of mean minimal frequency[5] (mm)	Difference between mean high and mean low song frequencies (kHz)
Pinaroloxias inornata	13.5	3	5	7.8 (7.5-8.0)	13.0 (12.7-13.2)	1347 (980-2000)	15.0 (14.1-15.9)	23	6.9 (4.7-8.4)	50	8.1
Certhidea olivacea	8.8	5	70	6.5 (6.3-6.8)	13.2 (12.8-13.7)						
(I. San Cristóbal)		0	4			1045 (775-1285)	14.0 (13.2-14.9)	25	10.6 (9.2-11.8)	24	-0.1
(I. Española)	7.6	1	25	6.3 (6.3)	12.8 (12.8)	744. (580-975)	11.6 (7.3-14.2)	30	9.0 (5.3-11.0)	38	2.6
(I. Santa Cruz)	9.5	4	22	6.6 (6.3-6.8)	13.3 (13.1-13.7)	487 (325-665)	13.3 (12.1-15.0)	26	10.3 (3.8-13.2)	33	3.0
(I. Genovesa)	8.0	0	13			3256 (1630-4420)	13.9 (9.9-15.3)	25	8.4 (4.6-11.7)	41	5.5
(I. Marchena)		0	7			1410 (1030-1875)	12.7 (10.8-14.9)	27	10.0 (6.8-11.3)	34	2.7
(I. Pinta)		0	3			820 (680-995)	11.6 (11.1-12.1)	30	7.5 (7.1-7.8)	46	4.1
(I. Wolf)	9.0	0	3			822 (455-1100)	13.3 (12.1-14.3)	26	10.0 (9.8-10.3)	34	3.3
All species and populations (mean of means and range thereof)				8.5 (6.3-12.9) mm	15.3 (13.0-20.4) mm	1891 (744-3792) msec	14.0 (11.6-15.9) kHz	25 (22-30) mm	10.0 (6.9-14.1) kHz	35 (27-50) mm	3.9 (0.0-6.2) kHz

[1] Sources for body weights: Bowman 1961, 1979; Cutler 1970; study skins in Vertebrate Museum, San Francisco State University.

[2] Minimal distance between left and right medial edge of tympanic recess, measured on ventral surface of skull across basisphenoidal plate, caudal to osseous eustachian tube. See Fig. 108.

[3] Maximal diameter of skull at the parietal region or at the quadratojugal-quadrate joint, whichever is greater. See Fig. 108.

[4] Measured on narrow-band, half-speed "songrams."

[5] Approximate wavelength of frequency calculated as follows: $\frac{\text{velocity of sound in air at 15° C (344.1192 M/sec)}}{\text{frequency of sound (Hz)}}$

TABLE 14. RELATIVE FREQUENCY OF SONG TYPES IN REPERTOIRES OF 10 SPECIES OF DARWIN'S FINCHES, ACCORDING TO STAGE OF VOCAL ONTOGENY

Species	No. of ind.	Island population	Ontogenetic stage[1]	Whistle song	Basic or derived song	Total
Geospiza						
magnirostris	1	Genovesa	subsong	7 (54%)	6 (46%)	13 (100%)
	3	Genovesa	rehearsed	23 (31%)	50 (69%)	73 (100%)
	10	Genovesa	definitive	23 (1%)	218 (99%)	241 (100%)
conirostris	1	Genovesa	rehearsed	34 (56%)	27 (44%)	61 (100%)
	11	Genovesa	definitive	24 (13%)	160 (87%)	184 (100%)
	43	Española	definitive	84 (6%)	1437 (94%)	1521 (100%)
fortis	3	Santa Cruz	subsong	38 (22%)	134 (88%)	172 (100%)
	8	Santa Cruz	rehearsed	78 (16%)	406 (84%)	484 (100%)
	17	Santa Cruz	definitive	9 (2%)	534 (98%)	543 (100%)
fuliginosa	2	Santa Cruz	subsong	20 (18%)	89 (82%)	109 (100%)
	4	Santa Cruz	rehearsed	16 (10%)	138 (90%)	154 (100%)
	16	Santa Cruz	definitive	10 (1%)	701 (99%)	711 (100%)
	14	Española	definitive	6 (1%)	957 (99%)	963 (100%)
difficilis	6	Genovesa	rehearsed	89 (34%)	168 (66%)	257 (100%)
	5	Genovesa	definitive	4 (2%)	185 (98%)	189 (100%)

Species	No. of ind.	Island population	Ontogenetic stage[1]	Whistle and basic songs[2]	Derived song	Total
Certhidea						
olivacea	4	Santa Cruz	rehearsed	292 (52%)	270 (48%)	562 (100%)
	34	Santa Cruz	definitive	102 (17%)	507 (83%)	609 (100%)
	2	Española	rehearsed	76 (45%)	92 (55%)	168 (100%)
	12	Española	definitive	46 (18%)	203 (82%)	249 (100%)
	20	Genovesa	definitive	82 (12%)	587 (88%)	669 (100%)

Species	No. of ind.	Island population	Ontogenetic stage[1]	Whistle song	Special basic	Derived song	Total
Cactospiza							
pallida	1	Santa Cruz	rehearsed	2 (23%)	4 (44%)	3 (33%)	9 (100%)
	8	Santa Cruz	definitive	6 (6%)	31 (31%)	64 (63%)	101 (100%)
Camarhynchus							
psittacula	7	Santa Cruz	definitive	6 (8%)	0 (0%)	74 (92%)	80 (100%)
pauper	2	Floreana	rehearsed	18 (32%)	17 (31%)	20 (36%)	55 (100%)
	16	Floreana	definitive	44 (10%)	145 (34%)	239 (56%)	428 (100%)
parvulus	1	Santa Cruz	subsong	1 (3%)	11 (38%)	17 (59%)	29 (100%)
	1	Santa Cruz	rehearsed	1 (0%)	4 (36%)	7 (64%)	11 (100%)
	11	Santa Cruz	definitive	11 (2%)	57 (9%)	574 (89%)	642 (100%)

[1] Based on criteria of Lanyon (1960).

[2] In *Certhidea olivacea*, whistle and basic songs are always given together.

TABLE 15. WAVELENGTHS OF MEAN MAXIMAL AND MINIMAL FREQUENCIES OF WHISTLE SONGS, EXPRESSED AS A PERCENTAGE OF INTERAURAL DISTANCE AND SKULL WIDTH[1]

Species	Interaural percentage[2]		Skull diameter percentage[3]	
	highest frequency	lowest frequency	highest frequency	lowest frequency
Platyspiza crassirostris	262	494	151	284
Geospiza magnirostris	193	286	122	181
Geospiza conirostris	230	346	128	193
Geospiza fortis	240	370	140	215
Geospiza fuliginosa	300	350	166	193
Geospiza difficilis (I. Genovesa)	320	426	175	234
Geospiza difficilis (I. Wolf)	300	337	166	186
Geospiza scandens	255	422	148	245
Cactospiza pallida	277	422	156	238
Camarhynchus psittacula	252	321	147	187
Camarhynchus pauper	289	361	161	201
Camarhynchus parvulus	306	386	162	204
Pinaroloxias inornata (I. Cocos, C. R.)	294	641	177	385
Certhidea olivacea (I. Santa Cruz)	393	500	195	248
Nesomimus[4]	299	420	136	191
Asio flammeus[4]	140	185	58	81
Buteo galapagoensis[4]	141	197	75	76

[1] In Darwin's finches, Galapagos mockingbirds, short-eared owl, and *Buteo* hawk. Percentages are based on mean maximal (highest) and mimimal (lowest) frequencies for each species as given in Table 13. Method of measuring skulls is shown in Fig. 108.

[2] $\frac{\text{Mean maximal (or minimal) wavelength in mm X 100}}{\text{Mean interaural distance in mm.}}$

[3] $\frac{\text{Mean maximal (or minimal) wavelength in mm X 100}}{\text{Mean skull diameter in mm.}}$

[4] Skull measurements based on the following specimens: *Nesomimus*, 3 male *parvulus* (I. Santa Cruz) and 2 male *macdonaldi* (I. Española); *Asio*, 1 male, 1 female, 1 unknown sex (I. Española, Genovesa and Santa Cruz); *Buteo* 1 male, 1 female, 1 unknown sex (I. Isabela, Pinzón and Santa Fe), and are expressed as a percentage of mean maximal (minimal) song wavelengths of all species of Darwin's finches combined (i.e. see means on bottom line of Table 13).

TABLE 16. CLUTCH SIZE, AGE AT FLEDGING, SELF-FEEDING AND VOICE CHANGE IN AVIARY-REARED NESTLINGS OF DARWIN'S FINCHES

Species population	Mean clutch size	Mean age (days) at fledging	Means of minimal and maximal ages (days) at self-feeding	Age (days) at voice change[1]
Geospiza				
difficilis (Isla Wolf)	2.08 (12)[2]	12.43 (21)	23.34-27.47 (17)	11.86 (7)
difficilis (Isla Darwin)	2.08 (8)	13.86 (7)	19.80-27.00 (5)	13.00 (2)
magnirostris (Isla Genovesa)	3.00 (5)	13.67 (3)	23.00-27.00 (2)	13.25 (4)
scandens intermedia (Isla Santa Cruz)	2.60 (9)	13.00 (8)	21.00-28.33 (3)	14.00 (2)
conirostris (Isla Española)	3.67 (6)	12.25 (4)	20.00-28.50 (2)	12.00 (4)

[1] See Fig. 116 for examples of sound spectrograms of nestling and fledgling food calls.
[2] Sample size in parenthesis.

TABLE 17A. CORRELATION OF WHISTLE AND SPECIAL BASIC SONGS OF *GEOSPIZA DIFFICILIS* WITH VEGETATION CHARACTERISTICS ON FIVE ISLANDS OF THE GALAPAGOS ARCHIPELAGO

Island[1]	Whistle song separate from basic song (Table 10)	Typical basic song present (Fig. 61)	Region 5 of special basic song (Fig. 62)		Vegetation of nesting habitat	
			Whistle-like	"Normal"	Type	Density
Genovesa	yes	yes	special basic song absent		xeric	open (Fig. 15)
Darwin	yes	yes	special basic song absent		xeric to semi-xeric	semi-open (Fig. 11)
Wolf	whistle song absent	yes, but rarely	yes	no	xeric to semi-xeric	semi-open to dense (Fig. 14)
Santiago	whistle song absent	yes	yes	no	semi-xeric to mesic	dense to very dense (Fig. 13b)
Pinta	whistle song absent	yes	no	yes	semi-xeric to mesic	dense to very dense

[1] Islands are arranged from top to bottom in order of decreasing xeric condition and increasing density of vegetation of nesting habitat.

TABLE 17B. GENERAL CLASSIFICATION OF SONG FEATURES OF DARWIN'S FINCHES

Song Feature	Whistle Song	Special Basic and *Certhidea* Basic Songs	Basic, Abbreviated Basic and Derived Song
Structure	Pure-tone	Wideband "buzzy" FM	Variable: strong to weak FM, to pure-tone
Locatability	Binaurally concealing	Binaurally revealing	Binaurally revealing
Behavioral context	Pair-bonding; nest invitation	Close -up aggression toward intruding males near nest.	Territorial repulsion of conspecific males; attraction of conspecific females
Presumed motivational state	Submissive and friendly	Aggressive (i.e. "growl")	Aggressive
Species distribution	All species[1]	*Certhidea olivacea* *Cactospiza pallida* *Camarhynchus* (all species) *Geospiza difficilis* (Isla Wolf and possibly other populations)	All species (but not including *Certhidea* basic)

[1] Including whistle-like song region 5 in *Geospiza difficilis*, Isla Wolf. According to Dr. L. Ratcliffe (pers. comm.), the special basic song of *G. difficilis*, Isla Pinta, has the same function as the whistle song alone in other populations of the species, e.g. Isla Genovesa.

TABLE 18. SOUND-PRESSURE LEVELS OF ADVERTISING SONGS OF FOUR SPECIES OF DARWIN'S FINCHES

Species	Island	Song type	Mean body weight (g)	No. of songs	Mean dB level by song regions[1] 1	2	3	4	5	Song spectrogram
Geospiza										
magnirostris	Genovesa	Basic	35	4	91	93	--	104	105	Fig. 124B
conirostris	Genovesa	Basic	25	4	100	100	102	100	101	Fig. 124A
difficilis	Genovesa	Basic	11	6	73	74	95	94	78	Fig. 125
difficilis	Wolf	Derived & special basic	21	1	104[2]	--	92	94	92	Fig. 126
Certhidea										
olivacea	Genovesa	Derived	3	2	82	92	91	97	--	Fig. 123

[1] Regions refer to points in time along the song, as shown in Figs. 123-126. Decibel values are adjusted so as to represent sound-pressure levels at approximately one inch from the bill of the bird. See text for details.

[2] Region 1 dB value is that of the derived song; regions 3, 4 and 5 are dB values for the special basic song.

TABLE 19. EXAMPLES OF CUMULATIVE SONG TRANSMISSION LOSSES (in dB) FOR FIVE PLANT COMMUNITIES IN THE GALAPAGOS ISLANDS, ACCORDING TO FREQUENCY AND DISTANCE FROM SOUND SOURCE. DATA ADJUSTED TO COMPENSATE FOR FREQUENCY-DEPENDENT AUDITORY SENSITIVITIES OF THE CANARY

Distance from sound source	25 ft.						25-50 ft.						25-100 ft.						25-200 ft.						25-300 ft.					
Frequency (kHz)	2	3	4	6	8	10	2	3	4	6	8	10	2	3	4	6	8	10	2	3	4	6	8	10	2	3	4	6	8	10
Auditory sensitivity factor (dB)[1]	16	8	15	24	40	53	16	8	15	24	40	53	16	8	15	24	40	53	16	8	15	24	40	53	16	8	15	24	40	53
Locality:																														
Isla Santa Cruz																														
Scalesia forest zone[2]	85	85	83	82	78	75	75	76	73	74	74	65	66	60	59	50	53	44	52	45	43	40	40	38	45	37	34	30	28	26
Adjusted SPL's[3]	69	77	68	58	38	22	59	68	58	50	34	12	50	52	44	26	14	-9	36	37	28	16	0	-15	29	29	19	6	-12	-27
Adjusted cumulative dB loss[4]							10[4]	9	10	8	4	10	19	25	24	32	24	31	33	37	40	42	38	37	40	45	49	52	50	49
Outer coastal zone	84	84	85	83	81	72	77	78	79	77	73	66	69	67	69	65	64	55	60	59	59	55	51	42	50	50	49	45	41	32
Adjusted SPL's	68	76	70	59	41	19	61	70	64	53	33	13	53	59	54	41	24	2	44	51	44	31	11	-11	34	42	34	21	1	-21
Adjusted cumulative dB loss							7	6	6	6	8	6	15	17	16	18	17	17	24	25	26	28	30	30	34	34	36	38	40	40
Isla Española	84	81	82	75	71	71	78	74	74	68	63	64	73	69	67	61	56	57	61	59	59	50	45	42	53	51	52	42	37	34
Adjusted SPL's	68	73	67	51	31	18	62	66	59	44	23	11	57	61	52	37	16	4	45	51	44	26	5	-11	37	43	37	18	-3	-18
Adjusted cumulative dB loss							6	7	8	7	8	7	11	12	15	14	15	14	23	22	23	25	26	29	31	30	30	33	34	37
Isla Genovesa	84	83	85	82	80	74	77	74	74	69	67	61	73	64	61	55	53	50	59	53	48	38	35	29	49	43	40	27	25	23
Adjusted SPL's	68	75	70	58	40	21	61	66	59	45	27	8	57	56	46	31	13	-3	43	45	33	14	-5	-24	33	35	25	3	-15	-30
Adjusted cumulative dB loss							7	9	11	13	13	13	11	19	24	27	27	24	25	30	37	44	45	45	35	40	45	55	55	51
Isla Wolf	81	81	83	77	74	71	74	68	66	51	58	54	63	53	47	37	36	36	49	39	36	33	34	34	46	34	32	31	32	32
Adjusted SPL's	65	73	68	53	34	18	58	60	51	27	18	1	47	45	32	13	-4	-17	33	31	21	9	-6	-19	30	26	17	7	-8	-21
Adjusted cumulative dB loss							7	13	17	26	16	17	18	28	36	40	38	35	32	42	47	44	40	37	35	47	51	46	42	39

[1] Auditory sensitivity factors for *Serinus canarius* from Dooling et al. (1971; Table 1, mean threshold of four birds).

[2] Numbers following the plant community name, e.g. *Scalesia* forest zone, are the absolute dB values of sound at frequencies of 2, 3, 4, 6, 8, and 10 kHz, at distances 25, 50, 100, 200, and 300 feet from sound source. Data from Tables 3-5.

[3] Absolute dB values of sound minus auditory sensitivity factors, e.g. 85 minus 16 equals 69 dB.

[4] Example: between 25 and 50 ft. from sound source and at a frequency of 2 kHz, the auditory sensitivity factor is 16 dB. The adjusted cumulative dB loss for the *Scalesia* forest zone is 10 dB, which represents the cumulative dB loss at 2 kHz between 25 and 50 feet from the sound source, i.e. 69 minus 59 equals 10 dB.

TABLE 20. CUMULATIVE SOUND TRANSMISSION LOSSES (dB's) AND SONG BANDWIDTHS OF *GEOSPIZA CONIROSTRIS* ON ISLAS GENOVESA AND ESPANOLA[1]

Frequency (kHz)		50			100			200			300	
	Cumulative transmission loss (dB's) Distance from sound source (ft.):											
Isla Genovesa												
8		13			27			45			55	
6		13			27			44			55	
4		11			24			37			45	
M–3		9	4		19	13		30	12		40	10
2–M[3]	2[2]	7		8	11		5	25		5	35	
Isla Española												
8		8			15			26			34	
6		7			14			25			33	
4		8			15			23			30	
3–M	2	7		4	12		1	22		1	30	
M–2		6	1		11	1		23	1		31	1

[1] Data from Table 19 (see also Fig. 130) are adjusted to the auditory sensitivity spectrum of the canary. Modal amplitudes and energy spectra of song dialects of *Geospiza conirostris* are shown for concordant and discordant island environments (i.e. brackets at left and right sides of columns, respectively).

[2] Difference in cumulative dB losses between upper and lower frequencies of song dialects containing 82-86% of sound energy as indicated by brackets.

[3] M equals modal amplitude of songs of *Geospiza conirostris* for concordant environment (left side of column) and discordant environment (right side of column).

TABLE 21. TERRITORY SIZE AND BODY WEIGHT FOR FOUR SPECIES OF DARWIN'S FINCHES ON ISLA GENOVESA

Species	Body weight (g)	Number of territories measured	Maximum diameter of territory[1] Range m	Mean m	Mean ft.
Geospiza magnirostris	35	9	61 - 117	78	256
Geospiza conirostris	25	6	52 - 104	78	256
Geospiza difficilis	11	13	22 - 52	40	131
Certhidea olivacea	8	5	26 - 87	56	184

[1] These figures are approximate, and were calculated from small-scale territory maps in Grant and Grant (1980; Fig. 5).

TABLE 22. FACTORS FAVORING THE OCCURRENCE OF HIGH FREQUENCIES IN TERRITORIAL SONGS OF DARWIN'S FINCHES

Category	Factor	Explanation
1. Anatomical	Syringeal structure	Through possession of a heavily muscularized syrinx of unique construction (Cutler 1970), all species are adapted to sing high frequency song, as in whistle song.
2. Physical	Sound-transmission field	There is no physical disadvantage in singing high frequencies over low, as in certain Galapagos environments (e. g. Isla Wolf) where there is a fairly uniform cumulative (adjusted) transmission loss over a broad bandwidth (i.e. 3.5-10.0 kHz) with similar cumulative dB losses throughout at a distance of 100 feet from sound source (see Table 19). Additionally, background noise levels are significantly lower in the higher frequencies as compared to lower frequencies (i.e. 20 dB versus 30 dB at 8 and 2 kHz, respectively; see Fig. 134A).
3. Psychological	Binaural localization of sound	Detection of intensity differences at left and right ears is enhanced by small wavelengths (high frequencies), which are better blocked (i.e. diffracted) than large wavelengths (low frequencies) by the head.
	Auditory contrast	Alternating high and low frequency notes or a sequence of notes of significantly different pitch are more effective "attention-getters" than a monotonous signal, continuous or discontinuous. See examples of song: *Camarhynchus parvulus*, Fig. 65; and *Geospiza magnirostris*, Fig. 53 (R-119 JLG).
4. Ecological	Small territory size	In food-resource-rich environments during the breeding season, territories may be relatively small. Frequency-dependent disparities in transmission loss over short distances are probably minimal in the higher frequencies. Smaller transmission losses resulting from smaller territories would tend to favor audition in the higher frequencies despite sharp ear-sensitivity fall-offs (Dooling et al. 1971).

TABLE 23. COMPARISON OF TERRITORY SIZES AND DISTANCES FROM SOUND SOURCE AT WHICH SONG AMPLITUDES ARE APPROXIMATELY 30 dB ABOVE BACKGROUND NOISE LEVELS IN FOUR SPECIES OF FINCH ON ISLA GENOVESA

Species	Mean body wt. (g)	Highest mean[1] adjusted[2] dB level of song at					Greatest width of territory (ft.)[3]	
		50′	100′		200′	300′	Range	Mean
Geospiza magnirostris	35	93	84		71	*63*[4]	200-383	256
Geospiza conirostris	25	96	87		74	*66*	170-341	256
Geospiza difficilis	11	73	*61*		44	37	72-171	131
Certhidea olivacea	8	82[5]	72	*58*[6]	50	41	85-285	184

[1] Data from Figs. 123-126.

[2] Frequencies "adjusted" to the auditory sensitivities of the canary as given in Table 19.

[3] Data from Table 21.

[4] Number in italics is the song amplitude at specified distance from source source having an average value of about 30 dB above the background noise level of 30 dB. Example: at 300 ft. from sound source, the dB level of the song is 63 dB. This value is arrived at as follows: from Fig. 124B we determine the average dB level of song using the values shown, i.e. 91 + 93 + 104 + 103 = 391. Divide 391 by 4 and we obtain a mean song dB of 98 dB. This value is "adjusted" by using data in Table 19 where we find that for Isla Genovesa, between 25 and 300 ft. from the sound source and at 2 kHz (the closest mean frequency of *G. magnirostris* song for which we have transmission data), the cumulative dB loss is indicated. We subtract this value, 35 dB, from the mean dB value of the song, 98, to obtain an "adjusted" value of 63 dB.

[5] Data from Table 25. Example: at 50 ft. from sound source, the highest dB levels of whistle, basic, and derived songs of *Certhidea olivacea* are 82, 83, and 80, respectively, with a mean dB value of 82.

[6] dB value at a distance of 150 ft. from sound source.

TABLE 24. CUMULATIVE SOUND-TRANSMISSION LOSSES (dB's) AND SONG BANDWIDTHS OF *CAMARHYNCHUS PARVULUS* IN THE *SCALESIA* FOREST AND OUTER COASTAL ZONES OF ISLA SANTA CRUZ[1]

Frequency (kHz)	*Cumulative transmission loss (dB's)* Distance from sound source (ft.): 50	100	200	300
Scalesia forest zone				
8	4	24	38	50
6 –M	8	32	42	52
4	10	20	40	49
[3]M–3–M	9	22	37	45
2	10	19	33	40
Left bracket (4–3)	1[2]	2	3	4
Right bracket (6–3)	1	10	5	7
Outer coastal zone				
8	8	17	30	40
M–6	6	18	28	38
4	6	16	26	36
M–3–M	6	17	25	34
2	7	15	24	34
Left bracket (6–3)	0	1	3	4
Right bracket (4–3)	0	1	1	2

[1] Data from Table 19 (see also Fig. 142) are adjusted to the auditory sensitivity spectrum of the canary. Modal amplitudes and energy spectra of song dialects of *Camarhynchus parvulus* are shown for concordant and discordant environments (i.e. brackets at left and right sides of columns, respectively).

[2] Difference in cumulative dB losses between upper and lower frequencies of song dialects containing 80-82% of sound energy, as indicated by brackets.

[3] M is the modal amplitude of song of *Camarhynchus parvulus* for concordant environment (left side of column) and discordant environment (right side of column).

TABLE 25. AMPLITUDES OF SONGS OF DARWIN'S FINCHES AT VARIOUS DISTANCES FROM THE SOUND SOURCE, ADJUSTED TO ACCOMMODATE FOR DIFFERING FREQUENCY-DEPENDENT AUDITORY SENSITIVITIES

Island/Species	Song/Regions[1]	Modal frequency[2] (Hz)	Center freq. nearest 1/3 octave (Hz)	Mean absolute amplitude of song[3] (dB)	Adjusted cumulative transmission loss (dB)[4] between 25 and: 50 (ft.)	100	200	300	Adjusted db level of song[5] at: 50 (ft.)	100	200	300	Mean diameter of territory[6] (ft.)
Genovesa													
Certhidea olivacea	Whistle	11.2	9920	95	13[7]	24	45	51	82	71	50	44	184
									(1)[8]	(8)	(1)	(3)	
	Basic	7.5	8000	96	13	27	45	55	[9][2]83	[5]79	[1]51	[6]41	
									(3)	(13)	(2)	(3)	
	Derived	6.0	6320	93	13	27	44	45	80	66	49	38	
Geospiza magnirostris	Basic: regions 1, 2, 3	2.5	2480	92	5	14	27	35	87	78	65	57	256
									(12)	(12)	(12)	(12)	
	Basic: regions 4, 5	2.5	2480	104	5	14	27	35	99	90	77	69	
Geospiza conirostris	Basic: regions 1, 2, 3	2.5	2480	100	5	14	27	35	95	86	73	65	256
									(1)	(1)	(1)	(1)	
	Basic: regions 4, 5	2.5	2480	101	5	14	27	35	96	87	74	66	
Geospiza difficilis	Basic: regions 1, 2, 5	4.0	4000	75	11	24	37	45	64	51	38	30	131
									(18)	(20)	(12)	(14)	
	Basic: regions 3, 4	9.5	9920	95	13	24	45	51	82	71	50	44	
Wolf													
Geospiza difficilis	Special basic regions 3, 4, 5	9.5	9920	93	16	35	37	39	76	58	56	54	---
									(11)	(10)	(1)	(1)	
	Derived: regions 1, 2	4.0	4000	104	17	36	47	51	87	68	57	53	

[1] Song types are illustrated in Figs. 42-47. Song regions are shown in Figs. 84-86 (cf. Table 18).
[2] Frequency (kHz) of modal amplitudes from Figs. 135-136 (advertising songs) and Table 13 (whistle song).
[3] dB values for song regions at sound source obtained from Figs. 130-135.
[4] Cumulative transmission losses are calculated from data in Table 19, and adjusted to compensate for frequency-dependent auditory sensitivities of the canary.
[5] Song amplitude (dB's) calculated by substracting adjusted cumulative transmission loss from mean absolute amplitude of song at source.
[6] Data on territory size from Table 21.
[7] Transmission losses for all frequencies above 10 kHz are calculated as if they were the same as for approximately 10 kHz (i.e. 9920 kHz, center frequency), whereas in reality they are probably much greater.
[8] Difference in amplitude (dB) between adjacent values at distances indicated.
[9] Difference in amplitude (dB) between whistle and derived songs at distances indicated.

TABLE 26. RELATIVE SIZE OF TERRITORIES OF *GEOSPIZA CONIROSTRIS* (ISLA GENOVESA), ACCORDING TO SONG TYPE

Song type[1]	No. of territories	Maximum diameter of territories[2] (mm)	Mean maximal diameter and range[3] of territories (mm)
A. *Mated males*			
Basic song	10	14.4, 15.9, 16.1, 18.1, 19.2, 25.4, 29.5, 30.9, 31.8, 32.2	23.35 ±7.32 ($S_{\bar{x}}$) (14.4-32.2)
Derived song	7	14.4, 15.8, 16.9, 18.4, 20.5, 26.3, 30.7	20.43 ±5.98 (14.4-30.7)
B. *Unmated males*			
Basic song	4	13.7, 16.1, 18.9, 30.0	19.68 ±7.20 (13.7-30.0)
Derived song	4	9.9, 18.6, 20.4, 40.1	22.25 ±12.75

[1] Basic and derived songs are equivalent names for songs B and A, respectively, of Grant and Grant 1979. Songs are illustrated in Fig. 94.

[2] As measured in mm from 6X magnifications of areas shown in Fig. 2 of B. R. Grant and P. R. Grant 1979. Territorial perimeters are not based on actual measured areas and therefore do not represent actual territorial sizes, nor do the authors present them as such (pers. comm. from L. Ratcliffe).

[3] There is no statistical significance between the means of any of the four song types. See footnote 2.

TABLE 27. COMPLEXITY OF *CERTHIDEA* DERIVED SONG ACCORDING TO GEOSPIZINE SPECIES DIVERSITY ON EIGHT ISLANDS OF THE GALAPAGOS ARCHIPELAGO

Island	No. species of Geospizinae[1]	Complexity of derived song[2]: Relative length	Complexity of derived song[2]: Phrase diversity[3]
Santa Cruz	9	short	2
Española	3	medium	2
San Cristóbal	7	medium	2
Santa Fe	4	long	1
Genovesa	4	long	3
Wolf	3	long	1
Pinta	9	long	1
Marchena	7	long	1

[1] See Fig. 3 and Table 2.

[2] See sound spectrograms of derived songs in Figs. 81-82. Subjective key to phrase diversity: 1 = low, 2 = modest, 3 = high.

[3] See Fig. 154 for examples of *Certhidea* phrases in three island populations. For remaining islands see Figs. 81-82 and 155-160.

TABLE 28. VARIATION IN FREQUENCY AND AMPLITUDE PARAMETERS OF SONGS OF THREE SPECIES OF *GEOSPIZA* AS A FUNCTION OF SYMPATRIC GEOSPIZINE DIVERSITY ON FOUR ISLANDS OF THE GALAPAGOS ARCHIPELAGO

Species	Island	No. of resident species	Modal amplitudes (kHz)	Limits of bandwidth[1] (kHz)	Bandwidth (kHz)
Geospiza magnirostris	Santa Cruz	9	1.75	1.0 - 2.75	1.75
	Genovesa	4	2.75	2.25 - 3.0	0.75
	Wolf	3	2.00	1.5 - 2.75	1.25
			5.00	4.0 - 5.25	1.25
			8.00	7.5 - 8.25	0.75
Geospiza conirostris	Española	3	2.25	1.5 - 4.0	2.5
	Genovesa	4	2.75	2.0 - 3.0	1.0
Geospiza scandens	Santa Cruz	9	3.00	2.5 - 3.75	1.25

[1] Bandwidths of *G. magnirostris* containing 81-88% of song energy. See Figs. 52-53 and 137. Bandwidths of *G. conirostris* and *G. scandens* containing 80-85% of song energy. See Figs. 54, 60, and 131.

TABLE 29. CORRELATION OF BILL VARIABILITY WITH SONG BANDWIDTH AND HABITAT DIVERSITY AND UTILIZATION IN *GEOSPIZA CONIROSTRIS*, *CAMARHYNCHUS PARVULUS*, AND *CERTHIDEA OLIVACEA*

Species	Island	Bill length: variability[1] No.	CV	Habitat diversity[2]	Habitat utilization	Song bandwidth[3] (kHz)	Acoustical diversity[4]	Acoustical aperture[5]
Geospiza conirostris	Española (Fig. 9)	87	6.08	79	All areas of patchy arid zone	2.5	Medium	Wide
	Genovesa (Fig. 11)	43	5.38	22	Only in dense *Opuntia* patches[6]	1.0	Low	Narrow
Camarhynchus parvulus (Isla Santa Cruz)	Coastal zone (Fig. 4B)	--	---	Species-poor,[7] patchy distribution	All areas	4.0	High	Wide
	Scalesia forest zone (Fig. 6)	--	---	Species-rich, uniform distribution	All areas	1.5	Low	Narrow
Certhidea olivacea	Genovesa (Fig. 11)	41	2.5	22	Patchy areas of arid zone	4.0	High	Wide
	Santa Cruz (Figs. 5-8)	44	4.5	193	Lower transition through moist zones	3.25	Medium	Wide
	Española (Fig. 9)	44	---	79	All zones of arid zone	2.75	Medium	Wide

1 Coefficients of variation from Bowman 1961, Table 61.

2 The numbers of species of vascular plants are from Stewart (1911). Comparable totals based on Wiggins and Porter (1971) have not been compiled, but relative differences in numbers should not differ significantly.

3 Data on *Geospiza conirostris* from Fig. 131, on *Camarhynchus parvulus* from Fig. 143, on *Certhidea olivacea* from Fig. 139.

4 Acoustical diversity is assumed to be high when the vegetation is patchy, strongly stratified, or distributed in altitudinal zones, and low when the vegetation is uniformly distributed, essentially unstratified, and contained within one vegetational zone.

5 See sound-transmission isopleths, Figs. 133-134. The width of the acoustical aperture is determined on the basis of known territory size (Isla Genovesa) but estimated (for islas Española and Santa Cruz) on the basis of relative size of the bird (see Fig. 140 and Table 21).

6 *Fide* Grant and Grant (1979).

7 Reeder and Riechert (1975).

TABLE 30. PRAGMATIC ANALYSIS OF SOME FACTORS AFFECTING THE DESIGN OF GEOSPIZINE VOCALIZATIONS

Feature	Physical Effect on	Consequence on song	Illustration
A. *BODY SIZE*	1. *Diameter of syringeal vibratory membranes*	*Frequency of modal amplitude*	*Figs. 128 and 129.*
Large	Large	Lower	Compare *Geospiza magnirostris* and *Certhidea olivacea* (Fig. 49) and 3 species of *Camarhynchus* (Fig. 69).
Small	Small	Higher	
	2. *Territory and population size*	*Amplitude*	*Figs. 137-138.*
Large	Large territory and small population size	Higher dB level	Compare *Geospiza magnirostris* and *G. difficilis* (Figs. 124-126).
Small	Small territory and large population size	Lower dB level	Compare *Certhidea, Camarhynchus parvulus*, and *Cactospiza pallida* (Fig. 70).
B. *VEGETATION DENSITY*	1. *Visibility*	*Temporal and tonal characteristics*	*Figs. 144, 146, and 153.*
High	Poor	FM signal with high repetition rate of sharp transients; of relatively long duration; buzzy quality.	Compare songs of *Geospiza fuliginosa* and *G. fortis* in brushy inner coastal zone of Academy Bay and coastal parkland zone of south James Bay (Figs. 151-152).
Low	Fair to good	Less note repetition and relatively more pure-tone whistle-like notes of variable form; relatively short song duration.	Compare *Certhidea* dialects on islas Santa Cruz and Genovesa (Figs. 81A-82A).
	2. *Sound transmission*	*Frequency of modal amplitude*	*Figs. 57-58.*
High	Selective attenuation of higher frequencies	Relatively less sound energy in higher frequencies and more concentrated about modal frequency.	Compare *Geospiza conirostris* on islas Española and Genovesa (Figs. 130-131).
Low	Attenuation less discriminatory of higher frequencies.	Relatively more sound energy in higher frequencies; polymodal frequency distribution of energy may appear.	Compare energy distribution in songs of *Camarhynchus parvulus* living in *Scalesia* forest and coastal zones of Isla Santa Cruz (Figs. 119-120 and 142-143).
C. *ATMOSPHERIC CONDITIONS* *Wind and temperature*	*Frequency-dependent energy spectrum*	*Amount of modulation and modal frequency of signal*	*See below*
1. Forest habitat (homogeneous)	Gradients less marked and slow to develop	Both AM and FM signal structures are effective.	Amplitude modulation in song region 4 of *G. magnirostris*, Isla Santa Cruz (Fig. 88); strong frequency modulation in other song regions.
2. Grassland and brush habitat (heterogeneous)	Wind and temperature gradients may be more marked, causing irregular transmission losses and degradation of features (via refraction); otherwise useful in binaural localization of signal source.	FM signal provides high repetition rate of sharp transients; AM avoided because of its greater susceptibility to distortion.	See songs of *Geospiza conirostris* (Figs. 55-57) recorded in semi-open brushland, Punta Suarez, I. Española. See Figs. 9 and 23B.

TABLE 30. PRAGMATIC ANALYSIS OF SOME FACTORS AFFECTING THE DESIGN OF GEOSPIZINE VOCALIZATIONS (Continued)

Feature	Physical Effect on	Consequence on song	Illustration
C. *ATMOSPHERIC CONDITIONS (Con'd.)*	*Frequency-dependent energy spectrum*	*Amount of modulation and modal frequency of signal*	*See below*
Relative humidity	Higher frequencies are attenuated less in moist air than in dry, but at any given humidity, lower frequencies are attenuated less than higher. With increasing distance from source, rate of sound attenuation for a given frequency increases more slowly in moist air than in dry.	Song energies are concentrated in lower frequencies.	This feature is not significant in explaining regional song differences in Galapagos environments during breeding (rainy) season, when relative humidities are similarly high in the *Scalesia* forest and coastal scrub (see Table 6).
D. *TRANSMISSION DISTANCE*	*Differential frequency-dependent attenuation*	*Signal bandwidth and frequency of modal amplitude.*	*See below.*
Long-distance	Large	Energy concentrated in low frequency, narrow bandwidth, FM signal, or pure tone.	Compare songs of *Geospiza magnirostris* and *G. conirostris* with *G. difficilis* and *Certhidea*, i.e large- and small-territoried species pairs, respectively, on I. Genovesa (Fig. 135). Also see Fig. 140.
Short-distance	Small	Broad frequency spread of song in FM signal. Energy spectrum may be polymodal.	See Figs. 134A and 136.
E. *ELEVATION OF SINGING PERCH*	*Broadcast area*	*Time of singing and modal frequency of song.*	*Fig. 135.*
Low	Relatively small	For small species with relatively small territories, there is no particular advantage in singing in early a.m. over other times of day, or in emphasizing a particular frequency.	*Geospiza difficilis*, I. Genovesa, sings at ground level and in low vegetation.
		Ditto for large species with relatively large territories. There may be no advantage in singing in early a.m. over other times of day, but of some advantage to emphasize lower frequencies.	*Geospiza magnirostris*, I. Wolf, sings in low vegetation, the only type present.
High	Relatively large	For small and large species with relatively large territories, there is an advantage in singing in early morning over other times of day, and in using relatively low frequencies.	No example of small species with large territory. *Geospiza magnirostris*, I. Genovesa, sings from tops of *Bursera* trees.

Sources: Bergmann (1976), Bowman (1979), Chappuis (1971), Henwood and Fabrick (1979), Hope (1980), Hunter (1980), Hunter and Krebs (1979), Konishi (1973), Linskens et al. (1976), Marler (1955, 1969), Marten and Marler (1977), Marten, Quine, and Marler (1977), Michelsen (1978), Morton (1975, 1977), Richards and Wiley (1980), Simkin (1973), Tremaine (1959), Waser and Waser (1977), Wilkenson and Howse (1975), and Wiley and Richards (1978).

TABLE 31. ANALYSIS OF SONG VARIATION IN THREE ISLAND POPULATIONS OF *CERTHIDEA OLIVACEA*

Song parameters	Populations			
	C. o. olivacea (I. Santa Cruz)	*C. o. cinerascens* (I. Española)	*C. o. mentalis* (I. Genovesa)	Average CV (3 populations)
Max. frequency (kHz)	9.54 ± 0.54[1] (5.66)	8.71 ± 0.62 (7.12)	9.69 ± 0.63 (6.50)	6.43
Min. frequency (kHz)	1.68 ± 0.17 (10.12)	1.86 ± 0.15 (8.06)	1.71 ± 0.087 (5.09)	7.76
Freq. spread (kHz)	7.86 ± 0.79 (10.06)	7.87 ± 0.67 (9.75)	7.98 ± 0.62 (7.77)	9.19
Song duration (sec.)	0.719 ± 0.122 (16.93)	0.953 ± 0.122 (12.75)	1.142 ± 0.229 (20.09)	16.59
Duration of phrase "A" (sec.)	0.268 ± 0.084 (31.42)	0.163 ± 0.075 (46.23)	0.418 ± 0.122 (29.28)	35.63
Duration of phrase "B" (sec.)	0.398 ± 0.130 (33.98)	0.531 ± 0.165 (31.14)	0.146 ± 0.035 (23.91)	29.48
Duration of phrase "C" (sec.)	-----	0.137 ± 0.025 (18.28)	0.598 ± 0.242 (40.52)	29.40
Syllable duration (sec.)	0.155 ± 0.055 (35.48)	0.084 ± 0.014 (17.20)	0.140 ± 0.026 (18.26)	23.65
Inter-syllable interval (sec.)[2]	0.048 ± 0.014 (29.17)	0.053 ± 0.014 (25.93)	0.047 ± 0.010 (22.01)	25.70
No. of syllables and phrases	3.21 ± 0.88 (27.41)	6.34 ± 1.30 (20.83)	8.25 ± 1.56 (18.91)	22.38
No. of syllables in phrase "A"	1 ± 0	1 ± 0	4.63 ± 1.38 (29.80)	---
No. of syllables in phrase "B"	2.21 ± 0.85 (38.46)	4.34 ± 1.20 (28.30)	1 ± 0	---
No. of syllables in phrase "C"	-----	1 ± 0	3.38 ± 1.56 (46.15)	---
Total no. notes	10.33 ± 2.54 (24.59)	13.14 ± 3.40 (25.88)	25.99 ± 2.54 (23.70)	24.72

[1] Mean ± standard deviation. Coefficient of variation (CV) in parenthesis.

[2] Calculated for repetitive parts of song only, i.e. phrase B in populations from islas Santa Cruz and Española, and phrase C from Isla Genovesa (see Fig. 154).

TABLE 32. AVERAGE COEFFICIENTS OF VARIATION OF SONG PARAMETERS FOR THREE ISLAND POPULATIONS OF *CERTHIDEA OLIVACEA*

Song parameters	Populations[1]			Average CV (3 populations)
	C. o. olivacea (I. Santa Cruz)	*C. o. cinerascens* (I. Española)	*C. o. mentalis* (I. Genovesa)	
Max. frequency (kHz)	3.45	5.75	5.13	4.46
Min. frequency (kHz)	9.19	8.82	11.36	9.67
Freq. spread (kHz)	4.20	6.83	7.19	5.64
Song duration (sec.)	6.03	9.92	12.87	8.79
Duration of phrase "A" (sec.)	4.34	8.48	3.09	5.03
Duration of phrase "B" (sec.)	10.04	14.11	4.50	9.58
Duration of phrase "C" (sec.)	---	10.96	13.13	12.09
Syllable duration (sec.)	4.54	7.82	4.44	5.32
Inter-syllable interval (sec.)[2]	14.63	13.77	14.72	14.44
No. of syllables and phrases	5.21	8.94	7.50	6.73
No. of syllables in phrase "A"	---	---	0.98	---
No. of syllables in phrase "B"	7.90	10.85	---	8.88
No. of syllables in phrase "C"	---	---	13.24	---
Total no. notes	10.01	11.87	13.68	11.44

[1] Sample sizes: Isla Santa Cruz, 26; Isla Española, 13; Isla Genovesa, 14.

[2] Calculated for repetitive parts of song only, i.e. phrase B in populations from islas Santa Cruz and Española, and phrase C from Isla Genovesa (see Fig. 154).

TABLE 33. COMPARISON OF SONG VARIATION IN POPULATIONS OF THE GALAPAGOS WARBLER-FINCH AND SPECIES OF MAINLAND FINCHES AND WRENS[1]

Song parameters	*Certhidea olivacea*[2]	*Junco oreganus*	*Junco caniceps*	*Pipilo fuscus*	*Zonotrichia leucophrys*	*Thryothorus sinaloa*	*Thryothorus felix*
No. of syllables	5.21 ± 2.57[3] (49.33)	14.1 ± 4.38 (31.10)	10.1 ± 2.9 (28.70)	10.4 ± 4.5 (43.30)	10.2 ± 1.08 (10.50)	16.02 ± 2.86 (18)	5.74 ± 1.36 (24)
Song duration (sec.)	0.888 ± 0.24 (27.03)	1.49 ± 0.203 (13.60)	1.63 ± 0.29 (17.80)	1.52 ± 0.31 (20.40)	1.1 ± 0.20 (18.20)	2.18 ± 0.48 (22)	1.01 ± 0.15 (15)
Interval between syllables (sec.)	0.049 ± 0.016 (32.65)	0.036 ± .0092 (25.60)	----	----	----	----	----
Syllable duration (sec.)	0.145 ± 0.051 (35.17)	0.080 ± .0293 (36.60)	0.138 ± 0.077 (55.80)	0.101 ± 0.057 (56.40)	----	0.05 ± 0.01 (26)	0.06 ± 0.03 (35)
Max. frequency (kHz)	9.38 ± 0.70 (7.46)	6.53 ± .0648 (9.90)	6.39 ± 0.51 (8.00)	6.50 ± 0.71 (10.90)	6.79 ± 0.054 (8.00)	6.6 ± 0.90 (14)	5.4 ± 0.63 (12)
Min. frequency (kHz)	1.73 ± 0.16 (9.25)	2.98 ± 0.12 (4.00)	2.09 ± 0.25 (12.00)	1.84 ± 0.35 (19.00)	2.36 ± 0.20 (8.50)	1.2 ± 0.13 (11)	1.6 ± 0.24 (15)
Frequency spread (kHz)	7.64 ± 0.84 (10.99)	3.52 ± 0.659 (18.80)	4.30 ± 0.58 (13.50)	4.01 ± 0.92 (22.90)	----	1.4 ± 0.4 (30)	1.8 ± 0.5 (25)
No. of songs analyzed	456	77	67	61	26	64	84
No. of birds	53	66	63	37	26	5	5

[1] Data on mainland species of finch are from Konishi (1965); data on mainland wrens are from Brown and Lemon (1979).

[2] Average of three island populations.

[3] Mean ± standard deviation. Coefficient of variation in parenthesis.

TABLE 34. SUMMARY OF EXPOSURE OF EXPERIMENTAL GEOSPIZINES TO PARENTAL AND TUTOR-TAPE MODEL SONGS

Species	Island	Nick-name	Text Figure	Reared by:		Age (in days) when exposed to song of:		Quality of song imitation
				parents alone	parents and hand	♂ parent in aviary	tutor-tape in isolation	
Males:								
Geospiza magnirostris	Genovesa	Junior	165	X		1-42		perfect
							150-179	no learning
Geospiza difficilis	Darwin	Perr	166		X	1-12		fair
							none	---
Geospiza magnirostris	Genovesa	J.L.G.	167		X	1-6		good
							23-69	good
Geospiza scandens	Santa Cruz	Eggbird-1	168		X	1-7		no learning
							none	---
Geospiza difficilis	Darwin	Rollo	169-170		X	1-8		poor
							27-39, 93-99	perfect
Geospiza difficilis	Darwin	George	171		X	1-12		fair
							33-35; 40-43; 94	poor
Geospiza difficilis	Wolf	Nureyev	172		X	1-12		fair
							33-35; 40-43; 94	poor
Females:								
Geospiza magnirostris	Genovesa	Thor	173		X	1-9		poor
							32-93	poor
Geospiza conirostris	Española	Snodgrass	174	X		1-31		poor
							none	---
Geospiza difficilis	Wolf	Duncan	175		X	108		no learning
							30-34	fair

TABLE 35. AGE OF HAND-REARED MALE DARWIN'S FINCHES AT FIRST SINGING OF SUBSONG AND DEFINITIVE SONG[1]

Species	Island	Subsong No. birds	Subsong Mean (days)	Subsong Range (days)	Definitive Song No. birds	Definitive Song Mean (days)	Definitive Song Range (days)
Geospiza difficilis	Wolf	9	93	49 - 153	7	246	138 - 349
	Darwin	6	75	50 - 105	2	173	143 - 202
Geospiza scandens	Santa Cruz	7	92	57 - 116	4	206	138 - 303
Geospiza conirostris	Española	2	95	75 - 115	–	––	–– ––
Geospiza magnirostris	Genovesa	3	73	66 - 84	1	181	–– ––

[1] Ages are approximate, i.e. they represent the bird's age on the day that it was first heard to sing during the 1-hour long monitoring period.

TABLE 36. AGE OF FEMALE HAND-REARED DARWIN'S FINCHES NEAR THE TIME OF EGG-LAYING

Species	Nick-name	Age at laying (days)	Notes[1]
Geospiza difficilis nigrescens	Baron-Eibl	–––––––––––	Brood patch detected on day 306
Geospiza difficilis nigrescens	Pepp	6 months (180 days)	ORETON (testosterone propionate) treatment on day 133. "Bloated" on day 161.
Geospiza conirostris conirostris	Snodgrass	First egg, 285 days; last egg, 304 days	5 eggs laid
Geospiza magnirostris (Genovesa)	Thor	177 days	One egg in sound chamber (no ORETON treatment)

[1] Birds were maintained individually in sound-isolation chambers.

TABLE 37. HYBRIDIZATION EXPERIMENTS ON DARWIN'S FINCHES

Females		*Males*	
A. Unsuccessful attempts at hybridization, i.e. pairs compatible, but no mating occurred.			
Pinaroloxias inornata (Cocos)	x	*Geospiza difficilis* (Wolf)	
Camarhynchus pauper (Floreana)	x	*Camarhynchus psittacula* (Santa Cruz)	
Geospiza fuliginosa (Santa Cruz)	x	*Geospiza difficilis* (Genovesa)	
Geospiza fuliginosa (Santa Cruz)	x	*Camarhynchus parvulus* (Santa Cruz)	
Geospiza fortis (Santa Cruz)	x	*Geospiza fuliginosa* (Santa Cruz)	
Geospiza conirostris (Española)	x	*Geospiza scandens* (Santa Cruz)	
Geospiza conirostris (Española)	x	*Geospiza fortis* (Santa Cruz)	
Geospiza magnirostris (Wolf)	x	*Geospiza magnirostris* (Genovesa)	
B. Hybridization resulting in infertile eggs.			
Geospiza fortis (Santa Cruz)	x	*Geospiza magnirostris* (Genovesa)	
C. Hybridization resulting in fertile eggs and one live young.			
Geospiza scandens (Santa Cruz)	x	*Geospiza difficilis* (Wolf)	2 days[1]
Geospiza difficilis (Wolf)	x	*Geospiza difficilis* (Darwin)	4 days
Geospiza difficilis (Genovesa)	x	*Geospiza difficilis* (Darwin)	15 days

[1] Age at which progeny died.

TABLE 38. COMPARISON OF WING AND BILL DIMENSIONS OF *CAMARHYNCHUS PARVULUS*, *"CAMARHYNCHUS CONJUNCTUS,"* AND *CERTHIDEA OLIVACEA*

Species	Specimen[1]	Sex	Wing length mm.	Bill depth at base mm.	Bill length from nostril mm.	Island	Reference
Camarhynchus parvulus	RIB 1636 (mate of RIB 1635)	F	59.8	6.8	7.1	Sta. Cruz	
	Average Range	F	61.3 (58-64)	7.1 (6.7-7.6)	7.4 (6.3-8.1)	Sta. Cruz	Lack 1945
	Average Range	M	64.0 (63-65)	7.3 (6.9-8.1)	7.5 (6.6-8.2)	Sta. Cruz	Lack 1945
"Camarhynchus conjunctus"	CAS 7713	M	59.0	5.2	7.9[2]	Floreana	Swarth 1929
	CAS 7714	M	58.2	5.8	7.8[2]	Floreana	Swarth 1929
	RIB 1635	M	58.5	5.4	7.8	Sta. Cruz	
	Average	M	58.6	5.5	7.8	Floreana & Sta. Cruz	
Certhidea olivacea	Average Range	M	54.1 (51.56)	4.3 (3.9-4.8)	7.6 (7.0-8.1)	Sta. Cruz	Lack 1945

[1] RIB = Robert I. Bowman specimen in Vertebrate Museum, San Francisco State University. CAS = California Academy of Sciences collection.

[2] Measurements from Lack 1947.

FIGURES

FIGURES

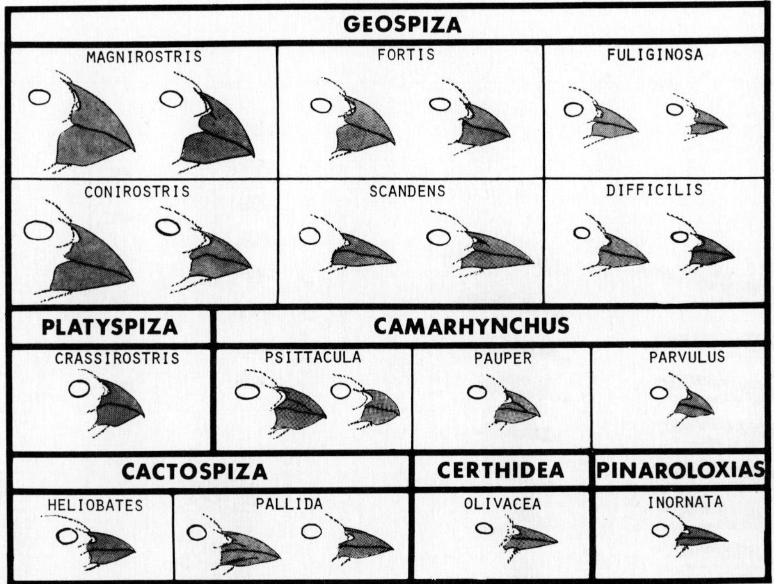

Fig. 1. Examples of variation in size and shape of the bills of 14 species of Darwin's finches. After Swarth 1931.

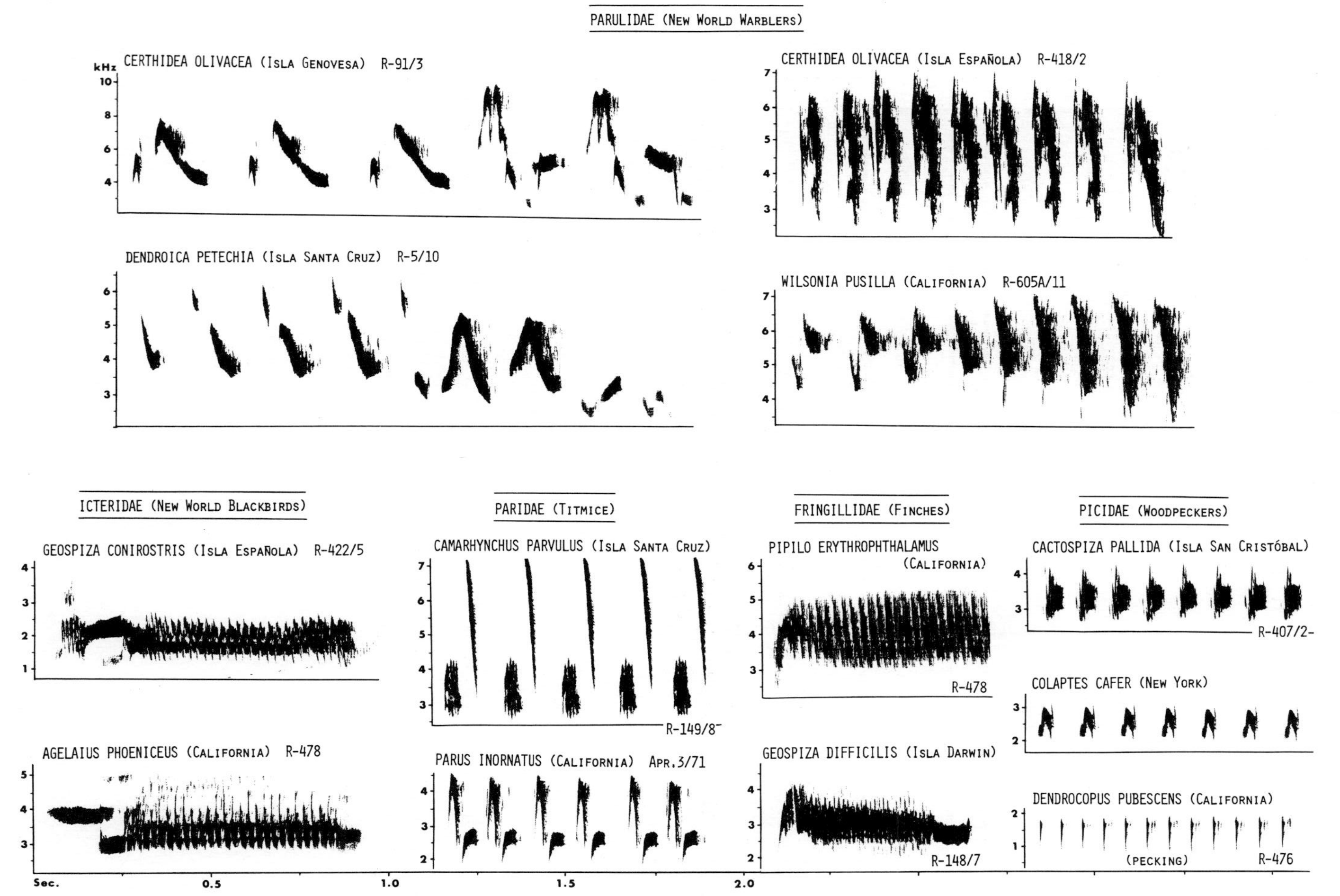

Fig. 2. Examples of adaptive radiation in the songs of Darwin's finches and convergence with sound signals of continental species of birds.

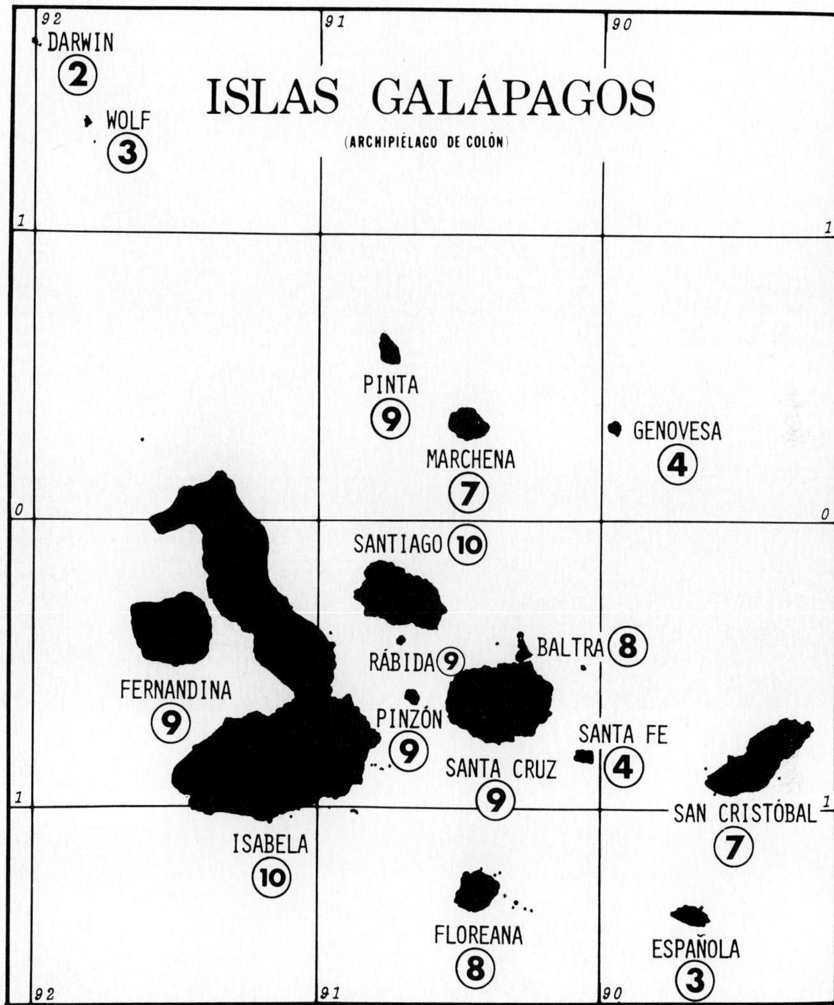

Fig. 3. Number of present-day breeding species of Darwin's finches on the principal islands of the Galapagos. For identification of species, see Table 2.

Fig. 4. Comparison of arid coastal zone vegetation at two locations in the Galapagos Archipelago. A, south shore of James Bay, Isla Santiago in the wet season. B, north shore of Academy Bay, Isla Santa Cruz in the dry season.

Fig. 5. Vegetation on the south side of Isla Santa Cruz. A, upper transition zone in the wet season. The large tree is *Psidium galapageium*. B, inner coastal zone in the dry season. The tree cactus is *Opuntia echios*.

Fig. 6. *Scalesia* forest zone in the interior highlands of Isla Santa Cruz during the wet season. A, leaf canopy of *Scalesia pedunculata*, about 20 feet high. B, shrubby undergrowth of *Psychotria*, *Tournefortia*, and *Chiococca*.

Fig. 7. Highlands vegetation on Isla Santa Cruz during the wet season. A, grassy upland zone with tree ferns, *Cyathea*, growing in protected depression (lower right). B, *Miconia* belt composed of the endemic melostome, *Miconia robinsoniana*, assorted ferns, and herbs.

Fig. 8. Transition zone vegetation during the wet season. A, Wittmer farm, Isla Floreana, showing dense woody tangle of naturalized guava, *Psidium guajava*, and sweet lime, *Citrus limetta*. B, mid-transition zone forest, south side of Isla Santa Cruz, showing admixture of *Psidium galapageium* and *Pisonia floribunda* (fallen trunk and large buttressed tree at far right).

Fig. 9. Coastal scrub, Punta Suarez, Isla Española, during the dry season. A, dormant stems of *Alternanthera echinocephala* and *Grabowskia boerhaaviaefolia*. B, *Cordia lutea* shrubs with nest of a Darwin's finch.

Fig. 10. A, nest and B, adult male of *Certhidea olivacea*, Isla Española.

Fig. 11. Arid zone vegetation near Darwin Bay, Isla Genovesa during the wet season. A, dwarf *Bursera graveolens* forest typical of the interior region. B, dense stand of *Opuntia helleri* near shore, which is most attractive to *Geospiza conirostris.*

Fig. 12. Arid zone vegetation on the south side of Isla Marchena in the wet season. A, coastal thicket of *Croton scouleri* and *Opuntia helleri* where *Geospiza scandens* was most common. B, interior forest dominated by *Bursera graveolens.*

Fig. 13. Vegetation on Isla Santiago during the wet season. A, *Bursera* parkland south of James Bay. B, forest clearing in the central highlands where *Geospiza difficilis* is most abundant. Photo courtesy of Daphne Gemmill.

Fig. 14. Isla Wolf during the wet season. A, aerial view of the northwest mesa. B, *Opuntia helleri* and *Croton scouleri* thicket, typical vegetation formation of the low-lying regions. *Croton* is replaced by *Scalesia incisa* on the elevated interior (cf. Wiggins and Porter 1971, color plate 54).

Fig. 15. Vegetation on Isla Darwin during the wet season. A, midget forest of *Croton scouleri* with ground cover of *Alternanthera helleri*, both plants providing nest sites for *Geospiza difficilis*. B. *Opuntia helleri*, the preferred nest site of *Certhidea olivacea*. Compare with Fig. 14.

Fig. 16. Mangrove "forest," Cartago Bay, Isla Isabela. A, trees of *Rhizophora mangle* in foreground; *Avicennia germinans* in background. B, stems and aerial roots of *Rhizophora*.

Fig. 17. Vegetation on Cocos Island, Costa Rica, March 1964. A, interior rain forest dominated by the tree *Cecropia pittieri*, lianas, and undergrowth of ferns. B, edge vegetation near Chatham Bay. Note the abundance of the epiphytic *Tillandsia* on tree trunk, and brushy growth of *Eugenia*, *Miconia*, and *Clibadium*, whose fruits are fed upon by the Cocos Island honeycreeper-finch, *Pinaroloxias inornata*.

Fig. 18. Vegetation of St. Lucia Island, West Indies in the region about Castries, home of the endemic black finch, *Melanospiza richardsoni*. March 1967.

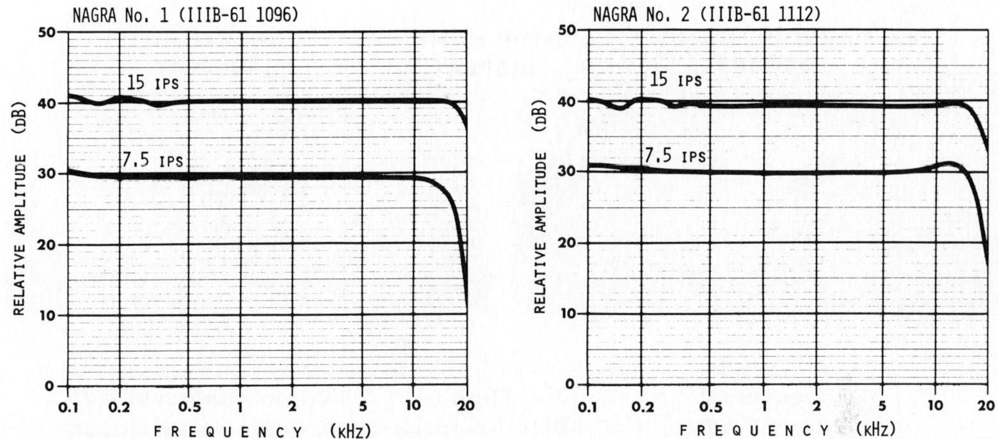

Fig. 19. Record-playback responses of Nagra III-B tape recorders at 38.1 cm/s and 19.05 cm/s using 3M Type 202 recording tape.

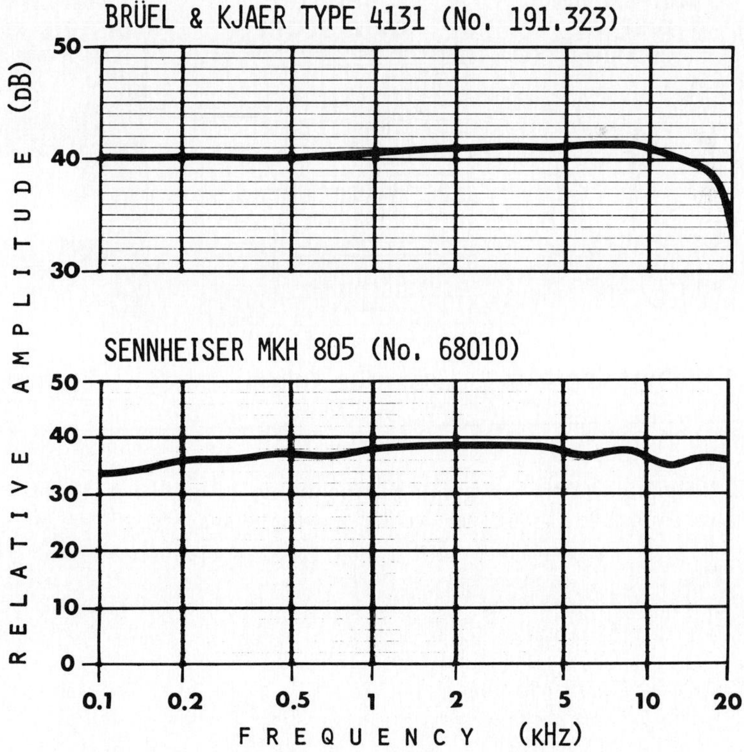

Fig. 20. Above: Individual frequency response curve for B & K microphone Type 4131 used with the B & K Sound Level Meter Type 2203. From 0.1 to 15 kHz, the response is linear within plus or minus 2 dB.

Below: Individual frequency response curve for Sennheiser "shotgun" microphone Type MKH 805 used for field recording finch songs. From 0.1 to 15 kHz, the response is linear within plus or minus 2 dB.

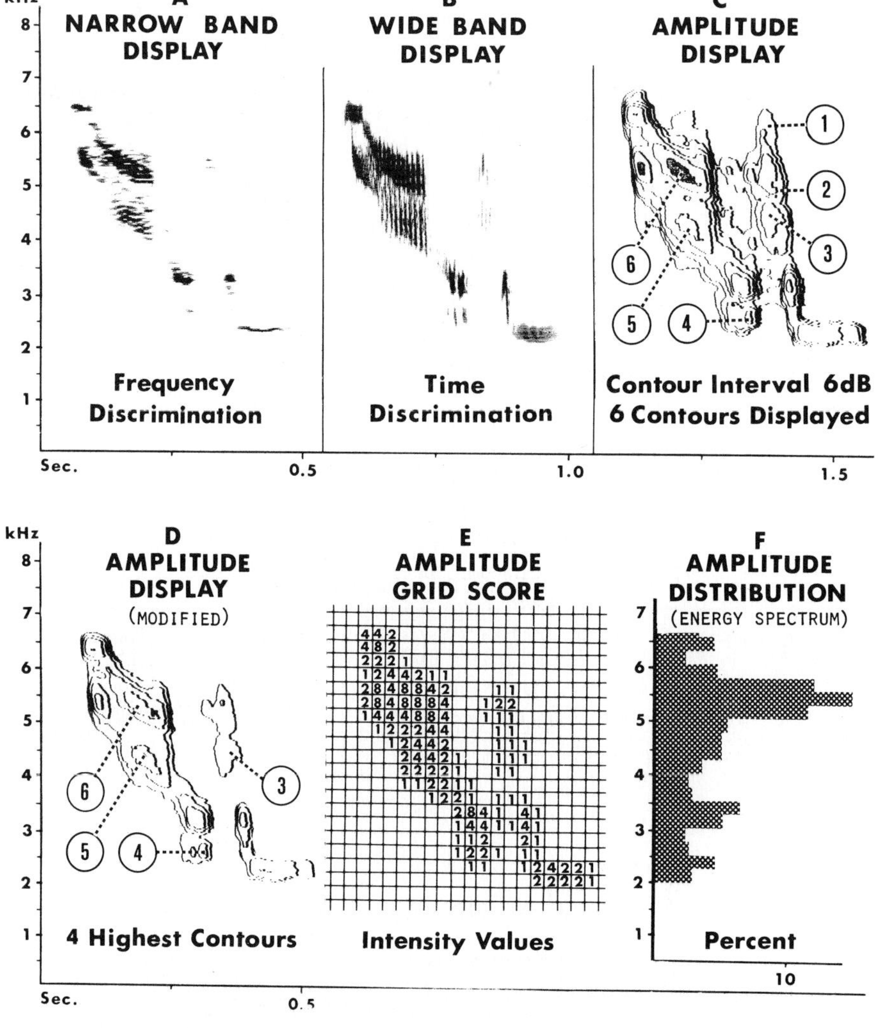

Fig. 21. Comparison of three types of graphic display of bird song (above) and methods of analysis of relative amplitude of song (below). See text for details. After Bowman 1979.

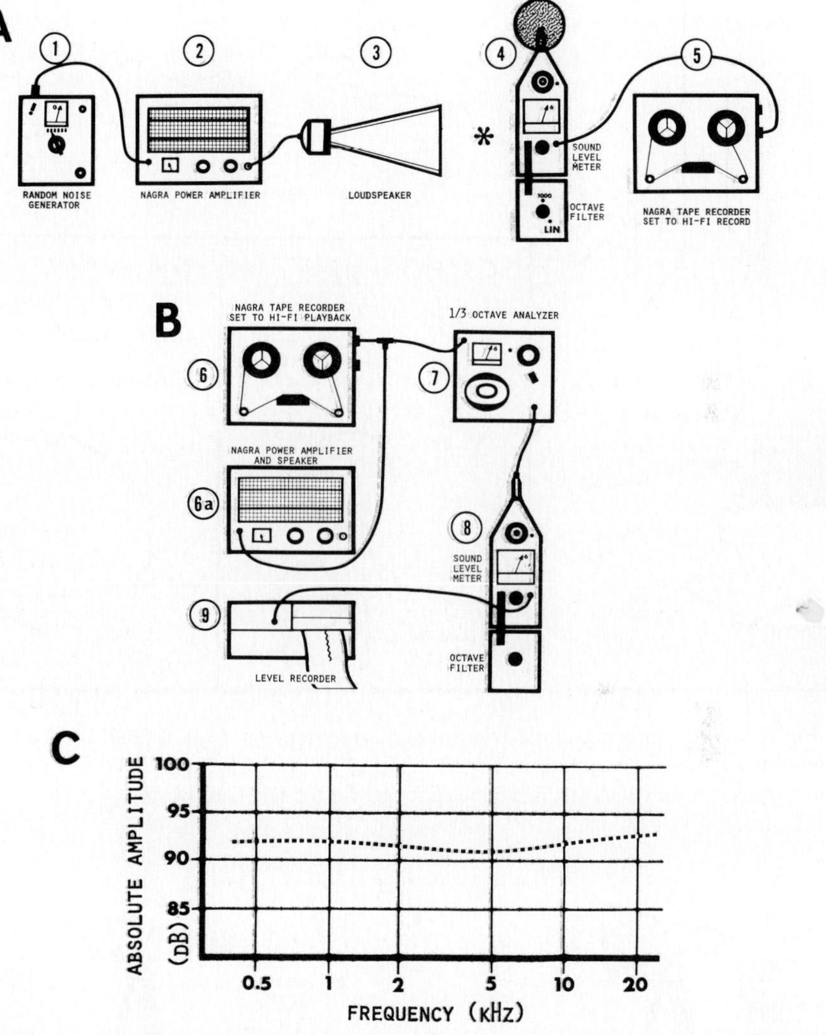

Fig. 22. Arrangement of electronic and acoustical pathways, and their combined performance under ideal conditions. A, equipment arrangement for generating (1, 2, and 3) and recording (4 and 5) random noise. The asterisk between 3 and 4 represents the acoustical pathway (environment) connecting sound-generating and sound-recording pathways. B, equipment arrangement for analyzing sound-pressure levels of the tape-recorded signals from 5. C, frequency response characteristics of the combined acoustical and electronic pathways under controlled test conditions.

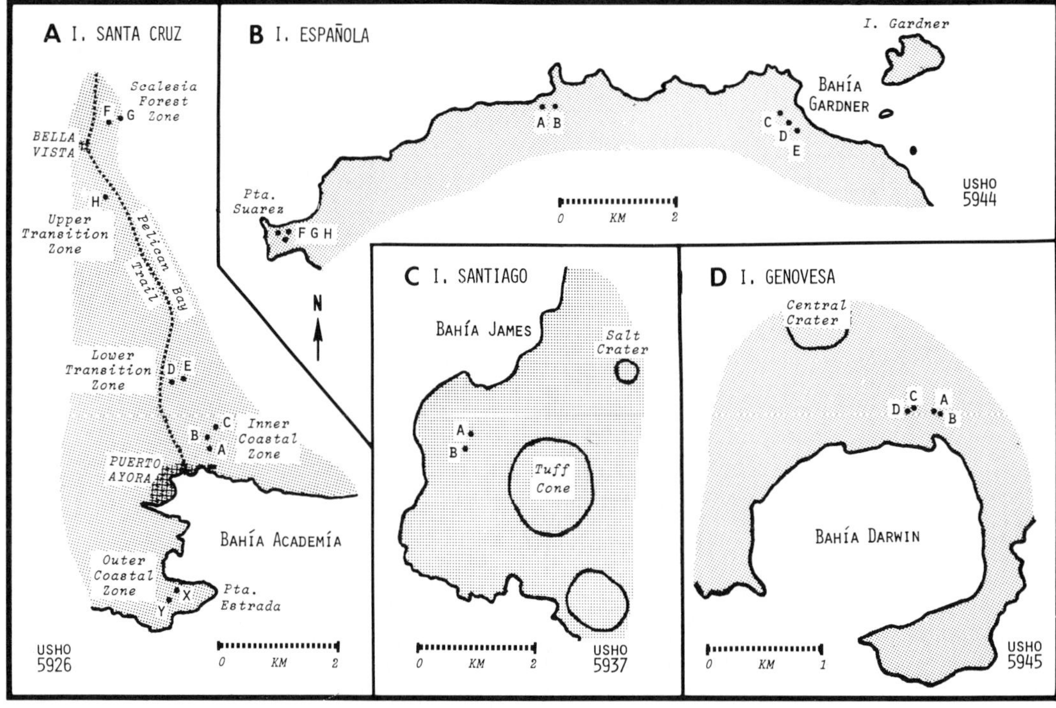

Fig. 23. Locations of sound-transmission transects on four islands of the Galapagos. For photographs of transect vegetation, see Figs. 4B, 5, 6, and 8B for Isla Santa Cruz; Fig. 9 for Isla Española; Figs. 4A and 13A for Isla Santiago; Fig. 11 for Isla Genovesa.

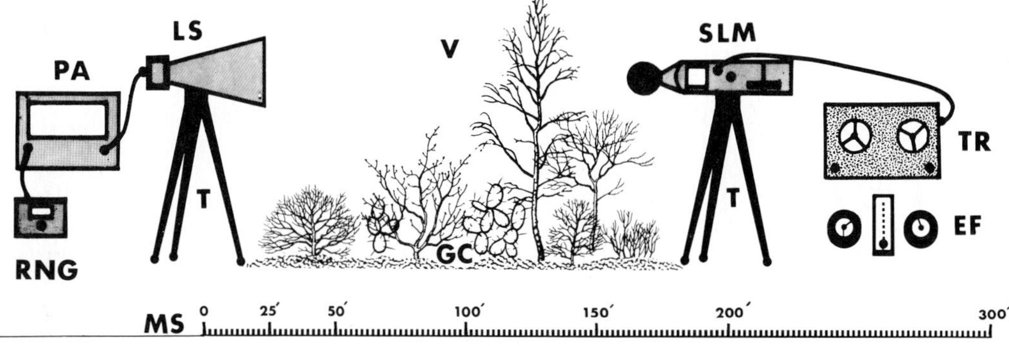

Fig. 24. Arrangement of equipment used for measuring sound transmission in Galapagos environments. Key to symbols: EF, environmental factors; GC, ground conditions; LS, loud speaker; MS, monitoring stations; PA, power amplifier; RNG, random noise generator; SIM, sound level meter; T, tripod; TR, tape recorder; and V, vegetation.

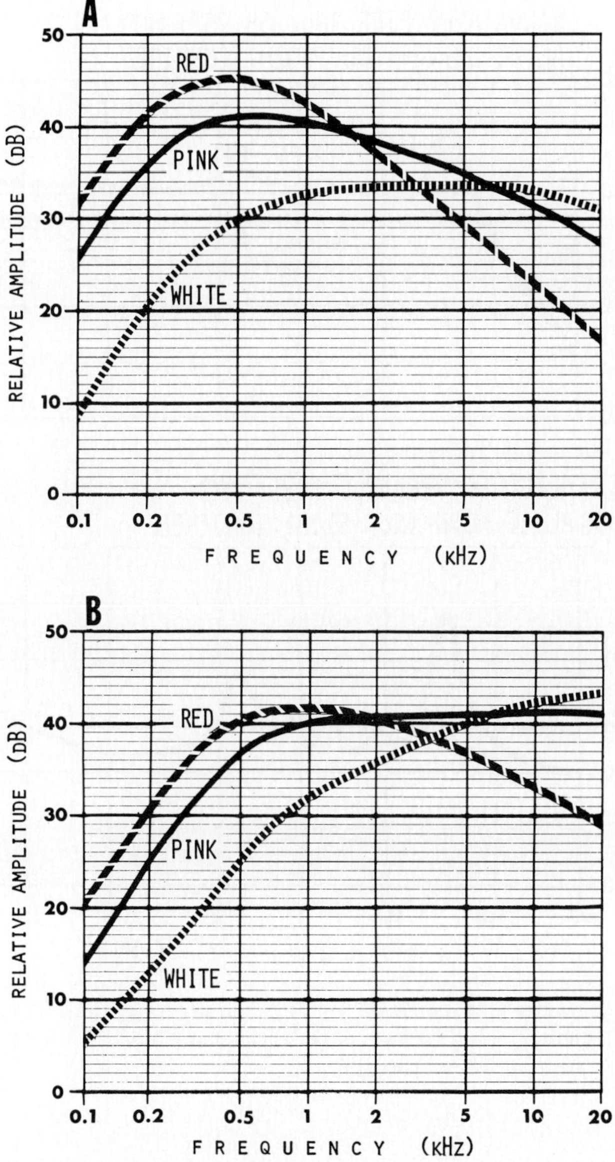

Fig. 25. Energy distribution as a function of frequency for red, pink, and white noises. Spectra produced by random noise generator before filtering (A), and after filtering (B), using a one-third octave constant percentage band sound analyzer. See Table 7 and Fig. 27.

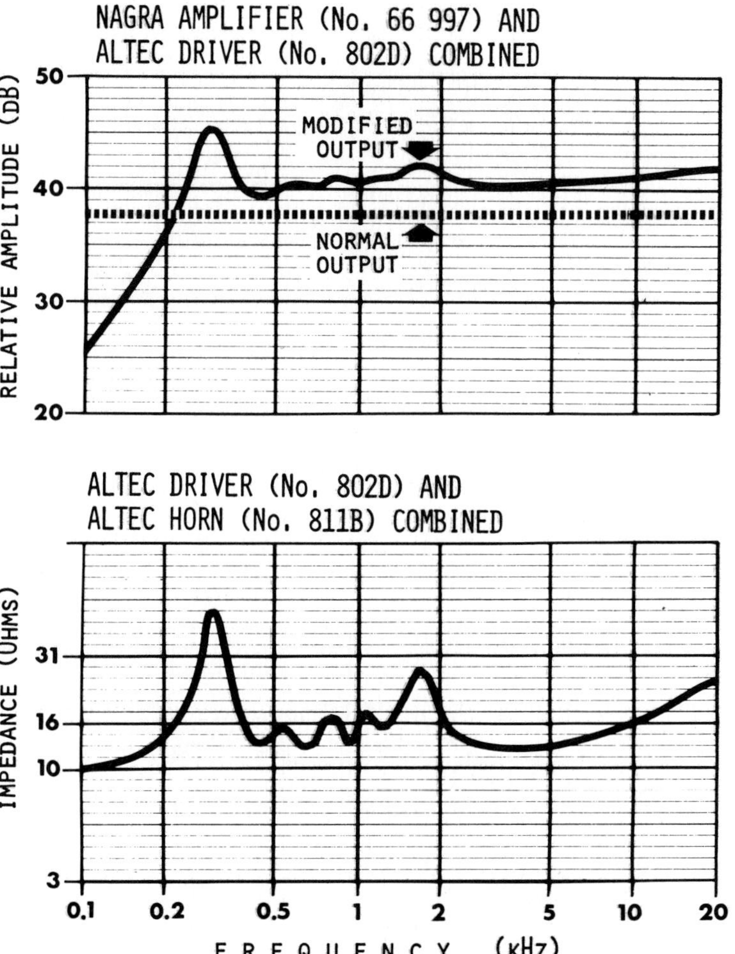

Fig. 26. Overall electrical response of the Nagra Power Amplifier–Altec Driver combination as a function of frequency (above), and impedance characteristics of Altec Driver and Horn combination (below). See text for explanation.

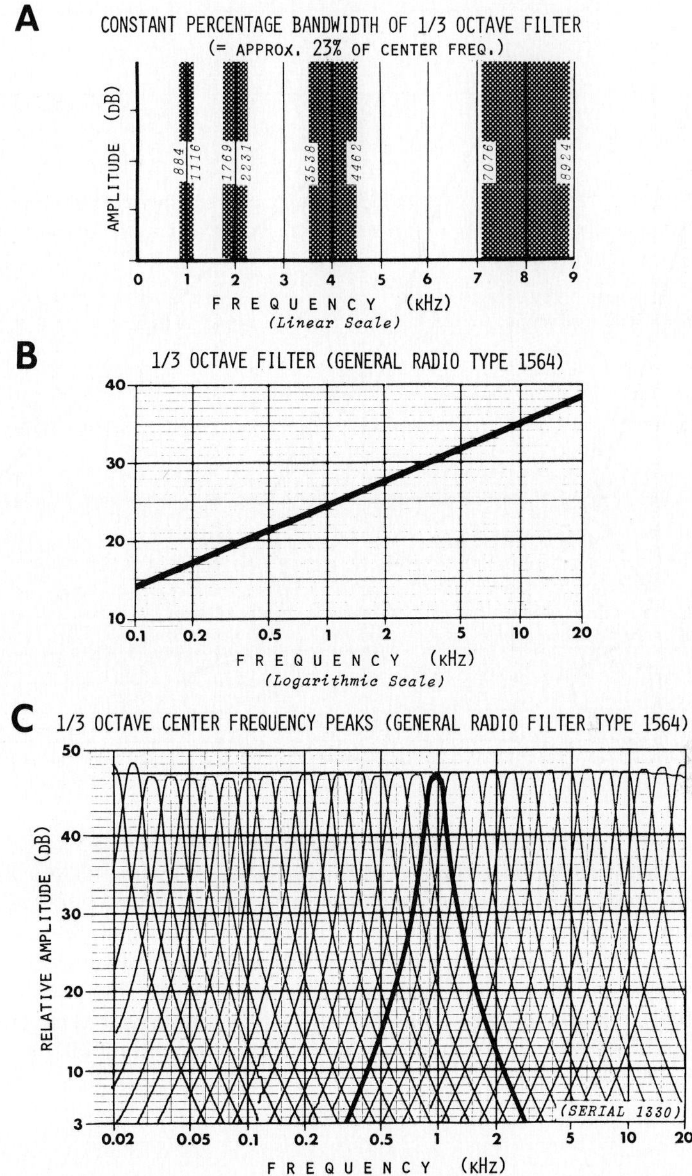

Fig. 27. Graphic representation of the resolution characteristics of a constant percentage bandwidth frequency analyzer. A: The one-third octave filter extracts a band of frequencies whose bandwidth is a constant percentage of the center frequency. When using this filter, upper and lower limits of the width of the band (indicated in Herz at the edges of the shaded areas) encompasses approximately 23% of the center frequency. Note that the frequency scale is linear. (After Peterson and Gross 1972:76). B: Output of a constant percentage bandwidth filter as a function of frequency when a noise signal of uniform spectral density (e.g. "white noise") is applied to the filter input. Because more energy is passed through the filter with increasing frequency (see A, above), the output also increases at the rate of approximaely 3dB per octave. C: Actual response characteristics of the one-third octave filter used in the analysis of the recorded sound-transmission signals. The curves represent the one-third octave pass bands whose center frequencies occur at standardized one-third octave steps.

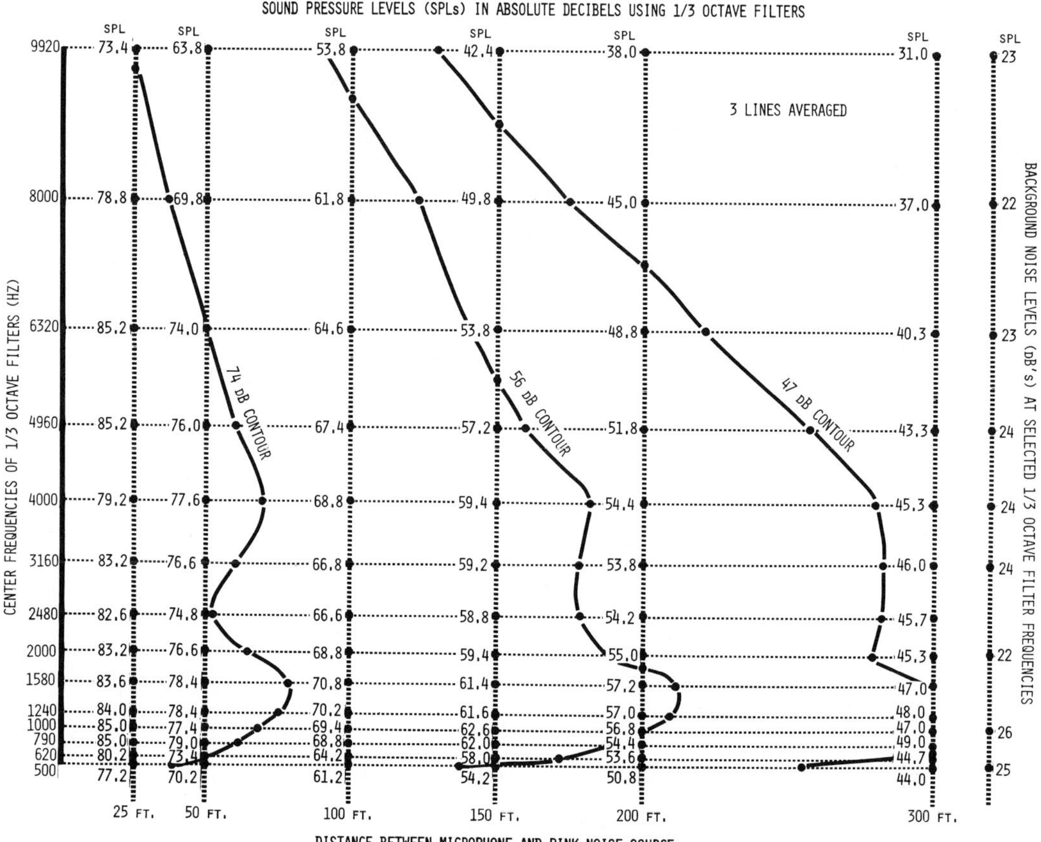

Fig. 28. Partially completed sound-transmission isopleth for the coastal zone of Isla Santa Cruz, showing the method of constructing isodecibel contour lines by connecting points on the grid of equal sound-pressure level (dB). Center frequencies of the one-third octave band filter are shown on the left vertical axis, and the distances between the sound source and six transect microphone positions are shown along the horizontal axis. At the right vertical axis are shown the average filtered background noise levels for nine center frequencies. Compare with completed isopleths (e.g. Figs. 133-134) where the contour interval is consistently 3 dB.

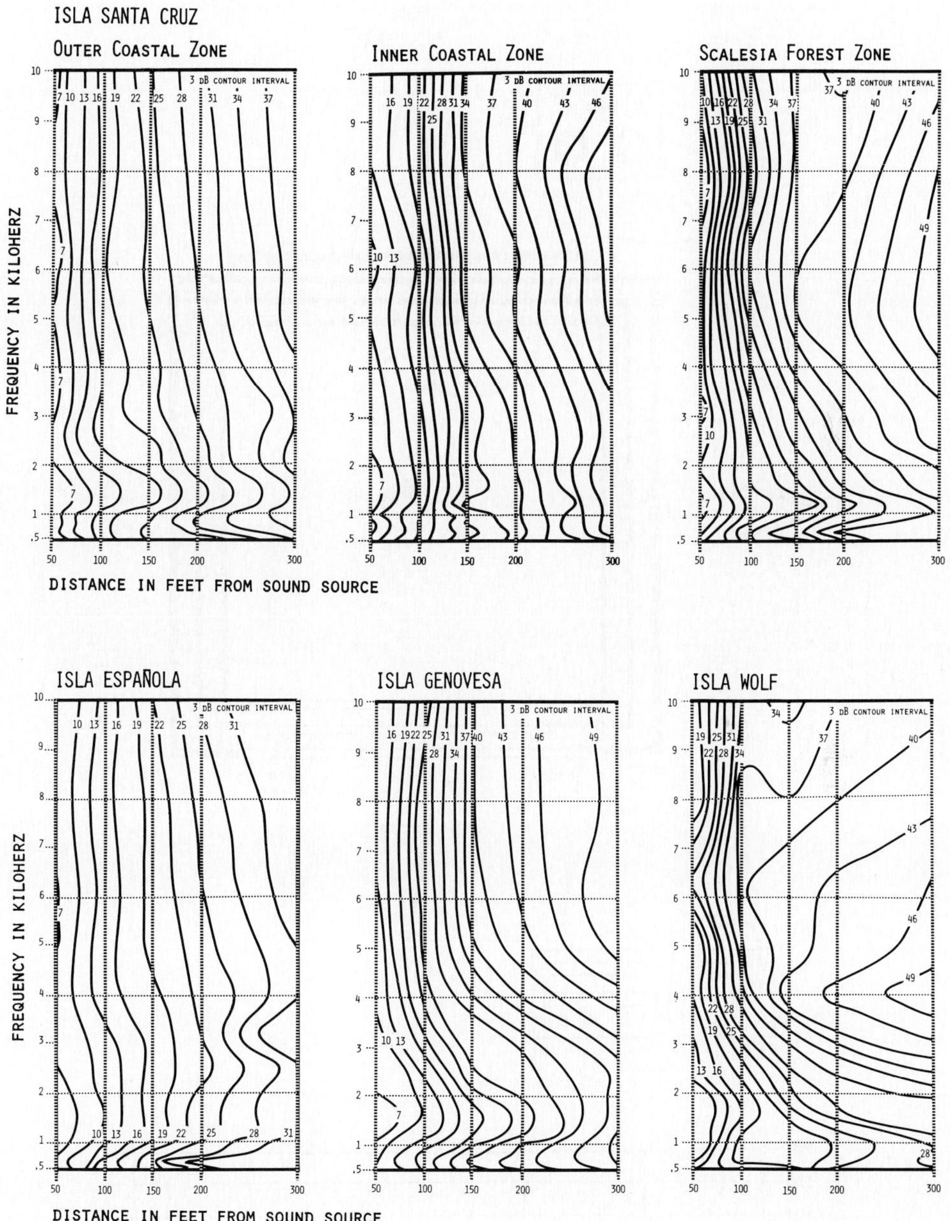

Fig. 29. Cumulative dB-loss isopleths for six vegetative environments of Darwin's finches. Contour interval is 3 dB.

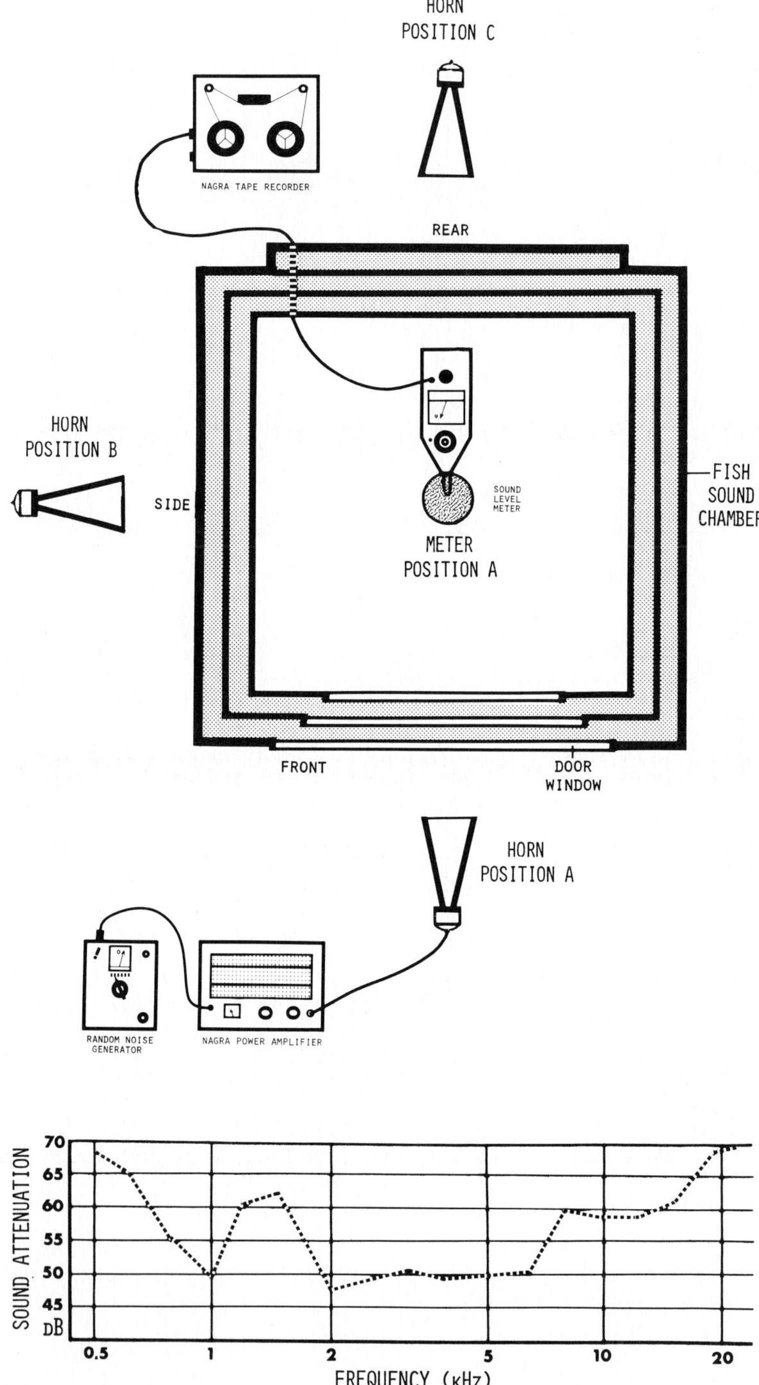

Fig. 30. Above: Arrangement of equipment used in measuring attenuation characteristics of the Fish Sound Isolation Chamber. Sound-level meter and horn were aligned in three positions during tests of insulation effectiveness of front, side, and rear walls. Below: Sound attenuation characteristics of a Fish Sound Isolation Chamber.

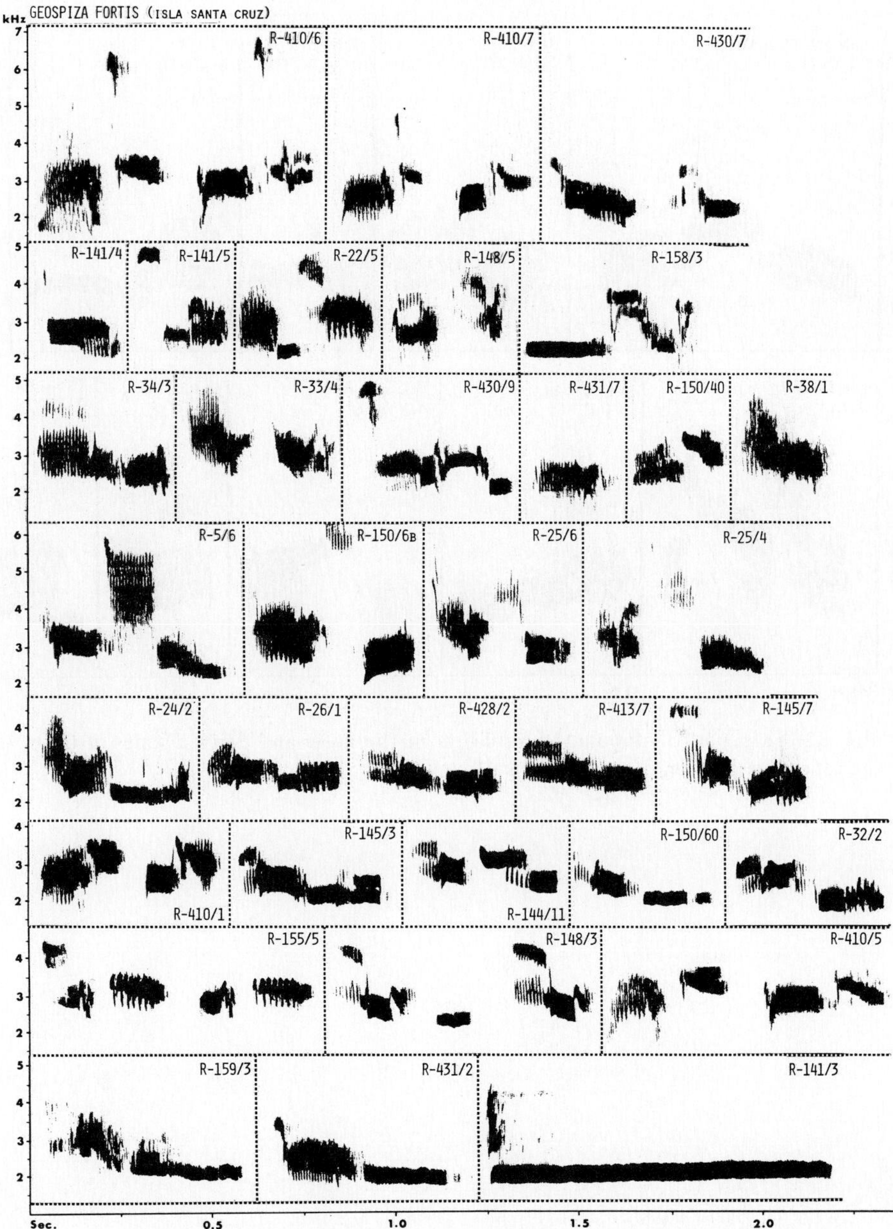

Fig. 31. Variation in the basic and derived songs of *Geospiza fortis*, Isla Santa Cruz. Only the repetitive portion of each song is displayed.

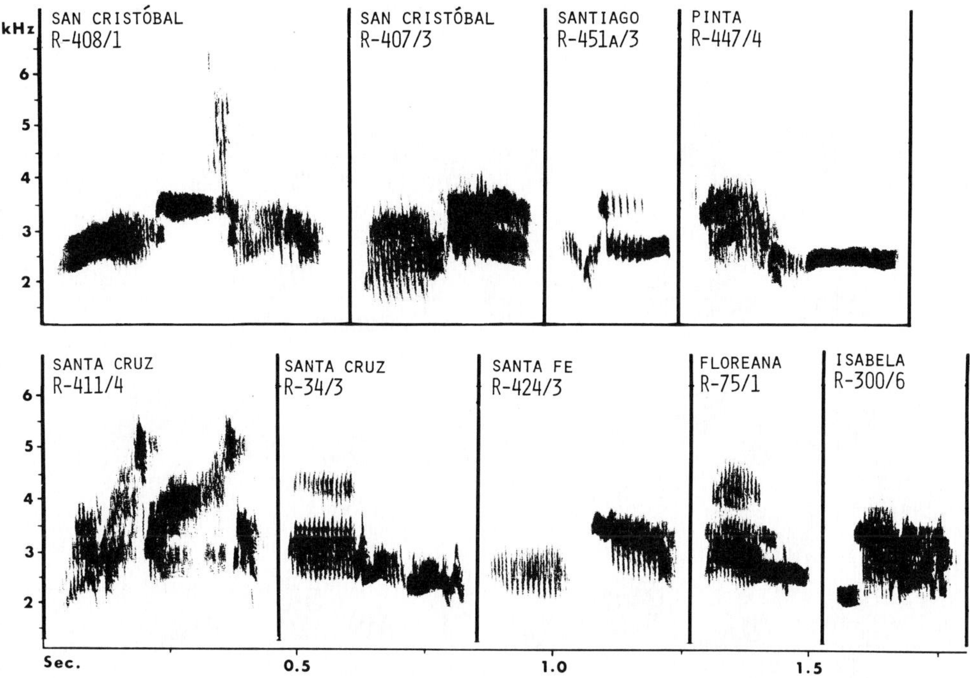

Fig. 32. Examples of population variation in the basic and derived songs of *Geospiza fortis*. Only the repetitive portion of each song is displayed.

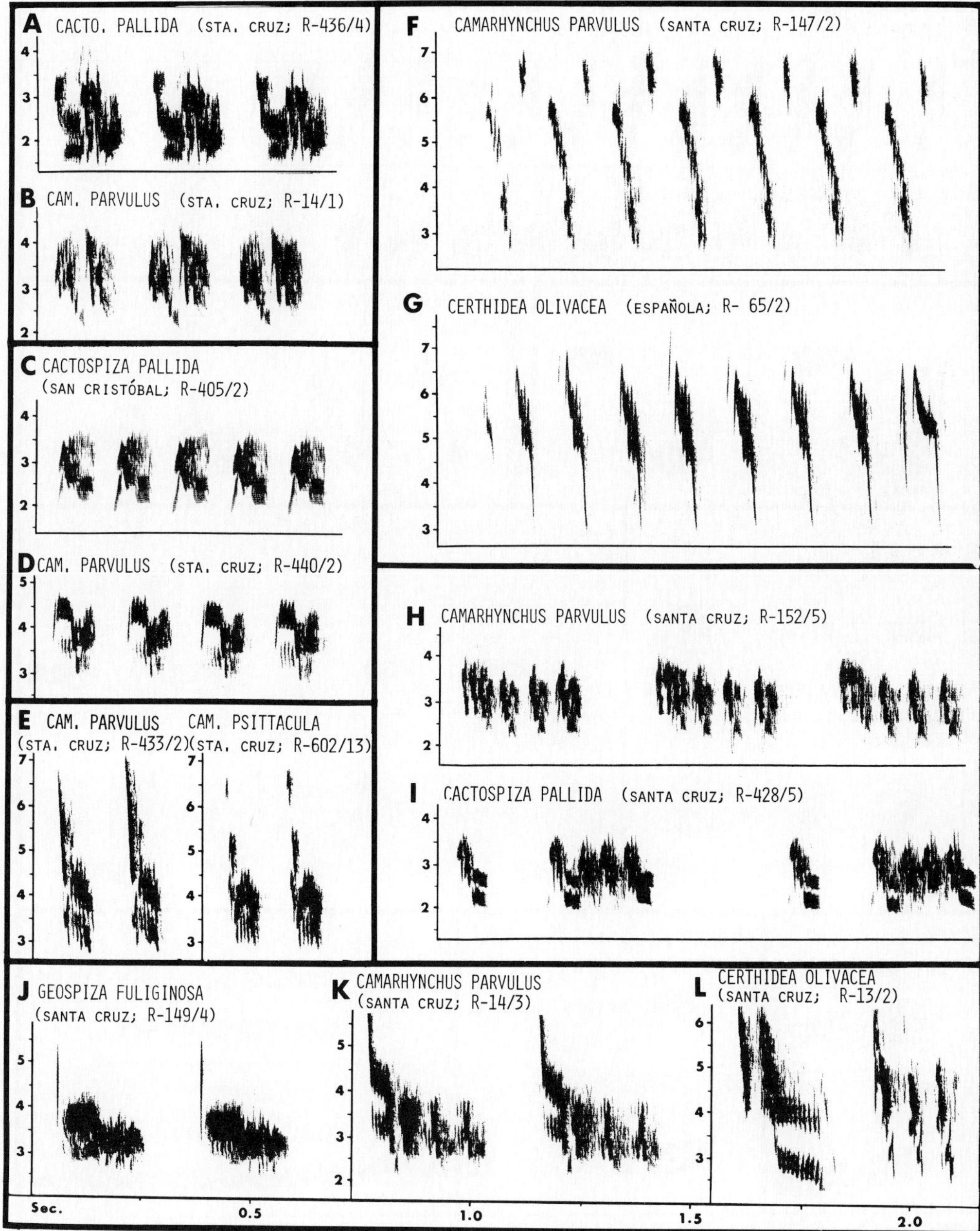

Fig. 33. Parallelism in the songs of Darwin's finches.

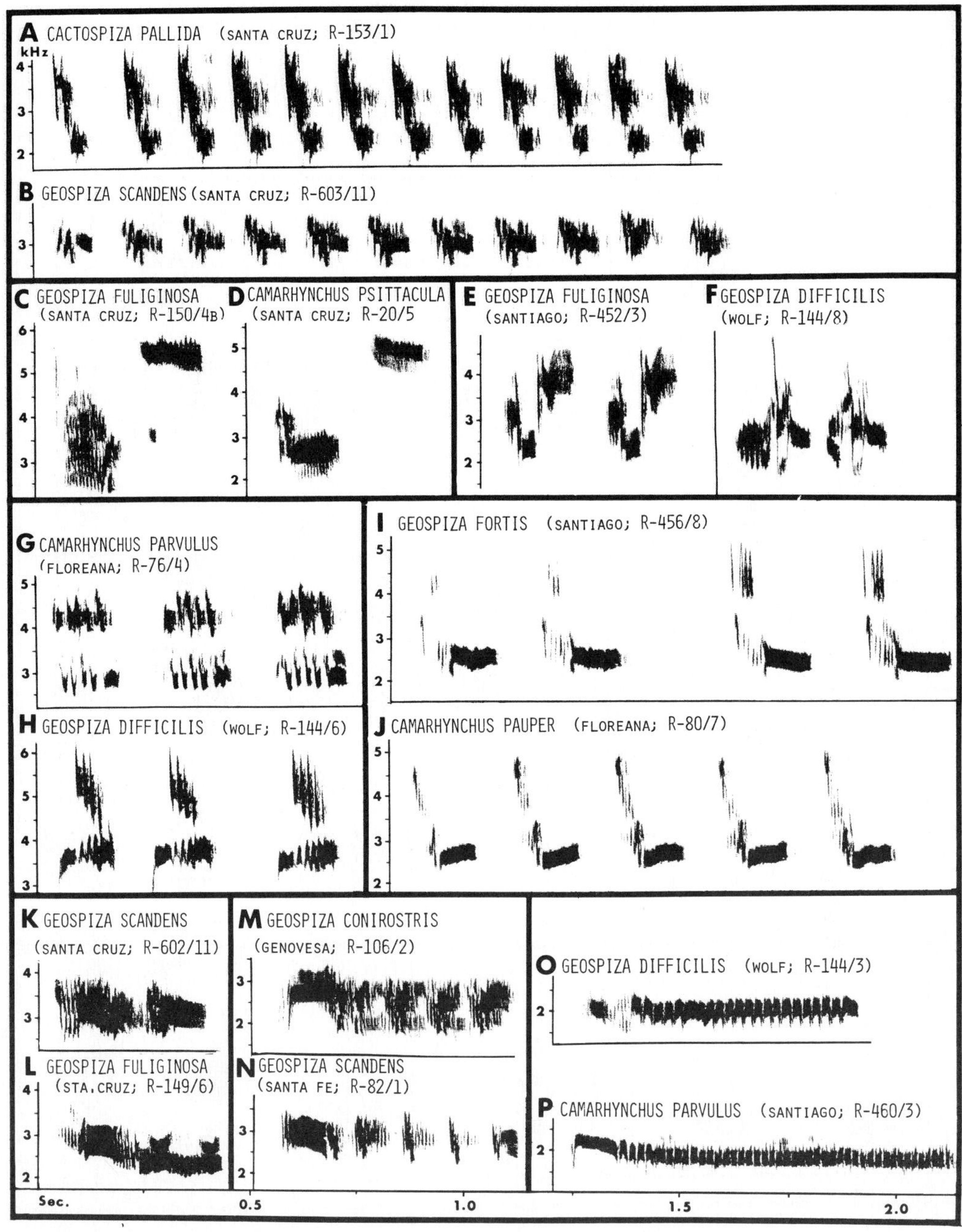

Fig. 34. Parallelism in the songs of Darwin's finches.

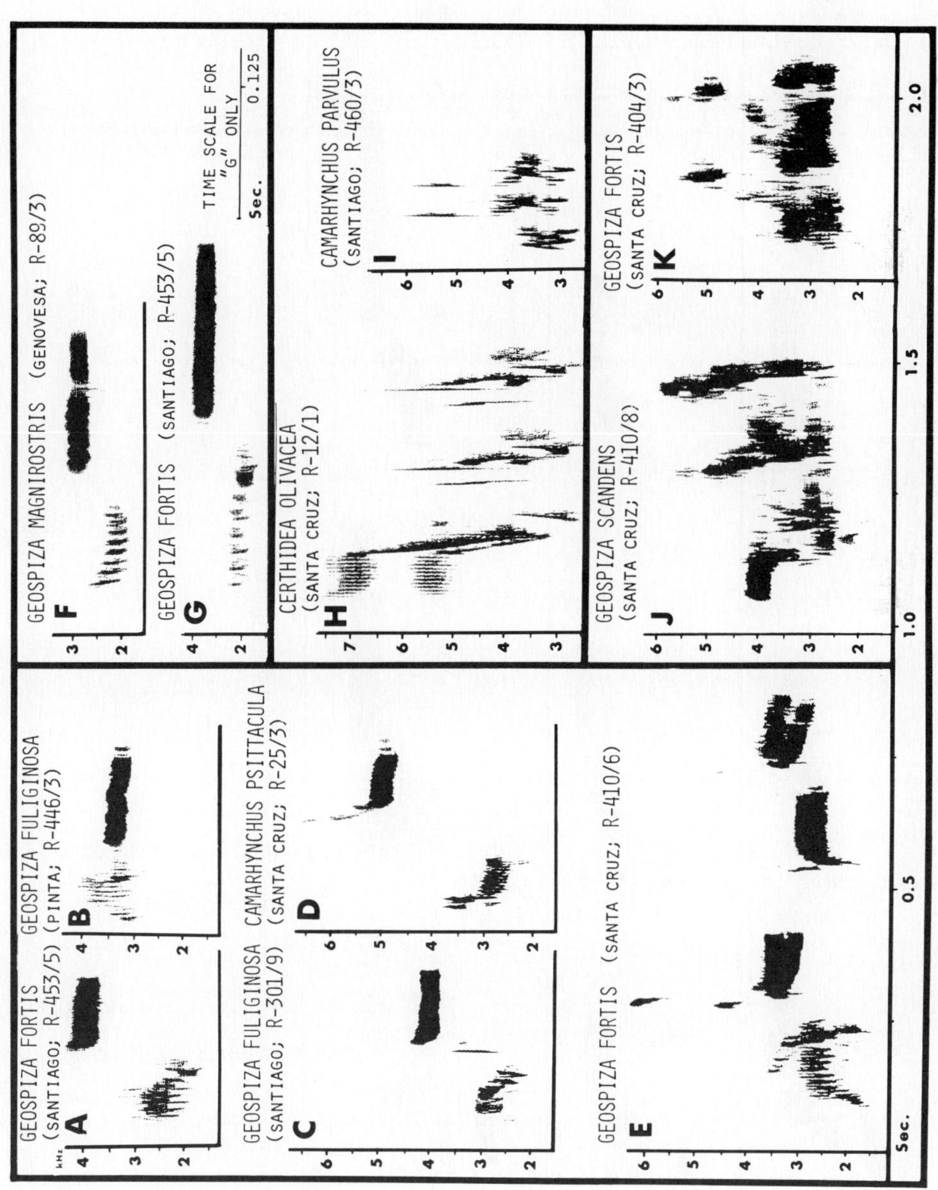

Fig. 35. Parallelism in the songs of Darwin's finches.

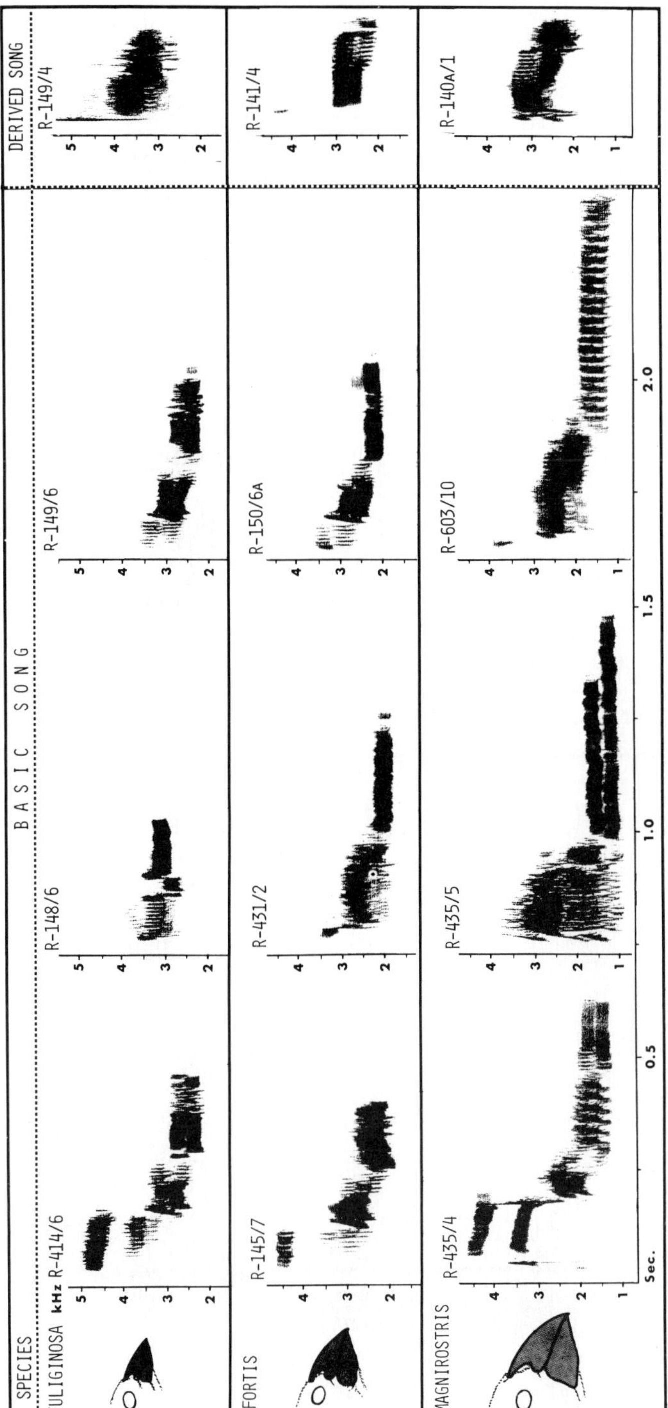

Fig. 36. Parallel structure in basic and derived songs of three sympatric songs of *Geospiza*, Academy Bay, Isla Santa Cruz.

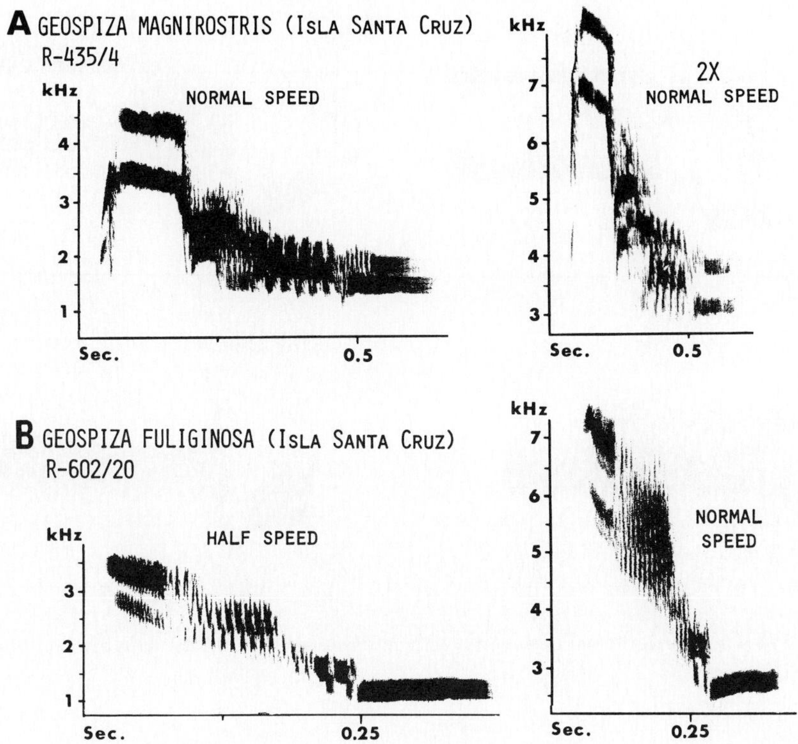

Fig. 37. Comparison of spectrograms of basic song of *Geospiza magnirostris* (A) displayed at normal and twice normal speeds, with those of *Geospiza fuliginosa* (B) displayed at half and normal speed, to emphasize pattern similarities of congenerics.

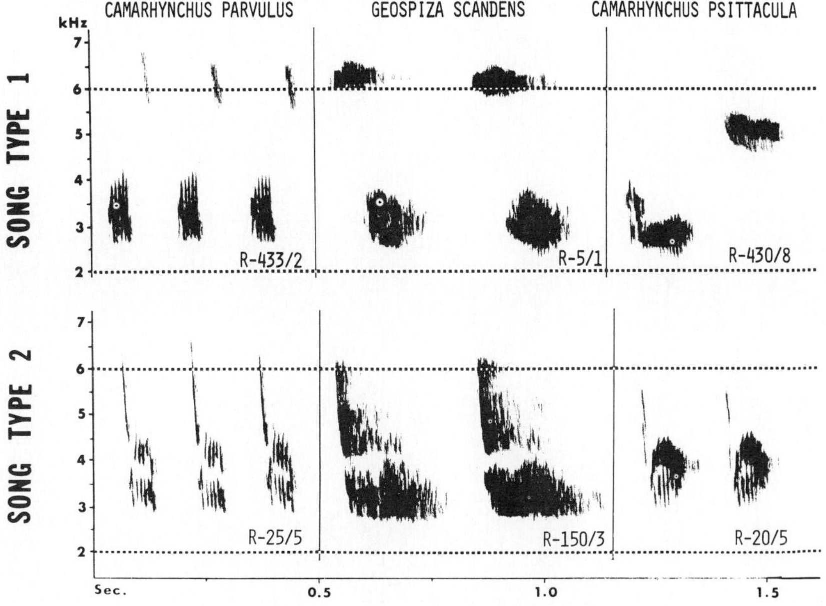

Fig. 38. Two types of parallel song pattern in three sympatric species of arboreal to semi-arboreal Darwin's finches, Academy Bay, Isla Santa Cruz.

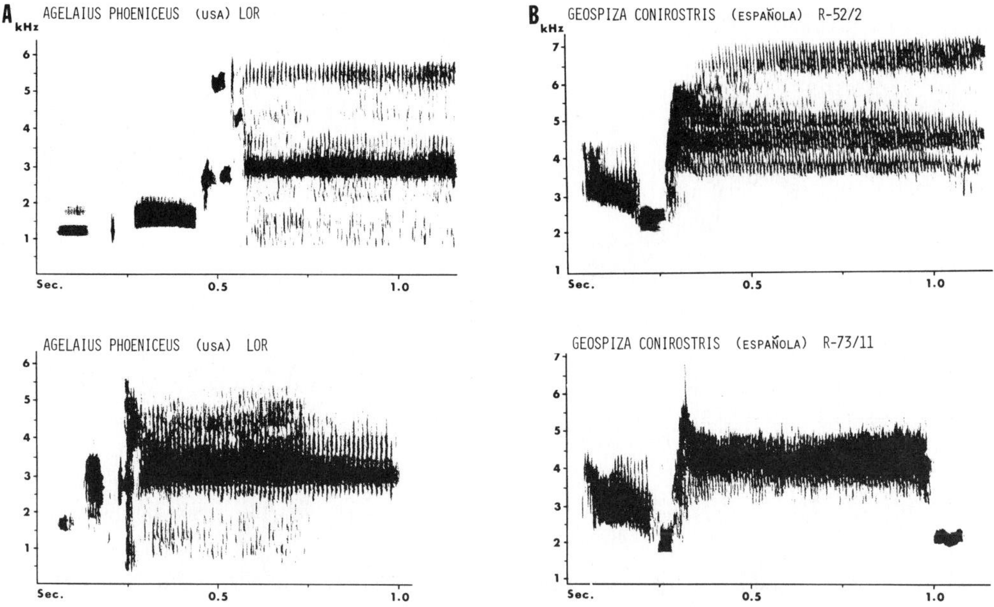

Fig. 39. Song convergence between *Agelaius phoenicius* (USA) and *Geospiza conirostris* (Isla Española, Galapagos).

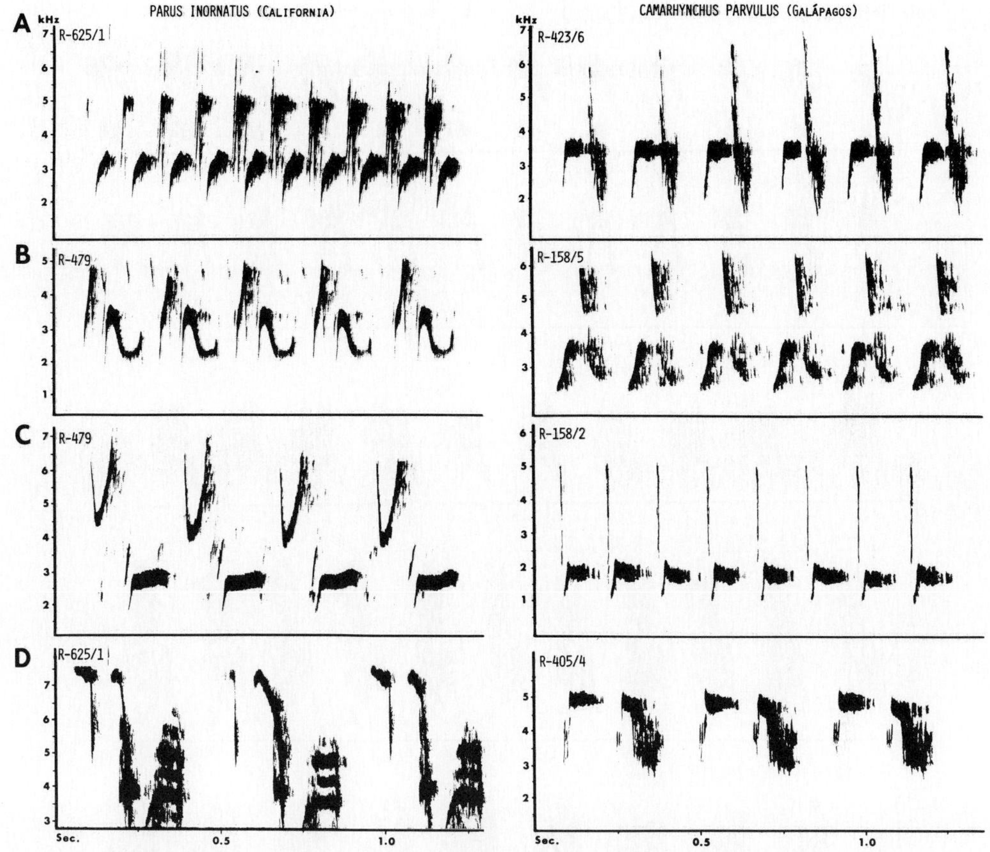

Fig. 40. Song convergence between *Parus inornatus* (California) and *Camarhynchus parvulus* (Galapagos).

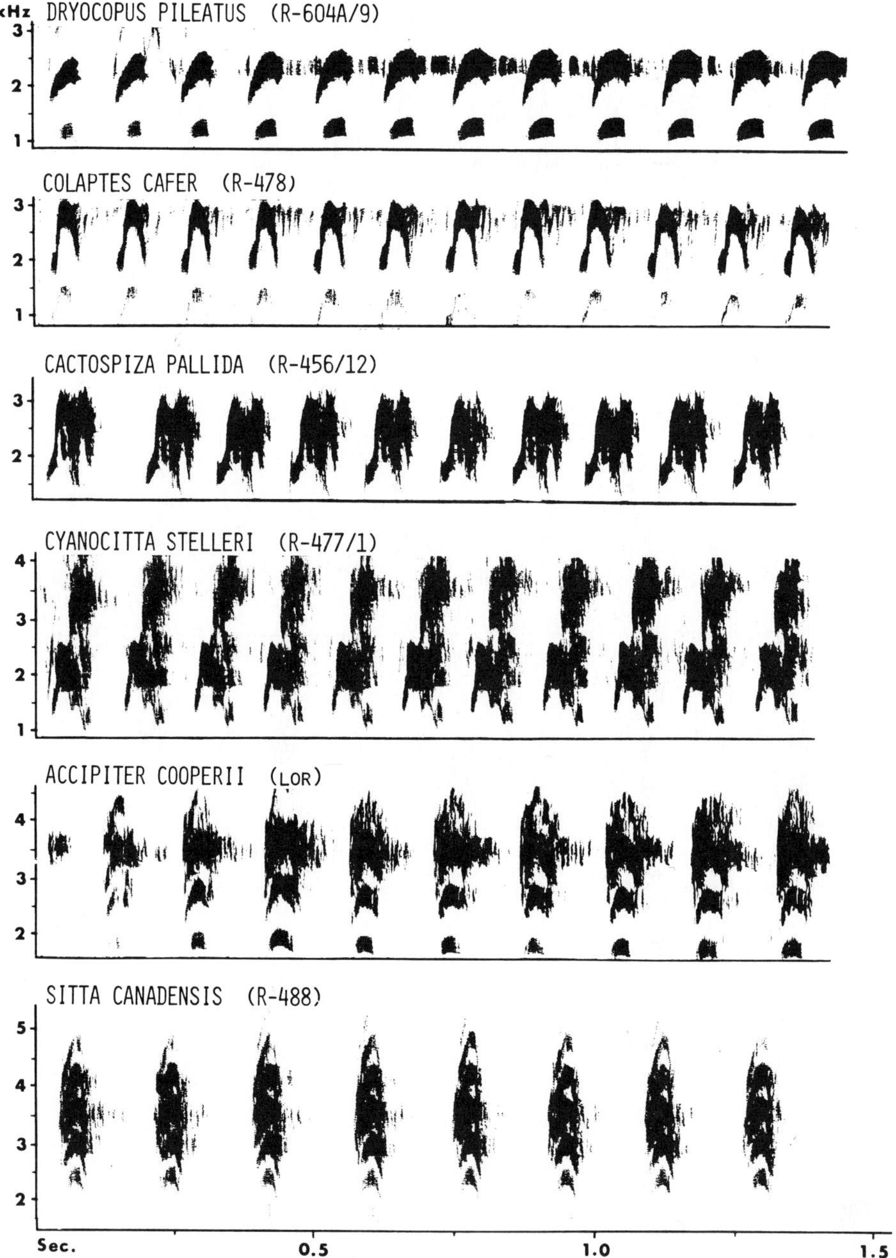

Fig. 41. Vocal similarities between *Cactospiza pallida* (Galapagos) and a variety of forest and tree-trunk foraging birds (North America).

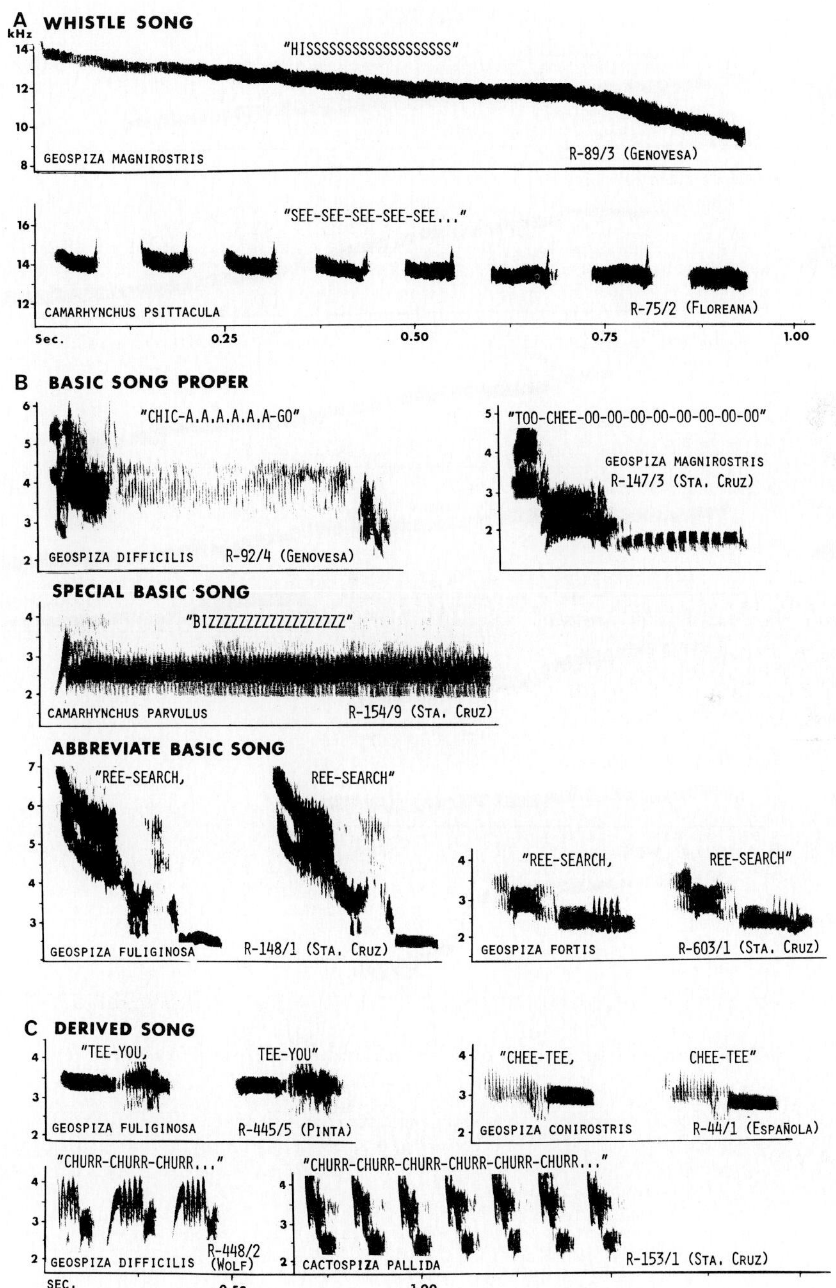

Fig. 42. Comparison of phonetic and audiospectrogrammic descriptions of principal song types of Darwin's finches.

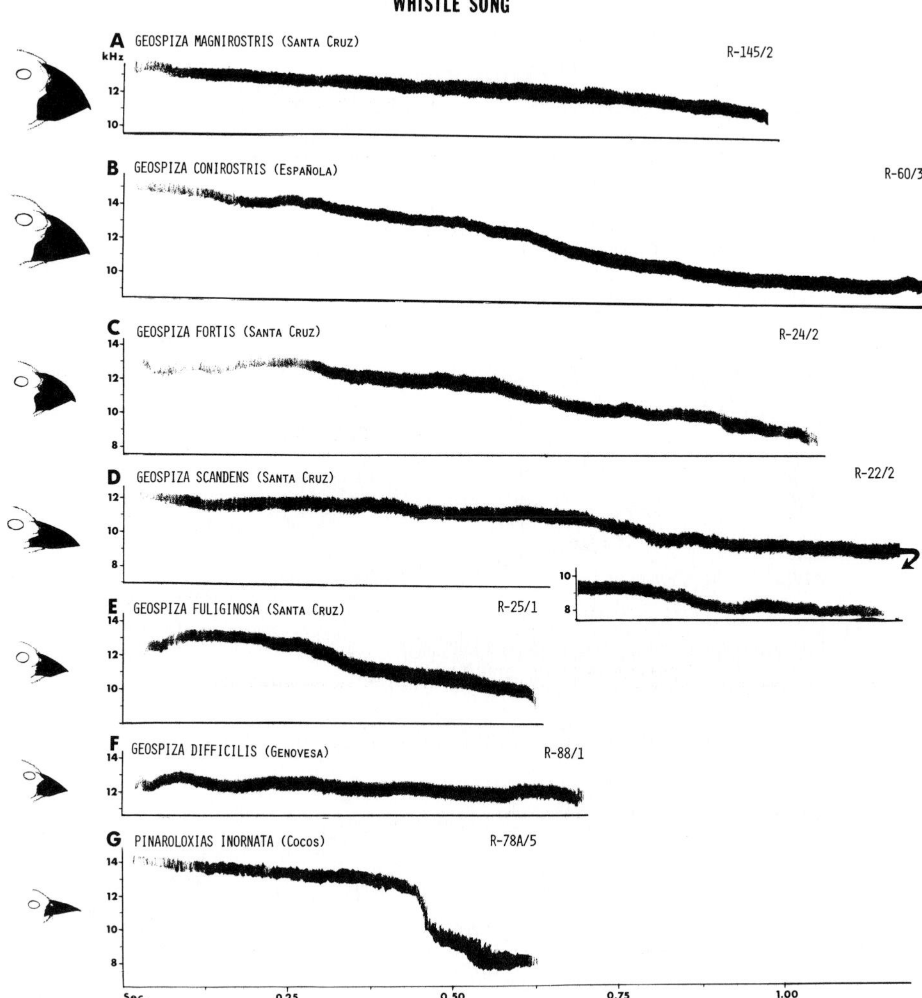

Fig. 43. Whistle songs of six species of *Geospiza* and *Pinaroloxias inornata.*

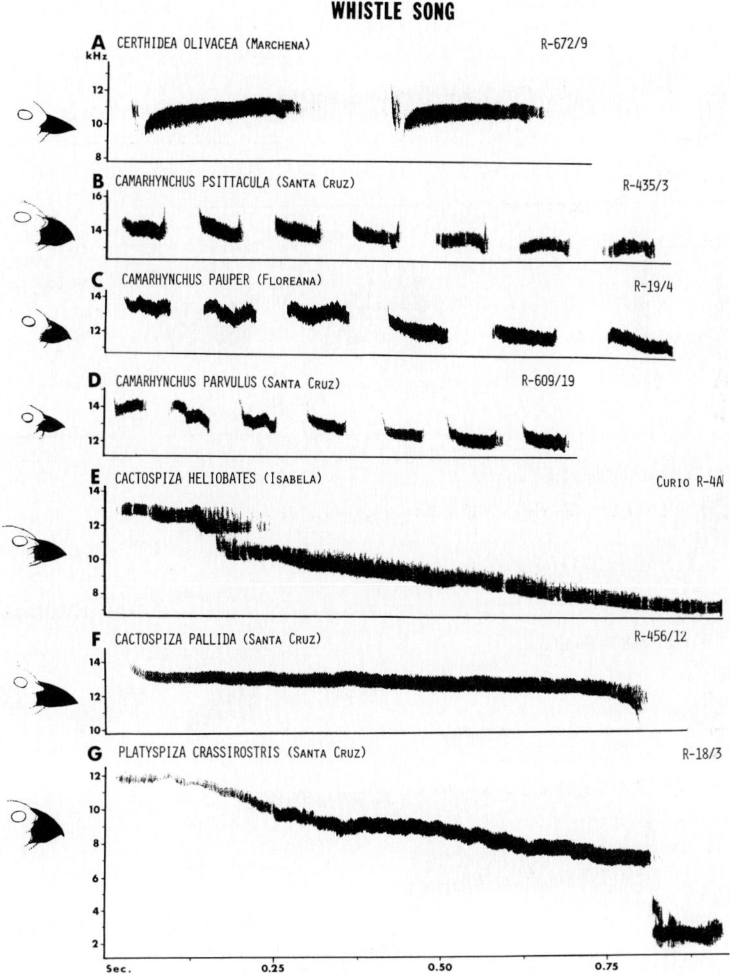

Fig. 44. Whistle songs of *Certhidea olivacea*, three species of *Camarhynchus*, two species of *Cactospiza*, and *Platyspiza crassirostris*.

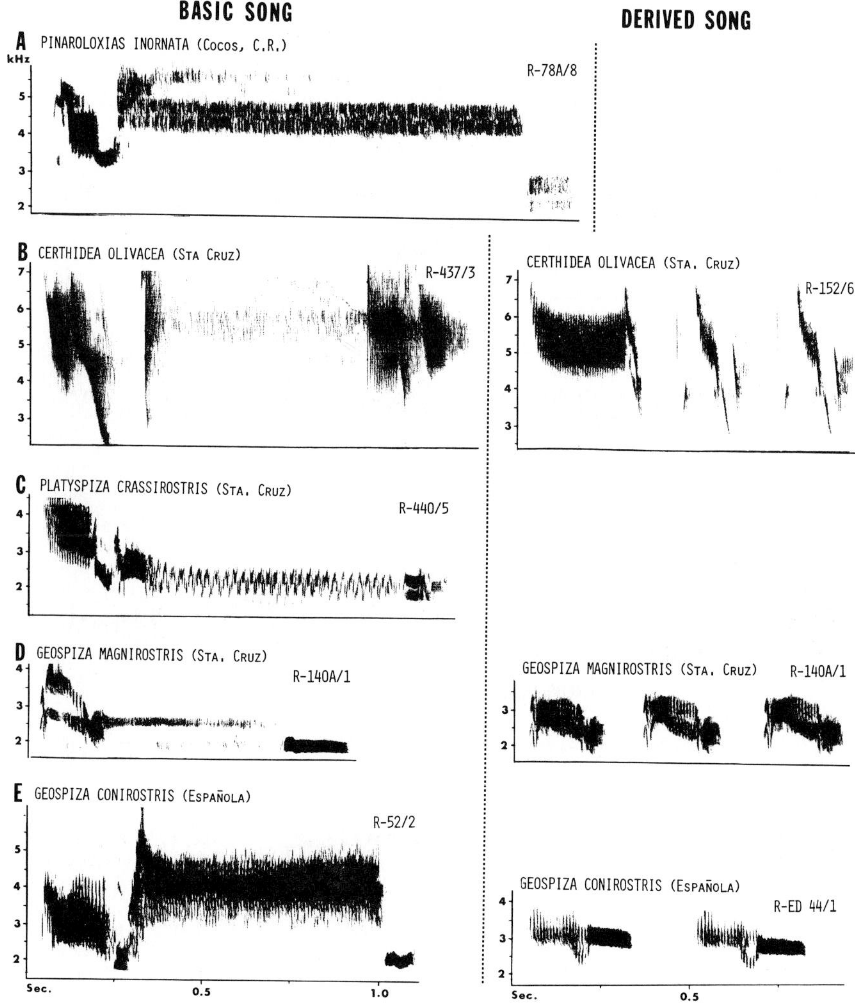

Fig. 45. Examples of basic and derived songs of five species of Darwin's finches.

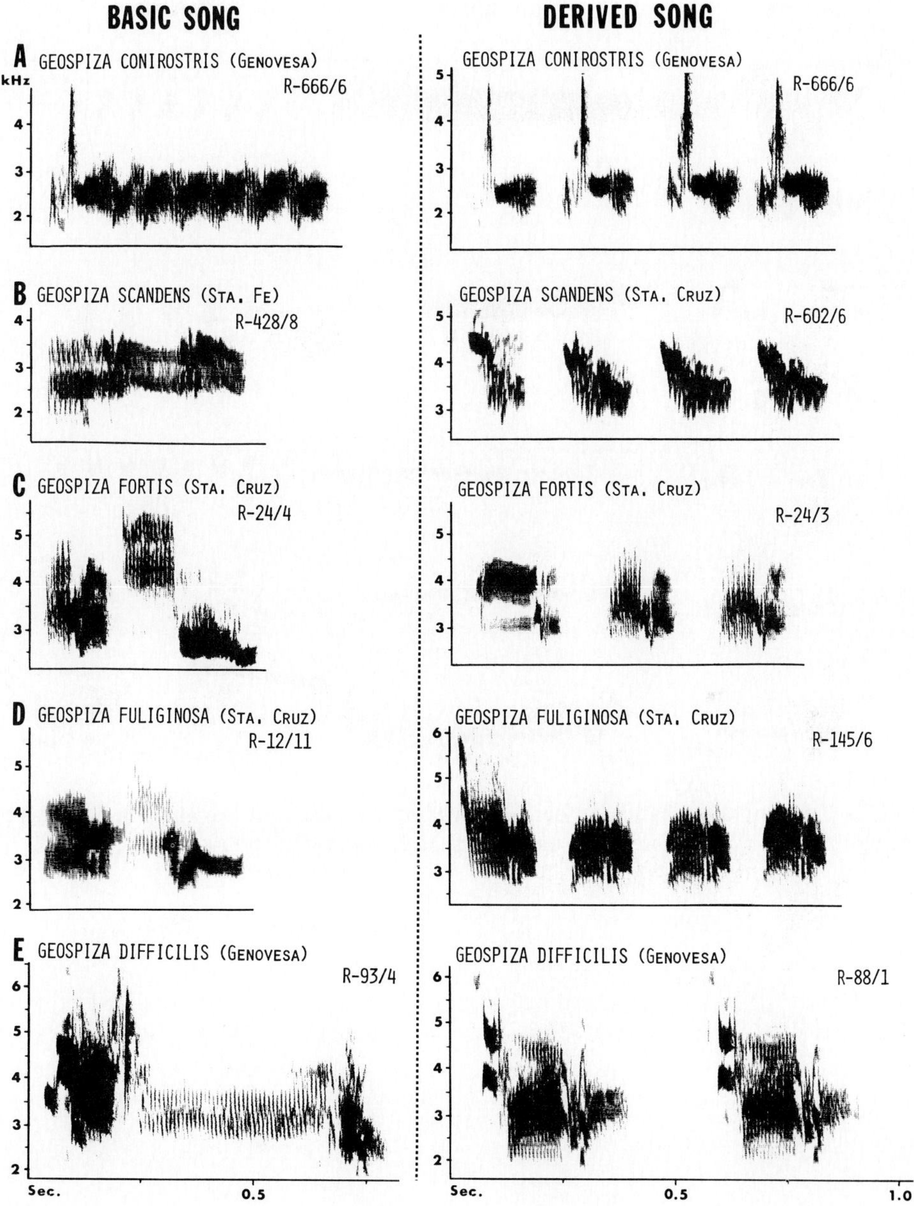

Fig. 46. Examples of basic and derived songs of five species of *Geospiza*. Basic songs include basic proper and abbreviate basic types. See text for details.

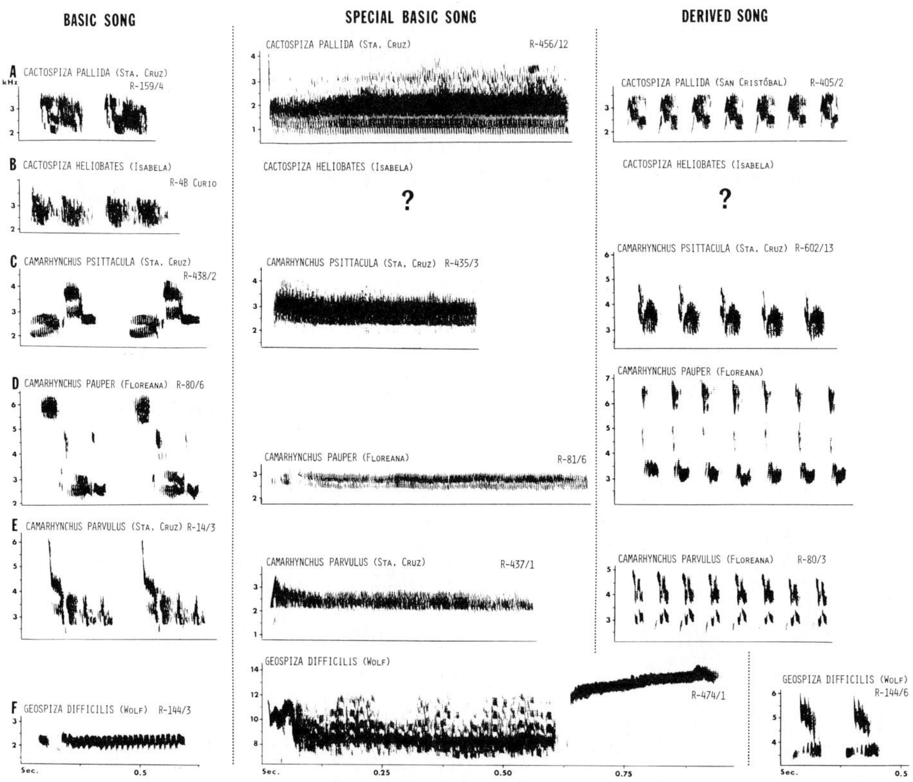

Fig. 47. Examples of basic and derived songs of six species of Darwin's finches. Basic songs include basic, proper, abbreviate basic, and special basic. See text for details.

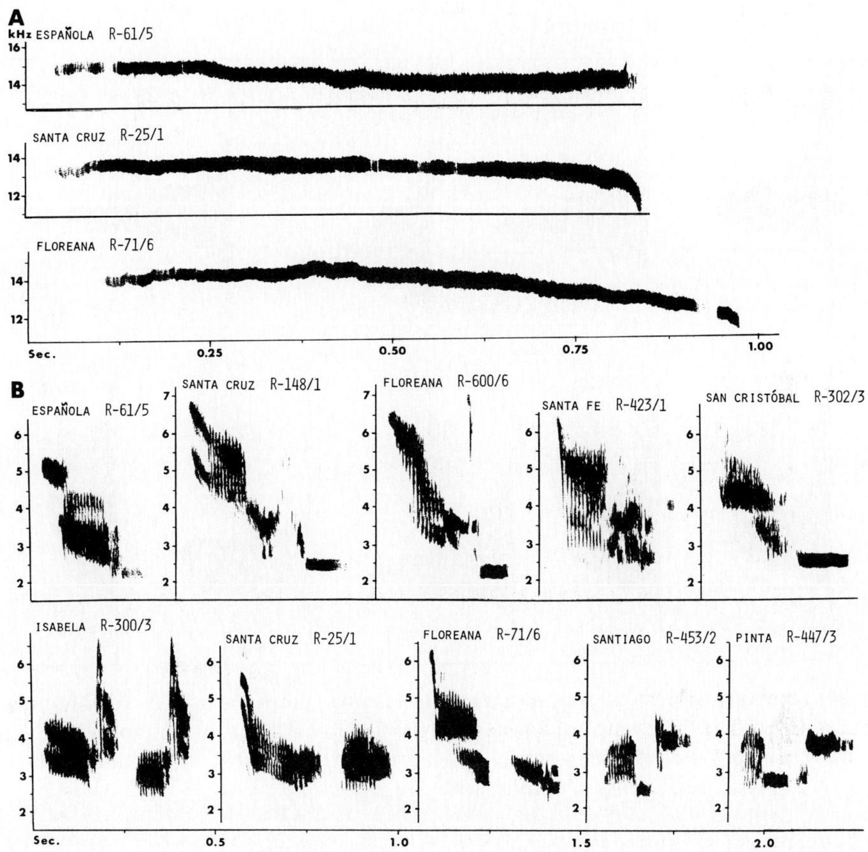

Fig. 48. Population variation in whistle songs (A) and basic and derived songs (B) of *Geospiza fuliginosa.*

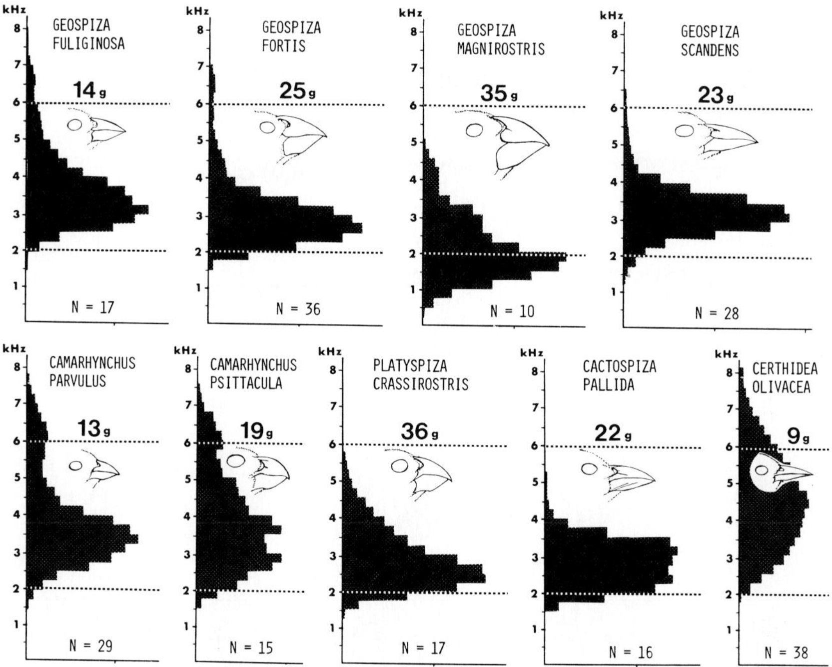

Fig. 49. Energy spectra of song populations of nine sympatric species of Darwin's finches on Isla Santa Cruz. The following song types are included: *Geospiza,* basic, abbreviate basic, and derived songs; *Camarhynchus, Cactospiza,* and *Certhidea*, abbreviate basic and derived songs; *Platyspiza crassirostris*, basic songs. Compare with Fig. 151.

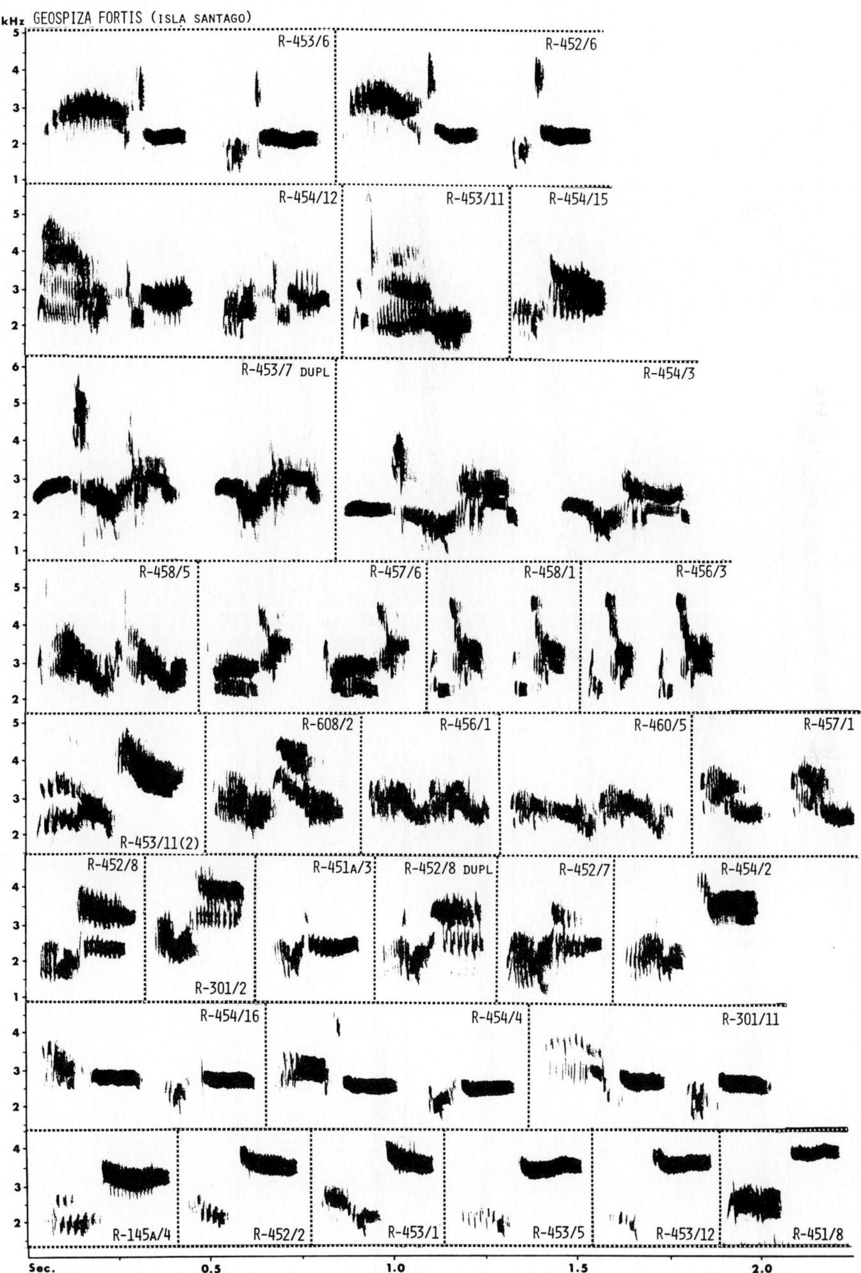

Fig. 50. Variation in basic and derived songs of *Geospiza fortis*, Isla Santiago. Only the repetitive portion of each song is displayed.

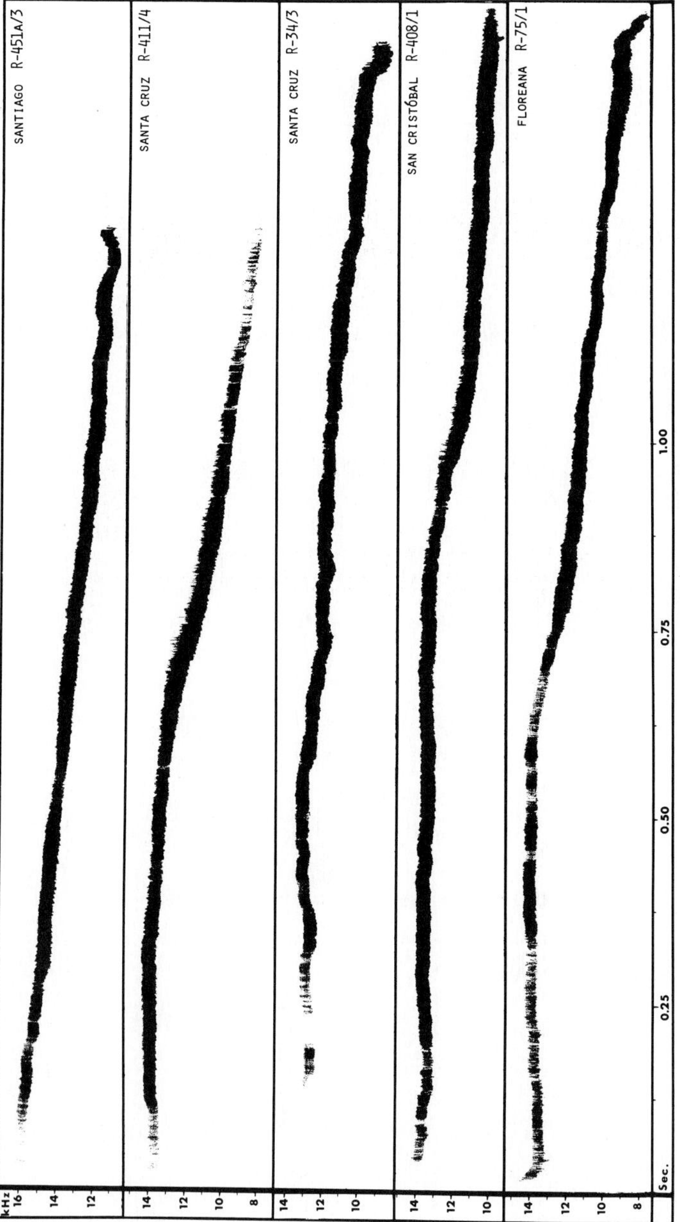

Fig. 51. Population variation in the whistle song of *Geospiza fortis*.

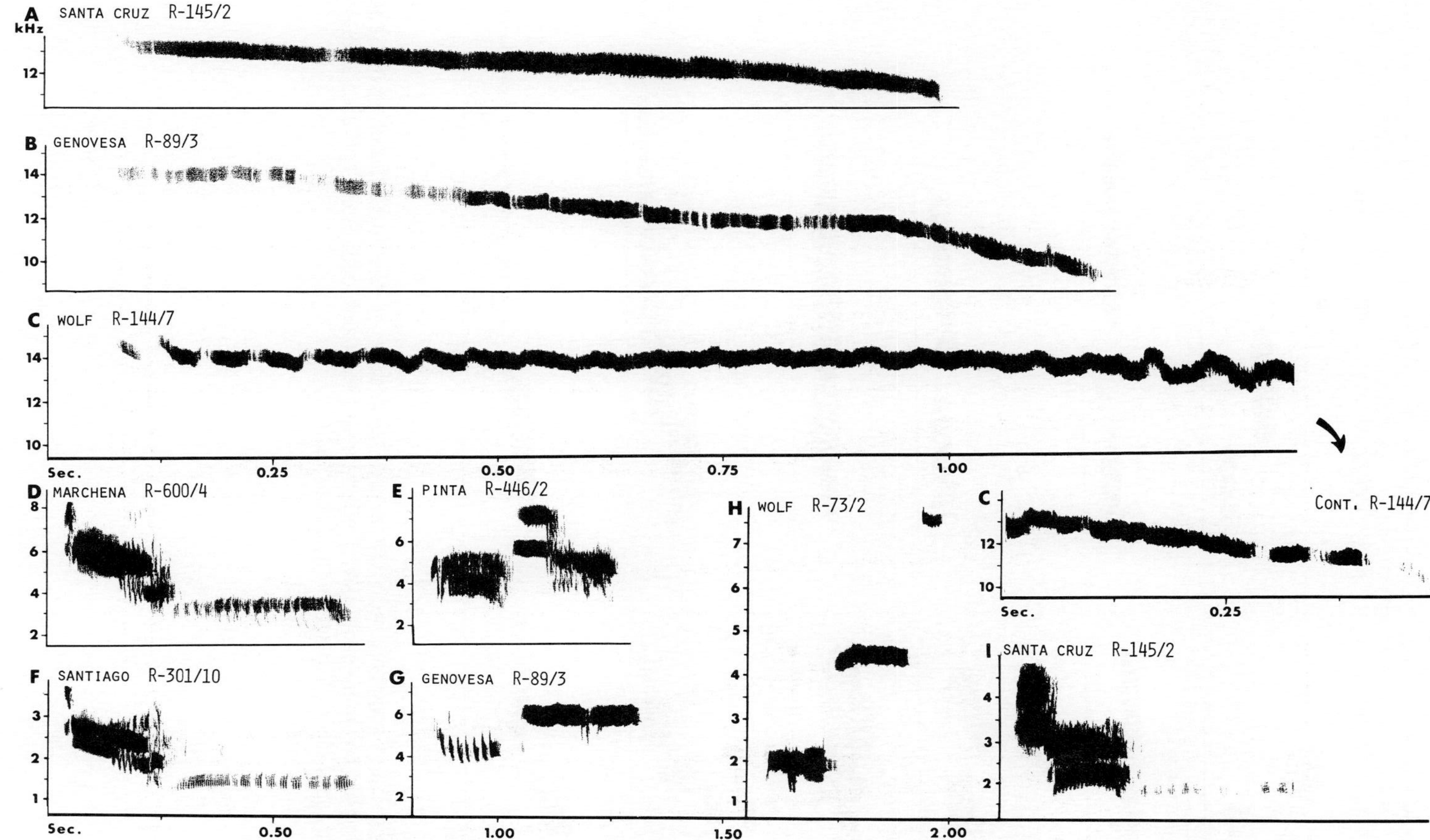

Fig. 52. Population variation in whistle and basic songs of *Geospiza magnirostris*.

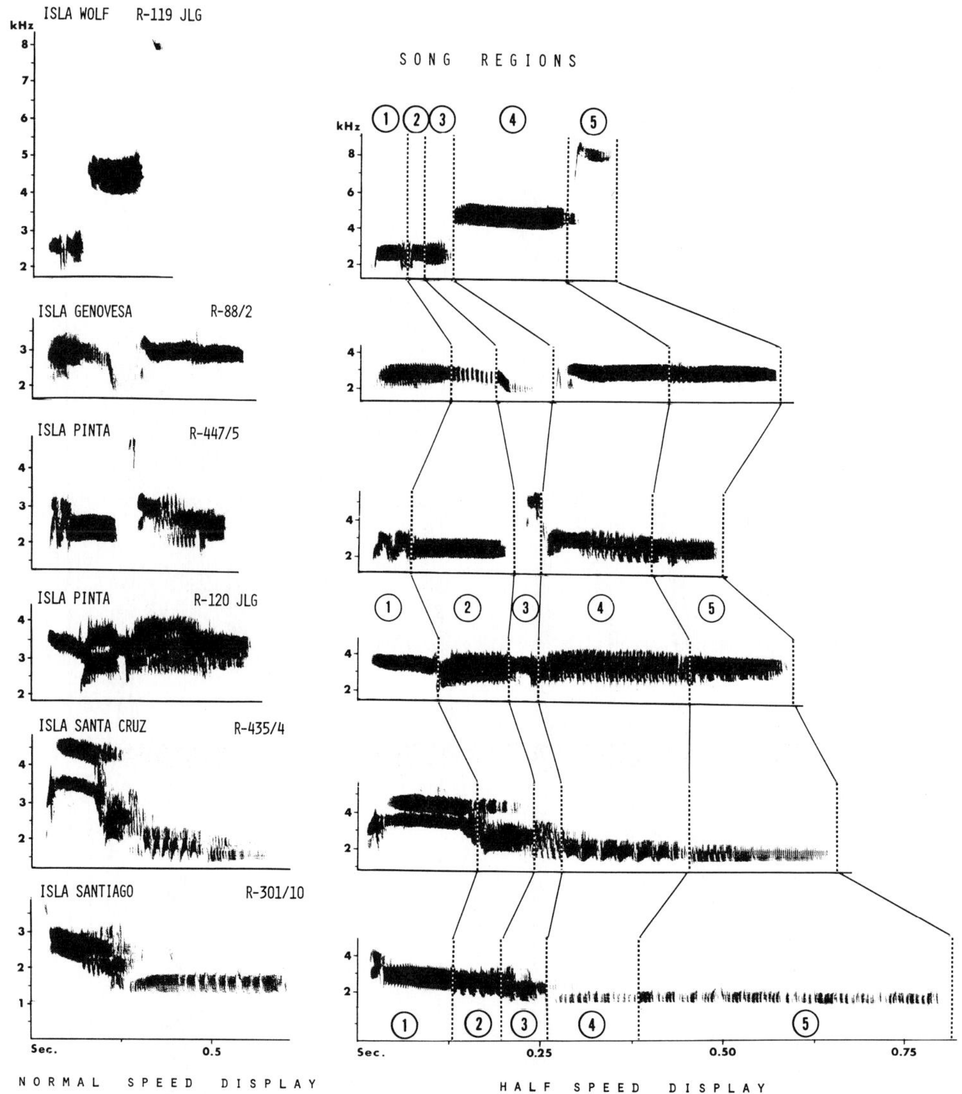

Fig. 53. Geographic variation in the basic song of *Geospiza magnirostris*. Song regions presumed to be homologous are similarly numbered and delineated by vertical lines. Normal speed displays at left; half speed displays at right.

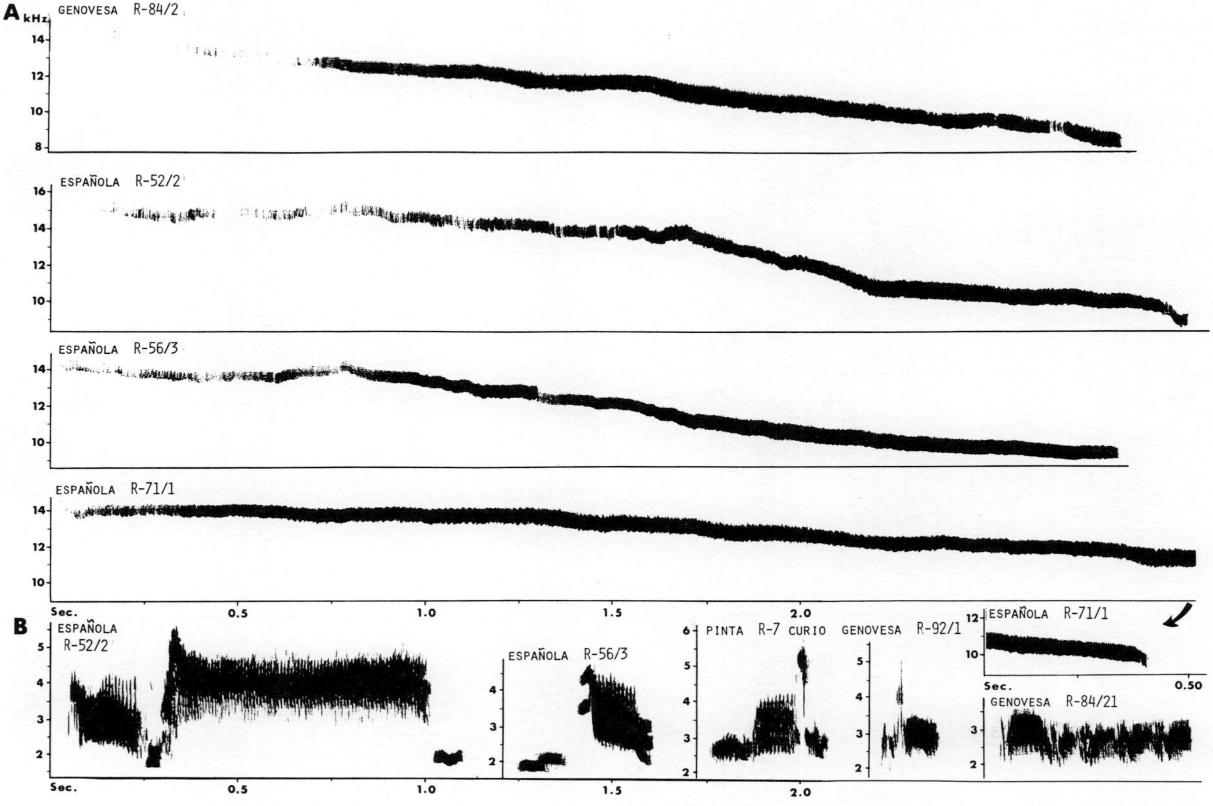

Fig. 54. Population variation in whistle, basic, and derived songs of *Geospiza conirostris*.

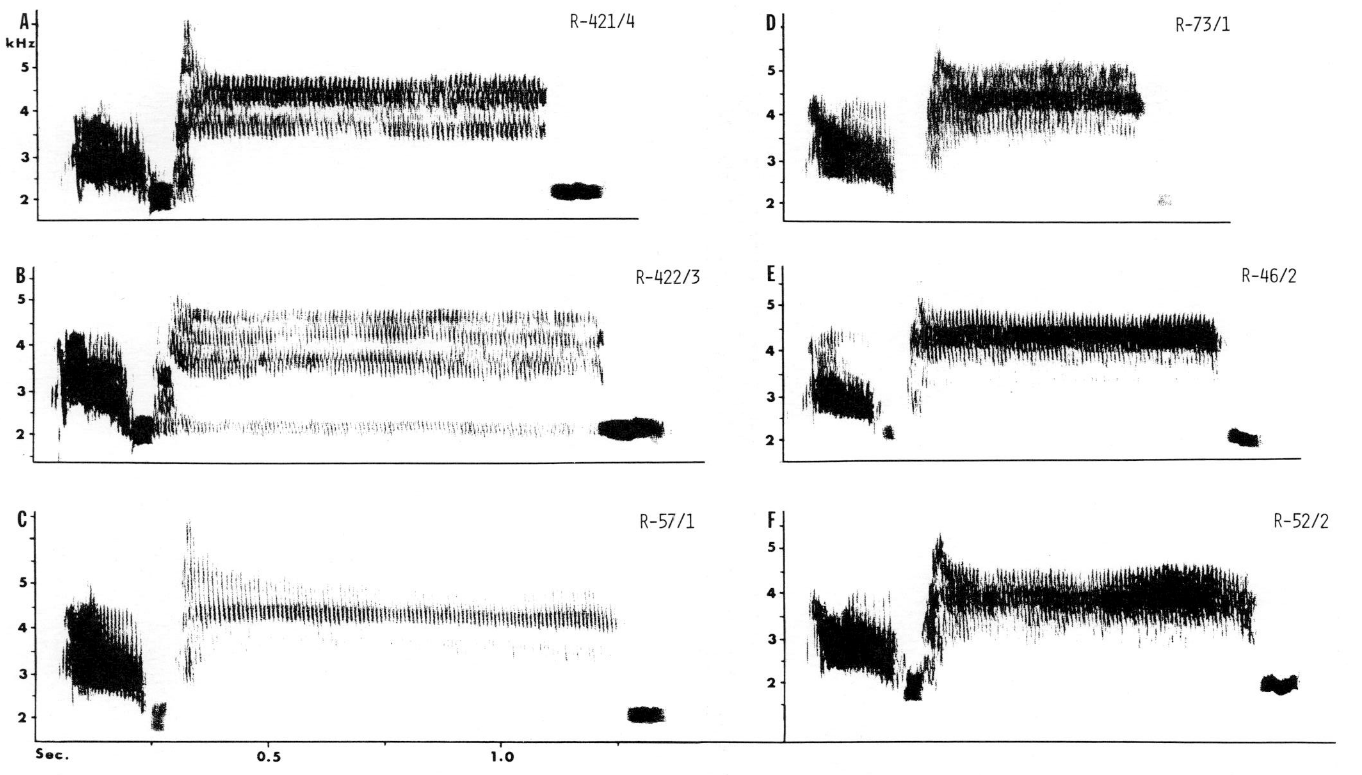

Fig. 55. Variation in the basic song of *Geospiza conirostris*, Isla Española. Note resemblance to songs of *Agelaius phoenicius* of North America (cf. Fig. 39).

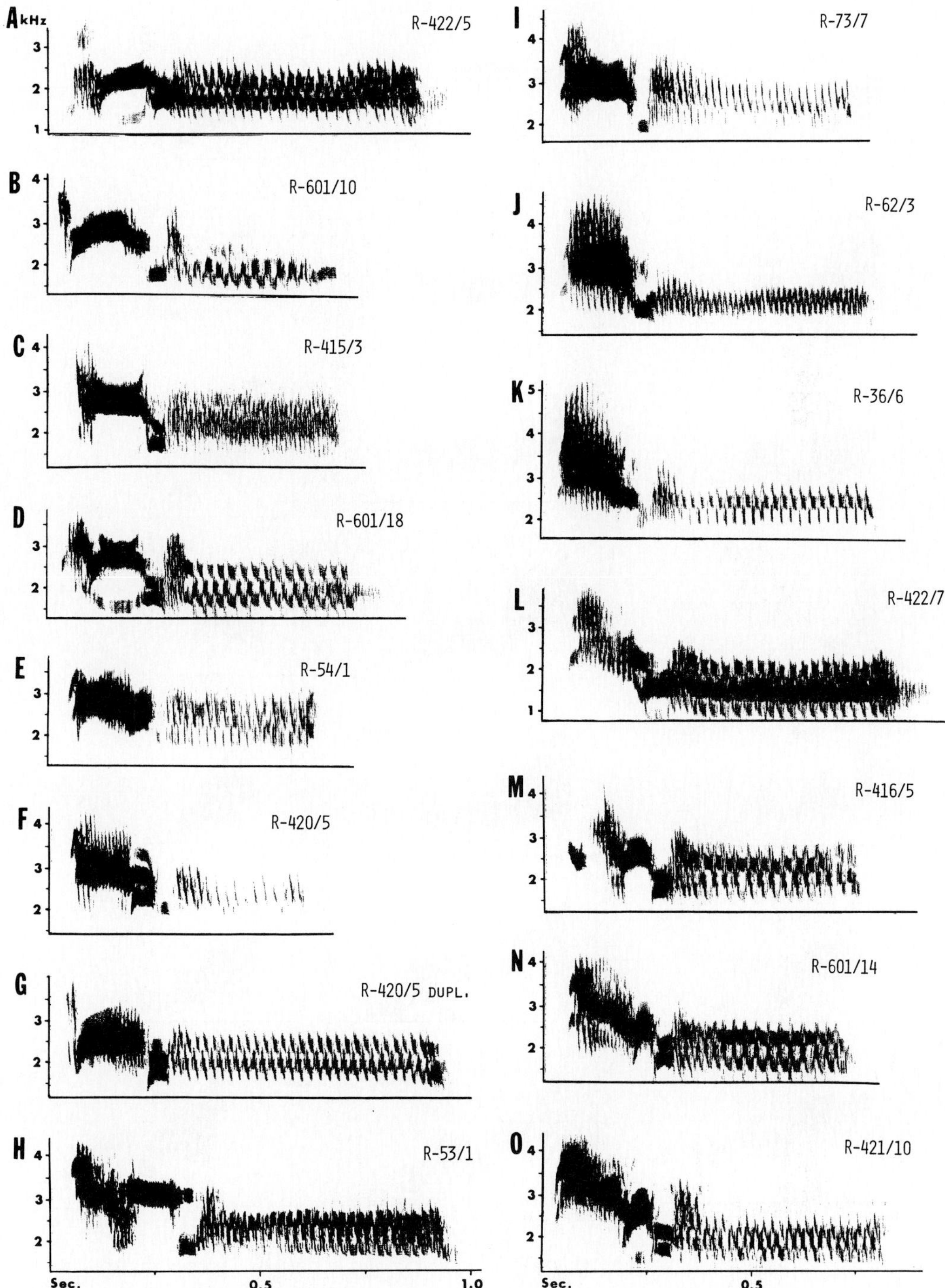

Fig. 56. Variation in the basic song of *Geospiza conirostris*, Isla Española.

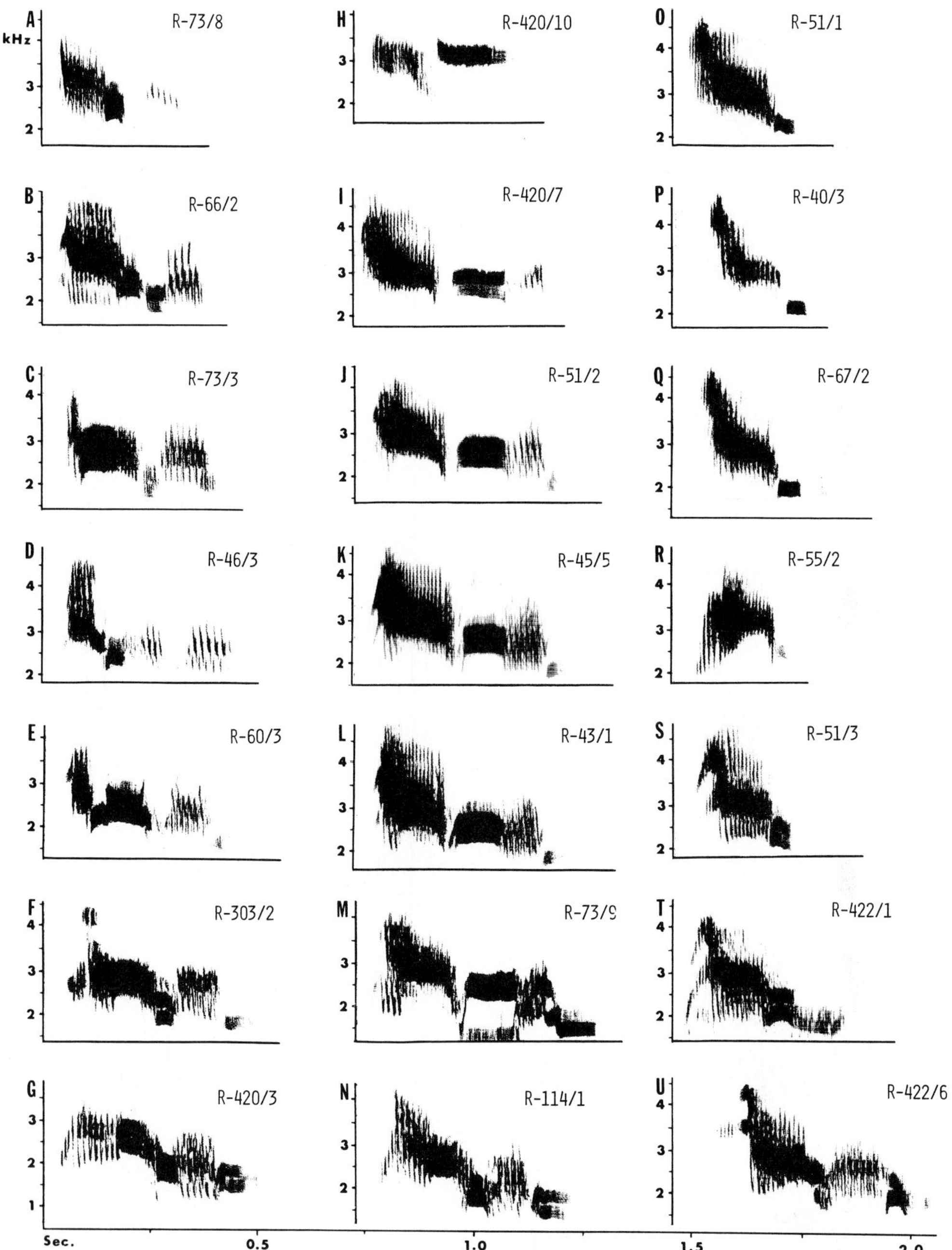

Fig. 57. Variation in the abbreviate basic and derived songs of *Geospiza conirostris*, Isla Española.

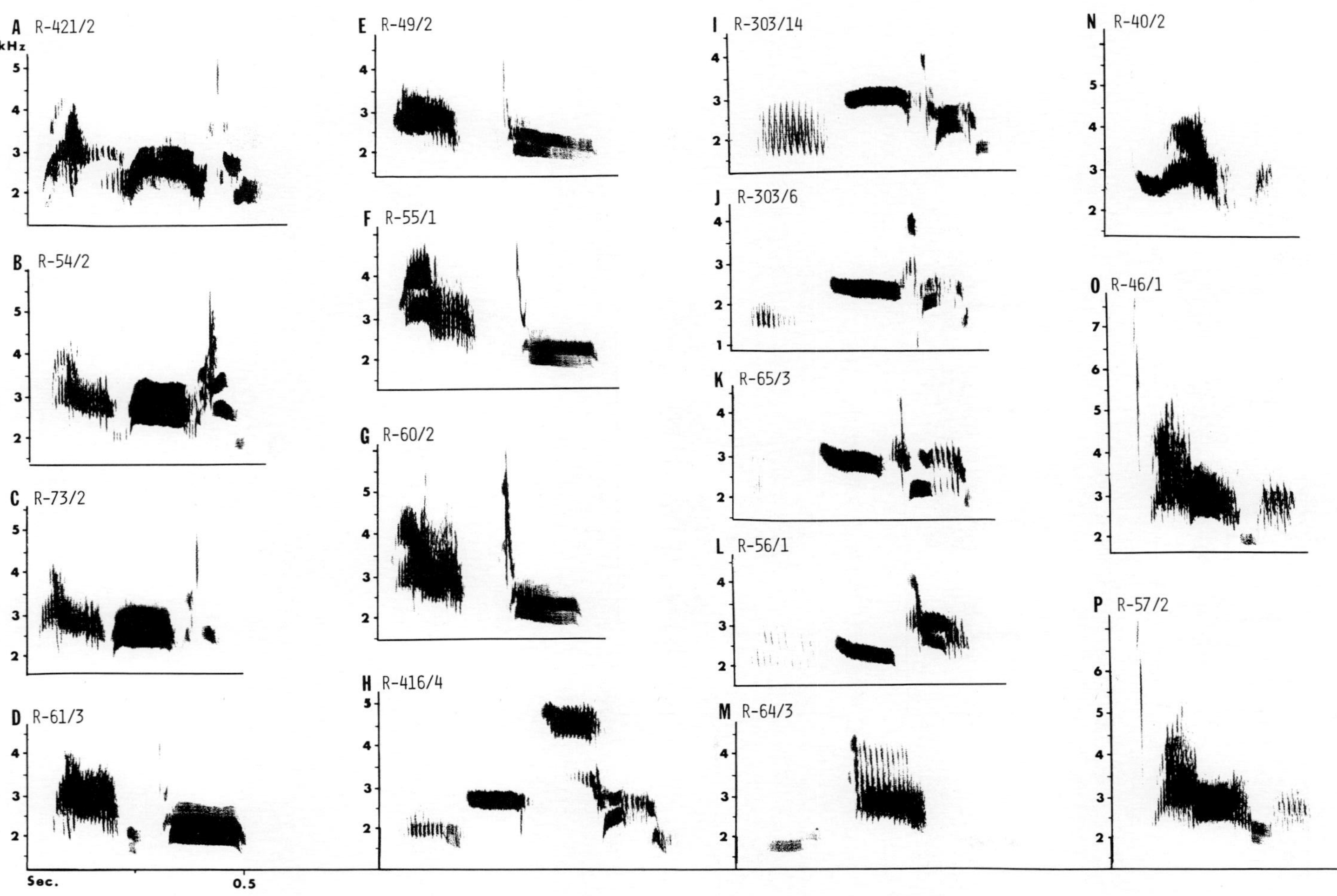

Fig. 58. Variation in the abbreviate basic and derived songs of *Geospiza conirostris*, Isla Española.

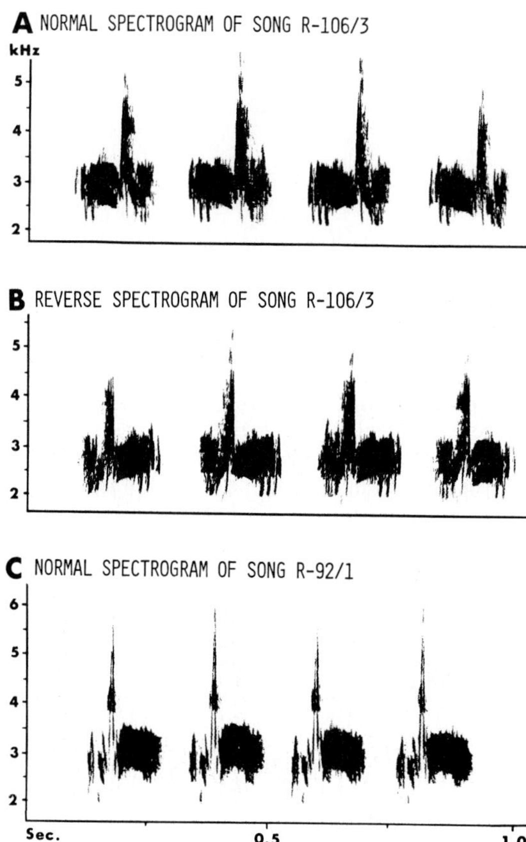

Fig. 59. Comparison of normal (A and C) and reverse (B) spectrograms of rare derived songs of *Geospiza conirostris*, Isla Española.

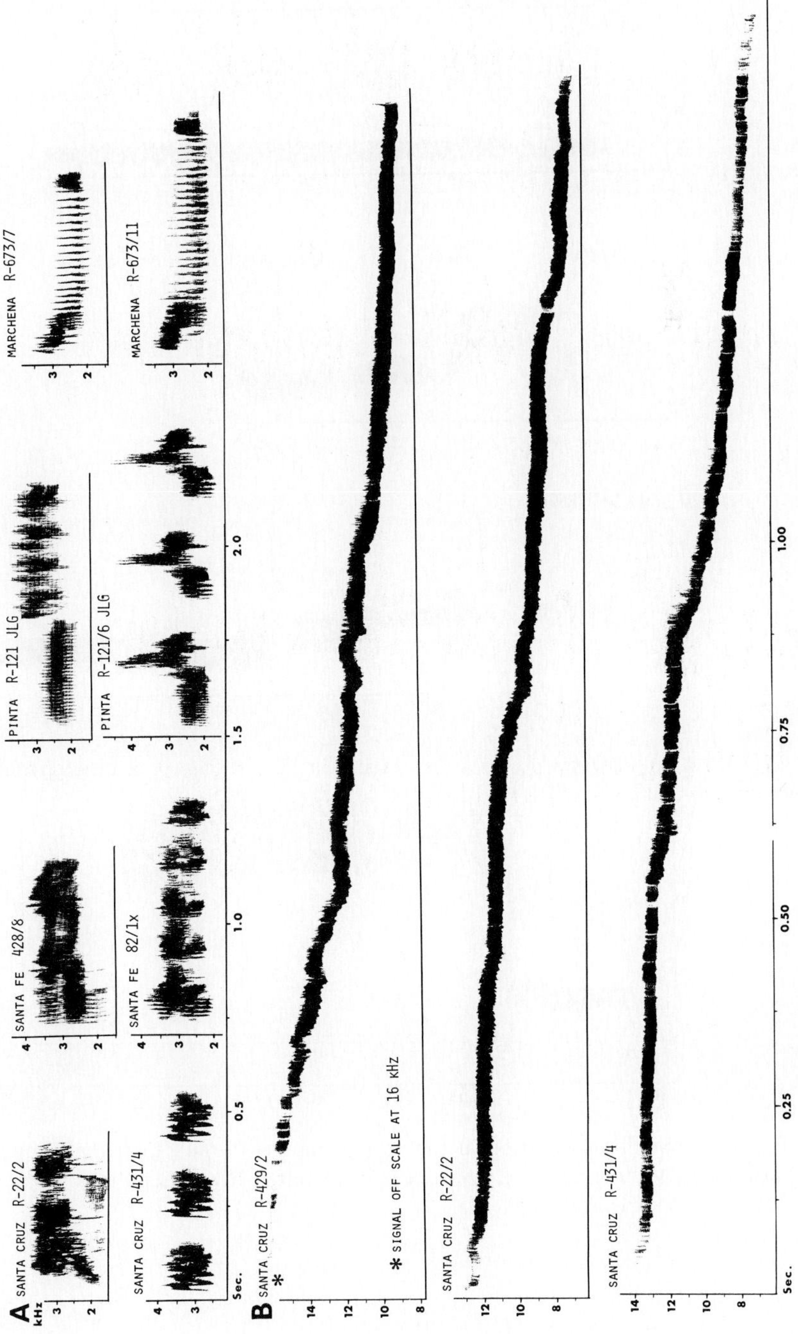

Fig. 60. Population variation in A, basic and derived songs, and B, whistle songs of *Geospiza scandens.*

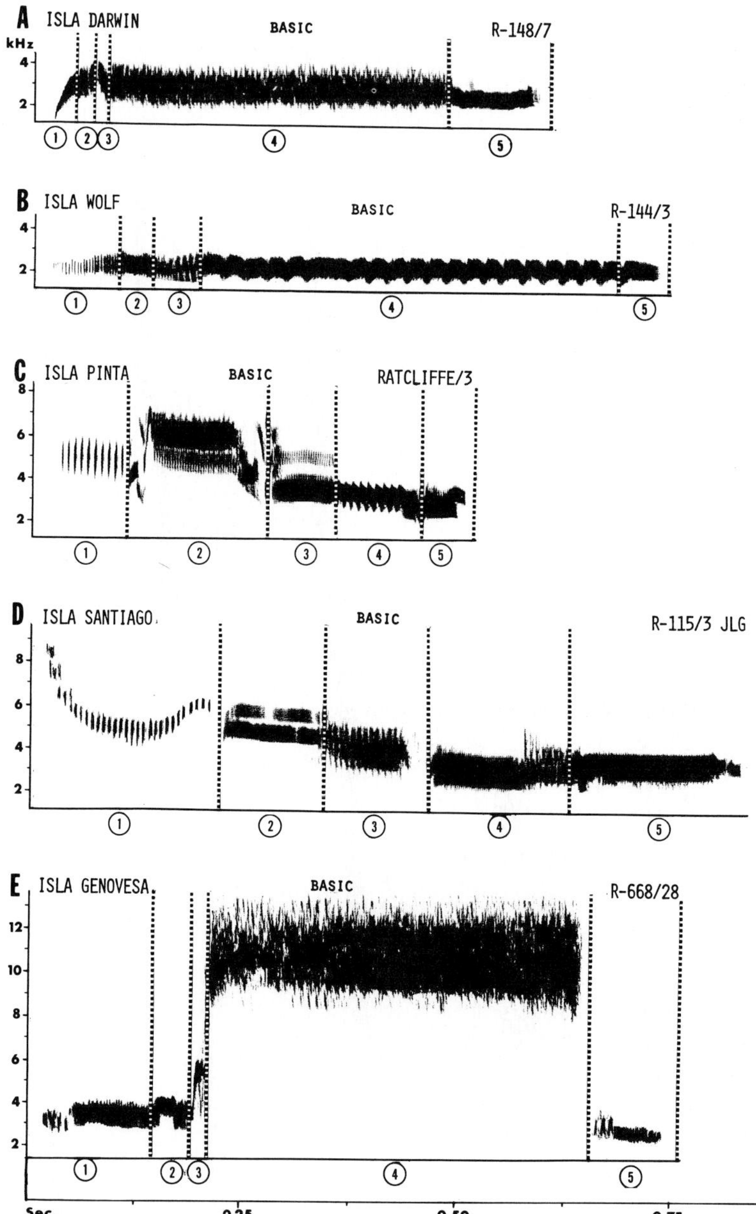

Fig. 61. Population variation in the basic song of *Geospiza difficilis*. Song regions presumed to be homologous are similarly numbered and delimited by vertical lines. Song sample from Isla Pinta (C) courtesy of L. Ratcliffe.

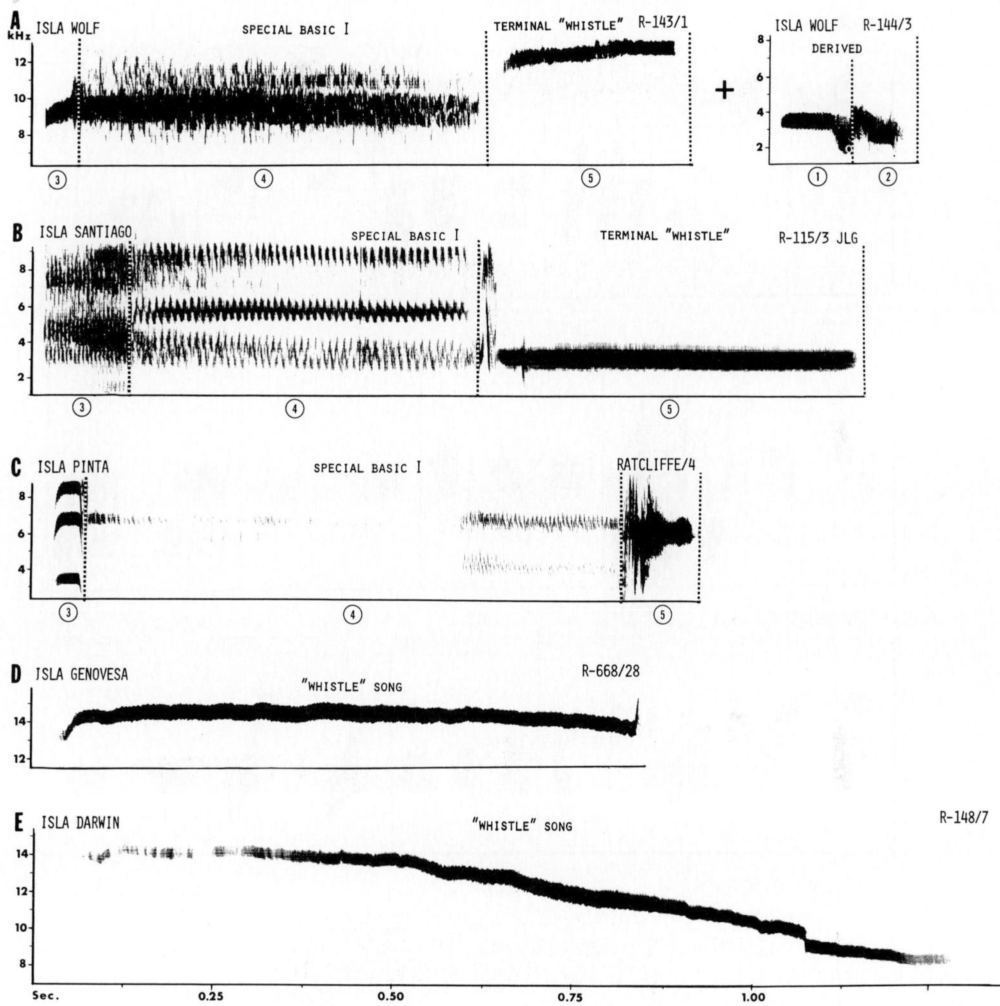

Fig. 62. Population variation in special basic and whistle songs of *Geospiza difficilis*. Song regions presumed to be homologous are similarly numbered and delimited by vertical lines. Example of a derived song from the Isla Wolf population is shown in A for comparison with special basic I song. Song sample from Isla Pinta (C) courtesy of L. Ratcliffe.

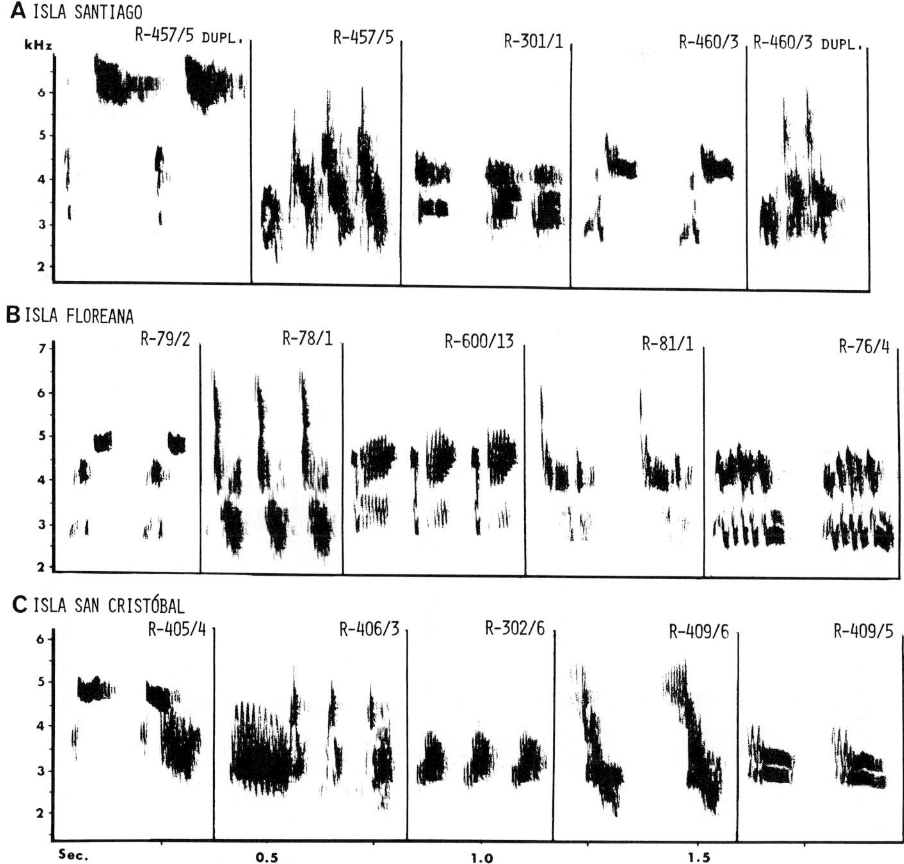

Fig. 63. Examples of population variation in songs of *Camarhynchus parvulus* from islas Santiago (A), Floreana (B) and San Cristóbal (C). Only a portion of the repetitive pattern of each song is displayed.

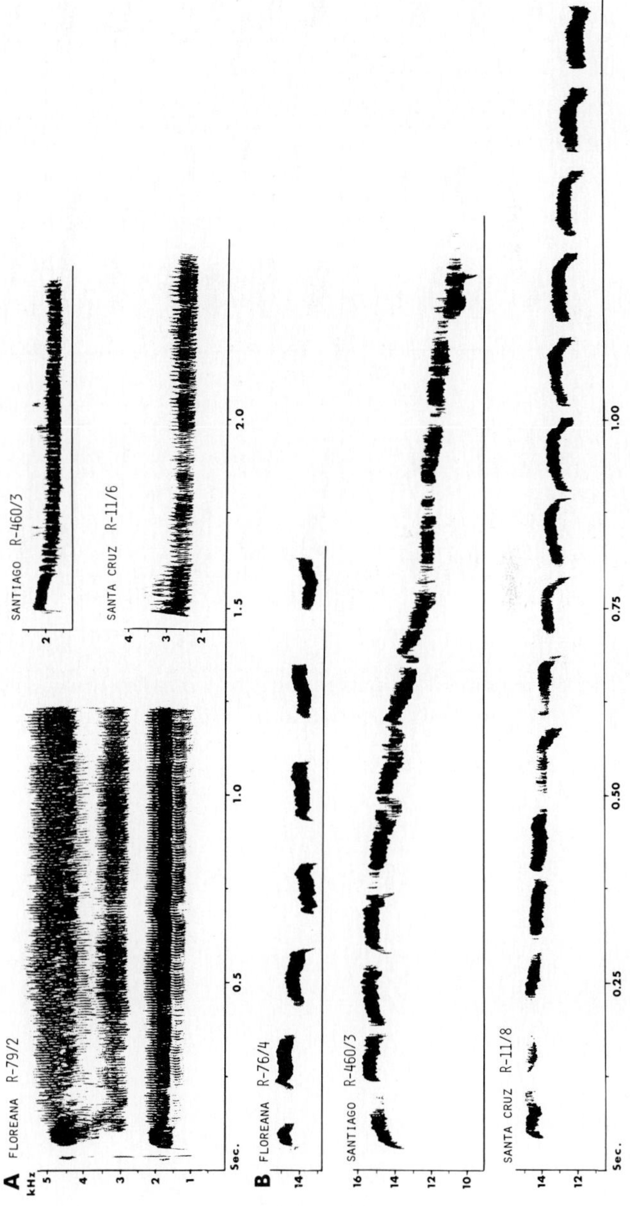

Fig. 64. Population variation in special basic and whistle songs of *Camarhynchus parvulus*.

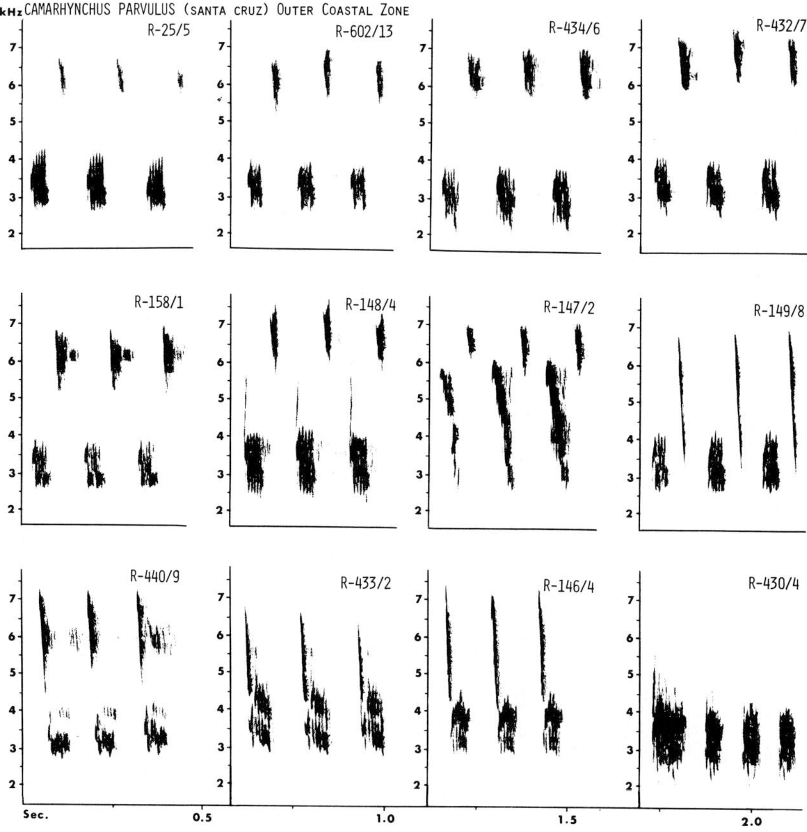

Fig. 65. Examples of derived songs of *Camarhynchus parvulus*, outer coastal zone, Academy Bay, Isla Santa Cruz. Only a portion of the repetitive pattern is displayed.

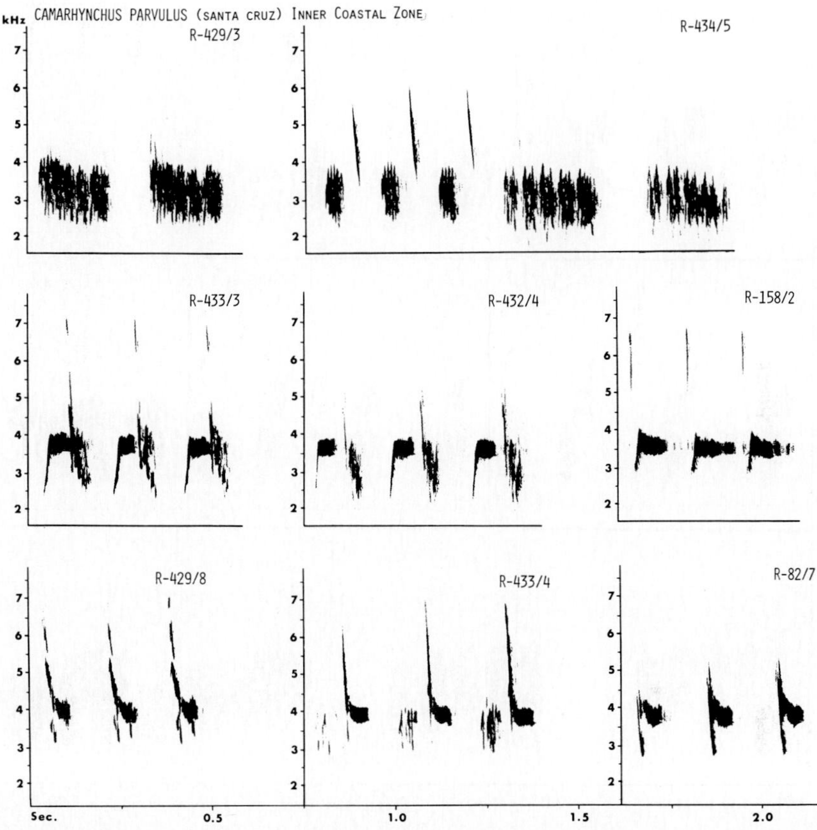

Fig. 66. Examples of derived songs of *Camarhynchus parvulus*, inner coastal zone, Academy Bay, Isla Santa Cruz. Only a portion of the repetitive pattern is displayed.

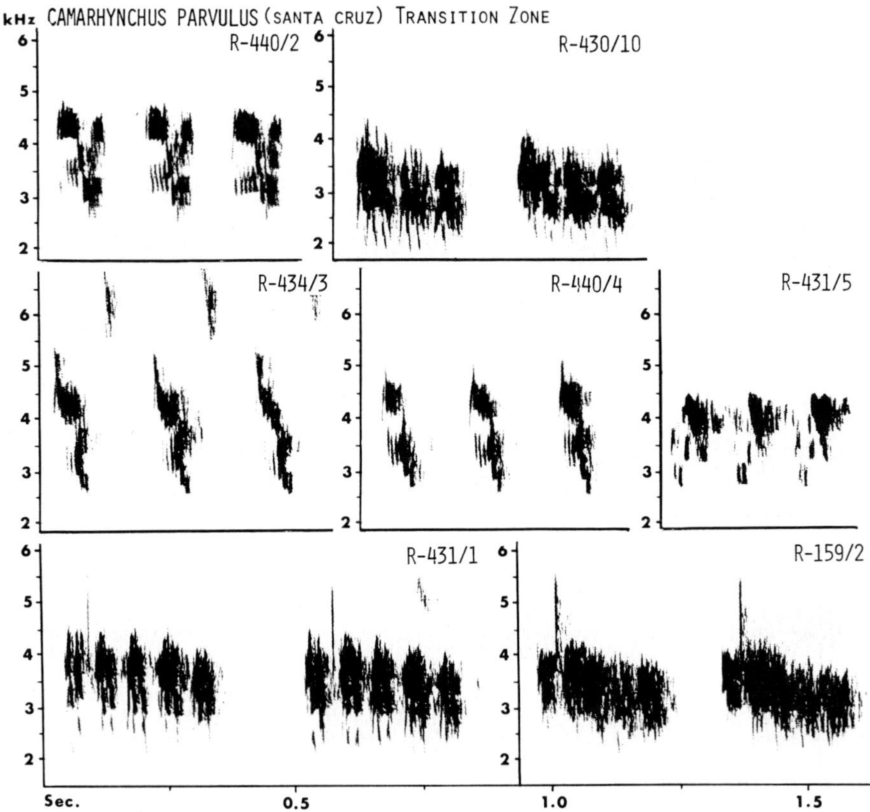

Fig. 67. Examples of derived and basic songs of *Camarhynchus parvulus*, transition zone, north of Academy Bay, Isla Santa Cruz. Only a portion of the repetitive pattern is displayed.

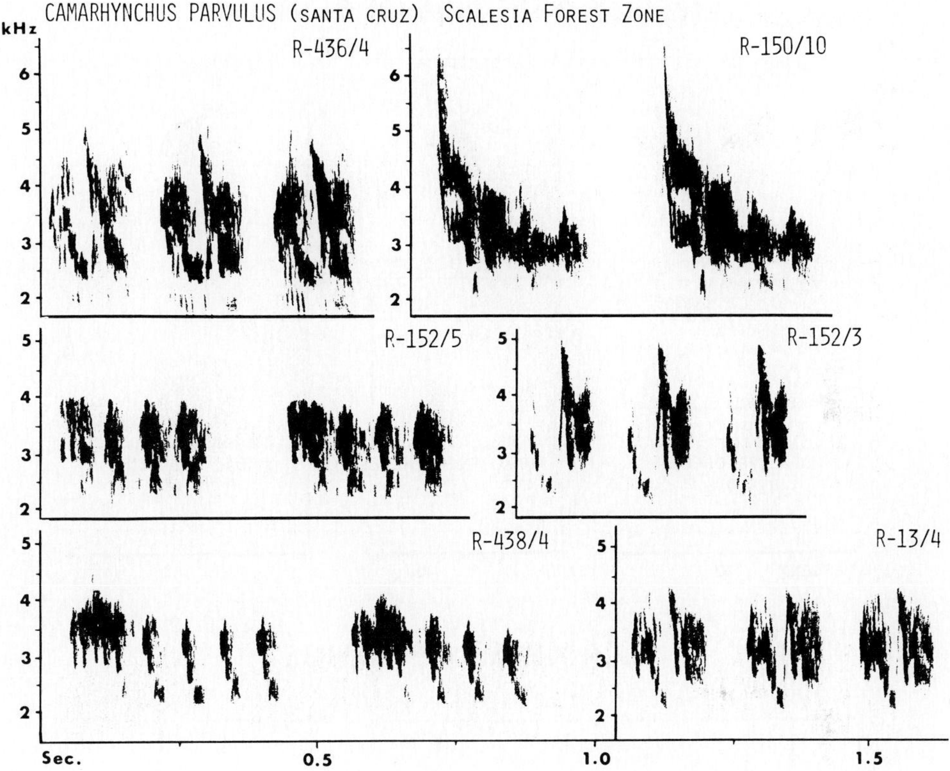

Fig. 68. Examples of derived and basic songs of *Camarhynchus parvulus, Scalesia* forest zone, near Bella Vista, Isla Santa Cruz. Only a portion of the repetitive pattern is displayed.

ENERGY SPECTRA OF SONGS

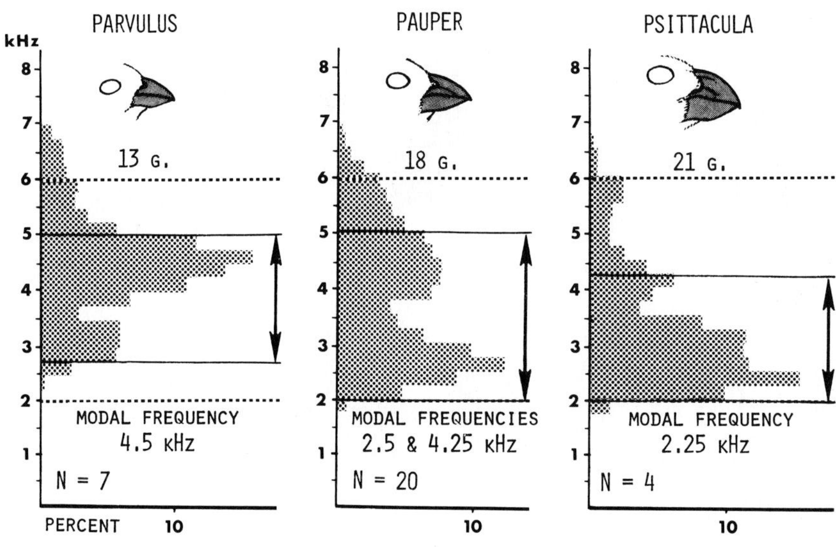

EXAMPLES OF SONGS

kHz

R-76/4

R-81/5

R-46/6

Sec. 0.5 1.0

Fig. 69. Comparison of energy spectra of derived songs, examples of songs, bills, and body weights of three sympatric species of *Camarhynchus* on Isla Floreana. Arrows indicate limits of song bandwidth containing 80-85% of song energy.

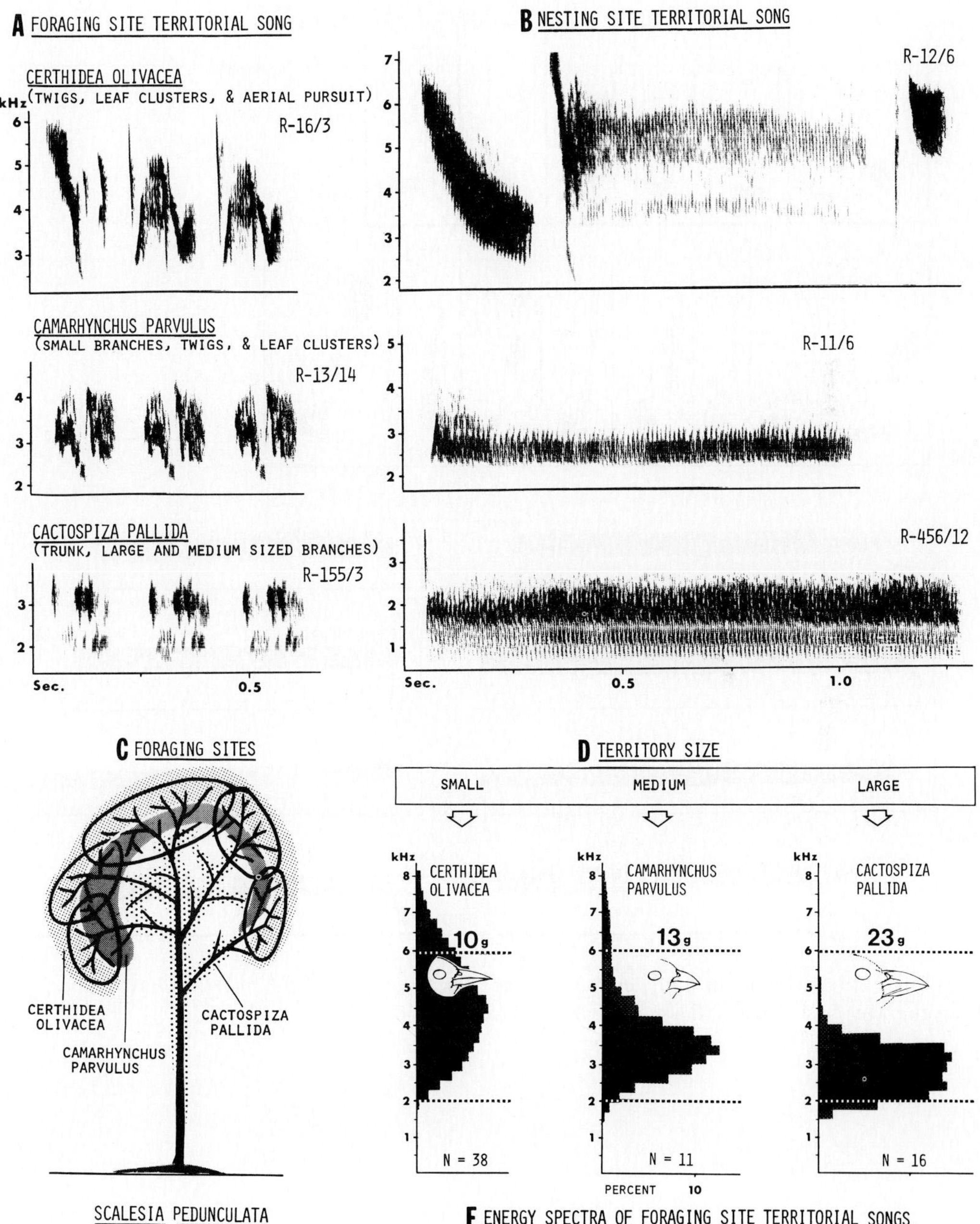

Fig. 70. Comparison of territorial songs, foraging sites, territory sizes, and energy spectra of songs of three sympatric species of "tree-finch" in the *Scalesia* forest of Isla Santa Cruz. Foraging site songs (A) are derived songs; nesting site songs (B) are basic (*Certhidea*) or special basic (*Camarhynchus* and *Cactospiza*) types.

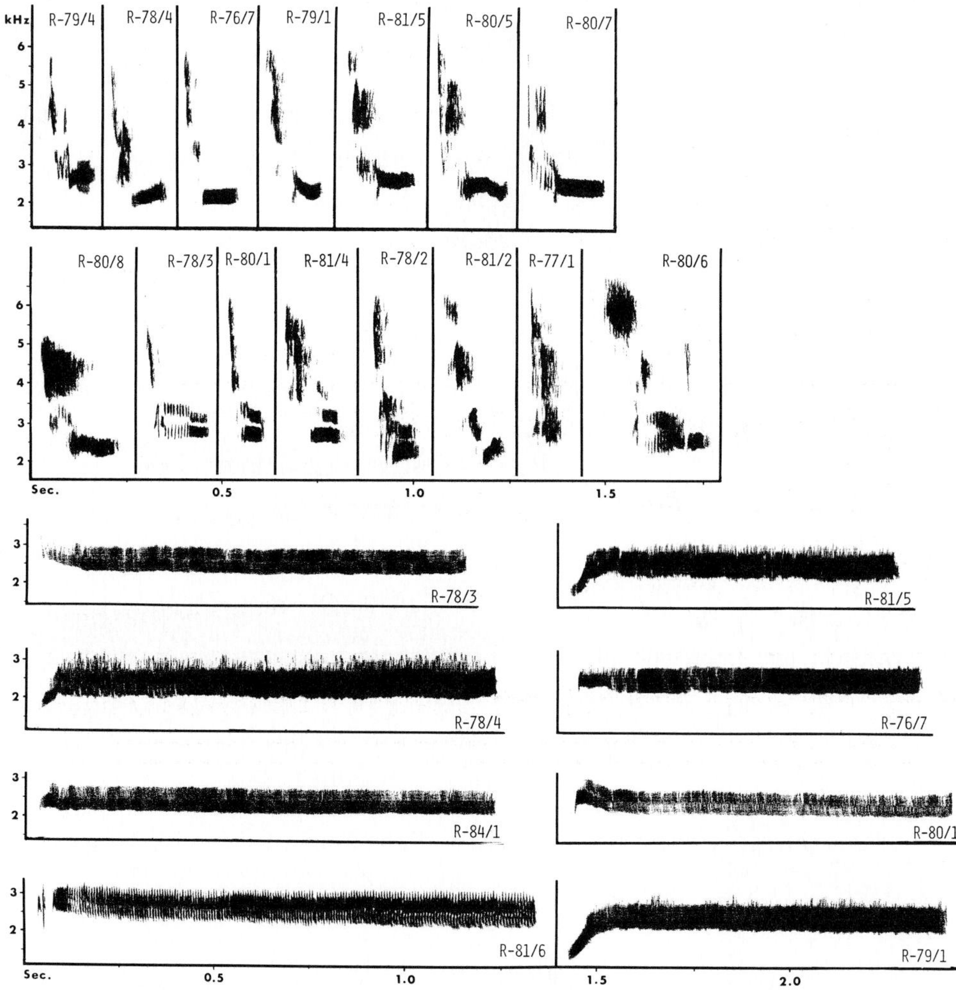

Fig. 71. Variation in the derived and special basic songs of *Camarhynchus pauper*, Isla Floreana. One basic song is illustrated, viz. R-80/6.

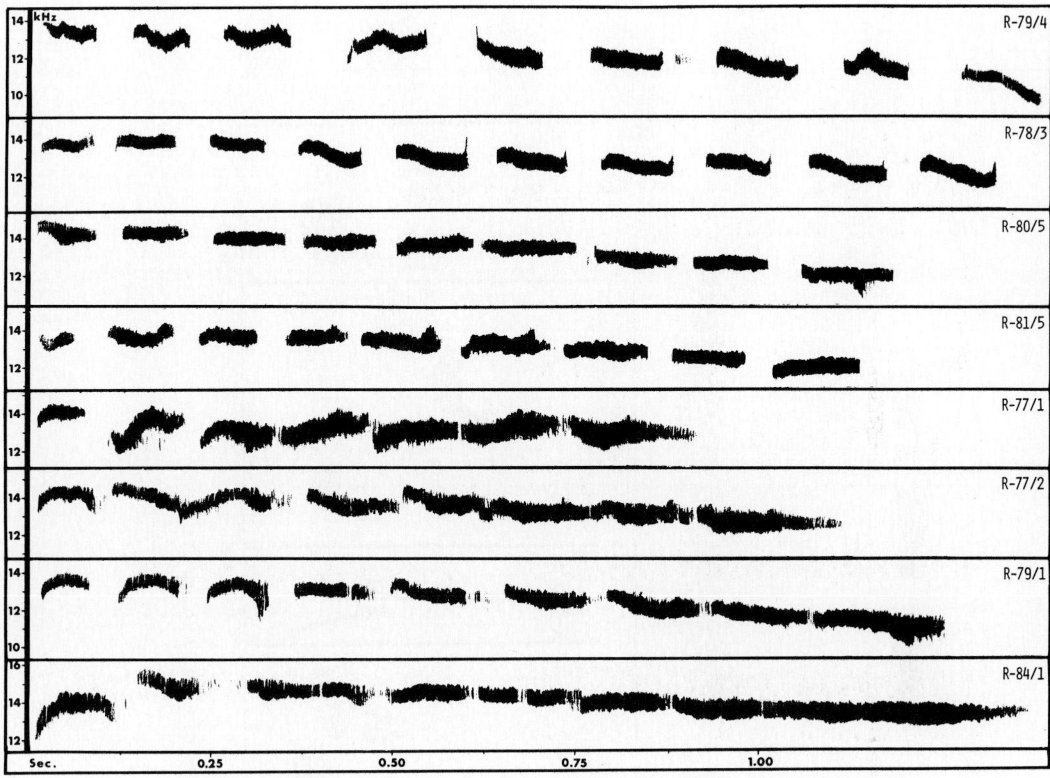

Fig. 72. Variation in the whistle song of *Camarhynchus pauper*, Isla Floreana.

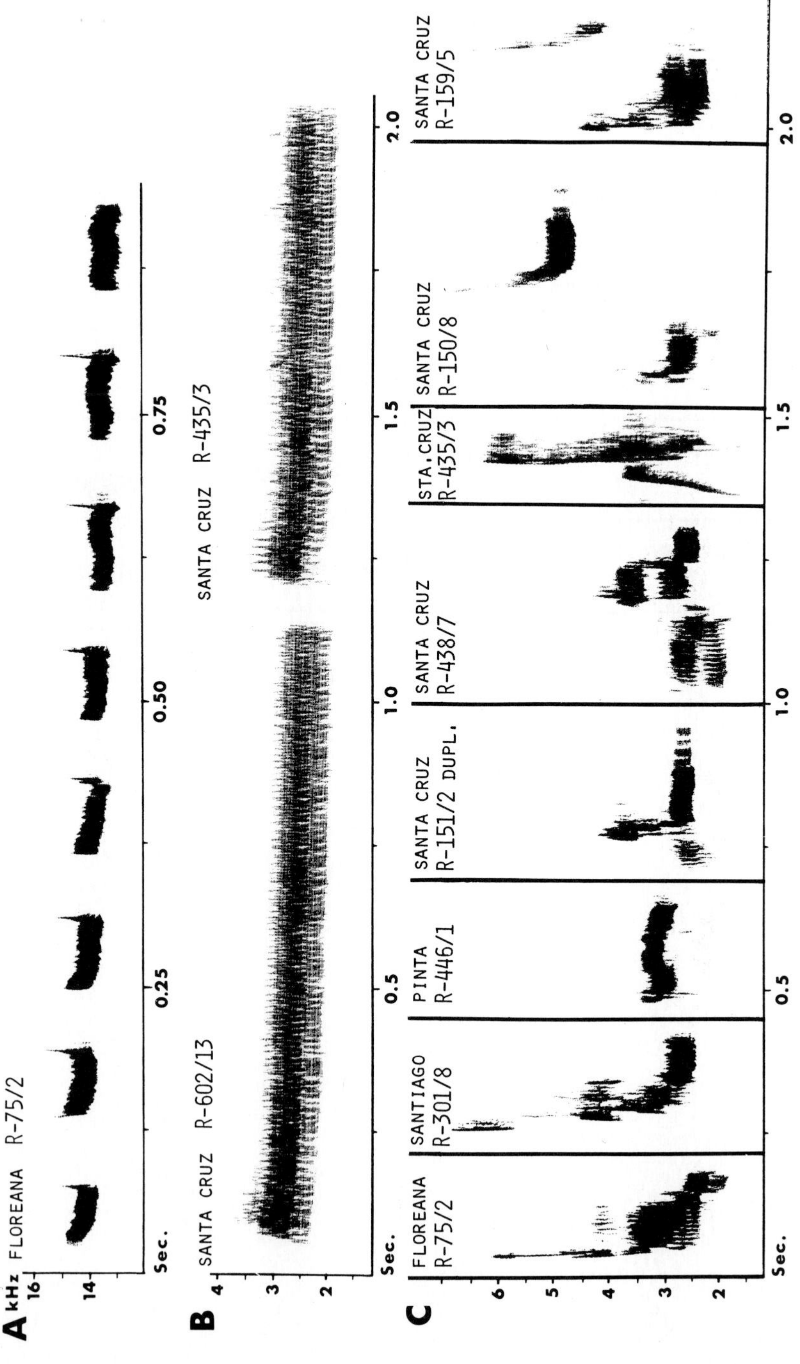

Fig. 73. Population variation in whistle, special basic, and derived songs of *Camarhynchus psittacula*.

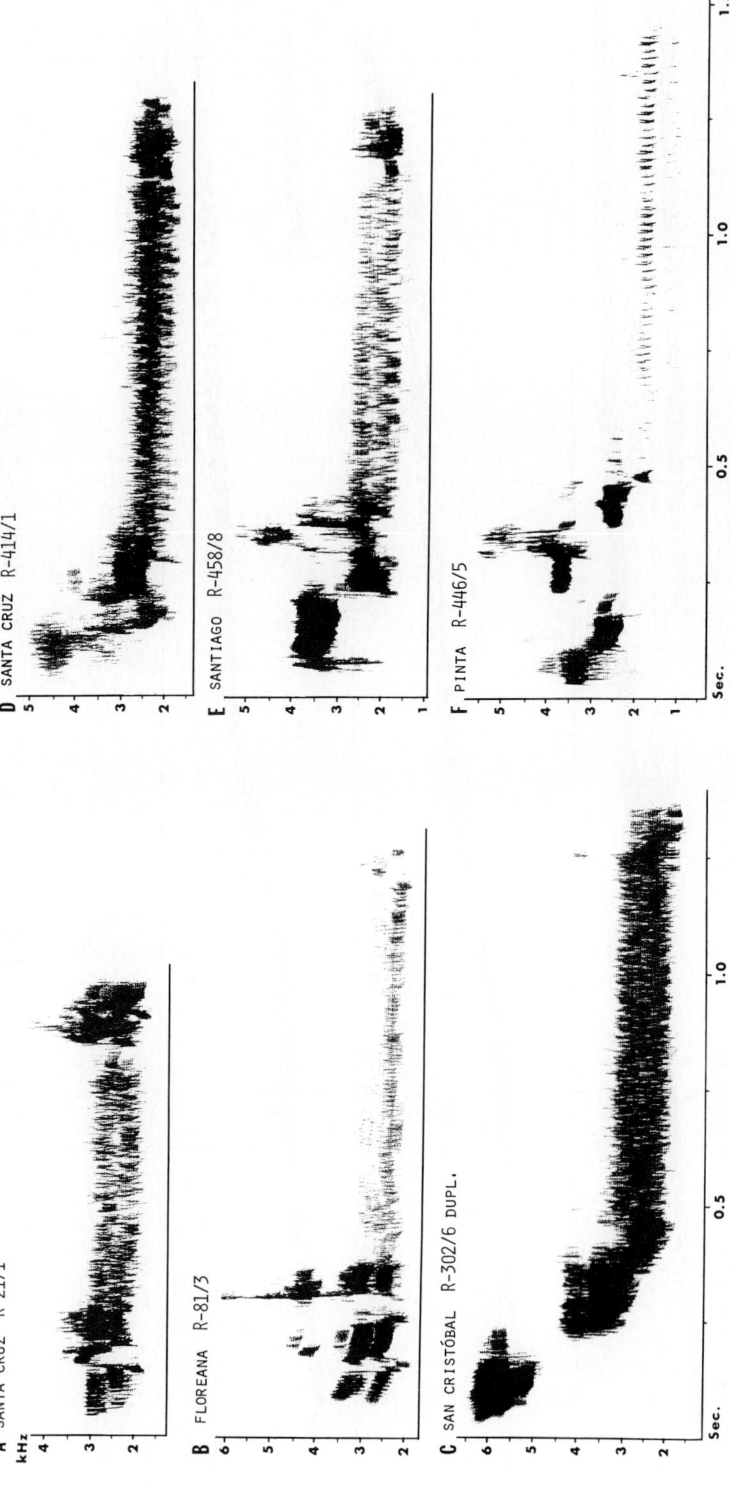

Fig. 74. Population variation in the basic song of *Platyspiza crassirostris.*

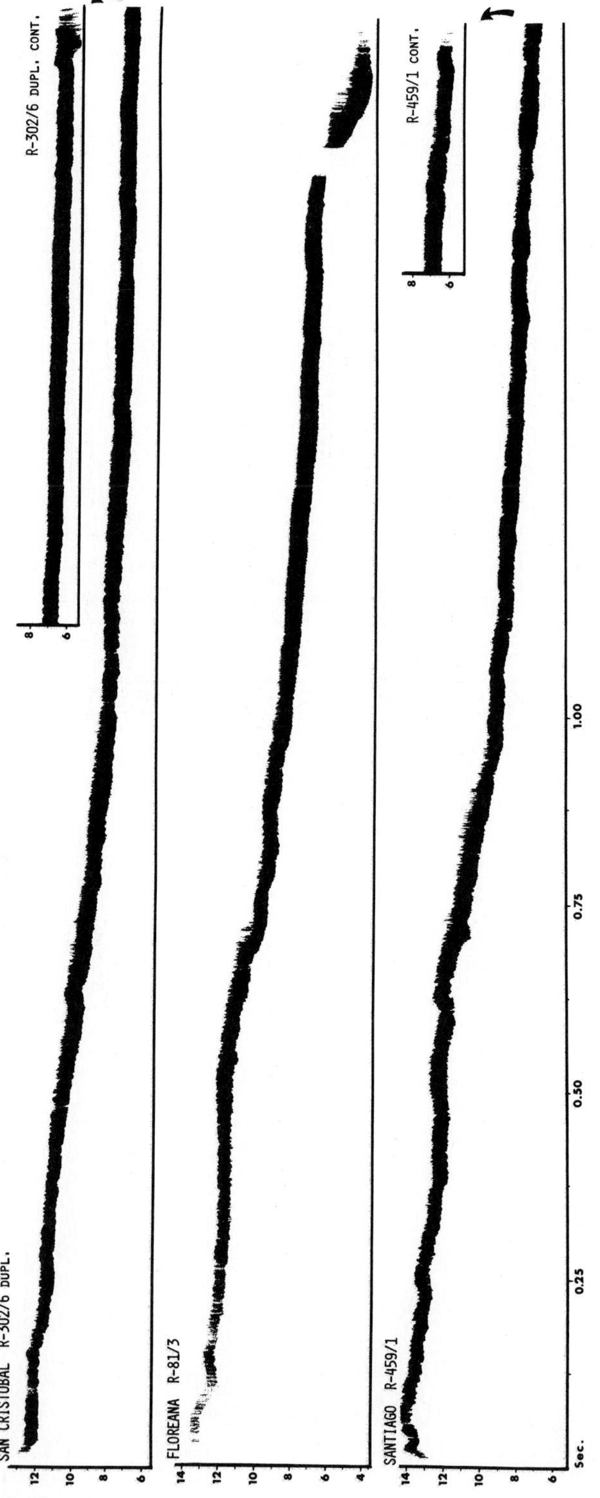

Fig. 75. Population variation in the whistle song of *Platyspiza crassirostris*.

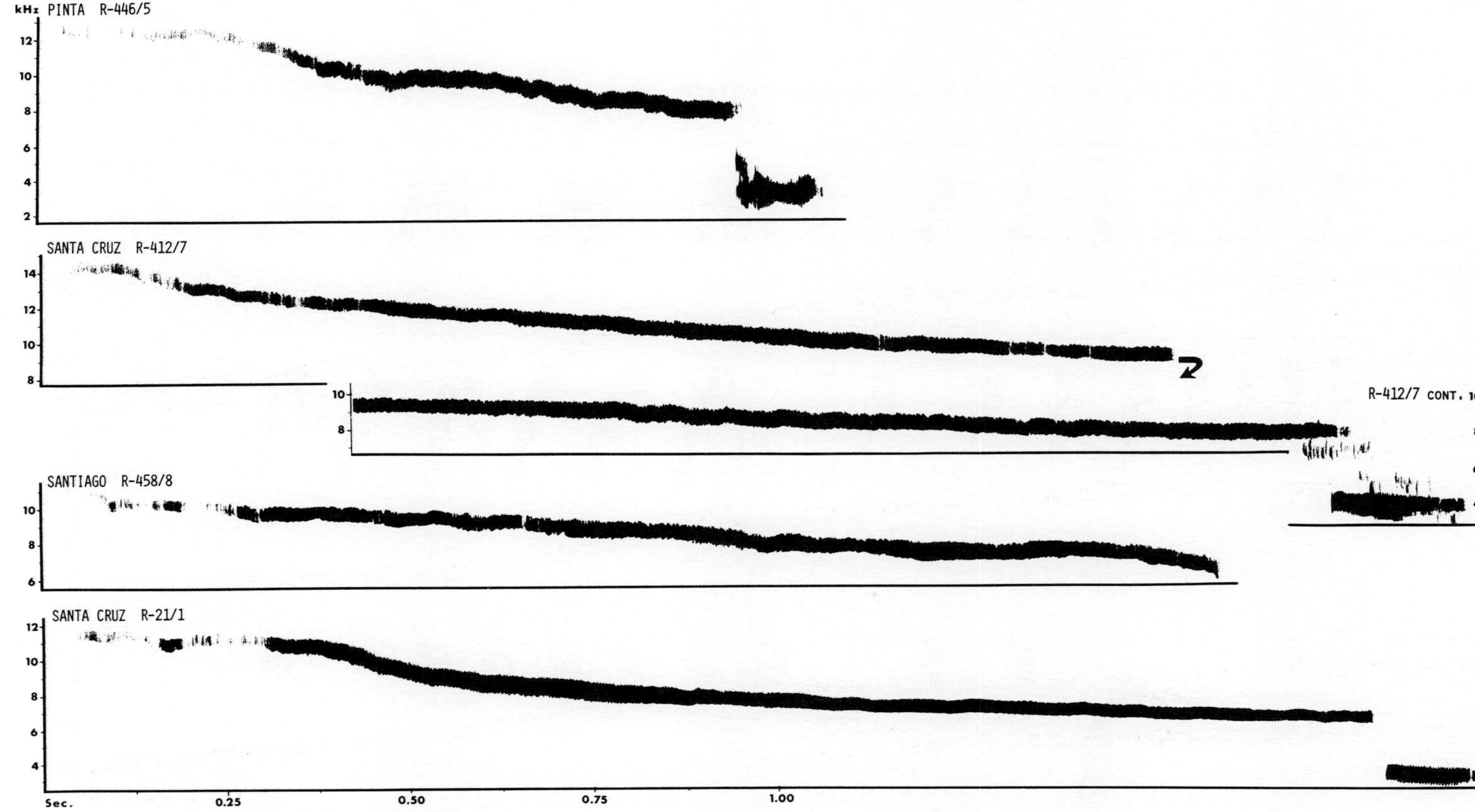

Fig. 76. Population variation in the whistle song of *Platyspiza crassirostris*.

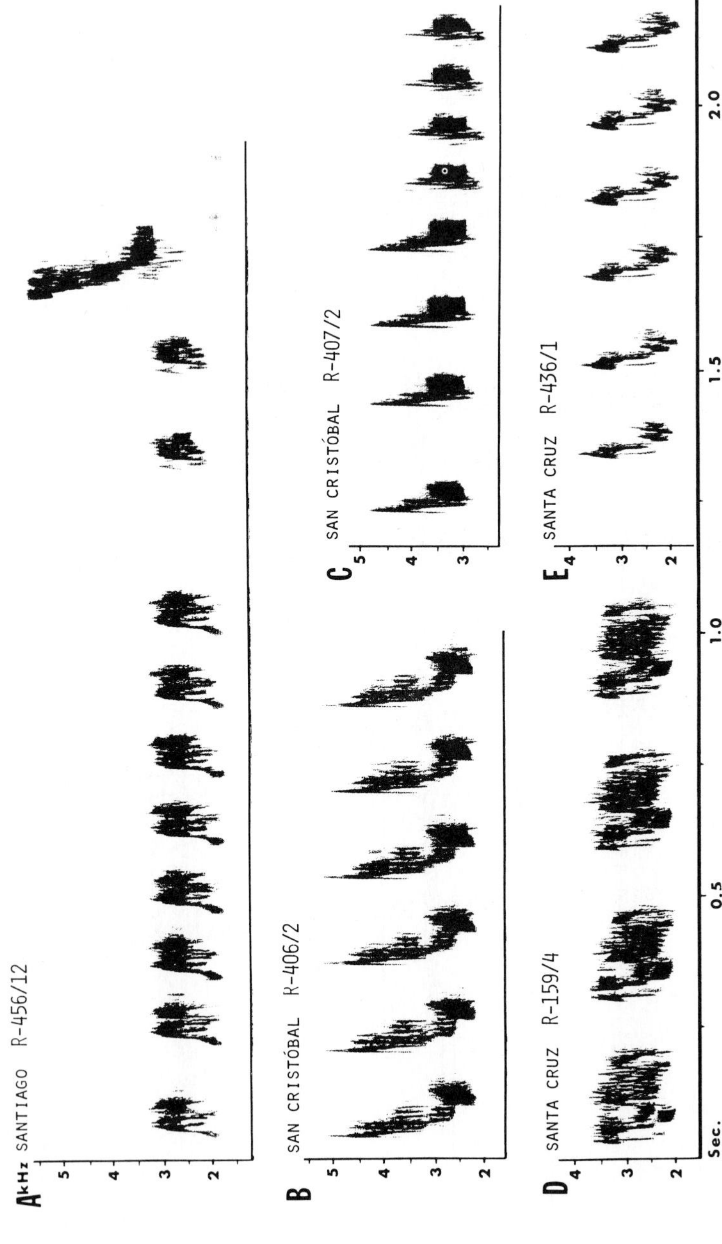

Fig. 77. Population variation in derived (A, B, C, and E) and abbreviate basic (D) songs of *Cactospiza pallida.*

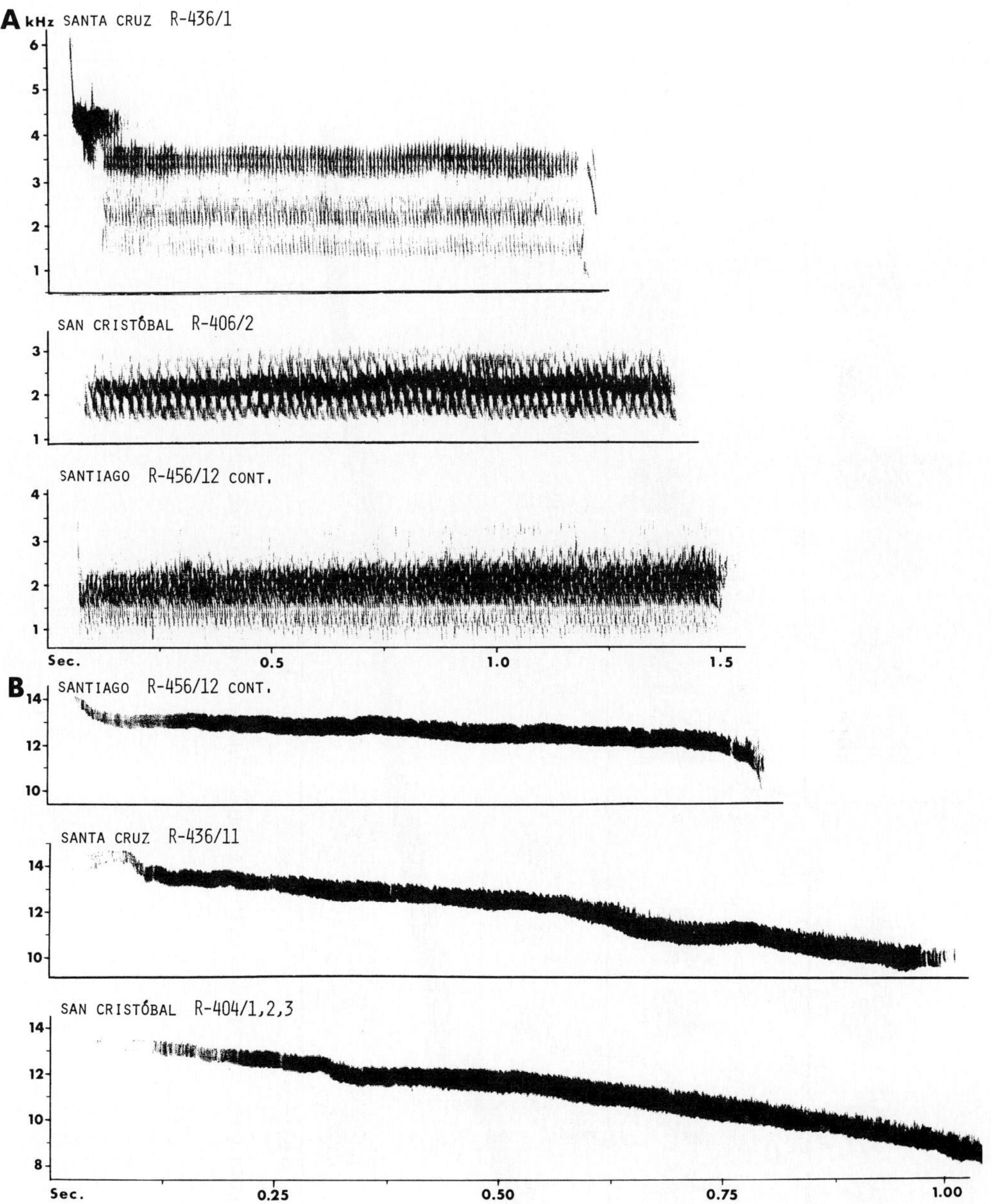

Fig. 78. Population variation in A, special basic, and B, whistle songs of *Cactospiza pallida*.

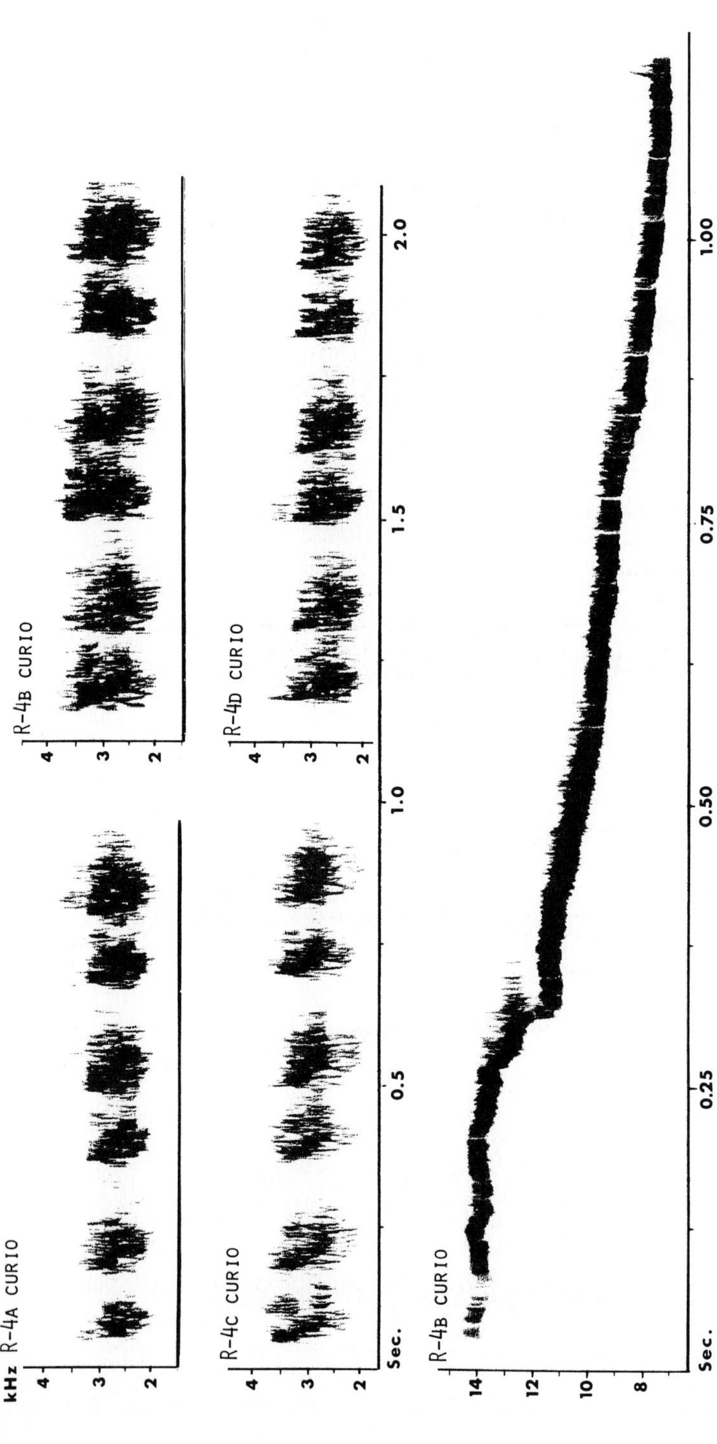

Fig. 79. Variation in abbreviate basic (cf. Fig. 91, pattern C) and whistle songs of *Cactospiza heliobates*, Isla Isabela. Recordings provided by E. Curio.

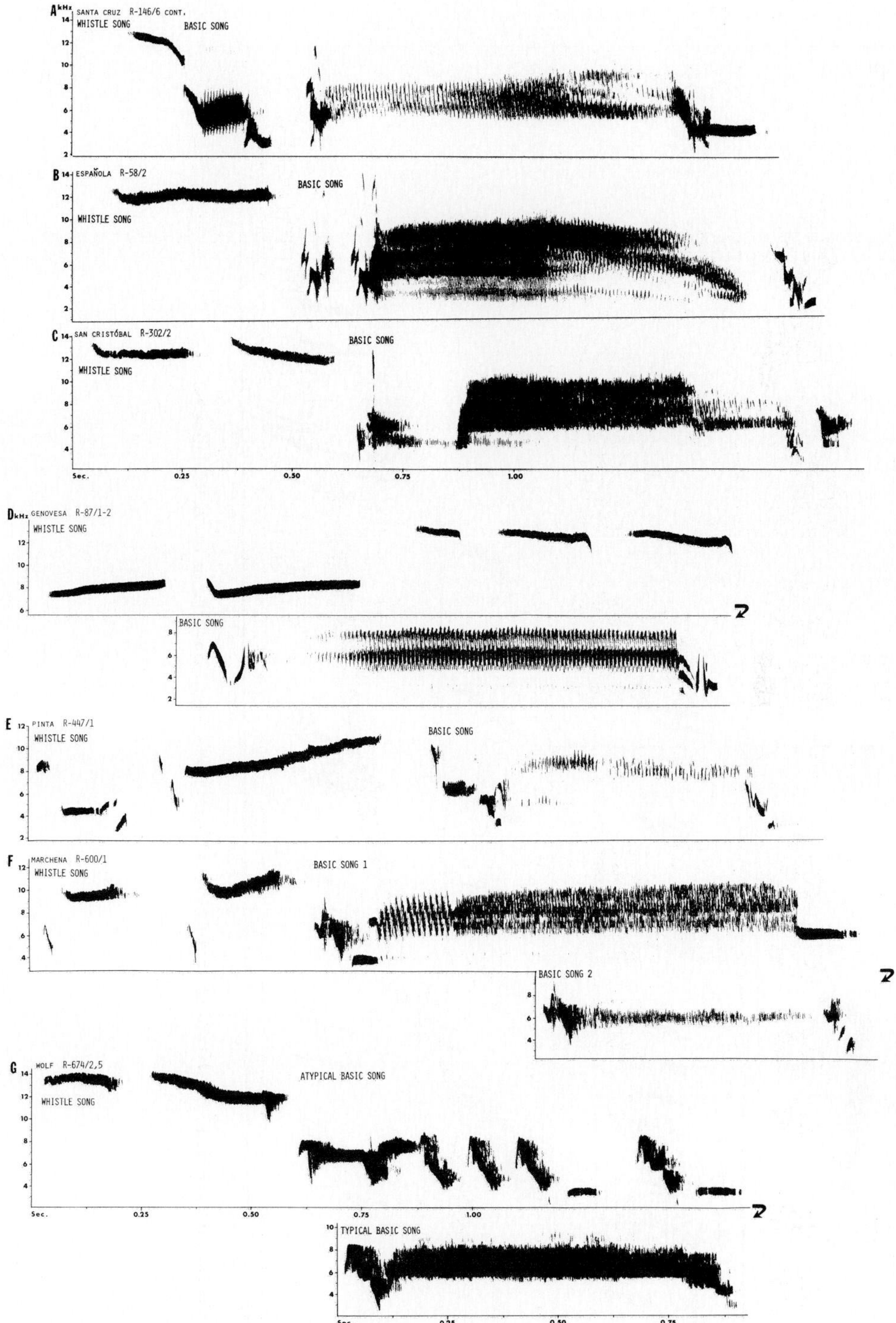

Fig. 80. Population variation in whistle and basic songs of *Certhidea olivacea* from seven islands in the Galapagos.

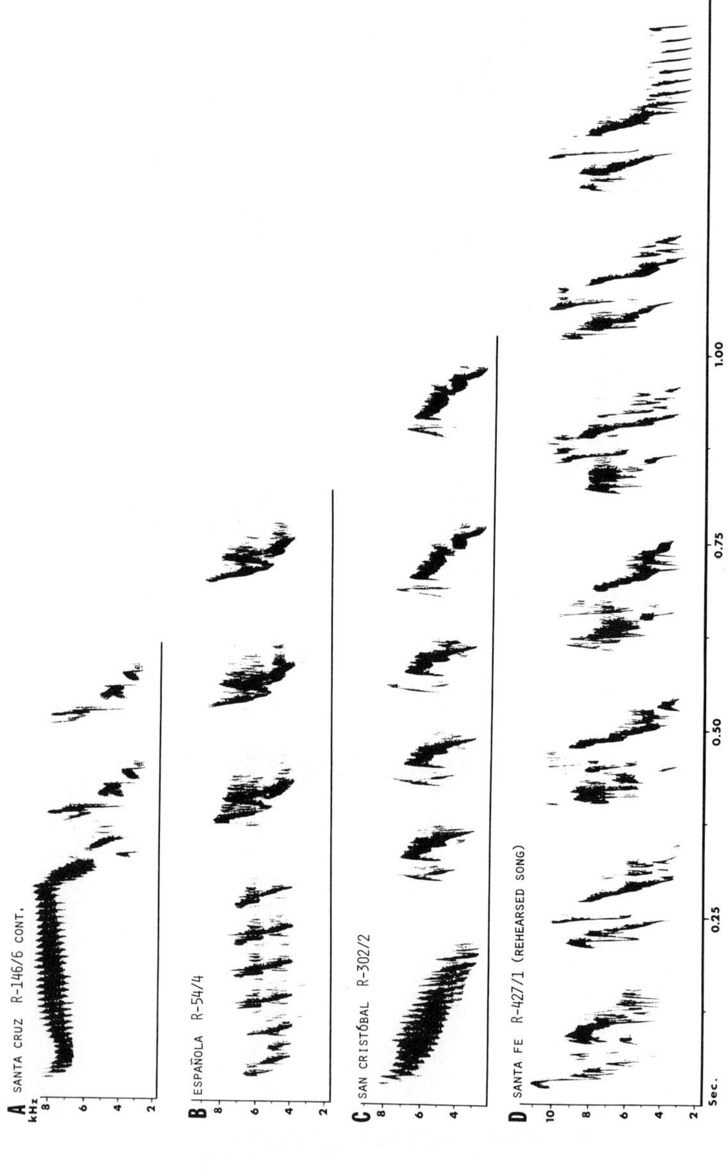

Fig. 81. Population variation in derived songs of *Certhidea olivacea* from four islands in the Galapagos.

Fig. 82. Population variation in derived songs of *Certhidea olivacea* from four islands in the Galapagos.

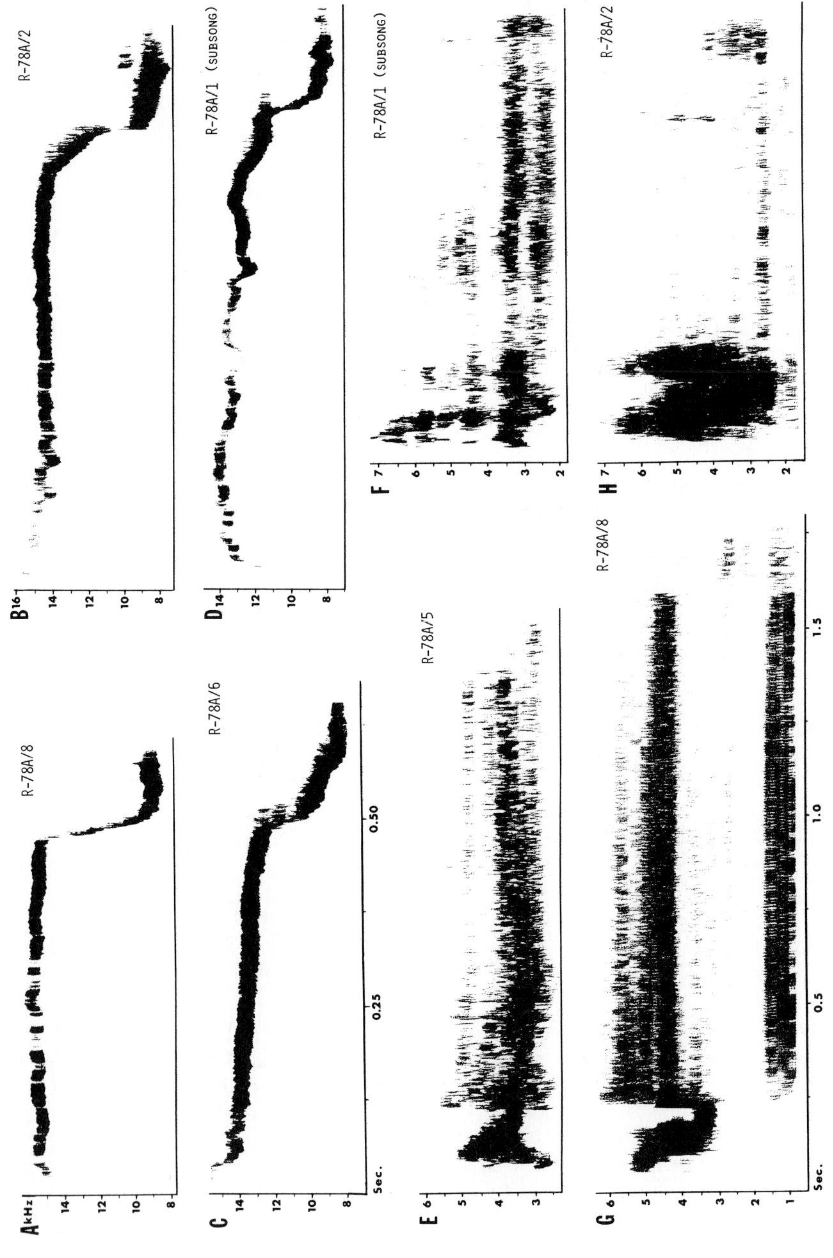

Fig. 83. Examples of whistle and basic songs of *Pinaroloxias inornata*, Isla Cocos, Costa Rica.

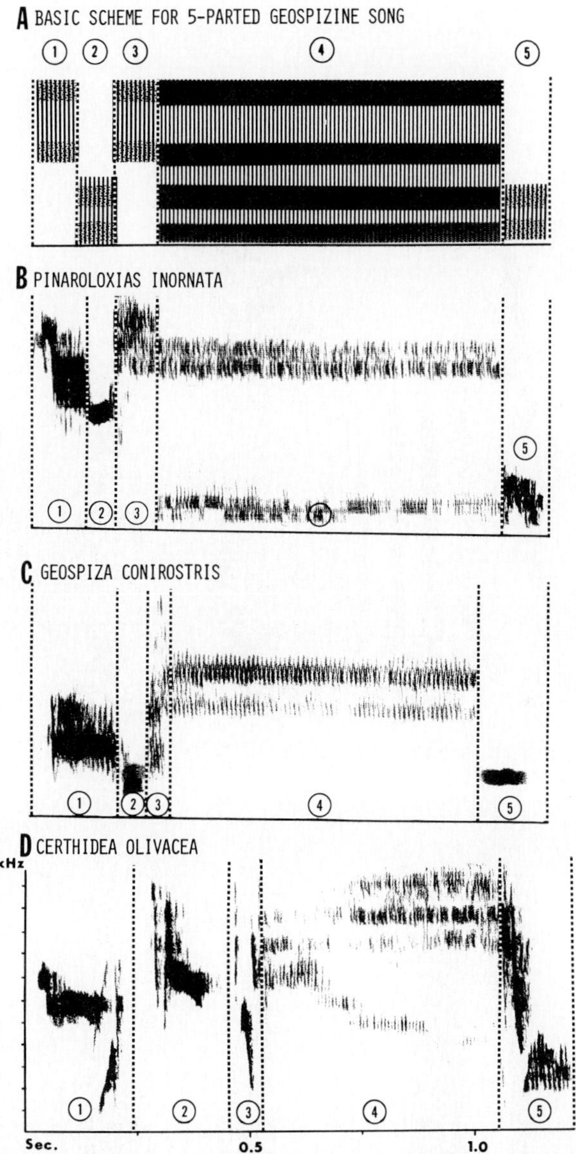

Fig. 84. Basic song pattern in Darwin's finches. A, basic scheme for five-parted song. B, C, and D show song regions of *Pinaroloxias inornata, Geospiza conirostris*, and *Certhidea olivacea*, respectively, with regions presumed to be homologous similarly numbered and delimited by vertical broken lines.

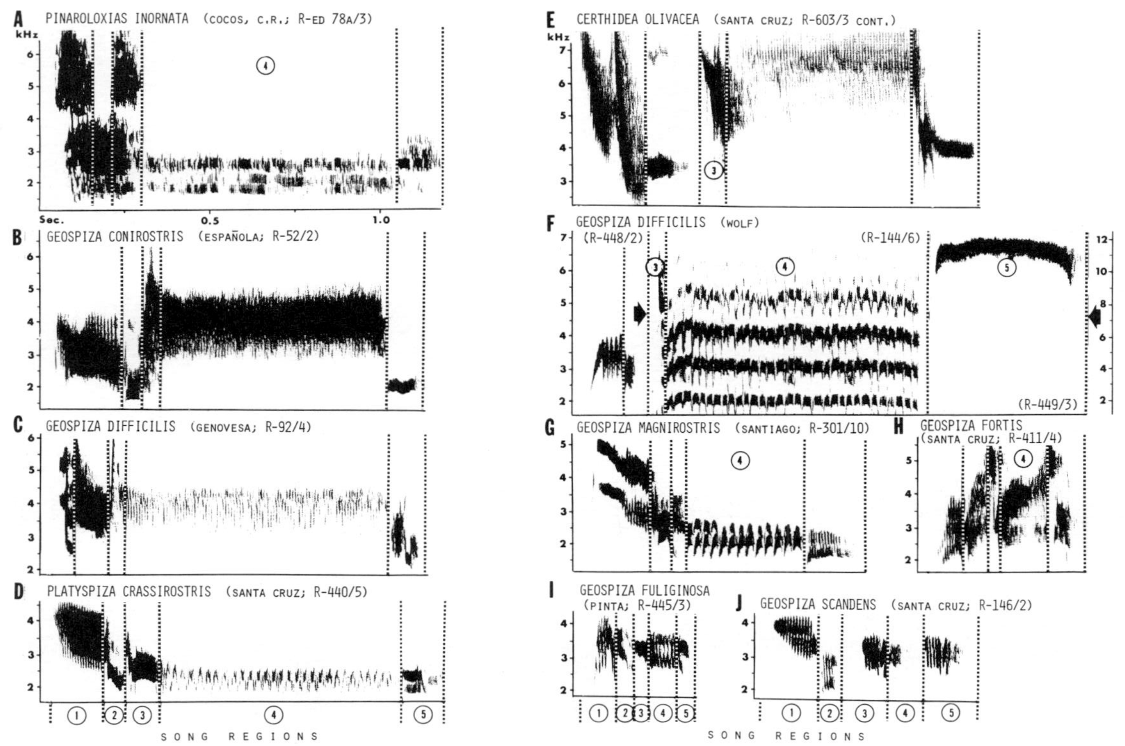

Fig. 85. Song regions of nine species of Darwin's finches. Regions presumed to be homologous are similarly numbered and delimited by vertical broken lines. Arrows in F indicate limits of song displayed at a half-speed time/frequency scale.

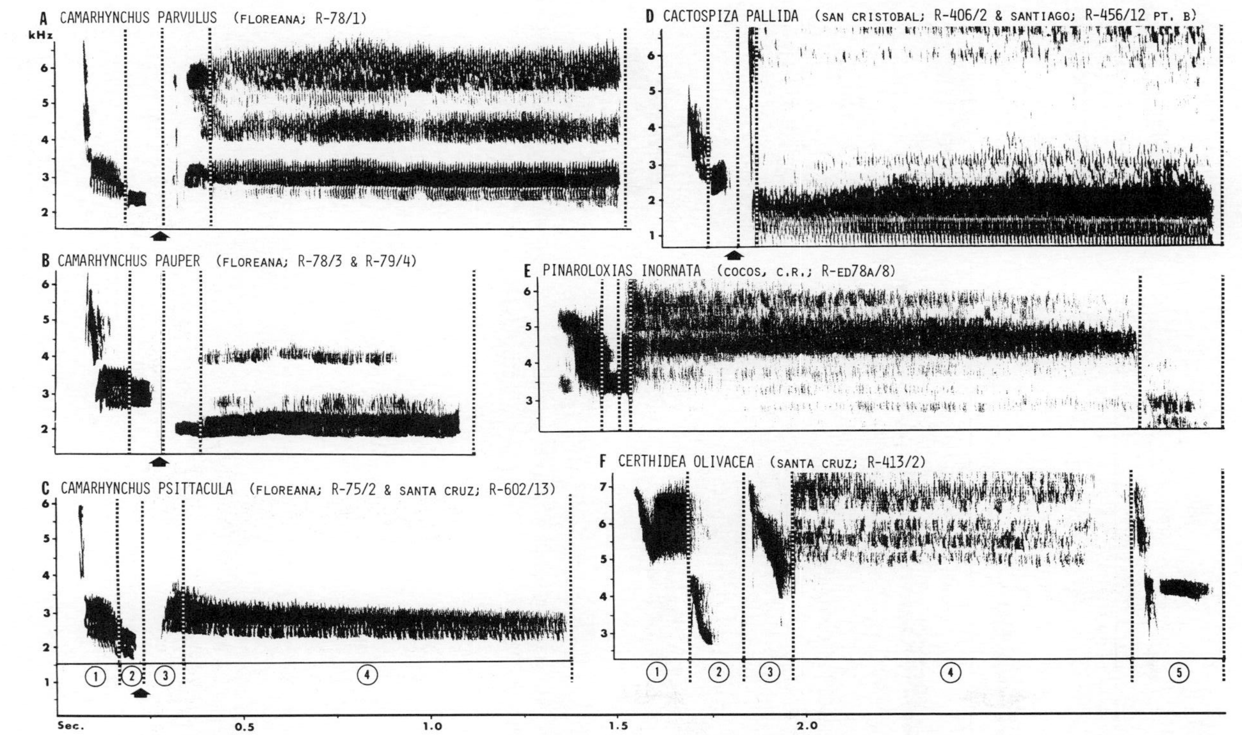

Fig. 86. Song regions of six species of Darwin's finches. Regions presumed to be homologous are similarly numbered and delimited by vertical broken lines. In species of *Camarhynchus* (A, B, and C) and *Cactospiza* (D), songs are composed of four regions only, the fifth having been lost. In *Pinaroloxias* (E) and *Certhidea* (F), all five song regions are present. Black arrows along the time axis indicate the point at which the ancestral basic song has been fractured to produce a derived song (using regions 1 and 2) and a special basic song (using regions 3 and 4).

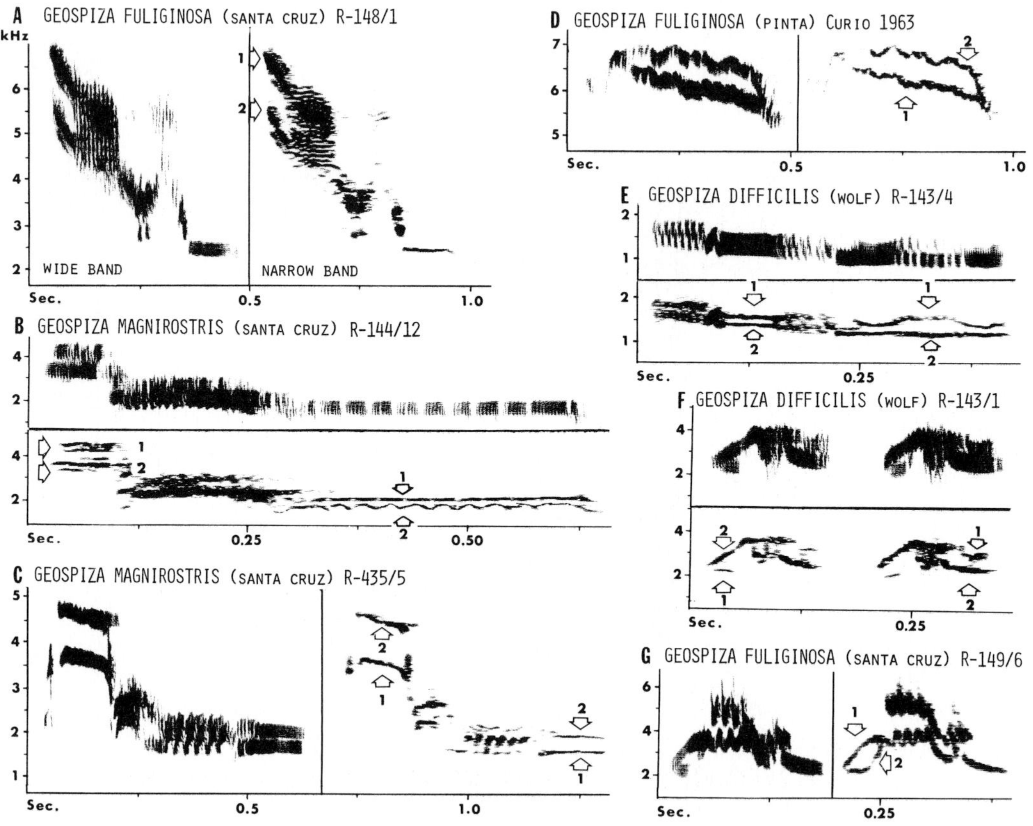

Fig. 87. Advertising songs of three species of *Geospiza* showing evidence of two independent oscillators (arrows 1 and 2 on the narrow-band displays).

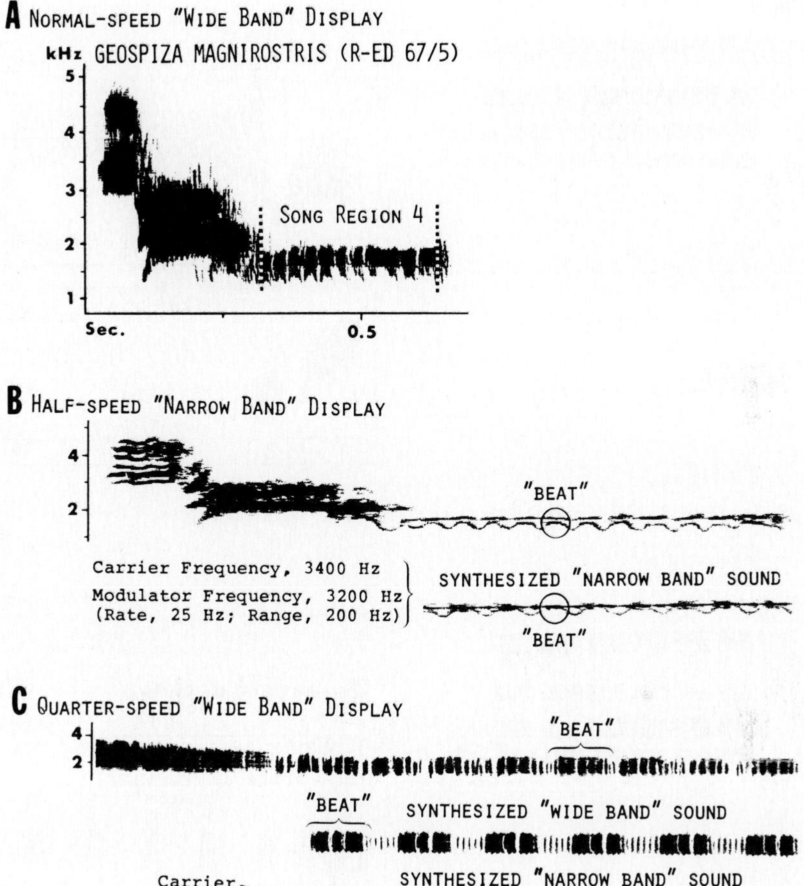

Fig. 88. Basic song of *Geospiza magnirostris*, Isla Santa Cruz. A, normal-speed display. B, half-speed display. C, quarter-speed display. "Beating" (i.e. amplitude modulation) in song region 4 is interpreted as an interference phenomenon between carrier and modulator oscillators whose frequencies periodically approach each other closely, but do not overlap.

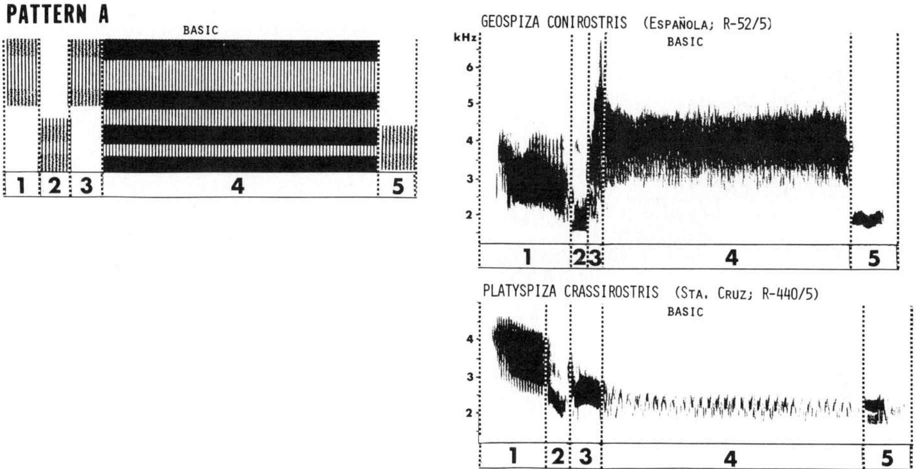

Fig. 89. Structural scheme for basic song pattern A, with examples.

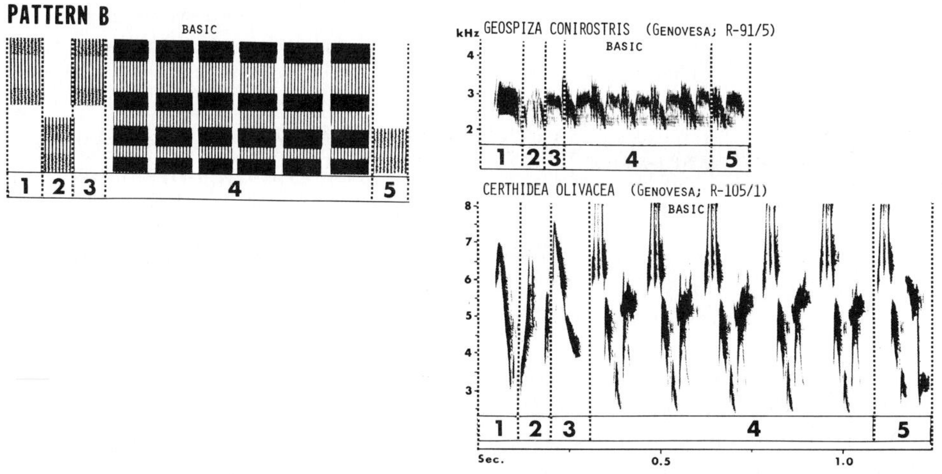

Fig. 90. Structural scheme for basic song pattern B, with examples.

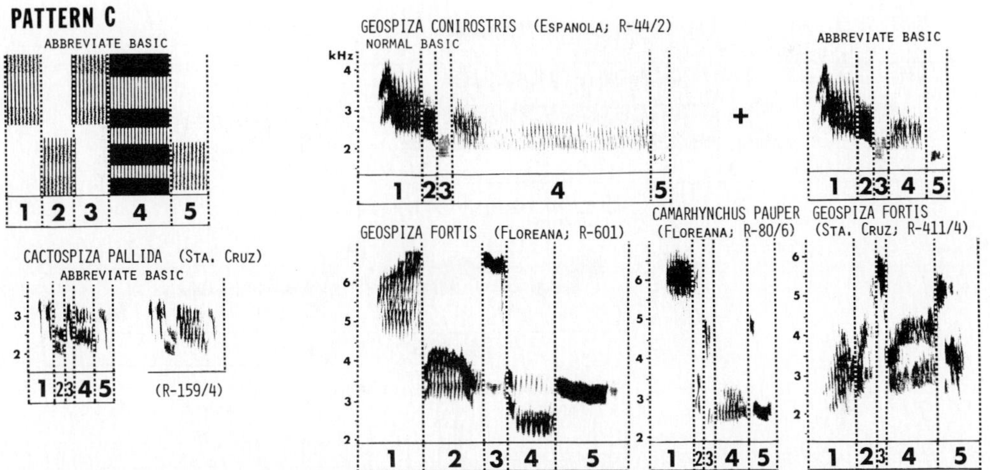

Fig. 91. Structural scheme for abbreviate basic song pattern C, with examples.

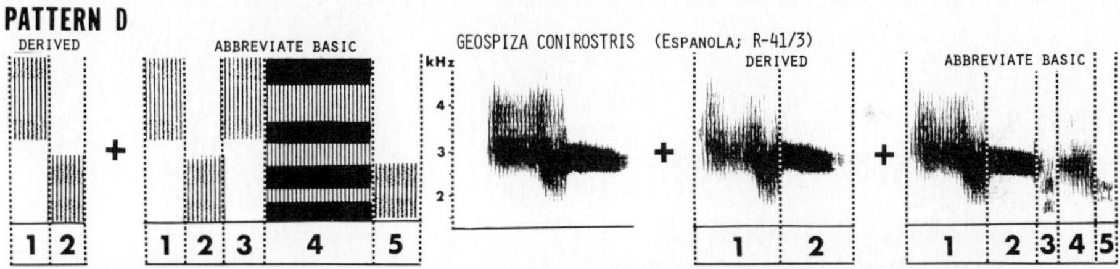

Fig. 92. Structural scheme for derived and abbreviate basic song pattern D, with example.

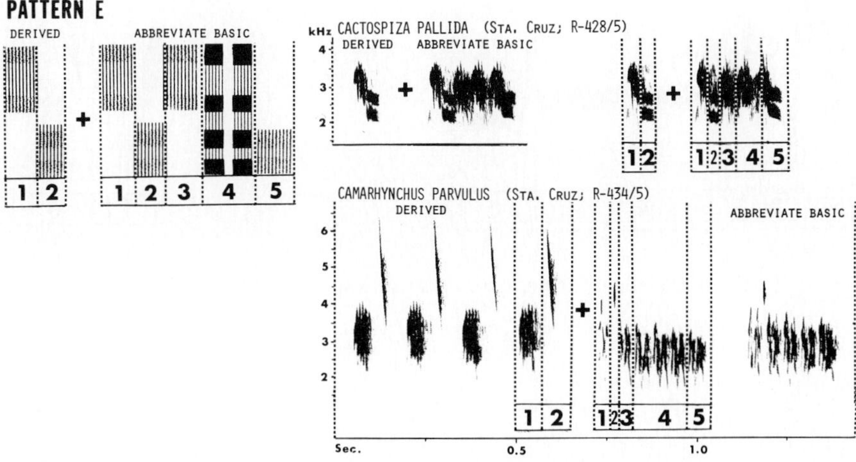

Fig. 93. Structural scheme for derived and abbreviate basic song pattern E, with examples.

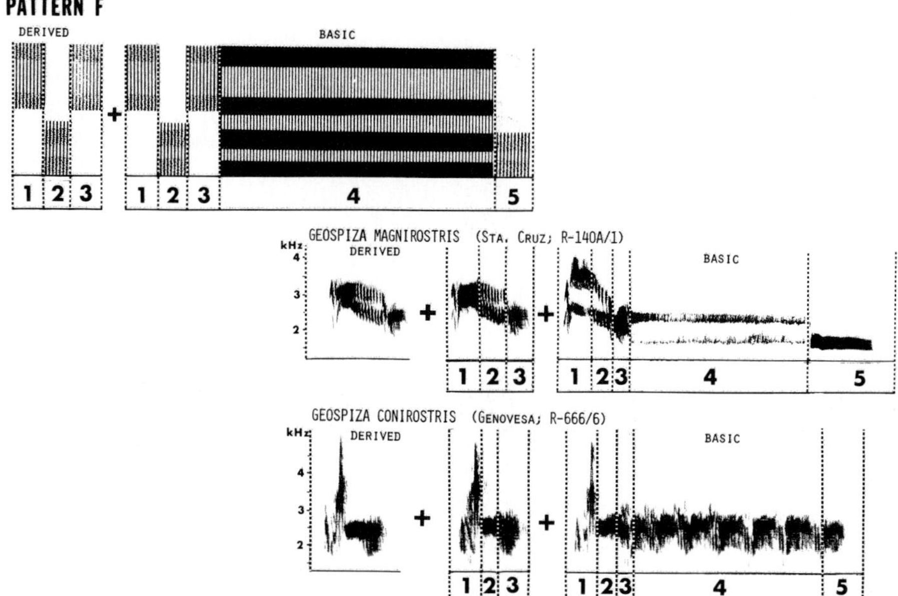

Fig. 94. Structural scheme for derived and basic song pattern F, with examples.

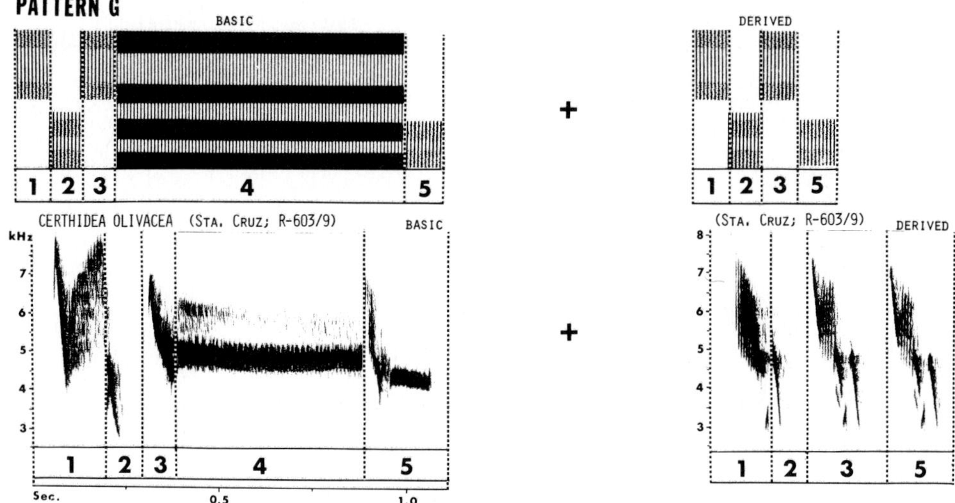

Fig. 95. Structural scheme for basic and derived song pattern G, with examples.

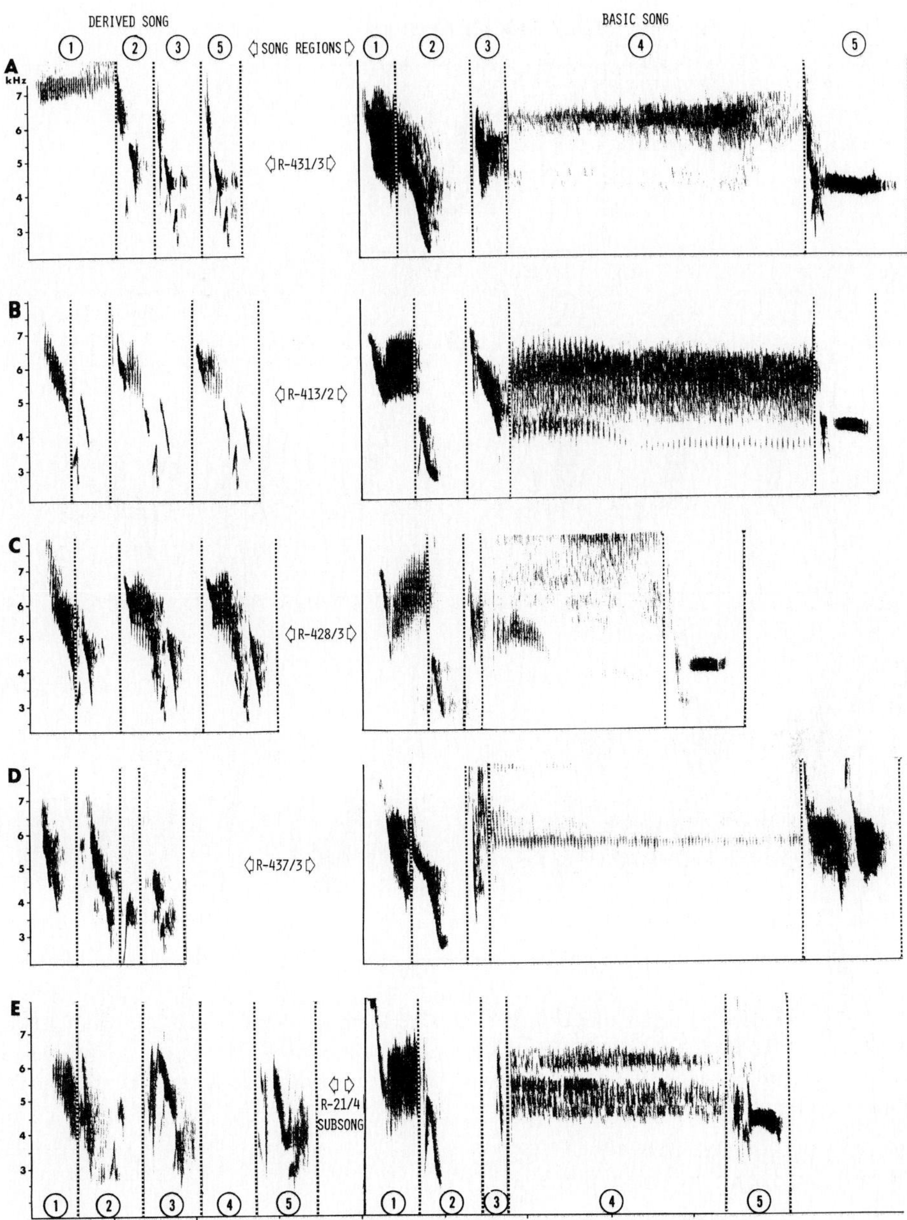

Fig. 96. Derived song (left) and basic song (right) of five individuals of *Certhidea olivacea* from Isla Santa Cruz. Regions of definitive songs (A through D) and subsongs (E) are delimited by broken vertical lines.

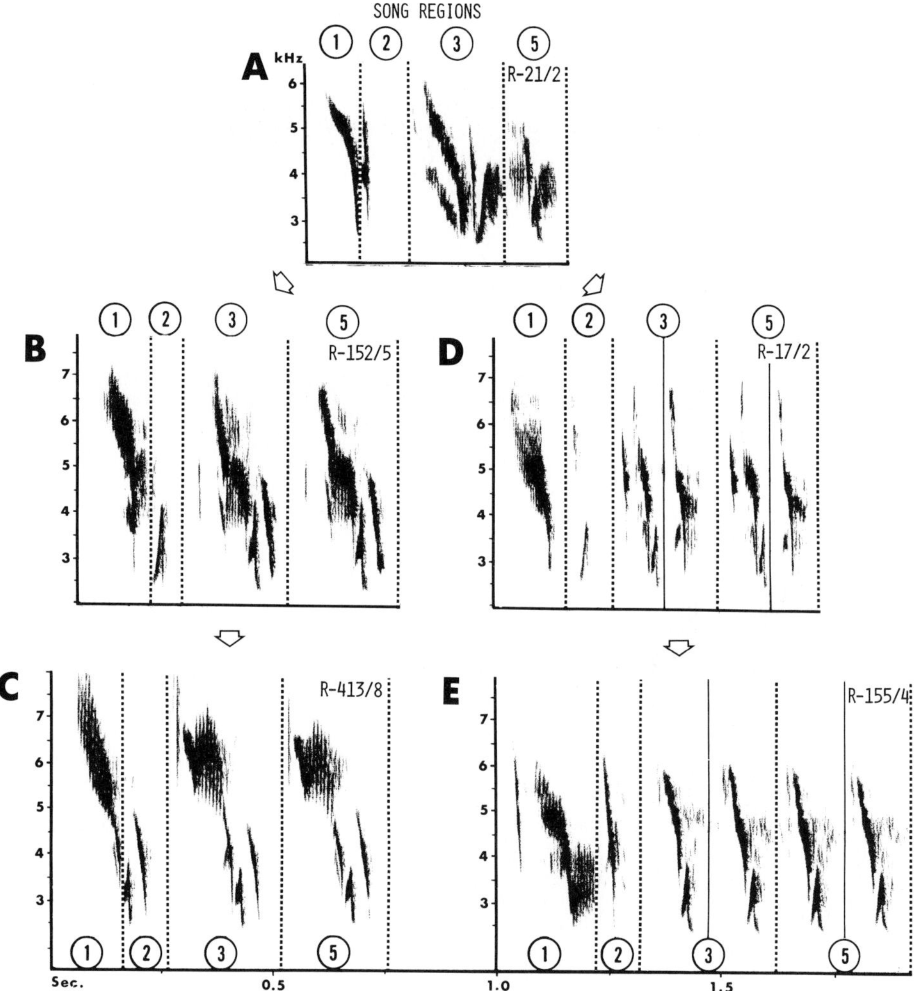

Fig. 97. Five derived songs of *Certhidea olivacea* from Isla Santa Cruz, arranged in two morphological series (A, B, C, and A, D, E). Both series begin with song type A, composed of four regions (1, 2, 3, and 5), each of different structure, and end with a song type (C or E) containing notes and syllables of very similar structure.

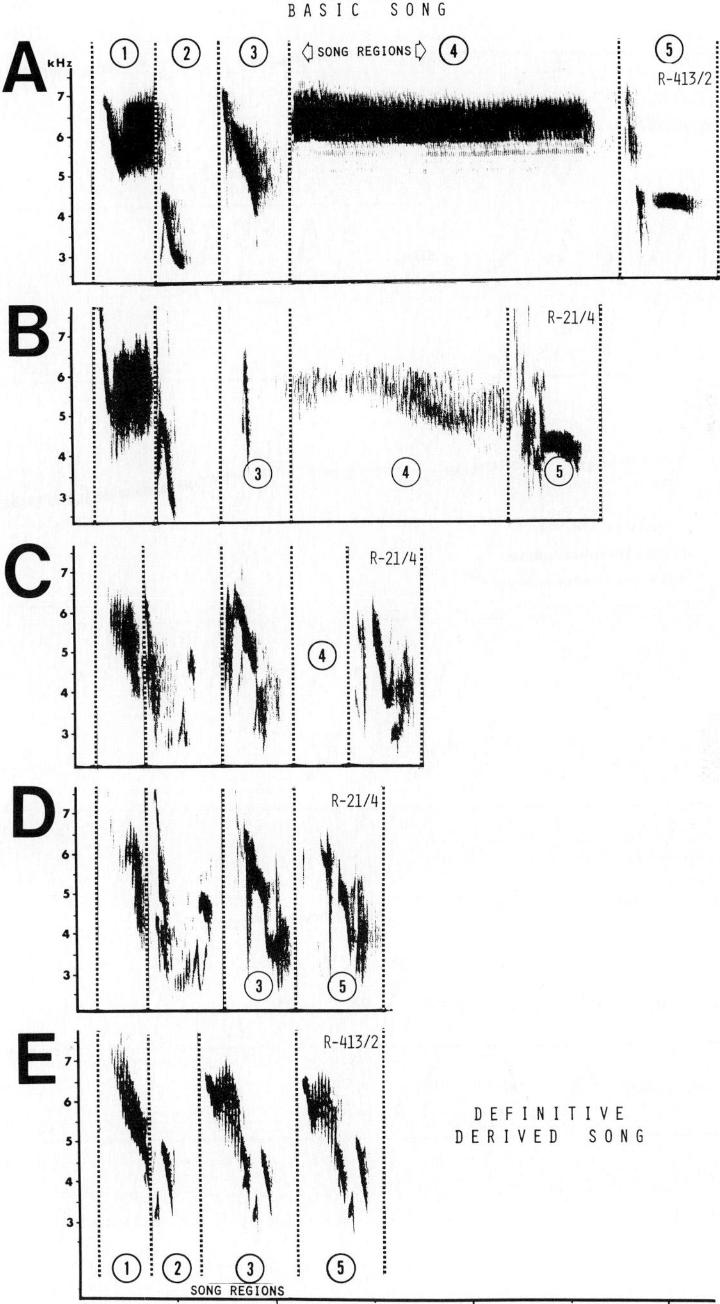

Fig. 98. Morphological series of song development in *Certhidea olivacea* (Isla Santa Cruz), suggesting how the basic song (A) has been transformed into the derived song (E) through loss of song region 4. Song regions presumed to be homologous are similarly numbered and delimited by broken vertical lines. Definitive songs A and E were sung by the same individual. Subsongs B, C, and D were sung by the same individual, but a different bird from that singing songs A and E.

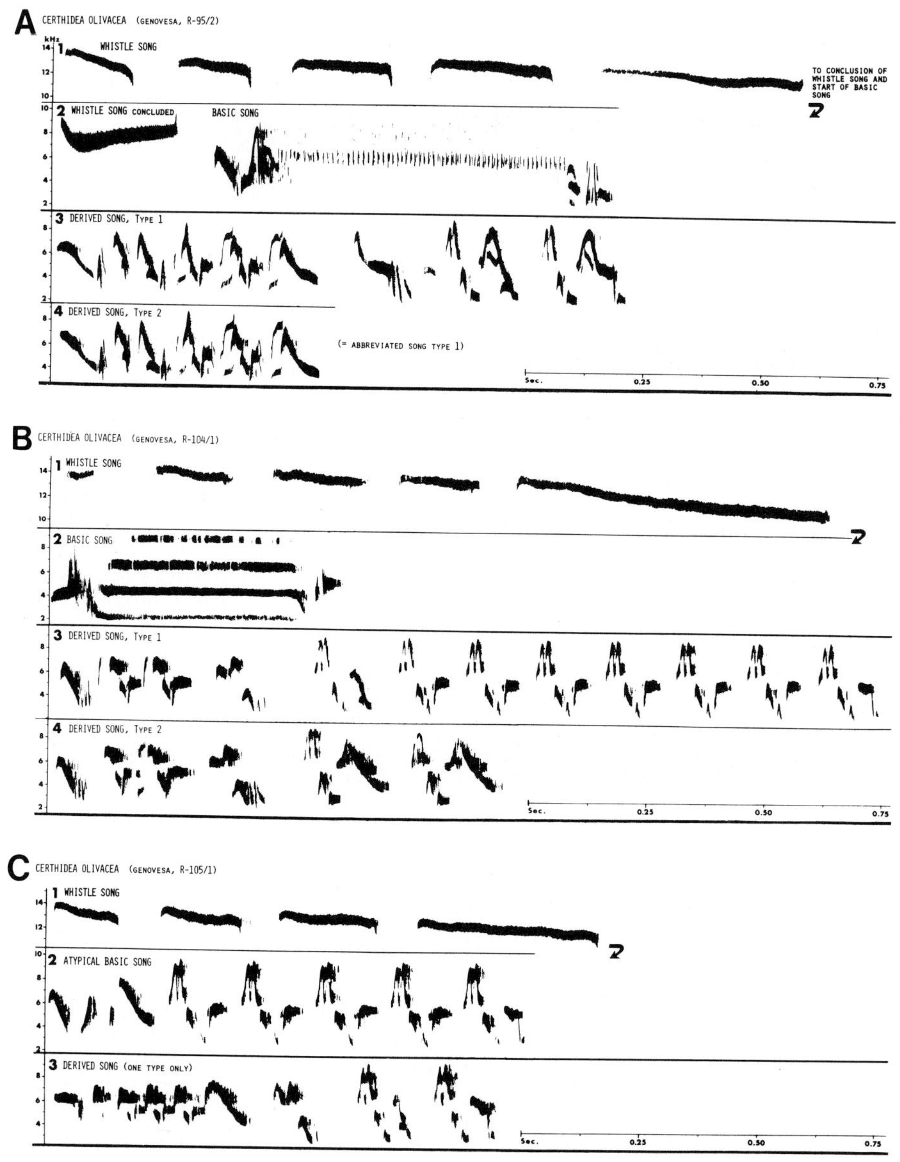

Fig. 99. Population variation in the whistle, basic, and derived songs of *Certhidea olivacea*, Isla Genovesa. Each suite of songs in A, B, and C was sung by the same individual.

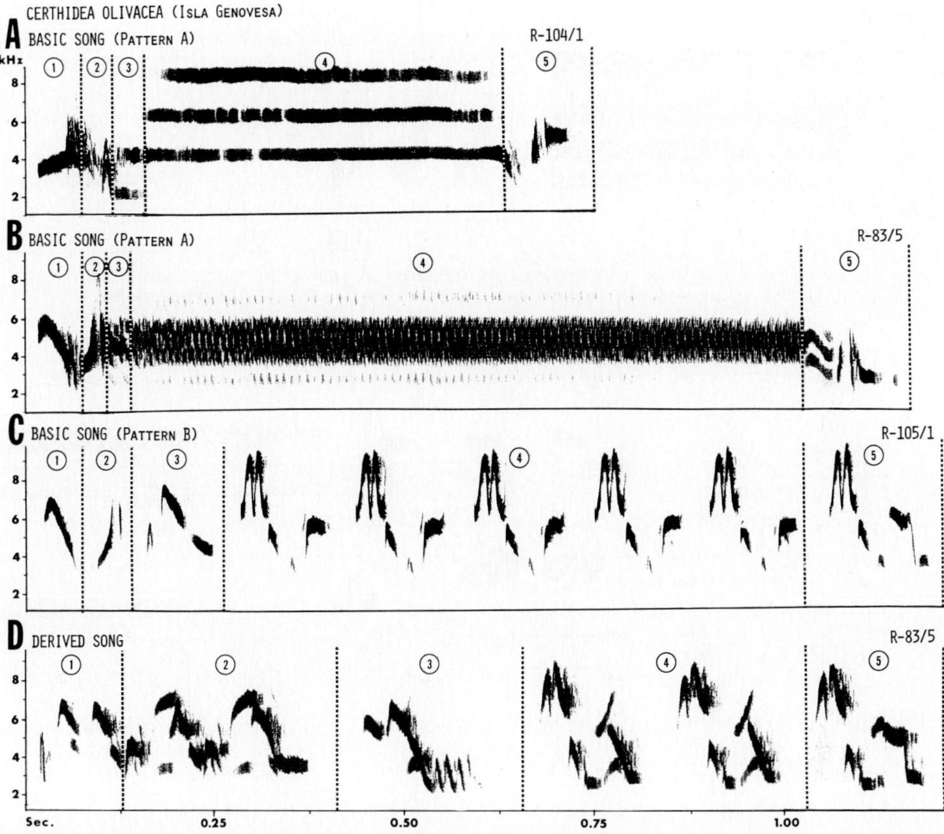

Fig. 100. Morphological series suggesting how the basic song pattern (A) of *Certhidea olivacea* might be transformed into the derived song pattern (D). Song regions presumed to be homologous are similarly numbered and delimited by broken vertical lines.

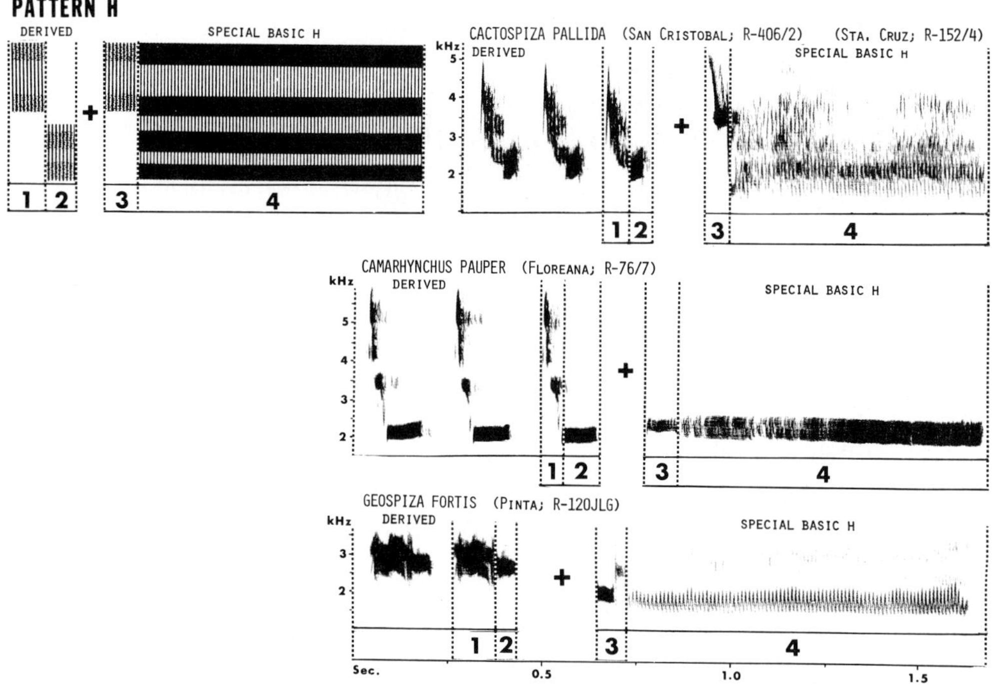

Fig. 101. Structural scheme for derived and special basic song pattern H, with examples.

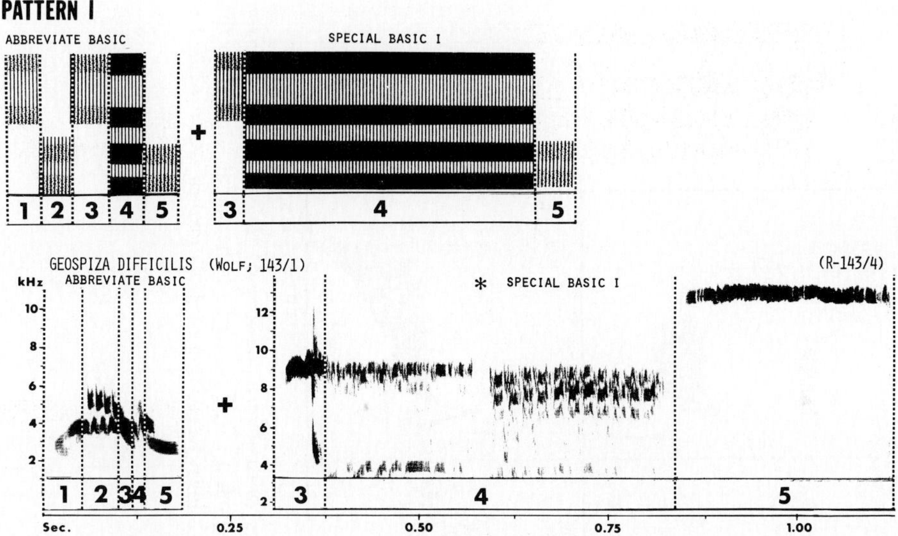

Fig. 102. Structural scheme for derived and special basic song pattern I, with an example.

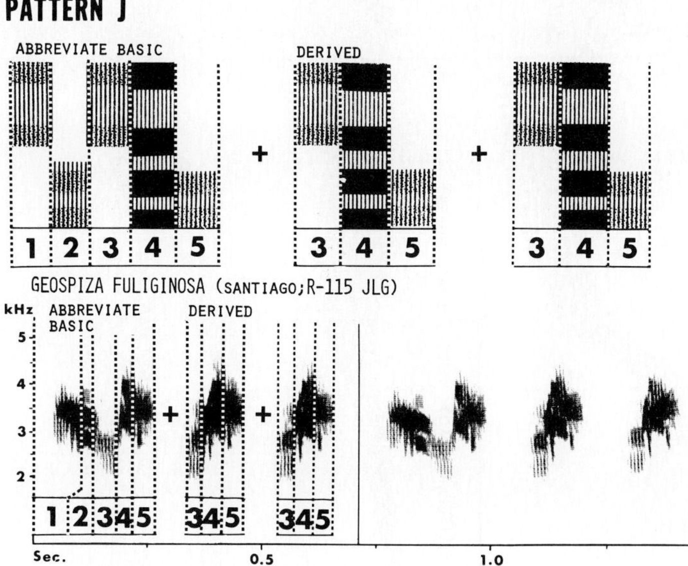

Fig. 103. Structural scheme for abbreviate basic and derived song pattern J, with an example.

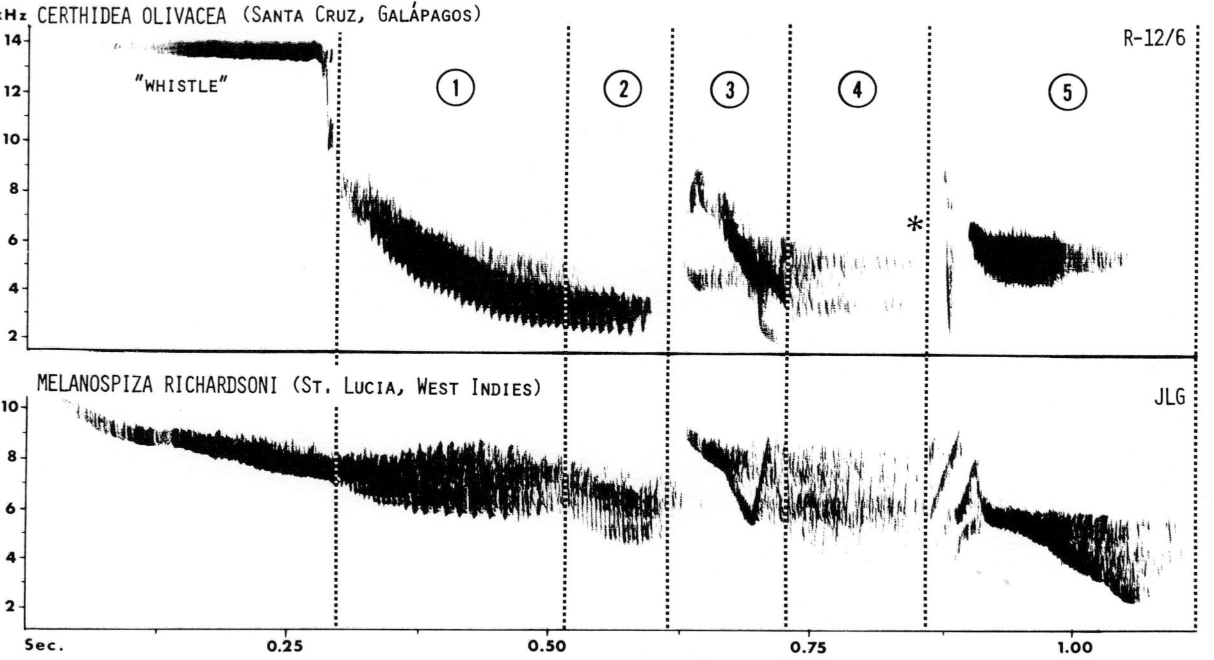

Fig. 104A. Comparison of the basic song of *Certhidea olivacea* (Isla Santa Cruz, Galapagos) with advertising song of *Melanospiza richardsoni* (St. Lucia, West Indies). Asterisk in region 4 of *Certhidea* song indicates the location from which a small portion of the signal (similar to that which remains) was removed in order to emphasize the close parallel construction of the two songs. Recording of *Melanospiza* was provided by J. L. Gulledge.

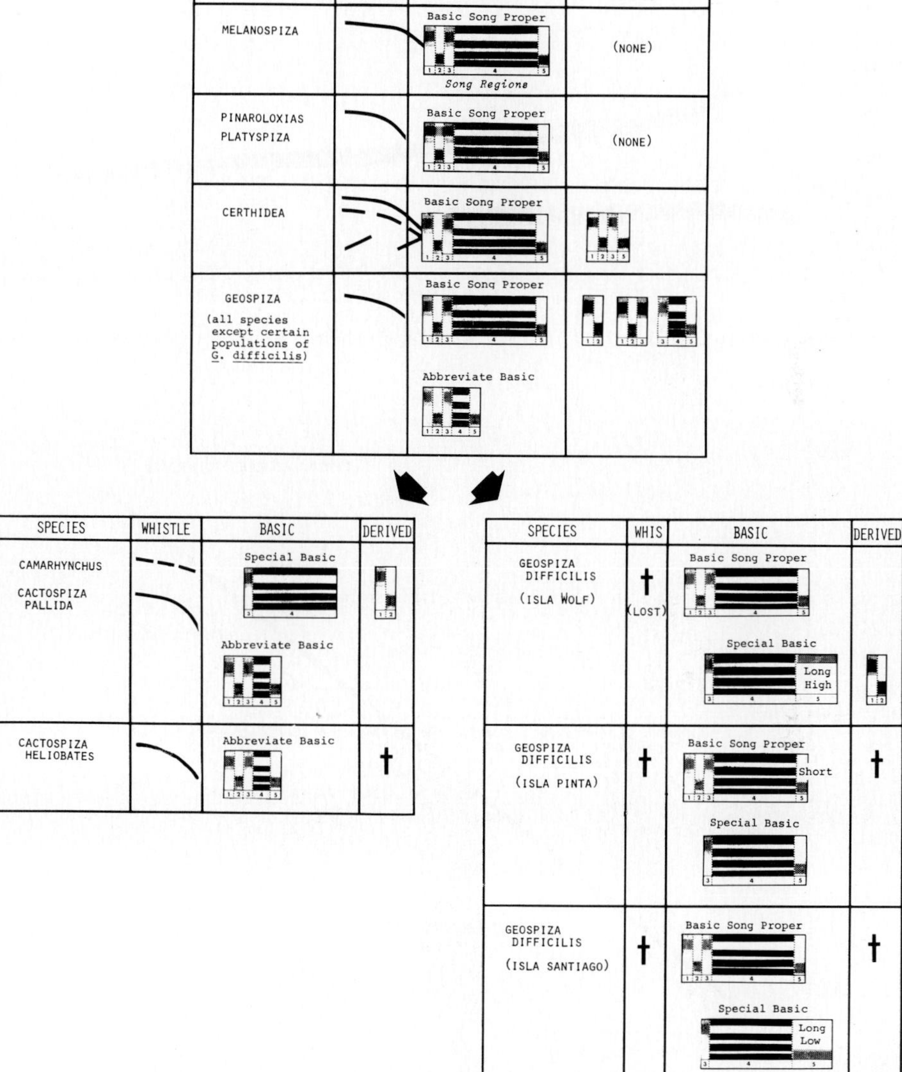

Fig. 104B. Schema suggesting morphological trends in the evolution of song patterns in Darwin's finches. *Melanospiza richardsoni* (top) is most clearly linked through similarities in whistle and basic song patterns to *Certhidea olivacea* (see Fig. 104A).

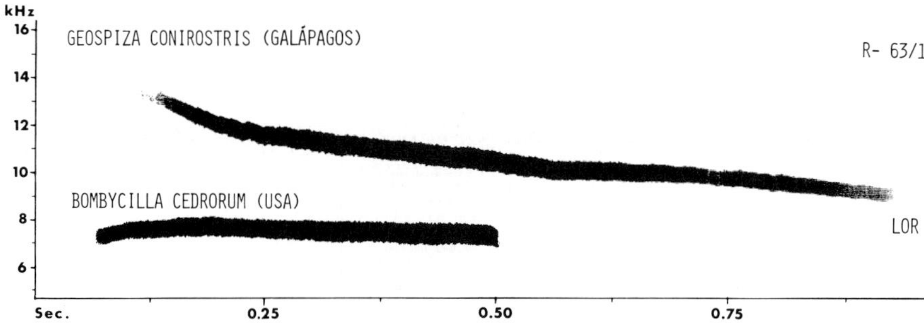

Fig. 105. Call note of *Bombycilla cedrorum* and whistle song of *Geospiza conirostris* compared.

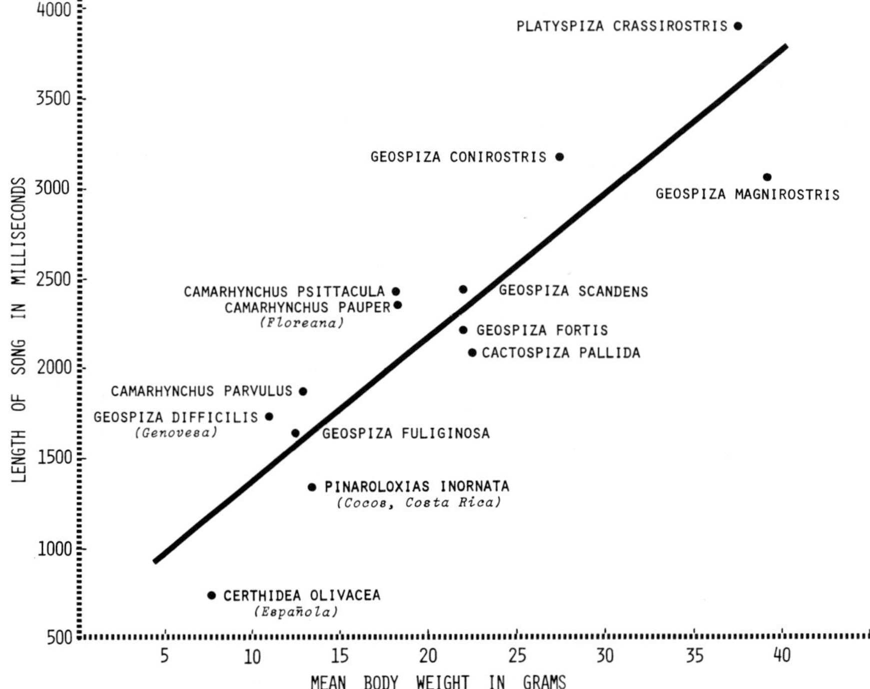

Fig. 106. Relationship between length of whistle song and mean body weight in 13 species of Darwin's finches. Data are from Table 13.

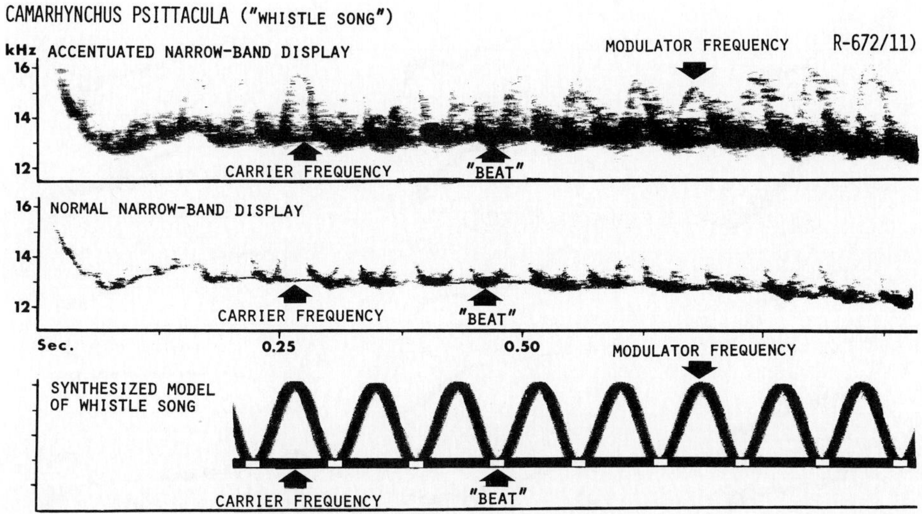

Fig. 107. Whistle song of *Camarhynchus psittacula* (Isla Santa Cruz). A, accentuated narrow-band display. B, normal narrow-band display. C, synthesized model of whistle song to demonstrate how the notes ("beats") of whistle song result from a periodic interaction of carrier and modulator frequencies.

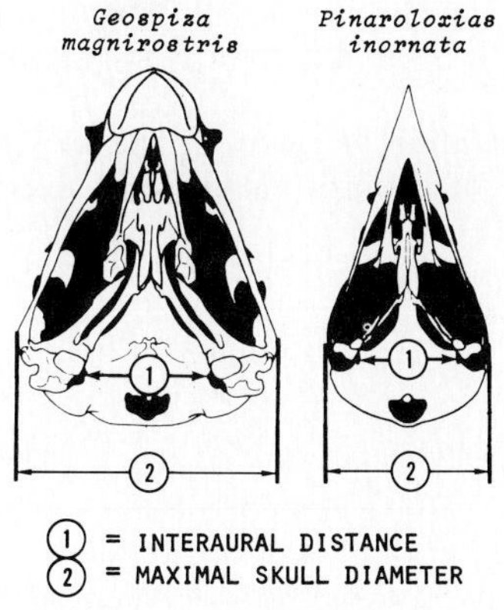

Fig. 108. Ventral view of the skulls of *Geospiza magnirostris* and *Pinaroloxias inornata* showing how interaural distance and maximal skull diameter were measured. Skull drawings from Tordoff 1954.

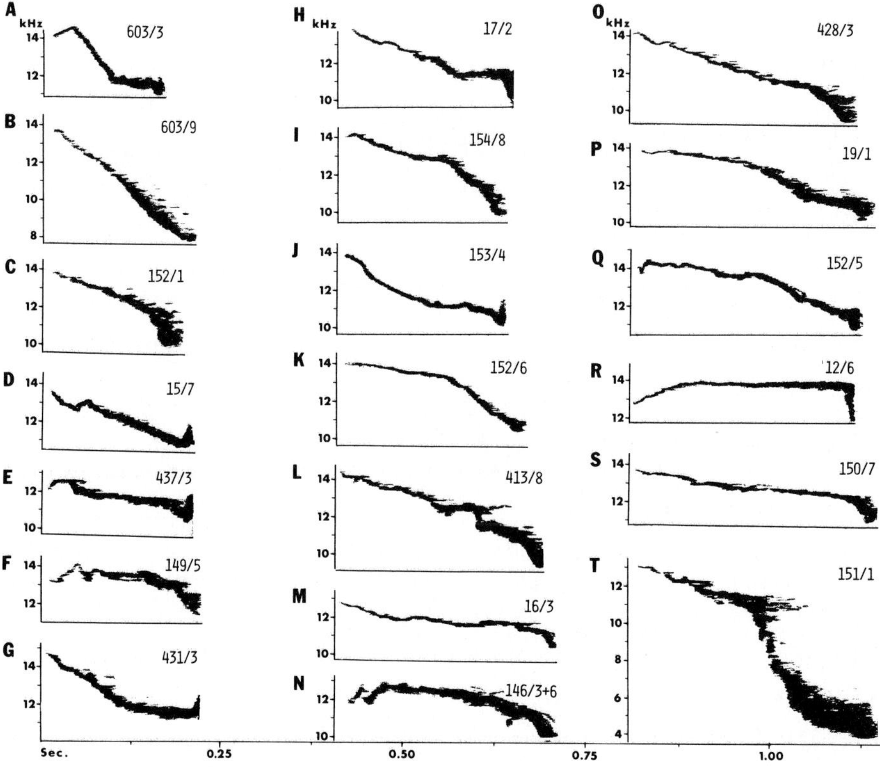

Fig. 109. Examples of population variation in the whistle song of *Certhidea olivacea*, Isla Santa Cruz. Narrow-band displays of definitive adult songs except T, which is a subsong whistle.

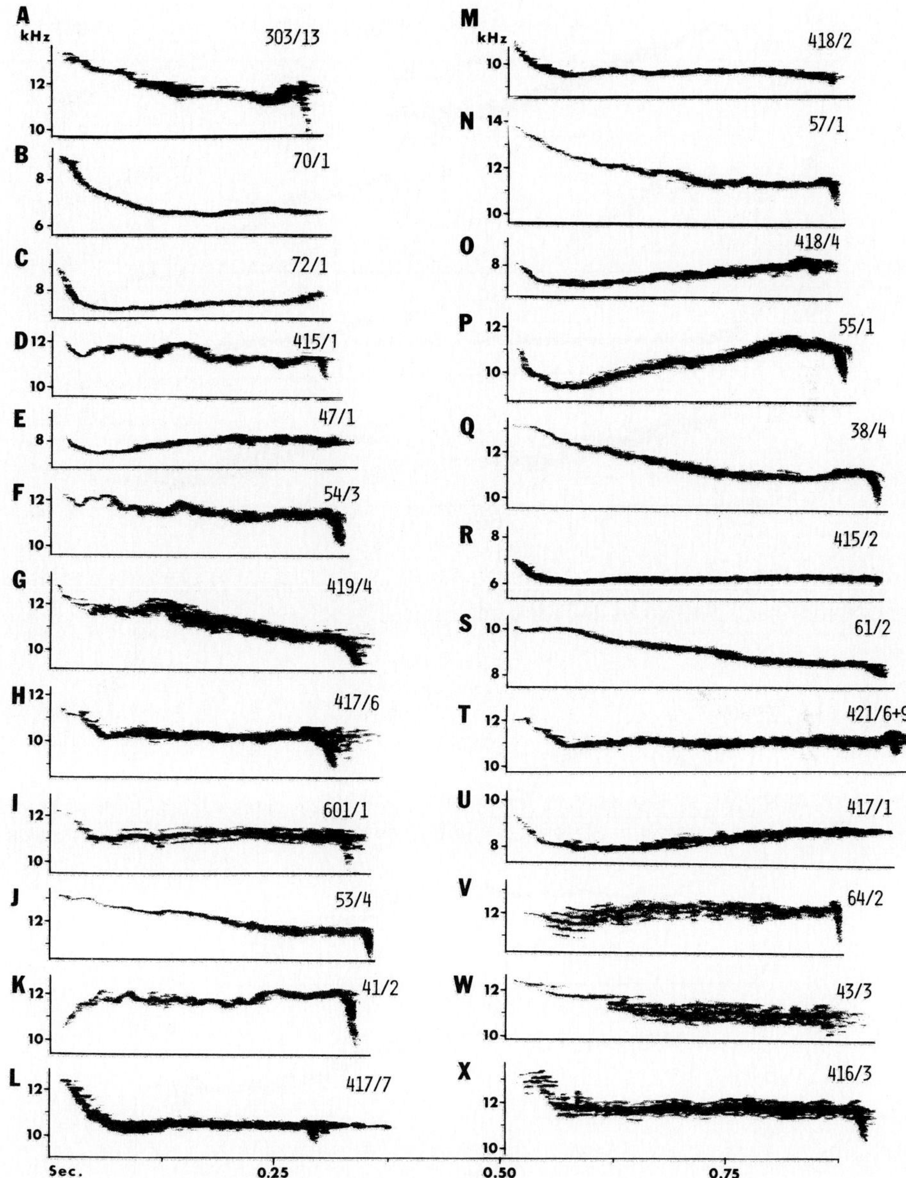

Fig. 110. Examples of population variation in the whistle song of *Certhidea olivacea*, Isla Española. Narrow-band displays of definitive adult songs.

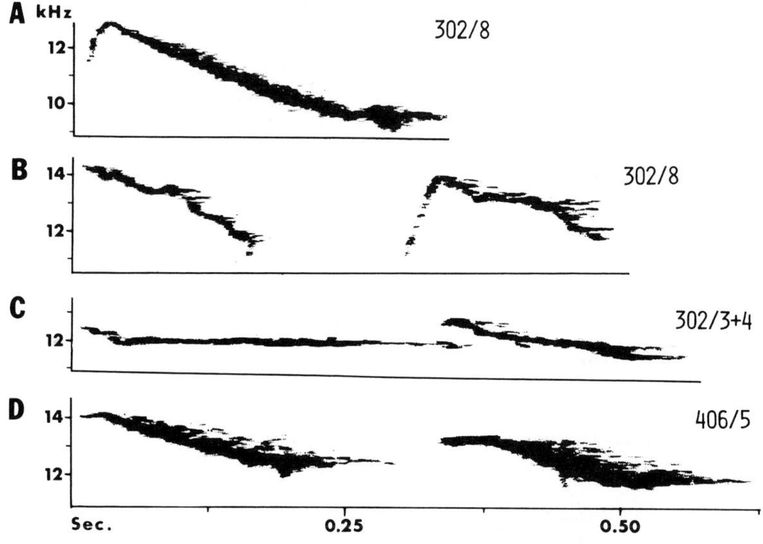

Fig. 111. Examples of population variation in the whistle song of *Certhidea olivacea*, Isla San Cristóbal. Narrow-band displays of definitive adult songs.

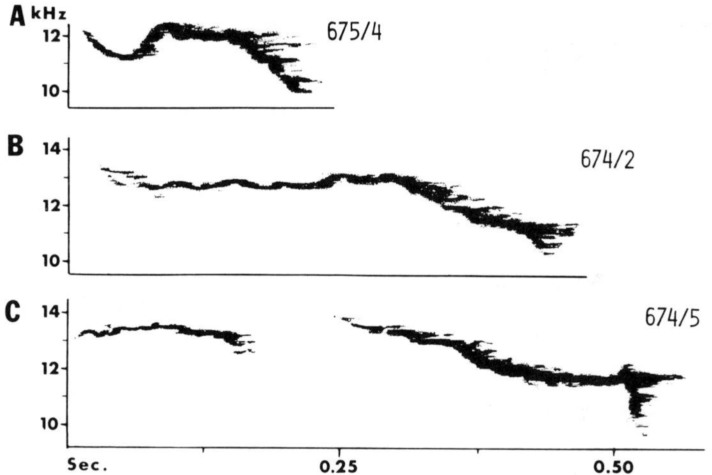

Fig. 112. Examples of population variation in the whistle song of *Certhidea olivacea*, Isla Wolf. Narrow-band displays of definitive adult song.

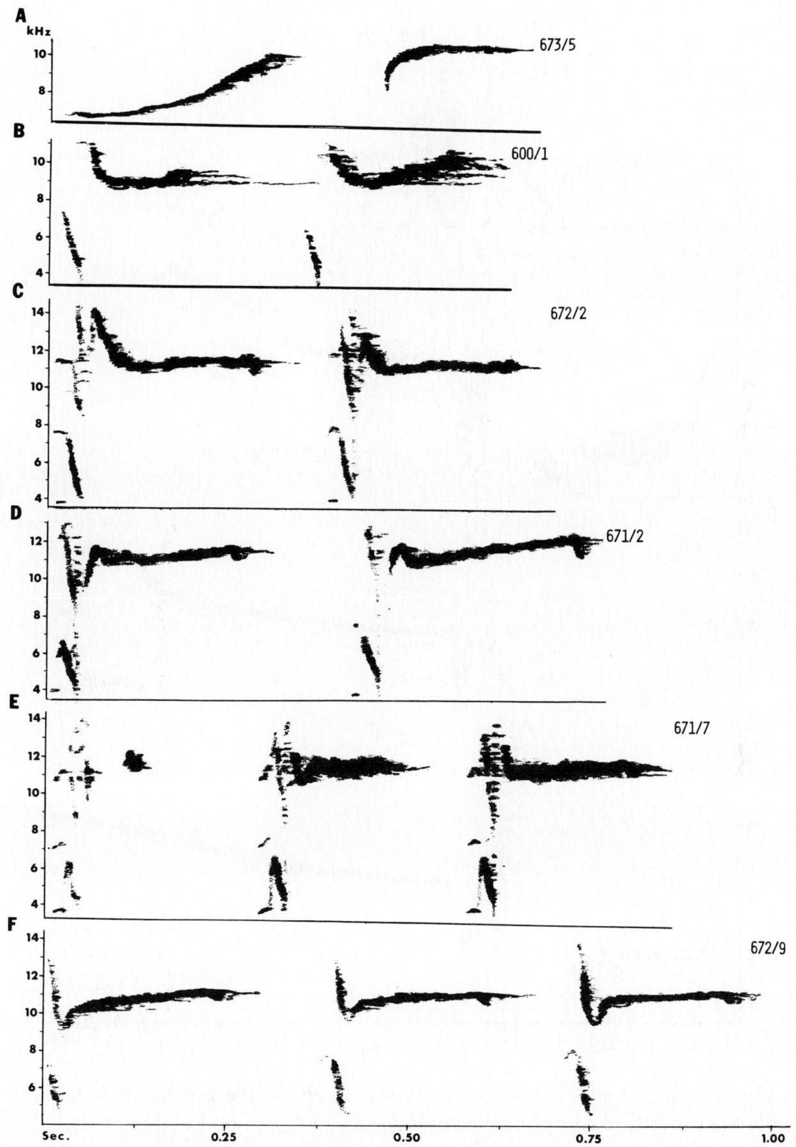

Fig. 113. Examples of population variation in the whistle song of *Certhidea olivacea*, Isla Marchena. Narrow-band displays of definitive adult songs.

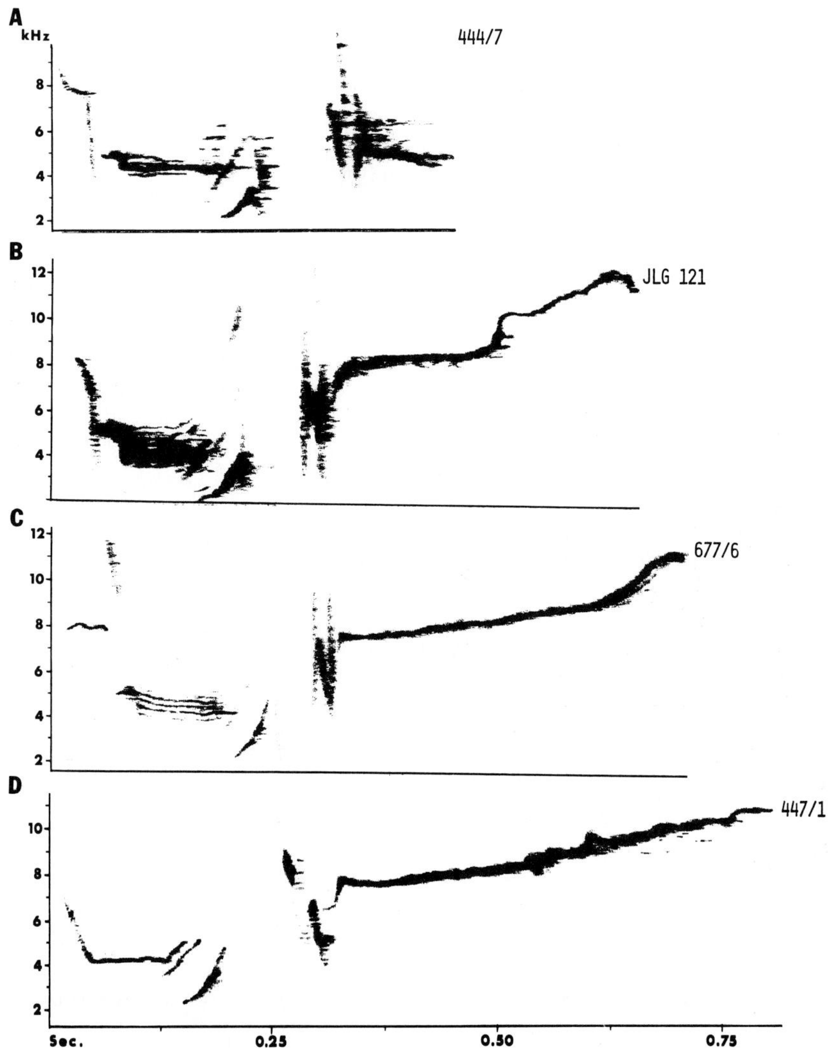

Fig. 114. Examples of population variation in the whistle song of *Certhidea olivacea*, Isla Pinta. Narrow-band displays of definitive adult songs.

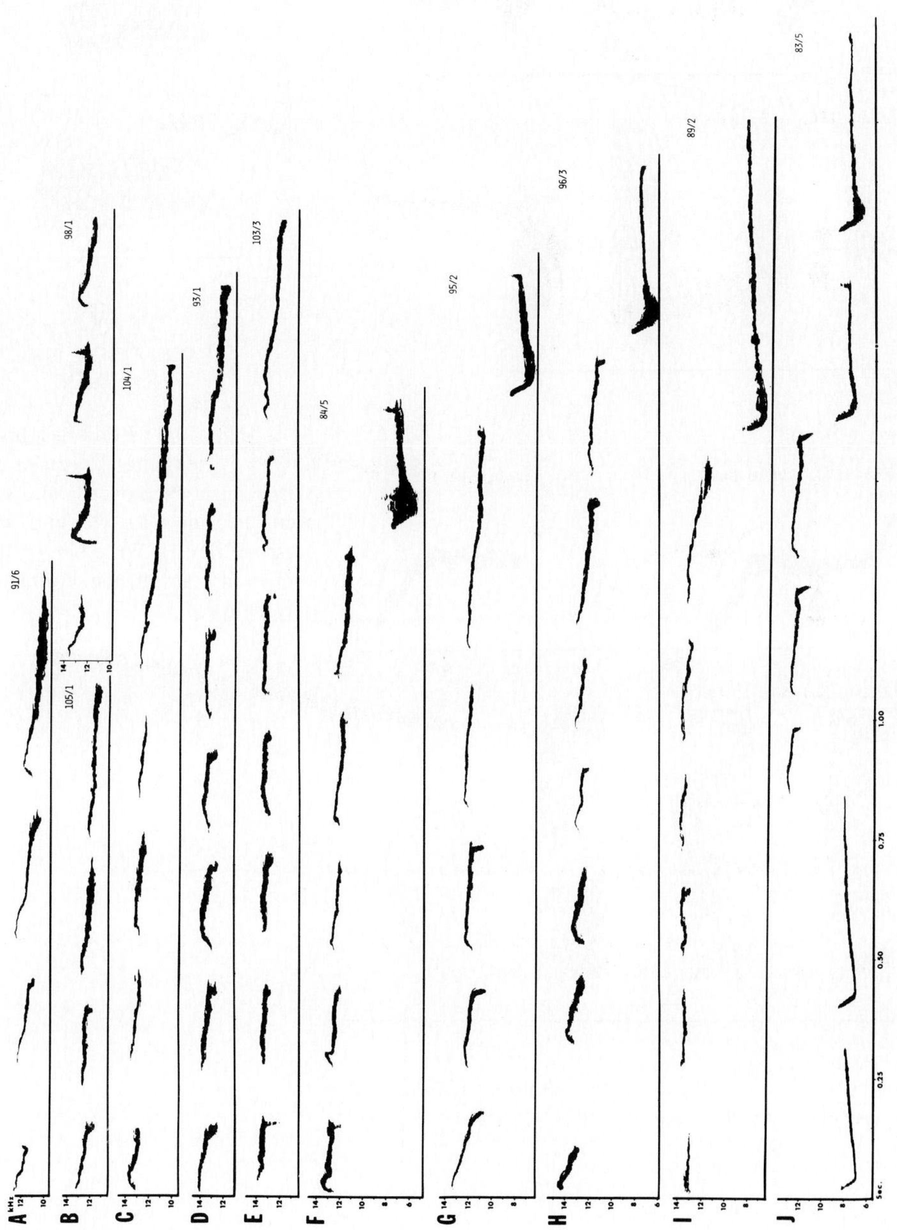

Fig. 115. Examples of population variation in the whistle song of *Certhidea olivacea*, Isla Genovesa. Narrow-band displays of definitive adult songs.

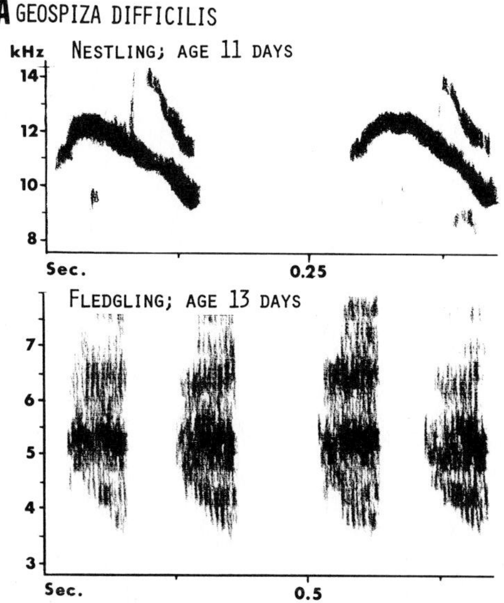

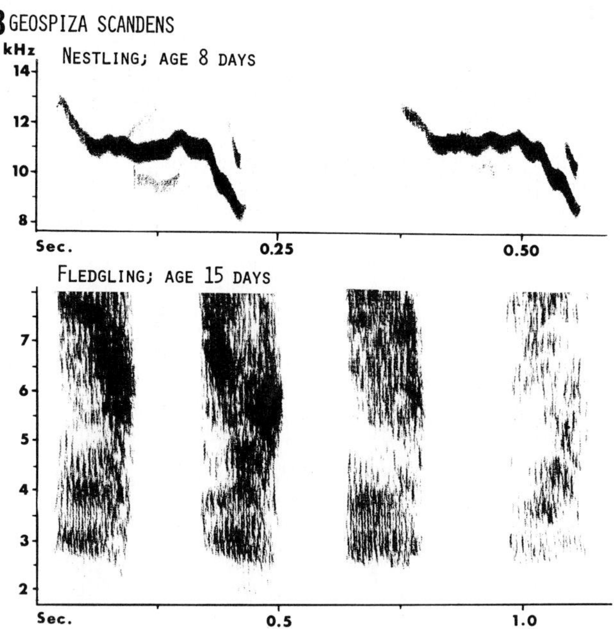

Fig. 116. Nestling and fledgling call notes of *Geospiza difficilis* (A) and *Geospiza scandens* (B).

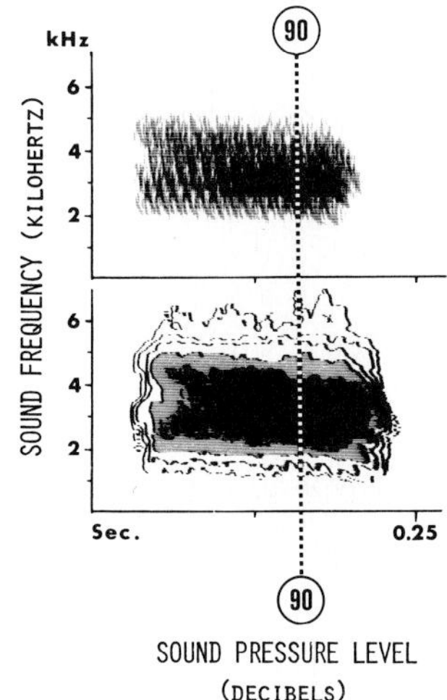

Fig. 117. Food-begging call note of fledgling *Geospiza conirostris*, Isla Genovesa, showing a point in time with maximal sound-pressure level. Wide-band display above and amplitude contour display below.

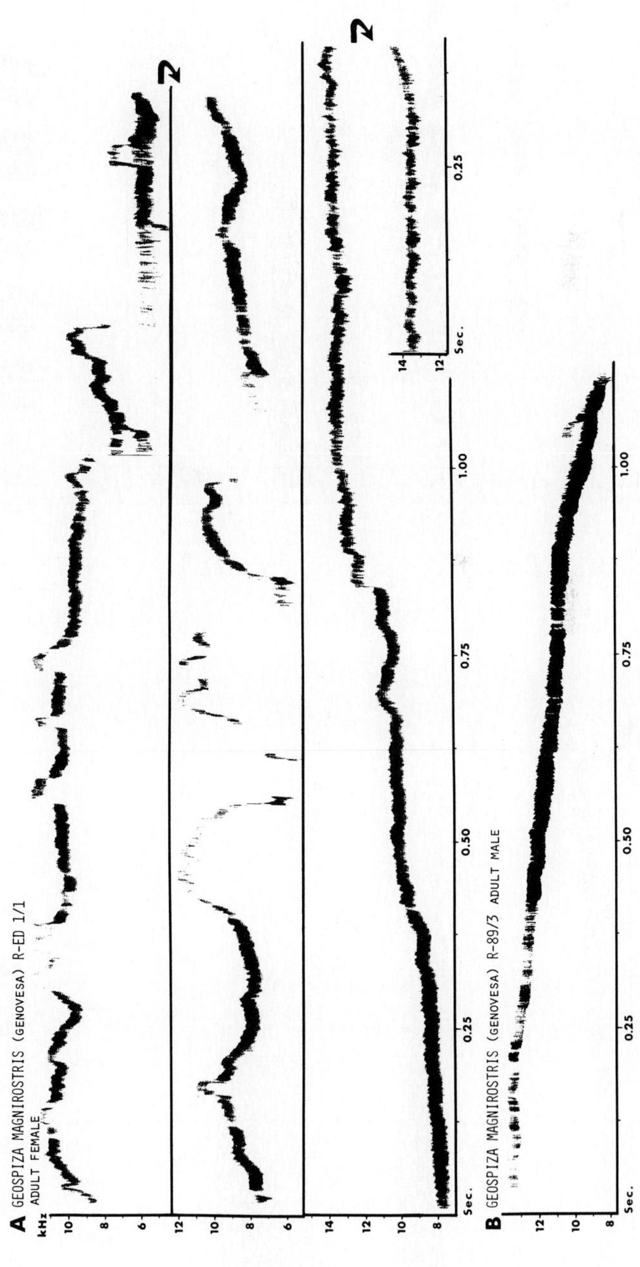

Fig. 118. Whistle songs of captive *Geospiza magnirostris* (Isla Genovesa). A, adult female; B, adult male. Both birds were captured in the wild and held captive in our San Francisco aviaries. Female whistle song (A) was induced by testosterone propionate injections. Male song (B) was spontaneous.

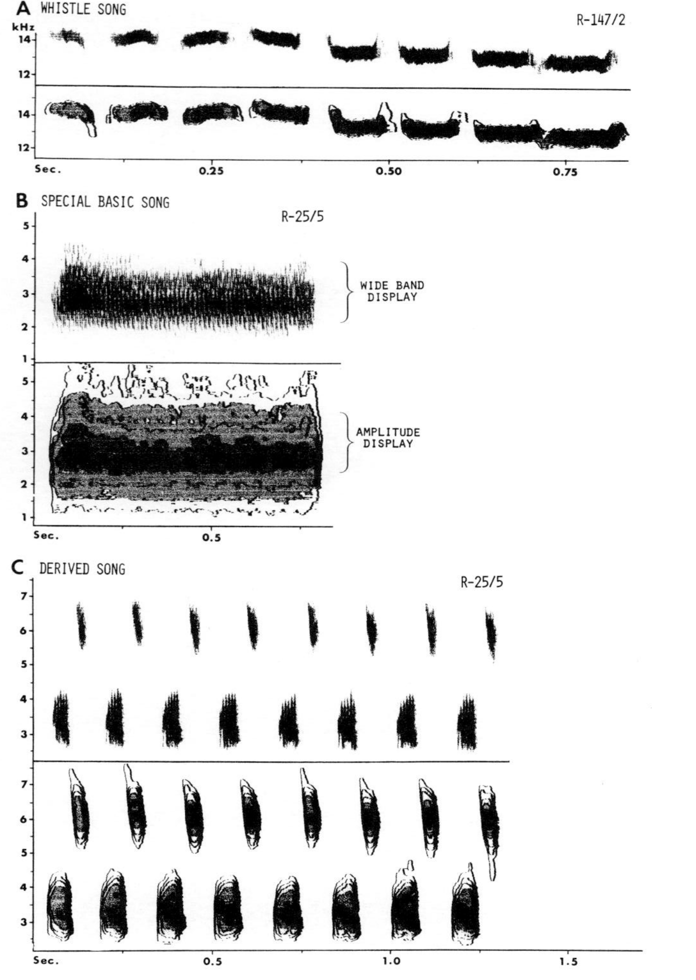

Fig. 119. As in Fig. 120, but from outer coastal zone, Academy Bay.

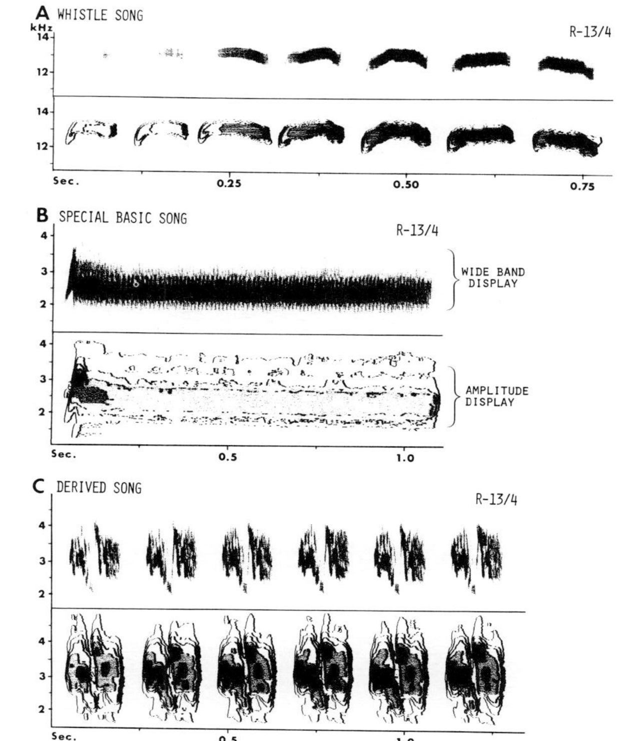

Fig. 120. Examples of three types of song of *Camarhynchus parvulus* recorded in *Scalesia* forest zone, I. Santa Cruz. Wide-band display (above) and amplitude contour display (below) are shown for whistle (A), special basic (B), and derived (C) songs.

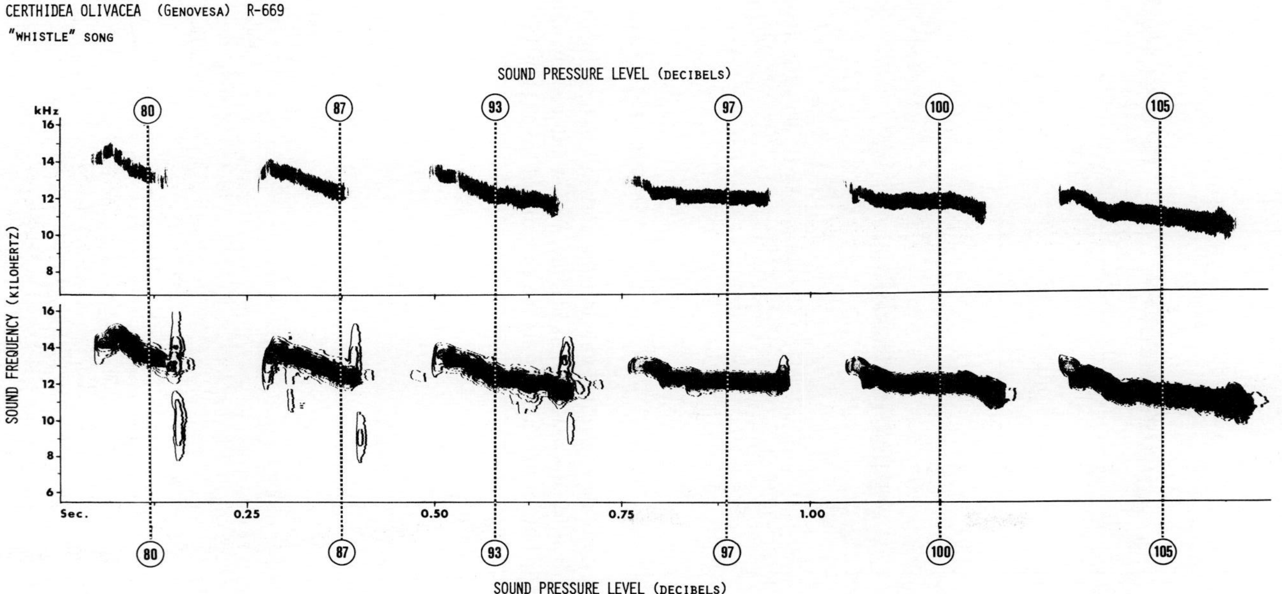

Fig. 121. Whistle song of *Certhidea olivacea*, Isla Genovesa, showing dB levels at several points in time. Last whistle note of song is shown in Fig. 122. Wide-band display above and amplitude contour display below.

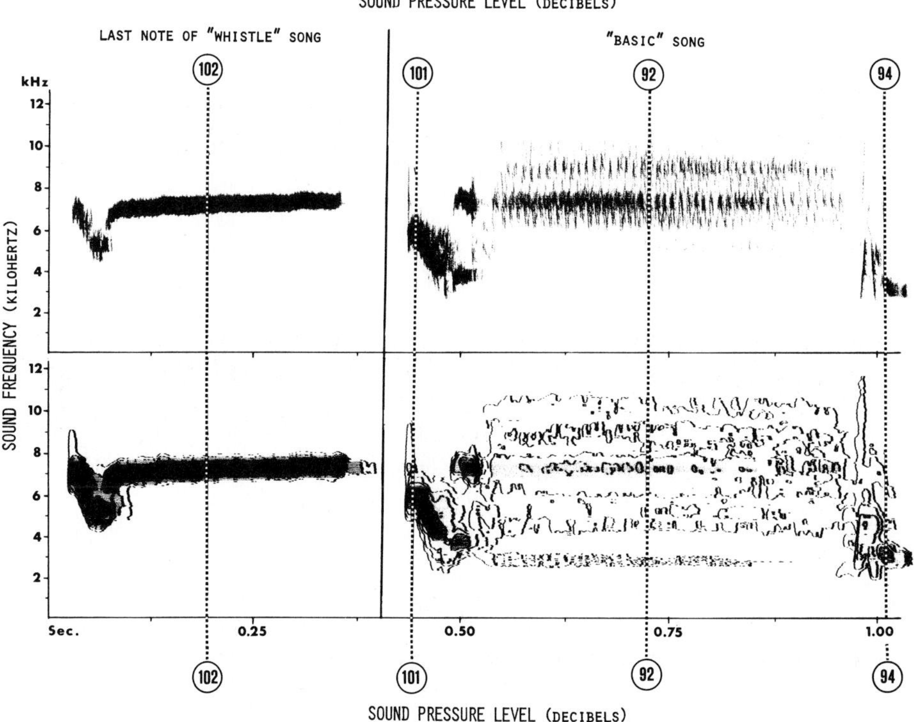

Fig. 122. Last note of whistle song and full basic song of *Certhidea olivacea*, Isla Genovesa, showing dB level at several points in time. Wide-band display above and amplitude contour display below. (First notes of whistle song are shown in Fig. 121.)

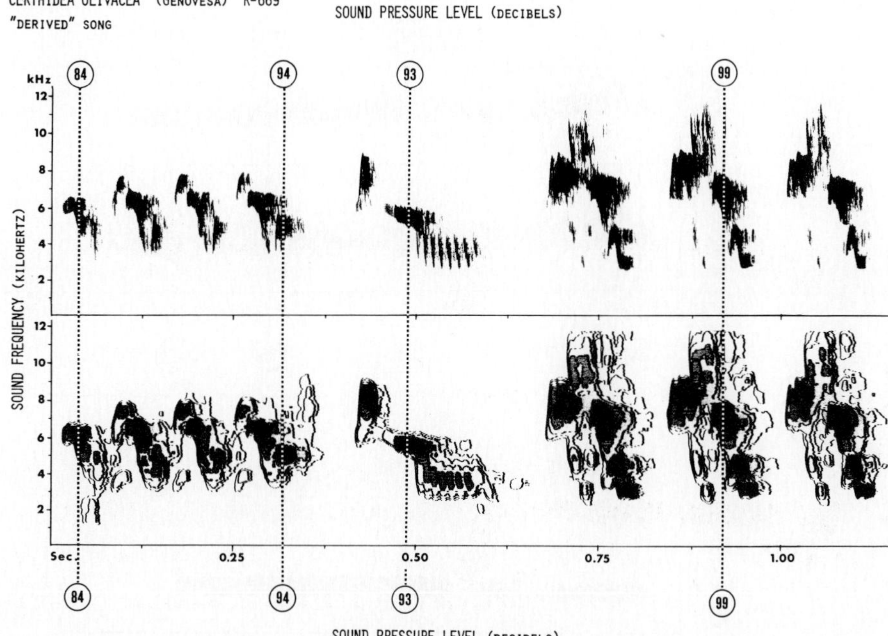

Fig. 123. Derived song of *Certhidea olivacea*, Isla Genovesa, showing dB levels at several points in time. Wide-band display above and amplitude contour display below.

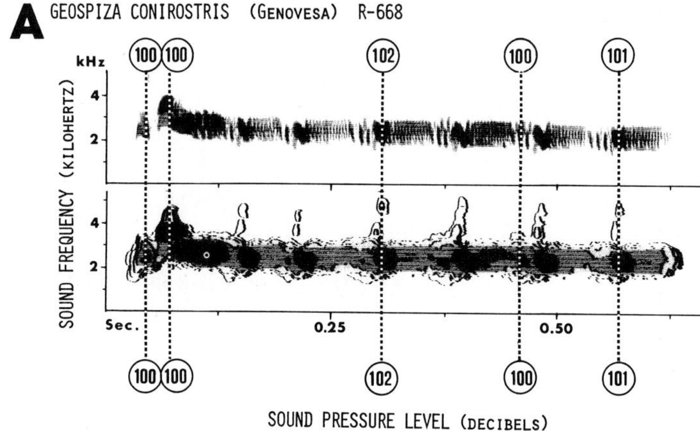

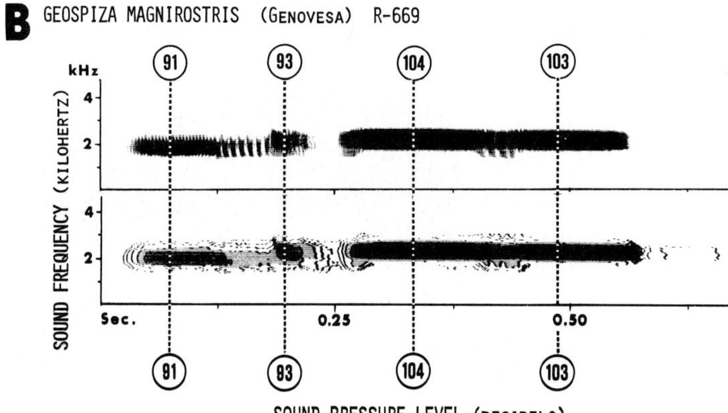

Fig. 124. Basic songs of *Geospiza conirostris* (A) and *Geospiza magnirostris* (B), Isla Genovesa, showing dB levels at several points in time. Wide-band display above and amplitude contour display below.

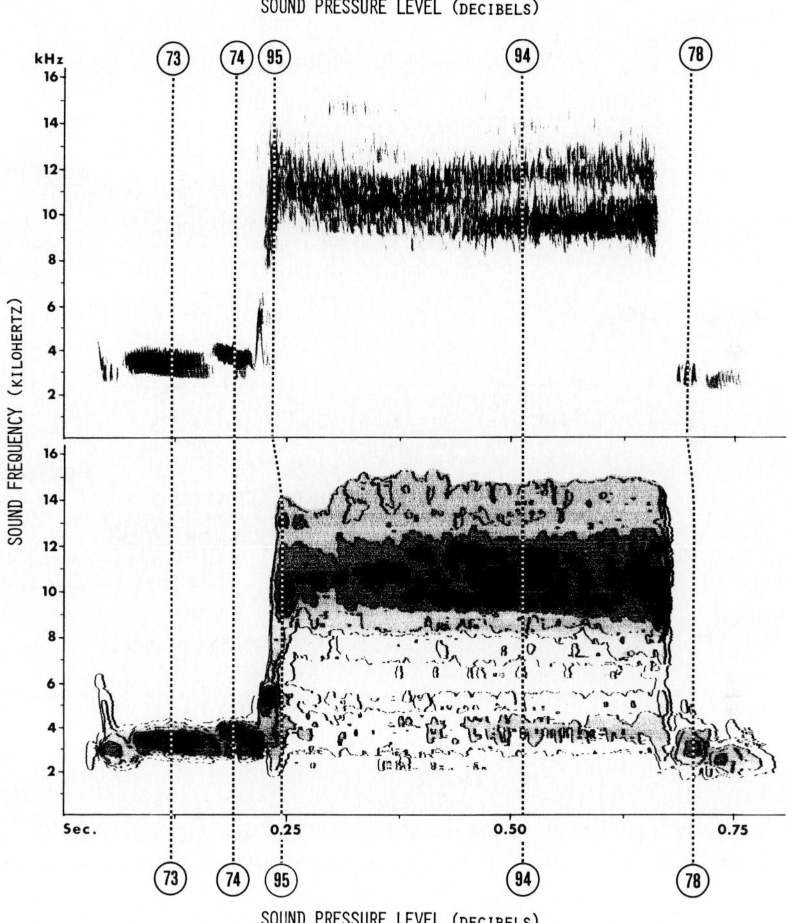

Fig. 125. Basic song of *Geospiza difficilis*, Isla Genovesa, showing dB levels at several points in time. Wide-band display above and amplitude contour display below.

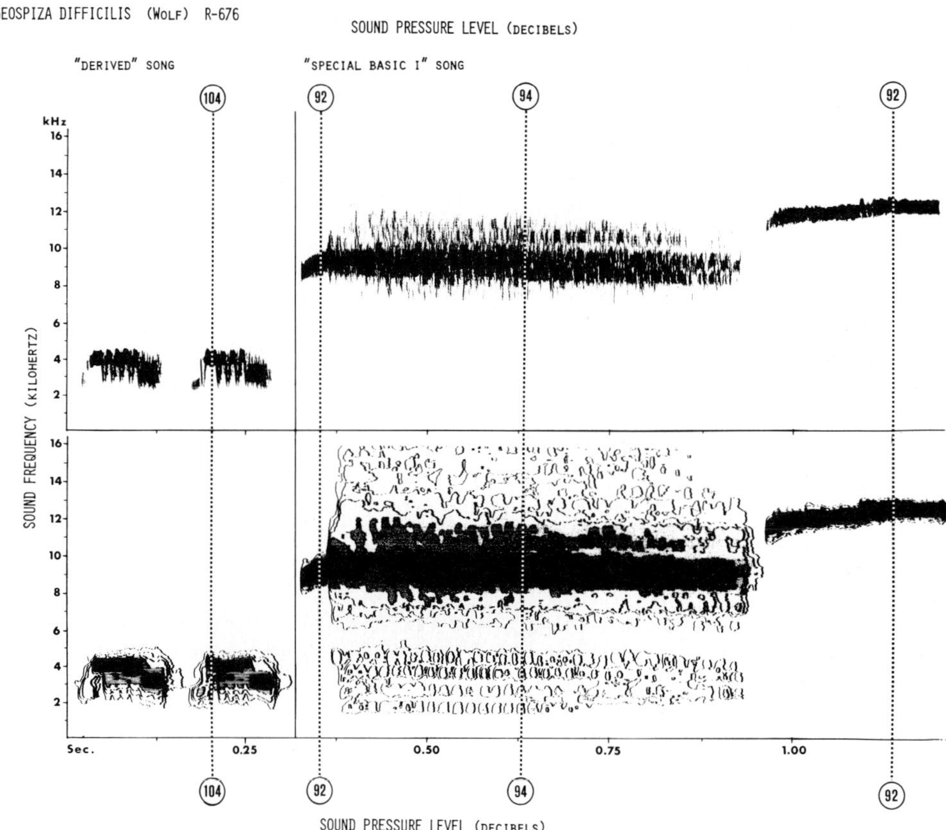

Fig. 126. Derived song (left) and basic song (right) of *Geospiza difficilis*, Isla Wolf, showing dB levels at several points in time. Wide-band display above and amplitude contour display below.

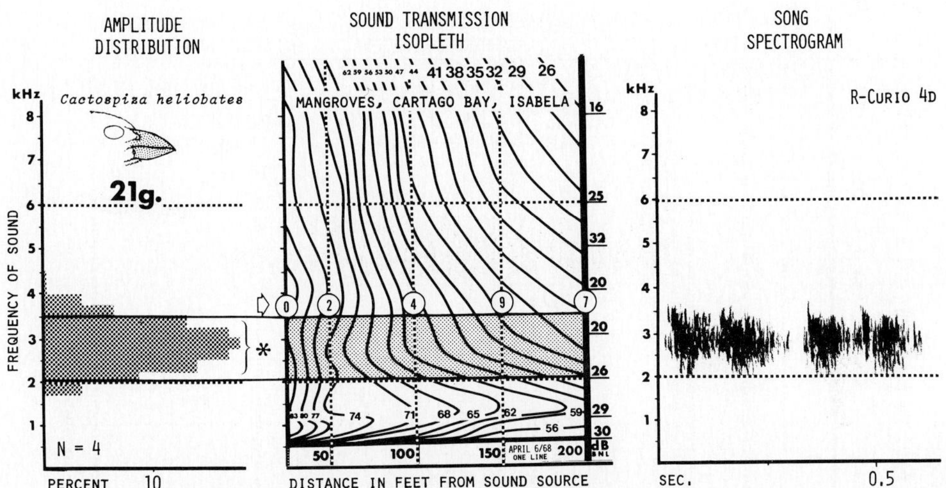

Fig. 127. Song energy spectrum, body weight, and sample song spectrograms of *Cactospiza heliobates* on Isla Isabela. Frequency band containing 80-85% of song energy is projected onto sound-transmission isopleth o the mangrove forest. Song recordings courtesy of E. Curio.

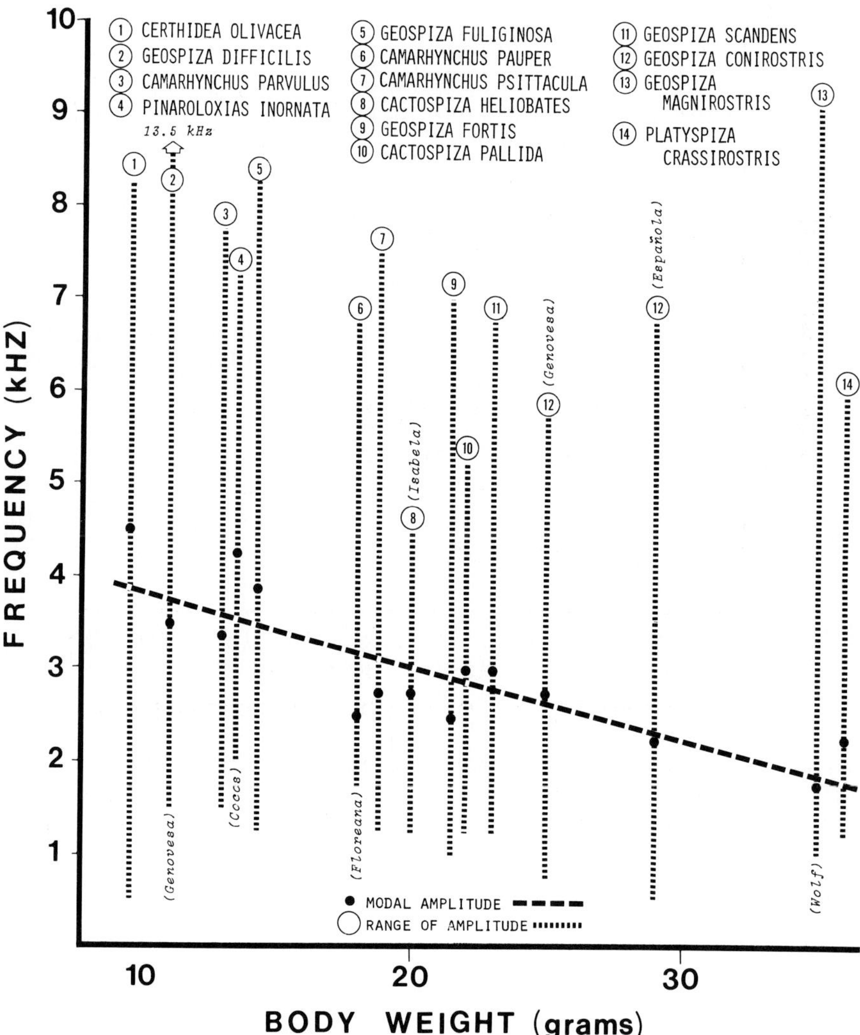

Fig. 128. Relationship between modal amplitude of song to frequency spread and mean body weight for 14 species of Darwin's finches. Data on males only are from Isla Santa Cruz, except as indicated.

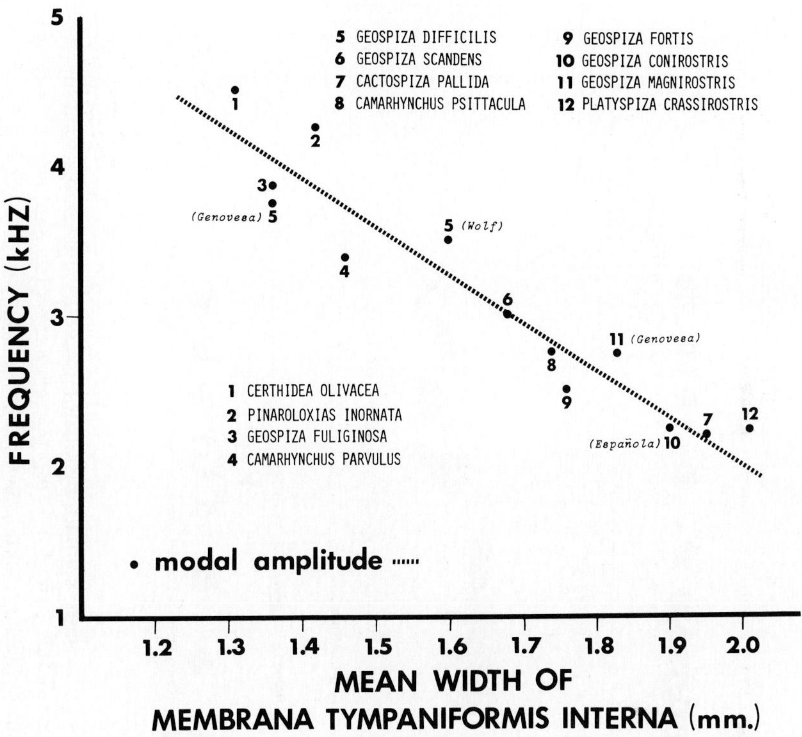

Fig. 129. Relationship of modal amplitude of song to frequency and mean width of the *Membrana tympaniformis interna* for 12 species of Darwin's finches. Data on males only are from Isla Santa Cruz, except as indicated. Membrane data are from males in singing condition (Cutler 1970).

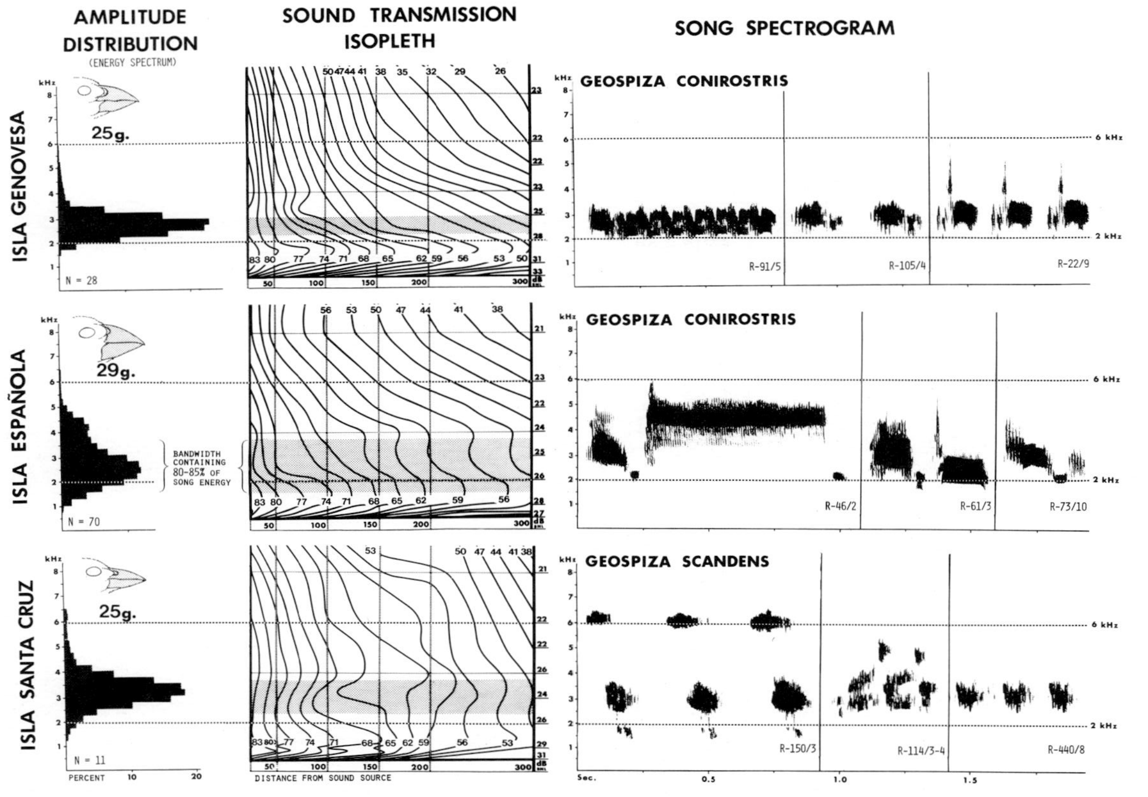

Fig. 130. Comparison of song amplitude distributions (energy spectra), body weights, sound-transmission isopleths and sample song spectrograms for *Geospiza conirostris* populations on Isla Genovesa (top), Isla Española (middle), and for *Geospiza scandens* on Isla Santa Cruz (bottom). Shaded bands on isopleths indicate song bandwidths containing approximately 80-85% of sound energy. Body weight datum for Isla Genovesa courtesy of P. R. Grant.

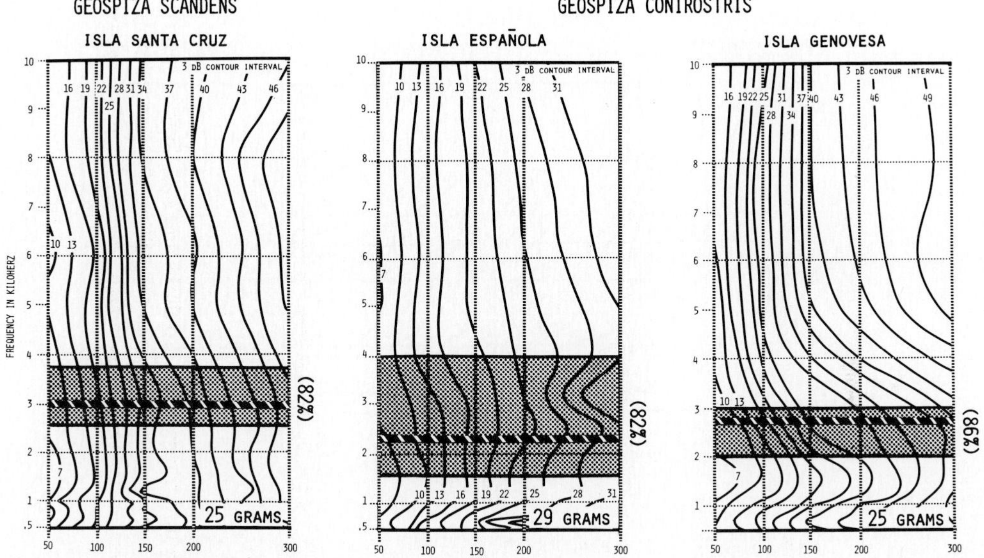

Fig. 131. Frequency bands of song of *Geospiza scandens* (Isla Santa Cruz) and *Geospiza conirostris* (islas Española and Genovesa), containing approximately 80-85% of sound energy, superimposed on cumulative dB-loss isopleths of concordant island environments. Frequencies of modal amplitudes are indicated by hatched lines.

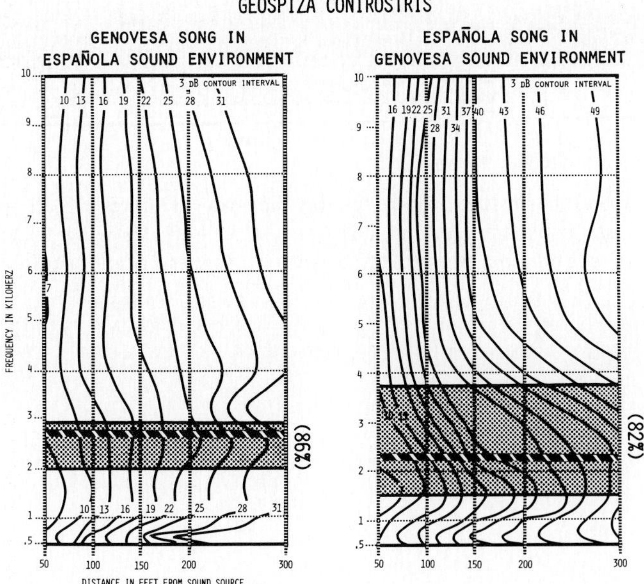

Fig. 132. Frequency bands of *Geospiza conirostris* songs containing 86% (Genovesa) and 82% (Española) of the sound energy, superimposed on discordant cumulative dB-loss isopleths of islas Española and Genovesa, respectively. Frequencies of modal amplitudes are indicated by hatched lines.

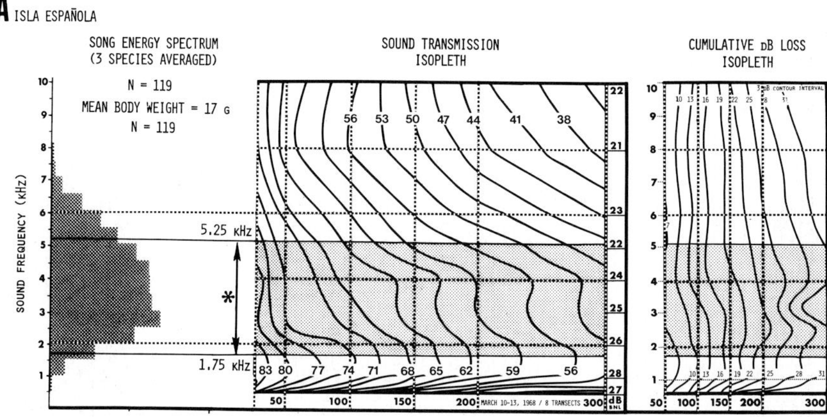

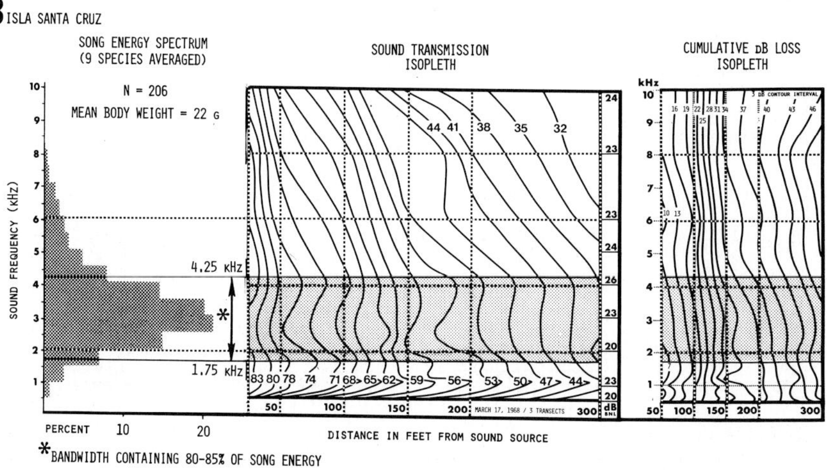

Fig. 133. Comparison of the average energy spectra of songs of all resident species of Darwin's finches on Isla Española (A) and Isla Santa Cruz (B), showing frequency bandwidths containing 80-85% of sound energy, projected onto transmission and cumulative dB isopleths for each island.

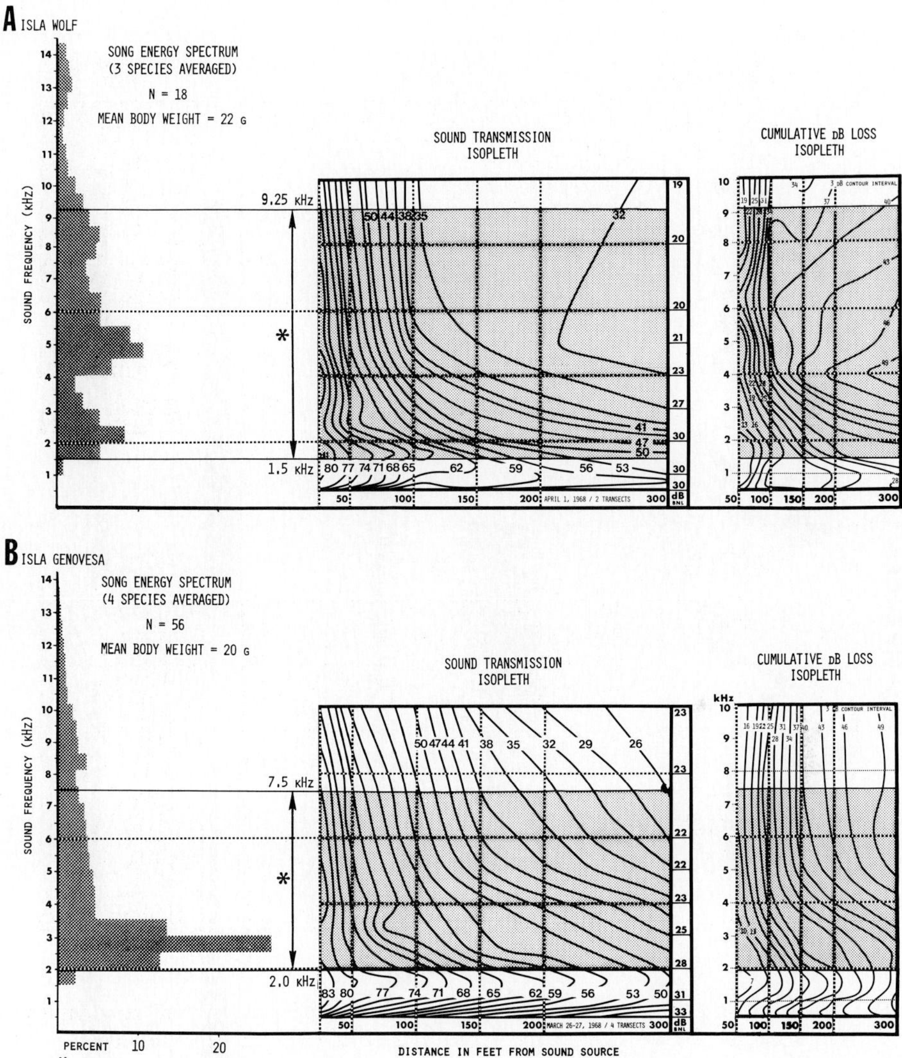

Fig. 134. Comparison of the average energy spectra of songs of all resident species of Darwin's finches on Isla Wolf (A) and Isla Genovesa (B), showing frequency bandwidths containing 80-85% of sound energy, projected onto transmission and cumulative dB loss isopleths for each island.

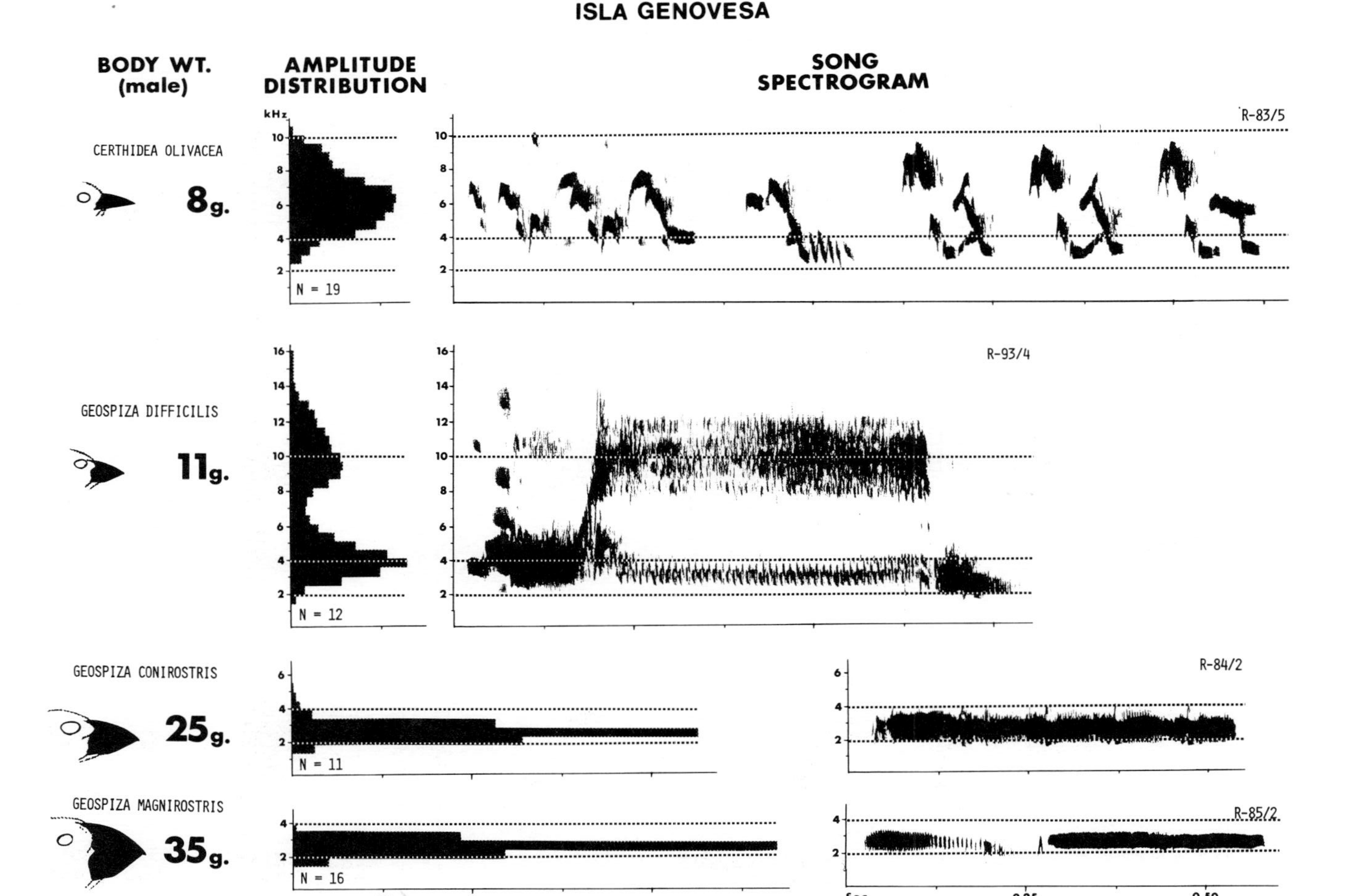

Fig. 135. Comparison of song spectrograms, song amplitude distributions, and body sizes in four species of Darwin's finches from Isla Genovesa. Body weight data courtesy of P. R. Grant.

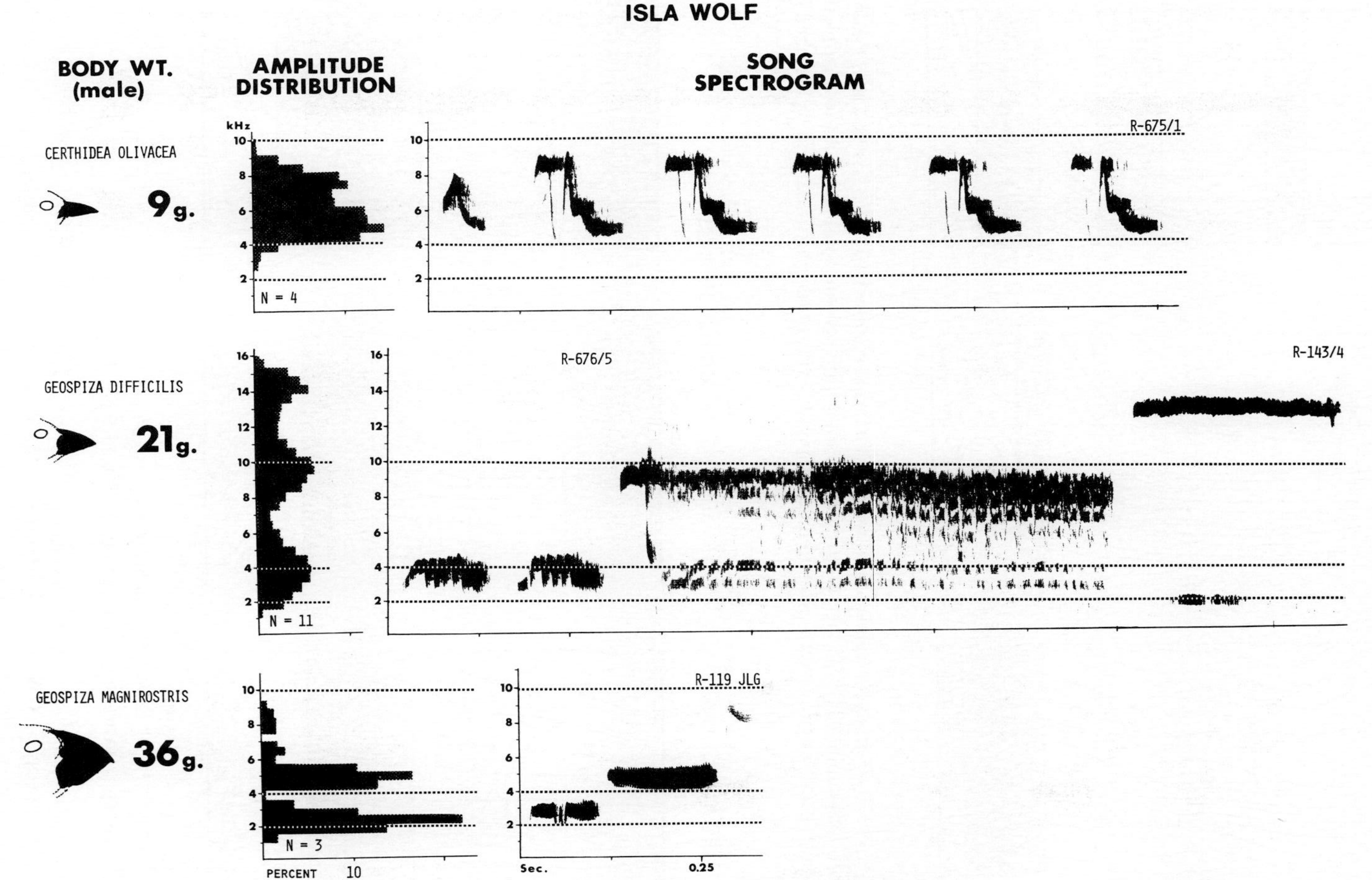

Fig. 136. Comparison of song spectrograms, song amplitude distributions, and body sizes in four species of Darwin's finches from Isla Wolf. Body weight data courtesy P. R. Grant.

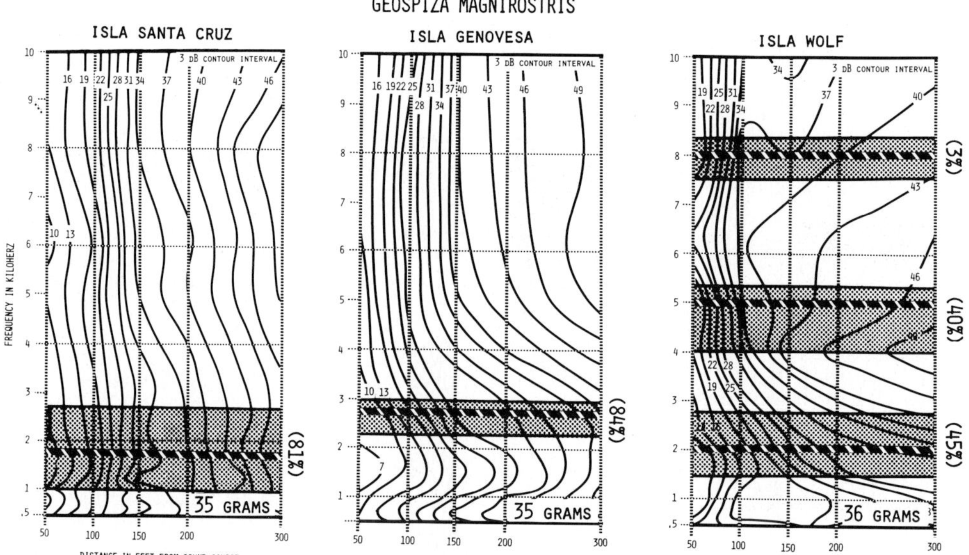

Fig. 137. Frequency bands of songs of *Geospiza magnirostris*, islas Santa Cruz, Genovesa, and Wolf, containing 81-88% of sound energy, superimposed on cumulative dB-loss isopleths of concordant island environments. Frequencies of modal amplitudes are indicated by hatched lines.

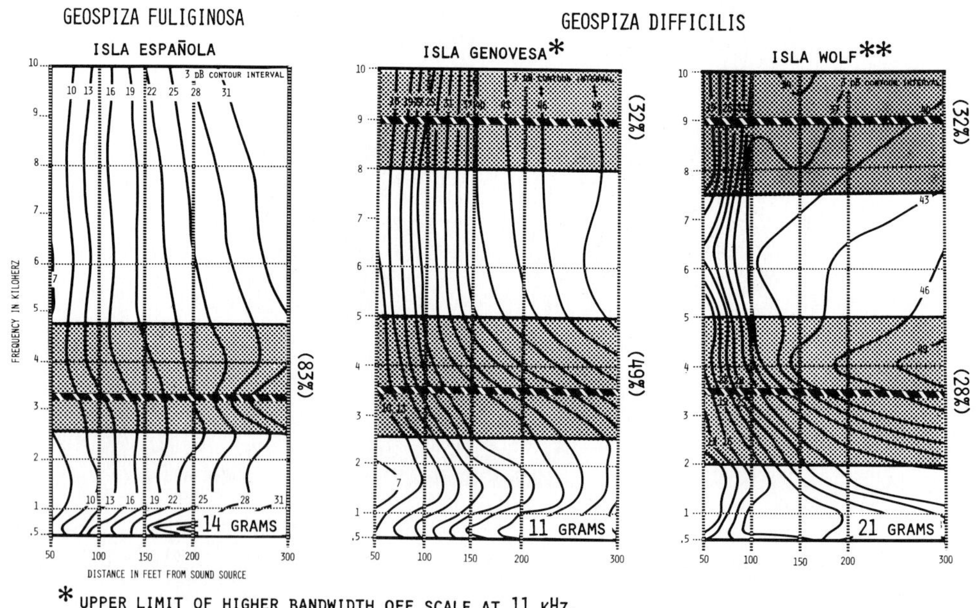

Fig. 138. Frequency bands of songs of *Geospiza fuliginosa*, Isla Española, and *Geospiza difficilis*, islas Genovesa and Wolf, containing 81-83% of sound energy, superimposed on cumulative dB-loss isopleths of concordant island environments. Frequencies of modal amplitudes are indicated by hatched lines.

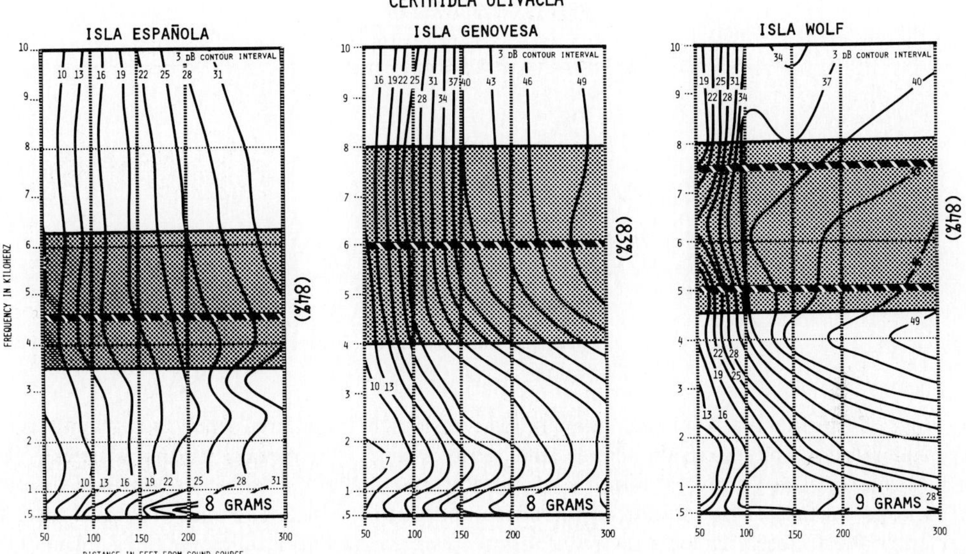

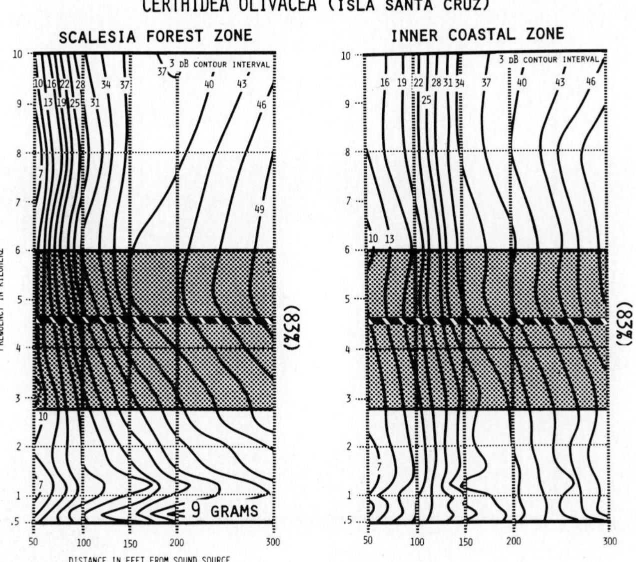

Fig. 139. Frequency bands of derived songs of *Certhidea olivacea*, islas Española, Genovesa, Wolf, and Santa Cruz (containing 83-84% of sound energy) superimposed on cumulative dB-loss isopleths of concordant island environments. Frequencies of modal amplitudes are indicated by hatched lines.

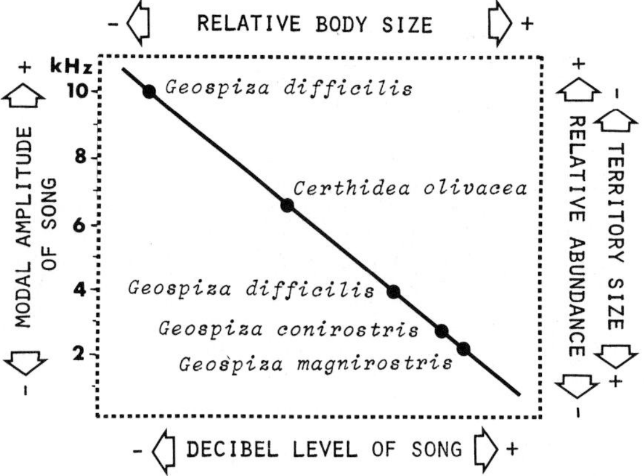

Fig. 140. Generalized scheme showing relationships between frequency and decibel level of song, and relative body size, abundance, and territory size, as it pertains to four species of Darwin's finches on Isla Genovesa. Modified from Bowman 1979. *Geospiza difficilis* appears twice on the slope because of a pronounced bimodal amplitude distribution, namely 10 and 4 kHz. The latter entry most closely reflects the relationship to weight and dB level of song; the former entry most closely reflects the relationships to territory size and relative abundance. Character states for each factor are indicated by plus and minus signs, i.e. + = high or large; - = low or small. Data on dB levels are from Fig. 141. Territory sizes were estimated from Grant and Grant 1980, Fig. 5 (see Table 21).

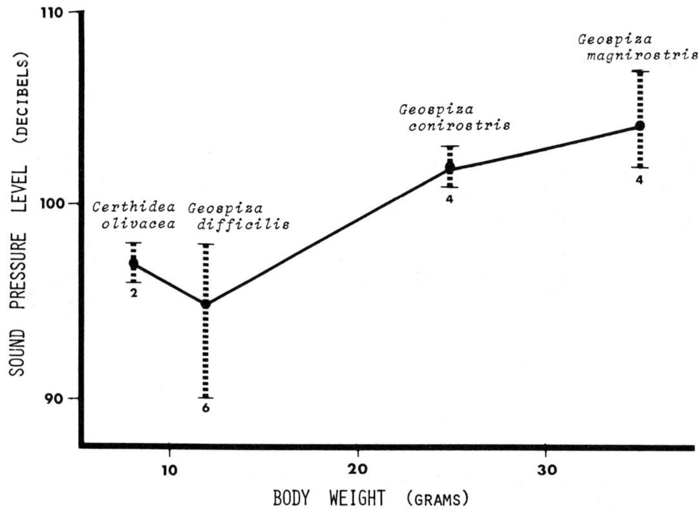

Fig. 141. Decibel values for the "loudest" region of the songs of four species of Darwin's finches on Isla Genovesa, arranged according to body weight. Solid line connects mean values and the broken vertical lines indicate ranges of variation in dB levels, with the number of songs analyzed shown at the lower end of each line. Compare with Table 18 and Figs. 123-126.

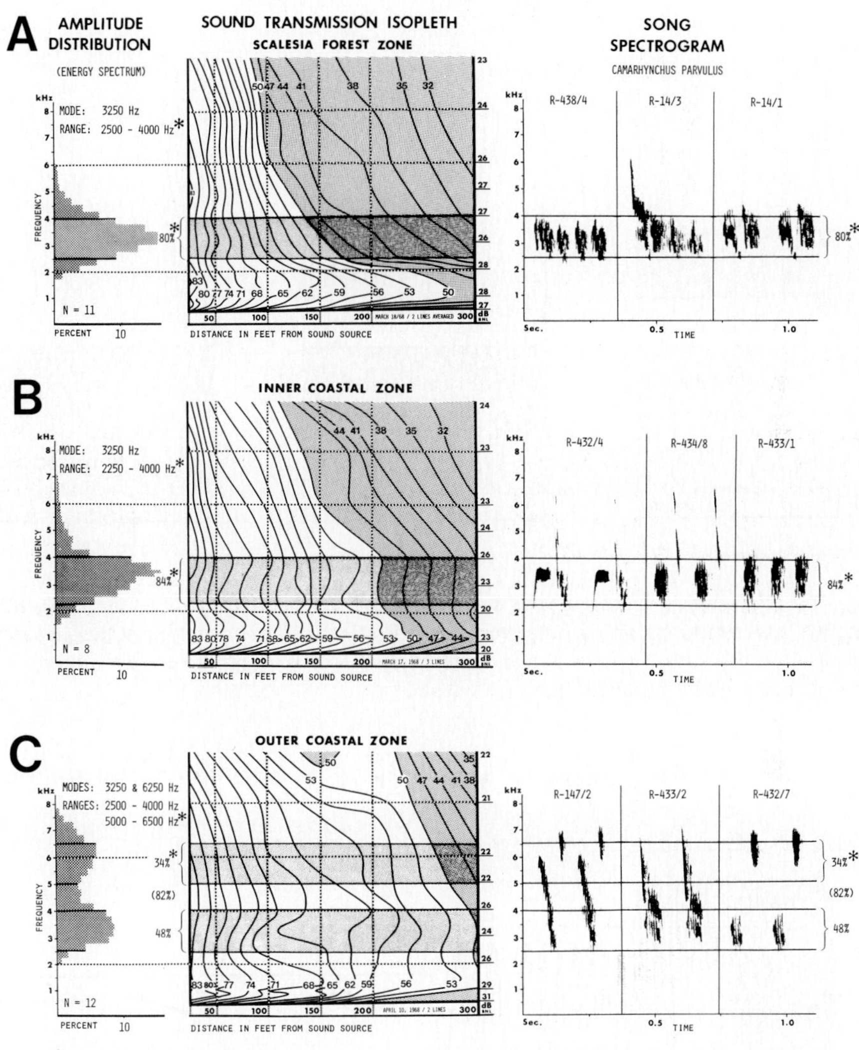

Fig. 142. Comparison of energy spectra, sound-transmission isopleths, and song spectrograms of *Camarhynchus parvulus* in three vegetation zones on Isla Santa Cruz. Frequency bands containing 82-84% of the song energy are shaded across the isopleths and are delimited on the song spectrograms by horizontal lines. Also shaded on the isopleths are the areas encompassing the 50 dB and below contour lines.

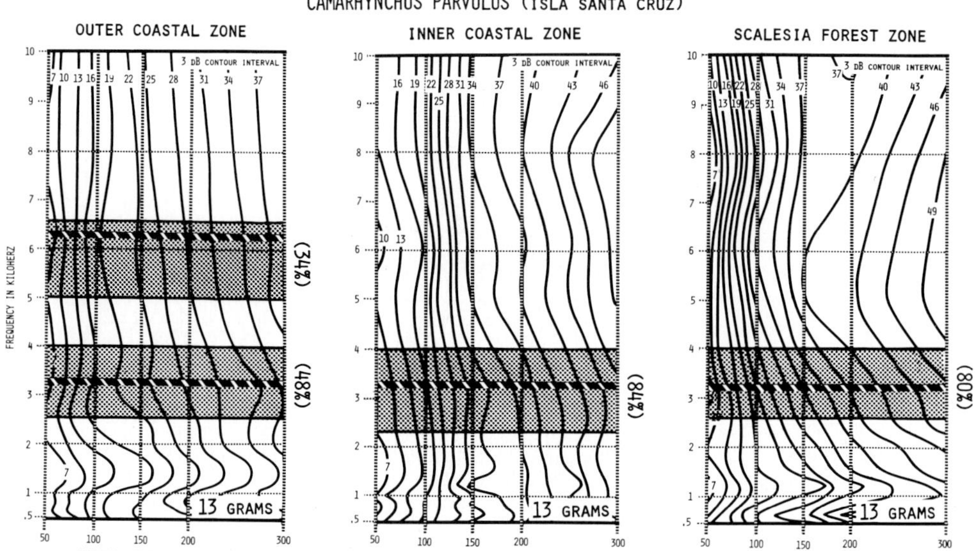

Fig. 143. Frequency bands of the songs of *Camarhynchus parvulus* containing 80-84% of sound energy, superimposed on cumulative dB-loss isopleths of the outer coastal zone (left), inner coastal zone (center), and *Scalesia* forest zone (right) of Isla Santa Cruz. Frequency of modal amplitudes is indicated by hatched lines.

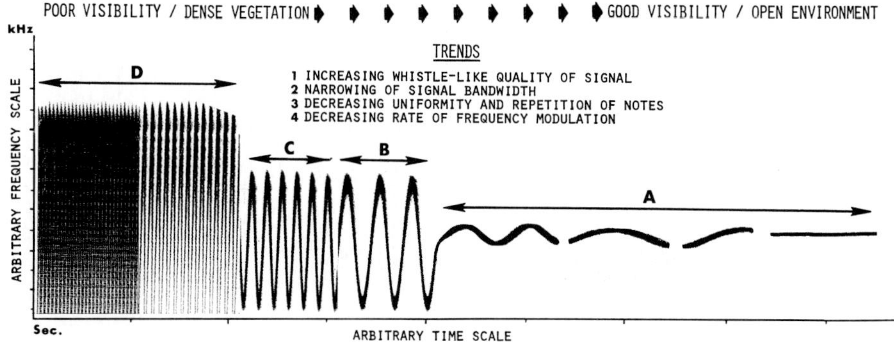

Fig. 144. Model of song structures to show correlation between amount of frequency modulation and environmental conditions. Regions A-D should be compared with examples of bird song in Fig. 145.

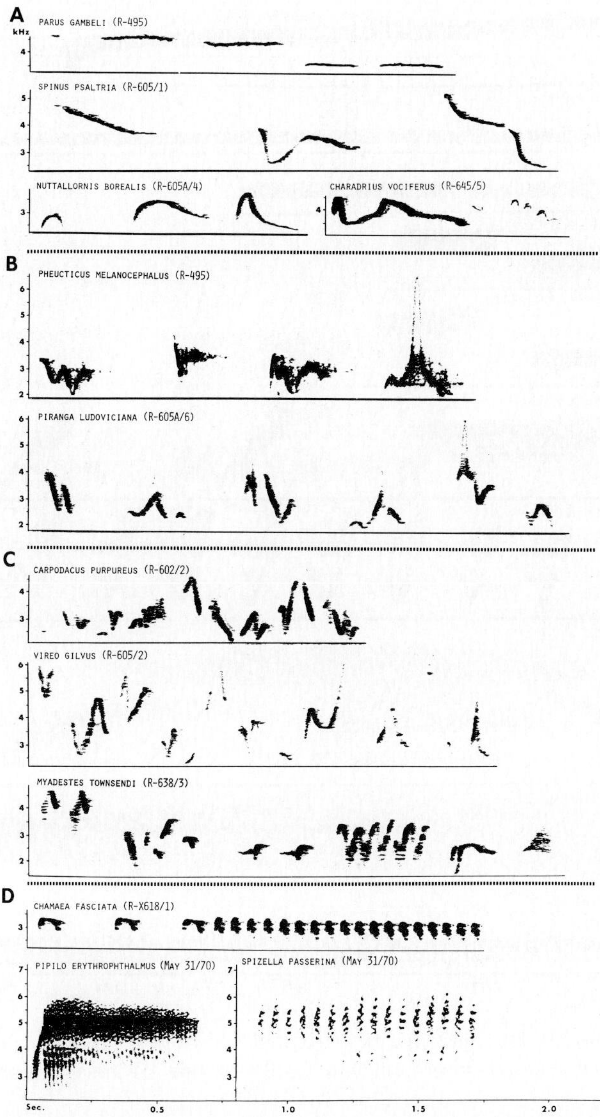

Fig. 145. Convergent vocalizations of western North American birds that occupy similar acoustical environments. A. Whistle-like songs of species living in fairly open vegetation where visibility is good. B. Moderately undulating whistle-like songs of species living partly within or beneath the leaf canopy of mixed sclerophyl-broadleaf trees. C. Strongly undulating whistle-like songs of species living in moderately dense stands of broadleaf or coniferous trees. D. Staccato-like or buzzy songs of species living in dense vegetation where visibility is poor. Compare songs with model FM signals of same group letters (A-D) in Fig. 144. Narrow-band display.

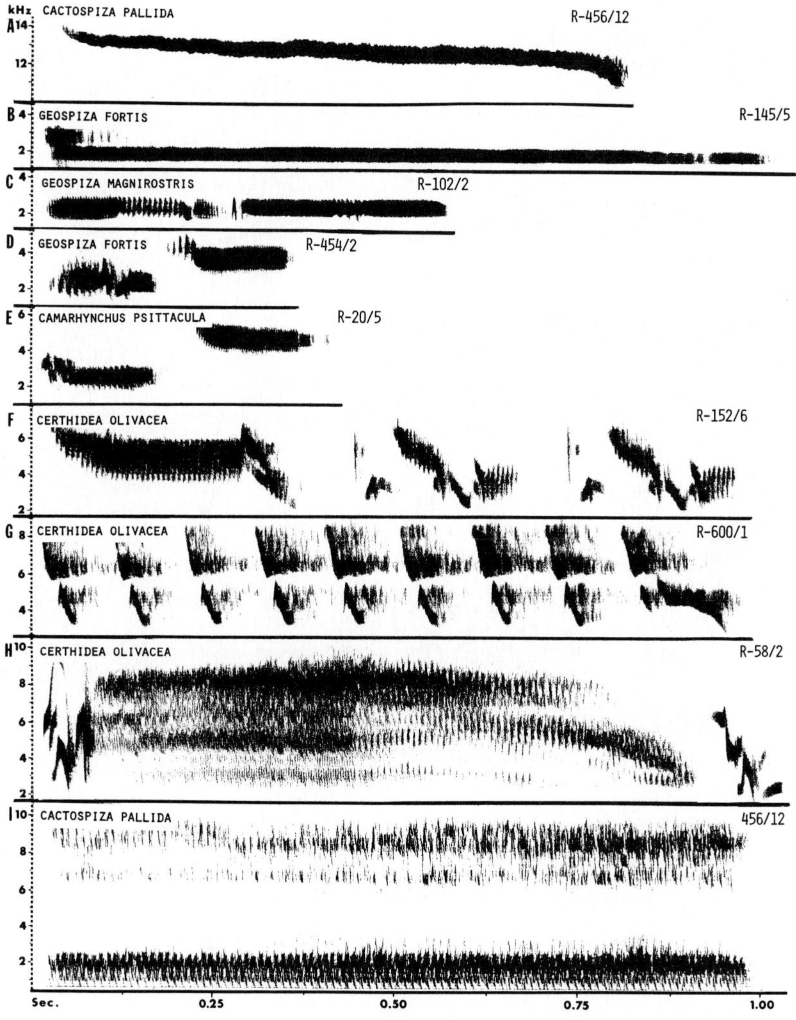

Fig. 146. Songs of Darwin's finches selected to show a morphological sequence from a condition of minimal frequency modulation (A,B) to one of maximal frequency modulation (H,I).

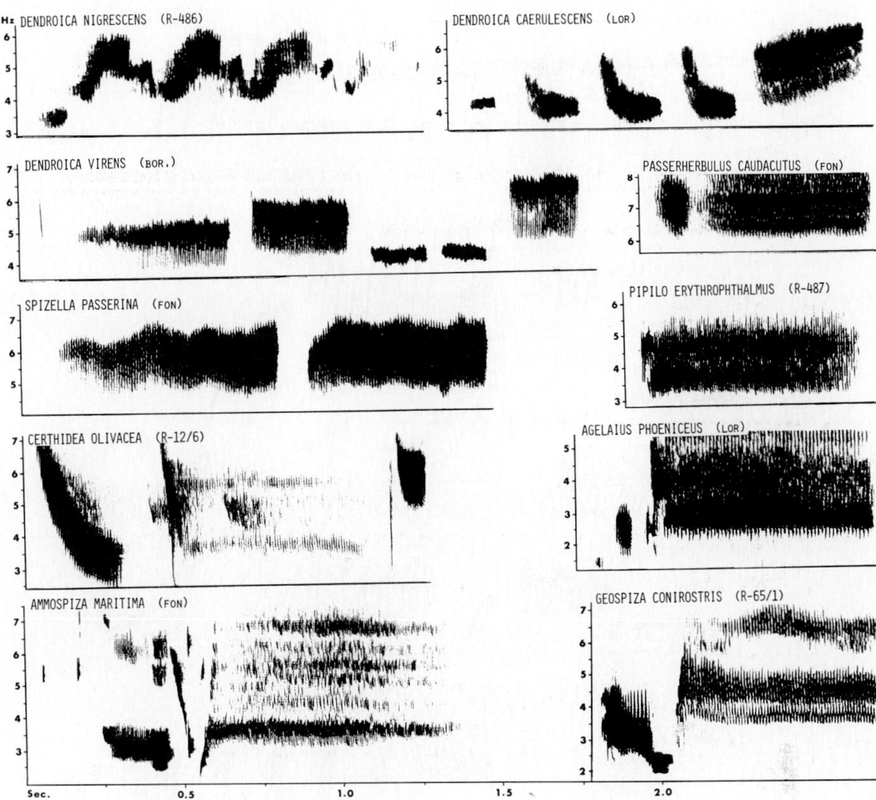

Fig. 147. Convergence in song structure of 10 species of songbirds living in fairly dense coarse grass, xerophytic foliage, brushy thickets, or boggy meadows and cattail swamps. Such habitats characteristically have obfuscated visibility.

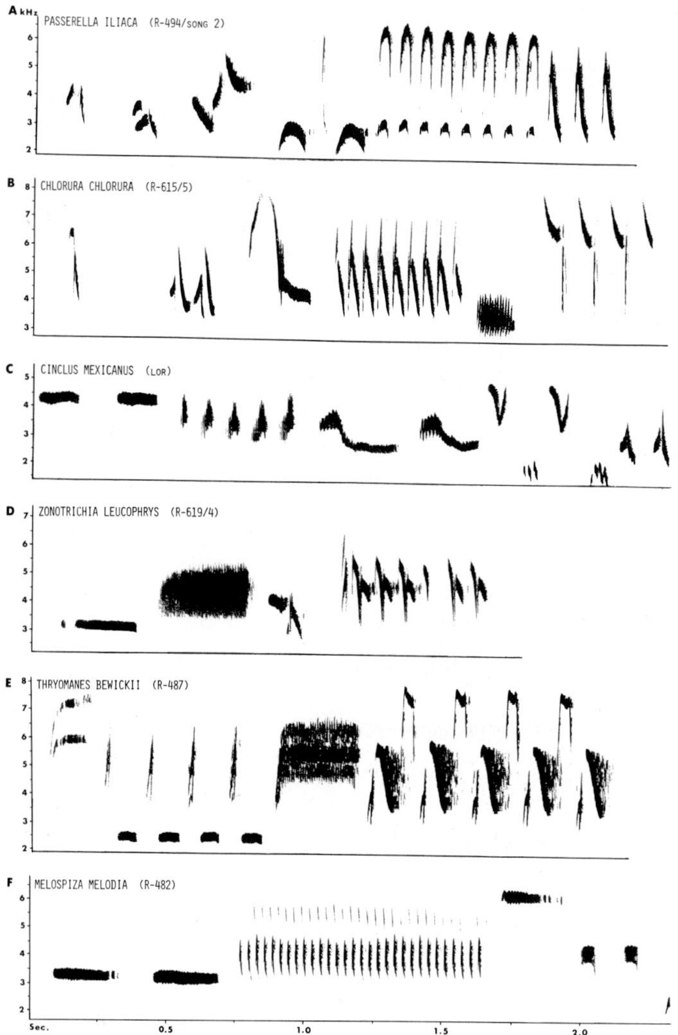

Fig. 148. Examples of the songs of six species of "edge" inhabiting birds.

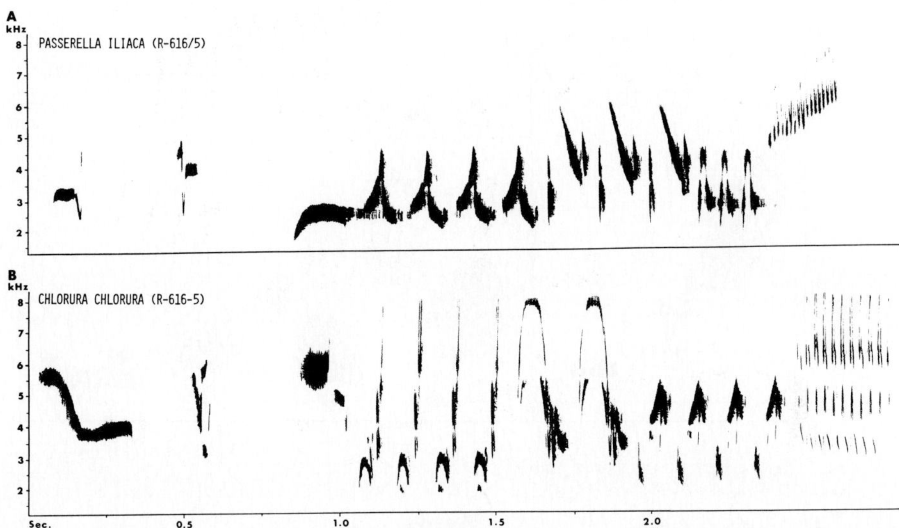

Fig. 149. Convergence in songs of two sympatric species of "edge" inhabiting songbirds in Alpine County, California, 7500 ft.

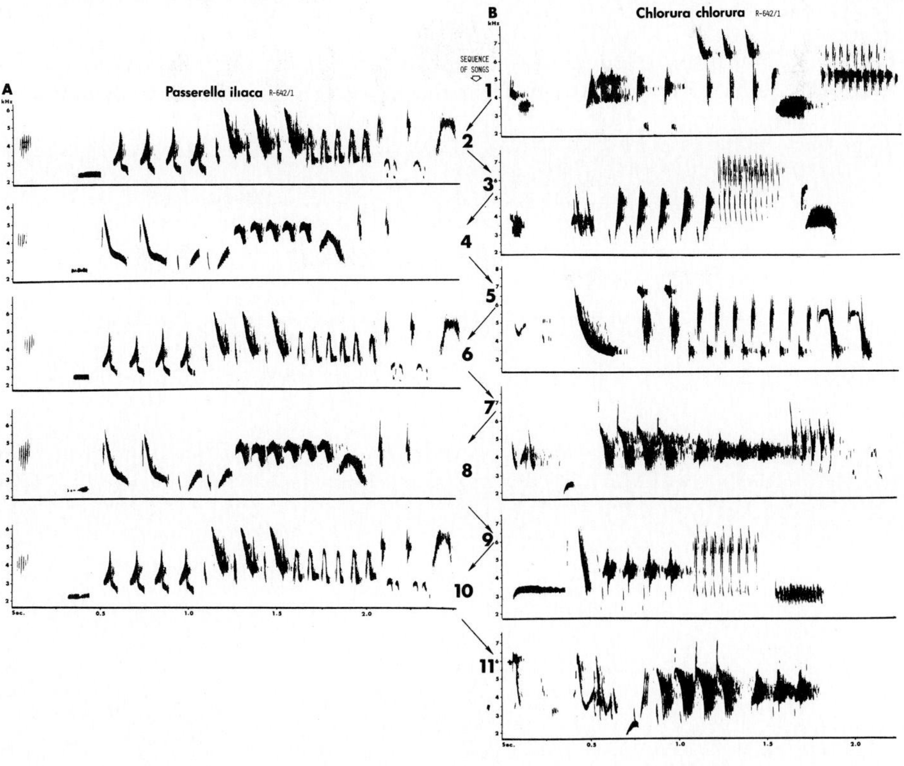

Fig. 150. Sequence of counter-singing between two sympatric species of songbird, Fox Sparrow (A) and Green-tailed Towhee (B), recorded in Alpine County, California, 7500 ft. Whereas the Fox Sparrow alternates between two songs, the Towhee songs are all different.

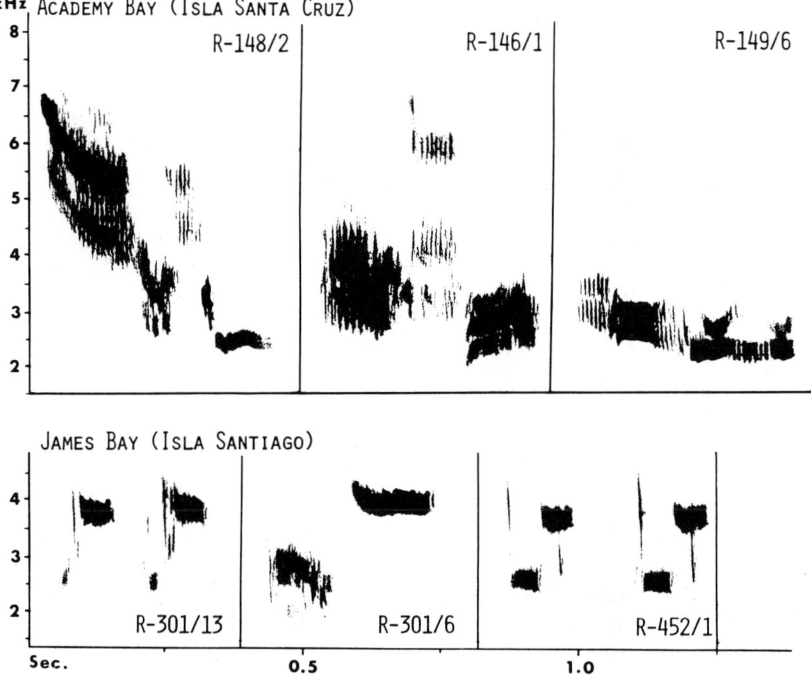

Fig. 151. Comparison of songs of *Geospiza fuliginosa* from the inner coastal zone of Academy Bay, Isla Santa Cruz (above) and from the parkland of south James Bay, Isla Santiago (below).

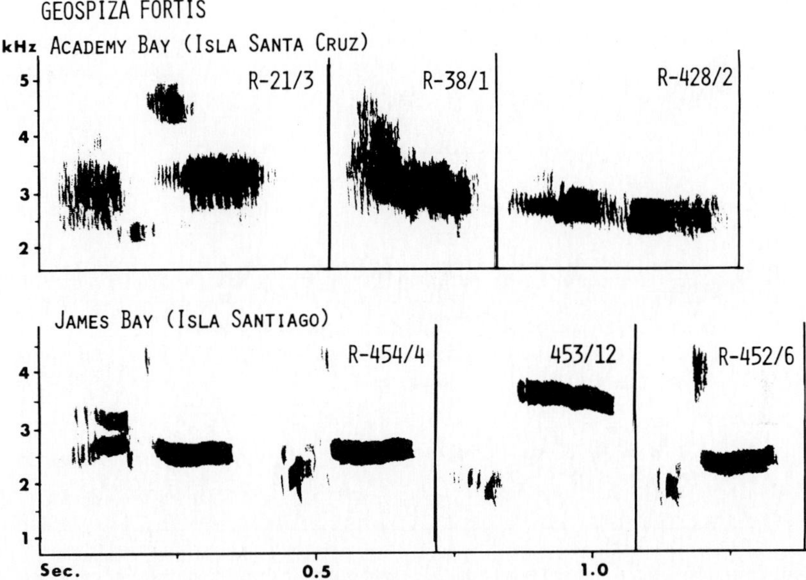

Fig. 152. Comparison of song of *Geospiza fortis* from the inner coastal zone of Academy Bay, Isla Santa Cruz (above) and from the parkland of south James Bay, Isla Santiago (below). Compare with full range of song of both islands in Figs. 31 and 50.

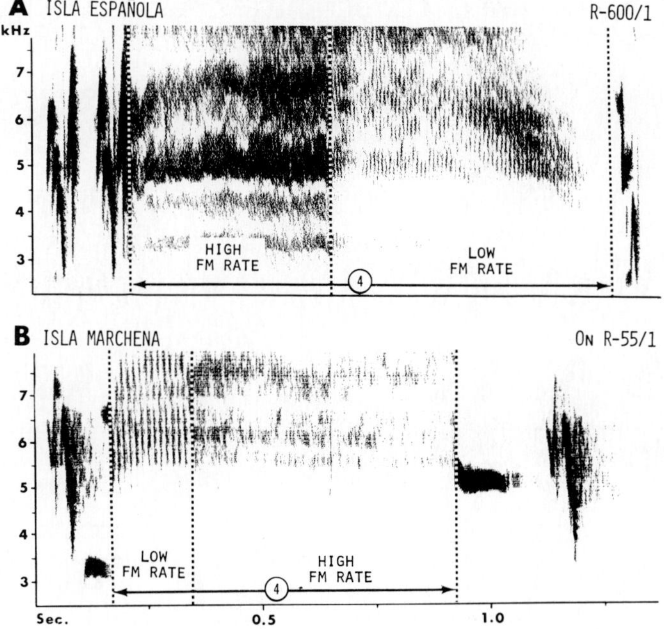

Fig. 153. Variation in frequency modulation rate in region 4 of the basic song of *Certhidea olivacea*, islas Española (A) and Marchena (B).

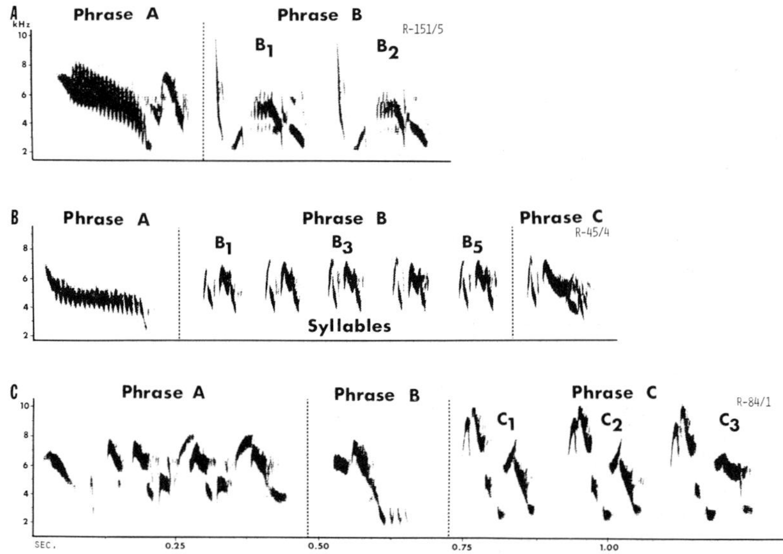

Fig. 154. Examples of the derived songs of *Certhidea olivacea* showing phrase complexities. A, Isla Santa Cruz, comparatively low complexity; B, I. Española, medium complexity; and C, I. Genovesa, high complexity.

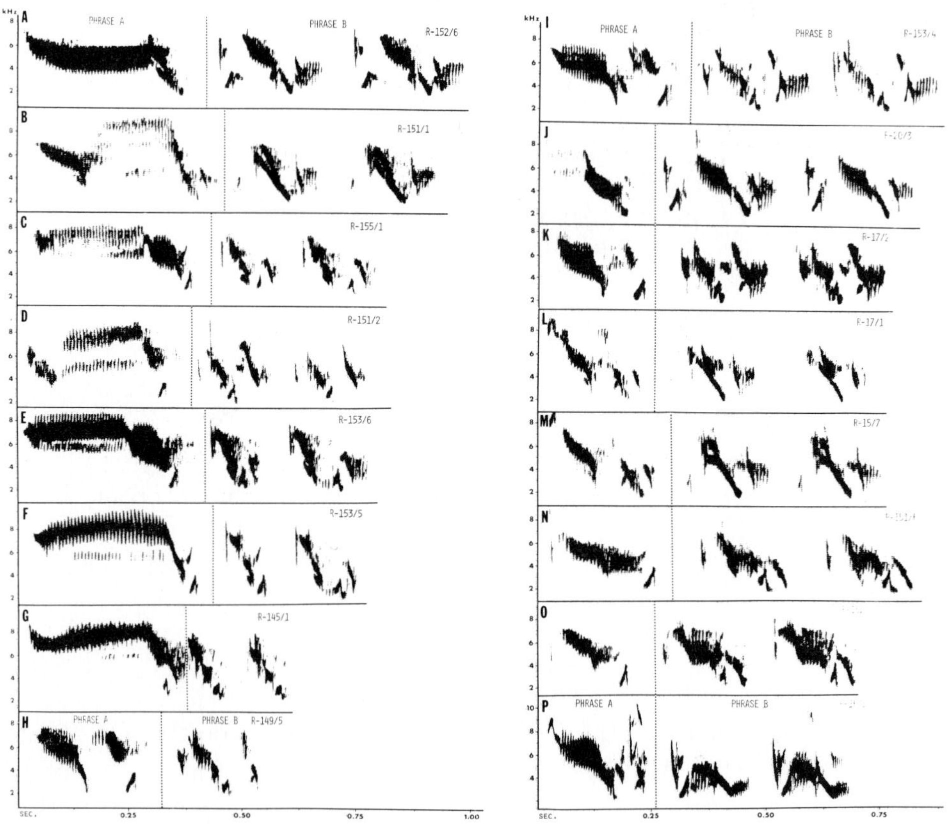

Fig. 155. Variation in the songs of *Certhidea olivacea* from Isla Santa Cruz, with phrases A and B delimited by broken vertical lines. All songs are essentially three-parted.

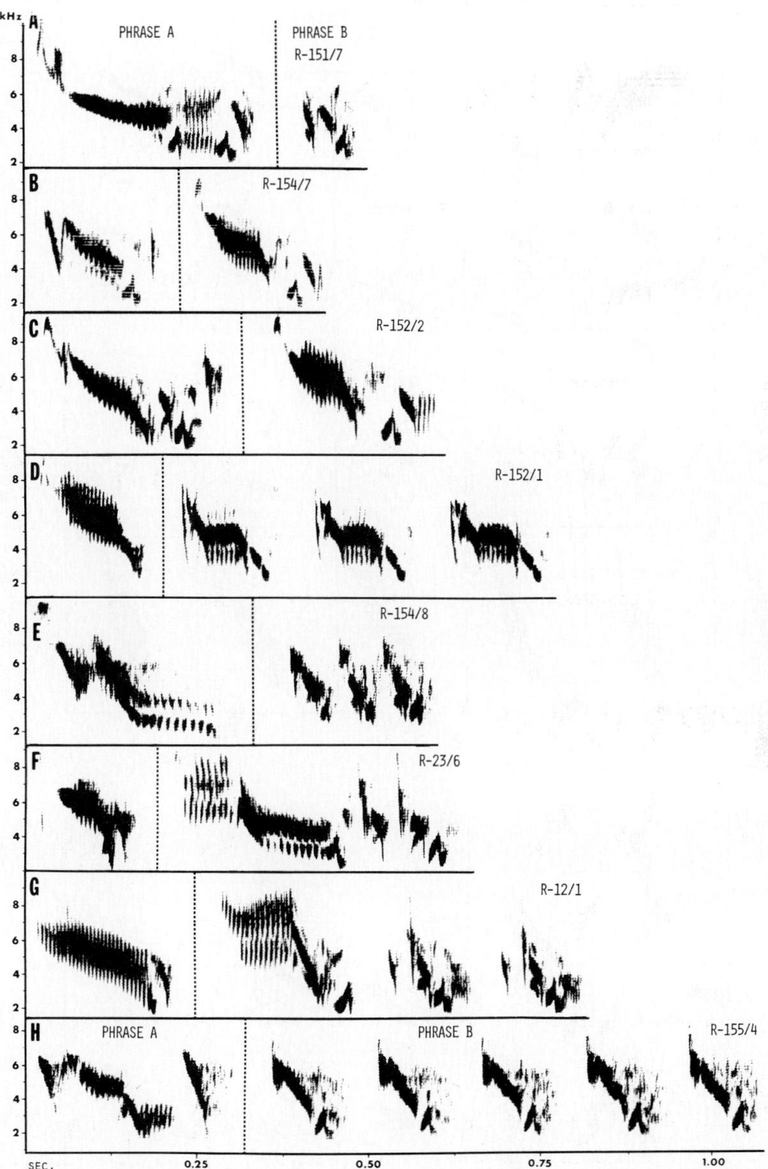

Fig. 156. Variation in the songs of *Certhidea olivacea* from Isla Santa Cruz, with phrases A and B delimited by broken vertical lines. These songs are two-parted (A-C), four-parted (D-G) and seven-parted (H).

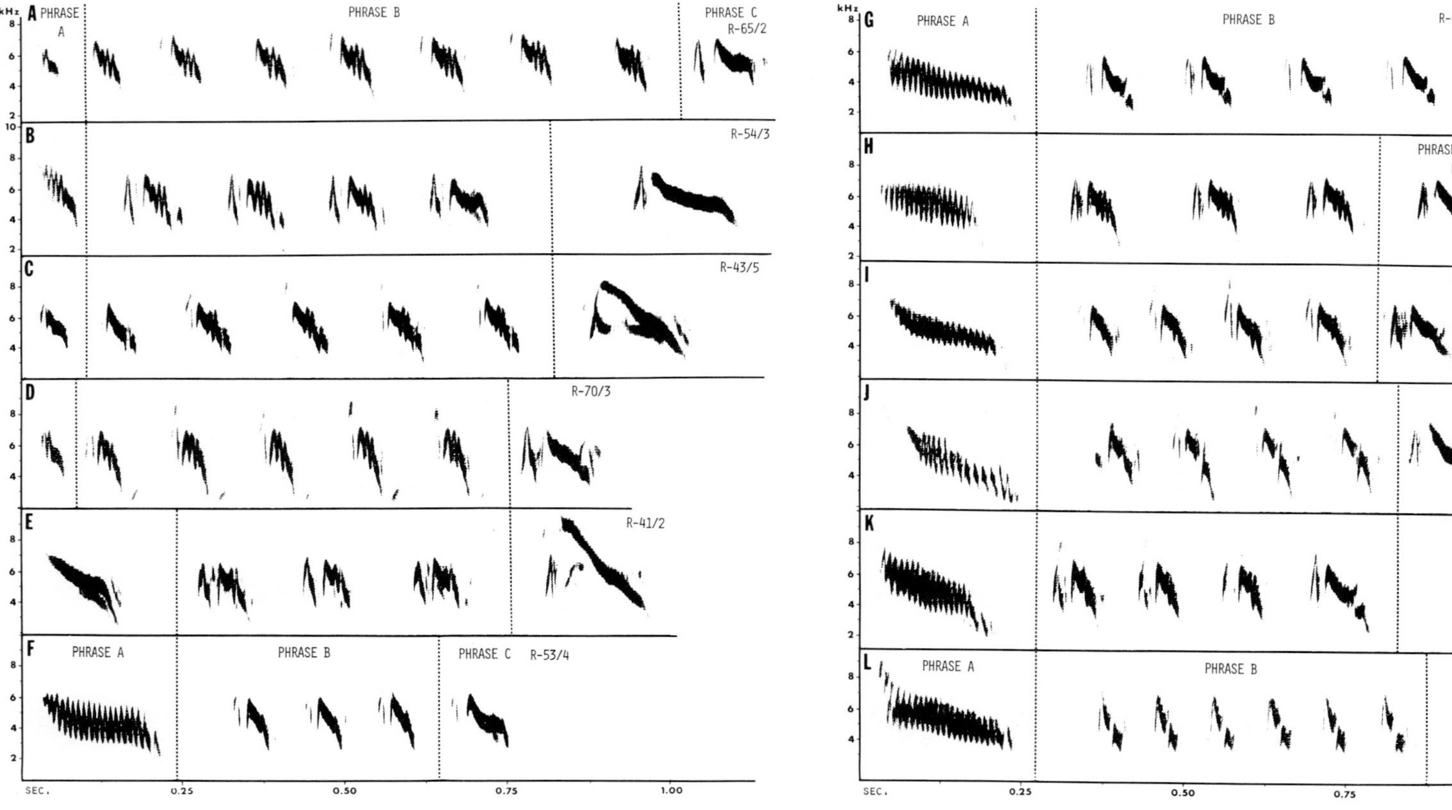

Fig. 157. Variation in the songs of *Certhidea olivacea* from Isla Española with phrases A, B, and C delimited by broken vertical lines.

Fig. 158. Variation in the songs of *Certhidea olivacea* from Isla Genovesa with phrases A, B, and C delimited by broken vertical lines.

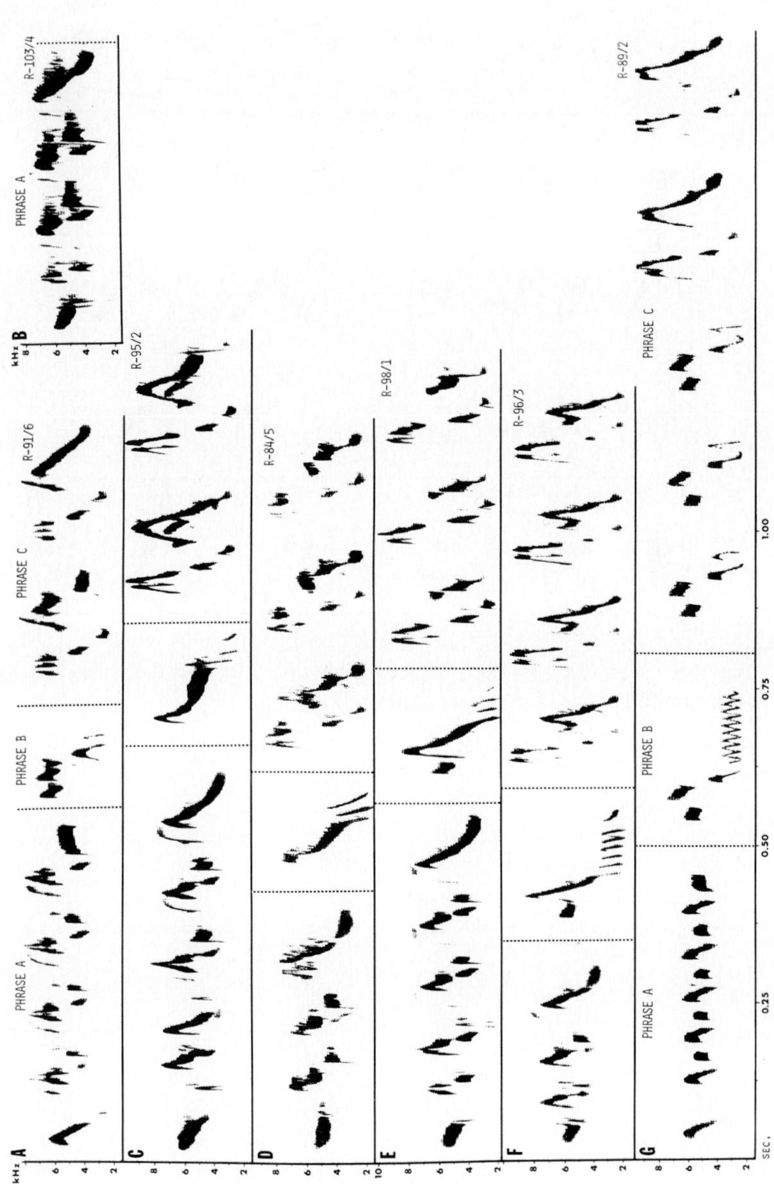

Fig. 159. Variation in the songs of *Certhidea olivacea* from Isla Genovesa with phrases A, B, and C delimited by broken vertical lines.

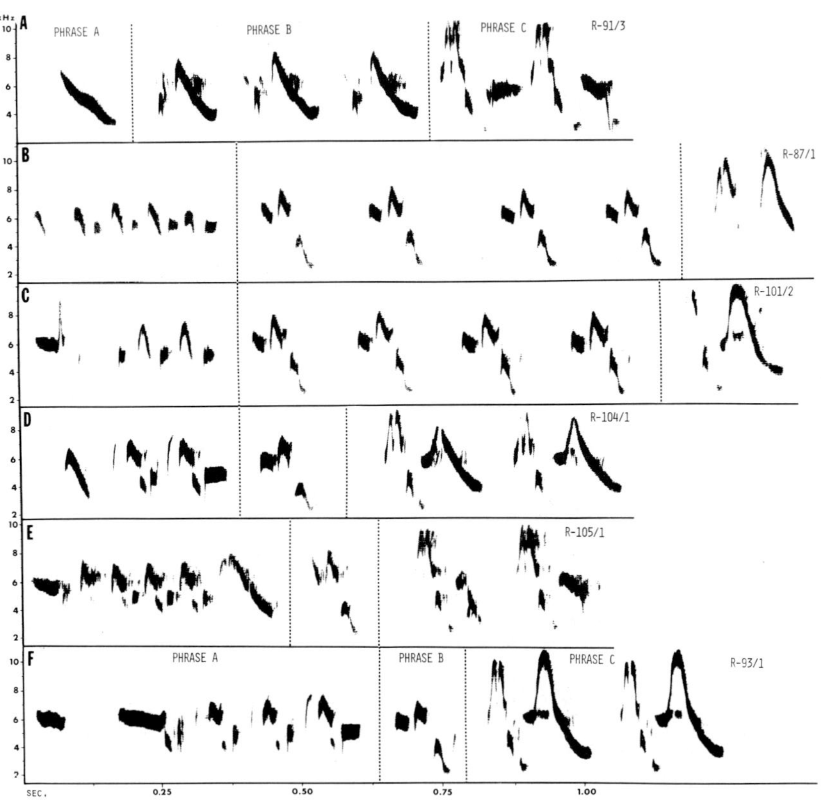

Fig. 160. Variation in the songs of *Certhidea olivacea* from Isla Genovesa with phrases A, B, and C delimited by broken vertical lines.

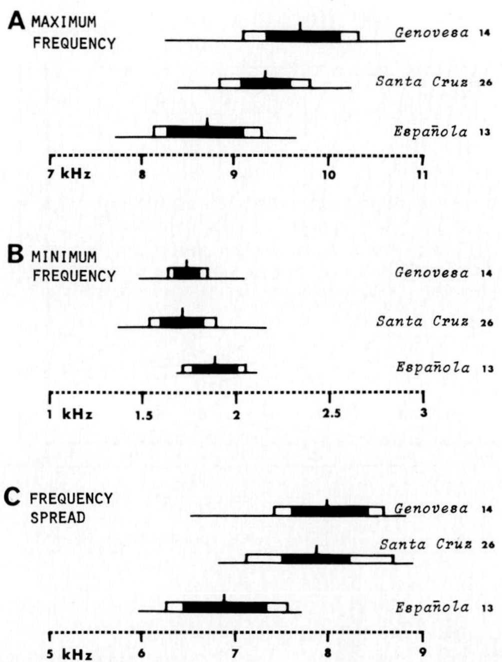

Fig. 161. Comparison of variation in frequency characteristics of the derived song of three island populations of *Certhidea olivacea*. Horizontal line represents observed range; open rectangles indicate standard deviation of the mean; black rectangles represent 95% confidence limits of the mean; vertical line indicates the mean. Number of specimens in each sample population is indicated after the name of the island.

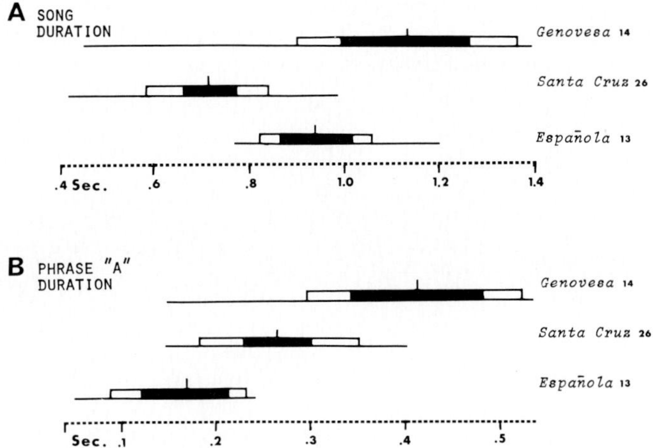

Fig. 162. Comparison of variation in duration of derived song (above) and phrase "A" below in three island populations of *Certhidea olivacea*. Horizontal line represents observed range; open rectangles indicate standard deviation of the mean; black rectangles represent 95% confidence limits of the mean; vertical line indicates the mean. Number of specimens in each sample population is indicated after the name of the island.

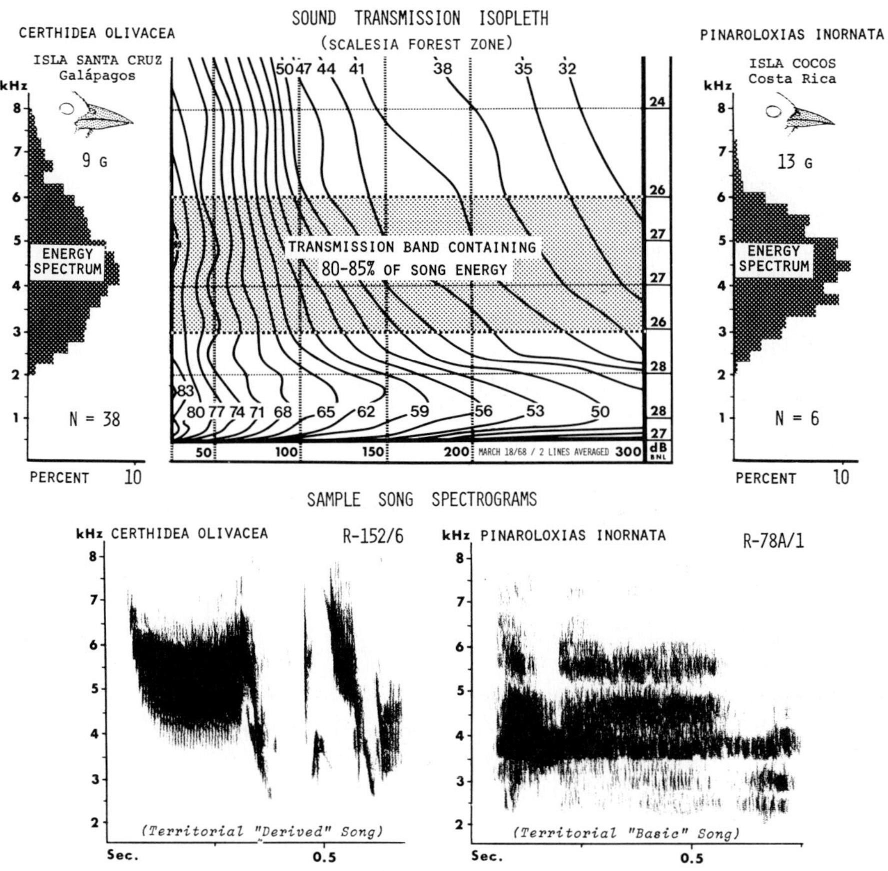

Fig. 163. Comparison of song energy spectra, body weights and song spectrograms of *Certhidea olivacea* and *Pinaroloxias inornata*. Frequency bandwidth containing 80-85% of song energy is projected onto the sound-transmission isopleth of the *Scalesia* forest, Isla Santa Cruz.

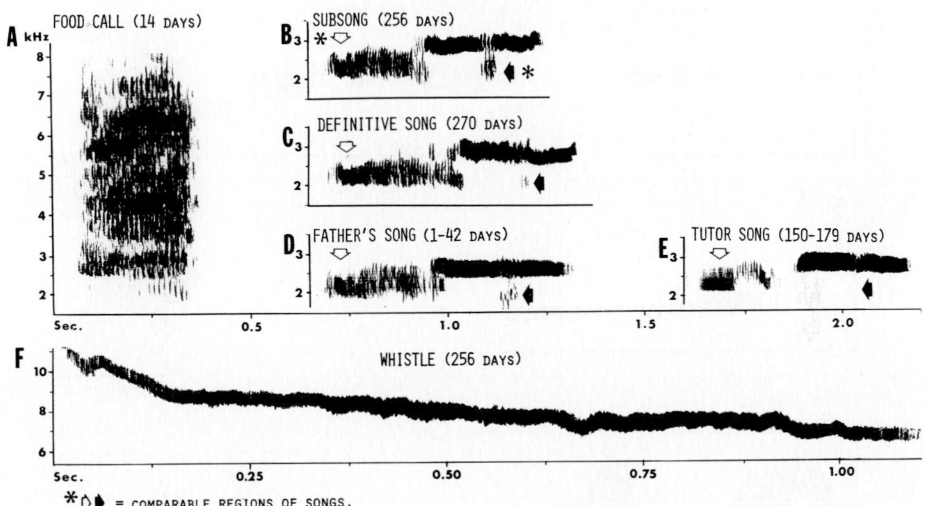

Fig. 164. Development of definitive song (C) of *Geospiza magnirostris* ("Junior"). Bird was reared by parents in aviary and exposed to father's song (D) up to age 42 days, and maintained thereafter in a sound isolation chamber. At age 150-179 days, bird was exposed to tutor-tape song (E). To facilitate comparisons, solid and open arrows indicate significant "landmarks" at similar points in time.

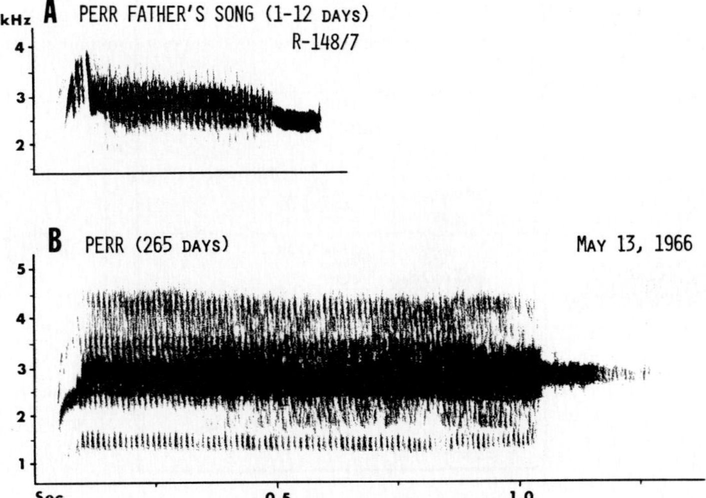

Fig. 165. Definitive song (B) of male *Geospiza difficilis* ("Perr"), which was hand-reared in sound isolation from day 13. Exposure to its father's song (A) occurred only up to 12 days of age.

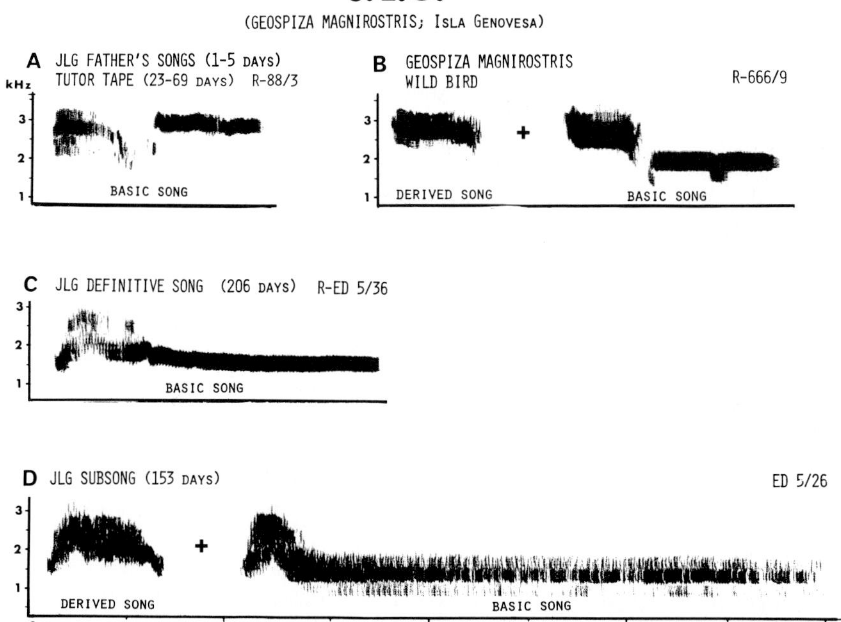

Fig. 166. Development of definitive song (C) in a male *Geospiza magnirostris* ("J.L.G."). Up to age six days, bird was exposed to father's song (A), after which it was placed in a sound isolation chamber where it was exposed to a tutor-tape recording of its father's song at age 23-69 days. At age 153 days, subsong (D) consisted of derived and basic songs (cf. Pattern F, Fig. 94). A definitive version of Pattern F song was recorded in the field (B).

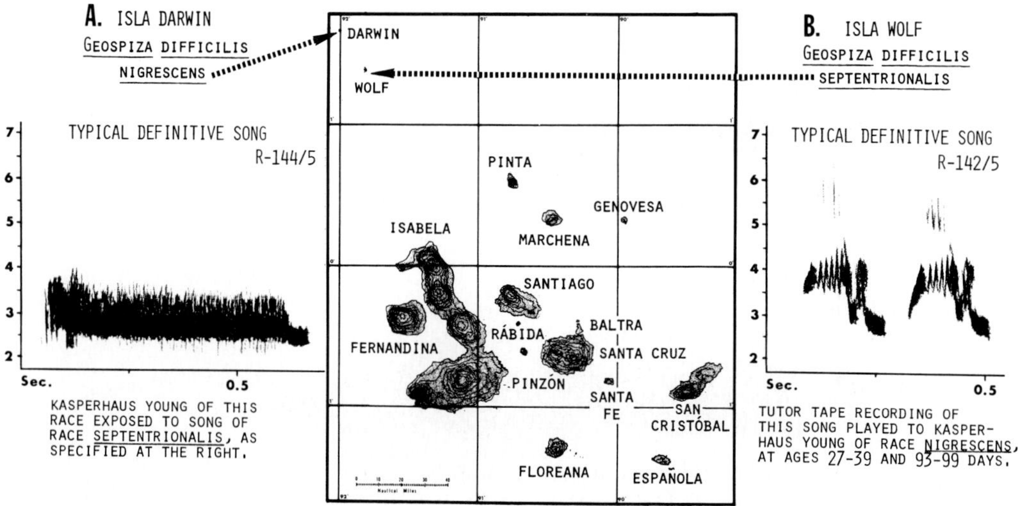

Fig. 168. Map of the Galapagos Archipelago showing locations of islas Darwin and Wolf, and sound spectrograms of typical male songs of *Geospiza difficilis negrescens* (A) and *G. d. septentrionalis* (B). Experimental conditions under which a hand-reared *G. d. nigrescens* ("Rollo") was raised are indicated below each spectrogram. See text for additional details.

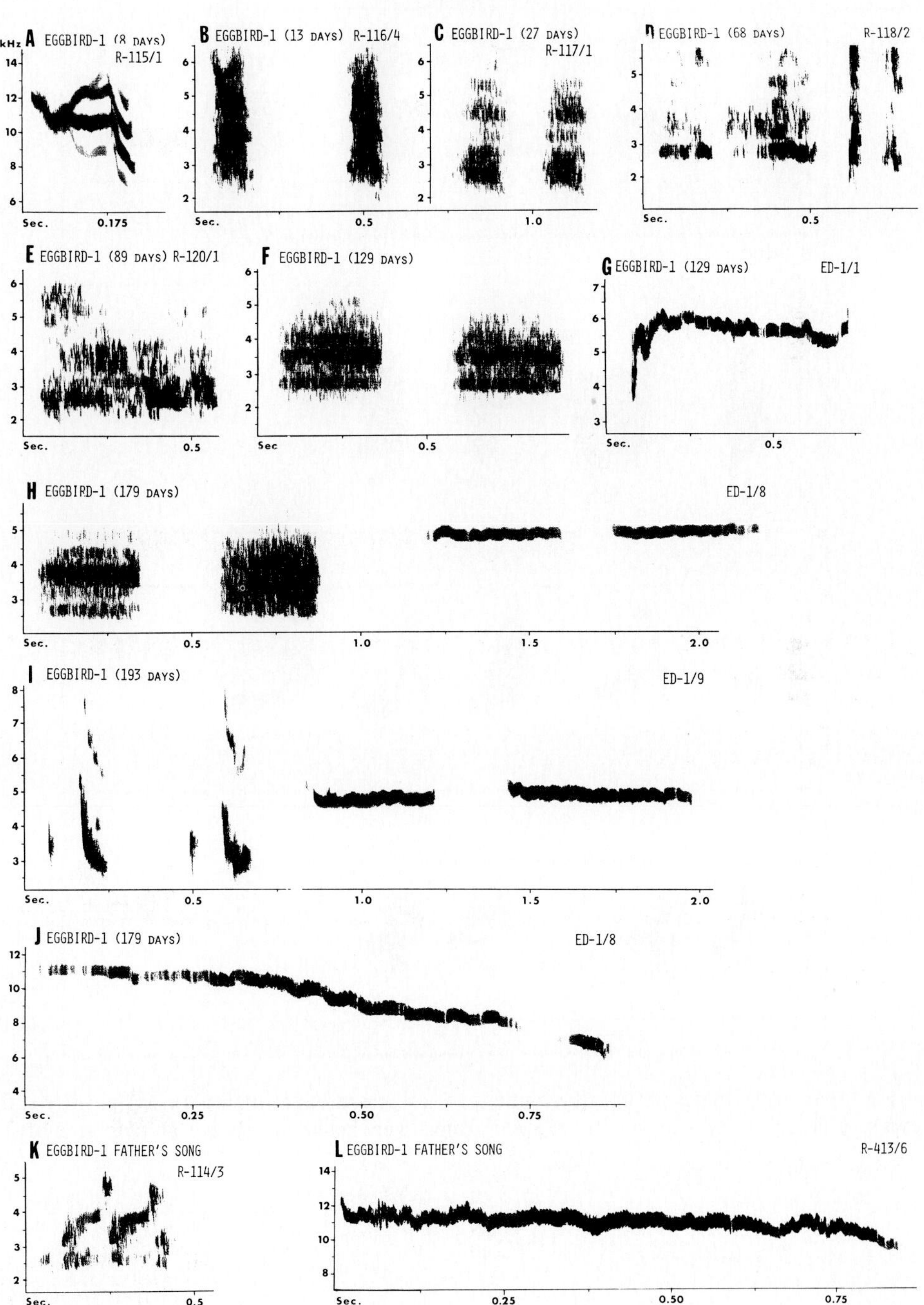

Fig. 167. Development of definitive song (H-J) in a male *Geospiza scandens* ("Eggbird-I"). Bird was orphaned at age 7 days and thereafter maintained in sound isolation without exposure to external song.

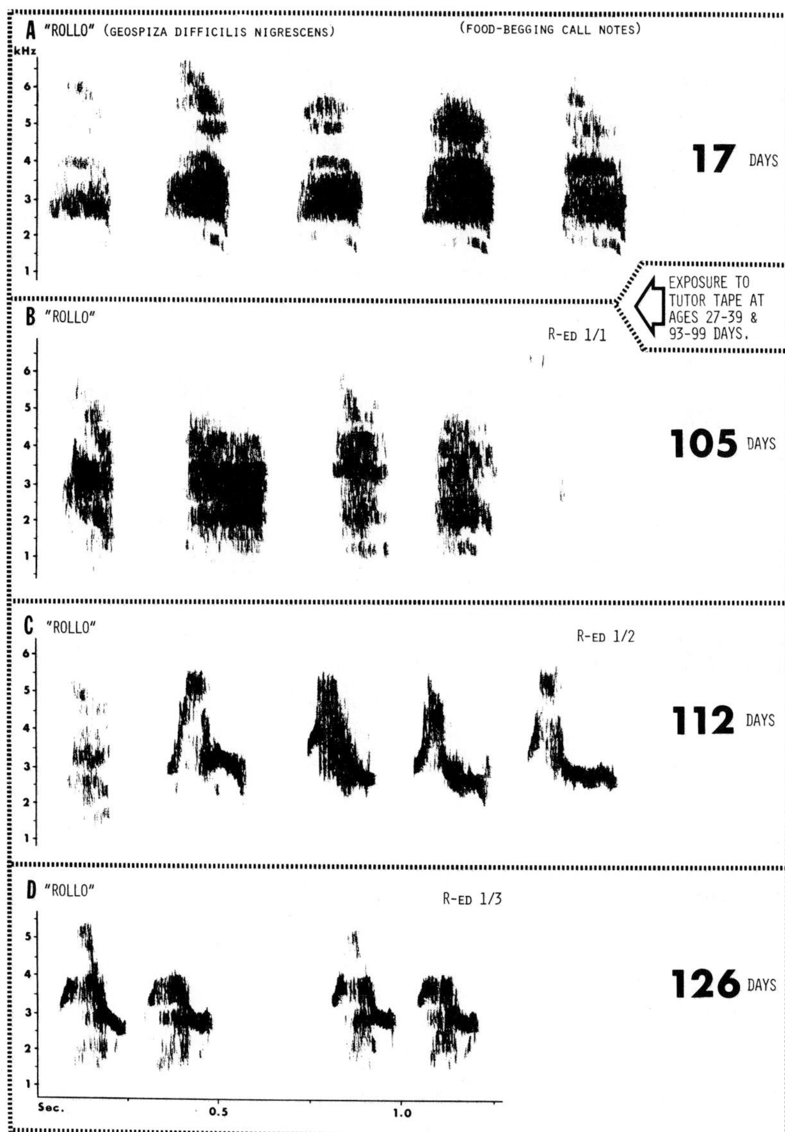

Fig. 169. Early stages in the development of song in an experimental male *Geospiza difficilis nigrescens* ("Rollo"). Ages at which song recordings were made are shown at right side of figure.

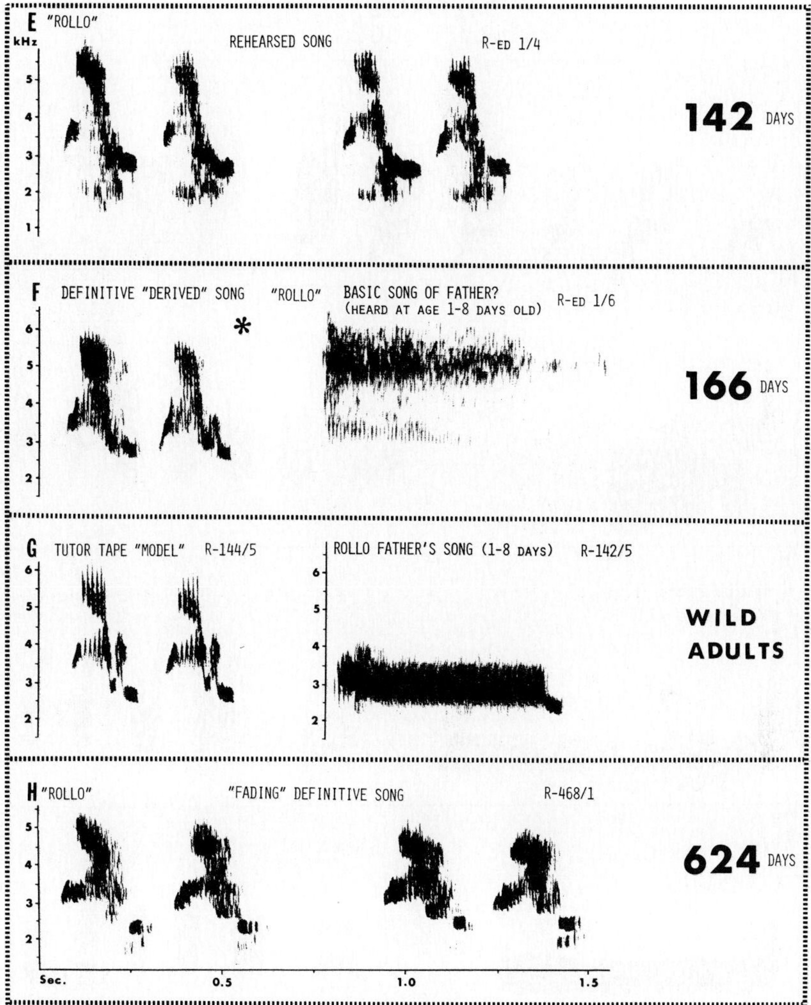

Fig. 169 (continued). Late stages in the development of song in an experimental male *Geospiza difficilis nigrescens* ("Rollo"). Ages at which song recordings were made are shown at right side of figure. Spectrograms of the tutor-tape model of Rollo's father are shown in G.

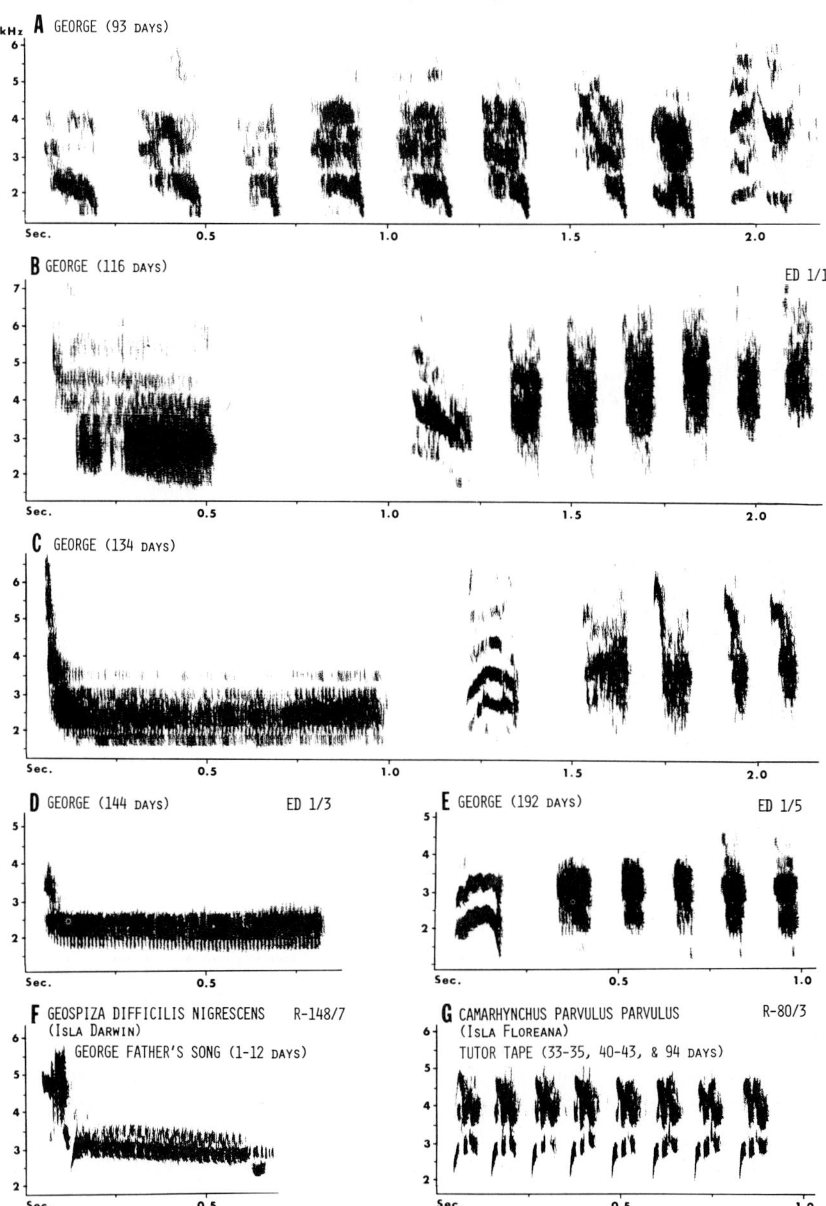

Fig. 170. Stages in the development of song in an experimental male *Geospiza difficilis nigrescens* ("George"). Ages at which song recordings were made are shown in the upper left hand corner of each spectrogram (A-F). Spectrograms of the songs of George's father and the tutor-tape model are shown in F and G, respectively, along with times of their exposure to George.

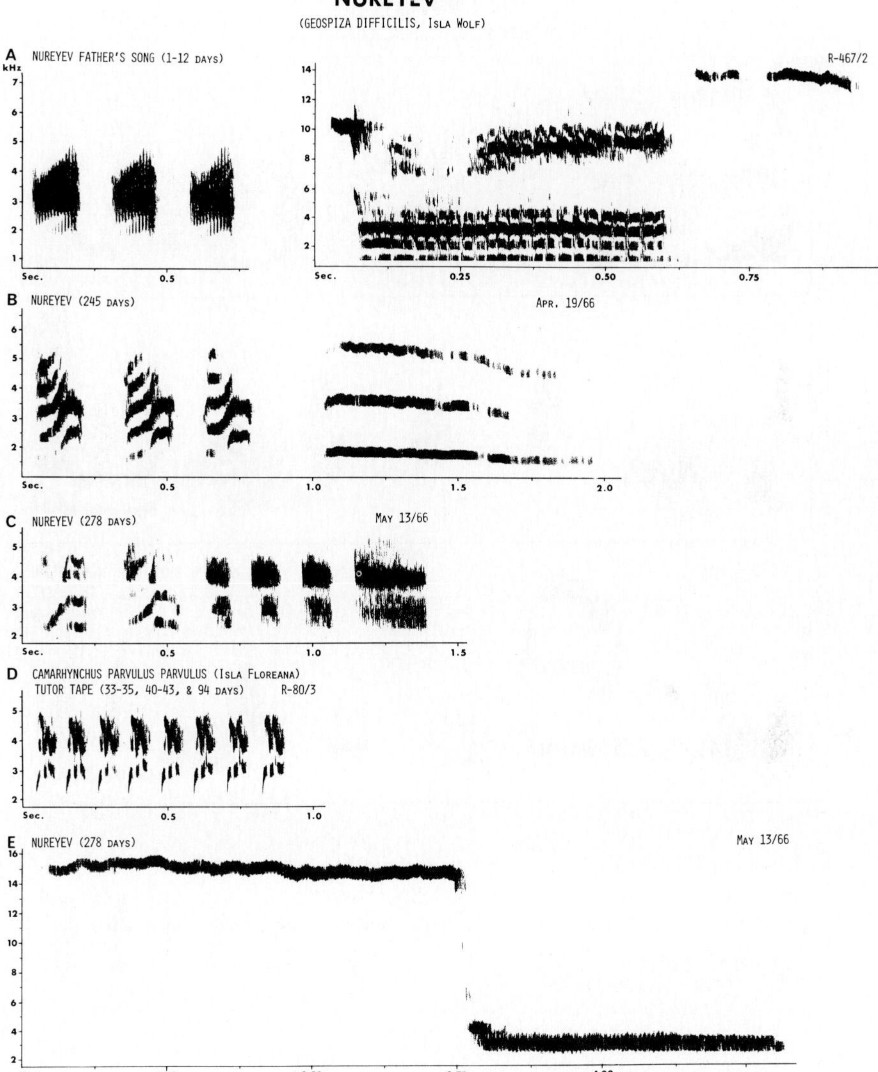

Fig. 171. Stages in the development of song in an experimental male *Geospiza difficilis septentrionalis* ("Nureyev"). Ages at which song recordings were made are indicated in parentheses after Nureyev's name (B, C, and E). Spectrograms of the songs of Nureyev's father and the tutor-tape model are shown in A and C, respectively, along with the times of their exposure to Nureyev.

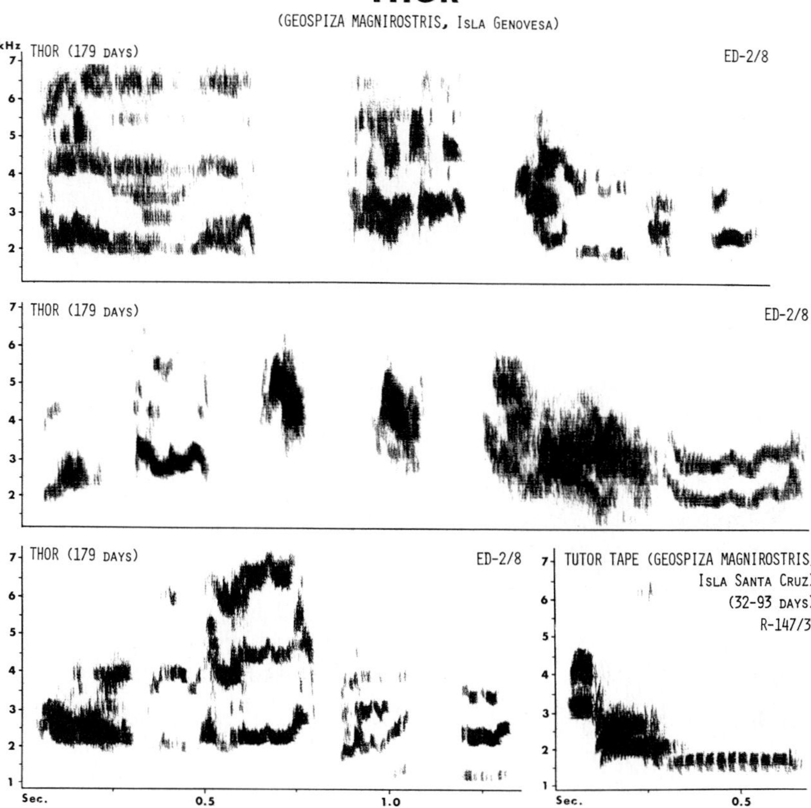

Fig. 172. Song of a female hand-reared *Geospiza magnirostris* ("Thor") at age 179 days, i.e. two days after spontaneous laying of first egg. Spectrograms of tutor-tape song and time of its exposure to Thor are shown at lower right. No testosterone propionate was administered.

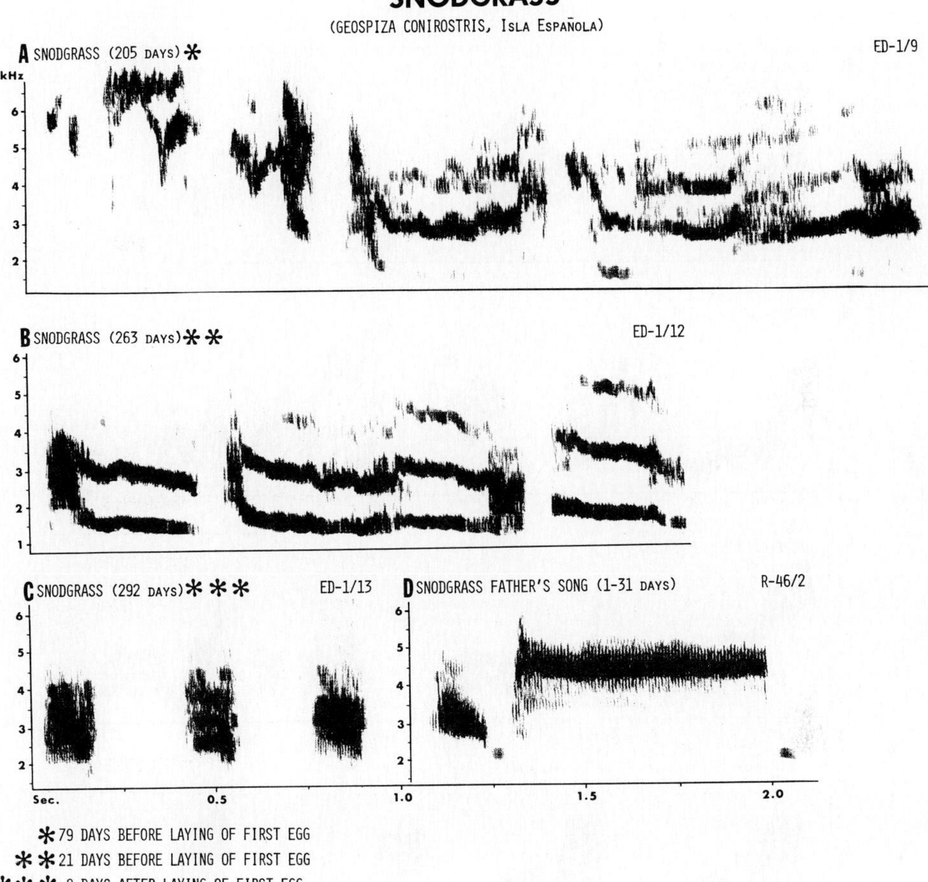

Fig. 173. Development of song in a female *Geospiza conirostris* ("Snodgrass") raised in captivity by wild parents from Isla Española. Songs A and B were recorded 79 and 21 days, respectively, before spontaneous laying of first egg. Song C was recorded 8 days after laying of first egg. Snodgrass was exposed to song of parental male (D) until age 31 days, after which she was placed in sound isolation. No testosterone propionate was administered.

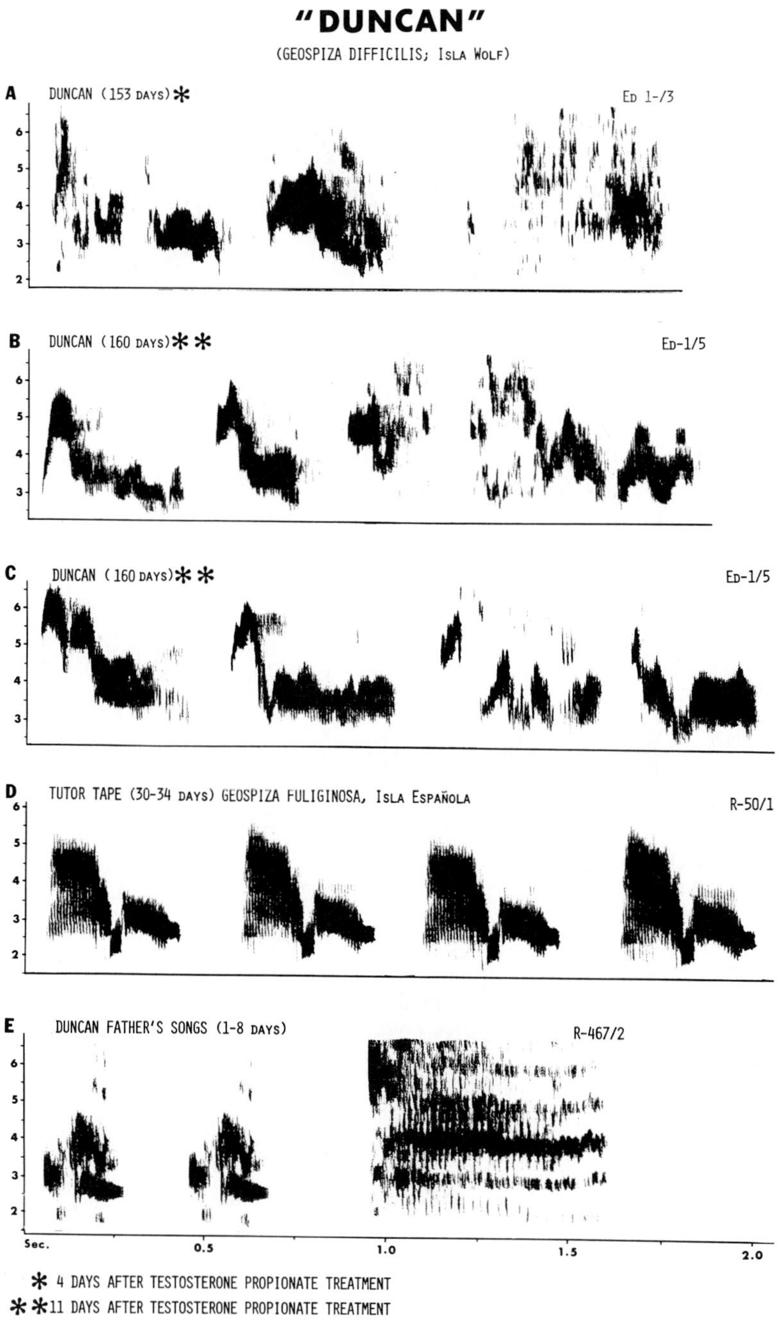

Fig. 174. Development of song in a female *Geospiza difficilis* ("Duncan") raised in captivity by wild parents from Isla Wolf. Songs in A, B, and C were the result of testosterone propionate treatment. Duncan was exposed to the song of parental male (E) to age 8 days, after which she was placed in sound isolation. From age 30 to 34 days she was exposed to tutor-tape song of *Geospiza fuliginosa*. Testosterone was administered at age 149 days.

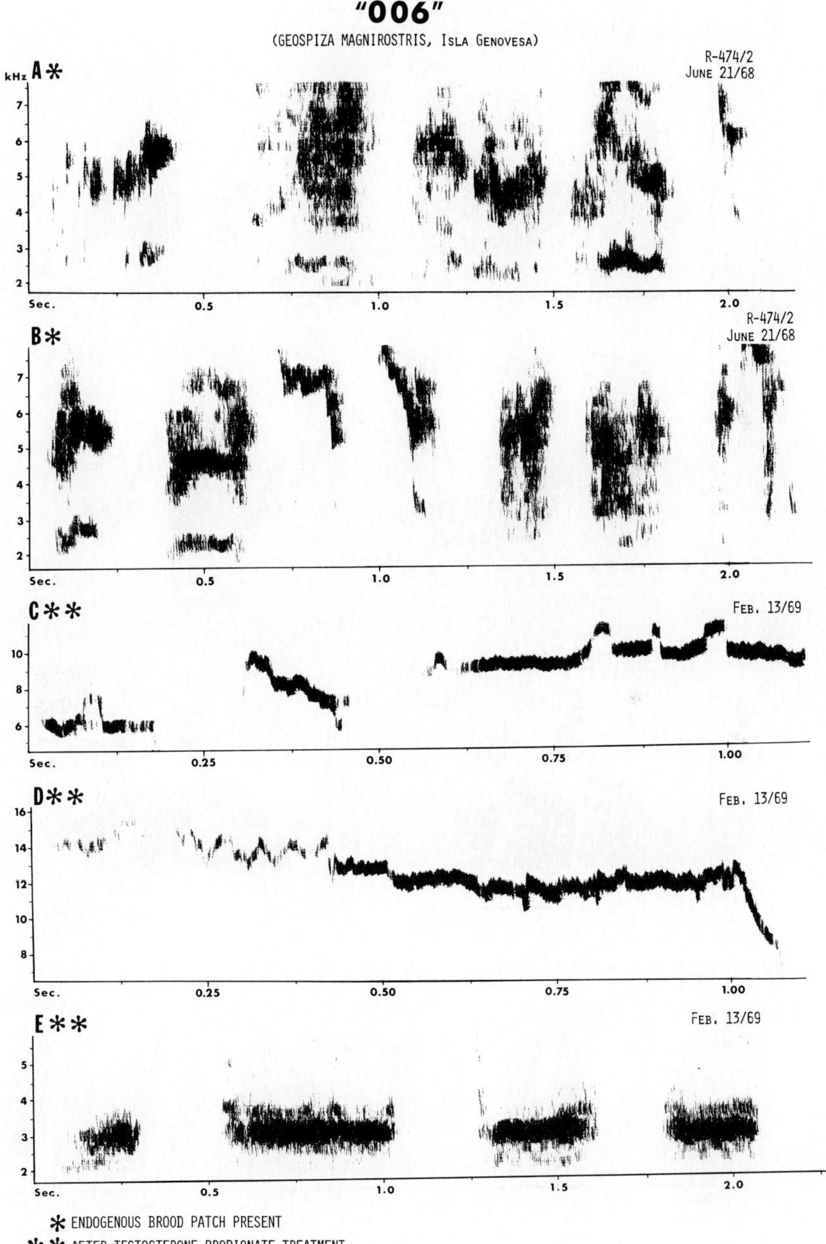

Fig. 175. Songs of a captive adult female *Geospiza magnirostris* ("006"). Vocalizations associated with the presence of an endogenous brood patch are shown in A and B. Those vocalizations induced by testosterone are shown in C, D, and E.

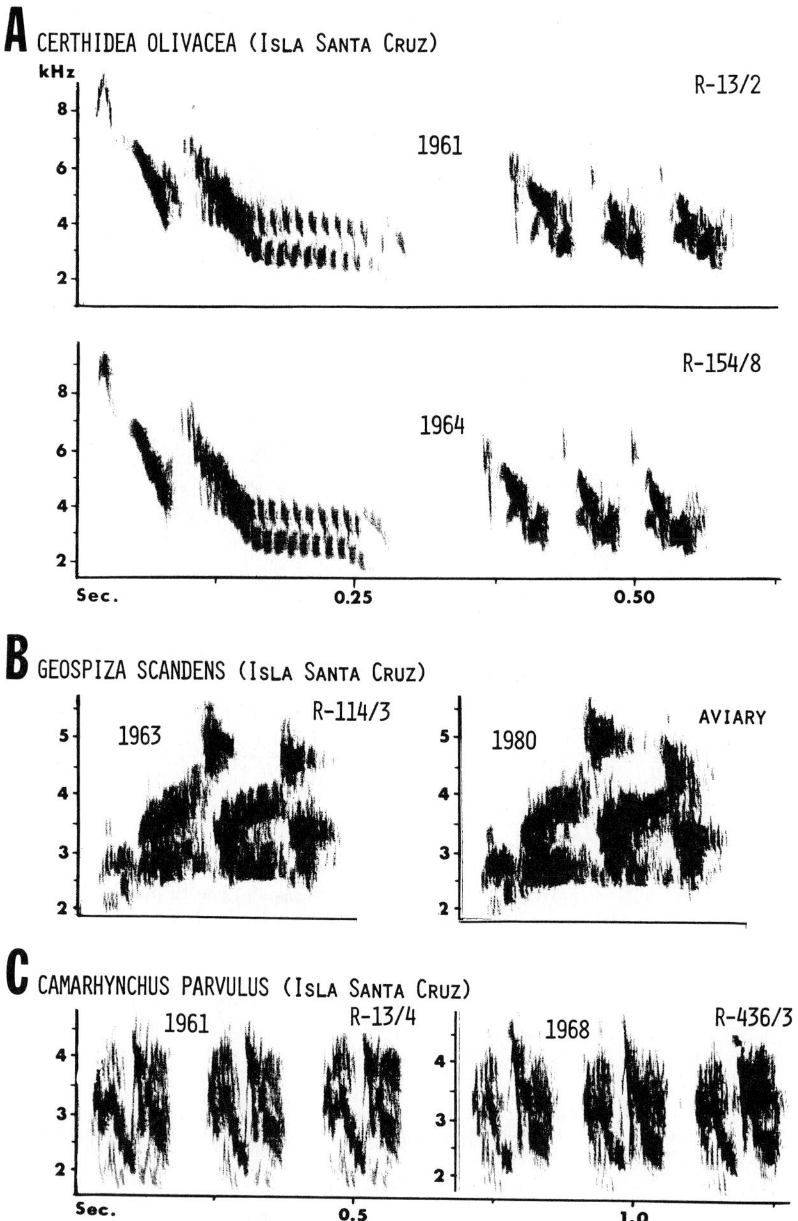

Fig. 176. Songs of *Certhidea olivacea, Geospiza scandens,* and *Camarhynchus parvulus*, recorded at intervals of 3, 17, and 7 years, respectively, and showing virtually no change with increasing age.

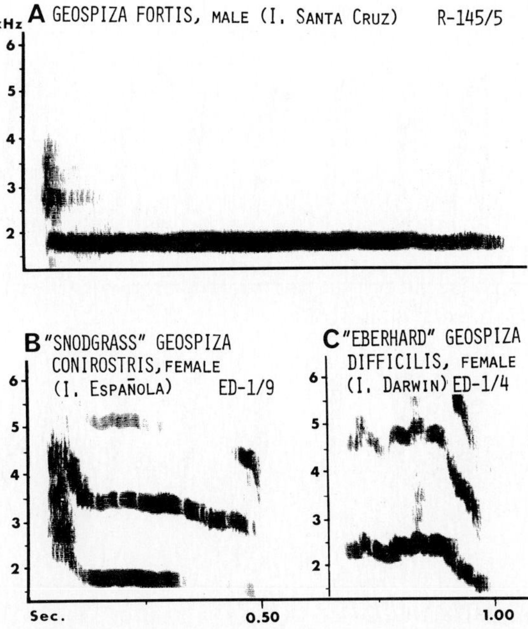

Fig. 177. Comparison of an atypical adult male song of *Geospiza fortis* (A), with female songs of parent-reared *Geospiza conirostris* (B), and a hand-reared *Geospiza difficilis* (C). See text for explanation.

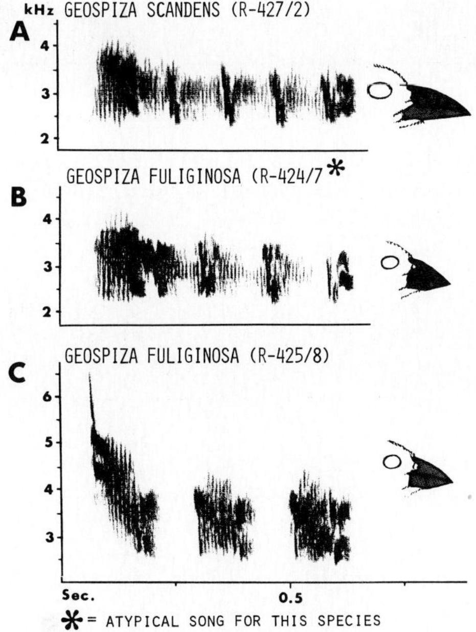

Fig. 179. Comparison of typical songs of *Geospiza scandens* (A) and *Geospiza fuliginosa* (C) with an atypical song of *Geospiza fuliginosa* (B). All songs recorded at northeast corner of Isla Santa Fé.

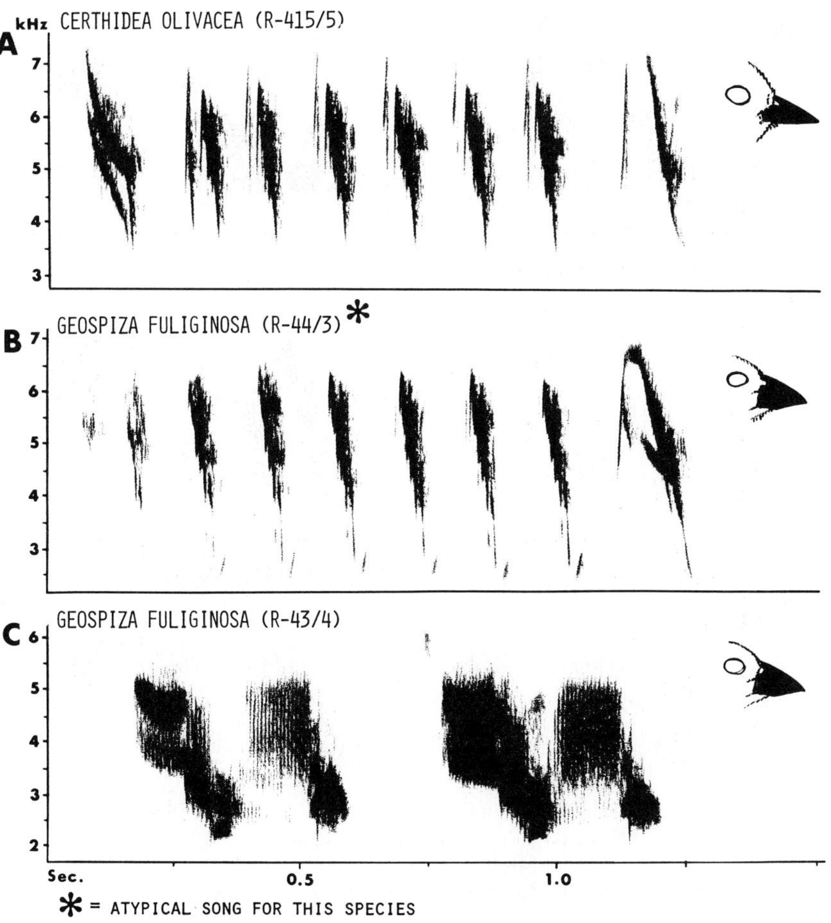

Fig. 178. Comparison of typical songs of *Certhidea olivacea* (A) and *Geospiza fuliginosa* (C) with atypical song of *Geospiza fuliginosa* (B). All songs recorded at Punta Suarez, Isla Española.

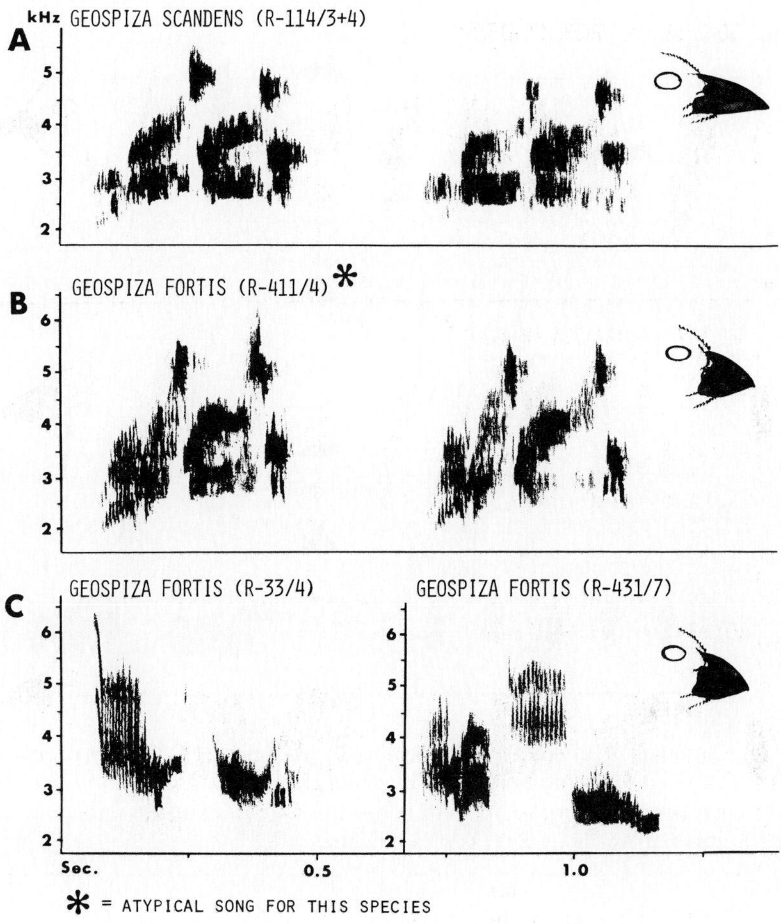

Fig. 180. Comparison of typical songs of *Geospiza scandens* (A) and *Geospiza fortis* (C) with an atypical song of *Geospiza fortis* (B). All songs recorded at Academy Bay, Isla Santa Cruz.

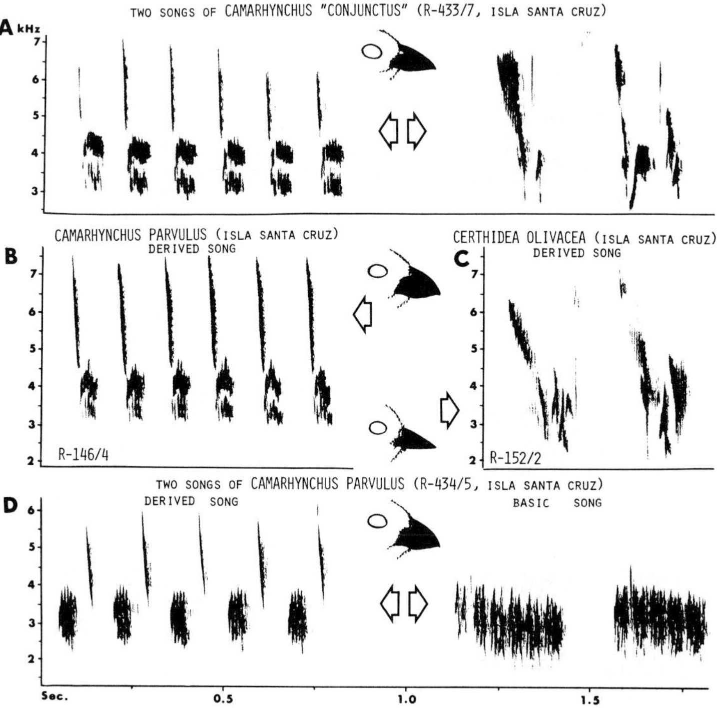

Fig. 181. Comparison of sound spectrograms of the bilingual "*Camarhynchus conjunctus*" (A), with typical derived songs of *Camarhynchus parvulus* (B) and *Certhidea olivacea* (C), and with the bilingual *Camarhynchus parvulus* (D). All songs were recorded in the inner coastal and lower transition zones north of Academy Bay, Isla Santa Cruz.

A PRESUMPTIVE PARENTS OF CAMARHYNCHUS "CONJUNCTUS"

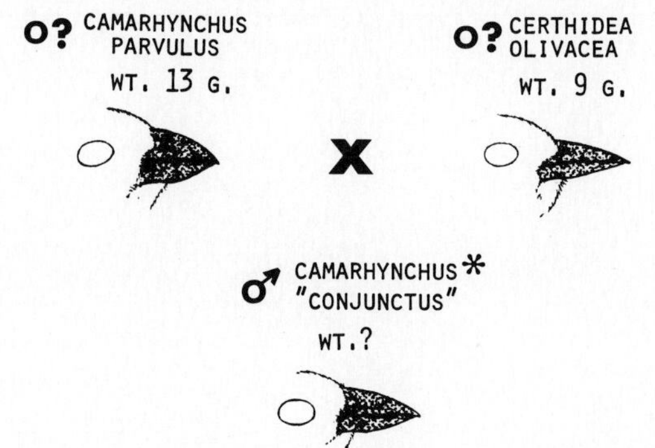

*1. Tawny colored throat feathers like CERTHIDEA.
2. Intermediate bill depth and wing length.
3. Sings typical songs of both parental species.

B KNOWN BACK-CROSS OF CAMARHYNCHUS "CONJUNCTUS"

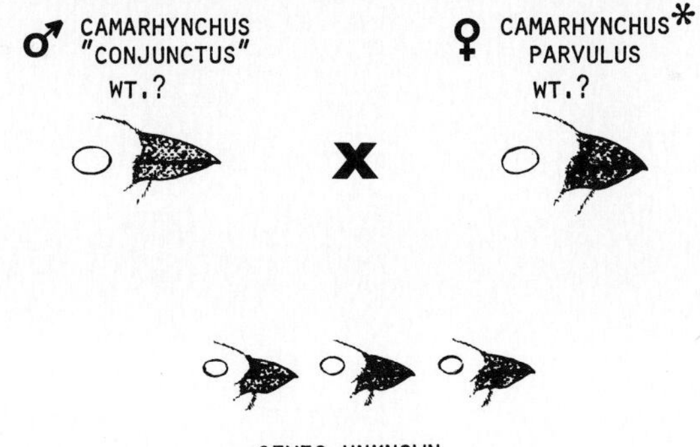

*Female larger than male in all known dimensions except bill length.

Fig. 182. Presumptive parents (A) and known back-cross (B) of hybrid "*Camarhynchus conjunctus*." See text for explanation.

BIOSYSTEMATICS OF THE NATIVE RODENTS OF THE GALAPAGOS ARCHIPELAGO, ECUADOR

JAMES L. PATTON AND MARK S. HAFNER[1]
Museum of Vertebrate Zoology, University of California, Berkeley, CA 94720

The native rodent fauna of the Galapagos Archipelago consists of seven species belonging to the generalized Neotropical rice rat (oryzomyine) stock of the family Cricetidae. These species comprise three rather distinct assemblages, each of which is varyingly accorded generic or subgeneric rank: (1) *Oryzomys* (*sensu stricto*), including *O. galapagoensis* [known only from Isla San Cristóbal] and *O. bauri* [from Isla Santa Fe]; (2) *Nesoryzomys*, including *N. narboroughi* [from Isla Fernandina], *N. swarthi* [from Isla Santiago], *N. darwini* [from Isla Santa Cruz], and *N. indefessus* [from both Islas Santa Cruz and Baltra]; and (3) *Megalomys curioi* [from Isla Santa Cruz]. *Megalomys* is only known from subfossil material and will not be treated here. Four of the remaining six species are now probably extinct as only *O. bauri* and *N. narboroughi* are known currently from viable populations.

The time and pattern of radiation, and the phylogenetic relationships of *Oryzomys* and *Nesoryzomys* are assessed by karyological, biochemical, and anatomical investigations of the two extant species, and by multivariate morphometric analyses of existing museum specimens of all taxa. These data suggest the following: (a) *Nesoryzomys* is a very unique entity and should be recognized at the generic level; (b) there were at least two separate invasions of the islands with *Nesoryzomys* representing an early entrant followed considerably later by *Oryzomys* (*s.s.*); (c) both taxa of *Oryzomys* are quite recent immigrants and are probably derived from *O. xantheolus* of the coastal Peruvian river valleys, or a common ancestor; (d) the origin of *Nesoryzomys* is ambiguous at the moment; (e) the three large forms of *Nesoryzomys* (*narboroughi, swarthi*, and *indefessus*) are best considered races of a single species, which differ primarily in pelage color; and (f) similarly, *O. galapagoensis* and *O. bauri* should probably be considered conspecific.

The fauna of the Galapagos Islands has certainly represented more of a cornerstone to the field of systematic and evolutionary biology than that of any other comparable area in the world. Since the initial visit by Darwin in 1835, countless scientific investigations have detailed the uniqueness and importance of this evolutionary theater. It is somewhat surprising, therefore, to note that the native mammalian fauna has received only cursory attention, an attention which has been almost exclusively in the form of taxonomic treatments. The list of native mammals includes but 12 species (2 bats, 3 pinnipeds, and 7 rodents). Although this complement is somewhat unremarkable when compared to other faunal elements of the archipelago, the rodent complex is more diverse than that on any similar group of oceanic islands and does include two major endemic taxa.

The seven species of native rodents are members of the rice rat, or oryzomyine, complex of the Neotropical assemblage of the family Cricetidae. The Galapagos species have been varyingly placed into one (*Oryzomys* [*s.l.*]) to three genera (*Oryzomys* [*s.s.*], 2 species; *Nesoryzomys*, 4 species; and *Megalomys*, 1 species) within this larger group. Beyond the original description of each and a few brief notes on natural history (e.g. Brosset 1963; Rosero Posso 1975), our knowledge of

[1] Present address: Museum of Zoology, Louisiana State University, Baton Rouge, LA 70893

this fauna is indeed poor. No comprehensive attempt has been made to assess the evolutionary relationships of these species, both among themselves and to their potential mainland relatives. The purpose of the present effort is to review these relationships and to develop an understanding of the course of evolution among the Galapagoan species.

History of Discovery of Galapagos Rodents

The first species from the Archipelago was collected by Charles Darwin in 1835 from Isla San Cristóbal (= Chatham) and was described as *Mus galapagoensis* by Waterhouse in 1839. J. A. Allen described a second species in 1892, *O. bauri* from Isla Santa Fe (= Barrington); this was followed in 1899 by Thomas' description of *O. indefessus* from Isla Santa Cruz (= Indefatigable). In 1904, Edmund Heller erected a new genus (*Nesoryzomys*) to include *O. indefessus* Thomas and another new species, from Isla Fernandina (= Narborough), which he named *N. narboroughi.* Two additional species of *Nesoryzomys* were added to the faunal list of the islands after Heller's report: *N. darwini* was described by Osgood in 1929 from Isla Santa Cruz; and *N. swarthi* from Isla Santiago (= James) was described by Orr in 1938. The only addition to the rodent fauna subsequently has been the discovery of subfossil remains of a giant cricetine from Isla Santa Cruz, described as *Megalomys curioi* by Niethammer in 1964. The distribution of these species is given in Fig. 1.

The genus *Oryzomys* is a widespread, highly diverse taxon ranging from the southern United States to Tierra del Fuego. It is most diverse in tropical habitats, and many workers consider it to represent the stem stock of all Neotropical cricetines in the Tribe Sigmodontini [e.g. Hershkovitz 1962]. *Nesoryzomys* is endemic to the Galapagos, but *Megalomys* has the curious distribution of both Galapagoan and Lesser Antillean members but with no known mainland representatives.

The status of the genus *Nesoryzomys* has been open to some debate since it was initially proposed. The characters distinguishing members of this group from other oryzomyines center on the elongate, narrow snout and hourglass-shaped interorbital region (when viewed dorsally) with rounded frontal edges. In contrast, the typical oryzomyine condition is one of a short, broad rostrum with a strongly directed, divergent interorbital region, the edges of which form a supraorbital bead or shelf (Fig. 2). While a cranial demarcation between Galapagoan species in these characters is quite strong (e.g. *galapagoensis* and *bauri* versus *indefessus, narboroughi, darwini* and *swarthi*), several authors (notably Goldman [1918]) have remarked that the alleged generic characters of *Nesoryzomys* are " . . . not widely different from some of the continental species of *Oryzomys*" (Goldman 1918:13). Hence, Ellerman (1941:340) and Hershkovitz (1962:84) list *Nesoryzomys* as a subgenus of *Oryzomys* while De Beaufort (1963) regards it as generally distinct. A thorough analysis of existing specimens relative to both the status of *Nesoryzomys* and its relationship with other oryzomyine genera or subgenera has never been attempted. Below we summarize the existing data base relative to these questions, a data base that is frustratingly incomplete because of the apparent extinction of four of the species in question. No attention will be given here to the subfossil *Megalomys curioi.* A detailed synopsis of the status and relationships of this form is being prepared by Dr. Clayton Ray, Division of Paleobiology, National Museum of Natural History, Washington, D. C.

MATERIALS AND METHODS

Specimens examined consisted primarily of conventional museum study skins and skulls supplemented by soft anatomical structures (e.g. glandes penes, male reproductive tracts, stomachs) where available. Details as to methodology and specifics as to number and kinds of specimens examined for those analyses other than standard morphometric approaches are given in their appropriate sections, below.

Twenty-eight cranial and external characters were quantified for each specimen: (1) total length [ToL]; (2) tail length [TaL]; (3) hind foot length [HF]; (4) ear height [E]; (5) occipito-nasal length [ON]; (6) basilar length of Hensel [BaL]; (7) breadth of braincase [BB]; (8) least interorbital width [IOC]; (9) greatest zygomatic breadth [ZB]; (10) rostral width [RW]; (11) rostral length [RL]; (12) width across maxillary tooth rows [MTRW]; (13) diastema length [DL]; (14) maxillary tooth row length [MTRL]; (15) bullar length [BuL]; (16) rostral depth [RD]; (17) cranial depth [CD]; (18) mandibular tooth row length [mTRL]; (19) ramus height at M^1 [RH]; (20) mandibular height from angle to condyle [ACH]; (21) braincase length [BCL]; (22) zygomatic plate width [ZPW]; (23) incisive foramen length [IFL]; (24) mestopterygoid fossa width [MPFW]; (25) mesopterygoid fossa length [MPFL]; (26) M^1 length [1L]; (27) M^2 length [2L]; (28) M^3 length [3L].

Measurements (1) through (4) were taken from the specimen label; measurements (25) through (28) were taken with the aid of a binocular measuring microscope; all others were taken with dial calipers.

In addition to the 28 mensural characters listed above, 23 qualitative characters of the skin and skull were scored for each specimen. Two to four states were recognized for every character with each state given a serial numerical score. The characters, states within, and scores are as follows:

Ventral view of skull. (1) shape of incisive foramina: teardrop shaped with lateral margins expanded posteriorly [1], lateral margins evenly rounded [2], or lateral margins straight and parallel [3]; (2) position of incisive foramina relative to M^1: posterior margin ends well anterior to M^1 [1] or posterior margin extends to or beyond anterior margin of M^1 [2]; (3) ventral width of maxillary septum of incisive foramina: very narrow [1], moderately broad [2], or very broad [3]; (4) relative size of ethmoid portion of incisive foramina septum: less than 1/2 length [1] or greater than 1/2 length [2]; (5) condition of posterior palatine pits: large and deep [1], large and shallow [2], or small and shallow [3]; (6) position of mesopterygoid fossa relative to M^3: anterior margin extends to or beyond M^3 [1] or anterior margin does not extend to M^3 [2]; (7) condition of sphenopalatine vacuity: open [1], mostly closed [2], or completely closed [3]; (8) relative size of foramen ovale (FO) and medial lacerate foramen (MLF): FO larger than MLF [1], FO and MLF subequal in size [2], or FO smaller than MLF [3]; (9) condition of petrotympanic fissure: completely closed, no visible fissure [1], moderately open [2], or greatly enlarged [3].

Lateral view of skull. (10) posterior shape of cranium: lambdoidal crest square, occiput flat [1], lambdoidal crest square, occiput rounded [2], or lambdoidal crest and occiput evenly rounded [3]; (11) prominence of anterior zygomatic plate: very prominent [1], moderately prominent [2], or not prominent [3]; (12) anterior profile of anterior zygomatic plate: square [1], weakly rounded [2], or strongly rounded [3].

Dorsal view of skull. (13) shape of supraorbital region: margins rounded [1] or margins divergent posteriorly [2]; (14) condition of supraorbital ridges: sharply shelved [1], beaded [2], or rounded [3].

Hind foot. (15) nature of hair covering claws: not covering claws [1] or covering claws [2]; (16) general foot proportions: short and broad [1], long and narrow [2], or long and broad [3]; (17) relative length of hallux: not reaching base of digit 2 [1], reaching base of digit 2 [2], or extending beyond base of digit 2 [3], (18) hairiness of heel: naked [1] or clothed in hair [2]; (19) presence of digital webbing; present [1] or absent [2].

Tail. (20) color pattern: bicolored [1] or unicolored [2]; (21) degree of hair covering: essentially naked [1], moderately haired with scales visible [2], or well haired with scales hidden [3]; (22) condition of scales: heavy and large [1] or light and small [2].

Pelage. (23) general quality of pelage: guard hairs not discernibly present [1], underfur soft and woolly with guard hairs present [2], underfur long and woolly with guard hairs present [3], or guard hairs thickly present, long, and somewhat bristle-like [4].

Samples of all Galapagoan species except *O. galapagoensis* (Waterhouse) were available for study. In addition, species representative of most other major oryzomyine genera and subgenera have been examined. Listed below are the 22 sampled taxa (operational taxonomic units, or OTU's) used in the morphometric analyses, along with general locality data and number of

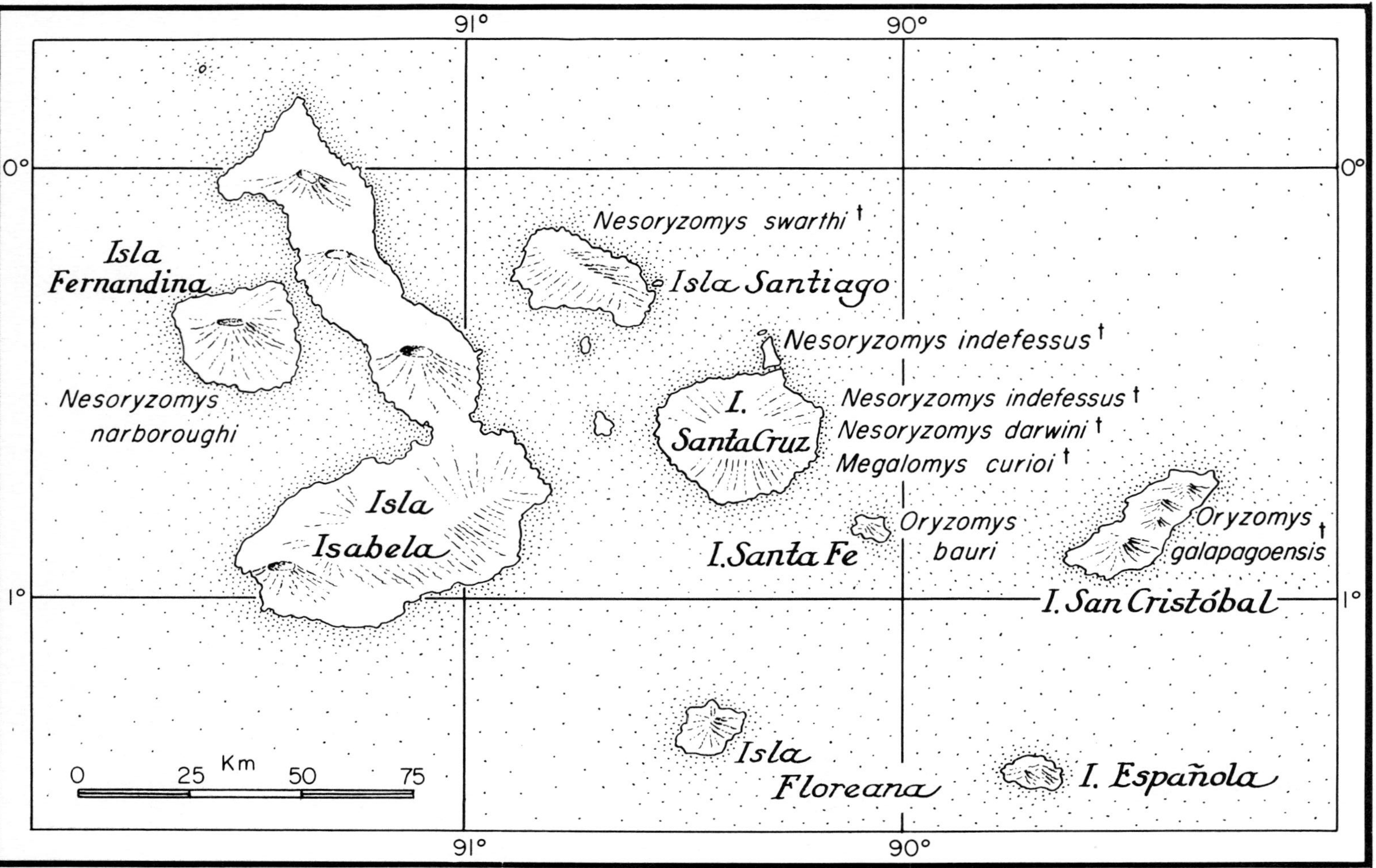

Fig. 1. Distribution of native rodents in the Galapagos Archipelago, Ecuador. A cross next to a name indicates an extinct taxon.

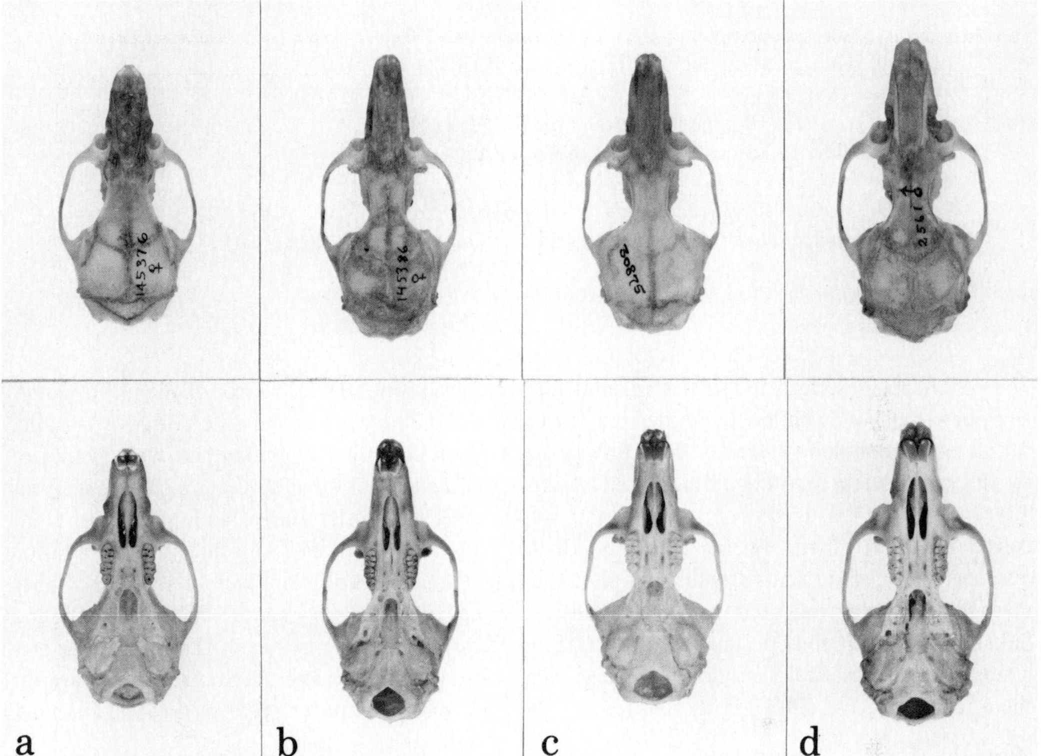

Fig. 2. Dorsal and ventral views of crania of four taxa of Galapagos rodents: (a) *Oryzomys bauri* J. A. Allen (♀, MVZ 145376); (b) *Nesoryzomys narboroughi* Heller (♀, MVZ 145386); (c) *Nesoryzomys indefessus* (Thomas) (♀, FMNH 30875); and (d) *Nesoryzomys swarthi* (♂, CAS 2561).

specimens available. All non-Galapagoan specimens are housed in the Museum of Vertebrate Zoology, University of California, Berkeley. More complete locality information with a list of all Galapagos specimens examined, catalogue numbers, and museum repositories is given in Appendix I.

Nesoryzomys

(1) *N. narboroughi* Heller: Isla Fernandina, Galapagos (57).
(2) *N. indefessus* (Thomas): Isla Santa Cruz (51) and Isla Baltra (25), Galapagos.
(3) *N. darwini* Osgood: Isla Santa Cruz, Galapagos (5).
(4) *N. swarthi* Orr: Isla Santiago, Galapagos (4).

Oryzomys (*Oryzomys*)

(5) *O. bauri* Allen: Isla Santa Fe, Galapagos (31).
(6) *O. xantheolus* Thomas: Depto. Arequipa, Peru (11).
(7) *O. keaysi* Allen: Depto. Puno, Peru (2).
(8) *O. albigularis* (Tomes): Deptos. Amazonas and Cajamarca, Peru (3).
(9) *O. palustris palustris* (Harlan): South Carolina, USA (3).
(10) *O. palustris peninsulae* Thomas: Baja California Sur, Mexico (3).
(11) *O. palustris regillus* Goldman: Michoacan, Mexico (3).
(12) *O. capito* (Olfers): Depto. Loreto, Peru (6).
(13) *O. yunganus* Thomas: Depto. Loreto, Peru (1).
(14) *O. nitidus* (Thomas): Depto. Loreto, Peru (5).

Oryzomys (*Melanomys*)

(15) *O. caliginosus* (Tomes): Cauca and Valle, Colombia (2).

Oryzomys (*Microryzomys*)
(16) *O. minutus* (Tomes): Depto. Ancash, Peru (3).
Oryzomys (*Oecomys*)
(17) *O. concolor* (Wagner): Depto. Loreto, Peru (1).
(18) *O. bicolor* (Tomes): Depto. Loreto, Peru (3).
Oryzomys (*Oligorozymys*)
(19) *O. longicaudatus longicaudatus* (Bennett): Santiago Prov., Chile (2).
(20) *O. longicaudatus destructor* (Tschudi): Depto. Loreto, Peru (10).
Neacomys
(21) *N. spinosus* (Thomas): Depto. Loreto, Peru (10).
Nectomys
(22) *N. squamipes* (Brants): Depto. Loreto, Peru (2).

Standard descriptive statistics (mean, standard deviation, standard error of the mean, range, and coefficient of variation) were derived for each of the 28 mensural and 23 qualitative variables for all taxa examined (Tables 1 and 2). Patterns of phenetic similarity among taxa were examined by the multivariate methods of factor analysis, discriminant function analysis, and cluster analysis. Taxa means served as the character states in all cases with quantitative and qualitative traits considered both separately and in unison. In the cluster analyses, both distance and correlation matrices were computed as measures of phenetic resemblance. Phenograms were derived from both matrices by the unweighted pair group method using arithmetic averages (UPGMA; Sneath and Sokal 1973), with the cophenetic correlation coefficient computed for each. The statistical programs of the Numerical Taxonomy Package written by W. W. Moss and the Statistical Package for the Social Sciences (SPSS), both adapted for the CDC 6400 computer, were used for all analyses.

DESCRIPTION AND ANALYSIS

Data from four sources representing three levels of biological organization (genic, gene packaging, and organismic) are available for the assessment of the phenetic and phylogenetic relationships of the Galapagos rats.The genic level was assayed by starch gel electrophoretic analysis; gene packaging by standard karyotypic analysis; and organismic by cranial and external morphometrics and by descriptive soft anatomical analysis.

Starch Gel Electrophoresis

Tissues for electrophoresis were available from 10 specimens each of *N. narboroughi* and *O. bauri* (kidney, liver, plasma, and hemolysate) and four *O. xantheolus* (kidney and liver only). Twenty-two enzymatic and non-enzymatic proteins representing 29 presumptive gene loci were scored for *N. narboroughi* and *O. bauri*. Since no blood was available from *O. xantheolus*, only 22 of these loci were scored for that species.

Loci scored for all three species include: lactate dehydrogenase (LDH-1 and 2), glutamic oxaloacetic transaminase (GOT-1 and 2), peptidase (Pept-1, 2, and 3), malate dehydrogenase (MDH-1 and 2), malic enzyme (ME), sorbitol dehydrogenase (SDH), isocitrate dehydrogenase (IDH-1 and 2), α-glycerophosphate dehydrogenase (αGPD), mucophosoisomerase (MPI), 6 phosphogluconate dehydrogenase (6PGD), xanthine dehydrogenase (SDH), indolphenol oxidase (IPO), alcohol dehydrogenase (ADH), phosphogluconate isomerase (PGI), and phosphoglucomutase (PGM-1 and 3). Systems scored from blood fractions included: hemoglobin (Hb), albumin (Alb), transferrin (Trf-1 and 2), and three general proteins (Pt-1, 2, and 3). In addition, six esterase loci were identifiable for each of the three species.

Based on the 22 loci for which all three species were compared, *N. narboroughi* shares a major or fixed allele at 13 loci with both *O. bauri* and *O. xantheolus* (overall genetic similarity = 59.1%). The latter two species share a major or fixed allele at all but three loci (86.4% similarity).

TABLE 1. MEAN CHARACTER STATES OF THE 23 QUALITATIVE CHARACTERS FOR EACH OF THE 22 OTU'S OF ORYZOMYINE RODENTS EXAMINED

CHARACTER	*Nectomys*	*Neacomys*	*O. keaysi*	*O. albigularis*	*O. yunganus*	*O. niditus*	*O. capito*	*O. palustris peninsulae*	*O. palustris palustris*	*O. palustris regillus*	*O. xantheolus*	*O. bauri*	*O. (Melanomys) caliginosus*	*(Microryzomys) minutus*	*(Oligoryzomys) l. destructor*	*(Oligoryzomys) l. longi*	*(Oecomys) concolor*	*(Oecomys) bicolor*	*N. indefessus*	*N. narboroughi*	*N. darwini*	*N. swarthi*
1	1.5	1.0	1.0	1.0	1.0	1.0	1.0	1.0	2.5	1.0	1.0	1.0	1.0	1.0	1.0	1.5	1.0	1.0	1.0	1.0	1.0	1.0
2	1.0	1.0	1.0	1.0	1.0	1.0	1.0	1.8	1.8	2.0	2.0	2.0	1.0	2.0	1.0	2.0	1.0	1.0	2.0	1.5	1.5	1.5
3	1.7	3.0	2.0	2.2	2.0	2.0	3.0	1.8	1.7	2.0	1.0	2.0	1.0	2.0	1.0	2.0	1.0	1.0	2.0	2.0	2.5	2.0
4	2.0	1.7	1.5	1.7	1.5	2.0	2.5	2.0	1.5	2.0	1.8	1.5	1.7	2.0	1.7	1.0	1.5	1.8	1.6	1.8	1.7	1.7
5	1.0	2.0	1.5	2.7	2.0	2.7	2.1	1.0	1.0	1.0	1.1	1.6	1.0	2.7	2.1	3.0	3.0	3.0	1.3	1.0	1.5	1.5
6	2.0	2.0	1.0	2.0	2.0	2.0	2.0	2.0	2.0	2.0	1.9	1.9	2.0	1.8	2.0	2.0	2.0	2.0	2.0	2.0	2.0	2.0
7	3.0	1.9	2.5	2.7	2.5	2.9	3.0	3.0	1.3	3.0	1.3	1.1	3.0	1.0	2.1	1.0	2.5	2.5	1.0	1.0	1.0	1.0
8	3.0	1.8	2.5	2.2	1.0	1.4	1.3	2.0	1.7	2.8	2.9	2.4	2.5	2.7	1.8	2.0	3.0	2.7	2.8	3.0	2.0	3.0
9	1.7	2.1	1.7	2.0	3.0	3.0	3.0	1.8	1.3	1.5	1.8	1.1	1.7	1.0	1.8	1.0	3.0	3.0	1.3	1.2	1.0	1.3
10	1.0	2.3	1.0	1.7	1.5	1.3	1.8	1.5	1.8	2.0	1.9	1.9	1.0	3.0	1.8	1.7	1.0	1.7	1.6	1.1	1.5	1.5
11	1.0	2.1	1.0	1.0	1.0	1.0	1.0	1.0	1.0	1.0	1.0	1.0	1.0	3.0	1.2	1.0	2.0	1.7	1.0	1.0	1.0	1.0
12	1.5	2.1	1.7	1.7	1.0	1.1	1.4	2.0	1.2	1.4	1.6	1.8	1.0	3.0	2.0	1.5	1.0	1.7	1.4	1.7	1.5	1.5
13	1.0	1.0	1.5	2.0	1.0	1.0	1.0	1.0	1.0	1.0	1.0	1.0	1.0	1.0	1.0	1.0	1.0	1.0	2.0	2.0	2.0	2.0
14	1.0	2.0	2.0	3.0	2.0	1.4	1.9	1.8	1.2	1.2	1.2	1.0	1.5	2.5	2.0	2.0	1.0	1.0	2.3	2.6	3.0	2.5
15	2.0	1.0	1.0	1.0	1.0	1.0	1.0	2.0	2.0	2.0	1.5	1.0	2.0	1.5	1.5	1.5	1.0	1.5	1.0	1.0	1.0	1.0
16	3.0	2.0	2.0	2.0	2.0	2.0	2.0	2.0	2.0	3.0	3.0	3.0	1.0	2.0	2.0	2.0	1.0	1.0	3.0	3.0	3.0	3.0
17	1.0	1.0	3.0	3.0	1.0	2.0	1.0	2.0	1.0	1.0	3.0	3.0	3.0	1.0	2.0	1.0	3.0	3.0	3.0	3.0	3.0	3.0
18	1.0	1.5	1.0	1.0	1.0	2.0	1.0	1.0	1.0	1.0	1.0	1.5	1.0	1.5	1.0	1.0	2.0	2.0	1.5	1.5	1.5	1.5
19	1.0	2.0	2.0	2.0	2.0	2.0	2.0	1.5	1.5	1.5	2.0	2.0	2.0	2.0	2.0	2.0	2.0	2.0	2.0	2.0	2.0	2.0
20	2.0	2.0	1.5	1.0	1.5	1.5	1.0	2.0	2.0	2.0	2.0	2.0	2.0	2.0	2.0	2.0	1.0	1.0	2.0	2.0	2.0	2.0
21	2.0	1.0	1.0	1.0	1.0	2.0	1.0	2.0	2.0	2.0	2.5	2.0	2.0	2.0	1.0	2.0	1.5	1.0	3.0	3.0	3.0	3.0
22	1.0	1.0	2.0	2.0	2.0	2.0	2.0	1.0	1.0	1.0	1.0	1.0	2.0	2.0	1.5	1.0	2.0	2.0	1.0	1.0	1.0	1.0
23	1.0	4.0	1.0	1.0	1.0	1.0	1.0	2.0	3.0	3.0	3.0	3.0	1.0	3.0	1.0	2.0	1.0	1.0	2.5	3.0	2.5	3.0

TABLE 2. TWENTY-EIGHT QUANTITATIVE CHARACTERS FOR THE SIX TAXA OF ENDEMIC GALAPAGOS RODENTS[1]

Character	*Oryzomys galapagoensis* [N=1]	*Oryzomys bauri* [N=31]	*Nesoryzomys indefessus* Santa Cruz [N=26]	*Nesoryzomys indefessus* Baltra [N=17]	*Nesoryzomys narboroughi* [N=31]	*Nesoryzomys darwini* [N=5]	*Nesoryzomys swarthi* [N=4]
ToL	- - -	290.9±2.90 260-335 5.52	256.0±3.90 222-297 7.97	245.7±2.90 220-264 4.86	280.8±2.50 243-303 4.87	193.0±8.00 177-202 9.28	307.5±14.3 267-334 9.32
TaL	- - -	145.2±1.50 129-165 5.94	107.3±1.70 91-121 7.86	99.4±1.60 88-114 6.70	121.9±1.60 101-136 7.14	85.8±1.90 79-90 5.04	132.0±3.90 124-140 5.84
HF	34	32.7±0.30 30-36 4.73	30.8±0.30 28-33 4.27	29.1±0.40 27-32 5.93	32.8±0.30 30-36 4.68	25.2±0.70 23-27 5.89	34.5±1.50 30-36 8.70
E	22	23.3±0.40 21-25 4.54	23.9±0.20 22-25 3.72	23.2±0.20 22-25 3.24	22.9±0.20 20-26 5.45	19.0±0.40 18-20 5.26	27.5±0.30 27-28 2.10
ON	32.9	34.03±0.21 31.4-36.8 3.38	36.77±0.26 34.5-39.1 3.60	35.92±0.16 34.8-36.9 1.79	38.39±0.23 34.4-41.5 3.35	29.58±0.29 28.6-30.1 2.22	38.98±1.36 34.9-40.4 6.97
BaL	27.1	26.68±0.22 24.3-29.3 4.64	27.35±0.25 25.1-29.6 4.64	26.79±0.14 25.7-27.9 2.14	28.92±0.23 25.1-31.3 4.42	21.36±0.30 20.2-21.8 3.12	29.37±1.32 25.8-31.4 8.85
MW	14.0	13.45±0.07 12.6-14.3 2.73	14.03±0.09 13.3-14.9 3.10	13.67±0.08 13.0-14.3 2.52	13.93±0.06 13.3-14.6 2.23	11.80±0.13 11.3-12.0 2.47	14.85±0.26 14.1-15.3 3.50
ZB	17.9	17.97±0.13 16.3-19.8 3.91	18.45±0.14 17.0-19.6 3.77	17.75±0.11 17.0-18.5 2.52	18.79±0.10 17.0-19.5 2.23	14.08±0.19 13.5-14.7 3.06	19.70±0.71 17.9-20.5 6.19
RL	- - -	13.83±0.12 12.3-14.9 4.90	15.99±0.17 14.8-17.7 5.48	15.43±0.11 14.7-16.2 2.86	16.63±0.13 14.5-18.3 4.28	12.62±0.25 12.0-13.3 4.46	16.50±0.80 14.1-17.5 9.75
DL	8.8	8.99±0.10 7.9-10.2 6.22	9.40±0.12 8.4-10.5 6.68	9.37±0.08 8.9-10.2 3.60	10.02±0.10 8.4-11.4 5.25	7.42±0.30 6.4-8.2 9.06	9.98±0.53 8.4-10.6 10.62
CD	- - -	11.97±0.08 11.1-13.0 3.89	12.85±0.10 11.6-13.7 3.61	12.85±0.08 12.3-13.5 2.64	13.47±0.08 12.5-14.5 3.31	10.66±0.12 10.2-10.9 2.54	14.10±0.41 12.9-14.8 5.88
RH	7.6	9.36±0.10 8.1-10.5 5.81	9.14±0.10 8.3-10.1 5.30	8.77±0.06 8.3-9.2 3.01	9.60±0.07 8.1-10.3 4.08	7.16±0.21 6.5-7.8 6.45	10.45±0.47 9.1-11.2 9.06
BCL	- - -	11.48±0.07 10.7-12.4 3.56	12.34±0.10 11.4-13.6 3.92	12.16±0.07 11.6-12.8 2.40	13.19±0.10 12.1-14.4 4.06	9.94±0.06 9.8-10.1 1.35	13.43±0.30 12.6-14.0 4.40

[1] Mean ± standard error of the mean; range; and coefficient of variation are given.

TABLE 2 (Continued). TWENTY-EIGHT QUANTITITATIVE CHARACTERS FOR THE SIX TAXA OF ENDEMIC GALAPAGOS RODENTS

Character	*Oryzomys galapagoensis* [N=1]	*Oryzomys bauri* [N=31]	*Nesoryzomys indefessus* Santa Cruz [N=26]	*Nesoryzomys indefessus* Baltra [N=17]	*Nesoryzomys narboroughi* [N=31]	*Nesoryzomys darwini* [N=5]	*Nesoryzomys swarthi* [N=4]
IOC	5.5	5.45±0.04 5.1-6.1 3.99	4.62±0.04 4.3-5.0 3.97	4.49±0.03 4.2-4.7 2.72	4.69±0.04 4.3-5.1 4.28	4.52±0.09 4.2-4.7 4.53	4.93±0.08 4.7-5.0 3.05
RW	6.1	6.24±0.06 5.6-7.0 5.37	6.25±0.08 5.6-6.9 6.17	6.26±0.05 6.06-6.6 3.05	6.42±0.06 5.6-7.2 4.93	5.32±0.20 4.8-5.9 8.34	7.33±0.31 6.4-7.7 8.52
MTRW	---	6.85±0.05 6.3-7.4 4.02	7.31±0.07 6.7-8.0 4.60	7.44±0.05 7.1-7.8 2.60	7.36±0.04 7.0-7.7 2.66	5.94±0.10 5.7-6.2 3.88	7.83±0.22 7.2-8.2 5.56
MTRL	5.5	5.67±0.04 5.3-6.4 3.52	5.58±0.03 5.3-5.9 3.10	5.33±0.05 5.0-5.7 3.56	5.51±0.03 5.2-6.0 3.41	4.94±0.07 4.7-5.1 3.07	6.15±0.12 5.8-6.3 3.87
BuL	---	5.87±0.04 5.4-6.3 3.67	6.71±0.05 5.8-7.1 4.11	6.35±0.05 6.0-6.7 2.95	6.57±0.04 6.0-7.1 3.61	5.40±0.10 5.1-5.7 4.14	6.95±0.12 6.6-7.4 4.92
RD	6.2	6.17±0.06 5.3-6.8 5.56	6.73±0.08 6.1-7.4 5.85	6.48±0.06 6.1-6.9 3.48	6.71±0.05 6.0-7.3 3.93	4.86±0.04 4.5-5.2 6.28	7.18±0.33 6.2-7.6 9.13
mTRL	5.6	5.77±0.03 5.4-6.0 2.61	5.56±0.04 5.2-5.9 3.64	5.35±0.04 5.1-5.8 3.31	5.36±0.03 5.0-6.0 3.00	4.88±0.04 4.8-5.0 1.71	6.20±0.11 6.0-6.5 3.48
ACH	---	6.40±0.08 5.6-7.5 6.65	6.52±0.10 5.5-7.3 7.43	6.29±0.08 5.8-7.1 5.21	6.45±0.06 5.4-7.1 5.50	4.68±0.07 4.5-4.9 3.17	7.28±0.40 6.2-8.1 11.08
ZPW	3.6	4.05±0.07 3.4-4.9 9.92	4.07±0.07 3.6-4.8 8.10	3.91±0.05 3.5-4.5 5.31	4.03±0.06 3.3-4.7 8.63	3.22±0.04 3.1-3.3 2.60	4.55±0.25 3.8-4.8 10.99
IFL	---	6.96±0.06 6.2-7.5 4.60	6.84±0.09 6.2-7.9 6.81	6.72±0.06 6.4-7.2 3.69	6.81±0.04 6.3-7.1 2.94	5.36±0.14 4.9-5.6 5.69	7.83±0.34 6.9-8.4 8.57
1L	---	2.56±0.03 2.3-2.8 5.95	2.56±0.02 2.3-2.8 4.43	2.51±0.03 2.3-2.7 4.20	2.47±0.02 2.2-2.7 4.81	2.16±0.07 2.0-2.3 7.02	2.73±0.05 2.6-2.8 3.51
2L	---	1.68±0.02 1.5-1.9 5.04	1.61±0.02 1.5-1.8 6.32	1.61±0.02 1.5-1.7 4.85	1.64±0.01 1.5-1.8 4.66	1.50±0.03 1.4-1.6 4.71	1.88±0.03 1.8-1.9 2.67
3L	---	1.27±0.02 1.1-1.5 7.09	1.20±0.01 1.1-1.3 4.41	1.22±0.02 1.1-1.3 5.22	1.20±0.01 1.1-1.4 6.09	1.08±0.04 1.0-1.2 7.75	1.50±0.03 1.4-1.6 5.44
MPFW	---	2.32±0.02 2.0-2.6 5.85	2.19±0.03 1.9-2.7 7.51	2.05±0.04 1.6-2.2 7.72	1.99±0.02 1.7-2.2 6.20	1.68±0.02 1.6-1.7 2.66	2.28±0.13 1.9-2.5 11.56
MPFL	---	5.57±0.06 4.7-6.1 5.81	4.91±0.06 4.4-5.4 5.94	4.87±0.04 4.4-5.2 3.76	4.75±0.04 4.0-5.1 5.18	3.84±0.08 3.6-4.0 4.73	5.48±0.20 4.9-5.8 7.21

The figure for *N. narboroughi* and *O. bauri* is considerably lower if the blood and esterase loci are included in the analysis. These represent an additional 13 loci for which the two species are fixed for different alleles at 10. Hence, a minimal estimate of overall genetic similarity for these species based on 35 loci is 45.7%.

There are 7 of the 22 loci which serve to differentiate *N. narboroughi* from both *O. bauri* and *O. xantheolus* (Fig. 3). *N. narboroughi* and *O. xantheolus* share an allele at one locus (XDH^a) which is not found in the sample of *O. bauri*, and *N. narboroughi* shares an allele at each of two loci with *O. bauri* ($MDH\text{-}1^b$ and ME^a) not found in *O. xantheolus*.

These data argue strongly that the Galapagoan *O. bauri* (and probably *O. galapagoensis*) shares a closer genic-based relationship with the coastal Peruvian *O. xantheolus* than it does with *N. narboroughi*, and undoubtedly with other species of *Nesoryzomys* as well. The only way to account for these data is to postulate a much earlier introduction and radiation of *Nesoryzomys* in the archipelago with the origin of the taxon at that time, or a derivation of *Nesoryzomys* on the mainland before introduction. In either event, clearly *O. bauri* has a close genetic relative on the mainland today in *O. xantheolus* while *Nesoryzomys* is not closely related to either of these species. A much more expanded data base is required to establish genic relationships of *Nesoryzomys.*

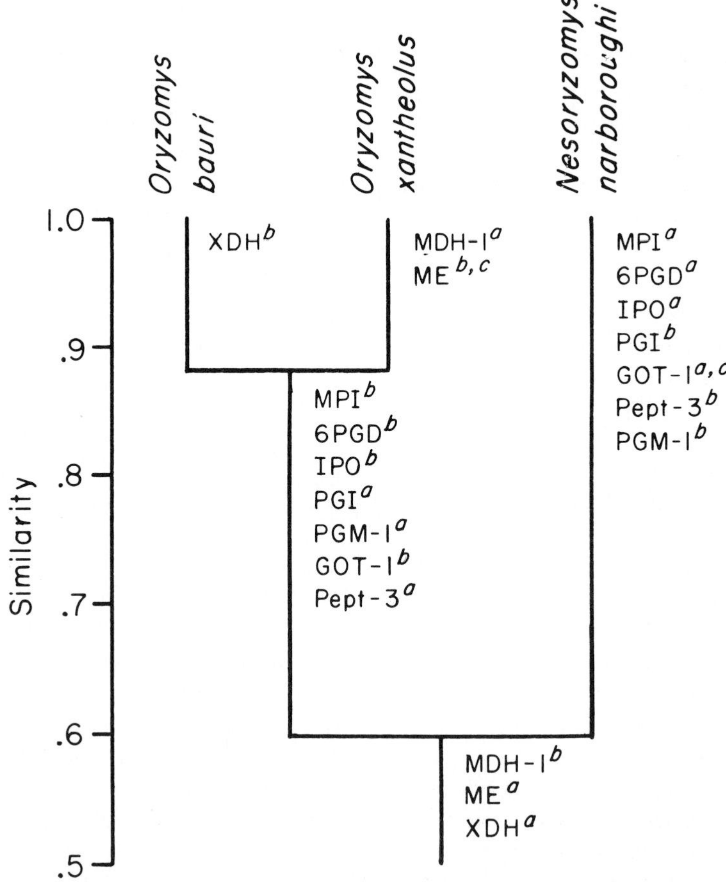

Fig. 3. Phenogram of relationships among the two extant Galapagos species (*O. bauri* and *N. narboroughi*) and the coastal Peruvian relative (*O. xantheolus*) based on electrophoretic analysis of 22 genetic loci (see text). Alleles at those loci which serve to differentiate each lineage are indicated.

Chromosomes

The pattern and extent of chromosomal variability among the oryzomyine complex of Neotropical cricetines has been summarized recently by Gardner and Patton (1976). This report presented karyotypes of *Nectomys, Neacomys*, and representatives of six subgenera of *Oryzomys*, including *Nesoryzomys*. These authors consider *N. narboroughi*, the only extant species of the group, to have the most strongly differentiated karyotype among the array of 34 oryzomyine taxa examined. It has the lowest combination of diploid and fundamental number of any oryzomyine with a karyotype composed primarily of biarmed chromosomes rather than the large number of acrocentrics characterizing nearly all other oryzomyines. The conclusion was reached that "*Nesoryzomys* is so aberrant chromosomally as to demand recognition as a full genus" (Gardner and Patton 1976:20). In a summary of hypothesized phylogenetic relationships among oryzomyines based on karyotypes, Gardner and Patton (1976) remarked that *Nesoryzomys* did not share a close or even obvious relationship with any examined taxon of the group. The karyotypic data at hand, therefore, only demonstrate significant differentiation for *Nesoryzomys* and do not really help in establishing phylogenetic affinities between it and other oryzomyine taxa.

Gross Stomach Morphology

The muroid rodent stomach has recently received attention from workers in mammalian systematics (e.g. Vorontsov 1957; Carleton 1973). Carleton has suggested relationships between 27 South American muroid genera based solely upon the type, location, and extent of stomach epithelial tissues. According to Carleton, 21 of the 27 genera (including several *Oryzomys* species) are fundamentally similar in gastric morphology and show the presumed ancestral unilocular-hemiglandular condition described below. Several other South American genera, representing more or less tight taxonomic units by other criteria, show various degrees of deviation from this basic condition, supporting the taxonomic usefulness of gross stomach morphology.

We surveyed the gross stomach morphology of *N. narboroughi* (4 specimens: MVZ 145382 - 145385), *O. bauri* (5 specimens: MVZ 125460, 145374, 145375, 145380, 145381) and two specimens of *O. palustris* (MVZ 98763 and 126831). The stomachs were excised from the specimens, longitudinally bisected, and preserved in 70% ethanol. Stomach contents were removed and saved. Anatomical observations using a Bausch and Lomb stereozoom microscope (10X-40X) focused on gross stomach shape and the type and extent of epithelial tissues. Although the general anatomical characteristics of the stomach were easily discerned regardless of the degree of stomach distention, only fully distended stomachs were used for illustrative purposes. Terminology follows Carleton (1973).

The gross stomach morphology of *O. bauri* (Fig. 4) is, in most respects, representative of the basic unilocular-hemiglandular condition characteristic of mainland *Oryzomys* species (e.g. *O. palustris*, Fig. 4). This basic type consists of a single large chamber with a cornified proximal portion (corpus) and a glandular distal portion (antrum). The incisura angularis roughly marks the division between the two epithelial zones. The stomach of *O. bauri* does show some noteworthy deviations from the basic and presumed ancestral (Carleton 1973) unilocular-hemiglandular condition of *O. palustris*. The antrum shows a considerably thicker glandular lining that is most apparent at the bordering fold. In all specimens, this hind-region of the gut contained numerous hairs and, in one specimen, sand and some unidentified chitinous material. Likewise, the cornified epithelium of the corpus appears to be somewhat thickened over the *O. palustris* condition. As in *O. palustris*, the antrum is maximally distensible to accommodate a volume of nearly one-half of the entire stomach volume.

The stomach of *N. narboroughi* (Fig. 4) is also of the unilocular-hemiglandular type. However, certain modifications of the basic *O. palustris* condition are noteworthy. First, the antrum is highly glandularized, even more so than in *O. bauri*. Second, the incisura angularis is deep and the

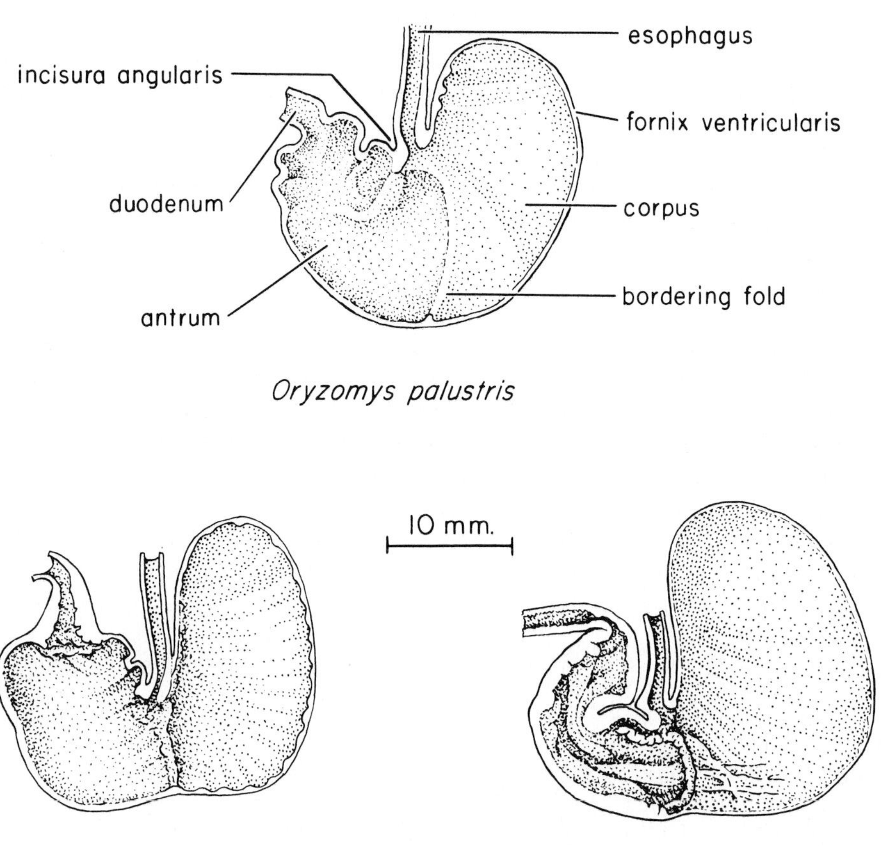

Fig. 4. Details of stomach morphology for two native Galapagos rats (*O. bauri*, MVZ 145374, and *N. narboroughi*, MVZ 145385) and the North American *O. palustris* (MVZ 98763).

bordering fold thus short, resulting in a narrow passageway between the corpus and antrum regions. Third, the antrum region is maximally distensible to accommodate considerably less than one-half of the entire stomach volume. The fornix ventricularis is high and broadly arched over the esophageal opening.

Judging from our specimens, it is evident that the stomachs of both species of native Galapagoan rats have undergone modification from the ancestral mainland type characterized by 21 of 27 genera examined by Carleton (1973). These changes are best interpreted as the result of dietary shifts concomitant with colonization of the islands. The apparent trend towards thickening of the glandular epithelium of the antrum may be related to the observed high incidence of abrasive material in the stomach contents.

As with the karyological survey, comparative gastric morphology does not aid in determining phylogenetic affinities between Galapagoan and mainland oryzomyine taxa. The derived gastric morphology of *Nesoryzomys* and the morphologically intermediate grade seen in *O. bauri* might, however, be interpreted as evidence of an earlier island invasion by *Nesoryzomys*. Considering the lack of knowledge of inter-island diet differences that could account for different rates of stomach modification, this interpretation as to the timing of the island invasions must be viewed in light of evidence from other sources. Certainly though, the stomach of *Nesoryzomys* is significantly differentiated from the basic oryzomyine condition.

Male Accessory Reproductive Glands

Arata (1964) reviewed the pattern and extent of variation in the male accessory reproductive glands of 23 genera of muroid rodents. We here use Arata's description of *Oryzomys palustris* to analyze, on a comparative basis, the degree of differentiation seen in the male reproductive system of the native Galapagos rats. Specimens available for examination were: *Nesoryzomys narboroughi* (3 specimens: MVZ 145382, 145384, 145385) and *Oryzomys bauri* (4 specimens: MVZ 145374, 145375, 145380, 145381). A single specimen of *O. palustris* (MVZ 126831) was used on occasion as a direct comparative reference. All specimens were adult with scrotal testes and enlarged tubules visible in the cauda epididymis. The entire reproductive tract was excised from each specimen and preserved in 70% ethanol. Anatomical observations were made using a Bausch and Lomb stereozoom microscope (10X-40X). Measurements of glands, when included, merely serve to indicate the approximate greatest length and width of the gland for comparative purposes. Determination of homologies within the prostate gland complement was particularly difficult. When in doubt as to whether a prostate element is bilobed or actually represents two separate glands, we have chosen to follow Arata's (1964) conservative approach and consider the element to constitute a single, bilobed gland.

Nesoryzomys narboroughi (Fig. 5). A single pair of preputial glands is present. The glands are smaller in size (10x2 mm) than those of *Oryzomys palustris* as examined by us and figured by Arata (1964). The main mass of each gland lies to the side of the glans penis. Each tapers distally and is drained by a single duct which enters the ventral edge of the preputial orifice.

The paired bulbo-urethral glands lie dorso-laterad to the urethral bulb. These glands are smaller in size than in the *Oryzomys* material examined (4x2 mm versus 8x4 mm in *Oryzomys*). Each gland is drained by a single, large duct that enters the urethra just caudad to the proximal penile urethra.

A single pair of ampullary glands is recognized, each gland intimately associated with its respective vas deferens. Numerous ducts drain each gland entering the lumen near the junction of the ampullary vestibule with the deferent duct. In *Nesoryzomys*, the ampullary glands are enlarged and entirely encircle the vasa deferentia.

The paired vesicular glands of *Nesoryzomys* are considerably smaller than those of *Oryzomys* (7 mm length versus 17 mm in *O. bauri*). Each gland is approximately pear-shaped, tapering somewhat near its junction with the prostatic urethra just laterad to the vas deferens. While the surface of the vesicular is quite smooth, transparent portions reveal extreme folding of mucous membrane within.

The prostate gland compliment consists of a single pair of dorsal prostates lying along the dorso-lateral aspect of the prostatic urethra. In 70% ethanol, the prostates are white in color. These glands encroach anteriorly onto the vesicular glands for approximately three-quarters of the latter's length. The dorsal prostates are multi-lobed structures that drain into the anterior dorso-lateral wall of the prostatic urethra.

Oryzomys bauri (Fig. 5). The single pair of preputial glands are reduced in size as in the *Nesoryzomys* material examined. Each tapers distally and is drained by a single duct opening at the preputial orifice.

The bulbo-urethral glands of *O. bauri* are less spheroid and more elongate in shape than those of both *Nesoryzomys* and *O. palustris* (8x2 mm in *O. bauri* vs. 8x4 mm in *O. palustris*). In other aspects of general morphology the bulbo-urethral glands are quite similar in all oryzomyine specimens examined.

The paired ampullary glands are compact, tubular structures lying adjacent to the vasa deferentia. These glands are of the same approximate size as those of *O. palustris* and are considerably smaller than those of *Nesoryzomys*. The ampullary glands entirely encircle the vasa deferentia and lie compressed between the prostate (ventrad) and vesicular (dorsad) elements. Each gland is

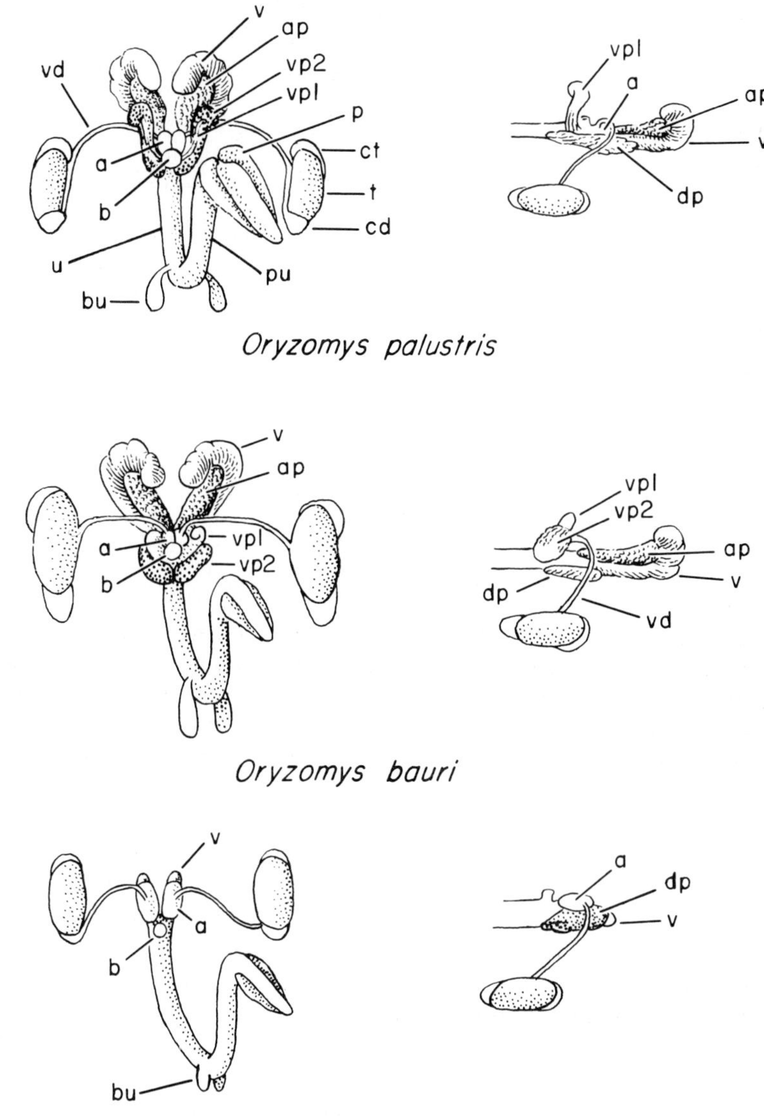

Fig. 5. Male reproductive tracts of the native Galapagos rats, *O. bauri* (MVZ 145374) and *N. narboroughi* (MVZ 145385) compared to the North American species *O. palustris* (MVZ 126831). a = ampullary gland; ap = anterior prostate; b = urinary bladder; bu = bulbo-urethral gland; cd = cauda epididymis; ct = caput epididymis; dp = dorsal prostate; p = preputial gland; pu = penile urethra t = testis; u = urethra; v = vesicular gland; vd = vas deferens; vp = ventral prostate.

drained by numerous ducts entering the vestibule of the ampulla near its junction with the vas deferens.

The vesicular glands are large, paired structures extending craniad from the prostatic urethra. Each gland is recurved postero-ventrally (and somewhat medially) for approximately the distal one-third of its length. These glands are highly rugose, being lobate along both the lesser and greater margins of the curvature. A single duct drains each gland into the prostatic urethra just laterad to the deferent duct.

Four pairs of prostate glands are recognized. This series closely resembles that described for *O. palustris* by Arata (1964). A large pair of ventrolateral prostates lies caudad and laterad to a smaller pair of ventromedial prostates, each gland draining independently into the prostatic urethra via single ducts. In 70% ethanol, the ventrolateral prostates are red in color, the ventromedial prostates are white. A single pair of elongate dorsal prostates (white in color) lies along the dorsal prostatic urethra extending largely onto the posterior portion of the vesicular glands. The dorsal prostate ducts enter the urethra just caudad to the vesicular ducts. A single pair of anterior prostates (white in color) lies embraced in the lesser curvature of the vesicular glands and is contained within the same connective tissue. A set of two ducts drains each gland into the antero-lateral wall of the prostatic urethra.

The accessory gland complement of the male reproductive system, as with the karyologic and stomach analyses above, sheds little light on the phylogenetic affinities of the endemic island rats. While *O. bauri* exhibits the pattern seen in most oryzomyines, the extreme morphologic divergence in the form of reduction or loss of gland elements in *Nesoryzomys* provides further evidence as to the distinctiveness of this form. In light of current knowledge, it is impossible to attach any degree of functional or taxonomic significance to the differences in glandular complements, save to document these differences and emphasize the uniqueness of *Nesoryzomys narboroughi*.

Glans Penis Morphology

The glans penis and associated bacular apparatus of the Neotropical cricetine rodents have found wide application in both general anatomical and systematic works (e.g. Arata et al. 1965; Hooper 1962; Hooper and Musser 1964). Based upon Hooper and Musser's work, the male phallus of all Neotropical cricetine species is of the "complex" type, that is, generally barrel-shaped with a terminal crater containing an osseous baculum armed distally with a three-pronged cartilaginous tip (see Hooper and Hart 1962 for a more complete description). In efforts to compare the phalli of certain native Galapagos rats with those of mainland species we have examined the glans penis of *Nesoryzomys narboroughi* (4 specimens: MVZ 133122, 133125, 133126 and 145385), *Oryzomys bauri* (2 specimens: MVZ 145375 and 145378), *O. xantheolus* (7 specimens: MVZ 135658, 135660, 135661, 135664, 135665, 135792, and 137943), and *O. palustris* (3 specimens: MVZ 98765, 98768, and 126381). All specimens were adults as determined by reproductive criteria mentioned above. The excised phalli were either preserved directly in 70% ethanol or cleared in KOH and stained with alizarin red as per the methods of Hooper (1958) and Lidicker (1968). Specimens were examined and figured with the aid of a Wild M5 stereomicroscope with a camera lucida attachment. Descriptive terminology follows that of previous workers.

The glans penis of *Oryzomys palustris* (Fig. 6) is of the basic complex type described by Hooper and Musser (1964). The phallus is short and barrel-shaped (length/diameter ratio ~ 1.2) with three relatively long cartilaginous digits. The three digits are nearly equal in length, each measuring approximately 80% of the osseous bacular length. The urethral lappets are large and each has a subapical lobule. Epidermal spines are relatively small and dense.

The phallus of *Oryzomys xantheolus* (Fig. 6) is elongate relative to the *O. palustris* condition (length/diameter ratio ~ 2.3). The terminal crater is shallow and encompasses only the proximal portion of the cartilaginous bacular apparatus. The osseous baculum is long and slender (length/diameter ratio ~ 2.2) and is tipped with three relatively short cartilaginous digits. The medial cartilaginous digit is shorter and more slender than the lateral pair. The length of the entire cartilaginous element is approximately 20% of the os bacular length. The urethral lappets are large and single lobed. Epidermal spines appear much as in *O. palustris*.

The glans penis of *Oryzomys bauri* (Fig. 6) is much like that described for *O. xantheolus*. The phallus is somewhat elongate (length/diameter ratio ~ 1.8) having a terminal crater slightly deeper and enclosing more of the bacular apparatus than in *O. xantheolus*. The osseous baculum is likewise elongate (length/diameter ratio ~2.0) with a much reduced terminal cartilaginous element. Unlike *O. xantheolus*, the medial digit of the latter structure is elongate and slender relative to the lateral pair which is slightly recurved medially. The urethral lappets are small and single lobed. Epidermal spines are as in *O. palustris* and *O. xantheolus*.

The phallus of *Nesoryzomys narboroughi* (Fig. 6) is of the elongate type (length/diameter ratio ~ 3.5) having a very shallow terminal crater. The entire cartilaginous bacular apparatus and the distal tip of the os baculum extend beyond the main body of the phallus. The osseous baculum is long and very slender (length/diameter ratio ~ 3.6) and is tipped with a very small cartilaginous apparatus. The latter element is three-pronged with a much reduced medial digit. The length of the lateral digits approximates only 10% that of the osseous baculum. The urethral lappets are small and narrow and extend beyond the tip of the small medial bacular digit. Epidermal spines are larger and more widely spaced in the *Nesoryzomys* specimens than in other taxa examined.

Based on phallic morphology, Hooper and Musser (1964) divided members of the genus *Oryzomys* into two subgroups: (1) the "*albigularis*" subgroup characterized by a robust phallus

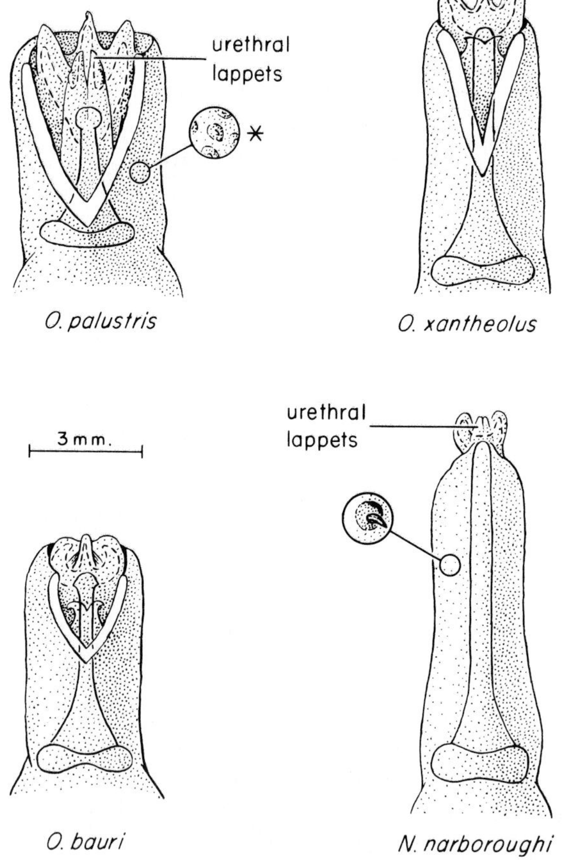

Fig. 6. Ventral views of male phalli of *O. palustris* (MVZ 98765), *O. xantheolus* (MVZ 137592), *O. bauri* (composite of MVZ 145375 and 145378), and *N. narboroughi* (MVZ 133122). A portion of each glans has been excised to reveal details of internal anatomy. Structure and position of the bacular apparatus is indicated by solid line (osseous baculum) and dashed line (cartilaginous baculum). The epidermal spines (*) of *O. xantheolus* and *O. bauri* are similar in structure and density to those figured for *O. palustris*.

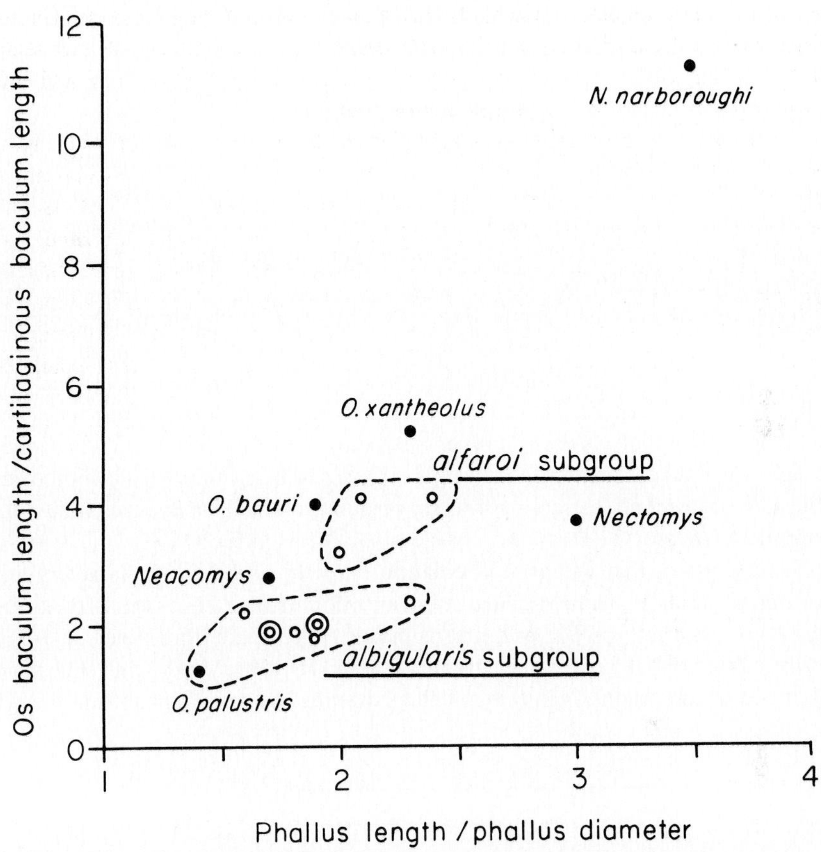

Fig. 7. Plot of bacular and phallus ratios for selected oryzomyine taxa based on data from Hooper and Musser (1964) except for *O. palustris, O. bauri, O. xantheolus*, and *N. narboroughi*. Species included within the "*alfaroi*" subgroup of Hooper and Musser (1964) are: *O. caliginosus, O. alfaroi*, and *O. melanotis*; those included within the "*albigularis*" subgroup are: *O. albigularis, O. devius, O. capito, O. concolor, O. flavescens, O. fulvescens, O. nigripes*, and *O. longicaudatus*.

with the cartilaginous bacular element long relative to the osseous baculum, and (2) the "*alfaroi*" subgroup characterized by a long, slender phallus with a much reduced cartilaginous bacular element. Figure 7 presents a bivariate plot comparing phallic robustness with the relative length of the cartilaginous baculum for the 14 oryzomyine taxa examined by Hooper and Musser (1964) and the three described here. Several aspects of this relationship among the included taxa are noteworthy. First, *Nesoryzomys* (as represented by *N. narboroughi*) is an extreme outlier in comparison to all other oryzomyines, including the genera *Neacomys* (as represented by *N. guianae*) and *Nectomys* (*N. alfaroi*). Second, of the other oryzomyine taxa only *O. xantheolus* shows tendencies of *Nesoryzomys* in terms of type and degree of phallic modification. This tendency is very slight indeed, as *O. xantheolus* is only slightly different from the "*alfaroi*" subgroup. Third, *O. bauri* is quite similar to "*alfaroi*" subgroup taxa but has a slightly stouter phallus than other members.

It is quite clear that *Nesoryzomys* is strongly differentiated and shows little resemblance in phallic structure to any other oryzomyine. While it is more similar to *O. xantheolus* than other taxa, the similarity is minimal and any phylogenetic connection must be remote. It is likely, however, that the basal stock leading to *Nesoryzomys* had a phallus of the type represented by the "*alfaroi*" subgroup. Slight modifications from this condition would lead to both *O. bauri* and *O.*

xantheolus, with change being in somewhat opposite directions: i.e. to a more slender condition in *O. xantheolus* and to a more robust condition in *O. bauri.*

Morphometric Analyses

The varied statistical approaches utilized to examine phenetic similarity among oryzomyine rodents describe two patterns of relationship. Both the cluster analyses based either on distance or correlation matrices and factor analysis show an obvious closeness among the four species of *Nesoryzomys*. However, the different approaches are not unanimous in the placement of *Nesoryzomys* relative to other oryzomyine taxa.

The cluster analyses actually depict three patterns of OTU placement, depending upon the method and character states used. Distance matrices based on both the 28 quantitative characters and the combination of quantitative-qualitative characters give nearly identical phenograms, with four groupings indicated (Fig. 8). There is, however, no association of the four species of *Nesoryzomys* nor other members of currently unified taxa (e.g. *O. palustris* or members of the subgenus *Oecomys*). This phenogram apparently reflects a strong size bias in the taxa examined as the four groups delineated correspond to rats with large, medium, or small body sizes rather than to potential phylogenetic units.

The second pattern, that based on correlation matrices of either all characters combined or quantitative characters only, indicates a marked association of the four *Nesoryzomys* taxa relative to all others (Fig. 9). *Nesoryzomys* as a unit is placed quite apart from other oryzomyines, but is phenetically closer to *Melanomys* than to any other OTU. *Oryzomys bauri* shows closest phenetic similarity to *O. xantheolus*, a species of the subgenus *Oryzomys* inhabiting the dry western

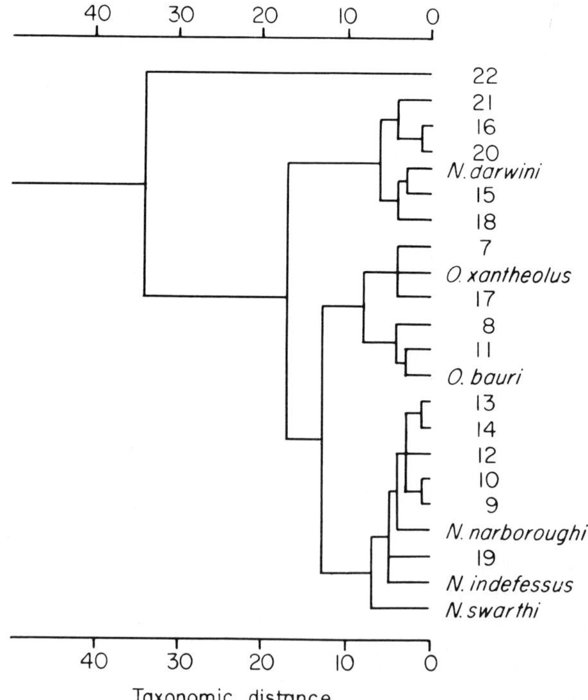

Fig. 8. Distance phenogram of 23 oryzomyine OTU's based on 28 quantitative characters. Numbers refer to OTU's as identified in Materials and Methods section of text. Cophenetic correlation coefficient = .701.

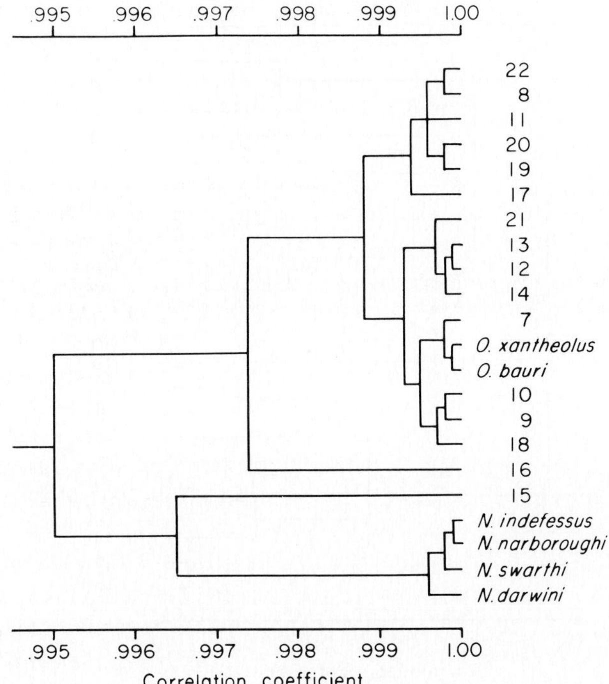

Fig. 9. Correlation phenogram of 23 oryzomyine OTU's based on 28 quantitative characters. Numbers refer to OTU's as identified in Materials and Methods section of text. Cophenetic correlation coefficient = .729.

coast of Peru. Both of these species are included within a larger gorup composed mostly of other medium-sized members of the subgenus *Oryzomys*.

The third pattern is based on both distance and correlation matrices of the 23 qualitative characters. The resultant phenogram (Fig. 10) again clusters all *Nesoryzomys* taxa as a tight-knit unit, but one linked to *O. bauri* and *O. xantheolus*. These taxa form a definite unit relative to other oryzomyines, not joining any of the latter until fairly far out on the dendrogram. The relative placement of OTUs on this phenogram is a very close approximation of most current views on their taxonomy. Such cannot be said for the other phenograms presented.

The factor analysis presents a picture of strong separation of *Nesoryzomys* from the other oryzomyines (Fig. 11). It is thus concordant with the correlation based phenogram for mensural characters. In general, all taxa of oryzomyines fall along a diagonal axis in the three-dimensional plot except for *Nesoryzomys* which is separated by a definite hiatus from this trend. It is apparent in Fig. 11 that members of the subgenus *Oryzomys* group in the center of the plot; species belonging to other subgenera of *Oryzomys* or to *Neacomys* are scattered close to that group; *Nectomys* is well differentiated but in the same directional trend; and *Nesoryzomys* is both separated and off the general trend. *Nesoryzomys darwini*, however, tends to bridge the gap between the main oryzomyine group and other *Nesoryzomys*.

A general size factor is indicated by the dispersion of OTUs along Factor I, which accounts for 76.8% of the total variance. Larger taxa are positioned on the positive side, smaller ones on the negative side (Fig. 11). All mensural characters except TaL and IOC contribute heavily and nearly equally to Factor I (Table 3). On the other hand, Factor II, accounting for 8.6% of the total variance, is most strongly influenced by TaL, IOC, BuL, and RL. The former two characters influence placement along Factor II in a direction opposite that of the latter two characters. Hence, Factor II largely separates out those OTUs with long tails and broad interorbital regions but with

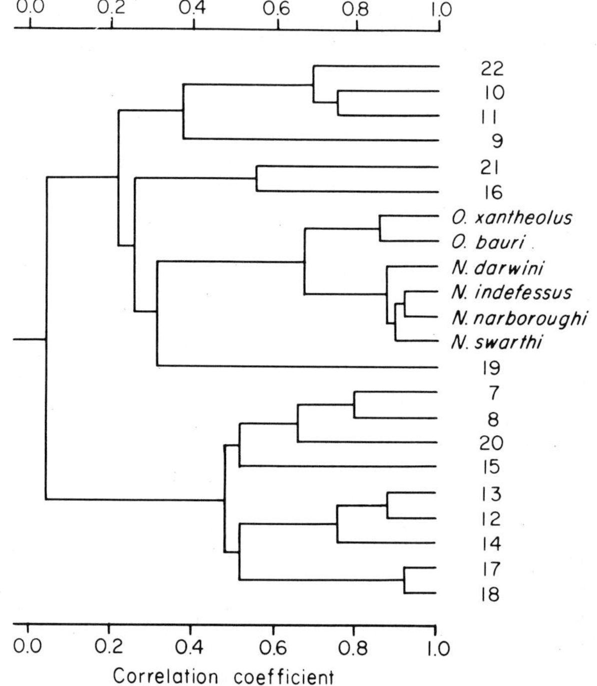

Fig. 10. Correlation phenogram of 22 oryzomyine OTU's based on 23 qualitative characters. Numbers refer to OTU's as identified in Materials and Methods section of text. Cophenetic correlation coefficient = .809.

short bullae and short rostra from those with the reverse combination of characters. *Nesoryzomys*, which is diagnosed by this particular combination of characters, is thus effectively separated along Factor II from all other oryzomyine OTU's examined.

The factor analysis permits us to evaluate the suggestion of Goldman (1918; quoted above)

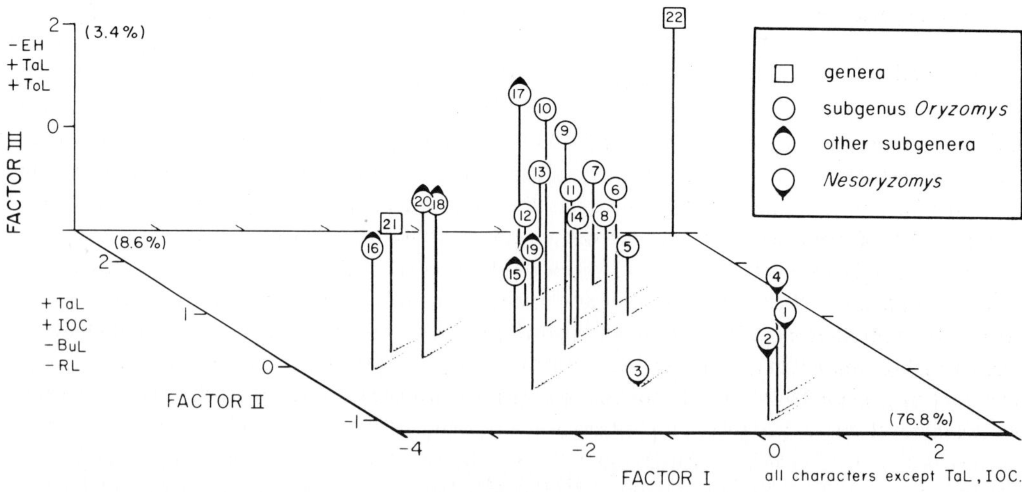

Fig. 11. Plot of the first three Factor axes for the 22 oryzomyine OTU's examined, numbered as in text. The percentage of total variance explained by each axis is given as are the characters which contribute to each axis.

TABLE 3. FACTOR ANALYSIS USING 28 MORPHOMETRIC VARIABLES FOR ALL 22 ORYZOMYINE OTU'S (SEE FIG. 11)

CHARACTER	I	II	III
ToL	.8191	.3942	.2990
TaL	.4882	.7328	.3302
HF	.8172	.3076	.2121
E	.7683	-.2080	-.3385
ON	.9413	-.2707	.1208
BaL	.9693	-.1035	.1517
BB	.9592	-.1621	.0365
ZB	.9730	-.0484	.1366
RL	.8745	-.4197	.0619
DL	.9286	-.2125	.1723
CD	.7947	-.3324	.1604
ACH	.9721	.0228	.1014
BCL	.8651	-.2690	.2368
IOC	.5683	.7254	-.0422
RW	.8958	.1330	.2457
MTRW	.9289	-.2580	-.0743
MTRL	.9489	.0489	-.2050
BuL	.7938	-.5224	-.0713
RD	.9198	-.1688	.2240
mTRL	.9375	.1685	-.2295
RH	.9567	-.0189	.1001
ZPW	.9176	-.0591	-.0377
IFL	.8320	-.1764	.0088
1L	.9291	.0556	-.1749
2L	.8992	.0889	-.1999
3L	.9083	.1894	-.1285
MFPW	.7522	.3586	-.2299
MFPL	.8449	.3721	-.1060
% total variance	76.8	8.6	3.4
Eigenvalue	23.82	2.66	1.07

and others that the diagnostic characters of *Nesoryzomys* are in reality shared by other oryzomyines, hence invalidating the generic status of these endemic Galapagos rats. Several oryzomyines were included in the present analysis which do indeed have features suggestive of *Nesoryzomys* (for example, *Melanomys caliginosus* and *O. xantheolus* have rather short tails and *O. keaysi* has a rounded, hourglass-shaped interorbital region). These taxa, however, fail either to cluster with *Nesoryzomys* in the phenograms or to be positioned with that form in the factor plot. None of the taxa of oryzomyines examined here encompasses the totality of cranial and external configuration characterizing *Nesoryzomys*. Indeed, the endemic rice rats of the Galapagos are the most strongly divergent in general body plan among all those oryzomyines examined, including OTU's currently given generic status.

DISCUSSION

Origin and Timing of Galapagos Endemic Radiation

The distinctiveness of *Nesoryzomys* as a morphologic and phylogenetic unit should no longer be questioned. In consideration of available data for the oryzomyine complex, *Nesoryzomys* is unique and quite divergent in a number of functionally unrelated morphological bases, including karyotype, male accessory reproductive structures, stomach, and glans penis. Indeed, even the nominal diagnostic features of the skin and skull segregate *Nesoryzomys* from other oryzomyines examined herein. While some of these features are seemingly shared with other taxa of oryzomyines, no single species or group of species combines the totality of features that separate *Nesoryzomys* as the most distinctive oryzomyine examined. The summation of data available, therefore, does support the proposal of Heller (1904) of generic status for *Nesoryzomys*.

This conclusion, however, does not aid one in an understanding of the phylogenetic relationships of *Nesoryzomys*. While on an overall phenetic basis *Nesoryzomys* is further from other genera of oryzomyines than the latter are among themselves, this does not mean that it necessarily shares a more distant common ancestor than that, for example of *Oryzomys, Neacomys*, and *Nectomys*. Indeed, an overview of the morphological data given above leaves the question of the relationships and origin of *Nesoryzomys* quite ambiguous. The uniqueness of the male reproductive tract, stomach, and karyotype provide little help to this problem, and the available biochemical data are too incomplete as yet. However, both the structure of the glans penis and certain of the exomorphological analyses provide suggestions as to affinities. A relationship between *Nesoryzomys* (as represented by *N. narboroughi*) and *O. xantheolus* is suggested by similar patterns in glans penis morphology, a pattern which is quite divergent relative to the oryzomyine complex as a whole (Hooper and Musser 1964). This alliance is also seen in the clustering pattern based on the qualitative skin and skull characters which link *Nesoryzomys* with *O. xantheolus* and *O. bauri*. We thus advance the hypothesis that *Nesoryzomys* owes its origin to a "*xantheolus*-like" ancestral stock inhabiting the xeric coastal regions of Peru and Chile. Significantly, this same pattern of origin is seen for *O. bauri* and *O. galapagoensis*, the other Galapagos endemics belonging to *Oryzomys* (*s.s.*). There is no evidence to date which suggests that any of the endemic Galapagos rats have had their origins among tropical representatives of the oryzomyine complex, as suggested by Orr (1966).

While we believe that both *Nesoryzomys* and the two forms of *Oryzomys* from the islands share a similar mode and place of origin, the timing of island invasion must have been considerably different. Several lines of evidence suggest that *Nesoryzomys* is an old immigrant to the archipelago while the *Oryzomys* species are quite recent. The high degree of phenetic distinctiveness of *Nesoryzomys* relative to other oryzomyines argues for a more ancient origin, especially since *O. bauri* is nearly identical in all respects to the mainland *O. xantheolus*. The available biochemical data also support this contention. Two estimates have been proposed as a basis for using the largely time dependent nature of protein change as an "evolutionary clock." One is based on the number and rate of amino acid substitutions in proteins detected by electrophoresis (see Nei 1975, for review) such that time in years (t) since divergence is estimated as $t = 5\text{x}10^6 D$, where D is Nei's genetic distance measure. The second is based on the concordance between distance measures based on electrophoresis and the albumin immunological distance (see Wilson et al. 1977; Sarich and Cronin 1976). In the latter, a Nei D-value of 1 is estimated to correspond to 20-25 million years.

The D-value for *N. narboroughi–O. bauri* or *N. narboroughi–O. xantheolus* comparisons is about 0.62 (an exact measure is not possible since the electrophoretic data for the three species are not totally equivalent). By Nei's methods, this suggests an origin of *Nesoryzomys* around 3 to 3.5 million years ago. The Sarich and Cronin method provides a considerably higher estimate of divergence time, on the order of 12.4 to 15.5 million years. We are inclined to favor the more recent of these two possibilities for the following reasons. For one, all current estimates based on magnetic reversal sequences and sea floor spreading place the origin of the islands at 4+ million years (see Cox, this volume). Hence, the Nei estimation falls well within this time limit. The alternative requires origin prior to the formation of the Galapagos and is considered less likely. This necessitates origin and radiation of *Nesoryzomys* on the mainland prior to colonization of the Galapagos with subsequent extinction in its place of origin, an hypothesis we find difficult to accept. In any event, the great morphological uniformity among the taxa of *Nesoryzomys* (see below) suggests but a single immigration to the islands, be it of pre-*Nesoryzomys* or *Nesoryzomys* form, with subsequent radiation.

The origin of *O. bauri–O. galapagoensis* is surely a more recent development. Electrophoretically, *O. bauri* differs in only a minor fashion at two loci from *O. xantheolus*, and in nearly all morphological analyses the two taxa are barely separable. To our knowledge, this close relationship was first observed by Gyldenstolpe (1932). *O. bauri* is so similar to *O. xantheolus* that we would not be surprised if future studies showed that it was introduced to the Galapagos within the last few hundred to a thousand years, perhaps by aboriginal sailors coursing the west coast of Peru.

Taxonomic Status of the Endemic Species

We have postponed to this point any discussion as to the validity of the various species of endemic rats in the archipelago. Each new island form discovered in the past has been accorded specific status as a matter of course, and no critical examination of the entire group has ever been made. The demonstration of the biological basis for the specific assignment of these forms is, however, impossible. In the first place, except for the sympatric nature of *N. darwini* and *N. indefessus* on Santa Cruz, all species are restricted to allopatric distributions on single islands. Hence, the "test of sympatry" has only been established once. Secondly, since only one species of each of the two endemic groups remains extant, it will never be possible to perform breeding or other experiments to assess the level of reproductive compatibility among the various island forms. We are left, therefore, with the necessity of assessing species status within the complex as a whole on purely morphological grounds. Since this is unsatisfactory in that the results remain equivocal, we here merely characterize the extent of variation among the included taxa and provide our personal biases as to the systematic meaning of this variation pattern.

The assessment of morphological variability within and between the various endemic forms was made by discriminant function analysis based on the 28 quantitative characters and by spectrophotometric analysis of pelage color. The latter analysis was limited to taxa in the genus *Nesoryzomys* since skins of *O. galapagoensis* were not available for study.

A plot of the first and second discriminant functions for the seven taxa examined is given in Fig. 12. Combined, these axes account for 84.2% of the variance seen in the analysis (Table 4). All of the Galapagoan rats are included along with *O. xantheolus* from coastal Peru; the single specimen of *O. galapagoensis* is the holotype from the British Museum (Natural History), kindly measured for us by Dr. John Pizzimenti. The strong separation of *Nesoryzomys* from *Oryzomys* proper is again apparent, but such is not the main point of the graph. It is clear that there are really three, and only three morphological groupings represented. First, the type of *O. galapagoensis* falls well within the cluster of *O. bauri* individuals and is thus inseparable from that form. These two also link closely with *O. xantheolus*, again a reflection of the overall high level of similarity between these species seen in other analyses. This group of three species is then separated from all *Nesoryzomys* along the first discriminant axis. Second, *N. darwini* is clearly differentiated from other members of that genus, with separation achieved along the second axis. The third group thus contains the remaining three forms of *Nesoryzomys* (*swarthi, indefessus*, and *narboroughi*). Among the latter group, *N. indefessus* and *N. narboroughi* are almost totally overlapping in individual placement while the four known individuals of *N. swarthi* are separate from that pair.

These results are fully consistent with the available published record of opinion on the status of these species. The likelihood of conspecificity of *O. bauri* and *O. galapagoensis* was intimated by Heller (1904:240) and Osgood (1929), and the two were placed in synonymy by Cabrera

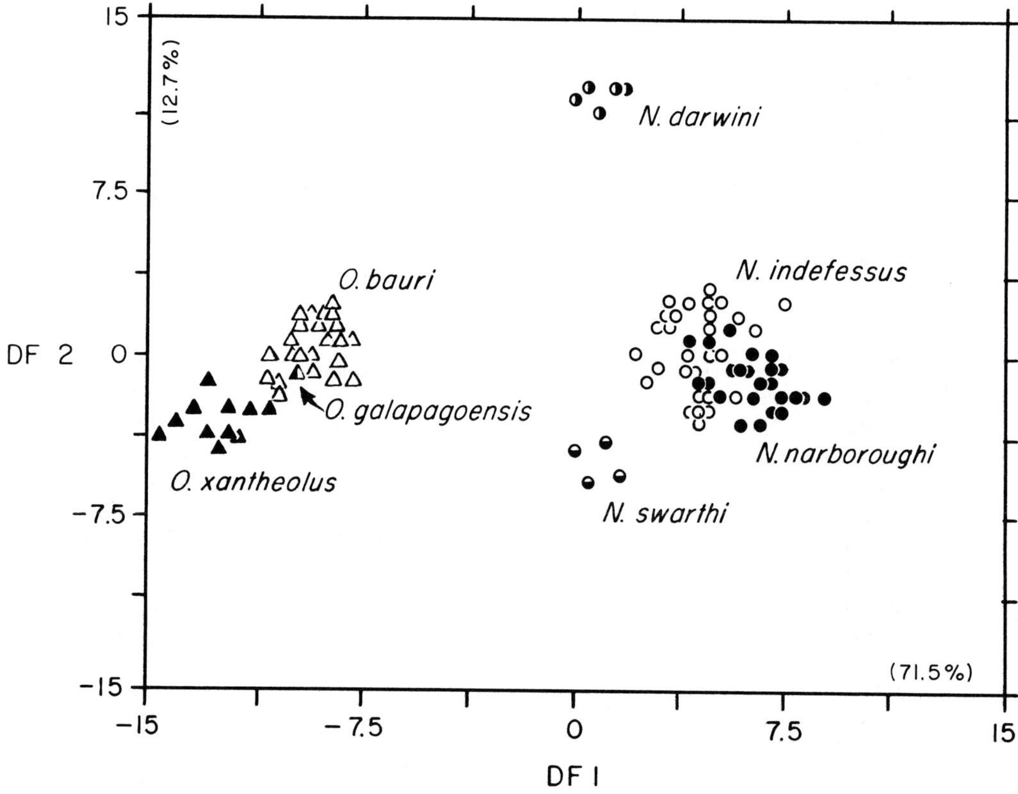

Fig. 12. Plot of the first two Discriminant Function axes comparing the six endemic Galapagos taxa with *O. xantheolus* from the Peruvian coast. The single specimen of *O. galapagoensis* is the holotype; its placement is based on analysis of only 14 of the 28 quantitative characters used for the remaining species.

(1961). Based on the present analysis, we see every reason to argue for this point of view. A similar stand can be made relative to the three large-bodied taxa of *Nesoryzomys*. Orr (1938) was the last author to characterize these species. He noted that *N. indefessus* and *N. narboroughi*, while virtually indistinguishable cranially, were separable primarily on the basis of pelage color. Color differences between the taxa are in the nature of a continuum (see Fig. 13). Complete overlap occurs in color characteristics between *N. indefessus* and *N. swarthi* and, while *N. narboroughi* is noticeably darker than the other taxa, some overlap between it and *N. indefessus* is apparent (Table 5 and Fig. 13). *N. swarthi* possesses certain characters in common with both of the others, being most distinct cranially. As a collective group, however, the three large forms differ much less among themselves than any differ from *N. darwini*. These statements are clearly supported by the discriminant and colorimetric analyses reported here. It is arguable, therefore, that the three large forms of *Nesoryzomys* should best be considered members of a single species characterized by a level of intraspecific variation expected of allopatric populations inhabiting ecologically quite distinct islands. For example, the blackish pelage of *N. narboroughi*, its major distinguishing feature, is to be expected for a form living largely on a black lava substrate. We are thus of the opinion that *N. narboroughi, N. indefessus,* and *N. swarthi* are most realistically considered only slightly to moderately delineated races of a single biological species, for which the name *indefessus* has priority.

TABLE 4. STANDARDIZED DISCRIMINANT FUNCTION COEFFICIENTS FOR THE FIRST THREE VECTORS

Character	I	II	III
ToL	- .6821	1.2174	.2567
TaL	-1.5331	-1.0539	-1.2329
HF	.7011	-1.1558	- .0457
E	.1903	- .5428	.5565
ON	3.8579	-1.9442	.4998
BaL	-2.0264	2.0423	-3.9496
BB	.1684	.5527	.7720
ZB	- .1490	-2.3254	.2986
RL	1.3083	.8201	-1.1713
DL	.7736	.5153	.6727
CD	.0512	- .0511	- .0856
ACH	- .3800	- .3991	- .4042
BCL	.2569	-1.4193	- .3778
IOC	- .4261	.3445	- .6799
RW	- .6997	.5934	.3418
MTRW	.7579	.2436	.5581
MTRL	.0075	.2381	.5364
BuL	- .1817	- .0219	.5875
RD	.6353	- .7008	.5875
mTRL	- .1290	- .5172	.9102
RH	.3747	.1840	- .2475
ZPW	- .8335	.2426	.7077
IFL	- .8904	- .4653	1.1189
1L	- .3230	- .5330	.5895
2L	- .2295	.0237	.0752
3L	.0561	.4336	-1.0261
MPFW	- .6686	- .6560	.5288
MPFL	-1.3695	.1760	.5788
% total variance	71.5	12.7	10.5
Eigenvalue	52.035	9.267	7.706

TABLE 5. THREE COLOR VARIABLES OF THE PELAGE OF THE FOUR TAXA OF *NESORYZOMYS* FROM THE GALAPAGOS ISLANDS[1]

CHARACTER	*Nesoryzomys indefessus* N=29	*Nesoryzomys narboroughi* N=26	*Nesoryzomys darwini* N=3	*Nesoryzomys swarthi* N=3
Brightness	8.3±0.19 6.46-10.67	5.57±0.11 4.30-6.59	7.52±0.74 6.60-8.99	7.99±0.57 7.11-9.05
Dominant wavelength	583.6±0.12 582-585	583.5±0.32 580-587	585.0±1.15 583-587	583.2±0.33 583-584
Purity	27.50±0.60 18.8-33.3	13.07±0.90 6.1-25.9	28.90±0.78 27.4-30.0	26.20±2.81 21.2-30.9

[1] Mean ± one standard error and range are given.

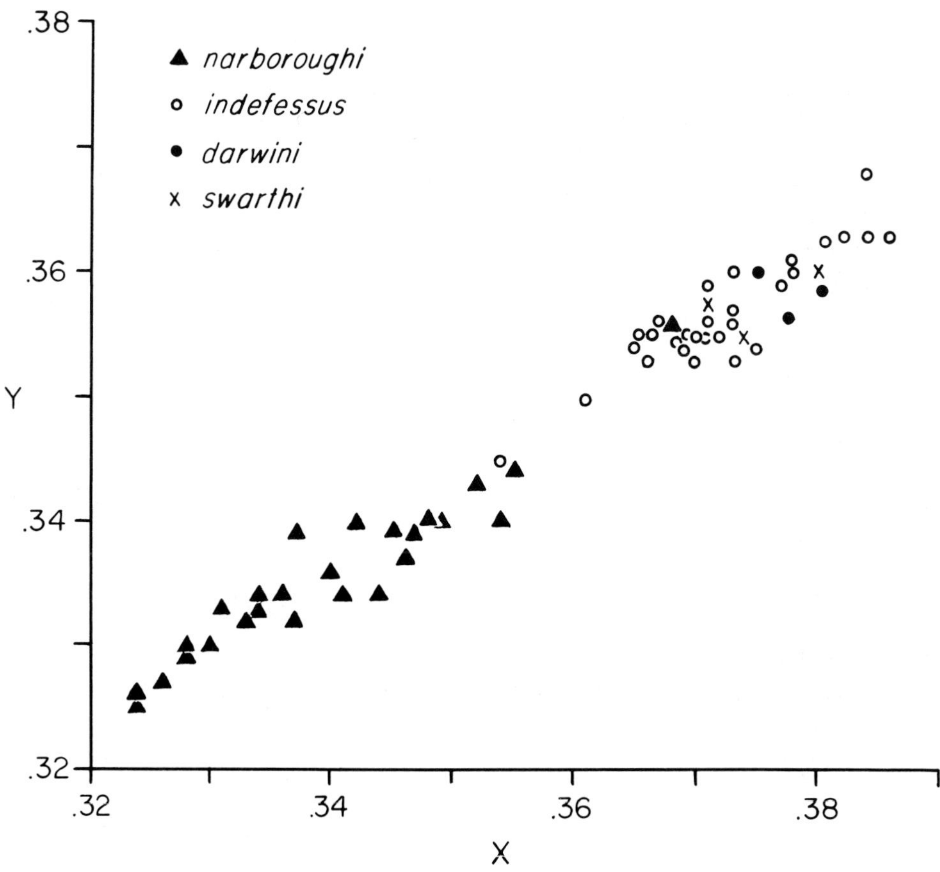

Fig. 13. Chromaticity diagram showing the distribution of trichromatic coefficients, *x* and *y*, for the four taxa of *Nesoryzomys*. Note the essentially linear spread of values with complete overlap between *N. indefessus, N. swarthi,* and *N. darwini*, and marginal overlap between *N. indefessus* and *N. narboroughi*. The white point (I.C.I. Illuminant C) is at x=.3163, y=.3101.

ACKNOWLEDGMENTS

This report is a contribution of the Charles Darwin Foundation. It could not have been completed without logistical and other support of the Direccion General de Desarrollo Forestal and Parque Nacional Galápagos, Ecuador, and the Charles Darwin Research Station, Galápagos. We are exceedingly grateful to Mrs. Carol P. Patton and Dr. Philip Myers for assistance in the field; Drs. Alfred L. Gardner, John W. Wright, and Philip Myers for relevant discussions; Dr. Peter Kramer and Mr. Craig MacFarland for logistical support at the Darwin Research Station; Dr. Luis de la Torre, Field Museum of Natural History, and Mrs. Jacqueline Schonewald, California Academy of Sciences, for permitting examination of specimens in their care; and Dr. John J. Pizzimenti for measuring the holotype of *O. galapagoensis* in the British Museum (Natural History). Illustrations were drawn by Mr. Gene M. Christman of the Museum of Vertebrate Zoology. Financial support was made available by the Janss Foundation, the Museum of Vertebrate Zoology, the Penrose Fund of the American Philosophical Society, and a Biomedical Sciences Support Grant from the U.S. Public Health Service.

RESUMEN

La fauna nativa de roedores en el archipiélago de las Galápagos consiste en siete especies pertenecientes al grupo generalizado de las "ratas de arroz" neotropicales de la familia Cricetidae. Esta especies forman tres complejos diferentes, siendo cada uno de ellos definido con rango genérico o subgenérico: (1) *Oryzomys* (*sensu stricto*), incluyendo *galapagoensis* (conocida solamenta en la Isla San Cristóbal) y *bauri* (de la Isla de Santa Fe); (2) *Nesoryzomys*, que incluye a las especies *narboroughi* (de la Isla Fernandina), *swarthi* (de la Isla Santiago), *darwini* (de la Isla Santa Cruz), y *indefessus* (de las islas Santa Cruz y Baltra); y (3) *Megalomys curioi* (de la Isla Santa Cruz). *Megalomys* conocido solamente por material subfósil no va ha ser tratado en este trabajo. Cuatro de las restantes seis especies están probablemente extintas ya que solo se conocen actualmente poblaciones activas de las especies *O. bauri* y *N. narboroughi*.

El tiempo, patrones de radiación biológica y relaciones filogenéticas de *Oryzomys* y *Nesoryzomys* son estudiados por medio de investigaciones cariológicas, bioquímicas y anatómicas de las dos únicas especies vivientes, y por análisis multivariable de caracteres morfométricos de ejemplares, preservados en colecciones de museos, pertenecientes a todas las especies. Nuestros datos sugieren lo siguiente: a) *Nesoryzomys* es una unidad claramente distinta y debe ser reconocida a nivel genérico; b) se pueden definir al menos dos invasiones, independientes una de la otra, a las islas, en donde *Nesoryzomys* representa un colonizador más temprano, seguido bastante más tarde por *Oryzomys* (*s. s.*); c) ambos grupos de *Oryzomys* son immigrantes bastante recientes y son indudablemente derivados de *O. xantheolus* de los valles fluviales de la región costera de Perú, o de un antepasado común; d) el origen de *Nesoryzomys* es poco claro actualmente; e) las especies de mayor tamaño del género *Nesoryzomys* (*narboroughi, swarthi* e *indefessus*) deberían ser consideradas razas de una misma especies que se diferencian solamente por el color del pelaje; f) similarmente, *O. galapagoensis* y *O. bauri* deberían ser consideradas conespecíficas.

LITERATURE CITED

Allen, J. A. 1892. On a small collection of mammals from the Galapagos Islands, collected by Dr. G. Baur. Bull. Amer. Mus. Nat. Hist. 4:47-50.

Arata, A. A. 1964. The anatomy and taxonomic significance of the male accessory reproductive glands of muroid rodents. Bull. Florida State Mus., Biol. Sci. 9:1-42.

Arata, A. A., N. C. Negus, and M. S. Downs. 1965. Histology, development, and individual variation of complex muroid bacula. Tulane Stud. Zool. 12:51-64.

Brosset, A. 1963. Statut actuel des mammifères des îles Galapagos. Mammalia 27:323-338.

Cabrera, A. 1961. Catalogo de los mamiferos de America del Sur. Rev. Mus. Argentino Cien. Nat. "Bernardino Rivadavia," Cien. Zool. 4(2):309-732.

Carleton, M. D. 1973. A survey of gross stomach morphology in New World Cricetinae (Rodentia, Muridae), with comments on functional interpretations. Misc. Publ. Mus. Zool., Univ. Michigan 146. 43 pp.

DeBeaufort, F. 1963. Les cricetines de Galapagos. Valeur du genre *Nesoryzomys*. Mammalia 27: 338-340.

Ellerman, J. R. 1941. The families and genera of living rodents. Vol. 2. British Museum (Natural History), London. 690 pp.

Gardner, A. L., and J. L. Patton. 1976. Karyotypic variation in oryzomyine rodents (Cricetinae) with comments on chromosomal evolution in the Neotropical Cricetine complex. Occas. Pap. Mus. Zool., Louisiana State Univ. 49. 48 pp.

Goldman, E. A. 1918. The rice rats of North America. North Amer. Fauna 43:1-100.

Gyldenstolpe, N. 1932. A manual of Neotropical sigmodont rodents. Kungl. Svensk. Vetenskapsakad. Handl. (3), 11:1-164.

Heller, E. 1904. Mammals of the Galápagos Archipelago, exclusive of the Cetacea. Proc. Calif. Acad. Sci., Ser. 3, 3:233-250.

Hershkovitz, P. 1962. Evolution of Neotropical cricetine rodents (Muridae) with special reference to the phyllotine group. Fieldiana: Zool. 46:1-524.

Hooper, E. T. 1958. The male phallus in mice of the genus *Peromyscus*. Misc. Publ. Mus. Zool., Univ. Michigan 105. 24 pp.

Hooper, E. T. 1962. The glans penis in *Sigmodon, Sigmomys*, and *Reithrodon* (Rodentia, Cricetinae). Occas. Pap. Mus. Zool., Univ. Michigan 625:1-11.

Hooper, E. T., and B. S. Hart. 1962. A synopsis of Recent North American microtine rodents. Misc. Publ. Mus. Zool., Univ. Michigan. 120. 68 pp.

Hooper, E. T., and G. G. Musser. 1964. The glans penis in Neotropical cricetines (Family Cricetidae) with comments on classification of muroid rodents. Misc. Publ. Mus. Zool., Univ. Michigan. 133. 57 pp.

Lidicker, W. Z., Jr. 1968. A phylogeny of New Guinea rodent genera based on phallic morphology. J. Mammal. 49:609-643.

Nei, M. 1975. Molecular population genetics and evolution. American Elsevier Publ. Co., New York, N. Y.

Niethammer, J. 1964. Contribution à la connaissance des mammifères terrestres de L'île Indefatigable (à Santa Cruz), Galápagos. Résultats de l'expédition allemande aux Galápagos 1962/63, No. VIII. Mammalia 28:593-606.

Orr, R. T. 1938. A new rodent of the genus *Nesoryzomys* from the Galapagos Islands. Proc. Calif. Acad. Sci., Ser. 4, 23:303-306.

Orr, R. T. 1966. Evolutionary aspects of the mammalian fauna of the Galápagos. Pages 276-281 *in* R. I. Bowman, ed. The Galápagos. University of California Press, Berkeley and Los Angeles, Calif.

Osgood, W. H. 1929. A new rodent from the Galápagos Islands. Field Mus. Nat. Hist., Zool. Ser., 17:21-24.

Peterson, R. L. 1966. Recent mammal records from the Galápagos Islands. Mammalia 30:441-445.

Rosero Posso, E. 1975. Peso, longitudes de colo y perineo y forma de vida de la rata endemica de la Isla Santa Fe, *Oryzomys bauri* (Cricetidae). Revista de la Universidad Catolica, Numero Monografico 3(8):185-217.

Sarich, V. M., and J. E. Cronin. 1976. Molecular systematics of the primates. Pages 141-170 *in* M. Goodman and R. E. Tashian, eds. Molecular Anthropology. Plenum Press, New York, N. Y.

Sneath, P. H. A., and R. R. Sokal. 1973. Numerical taxonomy. W. C. Freeman Co., San Francisco, Calif. 573 pp.

Thomas, O. 1899. Descriptions of new Neotropical mammals. Ann. Mag. Nat. Hist., Ser. 7, 4:278-288.

Waterhouse, G. R. 1839. The zoology of the voyage of H. M. S. Beagle, under the command of Captain Fitzroy, R. N., during the years 1832 to 1836. Part 2. Mammalia. Smith, Elder and Co., London. 97 pp.

Wilson, A. C., S. S. Carlson, and T. J. White. 1977. Biochemical evolution. Ann. Rev. Biochem. 46:573-639.

APPENDIX I

Specimens Examined

All specimens of Galapagos endemic rats utilized in this report are represented by standard museum preparations and are deposited in either the Museum of Vertebrate Zoology, University of California, Berkeley (MVZ); the California Academy of Sciences, San Francisco (CAS, or SU if part of the Stanford University collection housed by that institution); or the Field Museum of Natural History, Chicago (FMNH). Localities and sample sizes follow:

Nesoryzomys narboroughi Heller, 1904. Isla Fernandina: Punta Espinosa (23♂, 20♀ - MVZ 125476-125477, 133122-133129, 145382-145391; CAS 2505-2515, 2479, 2483, 2485-2488, 13273-13274, 13276, 13278-13279); Mangrove Point (9♂, 10♀ - FMNH 30832-30841, 30843-30844; SU 2468-2474).

Nesoryzomys indefessus (Thomas, 1899). Isla Santa Cruz: Academy Bay (22♂, 15♀ - FMNH 30847-30849, 30852-30855, 30847, 30869; CAS 2527-2532, 2534-2547, 2549-2553, 2575-2576); Conway Bay (7♂, 2♀ - FMNH 30869-20875, 20877, 30869); North Santa Cruz (3♂, 2♀ - SU 2463-2467). Isla Baltra: (16♂, 9♀ - FMNH 30859-30868; CAS 2490-2498; SU 2454, 2457-2461).

Nesoryomys darwini Osgood, 1929. Isla Santa Cruz: Academy Bay (4♂ - FMNH 30828-30829; CAS 2533, 2548); Conway Bay (1♂ - FMNH 30831).

Nesoryzomys swarthi Orr, 1938. Isla Santiago: Sullivan Bay (4♂ - CAS 2556, 2561-2563).

Oryzomys bauri J. A. Allen, 1892. Isla Santa Fe: northeast coast (18♂, 19♀ - MVZ 125469-125470, 145372-145381; FMNH 49012-49013, 51756-51757, 51761-51770; CAS 2478, 2480-2482, 2489; SU 2449-2453).

APPENDIX II

Remarks on the Current Status of Galapagos Endemic Rats

Oryzomys galapagoensis (Waterhouse, 1839)

This rat was collected by Darwin from Chatham (=San Cristóbal) Island during his visit in 1835 and was subsequently described by Waterhouse in 1839. Darwin noted that the species was abundant, but no subsequent expedition has secured specimens. Heller (1904) considered the species extinct, or if indeed extant, that it must be restricted to the barren eastern end of the island where Darwin secured his specimens. No mammalogical investigations of this section of the island have been made, to our knowledge, since Darwin's visit. Nevertheless, it is very doubtful that *O. galapagoensis* remains extant. Both *Rattus rattus* and *Mus musculus* have been introduced to the island, the former prior to 1891 (see Patton, et al. 1975).

Oryzomys bauri J. A. Allen, 1892

Specimens of this species were collected on Barrington (=Santa Fe) Island by Dr. G. Baur on the Salisbury Expedition in 1892, and subsequently described by Allen in 1892. Dr. Baur noted that the animal was common in all major habitats and all subsequent workers have held the same opinion. Brosset (1963) estimated a population size of from 1000-2000 individuals in 1962. The species breeds during the rainy season, from January through April (Rosero Posso 1975). No introduced rats have ever been recorded from the island. In its current abundant state, *O. bauri* is in no danger of extinction.

Nesoryzomys indefessus (Thomas, 1899)

This species was first collected by Webster and Harris of the Rothschild Expedition in 1897 on Indefatigable (=Santa Cruz) Island. It was originally described as *Oryzomys indefessus* by Oldfield Thomas in 1899. Heller (1904), as a member of the Hopkins-Stanford Expedition of